Oxford
Essential
Portuguese
Dictionary

PORTUGUESE–ENGLISH

ENGLISH–PORTUGUESE

PORTUGUÊS-INGLÊS

INGLÊS- PORTUGUÊS

OXFORD
UNIVERSITY PRESS

OXFORD
UNIVERSITY PRESS

Great Clarendon Street, Oxford OX2 6DP

Oxford University Press is a department of the University of Oxford.
It furthers the University's objective of excellence in research, scholarship,
and education by publishing worldwide in

Oxford New York

Auckland Cape Town Dar es Salaam Hong Kong Karachi
Kuala Lumpur Madrid Melbourne Mexico City Nairobi
New Delhi Shanghai Taipei Toronto

With offices in

Argentina Austria Brazil Chile Czech Republic France Greece
Guatemala Hungary Italy Japan Poland Portugal Singapore
South Korea Switzerland Thailand Turkey Ukraine Vietnam

Oxford is a registered trade mark of Oxford University Press
in the UK and in certain other countries

British Library Cataloguing in Publication Data

Data available

ISBN 978-0-19-957642-5

2

Typeset by SPI Publisher Services, Pondicherry, India
Printed in Great Britain by Clays Ltd, St. Ives plc

Contents/Índice

Preface

The *Oxford Essential Portuguese Dictionary* has been written for speakers of both Portuguese and English and contains the most useful words and expressions in use today.

The dictionary provides a handy and comprehensive reference work for tourists, students, and business people who require quick and reliable answers to their translation needs.

Thanks are due to: Dr John Sykes, Prof. A. W. Raitt, Commander Virgílio Correia, Marcelo Affonso, Eng. Pedro Carvalho, Eng. Vasco Carvalho, Dr Iva Correia, Dr Ida Reis de Carvalho, Eng. J. Reis de Carvalho, Prof. A. Falcão, Bishop Manuel Falcão, Dr M. Luísa Falcão, Prof. J. Ferraz, Prof. M. de Lourdes Ferraz, Drs Ana and Jorge Fonseca, Mr Robert Howes, Irene Lakhani, Eng. Hugo Pires, Prof. M. Kaura Pires, Dr M. Alexandre Pires, Ambassador L. Pazos Alonso, Dr Teresa Pinto Pereira, Dr Isabel Tully, Carlos Wallenstein, Ligia Xavier, and Dr H. Martins and the members of his Mesa Lusófona at St Anthony's College, Oxford.

Prefácio

O *Oxford Essential Portuguese Dictionary* foi escrito por pessoas de língua portuguesa e inglesa, e contém as palavras e expressões mais úteis em uso atualmente.

O dicionário constitui uma obra de referência prática e abrangente para turistas, estudantes e pessoas de negócios que necessitam de respostas rápidas e confiáveis para as suas traduções.

Agradecimentos a: Dr John Sykes, Prof. A. W. Raitt, Comandante Virgílio Correia, Marcelo Affonso, Eng. Pedro Carvalho, Eng. Vasco Carvalho, Dr Iva Correia, Dr Ida Reis de Carvalho, Eng. J. Reis de Carvalho, Prof. A. Falcão, Bispo Manuel Falcão, Dr M. Luísa Falcão, Prof. J. Ferraz, Prof. M. de Lourdes Ferraz, Drs Ana e Jorge Fonseca, Mr Robert Howes, Eng. Hugo Pires, Prof. M. Laura Pires, Dr M. Alexandre Pires, Embaixador L. Pazos Alonso, Dr Teresa Pinto Pereira, Dr Isabel Tully, Carlos Wallenstein, e Dr H. Martins e os membros de sua Mesa Lusófona do St Anthony's College, em Oxford.

Introduction

The swung dash (∼) is used to replace a headword, or that part of a headword preceding the vertical bar (|).

In both English and Portuguese, only irregular plural forms are given. Plural forms of Portuguese nouns and adjectives ending in a single vowel are formed by adding an *s* (e.g. *livro, livros*). Those ending in *n, r, s* where the stress falls on the final syllable, and *z*, add *es* (e.g. *mulher, mulheres, falaz, falazes*). Nouns and adjectives ending in *m* change the final *m* to *ns* (e.g. *homem, homens, bom, bons*). Most of those ending in *ão* change their ending to *ões* (e.g. *estação, estações*).

Portuguese nouns and adjectives ending in an unstressed *o* form the feminine by changing the *o* to *a* (e.g. *belo, bela*). Those ending in *or* become *ora* (e.g. *trabalhador, trabalhadora*). All other masculine-feminine changes are shown at the main headword.

English and Portuguese pronunciation is given by means of the International Phonetic Alphabet. It is shown for all headwords, and for those derived words whose pronunciation is not easily deduced from that of a headword.

Portuguese verb tables will be found in the appendix.

Introdução

O sinal (∼) é usado para substituir o verbete, ou parte deste precedendo a barra vertical (|).

Tanto em inglês como em português, somente as formas irregulares do plural são dadas. As formas regulares do plural dos substantivos ingleses recebem um *s* (ex. *teacher, teachers*), ou *es* quando terminarem em *ch, sh, s, ss, us, x* ou *z* (ex. *sash, sashes*). Os substantivos terminados em *y* e precedidos por uma consoante, mudam no plural para *ies* (ex. *baby, babies*).

O passado e o particípio passado dos verbos regulares ingleses são formados pelo acréscimo de *ed* à forma infinitiva (ex. *last, lasted*). Os verbos terminados em *e* recebem *d* (ex. *move, moved*). Aqueles terminados em *y* têm o *y* substituído por *ied* (*carry, carried*). As formas irregulares dos verbos aparecem no dicionário em ordem alfabética, remetidas à forma infinitiva, e também, na lista de verbos no apêndice.

As pronúncias inglesa e portuguesa são dadas em acordo com o Alfabeto Fonético Internacional. A pronúncia é dada para todos os verbetes, assim como para aquelas palavras derivadas cuja pronúncia não seja facilmente deduzida a partir do verbete.

Proprietary terms

This dictionary includes some words which are, or are asserted to be, proprietary names or trade marks. Their inclusion does not imply that they have acquired for legal purposes a non-proprietary or general significance, nor is any other judgement implied concerning their legal status. In cases where the editor has some evidence that a word is used as a proprietary name or trade mark this is indicated by the label *propr*, but no judgement concerning the legal status of such words is made or implied thereby.

Nomes comerciais

Este dicionário inclui algumas palavras que são, ou acredita-se ser, nomes comerciais ou marcas registradas. A sua inclusão no dicionário não implica que elas tenham adquirido para fins legais um significado geral ou não-comercial, assim como não afeta em nenhum dos conceitos implícitos o seu status legal.

Nos casos em que o editor tenha prova suficiente de que uma palavra seja usada como um nome comercial ou marca registrada, este emprego é indicado pela etiqueta *propr*, mas nenhuma apreciação relativa ao status legal de tais palavras é feita ou sugerida por esta indicação.

Portuguese Pronunciation

Vowels and Diphthongs

a, à, á, â	/ã/	cham*a*m, *a*mbos, *a*ntes	1) before *m* at the end of a word, or before *m* or *n* and another consonant, is nasalized
	/a/	*a*ba, *à*, *a*colá, desânimo	2) in other positions is like *a* in English r*a*ther
ã	/ã/	irm*ã*	is nasalized
e	/ẽ/	s*e*m, v*e*nda	1) before *m* at the end of a word, or before *m* or *n* and another consonant, is nasalized
	/i/	art*e*	2) at the end of a word is like *y* in English happ*y*
	/e/	m*e*nas	3) in other positions is like *e* in English th*e*y
é	/ɛ/	art*é*ria	is like *e* in English g*e*t
ê	/e/	f*ê*mur	is like *e* in English th*e*y
i	/ĩ/	s*í*m, v*i*ndo	1) before *m* at the end of a word, or before *m* or *n* and another consonant, is nasalized
	/i/	f*í*la	2) in other positions is like *ee* in English s*ee*
o	/õ/	c*o*m, s*o*mbra, *o*nda	1) before *m* at the end of a word, or before *m* or *n* and another consonant, is nasalized
	/u/	muit*o*	2) at the end of a word, unstressed, is like *u* in English r*u*le
	/o/	c*o*mover	3) in other positions, unstressed, is like *o* in English p*o*le
	/o/	b*o*bo	4) stressed, is like o in
	/ɔ/	l*o*ja	English p*o*le or *o* in sh*o*p
ó	/o/	*ó*pera	is like o in English sh*o*p
ô	/o/	t*ô*nica	is like o in English p*o*le

u, ú		*gue*rra, *gui*sado, *que*, *qui*lo	1) is silent in *gue*, *gui*, *que*, and *qui*
	/u/	m*u*la, púrp*u*ra	2) in other positions is like *u* in English r*u*le
ü, gü	/gw/	ung*üe*nto	in the combinations *güe* and *güi* is like *g* in English *g*ot, followed by English *w*
	/kw/	tranq*üi*lo	in the combinations *qüe* and *qüi* is like *qu* in English *qu*een
ãe	/ãj/	m*ãe*, p*ãe*s, alem*ãe*s	is like *y* in English b*y*, but nasalized
ai	/aj/	v*ai*, p*ai*, s*ai*, c*ai*ta	is like *y* in English b*y*
ao, au	/aw/	*ao*s, *au*todefesa	is like *ow* in English h*ow*
ão	/ãw/	n*ão*	is like *ow* in English h*ow*, but nasalized
ei	/ej/	l*ei*	is like *ey* in English th*ey*
eu	/ew/	d*eu*s, fl*eu*gma	both vowels pronounced separately
oẽ	/õj/	eleiç*õe*s	is like *oi* in English c*oi*n, but nasalized
oi	/oj/	n*oi*te	is like *oi* in English c*oi*n
ou	/o/	p*ou*co	is like *o* in English p*o*le

Consonants

b	/b/	*b*anho	is like *b* in English *b*all
c	/s/	*c*inza, *c*em	1) before *e* or *i* is like *s* in English *s*it
	/k/	*c*asa	2) in other positions is like *c* in English *c*at
ç	/s/	esta*ç*ão	is like *s* in English *s*it
ch	/ʃ/	*ch*á	is like *sh* in English *sh*out
d	/dʒ/	*d*izer, *d*onde	1) before *i* or final unstressed *e* is like *j* in English *j*oin
	/d/	*d*ar	2) in other positions is like *d* in English *d*og
f	/f/	*f*alar	is like *f* in English *f*all
g	/g/	a*g*ente, *g*iro	1) before *e* or *i* is like *s* in English vi*s*ion

	/g/	gato	2) in other positions is like g in English get
h		haver	is silent in Portuguese, but see ch, lh, nh
j	/ʒ/	junta	is like s in English vision
k	/k/	kit	is like English k in key
l	/w/	falta	1) between a vowel and a consonant, or following a vowel at the end of a word, is like w in English water
	/l/	lata	2) in other positions is like l in English like
l	/ʎ/	calhar	is like lli in English million
m		ambas/ãbuʃ/ com/kɪ/	1) between a vowel and a consonant, or after a vowel at the end of a word, m nasalizes the preceding vowel
	/m/	mato, mão	2) in other positions is like m in English mother
n		cinza/'sīza/	1) between a vowel and a consonant, n nasalizes the preceding vowel
	/n/	benigno	2) in other positions is like n in English near
nh	/ɲ/	banho	is like ni in English opinion
p	/p/	paz	is like p in English poor
q	/k/	que, inquieto	1) qu before e or i is like English k
	/kw/	quase, quórum	2) qu before a or o, or qü before e or i, is like qu in English queen
r	/r/	aparato, gordo	1) between two vowels, or between a vowel and a consonant, is trilled
	/x/	rato, garra, melro, genro, Israel	2) at the beginning of a word, or in rr, or after l, n, or s, is like ch in Scottish loch
s	/ʃ/	depois	at the end of a word is like sh in English shoot
	/z/	asa, desde, abismo, Israel	2) between two vowels, or before b, d, g, l, m, n, r, v, is like z in English zebra

	/s/	suave	3) in other positions is like *s* in English *sit*
t	/tʃ/	*tio, antes*	1) before *i* or final unstressed *e* is like *ch* in English *cheese*
	/tʃi/	*kit*	2) at the end of a word is like *chy* in English *itchy*
	/t/	*atar*	3) in other positions is like *t* in English *tap*
v	/v/	*luva*	is like *v* in English *vain*
w	/u/	*watt*	is shorter than English *w*
x	/z/	*exato, exemplo*	1) in the prefix *ex* before a vowel, is pronounced like *z* in *zero*
	/ʃ/	*xícara, baixo, peixe, frouxo*	2) at the beginning of a word or after *ai, ei* or *ou*, is pronounced like *sh* in *show*
	/s/	*explodir, auxiliar*	3) is like *s* in English *sit*
	/ks/	*axila, fixo*	4) is like *x* in English *exit*
			5) in the combination *xce, xci, x* is not pronounced in Portuguese e.g. *excelente, excitar*
z	/s/	*falaz*	1) at the end of a word, is like *s* in English *sit*
	/z/	*dizer*	2) in other positions, is like English *z*

Pronúncia Inglesa

Vogais e Ditongos

/iː/	see, tea	como i em giro
/ɪ/	sit, happy	é um som mais breve do que i em li
/e/	set	como e em tépido
/æ/	hat	é um som mais breve do que a em amor
/aː/	arm, calm	como a em cartaz
/ɒ/	got	como o em exótico
/ɔː/	saw, more	como o em corte
/ʊ/	put, look	como u em murro
/uː/	too, due	como u em duro
/ʌ/	cup, some	como a em pano
/ɜː/	firm, fur	como e em enxerto
/ə/	ago, weather	como e no português europeu parte
/eɪ/	page, pain, pay	como ei em leite
/əʊ/	home, roam	é um som mais longo do que o em coma
/aɪ/	fine, by, guy	como ai em sai
/aɪə/	fire, tyre	como ai em sai seguido por /ə/
/aʊ/	now, shout	como au em aula
/aʊə/	hour, flower	como au em aula seguido por /ə/
/ɔɪ/	join, boy	como oi em dói
/ɪə/	dear, here, beer	como ia em dia
/eə/	hair, care, bear, there	como e em etéreo
/ʊə/	poor, during	como ua em sua

Consoantes

/p/	snap	como p em pato
/b/	bath	como b em bala
/t/	tap	como t em tela
/d/	dip	como d em dar
/k/	cat, kite, stomach, pique	como c em casa
/ks/	exercise	como x em axila
/g/	got	como g em gato

/tʃ/	chin	como t em tio
/dʒ/	June, general, judge	como d em dizer
/f/	fall	como f em faca
/v/	vine, of	como v em vaca
/θ/	thin, moth	não tem equivalente, soa como um s entre os dentes
/ð/	this	não tem equivalente, soa com um z entre os dentes
/s/	so, voice	como s em suave
/z/	zoo, rose	como z em fazer
/ʃ/	she, lunch	como ch em chegar
/ʒ/	measure, vision	como j em jamais
/h/	how	h aspirado
/m/	man	como m em mala
/n/	none	como n em nada
/ŋ/	sing	como n em cinto
/l/	leg	como l em luva
/r/	red, write	como r em cara
/j/	yes, yoke	como i em ioga
/w/	weather, switch	como u em égua

' indica a sílaba tônica

European Portuguese

Brazilian Portuguese, which is used in this dictionary, differs in a number of respects from that used in Portugal and the rest of the Portuguese-speaking world. These differences affect both spelling and pronunciation. Spelling variations appear on the Portuguese-English side. In so far as they affect pronunciation, the main variants are:

Brazilian Portuguese often omits the letters *b, c, m,* and *p,* which are retained by European Portuguese:

	Brazilian	**European**
b	sutil	su*b*til
c	ação	ac*ç*ão
	ato	ac*t*o
	elétrico	elé*c*trico
m	indenizar	inde*m*nizar
p	batismo	ba*p*tismo
	exceção	exce*p*ção

Letters *c* and *p* in such variant forms are usually silent, hence acto /'atu/, baptismo/ba'tiʒmu/. However, *c* is pronounced in the combination *ect*, hence eléctrico/i'lektriku/.

The combinations *gü* and *qü* become *gu* and *qu*:

Brazilian	**European**
ung*ü*ento	ung*u*ento
tran*qü*ilo	tran*qu*ilo

However, they are still pronounced /gw/ and /kw/ respectively.

The other main differences in pronunciation are:

d	/d/	dar, dizer, balde, donde	1) at the beginning of a word, or after l, or n, is like d in English dog
	/ð/	cidade, medroso	2) in other positions is a sound between d in English dog and th in English this
e	/ə/	arte	at the end of a word, is like e in English quarrel
r	/rr/	rato, garra, melro, genro, Israel, guelra, tenro, israelense	at the beginning of a word, or in rr, or after l, n, or s, is strongly trilled
s	/ʃ/	depois, asco, raspar, costura	1) at the end of a word, or before c, f, p, qu, or t, is like English sh
	/ʒ/	desde, Islã, abismo, Israel	2) before b, d, g, l, m, n, r, or u is like s in English vision
t	/t/	atar, antes, tio	is like t in English tap
z	/ʃ/	falaz	at the end of a word, is like sh in English shake

Abbreviations/Abreviaturas

adjective	*a*	adjetivo
abbreviation	*abbr/abr*	abreviatura
something	*aco*	alguma coisa
adverb	*adv*	advérbio
somebody, someone	*alg*	algúem
article	*art*	artigo
American (English)	*Amer*	(inglês) americano
anatomy	*anat*	anatomia
architecture	*arquit*	arquitetura
astrology	*astr/astrol*	astrologia
motoring	*auto*	automobilismo
aviation	*aviat*	aviação
Brazilian Portuguese	*B*	português do Brasil
biology	*biol*	biologia
botany	*bot*	botânica
Brazilian Portuguese	*Bras*	português do Brasil
cinema	*cine*	cinema
colloquial	*colloq*	coloquial
commerce	*comm/com*	comércio
computing	*comput*	computação
conjunction	*conj*	conjunção
cookery	*culin*	cozinha
electricity	*electr/eletr*	eletricidade
feminine	*f*	feminina
familiar	*fam*	familiar
figurative	*fig*	figurativo
geography	*geog*	geografia
grammar	*gramm/gram*	gramática
infinitive	*inf*	infinitivo
interjection	*int*	interjeição
interrogative	*interr*	interrogativo
invariable	*invar*	invariável
legal, law	*jur/jurid*	jurídico
language	*lang*	linguagem
literal	*lit*	literal
masculine	*m*	masculino

thematics	*mat*	matemática
mechanics	*mech*	mecânica
medicine	*med*	medicina
military	*mil*	militar
music	*mus*	música
noun	*n*	substantivo
nautical	*naut*	náutico
negative	*neg*	negativo
oneself	*o.s.*	se, si mesmo
European Portuguese	*P*	português de Portugal
pejorative	*pej*	pejorativo
philosophy	*phil*	filosofia
plural	*pl*	plural
politics	*pol*	política
European Portuguese	*Port*	português de Portugal
past participle	*pp*	particípio passado
prefix	*pref*	prefixo
preposition	*prep*	preposição
present	*pres*	presente
present participle	*pres p*	particípio presente
pronoun	*pron*	pronome
psychology	*psych/psic*	psicologia
past tense	*pt*	pretérito
relative	*rel*	relativo
religion	*relig*	religião
somebody	*sb*	alguém
singular	*sing*	singular
slang	*sl*	gíria
someone	*s.o.*	alguém
something	*sth*	alguma coisa
subjunctive	*subj*	subjuntivo
technology	*techn/tecn*	tecnologia
theatre	*theat/teat*	teatro
television	*TV*	televisão
university	*univ*	universidade
auxiliary verb	*v aux*	verbo auxiliar
intransitive verb	*vi*	verbo intransitivo
pronominal verb	*vpr*	verbo pronominal
transitive verb	*vt*	verbo transitivo
transitive & intransitive verb	*vt/i*	verbo transitivo e intransitivo

a¹ /a/ *artigo* the □ *pron* (*mulher*) her; (*coisa*) it; (*você*) you

a² /a/ *prep* (*para*) to; (*em*) at; **às 3 horas** at 3 o'clock; **à noite** at night; **a lápis** in pencil; **a mão** by hand

à /a/ = **a²** + **a¹**

aba /'aba/ *f* (*de chapéu*) brim; (*de camisa*) tail; (*de mesa*) flap

abacate /aba'katʃi/ *m* avocado (pear)

abacaxi /abaka'ʃi/ *m* pineapple; (*fam: problema*) pain, headache

aba|de /a'badʒi/ *m* abbot; **~dia** *f* abbey

aba|fado /aba'fadu/ *a* (*tempo*) humid, close; (*quarto*) stuffy; **~far** *vt* (*asfixiar*) stifle; muffle <*som*>; smother <*fogo*>; suppress <*informação*>; cover up <*escândalo, assunto*>

abagunçar /abagu'sar/ *vt* mess up

abaixar /aba'ʃar/ *vt* lower; turn down <*som, rádio*> □ *vi* **~se** *vpr* bend down

abaixo /a'baʃu/ *adv* down; **~ de** below; **mais ~** further down; **~-assinado** *m* petition

abajur /aba'ʒur/ *m* (*quebra-luz*) lampshade; (*lâmpada*) (table) lamp

aba|lar /aba'lar/ *vt* shake; (*fig*) shock; **~lar-se** *vpr* be shocked, be shaken; **~lo** *m* shock

abanar /aba'nar/ *vt* shake, wave; wag <*rabo*>; (*com leque*) fan

abando|nar /abãdo'nar/ *vt* abandon; (*deixar*) leave; **~no** /o/ *m* abandonment; (*estado*) neglect

abarcar /abar'kar/ *vt* comprise, cover

abarro|tado /abaxo'tadu/ *a* crammed full; (*lotado*) crowded, packed; **~tar** *vt* cram full, stuff

abastado /abas'tadu/ *a* wealthy

abaste|cer /abaste'ser/ *vt* supply; fuel <*motor*>; fill up (with petrol) <*carro*>; refuel <*avião*>; **~cimento** *m* supply; (*de carro, avião*) refuelling

aba|ter /aba'ter/ *vt* knock down; cut down, fell <*árvore*>; shoot down <*avião, ave*>; slaughter <*gado*>; knock down, cut <*preço*>; **~ter alg** <*trabalho*> get s.o. down, wear s.o. out; <*má notícia*> sadden s.o.; <*doença*> lay s.o. low, knock the stuffing out of s.o.; **~tido** *a* dispirited, dejected; <*cara*> haggard, worn; **~timento** *m* dejection; (*de preço*) reduction

abaulado /abaw'ladu/ *a* convex; <*estrada*> cambered

abcesso /ab'sɛsu/ *m* (*Port*) *veja* **abscesso**

abdi|cação /abidʒika'sãw/ *f* abdication; **~car** *vt/i* abdicate

abdômen /abi'domẽ/ *m* abdomen

abecedário /abese'dariu/ *m* alphabet, ABC

abeirar-se /abe'rarsi/ *vr* draw near

abe|lha /a'beʎa/ *f* bee; **~lhudo** *a* inquisitive, nosy

abençoar /abẽso'ar/ *vt* bless

aber|to /a'bɛrtu/ *pp de* **abrir** □ *a* open; <*céu*> clear; <*gás, torneira*> on; <*sinal*> green; **~tura** *f* opening; (*foto*) aperture; (*pol*) liberalization

abeto /a'betu/ *m* fir (tree)

abis|mado /abiz'madu/ *a* astonished; **~mo** *m* abyss

abjeto /ab'ʒɛtu/ *a* abject

abóbada /a'bɔbada/ *f* vault

abobalhado /aboba'ʎadu/ *a* silly

abóbora /a'bɔbora/ *f* pumpkin

abobrinha /abo'briɲa/ *f* courgette, (*Amer*) zucchini

abo|lição /aboli'sãw/ *f* abolition; **~lir** *vt* abolish

abomi|nação /abomina'sãw/ *f* abomination; **~nável** (*pl* **~náveis**) *a* abominable

abo|nar /abo'nar/ *vt* guarantee <*dívida*>; give a bonus to <*empregado*>; **~no** /o/ *m* guarantee; (*no salário*) bonus; (*subsídio*) allowance, benefit; (*reforço*) endorsement

abordar /abor'dar/ *vt* approach <*pessoa*>; broach, tackle <*assunto*>; (*naut*) board

aborre|cer /aboxe'ser/ *vt* (*irritar*) annoy; (*entediar*) bore; **~cer-se** *vpr* get annoyed; get bored; **~cido** *a* annoyed; bored; **~cimento** *m* annoyance; boredom

abor|tar /abor'tar/ *vi* miscarry, have a miscarriage □ *vt* abort; **~to** /o/ *m* abortion; (*natural*) miscarriage

aboto|adura /abotoa'dura/ *f* cufflink; **~ar** *vt* button (up) □ *vi* bud

abra|çar /abra'sar/ *vt* hug, embrace; embrace <*causa*>; **~ço** *m* hug, embrace

abrandar /abrã'dar/ *vt* ease <*dor*>; temper <*calor, frio*>; mollify, appease, placate <*povo*>; tone down, smooth over <*escândalo*> □ *vi* <*dor*> ease; <*calor, frio*> become less extreme; <*tempestade*> die down

abranger /abrã'ʒer/ *vt* cover; (*entender*) take in, grasp; **~ a** extend to

abrasileirar /abrazile'rar/ *vt* Brazilianize

abre-|garrafas /abriga'xafas/ *m invar* (*Port*) bottle-opener; **~latas** *m invar* (*Port*) can-opener

abreugrafia /abrewgra'fia/ *f* X-ray

abrevi|ar /abrevi'ar/ *vt* abbreviate <*palavra*>; abridge <*livro*>; **~atura** *f* abbreviation

abridor /abri'dor/ *m* **~ (de lata)** can-opener; **~ de garrafa** bottle-opener

abri|gar /abri'gar/ *vt* shelter; house <*sem-teto*>; **~gar-se** *vpr* (take) shelter; **~go** *m* shelter

abril /a'briw/ *m* April

abrir /a'brir/ *vt* open; (*a chave*) unlock; turn on <*gás, torneira*>; make <*buraco, exceção*> □ *vi* open; <*céu, tempo*> clear (up); <*sinal*> turn green; **~-se** *vpr* open; (*desabafar*) open up

abrupto /a'bruptu/ *a* abrupt

abrutalhado /abruta'ʎadu/ *a* <*sapato*> heavy; <*pessoa*> coarse

abscesso /abi'sɛsu/ *m* abscess

absolu|tamente /abisoluta'mētʃi/ *adv* absolutely; (*não*) not at all; **~to** *a* absolute; **em ~to** not at all, absolutely not

absol|ver /abisow'ver/ *vt* absolve; (*jurid*) acquit; **~vição** *f* absolution; (*jurid*) acquittal

absor|ção /abisor'sãw/ *f* absorption; **~to** *a* absorbed; **~vente** *a* <*tecido*> absorbent; <*livro*> absorbing; **~ver** *vt* absorb; **~ver-se** *vpr* get absorbed

abs|têmio /abis'temiu/ *a* abstemious; (*de álcool*) teetotal □ *m* teetotaller; **~tenção** *f* abstention; **~tencionista** *a* abstaining □ *m/f* abstainer; **~ter-se** *vpr* abstain; **~ter-se de** refrain from; **~tinência** *f* abstinence

abstra|ção /abistra'sãw/ *f* abstraction; (*mental*) distraction; **~ir** *vt* separate; **~to** *a* abstract

absurdo /abi'surdu/ *a* absurd □ *m* nonsense

abun|dância /abū'dãsia/ *f* abundance; **~dante** *a* abundant; **~dar** *vi* abound

abu|sar /abu'zar/ *vi* go too far; **~sar de** abuse; (*aproveitar-se*) take advantage of; **~so** *m* abuse

abutre /a'butri/ *m* vulture

aca|bado /aka'badu/ *a* finished; (*exausto*) exhausted; (*velho*) decrepit; **~bamento** *m* finish; **~bar** *vt* finish □ *vi* finish, end; (*esgotar-se*) run out; **~bar-se** *vpr* end, be over; (*esgotar-se*) run out; **~bar com** put an end to, end; (*abolir, matar*) do away with; split up with <*namorado*>; wipe out <*adversário*>; **~bou de chegar** he has just arrived; **~bar fazendo** *or* **por fazer** end up doing

acabrunhado /akabru'ɲadu/ *a* dejected

aca|demia /akade'mia/ *f* academy; (*de ginástica etc*) gym; **~dêmico** *a* & *m* academic

açafrão /asa'frãw/ *m* saffron

acalentar /akalē'tar/ *vt* lull to sleep <*bebê*>; cherish <*esperanças*>; have in mind <*planos*>

acalmar /akaw'mar/ *vt* calm (down) □ *vi* <*vento*> drop; <*mar*> grow calm; **~-se** *vpr* calm down

acam|pamento /akãpa'mētu/ *m* camp; (*ato*) camping; **~par** *vi* camp

aca|nhado /aka'ɲadu/ *a* shy; **~nhamento** *m* shyness; **~nhar-se** *vpr* be shy

ação /a'sãw/ *f* action; (*jurid*) lawsuit; (*com*) share

acariciar /akarisi'ar/ *vt* (*com a mão*) caress, stroke; (*adular*) make a fuss of; cherish <*esperanças*>

acarretar /akaxe'tar/ *vt* bring, cause

acasalar /akaza'lar/ *vt* mate; **~-se** *vpr* mate

acaso /a'kazu/ *m* chance; **ao ~** at random; **por ~** by chance

aca|tamento /akata'mētu/ *m* respect, deference; **~tar** *vt* respect, defer to <*pessoa, opinião*>; obey, abide by <*leis, ordens*>; take in <*criança*>

acc-, acç- (*Port*) *veja* **ac-, aç-**

acautelar-se /akawte'larsi/ *vpr* be cautious

acei|tação /asejta'sãw/ *f* acceptance; **~tar** *vt* accept; **~tável** (*pl* **~táveis**) *a* acceptable

acele|ração /aselera'sãw/ *f* acceleration; **~rador** *m* accelerator; **~rar** *vi* accelerate □ *vt* speed up

acenar /ase'nar/ *vi* signal; (*saudando*) wave; **~ com** promise, offer

acender /asē'der/ *vt* light <*cigarro, fogo, vela*>; switch on <*luz*>; heat up <*debate*>

aceno /a'senu/ *m* signal; (*de saudação*) wave

acen|to /a'sētu/ *m* accent; **~tuar** *vt* accentuate; accent <*letra*>

acepção /asep'sãw/ *f* sense

acepipes /ase'pipʃ/ *m pl* (*Port*) cocktail snacks

acerca /a'serka/ **~ de** *prep* about, concerning

acercar-se /aser'karsi/ *vpr* **~ de** approach

acertar /aser'tar/ *vt* find <(*com o*) caminho, (*a*) casa>; put right, set <*relógio*>; get right <*pergunta*>; guess (correctly) <*solução*>; hit <*alvo*>; make <*acordo, negócio*>; fix, arrange

<*encontro*> ◻ *vi* (*ter razão*) be right; (*atingir o alvo*) hit the mark; **∼ com** find, happen upon; **∼ em** hit

acervo /a'servu/ *m* collection; (*jurid*) estate

aceso /a'sezu/ *pp de* **acender** ◻ *a* <*luz*> on; <*fogo*> alight

aces|sar /ase'sar/ *vt* access; **∼sível** (*pl* **∼síveis**) *a* accessible; affordable <*preço*>; **∼so** /ɛ/ *m* access; (*de raiva, tosse*) fit; (*de febre*) attack; **∼sório** *a* & *m* accessory

acetona /ase'tona/ *f* (*para unhas*) nail varnish remover

achado /a'ʃadu/ *m* find

achaque /a'ʃaki/ *m* ailment

achar /a'ʃar/ *vt* find; (*pensar*) think; **∼-se** *vpr* (*estar*) be; (*considerar-se*) think that one is; **acho que sim/não** I think so/I don't think so

achatar /aʃa'tar/ *vt* flatten; cut <*salário*>

aciden|tado /asidē'tadu/ *a* rough <*terreno*>; bumpy <*estrada*>; eventful <*viagem, vida*>; injured <*pessoa*>; **∼tal** (*pl* **∼tais**) *a* accidental; **∼te** *m* accident

acidez /asi'des/ *f* acidity

ácido /'asidu/ *a* & *m* acid

acima /a'sima/ *adv* above; **∼ de** above; **mais ∼** higher up

acio|nar /asio'nar/ *vt* operate; (*jurid*) sue; **∼nista** *m/f* shareholder

acirrado /asi'xadu/ *a* stiff, tough

acla|mação /aklama'sãw/ *f* acclaim; (*de rei*) acclamation; **∼mar** *vt* acclaim

aclarar /akla'rar/ *vt* clarify, clear up ◻ *vi* clear up; **∼-se** *vpr* become clear

aclimatar /aklima'tar/ *vt* acclimatize, (*Amer*) acclimate; **∼-se** *vpr* get acclimatized, (*Amer*) get acclimated

aço /'asu/ *m* steel; **∼ inoxidável** stainless steel

acocorar-se /akoko'rarsi/ *vpr* squat (down)

acolá /ako'la/ *adv* over there

acolcho|ado /akowʃo'adu/ *m* quilt; **∼ar** *vt* quilt; upholster <*móveis*>

aco|lhedor /akoʎe'dor/ *a* welcoming; **∼lher** *vt* welcome <*hóspede*>; take in <*criança, refugiado*>; accept <*decisão, convite*>; respond to <*pedido*>; **∼lhida** *f*, **∼lhimento** *m* welcome; (*abrigo*) refuge

acomodar /akomo'dar/ *vt* accommodate; (*ordenar*) arrange; (*tornar cômodo*) make comfortable; **∼-se** *vpr* make o.s. comfortable

acompa|nhamento /akõpaɲa-'mẽtu/ *m* (*mus*) accompaniment; (*prato*) side dish; (*comitiva*) escort; **∼nhante** *m/f*

companion; (*mus*) accompanist; **∼nhar** *vt* accompany, go with; watch <*jogo, progresso*>; keep up with <*eventos, caso*>; keep up with, follow <*aula, conversa*>; share <*política, opinião*>; (*mus*) accompany; **a estrada ∼nha o rio** the road runs alongside the river

aconche|gante /akõʃe'gãtʃi/ *a* cosy, (*Amer*) cozy; **∼gar** *vt* (*chegar a si*) cuddle; (*agasalhar*) wrap up; (*na cama*) tuck up; (*tornar cômodo*) make comfortable; **∼gar-se** *vpr* ensconce o.s.; **∼gar-se com** snuggle up to; **∼go** /e/ *m* cosiness, (*Amer*) coziness; (*abraço*) cuddle

acondicionar /akõdʒisio'nar/ *vt* condition; pack, package <*mercadoria*>

aconse|lhar /akõse'ʎar/ *vt* advise; **∼lhar-se** *vpr* consult; **∼lhar alg a** advise s.o. to; **∼lhar aco a alg** recommend sth to s.o.; **∼lhável** (*pl* **∼lháveis**) *a* advisable

aconte|cer /akõte'ser/ *vi* happen; **∼cimento** *m* event

acordar /akor'dar/ *vt/i* wake up

acorde /a'kɔrdʒi/ *m* chord

acordeão /akordʒi'ãw/ *m* accordion

acordo /a'kordu/ *m* agreement; **de ∼ com** in agreement with <*pessoa*>; in accordance with <*lei etc*>; **estar de ∼** agree

Açores /a'soris/ *m pl* Azores

açoriano /asori'ano/ *a* & *m* Azorean

acorrentar /akoxē'tar/ *vt* chain (up)

acossar /ako'sar/ *vt* hound, badger

acos|tamento /akosta'mẽtu/ *m* hard shoulder, (*Amer*) berm; **∼tar-se** *vpr* lean back

acostu|mado /akostu'madu/ *a* usual, customary; **estar ∼mado a** be used to; **∼mar** *vt* accustom; **∼mar-se a** get used to

acotovelar /akotove'lar/ *vt* (*empurrar*) jostle; (*para avisar*) nudge

açou|gue /a'sogi/ *m* butcher's (shop); **∼gueiro** *m* butcher

acovardar /akovar'dar/ *vt* cow, intimidate

acre /'akri/ *a* <*gosto*> bitter; <*aroma*> acrid, pungent; <*tom*> harsh

acredi|tar /akredʒi'tar/ *vt* believe; accredit <*representante*>; **∼tar em** believe <*pessoa, história*>; believe in <*Deus, fantasmas*>; (*ter confiança*) have faith in; **∼tável** (*pl* **∼táveis**) *a* believable

acre-doce /akri'dosi/ *a* sweet and sour

acrescentar /akresē'tar/ *vt* add

acres|cer /akre'ser/ *vt* (*juntar*) add; (*aumentar*) increase ◻ *vi* increase;

∼**cido de** with the addition of; ∼**ce que** add to that the fact that

acréscimo /a'krɛsimu/ *m* addition; (*aumento*) increase

acriançado /akriã'sadu/ *a* childish

acrílico /a'kriliku/ *a* acrylic

acroba|cia /akroba'sia/ *f* acrobatics; ∼**ta** *m/f* acrobat

act- (*Port*) *veja* **at-**

acuar /aku'ar/ *vt* corner

açúcar /a'sukar/ *m* sugar

açuca|rar /asuka'rar/ *vt* sweeten; sugar <*café, chá*>; ∼**reiro** *m* sugar bowl

açude /a'sudʒi/ *m* dam

acudir /aku'dʒir/ *vt/i* ∼ **(a)** come to the rescue (of)

acumular /akumu'lar/ *vt* accumulate; combine <*cargos*>

acupuntura /akupũ'tura/ *f* acupuncture

acu|sação /akuza'sãw/ *f* accusation; ∼**sar** *vt* accuse; (*jurid*) charge; (*revelar*) reveal, show up; acknowledge <*recebimento*>

acústi|ca /a'kustʃika/ *f* acoustics; ∼**co** *a* acoustic

adap|tação /adapta'sãw/ *f* adaptation; ∼**tado** *a* <*criança*> well-adjusted; ∼**tar** *vt* adapt; (*para encaixar*) tailor; ∼**tar-se** *vpr* adapt; ∼**tável** (*pl* ∼**táveis**) *a* adaptable

adega /a'dɛga/ *f* wine cellar

adentro /a'dẽtru/ *adv* inside; **selva** ∼ into the jungle

adepto /a'dɛptu/ *m* follower; (*Port: de equipa*) supporter

ade|quado /ade'kwadu/ *a* appropriate, suitable; ∼**quar** *vt* adapt, tailor

adereços /ade'resus/ *m pl* props

ade|rente /ade'rẽtʃi/ *m/f* follower; ∼**rir** *vi* (*colar*) stick; join <*a partido, causa*>; follow <*a moda*>; ∼**são** *f* adhesion; (*apoio*) support; ∼**sivo** *a* sticky, adhesive □ *m* sticker

ades|trado /ades'tradu/ *a* skilled; ∼**trador** *m* trainer; ∼**trar** *vt* train; break in <*cavalo*>

adeus /a'dews/ *int* goodbye □ *m* goodbye, farewell

adian|tado /adʒiã'tadu/ *a* advanced; <*relógio*> fast; **chegar** ∼**tado** be early; ∼**tamento** *m* progress; (*pagamento*) advance; ∼**tar** *vt* advance <*dinheiro*>; put forward <*relógio*>; bring forward <*data, reunião*>; get ahead with <*trabalho*> □ *vi* <*relógio*> gain; (*ter efeito*) be of use; ∼**tar-se** *vpr* progress, get ahead; **não** ∼**ta (fazer)** it's no use (doing); ∼**te** *adv* ahead

adia|r /adʒi'ar/ *vt* postpone; adjourn <*sessão*>; ∼**mento** *m* postponement, adjournment

adi|ção /adʒi'sãw/ *f* addition; ∼**cionar** *vt* add; ∼**do** *m* attaché

adivi|nhação /adʒiviɲa'sãw/ *f* guesswork; (*por adivinho*) fortune-telling; ∼**nhar** *vt* guess; tell <*futuro, sorte*>; read <*pensamento*>; ∼**nho** *m* fortune-teller

adjetivo /adʒe'tʃivu/ *m* adjective

adminis|tração /adʒiministra-'sãw/ *f* administration; (*de empresas*) management; ∼**trador** *m* administrator; manager; ∼**trar** *vt* administer; manage <*empresa*>

admi|ração /adʒimira'sãw/ *f* admiration; (*assombro*) wonder(ment); ∼**rado** *a* admired; (*surpreso*) amazed, surprised; ∼**rador** *m* admirer □ *a* admiring; ∼**rar** *vt* admire; (*assombrar*) amaze; ∼**rar-se** *vpr* be amazed; ∼**rável** (*pl* ∼**ráveis**) *a* admirable; (*assombroso*) amazing

admis|são /adʒimi'sãw/ *f* admission; (*de escola*) intake; ∼**sível** (*pl* ∼**síveis**) *a* admissible

admitir /adʒimi'tʃir/ *vt* admit; (*permitir*) permit, allow; (*contratar*) take on

adoção /ado'sãw/ *f* adoption

ado|çar /ado'sar/ *vt* sweeten; ∼**cicado** *a* slightly sweet

adoecer /adoe'ser/ *vi* fall ill □ *vt* make ill

adoles|cência /adole'sẽsia/ *f* adolescence; ∼**cente** *a & m* adolescent

adopt- (*Port*) *veja* **adot-**

adorar /ado'rar/ *vt* (*amar*) adore; worship <*deus*>; (*fam: gostar de*) love

adorme|cer /adorme'ser/ *vi* fall asleep; <*perna*> go to sleep, go numb; ∼**cido** *a* sleeping; <*perna*> numb

ador|nar /ador'nar/ *vt* adorn; ∼**no** /o/ *m* adornment

ado|tar /ado'tar/ *vt* adopt; ∼**tivo** *a* adopted

adquirir /adʒiki'rir/ *vt* acquire

adu|bar /adu'bar/ *vt* fertilize; ∼**bo** *m* fertilizer

adu|lação /adula'sãw/ *f* flattery; (*do público*) adulation; ∼**lar** *vt* make a fuss of; (*com palavras*) flatter

adulterar /aduwte'rar/ *vt* adulterate; cook, doctor <*contas*> □ *vi* commit adultery

adúltero /a'duwteru/ *m* adulterer (*f*-ess) □ *a* adulterous

adul|tério /aduw'tɛriu/ *m* adultery; ∼**to** *a & m* adult

advento /adʒi'vẽtu/ *m* advent

advérbio /adʒi'vɛrbiu/ *m* adverb

adver|sário /adʒiver'sariu/ *m* opponent; (*inimigo*) adversary; **~sidade** *f* adversity; **~so** *a* adverse; (*adversário*) opposed

adver|tência /adʒiver'tẽsia/ *f* warning; **~tir** *vt* warn

advo|cacia /adʒivoka'sia/ *f* legal practice; **~gado** *m* lawyer; **~gar** *vt* advocate; (*jurid*) plead □ *vi* practise law

aéreo /a'ɛriu/ *a* air

aero|dinâmica /aerodʒi'namika/ *f* aerodynamics; **~dinâmico** *a* aerodynamic; **~dromo** *m* airfield; **~moça** /o/ *f* air hostess; **~nauta** *m* airman (*f*-woman); **~náutica** *f* (*força*) air force; (*ciência*) aeronautics; **~nave** *f* aircraft; **~porto** /o/ *m* airport

aeros|sol /aero'sɔw/ (*pl* **~sóis**) *m* aerosol

afabilidade /afabili'dadʒi/ *f* friendliness, kindness

afagar /afa'gar/ *vt* stroke

afamado /afa'madu/ *a* renowned, famed

afas|tado /afas'tadu/ *a* remote; <*parente*> distant; **~tado de** (far) away from; **~tamento** *m* removal; (*distância*) distance; (*de candidato*) rejection; **~tar** *vt* move away; (*tirar*) remove; ward off <*perigo, ameaça*>; put out of one's mind <*idéia*>; **~tar-se** *vpr* move away; (*distanciar-se*) distance o.s.; (*de cargo*) step down

afá|vel /a'favew/ (*pl* **~veis**) *a* friendly, genial

afazeres /afa'zeris/ *m pl* business; **~domésticos** (household) chores

afect- (*Port*) *veja* **afet-**

Afeganistão /afeganis'tãw/ *m* Afghanistan

afe|gão /afe'gãw/ *a & m* (*f* **~gã**) Afghan

afeição /afej'sãw/ *f* affection, fondness

afeiçoado /afejsu'adu/ *a* (*devoto*) devoted; (*amoroso*) fond

afeminado /afemi'nadu/ *a* effeminate

aferir /afe'rir/ *vt* check, inspect <*pesos, medidas*>; (*avaliar*) assess; (*cotejar*) compare

aferrar /afe'xar/ *vt* grasp; **~se a** cling to

afe|tação /afeta'sãw/ *f* affectation; **~tado** *a* affected; **~tar** *vt* affect; **~tivo** *a* (*carinhoso*) affectionate; (*sentimental*) emotional; **~to** /ɛ/ *m* affection; **~tuoso** /o/ *a* affectionate

afi|ado /afi'adu/ *a* sharp; skilled <*pessoa*>; **~ar** *vt* sharpen

aficionado /afisio'nadu/ *m* enthusiast

afilhado /afi'ʎadu/ *m* godson (*f*-daughter)

afili|ação /afilia'sãw/ *f* affiliation; **~ada** *f* affiliate; **~ar** *vt* affiliate

afim /a'fĩ/ *a* related, similar

afinado /afi'nadu/ *a* in tune

afinal /afi'naw/ *adv* **~ (de contas)** (*por fim*) in the end; (*pensando bem*) after all

afinar /afi'nar/ *vt* tune □ *vi* taper

afinco /a'fĩku/ *m* perseverance, determination

afinidade /afini'dadʒi/ *f* affinity

afir|mação /afirma'sãw/ *f* assertion; **~mar** *vt* claim, assert; **~mativo** *a* affirmative

afivelar /afive'lar/ *vt* buckle

afixar /afik'sar/ *vt* stick, post

afli|ção /afli'sãw/ *f* (*física*) affliction; (*cuidado*) anxiety; **~gir** *vt* <*doença*> afflict; (*inquietar*) trouble; **~gir-se** *vpr* worry; **~to a** troubled, worried

afluente /aflu'ẽtʃi/ *m* tributary

afo|bação /afoba'sãw/ *f* fluster, flap; **~bado** *a* in a flap, flustered; **~bar** *vt* fluster; **~bar-se** *vpr* get flustered, get in a flap

afo|gado /afo'gadu/ *a* drowned; **morrer ~gado** drown; **~gador** *m* choke; **~gar** *vt/i* drown; (*auto*) flood; **~gar-se** *vpr* (*matar-se*) drown o.s.

afoito /a'fojtu/ *a* bold, daring

afora /a'fɔra/ *adv* **pelo mundo ~** throughout the world

afortunado /afortu'nadu/ *a* fortunate

afresco /a'fresku/ *m* fresco

África /'afrika/ *f* Africa; **~ do Sul** South Africa

africano /afri'kanu/ *a & m* African

afrodisíaco /afrodʒi'ziaku/ *a & m* aphrodisiac

afron|ta /a'frõta/ *f* affront, insult; **~tar** *vt* affront, insult

afrouxar /afro'ʃar/ *vt/i* loosen; (*de rapidez*) slow down; (*de disciplina*) relax

afta /'afta/ *f* (mouth) ulcer

afugentar /afuʒẽ'tar/ *vt* drive away; rout <*inimigo*>

afundar /afũ'dar/ *vt* sink; **~se** *vpr* sink

agachar /aga'ʃar/ *vi* **~se** *vpr* bend down

agarrar /aga'xar/ *vt* grab, snatch; **~se** *vpr* **~se a** cling to, hold on to

agasa|lhar /agaza'ʎar/ *vt* **~lhar-se** *vpr* wrap up (warmly); **~lho** *m* (*casaco*) coat; (*suéter*) sweater

agência /a'ʒẽsia/ *f* agency; **~ de correio** post office; **~ de viagens** travel agency

agenda /a'ʒẽda/ *f* diary

agente /a'ʒẽtʃi/ *m/f* agent

ágil /'aʒiw/ (*pl* **ágeis**) *a* <*pessoa*> agile; <*serviço*> quick, efficient

agili|dade /aʒili'dadʒi/ *f* agility; (*rapidez*) speed; **~zar** *vt* speed up, streamline

ágio /'aʒiu/ *m* premium

agiota /aʒi'ɔta/ *m/f* loan shark

agir /a'ʒir/ *vi* act

agi|tado /aʒi'tadu/ *a* agitated; <*mar*> rough; **~tar** *vt* wave <*braços*>; wag <*rabo*>; shake <*garrafa*>; (*perturbar*) agitate; **~tar-se** *vpr* get agitated; <*mar*> get rough

aglome|ração /aglomera'sãw/ *f* collection; (*de pessoas*) crowd; **~rar** collect; **~rar-se** *vpr* gather

agonia /ago'nia/ *f* anguish; (*da morte*) death throes

agora /a'gɔra/ *adv* now; (*há pouco*) just now; **~ mesmo** right now; **de ~ em diante** from now on; **até ~** so far, up till now

agosto /a'gostu/ *m* August

agouro /a'goru/ *m* omen

agraciar /agrasi'ar/ *vt* decorate

agra|dar /agra'dar/ *vt* please; (*fazer agrados*) be nice to, fuss over □ *vi* be pleasing, please; (*cair no gosto*) go down well; **~dável** (*pl* **~dáveis**) *a* pleasant

agrade|cer /agrade'ser/ *vt* **~cer aco a alg, ~cer a alg por aco** thank s.o. for sth □ *vi* say thank you; **~cido** *a* grateful; **~cimento** *m* gratitude; *pl* thanks

agrado /a'gradu/ *m* **fazer ~s a** be nice to, make a fuss of

agrafa|r /agra'far/ *vt* (*Port*) staple; **~dor** *m* stapler

agrário /a'grariu/ *a* land, agrarian

agra|vante /agra'vãtʃi/ *a* aggravating □ *f* aggravating circumstance; **~var** *vt* aggravate, make worse; **~var-se** *vpr* get worse

agredir /agre'dʒir/ *vt* attack

agregado /agre'gadu/ *m* (*em casa*) lodger

agres|são /agre'sãw/ *f* aggression; (*ataque*) assault; **~sivo** *a* aggressive; **~sor** *m* aggressor

agreste /a'grestʃi/ *a* rural

agrião /agri'ãw/ *m* watercress

agrícola /a'grikola/ *a* agricultural

agricul|tor /agrikuw'tor/ *m* farmer; **~tura** *f* agriculture, farming

agridoce /agri'dosi/ *a* bittersweet

agropecuá|ria /agropeku'aria/ *f* farming; **~rio** *a* agricultural

agru|pamento /agrupa'mētu/ *m* grouping; **~par** *vt* group; **~par-se** *vpr* group (together)

água /'agwa/ *f* water; **dar ~ na boca** be mouthwatering; **ir por ~ abaixo** go down the drain; **~ benta** holy water; **~ doce** fresh water; **~ mineral** mineral water; **~ salgada** salt water; **~ sanitária** household bleach

aguaceiro /agwa'seru/ *m* downpour

água-de-|coco /agwadʒi'koku/ *f* coconut water; **~-colônia** *f* eau de cologne

aguado /a'gwadu/ *a* watery

aguardar /agwar'dar/ *vt* wait for, await □ *vi* wait

aguardente /agwar'dētʃi/ *f* spirit

aguarrás /agwa'xas/ *m* turpentine

água-viva /agwa'viva/ *f* jellyfish

agu|çado /agu'sadu/ *a* pointed; <*sentidos*> acute; **~çar** *vt* sharpen; **~deza** *f* sharpness; (*mental*) perceptiveness; **~do** *a* sharp; <*som*> shrill; (*fig*) acute

agüentar /agwē'tar/ *vt* stand, put up with; hold <*peso*> □ *vi* <*pessoa*> hold out; <*suporte*> hold

águia /'agia/ *f* eagle

agulha /a'guʎa/ *f* needle

ai /aj/ *m* sigh; (*de dor*) groan □ *int* ah!; (*de dor*) ouch!

aí /a'i/ *adv* there; (*então*) then

aidético /aj'detʃiku/ *a* suffering from Aids □ *m* Aids sufferer

AIDS /'ajdʒis/ *f* Aids

ainda /a'ĩda/ *adv* still; **melhor ~** even better; **não ... ~** not ... yet; **~ assim** even so; **~ bem** just as well; **~ por cima** moreover, in addition; **~ que** even if

aipim /aj'pĩ/ *m* cassava

aipo /'ajpu/ *m* celery

ajeitar /aʒej'tar/ *vt* (*arrumar*) sort out; (*arranjar*) arrange; (*ajustar*) adjust; **~-se** *vpr* adapt; (*dar certo*) turn out right, sort o.s. out

ajoe|lhado /aʒoe'ʎadu/ *a* kneeling (down); **~lhar** *vi*, **~lhar-se** *vpr* kneel (down)

aju|da /a'ʒuda/ *f* help; **~dante** *m/f* helper; **~dar** *vt* help

ajuizado /aʒui'zadu/ *a* sensible

ajus|tar /aʒus'tar/ *vt* adjust; settle <*disputa*>; take in <*roupa*>; **~tar-se** *vpr* conform; **~tável** (*pl* **~táveis**) *a* adjustable; **~te** *m* adjustment; (*acordo*) settlement

ala /'ala/ *f* wing

ala|gação /alaga'sãw/ *f* flooding; **~gadiço** *a* marshy □ *m* marsh; **~gar** *vt* flood

alameda /ala'meda/ *f* avenue

álamo /'alamu/ *m* poplar (tree)

alarde /a'lardʒi/ *m* **fazer ~ de** flaunt; make a big thing of <*notícia*>; **~ar** *vt/i* flaunt

alargar /alar'gar/ *vt* widen; (*fig*) broaden; let out <*roupa*>

alarido /ala'ridu/ *m* outcry

alar|ma /a'larma/ *m* alarm; **∼mante** *a* alarming; **∼mar** *vt* alarm; **∼me** *m* alarm; **∼mista** *a & m* alarmist

alastrar /alas'trar/ *vt* scatter; (*disseminar*) □ *vi* spread

alavanca /ala'vãka/ *f* lever; **∼ de mudanças** gear lever

alban|ês /awba'nes/ *a & m* (*f* **∼esa**) Albanian

Albânia /aw'bania/ *f* Albania

albergue /aw'bɛrgi/ *m* hostel

álbum /'awbũ/ *m* album

alça /'awsa/ *f* handle; (*de roupa*) strap; (*de fusil*) sight

alcachofra /awka'ʃofra/ *f* artichoke

alçada /aw'sada/ *f* competence, power

álcali /'awkali/ *m* alkali

alcan|çar /awkã'sar/ *vt* reach; (*conseguir*) attain; (*compreender*) understand □ *vi* reach; **∼çável** (*pl* **∼çáveis**) *a* reachable; attainable; **∼ce** *m* reach; (*de tiro*) range; (*importância*) consequence; (*compreensão*) understanding

alcaparra /awka'paxa/ *f* caper

alcatra aw'katra/ *f* rump steak

alcatrão /awka'trãw/ *m* tar

álcool /'awkɔw/ *m* alcohol

alcoó|latra /awko'ɔlatra/ *m*/*f* alcoholic; **∼lico** *a & m* alcoholic

alcunha /aw'kuɲa/ *f* nickname

aldeia /aw'deja/ *f* village

aleatório /alia'tɔriu/ *a* random, arbitrary

alecrim /ale'krĩ/ *m* rosemary

ale|gação /alega'sãw/ *f* allegation; **∼gar** *vt* allege

ale|goria /alego'ria/ *f* allegory; **∼górico** *a* allegorical

ale|grar /ale'grar/ *vt* cheer up; brighten up <*casa*>; **∼grar-se** *vpr* cheer up; **∼gre** /ɛ/ *a* cheerful; <*cores*> bright; **∼gria** *f* joy

alei|jado /ale'ʒadu/ *a* crippled □ *m* cripple; **∼jar** *vt* cripple

alei|tamento /alejta'mẽtu/ *m* breast-feeding; **∼tar** *vt* breast-feed

além /a'lẽj/ *adv* beyond; **∼ de** (*ao lado de lá de*) beyond; (*mais de*) over; (*ademais de*) apart from

Alemanha /ale'maɲa/ *f* Germany

alemão /ale'mãw/ (*pl* **∼mães**) *a & m* (*f* **∼mã**) German

alen|tador /alẽta'dor/ *a* encouraging; **∼tar** *vt* encourage; **∼tar-se** *vpr* cheer up; **∼to** *m* courage; (*fôlego*) breath

alergia /aler'ʒia/ *f* allergy

alérgico /a'lɛrʒiku/ *a* allergic (**a** to)

aler|ta /a'lɛrta/ *a & m* alert □ *adv* on the alert; **∼tar** *vt* alert

alfa|bético /awfa'bɛtʃiku/ *a* alphabetical; **∼betização** *f* literacy; **∼betizar** *vt* teach to read and write; **∼beto** *m* alphabet

alface /aw'fasi/ *f* lettuce

alfaiate /awfaj'atʃi/ *m* tailor

al|fândega /aw'fãdʒiga/ *f* customs; **∼fandegário** *a* customs □ *m* customs officer

alfine|tada /awfine'tada/ *f* prick; (*dor*) stabbing pain; (*fig*) dig; **∼te** /e/ *m* pin; **∼te de segurança** safety pin

alforreca /alfo'xeka/ *f* (*Port*) jellyfish

alga /'awga/ *f* seaweed

algarismo /awga'rizmu/ *m* numeral

algazarra /awga'zaxa/ *f* uproar, racket

alge|mar /awʒe'mar/ *vt* handcuff; **∼mas** /e/*f pl* handcuffs

algibeira /alʒi'bejra/ *f* (*Port*) pocket

algo /'awgu/ *pron* something; (*numa pergunta*) anything □ *adv* somewhat

algodão /awgo'dãw/ *m* cotton; **∼(-doce)** candy floss, (*Amer*) cotton candy; **∼ (hidrófilo)** cotton wool, (*Amer*) absorbent cotton

alguém /aw'gẽj/ *pron* somebody, someone; (*numa pergunta*) anybody, anyone

al|gum /aw'gũ/ (*f* **∼guma**) *a* some; (*numa pergunta*) any; (*nenhum*) no, not one □ *pron pl* some; **∼guma coisa** something

algures /aw'guris/ *adv* somewhere

alheio /a'ʎeju/ *a* (*de outra pessoa*) someone else's; (*de outras pessoas*) other people's; **∼ a** foreign to; (*impróprio*) irrelevant to; (*desatento*) unaware of; **∼ de** removed from

alho /'aʎu/ *m* garlic; **∼-poró** *m* leek

ali /a'li/ *adv* (over) there

ali|ado /ali'adu/ *a* allied □ *m* ally; **∼ança** *f* alliance; (*anel*) wedding ring; **∼ar** *vt*, **∼ar-se** *vpr* ally

aliás /a'ljaʃ/ *adv* (*além disso*) what's more, furthermore; (*no entanto*) however; (*diga-se de passagem*) by the way, incidentally; (*senão*) otherwise

álibi /'alibi/ *m* alibi

alicate /ali'katʃi/ *m* pliers; **∼ de unhas** nail clippers

alicerce /ali'sɛrsi/ *m* foundation; (*fig*) basis

alie|nado /alie'nadu/ *a* alienated; (*demente*) insane; **∼nar** *vt* alienate; transfer <*bens*>; **∼nígena** *a & m*/*f* alien

alimen|tação /alimẽta'sãw/ *f* (*ato*) feeding; (*comida*) food; (*tecn*) supply; **∼tar** *a* food; <*hábitos*> eating □ *vt* feed; (*fig*) nurture; **∼tar-se de** live on;

~tício a gêneros ~tícios foodstuffs; ~to m food

ali|nhado /ali'naɖu/ a aligned; <pessoa> smart, (Amer) sharp; ~nhar vt align

alíquota /a'likwota/ f (de imposto) bracket

alisar /ali'zar/ vt smooth (out); straighten <cabelo>

alistar /alis'tar/ vt recruit; ~-se vpr enlist

aliviar /alivi'ar/ vt relieve

alívio /a'liviu/ m relief

alma /'awma/ f soul

almanaque /awma'naki/ m yearbook

almejar /awme'ʒar/ vt long for

almirante /awmi'rãtʃi/ m admiral

almo|çar /awmo'sar/ vi have lunch □ vt have for lunch; ~ço /o/ m lunch

almofada /awmo'fada/ f cushion; (Port: de cama) pillow

almôndega /aw'mõdʒiga/ f meatball

almoxarifado /awmoʃari'fadu/ m storeroom

alô /a'lo/ int hallo

alocar /alo'kar/ vt allocate

alo|jamento /aloʒa'mẽtu/ m accommodation, (Amer) accommodations; (habitação) housing; ~jar vt accommodate; house < sem-teto>; ~jar-se vpr stay

alongar /alõ'gar/ vt lengthen; extend, stretch out <braço>

alpendre /aw'pẽdri/ m shed; (pórtico) porch

Alpes /'awpis/ m pl Alps

alpinis|mo /awpi'nizmu/ m mountaineering; ~ta m/f mountaineer

alqueire /aw'keri/ m = 4.84 hectares, (in São Paulo = 2.42 hectares)

alquimi|a /awki'mia/ f alchemy; ~sta mf alchemist

alta /'awta/ f rise; dar ~ a discharge; ter ~ be discharged

altar /aw'tar/ m altar

alterar /awte'rar/ vt alter; (falsificar) falsify; ~-se vpr change; (zangar-se) get angry

alter|nado /awter'nadu/ a alternate; ~nar vt/i, ~nar-se vpr alternate; ~nativa f alternative; ~nativo a alternative; <corrente> alternating

al|teza /aw'teza/ f highness; ~titude f altitude

alti|vez /awtʃi'ves/ f arrogance; ~vo a arrogant; (elevado) majestic

alto /'awtu/ a high; <pessoa> tall; < barulho> loud □ adv high; <falar> loud(ly); <ler> aloud □ m top; os ~s e baixos the ups and downs □ int halt!; ~-falante m loudspeaker

altura /aw'tura/ f height; (momento) moment; ser à ~ de be up to

aluci|nação /alusina'sãw/ f hallucination; ~nante a mind-boggling, crazy

aludir /alu'dʒir/ vi allude (a to)

alu|gar /alu'gar/ vt rent <casa>; hire, rent <carro>; <locador> let, rent out, hire out; ~guel (Port), ~guer /ɛ/ m rent; (ato) renting

alumiar /alumi'ar/ vt light (up)

alumínio /alu'miniu/ m aluminium, (Amer) aluminum

aluno /a'lunu/ m pupil

alusão /alu'zãw/ f allusion (a to)

alvará /awva'ra/ m permit, licence

alve|jante /awve'ʒãtʃi/ m bleach; ~jar vt bleach; (visar) aim at

alvenaria /awvena'ria/ f masonry

alvo /'awvu/ m target

alvorada /awvo'rada/ f dawn

alvoro|çar /awvoro'sar/ vt stir up, agitate; (entusiasmar) excite; ~ço /o/ m (tumulto) uproar; (entusiasmo) excitement

amabilidade /amabili'dadʒi/ f kindness

amaci|ante /amasi'ãtʃi/ m (de roupa) (fabric) conditioner; ~ar vt soften; run in <carro>

amador /ama'dor/ a & m amateur; ~ismo m amateurism; ~ístico a amateurish

amadurecer /amadure'ser/ vt/i <fruta> ripen; (fig) mature

âmago /'amagu/ m heart, core; (da questão) crux

amaldiçoar /amawdʒiso'ar/ vt curse

amamentar /amamẽ'tar/ vt breast-feed

amanhã /ama'ɲã/ m & adv tomorrow; depois de ~ the day after tomorrow

amanhecer /amaɲe'ser/ vi & m dawn

amansar /amã'sar/ vt tame; (fig) placate < pessoa>

a|mante /a'mãtʃi/ m/f lover; ~mar vt/i love

amarelo /ama'rɛlu/ a & m yellow

amar|go /a'margu/ a bitter; ~gura f bitterness; ~gurar vt embitter; (sofrer) endure

amarrar /ama'xar/ vt tie (up); (naut) moor; ~ a cara frown, scowl

amarrotar /amaxo'tar/ vt crease

amassar /ama'sar/ vt crush, squash; screw up <papel>; crease <roupa>; dent <carro>; knead <pão>; mash <batatas>

amá|vel /a'mavew/ (pl ~veis) a kind

Ama|zonas /ama'zonas/ m Amazon; ~zônia f Amazonia

âmbar /'ābar/ m amber

ambi|ção /ăbi'sãw/ *f* ambition; **∼cionar** *vt* aspire to; **∼cioso** /o/ *a* ambitious

ambien|tal /ăbiẽ'taw/ (*pl* **∼tais**) *a* environmental; **∼tar** *vt* set <*filme, livro*>; set up <*casa*>; **∼tar-se** *vpr* settle in; **∼te** *m* environment; (*atmosfera*) atmosphere

am|bigüidade /ăbigwi'dadʒi/ *f* ambiguity; **∼bíguo** *a* ambiguous

âmbito /'ăbitu/ *m* scope, range

ambos /'ăbus/ *a & pron* both

ambu|lância /ăbu'lăsia/ *f* ambulance; **∼lante** *a* (*que anda*) walking; <*músico*> wandering; <*venda*> mobile; **∼latório** *m* out-patient clinic

amea|ça /ami'asa/ *f* threat; **∼çador** *a* threatening; **∼çar** *vt* threaten

ameba /a'mɛba/ *f* amoeba

amedrontar /amedrõ'tar/ *vt* scare; **∼-se** *vpr* get scared

ameixa /a'meʃa/ *f* plum; (*passa*) prune

amém /a'mẽj/ *int* amen □ *m* agreement; **dizer ∼ a** go along with

amêndoa /a'mẽdoa/ *f* almond

amendoim /amẽdo'ĩ/ *m* peanut

ame|nidade /ameni'dadʒi/ *f* pleasantness; *pl* pleasantries, small talk; **∼nizar** *vt* ease; calm <*ânimos*>; settle <*disputa*>; tone down <*repreensão*>; **∼no** /e/ *a* pleasant; mild <*clima*>

América /a'mɛrika/ *f* America; **∼ do Norte/Sul** North/South America

america|nizar /amerikani'zar/ *vt* Americanize; **∼no** *a & m* American

amestrar /ames'trar/ *vt* train

ametista /ame'tʃista/ *f* amethyst

amianto /ami'ãtu/ *m* asbestos

ami|gar-se /ami'garsi/ *vpr* make friends; **∼gável** (*pl* **∼gáveis**) *a* amicable

amígdala /a'migdala/ *f* tonsil

amigdalite /amigda'litʃi/ *f* tonsillitis

amigo /a'migu/ *a* friendly □ *m* friend; **∼ da onça** false friend

amistoso /amis'tozu/ *a & m* friendly

amiúde /ami'udʒi/ *adv* often

amizade /ami'zadʒi/ *f* friendship

amnésia /ami'nɛzia/ *f* amnesia

amnistia /amnis'tia/ *f* (*Port*) *veja* **anistia**

amo|lação /amola'sãw/ *f* annoyance; **∼lante** *a* annoying; **∼lar** *vt* annoy, bother; sharpen <*faca*>; **∼lar-se** *vpr* get annoyed

amolecer /amole'ser/ *vt/i* soften

amol|gadura /amowga'dura/ *f* dent; **∼gar** *vt* dent

amoníaco /amo'niaku/ *m* ammonia

amontoar /amõto'ar/ *vt* pile up; amass <*riquezas*>; **∼-se** *vpr* pile up

amor /a'mor/ *m* love; **∼ próprio** self-esteem

amora /a'mɔra/ *f* **∼ preta**, (*Port*) **silvestre** blackberry

amordaçar /amorda'sar/ *vt* gag

amoroso /amo'rozu/ *adj* loving

amor-perfeito /amorper'fejtu/ *m* pansy

amorte|cedor /amortese'dor/ *m* shock absorber; **∼cer** *vt* deaden; absorb <*impacto*>; break <*queda*> □ *vi* fade

amostra /a'mɔstra/ *f* sample

ampa|rar /ăpa'rar/ *vt* support; (*fig*) protect; **∼rar-se** *vpr* lean; **∼ro** *m* (*apoio*) support; (*proteção*) protection; (*ajuda*) aid

ampère /ă'pɛri/ *m* amp(ere)

ampli|ação /ăplia'sãw/ *f* (*de foto*) enlargement; (*de casa*) extension; **∼ar** *vt* enlarge <*foto*>; extend <*casa*>; broaden <*conhecimentos*>

amplifi|cador /ăplifika'dor/ *m* amplifier; **∼car** *vt* amplify

amplo /'ăplu/ *a* <*sala*> spacious; <*roupa*> full; <*sentido, conhecimento*> broad

ampola /ă'pola/ *f* ampoule

amputar /ăpu'tar/ *vt* amputate

Amsterdã /amister'dã/, (*Port*) **Amsterdão** /amiʃter'dãw/ *f* Amsterdam

amu|ado /amu'adu/ *a* in a sulk, sulky; **∼ar** *vi* sulk

amuleto /amu'leto/ *m* charm

amuo /a'muu/ *m* sulk

ana|crônico /ana'kroniku/ *a* anachronistic; **∼cronismo** *m* anachronism

anais /a'najs/ *m pl* annals

analfabeto /anawfa'bɛtu/ *a & m* illiterate

analisar /anali'zar/ *vt* analyse

análise /a'nalizi/ *f* analysis

ana|lista /ana'lista/ *m/f* analyst; **∼lítico** *a* analytical

analogia /analo'ʒia/ *f* analogy

análogo /a'nalogu/ *a* analogous

ananás /ana'naʃ/ *m invar* (*Port*) pineapple

anão /a'nãw/ *a & m* (*f* **anã**) dwarf

anarquia /anar'kia/ *f* anarchy; (*fig*) chaos

anárquico /a'narkiku/ *a* anarchic

anarquista /anar'kista/ *m/f* anarchist

ana|tomia /anato'mia/ *f* anatomy; **∼tômico** *a* anatomical

anca /'ăka/ *f* (*de pessoa*) hip; (*de animal*) rump

anchova /ă'ʃova/ *f* anchovy

ancinho /ă'siɲu/ *m* rake

âncora /'ăkora/ *f* anchor

a

anco|radouro /ãkora'doru/ *m* anchorage; ~**rar** *vt/i* anchor

andaime /ã'dajmi/ *m* scaffolding

an|damento /ãda'mẽtu/ *m* (*progresso*) progress; (*rumo*) course; **dar** ~**damento a** set in motion; ~**dar** *m* (*jeito de andar*) gait, walk; (*de prédio*) floor; (*Port: apartamento*) flat, (*Amer*) apartment □ *vi* (*ir a pé*) walk; (*de trem, ônibus*) travel; (*a cavalo, de bicicleta*) ride; (*funcionar, progredir*) go; **ele anda deprimido** he's been depressed lately

Andes /'ãdʒis/ *m pl* Andes

andorinha /ãdo'riɲa/ *f* swallow

anedota /ane'dɛta/ *f* anecdote

anel /a'nɛw/ (*pl* **anéis**) *m* ring; (*no cabelo*) curl; ~ **viário** ringroad

anelado /ane'ladu/ *a* curly

anemia /ane'mia/ *f* anaemia

anêmico /a'nemiku/ *a* anaemic

anes|tesia /aneste'zia/ *f* anaesthesia; (*droga*) anaesthetic; ~**tesiar** *vt* anaesthetize; ~**tésico** *a & m* anaesthetic; ~**tesista** *m/f* anaesthetist

ane|xar /anek'sar/ *vt* annex <*terras*>; (*em carta*) enclose; (*juntar*) attach; ~**xo** /ɛ/ *a* attached; (*em carta*) enclosed □ *m* annexe; (*em carta*) enclosure

anfíbio /ã'fibiu/ *a* amphibious □ *m* amphibian

anfiteatro /ãfitʃi'atru/ *m* amphitheatre; (*no teatro*) dress circle

anfi|trião /ãfitri'ãw/ *m* (*f* ~**triã**) host (*f* -ess)

angariar /ãgari'ar/ *vt* raise <*fundos*>; canvass for <*votos*>; win <*adeptos, simpatia*>

angli|cano /ãgli'kanu/ *a & m* Anglican; ~**cismo** *m* Anglicism

anglo-saxônico /ãglusak'soniku/ *a* Anglo-Saxon

Angola /ã'gɔla/ *f* Angola

angolano /ãgo'lanu/ *a & m* Angolan

angra /'ãgra/ *f* inlet, cove

angular /ãgu'lar/ *a* angular

ângulo /'ãgulu/ *m* angle

angústia /ã'gustʃia/ *f* anguish, anxiety

angustiante /ãgustʃi'ãtʃi/ *a* distressing; <*momento*> anxious

ani|mado /ani'madu/ *a* (*vivo*) lively; (*alegre*) cheerful; (*entusiasmado*) enthusiastic; ~**mador** *a* encouraging □ *m* presenter; ~**mal** (*pl* ~**mais**) *a & m* animal; ~**mar** *vt* encourage; liven up <*festa*>; ~**mar-se** *vpr* cheer up; <*festa*> liven up

ânimo /'animu/ *m* courage, spirit; *pl* tempers

animosidade /animozi'dadʒi/ *f* animosity

aniquilar /aniki'lar/ *vt* destroy; (*prostrar*) shatter

anis /a'nis/ *m* aniseed

anistia /anis'tʃia/ *f* amnesty

aniver|sariante /aniversari'ãtʃi/ *m/f* birthday boy (*f* girl); ~**sário** *m* birthday; (*de casamento etc*) anniversary

anjo /'ãʒu/ *m* angel

ano /'anu/ *m* year; **fazer** ~**s** have a birthday; ~ **bissexto** leap year; ~ **letivo** academic year; ~**-bom** *m* New Year

anoite|cer /anojte'ser/ *m* nightfall □ *vi* ~**ceu** night fell

anomalia /anoma'lia/ *f* anomaly

anonimato /anoni'matu/ *m* anonymity

anônimo /a'nonimu/ *a* anonymous

anor|mal /anor'maw/ (*pl* ~**mais**) *a* abnormal

ano|tação /anota'sãw/ *f* note; ~**tar** *vt* note down, write down

ânsia /'ãsia/ *f* anxiety; (*desejo*) longing; ~**s de vômito** nausea

ansi|ar /ãsi'ar/ *vi* ~ **por** long for; ~**edade** *f* anxiety; (*desejo*) eagerness; ~**oso** /o/ *a* anxious

antártico /ã'tartʃiku/ *a & m* Antarctic

antebraço /ãtʃi'brasu/ *m* forearm

antece|dência /ãtese'dẽsia/ *f* com ~**dência** in advance; ~**dente** *a* preceding; ~**dentes** *m pl* record, past

antecessor /ãtese'sor/ *m* (*f* ~**a**) predecessor

anteci|pação /ãtʃisipa'sãw/ *f* anticipation; **com** ~**pação** in advance; ~**padamente** *adv* in advance; ~**pado** *a* advance; ~**par** *vt* anticipate, forestall; (*adiantar*) bring forward; ~**par-se** *vpr* be previous

antena /ã'tena/ *f* aerial, (*Amer*) antenna; (*de inseto*) feeler

anteontem /ãtʃi'õtẽ/ *adv* the day before yesterday

antepassado /ãtʃipa'sadu/ *m* ancestor

anterior /ãteri'or/ *a* previous; (*dianteiro*) front

antes /'ãtʃis/ *adv* before; (*ao contrário*) rather; ~ **de/que** before

ante-sala /ãtʃi'sala/ *f* ante-room

anti|biótico /ãtʃibi'ɔtʃiku/ *a & m* antibiotic; ~**caspa** *a* anti-dandruff; ~**concepcional** (*pl* ~**concepcionais**) *a & m* contraceptive; ~**congelante** *m* antifreeze; ~**corpo** *m* antibody

antídoto /ã'tʃidotu/ *m* antidote

antiético /ãtʃi'ɛtʃiku/ *a* unethical

antigamente /ãtʃiga'mẽtʃi/ *adv* formerly

anti|go /ãˈtʃigu/ a old; (da antiguidade) ancient; <móveis etc> antique; (anterior) former; **~guidade** f antiquity; (numa firma) seniority; pl (monumentos) antiquities; (móveis etc) antiques

anti-|higiênico /ãtʃiʒiˈeniku/ a unhygienic; **~histamínico** a & m antihistamine; **~horário** a anticlockwise

antilhano /ãtʃiˈʎanu/ a & m West Indian

Antilhas /ãˈtʃiʎas/ f pl West Indies

anti|patia /ãtʃipaˈtʃia/ f dislike; **~pático** a unpleasant, unfriendly

antiquado /ãtʃiˈkwadu/ a antiquated, out-dated

anti-|semitismo /ãtʃisemi-ˈtʃizmu/ m anti-Semitism; **~séptico** a & m antiseptic; **~social** (pl **~sociais**) a antisocial

antítese /ãˈtʃitezi/ f antithesis

antologia /ãtoloˈʒia/ f anthology

antônimo /ãˈtonimu/ m antonym

antro /ˈãtru/ m cavern; (de animal) lair; (de ladrões) den

antro|pófago /ãtroˈpofagu/ a man-eating; **~pologia** f anthropology; **~pólogo** m anthropologist

anu|al /anuˈaw/ (pl **~ais**) a annual, yearly

anu|lação /anulaˈsãw/ f cancellation; **~lar** vt cancel; annul <casamento>; (compensar) cancel out □ m ring finger

anunciar /anũsiˈar/ vt announce; advertise <produto>

anúncio /aˈnũsiu/ m announcement; (propaganda, classificado) advert(isement); (cartaz) notice

ânus /ˈanus/ m invar anus

an|zol /ãˈzɔw/ (pl **~zóis**) m fish-hook

aonde /aˈõdʒi/ adv where

apadrinhar /apadriˈɲar/ vt be godfather to <afilhado>; be best man for <noivo>; (proteger) protect; (patrocinar) support

apa|gado /apaˈgadu/ a <fogo> out; <luz, TV>off; (indistinto) faint; < pessoa> dull; **~gar** vt put out <cigarro, fogo>; blow out <vela>; switch off <luz, TV>; rub out <erro>; clean <quadro-negro>; **~gar-se** vpr <fogo, luz> go out; <lembrança> fade; (desmaiar) pass out; (fam: dormir) nod off

apaixo|nado /apaʃoˈnadu/ a in love (por with); **~nante** a captivating; **~nar-se** vpr fall in love (por with)

apalpar /apawˈpar/ vt touch, feel; <médico> examine

apanhar /apaˈɲar/ vt catch; (do chão) pick up; pick <flores, frutas>; (ir

buscar) pick up; (alcançar) catch up □ vi be beaten

aparafusar /aparafuˈzar/ vt screw

apa|ra-lápis /aparaˈlapiʃ/ m invar (Port) pencil sharpener; **~rar** vt catch <bola>; parry <golpe>; trim <cabelo>; sharpen <lápis>

aparato /apaˈratu/ m pomp, ceremony

apare|cer /apareˈser/ vi appear; **~ça!** do drop in!; **~cimento** m appearance

apare|lhagem /apareˈʎaʒẽ/ f equipment; **~lhar** vt equip; **~lho** /e/ m apparatus; (máquina) machine; (de chá) set, service; (fone) phone

aparência /apaˈrẽsia/ f appearance; **na ~** apparently

aparen|tado /aparẽˈtadu/ a related; **~tar** vt show; (fingir) feign; **~te** a apparent

apar|tamento /apartaˈmẽtu/ m flat, (Amer) apartment; **~tar** vt, **~tar-se** vpr separate; **~te** m aside

apatia /apaˈtʃia/ f apathy

apático /aˈpatʃiku/ a apathetic

apavo|rante /apavoˈrãtʃi/ a terrifying; **~rar** vt terrify; **~rar-se** vpr be terrified

apaziguar /apaziˈgwar/ vt appease

apear-se /apiˈarsi/ vpr (de cavalo) dismount; (de ônibus) alight

ape|gar-se /apeˈgarsi/ vpr become attached (**a** to); **~go** /e/ m attachment

ape|lação /apelaˈsãw/ f appeal; (fig) exhibitionism; **~lar** vi appeal (**de** against); **~lar para** appeal to; (fig) resort to

apeli|dar /apeliˈdar/ vt nickname; **~do** m nickname

apelo /aˈpelu/ m appeal

apenas /aˈpenas/ adv only

apêndice /aˈpẽdʒisi/ m appendix

apendicite /apẽdʒiˈsitʃi/ f appendicitis

aperceber-se /aperseˈbersi/ vpr **~ (de)** notice, realize

aperfeiçoar /aperfejsoˈar/ vt perfect

aperitivo /aperiˈtʃivu/ m aperitif

aper|tado /aperˈtadu/ a tight; (sem dinheiro) hard-up; **~tar** vt (segurar) hold tight; tighten <cinto>; press <botão>; squeeze <esponja>; take in <vestido>; fasten <cinto de segurança>; step up <vigilância>; cut down on <despesas>; break <coração>; (fig) pressurize < pessoa> □ vi <sapato> pinch; <chuva, frio> get worse; <estrada> narrow; **~tar-se** vpr (gastar menos) tighten one's belt; (não o ter dinheiro) feel the pinch; **~tar a mão de alg** shake hands with s.o.; **~to** /e/ m pressure; (de botão) press; (dificuldade)

a

tight spot, jam; **~to de mãos**
handshake

apesar /ape'zar/ **~ de** *prep* in spite of

apeti|te /ape'tʃitʃi/ *m* appetite; **~toso** /o/
a appetizing

apetrechos /ape'treʃus/ *m pl* gear; (*de pesca*) tackle

apimentado /apimẽ'tadu/ *a* spicy, hot

apinhar /api'ɲar/ *vt* crowd, pack; **~-se**
vpr crowd

api|tar /api'tar/ *vi* whistle □ *vt* referee
<*jogo*>; **~to** *m* whistle

aplanar /apla'nar/ *vt* level <*terreno*>;
(*fig*) smooth <*caminho*>; smooth over
< *problema*>

aplau|dir /aplaw'dʒir/ *vt* applaud;
~so(s) *m* (*pl*) applause

apli|cação /aplika'sãw/ *f* application;
(*de dinheiro*) investment; (*de lei*)
enforcement; **~car** *vt* apply; invest
< *dinheiro*>; enforce <*lei*>; **~car-se**
vpr apply (**a** to); (*ao estudo etc*) apply o.s.
(**a** to); **~que** *m* hairpiece

apoderar-se /apode'rarsi/ *vpr* **~ de** take
possession of; <*raiva*> take hold of

apodrecer /apodre'ser/ *vt/i* rot

apoi|ar /apoj'ar/ *vt* lean; (*fig*) support;
(*basear*) base; **~ar-se** *vpr* **~ar-se em**
lean on; (*fig*) be based on, rest on; **~o**
m support

apólice /a'polisi/ *f* policy; (*ação*) bond

apon|tador /apõta'dor/ *m* pencil
sharpener; **~tar** *vt* (*com o dedo*) point
at, point to; point out <*erro, caso
interessante*>; aim <*arma*>; name
<*nomes*>; put forward <*razão*> □ *vi*
<*sol, planta*> come up; (*com o dedo*)
point (**para** to)

apoquentar /apokẽ'tar/ *vt* annoy

aporrinhar /apoxi'ɲar/ *vt* annoy

após /a'pɔs/ *adv* after; **loção ~-barba**
after-shave (lotion)

aposen|tado /apozẽ'tadu/ *a* retired □ *m*
pensioner; **~tadoria** *f* retirement;
(*pensão*) pension; **~tar** *vt*, **~tar-se** *vpr*
retire; **~to** *m* room

após-guerra /apɔz'gɛxa/ *m* post-war
period

apos|ta /a'pɔsta/ *f* bet; **~tar** *vt* bet (**em**
on); (*fig*) have faith (**em** in)

apostila /apos'tʃila/ *f* revision aid, book
of key facts

apóstolo /a'pɔstolu/ *m* apostle

apóstrofo /a'pɔstrofu/ *m* apostrophe

apre|ciação /apresia'sãw/ *f*
appreciation; **~ciar** *vt* appreciate;
think highly of <*pessoa*>; **~ciativo** *a*
appreciative; **~ciável** (*pl* **~ciáveis**) *a*
appreciable; **~ço** /e/ *m* regard

apreen|der /apriẽ'der/ *vt* seize
<*contrabando*>; apprehend

<*criminoso*>; grasp <*sentido*>; **~são** *f*
apprehension; (*de contrabando*)
seizure; **~sivo** *a* apprehensive

apregoar /aprego'ar/ *vt* proclaim; cry
<*mercadoria*>

apren|der /aprẽ'der/ *vt/i* learn; **~diz** *m/f*
(*de ofício*) apprentice; (*de direção*)
learner; **~dizado** *m*, **~dizagem** *f* (*de
ofício*) apprenticeship; (*de profissão*)
training; (*escolar*) learning

apresen|tação /aprezẽta'sãw/ *f*
presentation; (*teatral etc*) performance;
(*de pessoas*) introduction; **~tador** *m*
presenter; **~tar** *vt* present; introduce
<*pessoa*>; **~tar-se** *vpr* (*identificar-se*)
introduce o.s.; <*ocasião, problema*>
present o.s., arise; **~tar-se a** report to
<*polícia etc*>; go in for <*exame*>;
stand for <*eleição*>; **~tável** (*pl*
~táveis) *a* presentable

apres|sado /apre'sadu/ *a* hurried; **~sar**
vt hurry; **~sar-se** *vpr* hurry (up)

aprimorar /aprimo'rar/ *vt* perfect,
refine

aprofundar /aprofũ'dar/ *vt* deepen;
study carefully <*questão*>; **~-se** *vpr*
get deeper; **~-se em** go deeper into

aprontar /aprõ'tar/ *vt* get ready; pick
<*briga*> □ *vi* act up; **~-se** *vpr* get ready

apropriado /apropri'adu/ *a* appropriate,
suitable

apro|vação /aprova'sãw/ *f* approval;
(*num exame*) pass; **~var** *vt* approve of;
approve <*lei*> □ *vi* make the grade; **ser
~vado** (*num exame*) pass

aprovei|tador /aprovejta'dor/ *m*
opportunist; **~tamento** *m* utilization;
~tar *vt* take advantage of; take
<*ocasião*>; (*utilizar*) use □ *vi* make the
most of it; (*Port: adiantar*) be of use;
~tar-se *vpr* take advantage (**de** of);
~te! (*divirta-se*) have a good time!

aproxi|mação /aprosima'sãw/ *f*
(*chegada*) approach; (*estimativa*)
approximation; **~mado** *a* <*valor*>
approximate; **~mar** *vt* move nearer;
(*aliar*) bring together; **~mar-se** *vpr*
approach, get nearer (**de** to)

ap|tidão /aptʃi'dãw/ *f* aptitude,
suitability; **~to** *a* suitable

apunhalar /apuɲa'lar/ *vt* stab

apu|rado /apu'radu/ *a* refined; **~rar** *vt*
(*aprimorar*) refine; (*descobrir*)
ascertain; investigate <*caso*>; collect
<*dinheiro*>; count <*votos*>; **~rar-se**
vpr (*com a roupa*) dress smartly; **~ro** *m*
refinement; (*no vestir*) elegance;
(*dificuldade*) difficulty; *pl* trouble

aquarela /akwa'rɛla/ *f* watercolour

aquariano /akwari'anu/ *a & m*
Aquarian

aquário /a'kwariu/ *m* aquarium;
  Aquário Aquarius
aquartelar /akwarte'lar/ *vt* billet
aquático /a'kwatʃiku/ *a* aquatic, water
aque|cedor /akese'dor/ *m* heater; ∼**cer**
  vt heat □ *vi*, ∼**cer-se** *vpr* heat up;
  ∼**cimento** *m* heating
aqueduto /ake'dutu/ *m* aqueduct
aquele /a'keli/ *a* that; *pl* those □ *pron* that
  one; *pl* those; ∼ **que** the one that
àquele = a² + aquele
aqui /a'ki/ *adv* here
aquilo /a'kilu/ *pron* that
àquilo = a² + aquilo
aquisi|ção /akizi'sãw/ *f* acquisition;
  ∼**tivo** *a* **poder** ∼**tivo** purchasing
  power
ar /ar/ *m* air; (*aspecto*) look, air; (*Port: no
  carro*) choke; **ao** ∼ **livre** in the open
  air; **no** ∼ (*fig*) up in the air; (*TV*) on
  air; ∼ **condicionado** air conditioning
árabe /'arabi/ *a & m* Arab; (*ling*) Arabic
Arábia /a'rabia/ *f* Arabia; ∼ **Saudita**
  Saudi Arabia
arado /a'radu/ *m* plough, (*Amer*) plow
aragem /a'raʒẽ/ *f* breeze
arame /a'rami/ *m* wire; ∼ **farpado**
  barbed wire
aranha /a'raɲa/ *f* spider
arar /a'rar/ *vt* plough, (*Amer*) plow
arara /a'rara/ *f* parrot
arbi|trar /arbi'trar/ *vt/i* referee <*jogo*>;
  arbitrate <*disputa*>; ∼**trário** *a*
  arbitrary
arbítrio /ar'bitriu/ *m* judgement; **livre**
  ∼ free will
árbitro /'arbitru/ *m* arbiter <*da moda
  etc*>; (*jurid*) arbitrator; (*de futebol*)
  referee; (*de tênis*) umpire
arborizado /arbori'zadu/ *a* wooded,
  green; <*rua*> tree-lined
arbusto /ar'bustu/ *m* shrub
ar|ca /'arka/ *f* ∼**ca de Noé** Noah's Ark;
  ∼**cada** *f* (*galeria*) arcade; (*arco*) arch
arcaico /ar'kajku/ *a* archaic
arcar /ar'kar/ *vt* ∼ **com** deal with
arcebispo /arse'bispu/ *m* archbishop
arco /'arku/ *m* (*arquit*) arch; (*arma, mus*)
  bow; (*eletr, mat*) arc; ∼**-da-velha** *m*
  coisa do ∼**-da-velha** amazing thing;
  ∼**-íris** *m invar* rainbow
ar|dente /ar'dẽtʃi/ *a* burning; (*fig*)
  ardent; ∼**der** *vi* burn; <*olhos, ferida*>
  sting
ar|dil /ar'dʒiw/ (*pl* ∼**dis**) *m* trick, ruse
ardor /ar'dor/ *m* heat; (*fig*) ardour; **com**
  ∼ ardently
árduo /'arduu/ *a* strenuous, arduous
área /'aria/ *f* area; (**grande**) ∼ penalty
  area; ∼ (**de serviço**) yard

arear /ari'ar/ *vt* scour <*panela*>
areia /a'reja/ *f* sand
arejar /are'ʒar/ *vt* air □ *vi*, ∼**-se** *vpr* get
  some air; (*descansar*) have a breather
are|na /a'rena/ *f* arena; ∼**noso** /o/ *a*
  sandy
arenque /a'rẽki/ *m* herring
argamassa /arga'masa/ *f* mortar
Argélia /ar'ʒɛlia/ *f* Algeria
argelino /arʒe'linu/ *a & m* Algerian
Argentina /arʒẽ'tʃina/ *f* Argentina
argentino /arʒẽ'tʃinu/ *a & m*
  Argentinian
argila /ar'ʒila/ *f* clay
argola /ar'gɔla/ *f* ring
argumen|tar /argume'tar/ *vt/i* argue;
  ∼**to** *m* argument; (*de filme etc*) subject-
  matter
ariano /ari'anu/ *a & m* (*do signo Aries*)
  Arian
árido /'aridu/ *a* arid; barren <*deserto*>;
  (*fig*) dull, dry
Aries /'aris/ *f* Aries
arisco /a'risku/ *a* timid
aristo|cracia /aristokra'sia/ *f*
  aristocracy; ∼**crata** *m/f* aristocrat;
  ∼**crático** *a* aristocratic
aritmética /aritʃ'mɛtʃika/ *f* arithmetic
arma /'arma/ *f* weapon; *pl* arms; ∼ **de
  fogo** firearm
ar|mação /arma'sãw/ *f* frame; (*de óculos*)
  frames; (*naut*) rigging; ∼**madilha** *f*
  trap; ∼**madura** *f* suit of armour;
  (*armação*) framework; ∼**mar** *vt* (*dar
  armas a*) arm; (*montar*) put up,
  assemble; set up <*máquina*>; set, lay
  <*armadilha*>; fit out <*navio*>; hatch
  <*plano, complô*>; cause <*briga*>;
  ∼**mar-se** *vpr* arm o.s.
armarinho /arma'riɲu/ *m*
  haberdashery, (*Amer*) notions
armário /ar'mariu/ *m* cupboard; (*de
  roupa*) wardrobe
arma|zém /arma'zẽj/ *m* warehouse; (*loja*)
  general store; (*depósito*) storeroom;
  ∼**zenagem** *f*, ∼**zenamento** *m*
  storage; ∼**zenar** *vt* store
Armênia /ar'menia/ *f* Armenia
armênio /ar'meniu/ *a & m* Armenian
aro /'aru/ *m* (*de roda, óculos*) rim; (*de
  porta*) frame
aro|ma /a'roma/ *f* aroma; (*perfume*)
  fragrance; ∼**mático** *a* aromatic;
  fragrant
ar|pão /ar'pãw/ *m* harpoon; ∼**poar** *vt*
  harpoon
arquear /arki'ar/ *vt* arch; ∼**-se** *vpr* bend,
  bow
arque|ologia /arkiolo'ʒia/ *f*
  archaeology; ∼**lógico** *a*
  archaeological; ∼**ólogo** *m* archaeologist

arquétipo /ar'kɛtʃipu/ *m* archetype

arquibancada /arkibã'kada/ *f* terraces, (*Amer*) bleachers

arquipélago /arki'pɛlagu/ *m* archipelago

arquite|tar /arkite'tar/ *vt* think up; ∼**to** /ɛ/ *m* architect; ∼**tônico** *a* architectural; ∼**tura** *f* architecture

arqui|var /arki'var/ *vt* file <*papéis*>; shelve <*plano, processo*>; ∼**vista** *m*/*f* archivist; ∼**vo** *m* file; (*conjunto*) files; (*móvel*) filing cabinet; *pl* (*do Estado etc*) archives

arran|cada /axã'kada/ *f* lurch; (*de atleta, fig*) spurt; ∼**car** *vt* pull out <*botão etc*>; pull up <*erva daninha etc*>; take out <*dente*>; (*das mãos de alg*) wrench, snatch; extract <*confissão, dinheiro*> □ *vi* <*carro*> roar off; <*pessoa*> take off; (*dar solavanco*) lurch forward; ∼**car-se** *vpr* take off; ∼**co** *m* pull, tug; *veja* ∼**cada**

arranha-céu /axaɲa'sɛw/ *m* skyscraper

arra|nhadura /axaɲa'dura/ *f* scratch; ∼**nhão** *m* scratch; ∼**nhar** *vt* scratch; have a smattering of <*língua*>

arran|jar /axã'ʒar/ *vt* arrange; (*achar*) get, find; (*resolver*) settle, sort out; ∼**jar-se** *vpr* manage; ∼**jo** *m* arrangement

arrasar /axa'zar/ *vt* devastate; raze, flatten <*casa, cidade*>; ∼**se** *vpr* be devastated

arrastar /axas'tar/ *vt* drag; <*corrente, avalancha*> sweep away; (*atrair*) draw □ *vi* trail; ∼**se** *vpr* crawl; <*tempo*> drag; <*processo*> drag out

arreba|tador /axebata'dor/ *a* entrancing; shocking <*notícia*>; ∼**tar** *vt* (*enlevar*) entrance, send; (*chocar*) shock

arreben|tação /axebẽta'sãw/ *f* surf; ∼**tar** *vi* <*bomba*> explode; <*corda*> snap, break; <*balão, pessoa*> burst; <*onda*> break; <*guerra, incêndio*> break out □ *vt* snap, break <*corda*>; burst <*balão*>; break down <*porta*>

arrebitar /axebi'tar/ *vt* turn up <*nariz*>; prick up <*orelhas*>

arreca|dação /axekada'sãw/ *f* (*dinheiro*) tax revenue; ∼**dar** *vt* collect

arredar /axe'dar/ *vt* **não** ∼ **pé** stand one's ground

arredio /axe'dʒiu/ *a* withdrawn

arredondar /axedõ'dar/ *vt* round up <*quantia*>; round off <*ângulo*>

arredores /axe'dɔris/ *m pl* surroundings; (*de cidade*) outskirts

arrefecer /axefe'ser/ *vt*/*i* cool

arregaçar /axega'sar/ *vt* roll up

arrega|lado /axega'ladu/ *a* <*olhos*> wide; ∼**lar** *vt* ∼**lar os olhos** be wide-eyed with amazement

arreganhar /axega'ɲar/ *vt* bare <*dentes*>; ∼**se** *vpr* grin

arrema|tar /axema'tar/ *vt* finish off; (*no tricô*) cast off; ∼**te** *m* conclusion; (*na costura*) finishing off; (*no futebol*) finishing

arremes|sar /axeme'sar/ *vt* hurl; ∼**so** /e/ *m* throw

arrepen|der-se /axepẽ'dersi/ *vpr* be sorry; <*pecador*> repent; ∼**der-se de** regret; <*pecador*> repentant; ∼**dido** *a* sorry; <*pecador*> repentant; ∼**dimento** *m* regret; (*de pecado, crime*) repentance

arrepi|ado /axepi'adu/ *a* <*cabelo*> standing on end; <*pele, pessoa*> covered in goose pimples; ∼**ar** *vt* (*dar calafrios*) make shudder; make stand on end <*cabelo*>; **me** ∼**a (a pele)** it gives me goose pimples; ∼**ar-se** *vpr* (*estremecer*) shudder; <*cabelo*> stand on end; (*na pele*) get goose pimples; ∼**o** *m* shudder; **me dá** ∼**os** it makes me shudder

arris|cado /axis'kadu/ *a* risky; ∼**car** *vt* risk; ∼**car-se** *vpr* take a risk, risk it

arroba /a'xoba/ *m* (*comput*) @, at sign

arro|char /axo'ʃar/ *vt* tighten up □ *vi* be tough; ∼**cho** /o/ *m* squeeze

arro|gância /axo'gãsia/ *f* arrogance; ∼**gante** *a* arrogant

arro|jado /axo'ʒadu/ *a* bold; ∼**jar** *vt* throw

arrombar /axõ'bar/ *vt* break down <*porta*>; break into <*casa*>; crack <*cofre*>

arro|tar /axo'tar/ *vi* burp, belch; ∼**to** /o/ *m* burp

arroz /a'xoz/ *m* rice; ∼ **doce** rice pudding; ∼**al** (*pl* ∼**ais**) *m* rice field

arrua|ça /axu'asa/ *f* riot; ∼**ceiro** *m* rioter

arruela /axu'ɛla/ *f* washer

arruinar /axui'nar/ *vt* ruin; ∼**se** *vpr* be ruined

arru|madeira /axuma'dera/ *f* (*de hotel*) chambermaid; ∼**mar** *vt* tidy (up) <*casa*>; sort out <*papéis, vida*>; pack <*mala*>; (*achar*) find, get; make up <*desculpa*>; (*vestir*) dress up; ∼**mar-se** *vpr* (*aprontar-se*) get ready; (*na vida*) sort o.s. out

arse|nal /arse'naw/ (*pl* ∼**nais**) *m* arsenal

arsênio /ar'seniu/ *m* arsenic

arte /'artʃi/ *f* art; **fazer** ∼ <*criança*> get up to mischief; ∼**fato** *m* product, article

arteiro /ar'teru/ *a* mischievous

artéria /ar'tɛria/ f artery

artesa|nal /arteza'naw/ (pl ∼**nais**) a craft; ∼**nato** m craftwork

arte|são /arte'zãw/ (pl ∼**s**) m (f ∼**sã**) artisan, craftsman (f -woman)

ártico /'artʃiku/ a & m arctic

articu|lação /artʃikula'sãw/ f articulation; (anat, tecn) joint; ∼**lar** vt articulate

arti|ficial /artʃifisi'aw/ (pl ∼**ficiais**) a artificial; ∼**fício** m trick

artigo /ar'tʃigu/ m article; (com) item

arti|lharia /artʃiʎa'ria/ f artillery; ∼**lheiro** m (mil) gunner; (no futebol) striker

artimanha /artʃi'maɲa/ f trick; (método) clever way

ar|tista /ar'tʃista/ m/f artist; ∼**tístico** a artistic

artrite /ar'tritʃi/ f arthritis

árvore /'arvori/ f tree

arvoredo /arvo'redu/ m grove

as /as/ artigo & pron veja **a¹**

ás /as/ m ace

às = **a² + as**

asa /'aza/ f wing; (de xícara) handle; ∼**delta** f hang-glider

ascen|dência /asẽ'dẽsia/ f ancestry; (superioridade) ascendancy; ∼**dente** a rising; ∼**der** vi rise; ascend <ao trono>; ∼**são** f rise; (relig) Ascension; **em** ∼**são** rising; (fig) up and coming; ∼**sor** m lift, (Amer) elevator; ∼**sorista** m/f lift operator

asco /'asku/ m revulsion, disgust; **dar** ∼ be revolting

asfalto /as'fawtu/ m asphalt

asfixiar /asfiksi'ar/ vt/i asphyxiate

Asia /'azia/ f Asia

asiático /azi'atʃiku/ a & m Asian

asilo /a'zilu/ m (refúgio) asylum; (de velhos, crianças) home

as|ma /'azma/ f asthma; ∼**mático** a & m asthmatic

asneira /az'nera/ f stupidity; (uma) stupid thing

aspas /'aspas/ f pl inverted commas

aspargo /as'pargu/ m asparagus

aspecto /as'pɛktu/ m appearance, look; (de um problema) aspect

aspereza /aspe'reza/ f roughness; (do clima, de um som) harshness; (fig) rudeness

áspero /'asperu/ a rough; <clima, som> harsh; (fig) rude

aspi|ração /aspira'sãw/ f aspiration; (med) inhalation; ∼**rador** m vacuum cleaner; ∼**rar** vt inhale, breathe in <ar, fumaça>; suck up <líquido>; ∼**rar a** aspire to

aspirina /aspi'rina/ f aspirin

asqueroso /aske'rozu/ a revolting, disgusting

assa|do /a'sadu/ a & m roast; ∼**dura** f (na pele) sore patch

assalariado /asalari'adu/ a salaried ▢ m salaried worker

assal|tante /asaw'tãtʃi/ m robber; (na rua) mugger; (de casa) burglar; ∼**tar** vt rob; burgle, (Amer) burglarize <casa>; ∼**to** m (roubo) robbery; (a uma casa) burglary; (ataque) assault; (no boxe) round

assanhado /asa'ɲadu/ a worked up; <criança> excitable; (erótico) amorous

assar /a'sar/ vt roast

assassi|nar /asasi'nar/ vt murder; (pol) assassinate; ∼**nato** m murder; (pol) assassination; ∼**no** m murderer; (pol) assassin

asseado /asi'adu/ a well-groomed

as|sediar /asedʒi'ar/ vt besiege <cidade>; (fig) pester; ∼**sédio** m siege; (fig) pestering

assegurar /asegu'rar/ vt (tornar seguro) secure; (afirmar) guarantee; ∼ **a alg aco/que** assure s.o. of sth/that; ∼-**se de/que** make sure of/that

assembléia /asẽ'blɛja/ f (pol) assembly; (com) meeting

assemelhar /aseme'ʎar/ vt liken; ∼-**se** vpr be alike; ∼-**se a** resemble, be like

assen|tar /asẽ'tar/ vt (estabelecer) establish, define; settle <povo>; lay <tijolo> ▢ vi <pó> settle; ∼**tar-se** vpr settle down; ∼**tar com** go with; ∼**tar a** <roupa> suit; ∼**to** m seat; (fig) basis; **tomar** ∼**to** take a seat; <pó> settle

assen|tir /asẽ'tʃir/ vi agree; ∼**timento** m agreement

assessor /ase'sor/ m adviser; ∼**ar** vt advise

assexuado /aseksu'adu/ a asexual

assiduidade /asidui'dadʒi/ f (à escola) regular attendance; (diligência) diligence

assíduo /a'siduu/ a (que freqüenta) regular; (diligente) assiduous

assim /a'sĩ/ adv like this, like that; (portanto) therefore; **e** ∼ **por diante** and so on; ∼ **como** as well as; ∼ **que** as soon as

assimétrico /asi'mɛtriku/ a asymmetrical

assimilar /asimi'lar/ vt assimilate; ∼-**se** vpr be assimilated

assinalar /asina'lar/ vt (marcar) mark; (distinguir) distinguish; (apontar) point out

a

assi|nante /asiˈnãtʃi/ m/f subscriber; **~nar** vt/i sign; **~natura** f (nome) signature; (de revista) subscription

assis|tência /asisˈtẽsia/ f assistance; (presença) attendance; (público) audience; **~tente** a assistant □ m/f assistant; **~tente social** social worker; **~tir (a)** vt/i (ver) watch; (presenciar) attend; assist <doente>

assoalho /asoˈaʎu/ m floor

assoar /asoˈar/ vt **~ o nariz**, (Port) **~se** blow one's nose

assobi|ar /asobiˈar/ vt/i whistle; **~o** m whistle

associ|ação /asosiaˈsãw/ f association; **~ado** a & m associate; **~ar** vt associate (a with); **~ar-se** vpr associate; (com) go into partnership (a with)

assolar /asoˈlar/ vt devastate

assom|bração /asõbraˈsãw/ f ghost; **~brar** vt astonish, amaze; **~brar-se** vpr be amazed; **~bro** m amazement, astonishment; (coisa) marvel; **~broso** /o/ a astonishing, amazing

assoprar /asoˈprar/ vi blow □ vt blow; blow out <vela>

assovi- veja **assobi-**

assu|mido /asuˈmidu/ a (confesso) confirmed, self-confessed; **~mir** vt assume, take on; accept, admit <defeito> □ vi take office

assunto /aˈsũtu/ m subject; (negócio) matter

assus|tador /asustaˈdor/ a frightening; **~tar** vt frighten, scare; **~tar-se** vpr get frightened, get scared

asterisco /asteˈrisku/ m asterisk

as|tral /asˈtraw/ (pl **~trais**) m (fam) state of mind; **~tro** m star; **~trologia** f astrology; **~trólogo** m astrologer; **~tronauta** m/f astronaut; **~tronave** f spaceship; **~tronomia** f astronomy; **~tronômico** a astronomical; **~trônomo** m astronomer

as|túcia /asˈtusia/ f cunning; **~tuto** a cunning; <comerciante> astute

ata /ˈata/ f minutes

ataca|dista /atakaˈdʒista/ m/f wholesaler; **~do** m por **~do** wholesale

ata|cante /ataˈkãtʃi/ a attacking □ m/f attacker; **~car** vt attack; tackle <problema>

atadura /ataˈdura/ f bandage

ata|lhar /ataˈʎar/ vi take a shortcut; **~lho** m shortcut

ataque /aˈtaki/ m attack; (de raiva, riso) fit

atar /aˈtar/ vt tie

atarantado /atarãˈtadu/ a flustered, in a flap

atarefado /atareˈfadu/ a busy

atarracado /ataxaˈkadu/ a stocky

atarraxar /ataxaˈʃar/ vt screw

até /aˈtɛ/ prep (up) to, as far as; (tempo) until □ adv even; **~ logo** goodbye; **~ que** until

atéia /aˈtɛja/ a & f veja **ateu**

ateliê /ateliˈe/ m studio

atemorizar /atemoriˈzar/ vt frighten

Atenas /aˈtenas/ f Athens

aten|ção /atẽˈsãw/ f attention; pl (bondade) thoughtfulness; **com ~ção** attentively; **~cioso** a thoughtful, considerate

aten|der /atẽˈder/ **~der (a)** vt/i answer <telefone, porta>; answer to <nome>; serve <freguês>; see <paciente, visitante>; grant, meet <pedido>; heed <conselho>; **~dimento** m service; (de médico etc) consultation

aten|tado /atẽˈtadu/ m murder attempt; (pol) assassination attempt; (ataque) attack (contra on); **~tar** vi **~tar contra** make an attempt on

atento /aˈtẽtu/ a attentive; **~ a** mindful of

aterrador /atexaˈdor/ a terrifying

ater|ragem /ateˈxaʒẽ/ f (Port) landing; **~rar** vi (Port) land

aterris|sagem /atexiˈsaʒẽ/ f landing; **~sar** vi land

ater-se /aˈtersi/ vpr **~ a** keep to, go by

ates|tado /atesˈtadu/ m certificate; **~tar** vt attest (to)

ateu /aˈtew/ a & m (f **atéia**) atheist

atiçar /atʃiˈsar/ vt poke <fogo>; stir up <ódio, discórdia>; arouse <pessoa>

atinar /atʃiˈnar/ vt work out, guess; **~ com** find; **~ em** notice

atingir /atʃĩˈʒir/ vt reach; hit <alvo>; (conseguir) attain; (afetar) affect

atirar /atʃiˈrar/ vt throw □ vi shoot; **~ em** fire at

atitude /atʃiˈtudʒi/ f attitude; **tomar uma ~** take action

ati|va /aˈtʃiva/ f active service; **~var** vt activate; **~vidade** f activity; **~vo** a active □ m (com) assets

Atlântico /atˈlãtʃiku/ m Atlantic

atlas /ˈatlas/ m atlas

at|leta /atˈleta/ m/f athlete; **~lético** a athletic; **~letismo** m athletics

atmosfera /atʃimosˈfɛra/ f atmosphere

ato /ˈatu/ m act; (ação) action; **no ~** on the spot

ato|lar /atoˈlar/ vt bog down; **~lar-se** vpr get bogged down; **~leiro** m bog; (fig) fix, spot of trouble

atômico /aˈtomiku/ a atomic

atomizador /atomizaˈdor/ m atomizer spray

átomo /ˈatomu/ m atom

atônito /a'tonitu/ *a* astonished, stunned

ator /a'tor/ *m* actor

atordoar /atordo'ar/ *vt* <*golpe, notícia*> stun; <*som*> deafen; (*alucinar*) bewilder

atormentar /atormẽ'tar/ *vt* plague, torment

atração /atra'sãw/ *f* attraction

atracar /atra'kar/ *vt/i* (*naut*) moor; ~**-se** *vpr* grapple; (*fam*) neck

atractivo (*Port*) *veja* **atrativo**

atraente /atra'ẽtʃi/ *a* attractive

atraiçoar /atrajso'ar/ *vt* betray

atrair /atra'ir/ *vt* attract

atrapalhar /atrapa'ʎar/ *vt/i* (*confundir*) confuse; (*estorvar*) hinder; (*perturbar*) disturb; ~**-se** *vpr* get mixed up

atrás /a'traʃ/ *adv* behind; (*no fundo*) at the back; ~ **de** behind; (*depois de, no encalço de*) after; **um mês** ~ a month ago; **ficar** ~ be left behind

atra|sado /atra'zadu/ *a* late; <*país, criança*> backward; <*relógio*> slow; <*pagamento*> overdue; <*idéias*> old-fashioned; ~**sar** *vt* delay; put back <*relógio*> □ *vi* be late; <*relógio*> lose; ~**sar-se** *vpr* be late; (*num trabalho*) get behind; (*no pagar*) get into arrears; ~**so** *m* delay; (*de país etc*) backwardness; *pl* (*com*) arrears; **com** ~**so** late

atrativo /atra'tʃivu/ *m* attraction

através /atra'vɛs/ ~ **de** *prep* through; (*de um lado ao outro*) across

atravessado /atrave'sadu/ *a* <*espinha*> stuck; **estar com alg** ~ **na garganta** be fed up with s.o.

atravessar /atrave'sar/ *vt* go through; cross <*rua, rio*>

atre|ver-se /atre'versi/ *vpr* dare; ~**ver-se a** dare to; ~**vido** *a* daring; (*insolente*) impudent; ~**vimento** *m* daring, boldness; (*insolência*) impudence

atribu|ir /atribu'ir/ *vt* attribute (**a** to); confer <*prêmio, poderes*> (**a** on); attach <*importância*> (**a** to); ~**to** *m* attribute

atrito /a'tritu/ *m* friction; (*desavença*) disagreement

atriz /a'tris/ *f* actress

atrocidade /atrosi'dadʒi/ *f* atrocity

atrope|lar /atrope'lar/ *vt* run over, knock down <*pedestre*>; (*empurrar*) jostle; mix up <*palavras*>; ~**lamento** *m* (*de pedestre*) running over; ~**lo** /e/ *m* scramble

atroz /a'tros/ *a* awful, terrible; heinous <*crime*>; cruel <*pessoa*>

atuação /atua'sãw/ *f* (*ação*) action; (*desempenho*) performance

atu|al /atu'aw/ (*pl* ~**ais**) *a* current, present; <*assunto, interesse*> topical; <*pessoa, carro*> up-to-date; ~**alidade** *f* (*presente*) (time); (*de um livro*) topicality; *pl* current affairs; ~**alizado** *a* up-to-date; ~**alizar** *vt* update; ~**alizar-se** *vpr* bring o.s. up to date; ~**almente** *adv* at present, currently

atum /a'tũ/ *m* tuna

aturdir /atur'dʒir/ *vt veja* **atordoar**

audácia /aw'dasia/ *f* boldness; (*insolência*) audacity

audi|ção /awdʒi'sãw/ *f* hearing; (*concerto*) recital; ~**ência** *f* audience; (*jurid*) hearing

audiovisu|al /awdʒiovizu'aw/ (*pl* ~**ais**) *a* audiovisual

auditório /awdʒi'tɔriu/ *m* auditorium; **programa de** ~ variety show

auge /'awʒi/ *m* peak, height

aula /'awla/ *f* class, lesson; **dar** ~ teach

aumen|tar /awmẽ'tar/ *vt* increase; raise <*preço, salário*>; extend <*casa*>; (*com lente*) magnify; (*acrescentar*) add □ *vi* increase; <*preço, salário*> go up; ~**to** *m* increase; (*de salário*) rise, (*Amer*) raise

au|sência /aw'zẽsia/ *f* absence; ~**sente** *a* absent □ *m/f* absentee

aus|pícios /aws'pisius/ *m pl* auspices; ~**picioso** /o/ *a* auspicious

auste|ridade /awsteri'dadʒi/ *f* austerity; ~**ro** /ɛ/ *a* austere

Austrália /aws'tralia/ *f* Australia

australiano /awstrali'anu/ *a & m* Australian

Áustria /'awstria/ *f* Austria

austríaco /aws'triaku/ *a & m* Austrian

autarquia /awtar'kia/ *f* public authority

autêntico /aw'tẽtʃiku/ *a* authentic; genuine <*pessoa*>; true <*fato*>

autobio|grafia /awtobiogra'fia/ *f* autobiography; ~**gráfico** *a* autobiographical

autocarro /awto'kaxu/ *m* (*Port*) bus

autocrata /awto'krata/ *a* autocratic

autodefesa /awtode'feza/ *f* self-defence

autodidata /awtodʒi'data/ *a & m/f* self-taught (person)

autódromo /aw'tɔdromu/ *m* race track

auto-escola /awtois'kɔla/ *f* driving school

auto-estrada /awtois'trada/ *f* motorway, (*Amer*) expressway

autógrafo /aw'tɔgrafu/ *m* autograph

a

b

auto|mação /awtoma'sãw/ f automation; ~mático a automatic; ~matizar vt automate

auto|mobilismo /awtomobi'lizmu/ m motoring; (esporte) motor racing; ~móvel (pl ~móveis) m motor car, (Amer) automobile

au|tonomia /awtono'mia/ f autonomy; ~tônomo a autonomous; <trabalhador> selfemployed

autopeça /awto'pɛsa/ f car spare

autópsia /aw'topsia/ f autopsy

autor /aw'tor/ m (f ~a) author; (de crime) perpetrator; (jurid) plaintiff

auto-retrato /awtoxe'tratu/ m self-portrait

autoria /awto'ria/ f authorship; (de crime) responsibility (de for)

autori|dade /awtori'dadʒi/ f authority; ~zação f authorization; ~zar vt authorize

autuar /awtu'ar/ vt sue

au|xiliar /awsili'ar/ a auxiliary □ m/f assistant □ vt assist; ~xilio m assistance, aid

aval /a'vaw/ (pl avais) m endorsement; (com) guarantee

avali|ação /avalia'sãw/ f (de preço) valuation; (fig) evaluation; ~ar vt value <quadro etc> (em at); assess <danos, riscos>; (fig) evaluate

avan|çar /avã'sar/ vt move forward □ vi move forward; (mil, fig) advance; ~çar a (montar) amount to; ~ço m advance

avar|eza /ava'reza/ f meanness; ~ento a mean

ava|ria /ava'ria/ f damage; (de máquina) breakdown; ~riado a damaged; <máquina> out of order; <carro> broken down; ~riar vt damage □ vi be damaged; <máquina> break down

ave /'avi/ f bird; ~ de rapina bird of prey

aveia /a'veja/ f oats

avelã /ave'lã/ f hazelnut

avenida /ave'nida/ f avenue

aven|tal /avẽ'taw/ (pl ~tais) m apron

aventu|ra /avẽ'tura/ f adventure; (amorosa) fling; ~rar vt venture; ~rar-se vpr venture (a to); ~reiro a adventurous □ m adventurer

averiguar /averi'gwar/ vt check (out)

avermelhado /averme'ʎadu/ a reddish

aver|são /aver'sãw/ f aversion; ~so a averse (a to)

aves|sas /a'vɛsas/ às ~sas the wrong way round; (de cabeça para baixo) upside down; ~so /e/ m ao ~so inside out

avestruz /aves'trus/ m ostrich

avi|ação /avia'sãw/ f aviation; ~ão m (aero)plane, (Amer) (air)plane; ~ão a jato jet

avi|dez /avi'des/ f (cobiça) greediness; ~do a greedy

avi|sar /avi'zar/ vt (informar) tell, let know; (advertir) warn; ~so m notice; (advertência) warning

avistar /avis'tar/ vt catch sight of

avo /'avu/ m um doze ~s one twelfth

avó /a'vɔ/ f grandmother; ~s m pl grandparents

avô /a'vo/ m grandfather

avoado /avo'adu/ a dizzy, scatterbrained

avulso /a'vuwsu/ a loose, odd

avultado /avuw'tadu/ a bulky

axila /ak'sila/ f armpit

azaléia /aza'lɛja/ f azalea

azar /a'zar/ m bad luck; ter ~ be unlucky; ~ado, ~ento a unlucky

aze|dar /aze'dar/ vt sour □ vi go sour; ~do /e/ a sour

azei|te /a'zejtʃi/ m oil; ~tona /o/ f olive

azevinho /aze'viɲu/ m holly

azia /a'zia/ f heartburn

azucrinar /azukri'nar/ vt annoy

azul /a'zuw/ (pl azuis) a blue

azulejo /azu'leʒu/ m (ceramic) tile

azul-marinho /azuwma'riɲu/ a invar navy blue

....

Bb

....

babá /ba'ba/ f nanny; ~ eletrônica baby alarm

ba|bado /ba'badu/ m frill; ~bador m bib; ~bar vt/i, ~bar-se vpr drool (por over); <bebê> dribble; ~beiro (Port) m bib

baby-sitter /bejbi'siter/ (pl ~s) m/f babysitter

bacalhau /baka'ʎaw/ m cod

bacana /ba'kana/ (fam) a great

bacha|rel /baʃa'rɛw/ (pl ~réis) bachelor; ~relado m bachelor's degree; ~relar-se vpr graduate

bacia /ba'sia/ f basin; (da privada) bowl; (anat) pelvis

baço /'basu/ m spleen

bacon /'bejkõ/ m bacon

bactéria /bak'tɛria/ f bacterium; pl bacteria

bada|lado /bada'ladu/ *a* (*fam*) talked about; **~lar** *vt* ring <*sino*> □ *vi* ring; (*fam*) go out and about; **~lativo** (*fam*) *a* fun-loving, gadabout

badejo /ba'deʒu/ *m* sea bass

baderna /ba'dɛrna/ *f* (*tumulto*) commotion; (*desordem*) mess

badulaque /badu'laki/ *m* trinket

bafafá /bafa'fa/ (*fam*) *m* to-do, kerfuffle

ba|fo /'bafu/ *m* bad breath; **~fômetro** *m* Breathalyser; **~forada** *f* puff

bagaço /ba'gasu/ *m* pulp; (*Port: aguardente*) brandy

baga|geiro /baga'ʒeru/ *m* (*de carro*) roofrack; (*Port: homem*) porter; **~gem** *f* luggage; (*cultural etc*) baggage

bagatela /baga'tɛla/ *f* trifle

Bagdá /bagi'da/ *f* Baghdad

bago /'bagu/ *m* berry; (*de chumbo*) pellet

bagulho /ba'guʎu/ *m* piece of junk; *pl* junk; **ele é um ~** he's as ugly as sin

bagun|ça /ba'gũsa/ *f* mess; **~çar** *vt* mess up; **~ceiro** *a* messy

baía /ba'ia/ *f* bay

baiano /ba'janu/ *a* & *m* Bahian

baila /'bajla/ *f* **trazer/vir à ~** bring/come up

bai|lar /baj'lar/ *vt/i* dance; **~larino** *m* ballet dancer; **~le** *m* dance; (*de gala*) ball

bainha /ba'iɲa/ *f* (*de vestido*) hem; (*de arma*) sheath

baioneta /bajo'neta/ *f* bayonet

bairro /'bajxu/ *m* neighbourhood, area

baixa /'baʃa/ *f* drop, fall; (*de guerra*) casualty; (*dispensa*) discharge; **~mar** *f* low tide

baixar /ba'ʃar/ *vt* lower; issue <*ordem*>; pass <*lei*>; (*comput*) download □ *vi* drop, fall; (*fam: pintar*) turn up

baixaria /baʃa'ria/ *f* sordidness; (*uma*) sordid thing

baixela /ba'ʃɛla/ *f* set of cutlery

baixeza /ba'ʃeza/ *f* baseness

baixo /'baʃu/ *a* low; <*pessoa*> short; <*som, voz*> quiet, soft; <*cabeça, olhos*> lowered; (*vil*) sordid □ *adv* low; <*falar*> softly, quietly □ *m* bass; **em ~** underneath; (*em casa*) downstairs; **~ de** under; **para ~** down; (*em casa*) downstairs; **por ~ de** under(neath)

baju|lador /baʒula'dor/ *a* obsequious □ *m* sycophant; **~lar** *vt* fawn on

bala /'bala/ *f* (*de revólver*) bullet; (*doce*) sweet

balada /ba'lada/ *f* ballad

balaio /ba'laju/ *m* linen basket

balan|ça /ba'lãsa/ *f* scales; **Balança** (*signo*) Libra; **~ça de pagamentos** balance of payments; **~çar** *vt/i* (*no ar*) swing; (*numa cadeira etc*) rock; <*carro,*

avião> shake; <*navio*> roll; **~car-se** *vpr* swing; **~cete** /e/ *m* trial balance; **~ço** *m* (*com*) balance sheet; (*brinquedo*) swing; (*movimento no ar*) swinging; (*de carro, avião*) shaking; (*de navio*) rolling; (*de cadeira*) rocking; **fazer um ~ço de** (*fig*) take stock of

balangandã /balãgã'dã/ *m* bauble

balão /ba'lãw/ *m* balloon; **soltar um ~-de-ensaio** (*fig*) put out feelers

balar /ba'lar/ *vi* bleat

balbu|ciar /bawbusi'ar/ *vt/i* babble; **~cio** *m* babble, babbling

balbúrdia /baw'burdʒia/ *f* hubbub

bal|cão /baw'kãw/ *m* (*em loja*) counter; (*de informações, bilhetes*) desk; (*de cozinha*) worktop, (*Amer*) counter; (*no teatro*) circle; **~conista** *m/f* shop assistant

balde /'bawdʒi/ *m* bucket

baldeação /bawdʒia'sãw/ *f* **fazer ~** change (trains)

baldio /baw'dʒiu/ *a* fallow; **terreno ~** (piece of) waste ground

balé /ba'lɛ/ *m* ballet

balear /bali'ar/ *vt* shoot

baleia /ba'leja/ *f* whale

balido /ba'lidu/ *m* bleat, bleating

balísti|ca /ba'listʃika/ *f* ballistics; **~co** *a* ballistic

bali|za /ba'liza/ *f* marker; (*luminosa*) beacon; **~zar** *vt* mark out

balneário /bawni'ariu/ *m* seaside resort

balofo /ba'lofu/ *a* fat, tubby

baloiço, balouço /ba'lojsu, ba'losu/ (*Port*) *m* (*de criança*) swing

balsa /'bawsa/ *f* (*de madeira etc*) raft; (*que vai e vem*) ferry

bálsamo /'bawsamu/ *m* balm

báltico /'bawtʃiku/ *a* & *m* Baltic

baluarte /balu'artʃi/ *m* bulwark

bambo /'bãbu/ *a* loose, slack; <*pernas*> limp; <*mesa*> wobbly

bambo|lê /bãbo'le/ *m* hula hoop; **~lear** *vi* <*pessoa*> sway, totter; <*coisa*> wobble

bambu /bã'bu/ *m* bamboo

ba|nal /ba'naw/ (*pl* **~nais**) *a* banal; **~nalidade** *f* banality

bana|na /ba'nana/ *f* banana □ (*fam*) *m/f* wimp; **~nada** *f* banana fudge; **~neira** *f* banana tree; **plantar ~neira** do a handstand

banca /'bãka/ *f* (*de trabalho*) bench; (*de jornais*) newsstand; **~ examinadora** examining board; **~da** *f* (*pol*) bench

bancar /bã'kar/ *vt* (*custear*) finance; (*fazer papel de*) play; (*fingir*) pretend

bancário /bã'kariu/ *a* bank □ *m* bank employee

b

bancarrota /bãka'xota/ f bankruptcy; **ir à ~** go bankrupt

banco /'bãku/ m (com) bank; (no parque) bench; (na cozinha, num bar) stool; (de bicicleta) saddle; (de carro) seat; **~ de areia** sandbank; **~ de dados** database

banda /'bãda/ f band; (lado) side; **de ~** sideways on; **nestas ~s** in these parts; **~ desenhada** (Port) cartoon; **~ larga** broad band

bandei|ra /bã'dera/ f flag; (divisa) banner; **dar ~ra** (fam) give o.s. away; **~rante** m/f pioneer □ f girl guide; **~rinha** m linesman

bandeja /bã'deʒa/ f tray

bandido /bã'dʒidu/ m bandit

bando /'bãdu/ m (de pessoas) band; (de pássaros) flock

bandolim /bãdo'lĩ/ m mandolin

bangalô /bãga'lo/ m bungalow

Bangcoc /bã'koki/ f Bangkok

bangue-bangue /bãgi'bãgi/ (fam) m western

banguela /bã'gɛla/ a toothless

banha /'baɲa/ f lard

banhar /ba'ɲar/ vt (molhar) bathe; (lavar) bath; **~-se** vpr bathe

banhei|ra /ba'ɲera/ f bath, (Amer) bathtub; **~ro** m bathroom; (Port) lifeguard

banhista /ba'ɲista/ m/f bather

banho /'baɲu/ m bath; (no mar) bathe, dip; **tomar ~** have a bath; (no chuveiro) have a shower; **tomar um ~ de loja/cultura** go on a shopping/cultural spree; **~ de espuma** bubble bath; **~ de sol** sunbathing; **~-maria** (pl **~s-maria**) m bain marie

ba|nimento /bani'mẽtu/ m banishment; **~nir** vt banish

banjo /'bãʒu/ m banjo

banqueiro /bã'keru/ m banker

banqueta /bã'keta/ f foot-stool

banque|te /bã'ketʃi/ m banquet; **~teiro** m caterer

banzé /bã'zɛ/ (fam) m commotion, uproar

bapt- (Port) veja **bat-**

baque /'baki/ m thud, crash; (revés) blow; **~ar** vi topple over □ vt hit hard, knock for six

bar /bar/ m bar

barafunda /bara'fũda/ f jumble; (barulho) racket

bara|lhada /bara'ʎada/ f jumble; **~lho** m pack of cards, (Amer) deck of cards

barão /ba'rãw/ m baron

barata /ba'rata/ f cockroach

bara|tear /barat'ʃi'ar/ vt cheapen; **~teiro** a cheap

baratinar /baratʃi'nar/ vt fluster; (transtornar) rattle, shake up

barato /ba'ratu/ a cheap □ adv cheaply □ (fam) m **um ~** great; **que ~!** that's brilliant!

barba /'barba/ f beard; pl (de gato etc) whiskers; **fazer a ~** shave; **~da** f walkover; (cavalo) favourite; **~do** a bearded

barbante /bar'bãtʃi/ m string

bar|baridade /barbari'dadʒi/ f barbarity; (fam: muito dinheiro) fortune; **~bárie** f, **~barismo** m barbarism

bárbaro /'barbaru/ m barbarian □ a barbaric; (fam: forte, bom) terrific

barbatana /barba'tana/ f fin

bar|beador /barbia'dor/ m shaver; **~bear** vt shave; **~bear-se** vpr shave; **~bearia** f barber's shop; **~beiragem** (fam) f bit of bad driving; **~beiro** m barber; (fam: motorista) bad driver

bar|ca /'barka/ f barge; (balsa) ferry; **~caça** f barge; **~co** m boat; **~co a motor** motorboat; **~co a remo/vela** rowing/sailing boat, (Amer) rowboat/ sailboat

barga|nha /bar'gaɲa/ f bargain; **~nhar** vt/i bargain

barítono /ba'ritonu/ m baritone

barômetro /ba'rometru/ m barometer

baronesa /baro'neza/ f baroness

barra /'baxa/ f bar; (sinal gráfico) slash, stroke; (fam: situação) situation; **segurar a ~** hold out; **forçar a ~** force the issue

barra|ca /ba'xaka/ f (de acampar) tent; (na feira) stall; (casinha) hut; (guarda-sol) sunshade; **~cão** m shed; **~co** m shack, shanty

barragem /ba'xaʒẽ/ f (represa) dam

barra-pesada /baxape'zada/ (fam) a invar <bairro> rough; <pessoa> shady; (difícil) tough

bar|rar /ba'xar/ vt bar; **~reira** f barrier; (em corrida) hurdle; (em futebol) wall

barrento /ba'xẽtu/ a muddy

barricada /baxi'kada/ f barricade

barri|ga /ba'xiga/ f stomach, (Amer) belly; **~ga da perna** calf; **~gudo** a pot-bellied

bar|ril /ba'xiw/ (pl **~ris**) m barrel

barro /'baxu/ m (argila) clay; (lama) mud

barroco /ba'xoku/ a & m baroque

barrote /ba'xotʃi/ m beam, joist

baru|lheira /baru'ʎera/ f racket, din; **~lhento** a noisy; **~lho** m noise

base /'bazi/ f base; (fig: fundamento) basis; **com ~ em** on the basis of; **na ~ de** based on; **~ado** a based; (firme) well-founded □ (*fam*) *m* joint; ∼ar *vt* base; ∼ar-se em be based on

básico /'baziku/ *a* basic

basquete /bas'kɛtʃi/ *m*, **basquetebol** /basketʃi'bɔw/ *m* basketball

bas|ta /'basta/ *m* **dar um** ∼**ta em** call a halt to; ∼**tante** *a* (*muito*) quite a lot of; (*suficiente*) enough □ *adv* (*com adjetivo, advérbio*) quite; (*com verbo*) quite a lot; (*suficientemente*) enough

bastão /bas'tãw/ *m* stick; (*num revezamento, de comando*) baton

bastar /bas'tar/ *vi* be enough

bastidores /bastʃi'doris/ *m pl* (*no teatro*) wings; **nos** ∼ (*fig*) behind the scenes

bata /'bata/ *f* (*de mulher*) smock; (*de médico etc*) overall

bata|lha /ba'taʎa/ *f* battle; ∼**lhador** *a* plucky, feisty □ *m* fighter; ∼**lhão** *m* battalion; ∼**lhar** *vi* battle; (*esforçar-se*) fight hard □ *vt* fight hard to get

batata /ba'tata/ *f* potato; ∼ **doce** sweet potato; ∼ **frita** chips, (*Amer*) French fries; (*salgadinhos*) crisps, (*Amer*) potato chips

bate-boca /batʃi'boka/ *m* row, argument

bate|deira /bate'dera/ *f* whisk; (*de manteiga*) churn; ∼**dor** *m* (*policial etc*) outrider; (*no criquete*) batsman; (*no beisebol*) batter; (*de caça*) beater; ∼**dor de carteiras** pickpocket

batelada /bate'lada/ *f* batch; ∼**s de** heaps of

batente /ba'tẽtʃi/ *m* (*de porta*) doorway; **para o/no** ∼ (*fam: ao trabalho*) to/at work

bate-papo /batʃi'papu/ *m* chat.

bater /ba'ter/ *vt* beat; stamp <*pé*>; slam <*porta*>; strike <*horas*>; take <*foto*>; flap <*asas*>; (*datilografar*) type; (*lavar*) wash; (*usar muito*) wear a lot <*roupa*>; (*fam*) pinch <*carteira*> □ *vi* <*coração*> beat; <*porta*> slam; <*janela*> bang; <*horas*> strike; <*sino*> ring; (*à porta*) knock; (*com o carro*) crash; ∼**-se** *vpr* (*lutar*) fight; ∼ **à máquina** type; **à** *ou* **na porta** knock at the door; ∼ **em** hit; harp on <*assunto*>; <*luz, sol*> shine on; ∼ **com o carro** crash one's car, have a crash; ∼ **com a cabeça** bang one's head; **ele batia os dentes de frio** his teeth were chattering with cold; **ele não bate bem** (*fam*) he's not all there

bate|ria /bate'ria/ *f* (*eletr*) battery; (*mus*) drums; ∼**ria de cozinha** kitchen utensils; ∼**rista** *m/f* drummer

bati|da /ba'tʃida/ *f* beat; (*à porta*) knock; (*no carro*) crash; (*policial*) raid; (*bebida*) cocktail of rum, sugar and fruit juice; ∼**do** *a* beaten; <*roupa*>

well worn; <*assunto*> hackneyed □ *m* ∼**do de leite** (*Port*) milkshake

batina /ba'tʃina/ *f* cassock

ba|tismo /ba'tʃizmu/ *m* baptism; ∼**tizado** *m* christening; ∼**tizar** *vt* baptize; (*pôr nome*) christen

batom /ba'tõ/ *m* lipstick

batu|cada /batu'kada/ *f* samba percussion group; ∼**car** *vt/i* drum in a samba rhythm; ∼**que** *m* samba rhythm

batuta /ba'tuta/ *f* baton; **sob a** ∼ **de** under the direction of

baú /ba'u/ *m* trunk

baunilha /baw'niʎa/ *f* vanilla

bazar /ba'zar/ *m* bazaar; (*loja*) stationery and haberdashery shop

bê-a-bá /bea'ba/ *m* ABC

bea|titude /beatʃi'tudʒi/ *f* (*felicidade*) bliss; (*devoção*) piety, devoutness; ∼**to** *a* (*devoto*) pious, devout; (*feliz*) blissful

bêbado /'bebadu/ *a & m* drunk

bebê /be'be/ *m* baby; ∼ **de proveta** test-tube baby

bebe|deira /bebe'dera/ *f* (*estado*) drunkenness; (*ato*) drinking bout; ∼**dor** *m* drinker; ∼**douro** *m* drinking fountain

beber /be'ber/ *vt/i* drink

bebericar /beberi'kar/ *vt/i* sip

bebida /be'bida/ *f* drink

beca /'bɛka/ *f* gown

beça /'besa/ *f* **à** ∼ (*fam*) (*com substantivo*) loads of; (*com adjetivo*) really; (*com verbo*) a lot

beco /'beku/ *m* alley; ∼ **sem saída** dead end

bedelho /be'deʎu/ *m* **meter o** ∼ (**em**) stick one's oar in(to)

bege /'bɛʒi/ *a invar* beige

bei|cinho /bej'siɲu/ *m* **fazer** ∼**cinho** pout; ∼**ço** *m* lip; ∼**çudo** *a* thick-lipped

beija-flor /bejʒa'flor/ *m* hummingbird

bei|jar /be'ʒar/ *vt* kiss; ∼**jo** *m* kiss; ∼**joca** /ɔ/ *f* peck

bei|ra /'bera/ *f* edge; (*fig: do desastre etc*) verge, brink; **à** ∼**ra de** at the edge of, (*fig*) on the verge of; ∼**rada** *f* edge; ∼**ra-mar** *f* seaside; ∼**rar** *vt* (*ficar*) border (on); (*andar*) skirt; (*fig*) border on, verge on; **ele está** ∼**rando os 30 anos** he's nearing thirty

beisebol /bejzi'bɔw/ *m* baseball

belas-artes /bɛlaʃ'artʃiʃ/ *f pl* fine arts

beldade /bew'dadʒi/ *f*, **beleza** /be'leza/ *f* beauty

belga /'bɛwga/ *a & m* Belgian

Bélgica /'bɛwʒika/ *f* Belgium

beliche /be'liʃi/ *m* bunk

bélico /'bɛliku/ *a* war

belicoso /beli'kozu/ *a* warlike

belis|cão /belis'kãw/ *m* pinch; ~**car** *vt* pinch; nibble <*comida*>

Belize /be'lizi/ *m* Belize

belo /'bɛlu/ *a* beautiful

beltrano /bew'tranu/ *m* such-and-such

bem /bẽj/ *adv* well; (*bastante*) quite; (*muito*) very ◻ *m* good; *pl* goods, property; **está ~** (it's) fine, OK; **fazer ~ a** be good for; **tudo ~?** (*fam*) how's things?; **se ~ que** even though; **~ feito (por você)** (*fam*) it serves you right; **muito ~!** well done!; **de ~ com alg** on good terms with s.o.; **~ como** as well as

bem|-apessoado /bẽjapeso'adu/ *a* nice-looking; ~**-comportado** *a* well-behaved; ~**-disposto** *a* keen, willing; ~**-estar** *m* well-being; ~**-humorado** *a* good-humoured; ~**-intencionado** *a* well-intentioned; ~**-passado** *a* <*carne*> well-done; ~**-sucedido** *a* successful; ~**-vindo** *a* welcome; ~**-visto** *a* well thought of

bênção /'bẽsãw/ (*pl* ~**s**) *f* blessing

bendito /bẽ'dʒitu/ *a* blessed

benefi|cência /benefi'sẽsia/ *f* (*bondade*) goodness, kindness; (*caridade*) charity; ~**cente** *a* <*associação*> charitable; <*concerto, feira*> charity; ~**ciado** *m* beneficiary; ~**ciar** *vt* benefit; ~**ciar-se** *vpr* benefit (**de** from)

benefício /bene'fisiu/ *m* benefit; **em ~ de** in aid of

benéfico /be'nɛfiku/ *a* beneficial (**a** to)

benevolência /benevo'lẽsia/ *f* benevolence

benévolo /be'nɛvolu/ *a* benevolent

benfeitor /bẽfej'tor/ *m* benefactor

bengala /bẽ'gala/ *f* walking stick; (*pão*) French stick

benigno /be'niginu/ *a* benign

ben|to /'bẽtu/ *a* blessed; <*água*> holy; ~**zer** *vt* bless; ~**zer-se** *vpr* cross o.s.

berço /'bersu/ *m* (*de embalar*) cradle; (*caminha*) cot; (*fig*) birthplace; **ter ~** be from a good family

berimbau /berĩ'baw/ *m* Brazilian percussion instrument shaped like a bow

berinjela /berĩ'ʒɛla/ *f* aubergine, (*Amer*) eggplant

Berlim /ber'lĩ/ *f* Berlin

berma /'bɛrma/ (*Port*) *f* hard shoulder, (*Amer*) berm

bermuda /ber'muda/ *f* Bermuda shorts

Berna /'bɛrna/ *f* Berne

ber|rante /be'xãtʃi/ *a* loud, flashy; ~**rar** *vi* <*pessoa*> shout; <*criança*> bawl; <*boi*> bellow; ~**reiro** *m* (*gritaria*) yelling, shouting; (*choro*) crying, bawling; ~**ro** /ɛ/ *m* yell, shout; (*de boi*) bellow; **aos ~ros** shouting

besouro /be'zoru/ *m* beetle

bes|ta /'besta/ *a* (*idiota*) stupid; (*cheio de si*) full of o.s.; (*pedante*) pretentious ◻ *f* (*pessoa*) dimwit, numbskull; **ficar ~ta** (*fam*) be taken aback; ~**teira** *f* stupidity; (*uma*) stupid thing; **falar ~teira** talk rubbish; ~**tial** (*pl* ~**tiais**) *a* bestial; ~**tificar** *vt* astound, dumbfound

besuntar /bezũ'tar/ *vt* coat; (*sujar*) smear

betão /be'tãw/ (*Port*) *m* concrete

beterraba /bete'xaba/ *f* beetroot

betoneira /beto'nera/ *f* cement mixer

bexiga /be'ʃiga/ *f* bladder

bezerro /be'zeru/ *m* calf

bibelô /bibe'lo/ *m* ornament

Bíblia /'biblia/ *f* Bible

bíblico /'bibliku/ *a* biblical

biblio|grafia /bibliogra'fia/ *f* bibliography; ~**teca** /ɛ/ *f* library; ~**tecário** *m* librarian ◻ *a* library

bica /'bika/ *f* tap; (*Port: cafezinho*) espresso; **suar em ~s** drip with sweat

bicama /bi'kama/ *f* truckle bed

bicar /bi'kar/ *vt* peck

bíceps /'bisɛps/ *m invar* biceps

bicha /'biʃa/ *f* (*Port: fila*) queue; (*Bras: fam*) queer, fairy

bicheiro /bi'ʃeru/ *m* organizer of illegal numbers game, racketeer

bicho /'biʃu/ *m* animal; (*inseto*) insect, (*Amer*) bug; **que ~ te mordeu?** what's got into you?; ~**-da-seda** (*pl* ~**s-da-seda**) *m* silkworm; ~**-de-sete-cabeças** (*fam*) *m* big deal, big thing; ~**-do-mato** (*pl* ~**s-do-mato**) *m* very shy person

bicicleta /bisi'klɛta/ *f* bicycle, bike

bico /'biku/ *m* (*de ave*) beak; (*de faca*) point; (*de sapato*) toe; (*de bule*) spout; (*de caneta*) nib; (*do seio*) nipple; (*de gás*) jet; (*fam*) (*emprego*) odd job, sideline; (*boca*) mouth

bidê /bi'de/ *m* bidet

bidimensio|nal /bidʒimẽsio'naw/ (*pl* ~**nais**) *a* two-dimensional

biela /bi'ɛla/ *f* connecting rod

Bielo-Rússia /bielo'xusia/ *f* Byelorussia

bielo-russo /bielo'xusu/ *a & m* Byelorussian

bie|nal /bie'naw/ (*pl* ~**nais**) *a* biennial ◻ *f* biennial art exhibition

bife /'bifi/ *m* steak

bifo|cal /bifo'kaw/ (*pl* ~**cais**) *a* bifocal

bifur|cação /bifurka'sãw/ *f* fork; ~**car-se** *vpr* fork

bigamia /biga'mia/ *f* bigamy

bígamo /'bigamu/ *a* bigamous ◻ *m* bigamist

bigo|de /bi'gɔdʒi/ *m* moustache; ∼**dudo** *a* with a big moustache

bigorna /bi'gɔrna/ *f* anvil

bijuteria /biʒute'ria/ *f* costume jewellery

bilate|ral /bilate'raw/ (*pl* ∼**rais**) *a* bilateral

bilhão /bi'ʎãw/ *m* thousand million, (*Amer*) billion

bilhar /bi'ʎar/ *m* pool, billiards

bilhe|te /bi'ʎetʃi/ *m* ticket; (*recado*) note; ∼**te de ida e volta** return ticket, (*Amer*) round-trip ticket; ∼**te de identidade** (*Port*) identity card; **o** ∼**te azul** (*fam*) the sack; ∼**teria** *f*, (*Port*) ∼**teira** *f* (*no cinema, teatro*) box office; (*na estação*) ticket office

bilíngüe /bi'lĩgwi/ *a* bilingual

bilionário /bilio'nariu/ *a & m* billionaire

bilis /'bilis/ *f* bile

binário /bi'nariu/ *a* binary

bingo /'bĩgu/ *m* bingo

binóculo /bi'nɔkulu/ *m* binoculars

biodegradá|vel /biodegra'davew/ (*pl* ∼**veis**) *a* biodegradable

bio|grafia /biogra'fia/ *f* biography; ∼**gráfico** *a* biographical

biógrafo /bi'ɔgrafu/ *m* biographer

bio|logia /biolo'ʒia/ *f* biology; ∼**lógico** *a* biological

biólogo /bi'ɔlogu/ *m* biologist

biombo /bi'õbu/ *m* screen

biônico /bi'oniku/ *a* bionic; (*pol*) unelected

biópsia /bi'ɔpsia/ *f* biopsy

bioquími|ca /bioki'mika/ *f* biochemistry; ∼**co** *a* biochemical ◻ *m* biochemist

biquíni /bi'kini/ *m* bikini

birma|nês /birma'nes/ *a & m* (*f* ∼**nesa**) Burmese

Birmânia /bir'mania/ *f* Burma

birô /bi'ro/ *m* bureau

bir|ra /'bixa/ *f* wilfulness; **fazer** ∼**ra** have a tantrum; ∼**rento** *a* wilful

biruta /bi'ruta/ (*fam*) *a* crazy ◻ *f* windsock

bis /bis/ *int* encore!, more! ◻ *m invar* encore

bisa|vó /biza'vɔ/ *f* great-grandmother; ∼**vós** *m pl* great-grandparents; ∼**vô** *m* great-grandfather

bisbilho|tar /bizbiʎo'tar/ *vt* pry into ◻ *vi* pry; ∼**teiro** *a* prying ◻ *m* busybody;

bisca|te /bis'katʃi/ *m* odd job; ∼**teiro** *m* odd-job man

biscoito /bis'kojtu/ *m* biscuit, (*Amer*) cookie

bisnaga /biz'naga/ *f* (*pão*) bridge roll; (*tubo*) tube

bisne|ta /biz'nɛta/ *f* great-granddaughter; ∼**to** /ɛ/ *m* great-grandson; *pl* great-grandchildren

bis|pado /bis'padu/ *m* bishopric; ∼**po** *m* bishop

bissexto /bi'sestu/ *a* occasional; **ano** ∼ leap year

bissexu|al /biseksu'aw/ (*pl* ∼**ais**) *a & m/f* bisexual

bisturi /bistu'ri/ *m* scalpel

bito|la /bi'tɔla/ *f* gauge; ∼**lado** *a* narrow-minded

bizarro /bi'zaxu/ *a* bizarre

blablablá /blabla'bla/ (*fam*) *m* chitchat

black /'blɛki/ *m* black market; ∼**-tie** *m* evening dress

blas|femar /blasfe'mar/ *vi* blaspheme; ∼**fêmia** *f* blasphemy; ∼**femo** /e/ *a* blasphemous ◻ *m* blasphemer

blecaute /ble'kawtʃi/ *m* power cut

ble|far /ble'far/ *vi* bluff; ∼**fe** /ɛ/ *m* bluff

blin|dado /blĩ'dadu/ *a* armoured; ∼**dagem** *f* armour-plating

blitz /blits/ *f invar* police spot-check (on vehicles)

blo|co /'blɔku/ *m* block; (*pol*) bloc; (*de papel*) pad; (*no carnaval*) section; ∼**quear** *vt* block; (*mil*) blockade; ∼**queio** *m* blockage; (*psic*) mental block; (*mil*) blockade

blusa /'bluza/ *f* shirt; (*de mulher*) blouse; (*de lã*) sweater

boa /'boa/ *f de bom*; **numa** ∼ (*fam*) well; (*sem problemas*) easily; **estar numa** ∼ (*fam*) be doing fine; ∼**-gente** (*fam*) *a invar* nice; ∼**-pinta** (*pl* ∼**s-pintas**) (*fam*) *a* nice-looking; ∼**-praça** (*pl* ∼**s-praças**) (*fam*) *a* friendly, sociable

boate /bo'atʃi/ *f* nightclub

boato /bo'atu/ *m* rumour

boa|-nova /boa'nɔva/ (*pl* ∼**s-novas**) *f* good news; ∼**-vida** (*pl* ∼**s-vidas**) *m/f* good-for-nothing, waster; ∼**zinha** *a* sweet, kind

bo|bagem /bo'baʒẽ/ *f* silliness; (*uma*) silly thing; (*uma*) ∼ *f* slip-up; ∼**bear** *vi* slip up; ∼**beira** *f veja* **bobagem**

bobe /'bɔbi/ *m* curler, roller

bobina /bo'bina/ *f* reel; (*eletr*) coil

bobo /'bobu/ *a* silly ◻ *m* fool; (*da corte*) jester; ∼**ca** /ɔ/ (*fam*) *a* stupid ◻ *m/f* twit

bo|ca /'boka/ *f* mouth; (*no fogão*) ring; ∼**ca da noite** nightfall; ∼**cado** *m* (*na boca*) mouthful; (*pedaço*) piece, bit; ∼**cal** (*pl* ∼**cais**) *m* mouthpiece

boce|jar /bose'ʒar/ *vi* yawn; ∼**jo** /e/ *m* yawn

b

boche|cha /boˈʃeʃa/ f cheek; **~char** vi rinse one's mouth; **~cho** /e/ m mouthwash; **~chudo** a with puffy cheeks

bodas /ˈbodas/ f pl wedding anniversary; **~ de prata/ouro** silver/golden wedding

bode /ˈbɔdʒi/ m (billy) goat; **~ expiatório** scapegoat

bodega /boˈdɛga/ f (de bebidas) off-licence, (Amer) liquor store; (de secos e molhados) grocer's shop, corner shop

boêmio /boˈemiu/ a & m Bohemian

bofe|tada /bofeˈtada/ f, **bofe|tão** /bofeˈtãw/ m slap; **~tear** vt slap

boi /boj/ m bullock, (Amer) steer

bói /bɔj/ m office boy

bóia /ˈbɔja/ f (de balizamento) buoy; (de cortiça, isopor etc) float; (câmara de borracha) rubber ring; (de braço) armband, water wing; (na caixa-d'água) ballcock; (fam: comida) grub; **~ salva-vidas** lifebelt; **~fria** (pl **~s-frias**) m/f itinerant farm labourer

boiar /boˈjar/ vt/i float; (fam) be lost

boico|tar /bojkoˈtar/ vt boycott; **~te** /ɔ/ m boycott

boiler /ˈbojler/ (pl **~s**) m boiler

boina /ˈbojna/ f beret

bo|jo /ˈbɔʒu/ m bulge; **~judo** a (cheio) bulging; (arredondado) bulbous

bola /ˈbɔla/ f ball; **dar ~ para** (fam) give attention to <pessoa>; care about <coisa>; **~ de gude** marble; **~ de neve** snowball

bolacha /boˈlaʃa/ f (biscoito) biscuit, (Amer) cookie; (descanso) beermat; (fam: tapa) slap

bo|lada /boˈlada/ f large sum of money; **~lar** vt think up, devise

boléia /boˈlɛja/ f cab; (Port: carona) lift

boletim /boleˈtʃĩ/ m bulletin; (escolar) report

bolha /ˈboʎa/ f bubble; (na pele) blister □ (fam) m/f pain

boliche /boˈliʃi/ m skittles

Bolívia /boˈlivia/ f Bolivia

boliviano /boliviˈanu/ a & m Bolivian

bolo /ˈbolu/ m cake

bo|lor /boˈlor/ m mould, mildew; **~lorento** a mouldy

bolota /boˈlɔta/ f (glande) acorn; (bolinha) little ball

bol|sa /ˈbowsa/ f bag; **~sa (de estudo)** scholarship; **~sa (de valores)** stock exchange; **~sista** m/f, (Port) **~seiro** m scholarship student; **~so** /o/ m pocket

bom /bõ/ a (f **boa**) good; (de saúde) well; <comida> nice; **está ~** that's fine

bomba¹ /ˈbõba/ f (explosiva) bomb; (doce) eclair; (fig) bombshell; **levar ~** (fam) fail

bomba² /ˈbõba/ f (de bombear) pump

Bombaim /bõbaˈĩ/ f Bombay

bombar|dear /bõbardʒiˈar/ vt bombard; (do ar) bomb; **~deio** m bombardment; (do ar) bombing

bomba|-relógio /bõbaxeˈlɔʒiu/ (pl **~s-relógio**) f time bomb

bom|bear /bõbiˈar/ vt pump; **~beiro** m fireman; (encanador) plumber

bombom /bõˈbõ/ m chocolate

bombordo /bõˈbordu/ m port

bondade /bõˈdadʒi/ f goodness

bonde /ˈbõdʒi/ m tram; (teleférico) cable car

bondoso /bõˈdozu/ a good(-hearted)

boné /boˈnɛ/ m cap

bone|ca /boˈnɛka/ f doll; **~co** /ɛ/ m dummy

bonificação /bonifikaˈsãw/ f bonus

bonito /boˈnitu/ a <mulher> pretty; <homem> handsome; <tempo, casa etc> lovely

bônus /ˈbonus/ m invar bonus

boqui|aberto /bokiaˈbɛrtu/ a open-mouthed, flabbergasted; **~nha** f snack

borboleta /borboˈleta/ f butterfly; (roleta) turnstile

borbotão /borboˈtãw/ m spurt

borbu|lha /borˈbuʎa/ f bubble; **~lhar** vi bubble

borda /ˈbɔrda/ f edge; **~do** a edged; (à linha) embroidered □ m embroidery

bordão /borˈdãw/ m (frase) catchphrase

bordar /borˈdar/ vt (à linha) embroider

bor|del /borˈdɛw/ (pl **~déis**) m brothel

bordo /ˈbordu/ m **a ~** aboard

borra /ˈboxa/ f dregs; (de café) grounds

borra|cha /boˈxaʃa/ f rubber; **~cheiro** m tyre fitter

bor|rão /boˈxãw/ m (de tinta) blot; (rascunho) rough draft; **~rar** vt (sujar) blot; (riscar) cross out; (pintar) daub

borrasca /boˈxaska/ f squall

borri|far /boxiˈfar/ vt sprinkle; **~fo** m sprinkling

bosque /ˈbɔski/ m wood

bosta /ˈbɔsta/ f (de animal) dung; (chulo) crap

bota /ˈbɔta/ f boot

botâni|ca /boˈtanika/ f botany; **~co** a botanical □ m botanist

bo|tão /boˈtãw/ m button; (de flor) bud; **falar com os seus ~tões** say to o.s.

botar /bo'tar/ *vt* put; put on <*roupa*>; set <*mesa, despertador*>; lay <*ovo*>; find <*defeito*>

bote¹ /'bɔtʃi/ *m* (*barco*) dinghy; ~ **salva-vidas** lifeboat; (*de borracha*) liferaft

bote² /'bɔtʃi/ *m* (*de animal etc*) lunge

botequim /butʃi'kĩ/ *m* bar

botoeira /boto'era/ *f* buttonhole

boxe /'bɔksi/ *m* boxing; ~**ador** *m* boxer

brabo /'brabu/ *a* <*animal*> ferocious; <*calor, sol*> fierce; <*doença*> bad; <*prova, experiência*> tough; (*zangado*) angry

bra|cada /bra'sada/ *f* armful; (*em natação*) stroke; ~**cadeira** (*faixa*) armband; (*ferragem*) bracket; (*de atleta*) sweatband; ~**çal** (*pl* ~**çais**) *a* manual; ~**celete** *m* bracelet; ~**ço** *m* arm; ~**ço direito** (*fig: pessoa*) right-hand man

bra|dar /bra'dar/ *vt/i* shout; ~**do** *m* shout

braguilha /bra'giʎa/ *f* fly, flies

braile /'brajli/ *m* Braille

bra|mido /bra'midu/ *m* roar; ~**mir** *vi* roar

branco /'brãku/ *a* white ☐ *m* (*homem*) white man; (*espaço*) blank; **em** ~ <*cheque etc*> blank; **noite em** ~ sleepless night

bran|do /'brãdu/ *a* gentle; <*doença*> mild; (*indulgente*) lenient, soft; ~**dura** *f* gentleness; (*indulgência*) softness, leniency

brasa /'braza/ *f* **em** ~ red-hot; **mandar** ~ (*fam*) go to town

brasão /bra'zãw/ *m* coat of arms

braseiro /bra'zeru/ *m* brasier

Brasil /bra'ziw/ *m* Brazil

brasi|leiro /brazi'leru/ *a & m* Brazilian; ~**liense** *a & m/f* (*person*) from Brasília

bra|vata /bra'vata/ *f* bravado; ~**vio** *a* wild; <*mar*> rough; ~**vo** *a* (*corajoso*) brave; (*zangado*) angry; <*mar*> rough; ~**vura** *f* bravery

breca /'brɛka/ *f* **levado da** ~ very naughty

brecar /bre'kar/ *vt* stop <*carro*>; (*fig*) curb ☐ *vi* brake

brecha /'brɛʃa/ *f* gap; (*na lei*) loophole

bre|ga /'brɛga/ (*fam*) *a* tacky, naff; ~**guice** (*fam*) *f* tack, tackiness

brejo /'brɛʒu/ *m* marsh; **ir para o** ~ (*fig*) go down the drain

brenha /'brɛɲa/ *f* thicket

breque /'brɛki/ *m* brake

breu /brew/ *m* tar, pitch

bre|ve /'brɛvi/ *a* short, brief; **em** ~**ve** soon, shortly; ~**vidade** *f* shortness, brevity

briga /'briga/ *f* fight; (*bate-boca*) argument

briga|da /bri'gada/ *f* brigade; ~**deiro** *m* brigadier; (*doce*) chocolate truffle

bri|gão /bri'gãw/ *a* (*f* ~**gona**) belligerent; (*na fala*) argumentative ☐ *m* (*f* ~**gona**) troublemaker; ~**gar** *vi* fight; (*com palavras*) argue; <*cores*> clash

bri|lhante /bri'ʎãtʃi/ *a* (*reluzente*) shiny; (*fig*) brilliant; ~**lhar** *vi* shine; ~**lho** *m* (*de sapatos etc*) shine; (*dos olhos, de metais*) gleam; (*das estrelas*) brightness; (*de uma cor*) brilliance; (*fig: esplendor*) splendour

brin|cadeira /brĩka'dera/ *f* (*piada*) joke; (*brinquedo, jogo*) game; **de** ~**cadeira** for fun; ~**calhão** (*f* ~**calhona**) *a* playful ☐ *m* joker; ~**car** *vi* (*divertir-se*) play; (*gracejar*) joke

brinco /'brĩku/ *m* earring

brin|dar /brĩ'dar/ *vt* (*saudar*) toast, drink to; (*presentear*) give a gift to; ~**dar alg com aco** afford s.o. sth; (*de presente*) give s.o. sth as a gift; ~**de** *m* (*saudação*) toast; (*presente*) free gift

brinquedo /brĩ'kedu/ *m* toy

brio /'briu/ *m* self-esteem, character; ~**so** /o/ *a* self-confident

brisa /'briza/ *f* breeze

britadeira /brita'dera/ *f* pneumatic drill

britânico /bri'taniku/ *a* British ☐ *m* Briton; **os** ~**s** the British

broca /'brɔka/ *f* drill

broche /'brɔʃi/ *m* brooch

brochura /bro'ʃura/ *f* **livro de** ~ paperback

brócolis /'brɔkulis/ *m pl*, (*Port*) **brócolos** /'brɔkuluʃ/ *m pl* broccoli

bron|ca /'brɔka/ (*fam*) *f* telling-off; **dar uma** ~**ca em alg** tell s.o. off; ~**co** *a* coarse, rough

bronquite /brõ'kitʃi/ *f* bronchitis

bronze /'brõzi/ *m* bronze; ~**ado** *a* tanned, brown ☐ *m* (*sun*)tan; ~**ador** *a* tanning ☐ *m* suntan lotion; ~**amento** *m* tanning; ~**ar** *vt* tan; ~**ar-se** *vpr* go brown, tan

bro|tar /bro'tar/ *vt* sprout <*folhas, flores*>; spout <*lágrimas, palavras*> ☐ *vi* <*planta*> sprout; <*água*> spout; <*idéias*> pop up; ~**tinho** (*fam*) *m* youngster; ~**to** /o/ *m* shoot; (*fam*) youngster

broxa /'brɔʃa/ *f* (large) paint brush ☐ (*fam*) *a* impotent

bruços /'brusus/ **de** ~ face down

bru|ma /'bruma/ f mist; **~moso** /o/ a misty

brusco /'brusku/ a brusque, abrupt

bru|tal /bru'taw/ (pl **~tais**) a brutal; **~talidade** f brutality; **~to** a <feições> coarse; <homem> brutish; <tom, comentário> aggressive; <petróleo> crude; <peso, lucro, salário> gross □ m brute

bruxa /'bruʃa/ f witch; (feia) hag; **~ria** f witchcraft

Bruxelas /bru'ʃɛlas/ f Brussels

bruxo /'bruʃu/ m wizard

bruxulear /bruʃuli'ar/ vi flicker

bucha /'buʃa/ f (tampão) bung; (para paredes) rawlplug (R); **acertar na ~** (fam) hit the nail on the head

bucho /'buʃu/ m gut; **~ de boi** tripe

budis|mo /bu'dʒizmu/ m Buddhism; **~ta** a & m/f Buddhist

bueiro /bu'eru/ m storm drain

búfalo /'bufalu/ m buffalo

bu|fante /bu'fãtʃi/ a full, puffed; **~far** vi snort; (reclamar) grumble, moan

bufê /bu'fe/ m (refeição) buffet; (serviço) catering service; (móvel) sideboard

bugiganga /buʒi'gãga/ f knickknack

bujão /bu'ʒãw/ m **~ de gás** gas cylinder

bula /'bula/ f (de remédio) directions; (do Papa) bull

bulbo /'buwbu/ m bulb

bule /'buli/ m (de chá) teapot; (de café etc) pot

Bulgária /buw'garia/ f Bulgaria

búlgaro /'buwgaru/ a & m Bulgarian

bulhufas /bu'ʎufas/ (fam) pron nothing

bulício /bu'lisiu/ m bustle

bumbum /bũ'bũ/ (fam) m bottom, bum

bunda /'bũda/ f bottom

buquê /bu'ke/ m bouquet

buraco /bu'raku/ m hole; (de agulha) eye; (jogo de cartas) rummy; **~ da fechadura** keyhole

burburinho /burbu'riɲu/ m (de vozes) hubbub

bur|guês /bur'ges/ a & m (f **~guesa**) bourgeois; **~guesia** f bourgeoisie

burlar /bur'lar/ vt get round <lei>; get past <defesas, vigilância>

buro|cracia /burokra'sia/ f bureaucracy; **~crata** m/f bureaucrat; **~crático** a bureaucratic; **~cratizar** vt make bureaucratic

bur|rice /bu'xisi/ f stupidity; (uma) stupid thing; **~ro** a stupid; (ignorante) dim □ m (animal) donkey; (pessoa) halfwit, dunce; **~ro de carga** (fig) workhorse

bus|ca /'buska/ f search; **dar ~ca em** search; **~ca-pé** m banger; **~car** vt fetch; (de carro) pick up; **mandar ~car** send for

bússola /'busola/ f compass; (fig) guide

busto /'bustu/ m bust

butique /bu'tʃiki/ f boutique

buzi|na /bu'zina/ f horn; **~nada** f toot (of the horn); **~nar** vi sound the horn, toot the horn

....

Cc

....

cá /ka/ adv here; **o lado de ~** this side; **para ~** here; **de ~ para lá** back and forth; **de lá para ~** since then; **~ entre nós** between you and me

ca|bal /ka'baw/ (pl **~bais**) a complete, full; <prova> conclusive

cabana /ka'bana/ f hut; (casinha no campo) cottage

cabeça /ka'besa/ f head; (de lista) top; (pessoa inteligente) mind □ m/f (chefe) ringleader; (integrante mais inteligente) brains; **de ~** <saber> off the top of one's head; <calcular> in one's head; **de ~ para baixo** upside down; **deu-lhe na ~ de** he took it into his head to; **esquentar a ~** (fam) get worked up; **fazer a ~ de alg** convince s.o.; **quebrar a ~** rack one's brains; **subir à ~** go to s.o.'s head; **ter a ~ no lugar** have one's head screwed on; **~da** f (no futebol) header; (pancada) head butt; **dar uma ~da no teto** bang one's head on the ceiling; **~-de-porco** (pl **~s-de-porco**) f tenement; **~-de-vento** (pl **~s-de-vento**) m/f scatterbrain, airhead; **~lho** m heading

cabe|cear /kabesi'ar/ vt head <bola>; **~ceira** f head; **~çudo** a pigheaded

cabe|dal /kabe'daw/ (pl **~dais**) m wealth

cabelei|ra /kabe'lera/ f head of hair; (peruca) wig; **~reiro** m hairdresser

cabe|lo /ka'belu/ m hair; **cortar o ~lo** have one's hair cut; **~ludo** a hairy; (difícil) complicated; <palavra, piada> dirty

caber /ka'ber/ vi fit; (ter cabimento) be fitting; **~ a** <mérito, parte> be due to; <tarefa> fall to; **cabe a você ir** it is up to you to go; **~ em alg** <roupa> fit s.o.

cabide /ka'bidʒi/ m (peça de madeira, arame etc) hanger; (móvel) hat stand; (na parede) coat rack

cabimento /kabi'mẽtu/ *m* **ter** ~ be
fitting, be appropriate; **não ter** ~ be
out of the question
cabine /ka'bini/ *f* cabin; (*de avião*)
cockpit; (*de loja*) changing room; ~
telefônica phone box, (*Amer*) phone
booth
cabisbaixo /kabiz'baʃu/ *a* crestfallen
cabí|vel /ka'bivew/ (*pl* ~**veis**) *a*
appropriate, fitting
cabo[1] /'kabu/ *m* (*militar*) corporal; **ao** ~
de after; **levar a** ~ carry out; ~
eleitoral campaign worker
cabo[2] /'kabu/ *m* (*fio*) cable; (*de panela
etc*) handle; **TV por** ~ cable TV; ~ **de
extensão** extension lead; ~ **de força**
tug of war
caboclo /ka'boklu/ *a & m* mestizo
ca|bra /'kabra/ *f* goat; ~**brito** *m* kid
ca|ça /'kasa/ *f* (*atividade*) hunting;
(*caçada*) hunt; (*animais*) game □ *m*
(*avião*) fighter; **à** ~**ça de** in pursuit of;
~**ça das bruxas** (*fig*) witch hunt;
~**çador** *m* hunter; ~**ça-minas** *m invar*
minesweeper; ~**ça-níqueis** *m invar*
slot machine; ~**çar** *vt* hunt <*animais,
criminoso etc*>; (*procurar*) hunt for □ *vi*
hunt
cacareco /kaka'rɛku/ *m* piece of junk; *pl*
junk
cacare|jar /kakare'ʒar/ *vi* cluck; ~**jo** /e/
m clucking
caçarola /kasa'rɔla/ *f* saucepan
cacau /ka'kaw/ *m* cocoa
cace|tada /kase'tada/ *f* blow with a club;
(*fig*) annoyance; ~**te** /e/ *m* club
□ (*fam*) *int* damn
cachaça /ka'ʃasa/ *f* white rum
cachê /ka'ʃe/ *m* fee
cache|col /kaʃe'kɔw/ (*pl* ~**cóis**) *m* scarf
cachimbo /ka'ʃĩbu/ *m* pipe
cacho /'kaʃu/ *m* (*de banana, uva*) bunch;
(*de cabelo*) lock; (*fam: caso*) affair
cachoeira /kaʃo'era/ *f* waterfall
cachor|rinho /kaʃo'xĩnu/ *m* (*nado*)
doggy paddle; ~**ro** /o/ *m* dog; (*Port*)
puppy; (*pessoa*) scoundrel; ~**ro-
quente** (*pl* ~**ros-quentes**) *m* hot dog
cacife /ka'sifi/ *m* (*fig*) pull
caci|que /ka'siki/ *m* (*índio*) chief;
(*político*) boss; ~**quia** *f* leadership
caco /'kaku/ *m* shard; (*pessoa*) old crock
cacto /'kaktu/ *m* cactus
caçula /ka'sula/ *m/f* youngest child □ *a*
youngest
cada /'kada/ *a* each; ~ **duas horas** every
two hours; **custam £5** ~ (**um**) they
cost £5 each; ~ **vez mais** more and
more; ~ **vez mais fácil** easier and
easier; **ele fala** ~ **coisa** (*fam*) he says
the most amazing things

cadafalso /kada'fawsu/ *m* gallows
cadarço /ka'darsu/ *m* shoelace
cadas|trar /kadas'trar/ *vt* register; ~**tro**
m register; (*ato*) registration; (*policial,
bancário*) records, files; (*imobiliário*)
land register
ca|dáver /ka'daver/ *m* (dead)
body, corpse; ~**davérico** *a* cadaverous,
corpse-like; (*exame*) post-mortem
cadê /ka'de/ (*fam*) *adv* where is/are...?
cadeado /kadʒi'adu/ *m* padlock
cadeia /ka'deja/ *f* (*de eventos, lojas etc*)
chain; (*prisão*) prison; (*rádio, TV*)
network
cadeira /ka'dera/ *f* (*móvel*) chair; (*no
teatro*) stall; (*de político*) seat; (*função
de professor*) chair; (*matéria*) subject; *pl*
(*anat*) hips; ~ **de balanço** rocking
chair; ~ **de rodas** wheelchair;
~ **elétrica** electric chair
ca|dência /ka'dẽsia/ *f* (*mus, da voz*)
cadence; (*compasso*) rhythm;
~**denciado** *a* rhythmic; <*passos*>
measured
cader|neta /kader'neta/ *f* notebook; (*de
professor*) register; (*de banco*)
passbook; ~**neta de poupança**
savings account; ~**no** /ɛ/ *m* exercise
book; (*pequeno*) notebook; (*no jornal*)
section
cadete /ka'detʃi/ *m* cadet
cadu|car /kadu'kar/ *vi* <*pessoa*> become
senile; <*contrato*> lapse; ~**co** *a*
<*pessoa*> senile; <*contrato*> lapsed;
~**quice** *f* senility
cafajeste /kafa'ʒestʃi/ *m* swine
ca|fé /ka'fɛ/ *m* coffee; (*botequim*) café;
~**fé da manhã** breakfast; **tomar** ~**fé**
have breakfast; ~**fé-com-leite** *a invar*
coffee-coloured, light brown □ *m* white
coffee; ~**feeiro** *a* coffee □ *m* coffee
plant; ~**feicultura** *f* coffee-growing;
~**feína** *f* caffein(e)
cafetã /kafe'tã/ *m* caftan
cafetão /kafe'tãw/ *m* pimp
cafe|teira /kafe'tera/ *f* coffee pot; ~**zal**
(*pl* ~**zais**) *m* coffee plantation;
~**zinho** *m* small black coffee
cafo|na /ka'fona/ (*fam*) *a* naff, tacky;
~**nice** *f* tackiness; (*coisa*) tacky thing
cágado /'kagadu/ *m* turtle
caiar /kaj'ar/ *vt* whitewash
cãibra /'kãjbra/ *f* cramp
caí|da /ka'ida/ *f* fall; *veja* **queda**; ~**do** *a*
<*árvore etc*> fallen; <*beiços etc*>
drooping; (*deprimido*) dejected;
(*apaixonado*) smitten
caimento /kaj'mẽtu/ *m* fall
caipi|ra /kaj'pira/ *a* <*pessoa*>
countrified; <*festa, música*> country;
<*sotaque*> rural □ *m/f* country person;

C

(*depreciativo*) country bumpkin; ~rinha *f* cachaça with limes, sugar and ice

cair /ka'ir/ *vi* fall; <*dente, cabelo*> fall out; <*botão etc*> fall off; <*comércio, trânsito etc*> fall off; <*tecido, cortina*> hang; ~ **bem/mal** <*roupa*> go well/ badly; <*ato, dito*> go down well, badly; **estou caindo de sono** I'm really sleepy

cais /kajs/ *m* quay; (*Port: na estação*) platform

caixa /'kaʃa/ *f* box; (*de loja etc*) cashdesk □ *m/f* cashier; ~ **de correio** letter box; ~ **de mudanças**, (*Port*) ~ **de velocidades** gear box; ~ **postal** post office box, PO Box; ~**d'água** (*pl* ~**s-d'água**) *f* water tank; ~**forte** (*pl* ~**s-fortes**) *f* vault

cai|xão /ka'ʃãw/ *m* coffin; ~**xeiro** *m* (*em loja*) assistant; salesman; ~**xilho** *m* frame; ~**xote** /ɔ/ *m* crate

caju /ka'ʒu/ *m* cashew fruit; ~**eiro** *m* cashew tree

cal /kaw/ *f* lime

calado /ka'ladu/ *a* quiet

calafrio /kala'friu/ *m* shudder, shiver

calami|dade /kalami'dadʒi/ *f* calamity; ~**toso** /o/ *a* calamitous

calar /ka'lar/ *vi* be quiet □ *vt* keep quiet about <*segredo, sentimento*>; silence <*pessoa*>; ~**-se** *vpr* go quiet

calça /'kawsa/ *f* trousers, (*Amer*) pants

calça|da /kaw'sada/ *f* pavement, (*Amer*) sidewalk; (*Port: rua*) roadway; ~**dão** *m* pedestrian precinct; ~**deira** *f* shoe-horn; ~**do** *a* paved □ *m* shoe; *pl* footwear

calcanhar /kawka'ɲar/ *m* heel

calção /kaw'sãw/ *m* shorts; ~ **de banho** swimming trunks

calcar /kaw'kar/ *vt* (*pisar*) trample; (*comprimir*) press; ~ **aco em** (*fig*) base sth on, model sth on

calçar /kaw'sar/ *vt* put on <*sapatos, luvas*>; take <*número*>; pave <*rua*>; (*com calço*) wedge □ *vi* <*sapato*> fit; ~**-se** *vpr* put one's shoes on

calcário /kaw'kariu/ *m* limestone □ *a* <*água*> hard

calças /'kawsas/ *f pl veja* **calça**

calcinha /kaw'siɲa/ *f* knickers, (*Amer*) panties

cálcio /'kawsiu/ *m* calcium

calço /'kawsu/ *m* wedge

calcu|ladora /kawkula'dora/ *f* calculator; ~**lar** *vt/i* calculate; ~**lista** *a* calculating □ *m/f* opportunist

cálculo /'kawkulu/ *m* calculation; (*diferencial*) calculus; (*med*) stone

cal|da /'kawda/ *f* syrup; *pl* hot springs; ~**deira** *f* boiler; ~**deirão** *m* cauldron;

~**do** *m* (*sopa*) broth; (*suco*) juice; ~**do de carne/galinha** beef/chicken stock

calefação /kalefa'sãw/ *f* heating

caleidoscópio /kalejdos'kɔpiu/ *m* kaleidoscope

calejado /kale'ʒadu/ *a* <*mãos*> calloused; <*pessoa*> experienced

calendário /kalẽ'dariu/ *m* calendar

calha /'kaʎa/ *f* (*no telhado*) gutter; (*sulco*) gulley

calhamaço /kaʎa'masu/ *m* tome

calhambeque /kaʎã'bɛki/ (*fam*) *m* banger

calhar /ka'ʎar/ *vi* **calhou que** it so happened that; **calhou pegar em o mesmo trem** they happened to get the same train; ~ **de** happen to; **vir a** ~ come at the right time

cali|brado /kali'bradu/ *a* (*bêbado*) tipsy; ~**brar** *vt* calibrate; check (the pressure of) <*pneu*>; ~**bre** *m* calibre; **coisas desse** ~**bre** things of this order

cálice /'kalisi/ *m* (*copo*) liqueur glass; (*na missa*) chalice

caligrafia /kaligra'fia/ *f* (*letra*) handwriting; (*arte*) calligraphy

calista /ka'lista/ *m/f* chiropodist, (*Amer*) podiatrist

cal|ma /'kawma/ *f* calm; **com** ~**ma** calmly □ *int* calm down; ~**mante** *m* tranquilizer; ~**mo** *a* calm

calo /'kalu/ *m* (*na mão*) callus; (*no pé*) corn

calombo /ka'lõbu/ *m* bump

calor /ka'lor/ *m* heat; (*agradável, fig*) warmth; **estar com** ~ be hot

calo|rento /kalo'rẽtu/ *a* <*pessoa*> sensitive to heat; <*lugar*> hot; ~**ria** *f* calorie; ~**roso** /o/ *a* warm; <*protesto*> lively

calota /ka'lɔta/ *f* hubcap

calo|te /ka'lɔtʃi/ *m* bad debt; ~**teiro** *m* bad risk

calouro /ka'loru/ *m* (*na faculdade*) freshman; (*em outros ramos*) novice

ca|lúnia /ka'lunia/ *f* slander; ~**luniar** *vt* slander; ~**lunioso** /o/ *a* slanderous

cal|vície /kaw'visi/ *f* baldness; ~**vo** *a* bald

cama /'kama/ *f* bed; ~ **de casal/ solteiro** double/single bed; ~**beliche** (*pl* ~**s-beliches**) *f* bunk bed

camada /ka'mada/ *f* layer; (*de tinta*) coat

câmara /'kamara/ *f* chamber; (*fotográfica*) camera; ~ **digital** digital camera; **em** ~ **lenta** in slow motion; ~ **municipal** town council; (*Port*) town hall

camarada /kama'rada/ *a* friendly □ *m/f* comrade; ~**gem** *f* comradeship; (*convivência agradável*) camaraderie

câmara-de-ar /kamaradʒi'ar/ (*pl* **câmaras-de-ar**) *f* inner tube

camarão /kama'rãw/ *m* shrimp; (*maior*) prawn

cama|reira /kama'rera/ *f* chambermaid; ∼**rim** *m* dressing room; ∼**rote** /ɔ/ *m* (*no teatro*) box; (*num navio*) cabin

cambada /kã'bada/ *f* gang, horde

cambalacho /kãba'laʃu/ *m* scam

camba|lear /kãbali'ar/ *vi* stagger; ∼**lhota** *f* somersault

cambi|al /kãbi'aw/ (*pl* ∼**ais**) *a* exchange; ∼**ante** *m* shade; ∼**ar** *vt* change

câmbio /'kãbiu/ *m* exchange; (*taxa*) rate of exchange; ∼ **oficial/paralelo** official/black market exchange rate

cambista /kã'bista/ *m*/*f* (*de entradas*) ticket-tout, (*Amer*) scalper; (*de dinheiro*) money changer

Camboja /kã'bɔʒa/ *m* Cambodia

cambojano /kãbo'ʒanu/ *a* & *m* Cambodian

camburão /kãbu'rãw/ *m* police van

camelo /ka'melu/ *m* camel

camelô /kame'lo/ *m* street vendor

camião /kami'ãw/ (*Port*) *m veja* **caminhão**

caminhada /kami'nada/ *f* walk

caminhão /kami'nãw/ *m* lorry, (*Amer*) truck

cami|nhar /kami'nar/ *vi* walk; (*fig*) advance, progress; ∼**nho** *m* way; (*estrada*) road; (*trilho*) path; **a** ∼**nho** on the way; **a meio** ∼**nho** halfway; ∼**nho de ferro** (*Port*) railway, (*Amer*) railroad

caminho|neiro /kamiɲo'neru/ *m* lorry driver, (*Amer*) truck driver; ∼**nete** /ɛ/ *m* van

camio|neta /kamio'neta/ *f* van; ∼**nista** (*Port*) *m*/*f veja* **caminhoneiro**

cami|sa /ka'miza/ *f* shirt; ∼**sa-de-força** (*pl* ∼**sas-de-força**) *f* straitjacket; ∼**sa-de-vênus** (*pl* ∼**sas-de-vênus**) *f* condom; ∼**seta** /e/ *f* T-shirt; (*de baixo*) vest; ∼**sinha** (*fam*) *f* condom; ∼**sola** /ɔ/ *f* nightdress; (*Port*) sweater

camomila /kamo'mila/ *f* camomile

campainha /kãpa'iɲa/ *f* bell; (*da porta*) doorbell

campanário /kãpa'nariu/ *m* belfry

campanha /kã'paɲa/ *f* campaign

campe|ão /kãpi'ãw/ *m* (*f* ∼**ã**) champion; ∼**onato** *m* championship

cam|pestre /kã'pɛstri/ *a* rural; ∼**pina** *f* grassland

cam|ping /'kãpĩ/ *m* camping; (*lugar*) campsite; ∼**pismo** (*Port*) *m* camping

campo /'kãpu/ *m* field; (*interior*) country; (*de futebol*) pitch; (*de golfe*) course; ∼

de concentração concentration camp; ∼**nês** *m* (*f* ∼**nesa**) peasant

camu|flagem /kamu'flaʒẽ/ *f* camouflage; ∼**flar** *vt* camouflage

camundongo /kamũ'dõgu/ *m* mouse

cana /'kana/ *f* cane; ∼ **de açúcar** sugar cane

Canadá /kana'da/ *m* Canada

canadense /kana'dẽsi/ *a* & *m* Canadian

ca|nal /ka'naw/ (*pl* ∼**nais**) *m* channel; (*hidrovia*) canal

canalha /ka'naʎa/ *m*/*f* scoundrel

canali|zação /kanaliza'sãw/ *f* piping; ∼**zador** (*Port*) *m* plumber; ∼**zar** *vt* channel <*líquido, esforço, recursos*>; canalize <*rio*>; pipe for water and drainage <*cidade*>

canário /ka'nariu/ *m* canary

canastrão /kanas'trãw/ *m* (*f* ∼**trona**) ham actor (*f* actress)

canavi|al /kanavi'aw/ (*pl* ∼**ais**) *m* cane field; ∼**eiro** *a* sugar cane

canção /kã'sãw/ *f* song

cance|lamento /kãsela'mẽtu/ *m* cancellation; ∼**lar** *vt* cancel; (*riscar*) cross out

câncer /'kãser/ *m* cancer; **Câncer** (*signo*) Cancer

cance|riano /kãseri'anu/ *a* & *m* Cancerian; ∼**rígeno** *a* carcinogenic; ∼**roso** /o/ *a* cancerous □ *m* person with cancer

cancro /'kãkru/ *m* (*Port: câncer*) cancer; (*fig*) canker

candango /kã'dãgu/ *m* person from Brasília

cande|eiro /kãdʒi'eru/ *m* (oil-) lamp; ∼**labro** *m* candelabra

candida|tar-se /kãdʒida'tarsi/ *vpr* (*a vaga*) apply (**a** for); (*à presidência etc*) stand, (*Amer*) run (**a** for); ∼**to** *m* candidate (**a** for); (*a vaga*) applicant (**a** for); ∼**tura** *f* candidature; (*a vaga*) application (**a** for)

cândido /'kãdʒidu/ *a* innocent

candomblé /kãdõ'blɛ/ *m* Afro-Brazilian cult; (*reunião*) candomble meeting

candura /kã'dura/ *f* innocence

cane|ca /ka'nɛka/ *f* mug; ∼**co** /ɛ/ *m* tankard

canela[1] /ka'nɛla/ *f* (*condimento*) cinnamon

canela[2] /ka'nɛla/ *f* (*da perna*) shin; ∼**da** *f* **dar uma** ∼**da em alg** kick s.o. in the shins; **dar uma** ∼**da em aco** hit one's shins on sth

cane|ta /ka'nɛta/ *f* pen; ∼ **esferográfica** ballpoint pen; ∼**ta-tinteiro** (*pl* ∼**tas-tinteiro**) *f* fountain pen

cangote /kã'gotʃi/ *m* nape of the neck

canguru /kãgu'ru/ *m* kangaroo

C

canhão /ka'ɲãw/ m (*arma*) cannon; (*vale*) canyon

canhoto /ka'ɲotu/ a left-handed □ m (*talão*) stub

cani|bal /kani'baw/ (pl ~bais) m/f cannibal; ~**balismo** m cannibalism

caniço /ka'nisu/ m reed; (*pessoa*) skinny person

canícula /ka'nikula/ f heat wave

ca|nil /ka'niw/ (pl ~nis) m kennel

canivete /kani'vɛtʃi/ m penknife

canja /'kãʒa/ f chicken soup; (*fam*) piece of cake

canjica /kã'ʒika/ f corn porridge

cano /'kanu/ m pipe; (*de bota*) top; (*de arma de fogo*) barrel

cano|a /ka'noa/ f canoe; ~**agem** f canoeing; ~**ista** m/f canoeist

canonizar /kanoni'zar/ vt canonize

can|saço /kã'sasu/ m tiredness; ~**sado** a tired; ~**sar** vt tire; (*aborrecer*) bore □ vi, ~**sar-se** vpr get tired; ~**sativo** a tiring; (*aborrecido*) boring; ~**seira** f tiredness; (*lida*) toil

can|tada /kã'tada/ f (*fam*) chat-up; ~**tar** vt/i sing; (*fam*) chat up

cântaro /'kãtaru/ m **chover a ~s** pour down, bucket down

cantarolar /kãtaro'lar/ vt/i hum

cantei|ra /kã'tera/ f quarry; ~**ro** m (*de flores*) flowerbed; (*artífice*) stonemason; ~**ro de obras** site office

cantiga /kã'tʃiga/ f ballad

can|til /kã'tʃiw/ (pl ~tis) m canteen; ~**tina** f canteen

canto[1] /'kãtu/ m (*ângulo*) corner

can|to[2] /'kãtu/ m (*cantar*) singing; ~**tor** m singer; ~**toria** f singing

canudo /ka'nudu/ m (*de beber*) straw; (*tubo*) tube; (*fam: diploma*) diploma

cão /kãw/ (pl **cães**) m dog

caolho /ka'oʎu/ a one-eyed

ca|os /kaws/ m chaos; ~**ótico** a chaotic

capa /'kapa/ f (*de livro, revista*) cover; (*roupa sem mangas*) cape; **~ de chuva** raincoat

capacete /kapa'setʃi/ m helmet

capacho /ka'paʃu/ m doormat

capaci|dade /kapasi'dadʒi/ f capacity; (*aptidão*) ability; ~**tar** vt enable; (*convencer*) convince

capataz /kapa'tas/ m foreman

capaz /ka'pas/ a capable (**de** of); **ser ~ de** (*poder*) be able to; (*ser provável*) be likely to

cape|la /ka'pɛla/ f chapel; ~**lão** (pl ~**lães**) m chaplain

capen|ga /ka'pẽga/ a doddery; ~**gar** vi dodder

capeta /ka'peta/ m (*diabo*) devil; (*criança*) little devil

capilar /kapi'lar/ a hair

ca|pim /ka'pĩ/ m grass; ~**pinar** vt/i weed

capi|tal /kapi'taw/ (pl ~**tais**) a & m/f capital; ~**talismo** m capitalism; ~**talista** a & m/f capitalist; ~**talizar** vt (*com*) capitalize; (*aproveitar*) capitalize on

capi|tanear /kapitani'ar/ vt captain <*navio*>; (*fig*) lead; ~**tania** f captaincy; ~**tania do porto** port authority; ~**tão** (pl ~**tães**) m captain

capitulação /kapitula'sãw/ f capitulation, surrender

capítulo /ka'pitulu/ m chapter; (*de telenovela*) episode

capô /ka'po/ m bonnet, (*Amer*) hood

capoeira /kapo'era/ f Brazilian martial art

capo|ta /ka'pɔta/ f roof; ~**tar** vi overturn

capote /ka'pɔtʃi/ m overcoat

capri|char /kapri'ʃar/ vi excel o.s.; ~**cho** m (*esmero*) care; (*desejo*) whim; (*teimosia*) contrariness; ~**choso** /o/ a (*cheio de caprichos*) capricious; (*com esmero*) painstaking, meticulous

Capricórnio /kapri'kɔrniu/ m Capricorn

capricorniano /kaprikorni'anu/ a & m Capricorn

cápsula /'kapsula/ f capsule

cap|tar /kap'tar/ vt pick up <*emissão, sinais*>; tap <*água*>; catch, grasp <*sentido*>; win <*simpatia, admiração*>; ~**tura** f capture; ~**turar** vt capture

capuz /ka'pus/ m hood

caquético /ka'kɛtʃiku/ a broken-down, on one's last legs

caqui /ka'ki/ m persimmon

cáqui /'kaki/ a invar & m khaki

cara /'kara/ f face; (*aparência*) look; (*ousadia*) cheek □ (*fam*) m guy; **~ a ~** face to face; **de ~** straightaway; **dar de ~ com** run into; **está na ~** it's obvious; **fechar a ~** frown; **~ de pau** cheek; **~ de tacho** (*fam*) sheepish look

cara|col /kara'kɔw/ (pl ~**cóis**) m snail

caracte|re /karak'tɛri/ m character; ~**rística** f characteristic, feature; ~**rístico** a characteristic; ~**rizar** vt characterize; ~**rizar-se** vpr be characterized

cara-de-pau /karadʒi'paw/ (pl **caras-de-pau**) a cheeky, brazen

caramba /ka'rãba/ int (*de espanto*) wow; (*de desagrado*) damn

caramelo /kara'mɛlu/ *m* caramel; (*bala*) toffee

caramujo /kara'muʒu/ *m* water snail

caranguejo /karã'geʒu/ *m* crab

caratê /kara'te/ *m* karate

caráter /ka'rater/ *m* character

caravana /kara'vana/ *f* caravan

car|boidrato /karboi'dratu/ *m* carbohydrate; **~bono** /o/ *m* carbon

carbu|rador /karbura'dor/ *m* carburettor, (*Amer*) carburator; **~rante** *m* fuel

carcaça /kar'kasa/ *f* carcass; (*de navio etc*) frame

cárcere /'karseri/ *m* jail

carcereiro /karse'reru/ *m* jailer, warder

carcomido /karko'midu/ *a* worm-eaten; <*rosto*> pock-marked

cardápio /kar'dapiu/ *m* menu

carde|al /kardʒi'aw/ (*pl* **~ais**) *a* cardinal

cardíaco /kar'dʒiaku/ *a* cardiac; **ataque ~** heart attack

cardio|lógico /kardʒio'lɔʒiku/ *a* heart; **~logista** *m/f* heart specialist, cardiologist

cardume /kar'dumi/ *m* shoal

careca /ka'rɛka/ *a* bald □ *f* bald patch

ca|recer /kare'ser/ **~recer de** *vt* lack; **~rência** *f* lack; (*social*) deprivation; (*afetiva*) lack of affection; **~rente** *a* lacking; (*socialmente*) deprived; (*afetivamente*) in need of affection

carestia /kares'tʃia/ *f* high cost; (*geral*) high cost of living; (*escassez*) shortage

careta /ka'reta/ *f* grimace □ *a* (*fam*) straight, square

car|ga /'karga/ *f* load; (*mercadorias*) cargo; (*elétrica*) charge; (*de cavalaria*) charge; (*de caneta*) refill; (*fig*) burden; **~ga horária** workload; **~go** *m* (*função*) post, job; **a ~go de** in the charge of; **~gueiro** *m* (*navio*) cargo ship, freighter

cariar /kari'ar/ *vi* decay

Caribe /ka'ribi/ *m* Caribbean

caricatu|ra /karika'tura/ *f* caricature; **~rar** *vt* caricature; **~rista** *m/f* caricaturist

carícia /ka'risia/ *f* (*com a mão*) stroke, caress; (*carinho*) affection

cari|dade /kari'dadʒi/ *f* charity; **obra de ~dade** charity; **~doso** /o/ *a* charitable

cárie /'kari/ *f* tooth decay

carim|bar /karĩ'bar/ *vt* stamp; postmark <*carta*>; **~bo** *m* stamp; (*do correio*) postmark

cari|nho /ka'riɲu/ *m* affection; (*um*) caress; **~nhoso** /o/ *a* affectionate

carioca /kari'ɔka/ *a* from Rio de Janeiro □ *m/f* person from Rio de Janeiro □ (*Port*) *m* weak coffee

caris|ma /ka'rizma/ *m* charisma; **~mático** *a* charismatic

carna|val /karna'vaw/ (*pl* **~vais**) *m* carnival; **~valesco** /e/ *a* carnival; <*roupa*> over the top, overdone □ *m* carnival organizer

car|ne /'karni/ *f* (*humana etc*) flesh; (*comida*) meat; **~neiro** *m* sheep; (*macho*) ram; (*como comida*) mutton; **~niça** *f* carrion; **~nificina** *f* slaughter; **~nívoro** *a* carnivorous □ *m* carnivore; **~nudo** *a* fleshy

caro /'karu/ *a* expensive; (*querido*) dear □ *adv* <*custar, cobrar*> a lot; <*comprar, vender*> at a high price; **pagar ~** pay a high price (for)

caroço /ka'rosu/ *m* (*de pêssego etc*) stone; (*de maçã*) core; (*em sopa, molho etc*) lump

carona /ka'rona/ *f* lift

carpete /kar'pɛtʃi/ *m* fitted carpet

carpin|taria /karpĩta'ria/ *f* carpentry; **~teiro** *m* carpenter

carran|ca /ka'xãka/ *f* scowl; **~cudo** *a* <*cara*> scowling; <*pessoa*> sullen

carrapato /kaxa'patu/ *m* (*animal*) tick; (*fig*) hanger-on

carrasco /ka'xasku/ *m* executioner; (*fig*) butcher

carre|gado /kaxe'gadu/ *a* <*céu*> dark, black; <*cor*> dark; <*ambiente*> tense; **~gador** *m* porter; **~gamento** *m* loading; (*carga*) load; **~gar** *vt* load <*navio, arma, máquina fotográfica*>; (*levar*) carry; charge <*bateria, pilha*>; **~gar em** overdo; pronounce strongly <*letra*>; (*Port*) press

carreira /ka'xera/ *f* career

carre|tel /kaxe'tɛw/ (*pl* **~téis**) *m* reel

car|ril /ka'xiw/ (*pl* **~ris**) (*Port*) *m* rail

carrinho /ka'xiɲu/ *m* (*para bagagem, compras*) trolley; (*de criança*) pram; **~ de mão** wheel-barrow

carro /'kaxu/ *m* car; (*de bois*) cart; **~ alegórico** float; **~ esporte** sports car; **~ fúnebre** hearse; **~ça** /ɔ/ *f* cart; **~ceria** *f* bodywork; **~-chefe** (*pl* **~s-chefes**) *m* (*no carnaval*) main float; (*fig*) centrepiece; **~-forte** (*pl* **~s-fortes**) *m* security van

carros|sel /kaxo'sɛw/ (*pl* **~séis**) *m* merry-go-round

carruagem /kaxu'aʒẽ/ *f* coach

carta /'karta/ *f* letter; (*mapa*) chart; (*do baralho*) card; **~ branca** (*fig*) carte blanche; **~ de condução** (*Port*) driving licence, (*Amer*) driver's license; **~-bomba** (*pl* **~s-bomba**) *f* letter bomb; **~da** *f* (*fig*) move

cartão /kar'tãw/ *m* card; (*Port: papelão*) cardboard; **~ de crédito** credit card; **~ de visita** visiting card; **~ magnético**

swipe card; ~-postal (*pl* cartões-
postais) *m* postcard
car|taz /kar'tas/ *m* poster, (*Amer*) bill;
em ~ showing, (*Amer*) playing;
~teira *f* (*para dinheiro*) wallet;
(*cartão*) card; (*mesa*) desk; ~teira de
identidade identity card; ~teira de
motorista driving licence, (*Amer*)
driver's license; ~teiro *m* postman
car|tel /kar'tɛw/ (*pl* ~téis) *m* cartel
cárter /'karter/ *m* sump
carto|la /ka'tɔla/ *f* top hat □ *m* director;
~lina *f* card; ~mante *m/f* tarot
reader, fortune-teller
cartório /kar'tɔriu/ *m* registry office
cartucho /kar'tuʃu/ *m* cartridge; (*de
dinamite*) stick; (*de amendoim etc*) bag
car|tum /kar'tũ/ *m* cartoon; ~tunista
m/f cartoonist
caruncho /ka'rũʃu/ *m* woodcorm
carvalho /kar'vaʎu/ *m* oak
car|vão /kar'vãw/ *m* coal; (*de desenho*)
charcoal; ~voeiro *a* coal
casa /'kaza/ *f* house; (*comercial*) firm; (*de
tabuleiro*) square; (*de botão*) hole; em ~
at home; para ~ home; na ~ dos 30
anos in one's thirties; ~ da moeda
mint; ~ de banho (*Port*) bathroom; ~
de campo country house; ~ de saúde
private hospital; ~ decimal decimal
place; ~ popular council house
casaco /ka'zaku/ *m* (*sobretudo*) coat;
(*paletó*) jacket; (*de lã*) pullover
ca|sal /ka'zaw/ (*pl* ~sais) *m* couple;
~samento *m* marriage; (*cerimônia*)
wedding; ~sar *vt* marry; (*fig*) combine
□ *vi* get married; (*fig*) go together;
~sar-se *upr* get married; (*fig*)
combine; ~sar-se com marry
casarão /kaza'rãw/ *m* mansion
casca /'kaska/ *f* (*de árvore*) bark; (*de
laranja, limão*) peel; (*de banana*) skin;
(*de noz, ovo*) shell; (*de milho*) husk; (*de
pão*) crust; (*de ferida*) scab
cascalho /kas'kaʎu/ *m* gravel
cascata /kas'kata/ *f* waterfall; (*fam*) fib
casca|vel /kaska'vɛw/ (*pl* ~véis) *m*
(*cobra*) rattlesnake □ *f* (*mulher*) shrew
casco /'kasku/ *m* (*de cavalo etc*) hoof; (*de
navio*) hull; (*garrafa vazia*) empty
ca|sebre /ka'zebri/ *m* hovel, shack;
~seiro *a* <*comida*> home-made;
<*pessoa*> home-loving; <*vida*> home
□ *m* housekeeper
caserna /ka'zɛrna/ *f* barracks
casmurro /kaz'muxu/ *a* sullen
caso /'kazu/ *m* case; (*amoroso*) affair;
(*conto*) story □ *conj* in case; em todo *ou*
qualquer ~ in any case; fazer ~ de
take notice of; vir ao ~ be relevant; ~
contrário otherwise

casório /ka'zɔriu/ (*fam*) *m* wedding
caspa /'kaspa/ *f* dandruff
casquinha /kas'kiɲa/ *f* (*de sorvete*) cone,
cornet
cassar /ka'sar/ *vt* revoke, withdraw
<*direitos, autorização*>; ban
<*político*>
cassete /ka'sɛtʃi/ *m* cassette
cassetete /kase'tetʃi/ *m* truncheon,
(*Amer*) nightstick
cassino /ka'sinu/ *m* casino; ~ de oficiais
officers' mess
casta|nha /kas'taɲa/ *f* chestnut; ~nha
de caju cashew nut; ~nha-do-pará
(*pl* ~nhas-do-pará) *f* Brazil nut;
~nheiro *m* chestnut tree; ~nho *a*
chestnut (-coloured); ~nholas /ɔ/ *f pl*
castanets
castelhano /kaste'ʎanu/ *a* & *m* Castilian
castelo /kas'tɛlu/ *m* castle
casti|çal /kastʃi'saw/ (*pl* ~çais) *m*
candlestick
cas|tidade /kastʃi'dadʒi/ *f* chastity;
~tigar *vt* punish; ~tigo *m*
punishment; ~to *a* chaste
castor /kas'tor/ *m* beaver
castrar /kas'trar/ *vt* castrate
casu|al /kazu'aw/ (*pl* ~ais) *a* chance;
(*fortuito*) fortuitous; ~alidade *f*
chance
casulo /ka'zulu/ *m* (*de larva*) cocoon
cata /'kata/ *f* à ~ de in search of
cata|lão /kata'lãw/ (*pl* ~lães) *a* & *m*
(*f* ~lã) Catalan
catalisador /kataliza'dor/ *m* catalyst; (*de
carro*) catalytic converter
catalogar /katalo'gar/ *vt* catalogue
catálogo /ka'talogu/ *m* catalogue; (*de
telefones*) phone book
Catalunha /kata'luɲa/ *f* Catalonia
catapora /kata'pɔra/ *f* chicken pox
catar /ka'tar/ *vt* (*procurar*) search for;
(*recolher*) gather; (*do chão*) pick up; sort
<*arroz, café*>
catarata /kata'rata/ *f* waterfall; (*no olho*)
cataract
catarro /ka'taxu/ *m* catarrh
catástrofe /ka'tastrofi/ *f* catastrophe
catastrófico /katas'trɔfiku/ *a*
catastrophic
catecismo /kate'sizmu/ *m* catechism
cátedra /'katedra/ *f* chair
cate|dral /kate'draw/ (*pl* ~drais) *f*
cathedral; ~drático *m* professor
cate|goria /katego'ria/ *f* category;
(*social*) class; (*qualidade*) quality;
~górico *a* categorical; ~gorizar *vt*
categorize
catinga /ka'tʃĩga/ *f* body odour, stink

cati|vante /katʃi'vãtʃi/ *a* captivating; ∼**var** *vt* captivate; ∼**veiro** *m* captivity; ∼**vo** *a & m* captive

catolicismo /katoli'sizmu/ *m* Catholicism

católico /ka'tɔliku/ *a & m* Catholic

catorze /ka'torzi/ *a & m* fourteen

cau|da /'kawda/ *f* tail; ∼**dal** (*pl* ∼**dais**) *m* torrent

caule /'kawli/ *m* stem

cau|sa /'kawza/ *f* cause; (*jurid*) case; **por** ∼**sa de** because of; ∼**sar** *vt* cause

caute|la /kaw'tɛla/ *f* caution; (*documento*) ticket; ∼**loso** /o/ *a* cautious, careful

cava /'kava/ *f* armhole

cava|do /ka'vadu/ *a* <*vestido*> low-cut; <*olhos*> deep-set; ∼**dor** *a* hard-working □ *m* hard worker

cava|laria /kavala'ria/ *f* cavalry; ∼**lariça** *f* stable; ∼**leiro** *m* horseman; (*na Idade Média*) knight

cavalete /kava'letʃi/ *m* easel

caval|gadura /kavawga'dura/ *f* mount; ∼**gar** *vt/i* ride; sit astride <*muro, banco*>; (*saltar*) jump

cavalhei|resco /kavaʎe'resku/ *a* gallant, gentlemanly; ∼**ro** *m* gentleman □ *a* gallant, gentlemanly

cavalo /ka'valu/ *m* horse; **a** ∼ on horseback; ∼**-vapor** (*pl* ∼**s-vapor**) horsepower

cavanhaque /kava'ɲaki/ *m* goatee

cavaquinho /kava'kiɲu/ *m* ukulele

cavar /ka'var/ *vt* dig; (*fig*) go all out for □ *vi* dig; (*fig*) go all out; ∼ **em** (*vasculhar*) delve into; ∼ **a vida** make a living

caveira /ka'vera/ *f* skull

caverna /ka'vɛrna/ *f* cavern

caviar /kavi'ar/ *m* caviar

cavidade /kavi'dadʒi/ *f* cavity

cavilha /ka'viʎa/ *f* peg

cavo /'kavu/ *a* hollow

cavoucar /kavo'kar/ *vt* excavate

caxemira /kaʃe'mira/ *f* cashmere

caxumba /ka'ʃũba/ *f* mumps

cear /si'ar/ *vt* have for supper □ *vi* have supper

cebo|la /se'bola/ *f* onion; ∼**linha** *f* spring onion

ceder /se'der/ *vt* give up; (*dar*) give; (*emprestar*) lend □ *vi* (*não resistir*) give way; ∼ **a** yield to

cedilha /se'dʒiʎa/ *f* cedilla

cedo /'sedu/ *adv* early; **mais** ∼ **ou mais tarde** sooner or later

cedro /'sɛdru/ *m* cedar

cédula /'sedula/ *f* (*de banco*) note, (*Amer*) bill; (*eleitoral*) ballot paper

ce|gar /se'gar/ *vt* blind; blunt <*faca*>; ∼**go** /ɛ/ *a* blind; <*faca*> blunt □ *m* blind man; **às** ∼**gas** blindly

cegonha /se'goɲa/ *f* stork

cegueira /se'gera/ *f* blindness

ceia /'seja/ *f* supper

cei|fa /'sejfa/ *f* harvest; (*massacre*) slaughter; ∼**far** *vt* reap; claim <*vidas*>; (*matar*) mow down

cela /'sɛla/ *f* cell

cele|bração /selebra'sãw/ *f* celebration; ∼**brar** *vt* celebrate

célebre /'sɛlebri/ *a* celebrated

celebridade /selebri'dadʒi/ *f* celebrity

celeiro /se'leru/ *m* granary

célere /'sɛleri/ *a* swift, fast

celeste /se'lɛstʃi/ *a* celestial

celeuma /se'lewma/ *f* uproar

celibato /seli'batu/ *m* celibacy

celofane /selo'fani/ *m* cellophane

celta /'sɛwta/ *a* Celtic □ *m/f* Celt □ *m* (*língua*) Celtic

célula /'sɛlula/ *f* cell

celu|lar /selu'lar/ *a* cellular □ *m* mobile, (*Amer.*) cell phone ∼**lite** *f* cellulite; ∼**lose** /ɔ/ *f* cellulose

cem /sẽj/ *a & m* hundred

cemitério /semi'tɛriu/ *m* cemetery; (*fig*) graveyard

cena /'sena/ *f* scene; (*palco*) stage; **em** ∼ on stage

cenário /se'nariu/ *m* scenery; (*de crime etc*) scene

cênico /'seniku/ *a* stage

cenoura /se'nora/ *f* carrot

cen|so /'sẽsu/ *m* census; ∼**sor** *m* censor; ∼**sura** *f* (*de jornais etc*) censorship; (*órgão*) censor(s); (*condenação*) censure; ∼**surar** *vt* censor <*jornal, filme etc*>; (*condenar*) censure

centavo /sẽ'tavu/ *m* cent

centeio /sẽ'teju/ *m* rye

centelha /sẽ'teʎa/ *f* spark; (*fig: de gênio etc*) flash

cente|na /sẽ'tena/ *f* hundred; **uma** ∼**na de** about a hundred; **às** ∼**nas** in their hundreds; ∼**nário** *m* centenary

centésimo /sẽ'tɛzimu/ *a* hundredth

centí|grado /sẽ'tʃigradu/ *m* centigrade; ∼**litro** *m* centilitre; ∼**metro** *m* centimetre

cento /'sẽtu/ *a & m* hundred; **por** ∼ per cent

cen|tral /sẽ'traw/ (*pl* ∼**trais**) *a* central □ *f* switchboard; ∼**eólica** wind farm; ∼**tralizar** *vt* centralize; ∼**trar** *vt* centre; ∼**tro** *m* centre

cepti- (*Port*) *veja* **ceti-**

cera /'sera/ *f* wax; **fazer** ∼ waste time, faff about

cerâmi|ca /se'ramika/ *f* ceramics, pottery; **∼co** *a* ceramic

cer|ca /'serka/ *f* fence; **∼ca viva** hedge □ *adv* **∼ca de** around, about; **∼cado** *m* enclosure; (*para criança*) playpen; **∼car** *vt* surround; (*com muro, cerca*) enclose; (*assediar*) besiege

cercear /sersi'ar/ *vt* restrict

cerco /'serku/ *m* (*mil*) siege; (*policial*) dragnet

cere|al /seri'aw/ (*pl* **∼ais**) *m* cereal

cere|bral /sere'braw/ *a* cerebral

cérebro /'sɛrebru/ *m* brain; (*inteligência*) intellect

cere|ja /se'reʒa/ *f* cherry; **∼jeira** *f* cherry tree

cerimônia /seri'monia/ *f* ceremony; **sem ∼** unceremoniously; **fazer ∼** stand on ceremony

cerimoni|al /serimoni'aw/ (*pl* **∼ais**) *a* & *m* ceremonial; **∼oso** /o/ *a* ceremonious

cer|rado /se'xadu/ *a* <*barba, mata*> thick; <*punho, dentes*> clenched □ *m* scrubland; **∼rar** *vt* close; **∼rar-se** *vpr* close; <*noites, trevas*> close in

certeiro /ser'teru/ *a* well-aimed, accurate

certeza /ser'teza/ *f* certainty; **com ∼** certainly; **ter ∼** be sure (**de** of; **de que** that)

certidão /sertʃi'dãw/ *f* certificate; **∼ de nascimento** birth certificate

certifi|cado /sertʃifi'kadu/ *m* certificate; **∼car** *vt* certify; **∼car-se** make sure of

certo /'sɛrtu/ *a* (*correto*) right; (*seguro*) certain; (*algum*) a certain □ *adv* right; **dar ∼** work

cerveja /ser'veʒa/ *f* beer; **∼ria** *f* brewery; (*bar*) pub

cervo /'sɛrvu/ *m* deer

cer|zidura /serzi'dura/ *f* darning; **∼zir** *vt* darn

cesariana /sezari'ana/ *f* Caesarian

césio /'sɛziu/ *m* caesium

cessar /se'sar/ *vt/i* cease

ces|ta /'sesta/ *f* basket; (*de comida*) hamper; **∼to** /e/ *m* basket; **∼to de lixo** wastepaper basket

ceticismo /setʃi'sizmu/ *m* scepticism

cético /'sɛtʃiku/ *a* sceptical □ *m* sceptic

cetim /se'tʃĩ/ *m* satin

céu /sɛw/ *m* sky; (*na religião*) heaven; **∼ da boca** roof of the mouth

cevada /se'vada/ *f* barley

chá /ʃa/ *m* tea

chacal /ʃa'kaw/ (*pl* **∼cais**) *m* jackal

chácara /'ʃakara/ *f* smallholding; (*casa*) country cottage

chaci|na /ʃa'sina/ *f* slaughter; **∼nar** *vt* slaughter

chá|-de-bar /ʃadʒi'bar/ (*pl* **∼s-de-bar**) *m* bachelor party; **∼-de-panela** (*pl* **∼s-de-panela**) *m* hen night, (*Amer*) wedding shower

chafariz /ʃafa'ris/ *m* fountain

chaga /'ʃaga/ *f* sore

chaleira /ʃa'lera/ *f* kettle

chama /'ʃama/ *f* flame

cha|mada /ʃa'mada/ *f* call; (*dos presentes*) roll call; (*dos alunos*) register; **∼mado** *m* call □ *a* (*depois do substantivo*) called; (*antes do substantivo*) so-called; **∼mar** *vt* call; (*para sair etc*) ask, invite; attract <*atenção*> □ *vi* call; <*telefone*> ring; **∼mar-se** *vpr* be called; **∼mariz** *m* decoy; **∼mativo** *a* showy, flashy

chamejar /ʃame'ʒar/ *vi* flare

chaminé /ʃami'nɛ/ *f* (*de casa, fábrica*) chimney; (*de navio, trem*) funnel

champanhe /ʃã'paɲi/ *m* champagne

champu /ʃã'pu/ (*Port*) *m* shampoo

chamuscar /ʃamus'kar/ *vt* singe, scorch

chance /'ʃãsi/ *f* chance

chanceler /ʃãse'ler/ *m* chancellor

chanchada /ʃã'ʃada/ *f* (*peça*) second-rate play; (*filme*) B movie

chanta|gear /ʃãtaʒi'ar/ *vt* blackmail; **∼gem** *f* blackmail; **∼gista** *m/f* blackmailer

chão /ʃãw/ (*pl* **∼s**) *m* ground; (*dentro de casa etc*) floor

chapa /'ʃapa/ *f* sheet; (*foto*) plate; **∼ eleitoral** electoral list; **∼ de matrícula** (*Port*) number plate, (*Amer*) license plate □ (*fam*) *m* mate

chapéu /ʃa'pɛw/ *m* hat

charada /ʃa'rada/ *f* riddle

char|ge /'ʃarʒi/ *f* (political) cartoon; **∼gista** *m/f* cartoonist

charla|tanismo /ʃarlata'nizmu/ *m* charlatanism; **∼tão** (*pl* **∼tães**) *m* (*f* **∼tona**) charlatan

char|me /'ʃarmi/ *m* charm; **fazer ∼me** turn on the charm; **∼moso** /o/ *a* charming

charneca /ʃar'nɛka/ *f* moor

charuto /ʃa'rutu/ *m* cigar

chassi /ʃa'si/ *m* chassis

chata /'ʃata/ *f* (*barca*) barge

chate|ação /ʃatʃia'sãw/ *f* annoyance; **∼ar** *vt* annoy; **∼ar-se** *vpr* get annoyed

cha|tice /ʃa'tʃisi/ *f* nuisance; **∼to** *a* (*tedioso*) boring; (*irritante*) annoying; (*mal-educado*) rude; (*plano*) flat

chauvinis|mo /ʃovi'nizmu/ *m* chauvinism; **∼ta** *m/f* chauvinist □ *a* chauvinistic

cha|vão /ʃa'vãw/ *m* cliché; **∼ve** *f* key; (*ferramenta*) spanner; **∼ve de fenda** screwdriver; **∼ve inglesa** wrench;

~**veiro** *m* (*aro*) keyring; (*pessoa*) locksmith

chávena /'ʃavena/ *f* soup bowl; (*Port: xícara*) cup

checar /ʃe'kar/ *vt* check

che|fe /'ʃɛfi/ *m*/*f* (*patrão*) boss; (*gerente*) manager; (*dirigente*) leader; ~**fia** *f* leadership; (*de empresa*) management; (*sede*) headquarters; ~**fiar** *vt* lead; be in charge of <*trabalho*>

che|gada /ʃe'gada/ *f* arrival; ~**gado** *a* <*amigo, relação*> close; ~**gar** *vi* arrive; (*deslocar-se*) move up; (*ser suficiente*) be enough □ *vt* bring up <*prato, cadeira*>; ~**gar a fazer** go as far as doing; **aonde você quer** ~**gar?** what are you driving at?; ~**gar lá** (*fig*) make it

cheia /'ʃeja/ *f* flood

cheio /'ʃeju/ *a* full; (*fam: farto*) fed up

chei|rar /ʃe'rar/ *vt*/*i* smell (**a** of); ~**roso** /o/ *a* scented

cheque /'ʃɛki/ *m* cheque, (*Amer*) check; ~ **de viagem** traveller's cheque; ~ **em branco** blank cheque

chi|ado /ʃi'adu/ *m* (*de pneus, freios*) screech; (*de porta*) squeak; (*de vapor, numa fita*) hiss; ~**ar** *vi* <*porta*> squeak; <*pneus, freios*> screech; <*vapor, fita*> hiss; <*fritura*> sizzle; (*fam: reclamar*) grumble, moan

chiclete /ʃi'klɛtʃi/ *m* chewing gum; ~ **de bola** bubble gum

chico|tada /ʃiko'tada/ *f* lash; ~**te** /ɔ/ *m* whip; ~**tear** *vt* whip

chi|frar /ʃi'frar/ (*fam*) *vt* cheat on <*marido, esposa*>; two-time <*namorado, namorada*>; ~**fre** *m* horn; ~**frudo** *a* horned; (*fam*) cuckolded □ *m* cuckold

Chile /'ʃili/ *m* Chile

chileno /ʃi'lenu/ *a* & *m* Chilean

chilique /ʃi'liki/ (*fam*) *m* funny turn

chil|rear /ʃiwxi'ar/ *vi* chirp, twitter; ~**reio** *m* chirping, twittering

chimarrão /ʃima'xãw/ *m* unsweetened maté tea

chimpanzé /ʃĩpã'zɛ/ *m* chimpanzee

China /'ʃina/ *f* China

chinelo /ʃi'nɛlu/ *m* slipper

chi|nês /ʃi'nes/ *a* & *m* (*f* ~**nesa**) Chinese

chinfrim /ʃĩ'frĩ/ *a* tatty, shoddy

chio /'ʃiu/ *m* squeak; (*de pneus*) screech; (*de vapor*) hiss

chique /'ʃiki/ *a* <*pessoa, aparência, roupa*> smart, (*Amer*) sharp; <*hotel, bairro, loja etc*> smart, up-market, posh

chiqueiro /ʃi'keru/ *m* pigsty

chis|pa /'ʃispa/ *f* flash; ~**pada** *f* dash; ~**par** *vi* (*soltar chispas*) flash; (*correr*) dash

choca|lhar /ʃoka'ʎar/ *vt*/*i* rattle; ~**lho** *m* rattle

cho|cante /ʃo'kãtʃi/ *a* shocking; (*fam*) incredible; ~**car** *vt*/*i* hatch <*ovos*>; (*ultrajar*) shock; ~**car-se** *vpr* <*carros etc*> crash; <*teorias etc*> clash

chocho /'ʃoʃu/ *a* dull, insipid

chocolate /ʃoko'latʃi/ *m* chocolate

chofer /ʃo'fɛr/ *m* chauffeur

chope /'ʃopi/ *m* draught lager

choque /'ʃɔki/ *m* shock; (*colisão*) collision; (*conflito*) clash

cho|radeira /ʃora'dera/ *f* fit of crying; ~**ramingar** *vi* whine; ~**ramingas** *m*/*f invar* whiner; ~**rão** *m* (*salgueiro*) weeping willow □ *a* (~**rona**) tearful; ~**rar** *vi* cry; ~**ro** /o/ *m* crying; ~**roso** /o/ *a* tearful

chouriço /ʃo'risu/ *m* black pudding; (*Port*) sausage

chover /ʃo'ver/ *vi* rain

chuchu /ʃu'ʃu/ *m* chayote

chucrute /ʃu'krutʃi/ *m* sauerkraut

chumaço /ʃu'masu/ *m* wad

chum|bado /ʃũ'badu/ (*fam*) *a* knocked out; ~**bar** (*Port*) *vt* fill <*dente*>; fail <*aluno*> □ *vi* <*aluno*> fail; ~**bo** *m* lead; (*Port: obturação*) filling

chu|par /ʃu'par/ *vt* suck; <*esponja*> suck up; ~**peta** /e/ *f* dummy, (*Amer*) pacifier

churras|caria /ʃuxaska'ria/ *f* barbecue restaurant; ~**co** *m* barbecue; ~**queira** *f* barbecue; ~**quinho** *m* kebab

chu|tar /ʃu'tar/ *vt*/*i* kick; (*fam: adivinhar*) guess; ~**te** *m* kick; ~**teira** *f* football boot

chu|va /'ʃuva/ *f* rain; ~**va de pedra** hail; ~**varada** *f* torrential rainstorm; ~**veiro** *m* shower; ~**viscar** *vi* drizzle; ~**visco** *m* drizzle; ~**voso** /o/ *a* rainy

cica|triz /sika'tris/ *f* scar; ~**trizar** *vt* scar □ *vi* <*ferida*> heal

cic|lismo /si'klizmu/ *m* cycling; ~**lista** *m*/*f* cyclist; ~**lo** *m* cycle; ~**lone** /o/ *m* cyclone; ~**lovia** *f* cycle lane

cida|dania /sidada'nia/ *f* citizenship; ~**dão** (*pl* ~**dãos**) *m* (*f* ~**dã**) citizen; ~**de** *f* town; (*grande*) city; ~**dela** /ɛ/ *f* citadel

ciência /si'ẽsia/ *f* science

cien|te /si'ẽtʃi/ *a* aware; ~**tífico** *a* scientific; ~**tista** *m*/*f* scientist

ci|fra /'sifra/ *f* figure; (*código*) cipher; ~**frão** *m* dollar sign; ~**frar** *vt* encode

cigano /si'ganu/ *a* & *m* gypsy

cigarra /si'gaxa/ *f* cicada; (*dispositivo*) buzzer

cigar|reira /siga'xera/ f cigarette case; **~ro** m cigarette

cilada /si'lada/ f trap; (*estratagema*) trick

cilindrada /silĩ'drada/ f (engine) capacity

cilíndrico /si'lĩdriku/ a cylindrical

cilindro /si'lĩdru/ m cylinder; (*rolo*) roller

cílio /'siliu/ m eyelash

cima /'sima/ f **em ~** on top; (*na casa*) upstairs; **em ~ de** on, on top of; **para ~** up; (*na casa*) upstairs; **por ~** over the top; **por ~ de** over; **de ~** from above; **ainda por ~** moreover

címbalo /'sĩbalu/ m cymbal

cimeira /si'mera/ f crest; (*Port: cúpula*) summit

cimen|tar /simẽ'tar/ vt cement; **~to** m cement

cinco /'sĩku/ a & m five

cine|asta /sini'asta/ m/f film-maker; **~ma** /e/ m cinema

Cingapura /sĩga'pura/ f Singapore

cínico /'siniku/ a cynical □ m cynic

cinismo /si'nizmu/ m cynicism

cinqüen|ta /sĩ'kwẽta/ a & m fifty; **~tão** a & m (f **~tona**) fifty-year-old

cinti|lante /sĩtʃi'lãtʃi/ a glittering; **~lar** vi glitter

cin|to /'sĩtu/ m belt; **~to de segurança** seatbelt; **~tura** f waist; **~turão** m belt

cin|za /'sĩza/ f ash □ a invar grey; **~zeiro** m ashtray

cin|zel /sĩ'zɛw/ (pl **~zéis**) m chisel; **~zelar** vt carve

cinzento /sĩ'zẽtu/ a grey

cipó /si'pɔ/ m vine, liana; **~poal** (pl **~poais**) m jungle

cipreste /si'prɛstʃi/ m cypress

cipriota /sipri'ɔta/ a & m Cypriot

ciranda /si'rãda/ f (*fig*) merry-go-round

cir|cense /sir'sẽsi/ a circus; **~co** m circus

circu|ito /sir'kuitu/ m circuit; **~lação** f circulation; **~lar** a & f circular □ vt circulate □ vi (*dinheiro, sangue*) circulate; (*carro*) drive; (*ônibus*) run; (*trânsito*) move; (*pessoa*) go round

círculo /'sirkulu/ m circle

circunci|dar /sirkũsi'dar/ vt circumcise; **~ção** f circumcision

circun|dar /sirkũ'dar/ vt surround; **~ferência** f circumference; **~flexo** /ɛks/ a & m circumflex; **~scrição** f district; **~scrição eleitoral** constituency; **~specto** /ɛ/ a circumspect; **~stância** f circumstance; **~stanciado** a detailed; **~stancial** (pl **~stanciais**) a

circumstantial; **~stante** m/f bystander

cirrose /si'xɔzi/ f cirrhosis

cirur|gia /sirur'ʒia/ f surgery; **~gião** m (f **~giã**) surgeon

cirúrgico /si'rurʒiku/ a surgical

cisão /si'zãw/ f split, division

cisco /'sisku/ m speck

cisma[1] /'sizma/ m schism

cis|ma[2] /'sizma/ f (*mania*) fixation; (*devaneio*) imagining, daydream; (*prevenção*) irrational dislike; (*de criança*) whim; **~mar** vt/i be lost in thought; *<criança>* be insistent; **~mar em** brood over; **~mar de ou em fazer** insist on doing; **~mar que** insist on thinking that; **~mar com alg** take a dislike to s.o.

cisne /'sizni/ m swan

cistite /sis'tʃitʃi/ f cystitis

ci|tação /sita'sãw/ f quotation; (*jurid*) summons; **~tar** vt quote; (*jurid*) summon

ciúme /si'umi/ m jealousy; **ter ~s de** be jealous of

ciu|meira /siu'mera/ f fit of jealousy; **~mento** a jealous

cívico /'siviku/ a civic

ci|vil /si'viw/ (pl **~vis**) a civil □ m civilian; **~vilidade** f civility

civili|zação /siviliza'sãw/ f civilization; **~zado** a civilized; **~zar** vt civilize

civismo /si'vizmu/ m public spirit

cla|mar /kla'mar/ vt/i cry out, clamour (por for); **~mor** m outcry; **~moroso** /o/ a *<protesto>* loud, noisy; *<erro, injustiça>* blatant

clandestino /klãdes'tʃinu/ a clandestine

cla|ra /'klara/ f egg white; **~rabóia** f skylight; **~rão** m flash; **~rear** vt brighten; clarify *<questão>* □ vi brighten up; (*fazer-se dia*) become light; **~reira** f clearing; **~reza** /e/ f clarity; **~ridade** f brightness; (*do dia*) daylight

cla|rim /kla'rĩ/ m bugle; **~rinete** /e/ m clarinet

clarividente /klarivi'dẽtʃi/ m/f clairvoyant

claro /'klaru/ a clear; *<luz>* bright; *<cor>* light □ adv clearly □ int of course; **~ que sim/não** of course/of course not; **às claras** openly; **noite em ~** sleepless night; **já é dia ~** it's already daylight

classe /'klasi/ f class; **~ média** middle class

clássico /'klasiku/ a classical; (*famoso, exemplar*) classic □ m classic

classifi|cação /klasifika'sãw/ f classification; (*numa competição* *esportiva*) placing, place; ~**cado** *a* classified; <*candidato*> successful; <*esportista, time*> qualified; ~**car** *vt* classify; (*considerar*) describe (**de** as); ~**car-se** *vpr* <*candidato, esportista*> qualify; (*chamar-se*) describe o.s. (**de** as); ~**catório** *a* qualifying

classudo /kla'sudu/ (*fam*) *a* classy

claustro|fobia /klawstrofo'bia/ *f* claustrophobia; ~**fóbico** *a* claustrophobic

cláusula /'klawzula/ *f* clause

cla|ve /'klavi/ *f* clef; ~**vícula** *f* collar bone

cle|mência /kle'mẽsia/ *f* clemency; ~**mente** *a* <*pessoa*> lenient; <*tempo*> clement

cleptomaníaco /kleptoma'niaku/ *m* kleptomaniac

clérigo /'klɛrigu/ *m* cleric, clergyman

clero /'klɛru/ *m* clergy

clicar /kli'kar/ *vi* (*comput*) click

clien|te /kli'ẽtʃi/ *m*/*f*(*de loja*) customer; (*de advogado, empresa*) client; ~**tela** /ɛ/ *f* (*de loja*) customers; (*de restaurante, empresa*) clientele

cli|ma /'klima/ *m* climate; ~**mático** *a* climatic

clímax /'klimaks/ *m invar* climax

clíni|ca /'klinika/ *f* clinic; ~**ca geral** general practice; ~**co** *a* clinical □ *m* ~**co geral** general practitioner, GP

clipe /'klipi/ *m* clip; (*para papéis*) paper clip

clone /'kloni/ *m* clone

cloro /'klɔru/ *m* chlorine

close /'klozi/ *m* close-up

clube /'klubi/ *m* club

coação /koa'sãw/ *f* coercion

coadjuvante /koadʒu'vãtʃi/ *a* <*ator*> supporting □ *m*/*f* (*em peça, filme*) co-star; (*em crime*) accomplice

coador /koa'dor/ *m* strainer; (*de legumes*) colander; (*de café*) filter bag

coadunar /koadu'nar/ *vt* combine

coagir /koa'ʒir/ *vt* compel

coagular /koagu'lar/ *vt*/*i* clot; ~**-se** *vpr* clot

coágulo /ko'agulu/ *m* clot

coalhar /koa'ʎar/ *vt*/*i* curdle; ~**-se** *vpr* curdle

coalizão /koali'zãw/ *f* coalition

coar /ko'ar/ *vt* strain

coaxar /koa'ʃar/ *vi* croak □ *m* croaking

cobaia /ko'baja/ *f* guinea pig

cober|ta /ko'bɛrta/ *f* (*de cama*) bedcover; (*de navio*) deck; ~**to** /ɛ/ *a* covered □ *pp* **de cobrir**; ~**tor** *m* blanket; ~**tura** *f* (*revestimento*) covering; (*reportagem*) coverage; (*seguro*) cover; (*apartamento*) penthouse

cobi|ça /ko'bisa/ *f* greed, covetousness; ~**çar** *vt* covet; ~**çoso** /o/ *a* covetous

cobra /'kɔbra/ *f* snake

co|brador /kobra'dor/ *m* (*no ônibus*) conductor; ~**brança** *f* (*de dívida*) collection; (*de preço*) charging; ~**brança de pênalti/falta** penalty (kick)/free kick; ~**brar** *vt* collect <*dívida*>; ask for <*coisa prometida*>; take <*pênalti*>; ~**brar aco a alg** (*em dinheiro*) charge s.o. for sth; (*fig*) make s.o. pay for sth; ~**brar uma falta** (*no futebol*) take a free kick

cobre /'kɔbri/ *m* copper

cobrir /ko'brir/ *vt* cover; ~**-se** *vpr* <*pessoa*> cover o.s. up; <*coisa*> be covered

cocaína /koka'ina/ *f* cocaine

coçar /ko'sar/ *vt* scratch □ *vi* (*esfregar-se*) scratch; (*comichar*) itch; ~**-se** *vpr* scratch o.s.

coceira /ko'sera/ *f* itch

cochi|char /koʃi'ʃar/ *vt*/*i* whisper; ~**cho** *m* whisper

cochi|lada /koʃi'lada/ *f* doze; ~**lar** *vi* doze; ~**lo** *m* snooze

coco /'koku/ *m* coconut

cócoras /'kɔkoras/ *f pl* **de** ~ squatting; **ficar de** ~ squat

côdea /'kodʒia/ *f* crust

codificar /kodʒifi'kar/ *vt* encode <*mensagem*>; codify <*leis*>

código /'kɔdʒigu/ *m* code; ~ **de barras** bar code

codinome /kodʒi'nomi/ *m* codename

coeficiente /koefisi'ẽtʃi/ *m* coefficient; (*fig: fator*) factor

coelho /ko'eʎu/ *m* rabbit

coentro /ko'ẽtru/ *m* coriander

coerção /koer'sãw/ *f* coercion

coe|rência /koe'rẽsia/ *f* (*lógica*) coherence; (*conseqüência*) consistency; ~**rente** *a* (*lógico*) coherent; (*conseqüente*) consistent

coexis|tência /koezis'tẽsia/ *f* coexistence; ~**tir** *vi* coexist

cofre /'kɔfri/ *m* safe; (*de dinheiro público*) coffer

cogi|tação /koʒita'sãw/ *f* contemplation; **fora de** ~**tação** out of the question; ~**tar** *vt*/*i* contemplate

cogumelo /kogu'mɛlu/ *m* mushroom

coibir /koi'bir/ *vt* restrict; ~**-se de** keep o.s. from

coice /'kojsi/ *m* kick

coinci|dência /koĩsi'dẽsia/ *f* coincidence; ~**dir** *vi* coincide

coisa /'kojza/ *f* thing

coitado | combinação

coitado /koj'tadu/ *m* poor thing; ∼ **do pai** poor father

cola /'kɔla/ *f* glue; (*cópia*) crib

colabo|ração /kolabora'sãw/ *f* collaboration; (*de escritor etc*) contribution; ∼**rador** *m* collaborator; (*em jornal, livro*) contributor; ∼**rar** *vi* collaborate; (*em jornal, livro*) contribute (**em** to)

colagem /ko'laʒẽ/ *f* collage

colágeno /ko'laʒenu/ *m* collagen

colapso /ko'lapsu/ *m* collapse

colar¹ /ko'lar/ *m* necklace

colar² /ko'lar/ *vt* (*grudar*) stick; (*copiar*) crib □ *vi* stick; (*copiar*) crib; <*desculpa etc*> stand up, stick

colarinho /kola'riɲu/ *m* collar; (*de cerveja*) head

colate|ral /kolate'raw/ (*pl* ∼**rais**) *a* **efeito** ∼**ral** side effect

col|cha /'kowʃa/ *f* bedspread; ∼**chão** *m* mattress

colchete /kow'ʃetʃi/ *m* fastener; (*sinal de pontuação*) square bracket; ∼ **de pressão** press stud, popper

colchonete /kowʃo'nɛtʃi/ *m* (fold-away) mattress

coldre /'kɔwdri/ *m* holster

cole|ção /kole'sãw/ *f* collection; ∼**cionador** *m* collector; ∼**cionar** *vt* collect

colega /ko'lɛga/ *m*/*f* (*amigo*) friend; (*de trabalho*) colleague

colegi|al /koleʒi'aw/ (*pl* ∼**ais**) *a* school □ *m*/*f* schoolboy (*f*-girl)

colégio /ko'lɛʒiu/ *m* secondary school, (*Amer*) high school

coleira /ko'lera/ *f* collar

cólera /'kɔlera/ *f* (*doença*) cholera; (*raiva*) fury

colérico /ko'lɛriku/ *a* (*furioso*) furious □ *m* (*doente*) cholera victim

colesterol /koleste'rɔw/ *m* cholesterol

cole|ta /ko'lɛta/ *f* collection; ∼**tânea** *f* collection; ∼**tar** *vt* collect

colete /ko'letʃi/ *m* waistcoat, (*Amer*) vest; ∼ **salva-vidas** life-jacket, (*Amer*) life-preserver

coletivo /kole'tʃivu/ *a* collective; <*transporte*> public □ *m* bus

colheita /ko'ʎejta/ *f* harvest; (*produtos colhidos*) crop

colher¹ /ko'ʎɛr/ *f* spoon

colher² /ko'ʎer/ *vt* pick <*flores, frutos*>; gather <*informações*>

colherada /koʎe'rada/ *f* spoonful

colibri /koli'bri/ *m* hummingbird

cólica /'kɔlika/ *f* colic

colidir /koli'dʒir/ *vi* collide

coli|gação /koliga'sãw/ *f* (*pol*) coalition; ∼**gado** *m* (*pol*) coalition partner; ∼**gar** *vt* bring together; ∼**gar-se** *vpr* join forces; (*pol*) form a coalition

colina /ko'lina/ *f* hill

colírio /ko'liriu/ *m* eyewash

colisão /koli'zãw/ *f* collision

collant /ko'lã/ (*pl* ∼**s**) *m* body; (*de ginástica*) leotard

colmeia /kow'meja/ *f* beehive

colo /'kɔlu/ *f* (*regaço*) lap; (*pescoço*) neck

colo|cação /koloka'sãw/ *f* placing; (*emprego*) position; (*exposição de fatos*) statement; (*de aparelho, pneus, carpete etc*) fitting; ∼**cado** *a* placed; **o primeiro** ∼**cado** (*em ranking*) person in first place; ∼**cador** *m* fitter; ∼**car** put; fit <*aparelho, pneus, carpete etc*>; put forward, state <*opinião, idéias*>; (*empregar*) get a job for

Colômbia /ko'lõbia/ *f* Colombia

colombiano /kolõbi'anu/ *a* & *m* Colombian

cólon /'kɔlõ/ *m* colon

colônia¹ /ko'lonia/ *f* (*colonos*) colony

colônia² /ko'lonia/ *f* (*perfume*) cologne

coloni|al /koloni'aw/ (*pl* ∼**ais**) *a* colonial; ∼**alismo** *m* colonialism; ∼**alista** *a* & *m*/*f* colonialist; ∼**zar** *vt* colonize

colono /ko'lonu/ *m* settler, colonist; (*lavrador*) tenant farmer

coloqui|al /koloki'aw/ (*pl* ∼**ais**) *a* colloquial

colóquio /ko'lɔkiu/ *m* (*conversa*) conversation; (*congresso*) conference

colo|rido /kolo'ridu/ *a* colourful □ *m* colouring; ∼**rir** *vt* colour

colu|na /ko'luna/ *f* column; (*vertebral*) spine; ∼**nável** (*pl* ∼**náveis**) *a* famous □ *m*/*f* celebrity; ∼**nista** *m*/*f* columnist

com /kõ/ *prep* with; **o comentário foi comigo** the comment was meant for me; **você está** ∼ **a chave?** have you got the key?; ∼ **seis anos de idade** at six years of age

coma /'koma/ *f* coma

comadre /ko'madri/ *f* (*madrinha*) godmother of one's child; (*mãe do afilhado*) mother of one's godchild; (*urinol*) bedpan

coman|dante /komã'dãtʃi/ *m* commander; ∼**dar** *vt* lead; (*ordenar*) command; (*elevar-se acima de*) dominate; ∼**do** *m* command; (*grupo*) commando group

comba|te /kõ'batʃi/ *m* combat; (*a drogas, doença etc*) fight (**a** against); ∼**ter** *vt*/*i* fight; ∼**ter-se** *vpr* fight

combi|nação /kõbina'sãw/ *f* combination; (*acordo*) arrangement;

(*plano*) scheme; (*roupa*) petticoat; ~**nar** *vt* (*juntar*) combine; (*ajustar*) arrange □ *vi* go together, match; ~**nar com** go with, match; ~**nar de sair** arrange to go out; ~**nar-se** *vpr* (*juntar-se*) combine; (*harmonizar-se*) go together, match

comboio /kõ'boju/ *m* convoy; (*Port: trem*) train

combustí|vel /kõbus'tʃivew/ (*pl* ~**veis**) *m* fuel

come|çar /kome'sar/ *vt/i* start, begin; ~**ço** /e/ *m* beginning, start

comédia /ko'mɛdʒia/ *f* comedy

comediante /komedʒi'ãtʃi/ *m/f* comedian (*f* comedienne)

comemo|ração /komemora'sãw/ *f* (*celebração*) celebration; (*lembrança*) commemoration; ~**rar** *vt* (*festejar*) celebrate; (*lembrar*) commemorate

comen|tar /komē'tar/ *vt* comment on; (*falar mal de*) make comments about; ~**tário** *m* comment; (*de texto, na TV etc*) commentary; **sem** ~**tários** no comment; ~**tarista** *m/f* commentator

comer /ko'mer/ *vt* eat; <*ferrugem etc*> eat away; take <*peça de xadrez*> □ *vi* eat; ~**se** *vpr* (*de raiva etc*) be consumed (**de** with); **dar de** ~ **a** feed

comerci|al /komersi'aw/ (*pl* ~**ais**) *a & m* commercial; ~**alizar** *vt* market; ~**ante** *m/f* trader; ~**ar** *vi* do business, trade; ~**ário** *m* shopworker

comércio /ko'mɛrsiu/ *m* (*atividade*) trade; (*loja etc*) business; (*lojas*) shops: ~ **eletrônico** e-commerce

comes /'komis/ *m pl* ~ **e bebes** (*fam*) food and drink; ~**tíveis** *m pl* foods, food; ~**tível** (*pl* ~**tíveis**) *a* edible

cometa /ko'meta/ *m* comet

cometer /kome'ter/ *vt* commit <*crime*>; make <*erro*>

comichão /komi'ʃãw/ *f* itch

comício /ko'misiu/ *m* rally

cômico /'komiku/ *a* (*de comédia*) comic; (*engraçado*) comical

comida /ko'mida/ *f* food; (*uma*) meal

comigo = **com** + **mim**

comi|lão /komi'lãw/ *a* (*f* ~**lona**) greedy □ *m* (*f* ~**lona**) glutton

cominho /ko'miɲu/ *m* cummin

comiserar-se /komize'rarsi/ *vpr* commiserate (**de** with)

comis|são /komi'sãw/ *f* commission; ~**sário** *m* commissioner; ~**sário de bordo** (*aéreo*) steward; (*de navio*) purser; ~**sionar** *vt* commission

comi|tê /komi'te/ *m* committee; ~**tiva** *f* group; (*de uma pessoa*) retinue

como /'komu/ *adv* (*na condição de*) as; (*da mesma forma que*) like; (*de que maneira*) how □ *conj* as; ~? (*pedindo repetição*) pardon?; ~ **se** as if; **assim** ~ as well as

cômoda /'komoda/ *f* chest of drawers, (*Amer*) bureau

como|didade /komodʒi'dadʒi/ *f* comfort; (*conveniência*) convenience; ~**dismo** *m* complacency; ~**dista** *a* complacent

cômodo /'komodu/ *a* comfortable; (*conveniente*) convenient □ *m* (*aposento*) room

como|vente /komo'vētʃi/ *a* moving; ~**ver** *vt* move □ *vi* be moving; ~**ver-se** *vpr* be moved

compacto /kõ'paktu/ *a* compact □ *m* single

compadecer-se /kõpade'sersi/ *vpr* feel pity (**de** for)

compadre /kõ'padri/ *m* (*padrinho*) godfather of one's child; (*pai do afilhado*) father of one's godchild

compaixão /kõpaj'ʃãw/ *f* compassion

companhei|rismo /kõpaɲe-'rizmu/ *m* companionship; ~**ro** *m* (*de viagem etc*) companion; (*amigo*) friend, mate

companhia /kõpa'ɲia/ *f* company; **fazer** ~ **a alg** keep s.o. company

compa|ração /kõpara'sãw/ *f* comparison; ~**rar** *vt* compare; ~**rativo** *a* comparative; ~**rável** (*pl* ~**ráveis**) *a* comparable

compare|cer /kõpare'ser/ *vi* appear; ~**cer a** attend; ~**cimento** *m* attendance

comparsa /kõ'parsa/ *m/f* (*ator*) bit player; (*cúmplice*) sidekick

comparti|lhar /kõpartʃi'ʎar/ *vt/i* share (**de** in); ~**mento** *m* compartment

compassado /kõpa'sadu/ *a* (*medido*) measured; (*ritmado*) regular

compassivo /kõpa'sivu/ *a* compassionate

compasso /kõ'pasu/ *m* (*mus*) beat, time; (*instrumento*) compass, pair of compasses

compatí|vel /kõpa'tʃivew/ (*pl* ~**veis**) *a* compatible

compatriota /kõpatri'ɔta/ *m/f* compatriot, fellow countryman (*f*-woman)

compelir /kõpe'lir/ *vt* compel

compene|tração /kõpenetra'sãw/ *f* conviction; ~**trar** *vt* convince; ~**trar-se** *vpr* convince o.s.

compen|sação /kõpēsa'sãw/ *f* compensation; (*de cheques*) clearing; ~**sar** *vt* make up for

<*defeitos, danos*>; offset <*peso, gastos*>; clear <*cheques*> □ *vi* <*crime*> pay

compe|tência /kõpe'tẽsia/ *f* competence; **~tente** *a* competent

compe|tição /kõpetʃi'sãw/ *f* competition; **~tidor** *m* competitor; **~tir** *vi* compete; **~tir a** be up to; **~tividade** *f* competitiveness; **~titivo** *a* competitive

compla|cência /kõpla'sẽsia/ *f* complaisance; **~cente** *a* obliging

complemen|tar /kõplemẽ'tar/ *vt* complement □ *a* complementary; **~to** *m* complement

comple|tar /kõple'tar/ *vt* complete; top up <*copo, tanque etc*>; **~tar 20 anos** turn 20; **~to** /ɛ/ *a* complete; (*cheio*) full up; **por ~to** completely; **escrever por ~to** write out in full

comple|xado /kõplek'sadu/ *a* with a complex; **~xidade** *f* complexity; **~xo** /ɛ/ *a* & *m* complex

compli|cação /kõplika'sãw/ *f* complication; **~cado** *a* complicated; **~car** *vt* complicate; **~car-se** *vpr* get complicated

complô /kõ'plo/ *m* conspiracy, plot

com|ponente /kõpo'nẽtʃi/ *a* & *m* component; **~por** *vt/i* compose; **~por-se** *vpr* (*controlar-se*) compose o.s.; **~por-se de** be composed of

compor|tamento /kõporta'mẽtu/ *m* behaviour; **~tar** *vt* hold; bear <*dor, prejuízo*>; **~tar-se** *vpr* behave

composi|ção /kõpozi'sãw/ *f* composition; (*acordo*) conciliation; **~tor** *m* (*de música*) composer; (*gráfico*) compositor

compos|to /kõ'postu/ *pp de* **compor** □ *a* compound; <*pessoa*> level-headed □ *m* compound; **~to de** made up of; **~tura** *f* composure

compota /kõ'pɔta/ *f* fruit in syrup

com|pra /'kõpra/ *f* purchase; *pl* shopping; **fazer ~pras** go shopping; **~prador** *m* buyer; **~prar** *vt* buy; bribe <*oficial, juiz*>; pick <*briga*>

compreen|der /kõprié'der/ *vt* (*conter em si*) contain; (*estender-se a*) cover, take in; (*entender*) understand; **~são** *f* understanding; **~sível** (*pl* **~síveis**) *a* understandable; **~sivo** *a* understanding

compres|sa /kõ'prɛsa/ *f* compress; **~são** *f* compression; **~sor** *m* compressor; **rolo ~sor** steamroller

compri|do /kõ'pridu/ *a* long; **~mento** *m* length

compri|mido /kõpri'midu/ *m* pill, tablet □ *a* <*ar*> compressed; **~mir** *vt*

(*apertar*) press; (*reduzir o volume de*) compress

comprome|tedor /kõpromete'dor/ *a* compromising; **~ter** *vt* (*envolver*) involve; (*prejudicar*) compromise; **~ter alg a fazer** commit s.o. to doing; **~ter-se** *vpr* (*obrigar-se*) commit o.s.; (*prejudicar-se*) compromise o.s.; **~tido** *a* (*ocupado*) busy; (*noivo*) spoken for

compromisso /kõpro'misu/ *m* commitment; (*encontro marcado*) appointment; **sem ~** without obligation

compro|vação /kõprova'sãw/ *f* proof; **~vante** *m* receipt; **~var** *vt* prove

compul|são /kõpuw'sãw/ *f* compulsion; **~sivo** *a* compulsive; **~sório** *a* compulsory

compu|tação /kõputa'sãw/ *f* computation; (*matéria, ramo*) computing; **~tador** *m* computer; **~tadorizar** *vt* computerize; **~tar** *vt* compute

comum /ko'mũ/ *a* common; (*não especial*) ordinary; **fora do ~** out of the ordinary; **em ~** <*trabalho*> joint; <*atuar*> jointly; **ter muito em ~** have a lot in common

comungar /komũ'gar/ *vi* take communion

comunhão /komu'ɲãw/ *f* communion; (*relig*) (Holy) Communion

comuni|cação /komunika'sãw/ *f* communication; **~cação social /visual** media studies/ graphic design; **~cado** *m* notice; (*pol*) communiqué; **~car** *vt* announce; (*unir*) connect □ *vi*, **~car-se** *vpr* communicate; **~cativo** *a* communicative

comu|nidade /komuni'dadʒi/ *f* community; **~nismo** *m* communism; **~nista** *a* & *m/f* communist; **~nitário** *a* (*da comunidade*) community; (*para todos juntos*) communal

côncavo /'kõkavu/ *a* concave

conce|ber /kõse'ber/ *vt* conceive; (*imaginar*) conceive of □ *vi* conceive; **~bível** (*pl* **~bíveis**) *a* conceivable

conceder /kõse'der/ *vt* grant; **~ em** accede to

concei|to /kõ'sejtu/ *m* concept; (*opinião*) opinion; (*fama*) reputation; **~tuado** *a* highly thought of; **~tuar** *vt* (*imaginar*) conceptualize; (*avaliar*) assess

concen|tração /kõsẽtra'sãw/ *f* concentration; (*de jogadores*) training camp; **~trar** *vt* concentrate; **~trar-se** *vpr* concentrate

concepção /kõsep'sãw/ f conception; (*opinião*) view

concernir /kõser'nir/ vt ~ a concern

concerto /kõ'sertu/ m concert

conces|são /kõse'sãw/ f concession; ~**sionária** f dealership; ~**sionário** m dealer

concha /'kõʃa/ f (*de molusco*) shell; (*colher*) ladle

concili|ação /kõsilia'sãw/ f conciliation; ~**ador** a conciliatory; ~**ar** vt reconcile

concílio /kõ'siliu/ m council

conci|são /kõsi'zãw/ f conciseness; ~**so** a concise

conclamar /kõkla'mar/ vt call <*eleição, greve*>; call upon <*pessoa*>

conclu|dente /kõklu'dẽtʃi/ a conclusive; ~**ir** vt/i conclude; ~**são** f conclusion; ~**sivo** a concluding

concor|dância /kõkor'dãsia/ f agreement; ~**dante** a consistent; ~**dar** vi agree (em to) □ vt bring into line; ~**data** f abrir ~**data** go into liquidation

concórdia /kõ'kɔrdʒia/ f concord

concor|rência /kõko'xẽsia/ f competition (a for); ~**rente** a competing; ~**rer** vi compete (a for); ~**rer para** contribute to; ~**rido** a popular

concre|tizar /kõkretʃi'zar/ vt realize; ~**tizar-se** vpr be realized; ~**to** /ɛ/ a & m concrete

concurso /kõ'kursu/ m contest; (*prova*) competition

con|dado /kõ'dadu/ m county; ~**de** m count

condeco|ração /kõdekora'sãw/ f decoration; ~**rar** vt decorate

conde|nação /kõdena'sãw/ f condemnation; (*jurid*) conviction; ~**nar** vt condemn; convict

conden|sação /kõdẽsa'sãw/ f condensation; ~**sar** vt condense; ~**sar-se** vpr condense

condescen|dência /kõdesẽ'dẽsia/ f acquiescence; ~**dente** a acquiescent; ~**der** vi acquiesce; ~**der a** comply with <*pedido, desejo*>; ~**der a ir** condescend to go

condessa /kõ'desa/ f countess

condi|ção /kõdʒi'sãw/ f condition; (*qualidade*) capacity; **ter** ~**ção** ou ~**ções para** be able to; **em boas** ~**ções** in good condition; ~**cionado** a conditioned; ~**cional** (pl ~**cionais**) a conditional; ~**cionamento** m conditioning

condimen|tar /kõdʒimẽ'tar/ vt season; ~**to** m seasoning

condoer-se /kõdo'ersi/ vpr ~ **de** feel sorry for

condolência /kõdo'lẽsia/ f sympathy; pl condolences

condomínio /kõdo'miniu/ m (*taxa*) service charge

condu|ção /kõdu'sãw/ f (*de carro etc*) driving; (*transporte*) transport; ~**cente** a conducive (a to); ~**ta** f conduct; ~**to** m conduit; ~**tor** m driver; (*eletr*) conductor; ~**zir** vt lead; drive <*carro*>; (*eletr*) conduct □ vi (*de carro*) drive; (*levar*) lead (a to)

cone /'koni/ m cone

conecta|r /konek'tar/ vt connect; ~**do** a connected; (*comput*) on-line

cone|xão /konek'sãw/ f connection; ~**xo** /ɛ/ a connected

confec|ção /kõfek'sãw/ f (*roupa*) off-the-peg outfit; (*loja*) clothes shop, boutique; (*fábrica*) clothes manufacturer; ~**cionar** vt make

confederação /kõfedera'sãw/ f confederation

confei|tar /kõfej'tar/ vt ice; ~**taria** f cake shop; ~**teiro** m confectioner

confe|rência /kõfe'rẽsia/ f conference; (*palestra*) lecture; ~**rencista** m/f speaker

conferir /kõfe'rir/ vt check (**com** against); (*conceder*) confer (**a** on) □ vi (*controlar*) check; (*estar exato*) tally

confes|sar /kõfe'sar/ vt/i confess; ~**sar-se** vpr confess; ~**sionário** m confessional; ~**sor** m confessor

confete /kõ'fɛtʃi/ m confetti

confi|ança /kõfi'ãsa/ f (*convicção*) confidence; (*fé*) trust; ~**ante** a confident (**em** of); ~**ar** (*dar*) entrust; ~**ar em** trust; ~**ável** (pl ~**áveis**) a reliable; ~**dência** f confidence; ~**dencial** (pl ~**denciais**) a confidential; ~**denciar** vt tell in confidence; ~**dente** m/f confidant (f confidante)

configu|ração /kõfigura'sãw/ f configuration; ~**rar** vt (*representar*) represent; (*formar*) shape; (*comput*) configure

con|finar /kõfi'nar/ vi ~**finar com** border on; ~**fins** m pl borders

confir|mação /kõfirma'sãw/ f confirmation; ~**mar** vt confirm; ~**mar-se** vpr be confirmed

confis|car /kõfis'kar/ vt confiscate; ~**co** m confiscation

confissão /kõfi'sãw/ f confession

confla|gração /kõflagra'sãw/ f conflagration; ~**grar** vt set alight; (*fig*) throw into turmoil

confli|tante /kõfli'tãtʃi/ *a* conflicting; **~to** *m* conflict

confor|mação /kõforma'sãw/ *f* resignation; **~mado** *a* resigned (**com** to); **~mar** *vt* adapt (**a** to); **~mar-se com** conform to <*regra, política*>; resign o.s. to, come to terms with <*destino, evento*>; **~me** /ɔ/ *prep* according to □ *conj* depending on; **~me** it depends; **~midade** *f* conformity; **~mismo** *m* conformism; **~mista** *a & m/f* conformist

confor|tar /kõfor'tar/ *vt* comfort; **~tável** (*pl* **~táveis**) *a* comfortable; **~to** /o/ *m* comfort

confraternizar /kõfraterni'zar/ *vi* fraternize

confron|tação /kõfrõta'sãw/ *f* confrontation; **~tar** *vt* confront; (*comparar*) compare; **~to** *m* confrontation; (*comparação*) comparison

con|fundir /kõfũ'dʒir/ *vt* confuse; **~fundir-se** *vpr* get confused; **~fusão** *f* confusion; (*desordem*) mess; (*tumulto*) commotion; **~fuso** *a* (*confundido*) confused; (*que confunde*) confusing

conge|lador /kõʒela'dor/ *m* freezer; **~lamento** *m* (*de preços etc*) freeze; **~lar** *vt* freeze; **~lar-se** *vpr* freeze

congênito /kõ'ʒenitu/ *a* congenital

congestão /kõʒes'tãw/ *f* congestion

congestio|nado /kõʒestʃio'nadu/ *a* <*rua, cidade*> congested; <*pessoa, rosto*> flushed; <*olhos*> bloodshot; **~namento** *m* (*de trânsito*) traffic jam; **~nar** *vt* congest; **~nar-se** *vpr* <*rua*> get congested; <*rosto*> flush

conglomerado /kõglome'radu/ *m* conglomerate

congratular /kõgratu'lar/ *vt* congratulate (**por** on)

congre|gação /kõgrega'sãw/ *f* (*na igreja*) congregation; (*reunião*) gathering; **~gar** *vt* bring together; **~gar-se** *vpr* congregate

congresso /kõ'grɛsu/ *m* congress

conhaque /ko'ɲaki/ *m* brandy

conhe|cedor /koɲese'dor/ *a* knowing □ *m* connoisseur; **~cer** *vt* know; (*ser apresentado a*) get to know; (*visitar*) go to, visit; **~cido** *a* known; (*famoso*) well-known □ *m* acquaintance; **~cimento** *m* knowledge; **tomar ~cimento de** learn of; **travar ~cimento com alg** make s.o.'s acquaintance, become acquainted with s.o.

cônico /'koniku/ *a* conical

coni|vência /koni'vẽsia/ *f* connivance; **~vente** *a* conniving (**em** at)

conjetu|ra /kõʒe'tura/ *f* conjecture; **~rar** *vt/i* conjecture

conju|gação /kõʒuga'sãw/ *f* (*ling*) conjugation; **~gar** *vt* conjugate <*verbo*>

cônjuge /'kõʒuʒi/ *m/f* spouse

conjun|ção /kõʒũ'sãw/ *f* conjunction; **~tivo** *a & m* subjunctive; **~to** *a* joint □ *m* set; (*roupa*) outfit; (*musical*) group; **o ~to de** the body of; **em ~to** jointly; **~tura** *f* state of affairs; (*econômica*) state of the economy

conosco = **com** + **nós**

cono|tação /konota'sãw/ *f* connotation; **~tar** *vt* connote

conquanto /kõ'kwãtu/ *conj* although, even though

conquis|ta /kõ'kista/ *f* conquest; (*proeza*) achievement; **~tador** *m* conqueror □ *a* conquering; **~tar** *vt* conquer <*terra, país*>; win <*riqueza, independência*>; win over <*pessoa*>

consa|gração /kõsagra'sãw/ *f* (*de uma igreja*) consecration; (*dedicação*) dedication; **~grado** *a* <*artista, expressão*> established; **~grar** *vt* consecrate <*igreja*>; establish <*artista, estilo*>; (*dedicar*) dedicate (**a** to); **~grar-se a** dedicate o.s. to

consci|ência /kõsi'ẽsia/ *f* (*moralidade*) conscience; (*sentidos*) consciousness; (*no trabalho*) con-scientiousness; (*de um fato etc*) awareness; **~encioso** /o/ *a* conscientious; **~ente** *a* conscious; **~entizar** *vt* make aware (**de** of); **~entizar-se** *vpr* become aware (**de** of)

consecutivo /kõseku'tʃivu/ *a* consecutive

conse|guinte /kõse'gĩtʃi/ *a* **por ~guinte** consequently; **~guir** *vt* get; **~guir fazer** manage to do □ *vi* succeed

conse|lheiro /kõse'ʌeru/ *m* counsellor, adviser; **~lho** /e/ *m* piece of advice; *pl* advice; (*órgão*) council

consen|so /kõ'sẽsu/ *m* consensus; **~timento** *m* consent; **~tir** *vt* allow □ *vi* consent (**em** to)

conse|qüência /kõse'kwẽsia/ *f* consequence; **por ~qüência** consequently; **~qüente** *a* consequent; (*coerente*) consistent

conser|tar /kõser'tar/ *vt* repair; **~to** /e/ *m* repair

conser|va /kõ'sɛrva/ *f* (*em vidro*) preserve; (*em lata*) tinned food; **~vação** *f* preservation; **~vador** *a & m* conservative; **~vadorismo** *m* conservatism; **~vante** *a & m* preservative; **~var** *vt* preserve; (*manter, guardar*) keep; **~var-se** *vpr* keep; **~vatório** *m* conservatory

conside|ração /kõsidera'sãw/ *f*
consideration; *(estima)* esteem; **levar
em ~ração** take into consideration;
~rar *vt* consider; *(estimar)* think
highly of □ *vi* consider; **~rar-se** *vpr*
consider o.s.; **~rável** *(pl* **~ráveis)** *a*
considerable

consig|nação /kõsigna'sãw/ *f*
consignment; **~nar** *vt* consign

consigo = com + si

consis|tência /kõsis'tẽsia/ *f*
consistency; **~tente** *a* firm; **~tir** *vi*
consist (**em** in)

consoante /kõso'ãtʃi/ *f* consonant

conso|lação /kõsola'sãw/ *f* consolation;
~lador *a* consoling; **~lar** *vt* console;
~lar-se *vpr* console o.s.

consolidar /kõsoli'dar/ *vt* consolidate;
mend *<fratura>*

consolo /kõ'solu/ *m* consolation

consórcio /kõ'sɔrsiu/ *m* consortium

consorte /kõ'sɔrtʃi/ *m/f* consort

conspícuo /kõs'pikuu/ *a* conspicuous

conspi|ração /kõspira'sãw/ *f*
conspiracy; **~rador** *m* conspirator;
~rar *vi* conspire

cons|tância /kõs'tãsia/ *f* constancy;
~tante *a & f* constant; **~tar** *vi (em lista
etc)* appear; **não me ~ta** I am not
aware; **~ta que** it is said that; **~tar de**
consist of

consta|tação /kõstata'sãw/ *f*
observation; **~tar** *vt* note, notice;
certify *<óbito>*

conste|lação /kõstela'sãw/ *f*
constellation; **~lado** *a* star-studded

conster|nação /kõsterna'sãw/ *f*
consternation; **~nar** *vt* dismay

consti|pação /kõstʃipa'sãw/ *f (Port:
resfriado)* cold; **~pado** *a (resfriado)*
with a cold; *(no intestino)* constipated;
~par-se *vpr (Port: resfriar-se)* get a
cold

constitu|cional /kõstʃitusio'naw/ *(pl*
~cionais) *a* constitutional; **~ição** *f*
constitution; **~inte** *a* constituent □ *f*
Constituinte Constituent Assembly;
~ir *vt* form *<governo, sociedade>*;
(representar) constitute; *(nomear)*
appoint

constran|gedor /kõstrãʒe'dor/ *a*
embarrassing; **~ger** *vt* embarrass;
(coagir) constrain; **~ger-se** *vpr* get
embarrassed; **~gimento** *m (embaraço)*
embarrassment; *(coação)* constraint

constru|ção /kõstru'sãw/ *f*
construction; *(terreno)* building
site; **~ir** *vt* build *<casa, prédio>*;
(fig) construct; **~tivo** *a* constructive;
~tor *m* builder; **~tora** *f* building
firm

cônsul /'kõsuw/ *(pl* **~es)** *m* consul

consulado /kõsu'ladu/ *m* consulate

consul|ta /kõ'suwta/ *f* consultation;
~tar *vt* consult; **~tor** *m* consultant;
~toria *f* consultancy; **~tório** *m*
(médico) surgery, *(Amer)* office

consu|mação /kõsuma'sãw/ *f (taxa)*
minimum charge; **~mado** *a* fato
~mado fait accompli; **~mar** *vt*
accomplish *<projeto>*; carry out
<crime, sacrifício>; consummate
<casamento>

consu|midor /kõsumi'dor/ *a & m*
consumer; **~mir** *vt* consume; take up
<tempo>; **~mismo** *m* consumerism;
~mista *a & m/f* consumerist; **~mo** *m*
consumption

conta /'kõta/ *f (a pagar)* bill; *(bancária)*
account; *(contagem)* count; *(de vidro
etc)* bead; *pl (com)* accounts; **em ~**
economical; **por ~ de** on account of;
por ~ própria on one's own account;
ajustar ~s settle up; **dar ~ de** *(fig)*
be up to; **dar ~ do recado** *(fam)*
deliver the goods; **dar-se ~ de** realize;
fazer de ~ pretend; **ficar por ~ de** be
left to; **levar** *ou* **ter em ~** take into
account; **prestar ~s** account for;
tomar ~ de take care of; **~ bancária**
bank account; **~ corrente** current
account

contabi|lidade /kõtabili'dadʒi/ *f*
accountancy; *(contas)* accounts; *(seção)*
accounts department; **~lista** *(Port) m/
f* accountant; **~lizar** *vt* write up
<quantia>; *(fig)* notch up

contact- *(Port) veja* **contat-**

conta|dor /kõta'dor/ *m (pessoa)*
accountant; *(de luz etc)* meter; **~gem**
f counting; *(de pontos num jogo)*
scoring; **~gem regressiva**
countdown

contagi|ante /kõtaʒi'ãtʃi/ *a* infectious;
~ar *vt* infect; **~ar-se** *vpr* become
infected

contágio /kõ'taʒiu/ *m* infection

contagioso /kõtaʒi'ozu/ *a* contagious

contami|nação /kõtamina'sãw/ *f*
contamination; **~nar** *vt* contaminate

contanto /kõ'tãtu/ *adv* **~ que** provided
that

contar /kõ'tar/ *vt/i* count; *(narrar)* tell;
~ com count on

conta|tar /kõta'tar/ *vt* contact; **~to** *m*
contact; **entrar em ~to com** get in
touch with; **tomar ~to com** come into
contact with

contem|plação /kõtẽpla'sãw/ *f*
contemplation; **~plar** *vt (considerar)*
contemplate; *(dizer respeito a)* concern;
~plar alg com treat s.o. to □ *vi* ponder;
~plativo *a* contemplative

contemporâneo /kõtẽpo'raniu/ a & m
contemporary

contenção /kõtẽ'sãw/ f containment

conten|cioso /kõtẽsi'ozu/ a contentious;
~**da** f dispute

conten|tamento /kõtẽta'mẽtu/ m
contentment; ~**tar** vt satisfy; ~**tar-se**
vpr be content; ~**te** a (feliz) happy;
(satisfeito) content; ~**to** m **a** ~**to**
satisfactorily

conter /kõ'ter/ vt contain; ~-**se** vpr
contain o.s.

conterrâneo /kõte'xaniu/ m fellow
countryman (f -woman)

contestar /kõtes'tar/ vt question; (jurid)
contest

conteúdo /kõte'udu/ m (de recipiente)
contents; (fig: de carta etc) content

contexto /kõ'testu/ m context

contigo = **com** + **ti**

continência /kõtʃi'nẽsia/ f (mil)
salute

continen|tal /kõtʃinẽ'taw/ (pl ~**tais**) a
continental; ~**te** m continent

contin|gência /kõtʃĩ'ʒẽsia/ f
contingency; ~**gente** a (eventual)
possible; (incerto) contingent □ m
contingent

continu|ação /kõtʃinua'sãw/ f
continuation; ~**ar** vt/i continue; **eles**
~**am ricos** they are still rich; ~**idade**
f continuity

contínuo /kõ'tʃinuu/ a continuous □ m
office junior

con|tista /kõ'tʃista/ m/f (short) story
writer; ~**to** m (short) story; ~**to de**
fadas fairy tale; ~**to-do-vigário** (pl
~**tos-do-vigário**) m confidence trick,
swindle

contorcer /kõtor'ser/ vt twist; ~-**se** vpr
(de dor) writhe

contor|nar /kõtor'nar/ vt go round; (fig)
get round <obstáculo, problema>;
(cercar) surround; (delinear) outline;
~**no** /o/ m outline; (da paisagem)
contour

contra /'kõtra/ prep against

contra-|atacar /kõtrata'kar/ vt
counterattack; ~-**ataque** m
counterattack

contrabaixo /kõtra'baʃu/ m double bass

contrabalançar /kõtrabalã'sar/ vt
counterbalance

contraban|dear /kõtrabãdʒi'ar/ vt
smuggle; ~**dista** m/f smuggler; ~**do**
m (ato) smuggling; (artigos)
contraband

contração /kõtra'sãw/ f contraction

contracenar /kõtrase'nar/ vi ~ **com** play
up to

contraceptivo /kõtrasep'tʃivu/ a & m
contraceptive

contracheque /kõtra'ʃɛki/ m pay slip

contradi|ção /kõtradʒi'sãw/ f
contradiction; ~**tório** a contradictory;
~**zer** vt contradict; ~**zer-se** vpr
<pessoa> contradict o.s.; <idéias etc>
be contradictory

contragosto /kõtra'gostu/ m **a** ~
reluctantly

contrair /kõtra'ir/ vt contract; pick up
<hábito, vício>; ~-**se** vpr contract

contramão /kõtra'mãw/ f opposite
direction □ a invar one way

contramestre /kõtra'mɛstri/ m
supervisor; (em navio) bosun

contra-ofensiva /kõtraofẽ'siva/ f
counter-offensive

contrapartida /kõtrapar'tʃida/ f
(fig) compensation; **em** ~ on the other
hand

contraproducente /kõtraprodu'sẽtʃi/ a
counterproductive

contrari|ar /kõtrari'ar/ vt go against,
run counter to; (aborrecer) annoy;
~**edade** f adversity; (aborrecimento)
annoyance

contrário /kõ'trariu/ a opposite;
(desfavorável) adverse; ~ **a** contrary
to; <pessoa> opposed to □ m
opposite; **pelo** ou **ao** ~ on the contrary;
ao ~ **de** contrary to; **em** ~ to the
contrary

contras|tante /kõtras'tãtʃi/ a
contrasting; ~**tar** vt/i contrast; ~**te** m
contrast

contra|tante /kõtra'tãtʃi/ m/f
contractor; ~**tar** vt employ, take on
<operários>

contra|tempo /kõtra'tẽpu/ m hitch

contra|to /kõ'tratu/ m contract; ~**tual**
(pl ~**tuais**) a contractual

contraven|ção /kõtravẽ'sãw/ f
contravention; ~**tor** m offender

contribu|ição /kõtribui'sãw/ f
contribution; ~**inte** m/f contributor;
(pagador de impostos) taxpayer; ~**ir** vt
contribute □ vi contribute; (pagar
impostos) pay tax

contrição /kõtri'sãw/ f contrition

contro|lar /kõtro'lar/ vt control;
(fiscalizar) check; ~**le** /o/, (Port) ~**lo**
/o/ m control; (fiscalização) check

contro|vérsia /kõtro'vɛrsia/ f
controversy; ~**verso** /ɛ/ a
controversial

contudo /kõ'tudu/ conj nevertheless

contundir /kõtũ'dʒir/ vt (dar
hematoma em) bruise; injure
<jogador>; ~-**se** vpr bruise o.s.;
<jogador> get injured

conturbado /kõtur'badu/ *a* troubled

contu|são /kõtu'zãw/ *f* bruise; *(de jogador)* injury; **∼so** *a* bruised; *<jogador>* injured

convales|cença /kõvale'sẽsa/ *f* convalescence; **∼cer** *vi* convalesce

convenção /kõvẽ'sãw/ *f* convention

conven|cer /kõvẽ'ser/ *vt* convince; **∼cido** *a* (*convicto*) convinced; (*metido*) conceited; **∼cimento** *m* (*convicção*) conviction; (*imodéstia*) conceitedness

convencio|nal /kõvẽsio'naw/ (*pl* **∼nais**) *a* conventional

conveni|ência /kõveni'ẽsia/ *f* convenience; **∼ente** *a* convenient; (*cabível*) appropriate

convênio /kõ'veniu/ *m* agreement

convento /kõ'vẽtu/ *m* convent

convergir /kõver'ʒir/ *vi* converge

conver|sa /kõ'vɛrsa/ *f* conversation; **a ∼sa dele** the things he says; **∼sa fiada** idle talk; **∼sação** *f* conversation; **∼sado** *a* <*pessoa*> talkative; <*assunto*> talked about; **∼sador** *a* talkative

conversão /kõver'sãw/ *f* conversion

conversar /kõver'sar/ *vi* talk

conver|sível /kõver'sivew/ (*pl* **∼síveis**) *a & m* convertible; **∼ter** *vt* convert; **∼ter-se** *vpr* be converted; **∼tido** *m* convert

con|vés /kõ'vɛs/ (*pl* **∼veses**) *m* deck

convexo /kõ'veksu/ *a* convex

convic|ção /kõvik'sãw/ *f* conviction; **∼to** *a* convinced; (*ferrenho*) confirmed; <*criminoso*> convicted

convi|dado /kõvi'dadu/ *m* guest; **∼dar** *vt* invite; **∼dativo** *a* inviting

convincente /kõvĩ'sẽtʃi/ *a* convincing

convir /kõ'vir/ *vi* (*ficar bem*) be appropriate; (*concordar*) agree (**em** on); **∼ a** suit, be convenient for; **convém notar que** one should note that

convite /kõ'vitʃi/ *m* invitation

convi|vência /kõvi'vẽsia/ *f* coexistence; (*relação*) close contact; **∼ver** *vi* coexist; (*ter relações*) associate (**com** with)

convívio /kõ'viviu/ *m* association (**com** with)

convocar /kõvo'kar/ *vt* call <*eleições, greve*>; call upon <*pessoa*> (**a** to); (*ao serviço militar*) call up

convosco = **com** + **vós**

convul|são /kõvuw'sãw/ *f* (*do corpo*) convulsion; (*da sociedade etc*) upheaval; **∼sionar** *vt* convulse <*corpo*>; (*fig*) churn up; **∼sivo** *a* convulsive

cooper /'kuper/ *m* jogging; **fazer ∼** go jogging

coope|ração /koopera'sãw/ *f* cooperation; **∼rar** *vi* cooperate; **∼rativa** *f* cooperative; **∼rativo** *a* cooperative

coorde|nação /koordena'sãw/ *f* co-ordination; **∼nada** *f* coordinate; **∼nar** *vt* coordinate

copa /'kɔpa/ *f* (*de árvore*) top; (*aposento*) breakfast room; (*torneio*) cup; *pl* (*naipe*) hearts; **a Copa (do Mundo)** the World Cup; **∼-cozinha** (*pl* **∼s-cozinhas**) *f* kitchen-diner

cópia /'kɔpia/ *f* copy

copiar /kopi'ar/ *vt* copy

co-piloto /kopi'lotu/ *m* co-pilot

copioso /kopi'ozu/ *a* ample; <*refeição*> substantial

copo /'kɔpu/ *m* glass

coque /'kɔki/ *m* (*penteado*) bun

coqueiro /ko'keru/ *m* coconut palm

coqueluche /koke'luʃi/ *f* (*doença*) whooping cough; (*mania*) fad

coque|tel /koke'tɛw/ (*pl* **∼téis**) *m* cocktail; (*reunião*) cocktail party

cor¹ /kɔr/ *m* **de ∼** by heart

cor² /kor/ *f* colour; **TV a ∼es** colour TV; **pessoa de ∼** coloured person

coração /kora'sãw/ *m* heart

cora|gem /ko'raʒẽ/ *f* courage; **∼joso** /o/ *a* courageous

co|ral¹ /ko'raw/ (*pl* **∼rais**) *m* (*animal*) coral

co|ral² /ko'raw/ (*pl* **∼rais**) *m* (*de cantores*) choir □ *a* choral

co|rante /ko'rãtʃi/ *a & m* colouring; **∼rar** *vt* colour □ *vi* blush

cor|da /'kɔrda/ *f* rope; (*mus*) string; (*para roupa lavada*) clothes line; **dar ∼da em** wind <*relógio*>; **∼da bamba** tightrope; **∼das vocais** vocal chords; **∼dão** *m* cord; (*de sapatos*) lace; (*policial*) cordon

cordeiro /kor'deru/ *m* lamb

cor|del /kor'dɛw/ (*pl* **∼déis**) (*Port*) *m* string; **literatura de ∼del** trash

cor-de-rosa /kordʒi'rɔza/ *a invar* pink

cordi|al /kordʒi'aw/ (*pl* **∼ais**) *a & m* cordial; **∼alidade** *f* cordiality

cordilheira /kordʒi'ʎera/ *f* chain of mountains

coreano /kori'anu/ *a & m* Korean

Coréia /ko'rɛja/ *f* Korea

core|ografia /koriogra'fia/ *f* choreography; **∼ógrafo** *m* choreographer

coreto /ko'retu/ *m* bandstand

coriza /ko'riza/ *f* runny nose

corja /'kɔrʒa/ *f* pack; (*de pessoas*) rabble

córner /'kɔrner/ *m* (*futebol*) corner

coro /'koru/ *m* chorus

coro|a /ko'roa/ f crown; (de flores etc) wreath □ (fam) m/f old man (f woman); **~ação** f coronation; **~ar** vt crown

coro|nel /koro'nɛw/ (pl **~néis**) m colonel

coronha /ko'roɲa/ f butt

corpete /kor'petʃi/ m bodice

corpo /'korpu/ m body; (físico de mulher) figure; (físico de homem) physique; **~ de bombeiros** fire brigade; **~ diplomático** diplomatic corps; **~ docente** teaching staff, (Amer) faculty; **~a-~** m invar pitched battle; **~ral** (pl **~rais**) a physical; <pena> corporal

corpu|lência /korpu'lēsia/ f stoutness; **~lento** a stout

correção /koxe'sãw/ f correction

corre-corre /kɔxi'kɔxi/ m (debandada) stampede; (correria) rush

correct- (Port) veja **corret-**

corre|diço /koxe'dʒisu/ a <porta> sliding; **~dor** m (atleta) runner; (passagem) corridor

correia /ko'xeja/ f strap; (peça de máquina) belt; (para cachorro) lead, (Amer) leash

correio /ko'xeju/ m post, mail; (repartição) post office; **pôr no ~** post, (Amer) mail; **~ aéreo** air mail; **~ eletrônico** email

correlação /koxela'sãw/ f correlation

correligionário /koxeliʒio'nariu/ m party colleague

corrente /ko'xẽtʃi/ a <água> running; <mês, conta> current; <estilo> fluid; (usual) common □ f (de água, eletricidade) current; (cadeia) chain; **~ de ar** draught; **~za** /e/ f current; (de ar) draught

cor|rer /ko'xer/ vi (à pé) run; (de carro) drive fast, speed; (fazer rápido) rush; <água, sangue> flow; <tempo> elapse; <boato> go round □ vt draw <cortina>; run <risco>; **~reria** f rush

correspon|dência /koxespõ'dēsia/ f correspondence; **~dente** a corresponding □ m/f correspondent; (equivalente) equivalent; **~der** vi **~der a** correspond to; (retribuir) return; **~der-se** vpr correspond (com with)

corre|tivo /koxe'tʃivu/ a corrective □ m punishment; **~to** /ɛ/ a correct

corretor /koxe'tor/ m broker; **~ de imóveis** estate agent, (Amer) realtor

corrida /ko'xida/ f (prova) race; (ação de correr) run; (de taxi) ride

corrigir /koxi'ʒir/ vt correct

corrimão /koxi'mãw/ (pl **~s**) m handrail; (de escada) banister

corriqueiro /koxi'keru/ a ordinary, run-of-the-mill

corroborar /koxobo'rar/ vt corroborate

corroer /koxo'er/ vt corrode <metal>; (fig) erode; **~-se** vpr corrode; (fig) erode

corromper /koxõ'per/ vt corrupt; **~-se** vpr be corrupted

corro|são /koxo'zãw/ f (de metal) corrosion; (fig) erosion; **~sivo** a corrosive

corrup|ção /koxup'sãw/ f corruption; **~to** a corrupt

cor|tada /kor'tada/ f (em tênis) smash; (em pessoa) put-down; **~tante** a cutting; **~tar** vt cut; cut off <luz, telefone, perna etc>; cut down <árvore>; cut out <efeito, vício>; take away <prazer>; (com o carro) cut up; (desprezar) cut dead □ vi cut; **~tar o cabelo** (no cabeleireiro) get one's hair cut; **~te¹** /ɔ/ m cut; (gume) blade; (desenho) cross-section; **sem ~te** <faca> blunt; **~te de cabelo** haircut

cor|te² /'kortʃi/ f court; **~tejar** vt court; **~tejo** /e/ m (séquito) retinue; (fúnebre) cortège; **~tês** a (f **~tesa**) courteous, polite; **~tesão** (pl **~tesãos**) m courtier; **~tesia** f courtesy

corti|ça /kor'tʃisa/ f cork; **~ço** m (casa popular) slum tenement

cortina /kor'tʃina/ f curtain

cortisona /kortʃi'zona/ f cortisone

coruja /ko'ruʒa/ f owl □ a <pai, mãe> proud, doting

coruscar /korus'kar/ vi flash

corvo /'korvu/ m crow

cós /kɔs/ m invar waistband

coser /ko'zer/ vt/i sew

cosmético /koz'mɛtʃiku/ a & m cosmetic

cósmico /'kɔzmiku/ a cosmic

cosmo /'kɔzmu/ m cosmos; **~nauta** m/f cosmonaut; **~polita** a cosmopolitan □ m/f globetrotter

costa /'kɔsta/ f coast; pl (dorso) back; **Costa do Marfim** Ivory Coast; **Costa Rica** Costa Rica

costarriquenho /kostaxi'keɲu/ a & m Costa Rican

cos|teiro /kos'teru/ a coastal; **~tela** /ɛ/ f rib; **~teleta** /e/ f chop; pl (suíças) sideburns; **~telinha** f (de porco) spare rib

costu|mar /kostu'mar/ vt **~ma fazer** he usually does; **~mava fazer** he used to do; **~me** m (uso) custom; (traje) costume; **de ~me** usually; **como de ~me** as usual; **ter o ~me de** have a habit of; **~meiro** a customary

costu|ra /kos'tura/ *f* sewing; ~**rar** *vt/i* sew; ~**reira** *f* (*mulher*) dressmaker; (*caixa*) needlework box

co|ta /'kɔta/ *f* quota; ~**tação** *f* (*preço*) rate; (*apreço*) rating; ~**tado** *a* <*ação*> quoted; (*conceituado*) highly rated; ~**tar** *vt* rate; quote <*ações*>

cote|jar /kote'ʒar/ *vt* compare; ~**jo** /e/ *m* comparison

cotidiano /kotʃidʒi'anu/ *a* everyday □ *m* everyday life

cotonete /koto'nɛtʃi/ *m* cotton bud

cotove|lada /kotove'lada/ *f* (*para abrir caminho*) shove; (*para chamar atenção*) nudge; ~**lo** /e/ *m* elbow

coura|ça /ko'rasa/ *f* (*armadura*) breastplate; (*de navio, animal*) armour; ~**çado** (*Port*) *m* battleship

couro /'koru/ *m* leather; ~ **cabeludo** scalp

couve /'kovi/ *f* spring greens; ~**-de-bruxelas** (*pl* ~**s-de-bruxelas**) *f* Brussels sprout; ~**-flor** (*pl* ~**s-flores**) *f* cauliflower

couvert /ku'vɛr/ (*pl* ~**s**) *m* cover charge

cova /'kɔva/ *f* (*buraco*) pit; (*sepultura*) grave

covar|de /ko'vardʒi/ *m/f* coward □ *a* cowardly; ~**dia** *f* cowardice

coveiro /ko'veru/ *m* gravedigger

covil /ko'viw/ (*pl* ~**vis**) *m* den, lair

covinha /ko'viɲa/ *f* dimple

co|xa /'koʃa/ *f* thigh; ~**xear** *vi* hobble

coxia /ko'ʃia/ *f* aisle

coxo /'koʃu/ *a* hobbling; **ser** ~ hobble

co|zer /ko'zer/ *vt/i* cook; ~**zido** *m* stew, casserole

cozi|nha /ko'ziɲa/ *f* (*aposento*) kitchen; (*comida, ação*) cooking; (*arte*) cookery; ~**nhar** *vt/i* cook; ~**nheiro** *m* cook

crachá /kra'ʃa/ *m* badge, (*Amer*) button

crânio /'kraniu/ *m* skull; (*pessoa*) genius

crápula /'krapula/ *m/f* scoundrel

craque /'kraki/ *m* (*de futebol*) soccer star; (*fam*) expert

crase /'krazi/ *f* contraction; **a com** ~ a grave (à)

crasso /'krasu/ *a* crass

cratera /kra'tɛra/ *f* crater

cravar /kra'var/ *vt* drive in <*prego*>; dig <*unha*>; stick <*estaca*>; ~ **com os olhos** stare at; ~**-se** *vpr* stick

cravejar /krave'ʒar/ *vt* nail; (*com balas*) spray, riddle

cravo[1] /'kravu/ *m* (*flor*) carnation; (*condimento*) clove

cravo[2] /'kravu/ *m* (*na pele*) blackhead; (*prego*) nail

cravo[3] /'kravu/ *m* (*instrumento*) harpsichord

creche /'krɛʃi/ *f* crèche

credenci|ais /kredẽsi'ajs/ *f pl* credentials; ~**ar** *vt* qualify

credi|ário /kredʒi'ariu/ *m* hire purchase agreement, credit plan; ~**bilidade** *f* credibility; ~**tar** *vt* credit

cré|dito /'krɛdʒitu/ *m* credit; **a** ~ on credit

cre|do /'krɛdu/ *m* creed □ *int* heavens; ~**dor** *m* creditor □ *a* <*saldo*> credit

crédulo /'krɛdulu/ *a* gullible

cre|mação /krema'sãw/ *f* cremation; ~**mar** *vt* cremate; ~**matório** *m* crematorium

cre|me /'krɛmi/ *a invar* & *m* cream; ~**me Chantilly** whipped cream; ~**me de leite** (sterilized) cream; ~**moso** /o/ *a* creamy

cren|ça /'krẽsa/ *f* belief; ~**dice** *f* superstition; ~**te** *m* believer; (*protestante*) □ *a* religious; (*protestante*) Protestant; **estar** ~**te que** believe that

crepe /'krɛpi/ *m* crepe

crepitar /krepi'tar/ *vi* crackle

crepom /kre'põ/ *m* crepe; **papel** ~ tissue paper

crepúsculo /kre'puskulu/ *m* twilight

crer /krer/ *vt/i* believe (**em** in); **creio que** I think (that); ~**-se** *vpr* believe o.s. to be

cres|cendo /kre'sẽdu/ *m* crescendo; ~**cente** *a* growing □ *m* crescent; ~**cer** *vi* grow; <*bolo*> rise; ~**cido** *a* grown; ~**cimento** *m* growth

crespo /'krespu/ *a* <*cabelo*> frizzy; <*mar*> choppy

cretino /kre'tʃinu/ *m* cretin

cria /'kria/ *f* baby; *pl* young

criação /kria'sãw/ *f* creation; (*educação*) upbringing; (*de animais*) raising; (*gado*) livestock

criado /kri'adu/ *m* servant; ~**-mudo** (*pl* ~**s-mudos**) *m* bedside table

criador /kria'dor/ *m* creator; (*de animais*) farmer, breeder

crian|ça /kri'ãsa/ *f* child □ *a* childish; ~**çada** *f* kids; ~**cice** *f* childishness; (*uma*) childish thing

criar /kri'ar/ *vt* (*fazer*) create; bring up <*filhos*>; rear <*animais*>; grow <*planta*>; pluck up <*coragem*>; ~**-se** *vpr* be brought up, grow up

criati|vidade /kriatʃivi'dadʒi/ *f* creativity; ~**vo** *a* creative

criatura /kria'tura/ *f* creature

crime /'krimi/ *m* crime

crimi|nal /krimi'naw/ (*pl* ~**nais**) *a* criminal; ~**nalidade** *f* crime; ~**noso** *m* criminal

crina /'krina/ *f* mane

crioulo /kri'olu/ *a & m* creole; *(negro)* black

cripta /'kripta/ *f* crypt

crisálida /kri'zalida/ *f* chrysalis

crisântemo /kri'zãtemu/ *m* chrysanthemum

crise /'krizi/ *f* crisis

cris|ma /'krizma/ *f* confirmation; **∼mar** *vt* confirm; **∼mar-se** *vpr* get confirmed

crista /'krista/ *f* crest

cris|tal /kris'taw/ (*pl* **∼tais**) *m* crystal; *(vidro)* glass; **∼talino** *a* crystal-clear; **∼talizar** *vt/i* crystallize

cris|tandade /kristã'dadʒi/ *f* Christendom; **∼tão** (*pl* **∼tãos**) *a & m* (*f* **∼tã**) Christian; **∼tianismo** *m* Christianity

Cristo /'kristu/ *m* Christ

cri|tério /kri'tɛriu/ *m* discretion; *(norma)* criterion; **∼terioso** *a* perceptive, discerning

crítica /'kritʃika/ *f* criticism; *(análise)* critique; *(de filme, livro)* review; *(críticos)* critics

criticar /kritʃi'kar/ *vt* criticize; review <*filme, livro*>

crítico /'kritʃiku/ *a* critical □ *m* critic

crivar /kri'var/ *vt* (*furar*) riddle

crí|vel /'krivew/ (*pl* **∼veis**) *a* credible

crivo /'krivu/ *m* sieve; (*fig*) scrutiny

crocante /kro'kãtʃi/ *a* crunchy

crochê /kro'ʃe/ *m* crochet

crocodilo /kroko'dʒilu/ *m* crocodile

cromo /'kromu/ *m* chrome

cromossomo /kromo'somu/ *m* chromosome

crôni|ca /'kronika/ *f* *(histórica)* chronicle; *(no jornal)* feature; *(conto)* short story; **∼co** *a* chronic

cronista /kro'nista/ *m*/*f* *(de jornal)* feature writer; *(contista)* short story writer; *(historiador)* chronicler

crono|grama /krono'grama/ *m* schedule; **∼logia** *f* chronology; **∼lógico** *a* chronological; **∼metrar** *vt* time

cronômetro /kro'nometru/ *m* stopwatch

croquete /kro'kɛtʃi/ *m* savoury meatball in breadcrumbs

croqui /kro'ki/ *m* sketch

crosta /'krosta/ *f* crust; *(em ferida)* scab

cru /kru/ *a* (*f* **∼a**) raw; <*luz, tom, palavra*> harsh; <*linguagem*> crude; <*verdade*> unvarnished, plain

cruci|al /krusi'aw/ (*pl* **∼ais**) *a* crucial

crucifi|cação /krusifika'sãw/ *f* crucifixion; **∼car** *vt* crucify; **∼xo** /ks/ *m* crucifix

cru|el /kru'ɛw/ (*pl* **∼éis**) *a* cruel; **∼eldade** *f* cruelty; **∼ento** *a* bloody

crupe /'krupi/ *m* croup

crustáceos /krus'tasius/ *m pl* shellfish

cruz /krus/ *f* cross

cruza|da /kru'zada/ *f* crusade; **∼do¹** *m* *(soldado)* crusader

cru|zado² /kru'zadu/ *m* *(moeda)* cruzado; **∼zador** *m* cruiser; **∼zamento** *m* *(de ruas)* crossroads, junction, *(Amer)* intersection; *(de raças)* cross; **∼zar** *vt* cross □ *vi* <*navio*> cruise; **∼zar com** pass; **∼zar-se** *vpr* cross; <*pessoas*> pass each other; **∼zeiro** *m* *(moeda)* cruzeiro; *(viagem)* cruise; *(cruz)* cross

cu /ku/ *m* *(chulo)* arse, *(Amer)* ass

Cuba /'kuba/ *f* Cuba

cubano /ku'banu/ *a & m* Cuban

cúbico /'kubiku/ *a* cubic

cubículo /ku'bikulu/ *m* cubicle

cubis|mo /ku'bizmu/ *m* cubism; **∼ta** *a & m*/*f* cubist

cubo /'kubu/ *m* cube; *(de roda)* hub

cuca /'kuka/ (*fam*) *f* head

cuco /'kuku/ *m* cuckoo; *(relógio)* cuckoo clock

cu|-de-ferro /kudʒi'fɛxu/ (*pl* **∼s-de-ferro**) (*fam*) *m* swot

cueca /ku'ɛka/ *f* underpants; *pl* *(Port: de mulher)* knickers

cueiro /ku'eru/ *m* baby wrap

cuia /'kuia/ *f* gourd

cuidado /kui'dadu/ *m* care; **com ∼** carefully; **ter** *ou* **tomar ∼** be careful; **∼so** /o/ *a* careful

cuidar /kui'dar/ *vi* **∼ de** take care of; **∼-se** *vpr* look after o.s.

cujo /'kuʒu/ *pron* whose

culatra /ku'latra/ *f* breech; **sair pela ∼** (*fig*) backfire

culiná|ria /kuli'naria/ *f* cookery; **∼rio** *a* culinary

culmi|nância /kuwmi'nãsia/ *f* culmination; **∼nante** *a* culminating; **∼nar** *vi* culminate (**em** in)

cul|pa /'kuwpa/ *f* guilt; **foi ∼pa minha** it was my fault; **ter ∼pa de** be to blame for; **∼pabilidade** *f* guilt; **∼pado** *a* guilty □ *m* culprit; **∼par** *vt* blame (**de** for); *(na justiça)* find guilty (**de** of); **∼par-se** *vpr* take the blame (**de** for); **∼pável** (*pl* **∼páveis**) *a* culpable, guilty

culti|var /kuwtʃi'var/ *vt* cultivate; grow <*plantas*>; **∼vo** *m* cultivation; *(de plantas)* growing

cul|to /'kuwtu/ *a* cultured □ *m* cult; **∼tura** *f* culture; *(de terra)* cultivation; **∼tural** (*pl* **∼turais**) *a* cultural

cumbuca /kũ'buka/ *f* bowl

cume /'kumi/ *m* peak

cúmplice /'kũplisi/ *m/f* accomplice

cumplicidade /kũplisi'dadʒi/ *f* complicity

cumprimen|tar /kũprimẽ'tar/ *vt/i* (*saudar*) greet; (*parabenizar*) compliment; **~to** *m* (*saudação*) greeting; (*elogio*) compliment; (*de lei, ordem*) compliance (**de** with); (*de promessa, palavra*) fulfilment

cumprir /kũ'prir/ *vt* keep <*promessa, palavra*>; comply with <*lei, ordem*>; do <*dever*>; carry out <*obrigações*>; serve <*pena*>; **~ com** keep to □ *vi* **cumpre-nos ir** we should go; **~-se** *vpr* be fulfilled

cúmulo /'kumulu/ *m* height; **é o ~!** that's the limit!

cunha /'kuɲa/ *f* wedge

cunha|da /ku'ɲada/ *f* sister-in-law; **~do** *m* brother-in-law

cunhar /'kuɲar/ *vt* coin <*palavra, expressão*>; mint <*moedas*>

cunho /'kuɲu/ *m* hallmark

cupim /ku'pĩ/ *m* termite

cupom /ku'põ/ *m* coupon

cúpula /'kupula/ *f* (*abóbada*) dome; (*de abajur*) shade; (*chefia*) leadership; (**reunião de**) **~** summit (meeting)

cura /'kura/ *f* cure □ *m* curate, priest

curandeiro /kurã'deru/ *m* (*religioso*) faith-healer; (*índio*) medicine man; (*charlatão*) quack

curar /ku'rar/ *vt* cure; dress <*ferida*>; **~-se** *vpr* be cured

curativo /kura'tʃivu/ *m* dressing

curá|vel /ku'ravew/ (*pl* **~veis**) *a* curable

curin|ga /ku'rĩga/ *m* wild card; **~gão** *m* joker

curio|sidade /kuriozi'dadʒi/ *f* curiosity; **~so** /o/ *a* curious □ *m* (*espectador*) onlooker

cur|ral /ku'xaw/ (*pl* **~rais**) *m* pen

currículo /ku'xikulu/ *m* curriculum; (*resumo*) curriculum vitae, CV

cur|sar /kur'sar/ *vt* attend <*escola, aula*>; study <*matéria*>; **~so** *m* course; **~sor** *m* cursor

curta|-metragem /kurtame'traʒẽ/ (*pl* **~s-metragens**) *m* short (film)

cur|tição /kurtʃi'sãw/ (*pl* **~ções**) *f* enjoyment; **~tir** *vt* (*fam*) enjoy; tan <*couro*>

curto /'kurtu/ *a* short; <*conhecimento, inteligência*> limited; **~-circuito** (*pl* **~s-circuitos**) *m* short circuit

cur|va /'kurva/ *f* curve; (*de estrada, rio*) bend; **~va fechada** hairpin bend; **~var** *vt* bend; **~var-se** *vpr*

bend; (*fig*) bow (**a** to); **~vo** *a* curved; <*estrada*> winding

cus|parada /kuspa'rada/ *f* spit; **~pe** *m* spit, spittle; **~pir** *vt/i* spit

cus|ta /'kusta/ *f* **à ~ta de** at the expense of; **~tar** *vt* cost □ *vi* (*ser difícil*) be hard; **~tar a fazer** (*ter dificuldade*) find it hard to do; (*demorar*) take a long time to do; **~tear** *vt* finance, fund; **~teio** *m* funding; (*relação de despesas*) costing; **~to** *m* cost; **a ~to** with difficulty

custódia /kus'tɔdʒia/ *f* custody

cutelo /ku'tɛlu/ *m* cleaver

cutícula /ku'tʃikula/ *f* cuticle

cútis /'kutʃis/ *f invar* complexion

cutucar /kutu'kar/ *vt* (*com o cotovelo, joelho*) nudge; (*com o dedo*) poke; (*com instrumento*) prod

czar /zar/ *m* tsar

....

Dd

....

da = **de** + **a**

dádiva /'dadʒiva/ *f* gift; (*donativo*) donation

dado /'dadu/ *m* (*de jogar*) die, dice; (*informação*) fact, piece of information; *pl* data

daí /da'i/ *adv* (*no espaço*) from there; (*no tempo*) then; **~ por diante** from then on; **e ~?** (*fam*) so what?

dali /da'li/ *adv* from over there

dália /'dalia/ *f* dahlia

dal|tônico /daw'toniku/ *a* colour-blind; **~tonismo** *m* colour-blindness

dama /'dama/ *f* lady; (*em jogos*) queen; *pl* (*jogo*) draughts, (*Amer*) checkers; **~ de honra** bridesmaid

da|nado /da'nadu/ *a* damned; (*zangado*) angry; (*travesso*) naughty; **~nar-se** *vpr* get angry; **~ne-se!** (*fam*) who cares?

dan|ça /'dãsa/ *f* dance; **~çar** *vt* dance □ *vi* dance; (*fam*) <*pessoa*> miss out; <*coisa*> go by the board; <*crimonoso*> get caught; **~çarino** *m* dancer; **~ceteria** *f* discotheque

da|nificar /danifi'kar/ *vt* damage; **~ninho** *a* undesirable; **~no** *m* (*pl*) damage; **~noso** /o/ *a* damaging

dantes /'dãtʃis/ *adv* formerly

daquela(s), daquele(s) = **de** + **aquela(s), aquele(s)**

d

daqui /da'ki/ *adv* from here; ∼ **a 2 dias** in 2 days(' time); ∼ **a pouco** in a minute; ∼ **em diante** from now on

daquilo = de + aquilo

dar /dar/ *vt* give; have <*dormida, lida etc*>; do <*pulo, cambalhota etc*>; cause <*problemas*>; produce <*frutas, leite*>; deal <*cartas*>; (*lecionar*) teach □ *vi* (*ser possível*) be possible; (*ser suficiente*) be enough; ∼ **com** come across; ∼ **em** lead to; **ele dá para ator** he'd make a good actor; ∼ **por** (*considerar como*) consider to be; (*reparar em*) notice; ∼**-se** *vpr* <*coisa*> happen; <*pessoa*> get on

dardo /'dardu/ *m* dart; (*no atletismo*) javelin

das = de + as

da|ta /'data/ *f* date; **de longa** ∼ long since; ∼**tar** *vt/i* date

dati|lografar /datʃilogra'far/ *vt/i* type; ∼**lografia** *f* typing; ∼**lógrafo** *m* typist

de /dʒi/ *prep* of; (*procedência*) from; ∼ **carro** by car; **trabalho** ∼ **repórter** I work as a reporter

debaixo /dʒi'baʃu/ *adv* below; ∼ **de** under

debalde /dʒi'bawdʒi/ *adv* in vain

debandada /debã'dada/ *f* stampede

deba|te /de'batʃi/ *m* debate; ∼**ter** *vt* debate; ∼**ter-se** *vpr* grapple

debelar /debe'lar/ *vt* overcome

dé|bil /'dɛbiw/ (*pl* ∼**beis**) *a* feeble; ∼**bil mental** retarded (person)

debili|dade /debili'dadʒi/ *f* debility; ∼**tar** *vt* debilitate; ∼**tar-se** *vpr* become debilitated

debitar /debi'tar/ *vt* debit

débito /'dɛbitu/ *m* debit

debo|chado /debo'ʃadu/ *a* sardonic; ∼**char** *vt* mock; ∼**che** /ɔ/ *m* jibe

debruar /debru'ar/ *vt/i* edge

debruçar-se /debru'sarsi/ *vpr* bend over; ∼ **sobre** study

debrum /de'brũ/ *m* edging

debulhar /debu'ʎar/ *vt* thresh

debu|tante /debu'tãtʃi/ *f* debutante; ∼**tar** *vi* debut, make one's debut

década /'dɛkada/ *f* decade; **a** ∼ **dos 60** the sixties

deca|dência /deka'dẽsia/ *f* decadence; ∼**dente** *a* decadent

decair /deka'ir/ *vi* decline; (*degringolar*) go downhill; <*planta*> wilt

decal|car /dekaw'kar/ *vt* trace; ∼**que** *m* tracing

decapitar /dekapi'tar/ *vt* decapitate

decatlo /de'katlu/ *m* decathlon

de|cência /de'sẽsia/ *f* decency; ∼**cente** *a* decent

decepar /dese'par/ *vt* cut off

decep|ção /desep'sãw/ *f* disappointment; ∼**cionar** *vt* disappoint; ∼**cionar-se** *vpr* be disappointed

decerto /dʒi'sɛrtu/ *adv* certainly

deci|dido /desi'dʒidu/ *a* <*pessoa*> determined; ∼**dir** *vt/i* decide; ∼**dir-se** *vpr* make up one's mind; ∼**dir-se por** decide on

decíduo /de'sidu/ *a* deciduous

decifrar /desi'frar/ *vt* decipher

deci|mal /desi'maw/ (*pl* ∼**mais**) *a & m* decimal

décimo /'dɛsimu/ *a & m* tenth; ∼ **primeiro** eleventh; ∼ **segundo** twelfth; ∼ **terceiro** thirteenth; ∼ **quarto** fourteenth; ∼ **quinto** fifteenth; ∼ **sexto** sixteenth; ∼ **sétimo** seventeenth; ∼ **oitavo** eighteenth; ∼ **nono** nineteenth

deci|são /desi'zãw/ *f* decision; ∼**sivo** *a* decisive

decla|ração /deklara'sãw/ *f* declaration; ∼**rado** *a* <*inimigo*> sworn; <*crente*> avowed; <*ladrão*> self-confessed; ∼**rar** *vt* declare

decli|nação /deklina'sãw/ *f* declension; ∼**nar** *vt* ∼**nar (de)** decline □ *vi* decline; <*sol*> go down; <*chão*> slope down

declínio /de'kliniu/ *m* decline

declive /de'klivi/ *m* (downward) slope, incline

decodificar /dekodʒifi'kar/ *vt* decode

deco|lagem /deko'laʒẽ/ *f* take-off; ∼**lar** *vi* take off; (*fig*) get off the ground

decom|por /dekõ'por/ *vt* break down; contort <*feições*>; ∼**por-se** *vpr* break down; <*cadáver*> decompose; ∼**posição** *f* (*de cadáver*) decomposition

deco|ração /dekora'sãw/ *f* decoration; (*aprendizagem*) learning by heart; ∼**rar** *vt* (*adornar*) decorate; (*aprender*) learn by heart, memorize; ∼**rativo** *a* decorative; ∼**reba** /ɛ/ (*fam*) *f* rote-learning; ∼**ro** /o/ *m* decorum; ∼**roso** /o/ *a* decorous

deco|rrência /deko'xẽsia/ *f* consequence; ∼**rrente** *a* resulting (**de** from); ∼**rrer** *vi* <*tempo*> elapse; <*acontecimento*> pass off; (*resultar*) result (**de** from) □ *m* **no** ∼**rrer de** in the course of; **com o** ∼**rrer do tempo** in time, with the passing of time

deco|tado /deko'tadu/ *a* low-cut; ∼**te** /ɔ/ *m* neckline

decrépito /de'krɛpitu/ *a* decrepit

decres|cente /dekre'sẽtʃi/ *a* decreasing; ∼**cer** *vi* decrease

decre|tar /dekre'tar/ *vt* decree; declare <*estado de sítio*>; **~to** /ɛ/ *m* decree; **~to-lei** (*pl* **~tos-leis**) *m* act

decurso /de'kursu/ *m* course

de|dal /de'daw/ (*pl* **~dais**) *m* thimble; **~dão** *m* (*da mão*) thumb; (*do pé*) big toe

dedetizar /dedet∫i'zar/ *vt* spray with insecticide

dedi|cação /dedʒika'sãw/ *f* dedication; **~car** *vt* dedicate; devote <*tempo*>; **~car-se** *vpr* dedicate o.s. (**a** to); **~catória** *f* dedication

dedilhar /dedʒi'ʎar/ *vt* pluck

dedo /'dedu/ *m* finger; (*do pé*) toe; **cheio de ~s** all fingers and thumbs; (*sem graça*) awkward; **~-duro** (*pl* **~s-duros**) *m* sneak; (*político, criminoso*) informer

dedução /dedu'sãw/ *f* deduction

dedurar /dedu'rar/ *vt* sneak on; (*à polícia*) inform on

dedu|tivo /dedu't∫ivu/ *a* deductive; **~zir** *vt* (*descontar*) deduct; (*concluir*) deduce

defa|sado /defa'zadu/ *a* out of step; **~sagem** *f* gap, lag

defecar /defe'kar/ *vi* defecate

defei|to /de'fejtu/ *m* defect; **botar ~to em** find fault with; **~tuoso** /o/ *a* defective

defen|der /defẽ'der/ *vt* defend; **~der-se** *vpr* (*virar-se*) fend for o.s.; (*contra-atacar*) defend o.s. (**de** against); **~siva** *f* **na ~siva** on the defensive; **~sor** *m* defender; (*advogado*) defence counsel

defe|rência /defe'rẽsia/ *f* deference; **~rente** *a* deferential

defesa /de'feza/ *f* defence □ *m* defender

defici|ência /defisi'ẽsia/ *f* deficiency; **~ente** *a* deficient; (*física ou mentalmente*) handicapped □ *m*/*f* handicapped person

déficit /'dɛfisit∫i/ (*pl* **~s**) *m* deficit

deficitário /defisit∫i'ariu/ *a* in deficit; <*empresa*> loss-making

definhar /defi'ɲar/ *vi* waste away; <*planta*> wither

defi|nição /defini'sãw/ *f* definition; **~nir** *vt* define; **~nir-se** *vpr* (*descrever-se*) define o.s.; (*decidir-se*) come to a decision; (*explicar-se*) make one's position clear; **~nitivo** *a* definitive; **~nível** (*pl* **~níveis**) *a* definable

defla|ção /defla'sãw/ *f* deflation; **~cionário** *a* deflationary

deflagrar /defla'grar/ *vt* set off □ *vi* break out

defor|mar /defor'mar/ *vt* misshape; deform <*corpo*>; distort <*imagem*>; **~midade** *f* deformity

defraudar /defraw'dar/ *vt* defraud (**de** of)

defron|tar /defrõ'tar/ *vt* **~tar com** face; **~te** *adv* opposite; **~te de** opposite

defumar /defu'mar/ *vt* smoke

defunto /de'fũtu/ *a* & *m* deceased

dege|lar /deʒe'lar/ *vt/i* thaw; **~lo** /e/ *m* thaw

degeneração /deʒenera'sãw/ *f* degeneration

degenerar /deʒene'rar/ *vi* degenerate (**em** into)

degolar /dego'lar/ *vt* cut the throat of

degra|dação /degrada'sãw/ *f* degradation; **~dante** *a* degrading; **~dar** *vt* degrade

degrau /de'graw/ *m* step

degringolar /degrĩgo'lar/ *vi* deteriorate, go downhill

degustar /degus'tar/ *vt* taste

dei|tada /dej'tada/ *f* lie-down; **~tado** *a* lying down; (*dormindo*) in bed; (*fam: preguiçoso*) idle; **~tar** *vt* lay down; (*na cama*) put to bed; (*pôr*) put; (*Port: jogar*) throw □ *vi*, **~tar-se** *vpr* lie down; (*ir para cama*) go to bed

dei|xa /'dej∫a/ *f* cue; **~xar** *vt* leave; (*permitir*) let; **~xar de** (*parar*) stop; (*omitir*) fail; **não pôde ~xar de rir** he couldn't help laughing; **~xar alg nervoso** make s.o. annoyed; **~xar cair** drop; **~xar a desejar** leave a lot to be desired; **~xa (para lá)** (*fam*) never mind, forget it

dela(s) = **de** + **ela(s)**

delatar /dela'tar/ *vt* report

délavé /dela've/ *a invar* faded

dele(s) = **de** + **ele(s)**

dele|gação /delega'sãw/ *f* delegation; **~gacia** *f* police station; **~gado** *m* delegate; **~gado de polícia** police chief; **~gar** *vt* delegate

delei|tar /delej'tar/ *vt* delight; **~tar-se** *vpr* delight (**com** in); **~te** *m* delight; **~toso** /o/ *a* delightful

delgado /dew'gadu/ *a* slender

delibe|ração /delibera'sãw/ *f* deliberation; **~rar** *vt/i* deliberate

delica|deza /delika'deza/ *f* delicacy; (*cortesia*) politeness; **~do** *a* delicate; (*cortês*) polite

delícia /de'lisia/ *f* delight; **ser uma ~** <*comida*> be delicious; <*sol etc*> be lovely

delici|ar /delisi'ar/ *vt* delight; **~ar-se** delight (**com** in); **~oso** /o/ *a* delightful, lovely; <*comida*> delicious

deline|ador /delinia'dor/ *m* eye-liner; **~ar** *vt* outline

delin|qüência /delĩ'kwẽsia/ *f* delinquency; **~qüente** *a* & *m* delinquent

deli|rante /deli'rãtʃi/ *a* rapturous; (*med*) delirious; **~rar** *vi* go into raptures; <*doente*> be delirious

delírio /de'liriu/ *m* (*febre*) delirium; (*excitação*) raptures

delito /de'litu/ *m* crime

delonga /de'lõga/ *f* delay

delta /'dɛwta/ *f* delta

dema|gogia /demago'ʒia/ *f* demagogy; **~gógico** *a* demagogic; **~gogo** /o/ *m* demagogue

demais /dʒi'majs/ *a & adv* (*muito*) very much; (*em demasia*) too much; **os ~** the rest, the others; **é ~!** (*fam*) it's great!

deman|da /de'mãda/ *f* demand; (*jurid*) action; **~dar** *vt* sue

demão /de'mãw/ *f* coat

demar|car /demar'kar/ *vt* demarcate; **~catório** *a* demarcation

demasia /dema'zia/ *f* excess; **em ~** too (much, many)

de|mência /de'mẽsia/ *f* insanity; (*med*) dementia; **~mente** *a* insane; (*med*) demented

demissão /demi'sãw/ *f* sacking, dismissal; **pedir ~** resign

demitir /demi'tʃir/ *vt* sack, dismiss; **~-se** *vpr* resign

demo|cracia /demokra'sia/ *f* democracy; **~crata** *m/f* democrat; **~crático** *a* democratic; **~cratizar** *vt* democratize; **~grafia** *f* demography; **~gráfico** *a* demographic

demo|lição /demoli'sãw/ *f* demolition; **~lir** *vt* demolish

demônio /de'moniu/ *m* demon

demons|tração /demõstra'sãw/ *f* demonstration; **~trar** *vt* demonstrate; **~trativo** *a* demonstrative

demo|ra /de'mɔra/ *f* delay; **~rado** *a* lengthy; **~rar** *vi* (*levar*) take; (*tardar a voltar, terminar etc*) be long; (*levar muito tempo*) take a long time □ *vt* delay

dendê /dẽ'de/ *m* (*óleo*) palm oil

denegrir /dene'grir/ *vt* denigrate

dengoso /dẽ'gozu/ *a* coy

dengue /'dẽgi/ *m* dengue

denomi|nação /denomina'sãw/ *f* denomination; **~nar** *vt* name

denotar /deno'tar/ *vt* denote

den|sidade /dẽsi'dadʒi/ *f* density; **~so** *a* dense

den|tado /dẽ'tadu/ *a* serrated; **~tadura** *f* (set of) teeth; (*postiça*) dentures, false teeth; **~tal** (*pl* **~tais**) *a* dental; **~tário** *a* dental; **~te** *m* tooth; (*de alho*) clove; **~te do siso** wisdom tooth; **~tição** *f* teething; (*dentadura*) teeth; **~tífrico** *m* toothpaste; **~tista** *m/f* dentist

dentre = **de** + **entre**

dentro /'dẽtru/ *adv* inside; **lá ~** in there; **por ~** on the inside; **~ de** inside; (*tempo*) within

dentu|ça /dẽ'tusa/ *f* buck teeth; **~ço** *a* with buck teeth

denúncia /de'nũsia/ *f* (*à polícia etc*) report; (*na imprensa etc*) disclosure

denunciar /denũsi'ar/ *vt* (*à polícia etc*) report; (*na imprensa etc*) denounce

deparar /depa'rar/ *vi* **~ com** come across

departamento /departa'mẽtu/ *m* department

depauperar /depawpe'rar/ *vt* impoverish

depenar /depe'nar/ *vt* pluck <*aves*>; (*roubar*) fleece

depen|dência /depẽ'dẽsia/ *f* dependence; *pl* premises; **~dente** *a* dependent (**de** on) □ *m/f* dependant; **~der** *vi* depend (**de** on)

depi|lação /depila'sãw/ *f* depilation; **~lar** *vt* depilate; **~latório** *m* depilatory cream

deplo|rar /deplo'rar/ *vt* deplore; **~rável** (*pl* **~ráveis**) *a* deplorable

de|poente /depo'ẽtʃi/ *m/f* witness; **~poimento** *m* (*à polícia*) statement; (*na justiça, fig*) testimony

depois /de'pojs/ *adv* after(wards); **~ de** after; **~ que** after

depor /de'por/ *vi* (*na polícia*) make a statement; (*na justiça*) give evidence, testify □ *vt* lay down <*armas*>; depose <*rei, presidente*>

depor|tação /deporta'sãw/ *f* deportation; **~tar** *vt* deport

deposi|tante /depozi'tãtʃi/ *m/f* depositor; **~tar** *vt* deposit; cast <*voto*>; place <*confiança*>

depósito /de'pɔzitu/ *m* deposit; (*armazém*) warehouse

depra|vação /deprava'sãw/ *f* depravity; **~vado** *a* depraved; **~var** *vt* deprave

depre|ciação /depresia'sãw/ *f* (*perda de valor*) depreciation; (*menosprezo*) deprecation; **~ciar** *vt* (*desvalorizar*) devalue; (*menosprezar*) deprecate; **~ciar-se** *vpr* <*bens*> depreciate; <*pessoa*> deprecate o.s.; **~ciativo** *a* deprecatory

depre|dação /depreda'sãw/ *f* depredation; **~dar** *vt* wreck

depressa /dʒi'presa/ *adv* fast, quickly

depres|são /depre'sãw/ *f* depression; **~sivo** *a* depressive

depri|mente /depri'mẽtʃi/ *a* depressing; **~mido** *a* depressed; **~mir** *vt* depress; **~mir-se** *vpr* get depressed

depurar /depu'rar/ *vt* purify

depu|tação /deputa'sãw/ *f* deputation; **~tado** *m* deputy, MP, (*Amer*) congressman (*f*-woman); **~tar** *vt* delegate

deque /'dɛki/ *m* (sun)deck

deri|va /de'riva/ *f* à **~va** adrift; **andar à ~va** drift; **~vação** *f* derivation; **~var** *vt* derive; (*desviar*) divert □ *vi*, **~var-se** *vpr* derive, be derived (**de** from); <*navio*> drift

dermatolo|gia /dermato'ʒia/ *f* dermatology; **~gista** *m/f* dermatologist

derradeiro /dexa'deru/ *a* last, final

derra|mamento /dexama'mẽtu/ *m* spill, spillage; **~mamento de sangue** bloodshed; **~mar** *vt* spill; shed <*lágrimas*>; **~mar-se** *vpr* spill; **~me** *m* spill, spillage; **~me cerebral** stroke

derra|pagem /dexa'paʒẽ/ *f* skidding; (*uma*) skid; **~par** *vi* skid

derreter /dexe'ter/ *vt* melt; **~-se** *vpr* melt

derro|ta /de'xɔta/ *f* defeat; **~tar** *vt* defeat; **~tismo** *m* defeatism; **~tista** *a* & *m/f* defeatist

derrubar /dexu'bar/ *vt* knock down; bring down <*governo*>

desaba|far /dʒizaba'far/ *vi* speak one's mind; **~fo** *m* outburst

desa|bamento /dʒizaba'mẽtu/ *m* collapse; **~bar** *vi* collapse; <*chuva*> pour down

desabotoar /dʒiaboto'ar/ *vt* unbutton

desabri|gado /dʒizabri'gadu/ *a* homeless; **~gar** *vt* make homeless

desabrochar /dʒizabro'ʃar/ *vi* blossom, bloom

desaca|tar /dʒizaka'tar/ *vt* defy; **~to** *m* (*de pessoa*) disrespect; (*da lei etc*) disregard

desacerto /dʒiza'sertu/ *m* mistake

desacompanhado /dʒizakõpa'nadu/ *a* unaccompanied

desaconse|lhar /dʒizakõse'ʎar/ *vt* advise against; **~lhável** (*pl* **~lháveis**) *a* inadvisable

desacor|dado /dʒizakor'dadu/ *a* unconscious; **~do** /o/ *m* disagreement

desacostu|mado /dʒizakostu'madu/ *a* unaccustomed; **~mar** *vt* **~mar alg de** break s.o. of the habit of; **~mar-se de** get out of the habit of

desacreditar /dʒizakredʒi'tar/ *vt* discredit

desafeto /dʒiza'fɛtu/ *m* disaffection

desafi|ador /dʒizafia'dor/ *a* <*tarefa*> challenging; <*pessoa*> defiant; **~ar** *vt* challenge; (*fazer face a*) defy <*perigo, morte*>

desafi|nado /dʒizafi'nadu/ *a* out of tune; **~nar** *vi* (*cantando*) sing out of tune; (*tocando*) play out of tune □ *vt* put out of tune

desafio /dʒiza'fiu/ *m* challenge

desafivelar /dʒizafive'lar/ *vt* unbuckle

desafo|gar /dʒizafo'gar/ *vt* vent; (*despertar*) relieve; **~gar-se** *vpr* give vent to one's feelings; **~go** /o/ *m* (*alívio*) relief

desafo|rado /dʒizafo'radu/ *a* cheeky; **~ro** /o/ *m* cheek; (*um*) liberty

desafortunado /dʒizafortu'nadu/ *a* unfortunate

desagra|dar /dʒizagra'dar/ *vt* displease; **~dável** (*pl* **~dáveis**) *a* unpleasant; **~do** *m* displeasure

desagravo *m* redress, amends

desagregar /dʒizagre'gar/ *vt* split up; **~-se** *vpr* split up

desaguar /dʒiza'gwar/ *vt* drain □ *vi* <*rio*> flow (**em** into)

desajeitado /dʒizaʒej'tadu/ *a* clumsy

desajuizado /dʒizaʒui'zadu/ *a* foolish

desajus|tado /dʒizaʒus'tadu/ *a* (*psic*) maladjusted; **~te** *m* (*psic*) maladjustment

desalen|tar /dʒizalẽ'tar/ *vt* dishearten; **~tar-se** *vpr* get disheartened; **~to** *m* discouragement

desali|nhado /dʒizali'nadu/ *a* untidy; **~nho** *m* untidiness

desalojar /dʒizalo'ʒar/ *vt* turn out <*inquilino*>; flush out <*inimigo, ladrões*>

desamarrar /dʒizama'xar/ *vt* untie □ *vi* cast off

desamarrotar /dʒizamaxo'tar/ *vt* smooth out

desamassar /dʒizama'sar/ *vt* smooth out

desambientado /dʒizãbiẽ'tadu/ *a* unsettled

desampa|rar /dʒizãpa'rar/ *vt* abandon; **~ro** *m* abandonment

desandar /dʒizã'dar/ *vi* <*molho*> separate; **~ a** start to

de|sanimar /dʒizani'mar/ *vt* discourage □ *vi* <*pessoa*> lose heart; <*fato*> be discouraging; **~sânimo** *m* discouragement

desapaixonado /dʒizapaiʃo'nadu/ *a* dispassionate

desaparafusar /dʒizaparafu'zar/ *vt* unscrew

desapare|cer /dʒizapare'ser/ *vi* disappear; **~cimento** *m* disappearance

desapego /dʒiza'pegu/ *m* detachment; (*indiferença*) indifference

desapercebido /dʒizaperse'bidu/ *a* unnoticed

desapertar /dʒizaper'tar/ *vt* loosen

desapon|tamento /dʒizapõta'mẽtu/ *m* disapointment; **~tar** *vt* disappoint

desapropriar /dʒizapropri'ar/ vt expropriate

desapro|vação /dʒizaprova'sãw/ f disapproval; ~**var** vt disapprove of

desaproveitado /dʒizaprovej'tadu/ a wasted

desar|mamento /dʒizarma'mẽtu/ m disarmament; ~**mar** vt disarm; take down <barraca>

desarran|jar /dʒizaxã'ʒar/ vt mess up; upset <estômago>; ~**jo** m mess; (do estômago) upset

desarregaçar /dʒizaxega'sar/ vt roll down

desarru|mado /dʒizaxu'madu/ a untidy; ~**mar** vt untidy; unpack <mala>

desarticular /dʒizartʃiku'lar/ vt dislocate

desarvorado /dʒizarvo'radu/ a disoriented, at a loss

desassociar /dʒizasosi'ar/ vt disassociate; ~**-se** vpr disassociate o.s.

desas|trado /dʒizas'tradu/ a accident-prone; ~**tre** m disaster; ~**troso** /o/ a disastrous

desatar /dʒiza'tar/ vt untie; ~ **a chorar** dissolve in tears

desatarraxar /dʒizataxa'ʃar/ vt unscrew

desaten|cioso /dʒizatẽsi'ozu/ a inattentive; ~**to** a oblivious (**a to**)

desati|nar /dʒizatʃi'nar/ vt bewilder □ vi not think straight; ~**no** m bewilderment; (um) folly

desativar /dʒizatʃi'var/ vt deactivate; shut down <fábrica>

desatrelar /dʒizatre'lar/ vt unhitch

desatualizado /dʒizatuali'zadu/ a out-of-date

desavença /dʒiza'vẽsa/ f dispute

desavergonhado /dʒizavergo'ɲadu/ a shameless

desbancar /dʒizbã'kar/ vt outdo

desbaratar /dʒizbara'tar/ vt (desperdiçar) waste

desbocado /dʒizbo'kadu/ a outspoken

desbotar /dʒizbo'tar/ vt/i fade

desbra|vador /dʒizbrava'dor/ m explorer; ~**var** vt explore

desbun|dante /dʒizbũ'dãtʃi/ (fam) a mind-blowing; ~**dar** (fam) vt blow the mind of □ vi flip, freak out; ~**de** (fam) m knockout

descabido /dʒizka'bidu/ a inappropriate

descafeinado /dʒizkafej'nadu/ a decaffeinated

descalabro /dʒizka'labru/ m débâcle

descalço /dʒis'kawsu/ a barefoot

descambar /dʒizkã'bar/ vi deteriorate, degenerate

descan|sar /dʒizkã'sar/ vt/i rest; ~**so** m rest; (de prato, copo) mat

desca|rado /dʒiska'radu/ a blatant; ~**ramento** m cheek

descarga /dʒis'karga/ f (eletr) discharge; (da privada) flush

descarregar /dʒiskaxe'gar/ vt unload <mercadorias>; discharge <poluentes>; vent <raiva> □ vi <bateria> go flat; ~ **em cima de alg** take it out on s.o.

descarrilhar /dʒiskaxi'ʎar/ vt/i derail

descar|tar /dʒiskar'tar/ vt discard; ~**tável** (pl ~**táveis**) a disposable

descascar /dʒiskas'kar/ vt peel <frutas, batatas>; shell <nozes> □ vi <pessoa, pele> peel

descaso /dʒis'kazu/ m indifference

descen|dência /dʒesẽ'dẽsia/ f descent; ~**dente** a descended □ m/f descendant; ~**der** vi descend (**de** from)

descentralizar /dʒisẽtrali'zar/ vt decentralize

des|cer /de'ser/ vi go down; <avião> descend; (do ônibus, trem) get off; (do carro) get out □ vt go down <escada, ladeira>; scroll down <página>; ~**cida** f descent

desclassificar /dʒisklasifi'kar/ vt disqualify

desco|berta /dʒisko'berta/ f discovery; ~**berto** /ɛ/ a uncovered; <conta> overdrawn; **a** ~**berto** overdrawn; ~**bridor** m discoverer; ~**brimento** m discovery; ~**brir** vt discover; (expor) uncover

descolar /dʒisko'lar/ vt unstick; (fam) (dar) give; (arranjar) get hold of, rustle up; (Port) <avião> take off

descom|por /dʒiskõ'por/ vt (censurar) scold; ~**-se** vpr <pessoa> lose one's composure; ~**postura** f (estado) loss of composure; (censura) talking-to

descomprometido /dʒiskõprome'tʃidu/ a free

descomu|nal /dʒiskomu'naw/ (pl ~**nais**) a extraordinary; (grande) huge

desconcentrar /dʒiskõsẽ'trar/ vt distract

desconcer|tante /dʒiskõser'tãtʃi/ a disconcerting; ~**tar** vt disconcert

desconexo /dʒisko'neksu/ a incoherent

desconfi|ado /dʒiskõfi'adu/ a suspicious; ~**ança** f mistrust; ~**ar** vi suspect

desconfor|tável /dʒiskõfor'tavew/ (pl ~**táveis**) a uncomfortable; ~**to** /o/ m discomfort

descongelar /dʒiskõʒe'lar/ vt defrost <geladeira>; thaw <comida>

descongestio|nante /dʒiskõʒestʃio'nãtʃi/ a & m decongestant; ~**nar** vt decongest

desconhe|cer /dʒiskoɲe'ser/ *vt* not know; **∼cido** *a* unknown □ *m* stranger

desconsiderar /dʒiskõside'rar/ *vt* ignore

desconsolado /dʒiskõso'ladu/ *a* disconsolate

descontar /dʒiskõ'tar/ *vt* deduct; *(não levar em conta)* discount

desconten|tamento /dʒiskõtẽta'mẽtu/ *m* discontent; **∼te** *a* discontent

desconto /dʒis'kõtu/ *m* discount; **dar um ∼** *(fig)* make allowances

descontra|ção /dʒiskõtra'sãw/ *f* informality; **∼ído** *a* informal, casual; **∼ir** *vt* relax; **∼ir-se** *vpr* relax

descontro|lar-se /dʒiskõtro'larsi/ *vpr* *<pessoa>* lose control; *<coisa>* go out of control; **∼le** /o/ *m* lack of control

desconversar /dʒiskõver'sar/ *vi* change the subject

descortesia /dʒiskorte'zia/ *f* rudeness

descostu|rar /dʒiskostu'rar/ *vt* unrip; **∼rar-se** *vpr* come undone

descrédito /dʒis'krɛdʒitu/ *m* discredit

descren|ça /dʒis'krẽsa/ *f* disbelief; **∼te** *a* sceptical, disbelieving

des|crever /dʒiskre'ver/ *vt* describe; **∼crição** *f* description; **∼critivo** *a* descriptive

descui|dado /dʒiskui'dadu/ *a* careless; **∼dar** *vt* neglect; **∼do** *m* carelessness; *(um)* oversight

descul|pa /dʒis'kuwpa/ *f* excuse; **pedir ∼pas** apologize; **∼par** *vt* excuse; **∼pe!** sorry!; **∼par-se** *vpr* apologize; **∼pável** *(pl* **∼páveis)** *a* excusable

desde /'dezdʒi/ *prep* since; **∼ que** since

des|dém /dez'dêj/ *m* disdain; **∼denhar** *vt* disdain; **∼nhoso** /o/ *a* disdainful

desdentado /dʒizdẽ'tadu/ *a* toothless

desdita /dʒiz'dʒita/ *f* unhappiness

desdizer /dʒizdʒi'zer/ *vt* take back, withdraw □ *vi* take back what one said

desdo|bramento /dʒizdobra'mẽtu/ *m* implication; **∼brar** *vt (abrir)* unfold; break down *<dados, contas>*; **∼brar-se** *vpr* unfold; *(empenhar-se)* go to a lot of trouble, bend over backwards

dese|jar /deze'ʒar/ *vt* want; *(apaixonadamente)* desire; **∼jar aco a alg** wish s.o. sth; **∼jável** *(pl* **∼jáveis)** *a* desirable; **∼jo** /e/ *m* wish; *(forte)* desire; **∼joso** /o/ *a* desirous

deselegante /dʒizele'gãtʃi/ *a* inelegant

desemaranhar /dʒizemara'ɲar/ *vt* untangle

desembara|çado /dʒizĩbara'sadu/ *a* *<pessoa>* confident, nonchalant; **∼çar-se** *vpr* rid o.s. (**de** of); **∼ço** *m* confidence, ease

desembar|car /dʒizĩbar'kar/ *vt/i* disembark; **∼que** *m* disembarkation; *(seção do aeroporto)* arrivals

desembocar /dʒizĩbo'kar/ *vi* flow

desembol|sar /dʒizĩbow'sar/ *vt* spend, pay out; **∼so** /o/ *m* expenditure

desembrulhar /dʒizĩbru'ʎar/ *vt* unwrap

desembuchar /dʒizĩbu'ʃar/ *(fam) vi* *(desabafar)* get things off one's chest; *(falar logo)* spit it out

desempacotar /dʒizĩpako'tar/ *vt* unpack

desempatar /dʒizĩpa'tar/ *vt* decide *<jogo>*

desempe|nhar /dʒizĩpe'ɲar/ *vt* perform, play *<papel>*; **∼nho** *m* performance

desempre|gado /dʒizĩpre'gadu/ *a* unemployed; **∼go** /e/ *m* unemployment

desencadear /dʒizĩkadʒi'ar/ *vt* set off, trigger

desencaminhar /dʒizĩkami'ɲar/ *vt* lead astray; embezzle *<dinheiro>*

desencantar /dʒizĩkã'tar/ *vt* disenchant

desencon|trar-se /dʒizĩkõ'trarsi/ *vpr* miss each other, fail to meet; **∼tro** *m* failure to meet

desencorajar /dʒizĩkora'ʒar/ *vt* discourage

desenferrujar /dʒizĩfexu'ʒar/ *vt* derust *<metal>*; stretch *<pernas>*; brush up *<língua>*

desenfreado /dʒizĩfri'adu/ *a* unbridled

desenganar /dʒizĩga'nar/ *vt* disabuse; declare incurable *<doente>*

desengonçado /dʒizĩgõ'sadu/ *a* *<pessoa>* ungainly

desengre|nado /dʒizĩgre'nadu/ *a* *<carro>* in neutral; **∼nar** *vt* put in neutral *<carro>*; *(tec)* disengage

dese|nhar /deze'ɲar/ *vt* draw; **∼nhista** *m/f* drawer; *(industrial)* designer; **∼nho** /e/ *m* drawing

desenlace /dʒizẽ'lasi/ *m* dénouement, outcome

desenredar /dʒizĩxe'dar/ *vt* unravel

desenrolar /dʒizĩxo'lar/ *vt* unroll *<rolo>*

desenten|der /dʒizĩtẽ'der/ *vt* misunderstand; **∼der-se** *vpr* *(não se dar bem)* not get on; **∼dimento** *m* misunderstanding

desenterrar /dʒizĩte'xar/ *vt* dig up *<cadáver>*; unearth *<informação>*

desentortar /dʒizĩtor'tar/ *vt* straighten out

desentupir /dʒizĩtu'pir/ *vt* unblock

desenvol|to /dʒizĩ'vowtu/ *a* casual, nonchalant; **∼tura** *f* casualness, nonchalance; **com ∼tura** nonchalantly; **∼ver** *vt* develop; **∼ver-se** *vpr* develop; **∼vimento** *m* development

d

desequi|librado *a* unbalanced; **~librar** *vt* unbalance; **~librar-se** *vpr* become unbalanced; **~líbrio** *m* imbalance

deser|ção /dezer'sãw/ *f* desertion; **~tar** *vt/i* desert; **~to** /ɛ/ *a* deserted; **ilha ~ta** desert island □ *m* desert; **~tor** *m* deserter

desespe|rado /dʒizispe'radu/ *a* desperate; **~rador** *a* hopeless; **~rar** *vt* (*desesperançar*) make despair □ *vi*, **~rar-se** *vpr* despair; **~ro** /e/ *m* despair

desestabilizar /dʒizistabili'zar/ *vt* destabilize

desestimular /dʒizistʃimu'lar/ *vt* discourage

desfal|car /dʒisfaw'kar/ *vt* embezzle; **~que** *m* embezzlement

desfal|ecer /dʒisfale'ser/ *vt* (*desmaiar*) faint; **~ecimento** *m* faint

desfavor /dʒisfa'vor/ *m* disfavour

desfavo|rável /dʒisfavo'ravew/ (*pl* **~ráveis**) *a* unfavourable; **~recer** *vt* be unfavourable to; treat less favourably <*minorias etc*>

desfazer /dʒisfa'zer/ *vt* undo; unpack <*mala*>; strip <*cama*>; break <*contrato*>; clear up <*mistério*>; **~se** *vpr* come undone; <*casamento*> break up; <*sonhos*> crumble; **~se em lágrimas** dissolve into tears

desfe|char /dʒisfe'ʃar/ *vt* throw <*murro, olhar*>; **~cho** /e/ *m* outcome, dénouement

desfeita /dʒis'fejta/ *f* slight, insult

desferir /dʒisfe'rir/ *vt* give <*pontapé*>; launch <*ataque*>; fire <*flecha*>

desfiar /dʒisfi'ar/ *vt* pick the meat off <*frango*>; **~se** *vpr* <*tecido*> fray

desfigurar /dʒisfigu'rar/ *vt* disfigure; (*fig*) distort

desfi|ladeiro /dʒisfila'deru/ *m* pass; **~lar** *vi* parade; **~le** *m* parade; **~le de modas** fashion show

desflorestamento /dʒisfloresta'mẽtu/ *m* deforestation

desforra /dʒis'foxa/ *f* revenge

desfraldar /dʒisfraw'dar/ *vt* unfurl

desfrutar /dʒisfru'tar/ *vt* enjoy

desgas|tante /dʒizgas'tãtʃi/ *a* wearing, stressful; **~tar** *vt* wear out; **~te** *m* (*de máquina etc*) wear and tear; (*de pessoa*) stress and strain

desgosto /dʒiz'gostu/ *m* sorrow

desgovernar-se /dʒizgover'narsi/ *vpr* go out of control

desgraça /dʒiz'grasa/ *f* misfortune; **~do** *a* wretched □ *m* wretch

desgravar /dʒizgra'var/ *vt* erase

desgrenhado /dʒizgre'ɲadu/ *a* unkempt

desgrudar /dʒizgru'dar/ *vt* unstick; **~se** *vpr* <*pessoa*> tear o.s. away

desidra|tação /dʒizidrata'sãw/ *f* dehydration; **~tar** *vt* dehydrate

desig|nação /dezigna'sãw/ *f* designation; **~nar** *vt* designate

desi|gual /dʒizi'gwaw/ (*pl* **~guais**) *a* unequal; <*terreno*> uneven; **~gualdade** *f* inequality; (*de terreno*) unevenness

desilu|dir /dʒizilu'dʒir/ *vt* disillusion; **~são** *f* disillusionment

desinfe|tante /dʒizĩfe'tãtʃi/ *a* & *m* disinfectant; **~tar** *vt* disinfect

desinibido /dʒizini'bidu/ *a* uninhibited

desintegrar-se /dʒizĩte'grarsi/ *vpr* disintegrate

desinteres|sado /dʒizĩtere'sadu/ *a* uninterested; **~sante** *a* uninteresting; **~sar-se** *vpr* lose interest (**de** in); **~se** /e/ *m* disinterest

desis|tência /dezis'tẽsia/ *f* giving up; **~tir** *vt/i* **~tir (de)** give up

desle|al /dʒizle'aw/ (*pl* **~ais**) *a* disloyal; **~aldade** *f* disloyalty

deslei|xado /dʒizle'ʃadu/ *a* sloppy; (*no vestir*) scruffy; **~xo** *m* carelessness; (*no vestir*) scruffiness

desli|gado /dʒizli'gadu/ *a* <*luz, TV*> off; <*pessoa*> absent-minded; **~gar** *vt* turn off <*luz, TV, motor*>; hang up, put down <*telefone*> □ *vi* (*ao telefonar*) hang up, put the phone down

deslindar /dʒizlĩ'dar/ *vt* clear up, solve

desli|zante /dʒizli'zãtʃi/ *a* slippery; <*inflação*> creeping; **~zar** *vi* slip; **~zar-se** *vpr* creep; **~ze** *m* slip; (*fig: erro*) slip-up

deslo|cado *a* <*membro*> dislocated; (*fig*) out of place; **~car** *vt* move; (*med*) dislocate; **~car-se** *vpr* move

deslum|brado /dʒizlũ'bradu/ *a* (*fig*) starry-eyed; **~bramento** *m* (*fig*) wonderment; **~brante** *a* dazzling; **~brar** *vt* dazzle; **~brar-se** *vpr* (*fig*) be dazzled

desmai|ado /dʒizmaj'adu/ *a* unconscious; **~ar** *vi* faint; **~o** *m* faint

desman|cha-prazeres /dʒizmãʃapra'zeris/ *m/f invar* spoil-sport; **~char** *vt* break up; break off <*noivado*>; shatter <*sonhos*>; **~char-se** *vpr* break up; (*no ar, na água, em lágrimas*) dissolve

desmantelar /dʒizmãte'lar/ *vt* dismantle

desmarcar /dʒizmar'kar/ *vt* cancel <*encontro*>

desmascarar /dʒizmaske'rar/ *vt* unmask

desma|tamento /dʒizmata'mẽtu/ *m* deforestation; **~tar** *vt* clear (of forest)

desmedido /dʒizme'didu/ *a* excessive

desmemoriado /dʒizmemori'adu/ a forgetful

desmen|tido /dʒizmē'tʃidu/ m denial; **∼tir** vt deny

desmiolado /dʒizmio'ladu/ a brainless

desmontar /dʒizmõ'tar/ vt dismantle

desmorali|zante /dʒizmorali'zãtʃi/ a demoralizing; **∼zar** vt demoralize

desmoro|namento /dʒizmorona'mētu/ m collapse; **∼nar** vt destroy; **∼nar-se** vpr collapse

desnatar /dʒizna'tar/ vi skim <leite>

desnecessário /dʒiznese'sariu/ a unnecessary

desni|vel /dʒiz'nivew/ (pl **∼veis**) m difference in height

desnortear /dʒiznortʃi'ar/ vt disorientate, (Amer) disorient

desnutrição /dʒiznutri'sãw/ f malnutrition

desobe|decer /dʒizobede'ser/ vt/i **∼decer (a)** disobey; **∼diência** f disobedience; **∼diente** a disobedient

desobrigar /dʒizobri'gar/ vt release (de from)

desobstruir /dʒizobistru'ir/ vt unblock; empty <casa>

desocupado /dʒizoku'padu/ a unoccupied

desodorante /dʒizodo'rãtʃi/ m, (Port) **desodorizante** /dʒizoduri'zãtʃi/ m deodorant

deso|lação /dezola'sãw/ f desolation; **∼lado** a <lugar> desolate; <pessoa> desolated; **∼lar** vt desolate

desones|tidade /dʒizonestʃi'dadʒi/ f dishonesty; **∼to** /ɛ/ a dishonest

deson|ra /dʒi'zõxa/ f dishonour; **∼rar** vt dishonour; **∼roso** /o/ a dishonourable

desor|deiro /dʒizor'deru/ a trouble-making □ m troublemaker; **∼dem** f disorder; **∼denado** a disorganized; <vida> disordered; **∼denar** vt disorganize

desorgani|zação /dʒizorganiza'sãw/ f disorganization; **∼zar** vt disorganize; **∼zar-se** vpr get disorganized

desorientar /dʒizoriē'tar/ vt disorientate, (Amer) disorient

desossar /dʒizo'sar/ vt bone

deso|va /dʒi'zɔva/ f roe; **∼var** vi spawn

despa|chado /dʒispa'ʃadu/ a efficient; **∼chante** m/f (de mercadorias) shipping agent; (de documentos) documentation agent; **∼char** vt deal with; dispatch, forward <mercadorias>; **∼cho** m dispatch

desparafusar /dʒisparafu'zar/ vt unscrew

despedaçar /dʒispeda'sar/ vt (rasgar) tear to pieces; (quebrar) smash; **∼-se**

vpr <vidro, vaso> smash; <papel, tecido> tear

despe|dida /dʒispe'dʒida/ f farewell; **∼dida de solteiro** stag night, (Amer) bachelor party; **∼dir** vt dismiss; sack <empregado>; **∼dir-se** vpr say goodbye (**de** to)

despei|tado /dʒispej'tadu/ a spiteful; **∼to** m spite; **a ∼to de** despite, in spite of

despe|jar /dʒispe'ʒar/ vt pour out <líquido>; empty <recipiente>; evict <inquilino>; **∼jo** /e/ m (de inquilino) eviction

despencar /dʒispē'kar/ vi plummet

despender /dʒispē'der/ vt spend <dinheiro>

despensa /dʒis'pēsa/ f pantry, larder

despentear /dʒispētʃi'ar/ vt mess up <cabelo>; mess up the hair of <pessoa>

despercebido /dʒisperse'bidu/ a unnoticed

desper|diçar /dʒisperdʒi'sar/ vt waste; **∼dício** m waste

desper|tador /dʒisperta'dor/ m alarm clock; **∼tar** vt rouse <pessoa>; (fig) arouse <interesse, suspeitas etc> □ vi awake

despesa /dʒis'peza/ f expense

des|pido /des'pidu/ a bare, stripped (**de** of); **∼pir** vt strip (**de** of); strip off <roupa>; **∼pir-se** vpr strip (off), get undressed

despo|jar /dʒispo'ʒar/ vt strip (**de** of); **∼jar-se** vpr divest o.s. (**de** of); **∼jo** /o/ m spoils, booty; **∼jos mortais** mortal remains

despontar /dʒispõ'tar/ vi emerge

despor|tista /diʃpur'tiʃta/ (Port) m/f sportsman (f-woman); **∼tivo** (Port) a sporting; **∼to** /o/ (Port) m sport; **carro de ∼to** sports car

déspota /'dɛspota/ m/f despot

despótico /des'pɔtʃiku/ a despotic

despovoar /dʒispovo'ar/ vt depopulate

desprender /dʒisprē'der/ vt detach; (da parede) take down; **∼-se** vpr come off; (fig) detach o.s.

despreocupado /dʒisprioku'padu/ a unconcerned

despreparado /dʒisprepa'radu/ a unprepared

despretensioso /dʒispretēsi'ozu/ a unpretentious

desprestigiar /dʒisprestʃiʒi'ar/ vt discredit

desprevenido /dʒispreve'nidu/ a off one's guard, unprepared; **apanhar ∼** catch unawares despre|zar /dʒispre'zar/ vt despise; (ignorar) ignore; ~zível (pl ~zíveis) a despicable; ~zo /e/ m contempt

desproporção /dʒispropor'sãw/ f disproportion

desproporcio|nado / dʒisproporsio'nadu/ a disproportionate; ~nal (pl ~nais) a disproportional

despropositado /dʒispropozi'tadu/ a (absurdo) preposterous

desprovido /dʒispro'vidu/ a ~ de without

desqualificar /dʒiskwalifi'kar/ vt disqualify

desqui|tar-se /dʒiski'tarsi/ vpr (legally) separate; ~te m (legal) separation

desrespei|tar /dʒizxespej'tar/ vt not respect; (ignorar) disregard; ~to m disrespect; ~toso /o/ a disrespectful

dessa(s), desse(s) = de + essa(s), esse(s)

desta = de + esta

desta|camento /dʒistaka'mẽtu/ m detachment; ~car vt detach; (ressaltar) bring out, make stand out; ~car-se vpr (desprender-se) come off; <corredor> break away; (sobressair) stand out (sobre against); ~cável (pl ~cáveis) a detachable; <caderno> pull-out

destam|pado /dʒistã'padu/ a (panela) uncovered; ~par vt remove the lid of

destapar /dʒista'par/ vt uncover

destaque /dʒis'taki/ m prominence; (coisa, pessoa) highlight; (do notíciario) headline

destas, deste = de + estas, este

destemido /dʒiste'midu/ a intrepid, courageous

desterrar /dʒiste'xar/ vt (exilar) exile

destes = de + estes

destilar /desti'lar/ vt distil; ~ia f distillery

desti|nado /destʃi'nadu/ a (fadado) destined; ~nar vt intend, mean (para for); ~natário m addressee; ~no m (de viagem) destination; (sorte) fate

destituir /destʃitu'ir/ vt remove

desto|ante /dʒisto'ãtʃi/ a <sons> discordant; <cores> clashing; ~ar vi ~ar de clash with

destrancar /dʒistrã'kar/ vt unlock

destreza /des'treza/ f skill

destrinchar /dʒistrĩ'ʃar/ vt (expor) dissect; (resolver) sort out

destro /'destru/ a skilful

destro|çar /dʒistro'sar/ vt wreck; ~ços m pl wreckage

destronar /dʒistro'nar/ vt depose

destroncar /dʒistrõ'kar/ vt rick

destru|ição /dʒistrui'sãw/ f destruction; ~idor a destructive □ m destroyer; ~ir vt destroy

desumano /dʒizu'manu/ a inhuman; (cruel) inhumane

desunião /dʒizuni'ãw/ f disunity

desu|sado /dʒizu'zadu/ a disused; ~so m disuse

desvairado /dʒizvaj'radu/ a delirious, raving

desvalori|zação /dʒizvaloriza-'sãw/ f devaluation; ~zar vt devalue

desvanta|gem /dʒizvã'taʒẽ/ f disadvantage; ~joso /o/ a disadvantageous

desve|lar /dʒizve'lar/ vt unveil; uncover <segredo>; ~lar-se vpr go to a lot of trouble; ~lo /e/ m great care

desvencilhar /dʒizvẽsi'ʎar/ vt extricate, free

desvendar /dʒizvẽ'dar/ vt reveal <segredo>; solve <mistério>

desventura /dʒizvẽ'tura/ f misfortune; (infelicidade) unhappiness

desviar /dʒizvi'ar/ vt divert <trânsito, rio, atenção, dinheiro>; avert <golpe, suspeitas, olhos>; ~se vpr deviate; <do tema> digress

desvincular /dʒizvĩku'lar/ vt free

desvio /dʒiz'viu/ m diversion; (do trânsito) diversion, (Amer) detour; (linha ferroviária) siding

desvirtuar /dʒizvirtu'ar/ vt misrepresent <verdade>

deta|lhado /deta'ʎadu/ a detailed; ~lhar vt detail; ~lhe m detail

detec|tar /detek'tar/ vt detect; ~tive (Port) m veja detetive; ~tor m detector

de|tenção /detẽ'sãw/ f (prisão) detention; ~tentor m holder; ~ter vt (ter) hold; (prender) detain

detergente /deter'ʒẽtʃi/ m detergent

deterio|ração /deteriora'sãw/ f deterioration; ~rar vt damage; ~rar-se vpr deteriorate

determi|nação /determina'sãw/ f determination; ~nado a (certo) certain; (resoluto) determined; ~nar vt determine

detestar /detes'tar/ vt hate

detetive /dete'tʃivi/ m detective

detido /de'tʃidu/ pp de deter □ a thorough □ m detainee

detonar /deto'nar/ vt detonate; (fam: criticar) pull to pieces □ vi detonate

detrás /de'traʃ/ adv behind □ prep ~ de behind

detrito /de'tritu/ m detritus

deturpar /detur'par/ vt misrepresent, distort

deus /dews/ *m* (*f* **deusa**) god (*f* goddess); **∼dará** *m* **ao ∼-dará** at the mercy of chance

devagar /dʒiva'gar/ *adv* slowly

deva|near /devani'ar/ *vi* daydream; **∼neio** *m* daydream

devas|sar /deva'sar/ *vt* expose; **∼sidão** *f* debauchery; **∼so** *a* debauched

devastar /devas'tar/ *vt* devastate

de|vedor /deve'dor/ *a* debit □ *m* debtor; **∼ver** *vt* owe □ *vaux* **∼ve fazer** (*obrigação*) he has to do; **∼ve chegar** (*probabilidade*) he should arrive; **∼ve ser** (*suposição*) he must be; **∼ve ter ido** he must have gone; **∼v(er)ia fazer** he ought to do; **∼v(er)ia ter feito** he ought to have done; **∼vidamente** *adv* duly; **∼vido** *a* due (**a** to)

devoção /devo'sãw/ *f* devotion

de|volução /devolu'sãw/ *f* return; **∼volver** *vt* return

devorar /devo'rar/ *vt* devour

devo|tar /devo'tar/ *vt* devote; **∼tar-se** *vpr* devote o.s. (**a** to); **∼to** /ɔ/ *a* devout

dez /dɛs/ *a & m* ten

dezanove /dza'nɔv/ (*Port*) *a & m* nineteen

dezas|seis /dza'sejʃ/ (*Port*) *a & m* sixteen; **∼sete** /ɛ/ (*Port*) *a & m* seventeen

dezembro /de'zẽbru/ *m* December

deze|na /de'zena/ *f* ten; **uma ∼ (de)** about ten; **∼nove** /ɔ/ *a & m* nineteen

dezes|seis /dʒize'sejʃ/ *a & m* sixteen; **∼sete** /ɛ/ *a & m* seventeen

dezoito /dʒi'zojtu/ *a & m* eighteen

dia /'dʒia/ *m* day; **de ∼** by day; **(no) ∼ 20 de julho** (on) July 20th; **∼ de folga** day off; **∼ útil** working day; **∼-a-∼** *m* everyday life

dia|bete /dʒia'betʃi/ *f* diabetes; **∼bético** *a & m* diabetic

dia|bo /dʒi'abu/ *m* devil; **∼bólico** *a* diabolical, devilish; **∼brete** /e/ *m* little devil; **∼brura** *f* (*de criança*) bit of mischief; *pl* mischief

diadema /dʒia'dema/ *m* tiara

diafragma /dʒia'fragima/ *m* diaphragm

dia|gnosticar /dʒiagnostʃi'kar/ *vt* diagnose; **∼gnóstico** *m* diagnosis □ *a* diagnostic

diago|nal /dʒiago'naw/ (*pl* **∼nais**) *a & f* diagonal

diagra|ma /dʒia'grama/ *m* diagram; **∼mação** *f* design; **∼mador** *m* designer; **∼mar** *vt* design <*livro, revista*>

dialect- (*Port*) *veja* **dialet-**

dia|lética /dʒia'lɛtʃika/ *f* dialectics; **∼leto** /ɛ/ *m* dialect

dialogar /dʒialo'gar/ *vi* talk; (*pol*) hold talks

diálogo /dʒi'alogu/ *m* dialogue

diamante /dʒia'mãtʃi/ *m* diamond

diâmetro /dʒi'ametru/ *m* diameter

dian|te /dʒi'ãtʃi/ *adv* **de ... em ∼te** from ... on(wards); **∼te de** (*enfrentando*) faced with; (*perante*) before; **∼teira** *f* lead; **∼teiro** *a* front

diapasão /dʒiapa'zãw/ *m* tuning-fork

diapositivo /dʒiapozi'tʃivu/ *m* transparency

diá|ria /dʒi'aria/ *f* daily rate; **∼rio** *a* daily

diarista /dʒia'rista/ *m/f* day labourer; (*faxineira*) daily (help)

diarréia /dʒia'xɛja/ *f* diarrhoea

dica /'dʒika/ *f* tip, hint

dicção /dʒik'sãw/ *f* diction

dicionário /dʒisio'nariu/ *m* dictionary

didáti|ca /dʒi'datʃika/ *f* teaching methodology; **∼co** *a* teaching; <*livro*> educational; <*estilo*> didactic

die|ta /dʒi'ɛta/ *f* diet; **de ∼ta** on a diet; **∼tista** *m/f* dietician

difa|mação /dʒifama'sãw/ *f* defamation; **∼mar** *vt* defame; **∼matório** *a* defamatory

diferen|ça /dʒife'rẽsa/ *f* difference; **∼cial** (*pl* **∼ciais**) *a & f* differential; **∼ciar** *vt* differentiate; **∼ciar-se** *vpr* differ; **∼te** *a* different

dife|rimento /dʒiferi'mẽtu/ *m* deferment; **∼rir** *vt* defer □ *vi* differ

difí|cil /dʒi'fisiw/ (*pl* **∼ceis**) *a* difficult; (*improvável*) unlikely

dificilmente /dʒifisiw'mẽtʃi/ *adv* **∼ poderá fazê-lo** he's unlikely to be able to do it

dificul|dade /dʒifikuw'dadʒi/ *f* difficulty; **∼tar** *vt* make difficult

difteria /dʒifte'ria/ *f* diphtheria

difun|dir /dʒifũ'dʒir/ *vt* broadcast; (*pela rádio*) broadcast; diffuse <*luz, calor*>; **∼dir-se** *vpr* spread

difu|são /dʒifu'zãw/ *f* diffusion; **∼so** *a* diffuse

dige|rir /dʒiʒe'rir/ *vt* digest; **∼rível** (*pl* **∼ríveis**) *a* digestible

diges|tão /dʒiʒes'tãw/ *f* digestion; **∼tivo** *a* digestive

digi|tal /dʒiʒi'taw/ (*pl* **∼tais**) *a* digital; **impressão ∼tal** fingerprint; **∼tar** *vt* key

dígito /'dʒiʒitu/ *m* digit

digladiar /dʒigladʒi'ar/ *vi* do battle

dig|nar-se /dʒig'narsi/ *vpr* deign (**de** to); **∼nidade** *f* dignity; **∼nificar** *vt* dignify; **∼no** *a* worthy (**de** of); (*decoroso*) dignified

dilace|rante /dʒilase'rãtʃi/ *a* <*dor*> excruciating; **∼rar** *vt* tear to pieces

dilapidar /dʒilapi'dar/ *vt* squander

dilatar /dʒila'tar/ vt expand; (med)
dilate; ~-se vpr expand; (med) dilate

dilema /dʒi'lema/ m dilemma

diletante /dʒile'tãtʃi/ a & m/f dilettante

dili|gência /dʒili'ʒesia/ f diligence;
(carruagem) stagecoach; ~gente a
diligent, hard-working

diluir /dʒilu'ir/ vt dilute

dilúvio /dʒi'luviu/ m deluge

dimen|são /dʒime'sãw/ f dimension;
~sionar vt size up

diminu|ição /dʒiminui'sãw/ f
reduction; ~ir vt reduce ◻ vi lessen;
<carro, motorista> slow down; ~tivo a
& m diminutive; ~to a minute

Dinamarca /dʒina'marka/ f Denmark

dinamar|quês /dʒinamar'kes/ (f
~quesa) a Danish ◻ m Dane

dinâmi|ca /dʒi'namika/ f dynamics;
~co a dynamic

dina|mismo /dʒina'mizmu/ m
dynamism; ~mite f dynamite

dínamo /'dʒinamu/ m dynamo

dinastia /dʒinas'tʃia/ f dynasty

dinda /'dʒida/ (fam) f godmother

dinheiro /dʒi'ɲeru/ m money

dinossauro /dʒino'sawru/ m dinosaur

diocese /dʒio'sɛzi/ f diocese

dióxido /dʒi'ɔksidu/ m dioxide; ~ de
carbono carbon dioxide

diplo|ma /dʒi'ploma/ m
diploma; ~macia f diplomacy; ~mar-
se vpr take one's diploma; ~mata m/f
diplomat ◻ a diplomatic; ~mático a
diplomatic

direção /dʒire'sãw/ f (sentido) direction;
(de empresa) management; (condução
de carro) driving; (manuseio do volante)
steering

direct- (Port) veja **diret-**

direi|ta /dʒi'rejta/ f right; ~tinho adv
exactly right; ~tista a rightwing ◻ m/f
rightwinger, rightist; ~to a right;
(ereto) straight ◻ adv properly ◻ m
right

dire|tas /dʒi'rɛtas/ f pl direct
(presidential) elections; ~to a a direct
◻ adv directly; ~tor m director; (de
escola) headteacher; (de jornal) editor;
~tor-gerente managing director;
~toria f (diretores) board of directors;
(sala) boardroom; ~tório m directory;
~triz f directive

diri|gente /dʒiri'ʒetʃi/ a leading ◻ m/f
leader; ~gir vt direct; manage
<empresa>; drive <carro>; ~gir-se
vpr (ir) make one's way; ~gir-se a
(falar com) address

dis|cagem /dʒis'kaʒe/ f dialling; ~car
vt/i dial

discente /dʒi'setʃi/ a corpo ~ student
body

discer|nimento /dʒiserni'mẽtu/ m
discernment; ~nir vt discern

discipli|na /dʒisi'plina/ f discipline;
~nador a disciplinary; ~nar vt
discipline

discípulo /dʒi'sipulu/ m disciple

disc-jóquei /dʒisk'ʒɔkej/ m disc-jockey

disco /'dʒisku/ m disc; (de música)
record; (no atletismo) discus ◻ (fam) f
disco; ~ flexível/rígido floppy/hard
disk; ~ laser CD, compact disc;
~ voador flying saucer

discor|dante /dʒiskor'dãtʃi/ a
conflicting; ~dar vi disagree (de with)

discote|ca /dʒisko'tɛka/ f discotheque;
~cário m DJ

discre|pância /dʒiskre'pãsia/ f
discrepancy; ~pante a inconsistent;
~par vi diverge (de from)

dis|creto /dʒis'krɛtu/ a discreet;
~crição f discretion

discrimi|nação /dʒiskrimina'sãw/ f
discrimination; (descrição)
description; ~nar vt discriminate;
~natório a discriminatory

discur|sar /dʒiskur'sar/ vi speak; ~so m
speech

discussão /dʒisku'sãw/ f discussion;
(briga) argument

discu|tir /dʒisku'tʃir/ vt/i discuss;
(brigar) argue; ~tível (pl ~tíveis) a
debatable

disenteria /dʒizẽte'ria/ f dysentery

disfar|çar /dʒisfar'sar/ vt disguise;
~çar-se vpr disguise o.s.; ~ce m
disguise

dis|léxico /dʒiz'lɛtʃiku/ a & m dyslexic;
~lexia f dyslexia; ~léxico a & m
dyslexic

dispa|rada /dʒispa'rada/ f bolt; ~rado
adv o melhor ~rado the best by a long
way; ~rar vt fire <arma> ◻ vi (com
arma) fire; <preços, inflação> shoot
up; <corredor> surge ahead

disparate /dʒispa'ratʃi/ m piece of
nonsense; pl nonsense

dis|pêndio /dʒis'pẽdʒiu/ m expenditure;
~pendioso /o/ a costly

dispen|sa /dʒis'pẽsa/ f exemption; ~sar
vt (distribuir) dispense; (isentar)
exempt (de from); (prescindir de)
dispense with; ~sável (pl ~sáveis) a
dispensable

dispersar /dʒisper'sar/ vt disperse;
waste <energias> ◻ vi, ~-se vpr
disperse

disperso /dʒis'pɛrsu/ adj scattered

dispo|nibilidade /dʒisponibiliˈdadʒi/ f
availability; **~nível** (pl **~níveis**) a
available

dis|por /dʒisˈpor/ vt arrange □ vi **~por
de** have at one's disposal; **~por-se** vpr
form up □ m **ao seu ~por** at your
disposal; **~posição** f (vontade)
willingness; (arranjo) arrangement;
(de espírito) frame of mind; (de
testamento etc) provision; **à
~posição de alg** at s.o.'s disposal;
~positivo m device; **~posto** a
prepared, willing (**a** to)

dispu|ta /dʒisˈputa/ f dispute; **~tar** vt
dispute; (tentar ganhar) compete for

disquete /dʒisˈketʃi/ m diskette, floppy
(disk)

dissabores /dʒisaˈboris/ m pl troubles

disseminar /dʒisemiˈnar/ vt disseminate

dissertação /dʒisertaˈsãw/ f
dissertation, lecture

dissi|dência /dʒisiˈdẽsia/ f dissidence;
~dente a & m dissident

dissídio /dʒiˈsidʒiu/ m dispute

dissimular /dʒisimuˈlar/ vt hide □ vi
dissimulate

disso = **de** + **isso**

dissipar /dʒisiˈpar/ vt clear <nevoeiro>;
dispel <dúvidas, suspeitas, ilusões>;
dissipate <for·tuna>; **~se** vpr
<nevoeiro> clear; <dúvidas etc> be
dispelled

dissolu|ção /dʒisoluˈsãw/ f dissolution;
~to a dissolute

dissolver /dʒisowˈver/ vt dissolve; **~se**
vpr dissolve

dissuadir /dʒisuaˈdʒir/ vt dissuade (**de**
from)

distância /dʒisˈtãsia/ f distance

distan|ciar /dʒistãsiˈar/ vt distance;
~ciar-se vpr distance o.s.; **~te** a
distant

disten|der /dʒistẽˈder/ vt stretch
<pernas>; relax <músculo>; **~der-se**
vpr relax; **~são** f (med) pull; **~são
muscular** pulled muscle

distin|ção /dʒistʃĩˈsãw/ f distinction;
~guir vt distinguish (**de** from);
~guir-se vpr distinguish o.s.; **~tivo** a
distinctive □ m badge; **~to** a distinct;
<senhor> distinguished

disto = **de** + **isto**

distor|ção /dʒistorˈsãw/ f distortion;
~cer vt distort

distra|ção /dʒistraˈsãw/ f distraction;
~ído a absent-minded; **~ir** vt distract;
(divertir) amuse; **~ir-se** vpr be
distracted; (divertir-se) amuse o.s.

distribu|ição /dʒistribuiˈsãw/ f
distribution; **~idor** m distributor;
~idora f distributor, distribution
company; **~ir** vt distribute

distrito /dʒisˈtritu/ m district

distúrbio /dʒisˈturbiu/ m trouble

di|tado /dʒiˈtadu/ m dictation;
(provérbio) saying; **~tador** m dictator;
~tadura f dictatorship; **~tame** m
dictate; **~tar** vt dictate; **~tatorial** (pl
~tatoriais) a dictatorial

dito /ˈdʒitu/ a **~ e feito** no sooner said
than done □ m remark

ditongo /dʒiˈtõgu/ m diphthong

DIU /ˈdʒiu/ m IUD, coil

diurno /dʒiˈurnu/ a day

divã /dʒiˈvã/ m couch

divagar /dʒivaˈgar/ vi digress

diver|gência /dʒiverˈʒẽsia/ a divergence;
~gente a divergent; **~gir** vi diverge
(**de** from); **~são** f diversion;
(divertimento) amusement; **~sidade** f
diversity; **~sificar** vt/i diversify; **~so** /ɛ/
a (diferente) diverse; pl (vários) several;
~tido a (engraçado) funny; (que se curte)
enjoyable; **~timento** m enjoyment, fun;
(um) amusement; **~tir** vt amuse; **~tir-
se** vpr enjoy o.s., have fun

dívida /ˈdʒivida/ f debt; **~ externa**
foreign debt

divi|dendo /dʒiviˈdẽdu/ m dividend; **~dido**
a <pessoa> torn; **~dir** vt/i divide;
(compartilhar) share; **~dir-se** vpr be
divided

divindade /dʒivĩˈdadʒi/ f divinity

divino /dʒiˈvinu/ a divine

divi|sa /dʒiˈviza/ f (lema) motto; (galão)
stripes; (fronteira) border; pl foreign
currency; **~são** f division; **~sória** f
partition

divorci|ado /dʒivorsiˈadu/ a divorced
□ m divorcé; (f divorcée); **~ar** vt
divorce; **~ar-se** vpr get divorced;
~ar-se de divorce

divórcio /dʒiˈvorsiu/ m divorce

divul|gado /dʒivuwˈgadu/ a widespread;
~gar vt spread; publish (notícia);
divulge <segredo>; **~gar-se** vpr be
spread

dizer /dʒiˈzer/ vt say; **~ a alg que** tell sb
that; **~ para alg fazer** tell s.o. to do □ vi
~ com go with; **~se** vpr claim to be
□ m saying

dizimar /dʒiziˈmar/ vt decimate

do = **de** + **o**

dó /dɔ/ m pity; **dar ~** be pitiful; **ter ~ de**
feel sorry for

do|ação /doaˈsãw/ f donation; **~ador** m
donor; **~ar** vt donate

do|bra /ˈdɔbra/ f fold; (de calça) turn-up,
(Amer) cuff; **~bradiça** f hinge;
~bradiço a pliable; **~brado** a (duplo)
double; **~brar** vt (duplicar) double;
(fazer dobra em) fold; (curvar) bend; go
round <esquina>; ring <sinos>; (Port)

dub <*filme*> ▢ *vi* double; <*sinos*> ring; ∼**brar-se** *vpr* bend; ∼**bro** *m* double

doca /'dɔka/ *f* dock

doce /'dosi/ *a* sweet; <*água*> fresh ▢ *m* sweet; ∼ **de leite** fudge

docente /do'sẽtʃi/ *a* teaching; **corpo** ∼ teaching staff, (*Amer*) faculty

dó|cil /'dɔsiw/ (*pl* ∼**ceis**) *a* docile

documen|tação /dokumẽta'sãw/ *f* documentation; ∼**tar** *vt* document; ∼**tário** *a* & *m* documentary; ∼**to** *m* document

doçura /do'sura/ *f* sweetness

dodói /do'dɔj/ (*fam*) *m* **ter** ∼ have a pain ▢ *a* poorly, ill

doen|ça /do'ẽsa/ *f* illness; (*infecciosa, fig*) disease; ∼ **da vaca louca** mad cow disease; ∼**te** *a* ill; <*criança, aspecto*> sickly; <*interesse, curiosidade*> morbid

doer /do'er/ *vi* hurt; <*cabeça, músculo*> ache

dog|ma /'dɔgima/ *m* dogma; ∼**mático** *a* dogmatic

doido /'dojdu/ *a* crazy

dois /dojs/ *a* & *m* (*f* **duas**) two

dólar /'dɔlar/ *m* dollar

dolo|rido /dolo'ridu/ *a* sore; ∼**roso** /o/ *a* painful

dom /dõ/ *m* gift

do|mador /doma'dor/ *m* tamer; ∼**mar** *vt* tame

doméstica /do'mɛstʃika/ *f* housemaid

domesticar /domestʃi'kar/ *vt* domesticate

doméstico /do'mɛstʃiku/ *a* domestic

domi|ciliar /domisili'ar/ *a* home; ∼**cílio** *m* home

domi|nação /domina'sãw/ *f* domination; ∼**nador** *a* domineering; ∼**nante** *a* dominant; ∼**nar** *vt* dominate; have a command of <*língua*>; ∼**nar-se** *vpr* control o.s.

domin|go /do'mĩgu/ *m* Sunday; ∼**gueiro** *a* Sunday

domini|cal /domini'kaw/ (*pl* ∼**cais**) *a* Sunday; ∼**cano** *a* & *m* Dominican

domínio /do'miniu/ *m* command

dona /'dona/ *f* owner; **Dona** (*com nome*) Miss; ∼ **de casa** *f* housewife

donativo /dona'tʃivu/ *m* donation

donde /'dõdʒi/ *adv* from where; (*motivo*) from whence

dono /'donu/ *m* owner

donzela /dõ'zɛla/ *f* maiden

dopar /do'par/ *vt* drug

dor /dor/ *f* pain; (*menos aguda*) ache; ∼ **de cabeça** headache

dor|mente /dor'mẽtʃi/ *a* numb ▢ *m* sleeper; ∼**mida** *f* sleep; ∼**minhoco** /o/

m sleepyhead; ∼**mir** *vi* sleep; ∼**mitar** *vi* doze; ∼**mitório** *m* bedroom; (*comunitário*) dormitory

dorso /'dorsu/ *m* back; (*de livro*) spine

dos = **de** + **os**

do|sagem /do'zaʒẽ/ *f* dosage; ∼**sar** *vt* moderate; ∼**se** /ɔ/ *f* dose; (*de uísque etc*) shot, measure

dossiê /dosi'e/ *m* file

do|tação /dota'sãw/ *f* endowment; ∼**tado** *a* gifted; ∼**tado de** endowed with; ∼**tar** *vt* endow (**de** with); ∼**te** /ɔ/ *m* (*de noiva*) dowry; (*dom*) endowment

dou|rado /do'radu/ *a* (*de cor*) golden; (*revestido de ouro*) gilded, gilt ▢ *m* gilt; ∼**rar** *vt* gild

dou|to /'dotu/ *a* learned; ∼**tor** *m* doctor; ∼**torado** *m* doctorate, PhD; ∼**trina** *f* doctrine; ∼**trinar** *vt* indoctrinate

doze /'dozi/ *a* & *m* twelve

dragão /dra'gãw/ *m* dragon

dragar /dra'gar/ *vt* dredge

drágea /'draʒia/ *f* lozenge

dra|ma /'drama/ *m* drama; ∼**malhão** *m* melodrama; ∼**mático** *a* dramatic; ∼**matizar** *vt* dramatize; ∼**maturgo** *m* dramatist, playwright

drapeado /drapi'adu/ *a* draped

drástico /'drastʃiku/ *a* drastic

dre|nagem /dre'naʒẽ/ *f* drainage; ∼**nar** *vt* drain; ∼**no** /ɛ/ *m* drain

driblar /dri'blar/ *vt* (*em futebol*) dribble round, beat; (*fig*) get round

drinque /'drĩki/ *m* drink

drive /'drajvi/ *m* disk drive

dro|ga /'drɔga/ *f* drug; (*fam*) (*coisa sem valor*) dead loss; (*coisa chata*) drag ▢ *int* damn; ∼**gado** *a* on drugs ▢ *m* drug addict; ∼**gar** *vt* drug; ∼**gar-se** *vpr* take drugs; ∼**garia** *f* dispensing chemist's, pharmacy

duas /'duas/ *veja* **dois**

dúbio /'dubiu/ *a* dubious

dub|lagem /du'blaʒẽ/ *f* dubbing; ∼**lar** *vt* dub <*filme*>; mime <*música*>; ∼**lê** *m* double

ducentésimo /dusẽ'tɛzimu/ *a* two-hundredth

ducha /'duʃa/ *f* shower

ducto /'duktu/ *m* duct

duelo /du'ɛlu/ *m* duel

duende /du'ẽdʒi/ *m* elf

dueto /du'etu/ *m* duet

duna /'duna/ *f* dune

duodécimo /duo'dɛsimu/ *a* twelfth

duodeno /duo'dɛnu/ *m* duodenum

dupla /'dupla/ *f* pair, duo; <*no tênis*> doubles

dúplex /du'plɛks/ *a invar* two-floor □ *m invar* two-floor apartment, (*Amer*) duplex

dupli|car /dupli'kar/ *vt/i* double; **~cidade** *f* duplicity; **~cata** *f* duplicate

duplo /'duplu/ *a* double

duque /'duki/ *m* duke; **~sa** /e/ *f* duchess

du|ração /dura'sãw/ *f* duration; **~radouro** *a* lasting; **~rante** *prep* during; **~rar** *vi* last; **~rável** (*pl* **~ráveis**) *a* durable

durex /du'rɛks/ *m invar* sellotape

du|reza /du'reza/ *f* hardness; **~ro** *a* hard; (*fam: sem dinheiro*) hard up, broke

dúvida /'duvida/ *f* doubt; (*pergunta*) query

duvi|dar /duvi'dar/ *vt/i* doubt; **~doso** /o/ *a* doubtful

duzentos /du'zẽtus/ *a & m* two hundred

dúzia /'duzia/ *f* dozen

....

Ee

....

e /i/ *conj* and

ébano /'ɛbanu/ *m* ebony

ébrio /'ɛbriu/ *a* drunk □ *m* drunkard

ebulição /ebuli'sãw/ *f* boiling

eclesiástico /eklezi'astʃiku/ *a* ecclesiastical

eclético /e'klɛtʃiku/ *a* eclectic

eclip|sar /eklip'sar/ *vt* eclipse; **~se** *m* eclipse

eclodir /eklo'dʒir/ *vi* emerge; (*estourar*) break out; <*flor*> open

eco /'ɛku/ *m* echo; **ter ~** have repercussions; **~ar** *vt/i* echo

eco|logia /ekolo'ʒia/ *f* ecology; **~lógico** *a* ecological; **~logista** *m/f* ecologist

eco|nomia /ekono'mia/ *f* economy; (*ciência*) economics; *pl* (*dinheiro poupado*) savings; **~nômico** *a* economic; (*rentável, barato*) economical; **~nomista** *m/f* economist; **~nomizar** *vt* save □ *vi* economize

écran /ɛ'krã/ (*Port*) *m* screen

eczema /ek'zɛma/ *m* eczema

edição /edʒi'sãw/ *f* edition; (*de filmes*) editing

edificante /edʒifi'kãtʃi/ *a* edifying

edifício /edʒi'fisiu/ *m* building

Edimburgo /edʒi'burgu/ *f* Edinburgh

edi|tal /edʒi'taw/ (*pl* **~tais**) *m* announcement; **~tar** *vt* publish; (*comput*) edit; **~to** *m* edict; **~tor** *m*

publisher; **~tora** *f* publishing company; **~torial** (*pl* **~toriais**) *a* publishing □ *m* editorial

edredom /edre'dõ/ *m*, (*Port*) **edredão** /edre'dãw/ *m* quilt

educa|ção /eduka'sãw/ *f* (*ensino*) education; (*polidez*) good manners; **é falta de ~ção** it's rude; **~cional** (*pl* **~cionais**) *a* education

edu|cado /edu'kadu/ *a* polite; **~car** *vt* educate; **~cativo** *a* educational

EEB /ee'be/ *f* BSE

efeito /e'fejtu/ *m* effect; **fazer ~** have an effect; **para todos os ~s** to all intents and purposes; **~ colateral** side effect; **~ estufa** greenhouse effect

efêmero /e'fẽmeru/ *a* ephemeral

efeminado /efemi'nadu/ *a* effeminate

efervescente /eferve'sẽtʃi/ *a* effervescent

efe|tivar /efetʃi'var/ *vt* bring into effect; (*contratar*) make a permanent member of staff; **~tivo** *a* real, effective; <*cargo, empregado*> permanent; **~tuar** *vt* carry out, effect

efi|cácia /efi'kasia/ *f* effectiveness; **~caz** *a* effective

efici|ência /efisi'ẽsia/ *f* efficiency; **~ente** *a* efficient

efígie /e'fiʒi/ *f* effigy

Egeu /e'ʒew/ *a & m* Aegean

égide /'ɛʒidʒi/ *f* aegis

egípcio /e'ʒipsiu/ *a & m* Egyptian

Egito /e'ʒitu/ *m* Egypt

ego /'ɛgu/ *m* ego; **~cêntrico** *a* self-centred, egocentric; **~ísmo** *m* selfishness; **~ísta** *a* selfish □ *m/f* egoist □ *m* (*de rádio etc*) earplug

égua /'ɛgwa/ *f* mare

eis /ejs/ *adv* (*aqui está*) here is/are; (*isso é*) that is

eixo /'ejʃu/ *m* axle; (*mat, entre cidades*) axis; **pôr nos ~s** set straight

ela /'ɛla/ *pron* she; (*coisa*) it; (*com preposição*) her; (*coisa*) it

elaborar /elabo'rar/ *vt* (*fazer*) make, produce; (*desenvolver*) work out

elasticidade /elastʃisi'dadʒi/ *f* (*de coisa*) elasticity; (*de pessoa*) suppleness

elástico /e'lastʃiku/ *a* elastic □ *m* (*de borracha*) elastic band; (*de calcinha etc*) elastic

ele /'eli/ *pron* he; (*coisa*) it; (*com preposição*) him; (*coisa*) it

electr- (*Port*) *veja* **eletr-**

eléctrico /i'lɛktriku/ (*Port*) *m* tram, (*Amer*) streetcar □ *a veja* **elétrico**

elefante /ele'fãtʃi/ *m* elephant

ele|gância /ele'gãsia/ *f* elegance; **~gante** *a* elegant

d

e

eleger /ele'ʒer/ vt elect; ~**-se** vpr get elected

elegia /ele'ʒia/ f elegy

elei|ção /elej'sãw/ f election; ~**to** a elected, elect; <povo> chosen; ~**tor** m voter; ~**torado** m electorate; ~**toral** (pl ~**torais**) a electoral

elemen|tar /elemẽ'tar/ a elementary; ~**to** m element

elenco /e'lẽku/ m (de filme, peça) cast

eletri|cidade /eletrisi'dadʒi/ f electricity; ~**cista** m/f electrician

elétrico /e'lɛtriku/ a electric

eletri|ficar /eletrifi'kar/ vt electrify; ~**zar** vt electrify

eletro /e'lɛtru/ m ECG; ~**cutar** vt electrocute; ~**do** /o/ m electrode; ~**domésticos** m pl electrical appliances

eletrôni|ca /ele'tronika/ f electronics; ~**co** a electronic

ele|vação /eleva'sãw/ f elevation; (aumento) rise; ~**vado** a high; <sentimento, estilo> elevated; ~**vador** m lift, (Amer) elevator; ~**var** vt raise; (promover) elevate; ~**var-se** vpr rise

elimi|nar /elimi'nar/ vt eliminate; ~**natória** f heat; ~**natório** a eliminatory

elipse /e'lipsi/ f ellipse

elíptico /e'liptʃiku/ a elliptical

eli|te /e'litʃi/ f elite; ~**tismo** m elitism; ~**tista** a & m/f elitist

elmo /'ɛwmu/ m helmet

elo /'ɛlu/ m link

elo|giar /eloʒi'ar/ vt praise; ~**giar alg por** compliment s.o. on; ~**gio** m (louvor) praise; (um) compliment; ~**gioso** /o/ a complimentary

elo|quência /elo'kwẽsia/ f eloquence; ~**qüente** a eloquent

eluci|dar /elusi'dar/ vt elucidate; ~**dativo** a elucidatory

em /ẽj/ prep in; (sobre) on; **ela está no Eduardo** she's at Eduardo's (house); **de casa ~ casa** from house to house; **aumentar ~ 10%** increase by 10%

emagre|cer /emagre'ser/ vi lose weight, get thinner ▫ vt make thinner; ~**cimento** m slimming

emanar /ema'nar/ vi emanate (**de** from)

emanci|pação /emãsipa'sãw/ f emancipation; ~**par** vt emancipate; ~**par-se** vpr become emancipated

emara|nhado /emara'ɲadu/ a tangled ▫ m tangle; ~**nhar** vt tangle; (envolver) entangle; ~**nhar-se** vpr get tangled up; (envolver-se) become entangled (**em** in)

embaçar /ĩba'sar/, (Port) **embaciar** /ĩbasi'ar/ vt steam up <vidro> ▫ vi <vidro> steam up; <olhos> grow misty

embainhar /ĩbaj'ɲar/ vt hem <vestido, calça>

embaixa|da /ĩba'ʃada/ f embassy; ~**dor** m ambassador; ~**triz** f ambassador; (esposa) ambassador's wife

embaixo /ĩ'baʃu/ adv underneath; (em casa) downstairs; ~ **de** under

emba|lagem /ĩba'laʒẽ/ f packaging; ~**lar**[1] vt pack

emba|lar[2] /ĩba'lar/ vt rock <criança>; ~**lo** m (fig) excitement, thrill

embalsamar /ĩbawsa'mar/ vt embalm

embara|çar /ĩbara'sar/ vt embarrass; ~**çar-se** vpr get embarrassed (**com** by); ~**ço** m embarrassment; ~**çoso** /o/ a embarrassing

embaralhar /ĩbara'ʎar/ vt muddle up; shuffle <cartas>; ~**se** vpr get muddled up

embar|cação /ĩbarka'sãw/ f vessel; ~**cadouro** m wharf; ~**car** vt/i board, embark

embar|gado /ĩbar'gadu/ a <voz> faltering; ~**go** m embargo

embarque /ĩ'barki/ m boarding; (seção do aeroporto) departures

embasba|cado /ĩbazba'kadu/ a open-mouthed; ~**car-se** vpr be left open-mouthed

embate /ĩ'batʃi/ m (de carros etc) crash; (fig) clash

embebedar /ĩbebe'dar/ vt make drunk; ~**se** vpr get drunk

embeber /ĩbe'ber/ vt soak; ~**se de** soak up; ~**se em** get absorbed in

embele|zador /ĩbeleza'dor/ a <cirurgia> cosmetic; ~**zar** vt embellish; spruce up <casa>; ~**zar-se** vpr make o.s. beautiful

embevecer /ĩbeve'ser/ vt captivate, engross; ~**se** vpr get engrossed, be captivated

emblema /ẽ'blema/ m emblem

embocadura /ĩboka'dura/ f (de instrumento) mouthpiece; (de freio) bit; (de rio) mouth; (de rua) entrance

êmbolo /'ẽbulu/ m piston

embolsar /ĩbow'sar/ vt pocket; (reembolsar) reimburse

embora /ĩ'bɔra/ adv away ▫ conj although

emborcar /ĩbor'kar/ vi overturn; <barco> capsize

emboscada /ĩbos'kada/ f ambush

embrai|agem /ẽbraj'aʒẽ/ (Port) f veja **embreagem**; ~**ar** (Port) vi veja **embrear**

embre|agem /ẽbri'aʒẽ/ f clutch; ~**ar** vi let in the clutch

embria|gar /ẽbria'gar/ vt intoxicate; ~**gar-se** vpr get drunk, become intoxicated; ∼**guez** /e/ *f* drunkenness; ∼**guez no volante** drunken driving

embri|ão /ẽbri'ãw/ *m* embryo; ∼**onário** *a* embryonic

embro|mação /ĩbroma'sãw/ *f* flannel; ∼**mar** *vt* flannel, string along; (*enganar*) con □ *vi* stall, drag one's feet

embru|lhada /ĩbru'ʎada/ *f* muddle; ∼**lhar** *vt* wrap up <*pacote*>; upset <*estômago*>; (*confundir*) muddle up; ∼**lhar-se** *vpr* <*pessoa*> get muddled up; ∼**lho** *m* parcel; (*fig*) mix-up

embur|rado /ĩbu'xadu/ *a* sulky; ∼**rar** *vi* sulk

embuste /ĩ'bustʃi/ *m* hoax, put-up job

embu|tido /ĩbu'tʃidu/ *a* built-in, fitted; ∼**tir** *vt* build in, fit

emen|da /e'mẽda/ *f* correction, improvement; (*de lei*) amendment; ∼**dar** *vt* correct; amend <*lei*>; ∼**dar-se** *vpr* mend one's ways

ementa /i'mẽta/ (*Port*) *f* menu

emer|gência /emer'ʒẽsia/ *f* emergency; ∼**gente** *a* emergent; ∼**gir** *vi* surface

emi|gração /emigra'sãw/ *f* emigration; (*de aves etc*) migration; ∼**grado** *a* & *m* émigré; ∼**grante** *a* & *m*/*f* emigrant; ∼**grar** *vi* emigrate; <*aves, animais*> migrate

emi|nência /emi'nẽsia/ *f* eminence; ∼**nente** *a* eminent

emis|são /emi'sãw/ *f* (*de ações etc*) issue; (*na rádio, TV*) transmission, broadcast; (*de som, gases*) emission; ∼**sário** *m* emissary; ∼**sor** *m* transmitter; ∼**sora** *f* (*de rádio*) radio station; (*de TV*) TV station

emitir /emi'tʃir/ *vt* issue <*ações, selos etc*>; emit <*sons*>; (*pela rádio, TV*) transmit, broadcast

emoção /emo'sãw/ *f* emotion; (*excitação*) excitement

emocio|nal /emosio'naw/ (*pl* ∼**nais**) *a* emotional; ∼**nante** *a* (*excitante*) exciting; (*comovente*) touching, emotional; ∼**nar** *vt* (*excitar*) excite; (*comover*) move, touch; ∼**nar-se** *vpr* get emotional

emoldurar /emowdu'rar/ *vt* frame

emotivo /emo'tʃivu/ *a* emotional

empacar /ĩpa'kar/ *vi* <*cavalo*> baulk; <*negociações etc*> grind to a halt; <*orador*> dry up

empacotar /ĩpako'tar/ *vt* pack up; (*pôr em pacotes*) packet

empa|da /ẽ'pada/ *f* pie; ∼**dão** *m* (large) pie

empalhar /ĩpa'ʎar/ *vt* stuff

empalidecer /ĩpalide'ser/ *vi* turn pale

empanar[1] /ẽpa'nar/ *vt* tarnish, dull

empanar[2] /ẽpa'nar/ *vt* cook in batter <*carne etc*>

empanturrar /ĩpãtu'xar/ *vt* stuff; ∼**-se** *vpr* stuff o.s. (**de** with)

empapar /ĩpa'par/ *vt* soak

empa|tar /ẽpa'tar/ *vt* draw <*jogo*> □ *vi* <*times*> draw; <*corredores*> tie; ∼**te** *m* (*em jogo*) draw; (*em corrida, votação*) tie; (*em xadrez, fig*) stalemate

empatia /ẽpa'tʃia/ *f* empathy

empecilho /ẽpe'siʎu/ *m* hindrance

empenar /ẽpe'nar/ *vt*/*i* warp

empe|nhar /ĩpe'ɲar/ *vt* (*penhorar*) pawn; (*prometer*) pledge; ∼**-nhar-se** *vpr* do one's utmost (**em** to); ∼**nho** /e/ *m* (*compromisso*) pledge; (*diligência*) effort, commitment

emperrar /ĩpe'xar/ *vt* make stick □ *vi* stick

emperti|gado /ĩpertʃi'gadu/ *a* upright; ∼**gar-se** *vpr* stand up straight

empilhar /ĩpi'ʎar/ *vt* pile up

empi|nado /ĩpi'nadu/ *a* erect; (*íngreme*) sheer, steep; <*nariz*> turned-up; (*fig*) stuck-up; ∼**nar** *vt* stand upright; fly <*pipa*>; tip up <*copo*>

empírico /ẽ'piriku/ *a* empirical

emplacar /ĩpla'kar/ *vt* notch up <*pontos, sucessos, anos*>; license <*carro*>

emplastro /ĩ'plastru/ *m* surgical plaster; ∼ **de nicotina** nicotine patch

empobre|cer /ĩpobre'ser/ *vt* impoverish; ∼**cimento** *m* impoverishment

empoleirar /ĩpole'rar/ *vt* perch; ∼**-se** *vpr* perch

empol|gação /ĩpowga'sãw/ *f* fascination; ∼**gante** *a* fascinating; ∼**gar** *vt* fascinate

empossar /ĩpo'sar/ *vt* swear in

empreen|dedor /ẽpriẽde'dor/ *a* enterprising □ *m* entrepreneur; ∼**der** *vt* undertake; ∼**dimento** *m* undertaking

empre|gada /ĩpre'gada/ *f* (*doméstica*) maid; ∼**gado** *m* employee; ∼**gador** *m* employer; ∼**gar** *vt* employ; ∼**gar-se** *vpr* get a job; ∼**gatício** *a* **vínculo** ∼**gatício** contract of employment; ∼**go** /e/ *m* (*trabalho*) job; (*uso*) use

emprei|tada /ĩprej'tada/ *f* commission, contract; (*empreendimento*) venture; ∼**teira** *f* contractor, firm of contractors; ∼**teiro** *m* contractor

empre|sa /ĩ'preza/ *f* company; ∼ **dot.com** dot-com; ∼**sariado** *m* business community; ∼**sarial** (*pl* ∼**sariais**) *a* business; ∼**sário** *m* businessman; (*de cantor etc*) manager

empres|tado /ĩpres'tadu/ *a* on loan; **pedir** ∼**tado** (ask to) borrow; **tomar** ∼**tado** borrow; ∼**tar** *vt* lend

empréstimo /ĩ'prɛstʃimu/ *m* loan

empur|rão /ĩpu'xãw/ *m* push; **∼rar** *vt* push

emular /emu'lar/ *vt* emulate

enamorado /enamo'radu/ *a* (*apaixonado*) in love

encabeçar /ĩkabe'sar/ *vt* head

encabu|lado /ĩkabu'ladu/ *a* shy; **∼lar** *vt* embarrass; **∼lar-se** *vpr* be shy

encadear /ĩkade'ar/ *vt* chain *ou* link together

encader|nação /ĩkaderna'sãw/ *f* binding; **∼nado** *a* bound; (*com capa dura*) hardback; **∼nar** *vt* bind

encai|xar /ĩka'ʃar/ *vt/i* fit; **∼xe** *m* (*cavidade*) socket; (*juntura*) joint

encalço /ĩ'kawsu/ *m* pursuit; **no ∼ de** in pursuit of

encalhar /ĩka'ʎar/ *vi* <*barco*> run aground; (*fig*) get bogged down; <*mercadoria*> not sell; (*fam: ficar solteiro*) be left on the shelf

encaminhar /ĩkami'ɲar/ *vt* (*dirigir*) steer, direct; (*remeter*) pass on; set in motion <*processo*>; **∼-se** *vpr* set out

encana|dor /ĩkana'dor/ *m* plumber; **∼mento** *m* plumbing

encan|tador /ĩkãta'dor/ *a* enchanting; **∼tamento** *m* enchantment; **∼tar** *vt* enchant; **∼to** *m* charm

encaraco|lado /ĩkarako'ladu/ *a* curly; **∼lar** *vt* curl; **∼lar-se** *vpr* curl up

encarar /ĩka'rar/ *vt* confront, face

encarcerar /ĩkarse'rar/ *vt* imprison

encardido /ĩkar'dʒidu/ *a* grimy

encarecidamente /ĩkaresida-'mẽtʃi/ *adv* insistently

encargo /ĩ'kargu/ *m* task, responsibility

encar|nação /ĩkarna'sãw/ *f* (*do espírito*) incarnation; (*de um personagem*) embodiment; **∼nar** *vt* embody; play <*papel*>

encarre|gado /ĩkaxe'gadu/ *a* in charge (**de** of) □ *m* person in charge; (*de operários*) foreman; **∼gado de negócios** chargé d'affaires; **∼gar** *vt* **∼gar alg de** put s.o. in charge of; **∼gar-se de** undertake to

encarte /ĩ'kartʃi/ *m* insert

ence|nação /ĩsena'sãw/ *f* (*de peça*) production; (*fingimento*) playacting; **∼nar** *vt* put on □ *vi* put it on

ence|radeira /ĩsera'dera/ *f* floor polisher; **∼rar** *vt* wax

encer|rado /ĩse'xadu/ *a* <*assunto*> closed; **∼ramento** *m* close; **∼rar** *vt* close; **∼rar-se** *vpr* close

encharcar /ĩʃar'kar/ *vt* soak

en|chente /ẽ'ʃẽtʃi/ *f* flood; **∼cher** *vt* fill; (*fam*) annoy □ (*fam*) *vi* be annoying; **∼cher-se** *vpr* fill up; (*fam: fartar-se*) get fed up (**de** with)

enciclopédia /ẽsiklo'pɛdʒia/ *f* encyclopaedia

enco|berto /ĩko'bɛrtu/ *a* <*céu, tempo*> overcast; **∼brir** *vt* cover up □ *vi* <*tempo*> become overcast

encolher /ĩko'ʎer/ *vt* shrug <*ombros*>; pull up <*pernas*>; shrink <*roupa*> □ *vi* <*roupa*> shrink; **∼se** *vpr* (*de medo*) shrink; (*de frio*) huddle; (*espremer-se*) squeeze up

encomen|da /ĩko'mẽda/ *f* order; **de** *ou* **sob ∼da** to order; **∼dar** *vt* order (**a** from)

encon|trão /ĩkõ'trãw/ *m* bump; (*empurrão*) shove; **∼trar** *vt* (*achar*) find; (*ver*) meet; **∼trar com** meet; **∼trar-se** *vpr* (*ver-se*) meet; (*estar*) be; **∼tro** *m* meeting; (*mil*) encounter; **ir ao ∼tro de** go to meet; (*fig*) meet; **ir de ∼tro a** run into; (*fig*) go against

encorajar /ĩkora'ʒar/ *vt* encourage

encor|pado /ĩkor'padu/ *a* stocky; <*vinho*> full-bodied; **∼par** *vt/i* fill out

encos|ta /ĩ'kɔsta/ *f* slope; **∼tar** *vt* (*apoiar*) lean; park <*carro*>; leave on the latch <*porta*>; (*pôr de lado*) put aside □ *vi* <*carro*> pull in; **∼tar-se** *vpr* lean; **∼to** /o/ *m* back

encra|vado /ĩkra'vadu/ *a* <*unha, pêlo*> ingrowing; **∼var** *vt* stick

encren|ca /ĩ'krẽka/ *f* fix, jam; *pl* trouble; **∼car** *vt* get into trouble <*pessoa*>; complicate <*situação*> □ *vi* <*situação*> get complicated; <*carro*> break down; **∼car-se** *vpr* <*pessoa*> get into trouble; **∼queiro** *m* troublemaker

encres|pado /ĩkres'padu/ *a* <*mar*> choppy; **∼par** *vt* frizz <*cabelo*>; **∼par-se** *vpr* <*cabelo*> go frizzy; <*mar*> get choppy

encruzilhada /ĩkruzi'ʎada/ *f* crossroads

encurralar /ĩkuxa'lar/ *vt* hem in

encurtar /ĩkur'tar/ *vt* shorten

endere|çar /ĩdere'sar/ *vt* address; **∼ço** /e/ *m* address; (*comput*) **∼ço de e-mail** email address

endinheirado /ĩdʒiɲe'radu/ *a* well-off

endireitar /ĩdʒirej'tar/ *vt* straighten; **∼-se** *vpr* straighten up

endivi|dado /ĩdʒivi'dadu/ *a* in debt; **∼dar** *vt* put into debt; **∼dar-se** *vpr* get into debt

endoidecer /ĩdojde'ser/ *vi* get mad

endos|sar /ĩdo'sar/ *vt* endorse; **∼so** /o/ *m* endorsement

endurecer /ĩdure'ser/ *vt/i* harden

ener|gético /ener'ʒɛtʃiku/ *a* energy; **∼gia** *f* energy

enérgico /e'nɛrʒiku/ a vigorous; <*remédio, discurso*> powerful

enevoado /enevu'adu/ a (*com névoa*) misty; (*com nuvens*) cloudy

enfarte /ĩ'fartʃi/ m heart attack

ênfase /'ẽfazi/ f emphasis; **dar** ∼ **a** emphasize

enfático /ẽ'fatʃiku/ a emphatic

enfatizar /ẽfatʃi'zar/ vt emphasize

enfei|tar /ĩfej'tar/ vt decorate; ∼**tar-se** vpr dress up; ∼**te** m decoration

enfeitiçar /ĩfejtʃi'sar/ vt bewitch

enfer|magem /ĩfer'maʒẽ/ f nursing; ∼**maria** f ward; ∼**meira** f nurse; ∼**meiro** m male nurse; ∼**midade** f illness; ∼**mo** a sick □ m patient

enferru|jado /ĩfexu'ʒadu/ a rusty; ∼**jar** vt/i rust

enfezado /ĩfe'zadu/ a bad-tempered

enfiar /ẽfi'ar/ vt put; slip on <*roupa*>; thread <*agulha*>; string <*pérolas*>

enfileirar /ĩfilej'rar/ vt line up; ∼**-se** vpr line up

enfim /ẽ'fĩ/ adv (*finalmente*) finally; (*resumindo*) anyway

enfo|car /ĩfo'kar/ vt tackle; ∼**que** m approach

enfor|camento /ĩforka'mẽtu/ m hanging; ∼**car** vt hang; ∼**car-se** vpr hang o.s.

enfraquecer /ĩfrake'ser/ vt/i weaken

enfrentar /ĩfrẽ'tar/ vt face

enfumaçado /ĩfuma'sadu/ a smoky

enfurecer /ĩfure'ser/ vt infuriate; ∼**-se** vpr get furious

enga|jamento /ĩgaʒa'mẽtu/ m commitment; ∼**jado** a committed; ∼**jar-se** vpr get involved (**em** in)

engalfinhar-se /ĩgawfi'ɲarsi/ vpr grapple

enga|nado /ĩga'nadu/ a (*errado*) mistaken; ∼**nar** vt deceive; cheat on <*marido, esposa*>; stave off <*fome*>; ∼**nar-se** vpr be mistaken; ∼**no** m (*erro*) mistake; (*desonestidade*) deception

engarra|famento /ĩgaxafa'mẽtu/ m traffic jam; ∼**far** vt bottle <*vinho etc*>; block <*trânsito*>

engas|gar /ĩgaz'gar/ vt choke □ vi choke; <*motor*> backfire; ∼**go** m choking

engastar /ĩgaʃ'tar/ vt set <*jóias*>

engatar /ĩga'tar/ vt hitch <*reboque etc*> (**a** to); engage <*marcha*>

engatinhar /ĩgatʃi'ɲar/ vi crawl; (*fig*) start out

engave|tamento /ĩgaveta'mẽtu/ m pile-up; ∼**tar** vt shelve

engelhar /ĩʒe'ʎar/ vi (*pele*) wrinkle

enge|nharia /ĩʒeɲa'ria/ f engineering; ∼**nheiro** m engineer; ∼**nho** /e/ m (*de pessoa*) ingenuity; (*de açúcar*) sugar

mill; (*máquina*) device; ∼**nhoca** /ɔ/ f gadget; ∼**nhoso** a ingenious

engessar /ĩʒe'sar/ vt put in plaster

engodo /ĩ'godu/ m lure

engolir /ĩgo'lir/ vt/i swallow; ∼ **em seco** gulp

engomar /ĩgo'mar/ vt press; (*com goma*) starch

engordar /ĩgor'dar/ vt make fat; fatten <*animais*> □ vi <*pessoa*> put on weight; <*comida*> be fattening

engraçado /ĩgra'sadu/ a funny

engradado /ĩgra'dadu/ m crate

engravidar /ĩgravi'dar/ vt make pregnant □ vi get pregnant

engraxar /ĩgra'ʃar/ vt polish

engre|nado /ĩgre'nadu/ a <*carro*> in gear; ∼**nagem** f gear; (*fig*) mechanism; ∼**nar** vt put into gear <*carro*>; strike up <*conversa*>; ∼**nar-se** vpr mesh; (*fig*) <*pessoas*> get on

engrossar /ĩgro'sar/ vt thicken; raise <*voz*> □ vi thicken; <*pessoa*> turn nasty

enguia /ẽ'gia/ f eel

engui|çar /ẽgi'sar/ vi break down; ∼**ço** m breakdown

enig|ma /e'nigima/ m enigma; ∼**mático** a enigmatic

enjaular /ĩʒaw'lar/ vt cage

enjo|ar /ĩʒo'ar/ vt sicken □ vi, ∼**ar-se** vpr get sick (**de** of); ∼**ativo** a <*comida*> sickly; <*livro etc*> boring

enjôo /ĩ'ʒou/ m sickness

enlameado /ĩlami'adu/ a muddy

enlatado /ĩla'tadu/ a tinned, canned; ∼**s** m pl tinned foods

enle|var /ẽle'var/ vt enthral; ∼**vo** /e/ m rapture

enlouquecer /ĩloke'ser/ vt drive mad □ vi go mad

enluarado /ĩlua'radu/ a moonlit

enor|me /e'nɔrmi/ a enormous; ∼**midade** f enormity

enquadrar /ĩkwa'drar/ vt fit □ vi, ∼**-se** vpr fit in

enquanto /ĩ'kwãtu/ conj while; ∼ **isso** meanwhile; **por** ∼ for the time being

enquete /ã'kɛtʃi/ f survey

enraivecer /ĩxajve'ser/ vt enrage

enredo /ẽ'redu/ m plot

enrijecer /ĩxiʒe'ser/ vt stiffen; ∼**-se** vpr stiffen

enrique|cer /ĩxike'ser/ vt (*dar dinheiro a*) make rich; (*fig*) enrich □ vi get rich; ∼**cimento** m enrichment

enro|lado /ĩxo'ladu/ a complicated; ∼**lar** vt (*envolver*) roll up; (*complicar*) complicate; (*enganar*) cheat; ∼**lar-se** vpr (*envolver-se*) roll up; (*confundir-se*) get mixed up

enroscar /ĩxos'kar/ vt twist

enrouquecer /ĩxoke'ser/ vi go hoarse

enrugar /ĩxu'gar/ vt wrinkle <*pele, tecido*>; furrow <*testa*>

enrustido /ĩxus'tʃidu/ a repressed

ensaboar /ĩsabo'ar/ vt soap

ensai|ar /ĩsaj'ar/ vt (*provar*) try out; (*repetir*) rehearse; **~o** m (*prova*) test; (*repetição*) rehearsal; (*escrito*) essay

ensanguentado /ĩsãgwẽ'tadu/ a bloody, bloodstained

enseada /ĩsi'ada/ f inlet

ensebado /ĩse'badu/ a greasy

ensimesmado /ĩsimez'madu/ a lost in thought

ensi|nar /ẽsi'nar/ vt/i teach (**aco a alg** s.o. sth); **~nar alg a nadar** teach s.o. to swim; **~no** m teaching; (*em geral*) education

ensolarado /ĩsola'radu/ a sunny

enso|pado /ĩso'padu/ a soaked □ m stew; **~par** vt soak

ensurde|cedor /ĩsurdese'dor/ a deafening; **~cer** vt deafen □ vi go deaf

entabular /ĩtabu'lar/ vt open, start

entalar /ĩta'lar/ vt wedge, jam; (*em apertos*) get; **~se** vpr get wedged, get jammed; (*em apertos*) get caught up

entalhar /ĩta'ʎar/ vt carve

entanto /ĩ'tãtu/ m **no ~** however

então /ĩ'tãw/ adv then; (*nesse caso*) so

entardecer /ĩtarde'ser/ m sunset

ente /'ẽtʃi/ m being

entea|da /ẽtʃi'ada/ f stepdaughter; **~do** m stepson

entedi|ante /ĩtedʒi'ãtʃi/ a boring; **~ar** vt bore; **~ar-se** vpr get bored

enten|der /ĩtẽ'der/ vt understand; **~der-se** vpr (*dar-se bem*) get on (**com** with); **dar a ~der** give to understand; **~der de futebol** know about football; **~dimento** m understanding

enternecedor /ĩternese'dor/ a touching

enter|rar /ĩte'xar/ vt bury; **~ro** /e/ m burial; (*cerimônia*) funeral

entidade /ẽtʃi'dadʒi/ f entity; (*órgão*) body

entornar /ĩtor'nar/ vt tip over, spill

entorpe|cente /ĩtorpe'sẽtʃi/ m drug, narcotic; **~cer** vt numb

entortar /ĩtor'tar/ vt make crooked

entrada /ẽ'trada/ f entry; (*onde se entra*) entrance; (*bilhete*) ticket; (*prato*) starter; (*pagamento*) deposit; pl (*no cabelo*) receding hairline; **dar ~ a** enter; **~ proibida** no entry

entranhas /ĩ'traɲas/ f pl entrails

entrar /ẽ'trar/ vi go/come in; **~ com** enter <*dados*>; put in <*dinheiro*>; **~**

em detalhes go into details; **~ em vigor** come into force

entravar /ẽtra'var/ vt hamper

entre /'ẽtri/ prep between; (*em meio a*) among

entreaberto /ẽtria'bɛrtu/ a half-open

entrecortar /ẽtrikor'tar/ vt intersperse; (*cruzar*) intersect

entre|ga /ĩ'trɛga/ f delivery; (*rendição*) surrender; **~ga a domicílio** home delivery; **~gar** vt hand over; deliver <*mercadorias, cartas*>; hand in <*caderno, trabalho escolar*>; **~gar-se** vpr give o.s. up (**a** to); **~gue** pp de entregar

entrelaçar /ẽtrela'sar/ vt intertwine; clasp <*mãos*>

entrelinhas /ẽtri'liɲas/ f pl **ler nas ~** read between the lines

entremear /ẽtrimi'ar/ vt intersperse

entreolhar-se /ẽtrio'ʎarsi/ vpr look at one another

entretanto /ẽtre'tãtu/ conj however

entre|tenimento /ẽtreteni'mẽtu/ m entertainment; **~ter** vt entertain

entrever /ẽtre'ver/ vt glimpse

entrevis|ta /ẽtre'vista/ f interview; **~tador** m interviewer; **~tar** vt interview

entristecer /ĩtriste'ser/ vt sadden □ vi be saddened (**com** by)

entroncamento /ĩtrõka'mẽtu/ m junction

entrosar /ĩtro'zar/ vt/i integrate

entu|lhar /ĩtu'ʎar/ vt cram (**de** with); **~lho** m rubble

entupir /ĩtu'pir/ vt block; **~pir-se** vpr get blocked; (*de comida*) stuff o.s. (**de** with)

enturmar-se /ĩtur'marsi/ vpr mix in, fit in

entusias|mar /ĩtuziaz'mar/ vt fill with enthusiasm; **~mar-se** vpr get enthusiastic (**com** about); **~mo** m enthusiasm; **~ta** m/f enthusiast □ a enthusiastic

entusiástico /ĩtuzi'astʃiku/ a enthusiastic

enumerar /enume'rar/ vt enumerate

envelope /ẽve'lɔpi/ m envelope

envelhecer /ĩveʎe'ser/ vt/i age

envenenar /ĩvene'nar/ vt poison; (*fam*) soup up <*carro*>

envergadura /ĩverga'dura/ f wingspan; (*fig*) scale

envergo|nhado /ĩvergo'ɲadu/ a ashamed; (*constrangido*) embarrassed; **~nhar** vt disgrace; (*constranger*) embarrass; **~nhar-se** vpr be ashamed; (*acanhar-se*) get embarrassed

envernizar /ĩverni'zar/ vt varnish

en|viado /ẽvi'adu/ *m* envoy; **~viar** *vt* send; **~vio** *m* (*ato*) sending; (*remessa*) consignment

envidraçar /ĩvidra'sar/ *vt* glaze

enviesado /ĩvie'zadu/ *a* (*não vertical*) slanting; (*torto*) crooked

envol|vente /ĩvow'vẽtʃi/ *a* compelling, gripping; **~ver** *vt* (*embrulhar*) wrap; (*enredar*) involve; **~ver-se** *vpr* (*enrolar-se*) wrap o.s.; (*enredar-se*) get involved; **~vimento** *m* involvement

enxada /ẽ'ʃada/ *f* hoe

enxaguar /ẽʃa'gwar/ *vt* rinse

enxame /ẽ'ʃami/ *m* swarm

enxaqueca /ẽʃa'keka/ *f* migraine

enxergar /ĩʃer'gar/ *vt/i* see

enxer|tar /ĩʃer'tar/ *vt* graft; **~to** /e/ *m* graft

enxotar /ĩʃo'tar/ *vt* drive away

enxofre /ẽ'ʃofri/ *m* sulphur

enxo|val /ẽʃo'vaw/ (*pl* **~vais**) *m* (*de noiva*) trousseau; (*de bebê*) layette

enxugar /ĩʃu'gar/ *vt* dry; **~-se** *vpr* dry o.s.

enxurrada /ĩʃu'xada/ *f* torrent; (*fig*) flood

enxuto /ĩ'ʃutu/ *a* dry; <*corpo*> shapely

enzima /ẽ'zima/ *f* enzyme

epicentro /epi'sẽtru/ *m* epicentre

épico /'ɛpiku/ *a* epic

epidemia /epide'mia/ *f* epidemic

epi|lepsia /epilep'sia/ *f* epilepsy; **~léptico** *a* & *m* epileptic

epílogo /e'pilogu/ *m* epilogue

episódio /epi'zɔdʒiu/ *m* episode

epitáfio /epi'tafiu/ *m* epitaph

época /'ɛpoca/ *f* time; (*da história*) age, period; **fazer ~** make history; **móveis da ~** period furniture

epopéia /epo'pɛja/ *f* epic

equação /ekwa'sãw/ *f* equation

equador /ekwa'dor/ *m* equator; **o Equador** Ecuador

equatori|al /ekwatori'aw/ (*pl* **~ais**) *a* equatorial; **~ano** *a* & *m* Ecuadorian

equilibrar /ekili'brar/ *vt* balance; **~-se** *vpr* balance

equilíbrio /eki'libriu/ *m* balance

equipa /e'kipa/ (*Port*) *f* team

equi|pamento /ekipa'mẽtu/ *m* equipment; **~par** *vt* equip

equiparar /ekipa'rar/ *vt* equate (**com** with); **~-se** *vpr* compare (**a** with)

equipe /e'kipi/ *f* team

equitação /ekita'sãw/ *f* riding

equiva|lência /ekiva'lẽsia/ *f* equivalence; **~lente** *a* equivalent; **~ler** *vi* be equivalent (**a** to)

equivo|cado /ekivo'kadu/ *a* mistaken; **~car-se** *vpr* make a mistake

equívoco /e'kivoku/ *a* equivocal □ *m* mistake

era /'ɛra/ *f* era

erário /e'rariu/ *m* exchequer

ereção /ere'sãw/ *f* erection

eremita /ere'mita/ *m/f* hermit

ereto /e'rɛtu/ *a* erect

erguer /er'ger/ *vt* raise; erect <*monumento etc*>; **~-se** *vpr* rise

eri|çado /eri'sadu/ *a* bristling; **~çar-se** *vpr* bristle

ermo /'ermu/ *a* deserted □ *m* wilderness

erosão /ero'zãw/ *f* erosion

erótico /e'rɔtʃiku/ *a* erotic

erotismo /ero'tʃizmu/ *m* eroticism

er|rado /e'xadu/ *a* wrong; **~rante** *a* wandering; **~rar** *vt* (*não fazer certo*) get wrong; miss <*alvo*> □ *vi* (*enganar-se*) be wrong; (*vaguear*) wander; **~ro** /e/ *m* mistake; **fazer um ~ro** make a mistake; **~rôneo** *a* erroneous

erudi|ção /erudʒi'sãw/ *f* learning; **~to** *a* learned; <*música*> classical □ *m* scholar

erupção /erup'sãw/ *f* (*vulcânica*) eruption; (*cutânea*) rash

erva /'ɛrva/ *f* herb; **~ daninha** weed; **~-doce** *f* aniseed

ervilha /er'viʎa/ *f* pea

esban|jador /izbãʒa'dor/ *a* extravagant □ *m* spendthrift; **~jar** *vt* squander; burst with <*saúde, imaginação, energia etc*>

esbar|rão /izba'xãw/ *m* bump; **~rar** *vi* **~rar com** *ou* **em** bump into <*pessoa*>; come up against <*problema*>

esbelto /iz'bɛwtu/ *a* svelte

esbo|çar /izbo'sar/ *vt* sketch <*desenho etc*>; outline <*plano etc*>; **~çar um sorriso** give a hint of a smile; **~ço** /o/ *m* (*desenho*) sketch; (*plano*) outline; (*de um sorriso*) hint

esbofetear /izbofetʃi'ar/ *vt* slap

esborrachar /izboxa'ʃar/ *vt* squash; **~-se** *vpr* crash

esbravejar /izbrave'ʒar/ *vi* rant, rail

esbura|cado /izbura'kadu/ *a* full of holes; **~car** *vt* make holes in

esbuga|lhado /izbuga'ʎadu/ *a* <*olhos*> bulging; **~lhar-se** *vpr* <*olhos*> pop out

escabroso /iska'brozu/ *a* (*fig*) difficult, tough

escada /is'kada/ *f* (*dentro de casa*) stairs; (*na rua*) steps; (*de mão*) ladder; **~ de incêndio** fire escape; **~ rolante** escalator; **~ria** *f* staircase

escafan|drista /iskafã'drista/ *m/f* diver; **~dro** *m* diving suit

escala /is'kala/ *f* scale; (*de navio*) port of call; (*de avião*) stopover; **fazer ~** stop over; **sem ~** <*vôo*> non-stop

esca|lada /iska'lada/ f (fig) escalation; **∼lão** m echelon, level; **∼lar** vt (subir a) scale; (designar) select

escaldar /iskaw'dar/ vt scald; blanch <vegetais>

escalfar /iskaw'far/ vt poach

escalonar /iskalo'nar/ vt schedule <pagamento>

escama /is'kama/ f scale

escanca|rado /iskãka'radu/ a wide open; **∼rar** vt open wide

escandalizar /iskãdali'zar/ vt scandalize; **∼-se** vpr be scandalized

escândalo /is'kãdalu/ m (vexame) scandal; (tumulto) fuss, uproar; **fazer um ∼** make a scene

escandaloso /iskãda'lozu/ a (chocante) scandalous; (espalhafatoso) outrageous, loud

Escandinávia /iskãdʒi'navia/ f Scandinavia

escandinavo /iskãdʒi'navu/ a & m Scandinavian

escanga|lhado /iskãga'ʎadu/ a broken; **∼lhar** vt break up; **∼lhar-se** vpr fall to pieces; **∼lhar-se de rir** split one's sides laughing

escaninho /iska'niɲu/ m pigeonhole

escanteio /iskã'teju/ m corner

esca|pada /iska'pada/ f (fuga) escape; (aventura) escapade; **∼pamento** m exhaust; **∼par** vi **∼par a** ou **de** (livrar-se) escape from; (evitar) escape; **∼pou-lhe a palavra** the word slipped out; **o copo ∼pou-me das mãos** the glass slipped out of my hands; **o nome me ∼pa** the name escapes me; **∼par de boa** have a narrow escape; **∼patória** f way out; (desculpa) pretext; **∼pe** m escape; (de carro etc) exhaust; **∼pulir** vi escape (de from)

escaramuça /iskara'musa/ f skirmish

escaravelho /iskara'vɛʎu/ m beetle

escarcéu /iskar'sɛw/ m uproar, fuss

escarlate /iskar'latʃi/ a scarlet

escarnecer /iskarne'ser/ vt mock

escárnio /is'karniu/ m derision

escarpado /iskar'padu/ a steep

escarrado /iska'xadu/ m **ele é o pai ∼** he's the spitting image of his father

escarro /is'kaxu/ m phlegm

escas|sear /iskasi'ar/ vi run short; **∼sez** f shortage; **∼so** a (raro) scarce; (ralo) scant

esca|vadeira /iskava'dera/ f digger; **∼var** vt excavate

esclare|cer /isklare'ser/ vt explain <fatos>; enlighten <pessoa>; **∼cer-se** vpr <fato> be explained; <pessoa> find out; **∼cimento** m (de pessoas) enlightenment; (de fatos) explanation

esclerosado /isklero'zadu/ a senile

escoar /isko'ar/ vt/i drain

esco|cês /isko'ses/ a (f **∼cesa**) Scottish □ m (f **∼cesa**) Scot

Escócia /is'kɔsia/ f Scotland

esco|la /is'kɔla/ f school; **∼la de samba** samba school; **∼lar** a school □ m/f schoolchild; **∼laridade** f schooling

esco|lha /is'koʎa/ f choice; **∼lher** vt choose

escol|ta /is'kowta/ f escort; **∼tar** vt escort

escombros /is'kõbrus/ m pl debris

escon|de-esconde /iskõdʒis-'kõdʒi/ m hide-and-seek; **∼der** vt hide; **∼der-se** vpr hide; **∼derijo** m hiding place; (de bandidos) hideout; **∼didas** f pl **às ∼didas** secretly

esco|ra /is'kɔra/ f prop; **∼rar** vt prop up; **∼rar-se** vpr <argumento etc> be based (**em** on)

escore /is'kɔri/ m score

escória /is'kɔria/ f scum, dross

escori|ação /iskoria'sãw/ f graze, abrasion; **∼ar** vt graze

escorpião /iskorpi'ãw/ m scorpion; **Escorpião** Scorpio

escorredor /iskoxe'dor/ m drainer

escorrega /isko'xega/ m slide

escorre|gador /iskoxega'dor/ m slide; **∼gão** m slip; **∼gar** vi slip

escor|rer /isko'xer/ vt drain □ vi trickle; **∼rido** a <cabelo> straight

escoteiro /isko'teru/ m boy scout

escotilha /isko'tʃiʎa/ f hatch

esco|va /is'kova/ f brush; **fazer ∼va no cabelo** blow-dry one's hair; **∼va de dentes** toothbrush; **∼var** vt brush; **∼vinha** f **cabelo à ∼vinha** crew-cut

escra|chado /iskra'ʃadu/ a (fam) a outspoken; **∼char** (fam) vt tell off

escra|vatura /iskrava'tura/ f slavery; **∼vidão** f slavery; **∼vizar** vt enslave; **∼vo** m slave

escre|vente /iskre'vẽtʃi/ m/f clerk; **∼ver** vt/i write

escri|ta /is'krita/ f writing; **∼to** pp de **escrever** □ a written; **por ∼to** in writing; **∼tor** m writer; **∼tório** m office; (numa casa) study

escritu|ra /iskri'tura/ f (a Bíblia) scripture; (contrato) deed; **∼ração** f bookkeeping; **∼rar** vt keep, write up <contas>; draw up <documento>

escri|vaninha /iskriva'niɲa/ f bureau, writing desk; **∼vão** m (f **∼vã**) registrar

escrúpulo /is'krupulu/ m scruple

escrupuloso /iskrupu'lozu/ a scrupulous

escrutínio /iskru'tʃiniu/ m ballot

escu|dar /isku'dar/ vt shield; ~deria f team; ~do m shield; (moeda) escudo

escula|chado /iskula'ʃadu/ (fam) a sloppy; ~char (fam) vt mess up <coisa>; tell off <pessoa>; ~cho (fam) m (bagunça) mess; (bronca) telling-off

escul|pir /iskuw'pir/ vt sculpt; ~tor m sculptor; ~tura f sculpture; ~tural (pl ~turais) a statuesque

escuma /is'kuma/ f scum; ~deira f skimmer

escuna /is'kuna/ f schooner

escu|ras /is'kuras/ fpl às ~ras in the dark; ~recer vt darken □ vi get dark; ~ridão f darkness; ~ro a & m dark

escuso /is'kuzu/ a shady

escu|ta /is'kuta/ f listening; estar à ~ta be listening; ~ta telefônica phone tapping; ~tar vt (perceber) hear; (prestar atenção a) listen to □ vi (poder ouvir) hear; (prestar atenção) listen

esdrúxulo /iz'druʃulu/ a weird

esfacelar /isfase'lar/ vt wreck

esfalfar /isfaw'far/ vt wear out; ~-se vpr get worn out

esfaquear /isfaki'ar/ vt stab

esfarelar /isfare'lar/ vt crumble; ~-se vpr crumble

esfarrapado /isfaxa'padu/ a ragged; <desculpa> lame

es|fera /is'fɛra/ f sphere; ~férico a spherical

esferográfi|co /isfero'grafiku/ a caneta ~ca ball-point pen

esfiapar /isfia'par/ vt fray; ~-se vpr fray

esfinge /is'fĩʒi/ f sphinx

esfolar /isfo'lar/ vt skin; (fig) overcharge

esfomeado /isfomi'adu/ a starving, famished

esfor|çar-se /isfor'sarsi/ vpr make an effort; ~ço /o/ m effort; fazer ~ço make an effort

esfre|gaço /isfre'gasu/ m smear; ~gar vt rub; (para limpar) scrub

esfriar /isfri'ar/ vt cool □ vi cool (down); (sentir frio) get cold

esfumaçado /isfuma'sadu/ a smoky

esfuziante /isfuzi'ãtʃi/ a irrepressible, exuberant

esganar /izga'nar/ vt throttle

esganiçado /izgani'sadu/ a shrill

esgarçar /izgar'sar/ vt/i fray

esgo|tado /izgo'tadu/ a exhausted; <estoque, lotação> sold out; ~tamento m exhaustion; ~tamento nervoso nervous breakdown; ~tar vt exhaust; (gastar) use up; ~tar-se vpr <pessoa> become exhausted; <estoque, lotação> sell out; <recursos, provisões> run out; ~to /o/ m drain; (de detritos) sewer

esgri|ma /iz'grima/ f fencing; ~mir vt brandish □ vi fence; ~mista m/f fencer

esgrouvinhado /izgrovi'ɲadu/ a tousled, dishevelled

esgueirar-se /izge'rarsi/ vpr slip, sneak

esguelha /iz'geʎa/ f de ~ askew; <olhar> askance

esgui|char /izgi'ʃar/ vt/i spurt, squirt; ~cho m jet, spurt

esguio /iz'gio/ a slender

eslavo /iz'lavu/ a Slavic □ m Slav

esmaecer /izmaj'ser/ vi fade

esma|gador /izmaga'dor/ a <vitória, maioria> overwhelming; <provas> incontrovertible; ~gar vt crush

esmalte /iz'mawtʃi/ m enamel; ~ de unhas nail varnish

esmeralda /izme'rawda/ f emerald

esme|rar-se /izme'rarsi/ vpr take great care (em over); ~ro /e/ m great care

esmigalhar /izmiga'ʎar/ vt crumble <pão etc>; shatter <vidro, copo>; ~-se vpr <pão etc> crumble; <vidro, copo> shatter

esmiuçar /izmiu'sar/ vt examine in detail

esmo /'ezmu/ m a ~ <escolher> at random; <andar> aimlessly; <falar> nonsense

esmola /iz'mɔla/ f donation; pl charity

esmorecer /izmore'ser/ vi flag

esmurrar /izmu'xar/ vt punch

esno|bar /izno'bar/ vt snub □ vi be snobbish; ~be /iz'nɔbi/ a snobbish □ m/f snob; ~bismo m snobbishness

esotérico /ezo'tɛriku/ a esoteric

espa|çar /ispa'sar/ vt space out; make less frequent <visitas, consultas etc>; ~cial (pl ~ciais) a space; ~ço m space; (cultural etc) venue; ~çoso /o/ a spacious

espada /is'pada/ f sword; pl (naipe) spades; ~chim m swordsman

espádua /is'padua/ f shoulder blade

espaguete /ispa'getʃi/ m spaghetti

espaire|cer /ispajre'ser/ vt amuse □ vi relax; (dar uma volta) go for a walk; ~cimento m recreation

espaldar /ispaw'dar/ m back

espalhafato /ispaʎa'fatu/ m (barulho) fuss, uproar; (de roupa etc) extravagance; ~so /o/ a (barulhento) noisy, rowdy; (ostentoso) extravagant

espalhar /ispa'ʎar/ vt scatter; spread <notícia, terror etc>; shed <luz>; ~-se vpr spread; <pessoas> spread out

espa|nador /ispana'dor/ m feather duster; ~nar vt dust

espan|camento /ispãka'mẽtu/ *m*
beating; **~car** *vt* beat up

Espanha /is'paɲa/ *f* Spain

espa|nhol /ispa'ɲɔw/ (*pl* **~nhóis**) *a*
(*f* **~nhola**) Spanish □ *m* (*f* **~nhola**)
Spaniard; (*língua*) Spanish; **os**
~nhóis the Spanish

espan|talho /ispã'taʎu/ *m* scarecrow;
~tar *vt* (*admirar*) amaze; (*assustar*)
scare; (*afugentar*) drive away; **~tar-se**
vpr (*admirar-se*) be amazed; (*assustar-
se*) get scared; (*afugentar*) **~to m** (*susto*) fright;
(*admiração*) amazement; **~toso** /o/ *a*
amazing

esparadrapo /ispara'drapu/ *m* sticking
plaster

espargo /is'pargu/ (*Port*) *m* asparagus

esparramar /ispaxa'mar/ *vt* scatter;
~-se *vpr* be scattered, spread

espartano /ispar'tanu/ *a* spartan

espartilho /ispar'tʃiʎu/ *m* corset

espas|mo /is'pazmu/ *m* spasm; **~módico**
a spasmodic

espatifar /ispatʃi'far/ *vt* smash; **~-se** *vpr*
smash; <*carro, avião*> crash

especi|al /ispesi'aw/ (*pl* **~ais**) *a* special;
~alidade *f* speciality; **~alista** *m/f*
specialist

especiali|zado /ispesiali'zadu/ *a*
specialized; <*mão-de-obra*> skilled;
~zar-se *vpr* specialize (**em** in)

especiaria /ispesia'ria/ *f* spice

espécie /is'pɛsi/ *f* sort, kind; (*de
animais*) species

especifi|cação /ispesifika'sãw/ *f*
specification; **~car** *vt* specify

específico /ispe'sifiku/ *a* specific

espécime /is'pesimi/ *m* specimen

espectador /ispekta'dor/ *m* (*de TV*)
viewer; (*de jogo, espetáculo*) spectator;
(*de acidente etc*) onlooker

espectro /is'pektru/ *m* (*fantasma*)
spectre; (*de cores*) spectrum

especu|lação /ispekula'sãw/ *f*
speculation; **~lador** *m* speculator;
~lar *vi* speculate (**sobre** on); **~lativo**
a speculative

espe|lhar /ispe'ʎar/ *vt* mirror; **~lhar-se**
vpr be mirrored; **~lho** /e/ *m* mirror;
~lho retrovisor rear-view mirror

espelunca /ispe'lũka/ (*fam*) *f* dive

espera /is'pɛra/ *f* wait; **à ~ de** waiting
for

esperan|ça /ispe'rãsa/ *f* hope; **~çoso** /o/
a hopeful

esperar /ispe'rar/ *vt* (*aguardar*) wait for;
(*desejar*) hope for; (*contar com*) expect
□ *vi* wait (**por** for); **fazer alg** ~ keep
s.o. waiting; **espero que ele venha** I
hope (that) he comes; **espero que sim**
/não I hope so/not

esperma /is'pɛrma/ *m* sperm

espernear /isperni'ar/ *vi* kick; (*fig:
reclamar*) kick up

esper|talhão /isperta'ʎãw/ *m* (*f*
~talhona) wise guy; **~teza** /e/ *f*
cleverness; (*uma*) clever move; **~to** /e/
a clever

espes|so /is'pesu/ *a* thick; **~sura** *f*
thickness

espe|tacular /ispetaku'lar/ *a*
spectacular; **~táculo** *m* (*no teatro etc*)
show; (*cena impressionante*) spectacle;
~taculoso /o/ *a* spectacular

espe|tar /ispe'tar/ *vt* (*cravar*) stick;
(*furar*) skewer; **~tar-se** *vpr* (*cravar-se*)
stick; (*ferir-se*) prick o.s.; **~tinho** *m*
skewer; (*de carne etc*) kebab; **~to** /e/ *m*
spit

espevitado /ispevi'tadu/ *a* cheeky

espezinhar /ispezi'ɲar/ *vt* walk all over

espi|a /is'pia/ *m/f* spy; **~ão** *m* (*f* **~ã**) spy;
~ada *f* peep; **~ar** *vt* (*observar*) spy on;
(*aguardar*) watch for □ *vi* peer, peep

espicaçar /ispika'sar/ *vt* goad <*pessoa*>;
excite <*imaginação, curiosidade*>

espichar /ispi'ʃar/ *vt* stretch □ *vi* shoot
up; **~-se** *vpr* stretch out

espiga /is'piga/ *f* (*de trigo etc*) ear; (*de
milho*) cob

espina|fração /ispinafra'sãw/ (*fam*) *f*
telling-off; **~frar** (*fam*) *vt* tell off; **~fre**
m spinach

espingarda /ispĩ'garda/ *f* rifle, shotgun

espinha /is'piɲa/ *f* (*de peixe*) bone; (*na
pele*) spot; **~ dorsal** spine

espinho /is'piɲu/ *m* thorn; **~so** /o/ *a*
thorny; (*fig*) difficult, tough

espio|nagem /ispio'naʒẽ/ *f* espionage,
spying; **~nar** *vt* spy on □ *vi* spy

espi|ral /ispi'raw/ (*pl* **~rais**) *a & f* spiral

espírita /is'pirita/ *a & m/f* spiritualist

espiritismo /ispiri'tʃizmu/ *m*
spiritualism

espírito /is'piritu/ *m* spirit; (*graça*) wit

espiritu|al /ispiritu'aw/ (*pl* **~ais**) *a*
spiritual; **~oso** /o/ *a* witty

espir|rar /ispi'xar/ *vt* spurt □ *vi*
<*pessoa*> sneeze; <*lama, tinta etc*>
spatter; <*fogo, lenha, fritura etc*> spit;
~ro *m* sneeze

esplêndido /is'plẽdʒidu/ *a* splendid

esplendor /isplẽ'dor/ *m* splendour

espoleta /ispo'leta/ *f* fuse

espoliar /ispoli'ar/ *vt* plunder, pillage

espólio /is'pɔliu/ *m* (*herdado*) estate;
(*roubado*) spoils

espon|ja /is'põʒa/ *f* sponge; **~joso** /o/ *a*
spongy

espon|taneidade /ispõtanej-'dadʒi/ *f*
spontaneity; **~tâneo** *a* spontaneous

espora /is'pɔra/ *f* spur

esporádico /ispo'radʒiku/ *a* sporadic

esporear /ispori'ar/ *vt* spur on

espor|te /is'pɔrtʃi/ *m* sport □ *a invar* <*roupa*> casual; **carro ~te** sports car; **~tista** *m*/*f* sportsman (*f*-woman); **~tiva** *f* sense of humour; **~tivo** *a* sporting

espo|sa /is'poza/ *f* wife; **~so** *m* husband

espregui|çadeira /ispregisa'dera/ *f* (*tipo cadeira*) deckchair; (*tipo cama*) sun lounger; **~çar-se** *vpr* stretch

esprei|ta /is'prejta/ *f* **ficar à ~ta** lie in wait; **~tar** *vt* stalk <*caça, vítima*>; spy on <*vizinhos, inimigos etc*>; look out for <*ocasião*> □ *vi* peep, spy

espre|medor /ispreme'dor/ *m* squeezer; **~mer** *vt* squeeze; wring out <*roupa*>; squash <*pessoa*>; **~mer-se** *vpr* squeeze up

espu|ma /is'puma/ *f* foam; **~ma de borracha** foam rubber; **~mante** *a* <*vinho*> sparkling; **~mar** *vi* foam, froth

espúrio /is'puriu/ *a* spurious

esqua|dra /is'kwadra/ *f* squad; **~dra de polícia** (*Port*) police station; **~drão** *m* squadron; **~dria** *f* doors and windows; **~drinhar** *vt* explore; **~dro** *m* set square

esqualidez /iskwali'des/ *f* squalor

esquálido /is'kwalidu/ *a* squalid

esquartejar /iskwarte'ʒar/ *vt* chop up

esque|cer /iske'ser/ *vt*/*i* forget; **~cer-se de** forget; **~cido** *a* forgotten; (*com memória fraca*) forgetful; **~cimento** *m* oblivion; (*memória fraca*) forgetfulness

esque|lético /iske'lɛtʃiku/ *a* skinny, skeleton-like; **~leto** /e/ *m* skeleton

esque|ma /is'kema/ *m* outline, draft; (*operação*) scheme; **~ma de segurança** security operation; **~mático** *a* schematic

esquentar /iskẽ'tar/ *vt* warm up □ *vi* warm up; <*roupa*> be warm; **~-se** *vpr* get annoyed; **~ a cabeça** (*fam*) get worked up

esquer|da /is'kerda/ *f* left; **à ~da** (*posição*) on the left; (*direção*) to the left; **~dista** *a* left-wing □ *m*/*f* left-winger; **~do** /e/ *a* left

esqui /is'ki/ *m* ski; (*esporte*) skiing; **~ aquático** water skiing; **~ador** *m* skier; **~ar** *vi* ski

esquilo /is'kilu/ *m* squirrel

esquina /is'kina/ *f* corner

esquisi|tice /iskizi'tʃisi/ *f* strangeness; (*uma*) strange thing; **~to** *a* strange

esqui|var-se /iski'varsi/ *vpr* dodge out of the way; **~var-se de** dodge; **~vo** *a* elusive; <*pessoa*> aloof, antisocial

esquizo|frenia /iskizofre'nia/ *f* schizophrenia; **~frênico** *a* & *m* schizophrenic

es|sa /'ɛsa/ *pron* that (one); **~sa é boa** that's a good one; **~sa não** come off it; **por ~sas e outras** for these and other reasons; **~se** /e/ *a* that; *pl* those; (*fam: este*) this; *pl* these □ *pron* that one; *pl* those; (*fam: este*) this one; *pl* these

essência /e'sẽsia/ *f* essence

essenci|al /esẽsi'aw/ (*pl* **~ais**) *a* essential; **o ~al** what is essential

estabele|cer /istabele'ser/ *vt* establish; **~cer-se** *vpr* establish o.s.; **~cimento** *m* establishment

estabili|dade /istabili'dadʒi/ *f* stability; **~zar** *vt* stabilize; **~zar-se** *vpr* stabilize

estábulo /is'tabulu/ *m* cowshed

estaca /is'taka/ *f* stake; (*de barraca*) peg; **voltar à ~ zero** go back to square one

estação /ista'sãw/ *f* (*do ano*) season; (*ferroviária etc*) station; **~ balneária** seaside resort

estacar /ista'kar/ *vi* stop short

estacio|namento /istasiona'mẽtu/ *m* (*ação*) parking; (*lugar*) car park, (*Amer*) parking lot; **~nar** *vt*/*i* park

estada /is'tada/ *f*, **estadia** /ista-'dʒia/ *f* stay

estádio /is'tadʒiu/ *m* stadium

esta|dista /ista'dʒista/ *m*/*f* statesman (*f*-woman); **~do** *m* state; **~do civil** marital status; **~do de espírito** state of mind; **Estados Unidos da América** United States of America; **Estado-Maior** *m* Staff; **~dual** (*pl* **~duais**) *a* state

esta|fa /is'tafa/ *f* exhaustion; **~fante** *a* exhausting; **~far** *vt* tire out; **~far-se** *vpr* get tired out

estagi|ar /istaʒi'ar/ *vi* do a traineeship; **~ário** *m* trainee

estágio /is'taʒiu/ *m* traineeship

estag|nado /istagi'nadu/ *a* stagnant; **~nar** *vi* stagnate

estalagem /ista'laʒẽ/ *f* inn

estalar /ista'lar/ *vt* (*quebrar*) crack; (*fazer barulho com*) click □ *vi* crack

estaleiro /ista'leru/ *m* shipyard

estalo /is'talu/ *m* crack; (*de dedos, língua*) click; **me deu um ~** it clicked (in my mind)

estam|pa /is'tãpa/ *f* print; **~pado** *a* <*tecido*> patterned □ *m* (*desenho*) pattern; (*tecido*) print; **~par** *vt* print

estampido /istã'pidu/ *m* bang

estancar /istã'kar/ *vt* staunch; **~-se** *vpr* dry up

estância /is'tãsia/ *f* ~ hidromineral
spa

estandarte /istã'dartʃi/ *m* ban-ner

estanho /is'taɲu/ *m* tin

estanque /is'tãki/ *a* watertight

estante /is'tãtʃi/ *f* bookcase

estapafúrdio /istapa'furdʒiu/ *a* weird,
odd

estar /is'tar/ *vi* be; (~ em casa) be in;
está chovendo, (*Port*) está a
chover it's raining; ~ com have; ~
com calor/sono be hot/sleepy; ~
para terminar be about to finish;
ele não está para ninguém he's not
available to see anyone; o trabalho
está por terminar the work is yet to
be finished

estardalhaço /istarda'ʎasu/ *m* (*barulho*)
fuss; (*ostentação*) extravagance

estarre|cedor /istaxese'dor/ *a*
horrifying; ~cer *vt* horrify; ~cer-se
vpr be horrified

esta|tal /ista'taw/ (*pl* ~tais) *a* state-
owned □ *f* state company

estate|lado /istate'ladu/ *a* sprawling;
~lar *vt* knock down; ~lar-se *vpr* go
sprawling

estático /is'tatʃiku/ *a* static

estatísti|ca /ista'tʃistʃika/ *f* statistics;
~co *a* statistical

estati|zação /istatʃiza'sãw/ *f*
nationalization; ~zar *vt* nationalize

estátua /is'tatua/ *f* statue

estatueta /istatu'eta/ *f* statuette

estatura /ista'tura/ *f* stature

estatuto /ista'tutu/ *m* statute

está|vel /is'tavew/ (*pl* ~veis) *a* stable

este¹ /'estʃi/ *m a invar* & *m* east

este² /'estʃi/ *a* this; *pl* these □ *pron* this
one; *pl* these; (*mencionado por último*)
the latter

esteio /is'teju/ *m* prop; (*fig*) mainstay

esteira /is'tera/ *f* (*tapete*) mat; (*rastro*)
wake

estelionato /istelio'natu/ *m* fraud

estender /istẽ'der/ *vt* (*desdobrar*)
spread out; (*alongar*) stretch;
(*ampliar*) extend; hold out
<*mão*>; hang out <*roupa*>; roll out
<*massa*>; draw out <*conversa*>;
~-se *vpr* (*deitar-se*) stretch out; (*ir
longe*) stretch, extend; ~-se sobre
dwell on

esteno|datilógrafo /istenodatʃi-'lɔɡrafu/
m shorthand typist; ~grafia *f*
shorthand

estepe /is'tɛpi/ *m* spare wheel

esterco /is'terku/ *m* dung

estéreo /is'tɛriu/ *a invar* stereo

estere|otipado /isteriotʃi'padu/ *a*
stereotypical; ~ótipo *m* stereotype

esté|ril /is'tɛriw/ (*pl* ~reis) *a* sterile

esterili|dade /isterili'dadʒi/ *f* sterility;
~zar *vt* sterilize

esterli|no /ister'lino/ *a* libra ~na pound
sterling

esteróide /iste'rɔjdʒi/ *m* steroid

estética /is'tɛtʃika/ *f* aesthetics

esteticista /istetʃi'sista/ *m/f* beautician

estético /is'tɛtʃiku/ *a* aesthetic

estetoscópio /istetos'kɔpiu/ *m*
stethoscope

estiagem /istʃi'aʒẽ/ *f* dry spell

estibordo /istʃi'bordu/ *m* starboard

esti|cada /istʃi'kada/ *f* dar uma ~cada
go on; ~car *vt* stretch □ (*fam*) *vi* go on;
~car-se *vpr* stretch out

estigma /is'tʃigima/ *m* stigma; ~tizar *vt*
brand (de as)

estilha|çar /istʃiʎa'sar/ *vt* shatter; ~çar-
se *vpr* shatter; ~ço *m* shard, fragment

estilingue /istʃi'lĩɡi/ *m* catapult

estilis|mo /istʃi'lizmu/ *m* fashion
design; ~ta *m/f* fashion designer

esti|lístico /istʃi'listʃiku/ *a* stylistic;
~lizar *vt* stylize; ~lo *m* style; ~lo de
vida lifestyle

esti|ma /es'tʃima/ *f* esteem; ~mação *f*
estimation; cachorro de ~mação pet
dog; ~mado *a* esteemed; Estimado
Senhor Dear Sir; ~mar *vt* value
<*bens, jóias etc*> (em at); estimate
<*valor, preço etc*> (em at); think highly
of <*pessoa*>; ~mativa *f* estimate

estimu|lante /istʃimu'lãtʃi/ *a*
stimulating □ *m* stimulant; ~lar *vt*
stimulate; (*incentivar*) encourage

estímulo /is'tʃimulu/ *m* stimulus;
(*incentivo*) incentive

estio /is'tʃiu/ *m* summer

estipu|lação /istʃipula'sãw/ *f*
stipulation; ~lar *vt* stipulate

estirar /istʃi'rar/ *vt* stretch; ~-se *vpr*
stretch

estirpe /is'tʃirpi/ *f* stock, line

estivador /istʃiva'dor/ *m* docker

estocada /isto'kada/ *f* thrust

estocar /isto'kar/ *vt* stock □ *vi* stock up

Estocolmo /isto'kɔwmu/ *f* Stockholm

esto|far /isto'far/ *vt* upholster <*móveis*>;
~fo /o/ *m* upholstery

estóico /is'tɔjku/ *a* & *m* stoic

estojo /is'toʒu/ *m* case

estômago /is'tomagu/ *m* stomach

Estônia /is'tonia/ *f* Estonia

estonte|ante /istõtʃi'ãtʃi/ *a* stunning,
mind-boggling; ~ar *vt* stun

estopim /isto'pĩ/ *m* fuse; (*fig*) flashpoint

estoque /is'tɔki/ *m* stock

estore /is'tɔri/ *m* blind

estória /is'tɔria/ *f* story

estor|var /istor'var/ *vt* hinder; obstruct <*entrada, trânsito*>; **∼vo** /o/ *m* hindrance

estou|rado /isto'radu/ *a* <*pessoa*> explosive; **∼rar** *vi* <*bomba, escândalo, pessoa*> blow up; <*pneu*> burst; <*guerra*> break out; <*moda, cantor etc*> make it big; **∼ro** *m* (*de bomba, moda etc*) explosion; (*de pessoa*) outburst; (*de pneu*) blowout; (*de guerra*) outbreak

estrábico /is'trabiku/ *a* <*olhos*> squinty; <*pessoa*> squint-eyed

estrabismo /istra'bizmu/ *m* squint

estraçalhar /istrasa'ʎar/ *vt* tear to pieces

estrada /is'trada/ *f* road; **∼ de ferro** railway; (*Amer*) railroad; **∼ de rodagem** highway; **∼ de terra** dirt road

estrado /is'tradu/ *m* podium; (*de cama*) base

estraga-prazeres /istragapra'zeris/ *m/f invar* spoilsport

estragão /istra'gãw/ *m* tarragon

estra|gar /istra'gar/ *vt* (*tornar desagradável*) spoil; (*acabar com*) ruin □ *vi* (*quebrar*) break; (*apodrecer*) go off; **∼go** *m* damage; *pl* damage; (*da guerra, do tempo*) ravages

estrangeiro /istrã'ʒeru/ *a* foreign □ *m* foreigner; **do ∼** from abroad; **para o** /**no ∼** abroad

estrangular /istrãgu'lar/ *vt* strangle

estra|nhar /istra'ɲar/ *vt* (*achar estranho*) find strange; (*não se adaptar a*) find it hard to get used to; (*não se sentir à vontade com*) be shy with; **∼nhar que** find it strange that; **estou te ∼nhando** that's not like you; **não é de se ∼nhar** it's not surprising; **∼nheza** /e/ *f* (*esquisitice*) strangeness; (*surpresa*) surprise; **∼nho** *a* strange □ *m* stranger

estratagema /istrata'ʒema/ *m* stratagem

estraté|gia /istra'tɛʒia/ *f* strategy; **∼gico** *a* strategic

estrato /is'tratu/ *m* (*camada*) stratum; (*nuvem*) stratus; **∼sfera** *f* stratosphere

estre|ante /istri'ãtʃi/ *a* new □ *m/f* newcomer; **∼ar** *vt* première <*peça, filme*>; embark on <*carreira*>; wear for the first time <*roupa*> □ *vi* <*pessoa*> make one's début; <*filme, peça*> open

estrebaria /istreba'ria/ *f* stable

estréia /is'trɛja/ *f* (*de pessoa*) début; (*de filme, peça*) première

estrei|tar /istrej'tar/ *vt* narrow; take in <*vestido*>; make closer <*relações, laços*> □ *vi* narrow; **∼tar-se** *vpr* <*relações*> become closer; **∼to** *a* narrow; <*relações, laços*> close; <*saia*> straight □ *m* strait

estre|la /is'trela/ *f* star; **∼lado** *a* <*céu*> starry; <*ovo*> fried; **∼lado por** <*filme etc*> starring; **∼la-do-mar** (*pl* **∼las-do-mar**) *f* starfish; **∼lar** *vt* fry <*ovo*>; star in <*filme, peça*>; **∼lato** *m* stardom; **∼lismo** *m* star quality

estreme|cer /istreme'ser/ *vt* shake; strain <*relações, amizade*> □ *vi* shudder; <*relações, amizade*> become strained; **∼cimento** *m* shudder; (*de relações, amizade*) strain

estrepar-se /istre'parsi/ (*fam*) *vpr* come a cropper

estrépito /is'trɛpitu/ *m* noise; **com ∼** noisily

estrepitoso /istrepi'tozu/ *a* noisy; <*sucesso etc*> resounding

estres|sante /istre'sãtʃi/ *a* stressful; **∼sar** *vt* stress; **∼se** /ɛ/ *m* stress

estria /is'tria/ *f* streak; (*no corpo*) stretch mark

estribeira /istri'bera/ *f* stirrup; **perder as ∼s** lose control

estribilho /istri'biʎu/ *m* chorus

estribo /is'tribu/ *m* stirrup

estridente /istri'dẽtʃi/ *a* strident

estripulia /istripu'lia/ *f* antic

estrito /is'tritu/ *a* strict

estrofe /is'trɔfi/ *f* stanza, verse

estrogonofe /istrogo'nɔfi/ *m* stroganoff

estrógeno /is'trɔʒenu/ *m* oestrogen

estron|do /is'trõdu/ *m* crash; **∼doso** /o/ *a* loud; <*aplausos*> thunderous; <*sucesso, fracasso*> resounding

estropiar /istropi'ar/ *vt* cripple <*pessoa*>; mangle <*palavras*>

estrume /is'trumi/ *m* manure

estrutu|ra /istru'tura/ *f* structure; **∼ral** (*pl* **∼rais**) *a* structural; **∼rar** *vt* structure

estuário /istu'ariu/ *m* estuary

estudan|te /istu'dãtʃi/ *m/f* student; **∼til** (*pl* **∼tis**) *a* student

estudar /istu'dar/ *vt/i* study

estúdio /is'tudʒiu/ *m* studio

estu|dioso /istudʒi'ozu/ *a* studious □ *m* scholar; **∼do** *m* study

estufa /is'tufa/ *f* (*para plantas*) greenhouse; (*de aquecimento*) stove; **∼do** *m* stew

estupefato /istupe'fatu/ *a* dumbfounded

estupendo /istu'pẽdu/ *a* stupendous

estupidez /istupi'des/ *f* (*grosseria*) rudeness; (*uma*) rude thing; (*burrice*) stupidity; (*uma*) stupid thing

estúpido /is'tupidu/ *a* (*grosso*) rude, coarse; (*burro*) stupid □ *m* lout

estupor /istu'por/ *m* stupor

estu|prador /istupra'dor/ *m* rapist; **~prar** *vt* rape; **~pro** *m* rape

esturricar /istuxi'kar/ *vt* parch

esvair-se /izva'irsi/ *vpr* fade; **~ em sangue** bleed to death

esvaziar /izvazi'ar/ *vt* empty; **~-se** *vpr* empty

esverdeado /izverdʒi'adu/ *a* greenish

esvoa|çante /izvoa'sãtʃi/ *a* <*cabelo*> fly-away; **~çar** *vi* flutter

eta /'eta/ *int* what a

etapa /e'tapa/ *f* stage; (*de corrida, turnê etc*) leg

etário /e'tariu/ *a* age

éter /'ɛter/ *m* ether

etéreo /e'tɛriu/ *a* ethereal

eter|nidade /eterni'dadʒi/ *f* eternity; **~no** /ɛ/ *a* eternal

éti|ca /'ɛtʃika/ *f* ethics; **~co** *a* ethical

etimo|logia /etʃimolo'ʒia/ *f* etymology; **~lógico** *a* etymological

etíope /e'tʃiopi/ *a & m/f* Ethiopian

Etiópia /etʃi'ɔpia/ *f* Ethiopia

etique|ta /etʃi'keta/ *f* (*rótulo*) label; (*bons modos*) etiquette; **~tar** *vt* label

étnico /'ɛtʃiniku/ *a* ethnic

eu /ew/ *pron* I □ *m* self; **mais alto do que ~** taller than me; **sou ~** it's me

EUA *m pl* USA

eucalipto /ewka'liptu/ *m* eucalyptus

eufemismo /ewfe'mizmu/ *m* euphemism

euforia /ewfo'ria/ *f* euphoria

euro /'ewru/ *m* euro

Europa /ew'rɔpa/ *f* Europe

euro|peu /ewro'pew/ *a & m* (*f* **~péia**) European

eutanásia /ewta'nazia/ *f* euthanasia

evacu|ação /evakua'sãw/ *f* evacuation; **~ar** *vt* evacuate

evadir /eva'dʒir/ *vt* evade; **~-se** *vpr* escape (**de** from)

evan|gelho /evã'ʒɛʎu/ *m* gospel

evaporar /evapo'rar/ *vt* evaporate; **~-se** *vpr* evaporate

eva|são /eva'zãw/ *f* escape; (*fiscal etc*) evasion; **~são escolar** truancy; **~siva** *f* excuse; **~sivo** *a* evasive

even|to /e'vẽtu/ *m* event; **~tual** (*pl* **~tuais**) *a* possible; **~tualidade** *f* eventuality

evidência /evi'dẽsia/ *f* evidence

eviden|ciar /evidẽsi'ar/ *vt* show up; **~ciar-se** *vpr* show up; **~te** *a* obvious, evident

evi|tar /evi'tar/ *vt* avoid; **~tar de beber** avoid drinking; **~tável** (*pl* **~táveis**) *a* avoidable

evocar /evo'kar/ *vt* call to mind, evoke <*passado etc*>; call up <*espíritos etc*>

evolu|ção /evolu'sãw/ *f* evolution; **~ir** *vi* evolve

exacerbar /ezaser'bar/ *vt* exacerbate

exage|rado /ezaʒe'radu/ *a* over the top; **~rar** *vt* (*atribuir proporções irreais a*) exaggerate; (*fazer em excesso*) overdo □ *vi* (*ao falar*) exaggerate; (*exceder-se*) overdo it; **~ro** /e/ *m* exaggeration

exa|lação /ezala'sãw/ *f* fume; (*agradável*) scent; **~lar** *vt* give off <*perfume etc*>

exal|tação /ezawta'sãw/ *f* (*excitação*) agitation; (*engrandecimento*) exaltation; **~tar** *vt* (*excitar*) agitate; (*enfurecer*) infuriate; (*louvar*) exalt; **~tar-se** *vpr* (*excitar-se*) get agitated; (*enfurecer-se*) get furious

exa|me /e'zami/ *m* examination; (*na escola*) exam(ination); **~me de sangue** blood test; **~minar** *vt* examine

exaspe|ração /ezaspera'sãw/ *f* exasperation; **~rar** *vt* exasperate; **~rar-se** *vpr* get exasperated

exa|tidão /ezatʃi'dãw/ *f* exactness; **~to** *a* exact

exaurir /ezaw'rir/ *vt* exhaust; **~-se** *vpr* become exhausted

exaus|tivo /ezaws'tʃivu/ *a* <*estudo*> exhaustive; <*trabalho*> exhausting; **~to** *a* exhausted

exceção /ese'sãw/ *f* exception; **abrir ~** make an exception; **com ~ de** with the exception of

exce|dente /ese'dẽtʃi/ *a & m* excess, surplus; **~der** *vt* exceed; **~der-se** *vpr* overdo it

exce|lência /ese'lẽsia/ *f* excellence; (*tratamento*) excellency; **~lente** *a* excellent

excentricidade /esẽtrisi'dadʒi/ *f* eccentricity

excêntrico /e'sẽtriku/ *a & m* eccentric

excep|ção /iʃsɛ'sãw/ (*Port*) *f* veja **exceção**; **~cional** (*pl* **~cionais**) *a* exceptional; (*deficiente*) handicapped

exces|sivo /ese'sivu/ *a* excessive; **~so** /ɛ/ *m* excess; **~so de bagagem** excess baggage; **~so de velocidade** speeding

exce|to /e'sɛtu/ *prep* except; **~tuar** *vt* except

exci|tação /esita'sãw/ *f* excitement; **~tante** *a* exciting; **~tar** *vt* excite; **~tar-se** *vpr* get excited

excla|mação /isklama'sãw/ *f* exclamation; **~mar** *vt/i* exclaim

exclu|ir /isklu'ir/ *vt* exclude; **~são** *f* exclusion; **com ~são de** with the exclusion of; **~sividade** *f* exclusive rights; **com ~sividade** exclusively; **~sivo** a exclusive; **~so** a excluded

excomungar /iskomũ'gar/ vt excommunicate

excremento /iskre'mẽtu/ m excrement

excur|são /iskur'sãw/ f excursion; (a pé) hike, walk; **~sionista** m/f day-tripper; (a pé) hiker, walker

execu|ção /ezeku'sãw/ f execution; **~tante** m/f performer; **~tar** vt carry out <ordem, plano etc>; perform <papel, música>; execute <preso, criminoso etc>; **~tivo** a & m executive

exem|plar /ezẽ'plar/ a exemplary ◻ m (de espécie) example; (de livro, jornal etc) copy; **~plificar** vt exemplify

exemplo /e'zẽplu/ m example; **a ~ de** following the example of; **por ~** for example; **dar o ~** set an example

exeqüí|vel /eze'kwivew/ (pl **~veis**) a feasible

exer|cer /ezer'ser/ vt exercise; exert <pressão, influência>; carry on <profissão>; **~cício** m exercise; (mil) drill; (de profissão) practice; (financeiro) financial year; **~citar** vt exercise; practise <ofício>; **~citar-se** vpr train

exército /e'zɛrsitu/ m army

exibição /ezibi'sãw/ f (de filme, passaporte etc) showing; (de talento, força, ostentação) show

exibicionis|mo /ezibisio'nizmu/ m exhibitionism; **~ta** a & m/f exhibitionist

exi|bido /ezi'bidu/ a <pessoa> pretentious ◻ m show-off; **~bir** vt show; (ostentar) show off; **~bir-se** vpr (ostentar-se) show off

exi|gência /ezi'ʒẽsia/ f demand; **~gente** a demanding; **~gir** vt demand

exíguo /e'zigwu/ a (muito pequeno) tiny; (escasso) minimal

exi|lado /ezi'lado/ a exiled ◻ m exile; **~lar** vt exile; **~lar-se** vpr go into exile

exílio /e'ziliu/ m exile

exímio /e'zimiu/ a distinguished

eximir /ezi'mir/ vt exempt (de from); **~-se de** get out of

exis|tência /ezis'tẽsia/ f existence; **~tencial** (pl **~tenciais**) a existential; **~tente** a existing; **~tir** vi exist

êxito /'ezitu/ m success; (música, filme etc) hit; **ter ~** succeed

êxodo /'ezodu/ m exodus

exonerar /ezone'rar/ vt (de cargo) dismiss, sack; **~-se** vpr resign

exorbitante /ezorbi'tãtʃi/ a exorbitant

exor|cismo /ezor'sizmu/ m exorcism; **~cista** m/f exorcist; **~cizar** vt exorcize

exótico /e'zɔtʃiku/ a exotic

expan|dir /ispã'dʒir/ vt spread; **~dir-se** vpr spread; <pessoa> open up; **~dir-se sobre** expand upon; **~são** f expansion; **~sivo** a expansive, open

expatri|ado /ispatri'ado/ a & m expatriate; **~ar-se** vpr leave one's country

expectativa /ispekta'tʃiva/ f expectation; **na ~ de** expecting; **estar na ~** wait to see what happens; **~ de vida** life expectancy

expedição /espedʒi'sãw/ f (de encomendas, cartas) dispatch; (de passaporte, diploma etc) issue; (viagem) expedition

expediente /ispedʒi'ẽtʃi/ a <pessoa> resourceful ◻ m (horário) working hours; (meios) expedient; **meio ~** part-time

expe|dir /ispe'dʒir/ vt dispatch <encomendas, cartas>; issue <passaporte, diploma>; **~dito** a prompt, quick

expelir /ispe'lir/ vt expel

experi|ência /isperi'ẽsia/ f experience; (teste, tentativa) experiment; **~ente** a experienced

experimen|tação /isperimẽta'sãw/ f experimentation; **~tado** a experienced; **~tar** vt (provar) try out; try on <roupa>; try <comida>; (sentir, viver) experience; **~to** m experiment

expi|ar /espi'ar/ vt atone for; **~atório** a bode **~atório** scapegoat

expi|ração /espira'sãw/ f (vencimento) expiry; (de ar) exhalation; **~rar** vt exhale ◻ vi (morrer, vencer) expire; (expelir ar) breath out, exhale

expli|cação /isplika'sãw/ f explanation; **~car** vt explain; **~car-se** vpr explain o.s.; **~cável** (pl **~cáveis**) a explainable

explicitar /isplisi'tar/ vt set out

explícito /is'plisitu/ a explicit

explodir /isplo'dʒir/ vt explode ◻ vi explode; <ator etc> make it big

explo|ração /isplora'sãw/ f (uso, abuso) exploitation; (pesquisa) exploration; **~rar** vt (tirar proveito de) exploit; (esquadrinhar) explore

explo|são /isplo'zãw/ f explosion; **~sivo** a & m explosive

expor /es'por/ vt (sujeitar, arriscar) expose (a to); display <mercadorias>; exhibit <obras de arte>; (explicar) expound; **~ a vida** risk one's life; **~-se** vpr expose o.s. (a to)

expor|tação /isporta'sãw/ f export;
~**tador** a exporting □ m exporter;
~**tadora** f export company; ~**tar** vt
export

exposi|ção /ispozi'sãw/ f (de arte etc)
exhibition; (de mercadorias) display;
(de filme fotográfico) exposure;
(explicação) exposition; ~**tor** m
exhibitor

exposto /is'postu/ a exposed (**a**
to); <mercadoria, obra de arte>
on display

expres|são /ispre'sãw/ f expression;
~**sar** vt express; ~**sar-se** vpr express
o.s.; ~**sivo** a expressive; <número,
quantia> significant; ~**so** /ε/ a & m
express

exprimir /ispri'mir/ vt express; ~**-se** vpr
express o.s.

expropriar /ispropri'ar/ vt expropriate

expul|são /ispuw'sãw/ f expulsion;
(de jogador) sending off; ~**sar** vt
(de escola, partido, país etc) expel;
(de clube, bar, festa etc) throw out;
(de jogo) send off; ~**so** pp de
expulsar

expur|gar /ispur'gar/ vt purge;
expurgate <livro>; ~**go** m purge

êxtase /'estazi/ f ecstasy

extasiado /istazi'adu/ a ecstatic

exten|são /istẽ'sãw/ f extension;
(tamanho, alcance, duração) extent;
(de terreno) expanse; ~**sivo** a
extensive; ~**so** a extensive; **por** ~**so**
in full

extenu|ante /istenu'ãtʃi/ a wearing,
tiring; ~**ar** vt tire out; ~**ar-se** vpr tire
o.s. out

exterior /isteri'or/ a outside, exterior;
<aparência> outward; <relações,
comércio etc> foreign □ m outside,
exterior; (de pessoa) exterior; **o** ~
(outros países) abroad; **para o/no** ~
abroad

exter|minar /istermi'nar/ vt
exterminate; ~**mínio** m
extermination

exter|nar /ister'nar/ vt show; ~**na** /ε/ f
location shot; ~**no** /ε/ a external;
<dívida etc> foreign □ m day-pupil

extin|ção /istʃĩ'sãw/ f extinction;
~**guir** vt extinguish <fogo>; wipe out
<dívida, animal, povo>; ~**guir-se** vpr
<fogo, luz> go out; <animal, planta>
become extinct; ~**to** a extinct;
<organização, pessoa> defunct; ~**tor**
m fire extinguisher

extirpar /istʃir'par/ vt remove <tumor
etc>; uproot <ervas daninhas>;
eradicate <abusos>

extor|quir /istor'kir/ vt extort; ~**são** f
extortion

extra /'εstra/ a m/f extra; **horas** ~**s**
overtime

extração /istra'sãw/ f extraction; (da
loteria) draw

extraconju|gal /istrakõʒu'gaw/ (pl
~**gais**) a extramarital

extracurricular /istrakuxiku'lar/ a
extracurricular

extradi|ção /istradʒi'sãw/ f extradition;
~**tar** vt extradite

extrair /istra'ir/ vt extract; draw
<números da loteria>

extrajudici|al /estraʒudʒisi'aw/ (pl
~**ais**) a out-of-court; ~**almente** adv
out of court

extraordinário /istraordʒi'nariu/ a
extraordinary

extrapolar /istrapo'lar/ vt (exceder)
overstep; (calcular) extrapolate □ vi
overstep the mark, go too far

extra-sensori|al /estrasẽsori'aw/ (pl
~**ais**) a extra-sensory

extraterrestre /estrate'xestri/ a & m
extraterrestrial

extrato /is'trato/ m extract; (de conta)
statement

extrava|gância /istrava'gãsia/ f
extravagance; ~**gante** a extravagant

extravasar /istrava'zar/ vt release, let
out <emoções, sentimentos> □ vi
overflow

extra|viado /istravi'adu/ a lost; ~**viar** vt
lose, mislay <papéis, carta>; lead
astray <pessoa>; embezzle
<dinheiro>; ~**viar-se** vpr go astray;
<carta> get lost; ~**vio** m (perda)
misplacement; (de dinheiro)
embezzlement

extre|midade /estremi'dadʒi/ f end; (do
corpo) extremity; ~**mismo** m
extremism; ~**mista** a & m/f extremist;
~**mo** /e/ a & m extreme; **o Extremo
Oriente** the Far East; ~**moso** /o/ a
doting

extrovertido /istrover'tʃido/ a & m
extrovert

exube|rância /ezube'rãsia/ f
exuberance; ~**rante** a exuberant

exultar /ezuw'tar/ vi exult

exumar /ezu'mar/ vt exhume
<cadáver>; dig up <documentos etc>

Ff

fã /fã/ *m/f* fan

fábrica /'fabrika/ *f* factory

fabri|cação /fabrika'sãw/ *f* manufacture; **∼cante** *m/f* manufacturer; **∼car** *vt* manufacture; (*inventar*) fabricate

fábula /'fabula/ *f* fable; (*fam: dinheirão*) fortune

fabuloso /fabu'lozu/ *a* fabulous

faca /'faka/ *f* knife; **∼da** *f* knife blow; **dar uma ∼da em** (*fig*) get some money off

façanha /fa'saɲa/ *f* feat

facção /fak'sãw/ *f* faction

face /'fasi/ *f* face; (*do rosto*) cheek; **∼ta** /e/ *f* facet

fachada /fa'ʃada/ *f* façade

facho /'faʃu/ *m* beam

faci|al /fasi'aw/ (*pl* **∼ais**) *a* facial

fá|cil /'fasiw/ (*pl* **∼ceis**) *a* easy; <*pessoa*> easy-going

facili|dade /fasili'dadʒi/ *f* ease; (*talento*) facility; **∼tar** *vt* facilitate

fã-clube /fã'klubi/ *m* fan club

fac-símile /fak'simili/ *m* facsimile; (*fax*) fax

fact- (*Port*) *veja* **fat-**

facul|dade /fakuw'dadʒi/ *f* (*mental etc*) faculty; (*escola*) university, (*Amer*) college; **fazer ∼dade** go to university; **∼tativo** *a* optional

fada /'fada/ *f* fairy; **∼do** *a* destined, doomed; **∼-madrinha** (*pl* **∼s-madrinhas**) *f* fairy godmother

fadiga /fa'dʒiga/ *f* fatigue

fa|dista /fa'dʒista/ *m/f* fado singer; **∼do** *m* fado

fagote /fa'gɔtʃi/ *m* bassoon

fagulha /fa'guʎa/ *f* spark

faia /'faja/ *f* beech

faisão /faj'zãw/ *m* pheasant

faísca /fa'iska/ *f* spark

fais|cante /fajs'kãtʃi/ *a* sparkling; **∼car** *vi* spark; (*cintilar*) sparkle

faixa /'faʃa/ *f* strip; (*cinto*) sash; (*em karatê, judô*) belt; (*da estrada*) lane; (*de ônibus*) bus lane; (*para pedestres*) zebra crossing, (*Amer*) crosswalk; (*atadura*) bandage; (*de disco*) track; **∼ etária** age group

fajuto /fa'ʒutu/ (*fam*) *a* fake

fala /'fala/ *f* speech

falácia /fa'lasia/ *f* fallacy

fa|lado /fa'ladu/ *a* <*língua*> spoken; <*caso, pessoa*> talked about; **∼lante** *a* talkative; **∼lar** *vt/i* speak; (*dizer*) say; **∼lar com** talk to; **∼lar de** *ou* **em** talk about; **por ∼lar em** speaking of; **sem ∼lar em** not to mention; **∼lou!** (*fam*) OK!; **∼latório** *m* (*boatos*) talk; (*som de vozes*) talking

falaz /fa'las/ *a* fallacious

falcão /faw'kãw/ *m* falcon

falcatrua /fawka'trua/ *f* swindle

fale|cer /fale'ser/ *vi* die, pass away; **∼cido** *a & m* deceased; **∼cimento** *m* death

falência /fa'lẽsia/ *f* bankruptcy; **ir à ∼** go bankrupt

falésia /fa'lɛzia/ *f* cliff

fa|lha /'faʎa/ *f* fault; (*omissão*) failure; **∼lhar** *vi* fail; **∼lho** *a* faulty

fálico /'faliku/ *a* phallic

fa|lido /fa'lidu/ *a & m* bankrupt; **∼lir** *vi* go bankrupt; **∼lível** (*pl* **∼líveis**) *a* fallible

falo /'falu/ *m* phallus

fal|sário /faw'sariu/ *m* forger; **∼sear** *vt* falsify; **∼sete** *m* falsetto; **∼sidade** *f* falseness; (*mentira*) falsehood

falsifi|cação /fawsifika'sãw/ *f* forgery; **∼cador** *m* forger; **∼car** *vt* falsify; forge <*documentos, notas*>

falso /'fawsu/ *a* false

fal|ta /'fawta/ *f* lack; (*em futebol*) foul; **em ∼ta** at fault; **por ∼ta de** for lack of; **sem ∼ta** without fail; **fazer ∼ta** be needed; **sentir a ∼ta de** miss; **∼tar** *vi* be missing; <*aluno*> be absent; **∼tam dois dias para** it's two days until; **me ∼ta ...** I don't have ...; **∼tar a** miss <*aula etc*>; break <*palavra, promessa*>; **∼ to a** short (**de** of)

fa|ma /'fama/ *f* reputation; (*celebridade*) fame; **∼migerado** *a* notorious

família /fa'milia/ *f* family

famili|ar /famili'ar/ *a* familiar; (*de família*) family; **∼aridade** *f* familiarity; **∼arizar** *vt* familiarize; **∼arizar-se** *vpr* familiarize o.s.

faminto /fa'mĩtu/ *a* starving

famoso /fa'mozu/ *a* famous

fanático /fa'natʃiku/ *a* fanatical □ *m* fanatic

fanatismo /fana'tʃizmu/ *m* fanaticism

fanfarrão /fãfa'xãw/ *m* braggart

fanhoso /fa'ɲozu/ *a* nasal; **ser ∼** talk through one's nose

fanta|sia /fãta'zia/ *f* (*faculdade*) imagination; (*devaneio*) fantasy; (*roupa*) fancy dress; **∼siar** *vt* dream up

□ *vi* fantasize; ∼**siar-se** *vpr* dress up
(**de** as); ∼**sioso** /o/ *a* fanciful; <*pessoa*>
imaginative; ∼**sista** *a* imaginative

fantasma /fãˈtazma/ *m* ghost; ∼**górico** *a*
ghostly

fantástico /fãˈtastʃiku/ *a* fantastic

fantoche /fãˈtɔʃi/ *m* puppet

faqueiro /faˈkeru/ *m* canteen of cutlery

fara|ó /faraˈɔ/ *m* pharaoh; ∼**ônico** *a* (*fig*)
of epic proportions

farda /ˈfarda/ *f* uniform; ∼**do** *a*
uniformed

fardo /ˈfardu/ *m* (*fig*) burden

fare|jador /fareʒaˈdor/ *a* **cão** ∼**jador**
sniffer dog; ∼**jar** *vt* sniff out □ *vi* sniff

farelo /faˈrɛlu/ *m* bran; (*de pão*) crumb;
(*de madeira*) sawdust

farfalhar /farfaˈʎar/ *vi* rustle

farináceo /fariˈnasiu/ *a* starchy; ∼**s** *m pl*
starchy foods

farin|ge /faˈrĩʒi/ *f* pharynx; ∼**gite** *f*
pharyngitis

farinha /faˈriɲa/ *f* flour; ∼ **de rosca**
breadcrumbs

far|macêutico /farmaˈsewtʃiku/ *a*
pharmaceutical □ *m* (*pessoa*)
pharmacist; ∼**mácia** *f* (*loja*) chemist's,
(*Amer*) pharmacy; (*ciência*) pharmacy

faro /ˈfaru/ *m* sense of smell; (*fig*) nose

faroeste /faroˈɛstʃi/ *m* (*filme*) western;
(*região*) wild west

faro|fa /faˈrɔfa/ *f* fried manioc flour;
∼**feiro** (*fam*) *m* day-tripper

fa|rol /faˈrɔw/ (*pl* ∼**róis**) *m* (*de carro*)
headlight; (*de trânsito*) traffic light; (*à
beira-mar*) lighthouse; ∼**rol alto** full
beam; ∼**rol baixo** dipped
beam; ∼**roleiro** *a* boastful □ *m*
bighead; ∼**rolete** /e/ *m*, (*Port*) ∼**rolim**
m side-light; (*traseiro*) tail-light

farpa /ˈfarpa/ *f* splinter; (*de metal, fig*)
barb; ∼**do** *a* **arame** ∼**do** barbed wire

farra /ˈfaxa/ (*fam*) *f* partying; **cair na** ∼
go out and party

farrapo /faˈxapu/ *m* rag

far|rear /faxiˈar/ (*fam*) *vi* party; ∼**rista**
(*fam*) *m/f* raver

far|sa /ˈfarsa/ *f* (*peça*) farce;
(*fingimento*) pretence; ∼**sante** *m/f*
(*brincalhão*) joker; (*pessoa sem
seriedade*) unreliable character

far|tar /farˈtar/ *vt* satiate; ∼**tar-se** *vpr*
(*saciar-se*) gorge o.s. (**de** with); (*cansar*)
tire (**de** of); ∼**to** *a* (*abundante*)
plentiful; (*cansado*) fed up (**de** with);
∼**tura** *f* abundance

fascículo /faˈsikulu/ *m* instalment

fasci|nação /fasinaˈsãw/ *f* fascination;
∼**nante** *a* fascinating; ∼**nar** *vt*
fascinate

fascínio /faˈsiniu/ *m* fascination

fas|cismo /faˈsizmu/ *m* fascism; ∼**cista** *a*
& *m/f* fascist

fase /ˈfazi/ *f* phase

fa|tal /faˈtaw/ (*pl* ∼**tais**) *a* fatal;
∼**talismo** *m* fatalism; ∼**talista** *a*
fatalistic □ *m/f* fatalist; ∼**talmente**
adv inevitably

fatia /faˈtʃia/ *f* slice

fatídico /faˈtʃidʒiku/ *a* fateful

fati|gante /fatʃiˈgãtʃi/ *a* tiring; ∼**gar** *vt*
tire, fatigue

fato¹ /ˈfatu/ *m* fact; **de** ∼ as a matter of
fact, in fact; ∼ **consumado** fait
accompli

fato² /ˈfatu/ (*Port*) *m* suit

fator /faˈtor/ *m* factor

fátuo /ˈfatuu/ *a* fatuous

fatu|ra /faˈtura/ *f* invoice; ∼**ramento** *m*
turnover; ∼**rar** *vt* invoice for
<*encomenda*>; make <*dinheiro*>; (*fig*:
emplacar) notch up □ *vi* (*fam*) rake it in

fauna /ˈfawna/ *f* fauna

fava /ˈfava/ *f* broad bean; **mandar alg às**
∼**s** tell s.o. where to get off

favela /faˈvɛla/ *f* shanty town; ∼**do** *m*
shanty-dweller

favo /ˈfavu/ *m* honeycomb

favor /faˈvor/ *m* favour; **a** ∼ **de** in favour
of; **por** ∼ please; **faça** ∼ please

favo|rável /favoˈravew/ (*pl* ∼**ráveis**) *a*
favourable; ∼**recer** *vt* favour;
∼**ritismo** *m* favouritism; ∼**rito** *a* & *m*
favourite

faxi|na /faˈʃina/ *f* clean-up; ∼**neiro** *m*
cleaner

fazen|da /faˈzẽda/ *f* (*de café, gado etc*)
farm; (*tecido*) fabric, material;
(*pública*) treasury; ∼**deiro** *m* farmer

fazer /faˈzer/ *vt* do; (*produzir*) make; ask
<*pergunta*>; ∼**-se** *vpr* (*tornar-se*)
become; ∼**-se** make o.s. out to be; ∼
anos have a birthday; ∼ **20 anos**
twenty; **faz dois dias que ele está
aqui** he's been here for two days; **faz
dez anos que ele morreu** it's ten years
since he died; **tanto faz** it doesn't
matter

faz-tudo /fasˈtudu/ *m/f invar* jack of all
trades

fé /fɛ/ *f* faith

fe|bre /ˈfɛbri/ *f* fever; ∼**bre amarela**
yellow fever; ∼**bre do feno** hay fever;
∼**bril** (*pl* ∼**bris**) *a* feverish

fe|chado /feˈʃadu/ *a* closed; <*curva*>
sharp; <*sinal*> red; <*torneira*> off;
<*tempo*> overcast; <*cara*> stern;
<*pessoa*> reserved; ∼**chadura** *f* lock;
∼**chamento** *m* closure; ∼**char** *vt* close,
shut; turn off <*torneira*>; do up <*calça,
casaco*>; close <*negócio*> □ *vi* close,
shut; <*sinal*> go red; <*tempo*> cloud

over; ~char à chave lock; ~char a
cara frown; ~cho /e/ m fastener; ~cho
ecler zip

fécula /'fɛkula/ f starch

fecun|dar /fekũ'dar/ vt fertilize; ~do a
fertile

feder /fe'der/ vi stink

fede|ração /federa'sãw/ f federation;
~ral (pl ~rais) a federal; (fam) huge;
~rativo a federal

fedor /fe'dor/ m stink, stench; ~ento a
stinking

feérico /fe'ɛriku/ a magical

feições /fej'sõjs/ f pl features

fei|jão /fe'ʒãw/ m bean; (coletivo) beans;
~joada f bean stew; ~joeiro m bean
plant

feio /'feju/ a ugly; <palavra, situação,
tempo> nasty; <olhar> dirty; ~so /o/ a
plain

fei|ra /'fera/ f market; (industrial) trade
fair; ~rante m/f market trader

feiti|caria /fejtʃi'sera/ f magic; ~ceira
f witch; ~ceiro m wizard □ a
bewitching; ~ço m spell

fei|tio /fej'tʃiu/ m (de pessoa) make-up;
~to pp de fazer □ m (ato) deed;
(proeza) feat □ conj like; bem ~to por
ele (it) serves him right; ~tura f
making

feiúra /fej'ura/ f ugliness

feixe /'feʃi/ m bundle

fel /fɛw/ f gall; (fig) bitterness

felicidade /felisi'dadʒi/ f happiness

felici|tações /felisita'sõjs/ f pl
congratulations; ~tar vt congratulate
(por on)

felino /fe'linu/ a feline

feliz /fe'lis/ a happy; ~ardo a lucky;
~mente adv fortunately

fel|pa /'fewpa/ f (de pano) nap;
(penugem) down, fluff; ~pudo a fluffy

feltro /'fewtru/ m felt

fêmea /'femia/ a & f female

femi|nil /femi'niw/ (pl ~nis) a
feminine; ~nilidade f femininity;
~nino a female; <palavra> feminine;
~nismo m feminism; ~nista a & m/f
feminist

fêmur /'femur/ m femur

fen|da /'fẽda/ f crack; ~der vt/i split,
crack

feno /'fenu/ m hay

fenome|nal /fenome'naw/ (pl ~nais) a
phenomenal

fenômeno /fe'nomenu/ m phenomenon

fera /'fɛra/ f wild beast; ficar uma ~ get
really angry; ser ~ em (fam) be
brilliant at

féretro /'fɛretru/ m coffin

feriado /feri'adu/ m public holiday

férias /'fɛrias/ f pl holiday(s), (Amer)
vacation; de ~ on holiday; tirar ~ take
a holiday

feri|da /fe'rida/ f injury; (com arma)
wound; ~do a injured; (mil) wounded
□ m injured person; os ~dos the
injured; (mil) the wounded; ~r vt
injure; (com arma) wound; (magoar)
hurt

fermen|tar /fermẽ'tar/ vt/i ferment; ~to
m yeast; (fig) ferment; ~to em pó
baking powder

fe|rocidade /ferosi'dadʒi/ f ferocity;
~roz a ferocious

fer|rado /fe'xadu/ a estou ~rado (fam)
I've had it; ~rado no sono fast asleep;
~radura f horseshoe; ~ragem f
ironwork; pl hardware; ~ramenta f
tool; (coletivo) tools; ~rão m (de abelha)
sting; ~rar vt brand <gado>; shoe
<cavalo>; ~rar-se (fam) vpr come a
cropper; ~reiro m blacksmith;
~renho a <partidário etc> staunch;
<vontade> iron

férreo /'fɛxiu/ a iron

ferro /'fɛxu/ m iron; ~lho m bolt;
~-velho (pl ~s-velhos) m (pessoa)
scrap-metal dealer; (lugar) scrap-
metal yard; ~via f railway,
(Amer) railroad; ~viário a railway
□ m railway worker

ferrugem /fe'xuʒẽ/ f rust

fér|til /'fɛrtʃiw/ (pl ~teis) a fertile

fertili|dade /fertʃili'dadʒi/ f fertility;
~zante m fertilizer; ~zar vt fertilize

fer|vente /fer'vẽtʃi/ a boiling; ~ver vi
boil; (de raiva) seethe; ~vilhar vi
bubble; ~vilhar de swarm with; ~vor
m fervour; ~vura f boiling

fes|ta /'fɛsta/ f party; (religiosa) festival;
~tejar vt/i celebrate; (acolher) fete;
~tejo /e/ m celebration; ~tim m feast;
~tival (pl ~tivais) m festival;
~tividade f festivity; ~tivo a festive

feti|che /fe'tʃiʃi/ m fetish; ~-chismo m
fetishism; ~chista m/f fetishist □ a
fetishistic

fétido /'fɛtʃidu/ a fetid

feto[1] /'fɛtu/ m (no útero) foetus

feto[2] /'fɛtu/ (Port) m (planta) fern

feu|dal /few'daw/ (pl ~dais) a feudal;
~dalismo m feudalism

fevereiro /feve'reru/ m February

fezes /'fɛzis/ f pl faeces

fiação /fia'sãw/ f (eletr) wiring;
(fábrica) mill

fia|do /fi'adu/ a <conversa> idle □ adv
<comprar> on credit; ~dor m
guarantor

fiambre /fi'ãbri/ m cooked ham

fiança /fi'ãsa/ f surety; (jurid) bail

fiapo /fi'apu/ *m* thread

fiar /fi'ar/ *vt* spin <*lã etc*>

fiasco /fi'asku/ *m* fiasco

fibra /'fibra/ *f* fibre

ficar /fi'kar/ *vi* (*tornar-se*) become; (*estar, ser*) be; (*manter-se*) stay; ~ **fazendo** keep (on) doing; ~ **com** keep; get <*impressão, vontade*>; ~ **com medo** get scared; ~ **de fazer** arrange to do; ~ **para** be left for; ~ **bom** turn out well; (*recuperar-se*) get better; ~ **bem** look good

fic|ção /fik'sãw/ *f* fiction; ~**ção científica** science fiction; ~**-cionista** *m/f* fiction writer

fi|cha /'fiʃa/ *f* (*de telefone*) token; (*de jogo*) chip; (*da caixa*) ticket; (*de fichário*) file card; (*na polícia*) record; (*Port: tomada*) plug; ~**chário** *m*, (*Port*) ~**cheiro** *m* file; (*móvel*) filing cabinet

fictício /fik'tʃisiu/ *a* fictitious

fidalgo /fi'dalgu/ *m* nobleman

fide|digno /fide'dʒignu/ *a* trustworthy; ~**lidade** *f* fidelity

fiduciário /fidusi'ariu/ *a* fiduciary □ *m* trustee

fi|el /fi'ɛw/ (*pl* ~**éis**) *a* faithful □ *m* **os** ~**éis** (*na igreja*) the congregation

figa /'figa/ *f* talisman

fígado /'figadu/ *f* liver

fi|go /'figu/ *m* fig; ~**gueira** *f* fig tree

figu|ra /fi'gura/ *f* figure; (*carta de jogo*) face card; (*fam: pessoa*) character; **fazer (má)** ~**ra** make a (bad) impression; ~**rado** *a* figurative; ~**rante** *m/f* extra; ~**rão** *m* big shot; ~**rar** *vi* appear, figure; ~**rativo** *a* figurative; ~**rinha** *f* sticker; ~**rino** *m* fashion plate; (*de filme, peça*) costume design; (*fig*) model; **como manda o** ~**rino** as it should be

fila /'fila/ *f* line; (*de espera*) queue, (*Amer*) line; (*fileira*) row; **fazer** ~ queue up, (*Amer*) stand in line; ~ **indiana** single file

filamento /fila'mẽtu/ *m* filament

filante /fi'lãtʃi/ (*fam*) *m/f* sponger

filan|tropia /filãtro'pia/ *f* philanthropy; ~**trópico** *a* philanthropic; ~**tropo** /o/ *m* phil-anthropist

filão /fi'lãw/ *m* (*de ouro*) seam; (*fig*) money-spinner

filar /fi'lar/ (*fam*) *vt* sponge, cadge

filar|mônica /filar'monika/ *f* philharmonic (orchestra); ~**mônico** *a* philharmonic

filate|lia /filate'lia/ *f* philately; ~**lista** *m/f* philatelist

filé /fi'lɛ/ *m* fillet

fileira /fi'lera/ *f* row

filete /fi'lɛtʃi/ *m* fillet

fi|lha /'fiʎa/ *f* daughter; ~**lho** *m* son; *pl* (*crianças*) children; ~**lho da puta** (*chulo*) bastard, (*Amer*) son of a bitch; ~**lho de criação** foster child; ~**lho único** only child; ~**lhote** *m* (*de cão*) pup; (*de lobo etc*) cub; *pl* young

fili|ação /filia'sãw/ *f* affiliation; ~**al** (*pl* ~**ais**) *a* filial □ *f* branch

Filipinas /fili'pinas/ *f pl* Philippines

filipino /fili'pinu/ *a & m* Filipino

fil|madora /fiwma'dora/ *f* camcorder; ~**magem** *f* filming; ~**mar** *vt/i* film; ~**me** *m* film

fi|lologia /filolo'ʒia/ *f* philology; ~**lólogo** *m* philologist

filo|sofar /filozo'far/ *vi* philosophize; ~**sofia** *f* philosophy; ~**sófico** *a* philosophical

filósofo /fi'lɔzofu/ *m* philosopher

fil|trar /fiw'trar/ *vt* filter; ~**tro** *m* filter

fim /fĩ/ *m* end; **a** ~ **de** (*para*) in order to; **estar a** ~ **de** fancy; **por** ~ finally; **sem** ~ endless; **ter** ~ come to an end; ~ **de semana** weekend

fi|nado /fi'nadu/ *a & m* deceased, departed; ~**nal** (*pl* ~**nais**) *a* final □ *m* end □ *f* final; ~**nalista** *m/f* finalist; ~**nalizar** *vt/i* finish

finan|ças /fi'nãsas/ *f pl* finances; ~**ceiro** *a* financial □ *m* financier; ~**ciamento** *m* financing; (*um*) loan; ~**ciar** *vt* finance; ~**cista** *m/f* financier

fincar /fĩ'kar/ *vt* plant; ~ **o pé** (*fig*) dig one's heels in

findar /fĩ'dar/ *vt/i* end

fineza /fi'neza/ *f* finesse; (*favor*) kindness

fin|gido /fĩ'ʒidu/ *a* feigned; <*pessoa*> insincere; ~**gimento** *m* pretence; ~**gir** *vt* pretend; feign <*doença etc*> □ *vi* pretend; ~**gir-se de** pretend to be

finito /fi'nitu/ *a* finite

finlan|dês /fĩlã'des/ *a* (*f* ~**desa**) Finnish □ *m* (*f* ~**desa**) Finn; (*língua*) Finnish

Finlândia /fĩ'lãdʒia/ *f* Finland

fi|ninho /fi'niɲu/ *adv* **sair de** ~**ninho** slip away; ~**no** *a* (*não grosso*) thin; <*areia, pó etc*> fine; (*refinado*) refined; ~**nório** *a* crafty; ~**nura** *f* thinness; fineness

fio /'fiu/ *m* thread; (*elétrico*) wire; (*de sangue, água*) trickle; (*de luz, esperança*) glimmer; (*de navalha etc*) edge; **horas a** ~ hours on end

fir|ma /'firma/ *f* firm; (*assinatura*) signature; ~**mamento** *m* firmament; ~**mar** *vt* fix; (*basear*) base □ *vi* settle; ~**mar-se** *vpr* be based (**em** on); ~**me** *a* firm; <*tempo*> settled □ *adv* firmly; ~**meza** *f* firmness

fis|cal /fis'kaw/ (*pl* ~**cais**) *m* inspector; ~**calização** *f* inspection; ~**calizar** *vt* inspect; ~**co** *m* inland revenue, (*Amer*) internal revenue service

fis|gada /fiz'gada/ *f* stabbing pain; ~**gar** *vt* hook

físi|ca /'fizika/ *f* physics; ~**co** *a* physical □ *m* (*pessoa*) physicist; (*corpo*) physique

fisio|nomia /fiziono'mia/ *f* face; ~**nomista** *m/f* **ser** ~**nomista** have a good memory for faces; ~**terapeuta** *m/f* physiotherapist; ~**terapia** *f* physiotherapy

fissura /fi'sura/ *f* fissure; (*fam*) craving; ~**do** *a* ~**do em** (*fam*) mad about

fita /'fita/ *f* tape; (*fam: encenação*) playacting; **fazer** ~ (*fam*) put on an act; ~ **adesiva** (*Port*) adhesive tape; ~ **métrica** tape measure

fitar /fi'tar/ *vt* stare at

fivela /fi'vɛla/ *f* buckle

fi|xador /fiksa'dor/ *m* (*de cabelo*) setting lotion; (*de fotos*) fixative; ~**xar** *vt* fix; stick up <*cartaz*>; ~**xo** *a* fixed

flácido /'flasidu/ *a* flabby

flagelo /fla'ʒɛlu/ *m* scourge

fla|grante /fla'grãtʃi/ *a* flagrant; **apanhar em** ~**grante (delito)** catch in the act; ~**grar** *vt* catch

flame|jante /flame'ʒãtʃi/ *a* blazing; ~**jar** *vi* blaze

flamengo /fla'mẽgu/ *a* Flemish □ *m* Fleming; (*língua*) Flemish

flamingo /fla'mĩgu/ *m* flamingo

flâmula /'flamula/ *f* pennant

flanco /'flãku/ *m* flank

flanela /fla'nɛla/ *f* flannel

flanquear /flãki'ar/ *vt* flank

flash /flɛʃ/ *m* invar flash

flau|ta /'flawta/ *f* flute; ~**tista** *m/f* flautist

flecha /'flɛʃa/ *f* arrow

fler|tar /fler'tar/ *vi* flirt; ~**te** *m* flirtation

fleuma /'flewma/ *f* phlegm

fle|xão /flek'sãw/ *f* press-up, (*Amer*) push-up; (*ling*) inflection; ~**xibilidade** *f* flexibility; ~**xionar** *vt/i* flex <*perna, braço*>; (*ling*) inflect; ~**xível** (*pl* ~**xíveis**) *a* flexible

fliperama /flipe'rama/ *m* pinball machine

floco /'flɔku/ *m* flake

flor /flor/ *f* flower; **a fina** ~ the cream; **à** ~ **da pele** (*fig*) on edge

flo|ra /'flɔra/ *f* flora; ~**reado** *a* full of flowers; (*fig*) florid; ~**reio** *m* clever turn of phrase; ~**rescer** *vi* flower; ~**resta** /ɛ/ *f* forest; ~**restal** (*pl* ~**restais**) *a* forest; ~**rido** *a* in flower; (*fig*) florid; ~**rir** *vi* flower

flotilha /flo'tʃiʎa/ *f* flotilla

flu|ência /flu'ẽsia/ *f* fluency; ~**ente** *a* fluent

flui|dez /flui'des/ *f* fluidity; ~**do** *a & m* fluid

fluir /flu'ir/ *vi* flow

fluminense /flumi'nẽsi/ *a & m* (person) from Rio de Janeiro state

fluorescente /fluore'sẽtʃi/ *a* fluorescent

flutu|ação /flutua'sãw/ *f* fluctuation; ~**ante** *a* floating; ~**ar** *vi* float; <*bandeira*> flutter; (*hesitar*) waver

fluvi|al /fluvi'aw/ (*pl* ~**ais**) *a* river

fluxo /'fluksu/ *m* flow; ~**grama** *m* flowchart

fobia /fo'bia/ *f* phobia

foca /'fɔka/ *f* seal

focalizar /fokali'zar/ *vt* focus on

focinho /fo'siɲu/ *m* snout

foco /'fɔku/ *m* focus; (*fig*) centre

fofo /'fofu/ *a* soft; <*pessoa*> cuddly

fofo|ca /fo'fɔka/ *f* piece of gossip; *pl* gossip; ~**car** *vi* gossip; ~**queiro** *m* gossip □ *a* gossipy

fo|gão /fo'gãw/ *m* stove; (*de cozinhar*) cooker; ~**go** /o/ *m* fire; **tem** ~**go?** have you got a light?; **ser** ~**go** (*fam*) (*ser chato*) be a pain in the neck; (*ser incrível*) be amazing; ~**gos de artifício** fireworks; ~**goso** /o/ *a* fiery; ~**gueira** *f* bonfire; ~**guete** /e/ *m* rocket

foice /'fojsi/ *f* scythe

fol|clore /fow'klɔri/ *m* folklore; ~**clórico** *a* folk

fole /'fɔli/ *m* bellows

fôlego /'folegu/ *m* breath; (*fig*) stamina

fol|ga /'fɔwga/ *f* rest, break; (*fam: cara-de-pau*) cheek; ~**gado** *a* <*roupa*> full, loose; <*vida*> leisurely; (*fam: atrevido*) cheeky; ~**gar** *vt* loosen □ *vi* have time off

fo|lha /'foʎa/ *f* leaf; (*de papel*) sheet; **novo em** ~**lha** brand new; ~**lha de pagamento** payroll; ~**lhagem** *f* foliage; ~**lhear** *vt* leaf through; ~**lheto** /e/ *m* pamphlet; ~**linha** *f* tear-off calendar; ~**lhudo** *a* leafy

foli|a /fo'lia/ *f* revelry; ~**ão** *m* (*f* ~**ona**) reveller

folículo /fo'likulu/ *m* follicle

fome /'fomi/ *f* hunger; **estar com** ~ be hungry

fomentar /fomẽ'tar/ *vt* foment

fone /'foni/ *m* (*do telefone*) receiver; (*de rádio etc*) headphones

fonema /fo'nema/ *m* phoneme

fonéti|ca /fo'nɛtʃika/ *f* phonetics; ~**co** *a* phonetic

fonologia /fonolo'ʒia/ *f* phonology

fonte /'fõtʃi/ f (de água) spring; (fig) source

fora /'fɔra/ adv outside; (não em casa) out; (viajando) away □ prep except; **dar um ~** drop a clanger; **dar um ~ em alg** cut s.o. dead; chuck <namorado>; **por ~** on the outside; **~-de-lei** m/f invar outlaw

foragido /fora'ʒidu/ a at large, on the run □ m fugitive

forasteiro /foras'teru/ m outsider

forca /'fɔrka/ f gallows

for|ça /'fɔrsa/ f (vigor) strength; (violência) force; (elétrica) power; **dar uma ~ça a alg** help s.o. out; **fazer ~ça** make an effort; **~ças armadas** armed forces; **~çar** vt force; **~ça-tarefa** (pl **~ças-tarefa**) f task force

fórceps /'fɔrseps/ m invar forceps

forçoso /for'sozu/ a forced

for|ja /'fɔrʒa/ f forge; **~jar** vt forge

forma /'fɔrma/ f form; (contorno) shape; (maneira) way; **de qualquer ~** anyway; **manter a ~** keep fit

fôrma /'forma/ f mould; (de cozinha) baking tin

for|mação /forma'sãw/ f formation; (educação) education; (profissionalizante) training; **~-mado** m graduate; **~mal** (pl **~mais**) a formal; **~malidade** f formality; **~malizar** vt formalize; **~mar** vt form; (educar) educate; **~mar-se** vpr be formed; <estudante> graduate; **~mato** m format; **~matura** f graduation

formidá|vel /formi'davew/ (pl **~veis**) a formidable; (muito bom) tremendous

formi|ga /for'miga/ f ant; **~gamento** m pins and needles; **~gar** vi swarm (de with); <perna, mão etc> tingle; **~gueiro** m ants' nest

formosura /formo'zura/ f beauty

fórmula /'fɔrmula/ f formula

formu|lação /formula'sãw/ f formulation; **~lar** vt formulate; **~lário** m form

fornalha /for'naʎa/ f furnace

forne|cedor /forne'dor/ m supplier; **~cer** vt supply; **~cer aco a alg** supply s.o. with sth; **~cimento** m supply

forno /'fɔrnu/ m oven; (para louça etc) kiln

foro /'fɔru/ m forum

forra /'fɔxa/ f **ir à ~** get one's own back

for|ragem /fo'xaʒẽ/ f fodder; **~rar** vt line <roupa, caixa etc>; cover <sofá etc>; carpet <assoalho, sala etc>; **~ro** /o/ m (de roupa, caixa etc) lining; (de sofá etc) cover; (carpete) (fitted) carpet

forró /fo'xɔ/ m type of Brazilian dance

fortale|cer /fortale'ser/ vt strengthen; **~cimento** m strengthening; **~za** /e/ f fort-ress

for|te /'fɔrtʃi/ a strong; <golpe> hard; <chuva> heavy; <físico> muscular □ adv strongly; <bater, chover> hard □ m (militar) fort; (habilidade) strong point, forte; **~tificação** f fortification; **~tificar** vt fortify

fortu|ito /for'tuitu/ a chance; **~na** f fortune

fosco /'fosku/ a dull; <vidro> frosted

fosfato /fos'fatu/ m phosphate

fósforo /'fɔsforu/ m match; (elemento químico) phosphor

fossa /'fɔsa/ f pit; **na ~** (fig) miserable, depressed

fós|sil /'fɔsiw/ (pl **~seis**) m fossil

fosso /'fosu/ m ditch; (de castelo) moat

foto /'fɔtu/ f photo; **~cópia** f photocopy; **~copiadora** f photocopier; **~copiar** vt photocopy; **~gênico** a photogenic; **~grafar** vt photograph; **~grafia** f photography; **~gráfico** a photographic

fotógrafo /fo'tɔgrafu/ m photographer

foz /fɔs/ f mouth

fração /fra'sãw/ f fraction

fracas|sado /fraka'sadu/ a failed □ m failure; **~sar** vi fail; **~so** m failure

fracionar /frasio'nar/ vt break up

fraco /'fraku/ a weak; <luz, som> faint; <medíocre> poor □ m weakness, weak spot

fract- (Port) veja **frat-**

frade /'fradʒi/ m friar

fragata /fra'gata/ f frigate

frá|gil /'fraʒiw/ (pl **~geis**) a fragile; <pessoa> frail

fragilidade /fraʒili'dadʒi/ f fragility; (de pessoa) frailty

fragmen|tar /fragmẽ'tar/ vt fragment; **~tar-se** vpr fragment; **~to** m fragment

fra|grância /fra'grãsia/ f fragrance; **~grante** a fragrant

fralda /'frawda/ f nappy, (Amer) diaper

framboesa /frãbo'eza/ f raspberry

França /'frãsa/ f France

fran|cês /frã'ses/ a (f **~cesa**) French □ m (f **~cesa**) Frenchman (f -woman); (língua) French; **os ~ceses** the French

franco /'frãku/ a (honesto) frank; (óbvio) clear; (gratuito) free □ m franc; **~atirador** (pl **~atiradores**) m sniper; (fig) maverick

frangalho /frã'gaʎu/ m tatter

frango /'frãgu/ m chicken

franja /'frãʒa/ f fringe; (do cabelo) fringe, (Amer) bangs

fran|quear /frãki'ar/ vt frank <carta>; **~queza** /e/ f frankness; **~quia** f (de cartas) franking; (jur) franchise

fran|zino /frã'zinu/ a skinny; **~zir** vt gather <tecido>; wrinkle <testa>

fraque /'fraki/ m morning suit

fraqueza /fra'keza/ f weakness; (de luz, som) faintness

frasco /'frasku/ m bottle

frase /'frazi/ f (oração) sentence; (locução) phrase; **~ado** m phrasing

frasqueira /fras'kera/ f vanity case

frater|nal /frater'naw/ (pl **~nais**) a fraternal; **~nidade** f fraternity; **~nizar** vi fraternize; **~no** a fraternal

fratu|ra /fra'tura/ f fracture; **~rar** vt fracture; **~rar-se** vpr fracture

frau|dar /fraw'dar/ vt defraud; **~de** f fraud; **~dulento** a fraudulent

frear /fri'ar/ vt/i brake

freezer /'frizer/ m freezer

fre|guês /fre'ges/ m (f **~guesa**) customer; **~guesia** f (de loja etc) clientele; (paróquia) parish

frei /frej/ m brother

freio /'freju/ m brake; (de cavalo) bit

freira /'frera/ f nun

freixo /'frejʃu/ m ash

fremir /fre'mir/ vi shake

frêmito /'fremitu/ m wave

frenesi /frene'zi/ m frenzy

frenético /fre'nɛtʃiku/ a frantic

frente /'frẽtʃi/ f front; **em ~ a** ou **de** in front of; **para a ~** forward; **pela ~** ahead; **fazer ~ a** face

freqüência /fre'kwẽsia/ f frequency; (assiduidade) attendance; **com muita ~** often

freqüen|tador /frekwẽta'dor/ m regular visitor (de to); **~tar** vt frequent; (cursar) attend; **~te** a frequent

fres|cão /fres'kãw/ m air-conditioned coach; **~co** /e/ a <comida etc> fresh; <vento, água, quarto> cool; (fam) (afetado) affected; (exigente) fussy; **~cobol** m kind of racquetball; **~cor** m freshness; **~cura** f (fam) (afetação) affectation; (ser exigente) fussiness; (coisa sem importância) trifle

fresta /'frɛsta/ f slit

fre|tar /fre'tar/ vt charter <avião>; hire <caminhão>; **~te** /ɛ/ m freight; (aluguel de avião) charter; (de caminhão) hire

frevo /'frevu/ m type of Brazilian dance

fria /'fria/ (fam) f difficult situation, spot; **~gem** f chill

fric|ção /frik'sãw/ f friction; **~cionar** vt rub

fri|eira /fri'era/ f chilblain; **~eza** /e/ f coldness

frigideira /friʒi'dera/ f frying pan

frígido /'friʒidu/ a frigid

frigorífico /frigo'rifiku/ m cold store, refrigerator, fridge

frincha /'frĩʃa/ f chink

frio /'friu/ a & m cold; **estar com ~** be cold; **~rento** a sensitive to the cold

frisar /fri'zar/ vt (enfatizar) stress; crimp <cabelo>

friso /'frizu/ m frieze

fri|tada /fri'tada/ f fry-up; **~tar** vt fry; **~tas** f pl chips, (Amer) French fries; **~to** a fried; **está ~to** (fam) he's had it; **~tura** f fried food

frivolidade /frivoli'dadʒi/ f frivolity; **frívolo** a frivolous

fronha /'froɲa/ f pillowcase

fronte /'frõtʃi/ f forehead, brow

frontei|ra /frõ'tera/ f border; **~riço** a border

frota /'frɔta/ f fleet

frou|xidão /froʃi'dãw/ f looseness; (moral) laxity; **~xo** a loose; <regulamento> lax; <pessoa> lackadaisical

fru|gal /fru'gaw/ (pl **~gais**) a frugal; **~galidade** f frugality

frus|tração /frustra'sãw/ f frustration; **~trante** a frustrating; **~trar** vt frustrate

fru|ta /'fruta/ f fruit; **~ta-do-conde** (pl **~tas-do-conde**) f sweetsop; **~ta-pão** (pl **~tas-pão**) f breadfruit; **~teira** f fruitbowl; **~tífero** a (fig) fruitful; **~to** m fruit

fubá /fu'ba/ m maize flour

fu|çar /fu'sar/ vi nose around; **~ças** (fam) f pl face, chops

fu|ga /'fuga/ f escape; **~gaz** a fleeting; **~gida** f escape; **~gir** vi run away; (soltar-se) escape; **~gir a** avoid; **~gitivo** a & m fugitive

fulano /fu'lanu/ m whatever his name is

fuleiro /fu'leru/ a down-market, cheap and cheerful

fulgor /fuw'gor/ m brightness; (fig) splendour

fuligem /fu'liʒẽ/ f soot

fulmi|nante /fuwmi'nãtʃi/ a devastating; **~nar** vt strike down; (fig) devastate; **~nado por um raio** struck by lightning □ vi (criticar) rail

fu|maça /fu'masa/ f smoke; **~maceira** f cloud of smoke; **~mante**, (Port) **~mador** m smoker; **~mar** vt/i smoke; **~mê** a invar smoked; **~megar** vi smoke; **~mo** m (tabaco) tobacco; (Port: fumaça) smoke; (fumar) smoking

função /fũ'sãw/ f function; **em ~ de** as a result of; **fazer as funções de** function as

funcho /'fũʃu/ m fennel

funcio|nal /fũsio'naw/ (pl ~**nais**) a functional; ~**nalismo** m civil service; ~**namento** m working; ~**nar** vi work; ~**nário** m employee; ~**nário público** civil servant

fun|dação /fũda'sãw/ f foundation; ~**dador** m founder □ a founding

fundamen|tal /fũdamẽ'taw/ (pl ~**tais**) a fundamental; ~**tar** vt (basear) base; (justificar) substantiate; ~**to** m foundation

fun|dar /fũ'dar/ vt (criar) found; (basear) base; ~**dar-se** vpr be based (**em** on); ~**dear** vi drop anchor, anchor; ~**dilho** m seat

fundir /fũ'dʒir/ vt melt <ouro, ferro>; cast <sino, estátua>; (juntar) merge; ~**-se** vpr <ouro, ferro> melt; (juntar-se) merge

fundo /'fũdu/ a deep □ m (parte de baixo) bottom; (parte de trás) back; (de quadro, foto) background; (de dinheiro) fund; **no ~** basically; ~**s** m pl (da casa etc) back; (recursos) funds

fúnebre /'funebri/ a funereal

funerário /fune'rariu/ a funeral

funesto /fu'nɛstu/ a fatal

fungar /fũ'gar/ vt/i sniff

fungo /'fũgu/ m fungus

fu|nil /fu'niw/ (pl ~**nis**) m funnel; ~**nilaria** f panel-beating; (oficina) bodyshop

furacão /fura'kãw/ m hurricane

furado /fu'radu/ a **papo ~** (fam) hot air

furão /fu'rãw/ m (animal) ferret

furar /fu'rar/ vt pierce <orelha etc>; puncture <pneu>; make a hole in <roupa etc>; jump <fila>; break <greve> □ vi <roupa etc> go into a hole; <pneu> puncture; (fam) <programa> fall through

fur|gão /fur'gãw/ m van; ~**goneta** /e/ (Port) f van

fúria /'furia/ f fury

furioso /furi'ozu/ a furious

furo /'furu/ m hole; (de pneu) puncture; (jornalístico) scoop; (fam: gafe) blunder, faux pas; **dar um ~** put one's foot in it

furor /fu'ror/ m furore

fur|ta-cor /furta'kor/ a invar iridescent; ~**tar** vt steal; ~**-tivo** a furtive; ~**to** m theft

furúnculo /fu'rũkulu/ m boil

fusão /fu'zãw/ f fusion; (de empresas) merger

fusca /'fuska/ f VW beetle

fuselagem /fuze'laʒẽ/ f fuselage

fusi|vel /fu'zivew/ (pl ~**veis**) m fuse

fuso /'fuzu/ m spindle; ~ **horário** time zone

fustigar /fustʃi'gar/ vt lash; (fig: com palavras) lash out at

futebol /futʃi'bɔw/ m football; ~**ístico** a football

fú|til /'futʃiw/ (pl ~**teis**) a frivolous, inane

futilidade /futʃili'dadʒi/ f frivolity, inanity; (uma) frivolous thing

futu|rismo /futu'rizmu/ m futurism; ~**rista** a & m futurist; ~**rístico** a futuristic; ~**ro** a & m future

fu|zil /fu'ziw/ (pl ~**zis**) m rifle; ~**zilamento** m shooting; ~**zilar** vt shoot □ vi flash; ~**zileiro** m rifleman; ~**zileiro naval** marine

fuzuê /fuzu'e/ m commotion

Gg

gabar-se /ga'barsi/ vpr boast (**de** of)

gabarito /gaba'ritu/ m calibre

gabinete /gabi'netʃi/ m (em casa) study; (escritório) office; (ministros) cabinet

gado /'gadu/ m livestock; (bovino) cattle

gaélico /ga'ɛliku/ a & m Gaelic

gafanhoto /gafa'ɲotu/ m (pequeno) grasshopper; (grande) locust

gafe /'gafi/ f faux pas, gaffe

gafieira /gafi'era/ f dance; (salão) dance hall

gagá /ga'ga/ a (fam) senile

ga|go /'gagu/ a stuttering □ m stutterer; ~**gueira** f stutter; ~**guejar** vi stutter

gaiato /gaj'atu/ a funny

gaiola /gaj'ola/ f cage

gaita /'gajta/ f ~ **de foles** bagpipes

gaivota /gaj'vota/ f seagull

gajo /'gaʒu/ m (Port) guy, bloke

gala /'gala/ f **festa de ~** gala; **roupa de ~** formal dress

galã /ga'lã/ m leading man

galan|tear /galãtʃi'ar/ vt woo; ~**teio** m wooing; (um) courtesy

galão /ga'lãw/ m (enfeite) braid; (mil) stripe; (medida) gallon; (Port: café) white coffee

galáxia /ga'laksia/ f galaxy

galé /ga'lɛ/ f galley

galego /ga'legu/ *a & m* Galician
galera /ga'lɛra/ *f* (*fam*) crowd
galeria /gale'ria/ *f* gallery
Gales /'galis/ *m* **País de ~** Wales
ga|lês /ga'les/ *a* (*f* **~lesa**) Welsh □ *m* (*f* **~lesa**) Welshman (*f*-woman); (*língua*) Welsh
galeto /ga'letu/ *m* spring chicken
galgar /gaw'gar/ *vt* (*transpor*) jump over; climb *<escada>*
galgo /'gawgu/ *m* greyhound
galheteiro /gaʎe'teru/ *m* cruet stand
galho /'gaʎu/ *m* branch; **quebrar um ~** (*fam*) help out
galináceos /gali'nasius/ *m pl* poultry
gali|nha /ga'liɲa/ *f* chicken; **~nheiro** *m* chicken coop
galo /'galu/ *m* cock; (*inchação*) bump
galocha /ga'lɔʃa/ *f* Wellington boot
galo|pante /galo'pãtʃi/ *a* galloping; **~par** *vi* gallop; **~pe** /ɔ/ *m* gallop
galpão /gaw'pãw/ *m* shed
galvanizar /gawvani'zar/ *vt* galvanize
gama /'gama/ *f* (*musical*) scale; (*fig*) range
gamado /ga'madu/ *a* besotted (**por** with)
gamão /ga'mãw/ *m* backgammon
gamar /ga'mar/ *vi* fall in love (**por** with)
gana /'gana/ *f* desire
ganância /ga'nãsia/ *f* greed
ganancioso /ganãsi'ozu/ *a* greedy
gancho /'gãʃu/ *m* hook
gangorra /gã'goxa/ *f* seesaw
gangrena /gã'grena/ *f* gangrene
gangue /'gãgi/ *m* gang
ga|nhador /gaɲa'dor/ *m* winner □ *a* winning; **~nhar** *vt* win *<corrida, prêmio>*; earn *<salário>*; get *<presente>*; gain *<vantagem, tempo, amigo>* □ *vi* win; **~nhar a vida** earn a living; **~nha-pão** *m* livelihood; **~nho** *m* gain; *pl* (*no jogo*) winnings □ *pp de* **ganhar**
ga|nido *m* squeal; (*de cachorro*) yelp; **~nir** *vi* squeal; *<cachorro>* yelp
ganso /'gãsu/ *m* goose
gara|gem /ga'raʒẽ/ *f* garage; **~gista** *m/f* garage attendant
garanhão /gara'ɲãw/ *m* stallion
garan|tia /garã'tʃia/ *f* guarantee; **~tir** *vt* guarantee
garatujar /garatu'ʒar/ *vt* scribble
gar|bo /'garbu/ *m* grace; **~boso** *a* graceful
garça /'garsa/ *f* heron
gar|çom /gar'sõ/ *m* waiter; **~çonete** /ɛ/ *f* waitress
gar|fada /gar'fada/ *f* forkful; **~fo** *m* fork
gargalhada /garga'ʎada/ *f* gale of laughter; **rir às ~s** roar with laughter

gargalo /gar'galu/ *m* bottleneck; **tomar no ~** drink out of the bottle
garganta /gar'gãta/ *f* throat
gargare|jar /gargare'ʒar/ *vi* gargle; **~jo** /e/ *m* gargle
gari /ga'ri/ *m/f* (*lixeiro*) dustman, (*Amer*) garbage collector; (*varredor de rua*) roadsweeper, (*Amer*) streetsweeper
garim|par /garĩ'par/ *vi* prospect; **~peiro** *m* prospector; **~po** *m* mine
garo|a /ga'roa/ *f* drizzle; **~ar** *vi* drizzle
garo|ta /ga'rota/ *f* girl; **~to** /o/ *m* boy; (*Port: café*) coffee with milk
garoupa /ga'ropa/ *f* grouper
garra /'gaxa/ *f* claw; (*fig*) drive, determination; *pl* (*poder*) clutches
garra|fa /ga'xafa/ *f* bottle; **~fada** *f* blow with a bottle; **~fão** *m* flagon
garrancho /ga'xãʃu/ *m* scrawl
garrido /ga'xidu/ *a* (*alegre*) lively
garupa /ga'rupa/ *f* (*de animal*) rump; (*de moto*) pillion seat
gás /gas/ *m* gas; *pl* (*intestinais*) wind, (*Amer*) gas; **~ lacrimogêneo** tear gas
gasóleo /ga'zɔliu/ *m* diesel oil
gasolina /gazo'lina/ *f* petrol
gaso|sa /ga'zɔza/ *f* fizzy lemonade, (*Amer*) soda; **~so** *a* gaseous; *<bebida>* fizzy
gáspea /'gaspia/ *f* upper
gas|tador /gasta'dor/ *a & m* spendthrift; **~tar** *vt* spend *<dinheiro, tempo>*; use up *<energia>*; wear out *<roupa, sapatos>*; **~to** *m* expense; *pl* spending, expenditure; **dar para o ~to** do
gastrenterite /gastrẽte'ritʃi/ *f* gastroenteritis
gástrico /'gastriku/ *a* gastric
gastrite /gas'tritʃi/ *f* gastritis
gastronomia /gastrono'mia/ *f* gastronomy
ga|ta /'gata/ *f* cat; (*fam*) sexy woman; **~tão** *m* (*fam*) hunk
gatilho /ga'tʃiʎu/ *m* trigger
ga|tinha /ga'tʃiɲa/ *f* (*fam*) sexy woman; **~to** *m* cat; (*fam*) hunk; **fazer alg de ~to-sapato** treat s.o. like a doormat
gatuno /ga'tunu/ *m* crook □ *a* crooked
gaúcho /ga'uʃu/ *a & m* (person) from Rio Grande do Sul
gaveta /ga'veta/ *f* drawer
gavião /gavi'ãw/ *m* hawk
gaze /'gazi/ *f* gauze
gazela /ga'zɛla/ *f* gazelle
gazeta /ga'zeta/ *f* gazette
geada /ʒi'ada/ *f* frost

g

ge|ladeira /ʒela'dera/ f fridge; **~lado** a frozen; (muito frio) freezing □ m (Port) ice cream; **~lar** vt/i freeze

gelati|na /ʒela'tʃina/ f (sobremesa) jelly; (pó) gelatine; **~noso** /o/ a gooey

geléia /ʒe'lɛja/ f jam

ge|leira /ʒe'lera/ f glacier; **~lo** /e/ m ice

gema /'ʒema/ f (de ovo) yolk; (pedra) gem; **carioca da ~** carioca born and bred; **~da** f egg yolk whisked with sugar

gêmeo /'ʒemiu/ a & m twin; **Gêmeos** (signo) Gemini

ge|mer /ʒe'mer/ vi moan, groan; **~mido** m moan, groan

gene /'ʒɛni/ m gene; **~alogia** f genealogy; **~alógico** a genealogical; **árvore ~alógica** family tree

Genebra /ʒe'nɛbra/ f Geneva

gene|ral /ʒene'raw/ (pl **~rais**) m general; **~ralidade** f generality; **~ralização** f generalization; **~ralizar** vt/i generalize; **~ralizar-se** vpr become generalized

genérico /ʒe'nɛriku/ a generic

gênero /'ʒeneru/ m type, kind; (gramatical) gender; (literário) genre; pl goods; **~s alimentícios** foodstuffs; **ela não faz o meu ~** she's not my type

gene|rosidade /ʒenerozi'dadʒi/ f generosity; **~roso** /o/ a generous

genéti|ca /ʒe'nɛtʃika/ f genetics; **~co** a genetic

gengibre /ʒē'ʒibri/ m ginger

gengiva /ʒē'ʒiva/ f gum

geni|al /ʒeni'aw/ (pl **~ais**) a brilliant

gênio /'ʒeniu/ m genius; (temperamento) temperament

genioso /ʒeni'ozu/ a temperamental

geni|tal /ʒeni'taw/ (pl **~tais**) a genital

genitivo /ʒeni'tʃivu/ a & m genitive

genocídio /ʒeno'sidʒiu/ m genocide

genro /'ʒēxu/ m son-in-law

gente /'ʒētʃi/ f people; (fam) folks; **a ~** (sujeito) we; (objeto) us □ interj (fam) gosh

gen|til /ʒē'tʃiw/ (pl **~tis**) a kind; **~tileza** /e/ f kindness

genuíno /ʒenu'inu/ a genuine

geo|grafia /ʒeogra'fia/ f geography; **~gráfico** a geographical

geógrafo /ʒe'ɔgrafu/ m geographer

geo|logia /ʒeolo'ʒia/ f geology; **~lógico** a geological

geólogo /ʒe'ɔlogu/ m geologist

geo|metria /ʒeome'tria/ f geometry; **~métrico** a geometrical; **~político** a geopolitical

Geórgia /ʒi'ɔrʒia/ f Georgia

georgiano /ʒiorʒi'anu/ a & m Georgian

gera|ção /ʒera'sãw/ f generation; **~dor** m generator

ge|ral /ʒe'raw/ (pl **~rais**) a general □ f (limpeza) spring-clean; **em ~ral** in general

gerânio /ʒe'raniu/ m geranium

gerar /ʒe'rar/ vt create; generate <eletricidade>

gerência /ʒe'rēsia/ f management

gerenci|ador /ʒerēsia'dor/ m manager; **~al** (pl **~ais**) a management; **~ar** vt manage

gerente /ʒe'rētʃi/ m manager □ a managing

gergelim /ʒerʒe'lĩ/ m sesame

geri|atria /ʒeria'tria/ f geriatrics; **~átrico** a geriatric

geringonça /ʒerĩ'gõsa/ f contraption

gerir /ʒe'rir/ vt manage

germânico /ʒer'maniku/ a Germanic

ger|me /'ʒɛrmi/ m germ; **~me de trigo** wheatgerm; **~minar** vi germinate

gerúndio /ʒe'rũdʒiu/ m gerund

gesso /'ʒesu/ m plaster

ges|tação /ʒesta'sãw/ f gestation; **~tante** f pregnant woman

gestão /ʒes'tãw/ f management

ges|ticular /ʒes/ vi gesticulate; **~to** /'ʒɛstu/ m gesture

gibi /ʒi'bi/ m (fam) comic

Gibraltar /ʒibraw'tar/ f Gibraltar

gigan|te /ʒi'gãtʃi/ a & m giant; **~tesco** /e/ a gigantic

gilete /ʒi'lɛtʃi/ f razor blade □ a & m/f (fam) bisexual

gim /ʒĩ/ m gin

ginásio /ʒi'naziu/ m (escola) secondary school; (de ginástica) gymnasium

ginasta /ʒi'nasta/ m/f gymnast

ginásti|ca /ʒi'nastʃika/ f gymnastics; (aeróbica) aerobics; **~co** a gymnastic

ginecolo|gia /ʒinekolo'ʒia/ f gynaecology; **~gista** m/f gynaecologist

gingar /ʒĩ'gar/ vi sway

gira-discos /ʒira'diʃkuʃ/ m invar (Port) record player

girafa /ʒi'rafa/ f giraffe

gi|rar /ʒi'rar/ vt/i spin, revolve; **~rassol** (pl **~rassóis**) m sunflower; **~ratório** a revolving

gíria /'ʒiria/ f slang; (uma ~) slang expression

giro /'ʒiru/ m spin, turn □ a (Port fam) great

giz /ʒis/ m chalk

gla|cê /gla'se/ m icing; **~cial** (pl **~ciais**) a icy

glamour /gla'mur/ m glamour; **~oso** /o/ a glamorous

glândula /'glãdula/ *f* gland

glandular /glãdu'lar/ *a* glandular

glicerina /glise'rina/ *f* glycerine

glicose /gli'kɔzi/ *f* glucose

glo|bal /glo'baw/ (*pl* ~**bais**) *a* (*mundial*) global; <*preço etc*> overall; ~**bo** /o/ *m* globe; ~**bo ocular** eyeball

glóbulo /'glɔbulu/ *m* globule; (*do sangue*) corpuscle

glória /'glɔria/ *f* glory

glori|ficar /glorifi'kar/ *vt* glorify; ~**oso** /o/ *a* glorious

glossário /glo'sariu/ *m* glossary

glu|tão /glu'tãw/ *m* (*f* ~**tona**) glutton ◻ *a* (*f* ~**tona**) greedy

gnomo /gi'nomu/ *m* gnome

godê /go'de/ *a* flared

goela /go'ɛla/ *f* gullet

gogó /go'gɔ/ *m* (*fam*) Adam's apple

goia|ba /goj'aba/ *f* guava; ~**bada** *f* guava jelly; ~**beira** *f* guava tree

gol /'gow/ (*pl* ~**s**) *m* goal

gola /'gɔla/ *f* collar

gole /'gɔli/ *m* mouthful

go|lear /goli'ar/ *vt* thrash; ~**leiro** *m* goalkeeper

golfe /'gowfi/ *m* golf

golfinho /gow'fiɲu/ *m* dolphin

golfista /gow'fista/ *m/f* golfer

golo /'golu/ *m* (*Port*) goal

golpe /'gɔwpi/ *m* blow; (*manobra*) trick; ~ **(de estado)** coup (d'état); ~ **de mestre** masterstroke; ~ **de vento** gust of wind; ~ **de vista** glance; ~**ar** *vt* hit

goma /'goma/ *f* gum; (*para roupa*) starch

gomo /'gomu/ *m* segment

gôndola /'gõdola/ *f* rack

gongo /'gõgu/ *m* gong

gonorréia /gono'xɛja/ *f* gonorrhea

gonzo /'gõzu/ *m* hinge

gorar /go'rar/ *vi* go wrong, fail

gor|do /'gordu/ *a* fat; ~**ducho** *a* plump

gordu|ra /gor'dura/ *f* fat; ~**rento** *a* greasy; ~**roso** /u/ *a* fatty; <*pele*> greasy, oily

gorgolejar /gorgole'ʒar/ *vi* gurgle

gorila /go'rila/ *m* gorilla

gor|jear /gorʒi'ar/ *vi* twitter; ~**jeio** *m* twittering

gorjeta /gor'ʒeta/ *f* tip

gorro /'goxu/ *m* hat

gos|ma /'gɔzma/ *f* slime; ~**mento** *a* slimy

gos|tar /gos'tar/ *vi* ~**tar de** like; ~**to** /o/ *m* taste; (*prazer*) pleasure; **para o meu** ~**to** for my taste; **ter** ~**to de** taste of; ~**toso** *a* nice; <*comida*> nice, tasty; (*fam*) <*pessoa*> gorgeous

go|ta /'gota/ *f* drop; (*que cai*) drip; (*doença*) gout; **foi a** ~**ta d'água** (*fig*) it was the last straw; ~**teira** *f* (*buraco*) leak; (*cano*) gutter; ~**tejar** *vi* drip; <*telhado*> leak ◻ *vt* drip

gótico /'gɔtʃiku/ *a* Gothic

gotícula /go'tʃicula/ *f* droplet

gover|nador /governa'dor/ *m* governor; ~**namental** (*pl* ~**namentais**) *a* government; ~**nanta** *f* housekeeper; ~**nante** *a* ruling ◻ *m/f* ruler; ~**nar** *vt* govern; ~**nista** *a* government ◻ *m/f* government supporter; ~**no** /e/ *m* government

go|zação /goza'sãw/ *f* joking; (*uma*) send-up; ~**zado** *a* funny; ~**zar** *vt* ~**zar (de)** enjoy; (*fam: zombar de*) make fun of ◻ *vi* (*ter orgasmo*) come; ~**zo** *m* (*prazer*) enjoyment; (*posse*) possession; (*orgasmo*) orgasm; **ser um** ~**zo** be funny

Grã-Bretanha /grãbre'taɲa/ *f* Great Britain

graça /'grasa/ *f* grace; (*piada*) joke; (*humor*) humour, funny side; (*jur*) pardon; **de** ~ for nothing; **sem** ~ (*enfadonho*) dull; (*não engraçado*) unfunny; (*envergonhado*) embarrassed; **ser uma** ~ be lovely; **ter** ~ be funny; **não tem** ~ **sair sozinho** it's no fun to go out alone; ~**s a** thanks to

grace|jar /grase'ʒar/ *vi* joke; ~**jo** /e/ *m* joke

graci|nha /gra'siɲa/ *f* **ser uma** ~**nha** be sweet; ~**oso** /o/ *a* gracious

grada|ção /grada'sãw/ *f* gradation; ~**tivo** *a* gradual

grade /'gradʒi/ *f* grille, grating; (*cerca*) railings; **atrás das** ~**s** behind bars; ~**ado** *a* <*janela*> barred

grado /'gradu/ *m* **de bom/mau** ~ willingly/unwillingly

gradu|ação /gradua'sãw/ *f* graduation; (*mil*) rank; (*variação*) gradation; ~**ado** *a* <*escala*> graduated; <*estudante*> graduate; <*militar*> high-ranking; (*eminente*) respected; ~**al** (*pl* ~**ais**) *a* gradual; ~**ar** *vt* graduate <*escala*>; (*ordenar*) grade; (*regular*) regulate; ~**ar-se** *vpr* <*estudante*> graduate

grafia /gra'fia/ *f* spelling

gráfi|ca /'grafika/ *f* (*arte*) graphics; (*oficina*) print shop; ~**co** *a* graphic ◻ *m* (*pessoa*) printer; (*diagrama*) graph; *pl* (*de computador*) graphics

grã-fino /grã'finu/ (*fam*) *a* posh, upper-class ◻ *m* posh person

grafite /graˈfitʃi/ f (*mineral*) graphite; (*de lápis*) lead; (*pichação*) piece of graffiti

gra|fologia /grafoloˈʒia/ f graphology; **∼fólogo** m graphologist

grama¹ /ˈgrama/ m gramme

grama² /ˈgrama/ f grass; **∼do** m lawn; (*campo de futebol*) field

gramática /graˈmatʃika/ f grammar

gramati|cal /gramatʃiˈkaw/ (*pl* **∼cais**) a grammatical

gram|peador /grãpiaˈdor/ m stapler; **∼pear** vt staple <*papéis etc*>; tap <*telefone*>; **∼po** m (*de cabelo*) hairclip; (*para papéis etc*) staple; (*ferramenta*) clamp

grana /ˈgrana/ f (*fam*) cash

granada /graˈnada/ f (*projétil*) grenade; (*pedra*) garnet

gran|dalhão /grãdaˈʎãw/ a (f **∼dalhona**) enormous; **∼dão** a (f **∼dona**) huge; **∼de** a big; (*fig*) <*escritor, amor etc*> great; **∼deza** /e/ f greatness; (*tamanho*) magnitude; **∼dioso** /o/ a grand

granel /graˈnɛw/ m **a ∼** in bulk

granito /graˈnitu/ m granite

granizo /graˈnizu/ m hail

gran|ja /ˈgrãʒa/ f farm; **∼jear** vt win, gain

granulado /granuˈladu/ a granulated

grânulo /ˈgranulu/ m granule

grão /grãw/ (*pl* **∼s**) m grain; (*de café*) bean; **∼-de-bico** (*pl* **∼s-de-bico**) m chickpea

grasnar /grazˈnar/ vi <*pato*> quack; <*rã*> croak; <*corvo*> caw

grati|dão /gratʃiˈdãw/ f gratitude; **∼ficação** f (*dinheiro a mais*) gratuity; (*recompensa*) gratification; **∼ficante** a gratifying; **∼ficar** vt (*dar dinheiro a*) give a gratuity to; (*recompensar*) gratify

gratinado /gratʃiˈnadu/ a & m gratin

grátis /ˈgratʃis/ adv free

grato /ˈgratu/ a grateful

gratuito /graˈtuito/ a (*de graça*) free; (*sem motivo*) gratuitous

grau /graw/ m degree; **escola de 1°/2° ∼** primary/secondary school

graúdo /graˈudu/ a big; (*importante*) important

gra|vação /gravaˈsãw/ f (*de som*) recording; (*de desenhos etc*) engraving; **∼vador** m (*pessoa*) engraver; (*máquina*) tape recorder; **∼vadora** f record company; **∼var** vt record <*música, disco*>; (*fixar na memória*) memorize; (*estampar*) engrave

gravata /graˈvata/ f tie; (*golpe*) stranglehold; **∼ borboleta** bowtie

grave /ˈgravi/ a serious; <*voz, som*> deep; <*acento*> grave

grávida /ˈgravida/ f pregnant

gravidade /graviˈdadʒi/ f gravity

gravidez /graviˈdes/ f pregnancy

gravura /graˈvura/ f engraving; (*em livro*) illustration

graxa /ˈgraʃa/ f (*de sapatos*) polish; (*de lubrificar*) grease

Grécia /ˈgrɛsia/ f Greece

grego /ˈgregu/ a & m Greek

grei /grej/ f flock

gre|lha /ˈgrɛʎa/ f grill; **∼lhado** a grilled □ m grill; **∼lhar** vt grill

grêmio /ˈgremiu/ m guild, association

grená /greˈna/ a & m dark red

gre|ta /ˈgreta/ f crack; **∼tar** vt/i crack

gre|ve /ˈgrɛvi/ f strike; **entrar em ∼ve** go on strike; **∼ve de fome** hunger strike; **∼vista** m/f striker

gri|fado /griˈfadu/ a in italics; **∼far** vt italicize

griffe /ˈgrifi/ f label, line

gri|lado /griˈladu/ a (*fam*) hung-up; **∼lar** (*fam*) vt bug; **∼lar-se** vpr get hung-up (**com** about)

grilhão /griˈʎãw/ m fetter

grilo /ˈgrilu/ m (*bicho*) cricket; (*fam*) (*preocupação*) hang-up; (*problema*) hassle; (*barulho*) squeak

grinalda /griˈnawda/ f garland

gringo /ˈgrĩgu/ (*fam*) a foreign □ m foreigner

gri|pado /griˈpadu/ a **estar/ficar ∼pado** have/get the flu; **∼par-se** vpr get the flu; **∼pe** f flu, influenza; **∼pe das aves** bird flu

grisalho /griˈzaʎu/ a grey

gri|tante /griˈtãtʃi/ a <*erro*> glaring, gross; <*cor*> loud, garish; **∼tar** vt/i shout; (*de medo*) scream; **∼taria** f shouting; **∼to m** shout; (*de medo*) scream; **aos ∼tos** in a loud voice; **no ∼to** (*fam*) by force

grogue /ˈgrɔgi/ a groggy

grosa /ˈgrɔza/ f gross

groselha /groˈzɛʎa/ f (*vermelha*) redcurrant; (*espinhosa*) gooseberry; **∼ negra** blackcurrant

gros|seiro /groˈseru/ a rude; (*tosco, malfeito*) rough; **∼seria** f rudeness; (*uma*) rude thing; **∼so** /o/ a thick; <*voz*> deep; (*fam*) <*pessoa, atitude*> rude; **∼sura** f thickness; (*fam: grosseria*) rudeness

grotesco /groˈtesku/ a grotesque

grua /ˈgrua/ f crane

gru|dado /gruˈdadu/ a stuck; (*fig*) very attached (**em** to); **∼dar** vt/i stick; **∼de** m glue; **∼dento** a sticky

gru|nhido /gru'ɲidu/ *m* grunt; **~nhir** *vi* grunt

grupo /'grupu/ *m* group

gruta /'gruta/ *f* cave

guaraná /gwara'na/ *m* guarana

guarani /gwara'ni/ *a & m/f* Guarani

guarda /'gwarda/ *f* guard ◻ *m/f* guard; (*policial*) policeman (*f*-woman); **~ costeira** coastguard; **~-chuva** *m* umbrella; **~-costas** *m invar* bodyguard; **~dor** *m* parking attendant; **~florestal** (*pl* **~s-florestais**) *m/f* forest ranger; **~-louça** *m* china cupboard; **~napo** *m* napkin, serviette; **~-noturno** (*pl* **~s-noturnos**) *m* night watchman

guardar /gwar'dar/ *vt* (*pôr no lugar*) put away; (*conservar*) keep; (*vigiar*) guard; (*não esquecer*) remember; **~-se de** guard against

guarda|-redes /'gwarda-'xedʃ/ *m invar* (*Port*) goalkeeper; **~-roupa** *m* wardrobe; **~-sol** (*pl* **~-sóis**) *m* sunshade

guardi|ão /gwardʒi'ãw/ (*pl* **~ães** *ou* **~ões**) *m* (*f* **~ã**) guardian

guarita /gwa'rita/ *f* sentry box

guar|necer /gwarne'ser/ *vt* (*fortificar*) garrison; (*munir*) equip; (*enfeitar*) garnish; **~nição** *f* (*mil*) garrison; (*enfeite*) garnish

Guatemala /gwate'mala/ *f* Guatemala

guatemalteco /gwatemal'tɛku/ *a & m* Guatemalan

gude /'gudʒi/ *m* **bola de ~** marble

guelra /'gɛwxa/ *f* gill

guer|ra /'gɛxa/ *f* war; **~reiro** *m* warrior ◻ *a* warlike; **~rilha** *f* guerrilla war; **~rilheiro** *a & m* guerrilla

gueto /'getu/ *m* ghetto

guia /'gia/ *m/f* guide ◻ *m* guide(book) ◻ *f* delivery note

Guiana /gi'ana/ *f* Guyana

guianense /gia'nẽsi/ *a & m/f* Guyanan

guiar /gi'ar/ *vt* guide; drive <*veículo*> ◻ *vi* drive; **~-se** *vpr* be guided

guichê /gi'ʃe/ *m* window

guidom /gi'dõ/, (*Port*) **guidão** /gi'dãw/ *m* handlebars

guilhotina /giʎo'tʃina/ *f* guillotine

guimba /'gĩba/ *f* butt

guinada /gi'nada/ *f* change of direction; **dar uma ~** change direction

guinchar[1] /gĩ'ʃar/ *vi* squeal; <*freios*> screech

guinchar[2] /gĩ'ʃar/ *vt* tow <*carro*>; (*içar*) winch

guincho[1] /'gĩʃu/ *m* squeal; (*de freios*) screech

guincho[2] /'gĩʃu/ *m* (*máquina*) winch; (*veículo*) tow truck

guin|dar /gĩ'dar/ *vt* hoist; **~daste** *m* crane

Guiné /gi'nɛ/ *f* Guinea

gui|sado /gi'zadu/ *m* stew; **~sar** *vt* stew

guitar|ra /gi'taxa/ *f* (electric) guitar; **~rista** *m/f* guitarist

guizo /'gizu/ *m* bell

gu|la /'gula/ *f* greed; **~lodice** *f* greed; **~loseima** *f* delicacy; **~loso** /o/ *a* greedy

gume /'gumi/ *m* cutting edge

guri /gu'ri/ *m* boy; **~a** *f* girl

guru /gu'ru/ *m* guru

gutu|ral /gutu'raw/ (*pl* **~rais**) *a* guttural

g

h

Hh

há|bil /'abiw/ (*pl* **~beis**) *a* clever, skilful

habili|dade /abili'dadʒi/ *f* skill; **ter ~dade com** be good with; **~doso** /o/ *a* skilful; **~tação** *f* qualification; **~tar** *vt* qualify

habi|tação /abita'sãw/ *f* housing; (*casa*) dwelling; **~tacional** (*pl* **~tacionais**) *a* housing; **~tante** *m/f* inhabitant; **~tar** *vt* inhabit ◻ *vi* live; **~tável** (*pl* **~táveis**) *a* habitable

hábito /'abitu/ *m* habit

habitu|al /abitu'aw/ (*pl* **~ais**) *a* habitual; **~ar** *vt* accustom (**a** to); **~ar-se** *vpr* get accustomed (**a** to)

hadoque /a'dɔki/ *m* haddock

Haia /'aja/ *f* the Hague

Haiti /aj'tʃi/ *m* Haiti

haitiano /ajtʃi'anu/ *a & m* Haitian

hálito /'alitu/ *m* breath

halitose /ali'tɔzi/ *f* halitosis

hall /xɔw/ (*pl* **~s**) *m* hall; (*de hotel*) foyer

halte|re /aw'tɛri/ *m* dumbbell; **~rofilismo** *m* weight lifting; **~rofilista** *m/f* weight lifter

hambúrguer /ã'burger/ *m* hamburger

hangar /ã'gar/ *m* hangar

haras /'aras/ *m invar* stud farm

hardware /'xarduɛr/ *m* hardware

harmo|nia /armo'nia/ *f* harmony; **~nioso** /o/ *a* harmonious; **~nizar** *vt* harmonize; (*conciliar*) reconcile; **~nizar-se** *vpr* (*combinar*) tone in; (*concordar*) coincide

har|pa /'arpa/ *f* harp; **~pista** *m/f* harpist

haste /'astʃi/ *m* pole; (*de planta*) stem, stalk; ~**ar** *vt* hoist, raise

Havaí /ava'i/ *m* Hawaii

havaiano /avaj'anu/ *a & m* Hawaiian

haver /a'ver/ *m* credit; *pl* possessions □ *vt* (*auxiliar*) **havia sido** it had been; (*impessoal*) **há** there is/are; **ele trabalha aqui há anos** he's been working here for years; **ela morreu há vinte anos (atrás)** she died twenty years ago

haxixe /a'ʃiʃi/ *m* hashish

he|braico /e'brajku/ *a & m* Hebrew; ~**breu** *a & m* (*f* ~**bréia**) Hebrew

hectare /ek'tari/ *m* hectare

hediondo /edʒi'õdu/ *a* hideous

hein /ẽj/ *int* eh

hélice /'ɛlisi/ *f* propeller

helicóptero /eli'kɔpteru/ *m* helicopter

hélio /'ɛliu/ *m* helium

heliporto /eli'portu/ *m* heliport

hem /ẽj/ *int* eh

hematoma /ema'toma/ *m* bruise

hemisfério /emis'fɛriu/ *m* hemisphere; **Hemisfério Norte/Sul** Northern/ Southern Hemisphere

hemo|filia /emofi'lia/ *f* haemophilia; ~**fílico** *a & m* haemophiliac; ~**globina** *f* haemoglobin; ~**grama** *m* blood count

hemor|ragia /emoxa'ʒia/ *f* haemorrhage; ~**róidas** *f pl* haemorrhoids

henê /e'ne/ *m* henna

hepatite /epa'tʃitʃi/ *f* hepatitis

hera /'ɛra/ *f* ivy

heráldi|ca /e'rawdʒika/ *f* heraldry; ~**co** *a* heraldic

herança /e'rãsa/ *f* inheritance; (*de um povo etc*) heritage

her|bicida /erbi'sida/ *m* weedkiller; ~**bívoro** *a* herbivorous □ *m* herbivore

her|dar /er'dar/ *vt* inherit; ~**-deiro** *m* heir

hereditário /eredʒi'tariu/ *a* hereditary

here|ge /e'rɛʒi/ *m/f* heretic; ~**sia** *f* heresy

herético /e'rɛtʃiku/ *a* heretical

hermético /er'mɛtʃiku/ *a* airtight; (*fig*) obscure

hérnia /'ɛrnia/ *f* hernia

herói /e'rɔj/ *m* hero; ~**co** *a* heroic

hero|ína /ero'ina/ *f* (*mulher*) heroine; (*droga*) heroin; ~**ísmo** *m* heroism

herpes /'ɛrpis/ *m invar* herpes; ~**-zoster** *m* shingles

hesi|tação /ezita'sãw/ *f* hesitation; ~**tante** *a* hesitant; ~**tar** *vi* hesitate

hetero|doxo /etero'dɔksu/ *a* unorthodox; ~**gêneo** *a* heterogeneous

heterossexu|al /eteroseksu'aw/ (*pl* ~**ais**) *a & m* heterosexual

hexago|nal /eksago'naw/ (*pl* ~**nais**) *a* hexagonal

hexágono /ek'sagonu/ *m* hexagon

hiato /i'atu/ *m* hiatus

hiber|nação /iberna'sãw/ *f* hibernation; ~**nar** *vi* hibernate

híbrido /'ibridu/ *a & m* hybrid

hidrante /i'drãtʃi/ *m* fire hydrant

hidra|tante /idra'tãtʃi/ *a* moisturising □ *m* moisturizer; ~**tar** *vt* moisturize <*pele*>; ~**to** *m* ~**to de carbono** carbohydrate

hidráuli|ca /i'drawlika/ *f* hydraulics; ~**co** *a* hydraulic

hidrelétri|ca /idre'lɛtrika/ *f* hydroelectric power station; ~**co** *a* hydroelectric

hidro|avião /idroavi'ãw/ *m* seaplane; ~**carboneto** /e/ *m* hydrocarbon

hidrófilo /i'drɔfilu/ *a* absorbent; **algodão ~** cotton wool, (*Amer*) absorbent cotton

hidrofobia /idrofo'bia/ *f* rabies

hidro|gênio /idro'ʒeniu/ *m* hydrogen; ~**massagem** *f* banheira de ~**massagem** jacuzzi; ~**via** *f* waterway

hiena /i'ena/ *f* hyena

hierarquia /ierar'kia/ *f* hierarchy

hieróglifo /ie'rɔglifu/ *m* hieroglyphic

hífen /'ifẽ/ *m* hyphen

higi|ene /iʒi'eni/ *f* hygiene; ~**ênico** *a* hygienic

hilari|ante /ilari'ãtʃi/ *a* hilarious; ~**dade** *f* hilarity

Himalaia /ima'laja/ *m* Himalayas

hin|di /ĩ'dʒi/ *m* Hindi; ~**du** *a & m/f* Hindu; ~**duísmo** *m* Hinduism; ~**duísta** *a & m/f* Hindu

hino /'inu/ *m* hymn; ~ **nacional** national anthem

hipermercado /ipermer'kadu/ *m* hypermarket

hipersensí|vel /ipersẽ'sivew/ (*pl* ~**veis**) *a* hypersensitive

hipertensão /ipertẽ'sãw/ *f* hypertension

hípico /'ipiku/ *a* horseriding

hipismo /i'pizmu/ *m* horseriding; (*corridas*) horseracing

hip|nose /ipi'nɔzi/ *f* hypnosis; ~**nótico** *a* hypnotic; ~**notismo** *m* hypnotism; ~**notizador** *m* hypnotist; ~**notizar** *vt* hypnotize

hipocondríaco /ipokõ'driaku/ *a & m* hypochondriac

hipocrisia /ipokri'zia/ *f* hypocrisy

hipócrita /i'pɔkrita/ *m/f* hypocrite □ *a* hypocritical

hipódromo /i'pɔdromu/ *m* race course, (*Amer*) race track

hipopótamo /ipo'pɔtamu/ *m* hippopotamus

hipote|ca /ipo'tɛka/ *f* mortgage; ~**car** *vt* mortgage; ~**cário** *a* mortgage

hipotermia /ipoter'mia/ *f* hypothermia

hipótese /i'pɔtezi/ *f* hypothesis; **na ~ de** in the event of; **na pior das ~s** at worst

hipotético /ipo'tɛtʃiku/ *a* hypothetical

hirto /'irtu/ *adj* rigid, stiff

hispânico /is'paniku/ *a* Hispanic

histamina /ista'mina/ *f* histamine

his|terectomia /isterekto'mia/ *f* hysterectomy; ~**teria** *f* hysteria; ~**térico** *a* hysterical; ~**terismo** *m* hysteria

his|tória /is'tɔria/ *f* (*do passado*) history; (*conto*) story; *pl* (*amolação*) trouble; ~**toriador** *m* historian; ~**tórico** *a* historical; (*marcante*) historic □ *m* history

hoje /'oʒi/ *adv* today; ~ **em dia** nowadays; ~ **de manhã** this morning; ~ **à noite** tonight

Holanda /o'lãda/ *f* Holland

holan|dês /olã'des/ *a* (*f* ~**desa**) Dutch □ *m* (*f* ~**desa**) Dutchman (*f* -woman); (*língua*) Dutch; **os** ~**deses** the Dutch

holding /'xɔwdʒi/ (*pl* ~**s**) *f* holding company

holerite /ole'ritʃi/ *m* pay slip

holo|causto /olo'kawstu/ *m* holocaust; ~**fote** /ɔ/ *m* spotlight; ~**grama** *m* hologram

homem /'omẽ/ *m* man; ~ **de negócios** businessman; ~**rã** (*pl* **homens-rã**) *m* frogman

homena|gear /omenaʒi'ar/ *vt* pay tribute to; ~**gem** *f* tribute; **em** ~**gem a** in honour of

homeo|pata /omio'pata/ *m*/*f* homoeopath; ~**patia** *f* homoeopathy; ~**pático** *a* homoeopathic

homérico /o'mɛriku/ *a* (*estrondoso*) booming; (*extraordinário*) phenomenal

homi|cida /omi'sida/ *a* homicidal □ *m*/*f* murderer; ~**cídio** *m* homicide; ~**cídio involuntário** manslaughter

homo|geneizado /omoʒenej'zadu/ *a* <*leite*> homogenized; ~**gêneo** *a* homogeneous

homologar /omolo'gar/ *vt* ratify

homólogo /o'mɔlogu/ *m* opposite number □ *a* equivalent

homônimo /o'monimu/ *m* (*xará*) namesake; (*vocábulo*) homonym

homossexu|al /omoseksu'aw/ (*pl* ~**ais**) *a* & *m* homosexual; ~**alismo** *m* homosexuality

Honduras /õ'duras/ *f* Honduras

hondurenho /õdu'reɲu/ *a* & *m* Honduran

hones|tidade /onestʃi'dadʒi/ *f* honesty; ~**to** /ɛ/ *a* honest

hono|rário /ono'rariu/ *a* honorary; ~**rários** *m pl* fees; ~**rífico** *a* honorific

hon|ra /'õxa/ *f* honour; ~**radez** *f* honesty, integrity; ~**rado** *a* honourable; ~**rar** *vt* honour; ~**roso** /o/ *a* honourable

hóquei /'ɔkej/ *m* (field) hockey; ~ **sobre gelo** ice hockey; ~ **sobre patins** roller hockey

hora /'ɔra/ *f* (*unidade de tempo*) hour; (*ocasião*) time; **que ~s são?** what's the time?; **a que ~s?** at what time?; **às três ~s** at three o'clock; **dizer as ~s** tell the time; **tem ~s?** do you have the time?; **de ~ em ~** every hour; **em cima da ~** at the last minute; **na ~** (*naquele momento*) at the time; (*no ato*) on the spot; (*a tempo*) on time; **está na ~ de ir** it's time to go; **na ~ H** (*no momento certo*) at just the right moment; (*no momento crítico*) at the crucial moment; **meia ~** half an hour; **toda ~** all the time; **fazer ~** kill time; **marcar ~** make an appointment; **perder a ~** lose track of time; **não tenho ~** my time is my own; **não vejo a ~ de ir** I can't wait to go; ~**s extras** overtime; ~**s vagas** spare time

horário /o'rariu/ *a* hourly; **km** ~**s** km per hour □ *m* (*hora*) time; (*tabela*) timetable; (*de trabalho etc*) hours; ~ **nobre** prime time

horda /'ɔrda/ *f* horde

horista /o'rista/ *a* paid by the hour □ *m*/*f* worker paid by the hour

horizon|tal /orizõ'taw/ (*pl* ~**tais**) *a* & *f* horizontal; ~**te** *m* horizon

hor|monal /ormo'naw/ (*pl* ~**monais**) *a* hormonal; ~**mônio** *m* hormone

horóscopo /o'rɔskopu/ *m* horoscope

horrendo /o'xẽdu/ *a* horrid

horripi|lante /oxipi'lãtʃi/ *a* horrifying; ~**lar** *vt* horrify

horrí|vel /o'xivew/ (*pl* ~**veis**) *a* horrible, awful

horror /o'xor/ *m* horror (**a** of); (*coisa horrorosa*) horrible thing; **ser um** ~ be awful; **que** ~**!** how awful!

horro|rizar /oxori'zar/ *vt*/*i* horrify; ~**rizar-se** *vpr* be horrified; ~**roso** /o/ *a* horrible

horta /'ɔrta/ *f* vegetable plot; ~ **comercial** market garden, (*Amer*) truck farm; ~**liça** *f* vegetable

hortelã /orte'lã/ *f* mint; ~**-pimenta** peppermint

horti|cultor /ortʃikuw'tor/ *m* horticulturalist; ~**cultura** *f*

h

horticulture; **~frutigranjeiros** *m pl* fruit and vegetables; **~granjeiros** *m pl* vegetables

horto /'ɔrtu/ *m* market garden; (*viveiro*) nursery

hospe|dagem /ospe'daʒẽ/ *f* accommodation; **~dar** *vt* put up; **~dar-se** *vpr* stay

hóspede /'ɔspidʒi/ *m/f* guest

hospedei|ra /ospe'dera/ *f* landlady; **~ra de bordo** (*Port*) stewardess; **~ro** *m* landlord

hospício /os'pisiu/ *m* (*de loucos*) asylum

hospi|tal /ospi'taw/ (*pl* **~tais**) *m* hospital; **~talar** *a* hospital; **~taleiro** *a* hospitable; **~talidade** *f* hospitality; **~talizar** *vt* hospitalize

hóstia /'ɔstʃia/ *f* Host, Communion wafer

hos|til /os'tʃiw/ (*pl* **~tis**) *a* hostile; **~tilidade** *f* hostility; **~tilizar** *vt* antagonize

ho|tel /o'tɛw/ (*pl* **~téis**) *m* hotel; **~teleiro** *a* hotel □ *m* hotelier

huma|nidade /umani'dadʒi/ *f* humanity; **~nismo** *m* humanism; **~nista** *a & m/f* humanist; **~nitário** *a & m* humanitarian; **~nizar** *vt* humanize; **~no** *a* human; (*compassivo*) humane; **~nos** *m pl* humans

húmido /'umidu/ *adj* (*Port*) humid

humil|dade /umiw'dadʒi/ *f* humility; **~de** *a* humble

humi|lhação /umiʎa'sãw/ *f* humiliation; **~lhante** *a* humiliating; **~lhar** *vt* humiliate

humor /u'mor/ *m* humour; (*disposição do espírito*) mood; **de bom/mau ~** in a good/bad mood

humo|rismo /umo'rizmu/ *m* humour; **~rista** *m/f* (*no palco*) comedian; (*escritor*) humorist; **~rístico** *a* humorous

húngaro /'ũgaru/ *a & m* Hungarian

Hungria /ũ'gria/ *f* Hungary

hurra /'uxa/ *int* hurrah □ *m* cheer

··

Ii

··

ia|te /i'atʃi/ *m* yacht; **~tismo** *m* yachting; **~tista** *m/f* yachtsman (*f*-woman)

ibérico /i'bɛriku/ *a & m* Iberian

ibope /i'bɔpi/ *m* **dar ~** (*fam*) be popular

içar /i'sar/ *vt* hoist

iceberg /ajs'bɛrgi/ (*pl* **~s**) *m* iceberg

ícone /'ikoni/ *m* icon

iconoclasta /ikono'klasta/ *m/f* iconoclast □ *a* iconoclastic

icterícia /ikte'risia/ *f* jaundice

ida /'ida/ *f* going; **na ~** on the way there; **~ e volta** return, (*Amer*) round trip

idade /i'dadʒi/ *f* age; **meia ~** middle age; **homem de meia ~** middle-aged man; **senhor de ~** elderly man; **Idade Média** Middle Ages

ide|al /ide'aw/ (*pl* **~ais**) *a & m* ideal; **~alismo** *m* idealism; **~alista** *m/f* idealist □ *a* idealistic; **~alizar** *vt* (*criar*) devise; (*sublimar*) idealize; **~ar** *vt* devise; **~ário** *m* ideas

idéia /i'dɛja/ *f* idea; **mudar de ~** change one's mind

idem /'idẽ/ *adv* ditto

idêntico /i'dẽtʃiku/ *a* identical

identi|dade /idẽtʃi'dadʒi/ *f* identity; **~ficar** *vt* identify; **~ficar-se** *vpr* identify (**com** with)

ideo|logia /ideolo'ʒia/ *f* ideology; **~lógico** *a* ideological

idílico /i'dʒiliku/ *a* idyllic

idílio /i'dʒiliu/ *m* idyll

idio|ma /idʒi'oma/ *m* language; **~mático** *a* idiomatic

idio|ta /idʒi'ɔta/ *m/f* idiot □ *a* idiotic; **~tice** *f* stupidity; (*uma*) stupid thing

idola|trar /idola'trar/ *vt* idolize; **~tria** *f* idolatry

ídolo /'idulu/ *m* idol

idôneo /i'doniu/ *a* suitable

idoso /i'dozu/ *a* elderly

Iêmen /i'emẽ/ *m* Yemen

iemenita /ieme'nita/ *a & m/f* Yemeni

iene /i'ɛni/ *m* yen

iglu /i'glu/ *m* igloo

ignição /igni'sãw/ *f* ignition

ignomínia /igno'minia/ *f* ignominy

igno|rância /igno'rãsia/ *f* ignorance; **~rante** *a* ignorant; **~rar** (*desconsiderar*) ignore; (*desconhecer*) not know

igreja /i'greʒa/ *f* church

igu|al /i'gwaw/ (*pl* **~ais**) *a* equal; (*em aparência*) identical; (*liso*) even □ *m/f* equal; **por ~al** equally; **~alar** *vt* equal; level <*terreno*>; **~alar(-se) a** be equal to; **~aldade** *f* equality; **~alitário** *a* egalitarian; **~almente** *adv* equally; (*como resposta*) the same to you; **~alzinho a** exactly the same (**a** as)

iguaria /igwa'ria/ *f* delicacy

iídiche /i'idiʃi/ *m* Yiddish

ile|gal /ile'gaw/ (*pl* **~gais**) *a* illegal; **~galidade** *f* illegality

ilegítimo /ile'ʒitʃimu/ *a* illegitimate

ilegí|vel /ileˈʒivew/ (*pl* ~**veis**) *a* illegible

ileso /iˈlɛzu/ *a* unhurt

iletrado /ileˈtradu/ *adj* & *m* illiterate

ilha /ˈiʎa/ *f* island

ilharga /iˈʎarga/ *f* side

ilhéu /iˈʎɛw/ *m* (*f* **ilhoa**) islander

ilhós /iˈʎɔs/ *m invar* eyelet

ilhota /iˈʎɔta/ *f* small island

ilícito /iˈlisitu/ *a* illicit

ilimitado /ilimiˈtadu/ *a* unlimited

ilógico /iˈlɔʒiku/ *a* illogical

iludir /iluˈdʒir/ *vt* delude; ~**-se** *vpr* delude o.s.

ilumi|nação /iluminaˈsãw/ *f* lighting; (*inspiração*) enlightenment; ~**nar** *vt* light up, illuminate; (*inspirar*) enlighten

ilu|são /iluˈzãw/ *f* illusion; (*sonho*) delusion; ~**sionista** *m/f* illusionist; ~**sório** *a* illusory

ilus|tração /ilustraˈsãw/ *f* illustration; (*erudição*) learning; ~**trador** *m* illustrator; ~**trar** *vt* illustrate; ~**trativo** *a* illustrative; ~**tre** *a* illustrious; ~**tríssimo senhor** Dear Sir

ímã /ˈimã/ *m* magnet

imaculado /imakuˈladu/ *a* immaculate

imagem /iˈmaʒẽ/ *f* image; (*da TV*) picture

imagi|nação /imaʒinaˈsãw/ *f* imagination; ~**nar** *vt* imagine; ~**nário** *a* imaginary; ~**nativo** *a* imaginative; ~**nável** (*pl* ~**náveis**) *a* imaginable; ~**noso** /o/ *a* imaginative

imatu|ridade /imaturiˈdadʒi/ *f* immaturity; ~**ro** *a* immature

imbatí|vel /ĩbaˈtʃivew/ (*pl* ~**veis**) *a* unbeatable

imbe|cil /ĩbeˈsiw/ (*pl* ~**cis**) *a* stupid □ *m/f* imbecile

imberbe /ĩˈberbi/ *adj* (*sem barba*) beardless

imbricar /ĩbriˈkar/ *vt* overlap; ~**-se** *vpr* overlap

imedia|ções /imedʒiaˈsõjs/ *f pl* vicinity; ~**tamente** *adv* immediately; ~**to** *a* immediate

imemori|al /imemoriˈaw/ (*pl* ~**ais**) *a* immemorial

imen|sidão /imẽsiˈdãw/ *f* vastness; ~**so** *a* immense

imergir /imerˈʒir/ *vt* immerse

imi|gração /imigraˈsãw/ *f* immigration; ~**grante** *a* & *m/f* immigrant; ~**grar** *vi* immigrate

imi|nência /imiˈnẽsia/ *f* imminence; ~**nente** *a* imminent

imiscuir-se /imiskuˈirsi/ *vpr* interfere

imi|tação /imitaˈsãw/ *f* imitation; ~**tador** *m* imitator; ~**tar** *vt* imitate

imobili|ária /imobiliˈaria/ *f* estate agent's, (*Amer*) realtor; ~**ário** *a* property; ~**dade** *f* immobility; ~**zar** *vt* immobilize

imo|ral /imoˈraw/ (*pl* ~**rais**) *a* immoral; ~**ralidade** *f* immorality

imor|tal /imorˈtaw/ (*pl* ~**tais**) *a* immortal □ *m/f* member of the Brazilian Academy of Letters; ~**talidade** *f* immortality; ~**talizar** *vt* immortalize

imó|vel /iˈmɔvew/ (*pl* ~**veis**) *a* motionless, immobile □ *m* building, property; *pl* property, real estate

impaci|ência /ipasiˈẽsia/ *f* impatience; ~**entar-se** *vpr* get impatient; ~**ente** *a* impatient

impacto /ĩˈpaktu/, (*Port*) **impacte** /ĩˈpaktʃi/ *m* impact

impagá|vel /ĩpaˈgavew/ (*pl* ~**veis**) *a* priceless

ímpar /ˈĩpar/ *a* unique; <*número*> odd

imparci|al /ĩparsiˈaw/ (*pl* ~**ais**) *a* impartial; ~**alidade** *f* impartiality

impasse /ĩˈpasi/ *m* impasse

impassí|vel /ĩpaˈsivew/ (*pl* ~**veis**) *a* impassive

impecá|vel /ĩpeˈkavew/ (*pl* ~**veis**) *a* impeccable

impe|dido /ĩpeˈdʒidu/ *a* <*rua*> blocked; (*Port: ocupado*) engaged, (*Amer*) busy; (*no futebol*) offside; ~**dimento** *m* prevention; (*estorvo*) obstruction; (*no futebol*) offside position; ~**dir** *vt* stop; (*estorvar*) hinder; block <*rua*>; ~**dir alg de ir** *ou* **que alg vá** stop s.o. going

impelir /ĩpeˈlir/ *vt* drive

impenetrá|vel /ĩpeneˈtravew/ (*pl* ~**veis**) *a* impenetrable

impensá|vel /ĩpẽˈsavew/ (*pl* ~**veis**) *a* unthinkable

impe|rador /ĩperaˈdor/ *m* emperor; ~**rar** *vi* reign, rule; ~**rativo** *a* & *m* imperative; ~**ratriz** *f* empress

imperceptí|vel /ĩpersepˈtʃivew/ (*pl* ~**veis**) *a* imperceptible

imperdí|vel /ĩperˈdʒivew/ (*pl* ~**veis**) *a* unmissable

imperdoá|vel /ĩperdoˈavew/ (*pl* ~**veis**) *a* unforgivable

imperfei|ção /ĩperfejˈsãw/ *f* imperfection; ~**to** *a* & *m* imperfect

imperi|al /ĩperiˈaw/ (*pl* ~**ais**) *a* imperial; ~**alismo** *m* imperialism; ~**alista** *a* & *m/f* imperialist

império /ĩˈpɛriu/ *m* empire

imperioso /ĩperiˈozu/ *a* imperious; <*necessidade*> pressing

imperme|abilizar /ĩpermiabiliˈzar/ *vt* waterproof; ~**ável** (*pl* ~**áveis**) *a* waterproof; (*fig*) impervious (**a** to) □ *m* raincoat

imperti|nência /ĩpertʃi'nẽsia/ *f* impertinence; **∼nente** *a* impertinent

impesso|al /ĩpeso'aw/ (*pl* **∼ais**) *a* impersonal

ímpeto /'ĩpetu/ *m* (*vontade*) urge, impulse; (*de emoção*) surge; (*movimento*) start; (*na física*) impetus

impetuo|sidade /ĩpetuozi'dadʒi/ *f* impetuosity; **∼so** /o/ *a* impetuous

impiedoso /ĩpie'dozu/ *a* merciless

impingir /ĩpĩ'ʒir/ *vt* foist (**a** on)

implacá|vel /ĩpla'kavew/ (*pl* **∼veis**) *a* implacable

implan|tar /ĩplã'tar/ *vt* introduce; (*no corpo*) implant; **∼te** *m* implant

implemen|tar /ĩplemẽ'tar/ *vt* implement; **∼to** *m* implement

impli|cação /ĩplika'sãw/ *f* implication; **∼cância** *f* (*ato*) harassment; (*antipatia*) grudge; **estar de ∼cância com** have it in for; **∼cante** *a* troublesome □ *m/f* troublemaker; **∼car** *vt* (*comprometer*) implicate; **∼car (em)** (*dar a entender*) imply; (*acarretar, exigir*) involve; **∼car com** (*provocar*) pick on; (*antipatizar*) not get on with

implícito /ĩ'plisitu/ *a* implicit

implorar /ĩplo'rar/ *vt* plead for (**a** from)

imponente /ĩpo'nẽtʃi/ *a* imposing

impopular /ĩpopu'lar/ *a* unpopular

impor /ĩ'por/ *vt* impose (**a** on); command <*respeito*>; **∼-se** *vpr* assert o.s.

impor|tação /ĩporta'sãw/ *f* import; **∼tador** *m* importer; **∼tadora** *f* import company; **∼tados** *m pl* imported goods; **∼tância** *f* importance; (*quantia*) amount; **ter ∼tância** be important; **∼tante** *a* important; **∼tar** *vt* import <*mercadorias*> □ *vi* matter; **∼tar em** (*montar a*) amount to; (*resultar em*) lead to; **∼tar-se (com)** mind

importu|nar /ĩportu'nar/ *vt* bother; **∼no** *a* annoying

imposição /ĩpozi'sãw/ *f* imposition

impossibili|dade /ĩposibili'dadʒi/ *f* impossibility; **∼tar** *vt* make impossible; **∼tar alg de ir**, **∼tar a alg ir** prevent s.o. from going, make it impossible for s.o. to go

impossí|vel /ĩpo'sivew/ (*pl* **∼veis**) *a* impossible

impos|to /ĩ'postu/ *m* tax; **∼to de renda** income tax; **∼to sobre o valor acrescentado** (*Port*) VAT; **∼tor** *m* impostor; **∼tura** *f* deception

impo|tência /ĩpo'tẽsia/ *f* impotence; **∼tente** *a* impotent

impreci|são /ĩpresi'zãw/ *f* imprecision; **∼so** *a* imprecise

impregnar /ĩpreg'nar/ *vt* impregnate

imprensa /ĩ'prẽsa/ *f* press; **∼ marrom** gutter press

imprescindí|vel /ĩpresĩ'dʒivew/ (*pl* **∼veis**) *a* essential

impres|são /ĩpre'sãw/ *f* impression; (*no prelo*) printing; **∼são digital** fingerprint; **∼sionante** *a* (*imponente*) impressive; (*comovente*) striking; **∼sionar** *vt* (*causar admiração*) impress; (*co-mover*) make an impression on; **∼sionar-se** *vpr* be impressed (**com** by); **∼sionável** (*pl* **∼sionáveis**) *a* impressionable; **∼sionismo** *m* impressionism; **∼sionista** *a* & *m/f* impressionist; **∼so** *a* printed □ *m* printed sheet; *pl* printed matter; **∼sor** *m* printer; **∼sora** *f* printer

imprestá|vel /ĩpres'tavew/ (*pl* **∼veis**) *a* useless

impre|visível /ĩprevi'zivew/ (*pl* **∼visíveis**) *a* unpredictable; **∼visto** *a* unforeseen □ *m* unforeseen circumstance

imprimir /ĩpri'mir/ *vt* print

impropério /ĩpro'pɛriu/ *m* term of abuse; *pl* abuse

impróprio /ĩ'prɔpriu/ *a* improper; (*inadequado*) unsuitable (**para** for)

imprová|vel /ĩpro'vavew/ (*pl* **∼veis**) *a* unlikely

improvi|sação /ĩproviza'sãw/ *f* improvisation; **∼sar** *vt/i* improvise; **∼so** *m* **de ∼so** on the spur of the moment

impru|dência /ĩpru'dẽsia/ *f* recklessness; **∼dente** *a* reckless

impul|sionar /ĩpuwsio'nar/ *vt* drive; **∼sivo** *a* impulsive; **∼so** *m* impulse

impu|ne /ĩ'puni/ *a* unpunished; **∼nidade** *f* impunity

impu|reza /ĩpu'reza/ *f* impurity; **∼ra** *a* impure

imun|dície /imũ'dʒisi/ *f* filth; **∼do** *a* filthy

imu|ne /i'muni/ *a* immune (**a** to); **∼nidade** *f* immunity; **∼nizar** *vt* immunize

inabalá|vel /inaba'lavew/ (*pl* **∼veis**) *a* unshakeable

iná|bil /i'nabiw/ (*pl* **∼bis**) *a* (*desafeitado*) clumsy

inabitado /inabi'tadu/ *a* uninhabited

inacabado /inaka'badu/ *a* unfinished

inaceitá|vel /inasej'tavew/ (*pl* **∼veis**) *a* unacceptable

inacessí|vel /inase'sivew/ (*pl* **∼veis**) *a* inaccessible

inacreditá|vel /inakredʒi'tavew/ (*pl* ∼**veis**) *a* unbelievable

inadequado /inade'kwadu/ *a* unsuitable

inadmissí|vel /inadʒimi'sivew/ (*pl* ∼**veis**) *a* inadmissible

inadvertência /inadʒiver'têsia/ *f* oversight

inalar /ina'lar/ *vt* inhale

inalcançá|vel /inawkã'savew/ (*pl* ∼**veis**) *a* unattainable

inalterá|vel /inawte'ravew/ (*pl* ∼veis) *a* unchangeable

inanição /inani'sãw/ *f* starvation

inanimado /inani'madu/ *a* inanimate

inapto /i'naptu/ *a* (*incapaz*) unfit

inati|vidade /inatʃivi'dadʒi/ *f* inactivity; ∼**vo** *a* inactive

inato /i'natu/ *a* innate

inaudito /inaw'dʒitu/ *a* unheard of

inaugu|ração /inawgura'sãw/ *f* inauguration; ∼**ral** (*pl* ∼**rais**) *a* inaugural; ∼**rar** *vt* inaugurate

incabí|vel /ika'bivew/ (*pl* ∼**veis**) *a* inappropriate

incalculá|vel /īkawku'lavew/ (*pl* ∼**veis**) *a* incalculable

incandescente /īkãde'sētʃi/ *a* red-hot

incansá|vel /īkã'savew/ (*pl* ∼**veis**) *a* tireless

incapaci|tado /īkapasi'tadu/ *a* <*pessoa*> disabled; ∼**tar** *vt* incapacitate

incauto /ī'kawtu/ *a* reckless

incendi|ar /īsēdʒi'ar/ *vt* set alight; ∼**ar-se** *vpr* catch fire; ∼**ário** *a* incendiary; (*fig*) <*discurso*> inflammatory □ *m* arsonist; (*fig*) agitator

incêndio /ī'sēdʒiu/ *m* fire

incenso /ī'sēsu/ *m* incense

incenti|var /īsētʃi'var/ *vt* encourage; ∼**vo** *m* incentive

incer|teza /īser'teza/ *f* uncertainty; ∼**to** /ɛ/ *a* uncertain

inces|to /ī'sɛstu/ *m* incest; ∼**tuoso** /o/ *a* incestuous

incitar /īsi'tar/ *vt* incite

incli|nação /īklina'sãw/ *f* (*do chão*) incline; (*da cabeça*) nod; (*propensão*) inclination; ∼**nado** *a* <*chão*> sloping; <*edifício*> leaning; (*propenso*) inclined (**a** to); ∼**nar** *vt* tilt; nod <*cabeça*> □ *vi* <*chão*> slope;

<*edifício*> lean; (*tender*) incline (**para** towards); ∼**nar-se** *vpr* lean

inclu|ir /īklu'ir/ *vt* include; ∼**são** *f* inclusion; ∼**sive** *prep* including □ *adv* inclusive; (*até*) even; ∼**so** *a* included

incoe|rência /īkoe'rēsia/ *f* (*falta de nexo*) incoherence; (*inconseqüência*) inconsistency; ∼**rente** *a* (*sem nexo*) incoherent; (*inconseqüente*) inconsistent

incógni|ta /ī'kɔgnita/ *f* unknown; ∼**to** *adv* incognito

incolor /īko'lor/ *a* colourless

incólume /ī'kɔlumi/ *a* unscathed

incomodar /īkomo'dar/ *vt* bother □ *vi* be a nuisance; ∼**-se** *vpr* (*dar-se ao trabalho*) bother (**em** to); ∼**-se (com)** be bothered (by), mind

incômodo /ī'komodu/ *a* (*desagradável*) tiresome; (*sem conforto*) uncomfortable □ *m* nuisance

incompa|rável /īkõpa'ravew/ (*pl* ∼**ráveis**) *a* incomparable; ∼**tível** (*pl* ∼**tíveis**) *a* incompatible

incompe|tência /īkõpe'tēsia/ *f* incompetence; ∼**tente** *a* incompetent

incompleto /īkõ'plɛtu/ *a* incomplete

incompreensí|vel /īkõprië'sivew/ (*pl* ∼**veis**) *a* incomprehensible

inconcebí|vel /īkõse'bivew/ (*pl* ∼**veis**) *a* inconceivable

incondicio|nal /īkõdʒisio'naw/ (*pl* ∼**nais**) *a* unconditional; <*fã*, *partidário*> firm

inconformado /īkõfor'madu/ *a* unreconciled (**com** to)

inconfundí|vel /īkõfũ'dʒivew/ (*pl* ∼**veis**) *a* unmistakeable

inconsciente /īkõsi'ētʃi/ *a & m* unconscious

inconseqüente /īkõse'kwētʃi/ *a* inconsistent

incons|tância /īkõs'tãsia/ *f* changeability; ∼**tante** *a* changeable

inconstitucio|nal /īkõstʃitusio'naw/ (*pl* ∼**nais**) *a* unconstitutional

incontestá|vel /īkõtes'tavew/ (*pl* ∼**veis**) *a* indisputable

inconveniente /īkõveni'ētʃi/ *a* (*difícil*) inconvenient; (*desagradável*) annoying, tiresome; (*indecente*) unseemly □ *m* drawback

incorporar /īkorpo'rar/ *vt* incorporate

incorrer /īko'xer/ *vi* ∼ **em** <*multa etc*> incur

incorrigí|vel /īkoxi'ʒivew/ (*pl* ∼**veis**) *a* incorrigible

incrédulo /ī'krɛdulu/ *a* incredulous

incremen|tado /īkremē'tadu/ *a* (*fam*) stylish; ∼**tar** *vt* build up; (*fam*) jazz up; ∼**to** *m* development, growth

incriminar /ĩkrimi'nar/ *vt* incriminate

incrí|vel /ĩ'krivew/ (*pl* ~**veis**) *a* incredible

incu|bação /ĩkuba'sãw/ *f* incubation; ~**badora** *f* incubator; ~**bar** *vt/i* incubate

inculto /ĩ'kuwtu/ *a* <*pessoa*> uneducated; <*terreno*> uncultivated

incum|bência /ĩkũ'bẽsia/ *f* task; ~**bir** *vt* ~**bir alg de aco/de ir** assign s.o. sth/to go □ *vi* ~**bir a** be up to; ~**bir-se de** take on

incurá|vel /ĩku'ravew/ (*pl* ~**veis**) *a* incurable

incursão /ĩkur'sãw/ *f* incursion

incutir /ĩku'tʃir/ *vt* instil (**em** in)

indagar /ĩda'gar/ *vt* inquire (into)

inde|cência /ĩde'sẽsia/ *f* indecency; ~**cente** *a* indecent

indecifrá|vel /ĩdesi'fravew/ (*pl* ~**veis**) *a* indecipherable

indeciso /ĩde'sizu/ *a* undecided

indecoroso /ĩdeko'rozu/ *a* indecorous

indefi|nido /ĩdefi'nidu/ *a* indefinite; ~**nível** (*pl* ~**níveis**) *a* indefinable

indelé|vel /ĩde'lɛvew/ (*pl* ~**veis**) *a* indelible

indelica|deza /ĩdelika'deza/ *f* impoliteness; (*uma*) impolite thing; ~**do** *a* impolite

indeni|zação /ĩdeniza'sãw/ *f* compensation; ~**zar** *vt* compensate

indepen|dência /ĩdepẽ'dẽsia/ *f* independence; ~**dente** *a* independent

indescriti|vel /ĩdʒiskri'tʃivew/ (*pl* ~**veis**) *a* indescribable

indesculpá|vel /ĩdʒiskuw'pavew/ (*pl* ~**veis**) *a* inexcusable

indesejá|vel /ĩdeze'ʒavew/ (*pl* ~**veis**) *a* undesirable

indestruti|vel /ĩdʒistru'tʃivew/ (*pl* ~**veis**) *a* indestructible

indeterminado /ĩdetermi'nadu/ *a* indeterminate

indevido /ĩde'vidu/ *a* undue

indexar /ĩdek'sar/ *vt* index; index-link <*salário, preços*>

ndia /'ĩdʒia/ *f* India

indiano /ĩdʒi'anu/ *a & m* Indian

indi|cação /ĩdʒika'sãw/ *f* indication; (*do caminho*) directions; (*nomeação*) nomination; (*recomendação*) recommendation; ~**cador** *m* indicator; (*dedo*) index finger □ *a* indicative (**de** of); ~**car** *vt* indicate; (*para cargo, prêmio*) nominate (**para** for); (*recomendar*) recommend; ~**cativo** *a & m* indicative

índice /'ĩdʒisi/ *m* (*taxa*) rate; (*em livro etc*) index; ~ **de audiência** ratings

indiciar /ĩdʒisi'ar/ *vt* charge

indício /ĩ'dʒisiu/ *m* sign, indication; (*de crime*) clue

indife|rença /ĩdʒife'rẽsa/ *f* indifference; ~**rente** *a* indifferent

indígena /ĩ'dʒiʒena/ *a* indigenous, native □ *m/f* native

indiges|tão /ĩdʒiʒes'tãw/ *f* indigestion; ~**to** *a* indigestible; (*fig*) heavy-going

indig|nação /ĩdʒigna'sãw/ *f* indignation; ~**nado** *a* indignant; ~**nar** *vt* make indignant; ~**nar-se** *vpr* get indignant (**com** about)

indig|nidade /ĩdʒigni'dadʒi/ *f* indignity; ~**no** *a* <*pessoa*> unworthy; <*ato*> despicable

índio /'ĩdʒiu/ *a & m* Indian

indire|ta /ĩdʒi'rɛta/ *f* hint; ~**to** /ɛ/ *a* indirect

indis|creto /ĩdʒis'krɛtu/ *a* indiscreet; ~**crição** *f* indiscretion

indiscriminado /ĩdʒiskrimi'nadu/ *a* indiscriminate

indiscuti|vel /ĩdʒisku'tʃivew/ (*pl* ~**veis**) *a* unquestionable

indispensá|vel /ĩdʒispẽ'savew/ (*pl* ~**veis**) *a* indispensable

indisponí|vel /ĩdʒispo'nivew/ (*pl* ~**veis**) *a* unavailable

indis|por /ĩdʒis'por/ *vt* upset; ~**por alg contra** turn s.o. against; ~**por-se** *vpr* fall out (**com** with); ~**posição** *f* indisposition; ~**posto** *a* (*doente*) indisposed

indistinto /ĩdʒis'tʃĩtu/ *a* indistinct

individu|al /ĩdʒividu'aw/ (*pl* ~**ais**) *a* individual; ~**alidade** *f* individuality; ~**alismo** *m* individualism; ~**alista** *a & m/f* individualist

indivíduo /ĩdʒi'viduu/ *m* individual

indizí|vel /ĩdʒi'zivew/ (*pl* ~**veis**) *a* unspeakable

índole /'ĩdoli/ *f* nature

indo|lência /ĩdo'lẽsia/ *f* indolence; ~**lente** *a* indolent

indolor /ĩdo'lor/ *a* painless

Indonésia /ĩdo'nɛzia/ *f* Indonesia

indonésio /ĩdo'nɛziu/ *a & m* Indonesian

indubitá|vel /ĩdubi'tavew/ (*pl* ~**veis**) *a* undoubted

indul|gência /ĩduw'ʒẽsia/ *f* indulgence; ~**gente** *a* indulgent

indulto /ĩ'duwtu/ *m* pardon

indumentária /ĩdumẽ'taria/ *f* outfit

indústria /ĩ'dustria/ *f* industry

industri|al /ĩdustri'aw/ (*pl* ~**ais**) *a* industrial □ *m/f* industrialist; ~**alizado** *a* <*país*> industrialized; <*mercadoria*> manufactured; <*comida*> processed; ~**alizar** *vt* industrialize <*país, agricultura etc*>;

process <*comida, lixo etc*>; ~**oso** /o/ *a* industrious

induzir /ĩdu'zir/ *vt* (*persuadir*) induce; (*inferir*) infer (**de** from); ~ **em erro** lead astray, mislead s.o.

inebriante /inebri'ãtʃi/ *a* intoxicating

inédito /i'nedʒitu/ *a* unheard-of, unprecedented; (*não publicado*) unpublished

ineficaz /inefi'kas/ *a* ineffective

inefici|ência /inefisi'ẽsia/ *f* inefficiency; ~**ente** *a* inefficient

inegá|vel /ine'gavew/ (*pl* ~**veis**) *a* undeniable

inépcia /i'nɛpsia/ *f* ineptitude

inepto /i'nɛptu/ *a* inept

inequívoco /ine'kivoku/ *a* unmistakeable

inércia /i'nɛrsia/ *f* inertia

inerente /ine'rẽtʃi/ *a* inherent (**a** in)

inerte /i'nɛrtʃi/ *a* inert

inesgotá|vel /inezgo'tavew/ (*pl* ~**veis**) *a* inexhaustible

inesperado /inespe'radu/ *a* unexpected

inesquecí|vel /ineske'sivew/ (*pl* ~**veis**) *a* unforgettable

inevitá|vel /inevi'tavew/ (*pl* ~**veis**) *a* inevitable

inexato /ine'zatu/ *a* inaccurate

inexis|tência /inezis'tẽsia/ *f* lack; ~**tente** *a* non-existent

inexperi|ência /inisperi'ẽsia/ *f* inexperience; ~**ente** *a* inexperienced

inexpressivo /inespre'sivu/ *a* expressionless

infalí|vel /ĩfa'livew/ (*pl* ~**veis**) *a* infallible

infame /ĩ'fami/ *a* despicable; (*péssimo*) dreadful

infâmia /ĩ'famia/ *f* disgrace

infância /ĩ'fãsia/ *f* childhood

infantaria /ĩfãta'ria/ *f* infantry

infan|til /ĩfã'tʃiw/ *a* <*roupa, livro*> children's; (*bobo*) childish; ~**tilidade** *f* childishness; (*uma*) childish thing

infarto /ĩ'fartu/ *m* heart attack

infec|ção /ĩfek'sãw/ *f* infection; ~**cionar** *vt* infect; ~**cioso** *a* infectious

infeliz /ĩfe'lis/ *a* (*não contente*) unhappy; (*inconveniente*) unfortunate; (*desgraçado*) wretched ☐ *m* (*desgraçado*) wretch; ~**mente** *adv* unfortunately

inferi|or /ĩferi'or/ *a* lower; (*em qualidade*) inferior (**a** to); ~**oridade** *f* inferiority

inferir /ĩfe'rir/ *vt* infer

infer|nal /ĩfer'naw/ (*pl* ~**nais**) *a* infernal; ~**nizar** *vt* ~**nizar a vida dele** make his life hell; ~**no** /ɛ/ *m* hell

infér|til /ĩ'fɛrtʃiw/ (*pl* ~**teis**) *a* infertile

infertilidade /ĩfertʃili'dadʒi/ *f* infertility

infestar /ĩfes'tar/ *vt* infest

infetar /ĩfe'tar/ *vt* infect

infidelidade /ĩfideli'dadʒi/ *f* infidelity

infi|el /ĩfi'ɛw/ (*pl* ~**éis**) *a* unfaithful

infiltrar /ĩfiw'trar/ *vt* infiltrate; ~**-se em** infiltrate

ínfimo /'ĩfimu/ *a* lowest; (*muito pequeno*) tiny

infindá|vel /ĩfi'davew/ (*pl* ~**veis**) *a* unending

infinidade /ĩfini'dadʒi/ *f* infinity; **uma** ~ **de** an infinite number of

infini|tesimal /ĩfinitezi'maw/ (*pl* ~**tesimais**) *a* infinitesimal; ~**tivo** *a* & *m* infinitive; ~**to** *a* infinite ☐ *m* infinity

infla|ção /ĩfla'sãw/ *f* inflation; ~**cionar** *vt* inflate; ~**cionário** *a* inflationary; ~**cionista** *a* & *m/f* inflationist

infla|mação /ĩflama'sãw/ *f* inflammation; ~**mar** *vt* inflame; ~**mar-se** *upr* become inflamed; ~**matório** *a* inflammatory; ~**mável** (*pl* ~**máveis**) *a* inflammable

in|flar *vt* inflate; ~**flar-se** *upr* inflate; ~**flável** (*pl* ~**fláveis**) *a* inflatable

infle|xibilidade /ĩfleksibili'dadʒi/ *f* inflexibility; ~**xível** (*pl* ~**xíveis**) *a* inflexible

infligir /ĩfli'ʒir/ *vt* inflict (**a** on)

influência /ĩflu'ẽsia/ *f* influence

influen|ciar /ĩfluẽsi'ar/ *vt* ~**ciar (em)** influence; ~**ciar-se** *upr* be influenced; ~**ciável** (*pl* ~**ciáveis**) *a* open to influence; ~**te** *a* influential

influir /ĩflu'ir/ *vi* ~ **em** *ou* **sobre** influence

informação /ĩforma'sãw/ *f* information; (*uma*) a piece of information; (*mil*) intelligence; *pl* information

infor|mal /ĩfor'maw/ (*pl* ~**mais**) *a* informal; ~**malidade** *f* informality

infor|mar /ĩfor'mar/ *vt* inform; ~**mar-se** *upr* find out (**de** about); ~**mática** *f* information technology; ~**mativo** *a* informative; ~**matizar** *vt* computerize; ~**me** *m* (*mil*) piece of intelligence

infortúnio /ĩfor'tuniu/ *m* misfortune

infração /ĩfra'sãw/ *f* infringement

infra-estrutura /ĩfraistru'tura/ *f* infrastructure

infrator /ĩfra'tor/ *m* offender

infravermelho /ĩfraver'meʎu/ a
infrared

infringir /ĩfrĩ'ʒir/ vt infringe

infrutífero /ĩfru'tʃiferu/ a fruitless

infundado /ĩfũ'dadu/ a unfounded

infundir /ĩfũ'dʒir/ vt (insuflar) infuse;
(incutir) instil

infusão /ĩfu'zãw/ f infusion

ingenuidade /ĩʒenui'dadʒi/ f naivety

ingênuo /ĩ'ʒenuu/ a naive

Inglaterra /ĩgla'texa/ f England

ingerir /ĩʒe'rir/ vt ingest; (engolir)
swallow

in|glês /ĩ'gles/ a (f ~glesa) English □ m
(f ~glesa) Englishman (f-woman);
(língua) English; os ~gleses the
English

ingra|tidão /ĩgratʃi'dãw/ f ingratitude;
~to a ungrateful

ingrediente /ĩgredʒi'ẽtʃi/ m ingredient

íngreme /'ĩgrimi/ a steep

ingres|sar /ĩgre'sar/ vi ~sar em join;
~so m entry; (bilhete) ticket

inhame /i'ɲami/ m yam

ini|bição /inibi'sãw/ f inhibition; ~bir
vt inhibit

inici|ado /inisi'adu/ m initiate; ~al (pl
~ais) a & f initial; ~ar vt (começar)
begin; (em ciência, seita etc) initiate
(em into) □ vi begin; ~ativa f
initiative

início /i'nisiu/ m beginning

igualá|vel /inigwa'lavew/ (pl ~veis) a
unparalleled

inimaginá|vel /inimaʒi'navew/ (pl
~veis) a unimaginable

inimi|go /ini'migu/ a & m enemy;
~zade f enmity

ininterrupto /inĩte'xuptu/ a continuous

inje|ção /ĩʒe'sãw/ f injection; ~tado a
<olhos> bloodshot; ~tar vt inject;
~tável (pl ~táveis) a <droga>
intravenous

injúria /ĩ'ʒuria/ f insult

injuriar /ĩʒuri'ar/ vt insult

injus|tiça /ĩʒus'tʃisa/ f injustice;
~tiçado a wronged; ~to a unfair, unjust

ino|cência /ino'sẽsia/ f innocence;
~centar vt clear (de of); ~cente a
innocent

inocular /inoku'lar/ vt inoculate

inócuo /i'nɔkuu/ a harmless

inodoro /ino'dɔru/ a odourless

inofensivo /inofẽ'sivu/ a harmless

inoportuno /inopor'tunu/ a inopportune

inorgânico /inor'ganiku/ a inorganic

inóspito /i'nɔspitu/ a inhospitable

ino|vação /inova'sãw/ f innovation;
~var vt/i innovate

inoxidá|vel /inoksi'davew/ (pl ~veis) a
<aço> stainless

inquérito /ĩ'kɛritu/ m inquiry

inquie|tação /ĩkieta'sãw/ f concern;
~tador, ~tante a worrying; ~tar vt
worry; ~tar-se vpr worry; ~to /ɛ/ a
uneasy

inquili|nato /ĩkili'natu/ m tenancy; ~no
m tenant

inquirir /ĩki'rir/ vt cross-examine
<testemunha>

Inquisição /ĩkizi'sãw/ f a ~ the
Inquisition

insaciá|vel /ĩsasi'avew/ (pl ~veis) a
insatiable

insalubre /ĩsa'lubri/ a unhealthy

insatis|fação /ĩsatʃisfa'sãw/ f
dissatisfaction; ~fatório a
unsatisfactory; ~feito a dissatisfied

ins|crever /ĩskre'ver/ vt (registrar)
register; (gravar) inscribe; ~crever-
se vpr register; (em escola etc) enrol;
~crição f (registro) registration;
(em clube, escola) enrolment;
(em monumento etc) inscription

insegu|rança /ĩsegu'rãsa/ f insecurity;
~ro a insecure

insemi|nação /ĩsemina'sãw/ f
insemination; ~nar vt inseminate

insen|satez /ĩsẽsa'tes/ f folly; ~sato a
foolish; ~sibilidade f insensitivity;
~sível (pl ~síveis) a insensitive

inseparᬀ|vel /ĩsepa'ravew/ (pl ~veis) a
inseparable

inserção /ĩser'sãw/ f insertion

inserir /ĩse'rir/ vt insert; enter <dados>

inse|ticida /ĩsetʃi'sida/ m insecticide;
~to /ɛ/ m insect

insígnia /ĩ'signia/ f insignia

insignifi|cância /ĩsignifi'kãsia/ f
insignificance; ~cante a insignificant

insincero /ĩsĩ'sɛru/ a insincere

insinu|ante /ĩsinu'ãtʃi/ a suggestive;
~ar vt/i insinuate

insípido /ĩ'sipidu/ a insipid

insis|tência /ĩsis'tẽsia/ f insistence;
~tente a insistent; ~tir vt/i insist
(em on)

insolação /ĩsola'sãw/ f sunstroke

inso|lência /ĩso'lẽsia/ f insolence;
~lente a insolent

insólito /ĩ'sɔlitu/ a unusual

insolú|vel /ĩso'luvew/ (pl ~veis) a
insoluble

insone /ĩ'sɔni/ a <noite> sleepless;
<pessoa> insomniac □ m/f insomniac

insônia /ĩ'sonia/ f insomnia

insosso /ĩ'sosu/ a bland; (sem sabor)
tasteless; (sem sal) unsalted

inspe|ção /ĩspe'sãw/ f inspection;
~cionar vt inspect; ~tor m inspector

inspi|ração /ĩspira'sãw/ f inspiration; ~**rar** vt inspire; ~**rar-se** vpr take inspiration (**em** from)

instabilidade /ĩstabili'dadʒi/ f instability

insta|lação /ĩstala'sãw/ f installation; ~**lar** vt install; ~**lar-se** vpr install o.s.

instan|tâneo /ĩstã'taniu/ a instant; ~**te** m instant

instaurar /ĩstaw'rar/ vt set up

instá|vel /ĩ'stavew/ (pl ~**veis**) a unstable; <tempo> unsettled

insti|gação /ĩstʃiga'sãw/ f instigation; ~**gante** a stimulating; ~**gar** vt incite

instin|tivo /ĩstʃĩ'tʃivu/ a instinctive; ~**to** m instinct

institu|cional /ĩstʃitusio'naw/ (pl ~**cionais**) a institutional; ~**ição** f institution; ~**ir** vt set up; set <prazo>; ~**to** m institute

instru|ção /ĩstru'sãw/ f instruction; ~**ir** vt instruct; train <recrutas>; (informar) advise (**sobre** of)

instrumen|tal /ĩstrumẽ'taw/ (pl ~**tais**) a instrumental; ~**tista** m/f instrumentalist; ~**to** m instrument

instru|tivo /ĩstru'tʃivu/ a instructive; ~**tor** m instructor

insubstituí|vel /ĩsubistʃitu'ivew/ (pl ~**veis**) a irreplaceable

insucesso /ĩsu'sesu/ m failure

insufici|ência /ĩsufisi'ẽsia/ f insufficiency; (dos órgãos) failure; ~**ente** a insufficient

insulina /ĩsu'lina/ f insulin

insul|tar /ĩsuw'tar/ vt insult; ~**to** m insult

insuperá|vel /ĩsupe'ravew/ (pl ~**veis**) a <problema> insurmountable; <qualidade> unsurpassed

insuportá|vel /ĩsupor'tavew/ (pl ~**veis**) a unbearable

insur|gente /ĩsur'ʒẽtʃi/ a & m/f insurgent; ~**gir-se** vpr rise up, revolt; ~**reição** f insurrection

intato /ĩ'tatu/ a intact

íntegra /'ĩtegra/ f full text; **na** ~ in full

inte|gração /ĩtegra'sãw/ f integration; ~**gral** (pl ~**grais**) a whole; **arroz /pão** ~**gral** brown rice/bread; ~**grante** a integral □ m/f member; ~**grar** vt make up, form; ~**grar-se em** become a part of; ~**gridade** f integrity

íntegro /'ĩtegru/ a honest

intei|ramente /ĩtera'mẽtʃi/ adv completely; ~**rar** vt (informar) fill in, inform (**de** about); ~**rar-se** vpr find out (**de** about); ~**riço** a in one piece; ~**ro** a whole

intelec|to /ĩte'lɛktu/ m intellect; ~**tual** (pl ~**tuais**) a & m/f intellectual

inteli|gência /ĩteli'ʒẽsia/ f intelligence; ~**gente** a clever, intelligent; ~**gível** (pl ~**gíveis**) a intelligible

intem|périe /ĩtẽ'pɛri/ f bad weather; ~**pestivo** a ill-timed

inten|ção /ĩtẽ'sãw/ f intention; **segundas** ~**ções** ulterior motives

intencio|nado /ĩtẽsio'nadu/ a **bem** ~**nado** well-meaning; ~**nal** (pl ~**nais**) a intentional; ~**nar** vt intend

inten|sidade /ĩtẽsi'dadʒi/ f intensity; ~**sificar** vt intensify; ~**sificar-se** vpr intensify; ~**sivo** a intensive; ~**so** a intense

intento /ĩ'tẽtu/ m intention

intera|ção /ĩtera'sãw/ f interaction; ~**gir** vi interact; ~**tivo** a interactive

inter|calar /ĩterka'lar/ vt insert; ~**câmbio** m exchange; ~**ceptar** vt intercept

intercontinen|tal /ĩterkõtʃinẽ'taw/ (pl ~**tais**) a intercontinental

interdepen|dência /ĩterdepẽ'dẽsia/ f interdependence; ~**dente** a interdependent

interdi|ção /ĩterdʒi'sãw/ f closure; (jurid) injunction; ~**tar** vt close <rua etc>; (proibir) ban

interes|sante /ĩtere'sãtʃi/ a interesting; ~**sar** vt interest □ vi be relevant; ~**sar-se** vpr be interested (**em** ou **por** in); ~**se** /e/ m interest; (próprio) self-interest; ~**seiro** a self-seeking

interestadu|al /ĩteristadu'aw/ (pl ~**ais**) a interstate

interface /ĩter'fasi/ f interface

interfe|rência /ĩterfe'rẽsia/ f interference; ~**rir** vi interfere

interfone /ĩter'fɔni/ m intercom

ínterim /'ĩterĩ/ m interim; **nesse** ~ in the interim

interino /ĩte'rinu/ a temporary

interior /ĩteri'or/ a inner; (dentro do país) internal, domestic □ m inside; (do país) country, interior

inter|jeição /ĩterʒej'sãw/ f interjection; ~**ligar** vt interconnect; ~**locutor** m interlocutor; ~**mediário** a & m intermediary

intermédio /ĩter'mɛdʒiu/ m **por de** through

intermina|vel /ĩtermi'navew/ (pl ~**veis**) a interminable

internacio|nal /ĩternasio'naw/ (pl ~**nais**) a international

inter|nar /ĩter'nar/ vt intern <preso>; admit to hospital <doente>; ~**nato** m boarding school

internauta /ĩter'nawta/ m/f (comput) netsurfer

Internet /ĩter'nɛt/ f Internet

interno /ĩ'tɛrnu/ a internal

interpelar /ĩterpe'lar/ vt question

interpor /ĩter'por/ vt interpose; ~-se vpr intervene

interpre|tação /ĩterpreta'sãw/ f interpretation; ~tar vt interpret; perform <papel, música>; **intérprete** m/f (de línguas) interpreter; (de teatro etc) performer

interro|gação /ĩtexoga'sãw/ f interrogation; ~gar vt interrogate, question; ~gativo a interrogative; ~gatório m interrogation

inter|romper /ĩtexõ'per/ vt interrupt; ~rupção f interruption; ~ruptor m switch

interurbano /ĩterur'banu/ a long-distance □ m trunk call

intervalo /ĩter'valu/ m interval

inter|venção /ĩtervẽ'sãw/ f intervention; ~vir vi intervene

intesti|nal /ĩtestʃi'naw/ (pl ~nais) a intestinal; ~no m intestine

inti|mação /ĩtʃima'sãw/ f (da justiça) summons; ~mar vt order; (à justiça) summon

intimidade /ĩtʃimi'dadʒi/ f intimacy; (entre amigos) closeness; (vida íntima) private life; **ter ~ com** be close to

intimidar /ĩtʃimi'dar/ vt intimidate; ~-se vpr be intimidated

íntimo /'ĩtʃimu/ a intimate; <amigo> close; <vida> private □ m close friend

intitular /ĩtʃitu'lar/ vt entitle

intocá|vel /ĩto'kavew/ (pl ~veis) a untouchable

intole|rância /ĩtole'rãsia/ f intolerance; ~rável (pl ~ráveis) a intolerable

intoxi|cação /ĩtoksika'sãw/ f poisoning; ~cação alimentar food poisoning; ~car vt poison

intragá|vel /ĩtra'gavew/ (pl ~veis) a <comida> inedible; <pessoa> unbearable

intransigente /ĩtrãzi'ʒẽtʃi/ a uncompromising

intransi|tável /ĩtrãzi'tavew/ (pl ~táveis) a impassable; ~tivo a intransitive

intratá|vel /ĩtra'tavew/ (pl ~veis) a <pessoa> difficult

intra-uterino /ĩtraute'rinu/ a **dispositivo ~** intra-uterine device, IUD

intrépido /ĩ'trɛpidu/ a intrepid

intri|ga /ĩ'triga/ f intrigue; (enredo) plot; ~gante a intriguing; ~gar vt intrigue

intrincado /ĩtrĩ'kadu/ a intricate

intrínseco /ĩ'trĩsiku/ a intrinsic

introdu|ção /ĩtrodu'sãw/ f introduction; ~tório a introductory; ~zir vt introduce

introme|ter-se /ĩtrome'tersi/ vpr interfere; ~tido a interfering □ m busybody

introspec|ção /ĩtrospek'sãw/ f introspection; ~tivo a introspective

introvertido /ĩtrover'tʃidu/ a introverted □ m introvert

intruso /ĩ'truzu/ a intrusive □ m intruder

intu|ição /ĩtui'sãw/ f intuition; ~ir vt intuit; ~itivo a intuitive; ~to m purpose

inumano /inu'manu/ a inhuman

inumerá|vel /inume'ravew/ (pl ~veis) a innumerable

inúmero /i'numeru/ a countless

inun|dação /inũda'sãw/ f flood; ~dar vt/i flood

inusitado /inuzi'tadu/ a unusual

inú|til /i'nutʃiw/ (pl ~teis) a useless

inutilmente /inutʃiw'mẽtʃi/ adv in vain

inutilizar /inutʃili'zar/ vt render useless; damage <aparelho>; thwart <esforços>

invadir /ĩva'dʒir/ vt invade

invali|dar /ĩvali'dar/ vt invalidate; disable <pessoa>; ~dez /e/ f disability

inválido /ĩ'validu/ a & m invalid

invariá|vel /ĩvari'avew/ (pl ~veis) a invariable

inva|são /ĩva'zãw/ f invasion; ~sor m invader □ a invading

inve|ja /ĩ'vɛʒa/ f envy; ~jar vt envy; ~jável (pl ~jáveis) a enviable; ~joso /o/ a envious

inven|ção /ĩvẽ'sãw/ f invention; ~tar vt invent; ~tário m inventory; ~tivo a inventive; ~tor m inventor

inver|nar /ĩver'nar/ vi winter, spend the winter; ~no /ɛ/ m winter

inverossí|mil /ĩvero'simiw/ (pl ~meis) a improbable

inver|são /ĩver'sãw/ f inversion; ~so a inverse; <ordem> reverse □ m reverse; ~ter vt reverse; (colocar de cabeça para baixo) invert

invertebrado /ĩverte'bradu/ a & m invertebrate

invés /ĩ'vɛs/ m **ao ~ de** instead of

investida /ĩves'tʃida/ f attack

investidura /ĩvestʃi'dura/ f investiture

investi|gação /ĩvestʃiga'sãw/ *f* investigation; **∼gar** *vt* investigate

inves|timento /ĩvestʃi'mẽtu/ *m* investment; **∼tir** *vt/i* invest; **∼tir contra** attack

inveterado /ĩvete'radu/ *a* inveterate

inviá|vel /ĩvi'avew/ (*pl* **∼veis**) *a* impracticable

invicto /ĩ'viktu/ *a* unbeaten

invisí|vel /ĩvi'zivew/ (*pl* **∼veis**) *a* invisible

invocar /ĩvo'kar/ *vt* invoke; (*fam*) pester

invólucro /ĩ'vɔlukru/ *m* covering

involuntário /ĩvolũ'tariu/ *a* involuntary

invulnerá|vel /ĩvuwne'ravew/ (*pl* **∼veis**) *a* invulnerable

iodo /i'odu/ *m* iodine

ioga /i'ɔga/ *f* yoga

iogurte /io'gurtʃi/ *m* yoghurt

ir /ir/ *vi* go; **∼-se** *vpr* go away; **vou voltar** I will come back; **vou melhorando** I am (gradually) getting better

ira /'ira/ *f* wrath

Irã /i'rã/ *m* Iran

iraniano /irani'anu/ *a & m* Iranian

Irão /i'rãw/ *m* (*Port*) Iran

Iraque /i'raki/ *m* Iraq

iraquiano /iraki'anu/ *a & m* Iraqi

Irlanda /ir'lãda/ *f* Ireland

irlan|dês /irlã'des/ *a* (*f* **∼desa**) Irish □ *m* (*f* **∼desa**) Irishman (*f* -woman); (*língua*) Irish; **os ∼deses** the Irish

irmã /ir'mã/ *f* sister

irmandade /irmã'dadʒi/ *f* (*associação*) brotherhood

irmão /ir'mãw/ (*pl* **∼s**) *m* brother

ironia /iro'nia/ *f* irony

irônico /i'roniku/ *a* ironic

irracio|nal /ixasio'naw/ (*pl* **∼nais**) *a* irrational

irradiar /ixadʒi'ar/ *vt* radiate; (*pelo rádio*) broadcast □ *vi* shine; **∼-se** *vpr* spread, radiate

irre|al /ixe'aw/ (*pl* **∼ais**) *a* unreal

irreconheci|vel /ixekoɲe'sivew/ (*pl* **∼veis**) *a* unrecognizable

irrecuperá|vel /ixekupe'ravew/ (*pl* **∼veis**) *a* irretrievable

irrefletido /ixefle'tʃidu/ *a* rash

irregu|lar /ixegu'lar/ *a* irregular; (*inconstante*) erratic; **∼laridade** *f* irregularity

irrelevante /ixele'vãtʃi/ *a* irrelevant

irrepará|vel /ixepa'ravew/ (*pl* **∼veis**) *a* irreparable

irrepreensí|vel /ixeprië'sivew/ (*pl* **∼veis**) *a* irreproachable

irrequieto /ixeki'ɛtu/ *a* restless

irresistí|vel /ixezis'tʃivew/ (*pl* **∼veis**) *a* irresistible

irresoluto /ixezo'lutu/ *a* <*questão*> unresolved; <*pessoa*> indecisive

irresponsá|vel /ixespõ'savew/ (*pl* **∼veis**) *a* irresponsible

irreverente /ixeve'rẽtʃi/ *a* irreverent

irri|gação /ixiga'sãw/ *f* irrigation; **∼gar** *vt* irrigate

irrisório /ixi'zɔriu/ *a* derisory

irri|tação /ixita'sãw/ *f* irritation; **∼tadiço** *a* irritable; **∼tante** *a* irritating; **∼tar** *vt* irritate; **∼-tar-se** *vpr* get irritated

irromper /ixõ'per/ *vi* **∼ em** burst into

isca /'iska/ *f* bait

isen|ção /izẽ'sãw/ *f* exemption; **∼tar** *vt* exempt; **∼to** *a* exempt

Islã /iz'lã/ *m* Islam

islâmico /iz'lamiku/ *a* Islamic

isla|mismo /izla'mizmu/ *m* Islam; **∼mita** *a & m/f* Muslim

islan|dês /izlã'des/ *a* (*f* **∼desa**) Icelandic □ *m* (*f* **∼desa**) Icelander; (*língua*) Icelandic

Islândia /iz'lãdʒia/ *f* Iceland

iso|lamento /izola'mẽtu/ *m* isolation; (*eletr*) insulation; **∼lante** *a* insulating; **∼lar** *vt* isolate; (*eletr*) insulate □ *vi* (*contra azar*) touch wood, (*Amer*) knock on wood

isopor /izo'por/ *m* polystyrene

isqueiro /is'keru/ *m* lighter

Israel /izxa'ɛw/ *m* Israel

israe|lense /izraj'lẽsi/ *a & m/f* Israeli; **∼lita** *a & m/f* Israelite

isso /'isu/ *pron* that; **por ∼** therefore

isto /'istu/ *pron* this; **∼ é** that is

Itália /i'talia/ *f* Italy

italiano /itali'anu/ *a & m* Italian

itálico /i'taliku/ *a & m* italic

item /'itẽ/ *m* item

itine|rante /itʃine'rãtʃi/ *a* itinerant; **∼rário** *m* itinerary

Iugoslávia /iugoz'lavia/ *f* Yugoslavia

iugoslavo /iugoz'lavu/ *a & m* Yugoslavian

Jj

já /ʒa/ *adv* already; (*agoraâ*) right away
□ *conj* on the other hand; **desde ~** from
now on; **~ não** no longer; **~ que** since;
~, ~ in no time

jabuticaba /ʒabutʃi'kaba/ *f* jaboticaba

jaca /'ʒaka/ *f* jack fruit

jacaré /ʒaka'rɛ/ *m* alligator

jacinto /ʒa'sĩtu/ *m* hyacinth

jactância /ʒak'tãsia/ *f* boasting

jade /'ʒadʒi/ *m* jade

jaguar /ʒagu'ar/ *m* jaguar

jagunço /ʒa'gũsu/ *m* hired gunman

jamais /ʒa'majs/ *adv* never

Jamaica /ʒa'majka/ *f* Jamaica

jamaicano /ʒamaj'kanu/ *a & m*
Jamaican

jamanta /ʒa'mãta/ *f* juggernaut

janeiro /ʒa'neru/ *m* January

janela /ʒa'nɛla/ *f* window

jangada /ʒã'gada/ *f* (fishing) raft

janta /'ʒãta/ *f* (*fam*) dinner

jantar /ʒã'tar/ *m* dinner □ *vi* have dinner
□ *vt* have for dinner

Japão /ʒa'pãw/ *m* Japan

japo|na /ʒa'pona/ *f* pea jacket □ *m/f*
(*fam*) Japanese; **~nês** *a & m* (*f* **~nesa**)
Japanese

jaqueira /ʒa'kera/ *f* jack-fruit tree

jaqueta /ʒa'keta/ *f* jacket

jarda /'ʒarda/ *f* yard

jar|dim /ʒar'dʒĩ/ *m* garden;
~dim-de-infância (*pl* **~dins-de-
infância**) *f* kindergarten

jardi|nagem /ʒardʒi'naʒẽ/ *f* gardening;
~nar *vi* garden; **~neira** *f* (*calça*)
dungarees; (*vestido*) pinafore dress,
(*Amer*) jumper; (*ônibus*) open-sided
bus; (*para flores*) flower stand; **~neiro**
m gardener

jargão /ʒar'gãw/ *m* jargon

jar|ra /'ʒaxa/ *f* pot; **~ro** *m* jug

jasmim /ʒaz'mĩ/ *m* jasmine

jato /'ʒatu/ *m* jet

jaula /'ʒawla/ *f* cage

ja|zer /ʒa'zer/ *vi* lie; **~zida** *f* deposit;
~zigo *m* grave

jazz /dʒaz/ *m* jazz; **~ista** *m/f* jazz artist;
~ístico *a* jazzy

jeca /'ʒɛka/ *m/f* country bumpkin □ *a*
countrified; (*cafona*) tacky; **~tatu** *m/f*
country bumpkin

jei|tão /ʒej'tãw/ *m* (*fam*) individual style;
~tinho *m* knack; **~to** *m* way; (*de
pessoa*) manner; (*habilidade*) skill; **de
qualquer ~to** anyway; **de ~to**

nenhum no way; **pelo ~to** by the looks
of things; **sem ~to** awkward; **dar um
~to** find a way; **dar um ~to em**
(*arrumar*) tidy up; (*consertar*) fix;
(*torcer*) twist <*pé etc*>; **ter ~to de** look
like; **ter ou levar ~to para** be good at;
tomar ~to pull one's socks up; **~toso**
/o/ *a* skilful; (*de aparência*) elegant

je|juar /ʒeʒu'ar/ *vi* fast; **~jum** *m* fast

Jeová /ʒio'va/ *m* **testemunha de
~** Jehovah's witness

jérsei /'ʒersej/ *m* jersey

jesuíta /ʒezu'ita/ *a & m/f* Jesuit

Jesus /ʒe'zus/ *m* Jesus

jibóia /ʒi'bɔja/ *f* boa constrictor

jiboiar /ʒiboj'ar/ *vi* have a rest to let one's
dinner go down

jiló /ʒi'lɔ/ *m* okra

jipe /'ʒipi/ *m* jeep

jiu-jitsu /ʒiu'ʒitsu/ *m* jiu-jitsu

joa|lheiro /ʒoa'ʎeru/ *m* jeweller;
~lheria *f* jeweller's (shop)

joaninha /ʒoa'niɲa/ *f* ladybird, (*Amer*)
ladybug; (*alfinete*) safety pin

joão-ninguém /ʒoãwnĩ'gẽj/ (*pl
joões-ninguém*) *m* nobody

jocoso /ʒo'kozu/ *a* jocular

joe|lhada /ʒoe'ʎada/ *f* blow with the
knee; **~lheira** *f* kneepad; **~lho** /e/ *m*
knee; **de ~lhos** kneeling

jo|gada /ʒo'gada/ *f* move; **~gado** *a*
<*pessoa*> flat out; <*papéis, roupa etc*>
lying around; **~gador** *m* player; (*no
cassino etc*) gambler; **~gar** *vt* play;
(*atirar*) throw; (*arriscar no jogo*)
gamble □ *vi* play; (*no cassino etc*)
gamble; (*balançar*) toss; **~gar fora**
throw away; **~gatina** *f* gambling

jogging /'ʒɔgĩ/ *m* (*cooper*) jogging;
(*roupa*) track suit

jogo /'ʒogu/ *m* (*partida*) game; (*ação de
jogar*) play; (*jogatina*) gambling;
(*conjunto*) set; **em ~** at stake; **~ de
cintura** (*fig*) flexibility, room to
manoeuvre; **~ de luz** lighting effects;
~ do bicho illegal numbers game;
Jogos Olímpicos Olympic Games;
~-da-velha *m* noughts and crosses

joguete /ʒo'getʃi/ *m* plaything

jóia /'ʒɔja/ *f* jewel; (*propina*) entry fee
□ *a* (*fam*) great

joio /'ʒoju/ *m* chaff; **separar o ~ do trigo**
separate the wheat from the chaff

jóquei /'ʒɔkej/ *m* (*pessoa*) jockey; (*lugar*)
race course

Jordânia /ʒor'dania/ *f* Jordan

jordaniano /ʒordani'anu/ *a & m* Jordanian

jor|nada /ʒor'nada/ *f* (*viagem*) journey; **~nada de trabalho** working day; **~nal** (*pl* **~nais**) *m* newspaper; (*na TV*) news

jorna|leco /ʒorna'lɛku/ *m* rag, scandal sheet; **~leiro** *m* (*vendedor*) newsagent, (*Amer*) newsdealer; (*entregador*) paperboy; **~lismo** *m* journalism; **~lista** *m/f* journalist; **~lístico** *a* journalistic

jor|rar /ʒo'xar/ *vi* gush, spurt; **~ro** /'ʒoxu/ *m* spurt

jota /'ʒɔta/ *m* letter J

jovem /'ʒovẽ/ *a* young; (*criado por jovens*) youth ▫ *m/f* young man (*f* -woman); *pl* young people

jovi|al /ʒovi'aw/ (*pl* **~ais**) *a* jovial

juba /'ʒuba/ *f* mane

jubileu /ʒubi'lew/ *m* jubilee

júbilo /'ʒubilu/ *m* joy

ju|daico /ʒu'dajku/ *a* Jewish; **~daísmo** *m* Judaism; **~deu** *a* (*f* **~dia**) Jewish ▫ *m* (*f* **~dia**) Jew; **~diação** *f* ill-treatment; (*uma*) terrible thing; **~diar** *vi* **~diar de** ill-treat

judici|al /ʒudʒisi'aw/ (*pl* **~ais**) *a* judicial; **~ário** *a* judicial ▫ *m* judiciary; **~oso** /o/ *a* judicious

judô /ʒu'do/ *m* judo

judoca /ʒu'dɔka/ *m/f* judo player

jugo /'ʒugu/ *m* yoke

juiz /ʒu'is/ *m* (*f* **juíza**) judge; (*em jogos*) referee

juizado /ʒui'zadu/ *m* court

juízo /ʒu'izu/ *m* judgement; (*tino*) sense; (*tribunal*) court; **perder o ~** lose one's head; **ter ~** be sensible; **tomar** *ou* **criar ~** come to one's senses

jujuba /ʒu'ʒuba/ *f* (*bala*) fruit jelly

jul|gamento /ʒuwga'mẽtu/ *m* judgement; **~gar** *vt* judge; pass judgement on <*réu*>; (*imaginar*) think; **~gar-se** *vpr* consider o.s.

julho /'ʒuʎu/ *m* July

jumento /ʒu'mẽtu/ *m* donkey

junção /ʒũ'sãw/ *f* join; (*ação*) joining

junco /'ʒũku/ *m* reed

junho /'ʒuɲu/ *m* June

juni|no /ʒu'ninu/ *a* **festa ~na** St John's Day festival

júnior /'ʒunior/ *a & m* junior

jun|ta /'ʒũta/ *f* board; (*pol*) junta; **~tar** *vt* (*acrescentar*) add; (*uma coisa a outra*)

join; (*uma coisa com outra*) combine; save up <*dinheiro*>; gather up <*papéis, lixo etc*> ▫ *vi* gather; **~tar-se** *vpr* join together; <*multidão*> gather; <*casal*> live together; **~tar-se a** join; **~to** *a* together ▫ *adv* together; **~to a** next to; **~to com** together with

ju|ra /'ʒura/ *f* vow; **~rado** *m* juror; **~ramentado** *a* accredited; **~ramento** *m* oath; **~rar** *vt/i* swear; **~ra?** (*fam*) really?

júri /'ʒuri/ *m* jury

jurídico /ʒu'ridʒiku/ *a* legal

juris|consulto /ʒuriskõ'suwtu/ *m* legal advisor; **~dição** *f* jurisdiction; **~prudência** *f* jurisprudence; **~ta** *m/f* jurist

juros /'ʒurus/ *m pl* interest

jus /ʒus/ *m* **fazer ~ a** live up to

jusante /ʒu'zãtʃi/ *f* **a ~** downstream

justamente /ʒusta'mẽtʃi/ *adv* exactly; (*com justiça*) fairly

justapor /ʒusta'por/ *vt* juxtapose

justi|ça /ʒus'tʃisa/ *f* (*perante a lei*) justice; (*para com outros*) fairness; (*tribunal*) court; **~ceiro** *a* fair-minded ▫ *m* vigilante

justifi|cação /ʒustʃifika'sãw/ *f* justification; **~car** *vt* justify; **~cativa** *f* justification; **~cável** (*pl* **~cáveis**) *a* justifiable

justo /'ʒustu/ *a* fair; (*apertado*) tight ▫ *adv* just

juve|nil /ʒuve'niw/ (*pl* **~nis**) *a* youthful; (*para jovens*) for young people; <*time, torneio*> junior ▫ *m* junior championship

juventude /ʒuvẽ'tudʒi/ *f* youth

Kk

karaokê /karao'ke/ *m* karaoke

kart /'kartʃi/ (*pl* **~s**) *m* go-kart

ketchup /ke'tʃupi/ *m* ketchup

kit /'kitʃi/ (*pl* **~s**) *m* kit

kitchenette /kitʃe'netʃi/ *f* bedsitter

Kuwait /ku'wajtʃi/ *m* Kuwait

kuwaitiano /kuwajtʃi'anu/ *a & m* Kuwaiti

lá /la/ *adv* there; **até ~** <*ir*> there; <*esperar etc*> until then; **por ~** (*naquela direão*) that way; (*naquele lugar*) around there; **~ fora** outside; **sei ~** how should I know?

lã /lã/ *f* wool

labareda /laba'reda/ *f* flame

lábia /'labia/ *f* flannel; **ter ~** have the gift of the gab

lábio /'labio/ *m* lip

labirinto /labi'rĩtu/ *m* labyrinth

laboratório /labora'tɔriu/ *m* laboratory

laborioso /labori'ozu/ *a* hard-working

labu|ta /la'buta/ *f* drudgery; **~tar** *vi* slog

laca /'laka/ *f* lacquer

laçada /la'sada/ *f* slipknot

lacaio /la'kaju/ *m* lackey

la|çar /la'sar/ *vt* lasso <*boi*>; **~ço** *m* bow; (*de vaqueiro*) lasso; (*vínculo*) tie

lacônico /la'koniku/ *a* laconic

lacraia /la'kraja/ *f* centipede

la|crar /la'krar/ *vt* seal; **~cre** *m* (*substância*) sealing wax; (*fechamento*) seal

lacri|mejar /lakrime'ʒar/ *vi* water; **~mogêneo** *a* <*gás*> tear; <*filme*> tearjerking; **~moso** /o/ *a* tearful

lácteo /'laktʃiu/ *a* milk; **Via Láctea** Milky Way

laticínio /laktʃi'siniu/ *m veja* **laticínio**

lacuna /la'kuna/ *f* gap

ladainha /lada'ina/ *f* litany

la|dear /ladʒi'ar/ *vt* flank; sidestep <*dificuldade*>; **~deira** *f* slope

lado /'ladu/ *m* side; **o ~ de cá/lá** this/that side; **ao ~ de** beside; **~ a ~** side by side; **para este ~** this way; **por outro ~** on the other hand

la|drão /la'drãw/ *m* (*f* **~dra**) thief; (*tubo*) overflow pipe □ *a* thieving

ladrar /la'drar/ *vi* bark

ladri|lhar /ladri'ʎar/ *vt* tile; **~lho** *m* tile

ladroagem /ladro'aʒẽ/ *f* stealing

lagar|ta /la'garta/ *f* caterpillar; (*numa roda*) caterpillar track; **~tear** *vi* bask in the sun; **~tixa** *f* gecko; **~to** *m* lizard

lago /'lagu/ *m* lake

lagoa /la'goa/ *f* lagoon

lagos|ta /la'gosta/ *f* lobster; **~tim** *m* crayfish, (*Amer*) crawfish

lágrima /'lagrima/ *f* tear

laia /'laja/ *f* kind

laico /'lajku/ *adj* <*pessoa*> lay; <*ensino*> secular

laivos /'lajvus/ *m pl* traces

laje /'laʒi/ *m* flagstone; **~ar** *vt* pave

lajota /la'ʒɔta/ *f* small paving stone

lama /'lama/ *f* mud; **~çal** (*pl* **~çais**) *m* bog; **~cento** *a* muddy

lamba|da /lã'bada/ *f* lambada; **~teria** *f* lambada club

lam|ber /lã'ber/ *vt* lick; **~bida** *f* lick

lambreta /lã'breta/ *f* moped

lambris /lã'bris/ *m pl* panelling

lambuzar /lãbu'zar/ *vt* smear; **~-se** *vpr* get sticky

lamen|tar /lamẽ'tar/ *vt* (*lastimar*) lament; (*sentir*) be sorry; **~tar-se de** lament; **~tável** (*pl* **~táveis**) *a* lamentable; **~to** *m* lament

lâmina /'lamina/ *f* blade; (*de persiana*) slat

laminar /lami'nar/ *vt* laminate

lâmpada /'lãpada/ *f* light bulb; (*abajur*) lamp

lampe|jar /lãpe'ʒar/ *vi* flash; **~jo** /e/ *m* flash

lampião /lãpi'ãw/ *m* lantern

lamúria /la'muria/ *f* moaning

lamuriar-se /lamuri'arsi/ *vpr* moan (**de** about)

lan|ça /'lãsa/ *f* spear; **~çamento** *m* (*de navio, foguete, produto*) launch; (*de filme, disco*) release; (*novo produto*) new line; (*novo filme, disco*) release; (*novo livro*) new title; (*em livro comercial*) entry; **~çar** *vt* (*atirar*) throw; launch <*navio, foguete, novo produto, livro*>; release <*filme, disco*>; (*em livro comercial*) enter; (*em leilão*) bid; **~çar mão de** make use of; **~ce** *m* (*num filme, jogo*) bit, moment; (*episódio*) episode; (*questão*) matter; (*jogada*) move; (*em leilão*) bid; (*de escada*) flight; (*de casas*) row

lancha /'lãʃa/ *f* launch

lan|char /lã'ʃar/ *vi* have a snack □ *vt* have a snack of; **~che** *m* snack; **~chonete** /ɛ/ *f* snack bar

lancinante /lãsi'nãtʃi/ *a* <*dor*> shooting; <*grito*> piercing

lânguido /'lãgidu/ *a* languid

lantejoula /lãte'ʒola/ *f* sequin

lanter|na /lã'terna/ *f* lantern; (*de bolso*) torch, (*Amer*) flashlight; **~nagem** *f* panel-beating; (*oficina*) body-shop; **~ninha** *m/f* usher (*f* usherette)

lanugem /la'nuʒẽ/ *f* down

lapela /la'pɛla/ *f* lapel

lapidar /lapi'dar/ *vt* cut <*pedra preciosa*>; (*fig*) polish

lápide /'lapidʒi/ *f* tombstone

lápis /'lapis/ *m invar* pencil

lapiseira /lapi'zera/ *f* propelling pencil; (*caixa*) pencil box

Lapônia /la'ponia/ *f* Lappland

lapso /'lapsu/ *m* lapse

la|quê /la'ke/ *m* lacquer; ∼**quear** *vt* lacquer

lar /lar/ *m* home

laran|ja /la'rãʒa/ *f* orange □ *a invar* orange; ∼**jada** *f* orangeade; ∼**jeira** *f* orange tree

lareira /la'rera/ *f* hearth, fireplace

lar|gada /lar'gada/ *f* start; **dar a** ∼**gada** start off; ∼**gar** *vt* (*soltar*) let go of; give up <*estudos, emprego etc*>; ∼**gar de fumar** give up smoking; ∼**go** *a* wide; <*roupa*> loose □ *m* (*praça*) square; **ao** ∼**go** (*no alto-mar*) out at sea; ∼**gura** *f* width

larin|ge /la'rĩʒi/ *f* larynx; ∼**gite** *f* laryngitis

larva /'larva/ *f* larva

lasanha /la'zaɲa/ *f* lasagna

las|ca /'laska/ *f* chip; ∼**car** *vt/i* chip; **de** ∼**car** (*fam*) awful

lástima /'lastʃima/ *f* shame

lastro /'lastru/ *m* ballast

la|ta /'lata/ *f* (*material*) tin; (*recipiente*) tin, (*Amer*) can; ∼**ta de lixo** dustbin, (*Amer*) trash can; ∼**tão** *m* brass

late|jante /late'ʒãtʃi/ *a* throbbing; ∼**jar** *vi* throb

latente /la'tẽtʃi/ *a* latent

late|ral /late'raw/ (*pl* ∼**rais**) *a* side, lateral

laticínio /latʃi'siniu/ *m* dairy product

latido /la'tʃidu/ *m* bark

lati|fundiário /latʃifũdʒi'ariu/ *a* landowning □ *m* landowner; ∼**-fúndio** *m* estate

latim /la'tʃĩ/ *m* Latin

latino /la'tʃinu/ *a & m* Latin; ∼**-americano** *a & m* Latin American

latir /la'tʃir/ *vi* bark

latitude /latʃi'tudʒi/ *f* latitude

lauda /'lawda/ *f* side

laudo /'lawdu/ *m* report, findings

lava /'lava/ *f* lava

lava|bo /la'vabu/ *m* toilet; ∼**dora** *f* washing machine; ∼**gem** *f* washing; ∼**gem a seco** dry cleaning; ∼**gem cerebral** brainwashing

lavanda /la'vãda/ *f* lavender

lavanderia /lavãde'ria/ *f* laundry

lavar /la'var/ *vt* wash; ∼ **a seco** dry-clean; ∼**-se** *vpr* wash

lavatório /lava'tɔriu/ *m* (*Port*) washbasin

lavoura /la'vora/ *f* (*agricultura*) farming; (*terreno*) field

lav|rador /lavra'dor/ *m* farmhand; ∼**rar** *vt* work; draw up <*documento*>

laxante /la'ʃãtʃi/ *a & m* laxative

lazer /la'zer/ *m* leisure

le|al /le'aw/ (*pl* ∼**ais**) *a* loyal; ∼**aldade** *f* loyalty

leão /le'ãw/ *m* lion; **Leão** (*signo*) Leo; ∼**-de-chácara** (*pl* **leões-de-chácara**) *m* bouncer

lebre /'lɛbri/ *f* hare

lecionar /lesio'nar/ *vt/i* teach

le|gação /lega'sãw/ *f* legation; ∼**gado** *m* (*pessoa*) legate; (*herança*) legacy

le|gal /le'gaw/ (*pl* ∼**gais**) *a* legal; (*fam*) good; <*pessoa*> nice; **tá** ∼**gal** OK; ∼**galidade** *f* legality; ∼**galizar** *vt* legalize

legar /le'gar/ *vt* bequeath

legenda /le'ʒẽda/ *f* (*de quadro*) caption; (*de filme*) subtitle; (*inscrição*) inscription

legi|ão /leʒi'ãw/ *f* legion; ∼**-onário** *m* (*romano*) legionary; (*da legião estrangeira*) legionnaire

legis|lação /leʒizla'sãw/ *f* legislation; ∼**lador** *m* legislator; ∼**lar** *vi* legislate; ∼**lativo** *a* legislative □ *m* legislature; ∼**latura** *f* legislature; ∼**ta** *m/f* legal expert

legiti|mar /leʒitʃi'mar/ *vt* legitimize; ∼**midade** *f* legitimacy

legítimo /le'ʒitʃimu/ *a* legitimate

legí|vel /le'ʒivew/ (*pl* ∼**veis**) *a* legible

légua /'lɛgwa/ *f* league

legume /le'gumi/ *m* vegetable

lei /lej/ *f* law

leigo /'lejgu/ *a* lay □ *m* layman

lei|lão /lej'lãw/ *m* auction; ∼**loar** *vt* auction; ∼**loeiro** *m* auctioneer

leitão /lej'tãw/ *m* sucking pig

lei|te /'lejtʃi/ *m* milk; ∼**te condensado /desnatado** condensed/skimmed milk; ∼**teira** *f* (*jarro*) milk jug; (*panela*) milk saucepan; ∼**teiro** *m* milkman □ *a* <*vaca*> dairy

leito /'lejtu/ *m* bed

leitor /lej'tor/ *m* reader

leitoso /lej'tozu/ *a* milky

leitura /lej'tura/ *f* (*ação*) reading; (*material*) reading matter

lema /'lema/ *m* motto

lem|brança /lẽ'brãsa/ *f* memory; (*presente*) souvenir; ∼**brar** *vt/i* remember; ∼**brar-se de** remember; ∼**brar aco a alg** remind s.o. of sth; ∼**brete** /e/ *m* reminder

leme /'lemi/ *m* rudder

len|ço /'lẽsu/ *m* (*para o nariz*) handkerchief; (*para vestir*) scarf; ∼col /ɔ/ (*pl* ∼cóis) *m* sheet

len|da /'lẽda/ *f* legend; ∼dário *a* legendary

lenha /'leɲa/ *f* firewood; (*uma*) log; ∼dor *m* woodcutter

lente /'lẽtʃi/ *f* lens; ∼ de contato contact lens

lentidão /lẽtʃi'dãw/ *f* slowness

lentilha /lẽ'tʃiʎa/ *f* lentil

lento /'lẽtu/ *a* slow

leoa /le'oa/ *f* lioness

leopardo /lio'pardu/ *m* leopard

le|pra /'lɛpra/ *f* leprosy; ∼proso /o/ *a* leprous □ *m* leper

leque /'lɛki/ *m* fan; (*fig*) array

ler /ler/ *vt/i* read

ler|deza /ler'deza/ *f* sluggishness; ∼do /ɛ/ *a* sluggish

le|são /le'zãw/ *f* lesion, injury; ∼sar *vt* damage

lésbi|ca /'lɛzbika/ *f* lesbian; ∼co *a* lesbian

lesionar /lezio'nar/ *vt* injure

lesma /'lezma/ *f* slug

leste /'lɛstʃi/ *m* east

le|tal /le'taw/ (*pl* ∼tais) *a* lethal

le|tão /le'tãw/ *a & m* (*f* ∼tã) Latvian

letargia /letar'ʒia/ *f* lethargy

letivo /le'tʃivu/ *a* ano ∼ academic year

Letônia /le'tonia/ *f* Latvia

letra /'letra/ *f* letter; (*de música*) lyrics, words; (*caligrafia*) writing; **Letras** Modern Languages; **ao pé da** ∼ literally; **com todas as** ∼**s** in no uncertain terms; **tirar de** ∼ take in one's stride; ∼ **de fôrma** block letter

letreiro /le'treru/ *m* sign

leucemia /lewse'mia/ *f* leukaemia

leva /ɛ/ *f* batch

levado /le'vadu/ *a* naughty

levan|tamento /levãta'mẽtu/ *m* (*enquete*) survey; (*rebelião*) uprising; ∼tamento de pesos weightlifting; ∼tar *vt* raise; lift <*peso*> □ *vi* get up; ∼tar-se *vpr* get up; (*revoltar-se*) rise up

levante /le'vãtʃi/ *m* east

levar /le'var/ *vt* take; lead <*vida*>; get <*tapa, susto etc*> □ *vi* lead (a to)

leve /'lɛvi/ *a* light; (*não grave*) slight; de ∼ lightly

levedura /leve'dura/ *f* yeast

leveza /le'veza/ *f* lightness

levi|andade /leviã'dadʒi/ *f* frivolity; ∼ano *a* frivolous

levitar /levi'tar/ *vi* levitate

lexi|cal /leksi'kaw/ (*pl* ∼cais) *a* lexical

lêxico /'leksiku/ *m* lexicon

lexicografia /leksikogra'fia/ *f* lexicography

lhe /ʎi/ *pron* (*a ele*) to him; (*a ela*) to her; (*a você*) to you; ∼s *pron* to them; (*a vocês*) to you

liba|nês /liba'nes/ *a & m* (*f* ∼nesa) Lebanese

Líbano /'libanu/ *m* Lebanon

libélula /li'belula/ *f* dragonfly

libe|ração /libera'sãw/ *f* release; ∼ral (*pl* ∼rais) *a & m* liberal; ∼ralismo *m* liberalism; ∼ralizar *vt* liberalize; ∼rar *vt* release

liberdade /liber'dadʒi/ *f* freedom; pôr em ∼ set free; ∼ condicional probation

libero /'liberu/ *m* sweeper

liber|tação /liberta'sãw/ *f* liberation; ∼tar *vt* free

Líbia /'libia/ *f* Libya

líbio /'libiu/ *a & m* Libyan

libi|dinoso /libidʒi'nozu/ *a* lecherous; ∼do *f* libido

li|bra /'libra/ *f* pound; Libra (*signo*) Libra; ∼briano *a & m* Libran

lição /li'sãw/ *f* lesson

licen|ça /li'sẽsa/ *f* leave; (*documento*) licence; com ∼ça excuse me; de ∼ça on leave; sob ∼ça under licence; ∼ciar *vt* (*autorizar*) license; (*dar férias a*) give leave to; ∼ciar-se *vpr* (*tirar férias*) take leave; (*formar-se*) graduate; ∼ciatura *f* degree; ∼cioso /o/ *a* licentious

liceu /li'sew/ *m* (*Port*) secondary school, (*Amer*) high school

licor /li'kor/ *m* liqueur

lida /'lida/ *f* slog, grind; (*leitura*) read

lidar /li'dar/ *vt/i* ∼ com deal with

lide /'lidʒi/ *f* (*trabalho*) work

líder /'lider/ *m/f* leader

lide|rança /lide'rãsa/ *f* (*de partido etc*) leadership; (*em corrida, jogo etc*) lead; ∼rar *vt* lead

lido /'lidu/ *a* well-read

liga /'liga/ *f* (*aliança*) league; (*tira*) garter; (*presilha*) suspender; (*de metais*) alloy

li|gação /liga'sãw/ *f* connection; (*telefônica*) call; (*amorosa*) liaison; ∼gada *f* call, ring; ∼gado *a* <*luz, TV*> on; ∼gado em attached to <*pessoa*>; hooked on <*droga*>; ∼gamento *m* ligament; ∼gar *vt* join, connect; switch on <*luz, TV etc*>; start up <*carro*>; bind <*amigos*> □ *vi* ring up, call; ∼gar para (*telefonar*) ring, call; (*dar importância*) care about; (*dar atenção*) pay attention to; ∼gar-se *vpr* join

ligeiro /li'ʒeru/ *a* light; <*ferida, melhora*> slight; (*ágil*) nimble

lilás /li'las/ *m* lilac □ *a invar* mauve

lima¹ /'lima/ *f* (*ferramenta*) file

lima² /'lima/ *f* (*fruta*) sweet orange

limão /li'mãw/ *m* lime; (*amarelo*) lemon

limar /li'mar/ *vt* file

limeira /li'mera/ *f* sweet orange tree

limiar /limi'ar/ *m* threshold

limi|tação /limita'sãw/ *f* limitation; ~**tar** *vt* limit; ~**tar-se** *vpr* limit o.s.; ~**tar(-se) com** border on; ~**te** *m* limit; (*de terreno*) boundary; **passar dos** ~**tes** go too far; ~**te de velocidade** speed limit

limo|eiro /limo'eru/ *m* lime tree; ~**nada** *f* lemonade

lim|pador /lĩpa'dor/ *m* ~**pador de pára-brisas** windscreen wiper; ~**par** *vt* clean; wipe <*lágrimas, suor*>; (*fig*) clean up <*cidade, organização*>; ~**peza** /e/ *f* (*ato*) cleaning; (*qualidade*) cleanness; (*fig*) clean-up; ~**peza pública** sanitation; ~**po** *a* clean; <*céu, consciência*> clear; <*lucro*> net, clear; (*fig*) pure; **passar a** ~**po** write up <*trabalho*>; (*fig*) sort out <*vida*>; **tirar a** ~**po** get to the bottom of <*caso*>

limusine /limu'zini/ *f* limousine

lince /'lĩsi/ *m* lynx

lindo /'lĩdu/ *a* beautiful

linear /lini'ar/ *a* linear

lingote /lĩ'gɔtʃi/ *m* ingot

língua /'lĩgwa/ *f* (*na boca*) tongue; (*idioma*) language; ~ **materna** mother tongue

linguado /lĩ'gwadu/ *m* sole

lingua|gem /lĩ'gwaʒẽ/ *f* language; ~**jar** *m* speech, dialect

lingüeta /lĩ'gweta/ *f* bolt

lingüiça /lĩ'gwisa/ *f* pork sausage

lin|güista /lĩ'gwiʃta/ *m/f* linguist; ~**güística** *f* linguistics; ~**güístico** *a* linguistic

linha /'liɲa/ *f* line; (*fio*) thread; **perder a** ~ lose one's cool; ~ **aérea** airline; ~ **de fogo** firing line; ~ **de montagem** assembly line; ~**gem** *f* lineage

linho /'liɲu/ *m* linen; (*planta*) flax

linóleo /li'nɔliu/ *m* lino(leum)

lipoaspiração /lipoaspira'sãw/ *f* liposuction

liqui|dação /likida'sãw/ *f* liquidation; (*de loja*) clearance sale; (*de conta*) settlement; ~**dar** *vt* liquidate; settle <*conta*>; pay off <*dívida*>; sell off, clear <*mercadorias*>

liqüidificador /likwidʒifika'dor/ *m* liquidizer

líquido /'likidu/ *a* liquid; <*lucro, salário*> net □ *m* liquid

líri|ca /'lirika/ *f* (*mus*) lyrics; (*poesia*) lyric poetry; ~**co** *a* lyrical; <*poesia*> lyric

lírio /'liriu/ *m* lily

Lisboa /liz'boa/ *f* Lisbon

lisboeta /lizbo'eta/ *a & m/f* (person) from Lisbon

liso /'lizu/ *a* smooth; (*sem desenho*) plain; <*cabelo*> straight; (*fam: duro*) broke

lison|ja /li'zõʒa/ *f* flattery; ~**jear** *vt* flatter

lista /'lista/ *f* list; (*listra*) stripe; ~ **telefônica** telephone directory

listra /'listra/ *f* stripe; ~**do** *a* striped, stripey

lite|ral /lite'raw/ (*pl* ~**rais**) *a* literal; ~**rário** *a* literary; ~**ratura** *f* literature

litígio /li'tʃiʒiu/ *m* dispute; (*jurid*) lawsuit

lito|ral /lito'raw/ (*pl* ~**rais**) *m* coastline; ~**râneo** *a* coastal

litro /'litru/ *m* litre

Lituânia /litu'ania/ *f* Lithuania

lituano /litu'anu/ *a & m* Lithuanian

living /'livĩ/ (*pl* ~**s**) *m* living room

livrar /li'vrar/ *vt* free; (*salvar*) save; ~**-se** *vpr* escape; ~**-se de** get rid of

livraria /livra'ria/ *f* bookshop

livre /'livri/ *a* free; ~ **de impostos** tax-free; ~**-arbítrio** *m* free will

liv|reiro /li'vreru/ *m* bookseller; ~**ro** *m* book; ~**ro de consulta** reference book; ~**ro de cozinha** cookery book; ~**ro de texto** text book; ~**ro eletrônico** e-book

li|xa /'liʃa/ *f* (*de unhas*) emery board; (*para madeira etc*) sandpaper; ~**xar** *vt* sand <*madeira*>; file <*unhas*>; **estou me** ~**xando** (*fam*) I couldn't care less

li|xeira /li'ʃera/ *f* dustbin, (*Amer*) garbage can; ~**xeiro** *m* dustman, (*Amer*) garbage collector; ~**xo** rubbish, (*Amer*) garbage; (*atômico*) waste

lobisomem /lobi'zomẽ/ *m* werewolf

lobo /'lobu/ *m* wolf; ~**-marinho** (*pl* ~**s-marinhos**) *m* sea lion

lóbulo /'lɔbulu/ *m* lobe

lo|cação /loka'sãw/ *f* (*de imóvel*) lease; (*de carro*) rental; ~**cador** *m* (*de casa*) landlord; ~**cadora** *f* rental company; (*de vídeos*) video shop

lo|cal /lo'kaw/ (*pl* ~**cais**) *a* local □ *m* site; (*de um acidente etc*) scene; ~**calidade** *f* locality; ~**calização** *f* location; ~**calizar** *vt* locate; ~**calizar-se** *vpr* (*orientar-se*) get one's bearings

loção /lo'sãw/ *f* lotion; ~ **após-barba** aftershave lotion

I

locatário /loka'tariu/ *m* (*de imóvel*) tenant; (*de carro etc*) hirer

locomo|tiva /lokomo'tʃiva/ *f* locomotive; ~**ver-se** *vpr* get around

locu|ção /loku'sãw/ *f* phrase; ~**tor** *m* announcer

lodo /'lodu/ *m* mud; ~**so** /o/ *a* muddy

logaritmo /loga'ritʃimu/ *m* logarithm

lógi|ca /'lɔʒika/ *f* logic; ~**co** *a* logical

logo /'lɔgu/ *adv* (*em seguida*) straightaway; (*em breve*) soon; (*justamente*) just; ~ **mais** later; ~ **antes/depois** just before/straight after; ~ **que** as soon as; **até** ~ goodbye

logotipo /logo'tʃipu/ *m* logo

logradouro /logra'doru/ *m* public place

loiro /'lojru/ *a veja* **louro**

lo|ja /'lɔʒa/ *f* shop, (*Amer*) store; ~**ja de departamentos** department store; ~**ja maçônica** masonic lodge; ~**jista** *m/f* shopkeeper

lom|bada /lõ'bada/ *f* (*de livro*) spine; (*na rua*) speed bump; ~**binho** *m* tenderloin; ~**bo** *m* back; (*carne*) loin

lona /'lona/ *f* canvas

Londres /'lõdris/ *f* London

londrino /lõ'drinu/ *a* London □ *m* Londoner

longa-metragem /lõgame'traʒẽ/ (*pl* **longas-metragens**) *m* feature film

longe /'lõʒi/ *adv* far, a long way; **de** ~ from a distance; (*por muito*) by far; ~ **disso** far from it

longevidade /lõʒevi'dadʒi/ *f* longevity

longínquo /lõ'ʒĩkwu/ *a* distant

longitude /lõʒi'tudʒi/ *f* longitude

longo /'lõgu/ *a* long □ *m* long dress; **ao** ~ **de** along; (*durante*) through, over

lontra /'lõtra/ *f* otter

lorde /'lɔrdʒi/ *m* lord

lorota /lo'rɔta/ (*fam*) *f* fib

losango /lo'zãgu/ *m* diamond

lo|tação /lota'sãw/ *f* capacity; (*ônibus*) bus; ~**tação esgotada** full house; ~**tado** *a* crowded; <*teatro, ônibus*> full; ~**tar** *vt* fill □ *vi* fill up

lote /'lɔtʃi/ *m* (*quinhão*) portion; (*de terreno*) plot, (*Amer*) lot; (*em leilão*) lot; (*porção de coisas*) batch

loteria /lote'ria/ *f* lottery

louça /'losa/ *f* china; (*pratos etc*) crockery; **lavar a** ~ wash up, (*Amer*) do the dishes

lou|co /'loku/ *a* mad, crazy □ *m* madman; **estou** ~**co para ir** (*fam*) I'm dying to go; ~**cura** *f* madness; (*uma*) crazy thing

louro /'loru/ *a* blond □ *m* laurel; (*condimento*) bayleaf

lou|var /lo'var/ *vt* praise; ~**vável** (*pl* ~**váveis**) *a* praiseworthy; ~**vor** /o/ *m* praise

lua /'lua/ *f* moon; ~**-de-mel** *f* honeymoon

lu|ar /lu'ar/ *m* moonlight; ~**arento** *a* moonlit

lubrifi|cação /lubrifika'sãw/ *f* lubrication; ~**cante** *a* lubricating □ *m* lubricant; ~**car** *vt* lubricate

lucidez /lusi'des/ *f* lucidity

lúcido /'lusidu/ *a* lucid

lu|crar /lu'krar/ *vi* profit (**com** by); ~**cratividade** *f* profitability; ~**crativo** *a* profitable, lucrative; ~**cro** *m* profit

ludibriar /ludʒibri'ar/ *vt* cheat

lúdico /'ludʒiku/ *a* playful

lugar /lu'gar/ *m* place; (*espaço*) room; **em** ~ **de** in place of; **em primeiro** ~ in the first place; **em algum** ~ somewhere; **em todo** ~ everywhere; **dar** ~ **a** give rise to; **ter** ~ take place

lugarejo /luga'reʒu/ *m* village

lúgubre /'lugubri/ *a* gloomy, dismal

lula /'lula/ *f* squid

lume /'lumi/ *m* fire

luminária /lumi'naria/ *f* light, lamp; *pl* illuminations

luminoso /lumi'nozu/ *a* luminous; <*idéia*> brilliant

lunar /lu'nar/ *a* lunar □ *m* mole

lupa /'lupa/ *f* magnifying glass

lusco-fusco /lusku'fusku/ *m* twilight

lusitano /luzi'tanu/, **luso** /'luzu/ *a & m* Portuguese

lus|trar /lus'trar/ *vt* shine, polish; ~**tre** *m* shine; (*fig*) lustre; (*luminária*) light, lamp; ~**troso** /o/ *a* shiny

lu|ta /'luta/ *f* fight, struggle; ~**ta livre** wrestling; ~**tador** *m* fighter; (*de luta livre*) wrestler; ~**tar** *vi* fight □ *vt* do <*judô etc*>

luto /'lutu/ *m* mourning

luva /'luva/ *f* glove

luxação /luʃa'sãw/ *f* dislocation

Luxemburgo /luʃẽ'burgu/ *m* Luxembourg

luxembur|guês /luʃẽbur'ges/ *a* (*f* ~**guesa**) Luxemburg □ *m* (*f* ~**guesa**) Luxemburger; (*língua*) Luxemburgish

luxo /'luʃu/ *m* luxury; **hotel de** ~ luxury hotel; **cheio de** ~ (*fam*) fussy

luxuoso /luʃu'ozu/ *a* luxurious

luxúria /lu'ʃuria/ *f* lust

luxuriante /luʃuri'ãtʃi/ *a* lush

luz /lus/ *f* light; **à** ~ **de** by the light of <*velas etc*>; in the light of <*fatos etc*>; **dar à** ~ give birth to

luzidio /luzi'dʒio/ *a* shiny

luzir /lu'zir/ *vi* shine

Mm

maca /'maka/ f stretcher

maça /ma'sã/ f apple

macabro /ma'kabru/ a macabre

maca|cão /maka'kãw/ m (de trabalho) overalls, (Amer) coveralls; (tipo de calça) dungarees; (roupa inteiriça) jumpsuit; (para bebê) romper suit; ~co m monkey; (aparelho) jack

maçada /ma'sada/ f bore

maçaneta /masa'neta/ f doorknob

maçante /ma'sãtʃi/ a boring

macar|rão /maka'xãw/ m pasta; (espaguete) spaghetti; ~ronada f pasta with tomato sauce and cheese

macarrônico /maka'xoniku/ a broken

macete /ma'setʃi/ m trick

machado /ma'ʃadu/ m axe

ma|chão /ma'ʃãw/ a tough □ m tough guy; ~chismo m machismo; ~chista a chauvinistic □ m male chauvinist; ~cho a male; <homem> macho □ m male

machu|cado /maʃu'kadu/ m injury; (na pele) sore patch; ~car vt/i hurt; ~car-se vpr hurt o.s.

maciço /ma'sisu/ a solid; <dose etc> massive □ m massif

macieira /masi'era/ f apple tree

maciez /masi'es/ f softness

macilento /masi'lẽtu/ a haggard

macio /ma'siu/ a soft; <carne> tender

maço /'masu/ m (de cigarros) packet; (de notas) bundle

ma|çom /ma'sõ/ m freemason; ~çonaria f freemasonry

maconha /ma'koɲa/ f marijuana

maçônico /ma'soniku/ a masonic

má-criação /makria'sãw/ f rudeness

macrobiótico /makrobi'ɔtʃiku/ a macrobiotic

macum|ba /ma'kũba/ f Afro-Brazilian cult; (uma) spell; ~beiro m follower of macumba □ a macumba

madame /ma'dami/ f lady

Madeira /ma'dera/ f Madeira

madeira /ma'dera/ f wood □ m (vinho) Madeira; ~ de lei hardwood

madeirense /made'rẽsi/ a & m Madeiran

madeixa /ma'deʃa/ f lock

madrasta /ma'drasta/ f stepmother

madrepérola /madre'pɛrola/ f mother of pearl

madressilva /madre'siwva/ f honeysuckle

Madri /ma'dri/ f Madrid

madrinha /ma'driɲa/ f (de batismo) godmother; (de casamento) bridesmaid

madru|gada /madru'gada/ f early morning; ~gador m early riser; ~gar vi get up early

maduro /ma'duru/ a <fruta> ripe; <pessoa> mature

mãe /mãj/ f mother; ~-de-santo (pl ~s-de-santo) f macumba priestess

maes|tria /majs'tria/ f expertise; ~tro m conductor

máfia /'mafia/ f mafia

magazine /maga'zini/ m department store

magia /ma'ʒia/ f magic

mági|ca /'maʒika/ f magic; (uma) magic trick; ~co a magic □ m magician

magis|tério /maʒis'tɛriu/ m teaching; (professores) teachers; ~trado m magistrate

magnânimo /mag'nanimu/ a magnanimous

magnata /mag'nata/ m magnate

magnésio /mag'nɛziu/ m magnesium

mag|nético /mag'nɛtʃiku/ a magnetic; ~netismo m magnetism; ~netizar vt magnetize; (fig) mesmerize

mag|nificência /magnifi'sẽsia/ f magnificence; ~nífico a magnificent

magnitude /magni'tudʒi/ f magnitude

mago /'magu/ m magician; os reis ~s the Three Wise Men

mágoa /'magoa/ f sorrow

magoar /mago'ar/ vt/i hurt; ~-se vpr be hurt

ma|gricela /magri'sɛla/ a skinny; ~gro a thin; <leite> skimmed; <carne> lean; (fig) meagre

maio /'maju/ m May

maiô /ma'jo/ m swimsuit

maionese /majo'nɛzi/ f mayonnaise

maior /ma'jɔr/ a bigger; <escritor, amor etc> greater; o ~ carro the biggest car; o ~ escritor the greatest writer; ~ de idade of age

Maiorca /ma'jɔrka/ f Majorca

maio|ria /majo'ria/ f majority; a ~ria dos brasileiros most Brazilians; ~ridade f majority, adulthood

mais /majs/ adv & pron more; ~ dois two more; dois dias a ~ two more days; não trabalho ~ I don't work any more; ~ ou menos more or less

maisena /maj'zɛna/ f cornflour, (Amer) cornstarch

maître /mɛtr/ m head waiter

maiúscula /maˈjuskula/ f capital letter
majes|tade /maʒesˈtadʒi/ f majesty; **~toso** a majestic
major /maˈjɔr/ m major
majoritário /maʒoriˈtariu/ a majority
mal /maw/ adv badly; (quase não) hardly □ conj hardly □ m evil; (doença) sickness; **não faz ~** never mind; **levar a ~** take offence at; **passar ~** be sick
mala /ˈmala/ f suitcase; (do carro) boot, (Amer) trunk; **~ aérea** air courier
malabaris|mo /malabaˈrizmu/ m juggling act; **~ta** m/f juggler
malagradecido /malagradeˈsidu/ a ungrateful
malagueta /malaˈgeta/ f chilli pepper
malaio /maˈlaju/ a & m Malay
Malaísia /malaˈizia/ f Malaysia
malaísio /malaˈiziu/ a & m Malaysian
malan|dragem /malãˈdraʒẽ/ f hustling; (uma) clever trick; **~dro** a cunning □ m hustler
malária /maˈlaria/ f malaria
mal-assombrado /malasõˈbradu/ a haunted
Malavi /malaˈvi/ m Malawi
malcriado /mawkriˈadu/ a rude
mal|dade /mawˈdadʒi/ f wickedness; (uma) wicked thing; **por ~dade** out of spite; **~dição** f curse; **~dito** a cursed, damned; **~doso** /o/ a wicked
maleá|vel /maliˈavew/ (pl **~veis**) a malleable
maledicência /malediˈsẽsia/ f malicious gossip
maléfico /maˈlɛfiku/ a evil; (prejudicial) harmful
mal-encarado /malĩkaˈradu/ a shady, dubious □ m shady character
mal-entendido /malĩtẽˈdʒidu/ m misunderstanding
mal-estar /malisˈtar/ m (doença) ailment; (constrangimento) discomfort
maleta /maˈleta/ f overnight bag
malévolo /maˈlɛvolu/ a malevolent
malfei|to /mawˈfejtu/ a badly done; (roupa etc) badly made; (fig) wrongful; **~tor** m wrongdoer; **~toria** f wrongdoing
ma|lha /ˈmaʎa/ f (ponto) stitch; (tricô) knitting; (tecido) jersey; (casaco) jumper, (Amer) sweater; (para ginástica) leotard; (de rede) mesh; **fazer ~lha** knit; **~lhado** a <animal> dappled; <roque> heavy; **~lhar** vt beat; thresh <trigo etc> □ vi (fam) work out
mal-humorado /malumoˈradu/ a in a bad mood, grumpy
malícia /maˈlisia/ f (má índole) malice; (astúcia) guile; (humor) innuendo

malicioso /malisiˈozu/ a (mau) malicious; (astuto) crafty; (que põe malícia) dirty-minded
maligno /maˈliginu/ a malignant
malmequer /mawmeˈker/ m marigold
maloca /maˈlɔka/ f Indian village
malo|grar-se /maloˈgrarsi/ vpr go wrong, fail; **~gro** /o/ m failure
mal-passado /mawpaˈsadu/ a <carne> rare
Malta /ˈmawta/ f Malta
malte /ˈmawtʃi/ m malt
maltrapilho /mawtraˈpiʎu/ a scruffy
maltratar /mawtraˈtar/ vt ill-treat, mistreat
malu|co /maˈluku/ a mad, crazy □ m madman; **~quice** f madness; (uma) crazy thing
malvado /mawˈvadu/ a wicked
malver|sação /mawversaˈsãw/ f mismanagement; (de fundos) misappropriation; **~sar** vt mismanage; misappropriate <dinheiro>
Malvinas /mawˈvinas/ f pl Falklands
mamadeira /mamaˈdera/ f (baby's) bottle
mamãe /maˈmãj/ f mum
mamão /maˈmãw/ m papaya
ma|mar /maˈmar/ vi suckle; **~mata** f (fam) fiddle
mamífero /maˈmiferu/ m mammal
mamilo /maˈmilu/ m nipple
mamoeiro /mamoˈeru/ m papaya tree
manada /maˈnada/ f herd
mananci|al /manãsiˈaw/ (pl **~ais**) m spring; (fig) rich source
man|cada /mãˈkada/ f blunder; **~car** vi limp; **~car-se** vpr (fam) take the hint, get the message
Mancha /ˈmãʃa/ f **o canal da ~** the English Channel
man|cha /ˈmãʃa/ f stain; (na pele) mark; **~char** vt stain
manchete /mãˈʃɛtʃi/ f headline
manco /ˈmãku/ a lame □ m cripple
mandachuva /mãdaˈʃuva/ m (fam) bigwig; (chefe) boss
man|dado /mãˈdadu/ m order; **~dado de busca** search warrant; **~dado de prisão** arrest warrant; **~damento** m commandment; **~dante** m/f person in charge; **~dão** a (f **~dona**) bossy; **~dar** vt (pedir) order; (enviar) send □ vi be in charge; **~dar-se** vpr (fam) take off; **~dar buscar** fetch; **~dar dizer** send word; **~dar alg ir** tell s.o. to go; **~dar ver** (fam) go to town; **~dar em alg** order s.o. about; **~dato** m mandate
mandíbula /mãˈdʒibula/ f (lower) jaw

mandioca /mãdʒiˈɔka/ f manioc

maneira /maˈnera/ f way; pl (boas) manners; **desta ~** in this way; **de qualquer ~** anyway

mane|jar /maneˈʒar/ vt handle; operate <máquina>; **~jável** (pl **~jáveis**) a manageable; **~jo** /e/ m handling

manequim /maneˈkĩ/ m (boneco) dummy; (medida) size □ m/f mannequin, model

maneta /maˈneta/ a one-armed □ m/f person with one arm

manga¹ /ˈmãga/ f (de roupa) sleeve

manga² /ˈmãga/ f (fruta) mango

manganês /mãgaˈnes/ m manganese

mangue /ˈmãgi/ m mangrove swamp

mangueira¹ /mãˈgera/ f (tubo) hose

mangueira² /mãˈgera/ f (árvore) mango tree

manha /ˈmaɲa/ f tantrum

manhã /maˈɲã/ f morning; **de ~** in the morning

manhoso /maˈɲozu/ a wilful

mania /maˈnia/ f (moda) craze; (doença) mania

maníaco /maˈniaku/ a manic □ m maniac; **~-depressivo** a & m manic depressive

manicômio /maniˈkomiu/ m lunatic asylum

manicura /maniˈkura/ f manicure; (pessoa) manicurist

manifes|tação /manifestaˈsãw/ f manifestation; (passeata) demonstration; **~tante** m/f demonstrator; **~tar** vt manifest, demonstrate; **~tar-se** vpr (revelar-se) manifest o.s.; (exprimir-se) express an opinion; **~to** /ɛ/ a manifest, clear □ m manifesto

manipular /manipuˈlar/ vt manipulate

manjedoura /mãʒeˈdora/ f manger

manjericão /mãʒeriˈkãw/ m basil

mano|bra /maˈnɔbra/ f manoeuvre; **~brar** vt manoeuvre; **~brista** m/f parking valet

mansão /mãˈsãw/ f mansion

man|sidão /mãsiˈdãw/ f gentleness; (do mar) calm; **~sinho** adv **de ~sinho** (devagar) slowly; (de leve) gently; (de fininho) stealthily; **~so** a gentle; <mar> calm; <animal> tame

manta /ˈmãta/ f blanket; (casaco) cloak

mantei|ga /mãˈtejga/ f butter; **~gueira** f butter dish

manter /mãˈter/ vt keep; **~-se** vpr keep; (sustentar-se) keep o.s.

mantimentos /mãtʃiˈmẽtus/ m pl provisions

manto /ˈmãtu/ m mantle

manu|al /manuˈaw/ (pl **~ais**) a & m manual; **~fatura** f manufacture; (fábrica) factory; **~faturar** vt manufacture

manuscrito /manusˈkritu/ a handwritten □ m manuscript

manu|sear /manuziˈar/ vt handle; **~seio** m handling

manutenção /manuteˈsãw/ f maintenance; (de prédio) upkeep

mão /mãw/ (pl **~s**) f hand; (do trânsito) direction; (de tinta) coat; **abrir ~ de** give up; **agüentar a ~** hang on; **dar a ~ a alg** hold s.o.'s hand; (cumprimentando) shake s.o.'s hand; **deixar alg na ~** let s.o. down; **enfiar ou meter a ~ em** hit, slap; **lançar ~ de** make use of; **escrito à ~** written by hand; **ter à ~** have to hand; **de ~s dadas** hand in hand; **em segunda ~** second-hand; **fora de ~** out of the way; **~ única** one way; **~-de-obra** f labour

mapa /ˈmapa/ m map

maquete /maˈkɛtʃi/ f model

maqui|agem /makiˈaʒẽ/ f make-up; **~ar** vt make up; **~ar-se** vpr put on make-up

maquiavélico /makiaˈveliku/ a Machiavellian

maqui|lagem, ~lar, (Port) **~lhagem, ~lhar** veja **maqui|agem, ~ar**

máquina /ˈmakina/ f machine; (ferroviária) engine; **escrever à ~** type; **~ de costura** sewing machine; **~ de escrever** typewriter; **~ de lavar (roupa)** washing machine; **~ de lavar pratos** dishwasher; **~ fotográfica** camera

maqui|nação /makinaˈsãw/ f machination; **~nal** (pl **~nais**) a mechanical; **~nar** vt/i plot; **~naria** f machinery; **~nista** m/f (ferroviário) engine driver; (de navio) engineer

mar /mar/ m sea

maracu|já /marakuˈʒa/ m passion fruit; **~jazeiro** m passion-fruit plant

marasmo /maˈrazmu/ m stagnation

marato|na /maraˈtona/ f marathon; **~nista** m/f marathon runner

maravi|lha /maraˈviʎa/ f marvel; **às mil ~lhas** wonderfully; **~lhar** vt amaze; **~lhar-se** vpr marvel (**de** at); **~lhoso** /o/ a marvellous

mar|ca /ˈmarka/ f (sinal) mark; (de carro, máquina) make; (de cigarro, sabão etc) brand; **~ca registrada** registered trademark; **~cação** f marking; (Port: discagem) dialling; **~cador** m marker; (em livro) bookmark; (placar) scoreboard; (jogador) scorer; **~cante** a outstanding; **~capasso** m pacemaker; **~car** vt mark; arrange <hora,

encontro, jantar etc>; score *<gol, ponto>*; *(Port: discar)* dial; *<relógio, termômetro>* show; brand *<gado>*; *(observar)* keep a close eye on; *(impressionar)* leave one's mark on □ *vi* make one's mark; ~**car época** make history; ~**car hora** make an appointment; ~**car o compasso** beat time; ~**car os pontos** keep the score

marce|naria /marsena'ria/ *f* cabinet-making; *(oficina)* cabinet maker's workshop; ~**neiro** *m* cabinet maker

mar|cha /'marʃa/ *f* march; *(de carro)* gear; **pôr-se em ~cha** get going; ~**cha à ré**, *(Port)* ~**cha atrás** reverse; ~**char** *vi* march

marci|al /marsi'aw/ *(pl* ~**ais)** *a* martial; ~**ano** *a & m* Martian

marco¹ /'marku/ *m (sinal)* landmark

marco² /'marku/ *m (moeda)* mark

março /'marsu/ *m* March

maré /ma'rɛ/ *f* tide

mare|chal /mare'ʃaw/ *(pl* ~**chais)** *m* marshal

maresia /mare'zia/ *f* smell of the sea

marfim /mar'fĩ/ *m* ivory

margarida /marga'rida/ *f* daisy; *(para impressora)* daisywheel

margarina /marga'rina/ *f* margarine

mar|gem /'marʒẽ/ *f (de rio)* bank; *(de lago)* shore; *(parte em branco, fig)* margin; ~**ginal** *(pl* ~**ginais)** *a* marginal; *(delinqüente)* delinquent □ *m/f* delinquent □ *f (rua)* riverside road; ~**ginalidade** *f* delinquency; ~**ginalizar** *vt* marginalize

marido /ma'ridu/ *m* husband

marimbondo /marĩ'bõdu/ *m* hornet

marina /ma'rina/ *f* marina

mari|nha /ma'riɲa/ *f* navy; ~**nha mercante** merchant navy; ~**-nheiro** *m* sailor; ~**nho** *a* marine

marionete /mario'nɛtʃi/ *f* puppet

mariposa /mari'poza/ *f* moth

mariscos /ma'riskus/ *m* seafood

mari|tal /mari'taw/ *(pl* ~**tais)** *a* marital

marítimo /ma'ritʃimu/ *a* sea; *<cidade>* seaside

marmanjo /mar'mãʒu/ *m* grown-up

marme|lada /marme'lada/ *f (fam)* fix; ~**lo** /ɛ/ *m* quince

marmita /mar'mita/ *f (de soldado)* mess tin; *(de trabalhador)* lunchbox

mármore /'marmori/ *m* marble

marmóreo /mar'mɔriu/ *a* marble

marquise /mar'kizi/ *f* awning

marreco /ma'xɛku/ *m* wild duck

Marrocos /ma'xɔkus/ *m* Morocco

marrom /ma'xõ/ *a & m* brown

marroquino /maxo'kinu/ *a & m* Moroccan

Marte /'martʃi/ *m* Mars

marte|lada /marte'lada/ *f* hammer blow; ~**lar** *vt/i* hammer; ~**lar em** *(fig)* go on and on about; ~**lo** /ɛ/ *m* hammer

mártir /'martʃir/ *m/f* martyr

mar|tírio /mar'tʃiriu/ *m* martyrdom; *(fig)* torture; ~**tirizar** *vt* martyr; *(fig)* torture

marujo /ma'ruʒu/ *m* sailor

mar|xismo /mark'sizmu/ *m* Marxism; ~**xista** *a & m/f* Marxist

mas /mas/ *conj* but

mascar /mas'kar/ *vt* chew

máscara /'maskara/ *f* mask; *(tratamento facial)* face-pack

mascarar /maska'rar/ *vt* mask

mascate /mas'katʃi/ *m* street vendor

mascavo /mas'kavu/ *a* **açúcar** ~ brown sugar

mascote /mas'kɔtʃi/ *f* mascot

masculino /masku'linu/ *a* male; *(para homens)* men's; *<palavra>* masculine □ *m* masculine

másculo /'maskulu/ *a* masculine

masmorra /maz'moxa/ *f* dungeon

masoquis|mo /mazo'kizmu/ *m* masochism; ~**ta** *m/f* masochist □ *a* masochistic

massa /'masa/ *f* mass; *(de pão)* dough; *(de torta, empada)* pastry; *(macarrão etc)* pasta; **cultura de ~** mass culture; **em ~** en masse; **as ~s** the masses

massa|crante /masa'krãtʃi/ *a* gruelling; ~**crar** *vt* massacre; *(fig: maçar)* wear out; ~**cre** *m* massacre

massa|gear /masaʒi'ar/ *vt* massage; ~**gem** *f* massage; ~**gista** *m/f* masseur *(f* masseuse)

mastigar /mastʃi'gar/ *vt* chew; *(ponderar)* chew over

mastro /'mastru/ *m* mast; *(de bandeira)* flagpole

mastur|bação /masturba'sãw/ *f* masturbation; ~**bar-se** *vpr* masturbate

mata /'mata/ *f* forest

mata-borrão /matabo'xãw/ *m* blotting paper

matadouro /mata'doru/ *m* slaughterhouse

mata|gal /mata'gaw/ *(pl* ~**gais)** *m* thicket

mata-moscas /mata'moskas/ *m invar* fly spray

ma|tança /ma'tãsa/ *f* slaughter; ~**tar** *vt* kill; satisfy *<fome>*; quench *<sede>*; guess *<charada>*; *(fazer nas coxas)* dash off; *(fam)* skive off *<aula, serviço>* □ *vi* kill

mata-ratos /mata'xatuſ/ *m invar* rat poison

mate[1] /'matʃi/ *m* (*chá*) maté

mate[2] /'matʃi/ *a invar* matt

matemáti|ca /mate'matʃika/ *f* mathematics; **∼co** *a* mathematical □ *m* mathematician

matéria /ma'tɛria/ *f* (*assunto, disciplina*) subject; (*no jornal*) article; (*substância*) matter; (*usada para fazer algo*) material; **em ∼ de** in the way of

materi|al /materi'aw/ (*pl* **∼ais**) *m* materials □ *a* material; **∼alismo** *m* materialism; **∼alista** *a* materialistic □ *m/f* materialist; **∼alizar-se** *vpr* materialize

matéria-prima /ma'tɛria'prima/ (*pl* **matérias-primas**) *f* raw material

mater|nal /mater'naw/ (*pl* **∼nais**) *a* maternal; **∼nidade** *f* maternity; (*clínica*) maternity hospital; **∼no** /ɛ/ *a* maternal; **língua ∼na** mother tongue

mati|nal /matʃi'naw/ (*pl* **∼nais**) *a* morning; **∼nê** *f* matinée

matiz /ma'tʃis/ *m* shade; (*político*) colouring; (*pontinha: de ironia etc*) tinge

matizar /matʃi'zar/ *vt* tinge (**de** with)

mato /'matu/ *m* scrubland, bush

matraca /ma'traka/ *f* rattle; (*tagarela*) chatterbox

matreiro /ma'treru/ *a* cunning

matriar|ca /matri'arka/ *f* matriarch; **∼cal** (*pl* **∼cais**) *a* matriarchal

matrícula /ma'trikula/ *f* enrolment; (*taxa*) enrolment fee; (*Port: de carro*) number plate, (*Amer*) license plate

matricular /matriku'lar/ *vt* enrol; **∼-se** *vpr* enrol

matri|monial /matrimoni'aw/ (*pl* **∼moniais**) *a* marriage; **∼mônio** *m* marriage

matriz /ma'tris/ *f* matrix; (*útero*) womb; (*sede*) head office

maturidade /maturi'dadʒi/ *f* maturity

matutino /matu'tʃinu/ *a* morning □ *m* morning paper

matuto /ma'tutu/ *a* countrified □ *m* country bumpkin

mau /maw/ *a* (*f* **má**) bad; **∼-caráter** *m invar* bad lot □ *a invar* no-good; **∼-olhado** *m* evil eye

mausoléu /mawzo'lɛw/ *m* mausoleum

maus-tratos /maws'tratus/ *m pl* ill-treatment

maxilar /maksi'lar/ *m* jaw

máxima /'masima/ *f* maxim

maximizar /masimi'zar/ *vt* maximize; (*exagerar*) play up

máximo /'masimu/ *a* (*antes do substantivo*) utmost, greatest; (*depois do substantivo*) maximum □ *m* maximum; **o ∼** (*fam: o melhor*) really something; **ao ∼** to the maximum; **no ∼** at most

maxixe /ma'ʃiʃi/ *m* gherkin

me /mi/ *pron* me; (*indireto*) (to) me; (*reflexivo*) myself

meada /mi'ada/ *f* skein; **perder o fio da ∼** lose one's thread

meados /mi'adus/ *m pl* **∼ de maio** mid-May

meandro /mi'ãdru/ *f* meander; *pl* (*fig*) twists and turns

mecâni|ca /me'kanika/ *f* mechanics; **∼co** *a* mechanical □ *m* mechanic

meca|nismo /meka'nizmu/ *m* mechanism; **∼nizar** *vt* mechanize

mecenas /me'sɛnas/ *m invar* patron

mecha /'mɛʃa/ *f* (*de vela*) wick; (*de bomba*) fuse; (*porção de cabelos*) lock; (*cabelo tingido*) highlight; **∼do** *a* highlighted

meda|lha /me'daʎa/ *f* medal; **∼lhão** *m* medallion; (*jóia*) locket

média /'mɛdʒia/ *f* average; (*café*) white coffee; **em ∼** on average

medi|ação /medʒia'sãw/ *f* mediation; **∼ador** *m* mediator; **∼ante** *prep* through, by; **∼ar** *vi* mediate

medica|ção /medʒika'sãw/ *f* medication; **∼mento** *m* medicine

medição /medʒi'sãw/ *f* measurement

medicar /medʒi'kar/ *vt* treat □ *vi* practise medicine; **∼-se** *vpr* dose o.s. up

medici|na /medʒi'sina/ *f* medicine; **∼na legal** forensic medicine; **∼nal** (*pl* **∼nais**) *a* medicinal

médico /'mɛdʒiku/ *m* doctor □ *a* medical; **∼-legal** (*pl* **∼-legais**) *a* forensic; **∼-legista** (*pl* **∼-s-legistas**) *m/f* forensic scientist

medi|da /me'dʒida/ *f* measure; (*dimensão*) measurement; **à ∼da que** as; **sob ∼da** made to measure; **tirar as ∼das de alg** take s.o.'s measurements; **∼dor** *m* meter

medie|val /medʒie'vaw/ (*pl* **∼vais**) *a* medieval

médio /'mɛdʒiu/ *a* (*típico*) average; <*tamanho, prazo*> medium; <*classe, dedo*> middle

mediocre /me'dʒiokri/ *a* mediocre

mediocridade /medʒiokri'dadʒi/ *f* mediocrity

medir /me'dʒir/ *vt* measure; weigh <*palavras*> □ *vi* measure; **∼-se** *vpr* measure o.s.; **quanto você mede?** how tall are you?

medi|tação /medʒita'sãw/ *f* meditation; **∼tar** *vi* meditate

mediterrâneo /medʒite'xaniu/ a
Mediterranean □ m o **Mediterrâneo**
the Mediterranean
médium /'mɛdʒiũ/ m/f medium
medo /'medu/ m fear; **ter ~ de** be afraid
of; **com ~** afraid; **~nho** /o/ a frightful
medroso /me'drozu/ a fearful, timid
medula /me'dula/ f marrow
megalomania /megaloma'nia/ f
megalomania
meia /'meja/ f (comprida) stocking;
(curta) sock; (seis) six; **~-calça** (pl
~s-calças) f tights, (Amer) pantihose;
~-idade f middle age; **~-noite** f
midnight; **~-volta** (pl **~s-voltas**) f
about-turn
mei|go /'mejgu/ a sweet; **~guice** f
sweetness
meio /'meju/ a half □ adv rather □ m
(centro) middle; (ambiente)
environment; (recurso) means; **~ litro**
half a litre; **dois meses e ~** two and
a half months; **em ~ a** amid; **por ~
de** through; **o ~ ambiente** the
environment; **os ~s de comunicação**
the media; **~-dia** m midday; **~-fio** m
kerb; **~-termo** m (acordo) compromise
mel /mɛw/ m honey
mela|ço /me'lasu/ m molasses; **~do** a
treacly □ m treacle
melancia /melã'sia/ f watermelon
melan|colia /melãko'lia/ f melancholy;
~cólico a melancholy
melão /me'lãw/ m melon
melar /me'lar/ vt make sticky
melhor /me'ʎɔr/ a & adv better; **o ~** the
best
melho|ra /me'ʎɔra/ f improvement;
~ras! get well soon!; **~ramento** m
improvement; **~rar** vt improve □ vi
improve; <doente> get better
melin|drar /melĩ'drar/ vt hurt;
~drar-se vpr be hurt; **~droso** /o/ a
delicate; <pessoa> sensitive
melodi|a /melo'dʒia/ f melody; **~oso** /o/
a melodious
melodra|ma /melo'drama/ m
melodrama; **~mático** a melodramatic
meloso /me'lozu/ a sickly sweet
melro /'mɛwxu/ m blackbird
membrana /mẽ'brana/ f membrane
membro /'mẽbru/ m member; (braço,
perna) limb
memo|rando /memo'rãdu/ m memo;
~rável (pl **~ráveis**) a memorable
memória /me'mɔria/ f memory; pl
(autobiografia) memoirs
men|ção /mẽ'sãw/ f mention; **fazer
~ção de** mention; **~cionar** vt mention
mendi|cância /mẽdʒi'kãsia/ f begging;
~gar vi beg; **~go** m beggar

menina /me'nina/ f girl; **a ~ dos olhos
de alg** the apple of s.o.'s eye
meningite /menĩ'ʒitʃi/ f meningitis
meni|nice /meni'nisi/ f (idade)
childhood; **~no** m boy
menopausa /meno'pawza/ f menopause
menor /me'nɔr/ a smaller □ m/f minor;
o/a ~ the smallest; (mínimo) the
slightest, the least
menos /'menos/ adv & pron less □ prep
except; **dois dias a ~** two days less; **a
~ que** unless; **ao ou pelo ~** at least;
o ~ bonito the least pretty; **~prezar** vt
look down upon
mensa|geiro /mẽsa'ʒeru/ m messenger;
~gem f message; **~gem de texto**
(telec) text message
men|sal /mẽ'saw/ (pl **~sais**) a monthly;
~salidade f monthly payment;
~salmente adv monthly
menstru|ação /mẽstrua'sãw/ f
menstruation; **~ada a estar ~ada** be
having one's period; **~al** (pl **~ais**) a
menstrual; **~ar** vi menstruate
menta /'mẽta/ f mint
men|tal /mẽ'taw/ (pl **~tais**) a mental;
~talidade f mentality; **~te** f mind
men|tir /mẽ'tʃir/ vi lie; **~tira** f lie;
~tiroso /o/ a lying □ m liar
mentor /mẽ'tor/ m mentor
mercado /mer'kadu/ m market; **~ria** f
commodity; pl goods
mercan|te /mer'kãtʃi/ a merchant; **~til**
(pl **~tis**) a mercantile
mercê /mer'se/ f à **~ de** at the mercy of
merce|aria /mersia'ria/ f grocer's;
~eiro m grocer
mercenário /merse'nariu/ a & m
mercenary
mercúrio /mer'kuriu/ m mercury;
Mercúrio Mercury
merda /'mɛrda/ f (chulo) shit
mere|cedor /merese'dor/ a deserving;
~cer vt deserve □ vi be deserving;
~cimento m merit
merenda /me'rẽda/ f packed lunch;
~ escolar school dinner
mere|trício /mere'trisiu/ m
prostitution; **~triz** f prostitute
mergu|lhador /merguʎa'dor/ m diver;
~lhar vt dip (**em** into) □ vi (na água)
dive; (no trabalho) bury o.s.; **~lho** m
dive; (esporte) diving; (banho de mar)
dip
meridi|ano /meridʒi'anu/ m meridian;
~onal (pl **~onais**) a southern
mérito /'mɛritu/ m merit
merluza /mer'luza/ f hake
mero /'mɛru/ a mere
mês /mes/ (pl **meses**) m month

mesa /'meza/ *f* table; (*de trabalho*) desk; ~ **de centro** coffee table; ~ **de jantar** dining table; ~ **telefônica** switchboard

mesada /me'zada/ *f* monthly allowance

mescla /'mɛskla/ *f* mixture, blend

mesmice /mez'misi/ *f* sameness

mesmo /'mezmu/ *a* same □ *adv* (*até*) even; (*justamente*) right; (*de verdade*) really; **você** ~ you yourself; **hoje** ~ this very day; ~ **assim** even so; ~ **que** even if; **dá no** ~ it comes to the same thing; **fiquei na mesma** I'm none the wiser

mesqui|nharia /meskiɲa'ria/ *f* meanness; (*uma*) mean thing; ~**nho** *a* mean

mesquita /mes'kita/ *f* mosque

Messias /me'sias/ *m* Messiah

mesti|çagem /mestʃi'saʒẽ/ *f* interbreeding; ~**ço** *a* <*pessoa*> of mixed race; <*animal*> crossbred □ *m* (*pessoa*) person of mixed race; (*animal*) mongrel

mes|trado /mes'tradu/ *m* master's degree; ~**tre** /ɛ/ *m* (*f* ~**tra**) master (*f* mistress); (*de escola*) teacher □ *a* main; <*chave*> master; ~**tre-de-obras** (*pl* ~**tres-de-obras**) *m* foreman; ~**tre-sala** (*pl* ~**tres-salas**) *m* master of ceremonies (*in carnival procession*); ~**tria** *f* expertise

meta /'mɛta/ *f* (*de corrida*) finishing post; (*gol, fig*) goal

meta|bólico /meta'bɔliku/ *a* metabolic; ~**bolismo** *m* metabolism

metade /me'tadʒi/ *f* half; **pela** ~ halfway

metafísi|ca /meta'fizika/ *f* metaphysics; ~**co** *a* metaphysical

metáfora /me'tafora/ *f* metaphor

metafórico /meta'fɔriku/ *a* metaphorical

me|tal /me'taw/ (*pl* ~**tais**) *m* metal; *pl* (*numa orquestra*) brass; ~**tálico** *a* metallic

meta|lurgia /metalur'ʒia/ *f* metallurgy; ~**lúrgica** *f* metal works; ~**lúrgico** *a* metallurgical □ *m* metalworker

metamorfose /metamor'fɔzi/ *f* metamorphosis

metano /me'tanu/ *m* methane

meteórico /mete'ɔriku/ *a* meteoric

meteoro /mete'ɔru/ *m* meteor; ~**logia** *f* meteorology; ~**lógico** *a* meteorological; ~**logista** *m/f* (*cientista*) meteorologist; (*na TV*) weather forecaster

meter /me'ter/ *vt* put; ~**se** *vpr* (*envolver-se*) get (**em** into); (*intrometer-se*) meddle (**em** in); ~ **medo** be frightening

meticuloso /metʃiku'lozu/ *a* meticulous

metido /me'tʃidu/ *a* snobbish; **ele é** ~ **a perito** he thinks he's an expert

metódico /me'tɔdʒiku/ *a* methodical

metodista /meto'dʒista/ *a & m/f* Methodist

método /'mɛtodu/ *m* method

metra|lhadora /metraʎa'dora/ *f* machine gun; ~**lhar** *vt* machine-gun

métri|co /'mɛtriku/ *a* metric; **fita** ~**ca** tape measure

metro[1] /'mɛtru/ *m* metre

metro[2] /'mɛtru/ *m* (*Port: metropolitano*) underground, (*Amer*) subway

metrô /me'tro/ *m* underground, (*Amer*) subway

metrópole /me'trɔpoli/ *f* metropolis

metropolitano /metropoli'tanu/ *a* metropolitan □ *m* (*Port*) underground, (*Amer*) subway

meu /mew/ *a* (*f* **minha**) my □ *pron* (*f* **minha**) mine; **um amigo** ~ a friend of mine; **fico na minha** (*fam*) I keep myself to myself

mexer /me'ʃer/ *vt* move; (*com colher etc*) stir □ *vi* move; ~**se** *vpr* move; (*apressar-se*) get a move on; ~ **com** (*comover*) affect, get to; (*brincar com*) tease; (*trabalhar com*) work with; ~ **em** touch

mexeri|ca /meʃe'rika/ *f* tangerine; ~**car** *vi* gossip; ~**co** *m* piece of gossip; *pl* gossip; ~**queiro** *a* gossiping □ *m* gossip

mexicano /meʃi'kanu/ *a & m* Mexican

México /'mɛʃiku/ *m* Mexico

mexido /me'ʃidu/ *a* **ovos** ~**s** scrambled eggs

mexilhão /meʃi'ʎãw/ *m* mussel

mi|ado /mi'adu/ *m* miaow; ~**ar** *vi* miaow

micreiro /mi'krejru/ *m* pc hacker

micróbio /mi'krɔbiu/ *m* microbe

micro|cosmo /mikro'kɔzmu/ *m* microcosm; ~**empresa** /e/ *f* small business; ~**empresário** *m* small businessman; ~**filme** *m* microfilm; ~**fone** *m* microphone; ~**onda** *f* microwave; (**forno de**) ~**s** *m* microwave (oven); ~**ônibus** *m invar* minibus; ~**processador** *m* microprocessor

microrganismo /mikrorga-'nizmu/ *m* microorganism

microscó|pico /mikros'kɔpiku/ *a* microscopic; ~**pio** *m* microscope

mídia /'midʒia/ *f* media

migalha /mi'gaʎa/ *f* crumb

mi|gração /migra'sãw/ *f* migration; ~**grar** *vi* migrate

mi|jar /mi'ʒar/ *vi* (*fam*) pee; ~**jar-se** *vpr* wet o.s.; ~**jo** *m* (*fam*) pee

m

mil /miw/ *a & m invar* thousan **estar a ∼** be on top form

mila|gre /mi'lagri/ *m* miracle; **∼groso** /ɔ/ *a* miraculous

milênio /mi'leniu/ *m* millennium

milésimo /mi'lɛzimu/ *a* thousandth

milha /'miʎa/ *f* mile

milhão /mi'ʎãw/ *m* million; **um ∼ de dólares** a million dollars

milhar /mi'ʎar/ *m* thousand; **∼es de vezes** thousands of times; **aos ∼es** in their thousands

milho /'miʎo/ *m* maize, (*Amer*) corn

milico /mi'liku/ *m* (*fam*) military man; **os ∼s** the military

mili|grama /mili'grama/ *m* milligram; **∼litro** *m* millilitre; **∼-metro** /e/ *m* millimetre

milionário /milio'nariu/ *a & m* millionaire

mili|tante /mili'tãtʃi/ *a & m* militant; **∼tar** *a* military □ *m* soldier

mim /mĩ/ *pron* me

mimar /mi'mar/ *vt* spoil

mímica /'mimika/ *f* mime; (*brincadeira*) charades

mi|na /'mina/ *f* mine; **∼nar** *vt* mine; (*fig: prejudicar*) undermine

mindinho /mĩ'dʒiɲu/ *m* little finger, (*Amer*) pinkie

mineiro /mi'neru/ *a* mining; (*de MG*) from Minas Gerais □ *m* miner; (*de MG*) person from Minas Gerais

mine|ração /minera'sãw/ *f* mining; **∼ral** (*pl* **∼rais**) *a & m* mineral; **∼rar** *vt/i* mine

minério /mi'nɛriu/ *m* ore

mingau /mĩ'gaw/ *m* porridge

mingua /'mĩgwa/ *f* lack

minguante /mĩ'gwãtʃi/ *a* **quarto ∼** last quarter

minguar /mĩ'gwar/ *vi* dwindle

minha /'miɲa/ *a & pron veja* **meu**

minhoca /mi'ɲɔka/ *f* worm

miniatura /minia'tura/ *f* miniature

mini|malista /minima'lista/ *a & m/f* minimalist; **∼mizar** *vt* minimize; (*subestimar*) play down

mínimo /'minimu/ *a* (*muito pequeno*) tiny; (*mais baixo*) minimum □ *m* minimum; **a mínima idéia** the slightest idea; **no ∼** at least

minissaia /mini'saja/ *f* miniskirt

minis|terial /ministeri'aw/ (*pl* **∼teriais**) *a* ministerial; **∼tério** *m* ministry; **Ministério do Interior** Home Office, (*Amer*) Department of the Interior

minis|trar /minis'trar/ *vt* administer; **∼tro** *m* minister; **primeiro ∼tro** prime minister

Minorca /mi'nɔrka/ *f* Menorca

mino|ritário /minori'tariu/ *a* minority; **∼ria** *f* minority

minúcia /mi'nusia/ *f* detail

minucioso /minusi'ozu/ *a* thorough

minúscu|la /mi'nuskula/ *f* small letter; **∼lo** *a* <*letra*> small; (*muito pequeno*) minuscule

minuta /mi'nuta/ *f* (*rascunho*) rough draft

minuto /mi'nutu/ *m* minute

miolo /mi'olu/ *f* (*de fruta*) flesh; (*de pão*) crumb; *pl* brains

míope /'miopi/ *a* short-sighted

miopia /mio'pia/ *f* myopia

mira /'mira/ *f* sight; **ter em ∼** have one's sights on

mirabolante /mirabo'lãtʃi/ *a* amazing; <*idéias, plano*> grandiose

mi|ragem /mi'raʒẽ/ *f* mirage; **∼rante** *m* lookout; **∼rar** *vt* look at; **∼rar-se** *vpr* look at o.s.

mirim /mi'rĩ/ *a* little

miscelânea /mise'lania/ *f* miscellany

miscigenação /misiʒena'sãw/ *f* interbreeding

mise-en-plis /mizã'pli/ *m* shampoo and set

miserá|vel /mize'ravew/ (*pl* **∼veis**) *a* miserable

miséria /mi'zɛria/ *f* misery; (*pobreza*) poverty; **uma ∼** (*pouco dinheiro*) a pittance; **chorar ∼** claim poverty

miseri|córdia /mizeri'kɔrdʒia/ *f* mercy; **∼cordioso** *a* merciful

misógino /mi'zɔʒinu/ *m* misogynist □ *a* misogynistic

miss /'misi/ *f* beauty queen

missa /'misa/ *f* mass

missão /mi'sãw/ *f* mission

mís|sil /'misiw/ (*pl* **∼seis**) *m* missile; **∼sil de longo alcance** long-range missile

missionário /misio'nariu/ *m* missionary

missiva /mi'siva/ *f* missive

mis|tério /mis'tɛriu/ *m* mystery; **∼terioso** /o/ *a* mysterious; **∼ticismo** *m* mysticism

místico /'mistʃiku/ *m* mystic □ *a* mystical

misto /'mistu/ *a* mixed □ *m* mix; **∼ quente** toasted ham and cheese sandwich

mistu|ra /mis'tura/ *f* mixture; **∼-rar** *vt* mix; (*confundir*) mix up; **∼rar-se** *vpr* mix (**com** with)

mítico /'mitʃiku/ *a* mythical

mito /'mitu/ *m* myth; **∼logia** *f* mythology; **∼lógico** *a* mythological

miudezas /miu'dezas/ *f pl* odds and ends

miúdo /mi'udu/ *a* tiny, minute; *<chuva>* fine; *<despesas>* minor □ *m* (*criança*) child, little one; *pl* (*de galinha*) giblets; **trocar em ~s** go into detail

mixaria /miʃa'ria/ *f* (*fam*) (*soma irrisória*) pittance

mixórdia /mi'ʃɔrdʒia/ *f* muddle

mnemônico /ne'moniku/ *a* mnemonic

mobilar /mobi'lar/ *vt* (*Port*) furnish

mobília /mo'bilia/ *f* furniture

mobili|ar /mobili'ar/ *vt* furnish; **~ário** *m* furniture

mobili|dade /mobili'dadʒi/ *f* mobility; **~zar** *vt* mobilize

moça /'mosa/ *f* girl

moçambicano /mosãbi'kanu/ *a & m* Mozambican

Moçambique /mosã'biki/ *m* Mozambique

moção /mo'sãw/ *f* motion

mochila /mo'ʃila/ *f* rucksack

moço /'mosu/ *a* young □ *m* boy, lad

moda /'mɔda/ *f* fashion; **na ~** fashionable

modalidade /modali'dadʒi/ *f* (*esporte*) event

mode|lagem /mode'laʒẽ/ *f* modelling; **~lar** *vt* model (**a** on); **~lar-se** *vpr* model o.s. (**a** on) □ *a* model; **~lo** /e/ *m* model

mode|ração /modera'sãw/ *f* moderation; **~rado** *a* moderate; **~rar** *vt* moderate; reduce *<velocidade, despesas>*; **~rar-se** *vpr* restrain oneself

moder|nidade /moderni'dadʒi/ *f* modernity; **~nismo** *m* modernism; **~nista** *a & m/f* modernist; **~nizar** *vt* modernize; **~no** /ɛ/ *a* modern

modess /'mɔdʒis/ *m invar* sanitary towel

modéstia /mo'dɛstʃia/ *f* modesty

modesto /mo'dɛstu/ *a* modest

módico /'mɔdʒiku/ *a* modest

modifi|cação /modʒifika'sãw/ *f* modification; **~car** *vt* modify

mo|dismo /mo'dʒizmu/ *m* idiom; **~dista** *f* dressmaker

modo /'mɔdu/ *m* way; (*ling*) mood; *pl* (*maneiras*) manners

modular /modu'lar/ *vt* modulate □ *a* modular

módulo /'mɔdulu/ *m* module

moeda /mo'ɛda/ *f* (*peça de metal*) coin; (*dinheiro*) currency

mo|edor /moe'dor/ *m* **~edor de café** coffee-grinder; **~edor de carne** mincer; **~er** *vt* grind *<café, trigo>*; squeeze *<cana>*; mince *<carne>*; (*bater*) beat

mofado /mo'fadu/ *a* mouldy; **~far** *vi* moulder; **~fo** /o/ *m* mould

mogno /'mɔgnu/ *m* mahogany

moinho /mo'iɲu/ *m* mill; **~ de vento** windmill

moisés /moj'zɛs/ *m invar* carry-cot

moita /'mojta/ *f* bush

mola /'mɔla/ *f* spring

mol|dar /mow'dar/ *vt* mould; cast *<metal>*; **~de** /ɔ/ *m* mould; (*para costura etc*) pattern

moldu|ra /mow'dura/ *f* frame; **~rar** *vt* frame

mole /'mɔli/ *a* soft; *<pessoa>* listless; (*fam*) (*fácil*) easy □ *adv* easily; **é ~?** (*fam*) can you believe it?

molécula /mo'lɛkula/ *f* molecule

moleque /mo'lɛki/ *m* (*menino*) lad; (*de rua*) urchin; (*homem*) scoundrel

molestar /moles'tar/ *vt* bother

moléstia /mo'lɛstʃia/ *f* disease

moletom /mole'tõ/ *m* (*tecido*) knitted cotton; (*blusa*) sweatshirt

moleza /mo'leza/ *f* softness; (*de pessoa*) laziness; **viver na ~** lead a cushy life; **ser ~** be easy

mo|lhado /mo'ʎadu/ *a* wet; **~lhar** *vt* wet; **~lhar-se** *vpr* get wet

molho¹ /'mɔʎu/ *m* (*de chaves*) bunch; (*de palha*) sheaf

molho² /'moʎu/ *m* sauce; (*para salada*) dressing; **deixar de ~** leave in soak *<roupa>*; **~ inglês** Worcester sauce

molusco /mo'lusku/ *m* mollusc

momen|tâneo /momẽ'taniu/ *a* momentary; **~to** *m* moment; (*força*) momentum

Mônaco /'monaku/ *m* Monaco

monar|ca /mo'narka/ *m/f* monarch; **~quia** *f* monarchy; **~-quista** *a & m/f* monarchist

monástico /mo'nastʃiku/ *a* monastic

monção /mõ'sãw/ *f* monsoon

mone|tário /mone'tariu/ *a* monetary; **~tarismo** *m* monetarism; **~tarista** *a & m/f* monetarist

monge /'mõʒi/ *m* monk

monitor /moni'tor/ *m* monitor; **~ de vídeo** VDU

monitorar /monito'rar/ *vt* monitor

mono|cromo /mono'krɔmu/ *a* monochrome; **~gamia** *f* monogamy

monógamo /mo'nɔgamu/ *a* monogamous

monograma /mono'grama/ *m* monogram

monólogo /mo'nɔlogu/ *m* monologue

mononucleose /mononukli'ɔzi/ *f* glandular fever

mono|pólio /mono'pɔliu/ *m* monopoly; **~polizar** *vt* monopolize

monossílabo /mono'silabu/ *a* monosyllabic □ *m* monosyllable

monotonia /monoto'nia/ *f* monotony

monótono /mo'nɔtonu/ *a* monotonous

monóxido /mo'nɔksidu/ *m* ~ **de carbono** carbon monoxide

mons|tro /'mõstru/ *m* monster; ~**truosidade** *f* monstrosity; ~**truoso** /o/ *a* monstrous

monta|dor /mõta'dor/ *m* (*de cinema*) editor; ~**dora** *f* assembly company; ~**gem** *f* assembly; (*de filme*) editing; (*de peça teatral*) production

monta|nha /mõ'taɲa/ *f* mountain; ~**nha-russa** (*pl* ~**nhas-russas**) *f* roller coaster; ~**nhismo** *m* mountaineering; ~**nhoso** /o/ *a* mountainous

mon|tante /mõ'tãtʃi/ *m* amount □ *a* rising; a ~**tante** upstream; ~**tão** *m* heap; ~**tar** *vt* ride <*cavalo, bicicleta*>; assemble <*peças, máquina*>; put up <*barraca*>; set up <*empresa, escritório*>; mount <*guarda, diamante*>; put on <*espetáculo, peça*>; edit <*filme*> □ *vi* ride; ~**tar a** <*dívidas etc*> amount to; ~**tar em** (*subir em*) mount; ~**taria** *f* mount; ~**te** *m* heap; **um** ~**te de coisas** (*fam*) loads of things; **o Monte Branco** Mont Blanc

Montevidéu /mõtʃivi'dɛw/ *f* Montevideo

montra /'mõtra/ *f* (*Port*) shop window

monumen|tal /monumẽ'taw/ (*pl* ~**tais**) *a* monumental; ~**to** *m* monument

mora|da /mo'rada/ *f* (*Port*) dwelling; address; ~**dia** *f* dwelling; ~**dor** *m* resident

mo|ral /mo'raw/ (*pl* ~**rais**) *a* moral □ *f* (*ética*) morals; (*de uma história*) moral □ *m* (*ânimo*) morale; (*de pessoa*) moral sense; ~**ralidade** *f* morality; ~**ralista** *a* moralistic □ *m/f* moralist; ~**ralizar** *vi* moralize

morango /mo'rãgu/ *m* strawberry

morar /mo'rar/ *vi* live

moratória /mora'tɔria/ *f* moratorium

mórbido /'mɔrbidu/ *a* morbid

morcego /mor'segu/ *m* bat

mor|daça /mor'dasa/ *f* gag; (*para cão*) muzzle; ~**daz** *a* scathing; ~**der** *vt/i* bite; ~**dida** *f* bite

mordo|mia /mordo'mia/ *f* (*no emprego*) perk; (*de casa etc*) comfort; ~**mo** /o/ *m* butler

more|na /mo'rena/ *f* brunette; ~**no** *a* dark; (*bronzeado*) brown □ *m* dark person

morfina /mor'fina/ *f* morphine

moribundo /mori'būdu/ *a* dying

moringa /mo'rĩga/ *f* water jug

morma|cento /morma'sẽtu/ *a* sultry; ~**ço** *m* sultry weather

morno /'mornu/ *a* lukewarm

moro|sidade /morozi'dadʒi/ *f* slowness; ~**so** /o/ *a* slow

morrer /mo'xer/ *vi* die; <*luz, dia, ardor, esperança etc*> fade; <*carro*> stall

morro /'moxu/ *m* hill; (*fig: favela*) slum

mortadela /morta'dɛla/ *f* mortadella, salami

mor|tal /mor'taw/ (*pl* ~**tais**) *a & m* mortal; ~**talha** *f* shroud; ~**talidade** *f* mortality; ~**tandade** *f* slaughter; ~**te** /ɔ/ *f* death; ~**tífero** *a* deadly; ~**tificar** *vt* mortify; ~**to** /o/ *a* dead

mosaico /mo'zajku/ *m* mosaic

mosca /'moska/ *f* fly

Moscou /mos'ku/, (*Port*) **Moscovo** /moʃ'kovu/ *f* Moscow

mosquito /mos'kitu/ *m* mosquito

mostarda /mos'tarda/ *f* mustard

mosteiro /mos'teru/ *m* monastery

mos|tra /'mɔstra/ *f* display; **dar** ~**tras de** show signs of; **pôr à** ~**tra** show up; ~**trador** *m* face, dial; ~**trar** *vt* show; ~**trar-se** *vpr* (*revelar-se*) show o.s. to be; (*exibir-se*) show off; ~**truário** *m* display case

mo|tel /mo'tɛw/ (*pl* ~**téis**) *m* motel

motim /mo'tʃĩ/ *m* riot; (*na marinha*) mutiny

moti|vação /motʃiva'sãw/ *f* motivation; ~**var** *vt* (*incentivar*) motivate; (*provocar*) cause; ~**vo** *m* (*razão*) reason; (*estímulo*) motive; (*na arte, música*) motif; **dar** ~**vo de** give cause for

moto /'mɔtu/ *f* motorbike; ~**ca** /mo'tɔka/ *f* (*fam*) motorbike

motoci|cleta /motosi'klɛta/ *f* motorcycle; ~**clismo** *m* motorcycling; ~**clista** *m/f* motorcyclist

motoqueiro /moto'keru/ *m* (*fam*) biker

motor /mo'tor/ *m* (*de carro, avião etc*) engine; (*elétrico*) motor □ *a* (*f* **motriz**) <*força*> driving; (*anat*) motor; ~ **de arranque** starter motor; ~ **de popa** outboard motor

moto|rista /moto'rista/ *m/f* driver; ~**rizado** *a* motorized; ~**rizar** *vt* motorize

movedi|ço /move'dʒisu/ *a* unstable, moving; **areia** ~**ça** quicksand

mó|vel /'mɔvew/ (*pl* ~**veis**) *a* <*peça, parte*> moving; <*tropas*> mobile; <*festa*> movable □ *m* piece of furniture; *pl* furniture

mo|ver /mo'ver/ *vt* move; (*impulsionar, fig*) drive; ~**ver-se** *vpr* move; ~**vido** *a* driven; ~**vido a álcool** alcohol-powered

movimen|tação /movimẽta'sãw/ *f*
bustle; **~tado** *a* <*rua, loja*> busy;
<*música*> up-beat, lively; <*pessoa,
sessão*> lively; **~tar** *vt* liven up;
~tar-se *vpr* move; **~to** *m* movement;
(*tecn*) motion; (*na rua etc*) activity

muam|ba /mu'ãba/ *f* contraband;
~beiro *m* smuggler

muco /'muku/ *m* mucus

muçulmano /musuw'manu/ *a & m*
Muslim

mu|da /'muda/ *f* (*planta*) seedling; **~da
de roupa** change of clothes; **~dança**
f change; (*de casa*) move; (*de carro*)
transmission; **~dar** *vt/i* change; **~dar
de assunto** change the subject; **~dar
(de casa)** move (house); **~dar de cor**
change colour; **~dar de idéia** change
one's mind; **~dar de lugar** change
places; **~dar de roupa** change
(clothes); **~dar-se** *vpr* move

mu|dez /mu'des/ *f* silence; **~do** *a* silent;
(*deficiente*) dumb; <*telefone*> dead □ *m*
mute

mu|gido /mu'ʒidu/ *m* moo; **~gir** *vi* moo

muito /'mũitu/ *a* a lot of; *pl* many □ *pron*
a lot □ *adv* (*com adjetivo, advérbio*)
very; (*com verbo*) a lot; **~ maior** much
bigger; **~ tempo** a long time

mula /'mula/ *f* mule

mulato /mu'latu/ *a & m* mulatto

muleta /mu'leta/ *f* crutch

mulher /mu'ʎɛr/ *f* woman; (*esposa*) wife

mulherengo /muʎe'rẽgu/ *a* womanizing
□ *m* womanizer, ladies' man

mul|ta /'muwta/ *f* fine; **~tar** *vt* fine

multicolor /muwtʃiko'lor/ *a*
multicoloured

multidão /muwtʃi'dãw/ *f* crowd

multinacio|nal /muwtʃinasio'naw/ (*pl
~nais*) *a & f* multinational

multipli|cação /muwtʃiplika-sãw/ *f*
multiplication; **~car** *vt* multiply;
~car-se *vpr* multiply; **~cidade** *f*
multiplicity

múltiplo /'muwtʃiplu/ *a & m* multiple

multirraci|al /muwtʃixasi'aw/ (*pl
~ais*) *a* multiracial

múmia /'mumia/ *f* mummy

mun|dano /mũ'danu/ *a* <*prazeres etc*>
worldly; <*vida, mulher*> society;
~dial (*pl ~diais*) *a* world □ *m* world
championship; **~do** *m* world; **todo (o)
~do** everybody

munição /muni'sãw/ *f* ammunition

muni|cipal /munisi'paw/ (*pl ~cipais*) *a*
municipal; **~cípio** *m* (*lugar*) borough,
community; (*prédio*) town hall;
(*autoridade*) local authority

munir /mu'nir/ *vt* provide (**de** with);
~-se *vpr* equip o.s. (**de** with)

mu|ral /mu'raw/ (*pl ~rais*) *a & m* mural;
~ralha *f* wall

mur|char /mur'ʃar/ *vi* <*planta*> wither,
wilt; <*salada*> go limp; <*beleza*> fade
□ *vt* wither, wilt <*planta*>; **~cho** *a*
<*planta*> wilting; <*pessoa*> broken

mur|murar /murmu'rar/ *vi* murmur;
(*queixar-se*) mutter □ *vt* murmur;
~múrio *m* murmur

muro /'muru/ *m* wall

murro /'muxu/ *m* punch

musa /'muza/ *f* muse

muscu|lação /muskula'sãw/ *f* weight-
training; **~lar** *a* muscular; **~latura** *f*
musculature

músculo /'muskulu/ *m* muscle

musculoso /musku'lozu/ *a* muscular

museu /mu'zew/ *m* museum

musgo /'muzgu/ *m* moss

música /'muzika/ *f* music; (*uma*) song; **~
de câmara** chamber music; **~ de
fundo** background music; **~ clássica
ou erudita** classical music

musi|cal /muzi'kaw/ (*pl ~cais*) *a & m*
musical; **~car** *vt* set to music

músico /'muziku/ *m* musician □ *a*
musical

musse /'musi/ *f* mousse

mutilar /mutʃi'lar/ *vt* mutilate; maim
<*pessoa*>

mutirão /mutʃi'rãw/ *m* joint effort

mútuo /'mutuu/ *a* mutual

muxoxo /mu'ʃoʃu/ *m* **fazer ~** tut

Nn

na = **em** + **a**

nabo /'nabu/ *m* turnip

nação /na'sãw/ *f* nation

nacio|nal /nasio'naw/ (*pl ~nais*) *a*
national; (*brasileiro*) home-
produced; **~nalidade** *f* nationality;
~nalismo *m* nationalism; **~nalista** *a
& m/f* nationalist; **~nalizar** *vt*
nationalize

naco /'naku/ *m* chunk

nada /'nada/ *pron* nothing □ *adv* not at
all; **de ~** (*não há de quê*) don't mention
it; **que ~!**, **~ disso!** no way!

na|dadeira /nada'dera/ *f* (*de peixe*) fin;
(*de mergulhador*) flipper; **~dador** *m*
swimmer; **~dar** *vi* swim

nádegas /'nadegas/ *f pl* buttocks

nado /'nadu/ *m* **~ borboleta** butterfly
stroke; **~ de costas** backstroke; **~ de**

m

n

peito breaststroke; **atravessar a ~** swim across

náilon /'najlõ/ *m* nylon

naipe /'najpi/ *m* (*em jogo de cartas*) suit

namo|rada /namo'rada/ *f* girlfriend; **~rado** *m* boyfriend; **~rador** *a* amorous □ *m* ladies' man; **~rar** *vt* (*ter relação com*) go out with; (*cobiçar*) eye up □ *vi* <*casal*> (*ter relação*) go out together; (*beijar-se etc*) kiss and cuddle; <*homem*> have a girlfriend; <*mulher*> have a boyfriend; **~ro** /o/ *m* relationship

nanar /na'nar/ *vi* (*col*) sleep

nanico /na'niku/ *a* tiny

não /nãw/ *adv* not; (*resposta*) no □ *m* no; **~-alinhado** *a* non-aligned; **~-conformista** *a & m/f* non-conformist

naquela, naquele, naquilo = em + aquela, aquele, aquilo

narci|sismo /narsi'zizmu/ *m* narcissism; **~sista** *m/f* narcissist □ *a* narcissistic; **~so** *m* narcissus

narcótico /nar'kɔtʃiku/ *a & m* narcotic

nari|gudo /nari'gudu/ *a* with a big nose; **ser ~gudo** have a big nose; **~na** *f* nostril

nariz /na'ris/ *m* nose

nar|ração /naxa'sãw/ *f* narration; **~rador** *m* narrator; **~rar** *vt* narrate; **~rativa** *f* narrative; **~rativo** *a* narrative

nas = em + as

na|sal /na'zaw/ (*pl* **~sais**) *a* nasal; **~salizar** *vt* nasalize

nas|cença /na'sẽsa/ *f* birth; **~cente** *a* nascent □ *f* source; **~cer** *vi* be born; <*dente, espinha*> grow; <*planta*> sprout; <*sol, lua*> rise; <*dia*> dawn; (*fig*) <*empresa, projeto etc*> come into being □ *m* o **~cer do sol** sunrise; **~cimento** *m* birth

nata /'nata/ *f* cream

natação /nata'sãw/ *f* swimming

Natal /na'taw/ *m* Christmas

na|tal /na'taw/ (*pl* **~tais**) *a* <*país, terra*> native

nata|lício /nata'lisiu/ *a & m* birthday; **~lidade** *f* índice de **~lidade** birth rate; **~lino** *a* Christmas

nati|vidade /natʃivi'dadʒi/ *f* nativity; **~vo** *a & m* native

nato /'natu/ *a* born

natu|ral /natu'raw/ (*pl* **~rais**) *a* natural; (*oriundo*) originating (**de** from) □ *m* native (**de** of)

natura|lidade /naturali'dadʒi/ *f* naturalness; **com ~lidade** matter-of-factly; **de ~lidade carioca** born in Rio de Janeiro; **~lismo** *m* naturalism;

~lista *a & m/f* naturalist; **~lizar** *vt* naturalize; **~lizar-se** *vpr* become naturalized

natureza /natu'reza/ *f* nature; **~ morta** still life

naturis|mo /natu'rizmu/ *m* naturism; **~ta** *m/f* naturist

nau|fragar /nawfra'gar/ *vi* <*navio*> be wrecked; <*tripulação*> be shipwrecked; (*fig*) <*plano, casamento etc*> founder; **~frágio** *m* shipwreck; (*fig*) failure

náufrago /'nawfragu/ *m* castaway

náusea /'nawzia/ *f* nausea

nauseabundo /nawzia'bũdu/ *a* nauseating

náuti|ca /'nawtʃika/ *f* navigation; **~co** *a* nautical

naval /na'vaw/ (*pl* **~vais**) *a* naval; **construção ~val** shipbuilding

navalha /na'vaʎa/ *f* razor; **~da** *f* cut with a razor

nave /'navi/ *f* nave; **~ espacial** spaceship

nave|gação /navega'sãw/ *f* navigation; (*tráfego*) shipping; **~gador** *m* navigator; (*comput*) browser; **~gante** *m/f* seafarer; **~gar** *vt* navigate; sail <*mar*> □ *vi* sail; (*traçar o rumo*) navigate; **~gável** (*pl* **~gáveis**) *a* navigable

navio /na'viu/ *m* ship; **~ cargueiro** cargo ship; **~ de guerra** warship; **~ petroleiro** oil tanker

nazista /na'zista/, (*Port*) **nazi** /na'zi/ *a & m/f* Nazi

neblina /ne'blina/ *f* mist

nebulo|sa /nebu'lɔza/ *f* nebula; **~sidade** *f* cloud; **~so** /o/ *a* cloudy; (*fig*) obscure

neces|saire /nese'sɛr/ *m* toilet bag; **~sário** *a* necessary; **~sidade** *f* necessity; (*que se impõe*) need; (*pobreza*) need; **~sitado** *a* needy □ *m* person in need; **~sitar** *vt* require; (*tornar necessário*) necessitate; **~sitar de** need

necro|lógio /nekro'lɔʒiu/ *m* obituary column; **~tério** *m* mortuary, (*Amer*) morgue

nectarina /nekta'rina/ *f* nectarine

nefasto /ne'fastu/ *a* fatal

ne|gação /nega'sãw/ *f* denial; (*ling*) negation; **ser uma ~gação em** be hopeless at; **~gar** *vt* deny; **~gar-se a** refuse to; **~gativa** *f* refusal; (*ling*) negative; **~gativo** *a & m* negative

negli|gência /negli'ʒẽsia/ *f* negligence; **~genciar** *vt* neglect; **~gente** *a* negligent

negoci|ação /negosia'sãw/ *f* negotiation; **~ador** *m* negotiator;

~**ante** *m/f* dealer (**de** in); ~**ar** *vt/i*
negotiate; ~**ar em** deal in; ~**ata** *f*
shady deal; ~**ável** (*pl* ~**áveis**) *a*
negotiable

negócio /ne'gɔsiu/ *m* deal; (*fam: coisa*)
thing; *pl* business; **a** *ou* **de** ~**s** <*viajar*>
on business

negocista /nego'sista/ *m* wheeler-dealer
□ *a* wheeler-dealing

ne|grito /ne'gritu/ *m* bold; ~**gro** /e/ *a &*
m black; (*de raça*) Negro

nela, nele = **em** + **ela, ele**

nem /nēj/ *adv* not even □ *conj* ~ ... ~ ...
neither ... nor ...; ~ **sempre** not always;
~ **todos** not all; ~ **que** not even if; **que**
~ **like**; ~ **eu** nor do I

nenê /ne'ne/, **neném** /ne'nēj/ *m* baby

nenhum /ne'ɲũ/ *a* (*f* **nenhuma**) no
□ *pron* (*f* **nenhuma**) not one; ~ **dos**
dois neither of them; ~ **erro** no
mistakes; **erro** ~ no mistakes at all,
not a single mistake; ~ **lugar** nowhere

nenúfar /ne'nufar/ *m* waterlily

neologismo /neolo'ʒizmu/ *m* neologism

néon /'nɛõ/ *m* neon

neozelan|dês /neozelā'des/ *a* (*f* ~**desa**)
New Zealand □ *m* (*f* ~**desa**) New
Zealander

Nepal /ne'paw/ *m* Nepal

nervo /'nervu/ *m* nerve; ~**sismo** *m*
(*chateação*) annoyance; (*medo*)
nervousness; ~**so** /o/ *a* <*sistema,*
doença> nervous; (*chateado*) annoyed;
(*medroso*) nervous; **deixar alg** ~**so** get
on s.o.'s nerves

nessa(s), nesse(s) = **em** + **essa(s), esse(s)**

nesta(s), neste(s) = **em** + **esta(s), este(s)**

ne|ta /'nɛta/ *f* granddaughter; ~**to** /ɛ/ *m*
grandson; *pl* grandchildren

neuro|logia /newrolo'ʒia/ *f* neurology;
~**lógico** *a* neurological; ~**logista** *m/f*
neurologist

neu|rose /new'rɔzi/ *f* neurosis; ~**rótico**
a neurotic

neutrali|dade /newtrali'dadʒi/ *f*
neutrality; ~**zar** *vt* neutralize

neutrão /new'trãw/ *m* (*Port*) *veja*
nêutron

neutro /'newtru/ *a* neutral

nêutron /'newtrõ/ *m* neutron

ne|vada /ne'vada/ *f* snowfall; ~**vado** *a*
snow-covered; ~**var** *vi* snow; ~**vasca**
f snowstorm; ~**ve** /ɛ/ *f* snow

névoa /'nɛvoa/ *f* haze

nevoeiro /nevo'eru/ *m* fog

nexo /'nɛksu/ *m* connection; **sem** ~
incoherent

Nicarágua /nika'ragwa/ *f* Nicaragua

nicaragüense /nikara'gwẽsi/ *a & m/f*
Nicaraguan

nicho /'niʃu/ *m* niche

nicotina /niko'tʃina/ *f* nicotine

Níger /'niʒer/ *m* Niger

Nigéria /ni'ʒɛria/ *f* Nigeria

nigeriano /niʒeri'anu/ *a & m* Nigerian

Nilo /'nilu/ *m* Nile

ninar /ni'nar/ *vt* lull to sleep

ninfa /'nĩfa/ *f* nymph

ninguém /nĩ'gēj/ *pron* no-one, nobody

ninhada /ni'ɲada/ *f* brood

ninharia /niɲa'ria/ *f* trifle

ninho /'niɲu/ *m* nest

níquel /'nikew/ *m* nickel

nisei /ni'sej/ *a & m/f* Japanese Brazilian

nisso = **em** + **isso**

nisto = **em** + **isto**

nitidez /nitʃi'des/ *f* (*de imagem etc*)
sharpness

nítido /'nitʃidu/ *a* <*imagem, foto*> sharp;
<*diferença, melhora*> distinct, clear

nitrogênio /nitro'ʒeniu/ *m* nitrogen

ní|vel /'nivew/ (*pl* ~**veis**) *m* level; **a** ~**vel**
de in terms of

nivelamento /nivela'mẽtu/ *m* levelling

nivelar /nive'lar/ *vt* level

no = **em** + **o**

nó /nɔ/ *m* knot; **dar um** ~ tie a knot; ~
dos dedos knuckle; **um** ~ **na**
garganta a lump in one's throat

nobre /'nɔbri/ *a* noble; <*bairro*>
exclusive □ *m/f* noble; ~**za** /e/ *f*
nobility

noção /no'sãw/ *f* notion; *pl* (*rudimentos*)
elements

nocaute /no'kawtʃi/ *m* knockout; **pôr**
alg ~ knock s.o. out; ~ *vt* knock out

nocivo /no'sivu/ *a* harmful

nódoa /'nodoa/ *f* (*Port*) stain

nogueira /no'gera/ *f* (*árvore*) walnut
tree

noi|tada /noj'tada/ *f* night; ~**te** *f* night;
(*antes de dormir*) evening; **à** *ou* **de** ~**te**
at night; (*antes de dormir*) in the
evening; **hoje à** ~**te** tonight; **ontem à**
~**te** last night; **boa** ~**te** (*ao chegar*)
good evening; (*ao despedir-se*) good
night; ~**te em branco** *ou* **claro**
sleepless night

noi|vado /noj'vadu/ *m* engagement; ~**va**
f fiancée; (*no casamento*) bride; ~**vo** *m*
fiancé; (*no casamento*) bridegroom;
os ~**vos** the engaged couple; (*no*
casamento) the bride and groom; **ficar**
~**vo** get engaged

no|jento /no'ʒẽtu/ *a* disgusting; ~**jo** /o/ *m*
disgust

nômade /'nomadʒi/ *m/f* nomad □ *a*
nomadic

nome /'nomi/ *m* name; **de** ~ by name; **em**
~ **de** in the name of; ~ **comercial**

n

trade name; ~ **de batismo** Christian name; ~ **de guerra** professional name

nome|ação /nomia'sãw/ *f* appointment; **~ar** *vt* (*para cargo*) appoint; (*chamar pelo nome*) name

nomi|nal /nomi'naw/ (*pl* **~nais**) *a* nominal

nonagésimo /nona'ʒezimu/ *a* ninetieth

nono /'nonu/ *a & m* ninth

nora /'nɔra/ *f* daughter-in-law

nordes|te /nor'dɛstʃi/ *m* northeast; **~tino** *a* Northeastern □ *m* person from the Northeast (*of Brazil*)

nórdico /'nɔrdʒiku/ *a* Nordic

nor|ma /'nɔrma/ *f* norm; **~mal** (*pl* **~mais**) *a* normal

normali|dade /normali'dadʒi/ *f* normality; **~zar** *vt* bring back to normal; normalize <*relações diplomáticas*>; **~zar-se** *vpr* return to normal

noroeste /noro'ɛstʃi/ *a & m* northwest

norte /'nɔrtʃi/ *a & m* north; **~-africano** *a & m* North African; **~-americano** *a & m* North American; **~-coreano** *a & m* North Korean

nortista /nor'tʃista/ *a* Northern □ *m/f* Northerner

Noruega /noru'ɛga/ *f* Norway

norue|guês /norue'ges/ *a & m* (*f* **~guesa**) Norwegian

nos¹ = **em + os**

nos² /nus/ *pron* us; (*indireto*) (to) us; (*reflexivo*) ourselves

nós /nɔs/ *pron* we; (*depois de preposição*) us

nos|sa /'nɔsa/ *int* gosh; **~so** /ɔ/ *a* our □ *pron* ours

nos|talgia /nostaw'ʒia/ *f* nostalgia; **~tálgico** *a* nostalgic

nota /'nɔta/ *f* note; (*na escola etc*) mark; (*conta*) bill; **custar uma ~** (**preta**) (*fam*) cost a bomb; **tomar ~** take note (**de** of); **~ fiscal** receipt

no|tação /nota'sãw/ *f* notation; **~tar** *vt* notice, note; **fazer ~tar** point out; **~tável** (*pl* **~táveis**) *a & m/f* notable

notícia /no'tʃisia/ *f* piece of news; *pl* news

notici|ar /notʃi'sjar/ *vt* report; **~ário** *m* (*na TV*) news; (*em jornal*) news section; **~arista** *m/f* (*na TV*) newsreader; (*em jornal*) news reporter; **~oso** /ɔ/ *a* **agência ~osa** news agency

notifi|cação /notʃifika'sãw/ *f* notification; **~car** *vt* notify

notívago /no'tʃivagu/ *a* nocturnal □ *m* night person

notório /no'tɔriu/ *a* well-known

noturno /no'turnu/ *a* night; <*animal*> nocturnal

nova /'nɔva/ *f* piece of news; **~mente** *adv* again

novato /no'vatu/ *m* novice

nove /'nɔvi/ *a & m* nine; **~centos** *a & m* nine hundred

novela /no'vɛla/ *f* (*na TV*) soap opera; (*livro*) novella

novembro /no'vẽbru/ *m* November

noventa /no'vẽta/ *a & m* ninety

noviço /no'visu/ *m* novice

novidade /novi'dadʒi/ *f* novelty; (*notícia*) piece of news; *pl* (*notícias*) news

novilho /no'viʎu/ *m* calf

novo /'novu/ *a* new; (*jovem*) young; **de ~** again; **~ em folha** brand new

noz /nɔs/ *f* walnut; **~ moscada** nutmeg

nu /nu/ *a* (*f* **~a**) <*corpo, pessoa*> naked; <*braço, parede, quarto*> bare □ *m* nude; **~ em pêlo** stark naked; **a verdade ~a e crua** the plain truth

nuança /nu'ãsa/ *f* nuance

nu|blado /nu'bladu/ *a* cloudy; **~blar** *vt* cloud; **~blar-se** *vpr* cloud over

nuca /'nuka/ *f* nape of the neck

nuclear /nukli'ar/ *a* nuclear

núcleo /'nukliu/ *m* nucleus

nu|dez /nu'des/ *f* nakedness; (*na TV etc*) nudity; (*da parede etc*) bareness; **~dismo** *m* nudism; **~dista** *m/f* nudist

nulo /'nulu/ *a* void

num, numa(s) = **em + um, uma(s)**

nume|ral /nume'raw/ (*pl* **~rais**) *a & m* numeral; **~rar** *vt* number

numérico /nu'mɛriku/ *a* numerical

número /'numeru/ *m* number; (*de jornal, revista*) issue; (*de sapatos*) size; (*espetáculo*) act; **fazer ~** make up the numbers

numeroso /nume'rozu/ *a* numerous

nunca /'nũka/ *adv* never; **~ mais** never again

nuns = **em + uns**

nupci|al /nupsi'aw/ (*pl* **~ais**) *a* bridal

núpcias /'nupsias/ *f pl* marriage

nu|trição /nutri'sãw/ *f* nutrition; **~trir** *vt* nourish; (*fig*) harbour <*ódio, esperança*>; **~tritivo** *a* nourishing; <*valor*> nutritional

nuvem /'nuvẽ/ *f* cloud

Oo

o /u/ *artigo* the □ *pron* (*homem*) him; (*coisa*) it; (*você*) you; **~ que** (*a coisa que*) what; (*aquele que*) the one that; **~ quê?** what?; **meu livro e ~ do João** my book and John's (one)

ó /ɔ/ *int* (*fam*) look

ô /o/ *int* oh

oásis /oˈazis/ *m invar* oasis

oba /ˈoba/ *int* great

obcecar /obiseˈkar/ *vt* obsess

obe|decer /obedeˈser/ *vt* ~decer a obey; ~diência *f* obedience; ~diente *a* obedient

obe|sidade /obeziˈdadʒi/ *f* obesity; ~so /e/ *a* obese

óbito /ˈɔbitu/ *m* death

obituário /obituˈariu/ *m* obituary

obje|ção /obiʒeˈsãw/ *f* objection; ~tar *vt*/ *i* object (a to)

objeti|va /obiʒeˈtʃiva/ *f* lens; ~vidade *f* objectivity; ~vo *a* & *m* objective

objeto /obiˈʒɛtu/ *m* object

oblíquo /oˈblikwu/ *a* oblique; <*olhar*> sidelong

obliterar /oblieˈrar/ *vt* obliterate

oblongo /oˈblõgu/ *a* oblong

obo|é /oboˈɛ/ *m* oboe; ~ísta *m*/*f* oboist

obra /ˈɔbra/ *f* work; em ~s being renovated; ~ de arte work of art; ~ de caridade charity; ~-prima (*pl* ~s-primas) *f* masterpiece

obri|gação /obrigaˈsãw/ *f* obligation; (*título*) bond; ~gado *int* thank you; (*não querendo*) no thank you; ~gar *vt* force, oblige (a to); ~gar-se *vpr* undertake (a to); ~gatório *a* obligatory, compulsory

obsce|nidade /obiseniˈdadʒi/ *f* obscenity; ~no /e/ *a* obscene

obscu|ridade /obiskuriˈdadʒi/ *f* obscurity; ~ro *a* obscure

obséquio /obiˈsɛkiu/ *m* favour

obsequioso /obisekiˈozu/ *a* obsequious

obser|vação /obiservaˈsãw/ *f* observation; ~vador *a* observant □ *m* observer; ~vância *f* observance; ~var *vt* observe; ~vatório *m* observatory

obses|são /obiseˈsãw/ *f* obsession; ~sivo *a* obsessive

obsoleto /obisoˈletu/ *a* obsolete

obstáculo /obisˈtakulu/ *m* obstacle

obstar /obisˈtar/ *vt* stand in the way (a of)

obs|tetra /obisˈtɛtra/ *m*/*f* obstetrician; ~tetrícia *f* obstetrics; ~tétrico *a* obstetric

obsti|nação /obistinaˈsãw/ *f* obstinacy; ~nado *a* obstinate; ~nar-se *vpr* insist (em on)

obstru|ção /obistruˈsãw/ *f* obstruction; ~ir *vt* obstruct

ob|tenção /obitẽˈsãw/ *f* obtaining; ~ter *vt* obtain

obtu|ração /obituraˈsãw/ *f* filling; ~rador *m* shutter; ~rar *vt* fill <*dente*>

obtuso /obiˈtuzu/ *a* obtuse

óbvio /ˈɔbviu/ *a* obvious

ocasi|ão /okaziˈãw/ *f* occasion; (*oportunidade*) opportunity; (*compra*) bargain; ~onal (*pl* ~onais) *a* chance; ~onar *vt* cause

Oceania /osiaˈnia/ *f* Oceania

oce|ânico /osiˈaniku/ *a* ocean; ~ano *m* ocean

ociden|tal /osidẽˈtaw/ (*pl* ~tais) *a* western □ *m*/*f* Westerner; ~te *m* West

ócio /ˈɔsiu/ *m* (*lazer*) leisure; (*falta de trabalho*) idleness

ocioso /osiˈozu/ *a* idle □ *m* idler

oco /ˈoku/ *a* hollow; <*cabeça*> empty

ocor|rência /okoˈxẽsia/ *f* occurrence; ~rer *vi* occur (a to)

ocu|lar /okuˈlar/ *a* testemunha ~lar eye witness; ~lista *m*/*f* optician

óculos /ˈɔkulus/ *m pl* glasses; ~ de sol sunglasses

ocul|tar /okuwˈtar/ *vt* conceal; ~to *a* hidden; (*sobrenatural*) occult

ocu|pação /okupaˈsãw/ *f* occupation; ~pado *a* <*pessoa*> busy; <*cadeira*> taken; <*telefone*> engaged, (*Amer*) busy; ~par *vt* occupy; take up <*tempo, espaço*>; hold <*cargo*>; ~par-se *vpr* keep busy; ~par-se com *ou* de be involved with <*política, literatura etc*>; take care of <*cliente, doente, problema*>; occupy one's time with <*leitura, palavras cruzadas etc*>

odiar /odʒiˈar/ *vt* hate

ódio /ˈɔdʒiu/ *m* hatred, hate; (*raiva*) anger

odioso /odʒiˈozu/ *a* hateful

odontologia /odõtoloˈʒia/ *f* dentistry

odor /oˈdor/ *m* odour

oeste /oˈɛstʃi/ *a* & *m* west

ofe|gante /ofeˈgãtʃi/ *a* panting; ~gar *vi* pant

ofen|der /ofẽˈder/ *vt* offend; ~der-se *vpr* take offence; ~sa *f* insult; ~siva *f* offensive; ~sivo *a* offensive

ofere|cer /ofereˈser/ *vt* offer; ~cer-se *vpr* <*pessoa*> offer o.s. (como as); <*ocasião*> arise; ~cer-se para ajudar offer to help; ~cimento *m* offer

oferenda /ofeˈrẽda/ *f* offering

oferta /oˈfɛrta/ *f* offer; em ~ on offer; a ~ e a demanda supply and demand

ofici|al /ofisiˈaw/ (*pl* ~ais) *a* official □ *m* officer; ~alizar *vt* make official; ~ar *vi* officiate

oficina /ofiˈsina/ *f* workshop; (*para carros*) garage, (*Amer*) shop

ofício /oˈfisiu/ *m* (*profissão*) trade; (*na igreja*) service

oficioso /ofisiˈozu/ *a* unofficial

ofus|cante /ofusˈkãtʃi/ *a* dazzling; ~car *vt* dazzle <*pessoa*>; obscure <*sol etc*>; (*fig: eclipsar*) outshine

o

OGM /oʒe'ɛm/ *m* (*biol*) GMO

oi /oj/ *int* (*cumprimento*) hi; (*resposta*) yes?

oi|tavo /oi'tavu/ *a & m* eighth; **~tenta** *a & m* eighty; **~to** *a & m* eight; **~tocentos** *a & m* eight hundred

olá /o'la/ *int* hello

olaria /ola'ria/ *f* pottery

óleo /'ɔliu/ *m* oil

oleo|duto /oliu'dutu/ *m* oil pipeline; **~so** /o/ *a* oily

olfato /ow'fatu/ *m* sense of smell

olhada /o'ʎada/ *f* look; **dar uma ~** have a look

olhar /o'ʎar/ *vt* look at; (*assistir*) watch □ *vi* look □ *m* look; **~ para** look at; **~ por** look after; **e olhe lá** (*fam*) and that's pushing it

olheiras /o'ʎeras/ *fpl* dark rings under one's eyes

olho /'oʎu/ *m* eye; **a ~ nu** with the naked eye; **custar os ~s da cara** cost a fortune; **ficar de ~** keep an eye out; **ficar de ~ em** keep an eye on; **pôr alg no ~ da rua** throw s.o. out; **não pregar o ~** not sleep a wink; **~ gordo** *ou* **grande** envy; **~ mágico** peephole; **~ roxo** black eye

Olimpíada /oli'piada/ *f* Olympic Games

olímpico /o'līpiku/ *a* <*jogos, vila*> Olympic; (*fig*) blithe

oliveira /oli'vera/ *f* olive tree

olmo /'owmu/ *m* elm

om|breira /ö'brera/ *f* (*para roupa*) shoulder pad; **~bro** *m* shoulder; **dar de ~bros** shrug one's shoulders

omelete /ome'letʃi/, (*Port*) **omeleta** /ome'leta/ *f* omelette

omis|são /omi'sãw/ *f* omission; **~so** *a* negligent, remiss

omitir /omi'tʃir/ *vt* omit

omni- (*Port*) *veja* **oni-**

omoplata /omo'plata/ *f* shoulder blade

onça¹ /'õsa/ *f* (*peso*) ounce

onça² /'õsa/ *f* (*animal*) jaguar

onda /'õda/ *f* wave; **pegar ~** (*fam*) surf

onde /'õdʒi/ *adv* where; **por ~?** which way?; **~ quer que** wherever

ondu|lação /õdula'sãw/ *f* undulation; (*do cabelo*) wave; **~lado** *a* wavy; **~lante** *a* undulating; **~lar** *vt* wave <*cabelo*> □ *vi* undulate

onerar /one'rar/ *vt* burden

ônibus /'onibus/ *m invar* bus; **~ espacial** space shuttle

onipotente /onipo'tẽtʃi/ *a* omnipotent

onírico /o'niriku/ *a* dreamlike

onisciente /onisi'ẽtʃi/ *a* omniscient

onomatopéia /onomato'pɛja/ *f* onomatopoeia

ontem /'õtẽ/ *adv* yesterday

onze /'õzi/ *a & m* eleven

opaco /o'paku/ *a* opaque

opala /o'pala/ *f* opal

opção /opi'sãw/ *f* option

ópera /'ɔpera/ *f* opera

ope|ração /opera'sãw/ *f* operation; (*bancária etc*) transaction; **~rador** *m* operator; **~rar** *vt* operate; operate on <*doente*>; work <*milagre*> □ *vi* operate; **~rar-se** *vpr* (*acontecer*) come about; (*fazer operação*) have an operation; **~rário** *a* working □ *m* worker

opereta /ope'reta/ *f* operetta

opinar /opi'nar/ *vt* think □ *vi* express one's opinion

opinião /opini'ãw/ *f* opinion; **na minha ~** in my opinion; **~ pública** public opinion

ópio /'ɔpiu/ *m* opium

opor /o'por/ *vt* put up <*resistência, argumento*>; (*pôr em contraste*) contrast (**a** with); **~-se** *a* (*não aprovar*) oppose; (*ser diferente*) contrast with

oportu|nidade /oportuni'dadʒi/ *f* opportunity; **~nista** *a & m/f* opportunist; **~no** *a* opportune

oposi|ção /opozi'sãw/ *f* opposition (**a** to); **~cionista** *a* opposition □ *m/f* opposition politician

oposto /o'postu/ *a & m* opposite

opres|são /opre'sãw/ *f* oppression; (*no peito*) tightness; **~sivo** *a* oppressive; **~sor** *m* oppressor

oprimir /opri'mir/ *vt* oppress; (*com trabalho*) weigh down □ *vi* be oppressive

optar /opi'tar/ *vi* opt (**por** for); **~ por ir** opt to go

óptica, óptico *veja* **ótica, ótico**

opu|lência /opu'lẽsia/ *f* opulence; **~lento** *a* opulent

ora /'ɔra/ *adv & conj* now □ *int* come; **~ essa!** come now!; **~ ..., ~ ...** first ..., then

oração /ora'sãw/ *f* (*prece*) prayer; (*discurso*) oration; (*frase*) clause

oráculo /o'rakulu/ *m* oracle

orador /ora'dor/ *m* orator

oral /o'raw/ (*pl* **orais**) *a & f* oral

orar /o'rar/ *vi* pray

órbita /'ɔrbita/ *f* orbit; (*do olho*) socket

orçamen|tário /orsamẽ'tariu/ *a* budgetary; **~to** *m* (*plano financeiro*) budget; (*previsão dos custos*) estimate

orçar /or'sar/ *vt* estimate (**em** at)

ordeiro /or'deru/ *a* orderly

ordem /'ordẽ/ *f* order; **por ~ alfabética** in alphabetical order; **~ de pagamento** banker's draft; **~ do dia** agenda

orde|nação /ordenaˈsãw/ *f* ordering; (*de padre*) ordination; **~nado** *a* ordered ▫ *m* wages; **~nar** *vt* order; put in order <*papéis, livros etc*>; ordain <*padre*>

ordenhar /ordeˈɲar/ *vt* milk

ordinário /ordʒiˈnariu/ *a* (*normal*) ordinary; (*grosseiro*) vulgar; (*de má qualidade*) inferior; (*sem caráter*) rough

ore|lha /oˈreʎa/ *f* ear; **~lhão** *m* phone booth; **~lhudo** *a* with big ears; **ser ~lhudo** have big ears

orfanato /orfaˈnatu/ *m* orphanage

ór|fão /ˈɔrfãw/ (*pl* **~fãos**) *a* & *m* (*f* **~fã**) orphan

orgânico /orˈganiku/ *a* organic

orga|nismo /orgaˈnizmu/ *m* organism; (*do Estado etc*) institution; **~ geneticamente modificado** GMO; **~nista** *m/f* organist

organi|zação /organizaˈsãw/ *f* organization; **~zador** *a* organizing ▫ *m* organizer; **~zar** *vt* organize

órgão /ˈɔrgãw/ (*pl* **~s**) *m* organ; (*do Estado etc*) body

orgasmo /orˈgazmu/ *m* orgasm

orgia /orˈʒia/ *f* orgy

orgu|lhar /orguˈʎar/ *vt* make proud; **~lhar-se** *vpr* be proud (**de** of); **~lho** *m* pride; **~lhoso** *a* proud

orien|tação /orientaˈsãw/ *f* orientation; (*direção*) direction; (*vocacional etc*) guidance; **~tador** *m* advisor; **~tal** (*pl* **~tais**) *a* eastern; (*da Asia*) oriental; **~tar** *vt* direct; (*aconselhar*) advise; (*situar*) position; **~tar-se** *vpr* get one's bearings; **~tar-se por** be guided by; **~te** *m* east; **Oriente Médio** Middle East; **Extremo Oriente** Far East

orifício /oriˈfisiu/ *m* opening; (*no corpo*) orifice

origem /oˈriʒẽ/ *f* origin; **dar ~ a** give rise to; **ter ~** originate

origi|nal /oriʒiˈnaw/ (*pl* **~nais**) *a* & *m* original; **~nalidade** *f* originality; **~nar** *vt* give rise to; **~nar-se** *vpr* originate; **~nário** *a* <*planta, animal*> native (**de** to); <*pessoa*> originating (**de** from)

oriundo /oˈrjũdu/ *a* originating (**de** from)

orla /ˈɔrla/ *f* border; **~ marítima** seafront

ornamen|tação /ornamẽtaˈsãw/ *f* ornamentation; **~tal** (*pl* **~tais**) *a* ornamental; **~tar** *vt* decorate; **~to** *m* ornament

orques|tra /orˈkɛstra/ *f* orchestra; **~tra sinfônica** symphony orchestra; **~tral** (*pl* **~trais**) *a* orchestral; **~trar** *vt* orchestrate

orquídea /orˈkidʒia/ *f* orchid

ortodoxo /ortoˈdɔksu/ *a* orthodox

orto|grafia /ortograˈfia/ *f* spelling, orthography; **~gráfico** *a* orthographic

orto|pedia /ortopeˈdʒia/ *f* orthopaedics; **~pédico** *a* orthopaedic; **~pedista** *m/f* orthopaedic surgeon

orvalho /orˈvaʎu/ *m* dew

os /us/ *artigo & pron veja* **o**

oscilar /osiˈlar/ *vi* oscillate

ósseo /ˈɔsiu/ *a* bone

os|so /ˈosu/ *m* bone; **~sudo** *a* bony

ostensivo /ostẽˈsivu/ *a* ostensible

osten|tação /ostẽtaˈsãw/ *f* ostentation; **~tar** *vt* show off; **~toso** *a* showy, ostentatious

osteopata /ostʃioˈpata/ *m/f* osteopath

ostra /ˈostra/ *f* oyster

ostracismo /ostraˈsizmu/ *m* ostracism

otário /oˈtariu/ *m* (*fam*) fool

óti|ca /ˈɔtʃika/ *f* (*ciência*) optics; (*loja*) optician's; (*ponto de vista*) viewpoint; **~co** *a* optical

otimis|mo /otʃiˈmizmu/ *m* optimism; **~ta** *m/f* optimist ▫ *a* optimistic

ótimo /ˈɔtʃimu/ *a* excellent

otorrino /otoˈxinu/ *m* ear, nose and throat specialist

ou /o/ *conj* or; **~ ... ~ ...** either ... or ...; **~ seja** in other words

ouriço /oˈrisu/ *m* hedgehog; **~-do-mar** (*pl* **~s-do-mar**) *m* sea urchin

ouri|ves /oˈrivis/ *m/f invar* jeweller; **~vesaria** *f* (*loja*) jeweller's

ouro /ˈoru/ *m* gold; *pl* (*naipe*) diamonds; **de ~** golden

ou|sadia /ozaˈdʒia/ *f* daring; (*uma*) daring step; **~sado** *a* daring; **~sar** *vt/i* dare

outdoor /ˈawtdor/ (*pl* **~s**) *m* billboard

outo|nal /otoˈnaw/ (*pl* **~nais**) *a* autumnal; **~no** /o/ *m* autumn, (*Amer*) fall

outorgar /otorˈgar/ *vt* grant

ou|trem /oˈtrẽj/ *pron* (*outro*) someone else; (*outros*) others; **~tro** *a* other ▫ *pron* (*um*) another (one); *pl* others; **~tro copo** another glass; **~tra coisa** something else; **~tro dia** the other day; **no ~tro dia** the next day; **~tra vez** again; **~trora** *adv* once upon a time; **~trossim** *adv* equally

outubro /oˈtubru/ *m* October

ou|vido /oˈvidu/ *m* ear; **de ~vido** by ear; **dar ~vidos a** listen to; **~vinte** *m/f* listener; (*atentamente*) listen to ▫ *vi* hear; **~vir** *vt* hear; **~vir dizer que** hear that; **~vir falar de** hear of

ovação /ovaˈsãw/ *f* ovation

oval /oˈvaw/ (*pl* **ovais**) *a* & *f* oval

ovário /oˈvariu/ *m* ovary

o

ovelha /o'veʎa/ *f* sheep

óvni /'ɔvni/ *m* UFO

ovo /'ovu/ *m* egg; ~ **cozido /frito/mexido/pochê** boiled/fried /scrambled/poached egg

oxi|genar /oksiʒe'nar/ *vt* bleach <*cabelo*>; ~**gênio** *m* oxygen

ozônio /o'zoniu/ *m* ozone

....

Pp

....

pá /pa/ *f* spade; (*de hélice*) blade; (*de moinho*) sail ▫ *m* (*Port: fam*) mate

pacato /pa'katu/ *a* quiet

paci|ência /pasi'ēsia/ *f* patience; ~**ente** *a* & *m/f* patient

pacificar /pasifi'kar/ *vt* pacify

pacífico /pa'sifiku/ *a* peaceful; **Oceano Pacífico** Pacific Ocean; **ponto** ~ undisputed point

pacifis|mo /pasi'fizmu/ *m* pacifism; ~**ta** *a* & *m/f* pacifist

paço /'pasu/ *m* palace

pacote /pa'kɔtʃi/ *m* (*de biscoitos etc*) packet; (*mandado pelo correio*) parcel; (*econômico, turístico, software*) package

pacto /'paktu/ *m* pact

padaria /pada'ria/ *f* baker's (shop), bakery

padecer /pade'ser/ *vt/i* suffer

padeiro /pa'deru/ *m* baker

padiola /padʒi'ɔla/ *f* stretcher

padrão /pa'drãw/ *m* standard; (*desenho*) pattern

padrasto /pa'drastu/ *m* stepfather

padre /'padri/ *m* priest

padrinho /pa'driɲu/ *m* (*de batismo*) godfather; (*de casamento*) best man

padroeiro /padro'eru/ *m* patron saint

padronizar /padroni'zar/ *vt* standardize

paga /'paga/ *f* pay; ~**mento** *m* payment

pa|gão /pa'gãw/ (*pl* ~**gãos**) *a* & *m* (*f* ~**gã**) pagan

pagar /pa'gar/ *vt* pay for <*compra, erro etc*>; pay <*dívida, conta, empregado etc*>; pay back <*empréstimo*>; repay <*gentileza etc*> ▫ *vi* pay; **eu pago para ver** I'll believe it when I see it

página /'paʒina/ *f* page; ~ **web** web page

pago /'pagu/ *a* paid ▫ *pp de* **pagar**

pagode /pa'gɔdʒi/ *m* (*torre*) pagoda; (*fam*) singalong

pai /paj/ *m* father; *pl* (*pai e mãe*) parents; ~**-de-santo** (*pl* ~**s-de-santo**) *m* macumba priest

pai|nel /paj'nɛw/ (*pl* ~**néis**) *m* panel; (*de carro*) dashboard

paio /'paju/ *m* pork sausage

pairar /paj'rar/ *vi* hover

país /pa'is/ *m* country; **País de Gales** Wales; **Países Baixos** Netherlands

paisa|gem /paj'zaʒē/ *f* landscape; ~**gista** *m/f* landscape gardener

paisana /paj'zana/ *f* à ~ <*policial*> in plain clothes; <*soldado*> in civilian clothes

paixão /pa'ʃãw/ *f* passion

pala /'pala/ *f* (*de bonê*) peak; (*de automóvel*) sun visor

palácio /pa'lasiu/ *m* palace

paladar /pala'dar/ *m* palate, taste

palanque /pa'lãki/ *m* stand

palavra /pa'lavra/ *f* word; **pedir a** ~ ask to speak; **ter** ~ be reliable; **tomar a** ~ start to speak; **sem** ~ <*pessoa*> unreliable; ~ **de ordem** watchword; ~**s cruzadas** crossword

palavrão /pala'vrãw/ *m* swearword

palco /'pawku/ *m* stage

palestino /pales'tʃinu/ *a* & *m* Palestinian

palestra /pa'lɛstra/ *f* lecture

paleta /pa'leta/ *f* palette

paletó /pale'tɔ/ *m* jacket

palha /'paʎa/ *f* straw

palha|çada /paʎa'sada/ *f* joke; ~**ço** *m* clown

paliativo /palia'tʃivu/ *a* & *m* palliative

palidez /pali'des/ *f* paleness

pálido /'palidu/ *a* pale

pali|tar /pali'tar/ *vt* pick ▫ *vi* pick one's teeth; ~**teiro** *m* toothpick holder; ~**to** *m* (*para dentes*) toothpick; (*de fósforo*) matchstick; (*pessoa magra*) beanpole

pal|ma /'pawma/ *f* palm; *pl* (*aplauso*) clapping; **bater** ~**mas** clap; ~**meira** *f* palm tree; ~**mito** *m* palm heart; ~**mo** *m* span; ~**mo a** ~**mo** inch by inch

palpá|vel /paw'pavew/ (*pl* ~**veis**) *a* palpable

pálpebra /'pawpebra/ *f* eyelid

palpi|tação /pawpita'sãw/ *f* palpitation; ~**tante** *a* (*fig*) thrilling; ~**tar** *vi* <*coração*> flutter; <*pessoa*> tremble; (*dar palpite*) stick one's oar in; ~**te** *m* (*pressentimento*) hunch; (*no jogo etc*) tip; **dar** ~**te** stick one's oar in

panacéia /pana'sɛja/ *f* panacea

Panamá /pana'ma/ *m* Panama

panamenho /pana'meɲu/ *a* & *m* Panamanian

pan-americano /panameri'kanu/ *a* Pan-American

pança /'pãsa/ *f* paunch

pancada /pã'kada/ *f* blow; **~ d'água** downpour; **~ria** *f* fight, punch-up

pâncreas /'pãkrias/ *m invar* pancreas

pançudo /pã'sudu/ *a* paunchy

panda /'pãda/ *f* panda

pandarecos /pãda'rɛkus/ *m pl* **aos** *ou* **em ~** battered

pandeiro /pã'deru/ *m* tambourine

pandemônio /pãde'moniu/ *m* pandemonium

pane /'pani/ *f* breakdown

panela /pa'nɛla/ *f* saucepan; **~ de pressão** pressure cooker

panfleto /pã'fletu/ *m* pamphlet

pânico /'paniku/ *m* panic; **em ~** in a panic; **entrar em ~** panic

panifica|ção /panifika'sãw/ *f* bakery; **~dora** *f* bakery

pano /'panu/ *m* cloth; **~ de fundo** backdrop; **~ de pó** duster; **~ de pratos** tea towel

pano|rama /pano'rama/ *m* panorama; **~râmico** *a* panoramic

panqueca /pã'kɛka/ *f* pancake

panta|nal /pãta'naw/ (*pl* **~nais**) *m* marshland

pântano /'pãtanu/ *m* marsh

pantanoso /pãta'nozu/ *a* marshy

pantera /pã'tɛra/ *f* panther

pão /pãw/ (*pl* **pães**) *m* bread; **~ de fôrma** sliced loaf; **~ integral** brown bread; **~-de-ló** *m* sponge cake; **~-duro** (*pl* **pães-duros**) (*fam*) *a* stingy, tight-fisted □ *m*/*f* skinflint; **~zinho** *m* bread roll

Papa /'papa/ *m* Pope

papa /'papa/ *f* (*de nenem*) food; (*arroz etc*) mush

papagaio /papa'gaju/ *m* parrot

papai /pa'paj/ *m* dad, daddy; **Papai No·l** Father Christmas

papar /pa'par/ *vt*/*i* (*fam*) eat

papari|car /papari'kar/ *vt* pamper; **~cos** *m pl* pampering

pa|pel /pa'pɛw/ (*pl* **~péis**) *m* (*de escrever etc*) paper; (*um*) piece of paper; (*numa peça, filme*) part; (*fig: função*) role; **de ~pel passado** officially; **~pel de alumínio** aluminium foil; **~pel higiênico** toilet paper; **~pelada** *f* paperwork; **~pelão** *m* cardboard; **~pelaria** *f* stationer's (shop); **~pelzinho** *m* scrap of paper

papo /'papu/ *f* (*fam: conversa*) talk; (*do rosto*) double chin; **bater um ~** (*fam*) have a chat; **~ furado** idle talk

papoula /pa'pola/ *f* poppy

páprica /'paprika/ *f* paprika

paque|ra /pa'kɛra/ *f* (*fam*) pick-up; **~rador** *a* flirtatious □ *m* flirt; **~rar** *vt* flirt with *<pessoa>*; eye up *<vestido, carro etc>* □ *vi* flirt

paquista|nês /pakista'nes/ *a & m* (*f* **~nesa**) Pakistani

Paquistão /pakis'tãw/ *m* Pakistan

par /par/ *a* even □ *m* pair; (*parceiro*) partner; **a ~ de** up to date with *<notícias etc>*; **sem ~** unequalled

para /'para/ *prep* for; (*a*) to; **~ que** so that; **~ quê?** what for?; **~ casa** home; **estar ~ sair** be about to leave; **era ~ eu ir** I was supposed to go

para|benizar /parabeni'zar/ *vt* congratulate (**por** on); **~béns** *m pl* congratulations

parábola /pa'rabola/ *f* (*conto*) parable; (*curva*) parabola

parabóli|co /para'bɔliku/ *a* **antena ~ca** satellite dish

pára|-brisa /para'briza/ *m* windscreen, (*Amer*) windshield; **~-choque** *m* bumper

para|da /pa'rada/ *f* stop; (*interrupção*) stoppage; (*militar*) parade; (*fam: coisa difícil*) ordeal, challenge; **~da cardíaca** cardiac arrest; **~deiro** *m* whereabouts

paradisíaco /paradʒi'ziaku/ *a* idyllic

parado /pa'radu/ *a* *<trânsito, carro>* at a standstill, stopped; (*fig*) *<pessoa>* dull; **ficar ~** *<pessoa>* stand still; *<trânsito>* stop; (*deixar de trabalhar*) stop work

parado|xal /paradok'saw/ (*pl* **~xais**) *a* paradoxical; **~xo** /ɔ/ *m* paradox

parafina /para'fina/ *f* paraffin

paráfrase /pa'rafrazi/ *f* paraphrase

parafrasear /parafrazi'ar/ *vt* paraphrase

parafuso /para'fuzu/ *f* screw; **entrar em ~** get into a state

para|gem /pa'raʒẽ/ *f* (*Port: parada*) stop; **nestas ~gens** in these parts

parágrafo /pa'ragrafu/ *m* paragraph

Paraguai /para'gwaj/ *m* Paraguay

paraguaio /para'gwaju/ *a & m* Paraguayan

paraíso /para'izu/ *m* paradise

pára-lama /para'lama/ *m* (*de carro*) wing, (*Amer*) fender; (*de bicicleta*) mudguard

parale|la /para'lɛla/ *f* parallel; *pl* (*aparelho*) parallel bars; **~lepípedo** *m* paving stone; **~lo** /ɛ/ *a & m* parallel

para|lisar /parali'zar/ *vt* paralyse; bring to a halt *<fábrica, produção>*; **~lisar-se** *vpr* become paralysed; *<fábrica, produção>* grind to a halt; **~lisia** *f* paralysis; **~lítico** *a & m* paralytic; **~médico** *m* paramedic

paranói|a /para'nɔja/ *f* paranoia; **~co** *a* paranoid

parapeito /para'pejtu/ *m* (*muro*) parapet; (*da janela*) window-sill

pára-que|das /para'kɛdas/ *m invar* parachute; **~dista** *m/f* parachutist; (*militar*) paratrooper

parar /pa'rar/ *vt/i* stop; **~ de fumar** stop smoking; **ir ~** end up

pára-raios /para'xajus/ *m invar* lightning conductor

parasita /para'zita/ *a & m/f* parasite

parceiro /par'seru/ *m* partner

parce|la /par'sɛla/ *f* (*de terreno*) plot; (*prestação*) instalment; **~lar** *vt* spread <*pagamento*>

parceria /parse'ria/ *f* partnership

parci|al /parsi'aw/ *a* (*pl* **~ais**) *a* partial; (*partidário*) biased; **~alidade** *f* bias

parco /'parku/ *a* frugal; <*recursos*> scant

par|dal /par'daw/ *a* (*pl* **~dais**) *m* sparrow; **~do** *a* <*papel*> brown; <*pessoa*> mulatto

pare|cer /pare'ser/ *vi* (*ter aparência de*) seem; (*ter semelhança com*) be like; **~cer-se com** look like, resemble □ *m* opinion; **~cido** *a* similar (**com** to)

parede /pa'redʒi/ *f* wall

paren|te /pa'rẽtʃi/ *m/f* relative, relation; **~tesco** /e/ *m* relationship

parêntese /pa'rẽtʃizi/ *f* parenthesis; *pl* (*sinais*) brackets

paridade /pari'dadʒi/ *f* parity

parir /pa'rir/ *vt* give birth to □ *vi* give birth

parlamen|tar /parlamẽ'tar/ *a* parliamentary □ *m/f* member of parliament; **~tarismo** *m* parliamentary system; **~to** *m* parliament

parmesão /parme'zãw/ *a & m* (**queijo**) ~ Parmesan (cheese)

paródia /pa'rɔdʒia/ *f* parody

parodiar /parodʒi'ar/ *vt* parody

paróquia /pa'rɔkia/ *f* parish

parque /'parki/ *m* park; **~ temático** theme park

parte /'partʃi/ *f* part; (*quinhão*) share; (*num litígio, contrato*) party; **a maior ~ de** most of; **à ~** (*de lado*) aside; (*separadamente*) separately; **um erro da sua ~** a mistake on your part; **em ~** in part; **em alguma ~** somewhere; **por toda ~** everywhere; **por ~ do pai** on one's father's side; **fazer ~ de** be part of; **tomar ~ em** take part in

parteira /par'tera/ *f* midwife

partici|pação /partʃisipa'sãw/ *f* participation; (*numa empresa, nos lucros*) share; **~pante** *a* participating

□ *m/f* participant; **~par** *vi* take part (**de** *ou* **em**)

particípio /partʃi'sipiu/ *m* participle

partícula /par'tʃikula/ *f* particle

particu|lar /partʃiku'lar/ *a* private; (*especial*) unusual □ *m* (*pessoa*) private individual; *pl* (*detalhes*) particulars; **em ~lar** (*especialmente*) in particular; (*a sós*) in private; **~laridade** *f* peculiarity

partida /par'tʃida/ *f* (*saída*) departure; (*de corrida*) start; (*de futebol, xadrez etc*) match; **dar ~ em** start up

par|tidário /partʃi'dariu/ *a* partisan □ *m* supporter; **~tido** *a* broken □ *m* (*político*) party; (*casamento, par*) match; **tirar ~tido de** benefit from; **tomar o ~tido de** side with; **~tilha** *f* division; **~tir** *vi* (*sair*) depart; <*corredor*> start □ *vt* break; **~tir-se** *vpr* break; **a ~tir de …** from … onwards; **~tir para** (*fam*) resort to; **~tir para outra** do something different, change direction; **~titura** *f* score

parto /'partu/ *m* birth

parvo /'parvu/ *a* (*Port*) stupid

Páscoa /'paskoa/ *f* Easter

pas|mar /paz'mar/ *vt* amaze; **~mar-se** *vpr* be amazed (**com** at); **~mo** *a* amazed □ *m* amazement

passa /'pasa/ *f* raisin

pas|sada /pa'sada/ *f* **dar uma ~sada em** call in at; **~sadeira** *f* (*mulher*) woman who irons; (*Port: faixa*) zebra crossing, (*Amer*) crosswalk; **~sado** *a* <*ano, mês, semana*> last; <*tempo, particípio etc*> past; <*fruta, comida*> off □ *m* past; **são duas horas ~sadas** it's gone two o'clock; **bem/mal ~sado** <*bife*> well done/rare

passa|geiro /pasa'ʒeru/ *m* passenger □ *a* passing; **~gem** *f* passage; (*bilhete*) ticket; **de ~gem** <*dizer etc*> in passing; **estar de ~gem** be passing through; **~gem de ida e volta** return ticket, (*Amer*) round trip ticket

passaporte /pasa'pɔrtʃi/ *m* passport

passar /pa'sar/ *vt* pass; spend <*tempo*>; cross <*ponte, rio*>; (*a ferro*) iron <*roupa etc*>; (*aplicar*) put on <*creme, batom etc*> □ *vi* pass; <*dor, medo, chuva etc*> go; (*ser aceitável*) be passable □ *m* passing; **~-se** *vpr* happen; **passou a beber muito** he started to drink a lot; **passei dos 30 anos** I'm over thirty; **não passa de um boato** it's nothing more than a rumour; **~ por** go through; go along <*rua*>; (*ser considerado*) be taken for; **fazer-se ~ por** pass o.s. off as; **~ por cima de** (*fig*) overlook; **~ sem** do without

passarela /pasa'rɛla/ *f* (*sobre rua*) footbridge; (*para desfile de moda*) catwalk

pássaro /'pasaru/ *m* bird

passatempo /pasa'tẽpu/ *m* pastime

passe /'pasi/ *m* pass

pas|sear /pasi'ar/ *vi* go out and about; (*viajar*) travel around □ *vt* take for a walk; ∼**eata** *f* protest march; ∼**seio** *m* outing; (*volta a pé*) walk; (*volta de carro*) drive; **dar um** ∼**seio** (*a pé*) go for a walk; (*de carro*) go for a drive

passio|nal /pasio'naw/ (*pl* ∼**nais**) *a* **crime** ∼**nal** crime of passion

passista /pa'sista/ *m/f* dancer

passí|vel /pa'sivew/ (*pl* ∼**veis**) *a* ∼**vel de** subject to

passi|vidade /pasivi'dadʒi/ *f* passivity; ∼**vo** *a* passive □ *m* (*com*) liabilities; (*ling*) passive

passo /'pasu/ *m* step; (*velocidade*) pace; (*barulho*) footstep; ∼ **a** ∼ step by step; **a dois** ∼**s de** a stone's throw from; **dar um** ∼ take a step

pasta /'pasta/ *f* (*matéria*) paste; (*bolsa*) briefcase; (*fichário*) folder; **ministro sem** ∼ minister without portfolio; ∼ **de dentes** toothpaste

pas|tagem /pas'taʒẽ/ *f* pasture; ∼**tar** *vi* graze

pas|tel /pas'tɛw/ (*pl* ∼**téis**) *m* (*para comer*) samosa; (*Port: doce*) pastry; (*para desenhar*) pastel; ∼**telão** *m* (*comédia*) slapstick; ∼**telaria** *f* (*loja*) samosa vendor, (*Port*) pastry shop; (*Port: pastéis*) pastries

pasteurizado /pastewri'zadu/ *a* pasteurized

pastilha /pas'tʃiʎa/ *f* pastille

pas|to /'pastu/ *m* (*erva*) fodder, feed; (*lugar*) pasture; ∼**tor** *m* (*de gado*) shepherd; (*clérigo*) vicar; ∼**tor alemão** (*cachorro*) Alsatian; ∼**toral** (*pl* ∼**torais**) *a* pastoral

pata /'pata/ *f* paw; ∼**da** *f* kick

patamar /pata'mar/ *m* landing; (*fig*) level

patê /pa'te/ *m* pâté

patente /pa'tẽtʃi/ *a* obvious □ *f* (*mil*) rank; (*de invenção*) patent; ∼**ar** *vt* patent <*produto, invenção*>

pater|nal /pater'naw/ (*pl* ∼**nais**) *a* paternal; ∼**nidade** *f* paternity; ∼**no** /ɛ/ *a* paternal

pate|ta /pa'tɛta/ *a* daft, silly □ *m/f* fool; ∼**tice** *f* stupidity; (*uma*) silly thing

patético /pa'tɛtʃiku/ *a* pathetic

patíbulo /pa'tʃibulu/ *m* gallows

pati|faria /patʃifa'ria/ *f* roguishness; (*uma*) dirty trick; ∼**fe** *m* scoundrel

patim /pa'tʃĩ/ *m* skate; ∼ **de rodas** roller skate

pati|nação /patʃina'sãw/ *f* skating; (*rinque*) skating rink; ∼**nador** *m* skater; ∼**nar** *vi* skate; <*carro*> skid; ∼**nete** /ɛ/ *m* skateboard

pátio /'patʃiu/ *m* courtyard; (*de escola*) playground

pato /'patu/ *m* duck

pato|logia /patolo'ʒia/ *f* pathology; ∼**lógico** *a* pathological; ∼**logista** *m/f* pathologist

patrão /pa'trãw/ *m* boss

pátria /'patria/ *f* homeland

patriar|ca /patri'arka/ *m* patriarch; ∼**cal** (*pl* ∼**cais**) *a* patriarchal

patrimônio /patri'moniu/ *m* (*bens*) estate, property; (*fig: herança*) heritage

patri|ota /patri'ɔta/ *m/f* patriot; ∼**ótico** *a* patriotic; ∼**otismo** *m* patriotism

patroa /pa'troa/ *f* boss; (*fam: esposa*) missus, wife

patro|cinador /patrosina'dor/ *m* sponsor; ∼**cinar** *vt* sponsor; ∼**cínio** *m* sponsorship

patru|lha /pa'truʎa/ *f* patrol; ∼**lhar** *vt/i* patrol

pau /paw/ *m* stick; (*fam: cruzeiro*) cruzeiro; (*chulo: pênis*) prick; *pl* (*naipe*) clubs; **a meio** ∼ at half mast; **rachar** ∼ (*fam: brigar*) row, fight like cat and dog; ∼**lada** *f* blow with a stick

paulista /paw'lista/ *a & m/f* (*person*) from (the state of) São Paulo; ∼**no** *a & m* (*person*) from (the city of) São Paulo

pausa /'pawza/ *f* pause; ∼**do** *a* slow

pauta /'pawta/ *f* (*em papel*) lines; (*de música*) stave; (*fig: de discussão etc*) agenda; ∼**do** *a* <*papel*> lined

pavão /pa'vãw/ *m* peacock

pavilhão /pavi'ʎãw/ *m* pavilion; (*no jardim*) summerhouse

pavimen|tar /pavimẽ'tar/ *vt* pave; ∼**to** *m* floor; (*de rua etc*) surface

pavio /pa'viu/ *m* wick

pavor /pa'vor/ *m* terror; **ter** ∼ **de** be terrified of; ∼**oso** /o/ *a* dreadful

paz /pas/ *f* peace; **fazer as** ∼**es** make up

pé /pɛ/ *m* foot; (*planta*) plant; (*de móvel*) leg; **a** ∼ on foot; **ao** ∼ **da letra** literally; **estar de** ∼ <*festa etc*> be on; **ficar de** ∼ stand up; **em** ∼ standing (up); **em** ∼ **de igualdade** on an equal footing

peão /pi'ãw/ *m* (*Port: pedestre*) pedestrian; (*no xadrez*) pawn

peça /'pɛsa/ *f* piece; (*de máquina, carro etc*) part; (*teatral*) play; **pregar uma** ∼ **em** play a trick on; ∼ **de reposição** spare part; ∼ **de vestuário** item of clothing

p

pe|cado /pe'kadu/ *m* sin; ~cador *m* sinner; ~caminoso /o/ *a* sinful; ~car *vi* (*contra a religião*) sin; (*fig*) fall down

pechin|cha /pe'ʃĩʃa/ *f* bargain; ~char *vt* bargain, haggle

peçonhento /peso'ɲẽtu/ *a* **animais** ~s vermin

pecu|ária /peku'aria/ *f* livestock-farming; ~ário *a* livestock; ~arista *m/f* livestock farmer

peculi|ar /pekuli'ar/ *a* peculiar; ~aridade *f* peculiarity

pecúlio /pe'kuliu/ *m* savings

pedaço /pe'dasu/ *m* piece; **aos** ~s in pieces; **cair aos** ~s fall to pieces

pedágio /pe'daʒiu/ *m* toll; (*cabine*) tollbooth

peda|gogia /pedago'ʒia/ *f* education; ~gógico *a* educational; ~gogo /o/ *m* educationalist

pe|dal /pe'daw/ (*pl* ~dais) *m* pedal; ~dalar *vt/i* pedal

pedante /pe'dãtʃi/ *a* pretentious □ *m/f* pseud

pé|-de-atleta /pɛdʒiat'lɛta/ *m* athlete's foot; ~de-meia (*pl* ~s-de-meia) *m* nest egg; ~-de-pato (*pl* ~s-de-pato) *m* flipper

pederneira /peder'nera/ *f* flint

pedes|tal /pedes'taw/ (*pl* ~tais) *m* pedestal

pedestre /pe'dɛstri/ *a & m/f* pedestrian

pé|-de-vento /pɛdʒi'vẽtu/ (*pl* ~s-de-vento) *m* gust of wind

pedia|tra /pedʒi'atra/ *m/f* paediatrician; ~tria *f* paediatrics

pedicuro /pedʒi'kuru/ *m* chiropodist, (*Amer*) podiatrist

pe|dido /pe'dʒidu/ *m* request; (*encomenda*) order; **a** ~**dido de** at the request of; ~**dido de demissão** resignation; ~**dido de desculpa** apology; ~**dir** *vt* ask for; (*num restaurante etc*) order □ *vi* ask; (*num restaurante etc*) order; ~**dir aco a alg** ask s.o. for sth; ~**dir para alg ir** ask s.o. to go; ~**dir desculpa** apologize; ~**dir em casamento** propose to

pedinte /pe'dʒĩtʃi/ *m/f* beggar

pedra /'pɛdra/ *stone*; ~ **de gelo** ice cube; **chuva de** ~ hail; ~ **pomes** pumice stone

pedregoso /pedre'gozu/ *a* stony

pedreiro /pe'dreru/ *m* builder

pegada /pe'gada/ *f* footprint; (*de goleiro*) save

pegajoso /pega'ʒozu/ *a* sticky

pegar /pe'gar/ *vt* get; catch <*bola, doença, ladrão, ônibus*>; (*segurar*) get hold of; pick up <*emissora, hábito, mania*> □ *vi* (*aderir*) stick; <*doença*> be catching; <*moda*> catch on; <*carro, motor*> start; <*mentira, desculpa*> stick; ~**-se** *vpr* come to blows; ~ **bem /mal** go down well/badly; ~ **fogo** catch fire; **pega essa rua** take that street; ~ **em grab**; ~ **no sono** get to sleep

pego /'pɛgu/ *pp de* **pegar**

pei|dar /pej'dar/ *vi* (*chulo*) fart; ~do *m* (*chulo*) fart

pei|to /'pejtu/ *m* chest; (*seio*) breast; (*fig: coragem*) guts; ~toril (*pl* ~toris) *m* window-sill; ~tudo *a* <*mulher*> busty; (*fig: corajoso*) gutsy

pei|xaria /pe'ʃaria/ *f* fishmonger's; ~xe *m* fish; **Peixes** (*signo*) Pisces; ~xeiro *m* fishmonger

pela = por + a

pelado /pe'ladu/ *a* (*nu*) naked, in the nude

pelan|ca /pe'lãka/ *f* roll of fat; *pl* flab; ~cudo *a* flabby

pelar /pe'lar/ *vt* peel <*fruta, batata*>; skin <*animal*>; (*fam: tomar dinheiro de*) fleece

pelas = por + as

pele /'pɛli/ *f* skin; (*como roupa*) fur; ~teiro *m* furrier; ~teria *f* furrier's

pelica /pe'lika/ *f* **luvas de** ~ kid gloves

pelicano /peli'kanu/ *m* pelican

película /pe'likula/ *f* skin

pelo = por + o

pêlo /'pelu/ *m* hair; (*de animal*) coat; **nu em** ~ stark naked; **montar em** ~ ride bareback

pelos = por + os

pelotão /pelo'tãw/ *m* platoon

pelúcia /pe'lusia/ *f* **bicho de** ~ soft toy, fluffy animal

peludo /pe'ludu/ *a* hairy

pena[1] /'pena/ *f* (*de ave*) feather; (*de caneta*) nib

pena[2] /'pena/ *f* (*castigo*) penalty; (*de amor etc*) pang; **é uma** ~ que it's a pity that; **que** ~! what a pity!; **dar** ~ be upsetting; **estar com** *ou* **ter** ~ **de** feel sorry for; (**não**) **vale a** ~ it's (not) worth it; **vale a** ~ **tentar** it's worth trying; ~ **de morte** death penalty

penada /pe'nada/ *f* stroke of the pen

pe|nal /pe'naw/ (*pl* ~nais) *a* penal; ~nalidade *f* penalty; ~nalizar *vt* penalize

pênalti /'penawtʃi/ *m* penalty

penar /pe'nar/ *vi* suffer

pen|dente /pẽ'dẽtʃi/ *a* hanging; (*fig: causa*) pending; ~der *vi* hang; (*inclinar-se*) slope; (*tender*) be inclined (**a** to); ~dor *m* inclination

pêndulo /'pẽdulu/ *m* pendulum

pendu|rado /pẽdu'radu/ *a* hanging; (*fam: por fazer, pagar*) outstanding;

~**rar** *vt* hang (up); (*fam*) put on the slate <*compra*> □ *vi* (*fam*) pay later; ~**ricalho** *m* pendant

penedo /pe'nedu/ *m* rock

penei|ra /pe'nera/ *f* sieve; ~**rar** *vt* sieve, sift □ *vi* drizzle

pene|tra /pe'nɛtra/ *m*/*f* (*fam*) gatecrasher; ~**tração** *f* penetration; (*fig*) perspicacity; ~**trante** *a* <*som, olhar*> piercing; <*dor*> sharp; <*ferida*> deep; <*frio*> biting; < *análise, espírito*> incisive, perceptive; ~**trar** *vt* penetrate □ *vi* ~**trar em** enter <*casa*>; (*fig*) penetrate

penhasco /pe'ɲasku/ *m* cliff

penhoar /peɲo'ar/ *m* dressing gown

penhor /pe'ɲor/ *m* pledge; **casa de** ~**es** pawnshop

penicilina /penisi'lina/ *f* penicillin

penico /pe'niku/ *m* potty

península /pe'nĩsula/ *f* peninsula

pênis /'penis/ *m invar* penis

penitência /peni'tẽsia/ *f* (*arrependimento*) penitence; (*expiação*) penance

penitenciá|ria /penitẽsi'aria/ *f* prison; ~**rio** *a* prison □ *m* prisoner

penoso /pe'nozu/ *a* <*experiência, tarefa, assunto*> painful; <*trabalho, viagem*> hard, difficult

pensa|dor /pẽsa'dor/ *m* thinker; ~**mento** *m* thought

pensão /pẽ'sãw/ *f* (*renda*) pension; (*hotel*) guesthouse; ~ **(alimentícia)** (*paga por ex-marido*) alimony; ~ **completa** full board

pen|sar /pẽ'sar/ *vt*/*i* think (**em** of *ou* about); ~**sativo** *a* thoughtful, pensive

pên|sil /'pẽsiw/ (*pl* ~**seis**) *a* **ponte** ~**sil** suspension bridge

penso /'pẽsu/ *m* (*curativo*) dressing

pentágono /pẽ'tagonu/ *m* pentagon

pentatlo /pẽ'tatlu/ *m* pentathlon

pente /'pẽtʃi/ *m* comb; ~**adeira** *f* dressing table; ~**ado** *m* hairstyle, hairdo; ~**ar** *vt* comb; ~**ar-se** *vpr* do one's hair; (*com pente*) comb one's hair

Pentecostes /pẽte'kɔstʃis/ *m* Whitsun

pente-fino /pẽtʃi'finu/ *m* **passar a** ~ go over with a fine-tooth comb

pente|lhar /pẽte'ʎar/ *vt* (*fam*) bother; ~**lho** /e/ *m* pubic hair; (*fam: pessoa inconveniente*) pain (in the neck)

penugem /pe'nuʒẽ/ *f* down

penúltimo /pe'nuwtʃimu/ *a* last but one, penultimate

penumbra /pe'nũbra/ *f* half-light

penúria /pe'nuria/ *f* penury, extreme poverty

pepino /pe'pinu/ *m* cucumber

pepita /pe'pita/ *f* nugget

peque|nez /peke'nes/ *f* smallness; (*fig*) pettiness; ~**nininho** *a* tiny; ~**no** /e/ *a* small; (*mesquinho*) petty

Pequim /pe'kĩ/ *f* Peking, Beijing

pequinês /peki'nes/ *m* Pekinese

pêra /'pera/ *f* pear

perambular /perãbu'lar/ *vi* wander

perante /pe'rãtʃi/ *prep* before

percalço /per'kawsu/ *m* pitfall

perceber /perse'ber/ *vt* realize; (*Port: entender*) understand; (*psiqu*) perceive

percen|tagem /persẽ'taʒẽ/ *f* percentage; ~**tual** (*pl* ~**tuais**) *a* & *m* percentage

percep|ção /persep'sãw/ *f* perception; ~**tível** (*pl* ~**tíveis**) *a* perceptible

percevejo /perse'veʒu/ *m* (*bicho*) bedbug; (*tachinha*) drawing pin, (*Amer*) thumbtack

per|correr /perko'xer/ *vt* cross; cover <*distância*>; (*viajar por*) travel through; ~**curso** *m* journey

percus|são /perku'sãw/ *f* percussion; ~**sionista** *m*/*f* percussionist

percutir /perku'tʃir/ *vt* strike

perda /'perda/ *f* loss; ~ **de tempo** waste of time

perdão /per'dãw/ *f* pardon

perder /per'der/ *vt* lose; (*não chegar a ver, pegar*) miss <*ônibus, programa na TV etc*>; waste <*tempo*> □ *vi* lose; ~**-se** *vpr* get lost; ~**-se de alg** lose s.o.; ~ **aco de vista** lose sight of sth

perdiz /per'dʒis/ *f* partridge

perdoar /perdo'ar/ *vt* forgive (**aco a alg** s.o. for sth)

perdulário /perdu'lariu/ *a* & *m* spendthrift

perdurar /perdu'rar/ *vi* endure; <*coisa ruim*> persist

pere|cer /pere'ser/ *vi* perish; ~**cível** (*pl* ~**cíveis**) *a* perishable

peregri|nação /peregrina'sãw/ *f* peregrination; (*romaria*) pilgrimage; ~**nar** *vi* roam; (*por motivos religiosos*) go on a pilgrimage; ~**no** *m* pilgrim

pereira /pe'rera/ *f* pear tree

peremptório /perẽp'tɔriu/ *a* peremptory

perene /pe'reni/ *a* perennial

perereca /pere'rɛka/ *f* tree frog

perfazer /perfa'zer/ *vt* make up

perfeccionis|mo /perfeksio'nizmu/ *m* perfectionism; ~**ta** *a* & *m*/*f* perfectionist

perfei|ção /perfej'sãw/ *f* perfection; ~**to** *a* & *m* perfect

per|fil /per'fiw/ (*pl* ~**fis**) *m* profile; ~**filar** *vt* line up; ~**filar-se** *vpr* line up

perfu|mado /perfu'madu/ *a* <*flor, ar*> fragrant; <*sabonete etc*> scented;

p

\<pessoa\> with perfume on; ~mar vt
perfume; ~mar-se vpr put perfume on;
~maria f perfumery; (fam)
trimmings, frills; ~me m perfume

perfu|rador /perfura'dor/ m punch;
~rar vt punch \<papel, bilhete\>; drill
through \<chão\>; perforate \<úlcera,
pulmão etc\>; ~ratriz f drill

pergaminho /perga'miɲu/ m parchment

pergun|ta /per'gũta/ f question; **fazer
uma ~ta** ask a question; ~tar vt/i ask;
~tar aco a alg ask s.o. sth; ~tar por
ask after

perícia /pe'risia/ f (mestria) expertise;
(inspeção) investigation; (peritos)
experts

perici|al /perisi'aw/ (pl ~ais) a expert

pericli|tante /perikli'tãtʃi/ a precarious;
~tar vi be at risk

peri|feria /perife'ria/ f periphery; (da
cidade) outskirts; ~férico a & m
peripheral

perigo /pe'rigu/ m danger; ~so /o/ a
dangerous

perímetro /pe'rimetru/ m perimeter

periódico /peri'ɔdʒiku/ a periodic ▢ m
periodical

período /pe'riodu/ m period; **trabalhar
meio ~** work part-time

peripécias /peri'pɛsias/ f pl ups and
downs, vicissitudes

periquito /peri'kitu/ m parakeet; (de
estimação) budgerigar

periscópio /peris'kɔpiu/ m periscope

perito /pe'ritu/ a & m expert (em at)

per|jurar /perʒu'rar/ vi commit perjury;
~júrio m perjury; ~juro m perjurer

perma|necer /permane'ser/ vi remain;
~nência f permanence; (estadia) stay;
~nente a permanent ▢ f perm

permeá|vel /permi'avew/ (pl ~veis) a
permeable

permis|são /permi'sãw/ f permission;
~sível (pl ~síveis) a permissible;
~sivo a permissive

permitir /permi'tʃir/ vt allow, permit; ~
a alg ir allow s.o. to go

permutar /permu'tar/ vt exchange

perna /'pɛrna/ f leg

pernicioso /pernisi'ozu/ a pernicious

per|nil /per'niw/ (pl ~nis) m leg

pernilongo /perni'lõgu/ m (large)
mosquito

pernoi|tar /pernoj'tar/ vi spend the
night; ~te m overnight stay

pérola /'pɛrola/ f pearl

perpendicular /perpẽdʒiku'lar/ a
perpendicular

perpetrar /perpe'trar/ vt perpetrate

perpetu|ar /perpetu'ar/ vt perpetuate;
~idade f perpetuity

perpétu|o /per'pɛtuu/ a perpetual;
prisão ~a life imprisonment

perple|xidade /perpleksi'dadʒi/ f
puzzlement; ~xo /ɛ/ a puzzled

persa /'pɛrsa/ a & m/f Persian

perse|guição /persegi'sãw/ f pursuit;
(de minorias etc) persecution; ~guidor
m pursuer; (de minorias etc)
persecutor; ~guir vt pursue;
persecute \<minoria, seita etc\>

perseve|rança /perseve'rãsa/ f
perseverance; ~rante a persevering;
~rar vi persevere

persiana /persi'ana/ f blind

pérsico /'pɛrsiku/ a **Golfo Pérsico**
Persian Gulf

persignar-se /persig'narsi/ vt cross o.s.

persis|tência /persis'tẽsia/ f
persistence; ~tente a persistent; ~tir
vi persist

perso|nagem /perso'naʒẽ/ m/f (pessoa
famosa) personality; (em livro, filme etc)
character; ~nalidade f personality;
~nalizar vt personalize; ~nificar vt
personify

perspectiva /perspek'tʃiva/ f (na arte,
ponto de vista) perspective;
(possibilidade) prospect

perspi|cácia /perspi'kasia/ f insight,
perceptiveness; ~caz a perceptive

persua|dir /persua'dʒir/ vt persuade
(alg a s.o. to); ~são f persuasion;
~sivo a persuasive

perten|cente /pertẽ'sẽtʃi/ a belonging (a
to); (que tem a ver com) pertaining (a to);
~cer vi belong (a to); (referir-se)
pertain (a to); ~ces m pl belongings

perto /'pɛrtu/ adv near (de to); **aqui ~**
near here, nearby; **de ~** closely; \<ver\>
close up

pertur|bação /perturba'sãw/ f
disturbance; (do espírito) anxiety;
~bado a \<pessoa\> unsettled;
troubled; ~bar vt disturb; ~bar-se vpr
get upset, be perturbed

Peru /pe'ru/ m Peru

peru /pe'ru/ m turkey

perua /pe'rua/ f (carro grande) estate
car, (Amer) station wagon;
(caminhonete) van; (para escolares etc)
minibus; (fam: mulher) brassy woman

peruano /peru'ano/ a & m Peruvian

peruca /pe'ruka/ f wig

perver|são /perver'sãw/ f perversion;
~so a perverse; ~ter vt pervert

pesadelo /peza'delu/ m nightmare

pesado /pe'zadu/ a heavy; \<estilo, livro\>
heavy-going ▢ adv heavily

pêsames /'pezamis/ m pl condolences

pesar¹ /pe'zar/ vt weigh; (fig: avaliar)
weigh up ▢ vi weigh; (influir) carry

weight; ~ **sobre** <*ameaça etc*> hang over; ~**-se** *vpr* weigh o.s.

pesar[2] /pe'zar/ *m* sorrow; ~**oso** /o/ *a* sorry, sorrowful

pes|ca /'pɛska/ *f* fishing; **ir à** ~**ca** go fishing; ~**cador** *m* fisherman; ~**car** *vt* catch; (*retirar da água*) fish out □ *vi* fish; (*fam*) (*entender*) understand; (*cochilar*) nod off; ~**car de** (*fam*) know all about

pescoço /pes'kosu/ *m* neck

peseta /pe'zeta/ *f* peseta

peso /'pezu/ *m* weight; **de** ~ (*fig*) <*pessoa*> influential; <*livro, argumento*> authoritative

pesqueiro /pes'keru/ *a* fishing

pesqui|sa /pes'kiza/ *f* research; (*uma*) study; *pl* research; ~**sa de mercado** market research; ~**sador** *m* researcher; ~**sar** *vt/i* research

pêssego /'pesigu/ *m* peach

pessegueiro /pesi'geru/ *m* peach tree

pessimis|mo /pesi'mizmu/ *m* pessimism; ~**ta** *a* pessimistic □ *m/f* pessimist

péssimo /'pɛsimu/ *a* terrible, awful

pesso|a /pe'soa/ *f* person; *pl* people; **em** ~**a** in person; ~**al** (*pl* ~**ais**) *a* personal □ *m* staff; (*fam*) folks

pesta|na /pes'tana/ *f* eyelash; **tirar uma** ~**na** (*fam*) have a nap; ~**nejar** *vi* blink; **sem** ~**nejar** (*fig*) without batting an eyelid

pes|te /'pɛstʃi/ *f* (*doença*) plague; (*criança etc*) pest; ~**ticida** *m* pesticide

pétala /'pɛtala/ *f* petal

peteca /pe'tɛka/ *f* kind of shuttlecock; (*jogo*) kind of badminton played with the hand

peteleco /pete'lɛku/ *m* flick

petição /petʃi'sãw/ *f* petition

petisco /pe'tʃisku/ *m* savoury, titbit

petrificar /petrifi'kar/ *vt* petrify; (*de surpresa*) stun; ~**-se** *vpr* be petrified; (*de surpresa*) be stunned

petroleiro /petro'leru/ *a* oil □ *m* oil tanker

petróleo /pe'trɔliu/ *m* oil, petroleum; ~ **bruto** crude oil

petrolífero /petro'liferu/ *a* oil-producing

petroquími|ca /petro'kimika/ *f* petrochemicals; ~**co** *a* petrochemical

petu|lância /petu'lãsia/ *f* cheek; ~**lante** *a* cheeky

peúga /pi'uga/ *f* (*Port*) sock

pevide /pe'vidʒi/ *f* (*Port*) pip

pia /'pia/ *f* (*do banheiro*) washbasin; (*da cozinha*) sink; ~ **batismal** font

piada /pi'ada/ *f* joke

pia|nista /pia'nista/ *m/f* pianist; ~**no** *m* piano; ~**no de cauda** grand piano

piar /pi'ar/ *vi* <*pinto*> cheep; <*coruja*> hoot

picada /pi'kada/ *f* (*de agulha, alfinete etc*) prick; (*de abelha, vespa*) sting; (*de mosquito, cobra*) bite; (*de heroína*) shot; (*de avião*) nosedive; **o fim da** ~ (*fig*) the limit

picadeiro /pika'deru/ *m* ring

picante /pi'kãtʃi/ *a* <*comida*> hot, spicy; <*piada*> risqué; <*filme, livro*> raunchy

pica-pau /pika'paw/ *m* woodpecker

picar /pi'kar/ *vt* (*com agulha, alfinete etc*) prick; <*abelha, vespa, urtiga*> sting; <*mosquito, cobra*> bite; <*pássaro*> peck; chop <*carne, alho etc*>; shred <*papel*> □ *vi* <*peixe*> bite; <*lã, cobertor*> prickle

picareta /pika'reta/ *f* pickaxe

pi|chação /piʃa'sãw/ *f* piece of graffiti; *pl* graffiti; ~**char** *vt* spray with graffiti <*muro, prédio*>; spray <*grafite, desenho*>; ~**che** *m* pitch

picles /'piklis/ *m pl* pickles

pico /'piku/ *m* peak; **20 anos e** ~ (*Port*) just over 20

picolé /piko'lɛ/ *m* ice lolly

pico|tar /piko'tar/ *vt* perforate; ~**te** /ɔ/ *m* perforations

pie|dade /pie'dadʒi/ *f* (*religiosidade*) piety; (*compaixão*) pity; ~**doso** /o/ *a* merciful, compassionate

pie|gas /pi'ɛgas/ *a invar* <*filme, livro*> sentimental, schmaltzy; <*pessoa*> soppy; ~**guice** *f* sentimentality

pifar /pi'far/ *vi* (*fam*) break down, go wrong

pigar|rear /pigaxi'ar/ *vi* clear one's throat; ~**ro** *m* frog in the throat

pigmento /pig'mẽtu/ *m* pigment

pig|meu /pig'mew/ *a* & *m* (*f* ~**méia**) pygmy

pijama /pi'ʒama/ *m* pyjamas

pilantra /pi'lãtra/ *m/f* (*fam*) crook

pilão /pi'lãw/ *m* (*na cozinha*) pestle; (*na construção*) ram

pilar /pi'lar/ *m* pillar

pilastra /pi'lastra/ *f* pillar

pileque /pi'lɛki/ *m* drinking session; **tomar um** ~ get drunk

pilha /'piʎa/ *f* (*monte*) pile; (*elétrica*) battery

pilhar /pi'ʎar/ *vt* pillage

pilhéria /pi'ʎɛria/ *f* joke

pilotar /pilo'tar/ *vt* fly, pilot <*avião*>; drive <*carro*>

pilotis /pilo'tʃis/ *m pl* pillars

piloto /pi'lotu/ *m* pilot; (*de carro*) driver; (*de gás*) pilot light □ *a invar* pilot

p

pílula /'pilula/ *f* pill

pimen|ta /pi'mẽta/ *f* pepper; **~ta de Caiena** cayenne pepper; **~ta-do-reino** *f* black pepper; **~ta-malagueta** (*pl* ~**tas-malagueta**) *f* chilli pepper; **~tão** *m* (bell) pepper; **~teira** *f* pepper pot

pinacoteca /pinako'tɛka/ *f* art gallery

pin|ça /'pĩsa/ (*para tirar pêlos*) tweezers; (*para segurar*) tongs; (*de siri etc*) pincer; **~çar** *vt* pluck <*sobrancelhas*>

pin|cel /pĩ'sɛw/ (*pl* ~**céis**) *m* brush; **~celada** *f* brush stroke; **~celar** *vt* paint

pin|ga /'pĩga/ *f* Brazilian rum; **~gado** *a* <*café*> with a dash of milk; **~gar** *vi* drip; (*começar a chover*) spit (with rain) □ *vt* drip; **~gente** *m* pendant; **~go** *m* drop; (*no i*) dot

pingue-pongue /pĩgi'põgi/ *m* table tennis

pingüim /pĩ'gwĩ/ *m* penguin

pi|nha /'pĩɲa/ *f* pine cone; **~nheiro** *f* pine tree; **~nho** *m* pine

pino /'pinu/ *m* pin; (*para trancar carro*) lock; **a ~** upright; **bater ~** <*carro*> knock

pin|ta /'pĩta/ *f* (*sinal*) mole; (*fam: aparência*) look; **~tar** *vt* paint; dye <*cabelo*>; put make-up on <*rosto, olhos*> □ *vi* paint; (*fam*) <*pessoa*> show up; <*problema, oportunidade*> crop up; **~tar-se** *vpr* put on make-up

pintarroxo /pĩta'xoʃu/ *m* robin

pinto /'pĩtu/ *m* chick

pin|tor /pĩ'tor/ *m* painter; **~tura** *f* painting

pio¹ /'piu/ *m* (*de pinto*) cheep; (*de coruja*) hoot

pio² /'piu/ *a* pious

piolho /pi'oʎu/ *m* louse

pioneiro /pio'neru/ *m* pioneer □ *a* pioneering

pior /pi'ɔr/ *a & adv* worse; **o ~** the worst

pio|ra /pi'ɔra/ *f* worsening; **~rar** *vt* make worse, worsen □ *vi* get worse, worsen

pipa /'pipa/ *f* (*que voa*) kite; (*de vinho*) cask

pipilar /pipi'lar/ *vi* chirp

pipo|ca /pi'pɔka/ *f* popcorn; **~car** *vi* spring up; **~queiro** *m* popcorn seller

pique /'piki/ *m* (*disposição*) energy; **a ~** vertically; **ir a ~** <*navio*> sink

piquenique /piki'niki/ *m* picnic

pique|te /pi'ketʃi/ *m* picket; **~teiro** *m* picket

pirado /pi'radu/ *a* (*fam*) crazy

pirâmide /pi'ramidʒi/ *f* pyramid

piranha /pi'raɲa/ *f* piranha; (*fam: mulher*) maneater

pirar /pi'rar/ (*fam*) *vi* flip out, go mad

pirata /pi'rata/ *a & m/f* pirate; **~ria** *f* piracy

pires /'piris/ *m invar* saucer

pirilampo /piri'lãpu/ *m* glow-worm

Pirineus /piri'news/ *m pl* Pyrenees

pirra|ça /pi'xasa/ *f* spiteful act; **fazer ~ça** be spiteful; **~cento** *a* spiteful

pirueta /piru'eta/ *f* pirouette

pirulito /piru'litu/ *m* lollipop

pi|sada /pi'zada/ *f* step; (*rastro*) footprint; **~sar** *vt* tread on; tread <*uvas, palco*>; (*esmagar*) trample on □ *vi* step; **~sar em** step on; (*entrar*) set foot in

pis|cadela /piska'dɛla/ *f* wink; **~ca-pisca** *m* indicator; **~car** *vi* (*com o olho*) wink; (*pestanejar*) blink; <*estrela, luz*> twinkle; <*motorista*> indicate □ *m num* **~car de olhos** in a flash

piscicultura /pisikuw'tura/ *f* fish farming; (*lugar*) fish farm

piscina /pi'sina/ *f* swimming pool

piso /'pizu/ *m* floor

pisotear /pizotʃi'ar/ *vt* trample

pista /'pista/ *f* track; (*da estrada*) carriageway; (*para aviões*) runway; (*de circo*) ring; (*dica*) clue; **~ de dança** dancefloor

pistache /pis'taʃi/ *m*, **pistacho** /pis'taʃu/ *m* pistachio (nut)

pisto|la /pis'tɔla/ *f* pistol; (*para pintar*) spray gun; **~lão** *m* influential contact; **~leiro** *m* gunman

pitada /pi'tada/ *f* pinch

piteira /pi'tera/ *f* cigarette-holder

pitoresco /pito'resku/ *a* picturesque

pitu /pi'tu/ *m* crayfish

pivete /pi'vɛtʃi/ *m/f* child thief

pivô /pi'vo/ *m* pivot

pixaim /piʃa'ĩ/ *a* frizzy

pizza /'pitsa/ *f* pizza; **~ria** *f* pizzeria

placa /'plaka/ *f* plate; (*de carro*) number plate, (*Amer*) license plate; (*comemorativa*) plaque; (*em computador*) board; **~ de sinalização** roadsign

placar /pla'kar/ *m* scoreboard; (*escore*) scoreline

plácido /'plasidu/ *a* placid

plagi|ário /plaʒi'ariu/ *m* plagiarist; **~ar** *vt* plagiarize

plágio /'plaʒiu/ *m* plagiarism

plaina /'plajna/ *f* plane

planador /plana'dor/ *m* glider

planalto /pla'nawtu/ *m* plateau

planar /pla'nar/ *vi* glide

planeamento, planear (*Port*) *veja* **planejamento, planejar**

plane|jamento /planeʒaˈmẽtu/ *m* planning; **∼jamento familiar** family planning; **∼jar** *vt* plan

planeta /plaˈneta/ *m* planet

planície /plaˈnisi/ *f* plain

planificar /planifiˈkar/ *vt* (*programar*) plan (out)

planilha /plaˈniʎa/ *f* spreadsheet

plano /ˈplanu/ *a* flat □ *m* plan; (*superfície, nível*) plane; **primeiro ∼** foreground

planta /ˈplãta/ *f* plant; (*do pé*) sole; (*de edifício*) ground plan; **∼ção** *f* (*ato*) planting; (*terreno*) plantation; **∼do** *a* **deixar alg ∼do** (*fam*) keep s.o. waiting around

plantão /plãˈtãw/ *m* duty; (*noturno*) night duty; **estar de ∼** be on duty

plantar /plãˈtar/ *vt* plant

plas|ma /ˈplazma/ *m* plasma; **∼mar** *vt* mould, shape

plásti|ca /ˈplastʃika/ *f* face-lift; **∼co** *a* & *m* plastic

plataforma /plataˈfɔrma/ *f* platform

plátano /ˈplatanu/ *m* plane tree

platéia /plaˈtɛja/ *f* audience; (*parte do teatro*) stalls, (*Amer*) orchestra

platina /plaˈtʃina/ *f* platinum; **∼dos** *m pl* points

platônico /plaˈtoniku/ *a* platonic

plausí|vel /plawˈzivew/ (*pl* **∼veis**) *a* plausible

ple|be /ˈplɛbi/ *f* common people; **∼beu** *a* (*f* **∼béia**) plebeian □ *m* (*f* **∼béia**) commoner; **∼biscito** *m* plebiscite

plei|tear /plejtʃiˈar/ *vt* contest; **∼to** *m* (*litígio*) case; (*eleitoral*) contest

ple|namente /plenaˈmẽtʃi/ *adv* fully; **∼nário** *a* plenary □ *m* plenary assembly; **∼no** /e/ *a* full; **em ∼no verão** in the middle of summer

plissado /pliˈsadu/ *a* pleated

pluma /ˈpluma/ *f* feather; **∼gem** *f* plumage

plu|ral /pluˈraw/ (*pl* **∼rais**) *a* & *m* plural

plutônio /pluˈtoniu/ *m* plutonium

pluvi|al /pluviˈaw/ (*pl* **∼ais**) *a* rain

pneu /piˈnew/ *m* tyre; **∼mático** *a* pneumatic □ *m* tyre

pneumonia /pineumoˈnia/ *f* pneumonia

pó /pɔ/ *f* powder; (*poeira*) dust; **leite em ∼** powdered milk

pobre /ˈpɔbri/ *a* poor □ *m/f* poor man (*f* woman); **os ∼s** the poor; **∼za** /e/ *f* poverty

poça /ˈposa/ *f* pool; (*deixada pela chuva*) puddle

poção /poˈsãw/ *f* potion

pocilga /poˈsiwga/ *f* pigsty

poço /ˈposu/ *f* (*de água, petróleo*) well; (*de mina, elevador*) shaft

podar /poˈdar/ *vt* prune

pó-de-arroz /pɔdʒiaˈxoz/ *m* (face) powder

poder /poˈder/ *m* power □ *v aux* can, be able; (*eventualidade*) may; **ele pode /podia/poderá vir** he can/could/ might come; **ele pôde vir** he was able to come; **pode ser que** it may be that; **∼ com** stand up to; **em ∼ de alg** in sb's possession; **estar no ∼** be in power

pode|rio /podeˈriu/ *m* might; **∼roso** /o/ *a* powerful

pódio /ˈpɔdʒiu/ *m* podium

podre /ˈpodri/ *a* rotten; (*fam*) (*cansado*) exhausted; (*doente*) grotty; **∼ de rico** filthy rich; **∼s** *m pl* faults

poei|ra /poˈera/ *f* dust; **∼rento** *a* dusty

poe|ma /poˈema/ *m* poem; **∼sia** *f* (*arte*) poetry; (*poema*) poem; **∼ta** *m* poet

poético /poˈɛtʃiku/ *a* poetic

poetisa /poeˈtʃiza/ *f* poetess

pois /pojs/ *conj* as, since; **∼ é** that's right; **∼ não** of course; **∼ não?** can I help you?; **∼ sim** certainly not

polaco /puˈlaku/ (*Port*) *a* Polish □ *m* Pole; (*língua*) Polish

polar /poˈlar/ *a* polar

polarizar /polariˈzar/ *vt* polarize; **∼-se** *vpr* polarize

pole|gada /poleˈgada/ *f* inch; **∼gar** *m* thumb

poleiro /poˈleru/ *m* perch

polêmi|ca /poˈlemika/ *f* controversy, debate; **∼co** *a* controversial

pólen /ˈpɔlẽ/ *m* pollen

polícia /poˈlisia/ *f* police □ *m/f* policeman (*f*-woman)

polici|al /poliˈsiaw/ (*pl* **∼ais**) *a* <*carro, inquérito etc*> police; <*romance, filme*> detective □ *m/f* policeman (*f*-woman); **∼amento** *m* policing; **∼ar** *vt* police

poli|dez /poliˈdes/ *f* politeness; **∼do** *a* polite

poli|gamia /poligaˈmia/ *f* polygamy; **∼glota** *a* & *m/f* polyglot

Polinésia /poliˈnɛzia/ *f* Polynesia

polinésio /poliˈnɛziu/ *a* & *m* Polynesian

pólio /ˈpɔliu/ *f* polio

polir /poˈlir/ *vt* polish

polissílabo /poliˈsilabu/ *m* polysyllable

políti|ca /poˈlitʃika/ *f* politics; (*uma*) policy; **∼co** *a* political □ *m* politician

pólo[1] /ˈpɔlu/ *m* pole

pólo[2] /ˈpɔlu/ *m* (*jogo*) polo; **∼ aquático** water polo

polo|nês /poloˈnes/ *a* (*f* **∼nesa**) Polish □ *m* (*f* **∼nesa**) Pole; (*língua*) Polish

Polônia /poˈlonia/ *f* Poland

polpa /'powpa/ f pulp

poltrona /pow'trona/ f armchair

polu|ente /polu'ẽtʃi/ a & m pollutant; ∼**ição** f pollution; ∼**ir** vt pollute

polvilhar /powvi'ʎar/ vt sprinkle

polvo /'powvu/ m octopus

pólvora /'powvora/ f gunpowder

polvorosa /powvo'rɔza/ f uproar; **em** ∼ in uproar; <pessoa> in a flap

pomada /po'mada/ f ointment

pomar /po'mar/ m orchard

pom|ba /'põba/ f dove; ∼**bo** m pigeon

pomo-de-Adão /pomudʃia'dãw/ m Adam's apple

pom|pa /'põpa/ f pomp; ∼**poso** /o/ a pompous

ponche /'põʃi/ m punch

ponderar /põde'rar/ vt/i ponder

pônei /'ponej/ m pony

ponta /'põta/ f end; (de faca, prego) point; (de nariz, dedo, língua) tip; (de sapato) toe; (Cin, Teat: papel curto) walk-on part; (no campo de futebol) wing; (jogador) winger; **na** ∼ **dos pés** on tip-toe; **uma** ∼ **de** a touch of <ironia etc>; **agüentar as** ∼ **s** (fam) hold on; ∼**cabeça** /e/ f **de** ∼**cabeça** upside down

pontada /põ'tada/ f (dor) twinge

pontapé /põta'pɛ/ m kick; ∼ **inicial** kick-off

pontaria /põta'ria/ f aim; **fazer** ∼ take aim

ponte /'põtʃi/ f bridge; ∼ **aérea** shuttle; (em tempo de guerra) airlift; ∼ **de safena** heart bypass; ∼ **pênsil** suspension bridge

ponteiro /põ'teru/ m pointer; (de relógio) hand

pontiagudo /põtʃia'gudu/ a sharp

pontilhado /põtʃi'ʎadu/ a dotted

ponto /'põtu/ m point; (de costura, tricô) stitch; (no final de uma frase) full stop, (Amer) period; (sinalzinho, no i) dot; (de ônibus) stop; (no teatro) prompter; **a** ∼ **de** on the point of; **ao** ∼ <carne> medium; **até certo** ∼ to a certain extent; **às duas em** ∼ at exactly two o'clock; **dormir no** ∼ (fam) miss the boat; **entregar os** ∼**s** (fam) give up; **fazer** ∼ (fam) hang out; **dois** ∼**s** colon; ∼ **de exclamação/interrogação** exclamation/question mark; ∼ **de táxi** taxi rank, (Amer) taxi stand; ∼ **de vista** point of view; ∼ **morto** neutral; ∼**-e-vírgula** m semicolon

pontu|ação /põtua'sãw/ f punctuation; ∼**al** (pl ∼**ais**) a punctual; ∼**alidade** f punctuality; ∼**ar** vt punctuate

pontudo /põ'tudu/ a pointed

popa /'popa/ f stern

popu|lação /popula'sãw/ f population; ∼**lacional** (pl ∼**lacionais**) a population; ∼**lar** a popular; ∼**laridade** f popularity; ∼**larizar** vt popularize; ∼**larizar-se** vpr become popular

pôquer /'poker/ m poker

por /por/ prep for; (através de) through; (indicando meio, agente) by; (motivo) out of; ∼ **ano/mês**/ etc per year/month/ etc; ∼ **cento** per cent; ∼ **aqui** (nesta área) around here; (nesta direção) this way; ∼ **dentro/fora** on the inside/ outside; ∼ **isso** for this reason; ∼ **sorte** luckily; ∼ **que** why; ∼ **mais caro que seja** however expensive it may be; **está** ∼ **acontecer/fazer** it is yet to happen/ to be done

pôr /por/ vt put; put on <roupa, chapéu, óculos>; lay <mesa, ovos> □ m o ∼ **do sol** sunset; ∼**-se** vpr <sol> set; ∼**-se a caminho** set off

porão /po'rãw/ m (de prédio) basement; (de casa) cellar; (de navio) hold

porca /'porka/ f (de parafuso) nut; (animal) sow

porção /por'sãw/ f portion; **uma** ∼ **de** (muitos) a lot of

porcaria /porka'ria/ f (sujeira) filth; (coisa malfeita) piece of trash; pl trash

porcelana /porse'lana/ f china

porcentagem /porsẽ'taʒẽ/ f percentage

porco /'porku/ a filthy □ m (animal, fig) pig; (carne) pork; ∼**-espinho** (pl ∼**s-espinhos**) m porcupine

porém /po'rẽj/ conj however

pormenor /porme'nɔr/ m detail

por|nô /por'no/ a porn □ m porn film; ∼**nografia** f pornography; ∼**nográfico** a pornographic

poro /'pɔru/ m pore; ∼**so** /o/ a porous

por|quanto /por'kwãtu/ conj since; ∼**que** /por'ki/ conj because; (Port: por quê?) why; ∼**quê** /por'ke/ adv (Port) why □ m reason why

porquinho|-da-índia /porkiɲuda'ĩdʒia/ (pl ∼**s-da-índia**) m guinea pig

porrada /po'xada/ f (fam) beating

porre /'pɔxi/ m (fam) drinking session, booze-up; **de** ∼ drunk; **tomar um** ∼ get drunk

porta /'pɔrta/ f door

porta-aviões /pɔrtavi'õjs/ m invar aircraft carrier

portador /pɔrta'dor/ m bearer

portagem /por'taʒẽ/ f (Port) toll

porta|chaves /pɔrta'ʃavis/ m invar key-holder ou key-ring; ∼**jóias** m invar jewellery box; ∼**lápis** m invar pencil holder; ∼**luvas** m invar glove compartment; ~**-malas** *m invar* boot, (*Amer*) trunk; ~**-níqueis** *m invar* purse

portanto /por'tãtu/ *conj* therefore

portão /por'tãw/ *m* gate

portar /por'tar/ *vt* carry; ~**-se** *vpr* behave

porta|-retrato /pɔrtaxe'tratu/ *m* photo frame; ~**-revistas** *m invar* magazine rack

portaria /porta'ria/ *f* (*entrada*) entrance; (*decreto*) decree

portá|til (*pl* ~**teis**) *a* portable

porta|-toalhas /pɔrtato'aʎas/ *m invar* towel rail; ~**-voz** *m/f* spokesman (*f*-woman)

porte /'pɔrtʃi/ *m* (*frete*) carriage; (*de cartas etc*) postage; (*de pessoa*) bearing; (*dimensão*) scale; **de grande/pequeno** ~ large-/small-scale

porteiro /por'teru/ *m* doorman; ~ **eletrônico** entryphone

porto /'pɔrtu/ *m* port; **o Porto** Oporto; ~ **de escala** port of call; **Porto Rico** *m* Puerto Rico; ~**-riquenho** /e/ *a* & *m* Puertorican; **porto USB** *m* USB port

portuense /portu'ẽsi/ *a* & *m/f* (person) from Oporto

Portugal /portu'gaw/ *m* Portugal

portu|guês /portu'ges/ *a* & *m* (*f* ~**guesa**) Portuguese

portuário /portu'ariu/ *a* port ⬚ *m* dock worker, docker

po|sar /po'zar/ *vi* pose; ~**se** /o/ *f* pose; (*de filme*) exposure

pós-datar /pɔzda'tar/ *vt* postdate

pós-escrito /pɔzis'kritu/ *m* postscript

pós-gradua|ção /pɔzgradua'sãw/ *f* postgraduation; ~**do** *a* & *m* postgraduate

pós-guerra /pɔz'gɛxa/ *m* post-war period; **a Europa do** ~ post-war Europe

posi|ção /pozi'sãw/ *f* position; ~**cionar** *vt* position; ~**tivo** *a* & *m* positive

posologia /pozolo'ʒia/ *f* dosage

pos|sante /po'sãtʃi/ *a* powerful; ~**se** /ɔ/ *f* (*de casa etc*) possession, ownership; (*do presidente etc*) swearing in; *pl* (*pertences*) possessions; **tomar** ~**se** take office; **tomar** ~**se de** take possession of

posses|são /pose'sãw/ *f* possession; ~**sivo** *a* possessive; ~**so** /ɛ/ *a* possessed; (*com raiva*) furious

possibili|dade /posibili'dadʒi/ *f* possibility; ~**tar** *vt* make possible

possí|vel /po'sivew/ (*pl* ~**veis**) *a* possible; **fazer todo o** ~**vel** do one's best

possuir /posu'ir/ *vt* possess; (*ser dono de*) own

posta /'pɔsta/ *f* (*de peixe*) steak

pos|tal /pos'taw/ (*pl* ~**tais**) *a* postal ⬚ *m* postcard

postar /pos'tar/ *vt* place; ~**se** *vpr* position o.s.

poste /'pɔstʃi/ *m* post

pôster /'poster/ *m* poster

posteri|dade /posteri'dadʒi/ *f* posterity; ~**or** *a* (*no tempo*) subsequent, later; (*no espaço*) rear; ~**ormente** *adv* subsequently

postiço /pos'tʃisu/ *a* false

posto /'pɔstu/ *m* post; ~ **de gasolina** petrol station, (*Amer*) gas station; ~ **de saúde** health centre ⬚ *pp de* **pôr**; ~ **que** although

póstumo /'pɔstumu/ *a* posthumous

postura /pos'tura/ *f* posture

potá|vel /po'tavew/ (*pl* ~**veis**) *a* **água** ~**vel** drinking water

pote /'pɔtʃi/ *m* pot; (*de vidro*) jar

potência /po'tẽsia/ *f* power

poten|cial /potẽsi'aw/ (*pl* ~**ciais**) *a* & *m* potential; ~**te** *a* potent

potro /'potru/ *m* foal

pouco /'poku/ *a* & *pron* little; *pl* few ⬚ *adv* not much ⬚ *m* **um** ~ a little; ~ **a** ~ little by little; **aos** ~**s** gradually; **daqui a** ~ shortly; **por** ~ almost; ~ **tempo** a short time

pouquinho /po'kiɲu/ *m* **um** ~ (**de**) a little

pou|sada /po'zada/ *f* inn; ~**sar** *vi* land; ~**so** *m* landing

po|vão /po'vãw/ *m* common people; ~**vo** /o/ *m* people

povo|ação /povoa'sãw/ *f* settlement; ~**ar** *vt* populate

poxa /'poʃa/ *int* gosh

pra /pra/ *prep* (*fam*) *veja* **para**

praça /'prasa/ *f* (*largo*) square; (*mercado*) market ⬚ *m* (*soldado*) private

prado /'pradu/ *m* meadow

pra-frente /pra'frẽtʃi/ *a invar* (*fam*) with it, modern

praga /'praga/ *f* curse; (*inseto, doença, pessoa*) pest

prag|mático /prag'matʃiku/ *a* pragmatic; ~**matismo** *m* pragmatism

praguejar /prage'ʒar/ *vt/i* curse

praia /'praja/ *f* beach

pran|cha /'prãʃa/ *f* plank; (*de surfe*) board; ~**cheta** /e/ *f* drawing board

pranto /'prãtu/ *m* weeping

pra|ta /'prata/ f silver; ~**taria** f (coisas de prata) silverware; ~**teado** a silver-plated; (cor) silver

prateleira /prate'lera/ f shelf

prática /'pratʃika/ f practice; **na** ~ in practice

prati|cante /pratʃi'kãtʃi/ a practising □ m/f apprentice; (de esporte etc) player; ~**car** vt practise; (cometer, executar) carry out □ vi practise; ~**cável** (pl ~**cáveis**) a practicable

prático /'pratʃiku/ a practical

prato /'pratu/ m (objeto) plate; (comida) dish; (parte de uma refeição) course; (do toca-discos) turntable; pl (instrumento) cymbals; ~ **fundo** dish; ~ **principal** main course

praxe /'praʃi/ f normal practice; **de** ~ usually

prazer /pra'zer/ m pleasure; **muito** ~ (**em conhecê-lo**) pleased to meet you; ~**oso** /o/ a pleasurable

prazo /'prazu/ m term, time; **a** ~ <compra etc> on credit; **a curto/longo** ~ in the short/long term; **último** ~ deadline

preâmbulo /pri'ãbulu/ m preamble

precário /pre'kariu/ a precarious

precaução /prekaw'sãw/ f precaution

preca|ver-se /preka'versi/ vpr take precautions (**de** against); ~**vido** a cautious

prece /'prɛsi/ f prayer

prece|dência /prese'dẽsia/ f precedence; ~**dente** a preceding □ m precedent; ~**der** vt/i precede

preceito /pre'sejtu/ m precept

precioso /presi'ozu/ a precious

precipício /presi'pisiu/ m precipice

precipi|tação /presipita'sãw/ f haste; (chuva etc) precipitation; ~**tado** a <fuga> headlong; <decisão, ato> hasty, rash; ~**tar** vt (lançar) throw; (antecipar) hasten; ~**tar-se** vpr (lançar-se) throw o.s.; (apressar-se) rush; (agir sem pensar) act rashly

precisão /presi'zãw/ f precision, accuracy

precisamente /presiza'mẽtʃi/ adv precisely

preci|sar /presi'zar/ vt (necessitar) need; (indicar com exatidão) specify □ vi be necessary; ~**sar de** need; ~**so** ir I have to go; ~**sa-se** wanted; ~**so** a (exato) precise; (necessário) necessary

preço /'presu/ m price; ~ **de custo** cost price; ~ **fixo** set price

precoce /pre'kɔsi/ a <fruto> early; <velhice, calvície etc> premature; <criança> precocious

precon|cebido /prekõse'bidu/ a preconceived; ~**ceito** m prejudice; ~**ceituoso** a prejudiced

preconizar /prekoni'zar/ vt advocate

precursor /prekur'sor/ m forerunner

preda|dor /preda'dor/ m predator; ~**tório** a predatory

predecessor /predese'sor/ m predecessor

predestinar /predestʃi'nar/ vt predestine

predeterminar /predetermi'nar/ vt predetermine

predição /predʒi'sãw/ f prediction

predile|ção /predʒile'sãw/ f preference; ~**to** /ɛ/ a favourite

prédio /'prɛdʒiu/ m building

predis|por /predʒis'por/ vt prepare (**para** for); (tornar parcial) prejudice (**contra** against); ~**por-se** vpr prepare o.s.; ~**posto** a predisposed; (contra) prejudiced

predizer /predʒi'zer/ vt predict, foretell

predomi|nância /predomi'nãsia/ f predominance; ~**nante** a predominant; ~**nar** vi predominate

predomínio /predo'miniu/ m predominance

preencher /priẽ'ʃer/ vt fill; fill in, (Amer) fill out <formulário>; meet <requisitos>

pré|-escola /prɛis'kɔla/ f infant school, (Amer) preschool; ~**escolar** a pre-school; ~**estréia** f preview; ~**fabricado** a prefabricated

prefácio /pre'fasiu/ m preface

prefei|to /pre'fejtu/ m mayor; ~**tura** f prefecture; (prédio) town hall

prefe|rência /prefe'rẽsia/ f preference; (direito no trânsito) right of way; de ~**rência** preferably; ~**rencial** (pl ~**renciais**) a preferential; <rua> main; ~**rido** a favourite; ~**rir** vt prefer (**a** to); ~**rível** (pl ~**ríveis**) a preferable

prefixo /pre'fiksu/ m prefix

prega /'prɛga/ f pleat

pregador[1] /prega'dor/ m (de roupa) peg

pre|gador[2] /prega'dor/ m (quem prega) preacher; ~**gão** m (de vendedor) cry; **o** ~**gão** (na bolsa de valores) trading; (em leilão) bidding

pregar[1] /pre'gar/ vt fix; (com prego) nail; sew on <botão>; **não** ~ **olho** not sleep a wink; ~ **uma peça em** play a trick on; ~ **um susto em alg** give s.o. a fright

pregar[2] /pre'gar/ vt/i preach

prego /'prɛgu/ m nail

pregui|ça /pre'gisa/ f laziness; (bicho) sloth; **estou com** ~**ça de ir** I can't be bothered to go; ~**çoso** a lazy

pré-histórico /prɛjs'tɔriku/ a prehistoric

preia-mar /preja'mar/ f high tide

prejudi|car /preʒudʒi'kar/ vt harm; damage <saúde>; ~**car-se** vpr harm o.s.; ~**cial** (pl ~**ciais**) a harmful, damaging (**a** to)

prejuízo /preʒu'izu/ m damage; (financeiro) loss; **em** ~ **de** to the detriment of

prejulgar /preʒuw'gar/ vt prejudge

preliminar /prelimi'nar/ a & m/f preliminary

prelo /'prɛlu/ m printing press; **no** ~ being printed

prelúdio /pre'ludʒiu/ m prelude

prematuro /prema'turu/ a premature

premeditar /premedʒi'tar/ vt premeditate

premente /pre'mẽtʃi/ a pressing

premi|ado /premi'adu/ a <romance, atleta etc> prize-winning; <bilhete, número etc> winning ◻ m prize-winner; ~**ar** vt award a prize to <romance, atleta etc>; reward <honestidade, mérito>

prêmio /'premiu/ m prize; (de seguro) premium; **Grande Prêmio** (de F1) Grand Prix

premissa /pre'misa/ f premiss

premonição /premoni'sãw/ f premonition

pré-na|tal /prɛna'taw/ (pl ~**tais**) a antenatal, (Amer) prenatal

prenda /'prẽda/ f (Port) present; ~**s domésticas** household chores; ~**do** a domesticated

pren|dedor /prẽde'dor/ m clip; ~**dedor de roupa** clothes peg; ~**der** vt (pregar) fix; (capturar) arrest; (atar) tie up <cachorro>; tie back <cabelo>; (restringir) restrict; (ligar afetivamente) bind; ~**der (a atenção de) alg** grab s.o.('s attention)

prenhe /'prɛɲi/ a pregnant

prenome /pre'nomi/ m first name

pren|sa /'prẽsa/ f press; ~**sar** vt press

preocu|pação /preokupa'sãw/ f concern; ~**pante** a worrying; ~**par** vt worry; ~**par-se** vpr worry (**com** about)

prepa|ração /prepara'sãw/ f preparation; ~**rado** a preparation; ~**rar** vt prepare; ~**rar-se** vpr prepare, get ready; ~**rativos** m pl preparations; ~**ro** m preparation; (competência) knowledge; ~**ro físico** physical fitness

preponderar /prepõde'rar/ vi prevail (**sobre** over)

preposição /prepozi'sãw/ f preposition

prerrogativa /prexoga'tʃiva/ f prerogative

presa /'preza/ f (de caça) prey; (de cobra) fang; (de elefante) tusk; ~ **de guerra** spoils of war

prescin|dir /presĩ'dʒir/ vi ~**dir de** dispense with; ~**dível** (pl ~**díveis**) a dispensable

pres|crever /preskre'ver/ vt prescribe; ~**crição** f prescription; (norma) rule

presen|ça /pre'zẽsa/ f presence; ~**ça de espírito** presence of mind; ~**ciar** vt (estar presente a) be present at; (testemunhar) witness; ~**te** a & m present; ~**tear** vt ~**tear alg (com aco)** give s.o. (sth as) a present

presépio /pre'zɛpiu/ m crib

preser|vação /prezerva'sãw/ f preservation; ~**var** vt preserve, protect; ~**vativo** m (em comida) preservative; (camisinha) condom

presi|dência /prezi'dẽsia/ f presidency; (de uma reunião) chair; ~**dencial** (pl ~**denciais**) a presidential; ~**dencialismo** m presidential system; ~**dente** m (f ~**denta**) president; (de uma reunião) chairperson

presidiário /prezidʒi'ariu/ m convict

presídio /pre'zidʒiu/ m prison

presidir /prezi'dʒir/ vi preside (**a** over)

presilha /pre'ziʎa/ f fastener; (de cabelo) slide

preso /'prezu/ pp de **prender** ◻ m prisoner; **ficar** ~ get stuck; <saia, corda etc> get caught

pressa /'prɛsa/ f hurry; **às** ~**s** in a hurry, hurriedly; **estar com** ou **ter** ~ be in a hurry

presságio /pre'sagiu/ m omen

pressão /pre'sãw/ f pressure; **fazer** ~ **sobre** put pressure on; ~ **arterial** blood pressure

pressen|timento /presẽtʃi'mẽtu/ m premonition, feeling; ~**tir** vt sense

pressionar /presio'nar/ vt press <botão>; pressure <pessoa>

pressupor /presu'por/ vt <pessoa> presume; <coisa> presuppose

pressurizado /presuri'zadu/ a pressurized

pres|tação /presta'sãw/ f repayment, instalment; ~**tar** vt render <contas, serviço>; ◻ vi be of use; **não** ~**ta** he/it is no good; ~**tar atenção** pay attention; ~**tar juramento** take an oath; ~**tativo** a helpful; ~**tável** (pl ~**táveis**) a serviceable

prestes /'prɛstʃis/ a invar ~ **a** about to

prestidigita|ção /prestʃidʒiʒita-'sãw/ f conjuring; ~**dor** m conjurer

p

pres|tigiar /prestʃiʒi'ar/ *vt* give prestige to; **~tígio** *m* prestige; **~tigioso** /o/ *a* prestigious

préstimo /'prɛstʃimu/ *m* merit

presumir /prezu'mir/ *vt* presume

presun|ção /prezũ'sãw/ *f* presumption; **~çoso** /o/ *a* presumptuous

presunto /pre'zũtu/ *m* ham

pretendente /pretẽ'dẽtʃi/ *m/f* (*candidato*) candidate, applicant

preten|der /pretẽ'der/ *vt* intend; **~são** *f* pretension; **~sioso** /o/ *a* pretentious

preterir /prete'rir/ *vt* disregard

pretérito /pre'tɛritu/ *m* preterite

pretexto /pre'testu/ *m* pretext

preto /'pretu/ *a & m* black; **~-e-branco** *a invar* black and white

prevalecer /prevale'ser/ *vi* prevail

prevenção /prevẽ'sãw/ *f* (*impedimento*) prevention; (*parcialidade*) bias

prevenir /preve'nir/ *vt* (*evitar*) prevent; (*avisar*) warn; **~-se** *vpr* take precautions

preventivo /prevẽ'tʃivu/ *a* preventive

prever /pre'ver/ *vt* foresee, predict

previdência /previ'dẽsia/ *f* foresight; **~ social** social security

prévio /'prɛviu/ *a* prior

previ|são /previ'zãw/ *f* prediction, forecast; **~são do tempo** weather forecast; **~sível** (*pl* **~síveis**) *a* predictable

pre|zado /pre'zadu/ *a* esteemed; **Prezado Senhor** Dear Sir; **~zar** *vt* think highly of; **~zar-se** *vpr* have self-respect

prima /'prima/ *f* cousin

primário /pri'mariu/ *a* primary; (*fundamental*) basic

primata /pri'mata/ *m* primate

primave|ra /prima'vɛra/ *f* spring; (*flor*) primrose; **~ril** (*pl* **~ris**) *a* spring

primazia /prima'zia/ *f* primacy

primei|ra /pri'mera/ *f* (*marcha*) first (gear); **de ~ra** first-rate; <*carne*> prime; **~ra-dama** (*pl* **~ras-damas**) *f* first lady; **~ranista** *m/f* first-year (student); **~ro** *a & adv* first; **no dia ~ro de maio** on the first of May; **em ~ro lugar** (*para começar*) in the first place; (*numa corrida, competição*) in first place; **~ro de tudo** first of all; **~ros socorros** first aid; **~ro-ministro** (*pl* **~ros-ministros**) *m* (*f* **~ra-ministra**) prime-minister

primitivo /primi'tʃivu/ *a* primitive

primo /'primu/ *m* cousin □ *a* **número ~** prime number; **~gênito** *a & m* first-born

primor /pri'mor/ *m* perfection

primordi|al /primordʒi'aw/ (*pl* **~ais**) *a* (*primitivo*) primordial; (*fundamental*) fundamental

primoroso /primo'rozu/ *a* exquisite

princesa /prĩ'seza/ *f* princess

princi|pado /prĩsipi'adu/ *m* principality; **~pal** (*pl* **~pais**) *a* main □ *m* principal

príncipe /'prĩsipi/ *m* prince

principiante /prĩsipi'ãtʃi/ *m/f* beginner

princípio /prĩ'sipiu/ *m* (*início*) beginning; (*regra*) principle; **em ~** in principle; **por ~** on principle

priori|dade /priori'dadʒi/ *f* priority; **~tário** *a* priority

prisão /pri'zãw/ *f* (*ato de prender*) arrest; (*cadeia*) prison; (*encarceramento*) imprisonment; **~ perpétua** life imprisonment; **~ de ventre** constipation

prisioneiro /prizio'neru/ *m* prisoner

prisma /'prizma/ *m* prism

privação /priva'sãw/ *f* deprivation

privacidade /privasi'dadʒi/ *f* privacy

pri|vada /pri'vada/ *f* toilet; **~vado** *a* private; **~vado de** deprived of; **~var** *vt* deprive (**de** of); **~var-se** *vpr* deprive o.s. (**de** of)

privati|vo /priva'tʃivu/ *a* private; **~zar** *vt* privatize

privi|legiado /privileʒi'adu/ *a* privileged; <*tratamento*> preferential; **~legiar** *vt* favour; **~légio** *m* privilege

pro (*fam*) = **para** + **o**

pró /prɔ/ *adv* for □ *m* **os ~s e os contras** the pros and cons

proa /'proa/ *f* bow, prow

probabilidade /probabili'dadʒi/ *f* probability

proble|ma /pro'blema/ *m* problem; **~mático** *a* problematic

proce|dência /prose'dẽsia/ *f* origin; **~dente** *a* logical; **~dente de** coming from; **~der** *vi* proceed; (*comportar-se*) behave; (*na justiça*) take legal action; **~der de** come from; **~dimento** *m* procedure; (*comportamento*) behaviour; (*na justiça*) proceedings

proces|sador /prosesa'dor/ *m* processor; **~sador de texto** word processor; **~samento** *m* processing; (*na justiça*) prosecution; **~samento de dados** data processing; **~sar** *vt* process; (*por crime*) prosecute; (*por causa civil*) sue; **~so** /ɛ/ *m* process; (*criminal*) trial; (*civil*) lawsuit

procla|mação /proklama'sãw/ *f* proclamation; **~mar** *vt* proclaim

procri|ação /prokria'sãw/ *f* procreation; **~ar** *vt/i* procreate

procu|ra /pro'kura/ *f* search; (*de produto*) demand; **à ~ra de** in search of; ~**ração** f power of attorney; ~**rado** a sought after, in demand; ~**rado pela polícia** wanted by the police; ~**rador** m (*mandatário*) proxy; (*advogado*) public prosecutor; ~**rar** vt look for; (*contatar*) get in touch with; (*ir visitar*) look up; ~**rar saber** try to find out

prodígio /proˈdʒiʒiu/ m wonder; (*pessoa*) prodigy

prodigioso /prodʒiʒiˈozu/ a prodigious

pródigo /ˈprɔdigu/ a lavish, extravagant

produ|ção /produˈsãw/ f production; ~**tividade** f productivity; ~**tivo** a productive; ~**to** m product; (*renda*) proceeds; ~**to nacional bruto** gross national product; ~**tos agrícolas** agricultural produce; ~**tor** m producer ▫ a **país** ~**tor de trigo** wheat-producing country; ~**zido** a (*fam: arrumado*) done up; ~**zir** vt produce

proeminente /proemiˈnẽtʃi/ a prominent

proeza /proˈeza/ f achievement

profa|nar /profaˈnar/ vt desecrate; ~**no** a profane

profecia /profeˈsia/ f prophecy

proferir /profeˈrir/ vt utter; give <*discurso, palestra*>; pass <*sentença*>

profes|sar /profeˈsar/ vt profess; ~**so** /ɛ/ a professed; <*político etc*> seasoned; ~**sor** m teacher; ~**sor catedrático** professor

pro|feta /proˈfɛta/ m prophet; ~**fético** a prophetic; ~**fetizar** vt prophesy

profissão /profiˈsãw/ f profession

profissio|nal /profisioˈnaw/ (*pl* ~**nais**) a & m/f professional; ~**nalismo** m professionalism; ~**nalizante** a vocational; ~**nalizar-se** vpr <*esportista etc*> turn professional

profun|didade /profũdʒiˈdadʒi/ f depth; ~**do** a deep; <*sentimento etc*> profound

profusão /profuˈzãw/ f profusion

prog|nosticar /prognostʃiˈkar/ vt forecast; ~**nóstico** m forecast; (*med*) prognosis

progra|ma /proˈgrama/ m programme; (*de computador*) program; (*diversão*) thing to do; ~**mação** f programming; ~**mador** m programmer; ~**mar** vt plan; program <*computador etc*>; ~**mável** (*pl* ~**máveis**) a programmable

progredir /progreˈdʒir/ vi progress

progres|são /progreˈsãw/ f progression; ~**sista** a & m/f progressive; ~**sivo** a progressive; ~**so** /ɛ/ m progress

proi|bição /proibiˈsãw/ f ban (**de** on); ~**bido** a forbidden; ~**bir** vt forbid (**alg**

de s.o. to); ban <*livro, importações etc*>; ~**bitivo** a prohibitive

proje|ção /proʒeˈsãw/ f projection; ~**tar** vt plan <*viagem, estrada etc*>; design <*casa, carro etc*>; project <*filme, luz*>

projé|til /proˈʒɛtʃiw/ (*pl* ~**teis**) m projectile

proje|tista /proʒeˈtʃista/ m/f designer; ~**to** /ɛ/ m project; (*de casa, carro*) design; ~**to de lei** bill; ~**tor** m projector

prol /prɔw/ m **em** ~ **de** on behalf of

prole /ˈprɔli/ f offspring; ~**tariado** m proletariat; ~**tário** a & m proletarian

prolife|ração /proliferaˈsãw/ f proliferation; ~**rar** vi proliferate

prolífico /proˈlifiku/ a prolific

prolixo /proˈliksu/ a verbose, long-winded

prólogo /ˈprɔlogu/ m prologue

prolon|gado /prolõˈgadu/ a prolonged; ~**gar** vt prolong; ~**gar-se** vpr go on

promessa /proˈmɛsa/ f promise

prome|tedor /prometeˈdor/ a promising; ~**ter** vt promise ▫ vi (*dar esperança*) show promise; ~**ter voltar** promise to return

promíscuo /proˈmiskuu/ a promiscuous

promis|sor /promiˈsor/ a promising; ~**sória** f promissory note

promoção /promoˈsãw/ f promotion

promontório /promõˈtɔriu/ m promontory

promo|tor /promoˈtor/ m promoter; (*advogado*) prosecutor; ~**ver** vt promote

promulgar /promuwˈgar/ vt promulgate

prono|me /proˈnomi/ m pronoun; ~**minal** (*pl* ~**minais**) a pronominal

pron|tidão /prõtʃiˈdãw/ f readiness; **com** ~**tidão** promptly; **estar de** ~**tidão** be at the ready; ~**tificar** vt get ready; ~**tificar-se** vpr volunteer (**a** to; **para** for); ~**to** a ready; (*rápido*) prompt ▫ int that's that; ~**to-socorro** (*pl* ~**tos-socorros**) m casualty department; (*Port: reboque*) towtruck; ~**tuário** m (*manual*) manual, handbook; (*médico*) notes; (*policial*) record, file

pronúncia /proˈnũsia/ f pronunciation

pronunci|ado /pronũsiˈadu/ a pronounced; ~**amento** m pronouncement; ~**ar** vt pronounce

propagar /propaˈgar/ vt propagate <*espécie*>; spread <*notícia, idéia, fé*>; ~**-se** vpr spread; <*espécie*> propagate

propen|são /propẽˈsãw/ f propensity; ~**so** a inclined (**a** to)

pro|piciar /propisiˈar/ vt provide; ~**pício** a propitious

p

propina /pro'pina/ f bribe; (*Port: escolar*) fee

propor /pro'por/ vt propose; ~**-se** vpr set o.s. <*objetivo*>; ~**-se a estudar** set out to study

proporção /propor'sãw/ f proportion

proporcio|nado /proporsio'nadu/ a proportionate (**a** to); **bem** ~**nado** well proportioned; ~**nal** (pl ~**nais**) a proportional; ~**nar** vt provide

proposi|ção /propozi'sãw/ f proposition; ~**tado** a, ~**tal** (pl ~**tais**) a intentional

propósito /pro'pozitu/ m intention; **a** ~ by the way; **a** ~ **de** on the subject of; **chegar a** ~ arrive at the right time; **de** ~ on purpose

proposta /pro'posta/ f proposal

propriamente /propria'mẽtʃi/ adv strictly; **a casa** ~ **dita** the house proper

proprie|dade /proprie'dadʒi/ f property; (*direito sobre bens*) ownership; ~**tário** m owner; (*de casa alugada*) landlord

próprio /'propriu/ a (*de si*) own; <*sentido*> literal; <*nome*> proper; **meu** ~ **carro** my own car; **um carro** ~ a car of my own; **o** ~ **rei** the king himself; ~ **a** peculiar to; ~ **para** suited to

prorro|gação /proxoga'sãw/ f extension; (*de dívida*) deferment; (*em futebol etc*) extra time; ~**gar** vt extend <*prazo*>; defer <*pagamento*>

pro|sa /'proza/ f prose; ~**sador** m prose writer; ~**saico** a prosaic

proscrever /proskre'ver/ vt proscribe

prospecto /pros'pɛktu/ m (*livro*) brochure; (*folheto*) leaflet

prospe|rar /prospe'rar/ vi prosper; ~**ridade** f prosperity

próspero /'prosperu/ a prosperous

prosse|guimento /prosegi'mẽtu/ m continuation; ~**guir** vt continue ◻ vi proceed, go on

prostitu|ição /prostʃitui'sãw/ f prostitution; ~**ta** f prostitute

pros|tração /prostra'sãw/ f debility; ~**trado** a prostrate; ~**trar** vt prostrate; (*enfraquecer*) debilitate; ~**trar-se** vpr prostrate o.s.

protago|nista /protago'nista/ m/f protagonist; ~**nizar** vt be at the centre of <*acontecimento*>; feature in <*peça, filme*>

prote|ção /prote'sãw/ f protection; ~**cionismo** m protectionism; ~**cionista** a & f protectionist; ~**ger** vt protect; ~**gido** m protégé

proteína /prote'ina/ f protein

protelar /prote'lar/ vt put off

protes|tante /protes'tãtʃi/ a & m/f Protestant; ~**tar** vt/i protest; ~**to** /ɛ/ m protest

protetor /prote'tor/ m protector ◻ a protective

protocolo /proto'kolu/ m protocol; (*registro*) register

protótipo /pro'totʃipu/ m prototype

protuberância /protube'rãsia/ f bulge

pro|va /'prova/ f (*que comprova*) proof; (*teste*) trial; (*exame*) exam; (*esportiva*) competition; (*de livro etc*) proof; pl (*na justiça*) evidence; **à** ~**va de bala** bulletproof; **pôr à** ~**va** put to the test; ~**vado** a proven; ~**var** vt try <*comida*>; try on <*roupa*>; try out <*carro, novo sistema etc*>; (*comprovar*) prove

prová|vel /pro'vavew/ (pl ~**veis**) a probable

proveito /pro'vejtu/ m profit, advantage; **tirar** ~ **de** (*beneficiar-se*) profit from; (*explorar*) take advantage of; ~**so** /o/ a useful

proveni|ência /proveni'ẽsia/ f origin; ~**ente** a originating (**de** from)

proventos /pro'vẽtus/ m pl proceeds

prover /pro'ver/ vt provide (**de** with)

provérbio /pro'verbiu/ m proverb

proveta /pro'veta/ f test tube; **bebê de** ~ test-tube baby

provi|dência /provi'dẽsia/ f (*medida*) measure, step; (*divina*) providence; **tomar** ~**dências** take steps, take action; ~**denciar** vt (*prover*) get hold of, provide; (*resolver*) see to, take care of ◻ vi take action

província /pro'vĩsia/ f province; (*longe da cidade*) provinces

provinci|al /provĩsi'aw/ (pl ~**ais**) a provincial; ~**ano** a & m provincial

provir /pro'vir/ vi come (**de** from); (*resultar*) be due (**de** to)

provi|são /provi'zãw/ f provision; ~**sório** a provisional

provo|cação /provoka'sãw/ f provocation; ~**cador**, ~**cante** a provocative; ~**car** vt provoke; (*ocasionar*) cause

proximidade /prosimi'dadʒi/ f closeness; pl (*imediações*) vicinity

próximo /'prosimu/ a (*no tempo*) next; (*perto*) near, close (**de** to); <*parente*> close; <*futuro*> near ◻ m neighbour, fellow man

pru|dência /pru'dẽsia/ f prudence; ~**dente** a prudent

prumo /'prumu/ m plumb line; **a** ~ vertically

prurido /pru'ridu/ m itch

pseudônimo /pisew'donimu/ *m* pseudonym

psica|nálise /pisika'nalizi/ *f* psychoanalysis; **~nalista** *m/f* psychoanalyst

psi|cologia /psikolo'ʒia/ *f* psychology; **~cológico** *a* psychological; **~cólogo** *m* psychologist

psico|pata /pisiko'pata/ *m/f* psychopath; **~se** /ɔ/ *f* psychosis; **~terapeuta** *m/f* psychotherapist; **~terapia** *f* psychotherapy

psicótico /pisi'kɔtʃiku/ *a & m* psychotic

psique /pi'siki/ *f* psyche

psiqui|atra /pisiki'atra/ *m/f* psychiatrist; **~atria** *f* psychiatry; **~átrico** *a* psychiatric

psíquico /pi'sikiku/ *a* psychological

pua /'pua/ *f* bit

puberdade /puber'dadʒi/ *f* puberty

publi|cação /publika'sãw/ *f* publication; **~car** *vt* publish

publici|dade /publisi'dadʒi/ *f* publicity; *(reclame)* advertising; **~tário** *a* publicity; *(de reclame)* advertising □ *m* advertising executive

público /'publiku/ *a* public □ *m* public; *(platéia)* audience; **em ~** in public; **o grande ~** the general public

pudera /pu'dɛra/ *int* no wonder!

pudico /pu'dʒiku/ *a* prudish

pudim /pu'dʒĩ/ *m* pudding

pudor /pu'dor/ *m* modesty, shame

pue|ril /pue'riw/ *(pl ~ris)* *a* puerile

pugilis|mo /puʒi'lizmu/ *m* boxing; **~ta** *m* boxer

pu|ído /pu'idu/ *a* worn through; **~ir** *vt* wear through

pujan|ça /pu'ʒãsa/ *f* power; **~te** *a* powerful; *(de saúde)* robust

pular /pu'lar/ *vt* jump (over); *(omitir)* skip □ *vi* jump; **~ de contente** jump for joy; **~ carnaval** celebrate Carnival; **~ corda** skip

pulga /'puwga/ *f* flea

pulmão /puw'mãw/ *m* lung

pulo /'pulu/ *m* jump; **dar um ~ em** drop by; **dar ~s** jump up and down

pulôver /pu'lover/ *m* pullover

púlpito /'puwpitu/ *m* pulpit

pul|sar /puw'sar/ *vi* pulsate; **~seira** *f* bracelet; **~so** *m* *(do braço)* wrist; *(batimento arterial)* pulse

pulular /pulu'lar/ *vi* swarm (**de** with)

pulveri|zador /puwveriza'dor/ *m* spray; **~zar** *vt* spray *<líquido>*; *(reduzir a pó, fig)* pulverize

pun|gente /pũ'ʒẽtʃi/ *a* consuming; **~gir** *vt* afflict

pu|nhado /pu'ɲadu/ *m* handful; **~nhal** *(pl ~nhais)* *m* dagger; **~nhalada** *f*

stab wound; **~nho** *m* fist; *(de camisa etc)* cuff; *(de espada)* hilt

pu|nição /puni'sãw/ *f* punishment; **~nir** *vt* punish; **~nitivo** *a* punitive

pupila /pu'pila/ *f* pupil

purê /pu're/ *m* purée; **~ de batata** mashed potato

pureza /pu'reza/ *f* purity

pur|gante /pur'gãtʃi/ *a & m* purgative; **~gar** *vt* purge; **~gatório** *m* purgatory

purificar /purifi'kar/ *vt* purify

puritano /puri'tanu/ *a & m* puritan

puro /'puru/ *a* pure; *<aguardente>* neat; **~ e simples** pure and simple; **~-sangue** *(pl ~s-sangues)* *a & m* thoroughbred

púrpura /'purpura/ *a* purple

purpurina /purpu'rina/ *f* glitter

purulento /puru'lẽtu/ *a* festering

pus /pus/ *m* pus

pusilânime /puzi'lanimi/ *a* faint-hearted

pústula /'pustula/ *f* pimple

puta /'puta/ *f* whore □ *a invar* (*fam*) **um ~ carro** one hell of a car; **filho da ~** *(chulo)* bastard; **~ que (o) pariu!** *(chulo)* fucking hell!

puto /'putu/ *a* (*fam*) furious

putrefazer /putrefa'zer/ *vi* putrefy

puxa /'puʃa/ *int* gosh

pu|xado /pu'ʃadu/ *a* (*fam*) *<exame>* tough; *<trabalho>* hard; *<aluguel, preço>* steep; **~xador** *m* handle; **~xão** *m* pull, tug; **~xa-puxa** *m* toffee; **~xar** *vt* pull; strike up *<conversa>*; bring up *<assunto>*; **~xar de uma perna** limp; **~xar para** *(parecer com)* take after; **~xar por** *(exigir muito de)* push (hard); **~xa-saco** *m* (*fam*) creep

Qq

QI /ke i/ *m* IQ

quadra /'kwadra/ *f* *(de tênis etc)* court; *(quarteirão)* block; **~do** *a & m* square

quadragésimo /kwadra'ʒɛzimu/ *a* fortieth

qua|dril /kwa'driw/ *(pl ~dris)* *m* hip

quadrilha /kwa'driʎa/ *f* *(bando)* gang; *(dança)* square dance

quadrinho /kwa'driɲu/ *m* frame; **história em ~s** comic strip

quadro /'kwadru/ *m* picture; *(pintado)* painting; *(tabela)* table; *(pessoal)* staff;

(*equipe*) team; (*de uma peça*) scene; **~-negro** (*pl* **~s-negros**) *m* blackboard

quadruplicar /kwadrupli'kar/ *vt/i* quadruple

quádruplo /'kwadruplu/ *a* quadruple; **~s** *m pl* (*crianças*) quads

qual /kwaw/ (*pl* **quais**) *pron* which (one); **o/a ~** (*coisa*) that, which; (*pessoa*) that, who; **~ é o seu nome?** what's your name?; **seja ~ for a decisão** whatever the decision may be

qualidade /kwali'dadʒi/ *f* quality; **na ~ de** in one's capacity as, as

qualifi|cação /kwalifika'sãw/ *f* qualification; **~car** *vt* qualify; (*descrever*) describe (**de** as); **~car-se** *vpr* qualify

qualitativo /kwalita'tʃivu/ *a* qualitative

qualquer /kwaw'kɛr/ (*pl* **quaisquer**) *a* any; **um livro ~** any old book; **~ um** any one

quando /'kwãdu/ *adv & conj* when; **~ quer que** whenever; **~ de** at the time of; **~ muito** at most

quantia /kwã'tʃia/ *f* amount

quanti|dade /kwãtʃi'dadʒi/ *f* quantity; **uma ~dade de** a lot of; **em ~dade** in large amounts; **~ficar** *vt* quantify; **~tativo** *a* quantitative

quanto /'kwãtu/ *adv & pron* how much; *pl* how many; **~ tempo?** how long?; **~ mais barato melhor** the cheaper the better; **tão alto ~ eu** as tall as me; **~ ri!** how I laughed!; **~ a** as for; **~ antes** as soon as possible

quaren|ta /kwa'rẽta/ *a & m* forty; **~tão** *a & m* (*f* **~tona**) forty-year-old; **~tena** /e/ *f* quarantine

quaresma /kwa'rɛzma/ *f* Lent

quarta /'kwarta/ *f* (*dia*) Wednesday; (*marcha*) fourth (gear); **~-de-final** (*pl* **~s-de-final**) *f* quarter final; **~-feira** (*pl* **~s-feiras**) *f* Wednesday

quartanista /kwarta'nista/ *m/f* fourth-year (student)

quarteirão /kwarte'rãw/ *m* block

quar|tel /kwar'tɛw/ (*pl* **~téis**) *m* barracks; **~tel-general** (*pl* **~téis-generais**) *m* headquarters

quarteto /kwar'tetu/ *m* quartet; **~ de cordas** string quartet

quarto /'kwartu/ *a* fourth □ *m* (*parte*) quarter; (*aposento*) bedroom; (*guarda*) watch; **são três e/menos um ~** (*Port*) it's quarter past/to three; **~ de banho** (*Port*) bathroom; **~ de hora** quarter of an hour; **~ de hóspedes** guest room

quartzo /'kwartzu/ *m* quartz

quase /'kwazi/ *adv* almost, nearly; **~ nada/nunca** hardly anything/ever

quatro /'kwatru/ *a & m* four; **de ~** (*no chão*) on all fours; **~- centos** *a & m* four hundred

que /ki/ *a* which, what; **~ dia é hoje?** what's the date today?; **~ homem!** what a man!; **~ triste!** how sad! □ *pron* what; **~ é ~ é?** what is it? □ *pron rel* (*coisa*) which, that; (*pessoa*) who, that; (*interrogativo*) what; **o dia em ~ ...** the day when/that ... □ *conj* that; (*porque*) because; **espero ~ sim/não** I hope so/not

quê /ke/ *pron* what □ *m* **um ~** something; **não tem de ~** don't mention it

quebra /'kɛbra/ *f* break; (*de empresa, banco*) crash; (*de força*) cut; **de ~** in addition; **~-cabeça** *m* jigsaw (puzzle); (*fig*) puzzle; **~diço** *a* breakable; **~do** *a* broken; <*carro*> broken down; **~dos** *m pl* small change; **~-galho** (*fam*) *m* stopgap; **~-mar** *m* breakwater; **~-molas** *m invar* speed bump; **~-nozes** *m invar* nutcrackers; **~-pau** (*fam*) *m* row; **~-quebra** *m* riot

quebrar /ke'brar/ *vt* break □ *vi* break; <*carro etc*> break down; <*banco, empresa etc*> crash, go bust; **~-se** *vpr* break

queda /'kɛda/ *f* fall; **ter uma ~ por** have a soft spot for; **~-de-braço** *f* arm wrestling

quei|jeira /ke'ʒera/ *f* cheese dish; **~jo** *m* cheese; **~jo prato** cheddar; **~jo-de-minas** *m* Cheshire cheese

queima /'kejma/ *f* burning; **~da** *f* forest fire; **~do** *a* burnt; (*bronzeado*) tanned, brown; **cheiro de ~do** smell of burning

queimar /kej'mar/ *vt* burn; (*bronzear*) tan □ *vi* burn; <*lâmpada*> go; <*fusível*> blow; **~-se** *vpr* burn o.s.; (*bronzear-se*) go brown

queima-roupa /kejma'xopa/ *f* à **~** point-blank

quei|xa /'keʃa/ *f* complaint; **~xar-se** *vpr* complain (**de** about)

queixo /'keʃu/ *m* chin; **bater o ~** shiver

queixoso /ke'ʃozu/ *a* plaintive □ *m* plaintiff

quem /kẽj/ *pron* who; (*a pessoa que*) anyone who, he who; **de ~ é este livro?** whose is this book?; **~ quer que** whoever; **seja ~ for** whoever it is; **~ falou isso fui eu** it was me who said that; **~ me dera (que) ...** I wish ..., if only

Quênia /'kenia/ *m* Kenya

queniano /keni'anu/ *a & m* Kenyan

quen|tão /kẽ'tãw/ *m* mulled wine; **~te** *a* hot; (*com calor agradável*) warm; **~tura** *f* heat

quepe /'kɛpi/ *m* cap

quer /kɛr/ *conj* ∼ ... ∼ ... whether ... or ...

querer /ke'rer/ *vt/i* want; **quero ir** I want to go; **quero que você vá** I want you to go; **eu queria falar com o Sr X** I'd like to speak to Mr X; **vai ∼ vir amanhã?** do you want to come tomorrow?; **vou ∼ um cafezinho** I'd like a coffee; **se você quiser** if you want; **queira sentar** do sit down; ∼ **dizer** mean; **quer dizer** (*isto é*) that is to say, I mean

querido /ke'ridu/ *a* dear □ *m* darling

quermesse /ker'mɛsi/ *f* fête, fair

querosene /kero'zeni/ *m* kerosene

questão /kes'tãw/ *m* question; (*assunto*) matter; **em ∼** in question; **fazer ∼ de** really want to; **não faço ∼ de ir** I don't mind not going

questio|nar /kestʃio'nar/ *vt/i* question; ∼**nário** *m* questionnaire; ∼**nável** (*pl* ∼**náveis**) *a* questionable

quiabo /ki'abu/ *m* okra

quibe /'kibi/ *m* savoury meatball

quicar /ki'kar/ *vt/i* bounce

quiche /'kiʃi/ *f* quiche

quie|to /ki'ɛtu/ *a* (*calado*) quiet; (*imóvel*) still; ∼**tude** *f* quiet

quilate /ki'latʃi/ *m* carat; (*fig*) calibre

quilha /'kiʎa/ *f* keel

quilo /'kilo/ *m* kilo; ∼**grama** *m* kilogram; ∼**metragem** *f* mileage; ∼**métrico** *a* mile-long

quilômetro /ki'lometru/ *m* kilometre

quimbanda /kĩ'bãda/ *m* Afro-Brazilian cult

qui|mera /ki'mɛra/ *f* fantasy; ∼**mérico** *a* fanciful

quími|ca /'kimika/ *f* chemistry; ∼**co** *a* chemical □ *m* chemist

quimioterapia /kimiotera'pia/ *f* chemotherapy

quimono /ki'monu/ *m* kimono

quina /'kina/ *f* **de ∼** edgeways

quindim /kĩ'dʒĩ/ *m* sweet made of coconut, sugar and egg yolks

quinhão /ki'ɲãw/ *m* share

quinhentos /ki'ɲẽtus/ *a & m* five hundred

quinina /ki'nina/ *f* quinine

qüinquagésimo /kwĩkwa'ʒɛzimu/ *a* fiftieth

quinquilharias /kĩkiʎa'rias/ *f pl* knick-knacks

quinta[1] /'kĩta/ *f* (*fazenda*) farm

quinta[2] /'kĩta/ *f* (*dia*) Thursday; ∼**-feira** (*pl* ∼**s-feiras**) *f* Thursday

quin|tal /kĩ'taw/ (*pl* ∼**tais**) *m* back yard

quinteiro /kĩ'tajru/ *m* (*Port*) farmer

quinteto /kĩ'tetu/ *m* quintet

quin|to /'kĩtu/ *a & m* fifth; ∼**tuplo** *a* fivefold; ∼**tuplos** *m pl* (*crianças*) quins

quinze /'kĩzi/ *a & m* fifteen; **às dez e ∼** at quarter past ten; **são ∼ para as dez** it's quarter to ten; ∼**na** /e/ *f* fortnight; ∼**nal** (*pl* ∼**nais**) *a* fortnightly; ∼**nalmente** *adv* fortnightly

quiosque /ki'ɔski/ *m* (*banca*) kiosk; (*no jardim*) gazebo

quiro|mância /kiro'mãsia/ *f* palmistry; ∼**mante** *m/f* palmist

quisto /'kistu/ *m* cyst

quitan|da /ki'tãda/ *f* grocer's (shop); ∼**deiro** *m* grocer

qui|tar /ki'tar/ *vt* pay off <*dívida*>; ∼**te** *a* **estar ∼te** be quits

quociente /kwosi'ẽtʃi/ *m* quotient

quórum /'kwɔrũ/ *m* quorum

....

Rr

....

rã /xã/ *f* frog

rabanete /xaba'netʃi/ *m* radish

rabear /xabi'ar/ *vi* <*caminhão*> jack-knife

rabino /xa'binu/ *m* rabbi

rabis|car /xabis'kar/ *vt* scribble □ *vi* (*escrever mal*) scribble; (*fazer desenhos*) doodle; ∼**co** *m* doodle

rabo /'xabu/ *m* (*de animal*) tail; **com o ∼ do olho** out of the corner of one's eye; ∼**-de-cavalo** (*pl* ∼**s-de-cavalo**) *m* pony tail

rabugento /xabu'ʒẽtu/ *a* grumpy

raça /'xasa/ *f* (*de homens*) race; (*de animais*) breed

ração /xa'sãw/ *f* (*de comida*) ration; (*para animal*) food

racha /'xaʃa/ *f* crack; ∼**dura** *f* crack

rachar /xa'ʃar/ *vt* (*dividir*) split; (*abrir fendas em*) crack; chop <*lenha*>; split <*despesas*> □ *vi* (*dividir-se*) split; (*apresentar fendas*) crack; (*ao pagar*) split the cost

raci|al /xasi'aw/ (*pl* ∼**ais**) *a* racial

racio|cinar /xasiosi'nar/ *vi* reason; ∼**cínio** *m* reasoning; ∼**nal** (*pl* ∼**nais**) *a* rational; ∼**nalizar** *vt* rationalize

racio|namento /xasiona'mẽtu/ *m* rationing; ∼**nar** *vt* ration

racis|mo /xa'sizmu/ *m* racism; ∼**ta** *a & m/f* racist

radar /xa'dar/ *m* radar; (*na estrada*) speed camera

radia|ção /xadʒia'sãw/ *f* radiation; ∼**dor** *m* radiator

radialista /xadʒia'lista/ *m/f* radio announcer

radiante /xadʒiˈãtʃi/ a (de alegria) overjoyed

radi|cal /xadʒiˈkaw/ (pl ∼cais) a & m radical; ∼car-se vpr settle

rádio¹ /ˈxadʒiu/ m radio ◻ f radio station

rádio² /ˈxadʒiu/ m (elemento) radium

radioati|vidade /xadioatʃiviˈdadʒi/ f radioactivity; ∼vo a radioactive

radiodifusão /xadʒiodʒifuˈzãw/ f broadcasting

radiogra|far /radʒiograˈfar/ vt X-ray <pulmões, osso etc>; radio <mensagem>; ∼fia f X-ray

radiolo|gia /radʒioloˈʒia/ f radiology; ∼gista m/f radiologist

radio|novela /xadʒionoˈvɛla/ f radio serial; ∼patrulha f patrol car; ∼táxi m radio taxi; ∼terapia f radiotherapy

raia /ˈxaja/ f (em corrida) lane; (peixe) ray

rainha /xaˈiɲa/ f queen; ∼-mãe f queen mother

raio /ˈxaju/ m (de luz etc) ray; (de círculo) radius; (de roda) spoke; (relâmpago) bolt of lightning; ∼ de ação range

rai|va /ˈxajva/ f rage; (doença) rabies; estar com ∼va be furious (de with); ter ∼va de alg have it in for s.o.; ∼voso a furious; <cachorro> rabid

raiz /xaˈiz/ f root; ∼ quadrada/cúbica square/cube root

rajada /xaˈʒada/ f (de vento) gust; (de tiros) burst

ra|lador /xalaˈdor/ m grater; ∼lar vt grate

ralé /xaˈlɛ/ f rabble

ralhar /xaˈʎar/ vi scold

ralo¹ /ˈxalu/ m (ralador) grater; (de escoamento) drain

ralo² /ˈxalu/ a <cabelo> thinning; <sopa, tecido> thin; <vegetação> sparse; <café> weak

ra|mal /xaˈmaw/ (pl ∼mais) m (telefone) extension; (de ferrovia) branch line

ramalhete /xamaˈʎetʃi/ m posy, bouquet

ramifi|cação /xamifikaˈsãw/ f branch; ∼car-se vi branch off

ramo /ˈxamu/ m branch; (profissional etc) field; (buquê) bunch; **Domingo de Ramos** Palm Sunday

rampa /ˈxãpa/ f ramp

rancor /xãˈkor/ m resentment; ∼oso /o/ a resentful

rançoso /xãˈsozu/ a rancid

ran|ger /xãˈʒer/ vt grind <dentes> ◻ vi creak; ∼gido m creak

ranhura /xaˈɲura/ f groove; (para moedas) slot

ranzinza /xãˈzĩza/ a cantankerous

rapariga /xapaˈriga/ f (Port) girl

rapaz /xaˈpas/ m boy

rapé /xaˈpɛ/ m snuff

rapidez /xapiˈdes/ f speed

rápido /ˈxapidu/ a fast ◻ adv (fazer) quickly; <andar> fast

rapina /xaˈpina/ f ave de ∼ bird of prey

rapo|sa /xaˈpoza/ f vixen; ∼so m fox

rapsódia /xapˈsɔdʒia/ f rhapsody

rap|tar /xapˈtar/ vt abduct, kidnap <criança>; ∼to m abduction, kidnapping (de criança)

raquete /xaˈkɛtʃi/ f, (Port) **raqueta** /xaˈketa/ f racquet

raquítico /xaˈkitʃiku/ a puny

ra|ramente /xaraˈmẽtʃi/ adv rarely; ∼ridade f rarity; ∼ro a rare ◻ adv rarely

rascunho /xasˈkuɲu/ m rough version, draft

ras|gado /xazˈgadu/ a torn; (fig) <elogios etc> effusive; ∼gão m tear; ∼gar vt tear; (em pedaços) tear up ◻ vi, ∼gar-se vpr tear; ∼go m tear; (fig) burst

raso /ˈxazu/ a <água> shallow; <sapato> flat; <colher etc> level

ras|pão /xasˈpãw/ m graze; atingir de ∼pão graze; ∼par vt shave <cabeça, pêlos>; plane <madeira>; (para limpar) scrape; (tocar de leve) graze; ∼par em scrape

ras|teiro /xasˈteru/ a <planta> creeping; <animal> crawling; ∼tejante a crawling; <voz> slurred; ∼tejar vi crawl

rasto /ˈxastu/ m veja **rastro**

ras|trear /xastriˈar/ vt track <satélite etc>; scan <céu, corpo etc>; ∼tro m trail

ratear¹ /xatʃiˈar/ vi <motor> miss

ra|tear² /xatʃiˈar/ vt share; ∼teio m sharing

ratifi|cação /xatʃifikaˈsãw/ f ratification; ∼car vt ratify

rato /ˈxatu/ m rat; (camundongo) mouse; ∼eira f mousetrap

ravina /xaˈvina/ f ravine

razão /xaˈzãw/ f reason; (proporção) ratio ◻ m ledger; à ∼ de at the rate of; em ∼ de on account of; ter ∼ be right; não ter ∼ be wrong

razoá|vel /xazoˈavew/ (pl ∼veis) a reasonable

ré¹ /xɛ/ f (na justiça) defendant

ré² /xɛ/ f (marcha) reverse; dar ∼ reverse

reabastecer /xeabasteˈser/ vt/i refuel

reabilitar /xeabiliˈtar/ vt rehabilitate

rea|ção /xeaˈsãw/ f reaction; ∼ção em cadeia chain reaction; ∼cionário a & m reactionary

readmitir /xeadʒimiˈtʃir/ vt reinstate <funcionário>

reagir /xea'ʒir/ *vi* react; <*doente*> respond

reajus|tar /xeaʒus'tar/ *vt* readjust; ∼**te** *m* adjustment

re|al /xe'aw/ (*pl* ∼**ais**) *a* (*verdadeiro*) real; (*da realeza*) royal

real|çar /xeaw'sar/ *vt* highlight; ∼**ce** *m* prominence

realejo /xea'leʒu/ *m* barrel organ

realeza /xea'leza/ *f* royalty

realidade /xeali'dadʒi/ *f* reality

realimentação /xealimẽta'sãw/ *f* feedback

realis|mo /xea'lizmu/ *m* realism; ∼**ta** *a* realistic ▫ *m/f* realist

reali|zado /xeali'zadu/ *a* <*pessoa*> fulfilled; ∼**zar** *vt* (*fazer*) carry out; (*tornar real*) realize <*sonho, capital*>; ∼**zar-se** *vpr* <*sonho*> come true; <*pessoa*> fulfil o.s.; <*casamento, reunião etc*> take place

realmente /xeaw'mẽtʃi/ *adv* really

reaparecer /xeapare'ser/ *vi* reappear

reativar /xeatʃi'var/ *vt* reactivate

reaver /xea'ver/ *vt* get back

reavivar /xeavi'var/ *vt* revive

rebaixar /xeba'ʃar/ *vt* lower <*preço*>; (*fig*) demean ▫ *vi* <*preços*> drop; ∼**-se** *vpr* demean o.s.

rebanho /xe'baɲu/ *m* herd; (*fiéis*) flock

reba|te /xe'batʃi/ *m* alarm; ∼**ter** *vt* return <*bola*>; refute <*acusação*>; (*à máquina*) retype

rebelar-se /xebe'larsi/ *vpr* rebel

rebel|de /xe'bɛwdʒi/ *a* rebellious ▫ *m/f* rebel; ∼**dia** *f* rebelliousness

rebelião /xebeli'ãw/ *f* rebellion

reben|tar /xebẽ'tar/ *vt/i veja* **arrebentar**; ∼**to** *m* (*de planta*) shoot; (*descendente*) offspring

rebite /xe'bitʃi/ *m* rivet

rebobinar /xebobi'nar/ *vt* rewind

rebo|cador /xeboka'dor/ *m* tug; ∼**car** *vt* (*tirar*) tow; (*cobrir com reboco*) plaster; ∼**co** /o/ *m* plaster

reboque /xe'bɔki/ *m* towing; (*veículo a* ∼) trailer; (*com guindaste*) towtruck; **a** ∼ on tow

rebuçado /xebu'sadu/ *m* (*Port*) sweet, (*Amer*) candy

rebuliço /xebu'lisu/ *m* commotion

rebuscado /xebus'kadu/ *a* récherché

recado /xe'kadu/ *m* message

reca|ída /xeka'ida/ *f* relapse; ∼**ir** *vi* relapse; <*acento, culpa*> fall

recal|cado /xekaw'kadu/ *a* repressed; ∼**car** *vt* repress

recanto /xe'kãtu/ *m* nook, recess

recapitular /xekapitu'lar/ *vt* review ▫ *vi* recap

recarregar /xekare'gar/ *vt* (*bateria*) recharge; (*crédito*) top up

reca|tado /xeka'tadu/ *a* reserved, withdrawn; ∼**to** *m* reserve

recear /xesi'ar/ *vt/i* fear (*por* for)

rece|ber /xese'ber/ *vt* receive; entertain <*convidados*> ▫ *vi* (∼**ber** *salário*) get paid; (∼**ber** *convidados*) entertain; ∼**bimento** *m* receipt

receio /xe'seju/ *m* fear

recei|ta /xe'sejta/ *f* (*de cozinha*) recipe; (*médica*) prescription; (*dinheiro*) revenue; ∼**tar** *vt* prescribe

recém|-casados /xesẽjka'zadus/ *m pl* newly-weds; ∼**-chegado** *m* newcomer; ∼**-nascido** *a* newborn ▫ *m* newborn child, baby

recente /xe'sẽtʃi/ *a* recent; ∼**mente** *adv* recently

receoso /xese'ozu/ *a* (*apreensivo*) afraid

recep|ção /xesep'sãw/ *f* reception; (*Port: de carta*) receipt; ∼**cionar** *vt* receive; ∼**cionista** *m/f* receptionist; ∼**táculo** *m* receptacle; ∼**tivo** *a* receptive; ∼**tor** *m* receiver

reces|são /xese'sãw/ *f* recession; ∼**so** /ɛ/ *m* recess

re|chear /xeʃi'ar/ *vt* stuff <*frango, assado*>; fill <*empada*>; ∼**cheio** *m* (*para frango etc*) stuffing; (*de empada etc*) filling

rechonchudo /xeʃõ'ʃudu/ *a* plump

recibo /xe'sibu/ *m* receipt

reciclar /xesik'lar/ *vt* recycle

recife /xe'sifi/ *m* reef

recinto /xe'sĩtu/ *m* enclosure

recipiente /xesipi'ẽtʃi/ *m* container

reciprocar /xesipro'kar/ *vt* reciprocate

recíproco /xe'siproku/ *a* reciprocal; <*sentimento*> mutual

reci|tal /xesi'taw/ (*pl* ∼**tais**) *m* recital; ∼**tar** *vt* recite

recla|mação /xeklama'sãw/ *f* complaint; (*no seguro*) claim; ∼**mar** *vt* claim ▫ *vi* complain (**de** about); (*no seguro*) claim; ∼**me** *m*, (*Port*) ∼**mo** *m* advertising

reclinar-se /xekli'narsi/ *vpr* recline

recluso /xe'kluzu/ *a* reclusive ▫ *m* recluse

recobrar /xeko'brar/ *vt* recover; ∼**-se** *vpr* recover

recolher /xeko'ʎer/ *vt* collect; (*retirar*) withdraw; ∼**-se** *vpr* retire

recomeçar /xekome'sar/ *vt/i* start again

recomen|dação /xekomẽda'sãw/ *f* recommendation; ∼**dar** *vt* recommend; ∼**dável** (*pl* ∼**dáveis**) *a* advisable

recompen|sa /xekõ'pẽsa/ *f* reward; ∼**sar** *vt* reward

r

reconcili|ação /xekõsilia'sãw/ f
reconciliation; **~ar** vt reconcile;
~ar-se vpr be reconciled

reconhe|cer /xekoɲe'ser/ vt recognize;
(admitir) acknowledge; (mil)
reconnoitre; identify <corpo>;
~cimento m recognition; (gratidão)
gratitude; (mil) reconnaissance; (de
corpo) identification; **~cível** (pl
~cíveis) a recognizable

reconsiderar /xekõside'rar/ vt/i
reconsider

reconstituinte /xekõstʃitu'ĩtʃi/ m tonic

reconstituir /xekõstʃitu'ir/ vt reform;
reconstruct <crime, cena>

reconstruir /xekõstru'ir/ vt rebuild

recor|dação /xekorda'sãw/ f
recollection; (objeto) memento; **~dar**
vt recollect; **~dar-se (de)** recall

recor|de /xe'kɔrdʒi/ a invar & m record;
~dista a record-breaking □ m/f
record-holder

recorrer /xeko'xer/ vi **~ a** turn to
<médico, amigo>; resort to <violência,
tática>; **~ de** appeal against

recor|tar /xekor'tar/ vt cut out; **~te** /ɔ/ m
cutting, (Amer) clipping

recostar /xekos'tar/ vt lean back; **~-se**
vpr lean back

recreio /xe'kreju/ m recreation; (na
escola) break

recriar /xekri'ar/ vt recreate

recriminação /xekrimina'sãw/ f
recrimination

recrudescer /xekrude'ser/ vi intensify

recru|ta /xe'kruta/ m/f recruit;
~tamento m recruitment; **~tar** vt
recruit

recu|ar /xeku'ar/ vi move back;
<tropas> retreat; (no tempo) go back;
(ceder) back down; (não cumprir) back
out (de of) □ vt move back; **~o** m
retreat; (fig: recuo) climbdown

recupe|ração /xekupera'sãw/ f
recovery; **~rar** vt recover; make up
<atraso, tempo perdido>; **~rar-se** vpr
recover (de from)

recurso /xe'kursu/ m resort; (coisa útil)
resource; (na justiça) appeal; pl
resources

recu|sa /xe'kuza/ f refusal; **~sar** vt
refuse; turn down <convite, oferta>;
~sar-se vpr refuse (a to)

reda|ção /xeda'sãw/ f (de livro, contrato)
draft; (pessoal) editorial staff; (seção)
editorial department; (na escola)
composition; **~tor** m editor

rede /'xedʒi/ f net; (para deitar)
hammock; (fig: sistema) network; **~
corporativa** (comput) intranet

rédea /'xɛdʒia/ f rein

redemoinho /xedemo'iɲu/ m veja
rodamoinho

reden|ção /xedẽ'sãw/ f redemption;
~tor a redeeming □ m redeemer

redigir /xedʒi'ʒir/ vt draw up
<contrato>; write <artigo>; edit
<dicionário>

redimir /xedʒi'mir/ vt redeem

redobrar /xedo'brar/ vt redouble

redon|deza /xedõ'deza/ f roundness; pl
vicinity; **~do** a round

redor /xe'dor/ m **ao** ou **em ~ de** around

redução /xedu'sãw/ f reduction

redun|dante /xedũ'dãtʃi/ a redundant;
~dar vi **~dar em** develop into

redu|zido /xedu'zidu/ a limited;
(pequeno) small; **~zir** vt reduce;
~zir-se vpr (ficar reduzido) be reduced
(a to); (resumir-se) come down (a to)

reeleger /xeele'ʒer/ vt re-elect

reeleição /xeelej'sãw/ f re-election

reembol|sar /xeẽbow'sar/ vt reimburse
<pessoa>; refund <dinheiro>; **~so** /o/
m refund; **~so postal** cash on delivery

reencarnação /xeẽkarna'sãw/ f
reincarnation

reentrância /xeẽ'trãsia/ f recess

reescalonar /xeeskalo'nar/ vt
reschedule

reescrever /xeeskre'ver/ vt rewrite

refastelar-se /xefaste'larsi/ vpr stretch
out

refazer /xefa'zer/ vt redo; rebuild
<vida>; **~-se** vpr recover (de from)

refei|ção /xefej'sãw/ f meal; **~tório** m
dining hall

refém /xe'fẽj/ m hostage

referência /xefe'rẽsia/ f reference; **com
~ a** with reference to

referendo /xefe'rẽdũ/ m referendum

refe|rente /xefe'rẽtʃi/ a **~rente a**
regarding; **~rir** vt report; **~rir-se** vpr
refer (a to)

refestelar-se /xefeste'larsi/ vpr (Port)
veja **refastelar-se**

re|fil /xe'fiw/ (pl **~fis**) m refill

refi|nado /xefi'nadu/ a refined;
~namento m refinement; **~nar** vt
refine; **~naria** f refinery

refle|tido /xefle'tʃidu/ a <decisão>
well-thought-out; <pessoa>
thoughtful; **~tir** vt/i reflect; **~tir-se**
vpr be reflected; **~xão** /ks/ f reflection;
~xivo /ks/ a reflexive; **~xo** /ɛks/ a
<luz> reflected; (ação) reflex □ m (de
luz etc) reflection; (físico) reflex; (no
cabelo) streak

refluxo /xe'fluksu/ m ebb

refo|gado /xefo'gadu/ m lightly fried
mixture of onions and garlic; **~gar** vt
fry lightly

refor|çar /xefor'sar/ vt reinforce; ∼**ço** /o/ m reinforcement

refor|ma /xe'fɔrma/ f (da lei etc) reform; (na casa etc) renovation; (de militar) discharge; (pensão) pension; ∼**ma ministerial** cabinet reshuffle; ∼**mado** a reformed; (Port: aposentado) retired □ m (Port) pensioner; ∼**mar** vt reform <lei, sistema etc>; renovate <casa, prédio>; (Port: aposentar) retire; ∼**mar-se** vpr (Port: aposentar-se) retire; <criminoso> reform; ∼**matório** m reform school; ∼**mista** a & m/f reformist

refratário /xefra'tariu/ a <tigela etc> ovenproof, heatproof

refrear /xefri'ar/ vt rein in <cavalo>; (fig) curb, keep in check <paixões etc>; ∼**-se** vpr restrain o.s.

refrega /xe'frɛga/ f clash, fight

refres|cante /xefres'kãtʃi/ a refreshing; ∼**car** vt freshen, cool <ar>; refresh <pessoa, memória etc> □ vi get cooler; ∼**car-se** vpr refresh o.s.; ∼**co** /e/ m (bebida) soft drink; pl refreshments

refrige|rado /xefriʒe'radu/ a cooled; <casa etc> air-conditioned; (na geladeira) refrigerated; ∼**rador** m refrigerator; ∼**rante** m soft drink; ∼**rar** vt keep cool; (na geladeira) refrigerate

refugi|ado /xefuʒi'adu/ m refugee; ∼**ar-se** vpr take refuge

refúgio /xe'fuʒiu/ m refuge

refugo /xe'fugu/ m waste, refuse

refutar /xefu'tar/ vt refute

regaço /xe'gasu/ m lap

regador /xega'dor/ m watering can

regalia /xega'lia/ f privilege

regar /xe'gar/ vt water

regata /xe'gata/ f regatta

regatear /xegatʃi'ar/ vi bargain, haggle

re|gência /xe'ʒẽsia/ f (de verbo etc) government; ∼**gente** m/f (de orquestra) conductor; ∼**ger** vt govern □ vi rule

região /xeʒi'ãw/ f region; (de cidade etc) area

regi|me /xe'ʒimi/ m regime; (dieta) diet; **fazer** ∼**me** diet; ∼**mento** m (militar) regiment; (regulamento) regulations

régio /'xɛʒiu/ a regal

regio|nal /xeʒio'naw/ (pl ∼**nais**) a regional

regis|trador /xeʒistra'dor/ a **caixa** ∼**tradora** cash register; ∼**trar** vt register; (anotar) record; ∼**tro** m (lista) register; (de um fato, em banco de dados) record; (ato de ∼**trar**) registration

rego /'xegu/ m (de arado) furrow; (de roda) rut; (para escoamento) ditch

regozi|jar /xegozi'ʒar/ vt delight; ∼**jar-se** vpr be delighted; ∼**jo** m delight

regra /'xɛgra/ f rule; pl (menstruações) periods; **em** ∼ as a rule

regres|sar /xegre'sar/ vi return; ∼**sivo** a regressive; **contagem** ∼**siva** countdown; ∼**so** /ɛ/ m return

régua /'xɛgwa/ f ruler

regu|lagem /xegu'laʒẽ/ f (de carro) tuning; ∼**lamento** m regulations; ∼**lar** a regular; <estatura, qualidade etc> average □ vt regulate; tune <carro, motor>; set <relógio> □ vi work; ∼**lar-se por** go by, be guided by; ∼**laridade** f regularity; ∼**larizar** vt regularize

regurgitar /xegurʒi'tar/ vt bring up

rei /xej/ m king; ∼**nado** m reign

reincidir /xeĩsi'dʒir/ vi <criminoso> reoffend

reino /'xejnu/ m kingdom; (fig: da fantasia etc) realm; **Reino Unido** United Kingdom

reiterar /xejte'rar/ vt reiterate

reitor /xej'tor/ m chancellor, (Amer) president

reivindi|cação /xejvĩdʒika'sãw/ f demand; ∼**car** vt claim, demand

rejei|ção /xeʒej'sãw/ f rejection; ∼**tar** vt reject

rejuvenescer /xeʒuvene'ser/ vt rejuvenate □ vi be rejuvenated

relação /xela'sãw/ f relationship; (relatório) account; (lista) list; pl relations; **com** ou **em** ∼ **a** in relation to, regarding

relacio|namento /xelasiona'mẽtu/ m relationship; ∼**nar** vt relate (**com** to); (listar) list; ∼**nar-se** vpr relate (**com** to)

relações-públicas /xelasõjs'publikas/ m/f invar public-relations person

relâmpago /xe'lãpagu/ m flash of lightning; pl lightning □ a lightning; **num** ∼ in a flash

relampejar /xelãpe'ʒar/ vi flash; **relampejou** there was a flash of lightning

relance /xe'lãsi/ m glance; **olhar de** ∼ glance (at)

rela|tar /xela'tar/ vt relate; ∼**tivo** a relative; ∼**to** m account; ∼**tório** m report

rela|xado /xela'ʃadu/ a relaxed; <disciplina> lax; <pessoa> lazy, complacent; ∼**xamento** m (físico) relaxation; (de pessoa) complacency; ∼**xante** a relaxing □ m tranquillizer; ∼**xar** vt relax □ vi (descansar) relax; (tornar-se omisso) get complacent; ∼**xar-se** vpr relax; ∼**xe** m relaxation

reles /'xɛlis/ a invar <gente> common; <ação> despicable

r

rele|vância /xele'vãsia/ f relevance;
~vante a relevant; ~-var vt
emphasize; ~vo /e/ m relief;
(importância) prominence

religi|ão /xeliʒi'ãw/ f religion; ~oso /o/
a religious

relin|char /xelĩ'ʃar/ vi neigh; ~cho m
neighing

relíquia /xe'likia/ f relic

relógio /xe'lɔʒiu/ m clock; (de pulso)
watch

relu|tância /xelu'tãsia/ f reluctance;
~tante a reluctant; ~-tar vi be
reluctant (em to)

reluzente /xelu'zẽtʃi/ a shining,
gleaming

relva /'xɛwva/ f grass; ~do m lawn

remador /xema'dor/ m rower

remanescente /xemane'sẽtʃi/ a
remaining □ m remainder

remar /xe'mar/ vt/i row

rema|tar /xema'tar/ vt finish off; ~te m
finish; (adorno) finishing touch; (de
piada) punch line

remediar /xemedʒi'ar/ vt remedy

remédio /xe'mɛdʒiu/ m (contra doença)
medicine, drug; (a problema etc)
remedy

remelento /xeme'lẽtu/ a bleary

remen|dar /xemẽ'dar/ vt mend; (com
pedaço de pano) patch; ~do m mend;
(pedaço de pano) patch

remessa /xe'mɛsa/ f (de mercadorias)
shipment; (de dinheiro) remittance

reme|tente /xeme'tẽtʃi/ m/f sender;
~ter vt send <mercadorias, dinheiro
etc>; refer <leitor> (a to)

remexer /xeme'ʃer/ vt shuffle <papéis>;
stir up <poeira, lama>; wave <braços>
□ vi rummage; ~-se vpr move around

reminiscência /xemini'sẽsia/ f
reminiscence

remir /xe'mir/ vt redeem; ~-se vpr
redeem o.s.

remissão /xemi'sãw/ f (de pecados)
redemption; (de doença, pena)
remission; (num livro) cross-reference

remo /'xemu/ m oar; (esporte) rowing

remoção /xemo'sãw/ f removal

remoinho /xemo'iɲu/ m (Port) veja
rodamoinho

remontar /xemõ'tar/ vi ~ a <coisa> date
back to; <pessoa> think back to

remorso /xe'mɔrsu/ m remorse

remo|to /xe'mɔtu/ a remote; ~ver vt
remove

remune|ração /xemunera'sãw/ f
payment; ~rador a profitable; ~rar vt
pay

rena /'xena/ f reindeer

re|nal /xe'naw/ (pl ~nais) a renal,
kidney

Renascença /xena'sẽsa/ f Renaissance

renas|cer /xena'ser/ vi be reborn;
~cimento m rebirth

renda¹ /'xẽda/ f (tecido) lace

ren|da² /'xẽda/ f income; (Port: aluguel)
rent; ~der bring in, yield <lucro>;
earn <juros>; fetch <preço>; bring
<resultado> □ vi <investimento,
trabalho, ação> pay off; <comida> go a
long way; <produto comprado> give
value for money; ~der-se vpr
surrender; ~dição f surrender;
~dimento m (renda) income; (de
investimento, terreno) yield; (de motor
etc) output; (de produto comprado)
value for money; ~doso /o/ a profitable

rene|gado /xene'gadu/ a & m renegade;
~gar vt renounce

renhido /xe'ɲidu/ a hard-fought

Reno /'xenu/ m Rhine

reno|mado /xeno'madu/ a renowned;
~me /o/ m renown

reno|vação /xenova'sãw/ f renewal;
~var vt renew

renque /'xẽki/ m row

ren|tabilidade /xẽtabili'dadʒi/ f
profitability; ~tável (pl ~táveis) a
profitable

rente /'xẽtʃi/ adv ~ a close to □ a
<cabelo> cropped

renúncia /xe'nũsia/ f renunciation (a
of); (a cargo) resignation (a from)

renunciar /xenũsi'ar/ vi <presidente
etc> resign; ~ a give up; waive
<direito>

reorganizar /xeorgani'zar/ vt
reorganize

repa|ração /xepara'sãw/ f reparation;
(conserto) repair; ~rar vt (consertar)
repair; make up for <ofensa, injustiça,
erro>; make good <danos, prejuízo>
□ vi ~rar (em) notice; ~ro m
(conserto) repair

repar|tição /xepartʃi'sãw/ f division;
(seção do governo) department; ~tir vt
divide up

repassar /xepa'sar/ vt revise <matéria,
lição>

repatriar /xepatri'ar/ vt repatriate

repe|lente /xepe'lẽtʃi/ a & m repellent;
~lir vt repel; reject <idéia, proposta
etc>

repensar /xepẽ'sar/ vt/i rethink

repen|te /xe'pẽtʃi/ m de ~te suddenly;
(fam: talvez) maybe; ~tino a sudden

reper|cussão /xeperku'sãw/ f
repercussion; ~cutir vi <som>
reverberate; (fig: ter efeito) have
repercussions

repertório /xeper'tɔriu/ *m* (*músico etc*) repertoire; (*lista*) list

repe|tição /xepetʃi'sãw/ *f* repetition; ∼**tido** *a* repeated; ∼**tidas vezes** repeatedly; ∼**tir** *vt* repeat □ *vi* (*ao comer*) have seconds; ∼**tir-se** *vpr* <*pessoa*> repeat o.s.; <*fato, acontecimento*> recur; ∼**titivo** *a* repetitive

repi|car /xepi'kar/ *vt/i* ring; ∼**que** *m* ring

replay /xe'plej/ (*pl* ∼s) *m* action replay

repleto /xe'plɛtu/ *a* full up

réplica /'xɛplika/ *f* reply; (*cópia*) replica

replicar /xepli'kar/ *vt* answer □ *vi* reply

repolho /xe'poʎu/ *m* cabbage

repor /xe'por/ *vt* (*num lugar*) put back; (*substituir*) replace

reportagem /xepor'taʒẽ/ *f* (*uma*) report; (*ato*) reporting

repórter /xe'pɔrter/ *m/f* reporter

reposição /xepozi'sãw/ *f* replacement

repou|sar /xepo'sar/ *vt/i* rest; ∼**so** *m* rest

repreen|der /xepriẽ'der/ *vt* rebuke, reprimand; ∼**são** *f* rebuke, reprimand; ∼**sível** (*pl* ∼**síveis**) *a* reprehensible

represa /xe'preza/ *f* dam

represália /xepre'zalia/ *f* reprisal

represen|tação /xeprezẽta'sãw/ *f* representation; (*espetáculo*) performance; (*ofício de ator*) acting; ∼**tante** *m/f* representative; ∼**tar** *vt* represent; (*no teatro*) perform <*peça*>; play <*papel, personagem*> □ *vi* <*ator*> act; ∼**tativo** *a* representative

repres|são /xepre'sãw/ *f* repression; ∼**sivo** *a* repressive

repri|mido /xepri'midu/ *a* repressed; ∼**mir** *vt* repress

reprise /xe'prizi/ *f* (*na TV*) repeat; (*de filme*) rerun

reprodu|ção /xeprodu'sãw/ *f* reproduction; ∼**zir** *vt* reproduce; ∼**zir-se** *vpr* (*multiplicar-se*) reproduce; (*repetir-se*) recur

repro|vação /xeprova'sãw/ *f* disapproval; (*em exame*) failure; ∼**var** *vt* (*rejeitar*) disapprove of; (*em exame*) fail; **ser** ∼**vado** <*aluno*> fail

rép|til /'xɛptʃiw/ (*pl* ∼**teis**) *m* reptile

república /xe'publika/ *f* republic; (*de estudantes*) hall of residence

republicano /xepubli'kanu/ *a & m* republican

repudiar /xepudʒi'ar/ *vt* disown; repudiate <*esposa*>

repug|nância /xepug'nãsia/ *f* repugnance; ∼**nante** *a* repugnant

repul|sa /xe'puwsa/ *f* repulsion; (*recusa*) rejection; ∼**sivo** *a* repulsive

reputação /xeputa'sãw/ *f* reputation

requebrar /xeke'brar/ *vt* swing; ∼**-se** *vpr* sway

requeijão /xeke'ʒãw/ *m* cheese spread, cottage cheese

reque|rer /xeke'rer/ *vt* (*pedir*) apply for; (*exigir*) require; ∼**-rimento** *m* application

requin|tado /xekĩ'tadu/ *a* refined; ∼**tar** *vt* refine; ∼**te** *m* refinement

requisi|ção /xekizi'sãw/ *f* requisition; ∼**tar** *vt* requisition; ∼**to** *m* requirement

rês /xes/ (*pl* **reses**) *m* head of cattle; *pl* cattle

rescindir /xesĩ'dʒir/ *vt* rescind

rés-do-chão /xɛzdu'ʃãw/ *m invar* (*Port*) ground floor, (*Amer*) first floor

rese|nha /xe'zeɲa/ *f* review; ∼**-nhar** *vt* review

reser|va /xe'zɛrva/ *f* reserve; (*em hotel, avião etc, ressalva*) reservation; ∼**var** *vt* reserve; ∼**vatório** *m* reservoir; ∼**vista** *m/f* reservist

resfri|ado /xesfri'adu/ *a* **estar** ∼**ado** have a cold □ *m* cold; ∼**ar** *vt* cool □ *vi* get cold; (*tornar-se morno*) cool down; ∼**ar-se** *vpr* catch a cold

resga|tar /xezga'tar/ *vt* (*salvar*) rescue; (*remir*) redeem; ∼**te** *m* (*salvamento*) rescue; (*pago por refém*) ransom; (*remissão*) redemption

resguardar /xezgwar'dar/ *vt* protect; ∼**-se** *vpr* protect o.s. (**de** from)

residência /xezi'dẽsia/ *f* residence

residen|cial /xezidẽsi'aw/ (*pl* ∼**ciais**) *a* <*bairro*> residential; <*telefone etc*> home; ∼**te** *a & m/f* resident

residir /xezi'dʒir/ *vi* reside

resíduo /xe'ziduu/ *m* residue

resig|nação /xezigna'sãw/ *f* resignation; ∼**nado** *a* resigned; ∼**nar-se** *vpr* resign o.s. (**com** to)

resina /xe'zina/ *f* resin

resis|tência /xezis'tẽsia/ *f* resistance; (*de atleta, mental*) endurance; (*de material, objeto*) toughness; ∼**tente** *a* strong, tough; <*tecido, roupa*> hard-wearing; <*planta*> hardy; ∼**tente** *a* resistant to; ∼**tir** *vi* (*opor* ∼**tência**) resist; (*agüentar*) <*pessoa*> hold out; <*objeto*> hold; ∼**tir a** (*combater*) resist; (*agüentar*) withstand; ∼**tir ao tempo** stand the test of time

resmun|gar /xezmũ'gar/ *vi* grumble; ∼**go** *m* grumbling

resolu|ção /xezolu'sãw/ *f* resolution; (*firmeza*) resolve; (*de problema*) solution; ∼**to** *a* resolute; ∼**to a** resolved to

resolver /xezow'ver/ *vt* (*esclarecer*) sort out; solve <*problema, enigma*>;

r

(*decidir*) decide; ~**-se** *vpr* make up one's mind (**a** to)

respaldo /xes'pawdu/ *m* (*de cadeira*) back; (*fig: apoio*) backing

respectivo /xespek'tʃivu/ *a* respective

respei|tabilidade /xespejtabili'dadʒi/ *f* respectability; ~**tador** *a* respectful; ~**tar** *vt* respect; ~**tável** (*pl* ~**táveis**) *a* respectable; ~**to** *m* respect (**por** for); **a** ~**to de** about; **a este** ~**to** in this respect; **com** ~**to a** with regard to; **dizer** ~**to a** concern; ~**toso** /o/ *a* respectful

respin|gar /xespĩ'gar/ *vt/i* splash; ~**go** *m* splash

respi|ração /xespira'sãw/ *f* breathing; ~**rador** *m* respirator; ~**rar** *vt/i* breathe; ~**ratório** *a* respiratory; ~**ro** *m* breath; (*descanso*) break, breather

resplande|cente /xesplãde'sẽtʃi/ *a* resplendent; ~**cer** *vi* shine

resplendor /xesplẽ'dor/ *m* brilliance; (*fig*) glory

respon|dão /xespõ'dãw/ *a* (*f* ~**dona**) cheeky; ~**der** *vt/i* answer; (*com insolência*) answer back; ~**der a** answer; ~**der por** answer for, take responsibility for

responsabili|dade /xespõsabili'dadʒi/ *f* responsibility; ~**zar** *vt* hold responsible (**por** for); ~**zar-se** *vpr* take responsibility (**por** for)

responsá|vel /xespõ'savew/ (*pl* ~**veis**) *a* responsible (**por** for)

resposta /xes'posta/ *f* answer

resquício /xes'kisiu/ *m* vestige, remnant

ressabiado /xesabi'adu/ *a* wary, suspicious

ressaca /xe'saka/ *f* (*depois de beber*) hangover; (*do mar*) undertow

ressaltar /xesaw'tar/ *vt* emphasize □ *vi* stand out

ressalva /xe'sawva/ *f* reservation, proviso; (*proteção*) safeguard

ressarcir /xesar'sir/ *vt* refund

resse|cado /xese'kadu/ *a* <*terra*> parched; <*pele*> dry; ~**car** *vt/i* dry up

ressen|tido /xesẽ'tʃidu/ *a* resentful; ~**timento** *m* resentment; ~**tir-se de** (*ofender-se*) resent; (*ser influenciado*) show the effects of

ressequido /xese'kidu/ *a veja* **ressecado**

resso|ar /xeso'ar/ *vi* resound; ~**nância** *f* resonance; ~**nante** *a* resonant; ~**nar** *vi* (*Port*) snore

ressurgimento /xesurʒi'mẽtu/ *m* resurgence

ressurreição /xesuxej'sãw/ *f* resurrection

ressuscitar /xesusi'tar/ *vt* revive

restabele|cer /xestabele'ser/ *vt* restore; restore to health <*doente*>; ~**cer-se** *vpr* recover; ~**cimento** *m* restoration; (*de doente*) recovery

res|tante /xes'tãtʃi/ *a* remaining □ *m* remainder; ~**tar** *vi* remain; ~**ta-me dizer que** ... it remains for me to say that ...

restau|ração /xestawra'sãw/ *f* restoration; ~**rante** *m* restaurant; ~**rar** *vt* restore

restitu|ição /xestʃitui'sãw/ *f* return, restitution; ~**ir** *vt* (*devolver*) return; restore <*forma, força etc*>; reinstate <*funcionário*>

resto /'xɛstu/ *m* rest; *pl* (*de comida*) left-overs; (*de cadáver*) remains; **de** ~ besides

restrição /xestri'sãw/ *f* restriction

restringir /xestrĩ'ʒir/ *vt* restrict

restrito /xes'tritu/ *a* restricted

resul|tado /xezuw'tadu/ *m* result; ~**tante** *a* resulting (**de** from); ~**tar** *vi* result (**de** from; **em** in)

resu|mir /xezu'mir/ *vt* (*abreviar*) summarize; (*conter em poucas palavras*) sum up; ~**mir-se** *vpr* (*ser expresso em poucas palavras*) be summed up; (*ser apenas*) come down to; ~**mo** *m* summary; **em** ~**mo** briefly

resvalar /xezva'lar/ *vi* (*sem querer*) slip; (*deslizar*) slide

reta /'xɛta/ *f* (*linha*) straight line; (*de pista etc*) straight; ~ **final** home straight

retaguarda /xeta'gwarda/ *f* rearguard

retalho /xe'taʎu/ *m* scrap; **a** ~ (*Port*) retail

retaliação /xetalia'sãw/ *f* retaliation

retangular /xetãgu'lar/ *a* rectangular

retângulo /xe'tãgulu/ *m* rectangle

retar|dado /xetar'dadu/ *a* retarded □ *m* retard; ~**dar** *vt* delay; ~**datário** *m* latecomer

retenção /xetẽ'sãw/ *f* retention

reter /xe'ter/ *vt* keep <*pessoa*>; hold back <*águas, riso, lágrimas*>; (*na memória*) retain; ~**se** *vpr* restrain o.s.

rete|sado /xete'zadu/ *a* taut; ~**sar** *vt* pull taut

reticência /xetʃi'sẽsia/ *f* reticence

reti|dão /xetʃi'dãw/ *f* rectitude; ~**ficar** *vt* rectify

reti|rada /xetʃi'rada/ *f* (*de tropas*) retreat; (*de dinheiro*) withdrawal; ~**rado** *a* secluded; ~**rar** *vt* withdraw; (*afastar*) move away; ~**rar-se** *vpr* <*tropas*> retreat; (*afastar-se*) withdraw; (*de uma atividade*) retire; ~**ro** *m* retreat

reto /'xɛtu/ *a* <*linha etc*> straight; <*pessoa*> honest

retocar /xeto'kar/ *vt* touch up <*desenho, maquiagem etc*>; alter <*texto*>

reto|mada /xeto'mada/ *f* (*continuação*) resumption; (*reconquista*) retaking; **∼mar** *vt* (*continuar com*) resume; (*conquistar de novo*) retake

retoque /xe'tɔki/ *m* finishing touch

retorcer /xetor'ser/ *vt* twist; **∼-se** *vpr* writhe

retóri|ca /xe'tɔrika/ *f* rhetoric; **∼co** *a* rhetorical

retor|nar /xetor'nar/ *vi* return; **∼no** *m* return; (*na estrada*) turning place; **dar ∼no** do a U-turn

retrair /xetra'ir/ *vt* retract, withdraw; **∼-se** *vpr* (*recuar*) withdraw; (*encolher-se*) retract

retrasa|do /xetra'zadu/ *a* **a semana ∼da** the week before last

retratar[1] /xetra'tar/ *vt* (*desdizer*) retract

retra|tar[2] /xetra'tar/ *vt* (*em quadro, livro*) portray, depict; **∼to** *m* portrait; (*foto*) photo; (*representação*) portrayal; **∼to falado** identikit picture

retribuir /xetribu'ir/ *vt* return <*favor, visita*>; repay <*gentileza*>

retroativo /xetroa'tʃivu/ *a* retroactive; <*pagamento*> backdated

retro|ceder /xetrose'der/ *vi* retreat; (*desistir*) back down; **∼cesso** /ɛ/ *m* retreat; (*ao passado*) regression

retrógrado /xe'trɔgradu/ *a* retrograde

retrospec|tiva /xetrospek'tʃiva/ *f* retrospective; **∼tivo** *a* retrospective; **∼to** /ɛ/ *m* look back; **em ∼to** in retrospect

retrovisor /xetrovi'zor/ *a & m* (**espelho**) **∼** rear-view mirror

retrucar /xetru'kar/ *vt/i* retort

retum|bante /xetũ'bātʃi/ *a* resounding; **∼bar** *vi* resound

réu /'xɛw/ *m* (*f* **ré**) defendant

reumatismo /xewma'tʃizmu/ *m* rheumatism

reu|nião /xeuni'ãw/ *f* meeting; (*descontra ida*) get-together; (*de fam ília*) reunion; **∼nião de cúpula** summit meeting; **∼nir** *vt* bring together <*pessoas*>; combine <*qualidades*>; **∼nir-se** *vpr* meet; <*amigos, familiares*> get together; **∼nir-se a** join

revanche /xe'vãʃi/ *f* revenge; (*jogo*) return match

reveillon /xeve'jõ/ (*pl* **∼s**) *m* New Year's Eve

reve|lação /xevela'sãw/ *f* revelation; (*de fotos*) developing; (*novo talento*) promising newcomer; **∼lar** *vt* reveal;

develop <*filme, fotos*>; **∼lar-se** *vpr* (*vir a ser*) turn out to be

revelia /xeve'lia/ *f* **à ∼** by default; **à ∼ de** without the knowledge of

reven|dedor /xevēde'dor/ *m* dealer; **∼der** *vt* resell

rever /xe'ver/ *vt* (*ver de novo*) see again; (*revisar*) revise; (*examinar*) check

reve|rência /xeve'resia/ *f* reverence; (*movimento do busto*) bow; (*dobrando os joelhos*) curtsey; **∼rente** *a* reverent

reverso /xe'vɛrsu/ *m* reverse; **o ∼ da medalha** the other side of the coin

revés /xe'vɛs/ (*pl* **reveses**) *m* setback

reves|timento /xevestʃi'mētu/ *m* covering; **∼tir** *vt* cover

reve|zamento /xeveza'mētu/ *m* alternation; **∼zar** *vt/i* alternate; **∼zar-se** *vpr* alternate

revi|dar /xevi'dar/ *vt* return <*golpe, insulto*>; refute <*crítica*>; (*retrucar*) retort □ *vi* hit back; **∼de** *m* response

revigorar /xevigo'rar/ *vt* strengthen □ *vi*, **∼-se** *vpr* regain one's strength

revi|rar /xevi'rar/ *vt* turn out <*bolsos, gavetas*>; turn over <*terra*>; turn inside out <*roupa*>; roll <*olhos*>; **∼rar-se** *vpr* toss and turn; **∼ravolta** /ɔ/ *f* (*na política etc*) about-face, about-turn; (*da situação*) turnabout, dramatic change

revi|são /xevi'zãw/ *f* (*de lições etc*) revision; (*de máquina, motor*) overhaul; (*de carro*) service; **∼são de provas** proofreading; **∼sar** *vt* revise <*provas, lições*>; service <*carro*>; **∼sor** *m* (*de bilhetes*) ticket inspector; **∼sor de provas** proofreader

revis|ta /xe'vista/ *f* (*para ler*) magazine; (*teatral*) revue; (*de tropas etc*) review; **passar ∼ta** a review; **∼tar** *vt* search

reviver /xevi'ver/ *vt* relive □ *vi* revive

revogar /xevo'gar/ *vt* revoke <*lei*>; cancel <*ordem*>

revol|ta /xe'vɔwta/ *f* (*rebelião*) revolt; (*indignação*) disgust; **∼tante** *a* disgusting; **∼tar** *vt* disgust; **∼tar-se** *vpr* (*rebelar-se*) revolt; (*indignar-se*) be disgusted; **∼to** /o/ *a* <*casa, gaveta*> upside down; <*cabelo*> dishevelled; <*mar*> rough; <*mundo, região*> troubled; <*anos*> turbulent

revolu|ção /xevolu'sãw/ *f* revolution; **∼cionar** *vt* revolutionize; **∼cionário** *a & m* re-volutionary

revolver /xevow'ver/ *vt* turn over <*terra*>; roll <*olhos*>; go through <*gavetas, arquivos*>

revólver /xe'vɔwver/ *m* revolver

re|za /'xɛza/ *f* prayer; **∼zar** *vi* pray □ *vt* say <*missa, oração*>; (*dizer*) state

r

riacho /xi'aʃu/ *m* stream

ribalta /xi'bawta/ *f* footlights

ribanceira /xibã'sera/ *f* embankment

ribombar /xibõ'bar/ *vi* rumble

rico /'xiku/ *a* rich □ *m* rich man; **os ~s** the rich

ricochete /xiko'ʃetʃi/ *m* ricochet; **~ar** *vi* ricochet

ricota /xi'kɔta/ *f* curd cheese, ricotta

ridicularizar /xidʒikulari'zar/ *vt* ridicule

ridículo /xi'dʒikulu/ *a* ridiculous

ri|fa /'xifa/ *f* raffle; **~far** *vt* raffle

rifão /xi'fãw/ *m* saying

rifle /'xifli/ *m* rifle

rigidez /xiʒi'des/ *f* rigidity

rígido /'xiʒidu/ *a* rigid

rigor /xi'gor/ *m* severity; *(meticulosidade)* rigour; **vestido a ~** evening dress; **de ~** essential

rigoroso /xigo'rozu/ *a* strict; *<inverno, pena>* severe, harsh; *<lógica, estudo>* rigorous

rijo /'xiʒu/ *a* stiff; *<músculos>* firm

rim /xĩ/ *m* kidney; *pl (parte das costas)* small of the back

ri|ma /'xima/ *f* rhyme; **~mar** *vt/i* rhyme

ri|mel /'ximew/ (*pl* **~meis**) *m* mascara

ringue /'xĩgi/ *m* ring

rinoceronte /xinose'rõtʃi/ *m* rhinoceros

rinque /'xĩki/ *m* rink

rio /'xio/ *m* river

riqueza /xi'keza/ *f* wealth; *(qualidade)* richness; *pl* riches

rir /xir/ *vi* laugh (**de** at)

risada /xi'zada/ *f* laugh, laughter; **dar ~** laugh

ris|ca /'xiska/ *f* stroke; *(listra)* stripe; *(do cabelo)* parting; **à ~ca** to the letter; **~car** *vt (apagar)* cross out *<erro>*; strike *<fósforo>*; scratch *<mesa, carro etc>*; write off *<amigo etc>*; **~co¹** *m (na parede etc)* scratch; *(no papel)* line; *(esboço)* sketch

risco² /'xisku/ *m* risk

riso /'xizu/ *m* laugh; **~nho** /o/ *a* smiling

ríspido /'xispidu/ *a* harsh

rítmico /'xitʃmiku/ *a* rhythmic

ritmo /'xitʃimu/ *m* rhythm

rito /'xitu/ *m* rite

ritu|al /xitu'aw/ (*pl* **~ais**) *a & m* ritual

ri|val /xi'vaw/ (*pl* **~vais**) *a & m/f* rival; **~validade** *f* rivalry; **~valizar** *vt* rival □ *vi* vie (**com** with)

rixa /'xiʃa/ *f* fight

robô /xo'bo/ *m* robot

robusto /xo'bustu/ *a* robust

roça /'xɔsa/ *f (campo)* country

rocambole /xokã'bɔli/ *m* roll

roçar /xo'sar/ *vt* graze; **~ em** brush against

ro|cha /'xɔʃa/ *f* rock; **~chedo** /e/ *m* cliff

roda /'xɔda/ *f (de carro etc)* wheel; *(de amigos etc)* circle; **~ dentada** cog; **~da** *f* round; **~ d'água** *f* full skirt; **~-gigante** (*pl* **~s-gigantes**) *f* big wheel, *(Amer)* ferris wheel; **~moinho** *m (de vento)* whirlwind; *(na água)* whirlpool; *(fig)* whirl, swirl; **~pé** *m* skirting board, *(Amer)* baseboard

rodar /xo'dar/ *vt (fazer girar)* spin; *(viajar por)* go round; do *<quilometragem>*; shoot *<filme>*; run *<programa>* □ *vi (girar)* spin; *(de carro)* drive round

rodear /xodʒi'ar/ *vt (circundar)* surround; *(andar ao redor de)* go round

rodeio /xo'deju/ *m (ao falar)* circumlocution; *(de gado)* round-up; **falar sem ~s** talk straight

rodela /xo'dɛla/ *f (de limão etc)* slice; *(peça de metal)* washer

rodízio /xo'dʒiziu/ *m* rota

rodo /'xodu/ *m* rake

rodopiar /xodopi'ar/ *vi* spin round

rodovi|a /xodo'via/ *f* highway; **~ária** *f* bus station; **~ário** *a* road; **polícia ~ária** traffic police

ro|edor /xoe'dor/ *m* rodent; **~er** *vt* gnaw; bite *<unhas>*; *(fig)* eat away

rogar /xo'gar/ *vi* request

rojão /xo'ʒãw/ *m* rocket

rol /xɔw/ (*pl* **róis**) *m* roll

rolar /xo'lar/ *vt* roll □ *vi* roll; *(fam) (acontecer)* happen

roldana /xow'dana/ *f* pulley

roleta /xo'leta/ *f (jogo)* roulette; *(borboleta)* turnstile

rolha /'xoʎa/ *f* cork

roliço /xo'lisu/ *a <objeto>* cylindrical; *<pessoa>* plump

rolo /'xolu/ *m (de filme, tecido etc)* roll; *(máquina, bobe)* roller; **~ compressor** steamroller; **~ de massa** rolling pin

Roma /'xoma/ *f* Rome

romã /xo'mã/ *f* pomegranate

roman|ce /xo'mãsi/ *m (livro)* novel; *(caso)* romance; **~cista** *m/f* novelist

romano /xo'manu/ *a & m* Roman

romântico /xo'mãtʃiku/ *a* romantic

romantismo /xomã'tʃizmu/ *m (amor)* romance; *(idealismo)* romanticism

romaria /xoma'ria/ *f* pilgrimage

rombo /'xõbu/ *m* hole

Romênia /xo'menia/ *f* Romania

romeno /xo'menu/ *a & m* Romanian

rom|per /xõ'per/ *vt* break; break off *<relações>* □ *vi* break; *<dia>* break; *<sol>* rise; **~per com** break up with;

~**pimento** *m* break; (*de relações*) breaking off

ron|car /xõ'kar/ *vi* (*ao dormir*) snore; <*estômago*> rumble; ~**co** *m* snoring; (*um*) snore; (*de motor*) roar

ron|da /'xõda/ *f* round, patrol; ~**dar** *vt* (*patrulhar*) patrol; (*espreitar*) prowl around □ *vi* <*vigia etc*> patrol; <*animal, ladrão*> prowl around

ronronar /xõxo'nar/ *vi* purr

roque[1] /'xɔki/ *m* (*em xadrez*) rook

ro|que[2] /'xɔki/ *m* (*música*) rock; ~**queiro** *m* rock musician

rosa /'xɔza/ *f* rose □ *a invar* pink; ~**do** *a* rosy; <*vinho*> rosé

rosário /xo'zariu/ *m* rosary

rosbife /xoz'bifi/ *m* roast beef

rosca /'xoska/ *f* (*de parafuso*) thread; (*biscoito*) rusk; **farinha de** ~ breadcrumbs

roseira /xo'zera/ *f* rosebush

roseta /xo'zeta/ *f* rosette

rosnar /xoz'nar/ *vi* <*cachorro*> growl; <*pessoa*> snarl

rosto /'xostu/ *m* face

rota /'xɔta/ *f* route

rota|ção /xota'sãw/ *f* rotation; ~**tividade** *f* turnround; ~**tivo** *a* rotating

rotei|rista /xote'rista/ *m/f* scriptwriter; ~**ro** *m* (*de viagem*) itinerary; (*de filme, peça*) script; (*de discussão etc*) outline

roti|na /xo'tʃina/ *f* routine; ~**neiro** *a* routine

rótula /'xɔtula/ *f* kneecap

rotular /xotu'lar/ *vt* label (**de** as)

rótulo /'xɔtulu/ *m* label

rou|bar /xo'bar/ *vt* steal <*dinheiro, carro etc*>; rob <*pessoa, loja etc*> □ *vi* steal; (*em jogo*) cheat; ~**bo** *m* theft, robbery

rouco /'xoku/ *a* hoarse; <*voz*> gravelly

rou|pa /'xopa/ *f* clothes; (*uma*) outfit; ~**pa de baixo** underwear; ~**pa de cama** bedclothes; ~**pão** *m* dressing gown

rouquidão /xoki'dãw/ *f* hoarseness

rouxi|nol /xoʃi'nɔw/ (*pl* ~**nóis**) *m* nightingale

roxo /'xoʃu/ *a* purple

rua /'xua/ *f* street

rubéola /xu'bɛola/ *f* German measles

rubi /xu'bi/ *m* ruby

rude /'xudʒi/ *a* rude

rudimentos /xudʒi'mẽtus/ *m pl* rudiments, basics

ruela /xu'ɛla/ *f* backstreet

rufar /xu'far/ *vi* <*tambor*> roll □ *m* roll

ruga /'xuga/ *f* (*na pele*) wrinkle; (*na roupa*) crease

ru|gido /xu'ʒidu/ *m* roar; ~**gir** *vi* roar

ruibarbo /xui'barbu/ *m* rhubarb

ruído /xu'idu/ *m* noise

ruidoso /xui'dozu/ *a* noisy

ruim /xu'ĩ/ *a* bad

ruína /xu'ina/ *f* ruin

ruivo /'xuivu/ *a* <*cabelo*> red; <*pessoa*> red-haired □ *m* redhead

rulê /xu'le/ *a* **gola** ~ roll-neck

rum /xũ/ *m* rum

ru|mar /xu'mar/ *vi* head (**para** for); ~**mo** *m* course; ~**mo a** heading for; **sem** ~**mo** <*vida*> aimless; <*andar*> aimlessly

rumor /xu'mor/ *m* (*da rua, de vozes*) hum; (*do trânsito*) rumble; (*boato*) rumour

ru|ral /xu'raw/ (*pl* ~**rais**) *a* rural

rusga /'xuzga/ *f* quarrel, disagreement

rush /xaʃ/ *m* rush hour

Rússia /'xusia/ *f* Russia

russo /'xusu/ *a & m* Russian

rústico /'xustʃiku/ *a* rustic

Ss

Saara /saa'ra/ *m* Sahara

sábado /'sabadu/ *m* Saturday

sabão /sa'bãw/ *m* soap; ~ **em pó** soap powder

sabatina /saba'tʃina/ *f* test

sabedoria /sabedo'ria/ *f* wisdom

saber /sa'ber/ *vt/i* know (**de** about); (*descobrir*) find out (**de** about) □ *m* knowledge; **eu sei cantar** I know how to sing, I can sing; **sei lá** I've no idea; **que eu saiba** as far as I know

sabiá /sabi'a/ *m* thrush

sabi|chão /sabi'ʃãw/ *a & m* (*f* ~**chona**) know-it-all

sábio /'sabiu/ *a* wise □ *m* wise man

sabone|te /sabo'netʃi/ *m* bar of soap; ~**teira** *f* soapdish

sabor /sa'bor/ *m* flavour; **ao** ~ **de** at the mercy of

sabo|rear /sabori'ar/ *vt* savour; ~**roso** *a* tasty

sabo|tador /sabota'dor/ *m* saboteur; ~**tagem** *f* sabotage; ~**tar** *vt* sabotage

saca /'saka/ *f* sack

sacada /sa'kada/ *f* balcony

sa|cal /sa'kaw/ (*pl* ~**cais**) *a* (*fam*) boring

saca|na /sa'kana/ (*fam*) *a* (*desonesto*) devious; (*lascivo*) dirty-minded, naughty □ *m/f* rogue; ~**nagem** (*fam*) *f* (*esperteza*) trickery; (*sexo*) sex; (*uma*) dirty trick; **~near** (*fam*) *vt* (*enganar*) do the dirty on; (*amolar*) take the mickey out of

sacar /sa'kar/ *vt/i* withdraw <*dinheiro*>; draw <*arma*>; (*em tênis, vôlei etc*) serve; (*fam*) (*entender*) understand

saçaricar /sasari'kar/ *vi* play around

sacarina /saka'rina/ *f* saccharine

saca-rolhas /saka'xoʎas/ *m invar* corkscrew

sacer|dócio /saser'dɔsiu/ *m* priesthood; **~dote** /ɔ/ *m* priest; **~dotisa** *f* priestess

sachê /sa'ʃe/ *m* sachet

saciar /sasi'ar/ *vt* satisfy

saco /'saku/ *m* bag; **que ~!** (*fam*) what a pain!; **estar de ~ cheio (de)** (*fam*) be fed up (with), be sick (of); **encher o ~ de alg** (*fam*) get on s.o.'s nerves; **puxar o ~ de alg** (*fam*) suck up to s.o.; **~ de dormir** sleeping bag; **~la** /ɔ/ *f* bag; **~lão** *m* wholesale fruit and vegetable market; **~lejar** *vt* shake

sacramento /sakra'mẽtu/ *m* sacrament

sacri|ficar /sakrifi'kar/ *vt* sacrifice; have put down <*cachorro etc*>; **~fício** *m* sacrifice; **~légio** *m* sacrilege

sacrílego /sa'krilegu/ *a* sacrilegious

sacro /'sakru/ *a* <*música*> religious

sacrossanto /sakro'sãtu/ *a* sacrosanct

sacu|dida /saku'dʒida/ *f* shake; **~dir** *vt* shake

sádico /'sadʒiku/ *a* sadistic □ *m* sadist

sadio /sa'dʒiu/ *a* healthy

sadismo /sa'dʒizmu/ *m* sadism

safa|deza /safa'deza/ *f* (*desonestidade*) deviousness; (*libertinagem*) indecency; (*uma*) dirty trick; **~do** *a* (*desonesto*) devious; (*lascivo*) dirty-minded; (*esperto*) quick; <*criança*> naughty

safena /sa'fɛna/ *f* **ponte de ~** heart bypass; **~do** *m* bypass patient

safira /sa'fira/ *f* sapphire

safra /'safra/ *f* crop

sagitariano /saʒitari'anu/ *a & m* Sagittarian

Sagitário /saʒi'tariu/ *m* Sagittarius

sagrado /sa'gradu/ *a* sacred

saguão /sa'gwãw/ *m* (*de teatro, hotel*) foyer, (*Amer*) lobby; (*de estação, aeroporto*) concourse

saia /'saja/ *f* skirt; **~calça** (*pl* **~s-calças**) *f* culottes

saída /sa'ida/ *f* (*partida*) departure; (*porta, fig*) way out; **de ~** at the outset; **estar de ~** be on one's way out

sair /sa'ir/ *vi* (*de dentro*) go/come out; (*partir*) leave; (*desprender-se*) come off; <*mancha*> come out; (*resultar*) turn out; **~se** *vpr* fare; **~se com** (*dizer*)

come out with; **~ mais barato** work out cheaper

sal /saw/ (*pl* **sais**) *m* salt; **~ de frutas** Epsom salts

sala /'sala/ *f* (*numa casa*) lounge; (*num lugar público*) hall; (*classe*) class; **fazer ~ a** entertain; **~ (de aula)** classroom; **~ de embarque** departure lounge; **~ de espera** waiting room; **~ de jantar** dining room; **~ de operação** operating theatre

sala|da /sa'lada/ *f* salad; (*fig*) jumble, mishmash; **~da de frutas** fruit salad; **~deira** *f* salad bowl

sala-e-quarto /sali'kwartu/ *m* two-room flat

sala|me /sa'lami/ *m* salami; **~minho** *m* pepperoni

salão /sa'lãw/ *m* hall; (*de cabeleireiro*) salon; (*de carros*) show; **~ de beleza** beauty salon

salari|al /salari'aw/ (*pl* **~ais**) *a* wage

salário /sa'lariu/ *m* salary

sal|dar /saw'dar/ *vt* settle; **~do** *m* balance

saleiro /sa'leru/ *m* salt cellar

sal|gadinhos /sawga'dʒiɲus/ *m pl* snacks; **~gado** *a* salty; <*preço*> exorbitant; **~gar** *vt* salt

salgueiro /saw'geru/ *m* willow; **~ chorão** weeping willow

saliência /sali'ẽsia/ *f* projection

salien|tar /saliẽ'tar/ *vt* (*deixar claro*) point out; (*acentuar*) highlight; **~tar-se** *vpr* distinguish o.s.; **~te** *a* prominent

saliva /sa'liva/ *f* saliva

salmão /saw'mãw/ *m* salmon

salmo /'sawmu/ *m* psalm

salmonela /sawmo'nɛla/ *f* salmonella

salmoura /saw'mora/ *f* brine

salpicar /sawpi'kar/ *vt* sprinkle; (*sem querer*) spatter

salsa /'sawsa/ *f* parsley

salsicha /saw'siʃa/ *f* sausage

saltar /saw'tar/ *vt* (*pular*) jump; (*omitir*) skip □ *vi* jump; **~ à vista** be obvious; **~ do ônibus** get off the bus

saltear /sawtʃi'ar/ *vt* sauté <*batatas etc*>

saltitar /sawtʃi'tar/ *vi* hop

salto /'sawtu/ *m* (*pulo*) jump; (*de sapato*) heel; **~ com vara** pole vault; **~ em altura** high jump; **~ em distância** long jump; **~mortal** (*pl* **~s-mortais**) *m* somersault

salu|bre /sa'lubri/ *a* healthy; **~tar** *a* salutary

salva[1] /'sawva/ *f* (*de canhões*) salvo; (*bandeja*) salver; **~ de palmas** round of applause

salva[2] /'sawva/ *f* (*erva*) sage

S

salva|ção /sawva'sãw/ *f* salvation; **~dor** *m* saviour

salvaguar|da /sawva'gwarda/ *f* safeguard; **~dar** *vt* safeguard

sal|vamento /sawva'mẽtu/ *m* rescue; (*de navio*) salvage; **~var** *vt* save; **~var-se** *vpr* escape; **~va-vidas** *m invar* (*bóia*) lifebelt □ *m/f* (*pessoa*) lifeguard □ *a* **barco ~va-vidas** lifeboat; **~vo** *a* safe □ *prep* save; **a ~vo** safe

samambaia /samã'baja/ *f* fern

sam|ba /'sãba/ *m* samba; **~ba-canção** (*pl* **~bas-canção**) *m* slow samba □ *a invar* **cueca ~ba-canção** boxer shorts; **~ba-enredo** (*pl* **~bas-enredo**) *m* samba story; **~bar** *vi* samba; **~bista** *m/f* (*dançarino*) samba dancer; (*compositor*) composer of sambas; **~bódromo** *m* Carnival parade ground

samovar /samo'var/ *m* tea urn

sanar /sa'nar/ *vt* cure

san|ção /sã'sãw/ *f* sanction; **~cionar** *vt* sanction

sandália /sã'dalia/ *f* sandal

sandes /'sãdiʃ/ *f invar* (*Port*) sandwich

sanduíche /sãdu'iʃi/ *m* sandwich

sane|amento /sania'mẽtu/ *m* (*esgotos*) sanitation; (*de finanças*) rehabilitation; **~ar** *vt* set straight <*finanças*>

sanfona /sã'fona/ *f* (*instrumento*) accordion; (*tricô*) ribbing; **~do** *a* <*porta*> folding; <*pulôver*> ribbed

san|grar /sã'grar/ *vt/i* bleed; **~grento** *a* bloody; <*carne*> rare; **~gria** *f* bloodshed; (*de dinheiro*) extortion

sangue /'sãgi/ *m* blood; **~ pisado** bruise; **~-frio** *m* cool, coolness

sanguessuga /sãgi'suga/ *f* leech

sanguinário /sãgi'nariu/ *a* bloodthirsty

sanguíneo /sã'giniu/ *a* blood

sanidade /sani'dadʒi/ *f* sanity

sanitário /sani'tariu/ *a* sanitary; **~s** *mpl* toilets

san|tidade /sãtʃi'dadʒi/ *f* sanctity; **~tificar** *vt* sanctify; **~to** *a* holy □ *m* saint; **todo ~to dia** every single day; **~tuário** *m* sanctuary

São /sãw/ *a* Saint

são /sãw/ (*pl* **~s**) *a* (*f* **sã**) healthy; (*mentalmente*) sane; <*conselho*> sound

sapato /sa'pato/ *m* shoe; **~ria** *f* shoe shop

sapate|ado /sapatʃi'adu/ *m* tap dancing; **~ador** *m* tap dancer; **~ar** *vi* tap one's feet; (*dançar*) tap-dance

sapa|teiro /sapa'teru/ *m* shoemaker; **~tilha** *f* pump; **~tilha de balé** ballet shoe; **~to** *m* shoe

sapeca /sa'pɛka/ *a* saucy

sa|pinho /sa'piɲu/ *m* thrush; **~po** *m* toad

saque¹ /'saki/ *m* (*do banco*) withdrawal; (*em tênis, vôlei etc*) serve

saque² /'saki/ *m* (*de loja etc*) looting; **~ar** *vt* loot

saraiva /sa'rajva/ *f* hail; **~da** *f* hailstorm; **uma ~da de** a hail of

sarampo /sa'rãpu/ *m* measles

sarar /sa'rar/ *vt* cure □ *vi* get better; <*ferida*> heal

sar|casmo /sar'kazmu/ *m* sarcasm; **~cástico** *a* sarcastic

sarda /'sarda/ *f* freckle

Sardenha /sar'deɲa/ *f* Sardinia

sardento /sar'dẽtu/ *a* freckled

sardinha /sar'dʒiɲa/ *f* sardine

sardônico /sar'doniku/ *a* sardonic

sargento /sar'ʒẽtu/ *m* sergeant

sarjeta /sar'ʒeta/ *f* gutter

Satanás /sata'nas/ *m* Satan

satânico /sa'taniku/ *a* satanic

satélite /sa'tɛlitʃi/ *a & m* satellite

sátira /'satʃira/ *f* satire

satírico /sa'tʃiriku/ *a* satirical

satirizar /satʃiri'zar/ *vt* satirize

satisfa|ção /satʃisfa'sãw/ *f* satisfaction; **dar ~ções a** answer to; **~tório** *a* satisfactory; **~zer** *vt* **~zer (a)** satisfy □ *vi* be satisfactory; **~zer-se** *vpr* be satis- fied

satisfeito /satʃis'fejtu/ *a* satisfied; (*contente*) content; (*de comida*) full

saturar /satu'rar/ *vt* saturate

Saturno /sa'turnu/ *m* Saturn

saudação /sawda'sãw/ *f* greeting

saudade /saw'dadʒi/ *f* longing; (*lembrança*) nostalgia; **estar com ~s de** miss; **matar ~s** catch up

saudar /saw'dar/ *vt* greet

saudá|vel /saw'davew/ (*pl* **~veis**) *a* healthy

saúde /sa'udʒi/ *f* health □ *int* (*ao beber*) cheers; (*ao espirrar*) bless you

saudo|sismo /sawdo'zizmu/ *m* nostalgia; **~so** /o/ *a* longing; **estar ~so de** miss; **o nosso ~so amigo** our much-missed friend

sauna /'sawna/ *f* sauna

saxofo|ne /sakso'foni/ *m* saxophone; **~nista** *m/f* saxophonist

sazo|nado /sazo'nadu/ *a* seasoned; **~nal** (*pl* **~nais**) *a* seasonal

se¹ /si/ *conj* if; **não sei ~ ...** I don't know if/whether

se² /si/ *pron* (*ele mesmo*) himself; (*ela mesma*) herself; (*você mesmo*) yourself; (*eles/elas*) themselves; (*vocês*) yourselves; (*um ao outro*) each other; **dorme-~ tarde no Brasil** people go to bed late in Brazil; **aqui ~ fala inglês** English is spoken here

sebo /'sebu/ *m* (*sujeira*) grease; (*livraria*) secondhand bookshop; **~so** /o/ *a* greasy; <*pessoa*> slimy

seca /'seka/ *f* drought; **~dor** *m* **~dor de cabelo** hairdryer; **~dora** *f* tumble dryer

seção /se'sãw/ *f* section; (*de loja*) department

secar /se'kar/ *vt/i* dry

sec|ção /sek'sãw/ *f veja* **seção**; **~cionar** *vt* split up

seco /'seku/ *a* dry; <*resposta, tom*> curt; <*pessoa, caráter*> cold; <*barulho, pancada*> dull; **estar ~ por** I'm dying for

secretaria /sekreta'ria/ *f* (*de empresa*) general office; (*ministério*) department

secretá|ria /sekre'taria/ *f* secretary; **~ria eletrônica** ansaphone; **~rio** *m* secretary

secreto /se'krɛtu/ *a* secret

secular /seku'lar/ *a* (*não religioso*) secular; (*antigo*) age-old

século /'sɛkulu/ *m* century; *pl* (*muito tempo*) ages

secundário /sekũ'dariu/ *a* secondary

secura /se'kura/ *f* dryness; **estar com uma ~ de** be longing for/to

seda /'seda/ *f* silk

sedativo /seda'tʃivu/ *a & m* sedative

sede¹ /'sedʒi/ *f* headquarters; (*local do governo*) seat

sede² /'sedʒi/ *f* thirst (**de** for); **estar com ~** be thirsty

sedentário /sedē'tariu/ *a* sedentary

sedento /se'dẽtu/ *a* thirsty (**de** for)

sediar /sedʒi'ar/ *vt* host

sedimen|tar /sedʒimē'tar/ *vt* consolidate; **~to** *m* sediment

sedoso /se'dozu/ *a* silky

sedu|ção /sedu'sãw/ *f* seduction; **~tor** *a* seductive; **~zir** *vt* seduce

segmento /seg'mẽtu/ *m* segment

segredo /se'gredu/ *m* secret; (*de cofre etc*) combination

segregar /segre'gar/ *vt* segregate

segui|da /se'gida/ *f em* **~da** (*imediatamente*) straight away; (*depois*) next; **~do** *a* followed (**de** by); **cinco horas ~das** five hours running; **~dor** *m* follower; **~mento** *m* continuation; **dar ~mento a** go on with

se|guinte /se'gĩtʃi/ *a* following; <*dia, semana etc*> next; **~guir** *vt/i* follow; (*continuar*) continue; **~guir-se** *vpr* follow; **~guir em frente** (*ir embora*) go; (*indicação na rua*) go straight ahead

segun|da /se'gũda/ *f* (*dia*) Monday; (*marcha*) second; **de ~da** second-rate; **~da-feira** (*pl* **~das-feiras**) *f* Monday; **~do** *a & m* second □ *adv* secondly

□ *prep* according to □ *conj* according to what; **~das intenções** ulterior motives; **de ~da mão** second-hand

segu|rança /segu'rãsa/ *f* security; (*estado de seguro*) safety; (*certeza*) assurance □ *m/f* security guard; **~rar** *vt* hold; **~rar-se** *vpr* (*controlar-se*) control o.s.; **~rar-se em** hold on to; **~ro** *a* secure; (*fora de perigo*) safe; (*com certeza*) sure □ *m* insurance; **estar no ~ro** <*bens*> be insured; **fazer ~ro de** insure; **~ro-desemprego** *m* unemployment benefit

seio /'seju/ *m* breast, bosom; **no ~ de** within

seis /sejs/ *a & m* six; **~centos** *a & m* six hundred

seita /'sejta/ *f* sect

seixo /'sejʃu/ *m* pebble

sela /'sɛla/ *f* saddle

selar¹ /se'lar/ *vt* saddle <*cavalo*>

selar² /se'lar/ *vt* seal; (*franquear*) stamp

sele|ção /sele'sãw/ *f* selection; (*time*) team; **~cionar** *vt* select; **~to** /ɛ/ *a* select

selim /se'lĩ/ *m* saddle

selo /'selu/ *m* seal; (*postal*) stamp; (*de discos*) label

selva /'sɛwva/ *f* jungle; **~gem** *a* wild; **~geria** *f* savagery

sem /sēj/ *prep* without; **~ eu saber** without me knowing; **ficar ~ dinheiro** run out of money

semáforo /se'maforu/ *m* (*na rua*) traffic lights; (*de ferrovia*) signal

sema|na /se'mana/ *f* week; **~nal** (*pl* **~nais**) *a* weekly; **~nalmente** *adv* weekly; **~nário** *m* weekly

semear /semi'ar/ *vt* sow

semelhan|ça /seme'ʎãsa/ *f* similarity; **~te** *a* similar; (*tal*) such

sêmen /'semẽ/ *m* semen

semente /se'mẽtʃi/ *f* seed; (*em fruta*) pip

semestre /se'mɛstri/ *m* six months; (*da faculdade etc*) term, (*Amer*) semester

semi|círculo /semi'sirkulu/ *m* semicircle; **~final** (*pl* **~finais**) *f* semifinal

seminário /semi'nariu/ *m* (*aula*) seminar; (*colégio religioso*) seminary

sem-número /sē'numeru/ *m* **um ~ de** innumerable

sempre /'sẽpri/ *adv* always; **como ~** as usual; **para ~** for ever; **~ que** whenever

sem|-terra /sē'tɛxa/ *m/f invar* landless labourer; **~-teto** *a* homeless □ *m/f* homeless person; **~-vergonha** *a invar* brazen □ *m/f invar* scoundrel

sena|do /se'nadu/ *m* senate; **~dor** *m* senator

senão /si'nãw/ *conj* otherwise; (*mas antes*) but rather □ *m* snag

senda /'sẽda/ *f* path

senha /'seɲa/ *f* (*palavra*) password; (*número*) code; (*sinal*) signal

senhor /se'ɲor/ *m* gentleman; (*homem idoso*) older man; (*tratamento*) sir □ *a* (*f* ~a) mighty; **Senhor** (*com nome*) Mr; (*Deus*) Lord; **o** ~ (*você*) you

senho|ra /se'ɲora/ *f* lady; (*mulher idosa*) older woman; (*tratamento*) madam; **Senhora** (*com nome*) Mrs; **a** ~**ra** (*você*) you; **nossa** ~**ra!** (*fam*) gosh; ~**ria** *f* **Vossa Senhoria** you; ~**rita** *f* young lady; (*tratamento*) miss; **Senhorita** (*com nome*) Miss

se|nil (*pl* ~**nis**) *a* senile; ~**nilidade** *f* senility

sensação /sẽsa'sãw/ *f* sensation

sensacio|nal /sẽsasio'naw/ (*pl* ~**nais**) *a* sensational; ~**nalismo** *m* sensationalism; ~**nalista** *a* sensationalist

sen|sato /sẽ'satu/ *a* sensible; ~**sibilidade** *f* sensitivity; ~**sível** (*pl* ~**síveis**) *a* sensitive; (*que se pode sentir*) noticeable; ~**so** *m* sense; ~**sual** (*pl* ~**suais**) *a* sensual

sen|tado /sẽ'tadu/ *a* sitting; ~**tar** *vt/i* sit; ~**tar-se** *upr* sit down

sentença /sẽ'tẽsa/ *f* sentence

sentido /sẽ'tʃidu/ *m* sense; (*direção*) direction □ *a* hurt; **fazer** *ou* **ter** ~ make sense

sentimen|tal /sẽtʃimẽ'taw/ (*pl* ~**tais**) *a* sentimental; **vida** ~**tal** love life; ~**to** *m* feeling

sentinela /sẽtʃi'nɛla/ *f* sentry

sentir /sẽ'tʃir/ *vt* feel; (*notar*) sense; smell <*cheiro*>; taste <*gosto*>; tell <*diferença*>; (*ficar magoado por*) be hurt by □ *vi* feel; ~**se** *upr* feel; **sinto muito** I'm very sorry

sepa|ração /separa'sãw/ *f* separation; ~**rado** *a* separate; <*casal*> separated; ~**rar** *vt* separate; ~**rar-se** *upr* separate

séptico /'sɛptʃiku/ *a* septic

sepul|tar /sepuw'tar/ *vt* bury; ~**tura** *f* grave

seqüência /se'kwẽsia/ *f* sequence

sequer /se'kɛr/ *adv* **nem** ~ not even

seqües|trador /sekwestra'dor/ *m* kidnapper; (*de avião*) hijacker; ~**trar** *vt* kidnap <*pessoa*>; hijack <*avião*>; sequestrate <*bens*>; ~**tro** /ɛ/ *m* (*de pessoa*) kidnapping; (*de avião*) hijack; (*de bens*) sequestration

ser /sɛr/ *vi* be □ *m* being; **é** (*como resposta*) yes; **você gosta, não é?** you like it, don't you?; **ele foi morto** he was killed; **será que ele volta?** I wonder if he's coming back; **ou seja** in other words; **a não** ~ except; **a não** ~ **que** unless; **não sou de fofocar** I'm not one to gossip

sereia /se'reja/ *f* mermaid

serenata /sere'nata/ *f* serenade

sereno /se'renu/ *a* serene; <*tempo*> fine

série /'sɛri/ *f* series; (*na escola*) grade; **fora de** ~ incredible

seriedade /serie'dadʒi/ *f* seriousness

serin|ga /se'rĩga/ *f* syringe; ~**gueiro** *m* rubber tapper

sério /'sɛriu/ *a* serious; (*responsável*) responsible; **é** ~? really?; **falar** ~ be serious; **levar a** ~ take seriously

sermão /ser'mãw/ *m* sermon

serpen|te /ser'pẽtʃi/ *f* serpent; ~**tear** *vi* wind; ~**tina** *f* streamer

serra[1] /'sɛxa/ *f* (*montanhas*) mountain range

serra[2] /'sɛxa/ *f* (*de serrar*) saw; ~**gem** *f* sawdust; ~**lheiro** *m* locksmith

serrano /se'xanu/ *a* mountain

serrar /se'xar/ *vt* saw

ser|tanejo /serta'neʒu/ *a* from the backwoods □ *m* backwoodsman; ~**tão** *m* backwoods

servente /ser'vẽtʃi/ *m/f* labourer

Sérvia /'sɛrvia/ *f* Serbia

servi|çal /servi'saw/ (*pl* ~**çais**) *a* helpful □ *m/f* servant; ~**ço** *m* service; (*trabalho*) work; (*tarefa*) job; **estar de** ~**ço** be on duty; ~**dor** *m* servant; (*comput*) server; ~ **público** civil servant

ser|vil /ser'viw/ (*pl* ~**vis**) *a* servile

sérvio /'sɛrviu/ *a & m* Serbian

servir /ser'vir/ *vt* serve □ *vi* serve; (*ser adequado*) do; (*ser útil*) be of use; <*roupa, sapato etc*> fit; ~**se** *upr* (*ao comer etc*) help o.s. (**de** to); ~**se de** make use of; ~ **como** *ou* **de** serve as; **para que serve isso?** what is this (used) for?

sessão /se'sãw/ *f* session; (*no cinema*) showing, performance

sessenta /se'sẽta/ *a & m* sixty

seta /'sɛta/ *f* arrow; (*de carro*) indicator

sete /'sɛtʃi/ *a & m* seven; ~**centos** *a & m* seven hundred

setembro /se'tẽbru/ *m* September

setenta /se'tẽta/ *a & m* seventy

sétimo /'sɛtʃimu/ *a* seventh

setuagésimo /setua'ʒɛzimu/ *a* seventieth

setor /se'tor/ *m* sector

seu /sew/ *a* (*f* **sua**) (*dele*) his; (*dela*) her; (*de coisa*) its; (*deles*) their; (*de você, de vocês*) your □ *pron* (*dele*) his; (*dela*) hers; (*deles*) theirs; (*de você, de vocês*) yours; ~ **idiota!** you idiot!; **seu João** Mr John

S

seve|ridade /severi'dadʒi/ f severity;
~**ro** /ε/ a severe

sexagésimo /seksa'ʒεzimu/ a sixtieth

sexo /'sεksu/ m sex; **fazer** ~ have sex

sex|ta /'sesta/ f Friday; ~**ta-feira** (pl
~**tas-feiras**) f Friday; **Sexta-feira
Santa** Good Friday; ~**to** /e/ a & m sixth

sexu|al /seksu'aw/ (pl ~**ais**) a sexual;
vida ~**al** sex life

sexy /'sεksi/ a invar sexy

shopping /'ʃɔpĩ/ (pl ~**s**) m shopping
centre, (Amer) mall

short /'ʃɔrtʃi/ m (pl ~**s**) shorts; **um** ~ a
pair of shorts

show /'ʃou/ (pl ~**s**) m show; (de música)
concert

si /si/ pron (ele) himself; (ela) herself;
(coisa) itself; (você) yourself; (eles)
themselves; (vocês) yourselves;
(qualquer pessoa) oneself; **em** ~ in
itself; **fora de** ~ beside o.s.; **cheio de** ~
full of o.s.; **voltar a** ~ come round

sibilar /sibi'lar/ vi hiss

SIDA /'sida/ f (Port) AIDS

side|ral /side'raw/ (pl ~**rais**) a **espaço**
~**ral** outer space.

siderurgia /siderur'ʒia/ f iron and steel
industry

siderúrgi|ca /side'rurʒika/ f
steelworks; ~**co** a iron and steel □ m
steelworker

sifão /si'fãw/ m syphon

sífilis /'sifilis/ f syphilis

sigilo /si'ʒilu/ m secrecy; ~**so** /o/ a secret

sigla /'sigla/ f acronym

signatário /signa'tariu/ m signatory

signifi|cação /signifika'sãw/ f
significance; ~**cado** m meaning; ~**car**
vt mean; ~**cativo** a significant

signo /'signu/ m sign

sílaba /'silaba/ f syllable

silenciar /silẽsi'ar/ vt silence

silêncio /si'lẽsiu/ m silence

silencioso /silẽsi'ozu/ a silent □ m
silencer, (Amer) muffler

silhueta /siʎu'eta/ f silhouette

silício /si'lisiu/ m silicon

silicone /sili'kɔni/ m silicone

silo /'silu/ m silo

silvar /siw'var/ vi hiss

sil|vestre /siw'vεstri/ a wild;
~**vicultura** f forestry

sim /sĩ/ adv yes; **acho que** ~ I think so

simbólico /sĩ'bɔliku/ a symbolic

simbo|lismo /sĩbo'lizmu/ m symbolism;
~**lizar** vt symbolize

símbolo /'sĩbolu/ m symbol

si|metria /sime'tria/ f symmetry;
~**métrico** a symmetrical

similar /simi'lar/ a similar

sim|patia /sĩpa'tʃia/ f (qualidade)
pleasantness; (afeto) fondness (**por** for);
(compreensão, apoio) sympathy; pl
sympathies; **ter** ~**patia por** be fond of;
~- **pático** a nice

simpati|zante /sĩpatʃi'zãtʃi/ a
sympathetic □ m/f sympathizer; ~**zar**
vi ~**zar com** take a liking to <pessoa>;
sympathize with <idéias, partido etc>

simples /'sĩplis/ a invar simple; (único)
single □ f (no tênis etc) singles;
~**mente** adv simply

simpli|cidade /sĩplisi'dadʒi/ f
simplicity; ~**ficar** vt simplify

simplório /sĩ'plɔriu/ a simple

simpósio /sĩ'pɔziu/ m symposium

simu|lação /simula'sãw/ f simulation;
~**lar** vt simulate

simultâneo /simuw'taniu/ a
simultaneous

sina /'sina/ f fate

sinagoga /sina'gɔga/ f synagogue

si|nal /si'naw/ (pl ~**nais**) m sign; (aviso,
de rádio etc) signal; (de trânsito) traffic
light; (no telefone) tone; (dinheiro)
deposit; (na pele) mole; **por** ~**nal** as a
matter of fact; ~**nal de pontuação**
punctuation mark; ~**naleira** f traffic
lights; ~**nalização** f (na rua) road
signs; ~**nalizar** vt signal; signpost
<rua, cidade>

since|ridade /sĩseri'dadʒi/ f sincerity;
~**ro** /ε/ a sincere

sincro|nia /sĩkro'nia/ f
synchronization; ~**nizar** vt
synchronize

sindi|cal /sĩdʒi'kaw/ (pl ~**cais**) a trade
union; ~**calismo** m trade unionism;
~**calista** m/f trade unionist; ~**calizar**
vt unionize; ~**cato** m trade union

síndico /'sĩdʒiku/ m house manager

síndrome /'sĩdromi/ f syndrome

sineta /si'neta/ f bell

sin|fonia /sĩfo'nia/ f symphony;
~**fônica** f symphony orchestra

singe|leza /sĩʒe'leza/ f simplicity; ~**lo**
/ε/ a simple

singu|lar /sĩgu'lar/ a singular;
(estranho) peculiar; ~**larizar** vt single
out

sinis|trado /sinis'tradu/ a damaged;
~**tro** a sinister □ m accident

sino /'sinu/ m bell

sinônimo /si'nonimu/ a synonymous
□ m synonym

sintaxe /sĩ'taksi/ f syntax

síntese /'sĩtezi/ f synthesis

sin|tético /sĩ'tεtʃiku/ a (artificial)
synthetic; (resumido) concise;
~**tetizar** vt summarize

sinto|ma /sĩ'toma/ *m* symptom;
~**mático** *a* symptomatic
sintoni|zador /sĩtoniza'dor/ *m* tuner;
~**zar** *vt* tune <*rádio, TV*>; tune in to
<*emissora*> □ *vi* be in tune (**com** with)
sinuca /si'nuka/ *f* snooker
sinuoso /sinu'ozu/ *a* winding
sinusite /sinu'zitʃi/ *f* sinusitis
siri /si'ri/ *m* crab
Síria /'siria/ *f* Syria
sírio /'siriu/ *a & m* Syrian
siso /'sizu/ *m* good sense
siste|ma /sis'tema/ *m* system; ~**mático** *a*
systematic
sisudo /si'zudu/ *a* serious
site /sajt/ *m* (*comput*) website
sítio /'sitʃiu/ *m* (*chácara*) farm; (*Port:
local*) place; **estado de** ~ state of siege
situ|ação /situa'sãw/ *f* situation; (*no
governo*) party in power; ~**ar** *vt*
situate; ~**ar-se** *vpr* be situated;
<*pessoa*> position o.s.
smoking /iz'mɔkĩ/ (*pl* ~**s**) *m* dinner
jacket, (*Amer*) tuxedo
só /sɔ/ *a* alone; (*sentindo solidão*) lonely
□ *adv* only; **um** ~ **voto** one single vote;
~ **um carro** only one car; **a** ~**s** alone;
imagina ~ just imagine; ~ **que** except
(that)
soalho /so'aʎu/ *m* floor
soar /so'ar/ *vt/i* sound
sob /'sobi/ *prep* under
sobera|nia /sobera'nia/ *f* sovereignty;
~**no** *a & m* sovereign
soberbo /so'berbu/ *a* <*pessoa*> haughty;
(*magnífico*) splendid
sobra /'sɔbra/ *f* surplus; *pl* leftovers;
tempo de ~ (*muito*) plenty of time;
ficar de ~ be left over; **ter aco de**
~ (*sobrando*) have sth left over
sobraçar /sobra'sar/ *vt* carry under one's
arm
sobrado /so'bradu/ *m* (*casa*) house;
(*andar*) upper floor
sobrancelha /sobrã'seʎa/ *f* eyebrow
so|brar /so'brar/ *vi* be left; ~**bram-me
dois** I have two left
sobre /'sobri/ *prep* (*em cima de*) on; (*por
cima de, acima de*) over; (*acerca de*)
about
sobreaviso /sobria'vizu/ *m* **estar de** ~
be on one's guard
sobrecapa /sobri'kapa/ *f* dust jacket
sobrecarregar /sobrikaxe'gar/ *vt*
overload
sobreloja /sobri'lɔʒa/ *f* mezzanine
sobremesa /sobri'meza/ *f* dessert
sobrenatu|ral /sobrinatu'raw/ (*pl* ~**rais**)
a supernatural
sobrenome /sobri'nomi/ *m* surname

sobrepor /sobri'por/ *vt* superimpose
sobrepujar /sobripu'ʒar/ *vt* (*em altura*)
tower over; (*em valor, número etc*)
surpass; overwhelm <*adversário*>;
overcome <*problemas*>
sobrescritar /sobriskri'tar/ *vt* address
sobressair /sobrisa'ir/ *vi* stand out; ~**-se**
vpr stand out
sobressalente /sobrisa'lẽtʃi/ *a* spare
sobressal|tar /sobrisaw'tar/ *vt* startle;
~**tar-se** *vpr* be startled; ~**to** *m*
(*movimento*) start; (*susto*) fright
sobretaxa /sobri'taʃa/ *f* surcharge
sobretudo /sobri'tudu/ *adv* above all □ *m*
overcoat
sobrevir /sobri'vir/ *vi* happen suddenly;
(*seguir*) ensue; ~ **a** follow
sobrevi|vência /sobrivi'vẽsia/ *f*
survival; ~**vente** *a* surviving □ *m/f*
survivor; ~**ver** *vt/i* ~**ver (a)** survive
sobrevoar /sobrivo'ar/ *vt* fly over
sobri|nha /so'briɲa/ *f* niece; ~**nho** *m*
nephew
sóbrio /'sɔbriu/ *a* sober
socar /so'kar/ *vt* (*esmurrar*) punch;
(*amassar*) crush
soci|al /sosi'aw/ (*pl* ~**ais**) *a* social;
camisa ~**al** dress shirt; ~**alismo** *m*
socialism; ~**alista** *a & m/f* socialist;
~**alite** /-a'lajtʃi/ *m/f* socialite; ~**ável**
(*pl* ~**áveis**) *a* sociable
sociedade /sosie'dadʒi/ *f* society;
(*parceria*) partnership; ~ **anônima**
limited company
sócio /'sɔsiu/ *m* (*de empresa*) partner; (*de
clube*) member
socio-econômico /sosioeko'nomiku/ *a*
socio-economic
soci|ologia /sosiolo'ʒia/ *f* sociology;
~**ológico** *a* sociological; ~**ólogo** *m*
sociologist
soco /'soku/ *m* punch; **dar um** ~ **em**
punch
socor|rer /soko'xer/ *vt* help; ~**ro** *m* aid
□ *int* help; ~**ros primeiros** ~**ros** first aid
soda /'sɔda/ *f* (*água*) soda water; ~
cáustica caustic soda
sódio /'sɔdʒiu/ *m* sodium
sofá /so'fa/ *m* sofa; ~**-cama** (*pl*
~**s-camas**) *m* sofa-bed
sofisticado /sofistʃi'kadu/ *a*
sophisticated
so|fredor /sofre'dor/ *a* martyred; ~**frer**
vt suffer <*dor, derrota, danos etc*>; have
<*acidente*>; undergo <*operação,
mudança etc*> □ *vi* suffer; ~**frer de**
suffer from <*doença*>; have trouble
with <*coração etc*>; ~**frido** *a* long-
suffering; ~**frimento** *m* suffering;
~**frível** (*pl* ~**fríveis**) *a* passable

S

soft /'sɔftʃi/ (pl ∼s) m software package; ∼**ware** m software; (um) software package

so|gra /'sɔgra/ f mother-in-law; ∼**gro** /o/ m father-in-law; ∼**- gros** /ɔ/ m pl in-laws

soja /'sɔʒa/ f soya, (Amer) soy

sol /sɔw/ (pl **sóis**) m sun; **faz** ∼ it's sunny

sola /'sɔla/ f sole; ∼**do** a <bolo> flat

solapar /sola'par/ vt undermine

solar[1] /so'lar/ a solar

solar[2] /so'lar/ vt sole <sapato> □ vi <bolo> go flat

solavanco /sola'vãku/ m jolt; **dar** ∼**s** jolt

soldado /sow'dadu/ m soldier

sol|dadura /sowda'dura/ f weld; ∼**dar** vt weld

soldo /'sowdu/ m pay

soleira /so'lera/ f doorstep

sole|ne /so'leni/ a solemn; ∼**nidade** f (cerimônia) ceremony; (qualidade) solemnity

soletrar /sole'trar/ vt spell

solici|tação /solisita'sãw/ f request (de for); (por escrito) application (de for); ∼**tante** m/f applicant; ∼**tar** vt request; (por escrito) apply for

solícito /so'lisitu/ a helpful

solidão /soli'dãw/ f loneliness

soli|dariedade /solidarie'dadʒi/ f solidarity; ∼**dário** a supportive (com of)

soli|dez /soli'des/ f solidity; ∼**dificar** vt solidify; ∼**dificar-se** vpr solidify

sólido /'solidu/ a & m solid

solista /so'lista/ m/f soloist

solitá|ria /soli'taria/ f (verme) tapeworm; (cela) solitary confinement; ∼**rio** a solitary

solo[1] /'sɔlu/ m (terra) soil; (chão) ground

solo[2] /'sɔlu/ m solo

soltar /sow'tar/ vt let go <prisioneiros, animal etc>; let loose <cães>; (deixar de segurar) let go of; loosen <gravata, corda etc>; let down <cabelo>; let out <grito, suspiro etc>; let off <foguetes>; tell <piada>; take off <freio>; ∼**-se** vpr <peça, parafuso> come loose; <pessoa> let o.s. go

soltei|ra /sow'tera/ f single woman; ∼**rão** m bachelor; ∼**ro** a single □ m single man; ∼**rona** f spinster

solto /'sowtu/ a (livre) free; <cães> loose; <cabelo> down; <arroz> fluffy; (frouxo) loose; (à vontade) relaxed; (abandonado) abandoned; **correr** ∼ run wild

solução /solu'sãw/ f solution

soluçar /solu'sar/ vi (ao chorar) sob; (engasgar) hiccup

solucionar /solusio'nar/ vt solve

soluço /so'lusu/ m (ao chorar) sob; (engasgo) hiccup; **estar com** ∼**s** have the hiccups

solú|vel /so'luvew/ (pl ∼**veis**) a soluble

solvente /sow'vẽtʃi/ a & m solvent

som /sõ/ m sound; (aparelho) stereo; **um** ∼ (fam) (música) a bit of music

so|ma /'soma/ f sum; ∼**mar** vt add up <números etc>; (ter como soma) add up to

sombra /'sõbra/ f shadow; (área abrigada do sol) shade; **à** ∼ **de** in the shade of; **sem** ∼ **de dúvida** without a shadow of a doubt

sombre|ado /sõbri'adu/ a shady □ m shading; ∼**ar** vt shade

sombrinha /sõ'briɲa/ f parasol

sombrio /sõ'briu/ a gloomy

somente /so'mẽtʃi/ adv only

sonâmbulo /so'nãbulu/ m sleepwalker

sonante /so'nãtʃi/ a **moeda** ∼ hard cash

sonata /so'nata/ f sonata

son|da /'sõda/ f probe; ∼**dagem** f (no mar) sounding; (de terreno) survey; ∼**dagem de opinião** opinion poll; ∼**dar** vt probe; sound <profundeza>; (fig) sound out <pessoas, opiniões etc>

soneca /so'nɛka/ f nap; **tirar uma** ∼ have a nap

sone|gação /sonega'sãw/ f (de impostos) tax evasion; ∼**gador** m tax dodger; ∼**gar** vt with-hold

soneto /so'netu/ m sonnet

so|nhador /soɲa'dor/ a dreamy □ m dreamer; ∼**nhar** vt/i dream (com about); ∼**nho** /'soɲu/ m dream; (doce) doughnut

sono /'sonu/ m sleep; **estar com** ∼ be sleepy; **pegar no** ∼ get to sleep; ∼**lento** a sleepy

sono|plastia /sonoplas'tʃia/ f sound effects; ∼**ridade** f sound quality; ∼**ro** /ɔ/ a sound; <voz> sonorous; <consoante> voiced

sonso /'sõsu/ a devious

sopa /'sopa/ f soup

sopapo /so'papu/ m slap; **dar um** ∼ **em** slap

sopé /so'pɛ/ m foot

sopeira /so'pera/ f soup tureen

soprano /so'pranu/ m/f soprano

so|prar /so'prar/ vt blow <folhas etc>; blow up <balão>; blow out <vela> □ vi blow; ∼**pro** m blow; (de vento) puff; **instrumento de** ∼**pro** wind instrument

soquete[1] /so'kɛtʃi/ f ankle sock

soquete[2] /so'ketʃi/ m socket

sordidez /sordʒi'des/ f sordidness; (imundície) squalor

sórdido /'sɔrdʒidu/ *a* (*reles*) sordid; (*imundo*) squalid

soro /'sɔru/ *m* (*remédio*) serum; (*de leite*) whey

sorrateiro /soxa'teru/ *a* crafty

sor|ridente /soxi'dētʃi/ *a* smiling; **~rir** *vi* smile; **~riso** *m* smile

sorte /'sɔrtʃi/ *f* luck; (*destino*) fate; **pessoa de ~** lucky person; **por ~** luckily; **ter** *ou* **dar ~** be lucky; **tive a ~ de conhecê-lo** I was lucky enough to meet him; **tirar a ~** draw lots; **trazer** *ou* **dar ~** bring good luck

sor|tear /sortʃi'ar/ *vt* draw for <*prêmio*>; select in a draw <*pessoa*>; **~teio** *m* draw

sorti|do /sor'tʃidu/ *a* assorted; **~mento** *m* assortment

sorumbático /sorū'batʃiku/ *a* sombre, gloomy

sorver /sor'ver/ *vt* sip <*bebida*>

sósia /'sɔzia/ *m*/*f* double

soslaio /soz'laju/ *m* **de ~** sideways; <*olhar*> askance

sosse|gado /sose'gadu/ *a* <*vida*> quiet; **ficar ~gado** <*pessoa*> rest assured; **~gar** *vt* reassure □ *vi* rest; **~go** /e/ *m* peace

sótão /'sɔtãw/ (*pl* **~s**) *m* attic, loft

sotaque /so'taki/ *m* accent

soterrar /sote'xar/ *vt* bury

soutien /suti'ã/ (*pl* **~s**) *m* (*Port*) bra

sova|co /so'vaku/ *m* armpit; **~queira** *f* BO, body odour

soviético /sovi'ɛtʃiku/ *a & m* Soviet

sovi|na /so'vina/ *a* stingy, mean, (*Amer*) cheap □ *m*/*f* cheapskate; **~nice** *f* stinginess, meanness, (*Amer*) cheapness

sozinho /so'ziɲu/ *a* (*sem ninguém*) alone, on one's own; (*por si próprio*) by o.s.; **falar ~** talk to o.s.

spray /is'prej/ (*pl* **~s**) *m* spray

squash /is'kwɛʃ/ *m* squash

stand /is'tãdʒi/ (*pl* **~s**) *m* stand

status /is'tatus/ *m* status

stripper /is'triper/ (*pl* **~s**) *m*/*f* stripper

strip-tease /istripi'tʃizi/ *m* striptease

sua /'sua/ *a & pron veja* **seu**

su|ado /su'adu/ *a* <*pessoa, roupa*> sweaty; (*fig*) hard-earned; **~ar** *vt*/*i* sweat; **~ar por/para** (*fig*) work hard for/to; **~ar frio** come out in a cold sweat

sua|ve /su'avi/ *a* <*toque, subida*> gentle; <*gosto, cheiro, dor, inverno*> mild; <*música, voz*> soft; <*vinho*> smooth; <*trabalho*> light; <*prestações*> easy; **~vidade** *f* gentleness; mildness; softness; smoothness; *veja* **suave**; **~vizar** *vt* soften; soothe <*dor, pessoa*>

subalterno /subaw'tɛrnu/ *a & m* subordinate

subconsciente /subikõsi'ētʃi/ *a & m* subconscious

subdesenvolvido /subidʒizĩvow'vidu/ *a* underdeveloped

súbdito /'subditu/ *m* (*Port*) *veja* **súdito**

subdividir /subidʒivi'dʒir/ *vt* subdivide

subemprego /subĩ'pregu/ *m* menial job

subemprei|tar /subĩprej'tar/ *vt* subcontract; **~teiro** *m* subcontractor

subenten|der /subĩtē'der/ *vt* infer; **~dido** *a* implied □ *m* insinuation

subestimar /subestʃi'mar/ *vt* underestimate

su|bida /su'bida/ *f* (*ação*) ascent; (*ladeira*) incline; (*de preços etc, fig*) rise; **~bir** *vi* go up; <*rio, águas*> rise □ *vt* go up, climb; **~bir em** climb <*árvore*>; get up onto <*mesa*>; get on <*ônibus*>

súbito /'subitu/ *a* sudden; **(de) ~** suddenly

subjacente /subiʒa'sētʃi/ *a* underlying

subjeti|vidade /subiʒetʃivi'dadʒi/ *f* subjectivity; **~vo** *a* subjective

subjugar /subiʒu'gar/ *vt* subjugate

subjuntivo /subiʒũ'tʃivu/ *a & m* subjunctive

sublevar-se /suble'varsi/ *vpr* rise up

sublime /su'blimi/ *a* sublime

subli|nhado /subli'ɲadu/ *m* underlining; **~nhar** *vt* underline

sublocar /sublo'kar/ *vt*/*i* sublet

submarino /subima'rinu/ *a* underwater □ *m* submarine

submer|gir /subimer'ʒir/ *vt* submerge; **~gir-se** *vpr* submerge; **~so** *a* submerged

submeter /subime'ter/ *vt* subject (**a** to); put down, subdue <*povo, rebeldes etc*>; submit <*projeto*>; **~se a** *vpr* (*render-se*) submit; **~se a** (*sofrer*) undergo

submis|são /subimi'sãw/ *f* submission; **~so** *a* submissive

submundo /subi'mũdu/ *m* underworld

subnutrição /subinutri'sãw/ *f* malnutrition

subordi|nado /subordʒi'nadu/ *a & m* subordinate; **~nar** *vt* subordinate (**a** to)

subor|nar /subor'nar/ *vt* bribe; **~no** /o/ *m* bribe

subproduto /subipro'dutu/ *m* by-product

subs|crever /subiskre'ver/ *vt* sign <*carta etc*>; subscribe to <*opinião*>; subscribe <*dinheiro*> (**para** to); **~crever-se** *vpr* sign one's name; **~crição** *f* subscription; **~crito** *pp de* **~crever**

subseqüente /subise'kwētʃi/ *a* subsequent

S

subserviente /subiservi'ẽtʃi/ *a* subservient

subsidiar /subisidʒi'ar/ *vt* subsidize

subsidiá|ria /subisidʒi'aria/ *f* subsidiary; **~rio** *a* subsidiary

subsídio /subi'sidʒiu/ *m* subsidy

subsistência /subisis'tẽsia/ *f* subsistence

subsolo /subi'sɔlu/ *m* (*porão*) basement

substância /subis'tãsia/ *f* substance

substan|cial /subistãsi'aw/ (*pl* **~ciais**) *a* substantial; **~tivo** *m* noun

substitu|ição /subistʃitui'sãw/ *f* replacement; substitution; **~ir** *vt* (*pôr B no lugar de A*) replace (**A por B** A with B); (*usar B em vez de A*) substitute (**A por B** B for A); **~to** *a & m* substitute

subterfúgio /subiter'fuʒiu/ *m* subterfuge

subterrâneo /subite'xaniu/ *a* underground

sub|til /sub'til/ (*pl* **~tis**) *a* (*Port*) *veja* **sutil**

subtra|ção /subitra'sãw/ *f* subtraction; **~ir** *vt* subtract <*números*>; (*roubar*) steal

suburbano /subur'banu/ *a* suburban

subúrbio /su'burbiu/ *m* suburbs

subven|ção /subivẽ'sãw/ *f* grant, subsidy; **~cionar** *vt* subsidize

subver|são /subiver'sãw/ *f* subversion; **~sivo** *a & m* subversive

suca|ta /su'kata/ *f* scrap metal; **~tear** *vt* scrap

sucção /suk'sãw/ *f* suction

suce|der /suse'der/ *vi* (*acontecer*) happen □ *vt* **~der a** succeed <*rei etc*>; (*vir depois*) follow; **~der-se** *vpr* follow on from one another; **~dido a bem ~dido** successful

suces|são /suse'sãw/ *f* succession; **~sivo** *a* successive; **~so** /ɛ/ *m* success; (*música*) hit; **fazer** *ou* **ter ~so** be successful; **~sor** *m* successor

sucinto /su'sĩtu/ *a* succinct

suco /'suku/ *m* juice

suculento /suku'lẽtu/ *a* juicy

sucumbir /sukũ'bir/ *vi* succumb (**a** to)

sucur|sal /sukur'saw/ (*pl* **~sais**) *f* branch

Sudão /su'dãw/ *m* Sudan

sudário /su'dariu/ *m* shroud

sudeste /su'dɛstʃi/ *a & m* southeast; **o Sudeste Asiático** Southeast Asia

súdito /'sudʒitu/ *m* subject

sudoeste /sudo'ɛstʃi/ *a & m* southwest

Suécia /su'ɛsia/ *f* Sweden

sueco /su'ɛku/ *a & m* Swedish

suéter /su'ɛter/ *m/f* sweater

sufici|ência /sufisi'ẽsia/ *f* sufficiency; **~ente** *a* enough, sufficient; **o ~ente** enough

sufixo /su'fiksu/ *m* suffix

suflê /su'fle/ *m* soufflé

sufo|cante /sufo'kãtʃi/ *a* stifling; **~car** *vt* (*asfixiar*) suffocate; (*fig*) stifle □ *vi* suffocate; **~co** /o/ *m* hassle; **estar num ~co** be having a tough time

sufrágio /su'fraʒiu/ *m* suffrage

sugar /su'gar/ *vt* suck

sugerir /suʒe'rir/ *vt* suggest

suges|tão /suʒes'tãw/ *f* suggestion; **dar uma ~tão** make a suggestion; **~tivo** *a* suggestive

Suíça /su'isa/ *f* Switzerland

suíças /su'isas/ *f pl* sideburns

sui|cida /sui'sida/ *a* suicidal □ *m/f* suicide (victim); **~cidar-se** *vpr* commit suicide; **~cídio** *m* suicide

suíço /su'isu/ *a & m* Swiss

suíno /su'inu/ *a & m* pig

suíte /su'itʃi/ *f* suite

su|jar /su'ʒar/ *vt* dirty; (*fig*) sully <*reputação etc*> □ *vi*, **~jar-se** *vpr* get dirty; **~jar-se com alg** queer one's pitch with s.o.; **~jeira** *f* dirt; (*uma*) dirty trick

suje|itar /suʒej'tar/ *vt* subject (**a** to); **~tar-se** *vpr* subject o.s. (**a** to); **~to** *a* subject (**a** to) □ *m* (*de oração*) subject; (*pessoa*) person

su|jidade /suʒi'dadʒi/ *f* (*Port*) dirt; **~jo** *a* dirty

sul /suw/ *a invar & m* south; **~-africano** *a & m* South African; **~-americano** *a & m* South American; **~-coreano** *a & m* South Korean

sul|car /suw'kar/ *vt* furrow <*testa*>; **~co** *m* furrow

sulfúrico /suw'furiku/ *a* sulphuric

sulista /su'lista/ *a* southern □ *m/f* southerner

sultão /suw'tãw/ *m* sultan

sumário /su'mariu/ *a* <*justiça*> summary; <*roupa*> skimpy, brief

su|miço /su'misu/ *m* disappearance; **dar ~miço em** spirit away; **tomar chá de ~miço** disappear; **~mido** *a* <*cor, voz*> faint; **ele anda ~mido** he's disappeared; **~mir** *vi* disappear

sumo /'sumu/ *m* (*Port*) juice

sumptuoso /sũtu'ozu/ *a* (*Port*) *veja* **suntuoso**

sunga /'sũga/ *f* swimming trunks

suntuoso /sũtu'ozu/ *a* sumptuous

suor /su'or/ *m* sweat

superar /supe'rar/ *vt* overcome <*dificuldade etc*>; surpass <*expectativa, pessoa*>

superá|vel /supe'ravew/ (*pl* ∼ **veis**) *a* surmountable; ∼**vit** (*pl* ∼**vits**) *m* surplus

superestimar /superestʃi'mar/ *vt* overestimate

superestrutura /superistru'tura/ *f* superstructure

superfici|al /superfisi'aw/ (*pl* ∼**ais**) *a* superficial

superfície /super'fisi/ *f* surface; (*medida*) area

supérfluo /su'pɛrfluu/ *a* superfluous

superintendência /superĩtẽ'dẽsia/ *f* bureau

superi|or /superi'or/ *a* (*de cima*) upper; <*ensino*> higher; <*número, temperatura etc*> greater (**a** than); (*melhor*) superior (**a** to) □ *m* superior; ∼**oridade** *f* superiority

superlativo /superla'tʃivu/ *a & m* superlative

superlota|ção /superlota'sãw/ *f* overcrowding; ∼**do** *a* overcrowded

supermercado /supermer'kadu/ *m* supermarket

superpotência /superpo'tẽsia/ *f* superpower

superpovoado /superpovo'adu/ *a* overpopulated

supersecreto /superse'krɛtu/ *a* top secret

supersensí|vel /supersẽ'sivew/ (*pl* ∼**veis**) *a* oversensitive

supersônico /super'soniku/ *a* supersonic

supersti|ção /superstʃi'sãw/ *f* superstition; ∼**cioso** /o/ *a* superstitious

supervi|são /supervi'zãw/ *f* supervision; ∼**sionar** *vt* supervise; ∼**sor** *m* supervisor

supetão /supe'tãw/ *m* de ∼ all of a sudden

suplantar /suplã'tar/ *vt* supplant

suplemen|tar /suplemẽ'tar/ *a* supplementary □ *vt* supplement; ∼**to** *m* supplement

suplente /su'plẽtʃi/ *a & m/f* substitute

supletivo /suple'tʃivu/ *a* supplementary; **ensino** ∼ adult education

súplica /'suplika/ *f* plea; **tom de** ∼ pleading tone

suplicar /supli'kar/ *vt* plead for; (*em juízo*) petition for

suplício /su'plisiu/ *m* torture; (*fig: aflição*) torment

supor /su'por/ *vt* suppose

supor|tar /supor'tar/ *vt* (*sustentar*) support; (*tolerar*) stand, bear; ∼**tável**

(*pl* ∼**táveis**) *a* bearable; ∼**te** /ɔ/ *m* support

suposição /supozi'sãw/ *f* supposition

supositório /supozi'tɔriu/ *m* suppository

supos|tamente /suposta'mẽtʃi/ *adv* supposedly; ∼**to** /o/e/ *a* supposed; ∼**to que** supposing that

supre|macia /suprema'sia/ *f* supremacy; ∼**mo** /e/ *a* supreme

supressão /supre'sãw/ *f* (*de lei, cargo, privilégio*) abolition; (*de jornal, informação, nomes*) suppression; (*de palavras, cláusula*) deletion

suprimento /supri'mẽtu/ *m* supply

suprimir /supri'mir/ *vt* abolish <*lei, cargo, privilégio*>; suppress <*jornal, informação, nomes*>; delete <*palavras, cláusula*>

suprir /su'prir/ *vt* provide for <*família, necessidades*>; make up for <*falta*>; make up <*quantia*>; supply <*o que falta*>; (*substituir*) take the place of; ∼ **alg de** provide s.o. with; ∼ **A por B** substitute B for A

supurar /supu'rar/ *vi* turn septic

sur|dez /sur'des/ *f* deafness; ∼**do** *a* deaf; <*consoante*> voiceless □ *m* deaf person; **os** ∼**dos** the deaf; ∼**do-mudo** (*pl* ∼**dos-mudos**) *a* deaf and dumb □ *m* deaf-mute

sur|fe /'surfi/ *m* surfing; ∼**fista** *m/f* surfer

sur|gimento /surʒi'mẽtu/ *m* appearance; ∼**gir** *vi* arise; ∼**gir à mente** spring to mind

Suriname /suri'nami/ *m* Surinam

surpreen|dente /surpriẽ'dẽtʃi/ *a* surprising; ∼**der** *vt* surprise □ *vi* be surprising; ∼**der-se** *vpr* be surprised (**de** at)

surpre|sa /sur'preza/ *f* surprise; **de** ∼**sa** by surprise; ∼**so** /e/ *a* surprised

sur|ra /'suxa/ *f* thrashing; ∼**rado** *a* <*roupa*> worn-out; ∼**rar** *vt* thrash <*pessoa*>; wear out <*roupa*>

surrealis|mo /suxea'lizmu/ *m* surrealism; ∼**ta** *a & m/f* surrealist

surtir /sur'tʃir/ *vt* produce; ∼ **efeito** be effective

surto /'surtu/ *m* outbreak

suscept- (*Port*) *veja* **suscet-**

susce|tibilidade /susetʃibili-'dadʒi/ *f* (*de pessoa*) sensitivity; ∼**tível** (*pl* ∼**tíveis**) *a* <*pessoa*> touchy, sensitive; ∼**tível de** open to

suscitar /susi'tar/ *vt* cause; raise <*dúvida, suspeita*>

suspei|ta /sus'pejta/ *f* suspicion; ∼**tar** *vt/i* ∼**tar (de)** suspect; ∼**to** *a*

S

suspicious; (*duvidoso*) suspect □ *m*
suspect; ~**toso** /o/ *a* suspicious
suspen|der /suspẽ'der/ *vt* suspend;
~**são** *f* suspension; ~**se** *m* suspense;
~**so** *a* suspended; ~**sórios** *m pl* braces,
(*Amer*) suspenders
suspi|rar /suspi'rar/ *vi* sigh; ~**rar por**
long for; ~**ro** *m* sigh; (*doce*) meringue
sussur|rar /susu'xar/ *vt/i* whisper; ~**ro**
m whisper
sustar /sus'tar/ *vt/i* stop
susten|táculo /sustē'takulu/ *m*
mainstay; ~**tar** *vt* support; (*afirmar*)
maintain; ~**to** *m* support; (*ganha-pão*)
livelihood
susto /'sustu/ *m* fright
sutiã /sutʃi'ã/ *m* bra
su|til /su'tʃiw/ (*pl* ~**tis**) *a* subtle;
~**tileza** /e/ *f* subtlety
sutu|ra /su'tura/ *f* suture; ~**rar** *vt*
suture

....

Tt

....

tá /ta/ *int* (*fam*) OK; *veja* **estar**
taba|caria /tabaka'ria/ *f* tobacconist's;
~**co** *m* tobacco
tabefe /ta'bɛfi/ *m* slap
tabe|la /ta'bɛla/ *f* table; ~**lar** *vt* tabulate
tablado /ta'bladu/ *m* platform
tabu /ta'bu/ *a & m* taboo
tábua /'tabua/ *f* board; ~ **de passar
roupa** ironing board
tabuleiro /tabu'leru/ *m* (*de xadrez etc*)
board
tabuleta /tabu'lɛta/ *f* (*letreiro*) sign
taça /'tasa/ *f* (*prêmio*) cup; (*de
champanhe etc*) glass
ta|cada /ta'kada/ *f* shot; **de uma** ~**cada**
in one go; ~**car** *vt* hit <*bola*>; (*fam*)
throw
tacha /'taʃa/ *f* tack
tachar /ta'ʃar/ *vt* brand (**de** as)
tachinha /ta'ʃiɲa/ *f* drawing pin,
(*Amer*) thumbtack
tácito /'tasitu/ *a* tacit
taciturno /tasi'turnu/ *a* taciturn
taco /'taku/ *m* (*de golfe*) club; (*de bilhar*)
cue; (*de hóquei*) stick
tact- (*Port*) *veja* **tat-**
tagare|la /taga'rɛla/ *a* chatty, talkative
□ *m/f* chatterbox; ~**lar** *vi* chatter
tailan|dês /tajlã'des/ *a & m* (*f* ~**desa**)
Thai
Tailândia /taj'lãdʒia/ *f* Thailand

tailleur /ta'jɛr/ (*pl* ~**s**) *m* suit
Taiti /taj'tʃi/ *m* Tahiti
tal /taw/ (*pl* **tais**) *a* such; **que** ~? what do
you think?, (*Port*) how are you?; **que** ~
uma cerveja? how about a beer?; ~
como such as; ~ **qual** just like; **um** ~
de João someone called John; **e** ~ and
so on
tala /'tala/ *f* splint
talão /ta'lãw/ *m* stub; ~ **de cheques**
chequebook
talco /'tawku/ *m* talc
talen|to /ta'lẽtu/ *m* talent; ~**-toso** /o/ *a*
talented
talhar /ta'ʎar/ *vt* slice <*dedo, carne*>;
carve <*pedra, imagem*>
talharim /taʎa'rĩ/ *m* tagliatelle
talher /ta'ʎɛr/ *m* set of cutlery; *pl* cutlery
talho /'taʎu/ *m* (*Port*) butcher's
talismã /taliz'mã/ *m* charm, talisman
talo /'talu/ *m* stalk
talvez /taw'ves/ *adv* perhaps; ~ **ele
venha amanhã** he may come
tomorrow
tamanco /ta'mãku/ *m* clog
tamanho /ta'maɲu/ *m* size □ *adj* such
tâmara /'tamara/ *f* date
tamarindo /tama'rĩdu/ *m* tamarind
também /tã'bẽj/ *adv* also; ~ **não** not ...
either, neither
tam|bor /tã'bor/ *m* drum; ~**-borilar** *vi*
<*dedos*> drum; <*chuva*> patter;
~**borim** *m* tambourine
Tâmisa /'tamiza/ *m* Thames
tam|pa /'tãpa/ *f* lid; ~**pão** *m* (*vaginal*)
tampon; ~**par** *vt* put the lid on
<*recipiente*>; (*tapar*) cover; ~**pinha** *f*
top □ *m/f* (*fam*) shorthouse
tampouco /tã'poku/ *adv* nor, neither
tanga /'tãga/ *f* G-string; (*avental*)
loincloth
tangente /tã'ʒẽtʃi/ *f* tangent; **pela** ~
(*fig*) narrowly
tangerina /tãʒe'rina/ *f* tangerine
tango /'tãgu/ *m* tango
tanque /'tãki/ *m* tank; (*para lavar roupa*)
sink
tanto /'tãtu/ *a & pron* so much; *pl* so
many □ *adv* so much; ~ ... **como** ...
both ... and ...; ~ **(...) quanto** as much
(...) as; ~ **melhor** so much the better; ~
tempo so long; **vinte e** ~**s anos** twenty
odd years; **nem** ~ not as much; **um** ~
difícil somewhat difficult; ~ **que** to
the extent that
Tanzânia /tã'zania/ *f* Tanzania
tão /tãw/ *adv* so; ~ **grande quanto** as big
as; ~**somente** *adv* solely
tapa /'tapa/ *m ou f* slap; **dar um** ~ **em**
slap

tapar /ta'par/ *vt* (*cobrir*) cover; block
<*luz, vista*>; cork <*garrafa*>

tapeçaria /tapesa'ria/ *f* (*pano*) tapestry;
(*loja*) carpet shop

tape|tar /tape'tar/ *vt* carpet; ∼**te** /e/ *m*
carpet

tapioca /tapi'ɔka/ *f* tapioca

tapume /ta'pumi/ *m* fence

taquicardia /takikar'dʒia/ *f*
palpitations

taquigra|far /takigra'far/ *vt/i* write in
shorthand; ∼**fia** *f* shorthand

tara /'tara/ *f* fetish; ∼**do** *a* sex-crazed
□ *m* sex maniac; **ser** ∼**do por** be crazy
about

tar|dar /tar'dar/ *vi* (*atrasar*) be late;
(*demorar muito*) be long □ *vt* delay;
∼**dar a responder** take a long time to
answer, be a long time answering; **o
mais** ∼**dar** at the latest; **sem mais**
∼**dar** without further delay; ∼**de** *adv*
late □ *f* afternoon; **hoje à** ∼**de** this
afternoon; ∼**de da noite** late at night;
∼**dinha** *f* late afternoon; ∼**dio** *a* late

tarefa /ta'rɛfa/ *f* task, job

tarifa /ta'rifa/ *f* tariff; ∼ **de embarque**
airport tax

tarimbado /tarĩ'badu/ *a* experienced

tarja /'tarʒa/ *f* strip

ta|rô /ta'ro/ *m* tarot; ∼**rólogo** *m* tarot
reader

tartamu|dear /tartamudʒi'ar/ *vi*
stammer; ∼**do** *a* stammering □ *m*
stammerer

tártaro /'tartaru/ *m* tartar

tartaruga /tarta'ruga/ *f* (*bicho*) turtle;
(*material*) tortoiseshell

tatear /tatʃi'ar/ *vt* feel □ *vi* feel one's way

táti|ca /'tatʃika/ *f* tactics; ∼**co** *a* tactical

tá|til /'tatʃiw/ (*pl* ∼**teis**) *a* tactile

tato /'tatu/ *m* (*sentido*) touch;
(*diplomacia*) tact

tatu /ta'tu/ *m* armadillo

tatu|ador /tatua'dor/ *m* tattooist;
∼**agem** *f* tattoo; ∼**ar** *vt* tattoo

tauromaquia /tawroma'kia/ *f*
bullfighting

taxa /'taʃa/ *f* (*a pagar*) charge; (*índice*)
rate; ∼ **de câmbio** exchange rate; ∼ **de
juros** interest rate; ∼ **rodoviária** road
tax

taxar /ta'ʃar/ *vt* tax

taxativo /taʃa'tʃivu/ *a* firm, categorical

táxi /'taksi/ *m* taxi

taxiar /taksi'ar/ *vi* taxi

taxímetro /tak'simetru/ *m* taxi meter

taxista /tak'sista/ *m/f* taxi driver

tchã /tʃã/ *m* (*fam*) special something

tchau /tʃaw/ *int* goodbye, bye

tcheco /'tʃɛku/ *a* & *m* Czech

Tchecoslováquia /tʃekoslo'vakia/ *f*
Czechoslovakia

te /tʃi/ *pron* you; (*a ti*) to you

tear /tʃi'ar/ *m* loom

tea|tral /tʃia'traw/ (*pl* ∼**trais**) *a*
theatrical; <*grupo*> theatre; ∼**tro** *m*
theatre; ∼**trólogo** *m* playwright

tece|lagem /tese'laʒẽ/ *f* (*trabalho*)
weaving; (*fábrica*) textile factory;
∼**lão** *m* (*f* ∼**lã**) weaver

te|cer /te'ser/ *vt/i* weave; ∼**cido** *m* cloth;
(*no corpo*) tissue

te|cla /'tɛkla/ *f* key; ∼**cladista** *m/f*
(*músico*) keyboard player; (*de
computador*) keyboard operator;
∼**clado** *m* keyboard; ∼**clar** *vt* key (in)

técni|ca /'tɛknika/ *f* technique; ∼**co** *a*
technical □ *m* specialist; (*de time*)
manager; (*que mexe com máquinas*)
technician

tecno|crata /tekno'krata/ *m/f*
technocrat; ∼**logia** *f*
technology; ∼**lógico** *a* technological

teco-teco /tɛku'tɛku/ *m* light aircraft

tecto /'tɛtu/ *m* (*Port*) *veja* **teto**

tédio /'tɛdʒiu/ *m* boredom

tedioso /tedʒi'ozu/ *a* boring, tedious

Teerã /tee'rã/ *f* Teheran

teia /'teja/ *f* web

tei|ma /'tejma/ *f* persistence; ∼**mar** *vi*
insist; ∼**mar em ir** insist on going;
∼**mosia** *f* stubbornness; ∼**moso** /o/ *a*
stubborn; <*ruído*> insistent

teixo /'tejʃu/ *m* yew

Tejo /'teʒu/ *m* Tagus

tela /'tɛla/ *f* (*de cinema, TV etc*) screen;
(*tecido, pintura*) canvas; ∼**plana** flat
screen

telecoman|dado /telekomã'dadu/ *a*
remote-controlled; ∼**do** *m* remote
control

telecomunicação /telekomunika'sãw/
f telecommunication

teleférico /tele'fɛriku/ *m* cable car

telefo|nar /telefo'nar/ *vi* telephone;
∼**nar para alg** phone s.o.; ∼**ne** /o/ *m*
telephone; (*número*) phone number;
∼**ne celular** cell phone; ∼**ne sem fio**
cordless phone; ∼**nema** /e/ *m* phone
call; ∼**nia** *f* telephone technology

telefôni|co /tele'foniku/ *a* telephone;
cabine ∼**ca** phone box, (*Amer*) phone
booth; **mesa** ∼**ca** switchboard

telefonista /telefo'nista/ *m/f* (*da
companhia telefônica*) operator; (*dentro
de empresa etc*) telephonist

tele|grafar /telegra'far/ *vt/i* telegraph;
∼**gráfico** *a* telegraphic

telégrafo /te'lɛgrafu/ *m* telegraph

tele|grama /tele'grama/ *m* telegram;
∼**guiado** *a* remote- controlled

t

telejor|nal /teleʒor'naw/ (*pl* ∼**nais**) *m* television news

telemóvel /tele'mɔvew/ *m* mobile phone, (*Amer.*) cell phone

tele|novela /teleno'vɛla/ *f* TV soap opera; ∼**objetiva** *f* telephoto lens

tele|patia /telepa'tʃia/ *f* telepathy; ∼**pático** *a* telepathic

telescó|pico /teles'kɔpiku/ *a* telescopic; ∼**pio** *m* telescope

telespectador /telespekta'dor/ *m* television viewer □ *a* viewing

teletrabalho /teletra'baʎu/ *m* teleworking

televi|são /televi'zãw/ *f* television; ∼**são a cabo** cable television; ∼**sionar** *vt* televise; ∼**sivo** *a* television; ∼**sor** *m* television set

telex /te'lɛks/ *m invar* telex

telha /'teʎa/ *f* tile; ∼**do** *m* roof

te|ma /'tema/ *m* theme; ∼**mático** *a* thematic

temer /te'mer/ *vt* fear □ *vi* be afraid; ∼ **por** fear for

teme|rário /teme'rariu/ *a* reckless; ∼**ridade** *f* recklessness; ∼**roso** /o/ *a* fearful

te|mido /te'midu/ *a* feared; ∼**mível** (*pl* ∼**míveis**) *a* fearsome; ∼**mor** *m* fear

tempão /tẽ'pãw/ *m* **um** ∼ a long time

temperado /tẽpe'radu/ *a* <*clima*> temperate □ *pp de* **temperar**

temperamen|tal /tẽperamẽ'taw/ (*pl* ∼**tais**) *a* temperamental; ∼**to** *m* temperament

temperar /tẽpe'rar/ *vt* season <*comida*>; temper <*aço*>

temperatura /tẽpera'tura/ *f* temperature

tempero /tẽ'peru/ *m* seasoning

tempestade /tẽpes'tadʒi/ *f* storm

templo /'tẽplu/ *m* temple

tempo /'tẽpu/ *m* (*período*) time; (*atmosférico*) weather; (*do verbo*) tense; (*de jogo*) half; **ao mesmo** ∼ at the same time; **nesse meio** ∼ in the meantime; **o** ∼ **todo** all the time; **de todos os** ∼**s** of all time; **quanto** ∼ how long; **muito** /**pouco** ∼ a long/short time; ∼ **integral** full time

tempo|rada /tẽpo'rada/ *f* (*sazão*) season; (*tempo*) while; ∼**ral** (*pl* ∼**rais**) *a* temporal □ *m* storm; ∼**rário** *a* temporary

te|nacidade /tenasi'dadʒi/ *f* tenacity; ∼**naz** *a* tenacious □ *f* tongs

tenção /tẽ'sãw/ *f* intention

tencionar /tẽsio'nar/ *vt* intend

tenda /'tẽda/ *f* tent

tendão /tẽ'dãw/ *m* tendon; ∼ **de Aquiles** Achilles tendon

tendência /tẽ'dẽsia/ *f* (*moda*) trend; (*propensão*) tendency

tendencioso /tẽdẽsi'ozu/ *a* tendentious

ten|der /tẽ'der/ *vi* tend (**para** towards); ∼**de a engordar** he tends to get fat; **o tempo** ∼**de a ficar bom** the weather is improving

tenebroso /tene'brozu/ *a* dark; (*fig: terrível*) dreadful

tenente /te'nẽtʃi/ *m*/*f* lieutenant

tênis /'tenis/ *m invar* (*jogo*) tennis; (*sapato*) trainer; **um** ∼ (*par*) a pair of trainers; ∼ **de mesa** table tennis

tenista /te'nista/ *m*/*f* tennis player

tenor /te'nor/ *m* tenor

tenro /'tẽxu/ *a* tender

ten|são /tẽ'sãw/ *f* tension; ∼**são (arterial)** blood pressure; ∼**so** *a* tense

tentação /tẽta'sãw/ *f* temptation

tentáculo /tẽ'taculu/ *m* tentacle

ten|tador /tẽta'dor/ *a* tempting; ∼**tar** *vt* try; (*seduzir*) tempt □ *vi* try; ∼**tativa** *f* attempt; ∼**tativo** *a* tentative

tênue /'tenui/ *a* faint

teo|logia /teolo'ʒia/ *f* theology; ∼**lógico** *a* theological

teólogo /te'ɔlogu/ *m* theologian

teor /te'or/ *m* (*de gordura etc*) content; (*de carta, discurso*) drift

teo|rema /teo'rema/ *m* theorem; ∼**ria** *f* theory

teórico /te'ɔriku/ *a* theoretical

teorizar /teori'zar/ *vt* theorize

tépido /'tɛpidu/ *a* tepid

ter /ter/ *vt* have; **tenho vinte anos** I am twenty (years old); ∼ **medo/sede** be afraid/thirsty; **tenho que** *ou* **de ir** I have to go; **tem** (*há*) there is/are; **não tem de quê** don't mention it; ∼ **a ver com** have to do with

tera|peuta /tera'pewta/ *m*/*f* therapist; ∼**pêutico** *a* therapeutic; ∼**pia** *f* therapy

terça /'tersa/ *f* Tuesday; ∼**-feira** (*pl* ∼**s-feiras**) *f* Tuesday; **Terça-Feira Gorda** Shrove Tuesday

tercei|ra /ter'sera/ *f* (*marcha*) third; ∼**ranista** *m*/*f* third-year; ∼**ro** *a* third □ *m* third party

terço /'tersu/ *m* third

ter|col (*pl* ∼**çóis**) *m* stye

tergal /ter'gaw/ *m* Terylene

térmi|co /'tɛrmiku/ *a* thermal; **garrafa** ∼**ca** Thermos flask

termi|nal /termi'naw/ (*pl* ∼**nais**) *a* & *m* terminal; ∼**nal de vídeo** VDU; ∼**nante** *a* definite; ∼**nar** *vt* finish □ *vi* <*pessoa, coisa*> finish; <*coisa*> end; ∼**nar com alg** (*cortar relação*) break up with s.o.

ter|minologia /terminolo'ʒia/ f terminology; **∼mo**[1] /'termu/ m term; **pôr ∼mo a** put an end to; **meio ∼mo** compromise

termo[2] /'termu / m (Port) Thermos flask

ter|mômetro /ter'mometru/ m thermometer; **∼mostato** m thermostat

terno[1] /'tɛrnu/ m suit

ter|no[2] /'tɛrnu/ a tender; **∼nura** f tenderness

terra /'texa/ f land; (solo, elétrico) earth; (chão) ground; **a Terra** Earth; **por ∼** on the ground; **∼ natal** homeland

terraço /te'xasu/ m terrace

terra|cota /texa'kɔta/ f terracotta; **∼moto** /texa'mɔtu/ m (Port) earthquake; **∼plenagem** f earth moving

terreiro /te'xeru/ m meeting place for Afro-Brazilian cults

terremoto /texe'mɔtu/ m earthquake

terreno /te'xenu/ a earthly ▢ m ground; (geog) terrain; (um) piece of land; **∼ baldio** piece of waste ground

térreo /'tɛxiu/ a ground-floor; **(andar) ∼** ground floor, (Amer) first floor

terrestre /te'xɛstri/ a <animal, batalha, forças> land; (da Terra) of the Earth, the Earth's; <alegrias etc> earthly

terrificante /texifi'kãtʃi/ a terrifying

terrina /te'xina/ f tureen

territori|al /texitori'aw/ (pl ∼ais) a territorial

território /texi'tɔriu/ m territory

terrí|vel /te'xivew/ (pl ∼veis) a terrible

terror /te'xor/ m terror; **filme de ∼** horror film

terroris|mo /texo'rizmu/ m terrorism; **∼ta** a & m/f terrorist

tese /'tɛzi/ f theory; (escrita) thesis

teso /'tezu/ a (apertado) taut; (rígido) stiff

tesoura /te'zora/ f scissors; **uma ∼ a** pair of scissors

tesou|reiro /tezo'reru/ m treasurer; **∼ro** m treasure; (do Estado) treasury

testa /'tɛsta/ f forehead; **∼-de-ferro** (pl ∼s-de-ferro) m frontman

testamento /testa'mẽtu/ m will; (na Bíblia) testament

tes|tar /tes'tar/ vt test; **∼te** /ɛ/ m test

testemu|nha /teste'muɲa/ f witness; **∼nha ocular** eye witness; **∼nhar** vt bear witness to ▢ vi testify; **∼nho** m evidence, testimony

testículo /tes'tʃikulu/ m testicle

teta /'teta/ f teat

tétano /'tɛtanu/ m tetanus

teto /'tɛtu/ m ceiling; **∼ solar** sun roof

tétrico /'tɛtriku/ a (triste) dismal; (medonho) horrible

teu /tew/ (f **tua**) a your ▢ pron yours

têx|til /'testʃiw/ (pl ∼teis) m textile

tex|to /'testu/ m text; **∼tura** f texture

texugo /te'ʃugu/ m badger

tez /tes/ f complexion

ti /tʃi/ pron you

tia /'tʃia/ f aunt; **∼-avó** (pl ∼s-vós) f great aunt

tiara /tʃi'ara/ f tiara

tíbia /'tʃibia/ f shinbone

ticar /tʃi'kar/ vt tick

tico /'tʃiku/ m **um ∼ de** a little bit of

tiete /tʃi'ɛtʃi/ m/f fan

tifo /'tʃifu/ m typhoid

tigela /tʃi'ʒɛla/ f bowl; **de meia ∼** smalltime

tigre /'tʃigri/ m tiger; **∼sa** /e/ f tigress

tijolo /tʃi'ʒolu/ m brick

til /tʃiw/ (pl **tis**) m tilde

tilintar /tʃili'tar/ vi jingle ▢ m jingling

timão /tʃi'mãw/ m tiller

timbre /'tʃibri/ m (insígnia) crest; (em papel) heading; (de som) tone; (de vogal) quality

time /'tʃimi/ m team

timidez /tʃimi'des/ f shyness

tímido /'tʃimidu/ a shy

tímpano /'tʃipanu/ m (tambor) kettledrum; (no ouvido) eardrum

tina /'tʃina/ f vat

tingir /tʃi'ʒir/ vt dye <tecido, cabelo>; (fig) tinge

ti|nido /tʃi'nidu/ m tinkling; **∼nir** vi tinkle; <ouvidos> ring; (tremer) tremble; **estar ∼nindo** (fig) be in peak condition

tino /'tʃinu/ m sense, judgement; **ter ∼ para** have a flair for

tin|ta /'tʃita/ f (para pintar) paint; (para escrever) ink; (para tingir) dye; **∼teiro** m inkwell

tintim /tʃi'tʃi/ m **contar ∼ por ∼** give a blow-by-blow account of

tin|to /'tʃitu/ a dyed; <vinho> red; **∼tura** f dye; (fig) tinge; **∼turaria** f dry cleaner's

tio /'tʃiu/ m uncle; pl (∼ e tia) uncle and aunt; **∼-avô** (pl ∼s-avôs) m great uncle

típico /'tʃipiku/ a typical

tipo /'tʃipu/ m type

tipóia /tʃi'pɔja/ f sling

tique /'tʃiki/ m (sinal) tick; (do rosto etc) twitch

tiquete /'tʃiketʃi/ m ticket

tiquinho /tʃi'kiɲu/ m **um ∼ de** a tiny bit of

tira /'tʃira/ f strip ▢ m/f (fam) copper, (Amer) cop

tiracolo /tʃira'kɔlu/ m **a ∼** <bolsa> over one's shoulder; <pessoa> in tow

tiragem /tʃiˈraʒẽ/ *f* (*de jornal*) circulation

tira|-gosto /tʃiraˈgostu/ *m* snack; **∼-manchas** *m invar* stain remover

ti|rania /tʃiraˈnia/ *f* tyranny; **∼rânico** *a* tyrannical; **∼rano** *m* tyrant

tirar /tʃiˈrar/ *vt* (*afastar*) take away; (*de dentro*) take out; take off <*roupa, sapato, tampa*>; take <*foto, cópia, férias*>; clear <*mesa*>; get <*nota, diploma, salário*>; get out <*mancha*>

tiritar /tʃiriˈtar/ *vi* shiver

tiro /ˈtʃiru/ *m* shot; **∼ ao alvo** shooting; **é ∼ e queda** (*fam*) it can't fail; **∼teio** *m* shoot-out

titânio /tʃiˈtaniu/ *m* titanium

títere /ˈtʃiteri/ *m* puppet

ti|tia /tʃiˈtʃia/ *f* auntie; **∼tio** *m* uncle

tititi /tʃitʃiˈtʃi/ *m* (*fam*) talk

titubear /tʃitubiˈar/ *vi* stagger, totter; (*fig: hesitar*) waver

titular /tʃituˈlar/ *m*/*f* title holder; (*de time*) captain □ *vt* title

título /ˈtʃitulu/ *m* title; (*obrigação*) bond; **a ∼ de** on the basis of; **a ∼ pessoal** on a personal basis

toa /ˈtoa/ *f* **à ∼** (*sem rumo*) aimlessly; (*ao acaso*) at random; (*sem motivo*) without reason; (*em vão*) for nothing; (*desocupado*) at a loose end; (*de repente*) out of the blue

toada /toˈada/ *f* melody

toalete /toaˈletʃi/ *m* toilet

toalha /toˈaʎa/ *f* towel; **∼ de mesa** tablecloth

tobogã /toboˈgã/ *m* (*rampa*) slide; (*trenó*) toboggan

toca /ˈtɔka/ *f* burrow

toca|-discos /tokaˈdʒiskus/ *m invar* record player; **∼fitas** *m invar* tape player

tocaia /toˈkaja/ *f* ambush

tocante /toˈkãtʃi/ *a* (*enternecedor*) moving

tocar /toˈkar/ *vt* touch; play <*piano, música, disco etc*>; ring <*campainha*> □ *vi* touch; <*pianista, música, disco etc*> play; <*campainha, telefone, sino*> ring; **∼-se** *vpr* touch; (*mancar-se*) take the hint; **∼ a** (*dizer respeito*) concern; **∼ em** touch; touch on <*assunto*>

tocha /ˈtɔʃa/ *f* torch

toco /ˈtoku/ *m* (*de árvore*) stump; (*de cigarro*) butt

toda /ˈtoda/ *f* **a ∼** at full speed

todavia /todaˈvia/ *conj* however

todo /ˈtodu/ *a* all; (*cada*) every; *pl* all; **∼ o dinheiro** all the money; **∼s os dias** every day; **∼s os alunos** all the pupils; **o dia ∼** all day; **em ∼ lugar** everywhere; **∼ mundo, ∼s** everyone; **∼s nós** all of us; **ao ∼** in all; **∼-poderoso** *a* almighty

tofe /ˈtɔfi/ *m* toffee

toga /ˈtɔga/ *f* gown; (*de romano*) toga

toicinho /tojˈsiɲu/ *m* bacon

toldo /ˈtowdu/ *m* awning

tole|rância /toleˈrãsia/ *f* tolerance; **∼rante** *a* tolerant; **∼rar** *vt* tolerate; **∼rável** (*pl* **∼ráveis**) *a* tolerable

to|lice /toˈlisi/ *f* foolishness; (*uma*) foolish thing; **∼lo** /o/ *a* foolish □ *m* fool

tom /tõ/ *m* tone

to|mada /toˈmada/ *f* (*conquista*) capture; (*elétrica*) plughole; (*de filme*) shot; **∼mar** *vt* take; (*beber*) drink; **∼mar café** have breakfast

tomara /toˈmara/ *int* I hope so; **∼ que** let's hope that; **∼-que-caia** *a invar* <*vestido*> strapless

tomate /toˈmatʃi/ *m* tomato

tom|bar /tõˈbar/ *vt* (*derrubar*) knock down; list <*edifício*> □ *vi* fall over; **∼bo** *m* fall; **levar um ∼bo** have a fall

tomilho /toˈmiʎu/ *m* thyme

tomo /ˈtomu/ *m* volume

tona /ˈtona/ *f* **trazer à ∼** bring up; **vir à ∼** emerge

tonalidade /tonaliˈdadʒi/ *f* (*de música*) key; (*de cor*) shade

to|nel /toˈnɛw/ (*pl* **∼néis**) *m* cask; **∼nelada** *f* tonne

tôni|ca /ˈtonika/ *f* tonic; (*fig: assunto*) keynote; **∼co** *a* & *m* tonic

tonificar /tonifiˈkar/ *vt* tone up

ton|tear /tõtʃiˈar/ *vt* **∼tear alg** make s.o.'s head spin; **∼teira** *f* dizziness; **∼to** *a* (*zonzo*) dizzy; (*bobo*) stupid; (*atrapalhado*) flustered; **∼tura** *f* dizziness

to|pada /toˈpada/ *f* trip; **dar uma∼pada em** stub one's toe on; **∼par** *vt* agree to, accept; **∼par com** bump into <*pessoa*>; come across <*coisa*>

topázio /toˈpaziu/ *m* topaz

topete /toˈpetʃi/ *m* quiff

tópico /ˈtɔpiku/ *a* topical □ *m* topic

topless /topiˈlɛs/ *a invar* & *adv* topless

topo /ˈtopu/ *m* top

topografia /topograˈfia/ *f* topography

topônimo /toˈponimu/ *m* place name

toque /ˈtɔki/ *m* touch; (*da campainha, do telefone*) ring; (*de instrumento*) playing; **dar um ∼ em** (*fam*) have a word with

Tóquio /ˈtɔkiu/ *f* Tokyo

tora /ˈtɔra/ *f* log

toranja /toˈrãʒa/ *f* grapefruit

tórax /ˈtɔraks/ *m invar* thorax

tor|ção /torˈsãw/ *f* (*do braço etc*) sprain; **∼cedor** *m* supporter; **∼cer** *vt* twist; (*machucar*) sprain; (*espremer*) wring

<roupa>; (*centrifugar*) spin *<roupa>* □ *vi* (*gritar*) cheer (**por** for); (*desejar sucesso*) keep one's fingers crossed (**por** for; **para que** that); ∼**cer-se** *vpr* twist about; ∼**cicolo** /ɔ/ *m* stiff neck; ∼**cida** *f* (*torção*) twist; (*torcedores*) supporters; (*gritaria*) cheering

tormen|ta /tor'mẽta/ *f* storm; ∼**to** *m* torment; ∼**toso** /o/ *a* stormy

tornado /tor'nadu/ *m* tornado

tornar /tor'nar/ *vt* make; ∼**se** *vpr* become

torne|ado /torni'adu/ *a* **bem** ∼**ado** shapely; ∼**ar** *vt* turn

torneio /tor'neju/ *m* tournament

torneira /tor'nera/ *f* tap, (*Amer*) faucet

torniquete /torni'ketʃi/ *m* (*para ferido*) tourniquet; (*Port: de entrada*) turnstile

torno /'tornu/ *m* lathe; (*de ceramista*) wheel; **em** ∼ **de** around

tornozelo /torno'zelu/ *m* ankle

toró /to'rɔ/ *m* downpour

torpe /'torpi/ *a* dirty

torpe|dear /torpedʒi'ar/ *vt* torpedo; ∼**do** /e/ *m* torpedo

torpor /tor'por/ *m* torpor

torra|da /to'xada/ *f* piece of toast; *pl* toast; ∼**deira** *f* toaster

torrão /to'xãw/ *m* (*de terra*) turf; (*de açúcar*) lump

torrar /to'xar/ *vt* toast *<pão>*; roast *<café>*; blow *<dinheiro>*; sell off *<mercadorias>*

torre /'toxi/ *f* tower; (*em xadrez*) rook; ∼ **de controle** control tower; ∼**ão** *m* turret

torrefação /toxefa'sãw/ *f* (*ação*) roasting; (*fábrica*) coffee-roasting plant

torren|cial /toxẽsi'aw/ (*pl* ∼**ciais**) *a* torrential; ∼**te** *f* torrent

torresmo /to'xezmu/ *m* crackling

tórrido /'tɔxidu/ *a* torrid

torrone /to'xoni/ *m* nougat

torso /'torsu/ *m* torso

torta /'tɔrta/ *f* pie, tart

tor|to /'tortu/ *a* crooked; **a** ∼ **e a direito** left, right and centre; ∼**tuoso** *a* winding

tortu|ra /tor'tura/ *f* torture; ∼**rador** *m* torturer; ∼**rar** *vt* torture

to|sa /'toza/ *f* (*de cachorro*) clipping; (*de ovelhas*) shearing; ∼**são** *m* fleece; ∼**sar** *vt* clip *<cachorro>*; shear *<ovelhas>*; crop *<cabelo>*

tosco /'tosku/ *a* rough, coarse

tosquiar /toski'ar/ *vt* shear *<ovelha>*

tos|se /'tɔsi/ *f* cough; ∼**se de cachorro** whooping cough; ∼**sir** *vi* cough

tostão /tos'tãw/ *m* penny

tostar /tos'tar/ *vt* brown *<carne>*; tan *<pele, pessoa>*; ∼**se** *vpr* (*ao sol*) go brown

to|tal /to'taw/ (*pl* ∼**tais**) *a* & *m* total

totali|dade /totali'dadʒi/ *f* entirety; ∼**tário** *a* totalitarian; ∼**zar** *vt* total

touca /'toka/ *f* bonnet; (*de freira*) wimple; ∼ **de banho** bathing cap; ∼**dor** *m* dressing table

toupeira /to'pera/ *f* mole

tou|rada /to'rada/ *f* bullfight; ∼**reiro** *m* bullfighter; ∼**ro** *m* bull; **Touro** (*signo*) Taurus

tóxico /'tɔksiku/ *a* toxic □ *m* toxic substance

toxicômano /toksi'komanu/ *m* drug addict

toxina /tok'sina/ *f* toxin

traba|lhador /trabaʎa'dor/ *a* *<pessoa>* hard-working; *<classe>* working □ *m* worker; ∼ **lhar** *vt* work □ *vi* work; (*numa peça, filme*) act; ∼**lheira** *f* big job; ∼**lhista** *a* labour; ∼**lho** *m* work; (*um*) job; (*na escola*) assignment; **dar-se o** ∼**lho de** go to the trouble of; ∼**lho de parto** labour; ∼**lhos forçados** hard labour; ∼**lhoso** *a* laborious

traça /'trasa/ *f* moth

tração /tra'sãw/ *f* traction

tra|çar /tra'sar/ *vt* draw; draw up *<plano>*; set out *<ordens>*; ∼**ço** *m* stroke; (*entre frases*) dash; (*vestígio*) trace; (*característica*) trait; *pl* (*do rosto*) features

tractor /tra'tor/ *m* (*Port*) *veja* **trator**

tradi|ção /tradʒi'sãw/ *f* tradition; ∼**cional** (*pl* ∼**cionais**) *a* traditional

tradu|ção /tradu'sãw/ *f* translation; ∼**tor** *m* translator; ∼**zir** *vt/i* translate (**de** from; **para** into)

trafe|gar /trafe'gar/ *vi* run; ∼**gável** (*pl* ∼**gáveis**) *a* open to traffic

tráfego /'trafegu/ *m* traffic

trafi|cância /trafi'kãsia/ *f* trafficking; ∼**cante** *m/f* trafficker; ∼**car** *vt/i* traffic (**com** in)

tráfico /'trafiku/ *m* traffic

tra|gada /tra'gada/ *f* (*de bebida*) swallow; (*de cigarro*) drag; ∼**gar** *vt* swallow; inhale *<fumaça>*

tragédia /tra'ʒedʒia/ *f* tragedy

trágico /'traʒiku/ *a* tragic

trago /'tragu/ *m* (*de bebida*) swallow; (*de cigarro*) drag; **de um** ∼ in one go

trai|ção /traj'sãw/ *f* (*ato*) betrayal; (*deslealdade*) treachery; (*da pátria*) treason; ∼**çoeiro** *a* treacherous; ∼**dor** *a* treacherous □ *m* traitor

trailer /'trejler/ (*pl* ∼**s**) *m* (*de filme etc*) trailer; (*casa móvel*) caravan, (*Amer*) trailer

t

traineira /traj'nera/ f trawler

training /'trejnĩ/ (pl ~s) m track suit

trair /tra'ir/ vt betray; be unfaithful to <marido, mulher>; ~-se vpr give o.s. away

tra|jar /tra'ʒar/ vt wear; ~jar-se vpr dress (de in); ~je m outfit; ~je a rigor evening dress; ~je espacial space suit

traje|to /tra'ʒetu/ m (percurso) journey; (caminho) route; ~-tória f trajectory; (fig) course

tralha /'traʎa/ f (trastes) junk

tra|ma /'trama/ f plot; ~mar vt/i plot

trambi|que /trã'biki/ (fam) m con; ~queiro (fam) m con artist

tramitar /trami'tar/ vi be processed

trâmites /'tramitʃis/ m pl channels

tramóia /tra'mɔja/ f scheme

trampolim /trãpo'lĩ/ m (de ginástica) trampoline; (de piscina, fig) springboard

tranca /'trãka/ f bolt; (em carro) lock

trança /'trãsa/ f (de cabelo) plait

tran|cafiar /trãkafi'ar/ vt lock up; ~car vt lock; cancel <matrícula>

trançar /trã'sar/ vt plait <cabelo>; weave <palha etc>

tranco /'trãku/ m jolt; aos ~s e barrancos in fits and starts

tranqueira /trã'kera/ f junk

tranqüi|lidade /trãkwili'dadʒi/ f tranquillity; ~lizador a reassuring; ~lizante m tranquillizer □ a reassuring; ~lizar vt reassure; ~lizar-se vpr be reassured; ~lo a <bairro, sono> peaceful; <pessoa, voz, mar> calm; <consciência> clear; <sucesso, lucro> sure-fire □ adv with no trouble

transa /'trãza/ f (fam) (negócio) deal; (caso) affair; ~ção f transaction; ~do a (fam) <roupa, pessoa, casa> stylish; <relação> healthy

Transamazônica /trãzama'zonika/ f trans-Amazonian highway

transar /trã'zar/ (fam) vt set up; do <drogas> □ vi (negociar) deal; (fazer sexo) have sex

transatlântico /trãzat'lãtʃiku/ a transatlantic □ m liner

transbordar /trãzbor'dar/ vi overflow

transcen|dental /trãsēdē'taw/ (pl ~dentais) a transcendental; ~der vt/i ~der (a) transcend

trans|crever /trãskre'ver/ vt transcribe; ~crição f transcription; ~crito a transcribed □ m transcript

transe /'trãzi/ m trance

transeunte /trãzi'ũtʃi/ m/f passer-by

transfe|rência /trãsfe'rēsia/ f transfer; ~ridor m protractor; ~rir vt transfer; ~rir-se vpr transfer

transfor|mação /trãsforma'sãw/ f transformation; ~mador m transformer; ~mar vt transform; ~mar-se vpr be transformed

trânsfuga /'trãsfuga/ m/f deserter; (de um país) defector

transfusão /trãsfu'zãw/ f transfusion

trans|gredir /trãzgre'dʒir/ vt infringe; ~gressão f infringement

transi|ção /trãzi'sãw/ f transition; ~cional (pl ~cionais) a transitional

transi|gente /trãzi'ʒētʃi/ a open to compromise; ~gir vi compromise

transis|tor /trãzis'tor/ m transistor; ~torizado a transistorized

transi|tar /trãzi'tar/ vi pass; ~tável (pl ~táveis) a passable; ~tivo a transitive

trânsito /'trãzitu/ m traffic; em ~ in transit

transitório /trãzi'toriu/ a transitory

translúcido /trãz'lusidu/ a translucent

transmis|são /trãzmi'sãw/ f transmission; ~sor m transmitter

transmitir /trãzmi'tʃir/ vt transmit <programa, calor, doença>; convey <notícia, ordens>; transfer <herança, direito>; ~-se vpr <doença> be transmitted

transpa|recer /trãspare'ser/ vi be visible; (fig) <emoção, verdade> come out; ~rência f transparency; ~rente a transparent

transpi|ração /trãspira'sãw/ f perspiration; ~rar vt exude □ vi (suar) perspire; <notícia> trickle through; <verdade> come out

transplan|tar /trãsplã'tar/ vt transplant; ~te m transplant

transpor /trãs'por/ vt cross <rio, fronteira>; get over <obstáculo, dificuldade>; transpose <letras, música>

transpor|tadora /trãsporta'dora/ f transport company; ~tar vt transport; (em contas) carry forward; ~te m transport; ~-te coletivo public transport

transposto /trãs'postu/ pp de **transpor**

transtor|nar /trãstor'nar/ vt mess up <papéis, casa>; disrupt <rotina, ambiente>; disturb, upset <pessoa>; ~nar-se vpr <pessoa> be rattled; ~no /o/ m (de casa, rotina) disruption; (de pessoa) disturbance; (contratempo) upset

transver|sal /trãzver'saw/ (pl ~sais) a (rua) ~sal cross street; ~so /ɛ/ a transverse

transvi|ado /trãzvi'adu/ *a* wayward; **∼ar** *vt* lead astray

trapa|ça /tra'pasa/ *f* swindle; **∼cear** *vi* cheat; **∼ceiro** *a* crooked □ *m* cheat

trapa|lhada /trapa'ʎada/ *f* bungle; **∼lhão** *a* (*f* **∼lhona**) bungling □ *m* (*f* **∼lhona**) bungler

trapézio /tra'pɛziu/ *m* trapeze

trapezista /trape'zista/ *m/f* trapeze artist

trapo /'trapu/ *m* rag

traquéia /tra'kɛja/ *f* windpipe, trachea

traquejo /tra'keʒu/ *m* knack

traquinas /tra'kinas/ *a invar* mischievous

trás /tras/ *adv* de **∼** from behind; **a roda de ∼** the back wheel; **de ∼ para frente** back to front; **para ∼** backwards; **deixar para ∼** leave behind; **por ∼ de** behind

traseiro /tra'zeru/ *a* rear, back □ *m* bottom

trasladar /trazla'dar/ *vt* transport

traspas|sado /traspa'sadu/ *a* <*paletó*> double-breasted; **∼sar** *vt* pierce

traste /'trastʃi/ *m* (*pessoa*) pain; (*coisa*) piece of junk

tra|tado /tra'tadu/ *m* (*pacto*) treaty; (*estudo*) treatise; **∼tamento** *m* treatment; (*título*) title; **∼tar** *vt* treat; negotiate <*preço, venda*> □ *vi* (*manter relações*) have dealings (**com** with); (*combinar*) negotiate (**com** with); **∼tar de** deal with; **∼tar alg de** *ou* **por** address s.o. as; **∼tar de voltar** (*tentar*) seek to return; (*resolver*) decide to return; **∼tar-se de** be a matter of; **∼tável** (*pl* **∼táveis**) *a* <*doença*> treatable; <*pessoa*> accommodating; **∼tos** *m pl* **maus ∼tos** ill-treatment

trator /tra'tor/ *m* tractor

trauma /'trawma/ *m* trauma; **∼- tizante** *a* traumatic; **∼tizar** *vt* traumatize

tra|vão /tra'vãw/ *m* (*Port*) brake; **∼var** *vt* lock <*rodas, músculos*>; stop <*carro*>; block <*passagem*>; strike up <*amizade, conversa*>; wage <*luta, combate*> □ *vi* (*Port*) brake

trave /'travi/ *f* beam, joist; (*do gol*) crossbar

traves|sa /tra'vɛsa/ *f* (*trave*) crossbar; (*rua*) side street; (*prato*) dish; (*pente*) slide; **∼são** *m* dash; **∼seiro** *m* pillow; **∼sia** *f* crossing; **∼so** /e/ *a* <*criança*> naughty; **∼sura** *f* prank; *pl* mischief

travesti /traves'tʃi/ *m* transvestite; (*artista*) drag artist; **∼do** *a* in drag

trazer /tra'zer/ *vt* bring; bear <*nome, ferida*>; wear <*barba, chapéu, cabelo curto*>

trecho /'treʃu/ *m* (*de livro etc*) passage; (*de rua etc*) stretch

treco /'trɛku/ (*fam*) *m* (*coisa*) thing; (*ataque*) turn

trégua /'trɛgwa/ *f* truce; (*fig*) respite

trei|nador /trejna'dor/ *m* trainer; **∼namento** *m* training; **∼nar** *vt* train <*atleta, animal*>; practise <*língua etc*> □ *vi* <*atleta*> train; <*pianista, principiante*> practise; **∼no** *m* training; (*um*) training session

trejeito /tre'ʒejtu/ *m* grimace

trela /'trɛla/ *f* lead, (*Amer*) leash

treliça /tre'lisa/ *f* trellis

trem /trẽj/ *m* train; **∼ de aterrissagem** undercarriage; **∼ de carga** goods train, (*Amer*) freight train

trema /'trema/ *m* dieresis

treme|deira /treme'dera/ *f* shiver; **∼licar** *vi* tremble; **∼luzir** *vi* glimmer, flicker

tremendo /tre'mẽdu/ *a* tremendous

tre|mer /tre'mer/ *vi* tremble; <*terra*> shake; **∼mor** *m* tremor; (*tremedeira*) shiver; **∼mular** *vi* <*bandeira*> flutter; <*luz, estrela*> glimmer, flicker

trêmulo /'tremulu/ *a* trembling; <*luz*> flickering

trena /'trena/ *f* tape measure

trenó /tre'nɔ/ *m* sledge, (*Amer*) sled; (*puxado a cavalos etc*) sleigh

tre|padeira /trepa'dera/ *f* climbing plant; **∼par** *vt* climb □ *vi* climb; (*chulo*) fuck

três /tres/ *a & m* three

tresloucado /trezlo'kadu/ *a* deranged

trevas /'trɛvas/ *f pl* darkness

trevo /'trevu/ *m* (*planta*) clover; (*rodoviário*) interchange

treze /'trezi/ *a & m* thirteen

trezentos /tre'zẽtus/ *a & m* three hundred

triagem /tri'aʒẽ/ *f* (*escolha*) selection; (*separação*) sorting; **fazer uma ∼ de** sort

tri|angular /triãgu'lar/ *a* triangular; **∼ângulo** *m* triangle

tri|bal /tri'baw/ (*pl* **∼bais**) *a* tribal; **∼bo** *f* tribe

tribu|na /tri'buna/ *f* rostrum; **∼nal** (*pl* **∼nais**) *m* court

tribu|tação /tributa'sãw/ *f* taxation; **∼tar** *vt* tax; **∼tário** *a* tax □ *m* tributary; **∼to** *m* tribute

tri|cô /tri'ko/ *m* knitting; **artigos de ∼cô** knitwear; **∼cotar** *vt/i* knit

tridimensio|nal /tridʒimẽsio'naw/ (*pl* **∼nais**) *a* three-dimensional

trigêmeo /tri'ʒemiu/ *m* triplet

trigésimo /tri'ʒɛzimu/ *a* thirtieth

tri|go /'trigu/ *m* wheat; **∼gueiro** *a* dark

trilha /'triʎa/ *f* path; (*pista, de disco*) track; **∼ sonora** soundtrack

trilhão /tri'ʎãw/ *m* billion, (*Amer*) trillion

trilho /'triʎu/ *m* track

trilogia /trilo'ʒia/ *f* trilogy

trimes|tral /trimes'traw/ (*pl* ~**trais**) *a* quarterly; ~**tre** /ɛ/ *m* quarter; (*do ano letivo*) term

trincar /trĩ'kar/ *vt/i* crack

trincheira /trĩ'ʃera/ *f* trench

trinco /'trĩku/ *m* latch

trindade /trĩ'dadʒi/ *f* trinity

trinta /'trĩta/ *a & m* thirty

trio /'triu/ *m* trio; ~ **elétrico** music float

tripa /'tripa/ *f* gut

tripé /tri'pɛ/ *m* tripod

tripli|car /tripli'kar/ *vt/i*, ~**car-se** *vpr* treble; ~**cata** *f* triplicate

triplo /'triplu/ *a & m* triple

tripu|lação /tripula'sãw/ *f* crew; ~**lante** *m/f* crew member; ~**lar** *vt* man

triste /'tristʃi/ *a* sad; ~**za** /e/ *f* sadness; **é uma** ~**za** (*fam*) it's pathetic

tritu|rador /tritura'dor/ *m* (*de papel*) shredder; ~**rador de lixo** waste disposal unit; ~**rar** *vt* shred <*legumes, papel*>; grind up <*lixo*>

triun|fal /triũ'faw/ (*pl* ~**fais**) *a* triumphal; ~**fante** *a* triumphant; ~**far** *vi* triumph; ~**fo** *m* triumph

trivi|al /trivi'aw/ (*pl* ~**ais**) *a* trivial; ~**alidade** *f* triviality; *pl* **trivia**

triz /tris/ *m* **por um** ~ narrowly, by a hair's breadth; **não foi atropelado por um** ~ he narrowly missed being knocked down

tro|ca /'trɔka/ *f* exchange; **em** ~**ca de** in exchange for; ~**cadilho** *m* pun; ~**cado** *m* change; ~**cador** *m* conductor; ~**car** *vt* (*dar e receber*) exchange (**por** for); change <*dinheiro, lençóis, lâmpada, lugares etc*>; (*transpor*) change round; (*confundir*) mix up; ~**car-se** *vpr* change; ~**car de roupa/trem/lugar** change clothes /trains/places; ~**ca-troca** *m* swap; ~**-co** /o/ *m* change; **a** ~**co de quê?** what for?; **dar o** ~**co em alg** pay s.o. back

troço /'trɔsu/ (*fam*) *m* (*coisa*) thing; (*ataque*) turn; **me deu um** ~ I had a funny turn

troféu /tro'fɛw/ *m* trophy

trólebus /'trɔlebus/ *m invar* trolley bus

trom|ba /'trõba/ *f* (*de elefante*) trunk; (*cara amarrada*) long face; ~**bada** *f* crash; ~**ba-d'água** (*pl* ~**bas-d'água**) *f* downpour; ~**badinha** *m* bag snatcher; ~**bar** *vi* ~**bar com** crash into <*poste, carro*>; bump into <*pessoa*>

trombo|ne /trõ'bɔni/ *m* trombone; ~**nista** *m/f* trombonist

trompa /'trõpa/ *f* French horn; ~ **de Falópio** fallopian tube

trompe|te /trõ'petʃi/ *m* trumpet; ~**tista** *m/f* trumpeter

tron|co /'trõku/ *m* trunk; ~**cudo** *a* stocky

trono /'tronu/ *m* throne

tropa /'trɔpa/ *f* troop; (*exército*) army; *pl* troops; ~ **de choque** riot police

trope|ção /trope'sãw/ *m* trip; (*erro*) slip-up; ~**çar** *vi* trip; (*errar*) slip up; ~**ço** /e/ *m* stumbling block

trôpego /'tropegu/ *a* unsteady

tropi|cal /tropi'kaw/ (*pl* ~**cais**) *a* tropical

trópico /'trɔpiku/ *m* tropic

tro|tar /tro'tar/ *vi* trot; ~**te** /ɔ/ *m* (*de cavalo*) trot; (*de estudantes*) practical joke; (*mentira*) hoax

trouxa /'troʃa/ *f* (*de roupa etc*) bundle □ *m/f* (*fam*) sucker □ *a* (*fam*) gullible

tro|vão /tro'vãw/ *m* clap of thunder; *pl* thunder; ~**vejar** *vi* thunder; ~**voada** *f* thunderstorm; ~**voar** *vi* thunder

trucidar /trusi'dar/ *vt* slaughter

trucu|lência /truku'lẽsia/ *f* barbarity; ~**lento** *a* (*cruel*) barbaric; (*brigão*) belligerent

trufa /'trufa/ *f* truffle

trunfo /'trũfu/ *m* trump; (*fig*) trump card

truque /'truki/ *m* trick

truta /'truta/ *f* trout

tu /tu/ *pron* you

tua /'tua/ *veja* **teu**

tuba /'tuba/ *f* tuba

tubarão /tuba'rãw/ *m* shark

tubá|rio /tu'bariu/ *a* **gravidez** ~**ria** ectopic pregnancy

tuberculose /tuberku'lɔzi/ *f* tuberculosis

tubo /'tubu/ *m* tube; (*no corpo*) duct

tubulação /tubula'sãw/ *f* ducting

tucano /tu'kanu/ *m* toucan

tudo /'tudu/ *pron* everything; ~ **bem?** (*cumprimento*) how are things?; ~ **de bom** all the best; **em** ~ **quanto é lugar** all over the place

tufão /tu'fãw/ *m* typhoon

tulipa /tu'lipa/ *f* tulip

tumba /'tũba/ *f* tomb

tumor /tu'mor/ *m* tumour; ~ **cerebral** brain tumour

túmulo /'tumulu/ *m* grave

tumul|to /tu'muwtu/ *m* commotion; (*motim*) riot; ~**tuado** *a* disorderly, rowdy; ~**tuar** *vt* disrupt □ *vi* cause a commotion; ~**tuoso** *a* tumultuous

tú|nel /'tunew/ (*pl* ~**neis**) *m* tunnel

túnica /'tunika/ f tunic
Tunísia /tu'nizia/ f Tunisia
tupiniquim /tupini'kĩ/ a Brazilian
turbante /tur'bãtʃi/ m turban
turbilhão /turbi'ʎãw/ m whirlwind
turbina /tur'bina/ f turbine
turbu|lência /turbu'lêsia/ f turbulence;
~**lento** a turbulent
turco /'turku/ a & m Turkish
turfa /'turfa/ f peat
turfe /'turfe/ m horse-racing
turis|mo /tu'rizmu/ m tourism; **fazer**
~**mo** go sightseeing; ~**ta** m/f tourist
turístico /tu'ristʃiku/ a <ponto,
indústria> tourist; <viagem>
sightseeing
turma /'turma/ f group; (na escola) class
turnê /tur'ne/ f tour
turno /'turnu/ m (de trabalho) shift; (de
competição, eleição) round
turquesa /tur'keza/ m/f & a invar
turquoise
Turquia /tur'kia/ f Turkey
turra /'tuxa/ f **às** ~**s com** at loggerheads
with
tur|var /tur'var/ vt cloud; ~**vo** a cloudy
tutano /tu'tanu/ m marrow
tutela /tu'tɛla/ f guardianship
tutor /tu'tor/ m guardian
tutu /tu'tu/ m (vestido) tutu; (prato)
beans with bacon and manioc flour
TV /te've/ f TV

Uu

ubíquo /u'bikwu/ a ubiquitous
Ucrânia /u'krania/ f Ukraine
ucraniano /ukrani'anu/ a & m Ukrainian
ué /u'ɛ/ int hang on
ufa /'ufa/ int phew
ufanis|mo /ufa'nizmu/ m chauvinism;
~**ta** a & m/f chauvinist
Uganda /u'gãda/ m Uganda
ui /ui/ int (de dor) ouch; (de nojo) ugh; (de
espanto) oh
uísque /u'iski/ m whisky
ui|var /ui'var/ vi howl; ~**vo** m howl
úlcera /'uwsera/ f ulcer
ulterior /uwteri'or/ a further
ulti|mamente /uwtʃima'mẽtʃi/ adv
recently; ~**mar** vt finalize; ~**mato** m
ultimatum
último /'uwtʃimu/ a last; <moda, notícia
etc> latest; **em** ~ **caso** as a last resort;

nos ~**s anos** in recent years; **por** ~
last
ultra|jante /uwtra'ʒãtʃi/ a offensive;
~**jar** vt offend; ~**je** m outrage
ultraleve /uwtra'lɛvi/ m microlite
ultra|mar /uwtra'mar/ m overseas;
~**marino** a overseas
ultrapas|sado /uwtrapa'sadu/ a
outdated; ~**sagem** f overtaking,
(Amer) passing; ~**sar** vt (de carro)
overtake, (Amer) pass; (ser superior a)
surpass; (exceder) exceed; (extrapolar)
go beyond □ vi overtake, (Amer) pass
ultra-sonografia /uwtrasonogra'fia/ f
ultrasound scan
ultravioleta /uwtravio'leta/ a
ultraviolet
ulu|lante /ulu'lãtʃi/ a (fig) blatant; ~**lar**
vi wail
um /ũ/ (f **uma**, m pl **uns**, f pl **umas**) art a,
an; pl some □ a & pron one; ~ **ao outro**
one another; **vieram umas 20
pessoas** about 20 people came
umbanda /ũ'bãda/ m Afro-Brazilian cult
umbigo /ũ'bigu/ m navel
umbili|cal /ũbili'kaw/ (pl ~ **cais**) a
umbilical
umedecer /umede'ser/ vt moisten; ~**se**
vpr moisten
umidade /umi'dadʒi/ f moisture;
(desagradável) damp; (do ar) humidity
úmido /'umidu/ a moist; <parede, roupa
etc> damp; <ar, clima> humid
unânime /u'nanimi/ a unanimous
unanimidade /unanimi'dadʒi/ f
unanimity
undécimo /ũ'dɛsimu/ a eleventh
ungüento /ũ'gwẽtu/ m ointment
unha /'uɲa/ f nail; (de animal, utensílio)
claw
união /uni'ãw/ f union; (concórdia)
unity; (ato de unir) joining; **União
Européia** European Union, EU
unicamente /unika'mẽtʃi/ adv only
único /'uniku/ a only; (ímpar) unique
uni|dade /uni'dadʒi/ f unit; ~**do** a
united; <família> close
unifi|cação /unifika'sãw/ f unification;
~**car** vt unify
unifor|me /uni'fɔrmi/ a uniform;
<superfície> even □ m uniform;
~**midade** f uniformity; ~**mizado** a
<policial etc> uniformed;
(padronizado) standardized; ~**zar** vt
(padronizar) standardize
unilate|ral /unilate'raw/ (pl ~**rais**) a
unilateral
unir /u'nir/ vt unite <povo, nações,
família etc>; (ligar, casar) join;
(combinar) combine (a ou com with);
~**se** vpr (aliar-se) unite (a with);

(*juntar-se*) join together; (*combinar-se*) combine (**a** *ou* **com** with)

unissex /uni'sɛks/ *a invar* unisex

uníssono /u'nisonu/ *m* **em ~** in unison

univer|sal /univer'saw/ (*pl* **~sais**) *a* universal

universi|dade /universi'dadʒi/ *f* university; **~tário** *a* university ▢ *m* university student

universo /uni'vɛrsu/ *m* universe

untar /ũ'tar/ *vt* grease *<fôrma>*; spread *<pão>*; smear *<corpo>*

upa /'upa/ *int* (*incentivando*) upsadaisy; (*ao cair algo etc*) whoops

urânio /u'raniu/ *m* uranium

Urano /u'ranu/ *m* Uranus

urbanis|mo /urba'nizmu/ *m* town planning; **~ta** *m/f* town planner

urbani|zado /urbani'zadu/ *a* built-up; **~zar** *vt* urbanize

urbano /ur'banu/ *a* (*da cidade*) urban; (*refinado*) urbane

urdir /ur'dʒir/ *vt* weave; (*maquinar*) hatch

urdu /ur'du/ *m* Urdu

ur|gência /ur'ʒesia/ *f* urgency; **~gente** *a* urgent; **~gir** *vi* be urgent; *<tempo>* press; **~ge irmos** we must go urgently

uri|na /u'rina/ *f* urine; **~nar** *vt* pass ▢ *vi* urinate; **~nol** (*pl* **~nóis**) *m* (*penico*) chamber pot; (*em banheiro*) urinal

urna /'urna/ *f* (*para cinzas*) urn; (*para votos*) ballot box; *pl* (*fig*) polls

ur|rar /u'xar/ *vt/i* roar; **~ro** *m* roar

urso /'ursu/ *m* bear; **~-branco** (*pl* **~s-brancos**) *m* polar bear

urti|cária /urtʃi'karia/ *f* nettle rash; **~ga** *f* nettle

urubu /uru'bu/ *m* black vulture

Uruguai /uru'gwaj/ *m* Uruguay

uruguaio /uru'gwaju/ *a & m* Uruguayan

urze /'urzi/ *f* heather

usado /u'zadu/ *a* used; *<roupa>* worn; *<palavra>* common

usar /u'zar/ *vt* wear *<roupa, óculos, barba etc>*; **~ (de)** (*utilizar*) use

usina /u'zina/ *f* plant; **~ termonuclear** nuclear power station

uso /'uzu/ *m* use; (*de palavras, linguagem*) usage; (*praxe*) practice

usu|al /uzu'aw/ (*pl* **~ais**) *a* common; **~ário** *m* user; **~fruir** *vt* enjoy *<coisas boas>*; have the use of *<prédio, jardim etc>*; **~fruto** *m* use

usurário /uzu'rariu/ *a* money-grabbing ▢ *m* money-lender

usurpar /uzur'par/ *vt* usurp

uten|sílio /utẽ'siliu/ *m* utensil; **~te** *m/f* (*Port*) user

útero /'uteru/ *m* uterus, womb

UTI /ute'i/ *f* intensive care unit

útil. /'utʃiw/ (*pl* **úteis**) *a* useful; **dia ~** workday

utili|dade /utʃili'dadʒi/ *f* usefulness; (*uma*) utility; **~tário** *a* utilitarian; **~zar** *vt* (*empregar*) use; (*tornar útil*) utilize; **~zável** (*pl* **~záveis**) *a* usable

utopia /uto'pia/ *f* Utopia

utópico /u'tɔpiku/ *a* Utopian

uva /'uva/ *f* grape

úvula /'uvula/ *f* uvula

....

V V

....

vaca /'vaka/ *f* cow

vaci|lante /vasi'lãtʃi/ *a* wavering; *<luz>* flickering; **~lar** *vi* waver; *<luz>* flicker; (*fam: bobear*) slip up

vaci|na /va'sina/ *f* vaccine; **~ nação** *f* vaccination; **~nar** *vt* vaccinate

vácuo /'vakuu/ *m* vacuum

va|diar /vadʒi'ar/ *vi* (*viver ocioso*) laze around; (*fazer cera*) mess about; **~dio** *a* idle ▢ *m* idler

vaga /'vaga/ *f* (*posto*) vacancy; (*para estacionar*) parking place

vagabun|dear /vagabũdʒi'ar/ *vi* (*perambular*) roam; (*vadiar*) laze around; **~do** *a* *<pessoa, vida>* idle; *<produto, objeto>* shoddy ▢ *m* tramp; (*pessoa vadia*) bum

vaga-lume /vaga'lumi/ *m* glow-worm

va|gão /va'gãw/ *m* (*de passageiros*) carriage, (*Amer*) car; (*de carga*) wagon; **~gão-leito** (*pl* **~gões-leitos**) *m* sleeping car; **~gão-restaurante** (*pl* **~gões-restaurantes**) *m* dining car

vagar[1] /va'gar/ *vi* *<pessoa>* wander about; *<barco>* drift

vagar[2] /va'gar/ *vi* *<cargo, apartamento>* become vacant

vagaroso /vaga'rozu/ *a* slow

vagem /'vaʒẽ/ *f* green bean

vagi|na /va'ʒina/ *f* vagina; **~nal** (*pl* **~nais**) *a* vaginal

vago[1] /'vagu/ *a* (*indefinido*) vague

vago[2] /'vagu/ *a* (*desocupado*) vacant; *<tempo>* spare

vaguear /vagi'ar/ *vi* roam

vai|a /'vaja/ *f* boo; **~ar** *vi* boo

vai|dade /vaj'dadʒi/ *f* vanity; **~doso** *a* vain

vaivém /vaj'vẽj/ *m* comings and goings, toing and froing

vala /'vala/ *f* ditch; **~ comum** mass grave

vale¹ /'vali/ *m* (*de rio etc*) valley

vale² /'vali/ *m* (*ficha*) voucher; ~ **postal** postal order

valen|tão /valẽ'tãw/ *a* (*f* ~**tona**) tough □ *m* tough guy; ~**te** *a* brave; ~**tia** *f* bravery; (*uma*) feat

valer /va'ler/ *vt* be worth □ *vi* be valid; ~ **aco a alg** earn s.o. sth; ~**-se de** avail o.s. of; ~ **a pena** be worth it; **vale a pena tentar** it's worth trying; **mais vale desistir** it's better to give up; **vale tudo** anything goes; **fazer** ~ enforce <*lei*>; stand up for <*direitos*>; **para** ~ (*a sério*) for real; (*muito*) really

vale|-refeição /valirefej'sãw/ (*pl* ~**s-refeição**) *m* luncheon voucher

valeta /va'leta/ *f* gutter

valete /va'lɛtʃi/ *m* jack

valia /va'lia/ *f* value

validar /vali'dar/ *vt* validate

válido /'validu/ *a* valid

valioso /vali'ozu/ *a* valuable

valise /va'lizi/ *f* travelling bag

valor /va'lor/ *m* value; (*valentia*) valour; *pl* (*títulos*) securities; **no** ~ **de** to the value of; **sem** ~ worthless; **objetos de** ~ valuables; ~ **nominal** face value

valori|zação /valoriza'sãw/ *f* (*apreciação*) valuing; (*aumento no valor*) increase in value; ~**zado** *a* highly valued; ~**zar** *vt* (*apreciar*) value; (*aumentar o valor de*) increase the value of; ~**zar-se** *vt* <*coisa*> increase in value; <*pessoa*> value o.s.

val|sa /'vawsa/ *f* waltz; ~**sar** *vi* waltz

válvula /'vawvula/ *f* valve

vampiro /vã'piru/ *m* vampire

vandalismo /vãda'lizmu/ *m* vandalism

vândalo /'vãdalu/ *m* vandal

vangloriar-se /vãglori'arsi/ *vpr* brag (**de** about)

vanguarda /vã'gwarda/ *f* vanguard; (*de arte*) avant-garde

vanta|gem /vã'taʒẽ/ *f* advantage; **contar** ~**gem** boast; **levar** ~**gem** have the advantage (**a** over); **tirar** ~**gem de** take advantage of; ~**joso** /o/ *a* advantageous

vão /vãw/ (*pl* ~**s**) *a* (*f* **vã**) vain □ *m* gap; **em** ~ in vain

vapor /va'por/ *m* (*fumaça*) steam; (*gás*) vapour; (*barco*) steamer; **máquina a** ~ steam engine; **a todo** ~ at full blast

vaporizar /vapori'zar/ *vt* vaporize; (*com spray*) spray

vaqueiro /va'keru/ *m* cowboy

vaquinha /va'kiɲa/ *f* collection, whip-round

vara /'vara/ *f* rod; ~ **cívil** civil district; ~ **mágica** *ou* **de condão** magic wand

va|ral /va'raw/ (*pl* ~**rais**) *m* washing line

varanda /va'rãda/ *f* veranda

varão /va'rãw/ *m* male

varar /va'rar/ *vt* (*furar*) pierce; (*passar por*) sweep through

varejão /vare'ʒãw/ *m* wholesale store

varejeira /vare'ʒera/ *f* bluebottle

vare|jista /vare'ʒista/ *a* retail □ *m/f* retailer; ~**jo** /e/ *m* retail trade; **vender a** ~**jo** sell retail

vari|ação /varia'sãw/ *f* variation; ~**ado** *a* varied; ~**ante** *a* & *f* variant; ~**ar** *vt/i* vary; **para** ~**ar** for a change; ~**ável** (*pl* ~**áveis**) *a* variable; <*tempo*> changeable

varicela /vari'sɛla/ *f* chickenpox

variedade /varie'dadʒi/ *f* variety

vários /'varius/ *a pl* several

varíola /va'riola/ *f* smallpox

variz /va'ris/ *f* varicose vein

varo|nil /varo'niw/ (*pl* ~**nis**) *a* manly

var|rer /va'xer/ *vt* sweep; (*fig*) sweep away; ~**rido** *a* **um doido** ~**rido** a raving lunatic

Varsóvia /var'sovia/ *f* Warsaw

vasculhar /vasku'ʎar/ *vt* search through

vasectomia /vazekto'mia/ *f* vasectomy

vaselina /vaze'lina/ *f* vaseline

vasilha /va'ziʎa/ *f* jug

vaso /'vazu/ *m* pot; (*para flores*) vase; ~ **sanguíneo** blood vessel

vassoura /va'sora/ *f* broom

vas|tidão /vastʃi'dãw/ *f* vastness; ~**to** /o/ *a* vast

vatapá /vata'pa/ *m* spicy North-Eastern dish

Vaticano /vatʃi'kanu/ *m* Vatican

vati|cinar /vatʃisi'nar/ *vt* prophesy; ~**cínio** *m* prophecy

va|zamento /vaza'mẽtu/ *m* leak; ~**zante** *f* ebb tide; ~**zão** *m* outflow; **dar** ~**zão a** (*fig*) give vent to; ~**zar** *vt/i* leak

vazio /va'ziu/ *a* empty □ *m* emptiness; (*um*) void

veado /vi'adu/ *m* deer

ve|dação /veda'sãw/ *f* (*de casa, janela*) insulation; (*em motor etc*) gasket; ~**dar** *vt* seal <*recipiente, abertura*>; stanch <*sangue*>; seal off <*saída, área*>; ~**dar aco (a alg)** prohibit sth (for s.o.)

vedete /ve'dɛte/ *f* star

vee|mência /vee'mẽsia/ *f* vehemence; ~**mente** *a* vehement

vege|tação /veʒeta'sãw/ *f* vegetation; ~**tal** (*pl* ~**tais**) *a* & *m* vegetable; ~**tar** *vi* vegetate; ~**tariano** *a* & *m* vegetarian

veia /'veja/ *f* vein

veicular /veiku'lar/ *vt* convey; place <anúncios>

veículo /ve'ikulu/ *m* vehicle; (*de comunicação etc*) medium

vela¹ /'vɛla/ *f* (*de barco*) sail; (*esporte*) sailing

vela² /'vɛla/ *f* candle; (*em motor*) spark plug; **segurar a** ~ (*fam*) play gooseberry

velar¹ /ve'lar/ *vt* (*cobrir*) veil

velar² /ve'lar/ *vt* watch over □ *vi* keep vigil

veleidade /velej'dadʒi/ *f* whim

ve|leiro /ve'leru/ *m* sailing boat; ~**lejar** *vi* sail

velhaco /ve'ʎaku/ *a* crooked □ *m* crook

ve|lharia /veʎa'ria/ *f* old thing; ~**lhice** *f* old age; ~**lho** /ɛ/ *a* old □ *m* old man; ~**lhote** /ɔ/ *m* old man

velocidade /velosi'dadʒi/ *f* speed; (*Port: marcha*) gear; **a toda** ~ at full speed; ~ **máxima** speed limit

velocímetro /velo'simetru/ *m* speedometer

velocista /velo'sista/ *m/f* sprinter

velório /ve'lɔriu/ *m* wake

veloz /ve'lɔs/ *a* fast

veludo /ve'ludu/ *m* velvet; ~ **cotelê** corduroy

ven|cedor /vẽse'dor/ *a* winning □ *m* winner; ~**cer** *vt* win over <adversário etc>; win <partida, corrida, batalha> □ *vi* (*triunfar*) win; <prestação, aluguel, dívida> fall due; <contrato, passaporte, prazo> expire; <apólice> mature; ~**cido** *a* dar-se por ~**cido** give in; ~**cimento** *m* (*de dívida, aluguel*) due date; (*de contrato, prazo*) expiry date; (*de alimento, remédio etc*) best before date; (*salário*) payment; *pl* earnings

venda¹ /'vẽda/ *f* sale; (*loja*) general store; **à** ~ on sale; **pôr à** ~ put up for sale

ven|da² /'vẽda/ *f* blindfold; ~**dar** *vt* blindfold

venda|val /vẽda'vaw/ (*pl* ~**vais**) *m* gale, storm

ven|dável /vẽ'davew/ (*pl* ~**dáveis**) *a* saleable; ~**dedor** *m* (*de loja*) shop assistant; (*em geral*) seller; ~**der** *vt/i* sell; **estar** ~**dendo saúde** be bursting with health

vendeta /vẽ'deta/ *f* vendetta

veneno /ve'nenu/ *m* poison; (*de cobra etc, malignidade*) venom; ~**so** /o/ *a* poisonous; (*maldoso*) venomous

vene|ração /venera'sãw/ *f* reverence; (*de Deus etc*) worship; ~**rar** *vt* revere; worship <Deus etc>

vené|reo /ve'nɛriu/ *a* **doença** ~**rea** venereal disease

Veneza /ve'neza/ *f* Venice

veneziana /venezi'ana/ *f* shutter

Venezuela /venezu'ɛla/ *f* Venezuela

venezuelano /venezue'lanu/ *a & m* Venezuelan

venta /'vẽta/ *f* nostril

ven|tania /vẽta'nia/ *f* gale; ~**tar** *vi* be windy; ~**tarola** /ɔ/ *f* fan

venti|lação /vẽtʃila'sãw/ *f* ventilation; ~**lador** *m* fan; ~**lar** *vt* ventilate; air <sala, roupa>

ven|to /'vẽtu/ *m* wind; **de** ~**to em popa** smoothly; ~**toinha** *f* (*cata-vento*) weather vane; (*Port: ventilador*) fan; ~**tosa** /ɔ/ *f* sucker; ~**toso** /o/ *a* windy

ven|tre /'vẽtri/ *m* belly; ~**tríloquo** *m* ventriloquist

Vênus /'venus/ *f* Venus

ver /ver/ *vt* see; watch <televisão>; (*resolver*) see to □ *vi* see □ *m* **a meu** ~ in my view; ~**-se** *vpr* (*no espelho etc*) see o.s.; (*em estado, condição*) find o.s.; (*um ao outro*) see each other; **ter a** ~ **com** have to do with; **vai** ~ **que ela não sabe** (*fam*) I bet she doesn't know; **vê se você não volta tarde** see you don't get back late; **viu?** (*fam*) right?

veracidade /verasi'dadʒi/ *f* truthfulness

vera|near /verani'ar/ *vi* spend the summer; ~**neio** *m* summer holiday, (*Amer*) summer vacation; ~**nista** *m/f* holidaymaker, (*Amer*) vacationer

verão /ve'rãw/ *m* summer

veraz /ve'ras/ *a* truthful

verbas /'vɛrbas/ *f pl* funds

ver|bal /ver'baw/ (*pl* ~**bais**) *a* verbal; ~**bete** /e/ *m* entry; ~**bo** *m* verb; ~**borragia** *f* waffle; ~**boso** /o/ *a* verbose

verda|de /ver'dadʒi/ *f* truth; **de** ~**de** <coisa> real; <fazer> really; **na** ~**de** actually; **para falar a** ~**de** to tell the truth; ~**deiro** *a* <declaração, pessoa> truthful; (*real*) true

verde /'verdʒi/ *a & m* green; **jogar** ~ **para colher maduro** fish for information; ~**-abacate** *a invar* avocado; ~**-amarelo** *a* yellow and green; (*brasileiro*) Brazilian; (*nacionalista*) nationalistic; ~**-esmeralda** *a invar* emerald green; ~**jar** *vi* turn green

verdu|ra /ver'dura/ *f* (*para comer*) greens; (*da natureza*) greenery; ~**reiro** *m* greengrocer, (*Amer*) produce dealer

vereador /veria'dor/ *m* councillor

vereda /ve'reda/ *f* path

veredito /vere'dʒitu/ *m* verdict

vergar /ver'gar/ *vt/i* bend

vergo|nha /ver'goɲa/ f (*pudor*) shame; (*constrangimento*) embarrassment; (*timidez*) shyness; (*uma*) disgrace; **ter ∼nha** be ashamed; be embarrassed; be shy; **cria** *ou* **tome ∼nha na cara!** you should be ashamed of yourself !; **∼nhoso** *a* shameful

verídico /ve'ridʒiku/ *a* true

verificar /verifi'kar/ *vt* check, verify <*fatos, dados etc*>; **∼ que** ascertain that; **∼ se** check that; **∼-se** *vpr* <*previsão etc*> come true; <*acidente etc*> happen

verme /'vɛrmi/ *m* worm

verme|lhidão /vermeʎi'dãw/ f redness; **∼lho** /e/ *a & m* red; **no ∼lho** (*endividado*) in the red

vernáculo /ver'nakulu/ *a & m* vernacular

verniz /ver'nis/ f varnish; (*couro*) patent leather

veros|símil /vero'simiw/ (*pl* **∼símeis**) *a* plausible; **∼similhança** f plausibility

verruga /ve'xuga/ f wart

ver|sado /ver'sadu/ *a* well-versed (**em** in); **∼são** f version; **∼sar** *vi* **∼sar sobre** concern; **∼sátil** (*pl* **∼sáteis**) *a* versatile; **∼satilidade** f versatility; **∼sículo** *m* (*da Bíblia*) verse; **∼so¹** /ɛ/ *m* verse

verso² /ɛ/ *m* (*de página*) reverse, other side; **vide ∼** see over

vértebra /'vɛrtebra/ f vertebra

verte|brado /verte'bradu/ *a & m* vertebrate; **∼bral** (*pl* **∼brais**) *a* spinal

ver|tente /ver'tẽtʃi/ f slope; **∼ter** *vt* (*derramar*) pour; shed <*lágrimas, sangue*>; (*traduzir*) render (**para** into)

verti|cal /vertʃi'kaw/ (*pl* **∼cais**) *a & f* vertical; **∼gem** /ʒ/ f dizziness; **∼ginoso** /o/ *a* dizzy

vesgo /'vezgu/ *a* cross-eyed

vesícula /ve'zikula/ f gall bladder

vespa /'vespa/ f wasp

véspera /'vɛspera/ f **a ∼ the** day before; **a ∼ de** the eve of; **a ∼ de Natal** Christmas Eve; **nas ∼s de** on the eve of

vespertino /vesper'tʃinu/ *a* evening

ves|te /'vestʃi/ f robe; **∼tiário** *m* (*para se trocar*) changing room; (*para guardar roupa*) cloakroom

vestibular /vestʃibu'lar/ *m* university entrance exam

vestíbulo /ves'tʃibulu/ *m* hall(way); (*do teatro*) foyer

vestido /ves'tʃidu/ *m* dress □ *a* dressed (**de** in)

vestígio /ves'tʃiʒiu/ *m* trace

ves|timenta /vestʃi'mẽta/ f (*de sacerdote*) vestments; **∼tir** *vt* (*pôr*) put on; (*usar*) wear; (*pôr roupa em*) dress;

(*dar roupa a*) clothe; **∼tir-se** *vpr* dress; **∼tir-se de branco/de padre** dress in white/as a priest; **∼tuário** *m* clothing

vetar /ve'tar/ *vt* veto

veterano /vete'ranu/ *a & m* veteran

veterinário /veteri'nariu/ *a* veterinary □ *m* vet

veto /'vɛtu/ *m* veto

véu /vɛw/ *m* veil

vexa|me /ve'ʃami/ *m* disgrace; **dar um ∼me** make a fool of o.s.; **∼minoso** /o/ *a* disgraceful

vexar /ve'ʃar/ *vt* shame; **∼-se** *vpr* be ashamed (**de** of)

vez /ves/ f (*ocasião*) time; (*turno*) turn; **às ∼es** sometimes; **cada ∼ mais** more and more; **de ∼** for good; **desta ∼** this time; **de ∼ em quando** now and again, from time to time; **de uma ∼** (*ao mesmo tempo*) at once; (*de um golpe*) in one go; **de uma ∼ por todas** once and for all; **duas ∼es** twice; **em ∼ de** instead of; **fazer as ∼es de** take the place of; **mais uma ∼, outra ∼** again; **muitas ∼es** (*com muita frequência*) often; (*repetidamente*) many times; **raras ∼es** seldom; **repetidas ∼es** repeatedly; **uma ∼** once; **uma ∼ que** since

via /'via/ f (*estrada*) road; (*rumo, meio*) way; (*exemplar*) copy; *pl* (*trâmites*) channels □ *prep* via; **em ∼s de** on the point of; **por ∼ aérea/marítima** by air/sea; **por ∼ das dúvidas** just in case; **por ∼ de regra** as a rule; **Via Láctea** Milky Way

viabili|dade /viabili'dadʒi/ f feasibility; **∼zar** *vt* make feasible

viação /via'sãw/ f (*transporte*) road transport; (*estradas*) road network; (*companhia*) bus company

viaduto /via'dutu/ *m* viaduct; (*rodoviário*) flyover, (*Amer*) overpass

via|gem /vi'aʒẽ/ f (*uma*) trip, journey; (*em geral*) travelling; *pl* (*de uma pessoa*) travels; (*em geral*) travel; **boa ∼gem!** have a good trip!; **∼gem de negócios** business trip; **∼jado** *a* well-travelled; **∼jante** *a* travelling □ *m/f* traveller; **∼jar** *vi* travel; **estar ∼jando** (*fam*) (*com o pensamento longe*) be miles away

viário /vi'ariu/ *a* road; **anel ∼** ring road

viatura /via'tura/ f vehicle

viá|vel /vi'avew/ (*pl* **∼veis**) *a* feasible

víbora /'vibora/ f viper

vi|bração /vibra'sãw/ f vibration; (*fig*) thrill; **∼brante** *a* vibrant; **∼brar** *vt* shake □ *vi* vibrate; (*fig*) be thrilled (**com** by)

vice /'visi/ *m/f* deputy

V

vice-cam|peão /visikãpi'ãw/ *m* (*f* ∼**peã**) runner-up

vicejar /vise'ʒar/ *vi* flourish

vice-presiden|te /visiprezi'dẽtʃi/ *m* (*f* ∼**ta**) vice-president

vice-rei /visi'xej/ *m* viceroy

vice-versa /visi'vɛrsa/ *adv* vice-versa

vici|ado /visi'adu/ *a* addicted (**em** to) □ *m* addict; **um** ∼**ado em drogas** a drug addict; ∼**ar** *vt* (*falsificar*) tamper with; (*estragar*) ruin □ *vi* <*droga*> be addictive; ∼**ar-se** *vpr* get addicted (**em** to)

vício /'visiu/ *m* vice

vicioso /visi'ozu/ *a* **círculo** ∼ vicious circle

vicissitudes /visisi'tudʒis/ *f pl* ups and downs

viço /'visu/ *m* (*de plantas*) exuberance; (*de pessoa, pele*) freshness; ∼**so** /o/ *a* <*planta*> lush; <*pele, pessoa*> fresh

vida /'vida/ *f* life; **sem** ∼ lifeless; **dar** ∼ **a** liven up

videira /vi'dera/ *f* vine

vidente /vi'dẽtʃi/ *m/f* clairvoyant

vídeo /'vidʒiu/ *m* video; (*tela*) screen

video|cassete /vidʒiuka'sɛtʃi/ *m* (*fita*) video tape; (*aparelho*) video, (*Amer*) VCR; ∼**clipe** *m* video; ∼**clube** *m* video club; ∼**game** *m* videogame; ∼**teipe** *m* video tape

vidra|ça /vi'drasa/ *f* window pane; ∼**çaria** *f* (*fábrica*) glassworks; (*vidraças*) glazing; ∼**ceiro** *m* glazier

vi|drado /vi'dradu/ *a* glazed; **estar** ∼**drado em** *ou* **por** (*fam*) love; ∼**drar** *vt* glaze □ *vi* (*fam*) fall in love (**em** *ou* **por** with); ∼**dro** *m* (*material*) glass; (*pote*) jar; (*janela*) window; ∼**dro fumê** tinted glass

viela /vi'ɛla/ *f* alley

Viena /vi'ɛna/ *f* Vienna

Vietnã /viet'ʃi'nã/ *m*, (*Port*) **Vietname** /viet'nam/ *m* Vietnam

vietnamita /vietna'mita/ *a & m/f* Vietnamese

viga /'viga/ *f* joist

vigarice /viga'risi/ *f* swindle

vigário /vi'gariu/ *m* vicar

vigarista /viga'rista/ *m/f* swindler, con artist

vi|gência /vi'ʒẽsia/ *f* (*qualidade*) force; (*tempo*) period in force; ∼**gente** *a* in force

vigésimo /vi'ʒɛzimu/ *a* twentieth

vigi|a /vi'ʒia/ *f* (*guarda*) watch; (*em navio*) porthole □ *m* night watchman; ∼**ar** *vt* (*observar*) watch; (*cuidar de*) watch over; (*como sentinela*) guard □ *vi* keep watch

vigi|lância /viʒi'lãsia/ *f* vigilance; ∼**lante** *a* vigilant

vigília /vi'ʒilia/ *f* vigil

vigor /vi'gor/ *m* vigour; **em** ∼ in force

vigo|rar /vigo'rar/ *vi* be in force; ∼**roso** *a* vigorous

vil /viw/ (*pl* **vis**) *a* base, despicable

vila /'vila/ *f* (*cidadezinha*) small town; (*casa elegante*) villa; (*conjunto de casas*) housing estate; ∼ **olímpica** Olympic village

vi|lania /vila'nia/ *f* villainy; ∼**lão** *m* (*f* ∼**lã**) villain

vilarejo /vila'reʒu/ *m* village

vilipendiar /vilipẽdʒi'ar/ *vt* disparage

vime /'vimi/ *m* wicker

vina|gre /vi'nagri/ *m* vinegar; ∼**grete** /ɛ/ *m* vinaigrette

vin|car /vĩ'kar/ *vt* crease; line <*rosto*>; ∼**co** *m* crease; (*no rosto*) line

vincular /vĩku'lar/ *vt* bond, tie

vínculo /'vĩkulu/ *m* link, bond; ∼ **empregatício** contract of employment

vinda /'vĩda/ *f* coming; **dar as boas** ∼**s a** welcome

vindicar /vĩdʒi'kar/ *vt* vindicate

vindima /vĩ'dʒima/ *f* vintage

vin|do /'vĩdu/ *pp e pres de* **vir**; ∼**douro** *a* coming

vin|gança /vĩ'gãsa/ *f* vengeance, revenge; ∼**gar** *vt* revenge □ *vi* <*flores*> thrive; <*criança*> survive; <*plano, empreendimento*> be successful; ∼**gar-se** *vpr* take one's revenge (**de** for; **em** on); ∼**gativo** *a* vindictive

vinha /'viɲa/ *f* vineyard

vinhedo /vi'ɲedu/ *m* vineyard

vinheta /vi'ɲeta/ *f* (*na TV etc*) sequence

vinho /'viɲu/ *m* wine □ *a invar* maroon; ∼ **do Porto** port

vinícola /vi'nikola/ *a* wine-growing

vinicul|tor /vinikuw'tor/ *m* wine grower; ∼**tura** *f* wine-growing

vinil /vi'niw/ *m* vinyl

vinte /'vĩtʃi/ *a & m* twenty; ∼**na** /e/ *f* score

viola /vi'ola/ *f* viola

violação /viola'sãw/ *f* violation

violão /vio'lãw/ *m* guitar

violar /vio'lar/ *vt* violate

vio|lência /vio'lẽsia/ *f* violence; (*uma*) act of violence; ∼**lentar** *vt* rape <*mulher*>; ∼**lento** *a* violent

violeta /vio'leta/ *f* violet □ *a invar* violet

violi|nista /violi'nista/ *m/f* violinist; ∼**no** *m* violin

violonce|lista /violõse'lista/ *m/f* cellist; ∼**lo** /ɛ/ *m* cello

vir /vir/ *vi* come; **o ano que vem** next year; **venho lendo os jornais** I have been reading the papers; **vem cá** come here; (*fam*) listen; **isso não vem ao caso** that's irrelevant; **~ a ser** turn out to be; **~ com** give <*argumento etc*>

virabrequim /virabre'kĩ/ *m* crankshaft

viração /vira'sãw/ *f* breeze

vira-casaca /viraka'zaka/ *m/f* turncoat

vira|da /vi'rada/ *f* turn; **~do** *a* <*roupa*> inside out; (*de cabeça para baixo*) upside down; **~do para** facing

vira-lata /vira'lata/ *m* mongrel

virar /vi'rar/ *vt* turn; turn over <*disco, barco etc*>; turn inside out <*roupa*>; turn out <*bolsos*>; tip <*balde, água etc*> □ *vi* turn; <*barco*> turn over; (*tornar-se*) become; **~-se** *vpr* turn round; (*na vida*) get by, cope; **~-se para** turn to; **vira e mexe** every so often

viravolta /vira'vɔwta/ *f* about-turn

virgem /'virʒẽ/ *a* <*fita*> blank; <*floresta, noiva etc*> virgin □ *f* virgin; **Virgem** (*signo*) Virgo

virgindade /virʒĩ'dadʒi/ *f* virginity

vírgula /'virgula/ *f* comma; (*decimal*) point

vi|ril /vi'riw/ (*pl* **~ris**) *a* virile

virilha /vi'riʎa/ *f* groin

virilidade /virili'dadʒi/ *f* virility

virtu|al /virtu'aw/ (*pl* **~ais**) *a* virtual

virtude /vir'tudʒi/ *f* virtue

virtuo|sismo /virtuo'zizmu/ *m* virtuosity; **~so** /o/ *a* virtuous □ *m* virtuoso

virulento /viru'lẽtu/ *a* virulent

vírus /'virus/ *m invar* virus

visão /vi'zãw/ *f* vision; (*aspecto, ponto de vista*) view

visar /vi'zar/ *vt* aim at <*caça, alvo*>; **~ (a)** aim for <*objetivo*>; <*medida, ação*> be aimed at

vísceras /'viseras/ *f pl* innards

viscon|de /vis'kõdʒi/ *m* viscount; **~dessa** /e/ *f* viscountess

viscoso /vis'kozu/ *a* viscous

viseira /vi'zera/ *f* visor

visibilidade /vizibili'dadʒi/ *f* visibility

visionário /vizio'nariu/ *a & m* visionary

visi|ta /vi'zita/ *f* visit; (*visitante*) visitor; **fazer uma ~ta a alg** pay s.o. a visit; **~tante** *a* visiting □ *m/f* visitor; **~tar** *vt* visit

visí|vel /vi'zivew/ (*pl* **~veis**) *a* visible

vislum|brar /vizlũ'brar/ *vt* (*entrever*) glimpse; (*imaginar*) envisage; **~bre** *m* glimpse

visom /vi'zõ/ *m* mink

visor /vi'zor/ *m* viewfinder

vis|ta /'vista/ *f* sight; (*dos olhos*) eyesight; (*panorama*) view; **à ~ta** (*visível*) in view; (*em dinheiro*) in cash; **à primeira ~ta** at first sight; **pôr à ~ta** put on show; **de ~ta** <*conhecer*> by sight; **em ~ta de** in view of; **ter em ~ta** have in view; **dar na ~ta** attract attention; **fazer ~ta** look nice; **fazer ~ta grossa** turn a blind eye (**a** to); **perder de ~ta** lose sight of; **a perder de ~ta** as far as the eye can see; **uma ~ta de olhos** a quick look; **~to** *a* seen □ *m* visa; **pelo ~to** by the looks of things; **~to que** seeing that

visto|ria /visto'ria/ *f* inspection; **~riar** *vt* inspect

vistoso /vis'tozu/ *a* eye-catching

visu|al /vizu'aw/ (*pl* **~ais**) *a* visual □ *m* look; **~alizar** *vt* visualize

vi|tal /vi'taw/ (*pl* **~tais**) *a* vital; **~talício** *a* for life; **~talidade** *f* vitality

vita|mina /vita'mina/ *f* vitamin; (*bebida*) liquidized fruit drink; **~minado** *a* with added vitamins; **~mínico** *a* vitamin

vitela /vi'tɛla/ *f* (*carne*) veal

viticultura /vitʃikuw'tura/ *f* viticulture

vítima /'vitʃima/ *f* victim

viti|mar /vitʃi'mar/ *vt* (*matar*) claim the life of; **ser ~mado por** fall victim to

vitória /vi'tɔria/ *f* victory

vitorioso /vitori'ozu/ *a* victorious

vi|tral /vi'traw/ (*pl* **~trais**) *m* stained glass window

vitrine /vi'trini/ *f* shop window

vitrola /vi'trɔla/ *f* jukebox

viú|va /vi'uva/ *f* widow; **~vo** *a* widowed □ *m* widower

viva /'viva/ *f* cheer □ *int* hurray; **~ a rainha** long live the queen

vivacidade /vivasi'dadʒi/ *f* vivacity

vivalma /vi'vawma/ *f* **não há ~ lá fora** there's not a soul outside

vivar /vi'var/ *vt/i* cheer

vivaz /vi'vas/ *a* lively, vivacious; <*planta*> hardy

viveiro /vi'veru/ *m* (*de plantas*) nursery; (*de peixes*) fishpond; (*de aves*) aviary; (*fig*) breeding ground

vivência /vi'vẽsia/ *f* experience

vívido /'vividu/ *a* vivid

viver /vi'ver/ *vt/i* live (**de** on) □ *m* life; **ele vive reclamando** he's always complaining

víveres /'viveris/ *m pl* provisions

vivissecção /vivisek'sãw/ *f* vivisection

vivo /'vivu/ *a* (*que vive*) living; (*animado*) lively; <*cor*> bright □ *m* **os ~s** the living; **ao ~** live; **estar ~** be alive; **dinheiro ~** cash

vizi|nhança /vizi'ɲãsa/ *f* neighbourhood; **~nho** *a* neighbouring □ *m* neighbour

V

vo|ador /voa'dor/ *a* flying; **∼ar** *vi* fly; (*explodir*) blow up; **sair ∼ando** rush off

vocabulário /vokabu'lariu/ *m* vocabulary

vocábulo /vo'kabulu/ *m* word

voca|ção /voka'sãw/ *f* vocation; **∼cional** (*pl* **∼cionais**) *a* vocational; **orientação ∼cional** careers guidance

vo|cal /vo'kaw/ (*pl* **∼cais**) *a* vocal

você /vo'se/ *pron* you; **∼s** *pron* you

vociferar /vosife'rar/ *vi* shout abuse

vodca /'vɔdʒka/ *f* vodka

voga /'vɔga/ *f* (*moda*) vogue

vo|gal /vo'gaw/ (*pl* **∼gais**) *f* vowel

volante /vo'lãtʃi/ *m* (*de carro*) steering wheel

volá|til /vo'latʃiw/ (*pl* **∼teis**) *a* volatile

vôlei /'volej/ *m*, **voleibol** /volej'bɔw/ *m* volleyball

volt /'vɔwtʃi/ (*pl* **∼s**) *m* volt

volta /'vɔwta/ *f* (*retorno*) return; (*da pista*) lap; (*resposta*) answer; **às ∼s com** tied up with; **de ∼** back; **em ∼ de** around; **na ∼** on the way back; **na ∼ do correio** by return of post; **por ∼ de** around; **dar a ∼ ao mundo** go round the world; **dar a ∼ por cima** make a comeback; **dar meia ∼** turn round; **dar uma ∼** (*a pé*) go for a walk; (*de carro*) go for a drive; **dar uma ∼ em** turn round; **dar ∼s** spin round; **ter ∼** get a response; **∼ e meia** every so often; **∼do a ∼do para** geared towards

voltagem /vow'taʒẽ/ *f* voltage

voltar /vow'tar/ *vi* go/come back, return ◻ *vt* rewind <*fita*>; **∼-se** *vpr* turn round; **∼se para/contra** turn to/against; **∼ a si** come to; **∼ a fazer** do again; **∼ atrás** backtrack

volu|me /vo'lumi/ *m* volume; **∼moso** *a* sizeable; <*som*> loud

voluntário /volũ'tariu/ *a & m* volunteer

volúpia /vo'lupia/ *f* sensuality, lust

voluptuoso /voluptu'ozu/ *a* sensual; <*mulher*> voluptuous

volú|vel /vo'luvew/ (*pl* **∼veis**) *a* fickle

vomitar /vomi'tar/ *vt/i* vomit

vômito /'vomitu/ *m* vomit; *pl* vomiting

vontade /võ'tadʒi/ *f* will; **à ∼** (*bem*) at ease; (*quanto quiser*) as much as one likes; **fique à ∼** make yourself at home; **tem comida à ∼** there's plenty of food; **estar com ∼ de** feel like; **isso me dá ∼ de chorar** it makes me feel like crying; **fazer a ∼ de alg** do what s.o. wants

vôo /'vou/ *m* flight; **levantar ∼** take off; **∼ livre** hang-gliding

voraz /vo'ras/ *a* voracious

vos /vus/ *pron* you; (*a vocês*) to you

vós /vɔs/ *pron* you

vosso /'vɔsu/ *a* your ◻ *pron* yours

vo|tação /vota'sãw/ *f* vote; **∼tante** *m/f* voter; **∼tar** *vt* vote on <*lei etc*>; (*dedicar*) devote; (*prometer*) vow ◻ *vi* vote (**em** for)

voto /'vɔtu/ *m* (*em votação*) vote; (*promessa*) vow; *pl* (*desejos*) wishes

vo|vó /vo'vɔ/ *f* grandma; **∼vô** *m* grandpa

voz /vɔs/ *f* voice; **dar ∼ de prisão a alg** place s.o. under arrest

vozerio /voze'riu/ *m* shouting

vul|cânico /vuw'kaniku/ *a* volcanic; **∼cão** *m* volcano

vul|gar /vuw'gar/ *a* ordinary; (*baixo*) vulgar; **∼garizar** *vt* popularize; (*tornar baixo*) vulgarize; **∼go** *adv* commonly known as

vulne|rabilidade /vuwnerabili'dadʒi/ *f* vulnerability; **∼rável** (*pl* **∼ráveis**) *a* vulnerable

vul|to /'vuwtu/ *m* (*figura*) figure; (*tamanho*) bulk; (*importância*) importance; **de ∼to** important; **∼toso** /o/ *a* bulky

W w

walkie-talkie /uɔki'tɔki/ (*pl* **∼s**) *m* walkie-talkie

walkman /uok'mɛn/ *m invar* walkman

WAP /uap/ *a* (*telec*) WAP

watt /u'ɔtʃi/ (*pl* **∼s**) *m* watt

web /uɛb/ *m* web,WWW

windsur|fe /uĩ'surfi/ *m* windsurfing; **∼fista** *m/f* windsurfer

X x

xadrez /ʃa'dres/ *m* (*jogo*) chess; (*desenho*) check; (*fam: prisão*) prison ◻ *a invar* check

xale /'ʃali/ *m* shawl

xampu /ʃã'pu/ *m* shampoo

xará /ʃa'ra/ *m/f* namesake

xarope /ʃa'rɔpi/ *m* syrup

xaxim /ʃa'ʃĩ/ *m* plant fibre

xenofobia /ʃenofo'bia/ *f* xenophobia

xenófobo /ʃe'nɔfobu/ *a* xenophobic ◻ *m* xenophobe

xepa /'ʃepa/ f scraps

xeque[1] /'ʃɛki/ m (*árabe*) sheikh

xeque[2] /'ʃɛki/ m (*no xadrez*) check;
~**-mate** m checkmate

xere|ta /ʃe'reta/ (*fam*) a nosy □ m/f nosy
parker; ~**tar** (*fam*) vi nose around

xerez /ʃe'res/ m sherry

xerife /ʃe'rifi/ m sheriff

xerocar /ʃero'kar/ vt photocopy

xerox /ʃe'rɔks/ m invar photocopy

xexelento /ʃeʃe'lẽtu/ (*fam*) a scruffy
□ m scruff

xícara /'ʃikara/ f cup

xiita /ʃi'ita/ a & m/f Shiite

xilofone /ʃilo'foni/ m xylophone

xingar /ʃĩ'gar/ vt swear at □ vi swear

xis /ʃis/ m invar letter X; **o** ~ **do**
problema the crux of the problem

xixi /ʃi'ʃi/ (*fam*) m wee; **fazer** ~ do a wee

xô /ʃo/ int shoo

xucro /'ʃukru/ a ignorant

Zz

zagueiro /za'geru/ m fullback

Zaire /'zajri/ m Zaire

Zâmbia /'zãbia/ f Zambia

zan|gado /zã'gadu/ a cross, annoyed;
~**gar** vt annoy; ~**gar-se** vpr get cross,
get annoyed (**com** with)

zanzar /zã'zar/ vi wander

zarpar /zar'par/ vi set off; (*de navio*) set
sail

zebra /'zebra/ f zebra; (*pessoa*) fool;
(*resultado*) upset

ze|lador /zela'dor/ m caretaker,
(*Amer*) janitor; ~**lar** vt ~**lar** (**por**)
take care of; ~**lo** /e/ m zeal; ~**lo por**
devotion to; ~**loso** /o/ a zealous

zero /'zɛru/ m zero; (*em escores*) nil;
~**-quilômetro** a invar brand new

ziguezague /zigi'zagi/ m zigzag; ~**ar** vi
zigzag

Zimbábue /zĩ'babui/ m Zimbabwe

zinco /'zĩku/ m zinc

ziper /'ziper/ m zip, zipper

zodíaco /zo'dʒiaku/ m zodiac

zoeira /zo'era/ f din

zom|bador /zõba'dor/ a mocking;
~**bar** vi ~**bar** (**de**) mock; ~**baria** f
mockery

zona /'zona/ f (*área*) zone; (*de cidade*)
district; (*desordem*) mess; (*tumulto*)
commotion; (*bairro do meretrício*) red-
light district

zonzo /'zõzu/ a dizzy

zôo /'zou/ m zoo

zoo|logia /zoolo'ʒia/ f zoology; ~**lógico**
a zoological

zoólogo /zo'ɔlogu/ m zoologist

zulu /zu'lu/ a & m/f Zulu

zum /zũ/ m zoom lens

zumbi /zũ'bi/ m zombie

zum|bido /zũ'bidu/ m buzz; (*no ouvido*)
ringing; ~**bir** vi buzz

zu|nido /zu'nidu/ m (*de vento, bala*)
whistle; (*de inseto*) buzz; ~**nir** vi
<*vento, bala*> whistle; <*inseto*> buzz

zunzum /zũ'zũ/ m rumour

Zurique /zu'riki/ f Zurich

zurrar /zu'xar/ vi bray

a /ə/; *emphatic* /eɪ/ (*before vowel* **an** /ən/; *emphatic* /æn/) *a* um. **two pounds a metre** duas libras por metro. **sixty miles an hour** sessenta milhas por hora, (P) à hora. **once a year** uma vez por ano

aback /ə'bæk/ *adv* **taken ∼** desconcertado, (P) surpreendido

abandon /ə'bændən/ *vt* abandonar ◻ *n* abandono *m*. **∼ed** *a* abandonado; (*behaviour*) livre, dissoluto. **∼ment** *n* abandono *m*

abashed /ə'bæʃt/ *a* confuso, (P) atrapalhado

abate /ə'beɪt/ *vt/i* abater, abrandar, diminuir. **∼ment** *n* abrandamento *m*, diminuição *f*

abattoir /'æbətwɑː(r)/ *n* matadouro *m*

abbey /'æbɪ/ *n* abadia *f*, mosteiro *m*

abbreviat|e /ə'briːvɪeɪt/ *vt* abreviar. **∼ion** /-'eɪʃn/ *n* abreviação *f*; (*short form*) abreviatura *f*

abdicat|e /'æbdɪkeɪt/ *vt/i* abdicar. **∼ion** /-'keɪʃn/ *n* abdicação *f*

abdom|en /'æbdəmən/ *n* abdómen *m*, (P) abdómen *m*. **∼inal** /-'dɒmɪnl/ *a* abdominal

abduct /æb'dʌkt/ *vt* raptar. **∼ion** /-ʃn/ *n* rapto *m*. **∼or** *n* raptor, -a *mf*

aberration /æbə'reɪʃn/ *n* aberração *f*

abet /ə'bet/ *vt* (*pt* **abetted**) (*jur*) instigar; (*aid*) auxiliar

abeyance /ə'beɪəns/ *n* **in ∼** (*matter*) em suspenso; (*custom*) em desuso

abhor /əb'hɔː(r)/ *vt* (*pt* **abhorred**) abominar, ter horror a. **∼rence** /-'hɒrəns/ *n* horror *m*. **∼rent** /-'hɒrənt/ *a* abominável, execrável

abide /ə'baɪd/ *vt* (*pt* **abided**) suportar, tolerar. **∼ by** (*promise*) manter; (*rules*) acatar

abiding /ə'baɪdɪŋ/ *a* eterno, perpétuo

ability /ə'bɪlətɪ/ *n* capacidade *f* (**to do** para *or* de fazer); (*cleverness*) habilidade *f*, esperteza *f*

abject /'æbdʒekt/ *a* abjeto, (P) abjecto

ablaze /ə'bleɪz/ *a* em chamas; (*fig*) aceso, (P) excitado

abl|e /'eɪbl/ *a* (**∼er**, **∼est**) capaz (**to** de). **be ∼e to** (*have power, opportunity*) ser capaz de, poder; (*know how to*) ser capaz de, saber. **∼y** *adv* habilmente

ablutions /ə'bluːʃnz/ *npl* ablução *f*, abluções *fpl*

abnormal /æb'nɔːml/ *a* anormal. **∼ity** /-'mælətɪ/ *n* anormalidade *f*. **∼ly** *adv* (*unusually*) excepcionalmente

aboard /ə'bɔːd/ *adv* a bordo ◻ *prep* a bordo de

abode /ə'bəʊd/ *n* (*old use*) habitação *f*. **place of ∼** domicílio *m*

aboli|sh /ə'bɒlɪʃ/ *vt* abolir, extinguir. **∼tion** /æbə'lɪʃn/ *n* abolição *f*, extinção *f*

abominable /ə'bɒmməbl/ *a* abominável, detestável

abominat|e /ə'bɒmmeɪt/ *vt* abominar, detestar. **∼ion** /-'neɪʃn/ *n* abominação *f*

abort /ə'bɔːt/ *vt/i* (fazer) abortar. **∼ive** *a* (*attempt etc*) abortado, malogrado

abortion /ə'bɔːʃn/ *n* aborto *m*. **have an ∼** fazer um aborto, ter um aborto. **∼ist** *n* abortad/or, -eira *mf*

abound /ə'baʊnd/ *vi* abundar (**in** em)

about /ə'baʊt/ *adv* (*approximately*) aproximadamente, cerca de; (*here and there*) aqui e ali; (*all round*) por todos os lados, em roda, em volta; (*in existence*) por aí ◻ *prep* acerca de, sobre; (*round*) em torno de; (*somewhere in*) em, por. **∼-face**, **∼-turn** *ns* reviravolta *f*. **∼ here** por aqui. **be ∼ to** estar prestes a. **he was ∼ to eat** ia comer. **how** *or* **what ∼ leaving?** e se nós fôssemos embora? **know/talk ∼** saber/falar sobre

above /ə'bʌv/ *adv* acima, por cima ◻ *prep* sobre. **he's not ∼ lying** ele não é de mentir. **∼ all** sobretudo. **∼-board** *a* franco, honesto ◻ *adv* com lisura. **∼-mentioned** *a* acima, supracitado

abrasion /ə'breɪʒn/ *n* atrito *m*; (*injury*) escoriação *f*, esfoladura *f*

abrasive /ə'breɪsɪv/ *a* abrasivo; (*fig*) agressivo ◻ *n* abrasivo *m*

abreast /ə'brest/ *adv* lado a lado. **keep ∼ of** manter-se a par de

abridge /ə'brɪdʒ/ *vt* abreviar. **∼ment** *n* abreviação *f*, abreviatura *f*, redução *f*; (*abridged text*) resumo *m*

abroad /ə'brɔːd/ *adv* no estrangeiro; (*far and wide*) por todo o lado. **go ∼** ir para o estrangeiro

abrupt /ə'brʌpt/ *a* (*sudden, curt*) brusco; (*steep*) abrupto. **∼ly** *adv* (*suddenly*) bruscamente; (*curtly*) com brusquidão. **∼ness** *n* brusquidão *f*; (*steepness*) declive *m*

abscess /'æbsɪs/ *n* abscesso *m*, (P) abcesso *m*

abscond /əb'skɒnd/ *vi* evadir-se, andar fugido

absen|t¹ /'æbsənt/ *a* ausente; (*look etc*) distraído. **∼ce** *n* ausência *f*; (*lack*) falta *f*. **∼t-minded** *a* distraído

~t-mindedness *n* distração *f*, (P)
distracção *f*

absent[2] /əb'sent/ *v refl* ~o.s. ausentar-se

absentee /æbsen'tiː/ *n* ausente *mf*, (P)
absentista *mf*. ~ism *n* absenteísmo *m*,
(P) absentismo *m*

absolute /'æbsəluːt/ *a* absoluto; (*colloq:
coward etc*) autêntico, (P) verdadeiro.
~ly *adv* absolutamente

absolution /æbsə'luːʃn/ *n* absolvição *f*

absolve /əb'zɒlv/ *vt* (*from sin*) absolver
(**from** de); (*from vow*) desligar
(**from** de)

absor|b /əb'sɔːb/ *vt* absorver. ~ption *n*
absorção *f*

absorbent /əb'sɔːbənt/ *a* absorvente.
~ cotton (*Amer*) algodão hidrófilo *m*

abst|ain /əb'steɪn/ *vi* abster-se (**from** de).
~ention /-'stenʃn/ *n* abstenção *f*

abstemious /əb'stiːmɪəs/ *a* abstêmio, (P)
abstémio, sóbrio

abstinen|ce /'æbstɪnəns/ *n* abstinência
f. ~t *a* abstinente

abstract[1] /'æbstrækt/ *a* abstrato, (P)
abstracto

abstract[2] /əb'strækt/ *vt* (*take out*) extrair;
(*separate*) abstrair. ~ed *a* distraído.
~ion /-ʃn/ *n* (*of mind*) distração *f*, (P)
distracção *f*; (*idea*) abstração *f*, (P)
abstracção *f*

absurd /əb'sɜːd/ *a* absurdo. ~ity *n*
absurdo *m*

abundan|t /ə'bʌndənt/ *a* abundante.
~ce *n* abundância *f*

abuse[1] /ə'bjuːz/ *vt* (*misuse*) abusar de; (*ill-
treat*) maltratar; (*insult*) injuriar,
insultar

abus|e[2] /ə'bjuːs/ *n* (*wrong use*) abuso *m*
(**of** de); (*insults*) insultos *m pl*. ~ive
a injurioso, ofensivo

abysmal /ə'bɪzməl/ *a* abismal; (*colloq:
bad*) abissal

abyss /ə'bɪs/ *n* abismo *m*

academic /ækə'demɪk/ *a* acadêmico, (P)
académico, universitário; (*scholarly*)
intelectual; (*pej*) acadêmico, (P)
teórico □ *n* universitário

academy /ə'kædəmɪ/ *n* academia *f*

accede /æk'siːd/ *vi* ~ **to** (*request*) aceder a;
(*post*) assumir; (*throne*) ascender a,
subir a

accelerat|e /ək'seləreɪt/ *vt* acelerar □ *vi*
acelerar-se; (*auto*) acelerar. ~ion
/-'reɪʃn/ *n* aceleração *f*

accelerator /ək'seləreɪtə(r)/ *n* (*auto*)
acelerador *m*

accent[1] /'æksənt/ *n* acento *m*; (*local
pronunciation*) sotaque *m*

accent[2] /æk'sent/ *vt* acentuar

accentuate /æk'sentʃʊeɪt/
vt acentuar

accept /ək'sept/ *vt* aceitar. ~able *a*
aceitável. ~ance *n* aceitação *f*;
(*approval*) aprovação *f*

access /'ækses/ *n* acesso *m* (**to** a). ~ible
/ək'sesəbl/ *a* acessível

accessory /ək'sesərɪ/ *a* acessório □ *n*
acessório *m*; (*jur: person*) cúmplice *m*

accident /'æksɪdənt/ *n* acidente *m*,
desastre *m*; (*chance*) acaso *m*. ~al
/-'dentl/ *a* acidental, fortuito. ~ally
/-'dentlɪ/ *adv* acidentalmente, por
acaso

acclaim /ə'kleɪm/ *vt* aclamar □ *n* aplauso
m, aclamações *fpl*

acclimatiz|e /ə'klaɪmətaɪz/ *vt/i*
aclimatar(-se). ~ation /-'zeɪʃn/ *n*
aclimatação *f*

accommodat|e /ə'kɒmədeɪt/ *vt*
acomodar; (*lodge*) alojar; (*adapt*)
adaptar; (*supply*) fornecer; (*oblige*)
fazer a vontade de. ~ing *a* obsequioso,
amigo de fazer vontades. ~ion /-'deɪʃn/
n acomodação *f*; (*rooms*) alojamento *m*,
quarto *m*

accompan|y /ə'kʌmpənɪ/ *vt* acompanhar.
~iment *n* acompanhamento *m*. ~ist *n*
(*mus*) acompanhad/or, (B) -eira *mf*

accomplice /ə'kʌmplɪs/ *n* cúmplice *mf*

accomplish /ə'kʌmplɪʃ/ *vt* (*perform*)
executar, realizar; (*achieve*) realizar,
conseguir fazer. ~ed *a* acabado.
~ment *n* realização *f*; (*ability*) talento
m, dote *m*

accord /ə'kɔːd/ *vi* concordar □ *vt* conceder
□ *n* acordo *m*. **of one's own** ~ por
vontade própria, espontaneamente.
~ance *n* in ~ance with em
conformidade com, de acordo com

according /ə'kɔːdɪŋ/ *adv* ~ **to** conforme.
~ly *adv* (*therefore*) por conseguinte,
por consequência; (*appropriately*)
conformemente

accordion /ə'kɔːdɪən/ *n* acordeão *m*

accost /ə'kɒst/ *vt* abordar, abeirar-se de

account /ə'kaʊnt/ *n* (*comm*) conta *f*;
(*description*) relato *m*; (*importance*)
importância *f* □ *vt* considerar. ~ **for**
dar contas de, explicar. **on** ~ **of** por
causa de. **on no** ~ em caso algum.
take into ~ ter *or* levar em
conta. ~able /-əbl/ *a* responsável
(**for** por). ~ability /-'bɪlətɪ/
n responsabilidade *f*

accountant /ə'kaʊntənt/ *n* contador(a)
m/f, (P) contabilista *mf*

accrue /ə'kruː/ *vi* acumular-se. ~ **to**
reverter em favor de

accumulat|e /ə'kjuːmjʊleɪt/ *vt/i*
acumular(-se). ~ion /-'leɪʃn/ *n*
acumulação *f*, acréscimo *m*

accumulator /ə'kjuːmjʊleɪtə(r)/ *n* (*electr*)
acumulador *m*

a

accura|te /ˈækjərət/ a exato, (P) exacto, preciso. ~**cy** n exatidão f, (P) exactidão f, precisão f. ~**tely** adv com exatidão, (P) exactidão

accus|e /əˈkjuːz/ vt acusar. **the** ~**ed** o acusado. ~**ation** /ækjuː-ˈzeɪʃn/ n acusação f

accustom /əˈkʌstəm/ vt acostumar, habituar. ~**ed** a acostumado, habituado. **get** ~**ed to** acostumar-se a, habituar-se a

ace /eɪs/ n ás m

ache /eɪk/ n dor f □ vi doer. **my leg** ~**s** dói-me a perna, tenho dores na perna

achieve /əˈtʃiːv/ vt realizar, efetuar; (success) alcançar. ~**ment** n realização f; (feat) feito m, façanha f, sucesso m

acid /ˈæsɪd/ a ácido; (wine) azedo; (words) áspero □ n ácido m. ~**ity** /əˈsɪdəti/ n acidez f

acknowledge /əkˈnɒlɪdʒ/ vt reconhecer. ~ **(receipt of)** acusar a recepção de. ~**ment** n reconhecimento m; (letter etc) acusação f de recebimento, (P) aviso m de recepção

acne /ˈækni/ n acne mf

acorn /ˈeɪkɔːn/ n bolota f, glande f

acoustic /əˈkuːstɪk/ a acústico. ~**s** npl acústica f

acquaint /əˈkweɪnt/ vt ~ **s.o. with sth** pôr alg a par de alg coisa. **be** ~**ed with** (person, fact) conhecer. ~**ance** n (knowledge, person) conhecimento m; (person) conhecido m

acquiesce /ækwiˈes/ vi consentir. ~**nce** /ækwiˈesns/ n aquiescência f, consentimento m

acqui|re /əˈkwaɪə(r)/ vt adquirir. ~**sition** /ækwɪˈzɪʃn/ n aquisição f

acquit /əˈkwɪt/ vt (pt **acquitted**) absolver. ~ **o.s. well** sair-se bem. ~**tal** n absolvição f

acrid /ˈækrɪd/ a acre

acrimon|ious /ækrɪˈməʊnɪəs/ a acrimonioso. ~**y** /ˈækrɪmənɪ/ n acrimónia f, (P) acrimónia f

acrobat /ˈækrəbæt/ n acrobata mf. ~**ic** /-ˈbætɪk/ a acrobático. ~**ics** /-ˈbætɪks/ npl acrobacia f

acronym /ˈækrənɪm/ n sigla f

across /əˈkrɒs/ adv & prep (side to side) de lado a lado (de), de um lado para o outro (de); (on the other side) do outro lado (de); (crosswise) através (de), de través. **go** or **walk** ~ atravessar. **swim** ~ atravessar a nado

act /ækt/ n (deed, theatr) ato m, (P) acto m; (in variety show) número m; (decree) lei f □ vi agir, atuar, (P) actuar; (theatr) representar; (function) funcionar; (pretend) fingir □ vt (part, role)

desempenhar. ~ **as** servir de. ~**ing** a interino □ n (theatr) desempenho m

action /ˈækʃn/ n ação f, (P) acção f; (mil) combate m. **out of** ~ fora de combate; (techn) avariado. **take** ~ agir, atuar, (P) actuar

activ|e /ˈæktɪv/ a ativo, (P) activo; (interest) vivo; (volcano) em atividade, (P) actividade. ~**ity** /-ˈtɪvəti/ n atividade f, (P) actividade f

ac|tor /ˈæktə(r)/ n ator m, (P) actor m. ~**tress** n atriz f, (P) actriz f

actual /ˈæktʃʊəl/ a real, verdadeiro; (example) concreto. **the** ~ **pen which** a própria caneta que. ~**ity** /-ˈælətɪ/ n realidade f. ~**ly** adv (in fact) na realidade

acumen /əˈkjuːmen/ n agudeza f, perspicácia f

acupunctur|e /ˈækjʊpʌŋktʃə(r)/ n acupuntura f, (P) acupunctura f. ~**ist** n acupunturador m, (P) acupuncturista mf

acute /əˈkjuːt/ a agudo; (mind) perspicaz; (emotion) intenso, vivo; (shortage) grande. ~**ly** adv vivamente.

ad /æd/ n (colloq) anúncio m

AD abbr dC

adamant /ˈædəmənt/ a inflexível

adapt /əˈdæpt/ vt/i adaptar(-se). ~**ation** /ædæpˈteɪʃn/ n adaptação f. ~**or** n (electr) n adaptador m

adaptab|le /əˈdæptəbl/ a adaptável. ~**ility** /-ˈbɪlətɪ/ n adaptabilidade f

add /æd/ vt/i acrescentar. ~ **(up)** somar. ~ **up to** (total) elevar-se a

adder /ˈædə(r)/ n víbora f

addict /ˈædɪkt/ n viciado m. **drug** ~ (B) viciado em droga, viciado da droga, (P) toxicodependente mf

addict|ed /əˈdɪktɪd/ a **be** ~**ed to** (drink, drugs; fig) ter o vício de. ~**ion** /-ʃn/ n (med) dependência f; (fig) vicio m. ~**ive** a que produz dependência

addition /əˈdɪʃn/ n adição f. **in** ~ além disso. **in** ~ **to** além de. ~**al** /-ʃənl/ a adicional, suplementar

address /əˈdres/ n endereço m; (speech) discurso m □ vt endereçar; (speak to) dirigir-se a

adenoids /ˈædmɔɪdz/ npl adenóides mpl

adept /ˈædept/ a & n especialista (mf), perito (m) (at em)

adequa|te /ˈædɪkwət/ a adequado; (satisfactory) satisfatório. ~**cy** n adequação f; (of person) competência f. ~**tely** adv adequadamente

adhere /ədˈhɪə(r)/ vi aderir (**to** a)

adhesive /əd'hi:sɪv/ a & n adesivo (m).
~ **plaster** esparadrapo m, (P)
adesivo m

adjacent /ə'dʒeɪsnt/ a adjacente,
contíguo (**to** a)

adjective /'ædʒektɪv/ n adjetivo m, (P)
adjectivo m

adjoin /ə'dʒɔɪn/ vt confinar com, ficar
contíguo a

adjourn /ə'dʒɜ:n/ vt adiar □ vi suspender
a sessão. ~ **to** (go) passar a, ir para

adjudicate /ə'dʒu:dɪkeɪt/ vt/i julgar;
(award) adjudicar

adjust /ə'dʒʌst/ vt/i (alter) ajustar,
regular; (arrange) arranjar. ~ (o.s.)
to adaptar-se a. ~**able** a regulável.
~**ment** n (techn) regulação f, afinação
f; (of person) adaptação f

ad lib /æd'lɪb/ vi (pt ad libbed) (colloq)
improvisar □ adv à vontade

administer /əd'mɪnɪstə(r)/ vt
administrar

administrat|e /əd'mɪnɪstreɪt/ vt
administrar, gerir. ~**ion** /-'streɪʃn/
n administração f. ~**or** n
administrador m

administrative /əd'mɪnɪstrətɪv/ a
administrativo

admirable /'ædmərəbl/ a admirável

admiral /'ædmərəl/ n almirante m

admir|e /əd'maɪə(r)/ vt admirar. ~**ation**
/-mɪ'reɪʃn/ n admiração f. ~**er**
/-'maɪərə(r)/ n admirador m

admission /əd'mɪʃn/ n admissão f; (to
museum, theatre, etc) ingresso m, (P)
entrada f; (confession) confissão f

admit /əd'mɪt/ vt (pt admitted) (let in)
admitir, permitir a entrada a;
(acknowledge) reconhecer, admitir.
~ **to** confessar. ~**tance** n admissão f

admoni|sh /əd'mɒnɪʃ/ vt admoestar.
~**tion** /-ə'nɪʃn/ n admoestação f

adolescen|t /ædə'lesnt/ a & n adolescente
(mf). ~**ce** n adolescência f

adopt /ə'dɒpt/ vt adotar, (P) adoptar. ~**ed
child** filho adotivo, (P) adoptivo. ~**ion**
/-ʃn/ n adoção f, (P) adopção f

ador|e /ə'dɔ:(r)/ vt adorar. ~**able** a
adorável. ~**ation** /ædə'reɪʃn/ n
adoração f

adorn /ə'dɔ:n/ vt adornar, enfeitar

adrenalin /ə'drenəlɪn/ n adrenalina f

adrift /ə'drɪft/ a & adv à deriva

adult /'ædʌlt/ a & n adulto (m). ~**hood** n
idade f adulta, (P) maioridade f

adulterat|e /ə'dʌltəreɪt/ vt adulterar.
~**ion** /-'reɪʃn/ n adulteração f

adulter|y /ə'dʌltərɪ/ n adultério m. ~**er**,
~**ess** ns adúltero/o, -a mf. ~**ous** a
adúltero

advance /əd'vɑ:ns/ vt/i avançar
□ n avanço m; (payment)
adiantamento m □ a (payment,
booking) adiantado. **in** ~ com
antecedência. ~**d** a avançado. ~**ment**
n promoção f, ascensão f

advantage /əd'vɑ:ntɪdʒ/ n vantagem f.
take ~ **of** aproveitar-se de, tirar
partido de; (person) explorar. ~**ous**
/ædvən'teɪdʒəs/ a vantajoso

adventur|e /əd'ventʃə(r)/ n aventura f.
~**er** n aventureiro m, explorador m.
~**ous** a aventuroso

adverb /'ædvɜ:b/ n advérbio m

adversary /'ædvəsərɪ/ n adversário m,
antagonista mf

advers|e /'ædvɜ:s/ a (contrary) adverso;
(unfavourable) desfavorável. ~**ity**
/əd'vɜ:sətɪ/ n adversidade f

advert /'ædvɜ:t/ n (colloq) anúncio m

advertise /'ædvətaɪz/ vt/i anunciar, fazer
publicidade (de); (sell) pôr um anúncio
(para). ~ **for** procurar. ~**r** /-ə(r)/ n
anunciante mf

advertisement /əd'vɜ:tɪsmənt/ n
anúncio m; (advertising) publicidade f

advice /əd'vaɪs/ n conselho(s) mpl;
(comm) aviso m

advis|e /əd'vaɪz/ vt aconselhar; (inform)
avisar, informar. ~ **against**
desaconselhar. ~**able** a aconselhável.
~**er** n conselheiro m; (in business)
consultor m. ~**ory** a consultivo

advocate[1] /'ædvəkət/ n (jur) advogado m;
(supporter) defensor(a) m/f

advocate[2] /'ædvəkeɪt/ vt advogar,
defender

aerial /'eərɪəl/ a aéreo □ n antena f

aerobatics /eərə'bætɪks/ npl acrobacia f
aérea

aerobics /eə'rəʊbɪks/ n ginástica f
aeróbica

aerodynamic /eərəʊdaɪ'næmɪk/ a
aerodinâmico

aeroplane /'eərəpleɪn/ n avião m

aerosol /'eərəsɒl/ n aerossol m

aesthetic /i:s'θetɪk/ a estético.

affair /ə'feə(r)/ n (business) negócio m;
(romance) ligação f, aventura f;
(matter) assunto m. **love** ~ paixão f

affect /ə'fekt/ vt afetar, (P) afectar.
~**ation** /æfek'teɪʃn/ n afetação f, (P)
afectação f. ~**ed** a afetado, (P)
afectado, pretencioso

affection /ə'fekʃn/ n afeição f, afeto m,
(P) afecto m

affectionate /ə'fekʃənət/ a afetuoso, (P)
afectuoso, carinhoso

affiliat|e /ə'fɪlɪeɪt/ vt afiliar. ~**ed
company** filial f. ~**ion** /-'eɪʃn/ n
afiliação f

affirm /ə'fɜ:m/ vt afirmar. **~ation** /æfə'meɪʃn/ n afirmação f

affirmative /ə'fɜ:mətɪv/ a afirmativo. □ n afirmativa f

afflict /ə'flɪkt/ vt afligir. **~ion** /-ʃn/ n aflição f

affluen|t /'æflʊənt/ a rico, afluente. **~ce** n riqueza f, afluência f

afford /ə'fɔ:d/ vt (have money for) permitir-se, ter meios (para). **can you afford the time?** você teria tempo? **I can't afford a car** eu não posso comprar um carro. **we can't afford to lose** não podemos perder

affront /ə'frʌnt/ n afronta f □ vt insultar

afield /ə'fi:ld/ adv **far ~** longe

afloat /ə'fləʊt/ adv & a à tona, a flutuar; (at sea) no mar; (business) lançado, (P) sem dívidas

afraid /ə'freɪd/ a **be ~** ter medo (**of,** to de; **that** que); (be sorry) lamentar, ter muita pena. **I'm ~ (that)** (regret to say) lamento or tenho muita pena de dizer que

afresh /ə'freʃ/ adv de novo

Africa /'æfrɪkə/ n África f. **~n** a & n africano (m)

after /ɑ:ftə(r)/ adv depois □ prep depois de □ conj depois que. **~ all** afinal de contas. **~ doing**, depois de fazer. **be ~** (seek) querer, pretender. **~-effect** n sequela f, (P) sequela f, efeito m retardado; (of drug) efeito m secundário

aftermath /'ɑ:ftəmæθ/ n consequências fpl

afternoon /ɑ:ftə'nu:n/ n tarde f

aftershave /'ɑ:ftəʃeɪv/ n loção f após-barba, (P) loção f para a barba

afterthought /'ɑ:ftəθɔ:t/ n reflexão f posterior. **as an ~** pensando melhor

afterwards /'ɑ:ftəwədz/ adv depois, mais tarde

again /ə'gen/ adv de novo, outra vez; (on the other hand) por outro lado. **then ~** além disso

against /ə'genst/ prep contra

age /eɪdʒ/ n idade f; (period) época f, idade f □ vt/i (pres p **ageing**) envelhecer. **~s** (colloq: very long time) há séculos mpl. **of ~** (jur) maior. **ten years of ~** com/de dez anos. **under ~** menor. **~-group** n faixa etária f. **~less** a sempre jovem

aged[1] /eɪdʒd/ a **~ six** de seis anos de idade

aged[2] /'eɪdʒɪd/ a idoso, velho

agen|cy /'eɪdʒənsɪ/ n agência f; (means) intermédio m. **~t** n agente mf

agenda /ə'dʒendə/ n ordem f do dia

aggravat|e /'ægrəveɪt/ vt agravar; (colloq: annoy) irritar. **~ion** /-'veɪʃn/ n (worsening) agravamento m; (exasperation) irritação f; (colloq: trouble) aborrecimentos mpl

aggregate /'ægrɪgeɪt/ vt/i agregar (-se) □ a /'ægrɪgət/ total, global □ n (total, mass, materials) agregado m. **in the ~** no todo

aggress|ive /ə'gresɪv/ a agressivo; (weapons) ofensivo. **~ion** /-ʃn/ n agressão f. **~iveness** n agressividade f. **~or** n agressor m

aggrieved /ə'gri:vd/ a (having a grievance) lesado

agil|e /'ædʒaɪl/ a ágil. **~ity** /ə'dʒɪlətɪ/ n agilidade f

agitat|e /'ædʒɪteɪt/ vt agitar. **~ion** /-'teɪʃn/ n agitação f. **~or** n agitador m

agnostic /æg'nɒstɪk/ a & n agnóstico (m)

ago /ə'gəʊ/ adv há. **a month ~** há um mês. **long ~** há muito tempo

agon|y /'ægənɪ/ n agonia f; (mental) angústia f. **~ize** vi atormentar-se, torturar-se. **~izing** a angustiante, (P) doloroso

agree /ə'gri:/ vt/i concordar; (of figures) acertar. **~ that** reconhecer que. **~ to do** concordar em or aceitar fazer. **~ to sth** concordar com alguma coisa. **seafood doesn't ~ with me** não me dou bem com mariscos. **~d** a (time, place) combinado. **be ~d** estar de acordo

agreeable /ə'gri:əbl/ a agradável. **be ~ to** estar de acordo com

agreement /ə'gri:mənt/ n acordo m; (gramm) concordância f; (contract) contrato m. **in ~** de acordo com

agricultur|e /'ægrɪkʌltʃə(r)/ n agricultura f. **~al** /-'kʌltʃərəl/ a agrícola

aground /ə'graʊnd/ adv **run ~** (of ship) encalhar

ahead /ə'hed/ adv à frente, adiante; (in advance) adiantado. **~ of sb** diante de alguém, à frente de alguém. **~ of time** antes da hora, adiantado. **straight ~** sempre em frente

aid /eɪd/ vt ajudar □ n ajuda f. **~ and abet** ser cúmplice de. **in ~ of** em auxílio de, a favor de

AIDS /eɪdz/ n (med) AIDS f, (P) sida m

ail /eɪl/ vt **what ~s you?** o que é que você tem? **~ing** a doente. **~ment** n doença f, achaque m

aim /eɪm/ vt (gun) apontar; (efforts) dirigir; (send) atirar (**at** para) □ vi visar □ n alvo m. **~ at** visar. **~ to** aspirar a, tencionar. **take ~** fazer pontaria. **~less** a, **~lessly** adv sem objetivo, (P) objectivo

air /eə(r)/ n ar m □ vt arejar;
(views) expor □ a (base etc) aéreo.
in the ~ (rumour) espalhado;
(plans) no ar. **on the ~** (radio) no
ar. **~-conditioned** a com ar
condicionado. **~-conditioning** n
condicionamento m do ar, (P) ar
m condicionado. **~ force** Força f
Aérea. **~ hostess** aeromoça f, (P)
hospedeira f de bordo. **~ raid** ataque
m aéreo

airborne /'eəbɔːn/ a (aviat: in flight) no
ar; (diseases) levado pelo ar; (freight)
por transporte aéreo

aircraft /'eəkrɑːft/ n (pl invar) avião m.
~-carrier n porta-aviões m

airfield /'eəfiːld/ n campo m de aviação

airgun /'eəɡʌn/ n espingarda f de
pressão

airlift /'eəlɪft/ n ponte f aérea □ vt
transportar em ponte aérea

airline /'eəlaɪn/ n linha f aérea

airlock /'eəlɒk/ n câmara f de vácuo; (in
pipe) bolha f de ar

airmail /'eəmeɪl/ n correio m aéreo. **by ~**
por avião

airport /'eəpɔːt/ n aeroporto m

airsick /'eəsɪk/ a enjoado. **~ness** /-nɪs/ n
enjôo m, (P) enjoo m

airstrip /'eəstrɪp/ n pista f de
aterrissagem, (P) pista f de aterragem

airtight /'eətaɪt/ a hermético

airy /'eərɪ/ a (-ier, -iest) arejado;
(manner) desenvolto

aisle /aɪl/ n (of church) nave f lateral;
(gangway) coxia f

ajar /ə'dʒɑː(r)/ adv & a entreaberto

alabaster /'æləbɑːstə(r)/ n alabastro m

à la carte /aːlaːˈkaːt/ adv & a à la carte,
(P) à lista

alarm /ə'lɑːm/ n alarme m; (clock)
campainha f □ vt alarmar. **~-clock**
n despertador m. **~-bell** n campainha
f de alarme. **~ing** a alarmante. **~ist**
n alarmista mf

alas /ə'læs/ int ai! ai de mim!

albatross /'ælbətrɒs/ n albatroz m

album /'ælbəm/ n álbum m

alcohol /'ælkəhɒl/ n álcool m. **~ic**
/-ˈhɒlɪk/ a (person, drink) alcoólico
□ n alcoólico m. **~ism** n
alcoolismo m

alcove /'ælkəʊv/ n recesso m, alcova f

ale /eɪl/ n cerveja f inglesa

alert /ə'lɜːt/ a (lively) vivo; (watchful)
vigilante □ n alerta m □ vt alertar. **be
on the ~** estar alerta

algebra /'ældʒɪbrə/ n álgebra f. **~ic**
/-ˈbreɪk/ a algébrico

Algeria /æl'dʒɪərɪə/ n Argélia f. **~n** a & n
argelino (m)

alias /'eɪlɪəs/ n (pl -ases) outro nome m,
nome falso m, (P) pseudónimo m □ adv
aliás

alibi /'ælɪbaɪ/ n (pl -is) álibi m, (P)
alibi m

alien /'eɪlɪən/ n & a estrangeiro (m). **~ to**
(contrary) contrário a; (differing) alheio
a, estranho a

alienat|e /'eɪlɪəneɪt/ vt alienar. **~ion**
/-ˈneɪʃn/ n alienação f

alight[1] /ə'laɪt/ vi descer; (bird) pousar

alight[2] /ə'laɪt/ a (on fire) em chamas;
(lit up) aceso

align /ə'laɪn/ vt alinhar. **~ment** n
alinhamento m

alike /ə'laɪk/ a semelhante, parecido
□ adv da mesma maneira. **look
or be ~** parecer-se

alimony /'ælɪmənɪ/ n pensão f
alimentar, (P) de alimentos

alive /ə'laɪv/ a vivo. **~ to** sensível a.
~ with fervilhando de, (P) a
fervilhar de

alkali /'ælkəlaɪ/ n (pl -is) álcali m, (P)
alcali m

all /ɔːl/ a & pron todo (f & pl -a, -os, -as)
□ pron (everything) tudo □ adv
completamente, de todo □ n tudo m.
~ the better/less/more/worse etc
tanto melhor/menos/mais/pior etc.
~ (the) men todos os homens. **~ of us**
todos nós. **~ but** quase, todos menos.
~ in (colloq: exhausted) estafado. **~-in**
a tudo incluído. **~ out** a fundo, (P)
completamente. **~-out** a (effort)
máximo. **~ over** (in one's body) todo;
(finished) acabado; (in all parts of) por
todo. **~ right** bem; (as a response) está
bem. **~ round** em tudo; (for all) para
todos. **~-round** a geral. **~ the same**
apesar de tudo. **it's ~ the same to me**
(para mim) tanto faz

allay /ə'leɪ/ vt acalmar

allegation /ælɪ'ɡeɪʃn/ n alegação f

allege /ə'ledʒ/ vt alegar. **~dly** /-ɪdlɪ/ adv
segundo dizem, alegadamente

allegiance /ə'liːdʒəns/ n fidelidade f,
lealdade f

allegor|y /'ælɪɡərɪ/ n alegoria f. **~ical**
/-ˈɡɒrɪkl/ a alegórico

allerg|y /'ælədʒɪ/ n alergia f. **~ic**
/ə'lɜːdʒɪk/ a alérgico

alleviate /ə'liːvɪeɪt/ vt aliviar

alley /'ælɪ/ n (pl -eys) (street) viela f;
(for bowling) pista f

alliance /ə'laɪəns/ n aliança f

allied /'ælaɪd/ a aliado

alligator /'ælɪɡeɪtə(r)/ n jacaré m

allocat|e /'æləkeɪt/ vt (share out)
distribuir; (assign) destinar. **~ion**
/-ˈkeɪʃn/ n atribuição f

allot /ə'lɒt/ *vt* (*pt* **allotted**) atribuir. **~ment** *n* atribuição *f*; (*share*) distribuição *f*; (*land*) horta *f* alugada

allow /ə'laʊ/ *vt* permitir; (*grant*) conceder, dar; (*reckon on*) contar com; (*agree*) admitir, reconhecer. **~ sb to** (+ *inf*) permitir a alg (+ *inf or que* + *subj*). **~ for** levar em conta

allowance /ə'laʊəns/ *n* (*for employees*) ajudas *fpl* de custo; (*monthly, for wife, child*) benefício *m*; (*tax*) desconto *m*. **make ~s for** (*person*) levar em consideração, ser indulgente para com; (*take into account*) atender a, levar em consideração

alloy /ə'lɔɪ/ *n* liga *f*

allude /ə'lu:d/ *vi* **~ to** aludir a

allure /ə'lʊə(r)/ *vt* seduzir, atrair

allusion /ə'lu:ʒn/ *n* alusão *f*

ally[1] /'ælaɪ/ *n* (*pl* **-lies**) aliado *m*

ally[2] /ə'laɪ/ *vt* aliar. **~ oneself with/to** aliar-se com/a

almanac /'ɔ:lmənæk/ *n* almanaque *m*

almighty /ɔ:l'maɪtɪ/ *a* todo- poderoso; (*colloq*) grande, formidável

almond /'a:mənd/ *n* amêndoa *f*. **~ paste** maçapão *m*

almost /'ɔ:lməʊst/ *adv* quase

alone /ə'ləʊn/ *a & adv* só. **leave ~** (*abstain from interfering with*) deixar em paz. **let ~** (*without considering*) sem *or* para não falar de

along /ə'lɒŋ/ *prep* ao longo de □ *adv* (*onward*) para diante. **all ~** durante todo o tempo. **~ with** com. **move ~, please** ande, por favor

alongside /əlɒŋ'saɪd/ *adv* (*naut*) atracado. **come ~** acostar □ *prep* ao lado de

aloof /ə'lu:f/ *adv* à parte □ *a* distante. **~ness** *n* reserva *f*

aloud /ə'laʊd/ *adv* em voz alta

alphabet /'ælfəbet/ *n* alfabeto *m*. **~ical** /-'betɪkl/ *a* alfabético

alpine /'ælpaɪn/ *a* alpino, alpestre

Alps /ælps/ *npl* **the ~** os Alpes *mpl*

already /ɔ:l'redɪ/ *adv* já

also /'ɔ:lsəʊ/ *adv* também

altar /'ɔ:ltə(r)/ *n* altar *m*

alter /'ɔ:ltə(r)/ *vt/i* alterar(-se), modificar(-se). **~ation** /-'reɪʃn/ *n* alteração *f*; (*to garment*) modificação *f*

alternate[1] /ɔ:l'tɜ:nət/ *a* alternado. **~ly** *adv* alternadamente

alternat|e[2] /'ɔ:ltəneɪt/ *vt/i* alternar(-se). **~ing current** (*elect*) corrente *f* alterna. **~or** *n* (*elect*) alternador *m*

alternative /ɔ:l'tɜ:nətɪv/ *a* alternativo □ *n* alternativa *f*. **~ly** *adv* em alternativa. **or ~ly** ou então

although /ɔ:l'ðəʊ/ *conj* embora, conquanto

altitude /'æltɪtju:d/ *n* altitude *f*

altogether /ɔ:ltə'geðə(r)/ *adv* (*completely*) completamente; (*in total*) ao todo; (*on the whole*) de modo geral

aluminium /æljʊ'mɪnɪəm/ (*Amer* **aluminum** /ə'lu:mɪnəm/) *n* alumínio *m*

always /'ɔ:lweɪz/ *adv* sempre

am /æm/ *see* **be**

a.m. /eɪ'em/ *adv* da manhã

amalgamate /ə'mælgəmeɪt/ *vt/i* amalgamar(-se); (*comm*) fundir

amass /ə'mæs/ *vt* amontoar, juntar

amateur /'æmətə(r)/ *n & a* amador (*m*). **~ish** *a* (*pej*) de amador, (*P*) amadorístico

amaz|e /ə'meɪz/ *vt* assombrar, espantar. **~ed** *a* assombrado. **~ement** *n* assombro *m*. **~ingly** *adv* espantosamente

Amazon /'æməzən/ *n* **the ~** o Amazonas

ambassador /æm'bæsədə(r)/ *n* embaixador *m*

amber /'æmbə(r)/ *n* âmbar *m*; (*traffic light*) luz *f* amarela

ambigu|ous /æm'bɪgjʊəs/ *a* ambíguo. **~ity** /-'gju:ətɪ/ *n* ambigüidade *f*, (*P*) ambiguidade *f*

ambiti|on /æm'bɪʃn/ *n* ambição *f*. **~ous** *a* ambicioso

ambivalen|t /æm'bɪvələnt/ *a* ambivalente. **~ce** *n* ambivalência *f*

amble /'æmbl/ *vi* caminhar sem pressa

ambulance /'æmbjʊləns/ *n* ambulância *f*

ambush /'æmbʊʃ/ *n* emboscada *f* □ *vt* fazer uma emboscada para, (*P*) fazer uma emboscada a

amenable /ə'mi:nəbl/ *a* **~ to** (*responsive*) sensível a

amend /ə'mend/ *vt* emendar, corrigir. **~ment** *n* (*to rule*) emenda *f*. **~s** *n* **make ~s for** reparar, compensar

amenities /ə'mi:nətɪz/ *npl* (*pleasant features*) atrativos *mpl*, (*P*) atractivos *mpl*; (*facilities*) confortos *mpl*, comodidades *fpl*

America /ə'merɪkə/ *n* América *f*. **~n** *a & n* americano (*m*). **~nism** /-nɪzəm/ *n* americanismo *m*. **~nize** *vt* americanizar

amiable /'eɪmɪəbl/ *a* amável

amicable /'æmɪkəbl/ *a* amigável, amigo

amid(st) /ə'mɪd(st)/ *prep* entre, no meio de

amiss /ə'mɪs/ *a & adv* mal. **sth ~** qq coisa que não está bem. **take sth ~** levar qq coisa a mal

ammonia /ə'məʊnɪə/ *n* amoníaco *m*

ammunition /æmjʊ'nɪʃn/ *n* munições *fpl*

amnesia /æm'ni:zɪə/ n amnésia f
amnesty /'æmnəstɪ/ n anistia f, (P) amnistia f
amok /ə'mɒk/ adv **run ~** enlouquecer; (crowd) correr desordenadamente
among(st) /ə'mʌŋ(st)/ prep entre, no meio de. **~ ourselves** (aqui) entre nós
amoral /eɪ'mɒrəl/ a amoral
amorous /'æmərəs/ a amoroso
amount /ə'maʊnt/ n quantidade f; (total) montante m; (sum of money) quantia f □ vi **~ to** elevar-se a; (fig) equivaler a
amp /æmp/ n (colloq) ampère m
amphibi|an /æm'fɪbɪən/ n anfíbio m. **~ous** a anfíbio
ampl|e /'æmpl/ a (-er, -est) (large, roomy) amplo; (enough) suficiente, bastante. **~y** adv amplamente
amplif|y /'æmplɪfaɪ/ vt ampliar, amplificar. **~ier** n amplificador m
amputat|e /'æmpjuteɪt/ vt amputar. **~ion** /-'teɪʃn/ n amputação f
amus|e /ə'mju:z/ vt divertir. **~ement** n divertimento m. **~ ing** a divertido
an /ən, æn/ see **a**
anachronism /ə'nækrənɪzəm/ n anacronismo m
anaem|ia /ə'ni:mɪə/ n anemia f. **~ic** a anêmico, (P) anémico
anaesthetic /ænɪs'θetɪk/ n anestético m, (P) anestésico m. **give an ~ to** anestesiar
anaesthetist /ə'ni:sθətɪst/ n anestesista mf
anagram /'ænəgræm/ n anagrama m
analog(ue) /'ænəlɒg/ a análogo
analogy /ə'nælədʒɪ/ n analogia f
analys|e /'ænəlaɪz/ vt analisar. **~t** /-ɪst/ n analista mf
analysis /ə'næləsɪs/ n (pl **-yses**) /-əsi:z/ análise f
analytic(al) /ænə'lɪtɪk(l)/ a analítico
anarch|y /'ænəkɪ/ n anarquia f. **~ist** n anarquista mf
anatom|y /ə'nætəmɪ/ n anatomia f. **~ical** /ænə'tɒmɪkl/ a anatômico, (P) anatómico
ancest|or /'ænsestə(r)/ n antepassado m. **~ral** /-'sestrəl/ a ancestral (pl -ais)
ancestry /'ænsestrɪ/ n ascendência f, estirpe f
anchor /'æŋkə(r)/ n âncora f □ vt/i ancorar. **~age** /-rɪdʒ/ n ancoradouro m
anchovy /'æntʃəvɪ/ n enchova f, (P) anchova f
ancient /'eɪnʃənt/ a antigo
ancillary /æn'sɪlərɪ/ a ancilar, (P) subordinado
and /ənd/; emphatic /ænd/ conj e. **go ~ see** vá ver. **better ~ better/less ~ less** etc cada vez melhor/menos etc

anecdote /'ænɪkdəʊt/ n anedota f
angel /'eɪndʒl/ n anjo m. **~ic** /æn'dʒelɪk/ a angélico, angelical
anger /'æŋgə(r)/ n cólera f, zanga f □ vt irritar
angle[1] /'æŋgl/ n ângulo m
angle[2] /'æŋgl/ vi (fish) pescar (à linha). **~ for** (fig: compliments, information) andar à procura de. **~r** /-ə(r)/ n pescador m
anglicism /'æŋglɪsɪzəm/ n anglicismo m
Anglo- /'æŋgləʊ/ pref anglo-
Anglo-Saxon /'æŋgləʊ'sæksn/ a & n anglo-saxão (m)
angr|y /'æŋgrɪ/ a (-ier, -iest) zangado. **get ~y** zangar-se (with com). **~ily** adv furiosamente
anguish /'æŋgwɪʃ/ n angústia f
angular /'æŋgjʊlə(r)/ a angular; (features) anguloso
animal /'ænɪml/ a & n animal (m)
animate[1] /'ænɪmət/ a animado
animat|e[2] /'ænɪmeɪt/ vt animar. **~ion** /-'meɪʃn/ n animação f. **~ed cartoon** filme m de bonecos animados, (P) de desenhos animados
animosity /ænɪ'mɒsətɪ/ n animosidade f
aniseed /'ænɪsi:d/ n semente f de anis
ankle /'æŋkl/ n tornozelo m. **~ sock** meia f soquete
annex /ə'neks/ vt anexar. **~ation** /ænek'seɪʃn/ n anexação f
annexe /'æneks/ n anexo m
annihilate /ə'naɪəleɪt/ vt aniquilar
anniversary /ænɪ'vɜːsərɪ/ n aniversário m
announce /ə'naʊns/ vt anunciar. **~ment** n anúncio m. **~r** /-ə(r)/ n (radio, TV) locutor m
annoy /ə'nɔɪ/ vt irritar, aborrecer. **~ance** n aborrecimento m. **~ed** a aborrecido (with com). **get ~ed** aborrecer-se. **~ing** a irritante
annual /'ænjʊəl/ a anual □ n (bot) planta f anual; (book) anuário m. **~ly** adv anualmente
annuity /ə'nju:ətɪ/ n anuidade f
annul /ə'nʌl/ vt (pt annulled) anular. **~ment** n anulação f
anomal|y /ə'nɒməlɪ/ n anomalia f. **~ous** a anômalo, (P) anómalo
anonym|ous /ə'nɒnɪməs/ a anônimo, (P) anónimo. **~ity** /ænə'nɪmətɪ/ n anonimato m
anorak /'ænəræk/ n anoraque m, anorak m
another /ə'nʌðə(r)/ a & pron (um) outro. **~ ten minutes** mais de dez minutos. **to one ~** um ao outro, uns aos outros

a

answer /'a:nsə(r)/ n resposta f; (solution) solução f □ vt responder a; (prayer) atender a □ vi responder. ∼ **the door** atender à porta. ∼ **back** retrucar, (P) responder torto. ∼ **for** responder por. ∼**able** a responsável (**for** por; **to** perante). ∼**ing machine** n secretária f eletrónica

ant /ænt/ n formiga f

antagonis|m /æn'tægənɪzəm/ n antagonismo m. ∼**t** n antagonista mf. ∼**tic** /-'nɪstɪk/ a antagónico, (P) antagónico, hostil

antagonize /æn'tægənaɪz/ vt antagonizar, hostilizar

Antarctic /æn'ta:ktɪk/ n Antártico, (P) Antárctico m □ a antártico, (P) antárctico

ante- /'æntɪ/ pref ante-

antecedent /æntɪ'si:dnt/ a & n antecedente (m)

antelope /'æntɪləʊp/ n antílope m

antenatal /æntɪ'neɪtl/ a pré-natal

antenna /æn'tenə/ n (pl -ae /-i:/) antena f

anthem /'ænθəm/ n cântico m. **national** ∼ hino m nacional

anthology /æn'θɒlədʒɪ/ n antologia f

anthropolog|y /ænθrə'pɒlədʒɪ/ n antropologia f. ∼**ist** n antropólogo m

anti- /ænti/ pref anti-. ∼**-aircraft** /-eəkra:ft/ a antiaéreo

antibiotic /æntɪbaɪ'ɒtɪk/ n antibiótico m

antibody /'æntɪbɒdɪ/ n anticorpo m

anticipat|e /æn'tɪsɪpeɪt/ vt (foresee, expect) prever; (forestall) antecipar-se a. ∼**ion** /-'peɪʃn/ n antecipação f; (expectation) expectativa f. **in** ∼**ion of** na previsão or expectativa de

anticlimax /æntɪ'klaɪmæks/ n anticlímax m; (let-down) decepção f. **it was an** ∼ não correspondeu à expectativa

anticlockwise /æntɪ'klɒkwaɪz/ adv & a no sentido contrário ao dos ponteiros dum relógio

antics /'æntɪks/ npl (of clown) palhaçadas fpl; (behaviour) comportamento m bizarro

anticyclone /ˌæntɪ'saɪkləʊn/ n anticiclone m

antidote /'æntɪdəʊt/ n antídoto m

antifreeze /'æntɪfri:z/ n anticongelante m

antihistamine /æntɪ'hɪstəmi:n/ a & n anti-histamínico (m)

antipathy /æn'tɪpəθɪ/ n antipatia f

antiquated /'æntɪkweɪtɪd/ a antiquado

antique /æn'ti:k/ a antigo □ n antiguidade f. ∼ **dealer** antiquário m. ∼ **shop** loja f de antiguidades, (P) antiquário m

antiquity /æn'tɪkwətɪ/ n antiguidade f

antiseptic /æntɪ'septɪk/ a & n antiséptico (m)

antisocial /æntɪ'səʊʃl/ a anti-social; (unsociable) insociável

antithesis /æn'tɪθəsɪs/ n (pl -eses) /-si:z/ antítese f.

antlers /'æntləz/ npl chifres mpl, esgalhos mpl

antonym /'æntənɪm/ n antônimo m, (P) antónimo m

anus /'eməs/ n ânus m

anvil /'ænvɪl/ n bigorna f

anxiety /æŋ'zaɪətɪ/ n ansiedade f; (eagerness) ânsia f

anxious /'æŋkʃəs/ a (worried, eager) ansioso (**to** de, por). ∼**ly** adv ansiosamente; (eagerly) impacientemente

any /'enɪ/ a & pron qualquer, quaisquer; (in neg and interr sentences) algum, alguns; (in neg sentences) nenhum, nenhuns; (every) todo. **at** ∼ **moment** a qualquer momento. **at** ∼ **rate** de qualquer modo, em todo o caso. **in** ∼ **case** em todo o caso. **have you** ∼ **money/friends?** você tem (algum) dinheiro/(alguns) amigos? **I don't have** ∼ **time** não tenho nenhum tempo or tempo nenhum or tempo algum. **has she** ∼? ela tem algum? **she doesn't have** ∼ ela não tem nenhum □ adv (at all) de modo algum or nenhum; (a little) um pouco. ∼ **the less/the worse** etc menos/pior etc

anybody /'enɪbɒdɪ/ pron qualquer pessoa; (somebody) alguém; (after negative) ninguém. **he didn't see** ∼ ele não viu ninguém

anyhow /'enɪhaʊ/ adv (no matter how) de qualquer modo; (badly) de qualquer maneira, ao acaso; (in any case) em todo o caso. **you can try,** ∼ em todo o caso, você pode tentar

anyone /'enɪwʌn/ pron = anybody

anything /'enɪθɪŋ/ pron (something) alguma coisa; (no matter what) qualquer coisa; (after negative) nada. **he didn't say** ∼ não disse nada. **it is** ∼ **but cheap** é tudo menos barato. ∼ **you do** tudo o que você fizer

anyway /'enɪweɪ/ adv de qualquer modo; (in any case) em todo o caso

anywhere /'enɪweə(r)/ adv (some-where) em qualquer parte; (after negative) em parte alguma/nenhuma. ∼ **else** em qualquer outro lado. ∼ **you go** quer que você vá. **he doesn't go** ∼ ele não vai a lado nenhum

apart /ə'pa:t/ adv à parte; (separated) separado; (into pieces) aos bocados. ∼ **from** à parte, além de. **ten metres** ∼ a dez metros de distância entre si.

come ~ desfazer-se. keep ~ manter separado. take ~ desmontar

apartment /ə'pɑ:tmənt/ n (Amer) apartamento m. ~s aposentos mpl

apath|y /'æpəθɪ/ n apatia f. ~etic /-'θetɪk/ a apático

ape /eɪp/ n macaco m □ vt macaquear

aperitif /ə'perətɪf/ n aperitivo m

aperture /'æpətʃə(r)/ n abertura f

apex /'eɪpeks/ n ápice m, cume m

apiece /ə'pi:s/ adv cada, por cabeça

apologetic /əpɒlə'dʒetɪk/ a (tone etc) apologético, de desculpas. be ~ desculpar-se. ~ally /-əlɪ/ adv desculpando-se

apologize /ə'pɒlədʒaɪz/ vi desculpar-se (for de, por; to junto de, perante), pedir desculpa (for, por; to, a)

apology /ə'pɒlədʒɪ/ n desculpa f; (defence of belief) apologia f

apostle /ə'pɒsl/ n apóstolo m

apostrophe /ə'pɒstrəfɪ/ n apóstrofe f

appal /ə'pɔ:l/ vt (pt appalled) estarrecer. ~ling a estarrecedor

apparatus /æpə'reɪtəs/ n aparelho m

apparent /ə'pærənt/ a aparente. ~ly adv aparentemente

apparition /æpə'rɪʃn/ n aparição f

appeal /ə'pi:l/ vi (jur) apelar (to para); (attract) atrair (to a); (for funds) angariar □ n apelo m; (at-tractiveness) atrativo m, (P) atractivo m; (for funds) angariação f. ~ to sb for sth pedir uma coisa a alg. ~ing a (attractive) atraente

appear /ə'pɪə(r)/ vi aparecer; (seem) parecer; (in court, theatre) apresentar-se. ~ance n aparição f; (aspect) aparência f; (in court) comparecimento m, (P) comparência f

appease /ə'pi:z/ vt apaziguar

appendage /ə'pendɪdʒ/ n apêndice m

appendicitis /əpendɪ'saɪtɪs/ n apendicite f

appendix /ə'pendɪks/ n (pl -ices /-si:z/) (of book) apêndice m; (pl -ixes /-ksɪz/) (anat) apêndice m

appetite /'æpɪtaɪt/ n apetite m

appetizer /'æpɪtaɪzə(r)/ n (snack) tira-gosto m, (drink) aperitivo m

appetizing /'æpɪtaɪzɪŋ/ a apetitoso

applau|d /ə'plɔ:d/ vt/i aplaudir. ~se n aplauso(s) m(pl)

apple /'æpl/ n maçã f. ~ tree macieira f

appliance /ə'plaɪəns/ n aparelho m, instrumento m, utensílio m. **household** ~s utensílios mpl domésticos

applicable /'æplɪkəbl/ a aplicável

applicant /'æplɪkənt/ n candidato m (for a)

application /æplɪ'keɪʃn/ n aplicação f; (request) pedido m; (form) formulário m; (for job) candidatura f

appl|y /ə'plaɪ/ vt aplicar □ vi ~y to (refer) aplicar-se a; (ask) dirigir-se a. ~y for (job, grant) candidatar-se a. ~y o.s. to aplicar-se a. ~ied a aplicado

appoint /ə'pɔɪnt/ vt (to post) nomear; (time, date) marcar. well-~ed a bem equipado, bem provido. ~ment n nomeação f; (meeting) entrevista f; (with friends) encontro m; (with doctor etc) consulta f, (P) marcação f; (job) posto m

apprais|e /ə'preɪz/ vt avaliar. ~al n avaliação f

appreciable /ə'pri:ʃəbl/ a apreciável

appreciat|e /ə'pri:ʃɪeɪt/ vt (value) apreciar; (understand) compreender; (be grateful for) estar/ficar grato por □ vi encarecer. ~ion /-'eɪʃn/ n apreciação f; (rise in value) encarecimento m; (gratitude) reconhecimento m. ~ive /ə'pri:ʃɪətɪv/ a apreciador; (grateful) reconhecido

apprehen|d /æprɪ'hend/ vt (seize, understand) apreender; (dread) recear. ~sion n apreensão f

apprehensive /æprɪ'hensɪv/ a apreensivo

apprentice /ə'prentɪs/ n aprendiz, -a mf □ vt pôr como aprendiz (to de). ~ship n aprendizagem f

approach /ə'prəʊtʃ/ vt aproximar; (with request or offer) abordar □ vi aproximar-se □ n aproximação f. ~ to (problem) abordagem f de; (place) acesso m a; (person) diligência junto de. ~able a acessível

appropriate[1] /ə'prəʊprɪət/ a apropriado, próprio. ~ly adv apropriadamente, a propósito

appropriate[2] /ə'prəʊprɪeɪt/ vt apropriar-se de

approval /ə'pru:vl/ n aprovação f. on ~ (comm) sob condição, à aprovação

approv|e /ə'pru:v/ vt/i aprovar. ~e of aprovar. ~ingly adv com ar de aprovação

approximate[1] /ə'prɒksɪmət/ a aproximado. ~ly adv aproximadamente

approximat|e[2] /ə'prɒksɪmeɪt/ vt/i aproximar(-se) de. ~ion /-'meɪʃn/ n aproximação f

apricot /'eɪprɪkɒt/ n damasco m

April /'eɪprəl/ n Abril m. ~ Fool's Day o primeiro de Abril, o dia das mentiras. **make an ~ fool of** pregar uma mentira em, (P) pregar uma mentira a

apron /'eɪprən/ n avential m

apt /æpt/ a apto; (*pupil*) dotado. **be ~ to** ser propenso a. **~ly** adv apropriadamente

aptitude /'æptɪtjuːd/ n aptidão f, (P) aptitude f

aqualung /'ækwəlʌŋ/ n escafandro autónomo, (P) autónomo m

aquarium /ə'kweərɪəm/ n (pl -**ums**) aquário m

Aquarius /ə'kweərɪəs/ n (astr) Aquário m

aquatic /ə'kwætɪk/ a aquático; (sport) náutico, aquático

aqueduct /'ækwɪdʌkt/ n aqueduto m

Arab /'ærəb/ a & n árabe (mf). **~ic** a & n (lang) árabe (m), arábico (m). **a~ic numerals** algarismos mpl árabes or arábicos

Arabian /ə'reɪbɪən/ a árabe

arable /'ærəbl/ a arável

arbitrary /'ɑːbɪtrərɪ/ a arbitrário

arbitrat|e /'ɑːbɪtreɪt/ vi arbitrar. **~ion** /-'treɪʃn/ n arbitragem f. **~or** n árbitro m

arc /ɑːk/ n arco m. **~ lamp** lâmpada f de arco. **~ welding** soldadura f a arco

arcade /ɑː'keɪd/ n (shop) arcada f. **amusement ~** fliperama m

arch /ɑːtʃ/ n arco m; (vault) abóbada f □ vt/i arquear(-se)

arch- /ɑːtʃ/ pref arqui-.

archaeolog|y /ɑːkɪ'ɒlədʒɪ/ n arqueologia f. **~ical** /-ə'lɒdʒɪkl/ a arqueológico. **~ist** n arqueólogo m

archaic /ɑː'keɪɪk/ a arcaico

archbishop /ɑːtʃ'bɪʃəp/ n arcebispo m

arch-enemy /ɑːtʃ'enəmɪ/ n inimigo m número um

archer /'ɑːtʃə(r)/ n arqueiro m. **~y** n tiro m ao arco

archetype /'ɑːkɪtaɪp/ n arquétipo m

architect /'ɑːkɪtekt/ n arquiteto m, (P) arquitecto m

architectur|e /'ɑːkɪtektʃə(r)/ n arquitetura f, (P) arquitectura f. **~al** /-'tektʃərəl/ a arquitetônico, (P) arquitectónico

archiv|es /'ɑːkaɪvz/ npl arquivo m. **~ist** /-ɪvɪst/ n arquivista mf

archway /'ɑːtʃweɪ/ n arcada f

Arctic /'ɑːktɪk/ n Ártico m, (P) Árctico m □ a ártico, (P) árctico. **~ weather** tempo m glacial

ardent /'ɑːdnt/ a ardente. **~ly** adv ardentemente

ardour /'ɑːdə(r)/ n ardor m

arduous /'ɑːdjʊəs/ a árduo

are /ə(r)/; emphatic /ɑː(r)/ see be

area /'eərɪə/ n área f

arena /ə'riːnə/ n arena f

aren't /ɑːnt/ = are not

Argentin|a /ɑːdʒən'tiːnə/ n Argentina f. **~ian** /-'tɪnɪən/ a & n argentino (m)

argu|e /'ɑːgjuː/ vi discutir; (reason) argumentar, arguir □ vt (debate) discutir. **~e that** alegar que. **~able** a alegável. **it's ~- able that** pode-se sustentar que

argument /'ɑːgjʊmənt/ n (dispute) disputa f; (reasoning) argumento m. **~ative** /-'mentətɪv/ a que gosta de discutir, argumentativo

arid /'ærɪd/ a árido

Aries /'eəriːz/ n (astr) Áries m, Carneiro m

arise /ə'raɪz/ vi (pt arose, pp arisen) surgir. **~ from** resultar de

aristocracy /ærɪ'stɒkrəsɪ/ n aristocracia f

aristocrat /'ærɪstəkræt/ n aristocrata mf. **~ic** /-'krætɪk/ a aristocrático

arithmetic /ə'rɪθmətɪk/ n aritmética f

ark /ɑːk/ n Noah's **~** arca f de Noé

arm[1] /ɑːm/ n braço m. **~ in ~** de braço dado

arm[2] /ɑːm/ vt armar □ n (mil) arma f. **~ed robbery** assalto m à mão armada

armament /'ɑːməmənt/ n armamento m

armchair /'ɑːmtʃeə(r)/ n cadeira f de braços, poltrona f

armistice /'ɑːmɪstɪs/ n armistício m

armour /'ɑːmə(r)/ n armadura f; (on tanks etc) blindagem f. **~ed** a blindado

armoury /'ɑːmərɪ/ n arsenal m

armpit /'ɑːmpɪt/ n axila f, sovaco m

arms /ɑːmz/ npl armas fpl. **coat of ~** brasão m

army /'ɑːmɪ/ n exército m

aroma /ə'rəʊmə/ n aroma m. **~tic** /ærə'mætɪk/ a aromático

arose /ə'rəʊz/ see arise

around /ə'raʊnd/ adv em redor, em volta; (here and there) por aí □ prep em redor de, em torno de, em volta de; (approximately) aproximadamente. **~ here** por aqui

arouse /ə'raʊz/ vt despertar; (excite) excitar

arrange /ə'reɪndʒ/ vt arranjar; (time, date) combinar. **~ to do sth** combinar fazer alg coisa. **~ment** n arranjo m; (agreement) acordo m. **make ~ments (for)** (plans) tomar disposições (para); (preparations) fazer preparativos (para)

array /ə'reɪ/ vt revestir □ n **an ~ of** (display) um leque de, uma série de

arrears /ə'rɪəz/ npl dívidas fpl em atraso, atrasos mpl. **in ~** em atraso

arrest /əˈrest/ vt (*by law*) deter, prender; (*process, movement*) deter □ n captura f. **under ~** sob prisão

arrival /əˈraɪvl/ n chegada f. **new ~** recém-chegado m

arrive /əˈraɪv/ vi chegar

arrogan|t /ˈærəgənt/ a arrogante. **~ce** n arrogância f. **~tly** adv com arrogância

arrow /ˈærəʊ/ n flecha f, seta f

arsenal /ˈɑːsənl/ n arsenal m

arsenic /ˈɑːsnɪk/ n arsénico m, (P) arsénico m

arson /ˈɑːsn/ n fogo m posto. **~ist** n incendiário m

art[1] /ɑːt/ n arte f. **the ~s** (*univ*) letras fpl. **fine ~s** belas-artes fpl. **~ gallery** museu m (de arte); (*private*) galeria f de arte

artery /ˈɑːtərɪ/ n artéria f

artful /ˈɑːtfl/ a manhoso. **~ness** n manha f

arthritis /ɑːˈθraɪtɪs/ n artrite f

artichoke /ˈɑːtɪtʃəʊk/ n alcachofra f. **Jerusalem ~** topinambo m

article /ˈɑːtɪkl/ n artigo m. **~d** a (*jur*) em estágio, (P) a estagiar

articulate[1] /ɑːˈtɪkjʊlət/ a que se exprime com clareza; (*speech*) bem articulado

articulat|e[2] /ɑːˈtɪkjʊleɪt/ vt/i articular. **~ed lorry** camião m articulado. **~ion** /-ˈleɪʃn/ n articulação f

artifice /ˈɑːtɪfɪs/ n artifício m

artificial /ɑːtɪˈfɪʃl/ a artificial

artillery /ɑːˈtɪlərɪ/ n artilharia f

artisan /ɑːtɪˈzæn/ n artífice mf, artesão m, artesã f

artist /ˈɑːtɪst/ n artista mf. **~ic** /-ˈtɪstɪk/ a artístico. **~ry** n arte f

artiste /ɑːˈtiːst/ n artista mf

artless /ˈɑːtlɪs/ a ingénuo, (P) ingénuo, simples

as /əz/; *emphatic* /æz/ adv & conj como; (*while*) enquanto; (*when*) quando. **~ a gift** de presente. **~ tall as** tão alto quanto, (P) tão alto como □ pron que. **I ate the same ~ he** comi o mesmo que ele. **~ for, ~ to** quanto a. **~ from** a partir de. **~ if** como se. **~ much** tanto, tantos. **~ many** quanto, quantos. **~ soon as** logo que. **~ well** (*also*) também. **~ well as** (*in addition to*) assim como

asbestos /æzˈbestəs/ n asbesto m, amianto m

ascend /əˈsend/ vt/i subir. **~ the throne** ascender or subir ao trono

ascent /əˈsent/ n ascensão f; (*slope*) subida f, rampa f

ascertain /æsəˈteɪn/ vt certificar-se de. **~ that** certificar-se de que

ascribe /əˈskraɪb/ vt atribuir

ash[1] /æʃ/ n **~(-tree)** freixo m

ash[2] /æʃ/ n cinza f. **A~Wednesday** Quarta-feira f de Cinzas. **~en** a pálido

ashamed /əˈʃeɪmd/ a **be ~** ter vergonha, ficar envergonhado (**of** de, por)

ashore /əˈʃɔː(r)/ adv em terra. **go ~** desembarcar

ashtray /ˈæʃtreɪ/ n cinzeiro m

Asia /ˈeɪʃə/ n Ásia f. **~n** a & n asiático (m)

aside /əˈsaɪd/ adv de lado, de parte □ n (*theat*) aparte m. **~ from** (*Amer*) à parte

ask /ɑːsk/ vt/i pedir; (*a question*) perguntar; (*invite*) convidar. **~ sb sth** pedir uma coisa a alguém. **~ about** informar-se de. **~ after sb** pedir noticias de alg, perguntar por alg. **~ for** pedir. **~ sb in** mandar entrar alg. **~ sb to do sth** pedir alguém para fazer alguma coisa

askew /əˈskjuː/ adv & a de través, de esguelha

asleep /əˈsliːp/ adv & a adormecido; (*numb*) dormente. **fall ~** adormecer

asparagus /əˈspærəgəs/ n (*plant*) aspargo m, (P) espargo m; (*culin*) aspargos mpl, (P) espargo m

aspect /ˈæspekt/ n aspecto m; (*direction*) exposição f

aspersions /əˈspɜːʃnz/ npl **cast ~ on** caluniar

asphalt /ˈæsfælt/ n asfalto m □ vt asfaltar

asphyxiat|e /əsˈfɪksɪeɪt/ vt/i asfixiar. **~ion** /-ˈeɪʃn/ n asfixia f

aspir|e /əsˈpaɪə(r)/ vi **~e to** aspirar a. **~ation** /æspəˈreɪʃn/ n aspiração f

aspirin /ˈæsprɪn/ n aspirina f

ass /æs/ n burro m. **make an ~ of o.s.** fazer papel de palhaço, (P) fazer figura de parvo

assail /əˈseɪl/ vt assaltar, agredir. **~ant** n assaltante mf, agressor m

assassin /əˈsæsɪn/ n assassino m

assassinat|e /əˈsæsɪneɪt/ vt assassinar. **~ion** /-ˈeɪʃn/ n assassinato m

assault /əˈsɔːlt/ n assalto m □ vt assaltar, atacar

assemble /əˈsembl/ vt (*people*) reunir; (*fit together*) montar □ vi reunir-se

assembly /əˈsemblɪ/ n assembleia f, (P) assembleia f. **~ line** linha f de montagem

assent /əˈsent/ n assentimento m □ vi **~ to** consentir em

assert /əˈsɜːt/ vt afirmar; (*one's rights*) reivindicar. **~ o.s.** impor-se. **~ion** /-ʃn/ n asserção f. **~ive** a dogmático, peremptório. **~iveness** n assertividade f, (P) firmeza f

a

assess /əˈses/ avaliar; (*payment*) estabelecer o montante de. **~ment** *n* avaliação *f*. **~or** *n* (*valuer*) avaliador *m*

asset /ˈæset/ *n* (*advantage*) vantagem *f*. **~s** (*comm*) ativo *m*, (*P*) activo *m*; (*possessions*) bens *mpl*

assiduous /əˈsɪdjʊəs/ *a* assíduo

assign /əˈsam/ *vt* atribuir, destinar; (*jur*) transmitir. **~ sb to** designar alg para

assignation /æsɪgˈneɪʃn/ *n* combinação *f* (de hora e local) de encontro

assignment /əˈsammənt/ *n* tarefa *f*, missão *f*; (*jur*) transmissão *f*

assimilat|e /əˈsɪmɪleɪt/ *vt/i* assimilar(-se). **~ion** /-ˈeɪʃn/ *n* assimilação *f*

assist /əˈsɪst/ *vt/i* ajudar. **~ance** *n* ajuda *f*, assistência *f*

assistant /əˈsɪstənt/ *n* (*helper*) assistente *mf*, auxiliar *mf*; (*in shop*) ajudante *mf*, empregado *m* ☐ *a* adjunto

associat|e[1] /əˈsəʊʃieɪt/ *vt* associar ☐ *vi* **~e with** conviver com. **~ion** /-ˈeɪʃn/ *n* associação *f*

associate[2] /əˈsəʊʃiət/ *a & n* associado (*m*)

assort|ed /əˈsɔːtɪd/ *a* variados; (*foods*) sortidos. **~ment** *n* sortimento *m*, (*P*) sortido *m*

assume /əˈsjuːm/ *vt* assumir; (*presume*) supor, presumir

assumption /əˈsʌmpʃn/ *n* suposição *f*

assurance /əˈʃʊərəns/ *n* certeza *f*, garantia *f*; (*insurance*) seguro *m*; (*self-confidence*) segurança *f*, confiança *f*

assure /əˈʃʊə(r)/ *vt* assegurar. **~d** *a* certo, garantido. **rest ~d that** ficar certo que

asterisk /ˈæstərɪsk/ *n* asterisco *m*

asthma /ˈæsmə/ *n* asma *f*. **~tic** /-ˈmætɪk/ *a & n* asmático (*m*)

astonish /əˈstɒnɪʃ/ *vt* espantar. **~ingly** *adv* espantosamente. **~ment** *n* espanto *m*

astound /əˈstaʊnd/ *vt* assombrar

astray /əˈstreɪ/ *adv & a* **go ~** perder-se, extraviar-se. **lead ~** desencaminhar

astride /əˈstraɪd/ *adv & prep* escarranchado (em)

astringent /əˈstrɪndʒənt/ *a & n* adstringente (*m*)

astrolog|y /əˈstrɒlədʒɪ/ *n* astrologia *f*. **~er** *n* astrólogo *m*

astronaut /ˈæstrənɔːt/ *n* astronauta *mf*

astronom|y /əˈstrɒnəmɪ/ *n* astronomia *f*. **~er** *n* astrônomo *m*, (*P*) astrónomo *m*. **~ical** /æstrəˈnɒmɪkl/ *a* astronômico, (*P*) astronómico

astute /əˈstjuːt/ *a* astuto, astucioso. **~ness** *n* astúcia *f*

asylum /əˈsaɪləm/ *n* asilo *m*

at /ət/; *emphatic* /æt/ *prep* a, em. **~ sign** *m* arroba. **~ home** em casa. **~ night** à noite. **~ once** imediatamente; (*simultaneously*) ao mesmo tempo. **~ school** na escola. **~ sea** no mar. **~ the door** na porta. **~ times** às vezes. **angry/ surprised ~** zangado/ surpreendido com. **not ~ all** de nada. **no wind ~ all** nenhum vento

ate /et/ *see* eat

atheis|t /ˈeɪθɪɪst/ *n* ateu *m*. **~m** /-zəm/ *n* ateísmo *m*

athlet|e /ˈæθliːt/ *n* atleta *mf*. **~ic** /-ˈletɪk/ *a* atlético. **~ics** /-ˈletɪks/ *n(pl)* atletismo *m*

Atlantic /ətˈlæntɪk/ *a* atlântico ☐ *n* **~ (Ocean)** Atlântico *m*

atlas /ˈætləs/ *n* atlas *m*

atmospher|e /ˈætməsfɪə(r)/ *n* atmosfera *f*. **~ic** /-ˈferɪk/ *a* atmosférico

atom /ˈætəm/ *n* átomo *m*. **~ic** /əˈtɒmɪk/ *a* atômico, (*P*) atómico. **~(ic) bomb** bomba *f* atômica

atomize /ˈætəmaɪz/ *vt* atomizar, vaporizar, pulverizar. **~r** /-ə(r)/ *n* pulverizador *m*, vaporizador *m*

atone /əˈtəʊn/ *vi* **~ for** expiar. **~ment** *n* expiação *f*

atrocious /əˈtrəʊʃəs/ *a* atroz

atrocity /əˈtrɒsətɪ/ *n* atrocidade *f*

atrophy /ˈætrəfɪ/ *n* atrofia *f* ☐ *vt/i* atrofiar(-se)

attach /əˈtætʃ/ *vt/i* (*affix*) ligar (-se), prender(-se); (*join*) juntar (-se). **~ed** *a* (*document*) junto, anexo. **be ~ed to** (*like*) estar apegado a. **~ment** *n* ligação *f*; (*affection*) apego *m*; (*accessory*) acessório *m*

attaché /əˈtæʃeɪ/ *n* (*pol*) adido *m*. **~ case** pasta *f*

attack /əˈtæk/ *n* ataque *m* ☐ *vt/i* atacar. **~er** *n* atacante *mf*

attain /əˈteɪn/ *vt* atingir. **~able** *a* atingível. **~ment** *n* consecução *f*. **~ments** *npl* conhecimentos *mpl*, talentos *mpl* adquiridos

attempt /əˈtempt/ *vt* tentar ☐ *n* tentativa *f*

attend /əˈtend/ *vt/i* atender (**to** a); (*escort*) acompanhar; (*look after*) tratar; (*meeting*) comparecer a; (*school*) freqüentar, (*P*) frequentar. **~ance** *n* comparecimento *m*; (*times present*) freqüência *f*, (*P*) frequência *f*; (*people*) assistência *f*

attendant /əˈtendənt/ *a* concomitante, que acompanha ☐ *n* empregado *m*; (*servant*) servidor *m*

attention /əˈtenʃn/ *n* atenção *f*. **~!** (*mil*) sentido! **pay ~** prestar atenção (**to** a)

attentive /əˈtentɪv/ *a* atento; (*considerate*) atencioso

attest /ə'test/ *vt/i* ~ **(to)** atestar. ~ **a signature** reconhecer uma assinatura. ~**ation** /ætə'steɪʃn/ *n* atestação *f*, prova *f*

attic /'ætɪk/ *n* sótão *m*, água-furtada *f*

attitude /'ætɪtjuːd/ *n* atitude *f*

attorney /ə'tɜːnɪ/ *n* (*pl* -**eys**) procurador *m*; (*Amer*) advogado *m*

attract /ə'trækt/ *vt* atrair. ~**ion** /-ʃn/ *n* atração *f*, (*P*) atracção *f*; (*charm*) atrativo *m*, (*P*) atractivo *m*

attractive /ə'træktɪv/ *a* atraente. ~**ly** *adv* atraentemente, agradavelmente

attribute[1] /ə'trɪbjuːt/ *vt* ~ **to** atribuir a

attribute[2] /'ætrɪbjuːt/ *n* atributo *m*

attrition /ə'trɪʃn/ *n* **war of** ~ guerra *f* de desgaste

aubergine /'əʊbəʒiːn/ *n* berinjela *f*

auburn /'ɔːbən/ *a* cor de acaju, castanho-avermelhado

auction /'ɔːkʃn/ *n* leilão *m* □ *vt* leiloar. ~**eer** /-'nɪə(r)/ *n* leiloeiro *m*, (*P*) pregoeiro *m*

audaci|ous /ɔː'deɪʃəs/ *a* audacioso, audaz. ~**ty** /-æsətɪ/ *n* audácia *f*

audible /'ɔːdəbl/ *a* audível

audience /'ɔːdɪəns/ *n* auditório *m*; (*theat, radio; interview*) audiência *f*

audiovisual /ɔːdɪəʊ'vɪʒʊəl/ *a* audiovisual

audit /'ɔːdɪt/ *n* auditoria *f* □ *vt* fazer uma auditoria

audition /ɔː'dɪʃn/ *n* audição *f* □ *vt* dar/ fazer uma audição

auditor /'ɔːdɪtə(r)/ *n* perito-contador *m*, (*P*) perito-contabilista *m*

auditorium /ɔːdɪ'tɔːrɪəm/ *n* auditório *m*

augment /ɔːg'ment/ *vt/i* aumentar(-se)

augur /'ɔːgə(r)/ *vi* ~ **well/ill** ser de bom ou mau agouro

August /'ɔːgəst/ *n* Agosto *m*

aunt /ɑːnt/ *n* tia *f*

au pair /əʊ'peə(r)/ *n* au pair *f*

aura /'ɔːrə/ *n* aura *f*, emanação *f*

auspices /'ɔːspɪsɪz/ *npl* **under the** ~ **of** sob os auspícios *or* o patrocínio de

auspicious /ɔː'spɪʃəs/ *a* auspicioso

auster|e /ɔː'stɪə(r)/ *a* austero. ~**ity** /-erətɪ/ *n* austeridade *f*

Australia /ɒ'streɪlɪə/ *n* Austrália *f*. ~**n** *a &n* australiano (*m*)

Austria /'ɒstrɪə/ *n* Áustria *f*. ~**n** *a & n* austríaco (*m*)

authentic /ɔː'θentɪk/ *a* autêntico. ~**ity** /-ən'tɪsətɪ/ *n* autenticidade *f*

authenticate /ɔː'θentɪkeɪt/ *vt* autenticar

author /'ɔːθə(r)/ *n* autor *m*, autora *f*. ~**ship** *n* (*origin*) autoria *f*

authoritarian /ɔːθɒrɪ'teərɪən/ *a* autoritário

authorit|y /ɔː'θɒrətɪ/ *n* autoridade *f*; (*permission*) autorização *f*. ~**ative** /-ɪtətɪv/ *a* (*trusted*) autorizado; (*manner*) autoritário

authoriz|e /'ɔːθəraɪz/ *vt* autorizar. ~**ation** /-'zeɪʃn/ *n* autorização *f*

autistic /ɔː'tɪstɪk/ *a* autista, autístico

autobiography /ɔːtə'baɪɒgrəfɪ/ *n* autobiografia *f*

autocrat /'ɔːtəkræt/ *n* autocrata *mf*. ~**ic** /-'krætɪk/ *a* autocrático

autograph /'ɔːtəgrɑːf/ *n* autógrafo *m* □ *vt* autografar

automat|e /'ɔːtəmeɪt/ *vt* automatizar. ~**ion** /ɔːtə'meɪʃn/ *n* automação *f*

automatic /ɔːtə'mætɪk/ *a* automático □ *n* (*car*) automático *m*. ~**ally** /-klɪ/ *adv* automaticamente

automobile /'ɔːtəməbiːl/ *n* (*Amer*) automóvel *m*

autonom|y /ɔː'tɒnəmɪ/ *n* autonomia *f*. ~**ous** *a* autônomo, (*P*) autónomo

autopsy /'ɔːtɒpsɪ/ *n* autópsia *f*

autumn /'ɔːtəm/ *n* outono *m*. ~**al** /-'tʌmnəl/ *a* outonal

auxiliary /ɔːg'zɪlɪərɪ/ *a & n* auxiliar (*mf*). ~ **verb** verbo *m* auxiliar

avail /ə'veɪl/ *vt* ~ **o.s. of** servir-se de □ *vi* (*be of use*) valer □ *n* **of no** ~ inútil. **to no** ~ sem resultado, em vão

availab|le /ə'veɪləbl/ *a* disponível. ~**ility** /-'bɪlətɪ/ *n* disponibilidade *f*

avalanche /'ævəlɑːnʃ/ *n* avalanche *f*

avaric|e /'ævərɪs/ *n* avareza *f*. ~**ious** /-'rɪʃəs/ *a* avarento

avenge /ə'vendʒ/ *vt* vingar

avenue /'ævənjuː/ *n* avenida *f*; (*fig: line of approach*) via *f*

average /'ævərɪdʒ/ *n* média *f* □ *a* médio □ *vt* tirar a média de; (*produce, do*) fazer em média □ *vi* ~ **out at** dar de média, dar uma média de. **on** ~ em média

avers|e /ə'vɜːs/ *a* **be** ~**e to** ser avesso a. ~**ion** /-ʃn/ *n* aversão *f*, repugnância *f*

avert /ə'vɜːt/ *vt* (*turn away*) desviar; (*ward off*) evitar

aviary /'eɪvɪərɪ/ *n* aviário *n*

aviation /eɪvɪ'eɪʃn/ *n* aviação *f*

avid /'ævɪd/ *a* ávido

avocado /ævə'kɑːdəʊ/ *n* (*pl* -**s**) abacate *m*

avoid /ə'vɔɪd/ *vt* evitar. ~**able** *a* que se pode evitar, evitável. ~**ance** *n* evitação *f*

await /ə'weɪt/ *vt* aguardar

awake /ə'weɪk/ *vt/i* (*pt* **awoke**, *pp* **awoken**) acordar □ *a* **be** ~ estar acordado

awaken /ə'weɪkən/ *vt/i* despertar. ~**ing** *n* despertar *m*

award /ə'wɔːd/ *vt* atribuir, conferir; (*jur*) adjudicar □ *n* recompensa *f*, prêmio *m*, (*P*) prémio *m*; (*scholarship*) bolsa *f*

a

b

aware /əˈweə(r)/ *a* ciente, cônscio. **be ~ of** estar consciente de *or* ter consciência de. **become ~ of** tomar consciência de. **make sb ~ of** sensibilizar alg para. **~ness** *n* consciência *f*

away /əˈweɪ/ *adv* (*at a distance*) longe; (*to a distance*) para longe; (*absent*) fora; (*persistently*) sem parar; (*entirely*) completamente. **eight miles ~** a oito milhas (de distância). **four days ~** daí a quatro dias □ *a & n* ~ (**match**) jogo *m* fora de casa

awe /ɔː/ *n* assombro *m*, admiração *f* reverente, terror *m* respeitoso. **~some** *a* assombroso. **~struck** *a* assombrado, aterrado

awful /ˈɔːfl/ *a* terrível. **~ly** *adv* muito, terrivelmente

awhile /əˈwaɪl/ *adv* por algum tempo

awkward /ˈɔːkwəd/ *a* difícil; (*clumsy, difficult to use*) desajeitado, maljeitoso; (*inconvenient*) inconveniente; (*embarrassing*) embaraçoso; (*embarrassed*) embaraçado. **an ~ customer** (*colloq*) um preguês perigoso *or* intratável

awning /ˈɔːnɪŋ/ *n* toldo *m*

awoke, awoken /əˈwəʊk, əˈwəʊkən/ *see* **awake**

awry /əˈraɪ/ *adv* torto. **go ~** dar errado. **be ~** estar torto

axe /æks/ *n* machado *m* □ *vt* (*pres p* **axing**) (*reduce*) cortar; (*dismiss*) despedir

axiom /ˈæksɪəm/ *n* axioma *m*

axis /ˈæksɪs/ *n* (*pl* **axes** /-iːz/) eixo *m*

axle /ˈæksl/ *n* eixo (de roda) *m*

Azores /əˈzɔːz/ *n* Açores *mpl*

....

Bb

....

BA *abbr see* **Bachelor of Arts**

babble /ˈbæbl/ *vi* balbuciar; (*baby*) palrar; (*stream*) murmurar □ *n* balbucio *m*; (*of baby*) palrice *f*; (*of stream*) murmúrio *m*

baboon /bəˈbuːn/ *n* babuíno *m*

baby /ˈbeɪbɪ/ *n* bebé *m*, (*P*) bebé *m*. **~ carriage** (*Amer*) carrinho *m* de bebê, (*P*) bebé. **~-sit** *vi* tomar conta de crianças. **~-sitter** *n* baby-sitter *mf*, babá *f*

babyish /ˈbeɪbɪʃ/ *a* infantil

bachelor /ˈbætʃələ(r)/ *n* solteiro *m*. **B~ of Arts/Science** Bacharel *m* em Letras/ Ciencias

back /bæk/ *n* (*of person, hand, chair*) costas *fpl*; (*of animal*) dorso *m*; (*of car, train*) parte *f* traseira; (*of house, room*) fundo *m*; (*of coin*) reverso *m*; (*of page*) verso *m*; (*football*) beque *m*; zagueiro *m*, (*P*) defesa *m* □ *a* traseiro, posterior; (*taxes*) em atraso □ *adv* atrás, para trás; (*returned*) de volta □ *vt* (*support*) apoiar; (*horse*) apostar em; (*car*) (fazer) recuar □ *vi* recuar. **at the ~ of beyond** em casa do diabo, no fim do mundo. **~-bencher** *n* (*pol*) deputado *m* sem pasta. **~ down** desistir (**from** de). **~ number** número *m* atrasado. **~ out** (*of an undertaking etc*) desistir. **~ up** (*auto*) fazer marcha à ré, (*P*) atrás; (*comput*) tirar um back-up de. **~-up** *n* apoio *m*; (*comput*) back-up *m*; (*Amer: traffic-jam*) engarrafamento *m* □ *a* de reserva; (*comput*) back-up

backache /ˈbækeɪk/ *n* dor *f* nas costas

backbiting /ˈbækbaɪtɪŋ/ *n* maledicência *f*

backbone /ˈbækbəʊn/ *n* espinha *f* dorsal

backdate /bækˈdeɪt/ *vt* antedatar

backer /ˈbækə(r)/ *n* (*of horse*) apostador *m*; (*of cause*) partidário *m*, apoiante *mf*; (*comm*) patrocinador *m*, financiador *m*

backfire /bækˈfaɪə(r)/ *vi* (*auto*) dar explosões no tubo de escape; (*fig*) sair o tiro pela culatra

background /ˈbækgraʊnd/ *n* (*of picture*) fundo *m*, segundo-plano *m*; (*context*) contexto *m*; (*environment*) meio *m*; (*experience*) formação *f*

backhand /ˈbækhænd/ *n* (*tennis*) esquerda *f*. **~ed** *a* com as costas da mão. **~ed compliment** cumprimento *m* ambéguo. **~er** /-ˈhændə(r)/ *n* (*sl: bribe*) suborno *m*, (*P*) luvas *fpl* (*colloq*)

backing /ˈbækɪŋ/ *n* apoio *m*; (*comm*) patrocínio *m*

backlash /ˈbæklæʃ/ *n* (*fig*) reação *f* violenta, repercussões *fpl*

backlog /ˈbæklɒg/ *n* acúmulo *m* (de trabalho *etc*)

backside /ˈbæksaɪd/ *n* (*colloq: buttocks*) traseiro *m*

backstage /bækˈsteɪdʒ/ *a & adv* por detrás dos bastidores

backstroke /ˈbækstrəʊk/ *n* nado *m* de costas

backtrack /ˈbæktræk/ *vi* (*fig*) voltar atrás

b

backward /'bækwəd/ a retrógrado; (*retarded*) atrasado; (*step, look, etc*) para trás

backwards /'bækwədz/ adv para trás; (*walk*) para trás; (*fall*) de costas, para trás; (*in reverse order*) de trás para diante, às avessas. **go ~ and forwards** ir e vir, andar para trás e para a frente. **know sth ~** saber alg coisa de trás para a frente

backwater /'bækwɔːtə(r)/ n (*pej: place*) lugar m atrasado

bacon /'beɪkən/ n toucinho m defumado; (*in rashers*) bacon m

bacteria /bæk'tɪərɪə/ npl bactérias fpl. ~l a bacteriano

bad /bæd/ a (*worse, worst*) mau; (*accident*) grave; (*food*) estragado; (*ill*) doente. **feel ~** sentir-se mal. **~ language** palavrões mpl. **~-mannered** a mal educado. **~-tempered** a mal humorado. **~ly** adv mal; (*seriously*) gravemente. **want ~ly** (*desire*) desejar imensamente, ter grande vontade de; (*need*) precisar muito de

badge /bædʒ/ n emblema m; (*policeman's*) crachá m, (P) distintivo m

badger /'bædʒə(r)/ n texugo m ▯ vt atormentar; (*pester*) importunar

badminton /'bædmɪntən/ n badminton m

baffle /'bæfl/ vt atrapalhar, desconcertar

bag /bæg/ n saco m; (*handbag*) bolsa f, carteira f. **~s** (*luggage*) malas fpl ▯ vt (*pt bagged*) ensacar; (*colloq: take*) embolsar

baggage /'bægɪdʒ/ n bagagem f

baggy /'bægɪ/ a (*clothes*) muito largo, bufante

bagpipes /'bægpaɪps/ npl gaita f de foles

Bahamas /bə'haːməz/ npl the ~ as Bahamas fpl

bail[1] /beɪl/ n fiança f ▯ vt pôr em liberdade sob fiança. **be out on ~** estar solto sob fiança

bail[2] /beɪl/ vt ~ (**out**) (*naut*) esgotar, tirar água de

bailiff /'beɪlɪf/ n (*officer*) oficial m de diligências; (*of estate*) feitor m

bait /beɪt/ n isca f ▯ vt pôr isca; (*fig*) atormentar (com insultos), atazanar

bak|e /beɪk/ vt/i cozer (no forno); (*bread, cakes, etc*) assar; (*in the sun*) torrar. **~er** n padeiro m; (*of cakes*) doceiro m. **~ing** n cozedura f, (*batch*) fornada f. **~ing-powder** n fermento m em pó. **~ing tin** forma f

bakery /'beɪkərɪ/ n padaria f, (*cakes*) confeitaria f

balance /'bæləns/ n equilíbrio m; (*scales*) balança f; (*sum*) saldo m; (*comm*)

balanço m. **~ of power** equilíbrio m político. **~ of trade** balança f comercial. **~-sheet** n balanço m ▯ vt equilibrar; (*weigh up*) pesar; (*budget*) equilibrar ▯ vi equilibrar-se. **~d** a equilibrado

balcony /'bælkənɪ/ n balcão m; (*in a house*) varanda f

bald /bɔːld/ a (*-er, -est*) calvo, careca; (*tyre*) careca. **~ing** a be ~ing ficar calvo. **~ly** adv a nu e cru, (P) secamente. **~ness** n calvície f

bale[1] /beɪl/ n (*of straw*) fardo m; (*of cotton*) balote m ▯ vt enfardar

bale[2] /beɪl/ vi ~ **out** saltar em páraquedas

balk /bɔːk/ vt frustrar, contrariar ▯ vi ~ **at** assustar-se com, recuar perante

ball[1] /bɔːl/ n bola f. **~-bearing** n rolamento m de esferas. **~-cock** n válvula f de depósito de água. **~-point** n esferográfica f

ball[2] /bɔːl/ n (*dance*) baile m

ballad /'bæləd/ n balada f

ballast /'bæləst/ n lastro m

ballerina /bælə'riːnə/ n bailarina f

ballet /'bæleɪ/ n balé m, (P) ballet m, bailado m

balloon /bə'luːn/ n balão m

ballot /'bælət/ n escrutínio m. **~(-paper)** n cédula f eleitoral, (P) boletim m de voto. **~-box** n urna f ▯ vi (*pt balloted*) (*pol*) votar ▯ vt (*members*) consultar por voto secreto

ballroom /'bɔːlruːm/ n salão m de baile

balm /baːm/ n bálsamo m. **~y** a balsâmico; (*mild*) suave

balustrade /bælə'streɪd/ n balaustrada f

bamboo /bæm'buː/ n bambu m

ban /bæn/ vt (*pt banned*) banir. **~ from** proibir de ▯ n proibição f

banal /bə'naːl/ a banal. **~ity** /-ælətɪ/ n banalidade f

banana /bə'naːnə/ n banana f

band /bænd/ n (*for fastening*) cinta f, faixa f; (*strip*) tira f, banda f; (*mus: mil*) banda f; (*mus: dance, jazz*) conjunto m; (*group*) bando m ▯ vi ~ **together** juntar-se

bandage /'bændɪdʒ/ n atadura f, (P) ligadura f ▯ vt ligar

bandit /'bændɪt/ n bandido m

bandstand /'bændstænd/ n coreto m

bandwagon /'bændwægən/ n **climb on the ~** (*fig*) apanhar o trem

bandy /'bændɪ/ vt trocar. **~ a story about** espalhar uma história

bandy-legged /'bændɪlegd/ a cambaio, de pernas tortas

bang /bæŋ/ n (*blow*) pancada f; (*loud noise*) estouro m, estrondo

b

m; *(of gun)* detonação *f* □ *vt/i (hit, shut)* bater □ *vi* explodir □ *int* pum. **~ in the middle** jogar no meio. **shut the door with a ~** bater (com) a porta

banger /'bæŋə(r)/ *n* (*firework*) bomba *f*; *(sl: sausage)* salsicha *f*. **(old)** ~ *(sl: car)* calhambeque *m* (*colloq*)

bangle /'bæŋgl/ *n* pulseira *f*, bracelete *m*

banish /'bænɪʃ/ *vt* banir, desterrar

banisters /'bænɪstəz/ *npl* corrimão *m*

banjo /'bændʒəʊ/ *pl* (-os) banjo *m*

bank¹ /bæŋk/ *n* (*of river*) margem *f*; (*of earth*) talude *m*; (*of sand*) banco *m* □ *vt* amontoar □ *vi* (*aviat*) inclinar-se numa curva

bank² /bæŋk/ *n* (*comm*) banco *m* □ *vt* depositar no banco. ~ **account** conta *f* bancária. ~ **holiday** feriado *m* nacional. ~ **on** contar com. ~ **rate** taxa *f* bancária. ~ **with** ter conta em

bank|er /'bæŋkə(r)/ *n* banqueiro *m*. ~**ing** /-ɪŋ/ *n* operações *fpl* bancárias; (*career*) carreira *f* bancária, banca *f*

banknote /'bæŋknəʊt/ *n* nota *f* de banco

bankrupt /'bæŋkrʌpt/ *a & n* falido (*m*). **go ~** falir □ *vt* levar à falência. ~**cy** *n* falência *f*, bancarrota *f*

banner /'bænə(r)/ *n* bandeira *f*, estandarte *m*

banns /bænz/ *npl* proclamas *mpl*, (*P*) banhos *mpl*

banquet /'bæŋkwɪt/ *n* banquete *m*

banter /'bæntə(r)/ *n* gracejo *m*, brincadeira *f* □ *vi* gracejar, brincar

baptism /'bæptɪzəm/ *n* batismo *m*, (*P*) baptismo *m*

Baptist /'bæptɪst/ *n* batista *mf*, (*P*) baptista *mf*

baptize /bæp'taɪz/ *vt* batizar, (*P*) baptizar

bar /bɑ:(r)/ *n* (*of chocolate*) tablette *f*, barra *f*; (*of metal, soap, sand etc*) barra *f*; (*of door, window*) tranca *f*; (*in pub*) bar *m*; (*counter*) balcão *m*, bar *m*; (*mus*) barra *f* de compasso; (*fig: obstacle*) barreira *f*; (*in lawcourt*) teia *f*. **the B~** a advocacia *f* □ *vt* (*pt* **barred**) (*obstruct*) barrar; (*prohibit*) proibir (**from** de); (*exclude*) excluir; (*door, window*) trancar □ *prep* salvo, exceto, (*P*) excepto. ~ **none** sem exceção, (*P*) excepção. ~ **code** código *m* de barra. **behind ~s** na cadeia

Barbados /bɑ:'beɪdɒs/ *n* Barbados *mpl*

barbarian /bɑ:'beərɪən/ *n* bárbaro *m*

barbari|c /bɑ:'bærɪk/ *a* bárbaro. ~**ty** /-ətɪ/ *n* barbaridade *f*

barbarous /'bɑ:bərəs/ *a* bárbaro

barbecue /'bɑ:bɪkju:/ *n* (*grill*) churrasqueira *f*; (*occasion, food*) churrasco *m* □ *vt* assar

barbed /bɑ:bd/ *a* ~ **wire** arame *m* farpado

barber /'bɑ:bə(r)/ *n* barbeiro *m*

barbiturate /bɑ:'bɪtjʊrət/ *n* barbitúrico *m*

bare /beə(r)/ *a* (**-er, -est**) nu; (*room*) vazio; (*mere*) mero □ *vt* pôr à mostra, pôr a nu, descobrir

bareback /'beəbæk/ *adv* em pêlo

barefaced /'beəfeɪst/ *a* descarado

barefoot /'beə(r)fʊt/ *adv* descalço

barely /'beəlɪ/ *adv* apenas, mal

bargain /'bɑ:gɪn/ *n* (*deal*) negócio *m*; (*good buy*) pechincha *f* □ *vi* negociar; (*haggle*) regatear. ~ **for** esperar

barge /bɑ:dʒ/ *n* barcaça *f* □ *vi* ~ **in** interromper (despropositadamente); (*into room*) irromper

bark¹ /bɑ:k/ *n* (*of tree*) casca *f*

bark² /bɑ:k/ *n* (*of dog*) latido *m* □ *vi* latir. **his ~ is worse than his bite** cão que ladra não morde

barley /'bɑ:lɪ/ *n* cevada *f*. ~ **sugar** *n* açúcar *m* de cevada. ~ **water** *n* água *f* de cevada

barmaid /'bɑ:meɪd/ *n* empregada *f* de bar

barman /'bɑ:mən/ *n* (*pl* **-men**) barman *m*, empregado *m* de bar

barmy /'bɑ:mɪ/ *a* (*sl*) maluco

barn /bɑ:n/ *n* celeiro *m*

barometer /bə'rɒmɪtə(r)/ *n* barômetro *m*, (*P*) barómetro *m*

baron /'bærən/ *n* barão *m*. ~**ess** *n* baronesa *f*

baroque /bə'rɒk/ *a & n* barroco (*m*)

barracks /'bærəks/ *n* quartel *m*, caserna *f*

barrage /'bærɑ:ʒ/ *n* barragem *f*; (*fig*) enxurrada *f*; (*mil*) fogo *m* de barragem

barrel /'bærəl/ *n* (*of oil, wine*) barril *m*; (*of gun*) cano *m*. ~-**organ** *n* realejo *m*

barren /'bærən/ *a* estéril; (*soil*) árido, estéril

barricade /bærɪ'keɪd/ *n* barricada *f* □ *vt* barricar

barrier /'bærɪə(r)/ *n* barreira *f*; (*hindrance*) entrave *m*, barreira *f*

barring /'bɑ:rɪŋ/ *prep* salvo, exceto, (*P*) excepto

barrister /'bærɪstə(r)/ *n* advogado *m*

barrow /'bærəʊ/ *n* carrinho *m* de mão

barter /'bɑ:tə(r)/ *n* troca *f* □ *vt* trocar

base /beɪs/ *n* base *f* □ *vt* basear (**on** em) □ *a* baixo, ignóbil. ~**less** *a* infundado

baseball /'beɪsbɔ:l/ *n* beisebol *m*

basement /'beɪsmənt/ *n* porão *m*, (*P*) cave *f*

bash /bæʃ/ *vt* bater com violência □ *n* pancada *f* forte. **have a ~ at** (*sl*) experimentar

bashful /'bæʃfl/ *a* tímido

basic /'beɪsɪk/ *a* básico, elementar, fundamental. ~**ally** *adv* basicamente, no fundo

basil /'bæzl/ *n* mangericão *m*

basin /'beɪsn/ n bacia f; (for food)
tigela f; (naut) ante-doca f; (for
washing) pia f
basis /'beɪsɪs/ n (pl **bases** /-si:z/) base f
bask /bɑ:sk/ vi ~ **in the sun** apanhar sol
basket /'bɑ:skɪt/ n cesto m
basketball /'bɑ:skɪtbɔ:l/ n
basquete(bol) m
Basque /bɑ:sk/ a & n basco (m)
bass[1] /bæs/ n (pl **bass**) (fish) perca f
bass[2] /beɪs/ a (mus) grave □ n (pl **basses**)
(mus) baixo m
bassoon /bə'su:n/ n fagote m
bastard /'bɑ:stəd/ n (illegitimate child)
bastardo m; (sl: pej) safado (sl) m;
(colloq: not pej) cara (colloq) m
baste /beɪst/ vt (culin) regar (com molho)
bastion /'bæstɪən/ n bastião m, baluarte m
bat[1] /bæt/ n (cricket) pá f; (baseball)
bastão m; (table tennis) rafuete f □ vt/i
(pt **batted**) bater (em). **without** ~**ting
an eyelid** sem pestanejar
bat[2] /bæt/ n (zool) morcego m
batch /bætʃ/ n (loaves) fornada f;
(people) monte m; (goods) remessa f;
(papers, letters etc) batelada f, monte m
bated /'beɪtɪd/ a **with** ~ **breath** com a
respiração em suspenso, com a
respiração suspensa
bath /bɑ:θ/ n (pl -s /bɑ:ðz/) banho m; (tub)
banheira f. ~**s** (washing) banho m
público; (swimming) piscina f □ vt dar
banho a □ vi tomar banho
bathe /beɪð/ vt dar banho em; (wound)
limpar □ vi tomar banho (de mar)
□ n banho m (de mar). ~**r** /-ə(r)/ n
banhista mf
bathing /'beɪðɪŋ/ n banho m de mar.
~**-costume/-suit** n traje m de banho,
(P) fato m de banho
bathrobe /'bɑ:θrəʊb/ n (Amer) roupão m
bathroom /'bɑ:θru:m/ n banheiro m, (P)
casa f de banho
baton /'bætən/ n (mus) batuta f;
(policeman's) cassetete m; (mil) bastão m
battalion /bə'tælɪən/ n batalhão m
batter /'bætə(r)/ vt bater, espancar,
maltratar □ n (culin: for cakes) massa
f de bolos; (culin: for frying) massa f de
empanar. ~**ed** a (car, pan) amassado;
(child, wife) maltratado, espancado.
~**ing** n **take a** ~**ing** levar pancada or
uma surra
battery /'bætərɪ/ n (mil, auto) bateria f;
(electr) pilha f
battle /'bætl/ n batalha f; (fig) luta f □ vi
combater, batalhar, lutar
battlefield /'bætlfi:ld/ n campo m de
batalha
battlements /'bætlmənts/ npl ameias fpl
battleship /'bætlʃɪp/ n couraçado m

baulk /bɔ:lk/ vt/i = **balk**
bawdy /'bɔ:dɪ/ a (-ier, -iest) obsceno,
indecente
bawl /bɔ:l/ vt/i berrar
bay[1] /beɪ/ n (bot) loureiro m
bay[2] /beɪ/ n (geog) baía f. ~ **window**
janela f saliente
bay[3] /beɪ/ n (bark) latido m □ vi latir. **at** ~
(animal; fig) cercado, (P) em apuros.
keep at ~ manter à distância
bayonet /'beɪənɪt/ n baioneta f
bazaar /bə'zɑ:(r)/ n bazar m
BC abbr (before Christ) a C
be /bi:/ vi (pres **am, are, is**; pt **was, were**;
pp **been**) (permanent quality/place) ser;
(temporary place/state) estar; (become)
ficar. ~ **hot/right** etc ter calor/razão
etc. **he's 30** (age) ele tem 30 anos. **it's
fine/cold** etc (weather) faz bom tempo/
frio etc. **how are you**? (health) como
está? **I'm a doctor** — yes I am? eu sou
médico — é mesmo? **it's pretty, isn't
it**? é bonito, não é? **he is to come** (must)
ele deve vir. **how much is it**? (cost)
quanto é? ~ **reading eating** etc estar
lendo/comendo etc. **the money was
found** o dinheiro foi encontrado. **have
been to** ter ido a, ter estado em
beach /bi:tʃ/ n praia f
beacon /'bi:kən/ n farol m; (marker)
baliza f
bead /bi:d/ n conta f. ~ **of sweat** gota f de
suor
beak /bi:k/ n bico m
beaker /'bi:kə(r)/ n copo m de plástico
com bico; (in lab) proveta f
beam /bi:m/ n (of wood) trave f, viga f;
(of light) raio m; (of torch) feixe m de luz
□ vt/i (radiate) irradiar; (fig) sorrir
radiante. ~**ing** a radiante
bean /bi:n/ n feijão m. **broad** ~ fava f.
coffee ~**s** café m em grão. **runner**
~ feijão m verde
bear[1] /beə(r)/ n urso m
bear[2] /beə(r)/ vt/i (pt **bore**, pp **borne**)
sustentar, suportar; (endure) agüentar,
(P) aguentar, suportar; (child) dar à
luz. ~ **in mind** ter em mente, lembrar.
~ **left** virar à esquerda. ~ **on**
relacionar-se com, ter a ver com. ~ **out**
confirmar. ~ **up!** coragem! ~**able** a
tolerável, suportável. ~**er** n portador m
beard /bɪəd/ n barba f. ~**ed** a barbado,
com barba
bearing /'beərɪŋ/ n (manner) porte m;
(relevance) relação f; (naut) marcação
f. **get one's** ~**s** orientar-se
beast /bi:st/ n (animal, person) besta f,
animal m; (in fables) fera f. ~ **of
burden** besta f de carga
beat /bi:t/ vt/i (pt **beat**, pp **beaten**) bater
□ n (med) batimento m; (mus)

compasso m, ritmo m; (of drum) toque m; (of policeman) ronda f, (P) giro m. ~ **about the bush** estar com rodeios. ~ **a retreat** bater em retirada. ~ **it** (sl: go away) pôr-se a andar. **it ~s me** (colloq) não consigo entender. ~ **up** espancar. ~**er** n (culin) batedeira f. ~**ing** n sova f

beautician /bjuːˈtɪʃn/ n esteticista mf

beautiful /ˈbjuːtɪfl/ a belo, lindo. ~**ly** adv lindamente

beautify /ˈbjuːtɪfaɪ/ vt embelezar

beauty /ˈbjuːtɪ/ n beleza f. ~ **parlour** instituto m de beleza. ~ **spot** sinal m no rosto, mosca f; (place) local m pitoresco

beaver /ˈbiːvə(r)/ n castor m

became /brˈkeɪm/ see **become**

because /brˈkɒz/ conj porque □ adv ~ **of** por causa de

beckon /ˈbekən/ vt/i ~ **(to)** fazer sinal (para)

become /brˈkʌm/ vt/i (pt **became**, pp **become**) tornar-se; (befit) ficar bem a. **what has ~ of her?** que é feito dela?

becoming /brˈkʌmɪŋ/ a que fica bem, apropriado

bed /bed/ n cama f; (layer) camada f; (of sea) fundo m; (of river) leito m; (of flowers) canteiro m □ vt/i (pt **bedded**) ~ **down** ir deitar-se. ~ **in** plantar. ~ **and breakfast (b & b)** quarto m com café da manhã. ~**sit(ter)** n (colloq) misto m de quarto e sala. **go to~** ir para cama. **in ~** na cama. ~**ding** n roupa f de cama

bedclothes /ˈbedkləʊðz/ n roupa f de cama

bedlam /ˈbedləm/ n confusão f, balbúrdia f

bedraggled /brˈdrægld/ a (wet) molhado; (untidy) desarrumado; (dishevelled) desgrenhado

bedridden /ˈbedrɪdn/ a preso ao leito, doente de cama

bedroom /ˈbedruːm/ n quarto m de dormir

bedside /ˈbedsaɪd/ n cabeceira f. ~ **manner** (doctor's) modos mpl que inspiram confiança

bedspread /ˈbedspred/ n colcha f

bedtime /ˈbedtaɪm/ n hora f de deitar, hora f de ir para a cama

bee /biː/ n abelha f. **make a ~line for** ir direto a

beech /biːtʃ/ n faia f

beef /biːf/ n carne f de vaca

beefburger /ˈbiːfbɜːɡə(r)/ n hambúrguer m

beehive /ˈbiːhaɪv/ n colméia f

been /biːn/ see **be**

beer /bɪə(r)/ n cerveja f

beet /biːt/ n beterraba f

beetle /ˈbiːtl/ n escaravelho m

beetroot /ˈbiːtruːt/ n (raiz de) beterraba f

before /brˈfɔː(r)/ prep (time) antes de; (place) em frente de □ adv antes; (already) já □ conj antes que. ~ **leaving** antes de partir. ~ **he leaves** antes que ele parta, antes de ele partir

beforehand /brˈfɔːhænd/ adv de antemão, antecipadamente

befriend /brˈfrend/ vt tornar-se amigo de; (be helpful to) auxiliar

beg /beg/ vt/i (pt **begged**) mendigar; (entreat) suplicar. ~ **sb's pardon** pedir desculpa a alg. ~ **the question** fazer uma petição de princípio. **it's going ~ging** está sobrando

began /brˈɡæn/ see **begin**

beggar /ˈbeɡə(r)/ n mendigo m, pedinte mf; (colloq: person) cara (colloq) m

begin /brˈɡɪn/ vt/i (pt **began**, pp **begun**, pres p **beginning**) começar, principiar. ~**ner** n principiante mf. ~**ning** n começo m, princípio m

begrudge /brˈɡrʌdʒ/ vt ter inveja de; (give) dar de má vontade. ~ **doing** fazer de má vontade or a contragosto

beguile /brˈɡaɪl/ vt enganar

begun /brˈɡʌn/ see **begin**

behalf /brˈhaːf/ n **on ~ of** em nome de; (in the interest of) em favor de

behave /brˈheɪv/ vi portar-se. ~ **(o.s.)** portar-se bem

behaviour /brˈheɪvjə(r)/ n conduta f, comportamento m

behead /brˈhed/ vt decapitar

behind /brˈhaɪnd/ prep atrás de □ adv atrás; (late) com atraso □ n (colloq: buttocks) traseiro (colloq) m. ~ **the times** antiquado, retrógrado. **leave ~** deixar para trás

behold /brˈhəʊld/ vt (pt **beheld**) (old use) ver

beholden /brˈhəʊldən/ a em dívida (**to** para com)

beige /beɪʒ/ a & n bege (m), (P) beige (m)

being /ˈbiːɪŋ/ n ser m. **bring into ~** criar. **come into ~** nascer, originar-se

belated /brˈleɪtɪd/ a tardio, atrasado

belch /beltʃ/ vi arrotar □ vt ~ **out** (smoke) vomitar, lançar □ n arroto m

belfry /ˈbelfrɪ/ n campanário m

Belgi|um /ˈbeldʒəm/ n Bélgica f. ~**an** a & n belga (mf)

belief /brˈliːf/ n crença f; (trust) confiança f; (opinion) convicção f

believ|e /brˈliːv/ vt/i acreditar. ~**e in** acreditar em. ~**able** a crível. ~**er** /-ə(r)/ n crente mf

belittle /brˈlɪtl/ vt depreciar

bell /bel/ *n* sino *m*; (*small*) sineta *f*; (*on door, of phone*) campainha *f*; (*on cat, toy*) guizo *m*

belligerent /bɪˈlɪdʒərənt/ *a & n* beligerante (*mf*)

bellow /ˈbeləʊ/ *vt/i* berrar, bramir. ~ **out** rugir

bellows /ˈbeləʊz/ *npl* fole *m*

belly /ˈbelɪ/ *n* barriga *f*, ventre *m*. ~**-ache** *n* dor *f* de barriga

bellyful /ˈbelɪfʊl/ *n* **have a** ~ estar com a barriga cheia

belong /bɪˈlɒŋ/ *vi* ~ (**to**) pertencer (a); (*club*) ser sócio (de)

belongings /bɪˈlɒŋɪŋz/ *npl* pertences *mpl*. **personal** ~ objetos *mpl* de uso pessoal

beloved /bɪˈlʌvɪd/ *a & n* amado (*m*)

below /bɪˈləʊ/ *prep* abaixo de, debaixo de □ *adv* abaixo, em baixo; (*on page*) abaixo

belt /belt/ *n* cinto *m*; (*techn*) correia *f*; (*fig*) zona *f* □ *vt* (*sl: hit*) zurzir □ *vi* (*sl: rush*) safar-se

bemused /bɪˈmjuːzd/ *a* estonteado, confuso; (*thoughtful*) pensativo

bench /bentʃ/ *n* banco *m*; (*seat, working-table*) bancada *f*. **the** ~ (*jur*) os magistrados (no tribunal)

bend /bend/ *vt/i* (*pt & pp* bent) curvar (-se); (*arm, leg*) dobrar; (*road, river*) fazer uma curva, virar □ *n* curva *f*. ~ **over** debruçar-se *or* inclinar-se sobre

beneath /bɪˈniːθ/ *prep* abaixo de, debaixo de; (*fig*) abaixo de □ *adv* debaixo, em baixo

benediction /benɪˈdɪkʃn/ *n* benção *f*

benefactor /ˈbenɪfæktə(r)/ *n* benfeitor *m*

beneficial /benɪˈfɪʃl/ *a* benéfico, proveitoso

benefit /ˈbenɪfɪt/ *n* (*advantage, performance*) benefício *m*; (*profit*) proveito *m*; (*allowance*) subsídio *m* □ *vt/i* (*pt* benefited, *pres p* benefiting) (*be useful to*) beneficiar (**by** de); (*do good to*) beneficiar, fazer bem a; (*receive benefit*) lucrar, ganhar (**by, from** com)

beneficiary /benɪˈfɪʃərɪ/ *n* beneficiário *m*

benevolen|t /bɪˈnevələnt/ *a* benevolente. ~**ce** *n* benevolência *f*

benign /bɪˈnaɪn/ *a* (*incl med*) benigno

bent /bent/ *see* **bend** □ *n* (**for** para) (*skill*) aptidão *f*, jeito *m*; (*liking*) queda *f* □ *a* curvado; (*twisted*) torcido; (*sl: dishonest*) desonesto. ~ **on** decidido a

bequeath /bɪˈkwiːð/ *vt* legar

bequest /bɪˈkwest/ *n* legado *m*

bereave|d /bɪˈriːvd/ *a* **the** ~**d wife**/*etc* a esposa/*etc* do falecido. **the** ~**d family** a família enlutada. ~**ment** *n* luto *m*

bereft /bɪˈreft/ *a* ~ **of** privado de

beret /ˈbereɪ/ *n* boina *f*

Bermuda /bəˈmjuːdə/ *n* Bermudas *fpl*

berry /ˈberɪ/ *n* baga *f*

berserk /bəˈsɜːk/ *a* **go** ~ ficar louco de raiva, perder a cabeça

berth /bɜːθ/ *n* (*in ship*) beliche *m*; (*in train*) couchette *f*; (*anchorage*) ancoradouro *m* □ *vi* atracar. **give a wide** ~ **to** passar ao largo, (*P*) de largo

beside /bɪˈsaɪd/ *prep* ao lado de, junto de. ~ **o.s.** fora de si. **be** ~ **the point** não ter nada a ver com o assunto, não vir ao caso

besides /bɪˈsaɪdz/ *prep* além de; (*except*) fora, salvo □ *adv* além disso

besiege /bɪˈsiːdʒ/ *vt* sitiar, cercar. ~ **with** assediar

best /best/ *a & n* (**the**) ~ (o/a) melhor (*mf*) □ *adv* melhor. ~ **man** padrinho *m* de casamento. **at** (**the**) ~ na melhor das hipóteses. **do one's** ~ fazer o (melhor) que se pode. **make the** ~ **of** tirar o melhor partido de. **the** ~ **part of** a maior parte de. **to the** ~ **of my knowledge** que eu saiba

bestow /bɪˈstəʊ/ *vt* conferir. ~ **praise** fazer *or* tecer elogios

best-seller /bestˈselə(r)/ *n* best-seller *m*

bet /bet/ *n* aposta *f* □ *vt/i* (*pt* bet *or* betted) apostar (**on** em)

betray /bɪˈtreɪ/ *vt* trair. ~**al** *n* traição *f*

better /ˈbetə(r)/ *a & adv* melhor □ *vt* melhorar □ *n* **our** ~**s** os nossos superiores *mpl*. **all the** ~ tanto melhor. ~ **off** (*richer*) mais rico. **he's** ~ **off at home** é melhor para ele ficar em casa. **I'd** ~ **go** é melhor ir-me embora. **the** ~ **part of it** a maior parte disso. **get** ~ melhorar. **get the** ~ **of sb** levar a melhor em relação a alg

betting-shop /ˈbetɪŋʃɒp/ *n* agência *f* de apostas

between /bɪˈtwiːn/ *prep* entre □ *adv* **in** ~ no meio, no intervalo. ~ **you and me** aqui entre nós

beverage /ˈbevərɪdʒ/ *n* bebida *f*

beware /bɪˈweə(r)/ *vi* acautelar-se (**of** com), tomar cuidado (**of** com)

bewilder /bɪˈwɪldə(r)/ *vt* desorientar. ~**ment** *n* desorientação *f*, confusão *f*

bewitch /bɪˈwɪtʃ/ *vt* encantar, cativar

beyond /bɪˈjɒnd/ *prep* além de; (*doubt, reach*) fora de □ *adv* além. **it's** ~ **me** isso ultrapassa-me. **he lives** ~ **his means** ele vive acima dos seus meios

bias /ˈbaɪəs/ *n* parcialidade *f*; (*pej: prejudice*) preconceito *m*; (*sewing*) viés *m* □ *vt* (*pt* biased) influenciar. ~**ed** *a* parcial. ~**ed against** de prevenção contra, (*P*) de pé atrás contra

bib /bɪb/ *n* babeiro *m*, babette *m*

Bible /'baɪbl/ *n* Bíblia *f*

biblical /'bɪblɪkl/ *a* bíblico

bibliography /bɪblɪ'ɒgrəfɪ/ *n* bibliografia *f*

bicarbonate /baɪ'ka:bənət/ *n* ~ **of soda** bicarbonato *m* de soda

biceps /'baɪseps/ *n* bíceps *m*

bicker /'bɪkə(r)/ *vi* questionar, discutir

bicycle /'baɪsɪkl/ *n* bicicleta *f* □ *vi* andar de bicicleta

bid /bɪd/ *n* oferta *f*, lance *m*; (*attempt*) tentativa *f* □ *vt/i* (*pt* **bid**, *pres p* **bidding**) fazer uma oferta, lançar, oferecer como lance. ~**der** *n* licitante *mf*. **the highest** ~**der** quem dá *or* oferece mais

bide /baɪd/ *vt* ~ **one's time** esperar pelo bom momento

bidet /'bi:deɪ/ *n* bidê *m*, (P) bidé *m*

biennial /baɪ'enɪəl/ *a* bienal

bifocals /baɪ'fəʊklz/ *npl* óculos *mpl* bifocais

big /bɪg/ *a* (**bigger**, **biggest**) grande; (*sl: generous*) generoso □ *adv* (*colloq*) em grande. ~**-headed** *a* pretensioso, convencido. ~ **shot** (*sl*) manda-chuva *m*. **talk** ~ gabar-se (*colloq*). **think** ~ (*colloq*) ter grandes planos

bigam|y /'bɪgəmɪ/ *n* bigamia *f*. ~**ist** *n* bígamo *m*. ~**ous** *a* bígamo

bigot /'bɪgət/ *n* fanático *m*, intolerante *mf*. ~**ed** *a* fanático, intolerante. ~**ry** *n* fanatismo *m*, intolerância *f*

bigwig /'bɪgwɪg/ *n* (*colloq*) manda-chuva *m*

bike /baɪk/ *n* (*colloq*) bicicleta *f*

bikini /bɪ'ki:nɪ/ *n* (*pl* **-is**) biquíni *m*

bilberry /'bɪlbərɪ/ *n* arando *m*

bile /baɪl/ *n* bílis *f*

bilingual /baɪ'lɪŋgwəl/ *a* bilíngüe

bilious /'bɪlɪəs/ *a* bilioso

bill[1] /bɪl/ *n* (*invoice*) fatura *f*, (P) factura *f*; (*in restaurant*) conta *f*; (*pol*) projeto *m*, (P) projecto *m* de lei; (*Amer: banknote*) nota *f* de banco; (*poster*) cartaz *m* □ *vt* faturar, (P) facturar; (*theatre*) anunciar, pôr no programa. ~ **of exchange** letra *f* de câmbio. ~ **sb for** apresentar a alg a conta de

bill[2] /bɪl/ *n* (*of bird*) bico *m*

billiards /'bɪlɪədz/ *n* bilhar *m*

billion /'bɪlɪən/ *n* (10^9) mil milhões; (10^{12}) um milhão de milhões

bin /bɪn/ *n* (*for storage*) caixa *f*, lata *f*; (*for rubbish*) lata *f* do lixo, (P) caixote *m*

bind /baɪnd/ *vt* (*pt* **bound**) (*tie*) atar; (*book*) encadernar; (*jur*) obrigar; (*cover the edge of*) debruar □ *n* (*sl: bore*) chatice *f* (*sl*). **be** ~**ing on** ser obrigatório para

binding /'baɪndɪŋ/ *n* encadernação *f*; (*braid*) debrum *m*

binge /bɪndʒ/ *n* (*sl*) **go on a** ~ cair na farra; (*overeat*) empanturrar-se

bingo /'bɪŋgəʊ/ *n* bingo *m* □ *int* acertei!

binoculars /bɪ'nɒkjʊləz/ *npl* binóculo *m*

biochemistry /baɪəʊ'kemɪstrɪ/ *n* bioquímica *f*

biodegradable /baɪəʊdɪ'greɪdəbl/ *a* biodegradável

biograph|y /baɪ'ɒgrəfɪ/ *n* biografia *f*. ~**er** *n* biógrafo *m*

biolog|y /baɪ'ɒlədʒɪ/ *n* biologia *f*. ~**ical** /-ə'lɒdʒɪkl/ *a* biológico. ~**ist** *n* biólogo *m*

biopsy /'baɪɒpsɪ/ *n* biópsia *f*

birch /bɜ:tʃ/ *n* (*tree*) bétula *f*

bird /bɜ:d/ *n* ave *f*, pássaro *m*; (*sl: girl*) garota *f* (*colloq*). ~ **flu** gripe *f* das aves. ~ **sanctuary** refúgio *m* ornitológico. ~**-watcher** *n* ornitófilo *m*

Biro /'baɪərəʊ/ *n* (*pl* **-os**) (caneta) esferográfica *f*, Bic *f*

birth /bɜ:θ/ *n* nascimento *m*. ~ **certificate** certidão *f* de nascimento. ~ **control/rate** controle *m*/índice *m* de natalidade. ~**-place** *n* lugar *m* de nascimento. **give** ~ **to** dar à luz

birthday /'bɜ:θdeɪ/ *n* aniversário *m*, (P) dia *m* de anos. **his** ~ **is on 9 July** ele faz anos no dia 9 de julho

birthmark /'bɜ:θma:k/ *n* sinal *m*

biscuit /'bɪskɪt/ *n* biscoito *m*, bolacha *f*

bisect /baɪ'sekt/ *vt* dividir ao meio

bishop /'bɪʃəp/ *n* bispo *m*

bit[1] /bɪt/ *n* (*small piece, short time*) pedaço *m*, bocado *m*; (*of bridle*) freio *m*; (*of tool*) broca *f*. **a** ~ um pouco

bit[2] /bɪt/ *see* **bite**

bitch /bɪtʃ/ *n* cadela *f*; (*sl: woman*) peste *f* (*fig*), cadela *f* (*sl*) □ *vt/i* (*colloq: criticize*) malhar, (P) cortar (em) (*colloq*); (*colloq: grumble*) resmungar. ~**y** *a* (*colloq*) maldoso

bite /baɪt/ *vt/i* (*pt* **bit**, *pp* **bitten**) morder; (*insect*) picar □ *n* mordida *f*; (*sting*) picada *f*. **have a** ~ (**to eat**) comer qualquer coisa

biting /'baɪtɪŋ/ *a* cortante

bitter /'bɪtə(r)/ *a* amargo; (*weather*) glacial. ~**ly** *adv* amargamente. **it's** ~**ly cold** está um frio de rachar. ~**ness** *n* amargura *f*; (*resentment*) ressentimento *m*

bizarre /bɪ'za:(r)/ *a* bizarro

black /blæk/ *a* (**-er**, **-est**) negro, preto □ *n* negro *m*, preto *m*. **a B**~ (*person*) um preto, um negro □ *vt* enegrecer; (*goods*) boicotar. ~ **and blue** coberto de nódoas negras. ~ **coffee** café *m* (sem leite). ~ **eye** olho *m* negro. ~ **ice** gelo *m* negro sobre o asfalto. ∼ **market** mercado *m* negro. ∼ **spot** *n* (*place*) local *m* perigoso, ponto *m* negro

blackberry /'blækbərı/ *n* amora *f* silvestre

blackbird /'blækbɜːd/ *n* melro *m*

blackboard /'blækbɔːd/ *n* quadro *m* preto

blackcurrant /'blækkʌrənt/ *n* groselha *f* negra

blacken /'blækən/ *vt/i* escurecer. ∼ **sb's name** difamar, denegrir

blackleg /'blækleg/ *n* fura-greves *m*

blacklist /'blæklɪst/ *n* lista *f* negra □ *vt* pôr na lista negra

blackmail /'blækmeɪl/ *n* chantagem *f* □ *vt* fazer chantagem. ∼**er** *n* chantagista *mf*

blackout /'blækaʊt/ *n* (*wartime*) blecaute *m*; (*med*) desmaio *m*; (*electr*) falta *f* de corrente; (*theatr*) apagar *m* de luzes

blacksmith /'blæksmɪθ/ *n* ferreiro *m*

bladder /'blædə(r)/ *n* bexiga *f*

blade /bleɪd/ *n* lâmina *f*; (*of oar, propeller*) pá *f*; (*of grass*) ervinha *f*, folhinha *f* de erva

blame /bleɪm/ *vt* culpar □ *n* culpa *f*. **be to** ∼ ser o culpado. ∼**less** *a* irrepreensível; (*innocent*) inocente

bland /blænd/ *a* (-**er**, -**est**) (*of manner*) suave; (*mild*) brando; (*insipid*) insípido

blank /blæŋk/ *a* (*space, cheque*) em branco; (*look*) vago; (*wall*) nu □ *n* espaço *m* em branco; (*cartridge*) cartucho *m* sem bala

blanket /'blæŋkɪt/ *n* cobertor *m*; (*fig*) manto *m* □ *vt* (*pt* **blanketed**) cobrir com cobertor; (*cover thickly*) encobrir, recobrir. **wet** ∼ desmancha-prazeres *mf*

blare /bleə(r)/ *vt/i* ressoar, atroar □ *n* clangor *m*; (*of horn*) buzinar *m*

blasé /'blɑːzeɪ/ *a* blasé

blaspheme /blæs'fiːm/ *vt/i* blasfemar

blasphem|**y** /'blæsfəmɪ/ *n* blasfêmia *f*, (*P*) blasfémia *f*. ∼**ous** *a* blasfemo

blast /blɑːst/ *n* (*gust*) rajada *f*; (*sound*) som *m*; (*explosion*) explosão *f* □ *vt* dinamitar. ∼! droga! ∼**ed** *a* maldito. ∼**-furnace** *n* alto forno *m*. ∼**-off** *n* (*of missile*) lançamento *m*, início *m* de combustão

blatant /'bleɪtnt/ *a* flagrante; (*shameless*) descarado

blaze /bleɪz/ *n* chamas *fpl*; (*light*) clarão *m*; (*outburst*) explosão *f* □ *vi* arder; (*shine*) resplandecer, brilhar. ∼ **a trail** abrir o caminho, ser pioneiro

blazer /'bleɪzə(r)/ *n* blazer *m*

bleach /bliːtʃ/ *n* descolorante, descorante *m*; (*household*) água *f* sanitária □ *vt/i* branquear; (*hair*) oxigenar

bleak /bliːk/ *a* (-**er**, -**est**) (*place*) desolado; (*chilly*) frio; (*fig*) desanimador

bleary-eyed /'blɪərɪaɪd/ *a* com olhos injetados

bleat /bliːt/ *n* balido *m* □ *vi* balir

bleed /bliːd/ *vt/i* (*pt* **bled**) sangrar

bleep /bliːp/ *n* bip *m*. ∼**er** *n* bip *m*

blemish /'blemɪʃ/ *n* defeito *m*; (*on reputation*) mancha *f* □ *vt* manchar

blend /blend/ *vt/i* misturar(-se); (*go well together*) combinar-se □ *n* mistura *f*. ∼**er** *n* (*culin*) liquidificador *m*

bless /bles/ *vt* abençoar. **be** ∼**ed with** ter a felicidade de ter. ∼**ing** *n* benção *f*; (*thing one is glad of*) felicidade *f*. **it's a** ∼**ing in disguise** há males que vêm para bem

blessed /'blesɪd/ *a* bem-aventurado; (*colloq: cursed*) maldito

blew /bluː/ *see* **blow**

blight /blaɪt/ *n* doença *f* de plantas; (*fig*) influência *f* maligna □ *vt* arruinar, frustrar

blind /blaɪnd/ *a* cego □ *vt* cegar □ *n* (*on window*) persiana *f*; (*deception*) ardil *m*. ∼ **alley** (*incl fig*) beco *m* sem saída. ∼ **man/woman** cego *m*/cega *f* vir. **be** ∼ **to** não ver. **turn a** ∼ **eye to** fingir não ver, fechar os olhos a. ∼**ly** *adv* às cegas. ∼**ness** *n* cegueira *f*

blindfold /'blaɪndfəʊld/ *a & adv* de olhos vendados □ *n* venda *f* □ *vt* vendar os olhos a

blink /blɪŋk/ *vi* piscar

blinkers /'blɪŋkəz/ *npl* antolhos *mpl*

bliss /blɪs/ *n* felicidade *f*, beatitude *f*. ∼**ful** *a* felicíssimo. ∼**fully** *adv* maravilhosamente

blister /'blɪstə(r)/ *n* bolha *f*, empola *f* □ *vi* empolar

blizzard /'blɪzəd/ *n* tempestade *f* de neve, nevasca *f*

bloated /'bləʊtɪd/ *a* inchado

bloater /'bləʊtə(r)/ *n* arenque *m* salgado e defumado

blob /blɒb/ *n* pingo *m* grosso; (*stain*) mancha *f*

bloc /blɒk/ *n* bloco *m*

block /blɒk/ *n* bloco *m*; (*buildings*) quarteirão *m*; (*in pipe*) entupimento *m*. ∼ (**of flats**) prédio *m* (de andares) □ *vt* bloquear, obstruir; (*pipe*) entupir. ∼ **letters** maiúsculas *fpl*. ∼**age** *n* obstrução *f*

b

blockade /blɒ'keɪd/ *n* bloqueio *m* □ *vt* bloquear

bloke /bləʊk/ *n* (*colloq*) sujeito *m* (*colloq*), cara *m* (*colloq*)

blond /blɒnd/ *a & n* louro (*m*)

blonde /blɒnd/ *a & n* loura (*f*)

blood /blʌd/ *n* sangue *m* □ *a* (*bank, donor, transfusion, etc*) de sangue; (*poisoning*) do sangue; (*group, vessel*) sangüíneo. **~-curdling** *a* horrendo. **~ pressure** tensão *f* arterial. **~ test** exame *m* de sangue. **~less** *a* (*fig*) pacífico

bloodhound /'blʌdhaʊnd/ *n* sabujo *m*

bloodshed /'blʌdʃed/ *n* derramamento *m* de sangue, carnificina *f*

bloodshot /'blʌdʃɒt/ *a* injetado *or* (*P*) injectado de sangue

bloodstream /'blʌdstri:m/ *n* sangue *m*, fluxo *m* sangüíneo

bloodthirsty /'blʌdθɜ:stɪ/ *a* sanguinário

bloody /'blʌdɪ/ *a* (**-ier, -iest**) ensangüentado; (*with much bloodshed*) sangrento; (*sl*) grande, maldito □ *adv* (*sl*) pra burro. **~-minded** *a* (*colloq*) do contra (*colloq*), chato (*sl*)

bloom /blu:m/ *n* flor *f*; (*beauty*) frescura *f*, viço *m* □ *vi* florir; (*fig*) vicejar. **in ~** em flor

blossom /'blɒsəm/ *n* flor *f*. **in ~** em flor □ *vi* (*flower*) florir, desabrochar; (*develop, flourish*) florescer, desabrochar

blot /blɒt/ *n* mancha *f* □ *vt* (*pt* **blotted**) manchar; (*dry*) secar. **~ out** apagar; (*hide*) tapar, toldar. **~ter**, **~ting-paper** *n* (papel) mata-borrão *m*

blotch /blɒtʃ/ *n* mancha *f*. **~y** *a* manchado

blouse /blaʊz/ *n* blusa *f*; (*in uniform*) blusão *m*

blow[1] /bləʊ/ *vt*/*i* (*pt* **blew**, *pp* **blown**) soprar; (*fuse*) fundir-se, queimar; (*sl: squander*) esbanjar; (*trumpet etc*) tocar. **~ a whistle** apitar. **~ away** *or* **off** *vt* levar, soprar □ *vi* roar, ir pelos ares (fora). **~-dry** *vt* (*hair*) fazer um brushing □ *n* brushing *m*. **~ one's nose** assoar o nariz. **~ out** (*candle*) apagar, soprar. **~-out** *n* (*colloq: of tyre*) rebentar *m*; (*colloq: large meal*) comilança *f* (*colloq*). **~ over** passar. **~ up** *vt* (*explode*) explodir; (*tyre*) encher; (*photograph*) ampliar □ *vi* (*explode*) explodir

blow[2] /bləʊ/ *n* pancada *f*; (*slap*) bofetada *f*; (*punch*) murro *m*; (*fig*) golpe *m*

blowlamp /'bləʊlæmp/ *n* maçarico *m*

blown /bləʊn/ *see* **blow**[1]

bludgeon /'blʌdʒən/ *n* moca *f* □ *vt* malhar em. **~ to death** matar à pancada

blue /blu:/ *a* (**-er, -est**) azul; (*indecent*) indecente □ *n* azul *m*. **come out of the ~** ser inesperado. **~s** *n* (*mus*) blues. **have the ~s** estar deprimido (*colloq*)

bluebell /'blu:bel/ *n* jacinto *m* dos bosques

bluebottle /'blu:bɒtl/ *n* mosca *f* varejeira

blueprint /'blu:prɪnt/ *n* cópia *f* fotográfica de planta; (*fig*) projeto *m*, (*P*) projecto *m*

bluff /blʌf/ *vi* blefar, (*P*) fazer bluff □ *vt* enganar (fingindo), blefar □ *n* blefe *m*, (*P*) bluff *m*

blunder /'blʌndə(r)/ *vi* cometer um erro crasso; (*move*) avançar às cegas *or* tateando □ *n* erro *m* crasso, (*P*) bronca *f*

blunt /blʌnt/ *a* (**-er, -est**) embotado; (*person*) direto, (*P*) directo □ *vt* embotar. **~ly** *adv* sem rodeios. **~ness** *n* **franqueza** *f* **rude**

blur /blɜ:(r)/ *n* mancha *f* □ *vt* (*pt* **blurred**) (*smear*) manchar; (*make indistinct*) toldar

blurb /blɜ:b/ *n* contracapa *f*, sinopse *f* de um livro

blurt /blɜ:t/ *vt* **~ out** deixar escapar

blush /blʌʃ/ *vi* corar □ *n* rubor *m*, vermelhidão *f*

bluster /'blʌstə(r)/ *vi* (*wind*) soprar em rajadas; (*swagger*) andar com ar fanfarrão. **~y** *a* borrascoso

boar /bɔ:(r)/ *n* varrão *m*. **wild ~** javali *m*

board /bɔ:d/ *n* tábua *f*; (*for notices*) quadro *m*, (*P*) placard *m*; (*food*) pensão *f*; (*admin*) conselho *m* □ *vt*/*i* cobrir com tábuas; (*aircraft, ship, train*) embarcar (em); (*bus, train*) subir (em). **full ~** pensão *f* completa. **half ~** meia-pensão *f*. **on ~** a bordo. **~ up** entaipar. **~ with** ser pensionista em casa de. **~er** *n* pensionista *mf*; (*at school*) interno *m*. **~ing-card** *n* cartão *m* de embarque. **~ing-house** *n* pensão *f*. **~ing-school** *n* internato *m*

boast /bəʊst/ *vi* gabar-se □ *vt* orgulhar-se de □ *n* gabarolice *f*. **~er** *n* gabola *mf*. **~ful** *a* vaidoso. **~fully** *adv* com vaidade, gabando-se

boat /bəʊt/ *n* barco *m*. **in the same ~** nas mesmas circunstâncias. **~ing** *n* passear de barco

bob /bɒb/ *vt*/*i* (*pt* **bobbed**) (*curtsy*) inclinar-se; (*hair*) cortar pelos ombros, (*P*) cortar à Joãozinho. **~ (up and down)** andar para cima e para baixo

bobbin /'bɒbɪn/ *n* bobina *f*; (*sewing-machine*) canela *f*, bobina *f*

bob-sleigh /'bɒbsleɪ/ *n* trenó *m*

bode /bəʊd/ *vi* **~ well/ill** ser de bom/mau agouro

bodice /'bɒdɪs/ *n* corpete *m*

bodily /'bɒdɪlɪ/ a corporal, físico. □ adv (*in person*) fisicamente, em pessoa; (*lift*) em peso

body /'bɒdɪ/ n corpo m; (*organization*) organismo m. ~**(work)** n (*of car*) carroçaria f. **in a** ~ em massa. **the main** ~ **of** o grosso de. ~**-building** n body building m

bodyguard /'bɒdɪɡɑːd/ n guarda-costas m; (*escort*) escolta f

bog /bɒɡ/ n pântano m □ vt **get** ~**ged down** atolar-se; (*fig*) ficar emperrado

boggle /'bɒɡl/ vi **the mind** ~**s** não da para imaginar

bogus /'bəʊɡəs/ a falso

boil[1] /bɔɪl/ n (*med*) furúnculo m

boil[2] /bɔɪl/ vt/i ferver. **come to the** ~ ferver. ~ **down to** resumir-se a. ~ **over** transbordar. ~**ing hot** fervendo. ~**ing point** ponto m de ebulição

boiler /'bɔɪlə(r)/ n caldeira f. ~ **suit** macacão m, (P) fato m de macaco

boisterous /'bɔɪstərəs/ a turbulento; (*noisy and cheerful*) animado

bold /bəʊld/ a (-er, -est) ousado; (*of colours*) vivo. ~**ness** n ousadia f

Bolivia /bə'lɪvɪə/ n Bolívia f. ~**n** a & n boliviano (m)

bollard /'bɒləd/ n (*ship*) abita f; (*road*) poste m

bolster /'bəʊlstə(r)/ n travesseiro m □ vt sustentar; ajudar. ~ **one's spirits** levantar o moral

bolt /bəʊlt/ n (*on door etc*) ferrolho m; (*for nut*) parafuso m; (*lightning*) relâmpago m □ vt aferrolhar; (*food*) engolir □ vi fugir, disparar. ~ **upright** reto como um fuso

bomb /bɒm/ n bomba f □ vt bombardear. ~**er** n (*aircraft*) bombardeiro m; (*person*) bombista mf

bombard /bɒm'bɑːd/ vt bombardear. ~**ment** n bombardeamento m

bombastic /bɒm'bæstɪk/ a bombástico

bombshell /'bɒmʃel/ n granada f; (*fig*) bomba f

bond /bɒnd/ n (*agreement*) compromisso m; (*link*) laço m, vínculo m; (*comm*) obrigação f. **in** ~ em depósito na alfândega

bondage /'bɒndɪdʒ/ n escravidão f, servidão f

bone /bəʊn/ n osso m; (*of fish*) espinha f □ vt desossar. ~**-dry** a completamente seco, ressecado. ~ **idle** preguiçoso

bonfire /'bɒnfaɪə(r)/ n fogueira f

bonnet /'bɒnɪt/ n chapéu m; (*auto*) capô m do motor, (P) capot m

bonus /'bəʊnəs/ n bônus m, (P) bónus m

bony /'bəʊnɪ/ a (-ier, -iest) ossudo; (*meat, fish*) cheio de ossos/de espinhas

boo /buː/ int fora □ vt/i vaiar □ n vaia f

boob /buːb/ n (*sl: mistake*) asneira f, disparate m □ vi (*sl*) fazer asneira(s)

booby /'buːbɪ/ n ~ **prize** prêmio m de consolação. ~ **trap** bomba f armadilhada

book /bʊk/ n livro m. ~**s** (*comm*) contas fpl, escrita f □ vt (*enter*) averbar, registrar; (*comm*) escriturar; (*reserve*) marcar, reservar. ~ **of matches** carteira f de fósforos. ~ **of tickets** (*bus, tube*) caderneta f de bilhetes. **be fully** ~**ed** ter a lotação esgotada. ~**ing office** bilheteria f, (P) bilheteira f

bookcase /'bʊkkeɪs/ n estante f

bookkeep|**er** /'bʊkkiːpə(r)/ n guarda-livros m. ~**ing** n contabilidade f, escrituração f

booklet /'bʊklɪt/ n brochura f

bookmaker /'bʊkmeɪkə(r)/ n book (maker) m

bookmark /'bʊkmɑːk/ n marca f de livro, marcador m de página

bookseller /'bʊkselə(r)/ n livreiro m

bookshop /'bʊkʃɒp/ n livraria f

bookstall /'bʊkstɔːl/ n quiosque m

boom /buːm/ vi ribombar; (*of trade*) prosperar □ n (*sound*) ribombo m; (*comm*) boom m, prosperidade f

boon /buːn/ n benção f, vantagem f

boost /buːst/ vt desenvolver, promover; (*morale*) levantar; (*price*) aumentar □ n força f (*colloq*). ~**er** n (*med*) dose suplementar f; (*vaccine*) revacinação f, (P) reforço m

boot /buːt/ n bota f; (*auto*) portamala m □ vt ~ (**up**) (*comput*) dar cargaem. **to** ~ (*in addition*) ainda por cima

booth /buːð/ n barraca f; (*telephone, voting*) cabine f

booty /'buːtɪ/ n saque m, pilhagem f

booze /buːz/ vi (*colloq*) embebedar-se (*colloq*), encharcar-se (*colloq*) □ n (*colloq*) pinga f (*colloq*)

border /'bɔːdə(r)/ n borda f, margem f; (*frontier*) fronteira f; (*garden bed*) canteiro m □ vi ~ **on** confinar com; (*be almost the same as*) atingir as raias de

borderline /'bɔːdəlaɪn/ n linha f divisória. ~ **case** caso m limite

bore[1] /bɔː(r)/ *see* **bear**[2]

bore[2] /bɔː(r)/ vt/i (*techn*) furar, perfurar □ n (*of gun barrel*) calibre m

bore[3] /bɔː(r)/ vt aborrecer, entediar □ n maçante m; (*thing*) chatice f. **be** ~**d** aborrecer-se, maçar-se. ~**dom** n tédio m. **boring** a tedioso, maçante

born /bɔːn/ a nascido. **be** ~ nascer

borne /bɔːn/ *see* **bear**[2]

borough /'bʌrə/ n município m

borrow /'bɒrəʊ/ vt pedir emprestado (**from** a)

bosom /'bʊzəm/ n peito m; (*woman's; fig: midst*) seio m. ~ **friend** amigo m íntimo

boss /bɒs/ n (*colloq*) patrão m, patroa f, manda-chuva (*colloq*) m □ vt mandar. ~ **sb about** (*colloq*) mandar em alg

bossy /'bɒsɪ/ a mandão, autoritário

botan|y /'bɒtənɪ/ n botânica f. ~**ical** /bə'tænɪkl/ a botânico. ~**ist** /-ɪst/ n botânico m

botch /bɒtʃ/ vt atamancar; (*spoil*) estragar, escangalhar

both /bəʊθ/ a & pron ambos, os dois □ adv ~ . . . and não só . . . mas também, tanto . . . como. ~ **of us** nós dois. ~ **the books** ambos os livros

bother /'bɒðə(r)/ vt/i incomodar (-se) □ n (*inconvenience*) incómodo m, (P) incómodo m, trabalho m; (*effort*) custo m, trabalho m; (*worry*) preocupação f. **don't** ~ não se incomode. **I can't be** ~**ed** não posso me dar o trabalho

bottle /'bɒtl/ n garrafa f; (*small*) frasco m; (*for baby*) mamadeira f, (P) biberão m □ vt engarrafar. ~**opener** n sacarolhas m. ~ **up** reprimir

bottleneck /'bɒtlnek/ n (*obstruction*) entrave m; (*traffic-jam*) engarrafamento m

bottom /'bɒtəm/ n fundo m; (*of hill*) sopé m; (*buttocks*) traseiro m □ a inferior; (*last*) último. **from top to** ~ de alto a baixo. ~**less** a sem fundo

bough /baʊ/ n ramo m

bought /bɔːt/ see **buy**

boulder /'bəʊldə(r)/ n pedregulho m

bounce /baʊns/ vi saltar; (*of person*) pular, dar pulos; (*sl: of cheque*) ser devolvido □ vt fazer saltar □ n (*of ball*) salto m, (P) ressalto m

bound¹ /baʊnd/ vi pular; (*move by jumping*) ir aos pulos □ n pulo m

bound² /baʊnd/ see **bind** □ a **be** ~ **for** ir com destino a, ir para. **be** ~ **to** (*obliged*) ser obrigado a; (*certain*) haver de. **she's** ~ **to like it** ela há de gostar disso

boundary /'baʊndrɪ/ n limite m

bound|s /baʊndz/ npl limites mpl. **out of** ~**s** interdito. ~**ed by** limitado por. ~**less** a sem limites

bouquet /bʊ'keɪ/ n ramo m de flores; (*wine*) aroma m

bout /baʊt/ n período m; (*med*) ataque m; (*boxing*) combate m

boutique /buː'tiːk/ n boutique f

bow¹ /bəʊ/ n (*weapon, mus*) arco m; (*knot*) laço m. ~**legged** a de pernas tortas. ~**tie** n gravata borboleta f, (P) laço m

bow² /baʊ/ n vênia f, (P) vénia f □ vt/i inclinar(-se), curvar-se

bow³ /baʊ/ n (*naut*) proa f

bowels /'baʊəlz/ npl intestinos mpl; (*fig*) entranhas fpl

bowl¹ /bəʊl/ n (*basin*) bacia f; (*for food*) tigela f; (*of pipe*) fornilho m

bowl² /bəʊl/ n (*ball*) boliche m, (P) bola f de madeira. ~**s** npl boliche m, (P) jogo m com bolas de madeira □ vt (*cricket*) lançar. ~ **over** siderar, varar. ~**ing** n boliche m, (P) bowling m. ~**ing-alley** n pista f

bowler¹ /'bəʊlə(r)/ n (*cricket*) lançador m

bowler² /'bəʊlə(r)/ n ~ (**hat**) (chapéu de) coco m

box¹ /bɒks/ n caixa f; (*theatr*) camarote m □ vt pôr dentro duma caixa. ~ **in** fechar. ~ **office** n bilheteria f, (P) bilheteira f. **Boxing Day** feriado m no primeiro dia útil depois do Natal

box² /bɒks/ vt/i (*sport*) lutar boxe. ~ **the ears of** esbofetear. ~**er** n pugilista m, boxeur m. ~**ing** n boxe m, pugilismo m

boy /bɔɪ/ n rapaz m. ~**friend** n namorado m. ~**hood** n infância f. ~**ish** a de menino

boycott /'bɔɪkɒt/ vt boicotar □ n boicote m

bra /braː/ n soutien m

brace /breɪs/ n braçadeira f; (*dental*) aparelho m; (*tool*) berbequim m; (*of birds*) par m. ~**s** npl (*for trousers*) suspensórios mpl □ vt apoiar, firmar. ~ **o.s.** concentrar as energias, fazer força; (*for blow*) preparar-se

bracelet /'breɪslɪt/ n bracelete m, pulseira f

bracing /'breɪsɪŋ/ a tonificante, estimulante

bracken /'brækən/ n (*bot*) samambaia f, (P) feto m

bracket /'brækɪt/ n suporte m; (*group*) grupo m □ vt (*pt* **bracketed**) pôr entre parênteses; (*put together*) pôr em pé de igualdade, agrupar. **age/income** ~ faixa f etária/salarial. **round** ~**s** parênteses mpl. **square** ~**s** parênteses mpl, colchetes mpl

brag /bræg/ vi (*pt* **bragged**) gabar-se (**about** de)

braid /breɪd/ n galão m; (*of hair*) trança f

Braille /breɪl/ n braile m

brain /breɪn/ n cérebro m, miolos mpl (*colloq*); (*fig*) inteligência f. ~**s** (*culin*) miolos mpl. ~**child** n invenção f. ~**less** a estúpido

brainwash /'breɪnwɒʃ/ vt fazer uma lavagem cerebral

brainwave /'breɪnweɪv/ n idéia f, (P) ideia f genial

brainy /'breɪnɪ/ a (-ier, -iest) inteligente, esperto

braise /breɪz/ vt (culin) estufar

brake /breɪk/ n travão m □ vt/i travar. ~ **light** farol m do freio

bran /bræn/ n (husks) farelo m

branch /brɑːntʃ/ n ramo m; (of road) ramificação f; (of railway line) ramal m; (comm) sucursal f; (of bank) balcão m □ vi ~ **(off)** bifurcar-se, ramificar-se

brand /brænd/ n marca f □ vt marcar. ~ **name** marca f de fábrica. ~**-new** a novo em folha. ~ **sb as** tachar alg de, (P) rotular alg de

brandish /'brændɪʃ/ vt brandir

brandy /'brændɪ/ n aguardente f, conhaque m

brass /brɑːs/ n latão m. **the** ~ (mus) os metais mpl □ a de cobre, de latão. **get down to** ~ **tacks** tratar das coisas sérias. **top** ~ (sl) os chefões (colloq)

brassière /'bræsɪə(r)/ n soutien m

brat /bræt/ n (pej) fedelho m

bravado /brə'vɑːdəʊ/ n bravata f

brave /breɪv/ a (-er, -est) bravo, valente □ vt arrostar. ~**ry** /-ərɪ/ n bravura f

brawl /brɔːl/ n briga f, rixa f, desordem f □ vi brigar

brawn /brɔːn/ n força f muscular, músculo m. ~**y** a musculoso

bray /breɪ/ n zurro m □ vi zurrar

brazen /'breɪzn/ a descarado

brazier /'breɪzɪə(r)/ n braseiro m

Brazil /brə'zɪl/ n Brasil m. ~**ian** a & n brasileiro (m). ~ **nut** castanha f do Pará

breach /briːtʃ/ n quebra f; (gap) brecha f □ vt abrir uma brecha em. ~ **of contract** quebra f de contrato. ~ **of the peace** perturbação f da ordem pública. ~ **of trust** abuso m de confiança

bread /bred/ n pão m. ~**-winner** n ganha-pão m

breadcrumbs /'bredkrʌmz/ npl migalhas fpl; (culin) farinha f de rosca

breadline /'bredlaɪn/ n **on the** ~ na miséria

breadth /bredθ/ n largura f; (of mind, view) amplitude f

break /breɪk/ vt (pt broke, pp broken) partir, quebrar; (vow, silence, etc) quebrar; (law) transgredir; (journey) interromper; (news) dar; (a record) bater □ vi partir-se, quebrar-se; (voice, weather) mudar □ n quebra f, ruptura f; (interval) intervalo m; (colloq: opportunity) oportunidade f, chance f. ~ **one's arm/leg** quebrar o braço/a perma ~ **down** vt analisar □ vi (of person) ir-se abaixo; (of machine)

avariar-se. ~ **in** forçar uma entrada. ~ **off** vt quebrar □ vi desligar-se. ~ **out** rebentar. ~ **up** vt/i terminar □ vi (of schools) entrar em férias. ~**able** a quebrável. ~**age** n quebra f

breakdown /'breɪkdaʊn/ n (techn) avaria f, pane f; (med) esgotamento m nervoso; (of figures) análise f □ a (auto) de pronto-socorro. ~ **van** pronto-socorro m

breaker /'breɪkə(r)/ n vaga f de rebentação

breakfast /'brekfəst/ n café m da manhã

breakthrough /'breɪkθruː/ n descoberta f decisiva, avanço m

breakwater /'breɪkwɔːtə(r)/ n quebra-mar m

breast /brest/ n peito m. ~**-feed** vt (pt -fed) amamentar. ~**-stroke** n estilo m bruços

breath /breθ/ n respiração f. **bad** ~ mau hálito m. **out of** ~ sem fôlego. **under one's** ~ num murmúrio, baixo. ~**less** a ofegante

breathalyser /'breθəlaɪzə(r)/ n aparelho m para medir o nível de álcool no sangue, bafômetro m (colloq)

breath|e /briːð/ vt/i respirar. ~**e in** inspirar. ~**e out** expirar. ~**ing** n respiração f. ~**ing-space** n pausa f

breather /'briːðə(r)/ n pausa f de descanso, momento m para respirar

breathtaking /'breθteɪkɪŋ/ a assombroso, arrebatador

bred /bred/ see **breed**

breed /briːd/ vt (pt bred) criar □ vi reproduzir-se □ n raça f. ~**er** n criador m. ~**ing** n criação f; (fig) educação f

breez|e /briːz/ n brisa f. ~**y** a fresco

brevity /'brevətɪ/ n brevidade f

brew /bruː/ vt (beer) fabricar; (tea) fazer; (fig) armar, tramar □ vi fermentar; (tea) preparar; (fig) armar-se, preparar-se □ n decocção f; (tea) infusão f. ~**er** n cervejeiro m. ~**ery** n cervejaria f

bribe /braɪb/ n suborno m, (P) peita f □ vt subornar. ~**ry** /-ərɪ/ n suborno m, corrupção f

brick /brɪk/ n tijolo m

bricklayer /'brɪkleɪə(r)/ n pedreiro m

bridal /'braɪdl/ a nupcial

bride /braɪd/ n noiva f

bridegroom /'braɪdgrʊm/ n noivo m

bridesmaid /'braɪdzmeɪd/ n dama f de honra, (P) honor

bridge[1] /brɪdʒ/ n ponte f; (of nose) cana f □ vt ~ **a gap** preencher uma lacuna

bridge[2] /brɪdʒ/ n (cards) bridge m

bridle /'braɪdl/ n cabeçada f, freio m □ vt refrear. ~**-path** n atalho m, carreiro m

brief[1] /briːf/ a (-er, -est) breve. ∼s npl (men's) cueca f, (P) slip m; (women's) calcinhas fpl, (P) cuecas fpl. ∼ly adv brevemente

brief[2] /briːf/ n (jur) sumário m; (case) causa f; (instructions) instruções fpl □ vt dar instruções a

briefcase /briːfkeɪs/ n pasta f

brigad|e /brɪˈɡeɪd/ n brigada f. ∼ier /-əˈdɪə(r)/ n brigadeiro m

bright /braɪt/ a (-er, -est) brilhante; (of colour) vivo; (of light) forte; (room) claro; (cheerful) alegre; (clever) inteligente. ∼ness n (sheen) brilho m; (clarity) claridade f; (intelligence) inteligência f

brighten /braɪtn/ vt alegrar □ vi (of weather) clarear; (of face) animar-se, iluminar-se

brillian|t /brɪljənt/ a brilhante. ∼ce n brilho m

brim /brɪm/ n borda f; (of hat) aba f □ vi (pt brimmed) ∼ over transbordar, cair por fora

brine /braɪn/ n salmoura f

bring /brɪŋ/ vt (pt brought) trazer. ∼ about causar. ∼ back trazer (de volta); (call to mind) relembrar. ∼ down trazer para baixo; (bird, plane) abater; (prices) baixar. ∼ forward adiantar, apresentar. ∼ it off ser bem sucedido (em alg coisa). ∼ out (take out) tirar; (show) revelar; (book) publicar. ∼ round or to reanimar, fazer voltar a si. ∼ to bear (pressure etc) exercer. ∼ up educar; (med) vomitar; (question) levantar

brink /brɪŋk/ n beira f, borda f

brisk /brɪsk/ a (-er, -est) (pace, movement) vivo, rápido; (business, demand) grande

bristl|e /brɪsl/ n pêlo m.

Britain /brɪtən/ n Grã-Bretanha f

British /brɪtɪʃ/ a britânico. the ∼ o povo m britânico, os britânicos mpl

brittle /brɪtl/ a frágil

broach /brəʊtʃ/ vt abordar, entabular, encetar

broad /brɔːd/ a (-er, -est) largo; (daylight) pleno. ∼ band banda f larga ∼ bean fava f. ∼-minded a tolerante, liberal. ∼ly adv de modo geral

broadcast /brɔːdkɑːst/ vt/i (pt broadcast) transmitir, fazer uma transmissão; (person) cantar, falar etc na rádio or na TV □ n emissão f. ∼ing a & n (de) rádiodifusão (f)

broaden /brɔːdn/ vt/i alargar (-se)

broccoli /brɒkəlɪ/ n inv brócolis mpl, (P) brócolos mpl

brochure /brəʊʃə(r)/ n brochura f

broke /brəʊk/ see **break** □ a (sl) depenado (sl), liso (sl), (P) teso (sl)

broken /brəʊkən/ see **break** □ a ∼ **English** inglês m estropeado. ∼-hearted a com o coração despedaçado

broker /brəʊkə(r)/ n corretor m, broker m

bronchitis /brɒŋˈkaɪtɪs/ n bronquite f

bronze /brɒnz/ n bronze m

brooch /brəʊtʃ/ n broche m

brood /bruːd/ n ninhada f □ vi chocar; (fig) cismar. ∼y a (hen) choca; (fig) sorumbático

brook /brʊk/ n regato m, ribeiro m

broom /bruːm/ n vassoura f; (bot) giesta f

broth /brɒθ/ n caldo m

brothel /brɒθl/ n bordel m

brother /brʌðə(r)/ n irmão m. ∼-in-law n (pl ∼s-in-law) cunhado m. ∼hood n irmandade f, fraternidade f. ∼ly a fraternal

brought /brɔːt/ see **bring**

brow /braʊ/ n (forehead) testa f; (of hill) cume m; (eyebrow) sobrancelha f

browbeat /braʊbiːt/ vt (pt -beat, pp -beaten) intimidar

brown /braʊn/ a (-er, -est) castanho □ n castanho m □ vt/i acastanhar; (in the sun) bronzear, tostar; (meat) alourar

browse /braʊz/ vi (through book) folhear; (of animal) pastar; (in a shop) olhar sem comprar. ∼r (comput) navegador m

bruise /bruːz/ n hematoma m, contusão f □ vt causar um hematoma. ∼d a coberto de hematomas, contuso; (fruit) machucado

brunette /bruːˈnet/ n morena f

brunt /brʌnt/ n the ∼ of o maior peso de, o pior de

brush /brʌʃ/ n escova f; (painter's) pincel m; (skirmish) escaramuça f. ∼ against roçar. ∼ aside não fazer caso de. ∼ off (colloq: reject) mandar passear (colloq). ∼ up (on) aperfeiçoar

brusque /bruːsk/ a brusco

Brussels /brʌslz/ n Bruxelas f. ∼ sprouts couve-de-Bruxelas f

brutal /bruːtl/ a brutal. ∼ity /-ˈtælətɪ/ n brutalidade f

brute /bruːt/ n & a (animal, person) bruto (m). by ∼ force por força bruta

BSc abbr see **Bachelor of Science**

BSE /biːesiː/ n EEB, encefalopatia espongiforma bovina

bubb|le /bʌbl/ n bolha f; (of soap) bola f de sabão □ vi borbulhar. ∼le gum n chiclete m, (P) pastilha f elástica. ∼le over transbordar. ∼ly a efervescente

buck[1] /bʌk/ n macho m □ vi dar galões, (P) corcovear. ∼ up vt/i (sl) animar(-se); (*sl: rush*) apressar-se, despachar-se

buck[2] /bʌk/ *n* (*Amer sl*) dólar *m*

buck[3] /bʌk/ *n* **pass the ~** (*sl*) fazer o jogo do empurra

bucket /'bʌkɪt/ *n* balde *m*

buckle /'bʌkl/ *n* fivela *f* □ *vt/i* afivelar(-se); (*bend*) torcer(-se), vergar. **~ down to** empenhar-se

bud /bʌd/ *n* botão *m*, rebento *m* □ *vi* (*pt* **budded**) rebentar. **in ~** em botão

Buddhis|t /'bʊdɪst/ *a & n* budista (*mf*). **~m** /-zəm/ *n* budismo *m*

budding /'bʌdɪŋ/ *a* nascente, em botão, incipiente

budge /bʌdʒ/ *vt/i* mexer(-se)

budgerigar /'bʌdʒərɪɡa:(r)/ *n* periquito *m*

budget /'bʌdʒɪt/ *n* orçamento *m* □ *vi* (*pt* **budgeted**) **~ for** prever no orçamento *m*

buff /bʌf/ *n* (*colour*) côr *f* de camurça; (*colloq*) fanático *m*, entusiasta *mf* □ *vt* polir

buffalo /'bʌfələʊ/ *n* (*pl* **-oes**) búfalo *m*; (*Amer*) bisão *m*

buffer /'bʌfə(r)/ *n* pára-choque *m*

buffet[1] /'bʊfeɪ/ *n* (*meal, counter*) bufê *m*, (*P*) bufete *m*

buffet[2] /'bʌfɪt/ *vt* (*pt* **buffeted**) esbofetear

buffoon /bə'fu:n/ *n* palhaço *m*

bug /bʌɡ/ *n* (*insect*) bicho *m*; (*bed-bug*) percevejo *m*; (*sl: germ*) vírus *m*; (*sl: device*) microfone *m* de escuta; (*sl: defect*) defeito *m* □ *vt* (*pt* **bugged**) grampear; (*Amer sl: annoy*) chatear (*sl*)

bugbear /'bʌɡbeə(r)/ *n* papão *m*

buggy /'bʌɡɪ/ *n* (*for baby*) carrinho *m*

bugle /'bju:ɡl/ *n* clarim *m*

build /bɪld/ *vt/i* (*pt* **built**) construir, edificar □ *n* físico *m*, compleição *f*. **~ up** *vt/i* criar; (*increase*) aumentar; (*accumulate*) acumular(-se). **~-up** *n* acumulação *f*; (*fig*) publicidade *f*. **~er** *n* construtor *m*, empreiteiro *m*; (*workman*) operário *m*

building /'bɪldɪŋ/ *n* edifício *m*, prédio *m*. **~ site** canteiro *m* de obras. **~ society** sociedade *f* de investimentos imobiliários

built /bɪlt/ *see* build. **~-in** *a* incorporado. **~-in wardrobe** armário *m* embutido na parede. **~-up** *a* urbanizado

bulb /bʌlb/ *n* bolbo *m*; (*electr*) lâmpada *f*. **~ous** *a* bolboso

Bulgaria /bʌl'ɡeərɪə/ *n* Bulgária *f*. **~n** *a & n* búlgaro (*m*)

bulge /bʌldʒ/ *n* bojo *m*, saliência *f* □ *vi* inchar; (*jut out*) fazer uma saliência. **~ing** *a* inchado; (*pocket etc*) cheio

bulk /bʌlk/ *n* quantidade *f*, volume *m*. **in ~** por grosso; (*loose*) a granel. **the ~ of** a maior parte de. **~y** *a* volumoso

bull /bʊl/ *n* touro *m*. **~'s-eye** *n* (*of target*) centro *m* do alvo, mosca *f*

bulldog /'bʊldɒɡ/ *n* buldogue *m*

bulldoze /'bʊldəʊz/ *vt* terraplanar. **~r** /-ə(r)/ *n* bulldozer *m*

bullet /'bʊlɪt/ *n* bala *f*. **~-proof** *a* à prova de balas; (*vehicle*) blindado

bulletin /'bʊlətɪn/ *n* boletim *m*

bullfight /'bʊlfaɪt/ *n* tourada *f*, corrida *f* de touros. **~er** *n* toureiro *m*. **~ing** *n* tauromaquia *f*

bullring /'bʊlrɪŋ/ *n* arena *f*, (*P*) praça *f* de touros

bully /'bʊlɪ/ *n* mandão *m*, pessoa *f* prepotente; (*schol*) terror *m*, o mau □ *vt* intimidar; (*treat badly*) atormentar; (*coerce*) forçar (**into** a)

bum[1] /bʌm/ *n* (*sl: buttocks*) traseiro *m*, bunda *f* (*sl*)

bum[2] /bʌm/ *n* (*Amer sl*) vagabundo *m*

bump /bʌmp/ *n* choque *m*, embate *m*; (*swelling*) inchaço *m*; (*on head*) galo *m* □ *vt/i* bater, chocar. **~ into** bater em, chocar com; (*meet*) esbarrar com, encontrar. **~y** *a* (*surface*) irregular; (*ride*) aos solavancos

bumper /'bʌmpə(r)/ *n* pára-choques *m inv* □ *a* excepcional

bun /bʌn/ *n* pãozinho *m* doce com passas; (*hair*) coque *m*

bunch /bʌntʃ/ *n* (*of flowers*) ramo *m*; (*of keys*) molho *m*; (*of people*) grupo *m*; (*of grapes*) cacho *m*

bundle /'bʌndl/ *n* molho *m* □ *vt* atar num molho; (*push*) despachar

bung /bʌŋ/ *n* batoque *m*, rolha *f* □ *vt* rolhar; (*sl: throw*) atirar, deitar. **~ up** entupir

bungalow /'bʌŋɡələʊ/ *n* chalé *m*; (*outside Europe*) bungalô *m*, (*P*) bungalow *m*

bungle /'bʌŋɡl/ *vt* fazer mal feito, estragar

bunion /'bʌnjən/ *n* (*med*) joanete *m*

bunk /bʌŋk/ *n* (*in train*) couchette *f*; (*in ship*) beliche *m*. **~-beds** *npl* beliches *mpl*

bunker /'bʌŋkə(r)/ *n* (*mil*) abrigo *m*, casamata *f*, bunker *m*; (*golf*) obstáculo *m* em cova de areia

buoy /bɔɪ/ *n* bóia *f* □ *vt* **~ up** animar

buoyan|t /'bɔɪənt/ *a* flutuante; (*fig*) alegre. **~cy** *n* (*fig*) alegria *f*, exuberância *f*

burden /'bɜ:dn/ *n* fardo *m* □ *vt* collegar, sobrecarregar. **~some** *a* pesado

bureau /'bjʊərəʊ/ *n* (*pl* **-eaux**) /-əʊz/ (*desk*) secretária *f*; (*office*) seção *f*, (*P*) secção *f*

bureaucracy /bjʊəˈrɒkrəsɪ/ *n* burocracia *f*

bureaucrat /ˈbjʊərəkræt/ *n* burocrata *mf*. **~ic** /-ˈkrætɪk/ *a* burocrático

burger /ˈbɜːɡə(r)/ *n*

burglar /ˈbɜːɡlə(r)/ *n* ladrão *m*, assaltante *mf*. **~ alarm** *n* alarme *m* contra ladrões. **~ize** *vt* (*Amer*) assaltar. **~y** *n* assalto *m*

burgle /ˈbɜːɡl/ *vt* assaltar

burial /ˈberɪəl/ *n* enterro *m*

burly /ˈbɜːlɪ/ *a* (-**ier**, -**iest**) robusto e corpulento, forte

Burm|a /ˈbɜːmə/ *n* Birmânia *f*. **~ese** /-ˈmiːz/ *a* & *n* birmanês (*m*)

burn /bɜːn/ *vt* (*pt* **burned** *or* **burnt**) queimar □ *vi* queimar (-se), arder □ *n* queimadura *f*. **~ down** reduzir a cinzas. **~er** *n* (*of stove*) bico *m* de gás. **~ing** *a* (*thirst, desire*) ardente; (*topic*) candente

burnt /bɜːnt/ *see* **burn**

burp /bɜːp/ *n* (*colloq*) arroto *m* □ *vi* (*colloq*) arrotar

burrow /ˈbʌrəʊ/ *n* toca *f* □ *vi* cavar, fazer uma toca

burst /bɜːst/ *vt/i* (*pt* **burst**) arrebentar □ *n* estouro *m*, rebentar *m*; (*of anger, laughter*) explosão *f*; (*of firing*) rajada *f*; (*of energy*) acesso *m*. **~ into** (*flames, room, etc*) irromper em. **~ into tears** desatar num choro, desfazer-se em lágrimas. **~ out laughing** desatar a rir

bury /ˈberɪ/ *vt* sepultar, enterrar; (*hide*) esconder; (*engross, thrust*) mergulhar

bus /bʌs/ *n* (*pl* **buses**) ônibus *m*, (*P*) autocarro *m*. **~lane** faixa *f* de ônibus, de autocarro (*p*). **~-stop** *n* paragem *f*

bush /bʊʃ/ *n* arbusto *m*; (*land*) mato *m*. **~y** *a* espesso

business /ˈbɪznɪs/ *n* (*trade, shop, affair*) negócio *m*; (*task*) função *f*; (*occupation*) ocupação *f*. **have no ~ to** não ter o direito de. **it's no ~ of yours** não é da sua conta. **mind your own ~** cuide da sua vida. **that's my ~** isso é meu problema. **~like** *a* eficiente, sistemático. **~man** *n* homem *m* de negócios, comerciante *m*

busker /ˈbʌskə(r)/ *n* músico *m* ambulante

bust[1] /bʌst/ *n* busto *m*

bust[2] /bʌst/ *vt/i* (*pt* **busted** *or* **bust**) (*sl*) = **burst, break** □ *a* falido. **~-up** *n* (*sl*) discussão *f*, (*P*) bulha *f*. **go ~** (*sl*) falir

bustl|e /ˈbʌsl/ *vi* andar numa azáfama; (*hurry*) apressar-se □ *n* azáfama *f*. **~ing** *a* animado, movimentado

bus|y /ˈbɪzɪ/ *a* (-**ier**, -**iest**) ocupado; (*street*) movimentado; (*day*) atarefado □ *vt* **~y o.s. with** ocupar-se com. **~ily** *adv* ativamente, atarefadamente

busybody /ˈbɪzɪbɒdɪ/ *n* intrometido *m*, pessoa *f* abelhuda

but /bʌt/ *conj* mas □ *prep* exceto, (*P*) excepto, senão □ *adv* apenas, só. **all ~** todos menos; (*nearly*) quaze, por pouco não. **~ for** sem, se não fosse. **last ~ one/two** penúltimo/antepenúltimo. **nobody ~** ninguém a não ser

butcher /ˈbʊtʃə(r)/ *n* açougueiro *m*, (*P*) homem *m* do talho; (*fig*) carrasco *m* □ *vt* chacinar. **the ~'s** açougue *m*, (*P*) talho *m*. **~y** *n* chacina *f*

butler /ˈbʌtlə(r)/ *n* mordomo *m*

butt /bʌt/ *n* (*of gun*) coronha *f*; (*of cigarette*) ponta *f*; (*target*) alvo *m* de troça, de ridículo *etc*; (*cask*) barril *m* □ *vt/i* dar cabeçada em. **~ in** interromper

butter /ˈbʌtə(r)/ *n* manteiga *f* □ *vt* pôr manteiga em. **~-bean** *n* feijão *m* branco

buttercup /ˈbʌtəkʌp/ *n* botão-de-ouro *m*

butterfly /ˈbʌtəflaɪ/ *n* borboleta *f*

buttock /ˈbʌtək/ *n* nádega *f*

button /ˈbʌtn/ *n* botão *m* □ *vt/i* abotoar(-se)

buttonhole /ˈbʌtnhəʊl/ *n* casa *f* de botão; (*in lapel*) botoeira *f* □ *vt* (*fig*) obrigar a ouvir

buttress /ˈbʌtrɪs/ *n* contraforte *m*; (*fig*) esteio *m* □ *vt* sustentar

buxom /ˈbʌksəm/ *a* roliço, rechonchudo

buy /baɪ/ *vt* (*pt* **bought**) comprar (**from** a); (*sl: believe*) engolir (*colloq*) □ *n* compra *f*. **~er** *n* comprador *m*

buzz /bʌz/ *n* zumbido *m* □ *vi* zumbir. **~ off** (*sl*) pôr-se a andar. **~er** *n* campainha *f*

by /baɪ/ *prep* (*near*) junto de, perto de; (*along, past, means*) por; (*according to*) conforme; (*before*) antes de. **~ land/sea/air** por terra/mar/ar. **~ bike/car** *etc* de bicicleta/carro *etc*. **~ day/night** de dia/noite. **~ the kilo** por quilo. **~ now** a esta hora. **~ accident/mistake** sem querer. **~ oneself** sozinho □ *adv* (*near*) perto. **~ and ~** muito em breve. **~ and large** no conjunto. **~-election** *n* eleição *f* suplementar. **~-law** *n* regulamento *m*. **~-product** *n* derivado *m*

bye(-bye) /ˈbaɪ(baɪ)/ *int* (*colloq*) adeus, adeusinho

bygone /ˈbaɪɡɒn/ *a* passado. **let ~s be ~s** o que passou, passou

bypass /ˈbaɪpɑːs/ *n* (*estrada*) secundária *f*, desvio *m*; (*med*) by-pass *m*, ponte *f* de safema □ *vt* fazer um desvio; (*fig*) contornar

bystander /ˈbaɪstændə(r)/ *n* circunstante *mf*, espectador *m*

byte /baɪt/ *n* byte *m*

cab /kæb/ n táxi m; (of lorry, train) cabina f, cabine f

cabaret /'kæbəreɪ/ n variedades fpl, cabaré m

cabbage /'kæbɪdʒ/ n couve f, repolho m

cabin /'kæbɪn/ n cabana f; (in plane) cabina f; (in ship) camarote m

cabinet /'kæbɪnɪt/ n armário m. **C~** (pol) gabinete m

cable /'keɪbl/ n cabo m. **~-car** n funicular m, teleférico m. **~ railway** funicular m. **~ television** televisão f a cabo

cache /kæʃ/ n (esconderijo m de) tesouro m, armas fpl, provisões fpl

cackle /'kækl/ n cacarejo m □ vi cacarejar

cactus /'kæktəs/ n (pl **~es** or **cacti** /-taɪ/) cacto m

caddie /'kædɪ/ n (golf) caddie m

caddy /'kædɪ/ n lata f para o chá

cadet /kə'det/ n cadete m

cadge /kædʒ/ vt/i filar, (P) cravar

Caesarean /sɪ'zeərɪən/ a **~ (section)** cesariana f

café /'kæfeɪ/ n café m

cafeteria /kæfɪ'tɪərɪə/ n cafeteria f, restaurante m self-service

caffeine /'kæfi:n/ n cafeína f

cage /keɪdʒ/ n gaiola f

cagey /'keɪdʒɪ/ a (colloq: secretive) misterioso, reservado

cajole /kə'dʒəʊl/ vt **~ sb into doing sth** convencer alguém (com lábia ou lisonjas) a fazer alg coisa

cake /keɪk/ n bolo m. **~d** a empastado. **his shoes were ~d with mud** tinha os sapatos cobertos de lama. **a piece of ~** (sl) canja f (sl)

calamity /kə'læmətɪ/ n calamidade f

calcium /'kælsɪəm/ n cálcio m

calculat|e /'kælkjʊleɪt/ vt/i calcular; (Amer: suppose) supor. **~ed** a (action) deliberado, calculado. **~ing** a calculista. **~ion** /-'leɪʃn/ n cálculo m. **~or** n calculador m, (P) maquina f de calcular

calendar /'kælɪndə(r)/ n calendário m

calf [1] /ka:f/ n (pl **calves**) (young cow or bull) vitelo m, bezerro m; (of other animals) cria f

calf [2] /ka:f/ n (pl **calves**) (of leg) barriga f da perna

calibrat|e /'kælɪbreɪt/ vt calibrar. **~ion** /-'breɪʃn/ n calibragem f

calibre /'kælɪbə(r)/ n calibre m

calico /'kælɪkəʊ/ n pano m de algodão; (printed) chita f, algodão m

call /kɔ:l/ vt/i chamar; (summon) convocar; (phone) telefonar. **~ (in or round)** (visit) passar por casa de □ n chamada f; (bird's cry) canto m; (shout) brado m, grito m. **be ~ed** (named) chamar-se. **be on ~** estar de serviço. **~ back** (phone) tornar a telefonar; (visit) voltar. **~ for** (demand) pedir, requerer; (fetch) ir buscar. **~ off** cancelar. **~ on** (visit) visitar, fazer uma visita a. **~ out (to)** chamar. **~ up** (mil) mobilizar, recrutar; (phone) telefonar. **~-box** n cabina f telefónica, (P) telefónica. **~centre** central f telefónica **~er** n visitante f, visita f; (phone) chamador m, (P) pessoa f que faz a chamada. **~ing** n vocação f

callous /'kæləs/ a insensível. **~ly** adv sem piedade.

callow /'kæləʊ/ a (-er, -est) inexperiente, verde

calm /ka:m/ a (-er, -est) calmo □ n calma f □ vt/i **~ (down)** acalmar(-se). **~ness** n calma f

calorie /'kælərɪ/ n caloria f

camber /'kæmbə(r)/ n (of road) abaulamento m

camcorder /'kæmkɔ:də(r)/ n câmera f de filmar

came /keɪm/ see **come**

camel /'kæml/ n camelo m

camera /'kæmərə/ n máquina f fotográfica; (cine, TV) câmera f. **~man** n (pl -men) operador m

camouflage /'kæməflɑ:ʒ/ n camuflagem f □ vt camuflar

camp [1] /kæmp/ n acampamento m □ vi acampar. **~-bed** n cama f de campanha. **~er** n campista mf; (car) auto-caravana f. **~ing** n campismo m

camp [2] /kæmp/ a afetado, efeminado

campaign /kæm'peɪn/ n campanha f □ vi fazer campanha

campsite /'kæmpsaɪt/ n área f de camping, (P) parque m de campismo

campus /'kæmpəs/ n (pl -puses /-pəsɪz/) campus m, (P) cidade f universitária

can [1] /kæn/ n vasilha f de lata; (for food) lata f (de conserva) □ vt (pt **canned**) enlatar. **~ned music** música f em fita para locais públicos. **~-opener** n abridor m de latas, (P) abrelatas m

can [2] /kæn/ v aux (be able to) poder, ser capaz de; (know how to) saber. **I ~not/~'t go** não posso ir

Canad|a /ˈkænədə/ *n* Canadá *m*. ∼**ian** /kəˈneɪdɪən/ *a* & *n* canadense (*mf*), (*P*) canadiano (*m*)

canal /kəˈnæl/ *n* canal *m*

canary /kəˈneərɪ/ *n* canário *m*. **C**∼ **Islands** *npl* as (Ilhas) Canárias

cancel /ˈkænsl/ *vt* (*pt* **cancelled**) cancelar; (*cross out*) riscar; (*stamps*) inutilizar. ∼ **out** *vi* (*fig*) neutralizar-se mutuamente. ∼**lation** /-ˈleɪʃn/ *n* cancelamento *m*

cancer /ˈkænsə(r)/ *n* câncer *m*, cancro *m*. **C**∼ (*astrol*) Caranguejo *m*, Câncer *m*. ∼**ous** *a* canceroso

candid /ˈkændɪd/ *a* franco. ∼**ly** *adv* francamente

candida|te /ˈkændɪdeɪt/ *n* candidato *m*. ∼**cy** /-əsɪ/ *n* candidatura *f*

candle /ˈkændl/ *n* vela *f*; (*in church*) vela *f*, círio *m*. ∼**-light** *n* luz *f* de velas

candlestick /ˈkændlstɪk/ *n* castiçal *m*

candour /ˈkændə(r)/ *n* franqueza *f*, candura *f*

candy /ˈkændɪ/ *n* bala *f*, (*P*) açúcar cândi; (*Amer: sweet, sweets*) doce(s) *m* (*pl*). ∼**-floss** *n* algodão-doce *m*

cane /keɪn/ *n* cana *f*; (*walking-stick*) bengala *f*; (*for baskets*) verga *f*; (*school: for punishment*) vergasta *f* □ *vt* vergastar

canine /ˈkeɪnaɪn/ *a* & *n* canino (*m*)

canister /ˈkænɪstə(r)/ *n* lata *f*

cannabis /ˈkænəbɪs/ *n* cânhamo *m*, maconha *f*

cannibal /ˈkænɪbl/ *n* canibal *mf*. ∼**ism** /-zəm/ *n* canibalismo *m*

cannon /ˈkænən/ *n inv* canhão *m*. ∼**-ball** *n* bala *f* de canhão

cannot /ˈkænət/ = **can not**

canny /ˈkænɪ/ *a* (**-ier, -iest**) astuto, manhoso

canoe /kəˈnuː/ *n* canoa *f* □ *vi* andar de canoa. ∼**ing** *n* (*sport*) canoagem *f*. ∼**ist** *n* canoeiro *m*, (*P*) canoísta *mf*

canon /ˈkænən/ *n* cônego *m*, (*P*) cónego *m*; (*rule*) cânone *m*

canonize /ˈkænənaɪz/ *vt* canonizar

canopy /ˈkænəpɪ/ *n* dossel *m*; (*over doorway*) toldo *m*, marquise *f*; (*fig*) abóbada *f*

can't /kɑːnt/ = **can not**

cantankerous /kænˈtæŋkərəs/ *a* irascível, intratável

canteen /kænˈtiːn/ *n* cantina *f*; (*flask*) cantil *m*; (*for cutlery*) estojo *m*

canter /ˈkæntə(r)/ *n* meio galope *m*, cânter *m* □ *vi* andar a meio galope

canton /ˈkæntɒn/ *n* cantão *m*

canvas /ˈkænvəs/ *n* lona *f*; (*for painting or tapestry*) tela *f*

canvass /ˈkænvəs/ *vt/i* angariar votos *or* fregueses

canyon /ˈkænjən/ *n* canhão *m*, (*P*) desfiladeiro *m*

cap /kæp/ *n* (*with peak*) boné *m*; (*without peak*) barrete *m*; (*of nurse*) touca *f*; (*of bottle, pen, tube, etc*) tampa *f*; (*mech*) tampa *f*, tampão *m* □ *vt* (*pt* **capped**) (*bottle, pen, tube, etc*) tapar, tampar; (*rates*) impôr um limite a; (*outdo*) suplantar; (*sport*) selecionar, (*P*) seleccionar. ∼**ped with** encimado de, coroado de

capab|le /ˈkeɪpəbl/ *a* (*person*) capaz (**of** de); (*things, situations*) suscetível, (*P*) susceptível (**of** de). ∼**ility** /-ˈbɪlətɪ/ *n* capacidade *f*. ∼**ly** *adv* capazmente

capacity /kəˈpæsətɪ/ *n* capacidade *f*. **in one's** ∼ **as** na (sua) qualidade de

cape[1] /keɪp/ *n* (*cloak*) capa *f*

cape[2] /keɪp/ *n* (*geog*) cabo *m*

caper[1] /ˈkeɪpə(r)/ *vi* andar aos pinotes

caper[2] /ˈkeɪpə(r)/ *n* (*culin*) alcaparra *f*

capillary /kəˈpɪlərɪ/ *n* (*pl* **-ies**) vaso *m* capilar

capital /ˈkæpɪtl/ *a* capital □ *n* (*town*) capital *f*; (*money*) capital *m*. ∼ (*letter*) maiúscula *f*. ∼ **punishment** pena *f* de morte

capitalis|t /ˈkæpɪtəlɪst/ *a* & *n* capitalista (*mf*). ∼**m** /-zəm/ *n* capitalismo *m*

capitalize /ˈkæpɪtəlaɪz/ *vi* capitalizar; (*finance*) financiar; (*writing*) escrever com maiúscula. ∼ **on** tirar partido de

capitulat|e /kəˈpɪtʃʊleɪt/ *vi* capitular. ∼**ion** /-ˈleɪʃn/ *n* capitulação *f*

capricious /kəˈprɪʃəs/ *a* caprichoso

Capricorn /ˈkæprɪkɔːn/ *n* (*astrol*) Capricórnio *m*

capsicum /ˈkæpsɪkəm/ *n* pimento *m*

capsize /kæpˈsaɪz/ *vt/i* virar(-se)

capsule /ˈkæpsjuːl/ *n* cápsula *f*

captain /ˈkæptɪn/ *n* capitão *m*; (*navy*) capitão-de-mar-e-guerra *m* □ *vt* capitanear, comandar

caption /ˈkæpʃn/ *n* legenda *f*; (*heading*) título *m*

captivate /ˈkæptɪveɪt/ *vt* cativar

captiv|e /ˈkæptɪv/ *a* & *n* cativo (*m*), prisioneiro (*m*). ∼**ity** /-ˈtɪvətɪ/ *n* cativeiro *m*

captor /ˈkæptə(r)/ *n* captor *m*

capture /ˈkæptʃə(r)/ *vt* capturar; (*attention*) prender □ *n* captura *f*

car /kɑː(r)/ *n* carro *m*. ∼ **ferry** barca *f* para carros. ∼**-park** *n* (parque *m* de) estacionamento (*m*). ∼ **phone** telefone *m* de carro. ∼**-wash** *n* estação *f* de lavagem

carafe /kəˈræf/ *n* garrafa *f* para água ou vinho

caramel /'kærəməl/ n caramelo m.

carat /'kærət/ n quilate m

caravan /'kærəvæn/ n caravana f, reboque m

caraway /'kærəweɪ/ n ~ **seed** cariz f

carbohydrate /ka:bəʊ'haɪdreɪt/ n hidrato m de carbono

carbon /'ka:bən/ n carbono m. ~ **copy** cópia f em papel carbono, (P) químico. ~ **monoxide** óxido m de carbono. ~ **paper** papel m carbono, (P) químico

carburettor /ka:bjʊ'retə(r)/ n carburador m

carcass /'ka:kəs/ n carcaça f

card /ka:d/ n cartão m; (*postcard*) postal m; (*playing card*) carta f. ~**game(s)** n(*pl*) jogo(s) m(*pl*) de cartas. ~ **index** n fichário m, (P) ficheiro m

cardboard /'ka:dbɔ:d/ n cartão m, papelão m

cardiac /'ka:dɪæk/ a cardíaco

cardigan /'ka:dɪgən/ n casaco m de lã

cardinal /'ka:dɪnl/ a cardeal, principal. ~ **number** numeral m cardinal ◻ n (*relig*) cardeal m

care /keə(r)/ n cuidado m; (*concern*) interesse m ◻ vi ~ **about** (*be interested*) estar interessado por; (*be worried*) estar preocupado com. ~ **for** (*like*) gostar de; (*look after*) tomar conta de. **take** ~ tomar cuidado. **take** ~ **of** cuidar de; (*deal with*) tratar de. **he couldn't** ~ **less** ele está pouco ligando, ele não dá a menor (colloq)

career /kə'rɪə(r)/ n carreira f ◻ vi ir a toda a velocidade, ir numa carreira

carefree /'keəfri:/ a despreocupado

careful /'keəfl/ a cuidadoso; (*cautious*) cauteloso. ~**!** cuidado! ~**ly** adv cuidadosamente; (*cautiously*) cautelosamente

careless /'keəlɪs/ a descuidado (**about** com). ~**ly** adv descuidadamente. ~**ness** n descuido m, negligência f

caress /kə'res/ n carícia f ◻ vt acariciar

caretaker /'keəteɪkə(r)/ n zelador m duma casa vizia; (*janitor*) zelador m, (P) porteiro m

cargo /'ka:gəʊ/ n (*pl* -**oes**) carregamento m, carga f

Caribbean /kærɪ'bi:ən/ a caraíba. **the** ~ as Caraíbas fpl

caricature /'kærɪkətjʊə(r)/ n caricatura f ◻ vt caricaturar

caring /'keərɪŋ/ a carinhoso, afetuoso, (P) afectuoso

carnage /'ka:nɪdʒ/ n carnificina f

carnation /ka:'neɪʃn/ n cravo m

carnival /'ka:nɪvl/ n carnaval m

carol /'kærəl/ n cântico m or canto m de Natal

carp[1] /ka:p/ n inv carpa f

carp[2] /ka:p/ vi ~ (**at**) criticar

carpent|er /'ka:pɪntə(r)/ n carpinteiro m. ~**ry** n carpintaria f

carpet /'ka:pɪt/ n tapete m ◻ vt (*pt* **carpeted**) atapetar. **with fitted** ~**s** (estar) atapetado. **be on the** ~ (*colloq*) ser chamado à ordem. ~**sweeper** n limpador m de tapetes

carport /'ka:pɔ:t/ n abrigo m, (P) telheiro m para automóveis

carriage /'kærɪdʒ/ n carruagem f; (*of goods*) frete m, transporte m; (*cost, bearing*) porte m

carriageway /'kærɪdʒweɪ/ n faixa f de rodagem, pista f

carrier /'kærɪə(r)/ n transportador m; (*company*) transportadora f; (*med*) portador m. ~ (**bag**) saco m de plástico

carrot /'kærət/ n cenoura f

carry /'kærɪ/ vt/i levar; (*goods*) transportar; (*involve*) acarretar; (*have for sale*) ter à venda. **be carried away** entusiasmar-se, deixar-se levar. ~**cot** n moisés m. ~ **off** levar à força; (*prize*) incluir. ~ **it off** sair-se bem (de). ~ **on** continuar; (*colloq: flirt*) flertar; (*colloq: behave*) portar-se (mal). ~ **out** executar; (*duty*) cumprir. ~ **through** levar a cabo

cart /ka:t/ n carroça f, carro m ◻ vt acarretar; (*colloq*) carregar com

cartilage /'ka:tɪlɪdʒ/ n cartilagem f

carton /'ka:tn/ n embalagem f de cartão or de plástico; (*of yogurt*) embalagem f, pote m; (*of milk*) pacote m

cartoon /ka:'tu:n/ n desenho m humorístico, caricatura f; (*strip*) estória f em quadrinhos, (P) banda f desenhada; (*film*) desenhos mpl animados. ~**ist** n caricaturista mf; (*of strip, film*) desenhador m

cartridge /'ka:trɪdʒ/ n cartucho m

carv|e /ka:v/ vt esculpir, talhar; (*meat*) trinchar. ~**ing** n obra f de talha; (*on tree-trunk*) incisão f. ~**ing knife** faca f de trinchar, trinchante m

cascade /kæs'keɪd/ n cascata f ◻ vi cair em cascata

case[1] /keɪs/ n caso m; (*jur*) causa f, processo m; (*phil*) argumentos mpl. **in any** ~ em todo caso. **in** ~ (**of**) no caso (de). **in that** ~ nesse caso

case[2] /keɪs/ n caixa f; (*crate*) caixa f, caixote m; (*for camera, jewels, spectacles, etc*) estojo m; (*suitcase*) mala f; (*for cigarettes*) cigarreira f

cash /kæʃ/ n dinheiro m, numerário m, cash m ◻ vt (*obtain money for*) cobrar, receber; (*give money for*) pagar. **be short of** ~ ter pouco dinheiro. ~ **a cheque** (*receive/give*) cobrar/descontar um cheque. ∼ **in** receber. ∼ **in (on)** aproveitar-se de. **in** ∼ em dinheiro. **pay** ∼ pagar em dinheiro. ∼ **desk** caixa *f*. ∼ **dispenser** caixa *f* electrónica. ∼**flow** *n* cash-flow *m*. ∼ **register** caixa *f* registadora, (*P*) registradora *f*

cashew /kæˈʃuː/ *n* caju *m*

cashier /kæˈʃɪə(r)/ *n* caixa *mf*

cashmere /kæʃˈmɪə(r)/ *n* caxemira *f*

casino /kəˈsiːnəʊ/ *n* (*pl* -**os**) casino *m*

cask /kɑːsk/ *n* casco *m*, barril *m*

casket /ˈkɑːskɪt/ *n* pequeno cofre *m*; (*Amer: coffin*) caixão *m*

casserole /ˈkæsərəʊl/ *n* caçarola *f*; (*stew*) estufado *m*

cassette /kəˈset/ *n* cassette *f*. ∼ **player** gravador *m*. ∼ **recorder** *n* gravador *m*

cast /kɑːst/ *vt* (*pt* **cast**) lançar, arremessar; (*shed*) despojar-se de; (*vote*) dar; (*metal*) fundir; (*shadow*) projetar, (*P*) projectar ▫ *n* (*theatr*) elenco *m*; (*mould*) molde *m*; (*med*) aparelho *m* de gesso. ∼ **iron** *n* ferro *m* fundido. ∼**-iron** *a* de ferro fundido; (*fig*) muito forte. ∼**-offs** *npl* roupa *f* velha

castanets /kæstəˈnets/ *npl* castanholas *fpl*

castaway /ˈkɑːstəweɪ/ *n* náufrago *m*

caste /kɑːst/ *n* casta *f*

castigate /ˈkæstɪɡeɪt/ *vt* castigar

castle /ˈkɑːsl/ *n* castelo *m*; (*chess*) torre *f*

castor /ˈkɑːstə(r)/ *n* roda *f* de pé de móvel. ∼ **sugar** açúcar *m* em pó

castrat|e /kæˈstreɪt/ *vt* castrar. ∼**ion** /-ʃn/ *n* castração *f*

casual /ˈkæʒʊəl/ *a* (*chance: meeting*) casual; (*careless, unmethodical*) descuidado; (*informal*) informal. ∼ **clothes** roupa *f* prática *or* de lazer. ∼ **work** trabalho *m* ocasional. ∼**ly** *adv* casualmente; (*carelessly*) sem cuidado

casualty /ˈkæʒʊəltɪ/ *n* (*dead*) morto *m*; (*death*) morte *f*; (*injured*) ferido *m*; (*victim*) vítima *f*; (*mil*) baixa *f*

cat /kæt/ *n* gato *m*. ∼**'s-eyes** *npl* (*P*) reflectores *mpl*

Catalonia /kætəˈləʊnɪə/ *n* Catalunha *f*

catalogue /ˈkætəlɒɡ/ *n* catálogo *m* ▫ *vt* catalogar

catalyst /ˈkætəlɪst/ *n* catalisador *m*

catapult /ˈkætəpʌlt/ *n* (*child's*) atiradeira *f*, (*P*) fisga *f* ▫ *vt* catapultar

cataract /ˈkætərækt/ *f* (*waterfall & med*) catarata *f*

catarrh /kəˈtɑː(r)/ *n* catarro *m*

catastroph|e /kəˈtæstrəfɪ/ *n* catástrofe *f*. ∼**ic** /kætəsˈtrɒfɪk/ *a* catastrófico

catch /kætʃ/ *vt* (*pt* **caught**) apanhar; (*grasp*) agarrar; (*hear*) perceber ▫ *vi*

prender-se (**in** em); (*get stuck*) ficar preso ▫ *n* apanha *f*; (*of fish*) pesca *f*; (*trick*) ratoeira *f*; (*snag*) problema *m*; (*on door*) trinco *m*; (*fastener*) fecho *m*. ∼ **fire** pegar fogo, (*P*) incendiar-se. ∼ **on** (*colloq*) pegar, tornar-se popular. ∼ **sb's eye** atrair a atenção de alg. ∼ **sight of** avistar. ∼ **up (with)** pôr-se a par (com); (*work*) pôr em dia. ∼**-phrase** *n* cliché *m*

catching /ˈkætʃɪŋ/ *a* contagioso, infeccioso

catchment /ˈkætʃmənt/ *n* ∼ **area** (*geog*) bacia *f* de captação; (*fig: of school, hospital*) área *f*

catchy /ˈkætʃɪ/ *a* que pega fácil

categorical /kætɪˈɡɒrɪkl/ *a* categórico

category /ˈkætɪɡərɪ/ *n* categoria *f*

cater /ˈkeɪtə(r)/ *vi* fornecer comida (para clubes, casamentos, etc). ∼ **for** (*pander to*) satisfazer; (*consumers*) dirigir-se a. ∼**er** *n* fornecedor *m*. ∼**ing** *n* catering *m*

caterpillar /ˈkætəpɪlə(r)/ *n* lagarta *f*

cathedral /kəˈθiːdrəl/ *n* catedral *f*

catholic /ˈkæθəlɪk/ *a* universal; (*eclectic*) eclético, (*P*) ecléctico. **C**∼ *a* & *n* católico (*m*). **C**∼**ism** /kəˈθɒlɪsɪzəm/ *n* catolicismo *m*

cattle /ˈkætl/ *npl* gado *m*

catty /ˈkætɪ/ *a* (*dissimuladamente*) maldoso, com perfídia

caught /kɔːt/ *see* **catch**

cauldron /ˈkɔːldrən/ *n* caldeirão *m*

cauliflower /ˈkɒlɪflaʊə(r)/ *n* couve-flor *f*

cause /kɔːz/ *n* causa *f* ▫ *vt* causar. ∼ **sth to grow/move** *etc* fazer crescer/mexer *etc* alg coisa

causeway /ˈkɔːzweɪ/ *n* estrada *f* elevada, caminho *m* elevado

caustic /ˈkɔːstɪk/ *a* cáustico

cauti|on /ˈkɔːʃn/ *n* cautela *f*; (*warning*) aviso *m* ▫ *vt* avisar. ∼**ous** /ˈkɔːʃəs/ *a* cauteloso. ∼**ously** *adv* cautelosamente

cavalry /ˈkævəlrɪ/ *n* cavalaria *f*

cave /keɪv/ *n* caverna *f*, gruta *f* ▫ *vi* ∼ **in** desabar, dar de si

caveman /ˈkeɪvmæn/ *n* (*pl* -**men**) troglodita *m*, homen *m* das cavernas; (*fig*) (*tipo*) primário *m*

cavern /ˈkævən/ *n* caverna *f*. ∼**ous** *a* cavernoso

caviare /ˈkævɪɑː(r)/ *n* caviar *m*

caving /ˈkeɪvɪŋ/ *n* espeleologia *f*

cavity /ˈkævətɪ/ *n* cavidade *f*

cavort /kəˈvɔːt/ *vi* curvetear; (*person*) andar aos pinotes

CD /siːˈdiː/ *see* **compact disc**

cease /siːs/ *vt/i* cessar. ∼**-fire** *n* cessar-fogo *m*. ∼**less** *a* incessante

cedar /ˈsiːdə(r)/ *n* cedro *m*

cedilla /sɪ'dɪlə/ n cedilha f
ceiling /'si:lɪŋ/ n (lit & fig) teto m, (P) tecto m
celebrat|e /'selɪbreɪt/ vt/i celebrar, festejar. ~**ion** /-'breɪʃn/ n celebração f, festejo m
celebrated /'selɪbreɪtɪd/ a célebre
celebrity /sɪ'lebrətɪ/ n celebridade f
celery /'selərɪ/ n aipo m
celiba|te /'selɪbət/ a celibatário. ~**cy** n celibato m
cell /sel/ n (of prison, convent) cela f; (biol, pol, electr) célula f ~**phone** (B) celular m, (p) telemóvel
cellar /'selə(r)/ n porão m, cave f; (for wine) adega f, cave f
cell|o /'tʃeləʊ/ n (pl -os) violoncelo m. ~**ist** n violoncelista mf
Cellophane /'seləfem/ n (P) celofane m
cellular /'seljʊlə(r)/ a celular
Celt /kelt/ n celta mf. ~**ic** a celta, céltico
cement /sɪ'ment/ n cimento m □ vt cimentar. ~**-mixer** n betoneira f
cemetery /'semətrɪ/ n cemitério m
censor /'sensə(r)/ n censor m □ vt censurar. ~**ship** n censura f
censure /'senʃə(r)/ n censura f, crítica f □ vt censurar, criticar
census /'sensəs/ n recenseamento m, censo m
cent /sent/ n cêntimo m
centenary /sen'ti:nərɪ/ n centenário m
centigrade /'sentɪgreɪd/ a centígrado
centilitre /'sentɪli:tə(r)/ n centilitro m
centimetre /'sentmi:tə(r)/ n centímetro m
centipede /'sentɪpi:d/ n centopéia f, (P) centopeia f
central /'sentrəl/ a central. ~ **heating** aquecimento m central. ~**ize** vt centralizar. ~**ly** adv no centro
centre /'sentə(r)/ n centro m □ vt (pt centred) centrar □ vi ~ **on** concentrar-se em, fixar-se em
centrifugal /sen'trɪfjʊgl/ a centrífugo
century /'sentʃərɪ/ n século m
ceramic /sɪ'ræmɪk/ a (object) em cerâmica. ~**s** n cerâmica f
cereal /'sɪərɪəl/ n cereal m
cerebral /'serɪbrəl/ a cerebral
ceremonial /serɪ'məʊnɪəl/ a de cerimônia □ n cerimonial m
ceremon|y /'serɪmənɪ/ n cerimônia f, (P) cerimónia f. ~**ious** /-'məʊnɪəs/ a cerimonioso
certain /'sə:tn/ a certo. **be** ~ ter a certeza. **for** ~ com certeza, ao certo. **make** ~ confirmar, verificar. ~**ly** adv com certeza, certamente. ~**ty** n certeza f

certificate /sə'tɪfɪkət/ n certificado m; (birth, marriage) certidão f; (health) atestado m
certif|y /'sɜ:tɪfaɪ/ vt/i certificar. ~**ied** a (as insane) declarado
cervical /sɜ:'vaɪkl/ a cervical; (of cervix) do útero
cesspit, cesspool /'sespɪt, 'sespu:l/ ns fossa f sanitária
chafe /tʃeɪf/ vt/i esfregar; (make/become sore) esfolar/ficar esfolado; (fig) irritar(-se)
chaff /tʃa:f/ vt brincar com □ n brincadeira f; (husk) casca f
chaffinch /'tʃæfɪntʃ/ n tentilhão m
chagrin /'ʃægrɪn/ n decepção f, desgosto m, aborrecimento m
chain /tʃeɪn/ n corrente f, cadeia f; (series) cadeia f □ vt acorrentar. ~ **reaction** reação f, (P) reacção f em cadeia. ~**-smoke** vi fumar cigarros um atrás do outro. ~ **store** loja f pertencente a uma cadeia
chair /tʃeə(r)/ n cadeira f; (position of chairman) presidência f; (univ) cátedra f □ vt presidir
chairman /'tʃeəmən/ n (pl -men) presidente mf
chalet /'ʃæleɪ/ n chalé m
chalk /tʃɔ:k/ n greda f, cal f; (for writing) giz m □ vt traçar com giz
challeng|e /'tʃælɪndʒ/ n desafio m; (by sentry) interpelação f □ vt desafiar; (question truth of) contestar. ~**er** n (sport) pretendente mf (ao título). ~**ing** a estimulante, que constitui um desafio
chamber /'tʃeɪmbə(r)/ n (old use) aposento m. ~**-maid** n arrumadeira f. ~ **music** música f de câmara. **C**~ **of Commerce** Câmara f de Comércio
chamois /'ʃæmɪ/ n. ~**(-leather)** camurça f
champagne /ʃæm'peɪn/ n champanhe m
champion /'tʃæmpɪən/ n campeão m, campeã f □ vt defender. ~**ship** n campeonato m
chance /tʃɑ:ns/ n acaso m; (luck) sorte f; (opportunity) oportunidade f, chance f; (likelihood) hipótese f, probabilidade f; (risk) risco m □ a casual, fortuito □ vi calhar □ vt arriscar. **by** ~ por acaso
chancellor /'tʃɑ:nsələ(r)/ n chanceler m. **C**~ **of the Exchequer** Ministro m das Finanças
chancy /'tʃɑ:nsɪ/ a arriscado
chandelier /ʃændə'lɪə(r)/ n lustre m
change /tʃeɪndʒ/ vt mudar; (exchange) trocar (**for** por); (clothes, house, trains, etc) mudar de □ vi mudar, (clothes) mudar-se, mudar de roupa □ n mudança f; (money) troco m. **a** ~ **of**

clothes uma muda de roupa. **~ hands** (*ownership*) mudar de dono. **~ into** (*a butterfly etc*) transformar-se em; (*evening dress etc*) pôr. **~ one's mind** mudar de idéia. **~ over** passar, mudar (**to** para). **~-over** *n* mudança *f*. **~able** *a* variável

channel /'tʃænl/ *n* canal *m* □ *vt* (*pt* **channelled**) canalizar. **the C~ Islands** as Ilhas do Canal da Mancha. **the (English) C~** o Canal da Mancha

chant /tʃɑːnt/ *n* cântico *m*; (*of crowd etc*) *vt/i* cantar, entoar

chao|s /'keɪɒs/ *n* caos *m*. **~tic** /-'ɒtɪk/ *a* caótico

chap /tʃæp/ *n* (*colloq*) sujeito *m*, (*B*) cara *m*, (*P*) tipo *m*

chapel /'tʃæpl/ *n* capela *f*

chaperon /'ʃæpərəʊn/ *n* pau-de-cabeleira *m*, chaperon *m* □ *vt* servir de pau-de-cabeleira *or* de chaperon

chaplain /'tʃæplɪn/ *n* capelão *m*. **~cy** *n* capelania *f*

chapter /'tʃæptə(r)/ *n* capítulo *m*

char /tʃɑː(r)/ *vt* (*pt* **charred**) carbonizar

character /'kærəktə(r)/ *n* caráter *m*, (*P*) carácter *m*; (*in novel, play*) personagem *m*; (*reputation*) fama *f*; (*eccentric person*) excêntrico *m*; (*letter*) caractere *m*, (*P*) carácter *m*. **~ize** *vt* caracterizar

characteristic /kærəktə'rɪstɪk/ *a* característico □ *n* característica *f*. **~ally** *adv* tipicamente

charade /ʃə'rɑːd/ *n* charada *f*

charcoal /'tʃɑːkəʊl/ *n* carvão *m* de lenha

charge /tʃɑːdʒ/ *n* preço *m*; (*electr, mil*) carga *f*; (*jur*) acusação *f*; (*task, custody*) cargo *m* □ *vt/i* (*price*) cobrar; (*enemy*) atacar; (*jur*) incriminar. **be in ~ of** ter a cargo. **take ~ of** encarregar-se de

chariot /'tʃærɪət/ *n* carro *m* de guerra *or* triunfal

charisma /kə'rɪzmə/ *n* carisma *m*. **~tic** /kærɪz'mætɪk/ *a* carismático

charit|y /'tʃærətɪ/ *n* caridade *f*; (*society*) instituição *f* de caridade. **~able** *a* caridoso

charlatan /'ʃɑːlətən/ *n* charlatão *m*

charm /tʃɑːm/ *n* encanto *m*, charme *m*; (*spell*) feitiço *m*; (*talisman*) amuleto *m* □ *vt* encantar. **~ing** *a* encantador

chart /tʃɑːt/ *n* (*naut*) carta *f*; (*table*) mapa *m*, gráfico *m*, tabela *f* □ *vt* fazer o mapa de

charter /'tʃɑːtə(r)/ *n* carta *f*. **~ (flight)** (voo) charter *m* □ *vt* fretar. **~ed accountant** *n* perito *m* contador, (*P*) perito *m* de contabilidade

charwoman /'tʃɑːwʊmən/ *n* (*pl* -**women**) faxineira *f*, (*P*) mulher *f* a dias

chase /tʃeɪs/ *vt* perseguir □ *vi* (*colloq*) correr (**after** atrás de) □ *n* caça *f*, perseguição *f*. **~ away** *or* **off** afugentar, expulsar

chasm /'kæzm/ *n* abismo *m*

chassis /'ʃæsɪ/ *n* chassi *m*

chaste /tʃeɪst/ *a* casto

chastise /tʃæs'taɪz/ *vt* castigar

chastity /'tʃæstətɪ/ *n* castidade *f*

chat /tʃæt/ *n* conversa *f* □ *vi* (*pt* **chatted**) conversar, cavaquear. **have a ~** bater um papo, (*P*) dar dois dedos de conversa. **~ty** *a* conversador

chatter /'tʃætə(r)/ *vi* tagarelar. **his teeth are ~ing** seus dentes estão tiritando □ *n* tagarelice *f*

chauffeur /'ʃəʊfə(r)/ *n* motorista *m*, chofer (particular) *m*, chauffeur *m*

chauvinis|t /'ʃəʊvɪnɪst/ *n* chauvinista *mf*. **male ~t** (*pej*) machista *m*. **~m** /-zəm/ *n* chauvinismo *m*

cheap /tʃiːp/ *a* (**-er, -est**) barato; (*fare, rate*) reduzido. **~(ly)** *adv* barato. **~ness** *n* barateza *f*

cheapen /'tʃiːpən/ *vt* depreciar

cheat /tʃiːt/ *vt* enganar, trapacear □ *vi* (*at games*) roubar, (*P*) fazer batota; (*in exams*) copiar □ *n* intrujão *m*; (*at games*) trapaceiro *m*, (*P*) batoteiro *m*

check¹ /tʃek/ *vt/i* (*examine*) verificar; (*tickets*) revisar; (*restrain*) controlar, refrear □ *n* verificação *f*; (*tickets*) controle *m*; (*curb*) freio *m*; (*chess*) xeque *m*; (*Amer: bill*) conta *f*; (*Amer: cheque*) cheque *m*. **~ in** assinar o registro; (*at airport*) fazer o check-in. **~-in** *n* check-in *m*. **~ out** pagar a conta. **~-out** *n* caixa *f*. **~-up** *n* exame *m* médico, check-up *m*

check² /tʃek/ *n* (*pattern*) xadrez *m*. **~ed** *a* de xadrez

checkmate /'tʃekmeɪt/ *n* xeque-mate *m*

cheek /tʃiːk/ *n* face *f*; (*fig*) descaramento *m*. **~y** *a* descarado

cheer /tʃɪə(r)/ *n* alegria *f*; (*shout*) viva *m* □ *vt/i* aclamar, aplaudir. **~s!** à sua, (*P*) vossa (saúde)!; (*thank you*) obrigadinho. **~ (up)** animar(-se). **~ful** *a* bem disposto; alegre

cheerio /tʃɪərɪ'əʊ/ *int* (*colloq*) até logo, (*P*) adeusinho

cheese /tʃiːz/ *n* queijo *m*

cheetah /'tʃiːtə/ *n* chita *f*, lobo-tigre *m*

chef /ʃef/ *n* cozinheiro-chefe *m*

chemical /'kemɪkl/ *a* químico □ *n* produto *m* químico

chemist /'kemɪst/ *n* farmacêutico *m*; (*scientist*) químico *m*. **~s (shop)** *n* farmácia *f*. **~ry** *n* química *f*

cheque /tʃek/ n cheque m. ~-**book** n talão m de cheques. ~-**card** n cartão m de banco

cherish /'tʃerɪʃ/ vt estimar, querer; (hope) acalentar

cherry /'tʃerɪ/ n cereja f. ~-**tree** n cerejeira f

chess /tʃes/ n jogo m de xadrez. ~-**board** n tabuleiro m de xadrez

chest /tʃest/ n peito m; (for money, jewels) cofre m. ~ **of drawers** cômoda f, (P) cómoda f

chestnut /'tʃesnʌt/ n castanha f. ~-**tree** n castanheiro m

chew /tʃu:/ vt mastigar. ~**ing-gum** n chiclete m, (P) pastilha f elástica

chic /ʃi:k/ a chique

chick /tʃɪk/ n pinto m

chicken /'tʃɪkɪn/ n galinha f □ vi ~ **out** (sl) acovardar-se. ~-**pox** n catapora f, (P) varicela f

chicory /'tʃɪkərɪ/ n (for coffee) chicória f; (for salad) endívia f

chief /tʃi:f/ n chefe m □ a principal. ~**ly** adv principalmente

chilblain /'tʃɪlbleɪn/ n frieira f

child /tʃaɪld/ n (pl **children** /'tʃɪldrən/) criança f; (son) filho m; (daughter) filha f. ~**hood** n infância f, meninice f; ~**ish** a infantil; (immature) acriançado, pueril. ~**less** a sem filhos. ~-**like** a infantil. ~-**minder** n babá f que cuida de crianças em sua propria casa

childbirth /'tʃaɪldbɜ:θ/ n parto m

Chile /'tʃɪlɪ/ n Chile m. ~**an** a & n chileno (m)

chill /tʃɪl/ n frio m; (med) resfriado m, (P) constipação f □ vt/i arrefecer; (culin) refrigerar. ~**y** a frio. **be** or **feel** ~**y** ter frio

chilli /'tʃɪlɪ/ n (pl -**ies**) malagueta f

chime /tʃaɪm/ n carrilhão m; (sound) música m de carrilhão □ vt/i tocar

chimney /'tʃɪmnɪ/ n (pl -**eys**) chaminé f. ~-**sweep** n limpador m de chaminés, (P) limpa-chaminés f

chimpanzee /tʃɪmpæn'zi:/ n chimpanzé m

chin /tʃɪn/ n queixo m

china /'tʃaɪnə/ n porcelana f; (crockery) louça f

Chin|a /'tʃaɪnə/ n China f. ~**ese** /-'ni:z/ a & n chinês (m)

chink¹ /tʃɪŋk/ n (crack) fenda f, fresta f

chink² /tʃɪŋk/ n tinir m □ vt/i (fazer) tinir

chip /tʃɪp/ n (broken piece) bocado m; (culin) batata f frita em palitos; (gambling) ficha f; (electronic) chip m, circuito m integrado □ vt/i (pt **chipped**) lascar(-se)

chipboard /'tʃɪpbɔ:d/ n compensado m (de madeira)

chiropodist /kɪ'rɒpədɪst/ n calista mf

chirp /tʃɜ:p/ n pipilar m; (of cricket) cricri m □ vi pipilar; (cricket) cantar, fazer cricri

chisel /'tʃɪzl/ n cinzel m, escopro m □ vt (pt **chiselled**) talhar

chivalr|y /'ʃɪvlrɪ/ n cavalheirismo m. ~**ous** a cavalheiresco

chive /tʃaɪv/ n cebolinho m

chlorine /'klɔ:ri:n/ n cloro m

chocolate /'tʃɒklɪt/ n chocolate m

choice /tʃɔɪs/ n escolha f □ a escolhido, seleto, (P) seleccionado

choir /'kwaɪə(r)/ n coro m

choirboy /'kwaɪəbɔɪ/ n menino m de coro, corista m, (P) coralista m

choke /tʃəʊk/ vt/i sufocar; (on food) engasgar(-se) □ n (auto) afogador m, (P) botão m do ar (colloq)

cholesterol /kə'lestərɒl/ n colesterol m

choose /tʃu:z/ vt/i (pt **chose**, pp **chosen**) escolher; (prefer) preferir. ~ **to do** decidir fazer

choosy /'tʃu:zɪ/ a (colloq) exigente, difícil de contentar

chop /tʃɒp/ vt/i (pt **chopped**) cortar □ n (wood) machadada f; (culin) costeleta f. ~ **down** abater. ~**per** n cutelo m; (sl: helicopter) helicóptero m

choppy /'tʃɒpɪ/ a (sea) picado

chopstick /'tʃɒpstɪk/ n fachi m, pauzinho m

choral /'kɔ:rəl/ a coral

chord /kɔ:d/ n (mus) acorde m

chore /tʃɔ:(r)/ n trabalho m; (unpleasant task) tarefa f maçante. **household** ~**s** afazeres mpl domésticos

choreograph|er /kɒrɪ'ɒɡrəfə(r)/ n coreógrafo m. ~**y** n coreografia f

chortle /'tʃɔ:tl/ n risada f □ vi rir alto

chorus /'kɔ:rəs/ n coro m; (of song) refrão m, estribilho m

chose, chosen /tʃəʊz, 'tʃəʊzn/ see **choose**

Christ /kraɪst/ n Cristo m

christen /'krɪsn/ vt batizar, (P) baptizar. ~**ing** n batismo m, (P) baptismo m

Christian /'krɪstʃən/ a & n cristão (m). ~ **name** nome m de batismo, (P) baptismo. ~**ity** /-strɪ'ænətɪ/ n cristandade f

Christmas /'krɪsməs/ n Natal m □ a do Natal. ~ **card** cartão m de Boas Festas. ~ **Day/Eve** dia m/véspera f de Natal. ~ **tree** árvore f de Natal

chrome /krəʊm/ n cromo m

chromosome /'krəʊməsəʊm/ n cromossoma m

chronic /'krɒnɪk/ a crônico, (P) crónico

chronicle /'krɒnɪkl/ n crônica f

chronological /krɒnə'lɒdʒɪkl/ a cronológico

chrysanthemum /krɪ'sænθəməm/ n crisântemo m

chubby /'tʃʌbɪ/ a (-ier, -iest) gorducho, rechonchudo

chuck /tʃʌk/ vt (colloq) deitar, atirar. ~ **out** (person) expulsar; (thing) jogar fora, (P) deitar fora

chuckle /'tʃʌkl/ n riso m abafado □ vi rir sozinho

chum /tʃʌm/ n (colloq) amigo m íntimo, camarada mf. ~my a amigável

chunk /tʃʌŋk/ n (grande) bocado m, naco m

church /tʃɜːtʃ/ n igreja f

churchyard /'tʃɜːtʃjɑːd/ n cemitério m

churlish /'tʃɜːlɪʃ/ a grosseiro, indelicado

churn /tʃɜːn/ n batedeira f; (milk can) vasilha f de leite □ vt bater. ~ **out** produzir em série

chute /ʃuːt/ n calha f; (for rubbish) conduta f de lixo

chutney /'tʃʌtnɪ/ n (pl -eys) chutney m

cider /'saɪdə(r)/ n sidra f, (P) cidra f

cigar /sɪ'gɑː(r)/ n charuto m

cigarette /sɪgə'ret/ n cigarro m. ~-**case** n cigarreira f

cinder /'sɪndə(r)/ n brasa f. burnt to a ~ estorricado

cinema /'sɪnəmə/ n cinema m

cinnamon /'sɪnəmən/ n canela f

cipher /'saɪfə(r)/ n cifra f

circle /'sɜːkl/ n círculo m; (theat) balcão m □ vt dar a volta a □ vi descrever círculos, voltear

circuit /'sɜːkɪt/ n circuito m

circuitous /sɜː'kjuːɪtəs/ a indireto, tortuoso

circular /'sɜːkjʊlə(r)/ a circular

circulat|e /'sɜːkjʊleɪt/ vt/i (fazer) circular. ~**ion** /-'leɪʃn/ n circulação f; (sales of newspaper) tiragem f

circumcis|e /'sɜːkəmsaɪz/ vt circuncidar. ~**ion** /-'sɪʒn/ n circuncisão f

circumference /sə'kʌmfərəns/ n circunferência f

circumflex /'sɜːkəmfleks/ n circunflexo m

circumstance /'sɜːkəmstəns/ n circunstância f. ~s (means) situação f econômica, (P) económica

circus /'sɜːkəs/ n circo m

cistern /'sɪstən/ n reservatório m; (of WC) autoclismo m

cit|e /saɪt/ vt citar. ~**ation** /-'teɪʃn/ n citação f

citizen /'sɪtɪzn/ n cidadão m, cidadã f; (of town) habitante mf. ~**ship** n cidadania f

citrus /'sɪtrəs/ n ~ **fruit** citrino m

city /'sɪtɪ/ n cidade f

civic /'sɪvɪk/ a cívico

civil /'sɪvl/ a civil; (rights) cívico; (polite) delicado. ~ **servant** funcionário m público. C~ **Service** Administração f Pública. ~ **war** guerra f civil. ~**ity** /-'vɪlətɪ/ n civilidade f, cortesia f

civilian /sɪ'vɪliən/ a & n civil (mf), paisano m

civiliz|e /'sɪvəlaɪz/ vt civilizar. ~**ation** /-'zeɪʃn/ n civilização f

claim /kleɪm/ vt reclamar; (assert) pretender □ vi (from insurance) reclamar □ n reivindicação f; (assertion) afirmação f; (right) direito m; (from insurance) reclamação f

clairvoyant /kleə'vɔɪənt/ n vidente mf □ a clarividente

clam /klæm/ n molusco m

clamber /'klæmbə(r)/ vi trepar

clammy /'klæmɪ/ a (-ier, -iest) úmido, (P) húmido e pegajoso

clamour /'klæmə(r)/ n clamor m, vociferação f □ vi ~ **for** exigir aos gritos

clamp /klæmp/ n grampo m; (for car) bloqueador m □ vt prender com grampo; (a car) bloquear. ~ **down on** apertar, suprimir; (colloq) cair em cima de (colloq)

clan /klæn/ n clã m

clandestine /klæn'destɪn/ a clandestino

clang /klæŋ/ n tinir m

clap /klæp/ vt/i (pt clapped) aplaudir; (put) meter □ n aplauso m; (of thunder) ribombo m. ~ **one's hands** bater palmas

claptrap /'klæptræp/ n parlapatice f

claret /'klærət/ n clarete m

clarif|y /'klærɪfaɪ/ vt esclarecer. ~**ication** /-ɪ'keɪʃn/ n esclarecimento m

clarinet /klærɪ'net/ n clarinete m

clarity /'klærətɪ/ n claridade f

clash /klæʃ/ n choque m; (sound) estridor m; (fig) conflito m □ vt/i entrechocar(-se); (of colours) destoar

clasp /klɑːsp/ n (fastener) fecho m; (hold, grip) aperto m de mão □ vt apertar, serrar

class /klɑːs/ n classe f □ vt classificar

classic /'klæsɪk/ a & n clássico (m). ~s npl letras fpl clássicas, (P) estudos mpl clássicos. ~**al** a clássico

classif|y /'klæsɪfaɪ/ vt classificar. ~**ication** /-ɪ'keɪʃn/ n classificação f. ~**ied advertisement** (anúncio m) classificado (m)

classroom /'klɑ:sru:m/ n sala f de aulas

clatter /'klætə(r)/ n estardalhaço m ▢ vi fazer barulho

clause /klɔːz/ n cláusula f; (gram) oração f

claustrophob|ia /klɔːstrə'fəʊbɪə/ n claustrofobia f. **~ic** a claustrofóbico

claw /klɔː/ n garra f; (of lobster) tenaz f, pinça f ▢ vt (seize) agarrar; (scratch) arranhar; (tear) rasgar

clay /kleɪ/ n argila f, barro m

clean /kliːn/ a (-er, -est) limpo ▢ adv completamente ▢ vt limpar ▢ vi **~ up** fazer a limpeza. **~-shaven** a de cara rapada. **~er** n faxineira f, (P) mulher f da limpeza; (of clothes) empregado m da tinturaria. **~ly** adv com limpeza, como deve ser

cleans|e /klenz/ vt limpar; (fig) purificar. **~ing cream** creme m de limpeza

clear /klɪə(r)/ a (-er, -est) claro; (glass) transparente; (without obstacles) livre; (profit) líquido; (sky) limpo ▢ adv claramente ▢ vt (snow, one's name, etc) limpar; (the table) tirar; (jump) transpor; (debt) saldar; (jur) absolver; (through customs) despachar ▢ vi (fog) dissipar-se; (sky) limpar. **~ of** (away from) afastado de. **~ off or out** (sl) sair andando, zarpar. **~ out** (clean) fazer a limpeza. **~ up** (tidy) arrumar; (mystery) desvendar; (of weather) clarear, limpar. **~ly** adv claramente

clearance /'klɪərəns/ n autorização f; (for ship) despacho m; (space) espaço m livre. **~ sale** liquidação f, saldos mpl

clearing /'klɪərɪŋ/ n clareira f

clearway /'klɪəweɪ/ n rodovia f de estacionamento proibido

cleavage /'kliːvɪdʒ/ n divisão f; (between breasts) rego m; (of dress) decote m

cleaver /'kliːvə(r)/ n cutelo m

clef /klef/ n (mus) clave f

cleft /kleft/ n fenda f

clench /klentʃ/ vt (teeth, fists) cerrar; (grasp) agarrar

clergy /'klɜːdʒɪ/ n clero m. **~man** n (pl -men) clérigo m, sacerdote m

cleric /'klerɪk/ n clérigo m. **~al** a (relig) clerical; (of clerks) de escritório

clerk /klɑːk/ n auxiliar m de escritório

clever /'klevə(r)/ a (-er, -est) esperto, inteligente; (skilful) hábil, habilidoso. **~ly** adv inteligentemente; (skilfully) habilmente, habilidosamente. **~ness** n esperteza f, inteligência f

cliché /'kliːʃeɪ/ n chavão m, lugar-comum m, clichê m

click /klɪk/ n estalido m, clique m ▢ vi dar um estalido; (comput) clicar

client /'klaɪənt/ n cliente mf

clientele /kliːən'tel/ n clientela f

cliff /klɪf/ n penhasco m. **~s** npl falésia f

climat|e /'klaɪmɪt/ n clima m. **~ic** /-'mætɪk/ a climático

climax /'klaɪmæks/ n clímax m, ponto m culminante

climb /klaɪm/ vt (stairs) subir; (tree, wall) subir em, trepar em; (mountain) escalar ▢ vi subir, trepar ▢ n subida f; (mountain) escalada f. **~ down** descer; (fig) dar a mão à palmatória (fig). **~er** n (sport) alpinista mf; (plant) trepadeira f

clinch /klɪntʃ/ vt (deal) fechar; (argument) resolver

cling /klɪŋ/ vi (pt **clung**) **~ (to)** agarrar-se (a); (stick) colar-se (a)

clinic /'klɪnɪk/ n clínica f

clinical /'klɪnɪkl/ a clínico

clink /klɪŋk/ n tinido m ▢ vt/i (fazer) tilintar

clip[1] /klɪp/ m (for paper) clipe m; (for hair) grampo m, (P) gancho m; (for tube) braçadeira f ▢ vt (pt **clipped**) prender

clip[2] /klɪp/ vt (pt **clipped**) cortar; (trim) aparar ▢ n tosquia f; (colloq: blow) murro m. **~ping** n recorte m

clique /kliːk/ n panelinha f, facção f, conventículo m

cloak /kləʊk/ n capa f, manto m

cloakroom /'kləʊkru:m/ n vestiário m; (toilet) toalete m, (P) lavabo m

clock /klɒk/ n relógio m ▢ vi **~ in/out** marcar o ponto (à entrada/à saída). **~ up** (colloq: miles etc) fazer

clockwise /'klɒkwaɪz/ a & adv no sentido dos ponteiros do relógio

clockwork /'klɒkwɜːk/ n mecanismo m. **go like ~** ir às mil maravilhas

clog /klɒg/ n tamanco m, soco m ▢ vt/i (pt **clogged**) entupir(-se)

cloister /'klɔɪstə(r)/ n claustro m

close[1] /kləʊs/ a (-er, -est) próximo (to de); (link, collaboration) estreito; (friend) íntimo; (weather) abafado ▢ adv perto. **~ at hand, ~ by** muito perto. **~ together** (crowded) espremido. **have a ~ shave** (fig) escapar por um triz. **~-up** n grande plano m. **~ly** adv de perto. **~ness** n proximidade f

close[2] /kləʊz/ vt/i fechar(-se); (end) terminar; (of shop etc) fechar ▢ n fim m. **~d shop** organização f que só admite trabalhadores sindicalizados

closet /'klɒzɪt/ n armário m

closure /'kləʊʒə(r)/ n encerramento m

clot /klɒt/ n coágulo m ▢ vi (pt **clotted**) coagular

cloth /klɒθ/ *n* pano *m*; (*tablecloth*) toalha *f* de mesa

cloth|e /kləʊð/ *vt* vestir. **~ing** *n* vestuário *m*, roupa *f*

clothes /kləʊðz/ *npl* roupa *f*, vestuário *m*. **~-line** *n* varal *m* para roupa

cloud /klaʊd/ *n* núvem *f* □ *vt/i* toldar(-se). **~y** *a* nublado, toldado; (*liquid*) turvo

clout /klaʊt/ *n* cascudo *m*, (*P*) carolo *m*; (*colloq: power*) poder *m* efectivo □ *vt* (*colloq*) bater

clove /kləʊv/ *n* cravo *m*. **~ of garlic** dente *m* de alho

clover /ˈkləʊvə(r)/ *n* trevo *m*

clown /klaʊn/ *n* palhaço *m* □ *vi* fazer palhaçadas

club /klʌb/ *n* clube *m*; (*weapon*) cacete *m*. **~s** (*cards*) paus *mpl* □ *vt/i* (*pt* **clubbed**) dar bordoadas *or* cacetadas (em). **~ together** (*share costs*) cotizar-se

cluck /klʌk/ *vi* cacarejar

clue /kluː/ *n* indício *m*, pista *f*; (*in crossword*) definição *f*. **not have a ~** (*colloq*) não fazer a menor idéia

clump /klʌmp/ *n* maciço *m*, tufo *m*

clumsy /ˈklʌmzɪ/ *a* (**-ier**, **-iest**) desajeitado

clung /klʌŋ/ *see* **cling**

cluster /ˈklʌstə(r)/ *n* (pequeno) grupo *m*; (*bot*) cacho *m* □ *vt/i* agrupar(-se)

clutch /klʌtʃ/ *vt* agarrar (em), apertar □ *vi* agarrar-se (**at a**) □ *n* (*auto*) embreagem *f*, (*P*) embraiagem *f*. **~es** *npl* garras *fpl*

clutter /ˈklʌtə(r)/ *n* barafunda *f*, desordem *f* □ *vt* atravancar

coach /kəʊtʃ/ *n* ônibus *m*, (*P*) camioneta *f*; (*of train*) carruagem *f*; (*sport*) treinador *m* □ *vt* (*tutor*) dar aulas a; (*sport*) treinar

coagulate /kəʊˈægjʊleɪt/ *vt/i* coagular(-se)

coal /kəʊl/ *n* carvão *m*

coalfield /ˈkəʊlfiːld/ *n* região *f* carbonífera

coalition /kəʊəˈlɪʃn/ *n* coligação *f*

coarse /kɔːs/ *a* (**-er**, **-est**) grosseiro

coast /kəʊst/ *n* costa *f* □ *vi* costear; (*cycle*) descer em roda-livre; (*car*) ir em ponto morto. **~al** *a* costeiro

coastguard /ˈkəʊstgaːd/ *n* polícia *f* marítima

coastline /ˈkəʊstlaɪn/ *n* litoral *m*

coat /kəʊt/ *n* casaco *m*; (*of animal*) pêlo *m*; (*of paint*) camada *f*, demão *f* □ *vt* cobrir. **~ of arms** brasão *m*. **~ing** *n* camada *f*

coax /kəʊks/ *vt* levar com afagos ou lisonjas, convencer

cobble /ˈkɒbl/ *n* **~(-stone)** *n* pedra *f* de calçada

cobweb /ˈkɒbweb/ *n* teia *f* de aranha

cocaine /kəʊˈkeɪn/ *n* cocaína *f*

cock /kɒk/ *n* (*male bird*) macho *m*; (*rooster*) galo *m* □ *vt* (*gun*) engatilhar; (*ears*) fitar. **~-eyed** *a* (*sl: askew*) de esguelha

cockerel /ˈkɒkərəl/ *n* frango *m*, galo *m* novo

cockle /ˈkɒkl/ *n* berbigão *m*

cockney /ˈkɒknɪ/ *n* (*pl* **-eys**) (*person*) londrino *m*; (*dialect*) dialeto *m* do leste de Londres

cockpit /ˈkɒkpɪt/ *n* cabine *f*

cockroach /ˈkɒkrəʊtʃ/ *n* barata *f*

cocktail /ˈkɒkteɪl/ *n* cocktail *m*, coquetel *m*. **fruit ~** salada *f* de fruta

cocky /ˈkɒkɪ/ *a* (**-ier**, **-iest**) convencido (*colloq*)

cocoa /ˈkəʊkəʊ/ *n* cacau *m*

coconut /ˈkəʊkənʌt/ *n* coco *m*

cocoon /kəˈkuːn/ *n* casulo *m*

cod /kɒd/ *n* (*pl invar*) bacalhau *m*. **~-liver oil** óleo *m* de figado de bacalhau

code /kəʊd/ *n* código *m* □ *vt* codificar

coeducational /kəʊedʒʊˈkeɪʃənl/ *a* misto

coerc|e /kəʊˈɜːs/ *vt* coagir. **~ion** /-ʃn/ *n* coação *f*, (*P*) coacção *f*

coexist /kəʊɪɡˈzɪst/ *vi* coexistir. **~ence** *n* coexistência *f*

coffee /ˈkɒfɪ/ *n* café *m*. **~ bar** café *m*. **~-pot** *n* cafeteira *f*. **~-table** *n* mesa *f* baixa

coffin /ˈkɒfɪn/ *n* caixão *m*

cog /kɒg/ *n* dente *m* de roda. **a ~ in the machine** (*fig*) uma rodinha numa engrenagem

cogent /ˈkəʊdʒənt/ *a* convincente; (*relevant*) pertinente

cognac /ˈkɒnjæk/ *n* conhaque *m*

cohabit /kəʊˈhæbɪt/ *vi* coabitar

coherent /kəˈhɪərənt/ *a* coerente

coil /kɔɪl/ *vt/i* enrolar(-se) □ *n* rolo *m*; (*electr*) bobina *f*; (*one ring*) espiral *f*; (*contraceptive*) dispositivo *m* intra-uterino, DIU

coin /kɔɪn/ *n* moeda *f* □ *vt* cunhar

coincide /kəʊɪnˈsaɪd/ *vi* coincidir

coinciden|ce /kəʊˈɪnsɪdəns/ *n* coincidência *f*. **~tal** /-ˈdentl/ *a* que acontece por coincidência

colander /ˈkʌləndə(r)/ *n* peneira *f*, (*P*) coador *m*

cold /kəʊld/ *a* (**-er**, **-est**) frio □ *n* frio *m*; (*med*) resfriado *m*, constipação *f*. **be or feel ~** estar com frio. **it's ~** está frio. **~-blooded** *a* (*person*) insensível; (*deed*) a sangue frio. **~ cream** creme *m* para a pele. **~ness** *n* frio *m*; (*of feeling*) frieza *f*

coleslaw /ˈkəʊlslɔː/ *n* salada *f* de repolho cru

colic /'kɒlɪk/ n cólica(s) f (pl)

collaborat|e /kə'læbəreɪt/ vi colaborar. ~ion /-'reɪʃn/ n colaboração f. ~or n colaborador m

collapse /kə'læps/ vi desabar; (med) ter um colapso □ n colapso m

collapsible /kə'læpsəbl/ a desmontável, dobrável

collar /'kɒlə(r)/ n gola f; (of shirt) colarinho m; (of dog) coleira f □ vt (colloq) pôr a mão a. ~-bone n clavícula f

colleague /'kɒliːg/ n colega mf

collect /kə'lekt/ vt (gather) juntar; (fetch) ir/vir buscar; (money, rent) cobrar; (as hobby) coleccionar, (P) coleccionar □ vi juntar-se. **call ~** (Amer) chamar a cobrar. ~ion /-ʃn/ n coleção f, (P) colecção f; (in church) coleta f, (P) colecta f; (of mail) tiragem f, coleta f, (P) abertura f. ~or n (as hobby) colecionador m, (P) coleccionador m

collective /kə'lektɪv/ a coletivo, (P) colectivo

college /'kɒlɪdʒ/ n colégio m

collide /kə'laɪd/ vi colidir

colliery /'kɒlɪərɪ/ n mina f de carvão

collision /kə'lɪʒn/ n colisão f, choque m; (fig) conflito m

colloquial /kə'ləʊkwɪəl/ a coloquial. ~ism n expressão f coloquial

collusion /kə'luːʒn/ n conluio m

colon /'kəʊlən/ n (gram) dois pontos mpl; (anat) cólon m

colonel /'kɜːnl/ n coronel m

colonize /'kɒlənaɪz/ vt colonizar

colon|y /'kɒlənɪ/ n colónia f, (P) colónia f. ~ial /kə'ləʊnɪəl/ a & n colonial (mf)

colossal /kə'lɒsl/ a colossal

colour /'kʌlə(r)/ n cor f □ a (photo, TV, etc) a cores; (film) colorido □ vt colorir, dar cor a □ vi (blush) corar. ~-blind a daltónico, (P) daltónico. ~ful a colorido. ~ing n (of skin) cor f; (in food) corante m. ~less a descolorido

coloured /'kʌləd/ a (pencil, person) de cor □ n pessoa f de cor

column /'kɒləm/ n coluna f

columnist /'kɒləmnɪst/ n colunista mf

coma /'kəʊmə/ n coma m

comb /kəʊm/ n pente m □ vt pentear; (search) vasculhar. **~ one's hair** pentear-se

combat /'kɒmbæt/ n combate m □ vt (pt **combated**) combater

combination /kɒmbɪ'neɪʃn/ n combinação f

combine /kəm'baɪn/ vt/i combinar(-se), juntar(-se), reunir(-se)

combustion /kəm'bʌstʃən/ n combustão f

come /kʌm/ vi (pt **came**, pp **come**) vir; (arrive) chegar; (occur) suceder. **~ about** acontecer. **~ across** encontrar, dar com. **~ away** or **off** soltar-se. **~ back** voltar. **~-back** n regresso m; (retort) réplica f. **~ by** obter. **~ down** descer; (price) baixar. **~-down** n humilhação f. **~ from** vir de. **~ in** entrar. **~ into** (money) herdar. **~ off** (succeed) ter êxito; (fare) sair-se. **~ on!** vamos! **~ out** sair. **~ round** (after fainting) voltar a si; (be converted) deixar-se convencer. **~ to** (amount to) montar a. **~ up** subir; (seeds) despontar; (fig) surgir. **~ up with** (idea) vir com, propor. **~-uppance** n castigo m merecido

comedian /kə'miːdɪən/ n comediante mf

comedy /'kɒmədɪ/ n comédia f

comet /'kɒmɪt/ n cometa m

comfort /'kʌmfət/ n conforto m □ vt confortar, consolar. **~able** a confortável

comic /'kɒmɪk/ a cômico, (P) cómico □ n cômico m, (P) cómico m; (periodical) estórias fpl em quadrinhos, (P) revista f de banda desenhada. **~ strip** estória f em quadrinhos, (P) banda f desenhada. **~al** a cômico, (P) cómico

coming /'kʌmɪŋ/ n vinda f □ a próximo. **~s and goings** idas e vindas fpl

comma /'kɒmə/ n vírgula f

command /kə'maːnd/ n (mil) comando m; (order) ordem f; (mastery) domínio m □ vt comandar; (respect) inspirar, impor. **~er** n comandante m. **~ing** a imponente

commandeer /kɒmən'dɪə(r)/ vt requisitar

commandment /kə'maːndmənt/ n mandamento m

commemorat|e /kə'meməreɪt/ vt comemorar. **~ion** /-'reɪʃn/ n comemoração f. **~ive** a comemorativo

commence /kə'mens/ vt/i começar. **~ment** n começo m

commend /kə'mend/ vt louvar; (entrust) confiar. **~able** a louvável. **~ation** /kɒmen'deɪʃn/ n louvor m

comment /'kɒment/ n comentário m □ vi comentar. **~ on** comentar, fazer comentários

commentary /'kɒməntrɪ/ n comentário m; (radio, TV) relato m

commentat|e /'kɒmənteɪt/ vi fazer um relato. **~or** n (radio, TV) comentarista mf, (P) comentador m

commerce /'kɒmɜːs/ n comércio m

commercial /kə'mɜː.ʃl/ a comercial □ n publicidade (comercial) f. ~**ize** vt comercializar

commiserat|e /kə'mɪzəreɪt/ vi ~ **with** compadecer-se de. ~**ion** /-'reɪʃn/ n comiseração f, pesar m

commission /kə'mɪʃn/ n comissão f; (order for work) encomenda f □ vt encomendar; (mil) nomear. ~ **to do** encarregar de fazer. **out of** ~ fora de serviço ativo, (P) activo. ~**er** n comissário m; (police) chefe m

commit /kə'mɪt/ vt (pt **committed**) cometer; (entrust) confiar. ~ **o.s.** comprometer-se, empenhar-se. ~ **suicide** suicidar-se. ~ **to memory** decorar. ~**ment** n compromisso m

committee /kə'mɪti/ n comissão f, comitê m, (P) comité m

commodity /kə'mɒdətɪ/ n artigo m, mercadoria f

common /'kɒmən/ a (-**er**, -**est**) comum; (usual) usual, corrente; (pej: ill-bred) ordinário □ n prado m público, (P) baldio m. ~ **law** direito m consuetudinário. **C~ Market** Mercado m Comum. ~-**room** n sala f dos professores. ~ **sense** bom senso m, senso m comum. **House of C~s** Câmara f dos Comuns. **in** ~ em comum. ~**ly** adv mais comum

commoner /'kɒmənə(r)/ n plebeu m

commonplace /'kɒmənpleɪs/ a banal □ n lugar-comum m

commotion /kə'məʊʃn/ n agitação f, confusão f, barulheira f

communal /'kɒmjʊnl/ a (of a commune) comunal; (shared) comum

commune /'kɒmjuːn/ n comuna f

communicat|e /kə'mjuːnɪkeɪt/ vt/i comunicar. ~**ion** /-'keɪʃn/ n comunicação f. ~**ion cord** sinal m de alarme. ~**ive** /-ətɪv/ a comunicativo

communion /kə'mjuːnɪən/ n comunhão f

communis|t /'kɒmjʊnɪst/ n comunista mf □ a comunista. ~**m** /-zəm/ n comunismo m

community /kə'mjuːnətɪ/ n comunidade f. ~ **centre** centro m comunitário

commute /kə'mjuːt/ vi viajar diariamente para o trabalho. ~**r** /-ə(r)/ n pessoa f que viaja diariamente para o trabalho

compact[1] /kəm'pækt/ a compacto. ~ **disc** /'kɒmpækt/ cd m

compact[2] /'kɒmpækt/ n estojo m de pó-de-arroz, (P) caixa f

companion /kəm'pænɪən/ n companheiro m. ~**ship** n companhia f, convívio m

company /'kʌmpənɪ/ n companhia f; (guests) visitas fpl. **keep sb** ~ fazer companhia a alg

comparable /'kɒmpərəbl/ a comparável

compar|e /kəm'peə(r)/ vt/i comparar(-se) (**to, with** com). ~**ative** /-'pærətɪv/ a comparativo; (comfort etc) relativo

comparison /kəm'pærɪsn/ n comparação f

compartment /kəm'pɑːtmənt/ n compartimento m

compass /'kʌmpəs/ n bússola f. ~**es** compasso m

compassion /kəm'pæʃn/ n compaixão f. ~**ate** a compassivo

compatib|le /kəm'pætəbl/ a compatível. ~**ility** /-'bɪlətɪ/ n compatibilidade f

compel /kəm'pel/ vt (pt **compelled**) compelir, forçar. ~**ling** a irresistível, convincente

compensat|e /'kɒmpənseɪt/ vt/i compensar. ~**ion** /-'seɪʃn/ n compensação f; (financial) indenização f, (P) indemnização f

compete /kəm'piːt/ vi competir. ~ **with** rivalizar com

competen|t /'kɒmpɪtənt/ a competente. ~**ce** n competência f

competition /kɒmpə'tɪʃn/ n competição f; (comm) concorrência f

competitive /kəm'petɪtɪv/ a (sport, prices) competitivo. ~ **examination** concurso m

competitor /kəm'petɪtə(r)/ n competidor m, concorrente mf

compile /kəm'paɪl/ vt compilar, coligir. ~**r** /-ə(r)/ n compilador m

complacen|t /kəm'pleɪsnt/ a satisfeito consigo mesmo, (P) complacente. ~**cy** n (auto-)satisfação f, (P) complacência f

complain /kəm'pleɪn/ vi queixar-se (**about, of** de)

complaint /kəm'pleɪnt/ n queixa f; (in shop) reclamação f; (med) doença f, achaque m

complement /'kɒmplɪmənt/ n complemento m □ vt completar, complementar. ~**ary** /-'mentrɪ/ a complementar

complet|e /kəm'pliːt/ a completo; (finished) acabado; (downright) perfeito □ vt completar; (a form) preencher. ~**ely** adv completamente. ~**ion** /-ʃn/ n conclusão f, feitura f, realização f

complex /'kɒmpleks/ a complexo □ n complexo m. ~**ity** /kəm'pleksətɪ/ n complexidade f

complexion /kəm'plekʃn/ n cor f da tez; (fig) caráter m, (P) carácter m, aspecto m

compliance /kəm'plaɪəns/ *n* docilidade *f*; (*agreement*) conformidade *f*. **in ~ with** em conformidade com

complicat|e /'kɒmplɪkeɪt/ *vt* complicar. **~ed** *a* complicado. **~ion** /-'keɪʃn/ *n* complicação *f*

compliment /'kɒmplɪmənt/ *n* cumprimento *m* □ *vt* /'kɒmplɪment/ cumprimentar

complimentary /kɒmplɪ'mentrɪ/ *a* amável, elogioso. **~ copy** oferta *f*. **~ ticket** bilhete *m* grátis

comply /kəm'plaɪ/ *vi* **~ with** agir em conformidade com

component /kəm'pəʊnənt/ *n* componente *m*; (*of machine*) peça *f* □ *a* componente, constituinte

compose /kəm'pəʊz/ *vt* compor. **~ o.s.** acalmar-se, dominar-se. **~d** *a* calmo, senhor de si. **~r** /-ə(r)/ *n* compositor *m*

composition /kɒmpə'zɪʃn/ *n* composição *f*

compost /'kɒmpɒst/ *n* húmus *m*, adubo *m*

composure /kəm'pəʊʒə(r)/ *n* calma *f*, domínio *m* de si mesmo

compound /'kɒmpaʊnd/ *n* composto *m*; (*enclosure*) cercado *m*, recinto *m* □ *a* composto. **~ fracture** fratura *f*, (*P*) fractura *f* exposta

comprehen|d /kɒmprɪ'hend/ *vt* compreender. **~sion** *n* compreensão *f*

comprehensive /kɒmprɪ'hensɪv/ *a* compreensivo, vasto; (*insurance*) contra todos os riscos. **~ school** escola *f* de ensino secundário técnico e académico, (*P*) académico

compress /kəm'pres/ *vt* comprimir. **~ion** /-ʃn/ *n* compressão *f*

comprise /kəm'praɪz/ *vt* compreender, abranger

compromise /'kɒmprəmaɪz/ *n* compromisso *m* □ *vt* comprometer □ *vi* chegar a um meio-termo

compulsion /kəm'pʌlʃn/ *n* (*constraint*) coação *f*; (*psych*) desejo *m* irresistível

compulsive /kəm'pʌlsɪv/ *a* (*psych*) compulsivo; (*liar, smoker etc*) inveterado

compulsory /kəm'pʌlsərɪ/ *a* obrigatório, compulsório

computer /kəm'pju:tə(r)/ *n* computador *m*. **~ science** informática *f*. **~ize** *vt* computerizar

comrade /'kɒmreɪd/ *n* camarada *mf*. **~ship** *n* camaradagem *f*

con[1] /kɒn/ *vt* (*pt* **conned**) (*sl*) enganar □ *n* (*sl*) intrujice *f*, vigarice *f*, burla *f*. **~ man** (*sl*) intrujão *m*, vigarista *m*, burlão *m*

con[2] /kɒn/ *see* **pro**

concave /'kɒŋkeɪv/ *a* côncavo

conceal /kən'si:l/ *vt* ocultar, esconder. **~ment** *n* encobrimento *m*

concede /kən'si:d/ *vt* conceder, admitir; (*in a game etc*) ceder

conceit /kən'si:t/ *n* presunção *f*. **~ed** *a* presunçoso, presumido, cheio de si

conceivabl|e /kən'si:vəbl/ *a* concebível. **~y** *adv* possivelmente

conceive /kən'si:v/ *vt/i* conceber

concentrat|e /'kɒnsntreɪt/ *vt/i* concentrar(-se). **~ion** /-'treɪʃn/ *n* concentração *f*

concept /'kɒnsept/ *n* conceito *m*

conception /kən'sepʃn/ *n* concepção *f*

concern /kən'sɜ:n/ *n* (*worry*) preocupação *f*; (*business*) negócio *m* □ *vt* dizer respeito a, respeitar. **~ o.s. with, be ~ed with** interessar-se por, ocupar-se de; (*regard*) dizer respeito a. **it's no ~ of mine** não me diz respeito. **~ing** *prep* sobre, respeitante a

concerned /kən'sɜ:nd/ *a* inquieto, preocupado (**about** com)

concert /'kɒnsət/ *n* concerto *m*

concerted /kən'sɜ:tɪd/ *a* concertado

concession /kən'seʃn/ *n* concessão *f*

concise /kən'saɪs/ *a* conciso. **~ly** *adv* concisamente

conclu|de /kən'klu:d/ *vt* concluir □ *vi* terminar. **~ding** *a* final. **~sion** *n* conclusão *f*

conclusive /kən'klu:sɪv/ *a* conclusivo. **~ly** *adv* de forma conclusiva

concoct /kən'kɒkt/ *vt* preparar por mistura; (*fig: invent*) fabricar. **~ion** /-ʃn/ *n* mistura *f*; (*fig*) invenção *f*, mentira *f*

concrete /'kɒŋkri:t/ *n* concreto *m*, (*P*) cimento *m* □ *a* concreto □ *vt* concretar, (*P*) cimentar

concur /kən'kɜ:(r)/ *vi* (*pt* **concurred**) concordar; (*of circumstances*) concorrer

concussion /kən'kʌʃn/ *n* comoção *f* cerebral

condemn /kən'dem/ *vt* condenar. **~ation** /kɒndem'neɪʃn/ *n* condenação *f*

condens|e /kən'dens/ *vt/i* condensar(-se). **~ation** /kɒnden'seɪʃn/ *n* condensação *f*

condescend /kɒndɪ'send/ *vi* condescender; (*lower o.s.*) rebaixar-se

condition /kən'dɪʃn/ *n* condição *f* □ *vt* condicionar. **on ~ that** com a condição de que. **~al** *a* condicional. **~er** *n* (*for hair*) condicionador *m*, creme *m* rinse

condolences /kən'dəʊlənsɪz/ *npl* condolências *fpl*, pêsames *mpl*, sentimentos *mpl*

condom /'kɒndəm/ *n* preservativo *m*

condone /kənˈdəʊn/ vt desculpar, fechar os olhos a

conducive /kənˈdjuːsɪv/ a be ∼ to contribuir para, ser propício a

conduct[1] /kənˈdʌkt/ vt conduzir, dirigir; (*orchestra*) reger

conduct[2] /ˈkɒndʌkt/ n conduta f

conductor /kənˈdʌktə(r)/ n maestro m; (*electr; of bus*) condutor m

cone /kəʊn/ n cone m; (*bot*) pinha f; (*for ice-cream*) casquinha f, (P) cone m

confectioner /kənˈfekʃnə(r)/ n confeiteiro m, (P) pasteleiro m. ∼y n confeitaria f, (P) pastelaria f

confederation /kənfedəˈreɪʃn/ n confederação f

confer /kənˈfɜː(r)/ (*pt* conferred) vt conferir, outorgar □ vi conferenciar

conference /ˈkɒnfərəns/ n conferência f. in ∼ em reunião f

confess /kənˈfes/ vt/i confessar; (*relig*) confessar(-se). ∼ion /-ʃn/ n confissão f. ∼ional n confessionário m. ∼or n confessor m

confetti /kənˈfetɪ/ n confetes mpl, (P) confetti mpl

confide /kənˈfaɪd/ vt confiar □ vi ∼ in confiar em

confiden|t /ˈkɒnfɪdənt/ a confiante, confiado. ∼ce n confiança f; (*boldness*) confiança f em si; (*secret*) confidência f. ∼ce trick vigarice f. in ∼ce em confidência

confidential /kɒnfrˈdenʃl/ a confidencial

confine /kənˈfaɪn/ vt fechar; (*limit*) limitar (to a). ∼ment n detenção f; (*med*) parto m

confirm /kənˈfɜːm/ vt confirmar. ∼ation /kɒnfəˈmeɪʃn/ n confirmação f. ∼ed a (*bachelor*) inveterado

confiscat|e /ˈkɒnfɪskeɪt/ vt confiscar. ∼ion /-ˈkeɪʃn/ n confiscação f

conflict[1] /ˈkɒnflɪkt/ n conflito m

conflict[2] /kənˈflɪkt/ vi estar em contradição. ∼ing a contraditório

conform /kənˈfɔːm/ vt/i conformar(-se)

confound /kənˈfaʊnd/ vt confundir. ∼ed a (*colloq*) maldito

confront /kənˈfrʌnt/ vt confrontar, defrontar, enfrentar. ∼ with confrontar-se com. ∼ation /kɒnfrʌnˈteɪʃn/ n confrontação f

confus|e /kənˈfjuːz/ vt confundir. ∼ed a confuso. ∼ing a que faz confusão. ∼ion /-ʒn/ n confusão f

congeal /kənˈdʒiːl/ vt/i congelar, solidificar

congenial /kənˈdʒiːnɪəl/ a (*agreeable*) simpático

congenital /kənˈdʒenɪtl/ a congênito, (P) congénito

congest|ed /kənˈdʒestɪd/ a congestionado. ∼ion /-tʃn/ n (*traffic*) congestionamento m; (*med*) congestão f

congratulat|e /kənˈɡrætjʊleɪt/ vt felicitar, dar os parabéns (on por). ∼ions /-ˈleɪʃnz/ npl felicitações fpl, parabéns mpl

congregat|e /ˈkɒnɡrɪɡeɪt/ vi reunir-se. ∼ion /-ˈɡeɪʃn/ n (*in church*) congregação f, fiéis mpl

congress /ˈkɒnɡres/ n congresso m. C∼ (*Amer*) Congresso m

conjecture /kənˈdʒektʃə(r)/ n conjetura f, (P) conjactura f □ vt/i conjeturar, (P) conjecturar

conjugal /ˈkɒndʒʊɡl/ a conjugal

conjugat|e /ˈkɒndʒʊɡeɪt/ vt conjugar. ∼ion /-ˈɡeɪʃn/ n conjugação f

conjunction /kənˈdʒʌŋkʃn/ n conjunção f

conjur|e /ˈkʌndʒə(r)/ vi fazer truques mágicos □ vt ∼e up fazer aparecer. ∼or n mágico m, prestidigitador m

connect /kəˈnekt/ vt/i ligar(-se); (*of train*) fazer ligação. ∼ed a ligado. be ∼ed with estar relacionado com

connection /kəˈnekʃn/ n relação f; (*rail; phone call*) ligação f; (*electr*) contacto m

connoisseur /kɒnəˈsɜː(r)/ n conhecedor m, apreciador m

connotation /kɒnəˈteɪʃn/ n conotação f

conquer /ˈkɒŋkə(r)/ vt vencer; (*country*) conquistar. ∼or n conquistador m

conquest /ˈkɒŋkwest/ n conquista f

conscience /ˈkɒnʃəns/ n consciência f

conscientious /kɒnʃɪˈenʃəs/ a consciencioso

conscious /ˈkɒnʃəs/ a consciente. ∼ly adv conscientemente. ∼ness n consciência f

conscript[1] /kənˈskrɪpt/ vt recrutar. ∼ion /-ʃn/ n serviço m militar obrigatório

conscript[2] /ˈkɒnskrɪpt/ n recruta m

consecrate /ˈkɒnsɪkreɪt/ vt consagrar

consecutive /kənˈsekjʊtɪv/ a consecutivo, seguido

consensus /kənˈsensəs/ n consenso m

consent /kənˈsent/ vi consentir (to em) □ n consentimento m

consequence /ˈkɒnsɪkwəns/ n consequência f, (P) consequência f

consequent /ˈkɒnsɪkwənt/ a resultante (on, upon de). ∼ly adv por consequência, (P) consequência, por consequinte

conservation /kɒnsəˈveɪʃn/ n conservação f

conservative /kənˈsɜːvətɪv/ a conservador; (*estimate*) moderado. C∼ a & n conservador (m)

conservatory /kən'sɜ:vətri/ n
(*greenhouse*) estufa f; (*house extension*)
jardim m de inverno

conserve /kən'sɜ:v/ vt conservar

consider /kən'sɪdə(r)/ vt considerar;
(*allow for*) levar em consideração.
~**ation** /-'reɪʃn/ n consideração f.
~**ing** prep em vista de, tendo em conta

considerabl|e /kən'sɪdərəbl/ a
considerável; (*much*) muito. ~**y** adv
consideravelmente

considerate /kən'sɪdərət/ a atencioso,
delicado

consign /kən'saɪn/ vt consignar. ~**ment**
n consignação f

consist /kən'sɪst/ vi consistir (**of**, **in**, em)

consisten|t /kən'sɪstənt/ a (*unchanging*)
constante; (*not contradictory*) coerente.
~**t with** conforme com. ~**cy** n
consistência f; (*fig*) coerência f. ~**tly**
adv regularmente

consol|e /kən'səʊl/ vt consolar. ~**ation**
/kɒnsə'leɪʃn/ n consolação f. ~**ation
prize** prêmio m de consolação

consolidat|e /kən'sɒlɪdeɪt/ vt/i
consolidar(-se). ~**ion** /-'deɪʃn/ n
consolidação f

consonant /'kɒnsənənt/ n consoante f

consortium /kən'sɔ:tɪəm/ n (pl -**tia**)
consórcio m

conspicuous /kən'spɪkjʊəs/ a conspícuo,
visível; (*striking*) notável. **make o.s.**
~ fazer-se notar, chamar a atenção

conspira|cy /kən'spɪrəsɪ/ n conspiração
f. ~**tor** n conspirador m

conspire /kən'spaɪə(r)/ vi conspirar

constable /'kʌnstəbl/ n polícia m

constant /'kɒnstənt/ a constante. ~**ly**
adv constantemente

constellation /kɒnstə'leɪʃn/ n
constelação f

consternation /kɒnstə'neɪʃn/ n
consternação f

constipation /kɒnstɪ'peɪʃn/ n prisão f de
ventre

constituency /kən'stɪtjʊənsɪ/ n (pl -**cies**)
círculo m eleitoral

constituent /kən'stɪtjʊənt/ a & n
constituinte (m)

constitut|e /'kɒnstɪtju:t/ vt constituir.
~**ion** /-'tju:ʃn/ n constituição f.
~**ional** /-'tju:ʃənl/ a constitucional

constrain /kən'streɪn/ vt constranger

constraint /kən'streɪnt/ n
constrangimento m

constrict /kən'strɪkt/ vt constringir,
apertar. ~**ion** /-ʃn/ n constrição f

construct /kən'strʌkt/ vt construir. ~**ion**
/-ʃn/ n construção f. **under** ~**ion** em
construção

constructive /kən'strʌktɪv/ a
construtivo

consul /'kɒnsl/ n cônsul m

consulate /'kɒnsjʊlət/ n consulado m

consult /kən'sʌlt/ vt consultar. ~**ation**
/kɒnsl'teɪʃn/ n consulta f

consultant /kən'sʌltənt/ n consultor m;
(*med*) especialista mf

consume /kən'sju:m/ vt consumir.
~**r** /-ə(r)/ n consumidor m

consumption /kən'sʌmpʃn/ n
consumo m

contact /'kɒntækt/ n contacto m;
(*person*) relação f. ~ **lenses** lentes fpl
de contacto ▫ vt contactar

contagious /kən'teɪdʒəs/ a contagioso

contain /kən'teɪn/ vt conter. ~ **o.s.**
conter-se. ~**er** n recipiente m; (*for
transport*) contentor m

contaminat|e /kən'tæmɪneɪt/ vt
contaminar. ~**ion** /-'neɪʃn/ n
contaminação f

contemplat|e /'kɒntempleɪt/ vt
contemplar; (*intend*) ter em vista;
(*consider*) esperar, pensar em. ~**ion**
/-'pleɪʃn/ n contemplação f

contemporary /kən'temprərɪ/ a & n
contemporâneo (m)

contempt /kən'tempt/ n desprezo m.
~**ible** a desprezível. ~**uous** /-tʃʊəs/ a
desdenhoso

contend /kən'tend/ vt afirmar, sustentar
▫ vi ~ **with** lutar contra. ~**er** n
adversário m, contendor m

content[1] /kən'tent/ a satisfeito, contente
▫ vt contentar. ~**ed** a satisfeito,
contente. ~**ment** n contentamento m,
satisfação f

content[2] /'kɒntent/ n conteúdo m. (**table
of**) ~**s** índice m

contention /kən'tenʃn/ n disputa f,
contenda f; (*assertion*) argumento m

contest[1] /'kɒntest/ n competição f;
(*struggle*) luta f

contest[2] /kən'test/ vt contestar; (*compete
for*) disputar. ~**ant** n concorrente mf

context /'kɒntekst/ n contexto m

continent /'kɒntɪnənt/ n continente m.
the C~ a Europa (continental) f. ~**al**
/-'nentl/ a continental; (*of mainland
Europe*) europeu ~**al breakfast** café m
da manhã europeu (P) pequeno almoço
m europeu. ~**al quilt** edredom m, (P)
edredão m

contingen|t /kən'tɪndʒənt/ a & n
contingente (m). ~**cy** n contingência f.
~**cy plan** plano m de emergência

continual /kən'tɪnjʊəl/ a contínuo. ~**ly**
adv continuamente

continu|e /kən'tɪnju:/ vt/i continuar.
~**ation** /-tɪnjʊ'eɪʃn/ n continuação f.

continuity /kɒntɪˈnjuːətɪ/ n
continuidade f

continuous /kənˈtɪnjʊəs/ a contínuo.
~ly adv continuamente

contort /kənˈtɔːt/ vt contorcer; (fig)
distorcer. ~ion /-ʃn/ n contorção f

contour /ˈkɒntʊə(r)/ n contorno m

contraband /ˈkɒntrəbænd/ n
contrabando m

contraception /kɒntrəˈsepʃn/ n
contracepção f

contraceptive /kɒntrəˈseptɪv/ a & n
contraceptivo (m)

contract[1] /ˈkɒntrækt/ n contrato m

contract[2] /kənˈtrækt/ vt/i contrair(-se);
(make a contract) contratar. ~ion /-ʃn/
n contração f, (P) contracção f

contractor /kənˈtræktə(r)/ n
empreiteiro m; (firm) firma f
empreiteira de serviços, (P)
recrutadora f de mão de obra
temporária

contradict /kɒntrəˈdɪkt/ vt contradizer.
~ion /-ʃn/ n contradição f. ~ory a
contraditório

contraflow /ˈkɒntrəfləʊ/ n fluxo m em
sentido contrátio

contrary[1] /ˈkɒntrərɪ/ a & n (opposite)
contrário (m) □ adv ~ to
contrariamente a. on the ~ ao ou pelo
contrário

contrary[2] /kənˈtreərɪ/ a (perverse) do
contra, embirrento

contrast[1] /ˈkɒntrɑːst/ n contraste m

contrast[2] /kənˈtrɑːst/ vt/i contrastar.
~ing a contrastante

contraven|e /kɒntrəˈviːn/ vt infringir.
~tion /-ˈvenʃn/ n contravenção f

contribut|e /kənˈtrɪbjuːt/ vt/i contribuir
(to para); (to newspaper etc) colaborar
(to em). ~ion /kɒntrɪˈbjuːʃn/ n
contribuição f. ~or /-ˈtrɪbjutə(r)/ n
contribuinte mf; (to newspaper)
colaborador m

contrivance /kənˈtraɪvəns/ n (invention)
engenho m; (device) engenhoca f; (trick)
maquinação f

contrive /kənˈtraɪv/ vt imaginar,
inventar. ~ to do conseguir fazer

control /kənˈtrəʊl/ vt (pt controlled)
(check, restrain) controlar; (firm etc)
dirigir □ n controle m; (management)
direção f, (P) direcção f. ~s (of car,
plane) comandos mpl; (knobs) botões
mpl. be in ~ of dirigir. under ~ sob
controle

controversial /kɒntrəˈvɜːʃl/ a
controverso, discutível

controversy /ˈkɒntrəvɜːsɪ/ n
controvérsia f

convalesce /kɒnvəˈles/ vi convalescer.
~nce n convalescença f. ~nt /-nt/ a &
n convalescente (mf). ~nt home casa
f de repouso

convene /kənˈviːn/ vt convocar □ vi
reunir-se

convenience /kənˈviːnɪəns/ n
conveniência f. ~s (appliances)
comodidades fpl; (lavatory) privada f,
(P) casa f de banho. at your ~ quando
(e como) lhe convier. ~ foods
alimentos mpl semiprontos

convenient /kənˈviːnɪənt/ a
conveniente. be ~ for convir a. ~ly
adv sem inconveniente; (situated) bem;
(arrive) a propósito

convent /ˈkɒnvənt/ n convento m.
~ school colégio m de freiras

convention /kənˈvenʃn/ n convenção f;
(custom) uso m, costume m. ~al a
convencional

converge /kənˈvɜːdʒ/ vi convergir

conversant /kənˈvɜːsnt/ a be ~ with
conhecer; (fact) saber; (machinery)
estar familiarizado com

conversation /kɒnvəˈseɪʃn/ n conversa
f. ~al a de conversa, coloquial

converse[1] /kənˈvɜːs/ vi conversar

converse[2] /ˈkɒnvɜːs/ a & n inverso (m).
~ly adv /kənˈvɜːslɪ/ adv ao invés,
inversamente

conver|t[1] /kənˈvɜːt/ vt converter; (house)
transformar. ~sion /-ʃn/ n conversão
f; (house) transformação f. ~tible a
convertível, conversível □ n (auto)
conversível m

convert[2] /ˈkɒnvɜːt/ n convertido m,
converso m

convex /ˈkɒnveks/ a convexo

convey /kənˈveɪ/ vt transmitir; (goods)
transportar; (idea, feeling) comunicar.
~ance n transporte m. ~or belt tapete
m rolante, correia f transportadora

convict[1] /kənˈvɪkt/ vt declarar culpado.
~ion /-ʃn/ n condenação f; (opinion)
convicção f

convict[2] /ˈkɒnvɪkt/ n condenado m

convinc|e /kənˈvɪns/ vt convencer. ~ing
a convincente

convoluted /ˈkɒnvəˈluːtɪd/ a retorcido;
(fig) complicado; (bot) convoluto

convoy /ˈkɒnvɔɪ/ n escolta f

convuls|e /kənˈvʌls/ vt convulsionar;
(fig) abalar. be ~ed with laughter
torcer-se de riso. ~ion /-ʃn/ n
convulsão f

coo /kuː/ vi (pt cooed) arrulhar □ n
arrulho m

cook /kʊk/ vt/i cozinhar □ n cozinheira f,
cozinheiro m. ~ up (colloq) cozinhar
(fig), fabricar

cooker /ˈkʊkə(r)/ n fogão m
cookery /ˈkʊkərɪ/ n cozinha f. ~ **book**
livro m de culinária
cookie /ˈkʊkɪ/ n (Amer) biscoito m
cool /kuːl/ a (-er, -est) fresco; (calm)
calmo; (unfriendly) frio □ n frescura f;
(sl: composure) sangue-frio m □ vt/i
arrefecer. ~-**box** n geladeira f portátil.
in the ~ no fresco. ~**ly** /ˈkuːllɪ/ adv
calmamente; (fig) friamente. ~**ness** n
frescura f; (fig) frieza f
coop /kuːp/ n galinheiro m □ vt ~ **up**
engaislar, fechar
co-operat|e /kəʊˈɒpəreɪt/ vi cooperar.
~**ion** /-ˈreɪʃn/ n cooperação f
cooperative /kəʊˈɒpərətɪv/ a
cooperativo □ n cooperativa f
coordinat|e /kəʊˈɔːdmeɪt/ vt co-
ordenar. ~**ion** /-ˈneɪʃn/ n coordenação f
cop /kɒp/ n (sl) porco m (sl), (P) xui m (sl)
cope /kəʊp/ vi aguentar-se, arranjar-se.
~ **with** poder com, dar conta de
copious /ˈkəʊpɪəs/ a copioso
copper[1] /ˈkɒpə(r)/ n cobre m □ a de cobre
copper[2] /ˈkɒpə(r)/ n (sl) porco m (sl), (P)
xui m (sl)
coppice /ˈkɒpɪs/, **copse** /kɒps/ ns mata f
de corte
copulat|e /ˈkɒpjʊleɪt/ vi copular. ~**ion**
/-ˈleɪʃn/ n cópula f
copy /ˈkɒpɪ/ n cópia f; (of book) exemplar
m; (of newspaper) número m □ vt/i
copiar
copyright /ˈkɒpɪraɪt/ n direitos mpl
autorais
coral /ˈkɒrəl/ n coral m
cord /kɔːd/ n cordão m; (electr) fio m
cordial /ˈkɔːdɪəl/ a & n cordial (m)
cordon /ˈkɔːdn/ n cordão m □ vt ~ **off**
fechar (com um cordão de isolamento)
corduroy /ˈkɔːdərɔɪ/ n veludo m cotelé
core /kɔː(r)/ n âmago m; (of apple, pear)
coração m
cork /kɔːk/ n cortiça f; (for bottle) rolha f
□ vt rolhar
corkscrew /ˈkɔːkskruː/ n saca-rolhas m
corn[1] /kɔːn/ n trigo m; (Amer: maize)
milho m; (seed) grão m. ~ **on the cob**
espiga f de milho
corn[2] /kɔːn/ n (hard skin) calo m
corned /kɔːnd/ a ~ **beef** carne f de vaca
enlatada
corner /ˈkɔːnə(r)/ n canto m; (of street)
esquina f; (bend in road) curva f □ vt
encurralar; (market) monopolizar □ vi
dar uma curva, virar
cornet /ˈkɔːnɪt/ n (mus) cornetim m; (for
ice-cream) casquinha f, (P) cone m
cornflakes /ˈkɔːnfleɪks/ npl cornflakes
mpl, cereais mpl

cornflour /ˈkɔːnflaʊə(r)/ n fécula f de
milho, maisena f
Corn|wall /ˈkɔːnwəl/ n Cornualha f.
~**ish** a da Cornualha
corny /ˈkɔːnɪ/ a (colloq) batido, (P)
estafado
coronary /ˈkɒrənrɪ/ n ~ (**thrombosis**)
infarto m, enfarte m
coronation /kɒrəˈneɪʃn/ n coroação f
coroner /ˈkɒrənə(r)/ n magistrado m que
investiga os casos de morte suspeita
corporal[1] /ˈkɔːpərəl/ n (mil) cabo m
corporal[2] /ˈkɔːpərəl/ a ~ **punishment**
castigo m corporal
corporate /ˈkɔːpərət/ a coletivo, (P)
colectivo; (body) corporativo
corporation /kɔːpəˈreɪʃn/ n corporação
f; (of town) municipalidade f
corps /kɔː(r)/ n (pl corps /kɔːz/) corpo m
corpse /kɔːps/ n cadáver m
corpuscle /ˈkɔːpʌsl/ n corpúsculo m
correct /kəˈrekt/ a correto, (P) correcto.
the ~ **time** a hora certa. **you are** ~
você tem razão □ vt corrigir. ~**ion** /-ʃn/
n correção f, (P) correcção f, emenda f
correlat|e /ˈkɒrəleɪt/ vt/i
correlacionar(-se). ~**ion** /-ˈleɪʃn/ n
correlação f
correspond /kɒrɪˈspɒnd/ vi
corresponder (**to, with**, a); (write
letters) corresponder-se (**with**, com).
~**ence** n correspondência f. ~**ent** n
correspondente mf. ~**ing** a
correspondente
corridor /ˈkɒrɪdɔː(r)/ n corredor m
corroborate /kəˈrɒbəreɪt/ vt corroborar
corro|de /kəˈrəʊd/ vt/i corroer (-se).
~**sion** n corrosão f
corrugated /ˈkɒrəgeɪtɪd/ a corrugado.
~ **cardboard** cartão m canelado.
~ **iron** chapa f ondulada
corrupt /kəˈrʌpt/ a corrupto □ vt
corromper. ~**ion** /-ʃn/ n corrupção f
corset /ˈkɔːsɪt/ n espartilho m;
(elasticated) cinta f elástica
Corsica /ˈkɔːsɪkə/ n Córsega f
cosmetic /kɒzˈmetɪk/ n cosmético m □ a
cosmético; (fig) superficial
cosmonaut /ˈkɒzmənɔːt/ n cosmonauta
mf
cosmopolitan /kɒzməˈpɒlɪtən/ a & n
cosmopolita (mf)
cosset /ˈkɒsɪt/ vt (pt cosseted) proteger
cost /kɒst/ vt (pt cost) custar; (pt costed)
fixar o preço de □ n custo m. ~**s** (jur)
custos mpl. **at all** ~**s** custe o que
custar. **to one's** ~ à sua custa. ~ **of
living** custo m de vida
costly /ˈkɒstlɪ/ a (-ier, -iest) a caro;
(valuable) precioso
costume /ˈkɒstjuːm/ n traje m

cos|y /'kəʊzı/ a (-ier, -iest) confortável, íntimo □ n abafador m (do bule do chá). ~iness n conforto m

cot /kɒt/ n cama f de bêbê, berço m

cottage /'kɒtɪdʒ/ n pequena casa f de campo. ~ cheese requeijão m, ricota f. ~ industry artesanato m. ~ pie empada f de carne picada

cotton /'kɒtn/ n algodão m; (thread) fio m, linha f. ~ wool algodão m hidrófilo

couch /kaʊtʃ/ n divã m

couchette /ku:'ʃet/ n couchette f

cough /kɒf/ vi tossir □ n tosse f

could /kʊd, kəd/ pt of can²

couldn't /'kʊdnt/ = could not

council /'kaʊnsl/ n conselho m. ~ house casa f de bairro popular

councillor /'kaʊnsələ(r)/ n vereador m

counsel /'kaʊnsl/ n conselho m; (pl invar) (jur) advogado m. ~lor n conselheiro m

count¹ /kaʊnt/ vt/i contar □ n conta f. ~-down n (rocket) contagem f regressiva. ~ on contar com

count² /kaʊnt/ n (nobleman) conde m

counter¹ /'kaʊntə(r)/ n (in shop) balcão m; (in game) ficha f, (P) tento m

counter² /'kaʊntə(r)/ adv ~ to em sentido contrário a; (in the opposite direction) em sentido contrário a □ a oposto □ vt opor; (blow) aparar □ vi ripostar

counter- /'kaʊntə(r)/ pref contra-

counteract /kaʊntər'ækt/ vt neutralizar, frustrar

counter-attack /'kaʊntərətæk/ n contra-ataque m □ vt/i contra-atacar

counterbalance /'kaʊntəbæləns/ n contrapeso m □ vt contrabalançar

counterfeit /'kaʊntəfɪt/ a falsificado, falso □ n falsificação f □ vt falsificar

counterfoil /'kaʊntəfɔɪl/ n talão m, canhoto m

counterpart /'kaʊntəpa:t/ n equivalente m; (person) homólogo m

counter-productive /'kaʊntəprədʌktɪv/ a contraproducente

countersign /'kaʊntəsam/ vt subscrever documento já assinado; (cheque) contrassinar

countess /'kaʊntıs/ n condessa f

countless /'kaʊntlıs/ a sem conta, incontável, inúmero

country /'kʌntrı/ n país m; (homeland) pátria f; (countryside) campo m

countryside /'kʌntrısaɪd/ n campo m

county /'kaʊntı/ n condado m

coup /ku:/ n ~ (d'état) golpe m (de estado)

couple /'kʌpl/ n par m, casal m □ vt/i unir(-se), ligar(-se); (techn) acoplar. a ~ of um par de

coupon /'ku:pɒn/ n cupão m

courage /'kʌrɪdʒ/ n coragem f. ~ous /kə'reɪdʒəs/ a corajoso

courgette /kʊə'ʒet/ n abobrinha f

courier /'kʊrɪə(r)/ n correio m; (for tourists) guia mf; (for parcels, mail) estafeta m

course /kɔ:s/ n curso m; (series) série f; (culin) prato m; (for golf) campo m; (fig) caminho m. in due ~ na altura devida, oportunamente. in the ~ of durante. of ~ está claro, com certeza

court /kɔ:t/ n (of monarch) corte f; (courtyard) pátio m; (tennis) court m, quadra f, (P) campo m; (jur) tribunal m □ vt cortejar; (danger) provocar. ~ martial (pl courts martial) conselho m de guerra

courteous /'kɜ:tɪəs/ a cortês, delicado

courtesy /'kɜ:təsɪ/ n cortesia f

courtship /'kɔ:tʃɪp/ n namoro m, corte f

courtyard /'kɔ:tja:d/ n pátio m

cousin /'kʌzn/ n primo m. first/second ~ primo m em primeiro/segundo grau

cove /kəʊv/ n angra f, enseada f

covenant /'kʌvənənt/ n convenção f, convénio m; (jur) contrato m; (relig) aliança f

cover /'kʌvə(r)/ vt cobrir □ n cobertura f; (for bed) colcha f; (for book, furniture) capa f; (lid) tampa f; (shelter) abrigo m. ~ charge serviço m. ~ up tapar; (fig) encobrir. ~-up n (fig) encobrimento m. take ~ abrigar-se. under separate ~ em separado. ~ing n cobertura f. ~ing letter carta f (que acompanha um documento)

coverage /'kʌvərɪdʒ/ n (of events) reportagem f, cobertura f

covet /'kʌvɪt/ vt cobiçar

cow /kaʊ/ n vaca f

coward /'kaʊəd/ n covarde mf. ~ly a covarde

cowardice /'kaʊədıs/ n covardia f

cowboy /'kaʊbɔɪ/ n cowboy m, vaqueiro m

cower /'kaʊə(r)/ vi encolher-se (de medo)

cowshed /'kaʊʃed/ n estábulo m

coy /kɔɪ/ a (-er, -est) (falsamente) tímido

crab /kræb/ n caranguejo m

crack /kræk/ n fenda f; (in glass) rachadura f; (noise) estalo m; (sl: joke) piada f; (drug) crack m □ a (colloq) de élite □ vt/i estalar; (nut) quebrar; (joke) contar; (problem) resolver; (voice) mudar. ~ down on (colloq) cair em cima de, arrochar. get ~ing (colloq) pôr mãos à obra

cracker /'krækə(r)/ n busca-pé m, bomba f de estalo; (culin) bolacha f de água e sal

crackers /'krækəz/ *a* (*sl*) desmiolado, maluco

crackle /'krækl/ *vi* crepitar □ *n* crepitação *f*

crackpot /'krækpɒt/ *n* (*sl*) desmiolado, maluco

cradle /'kreɪdl/ *n* berço *m* □ *vt* embalar

craft[1] /kra:ft/ *n* ofício *m*; (*technique*) arte *f*; (*cunning*) manha *f*, astúcia *f*

craft[2] /kra:ft/ *n* (*invar*) (*boat*) embarcação *f*

craftsman /'kra:ftsmən/ *n* (*pl* -**men**) artífice *mf*. ~**ship** *n* arte *f*

crafty /'kra:ftɪ/ *a* (-**ier**, -**iest**) manhoso, astucioso

crag /kræg/ *n* penhasco *m*. ~**gy** *a* escarpado, íngreme

cram /kræm/ *vt* (*pt* **crammed**) ~ (**for an exam**) decorar, (*P*) empinar. ~ **into/with** entulhar com

cramp /kræmp/ *n* cãimbra *f* □ *vt* restringir, tolher. ~**ed** *a* apertado

crane /kreɪn/ *n* grua *f*; (*bird*) grou *m* □ *vt* (*neck*) esticar

crank[1] /kræŋk/ *n* (*techn*) manivela *f*. ~**shaft** *n* (*techn*) cambota *f*

crank[2] /kræŋk/ *n* excêntrico *m*. ~**y** *a* excêntrico

crash /kræʃ/ *n* acidente *m*; (*noise*) estrondo *m*; (*comm*) falência *f*; (*financial*) colapso *m*, crash *m* □ *vt/i* (*fall/strike*) cair/bater com estrondo; (*two cars*) chocar, bater; (*comm*) abrir falência; (*plane*) cair □ *a* (*course, programme*) intensivo. ~**helmet** *n* capacete *m*. ~**land** *vi* fazer uma aterrissagem forçada

crate /kreɪt/ *n* engradado *m*

crater /'kreɪtə(r)/ *n* cratera *f*

crav|e /kreɪv/ *vt/i* ~**e** (**for**) ansiar por. ~**ing** *n* desejo *m* irresistível, ânsia *f*

crawl /krɔ:l/ *vi* rastejar; (*of baby*) engatinhar, (*P*) andar de gatas; (*of car*) mover-se lentamente □ *n* rastejo *m*; (*swimming*) crawl *m*. be ~**ing with** fervilhar de, estar cheio de

crayfish /'kreɪfɪʃ/ *n* (*pl invar*) lagostim *m*

crayon /'kreɪən/ *n* crayon *m*, lápis *m* de pastel

craze /kreɪz/ *n* moda *f*, febre *f*

craz|y /'kreɪzɪ/ *a* (-**ier**, -**iest**) doido, louco (**about** por). ~**iness** *n* loucura *f*

creak /kri:k/ *n* rangido *m* □ *vi* ranger

cream /kri:m/ *n* (*milk fat; fig*) nata *f*; (*cosmetic; culin*) creme *m* □ *a* creme *invar* □ *vt* desnatar. ~ **cheese** queijo-creme *m*. ~**y** *a* cremoso

crease /kri:s/ *n* vinco *m* □ *vt/i* amarrotar(-se)

creat|e /kri:'eɪt/ *vt* criar. ~**ion** /-ʃn/ *n* criação *f*. ~**ive** *a* criador. ~**or** *n* criador *m*

creature /'kri:tʃə(r)/ *n* criatura *f*

crèche /kreʃ/ *n* creche *f*

credentials /krɪ'denʃlz/ *npl* credenciais *fpl*; (*of competence etc*) referências *fpl*

credib|le /'kredəbl/ *a* crível, verosímil, (*P*) verossímil. ~**ility** /-'bɪlətɪ/ *n* credibilidade *f*

credit /'kredɪt/ *n* crédito *m*; (*honour*) honra *f*. ~**s** (*cinema*) créditos *mpl* □ *vt* (*pt* **credited**) acreditar em; (*comm*) creditar. ~ **card** cartão *m* de crédito. ~ **sb with** atribuir a alg. ~**or** *n* credor *m*

creditable /'kredɪtəbl/ *a* louvável, honroso

credulous /'kredjʊləs/ *a* crédulo

creed /kri:d/ *n* credo *m*

creek /kri:k/ *n* enseada *f* estreita. be up the ~ (*sl*) estar frito (*sl*)

creep /kri:p/ *vi* (*pt* **crept**) rastejar; (*move stealthily*) mover-se furtivamente □ *n* (*sl*) cara *m* nojento. give sb the ~**s** dar arrepios a alg. ~**er** *n* (*planta f*) trepadeira (*f*). ~**y** *a* arrepiante

cremat|e /krɪ'meɪt/ *vt* cremar. ~**ion** /-ʃn/ *n* cremação *f*

crematorium /kremə'tɔ:rɪəm/ *n* (*pl* -**ia**) crematório *m*

crêpe /kreɪp/ *n* crepe *m*. ~ **paper** papel *m* crepom, (*P*) plissado

crept /krept/ *see* **creep**

crescent /'kresnt/ *n* crescente *m*; (*street*) rua *f* em semicírculo

cress /kres/ *n* agrião *m*

crest /krest/ *n* (*of bird, hill*) crista *f*; (*on coat of arms*) timbre *m*

Crete /kri:t/ *n* Creta *f*

crevasse /krɪ'væs/ *n* fenda *f* (em geleira)

crevice /'krevɪs/ *n* racha *f*, fenda *f*

crew[1] /kru:/ *see* **crow**

crew[2] /kru:/ *n* tripulação *f*; (*gang*) bando *m*. ~**cut** *n* corte *m* à escovinha. ~**neck** *n* gola *f* redonda e um pouco subida

crib[1] /krɪb/ *n* berço *m*; (*Christmas*) presépio *m*

crib[2] /krɪb/ *vt/i* (*pt* **cribbed**) (*colloq*) colar (*sl*), (*P*) cabular (*sl*) □ *n* cópia *f*, plágio *m*; (*translation*) burro *m* (*sl*)

cricket[1] /'krɪkɪt/ *n* críquete *m*. ~**er** *n* jogador *m* de críquete

cricket[2] /'krɪkɪt/ *n* (*insect*) grilo *m*

crime /kraɪm/ *n* crime *m*; (*minor*) delito *m*; (*collectively*) criminalidade *f*

criminal /'krɪmɪnl/ *a & n* criminoso (*m*)

crimp /krɪmp/ *vt* preguear; (*hair*) frisar

crimson /'krɪmzn/ *a & n* carmesim (*m*)

cring|e /krɪndʒ/ *vi* encolher-se. ~**ing** *a* servil

crinkle /'krɪŋkl/ *vt/i* enrugar(-se) □ *n* vinco *m*, ruga *f*

cripple /'krɪpl/ *n* aleijado *m*, coxo *m* □ *vt* estropiar; (*fig*) paralisar

crisis /'kraɪsɪs/ *n* (*pl* **crises** /-si:z/) crise *f*

crisp /krɪsp/ *a* (**-er, est**) (*culin*) crocante; (*air*) fresco; (*manners, reply*) decidido. **~s** *npl* batatas *fpl* fritas redondas

criterion /kraɪˈtɪərɪən/ *n* (*pl* **-ia**) critério *m*

critic /'krɪtɪk/ *n* crítico *m*. **~al** *a* crítico. **~ally** *adv* de forma crítica; (*ill*) gravemente

criticism /'krɪtɪsɪzəm/ *n* crítica *f*

criticize /'krɪtɪsaɪz/ *vt/i* criticar

croak /krəʊk/ *n* (*frog*) coaxar *m*; (*raven*) crocitar *m*, crocito *m* □ *vi* (*frog*) coaxar; (*raven*) crocitar

crochet /'krəʊʃeɪ/ *n* crochê *m* □ *vt* fazer em crochê

crockery /'krɒkəri/ *n* louça *f*

crocodile /'krɒkədaɪl/ *n* crocodilo *m*

crocus /'krəʊkəs/ *n* (*pl*-**uses** /-sɪz/) croco *m*

crony /'krəʊni/ *n* camarada *mf*, amigão *m*, parceiro *m*

crook /krʊk/ *n* (*colloq: criminal*) vigarista *mf*; (*stick*) cajado *m*

crooked /'krʊkɪd/ *a* torcido; (*winding*) tortuoso; (*askew*) torto; (*colloq: dishonest*) desonesto. **~ly** *adv* de través

crop /krɒp/ *n* colheita *f*; (*fig*) quantidade *f*; (*haircut*) corte *m* rente □ *vt* (*pt* **cropped**) cortar □ *vi* **~ up** aparecer, surgir

croquet /'krəʊkeɪ/ *n* croquet *m*, croqué *m*

cross /krɒs/ *n* cruz *f* □ *vt/i* cruzar; (*cheque*) cruzar, (*P*) barrar; (*oppose*) contrariar; (*of paths*) cruzar-se □ *a* zangado. **~ off** *or* **out** riscar. **~ o.s.** benzer-se. **~ sb's mind** passar pela cabeça *or* pelo espírito de alg, ocorrer a alg. **talk at ~ purposes** falar sem se entender. **~-country** *a* & *adv* a corta-mato. **~-examine** *vt* fazer o contra-interrogatório (de testemunhas). **~-eyed** *a* vesgo, estrábico. **~-fire** *n* fogo *m* cruzado. **~-reference** *n* nota *f* remissiva. **~-section** *n* corte *m* transversal; (*fig*) grupo *m* or sector *m* representativo. **~ly** *adv* irritadamente

crossbar /'krɒsbɑ:(r)/ *n* barra *f* transversal *f*; (*of bicycle*) travessão *m*

crossing /'krɒsɪŋ/ *n* cruzamento *m*; (*by boat*) travessia *f*; (*on road*) passagem *f*

crossroads /'krɒsrəʊdz/ *n* encruzilhada *f*, cruzamento *m*

crossword /'krɒswɜ:d/ *n* palavras *fpl* cruzadas

crotch /krɒtʃ/ *n* entrepernas *fpl*

crotchet /'krɒtʃɪt/ *n* (*mus*) semínima *f*

crouch /kraʊtʃ/ *vi* agachar-se

crow /krəʊ/ *n* corvo *m* □ *vi* (*cock*) (*pt* **crew**) cantar; (*fig*) rejubilar-se (**over** com). **as the ~ flies** em linha reta, (*P*) recta

crowbar /'krəʊbɑ:(r)/ *n* alavanca *f*, pé-de-cabra *m*

crowd /kraʊd/ *n* multidão *f* □ *vi* afluir □ *vt* encher. **~ into** apinhar-se em. **~ed** *a* cheio, apinhado

crown /kraʊn/ *n* coroa *f*; (*of hill*) topo *m*, cume *m* □ *vt* coroar; (*tooth*) pôr uma coroa em

crucial /'kru:ʃl/ *a* crucial

crucifix /'kru:sɪfɪks/ *n* crucifixo *m*

crucif|y /'kru:sɪfaɪ/ *vt* crucificar. **~ixion** /-'fɪkʃn/ *n* crucificação *f*

crude /kru:d/ *a* (**-er, -est**) (*raw*) bruto; (*rough, vulgar*) grosseiro. **~ oil** petróleo *m* bruto

cruel /krʊəl/ *a* (**crueller, cruellest**) cruel. **~ty** *n* crueldade *f*

cruis|e /kru:z/ *n* cruzeiro *m* □ *vi* cruzar; (*of tourists*) fazer um cruzeiro; (*of car*) ir a velocidade de cruzeiro. **~er** *n* cruzador *m*. **~ing speed** velocidade *f* de cruzeiro

crumb /krʌm/ *n* migalha *f*, farelo *m*

crumble /'krʌmbl/ *vt/i* desfazer (-se); (*bread*) esmigalhar(-se); (*collapse*) desmoronar-se

crumple /'krʌmpl/ *vt/i* amarrotar (-se)

crunch /krʌntʃ/ *vt* trincar; (*under one's feet*) fazer ranger

crusade /kru:'seɪd/ *n* cruzada *f*. **~r** /-ə(r)/ *n* cruzado *m*; (*fig*) militante *mf*

crush /krʌʃ/ *vt* esmagar; (*clothes, papers*) amassar, amarrotar □ *n* aperto *m*. **a ~ on** (*sl*) uma paixonite, (*P*) paixoneta por.

crust /krʌst/ *n* côdea *f*, crosta *f*. **~y** *a* crocante

crutch /krʌtʃ/ *n* muleta *f*; (*crotch*) entrepernas *fpl*

crux /krʌks/ *n* (*pl* **cruxes**) o ponto crucial

cry /kraɪ/ *n* grito *m* □ *vi* (*weep*) chorar; (*call out*) gritar. **a far ~ from** muito diferente de.

crying /'kraɪɪŋ/ *a* **a ~ shame** uma grande vergonha

crypt /krɪpt/ *n* cripta *f*

cryptic /'krɪptɪk/ *a* críptico, enigmático

crystal /'krɪstl/ *n* cristal *m*. **~lize** *vt/i* cristalizar(-se)

cub /kʌb/ *n* cria *f*, filhote *m*. **C~ (Scout)** lobito *m*

Cuba /'kju:bə/ *n* Cuba *f*. **~n** *a* & *n* cubano (*m*)

cubby-hole /'kʌbɪhəʊl/ n cochicho m; (*snug place*) cantinho m

cub|e /kju:b/ n cubo m. **~ic** a cúbico

cubicle /'kju:bɪkl/ n cubículo m, compartimento m; (*at swimming pool*) cabine f

cuckoo /'kʊku:/ n cuco m

cucumber /'kju:kʌmbə(r)/ n pepino m

cuddl|e /'kʌdl/ vt/i abraçar com carinho; (*nestle*) aninhar(-se) □ n abracinho m, festinha f. **~y** a fofo, aconchegante

cudgel /'kʌdʒl/ n cacete m, moca f □ vt (pt **cudgelled**) dar cacetadas em

cue[1] /kju:/ n (*theat*) deixa f; (*hint*) sugestão f, sinal m

cue[2] /kju:/ n (*billiards*) taco m

cuff /kʌf/ n punho m; (*blow*) sopapo m □ vt dar um sopapo. **~-link** n botão m de punho. **off the ~** de improviso

cul-de-sac /'kʌldəsæk/ n (pl **culs-de-sac**) beco m sem saída

culinary /'kʌlɪnərɪ/ a culinário

cull /kʌl/ vt (*select*) escolher; (*kill*) abater seletivamente, (P) selectivamente □ n abate m

culminat|e /'kʌlmɪneɪt/ vi **~e in** acabar em. **~ion** /-'neɪʃn/ n auge m, ponto m culminante

culprit /'kʌlprɪt/ n culpado m

cult /kʌlt/ n culto m

cultivat|e /'kʌltɪveɪt/ vt cultivar. **~ion** /-'veɪʃn/ n cultivo m, cultivação f

cultural /'kʌltʃərəl/ a cultural

culture /'kʌltʃə(r)/ n cultura f. **~d** a culto

cumbersome /'kʌmbəsəm/ a (*unwieldy*) pesado, incômodo, (P) incómodo

cumulative /'kju:mjʊlətɪv/ a cumulativo

cunning /'kʌnɪŋ/ a astuto, manhoso □ n astúcia f, manha f

cup /kʌp/ n xícara f, (P) chávena f; (*prize*) taça f. **C~ Final** Final de Campeonato f

cupboard /'kʌbəd/ n armário m

cupful /'kʌpfʊl/ n xícara f cheia, (P) chávena f (cheia)

curable /'kjʊərəbl/ a curável

curator /kjʊə'reɪtə(r)/ n (*museum*) conservador m; (*jur*) curador m

curb /kɜ:b/ n freio m □ vt refrear; (*price increase etc*) sustar

curdle /'kɜ:dl/ vt/i coalhar

cure /kjʊə(r)/ vt curar □ n cura f

curfew /'kɜ:fju:/ n toque m de recolher

curio /'kjʊərɪəʊ/ n (pl -os) curiosidade f

curi|ous /'kjʊərɪəs/ a curioso. **~osity** /-'ɒsətɪ/ n curiosidade f

curl /kɜ:l/ vt/i encaracolar(-se) □ n caracol m. **~ up** enroscar(-se)

curler /'kɜ:lə(r)/ n rolo m

curly /'kɜ:lɪ/ a (-ier, -iest) encaracolado, crespo

currant /'kʌrənt/ n passa f de Corinto

currency /'kʌrənsɪ/ n moeda f corrente; (*general use*) circulação f. **foreign ~** moeda f estrangeira

current /'kʌrənt/ a (*common*) corrente; (*event, price, etc*) atual, (P) actual □ n corrente f. **~ account** conta f corrente. **~ affairs** atualidades fpl, (P) actualidades fpl. **~ly** adv atualmente, (P) actualmente

curriculum /kə'rɪkjʊləm/ n (pl -la) currículo m, programa m de estudos. **~ vitae** n curriculum vitae m

curry[1] /'kʌrɪ/ n caril m

curry[2] /'kʌrɪ/ vt **~ favour with** procurar agradar a

curse /kɜ:s/ n maldição f, praga f; (*bad language*) palavrão m □ vt amaldiçoar, praguejar contra □ vi praguejar; (*swear*) dizer palavrões

cursor /'kɜ:sə(r)/ n cursor m

cursory /'kɜ:sərɪ/ a apressado, superficial. **a ~ look** uma olhada superficial

curt /kɜ:t/ a brusco

curtail /kɜ:'teɪl/ vt abreviar; (*expenses etc*) reduzir

curtain /'kɜ:tn/ n cortina f; (*theat*) pano m

curtsy /'kɜ:tsɪ/ n reverência f □ vi fazer uma reverência

curve /kɜ:v/ n curva f □ vt/i curvar(-se); (*of road*) fazer uma curva

cushion /'kʊʃn/ n almofada f □ vt (a *blow*) amortecer; (*fig*) proteger

cushy /'kʊʃɪ/ a (-ier, -iest) (*colloq*) fácil, agradável. **~ job** sinecura f, boca f (*fig*)

custard /'kʌstəd/ n creme m

custodian /kʌ'stəʊdɪən/ n guarda m

custody /'kʌstədɪ/ n (*safe keeping*) custódia f; (*jur*) detenção f; (*of child*) tutela f

custom /'kʌstəm/ n costume m; (*comm*) freguesia f, clientela f. **~ary** a habitual

customer /'kʌstəmə(r)/ n freguês m, cliente mf

customs /'kʌstəmz/ npl alfândega f □ a alfandegário. **~ clearance** desembaraço m alfandegário. **~ officer** funcionário m da alfândega

cut /kʌt/ vt/i (pt **cut**, pres p **cutting**) cortar; (*prices etc*) reduzir □ n corte m, golpe m; (*of clothes, hair*) corte m; (*piece*) pedaço m; (*prices etc*) redução f, corte m; (*sl: share*) comissão f, (P) talhada f (sl). **~ back** or **down (on)** reduzir. **~back** n corte m. **~ in** intrometer-se; (*auto*) cortar. **~ off** cortar; (*fig*) isolar. **~ out** recortar;

cute | dart

(*leave out*) suprimir. **~-out** *n* figura *f* para recortar. **~-price** *a* a preço(s) reduzido(s). **~ short** encurtar, (*P*) atalhar

cute /kjuːt/ *a* (**-er, -est**) (*colloq: clever*) esperto; (*attractive*) bonito, (*P*) giro (*colloq*)

cuticle /'kjuːtɪkl/ *n* cutícula *f*

cutlery /'kʌtlərɪ/ *n* talheres *mpl*

cutlet /'kʌtlɪt/ *n* costeleta *f*

cutting /'kʌtɪŋ/ *a* cortante □ *n* (*from newspaper*) recorte *m*; (*plant*) estaca *f*. **~ edge** gume *m*

CV *abbr see* **curriculum vitae**

cyanide /'saɪənaɪd/ *n* cianeto *m*

cycl|e /'saɪkl/ *n* ciclo *m*; (*bicycle*) bicicleta *f* □ *vi* andar de bicicleta. **~lane** cicloria *f*. **~ing** *n* ciclismo *m*. **~ist** *n* ciclista *mf*

cyclone /'saɪkləʊn/ *n* ciclone *m*

cylind|er /'sɪlɪndə(r)/ *n* cilindro *m*. **~rical** *a* cilíndrico

cymbals /'sɪmblz/ *npl* (*mus*) pratos *mpl*

cynic /'sɪnɪk/ *n* cínico *m*. **~al** *a* cínico. **~ism** /-sɪzəm/ *n* cinismo *m*

Cypr|us /'saɪprəs/ *n* Chipre *m*. **~iot** /'sɪprɪət/ *a* & *n* cipriota (*mf*)

cyst /sɪst/ *n* quisto *m*

Czech /tʃek/ *a* & *n* tcheco (*m*), (*P*) checo (*m*)

Dd

dab /dæb/ *vt* (*pt* **dabbed**) aplicar levemente □ *n* **a ~ of** uma aplicaçãozinha de. **~ sth on** aplicar qq coisa em gestos leves

dabble /'dæbl/ *vi* **~ in** interessar-se por, fazer um pouco de (como amador). **~r** /-ə(r)/ *n* amador *m*

dad /dæd/ *n* (*colloq*) paizinho *m*. **~dy** *n* (*children's use*) papai *m*, (*P*) papá *m*. **~dy-long-legs** *n* pernilongo *m*

daffodil /'dæfədɪl/ *n* narciso *m*

daft /daːft/ *a* (**-er, -est**) doido, maluco

dagger /'dægə(r)/ *n* punhal *m*. **at ~s drawn** prestes a lutar (**with** com)

daily /'deɪlɪ/ *a* diário, quotidiano □ *adv* diariamente, todos os dias □ *n* (*newspaper*) diário *m*; (*colloq: charwoman*) faxineira *f*, (*P*) mulher *f* a dias

dainty /'deɪntɪ/ *a* (**-ier, -iest**) delicado; (*pretty, neat*) gracioso

dairy /'deərɪ/ *n* leiteria *f*. **~ products** laticínios *mpl*

daisy /'deɪzɪ/ *n* margarida *f*

dam /dæm/ *n* barragem *f*, represa *f* □ *vt* (*pt* **dammed**) represar

damag|e /'dæmɪdʒ/ *n* estrago(s) *mpl*. **~es** (*jur*) perdas *fpl* e danos *mpl* □ *vt* estragar, danificar; (*fig*) prejudicar. **~ing** *a* prejudicial

dame /deɪm/ *n* (*old use*) dama *f*; (*Amer sl*) mulher *f*

damn /dæm/ *vt* (*relig*) condenar aõ inferno; (*swear at*) amaldiçoar, maldizer; (*fig: condemn*) condenar □ *int* raios!, bolas! □ *n* **not care a ~** (*colloq*) estar pouco ligando (*colloq*), (*P*) estar-se marimbando (*colloq*) □ *a* (*colloq*) do diabo, danado □ *adv* (*colloq*) muitíssimo. **I'll be ~ed if** que um raio me atinja se. **~ation** /-'neɪʃn/ *n* danação *f*, condenação *f*. **~ing** *a* comprometedor, condenatório

damp /dæmp/ *n* umidade *f*, (*P*) humidade *f* □ *a* (**-er, -est**) úmido, (*P*) húmido □ *vt* umedecer, (*P*) humedecer. **~en** *vt* = **damp**. **~ness** *n* umidade *f*, (*P*) humidade *f*

dance /daːns/ *vt/i* dançar □ *n* dança *f*. **~ hall** sala *f* de baile. **~r** /-ə(r)/ *n* dançarino *m*; (*professional*) bailarino *m*

dandelion /'dændɪlaɪən/ *n* dente-de-leão *m*

dandruff /'dændrʌf/ *n* caspa *f*

Dane /deɪn/ *n* dinamarquês *m*

danger /'deɪndʒə(r)/ *n* perigo *m*. **be in ~ of** correr o risco de. **~ous** *a* perigoso

dangle /'dæŋgl/ *vi* oscilar, pender □ *vt* ter or trazer dependurado; (*hold*) balançar; (*fig: hopes, etc*) acenar com

Danish /'deɪnɪʃ/ *a* dinamarquês □ *n* (*lang*) dinamarquês *m*

dank /dæŋk/ *a* (**-er, -est**) frio e úmido, (*P*) húmido

dare /deə(r)/ *vt* **~ to do** ousar fazer. **~ sb to do** desafiar alg a fazer □ *n* desafio *m*. **I ~ say** creio

daredevil /'deədevl/ *n* louco *m*, temerário *m*

daring /'deərɪŋ/ *a* audacioso □ *n* audácia *f*

dark /daːk/ *a* (**-er, -est**) escuro, sombrio; (*gloomy*) sombrio; (*of colour*) escuro; (*of skin*) moreno □ *n* escuridão *f*, escuro *m*; (*nightfall*) anoitecer *m*, cair *m* da noite. **~ horse** concorrente *mf* que é uma incógnita. **~-room** *n* câmara *f* escura. **be in the ~ about** (*fig*) ignorar. **~ness** *n* escuridão *f*

darken /'daːkən/ *vt/i* escurecer

darling /'daːlɪŋ/ *a* & *n* querido (*m*)

darn /daːn/ *vt* serzir, remendar

dart /daːt/ *n* dardo *m*, flecha *f*. **~s** (*game*) jogo *m* de dardos □ *vi* lançar-se

dartboard /'da:tbɔ:d/ *n* alvo *m*

dash /dæʃ/ *vi* precipitar-se □ *vt* arremessar; (*hopes*) destruir □ *n* corrida *f*; (*stroke*) travessão *m*; (*Morse*) traço *m*. **a ~ of** um pouco de. **~ off** partir a toda a velocidade; (*letter*) escrever às pressas

dashboard /'dæʃbɔ:d/ *n* painel *m* de instrumentos, quadro *m* de bordo

data /'deɪtə/ *npl* dados *mpl*. **~ capture** aquisição *f* de informações, recolha *f* de dados. **~base** *n* base *f* de dados. **~ processing** processamento *m or* tratamento *m* de dados

date[1] /deɪt/ *n* data *f*; (*colloq*) encontro *m* marcado □ *vt/i* datar; (*colloq*) andar com. **out of ~** desatualizado, (*P*) desactualizado. **to ~** até à data. **up to ~** (*style*) moderno; (*information etc*) em dia. **~d** *a* antiquado

date[2] /deɪt/ *n* (*fruit*) tâmara *f*

daub /dɔ:b/ *vt* borrar, pintar toscamente

daughter /'dɔ:tə(r)/ *n* filha *f*. **~-in-law** *n* (*pl* **~s-in-law**) nora *f*

daunt /dɔ:nt/ *vt* assustar, intimidar, desencorajar

dawdle /'dɔ:dl/ *vi* perder tempo

dawn /dɔ:n/ *n* madrugada *f* □ *vi* madrugar, amanhecer. **~ on** (*fig*) fazer-se luz no espírito de, começar a perceber

day /deɪ/ *n* dia *m*; (*period*) época *f*, tempo *m*. **~-dream** *n* devaneio *m* □ *vi* devanear. **the ~ before** a véspera

daybreak /'deɪbreɪk/ *n* romper *m* do dia, aurora *f*, amanhecer *m*

daylight /'deɪlaɪt/ *n* luz *f* do dia. **~ robbery** roubar descaradamente

daytime /'deɪtaɪm/ *n* dia *m*, dia *m* claro

daze /deɪz/ *vt* aturdir □ *n* **in a ~** aturdido

dazzle /'dæzl/ *vt* deslumbrar; (*with headlights*) ofuscar

dead /ded/ *a* morto; (*numb*) dormente □ *adv* completamente, de todo □ *n* **in the ~ of the night** a horas mortas, na calada da noite. **the ~** os mortos. **in the ~ centre** bem no meio. **stop ~** estacar. **~ beat** *a* (*colloq*) morto de cansaço. **~ end** beco *m* sem saída. **~-pan** *a* inexpressivo

deaden /'dedn/ *vt* (*sound, blow*) amortecer; (*pain*) aliviar

deadline /'dedlaɪn/ *n* prazo *m* final

deadlock /'dedlɒk/ *n* impasse *m*

deadly /'dedlɪ/ *a* (**-ier, -iest**) mortal; (*weapon*) mortífero

deaf /def/ *a* (**-er, -est**) surdo. **turn a ~ ear** fingir que não ouve. **~ mute** surdo-mudo *m*. **~ness** *n* surdez *f*

deafen /'defn/ *vt* ensurdecer. **~ing** *a* ensurdecedor

deal /di:l/ *vt* (*pt* **dealt**) distribuir; (*a blow, cards*) dar □ *vi* negociar □ *n* negócio *m*; (*cards*) vez de dar *f*. **a great ~** muito (**of** de). **~ in** negociar em. **~ with** (*person*) tratar (com); (*affair*) tratar de. **~er** *n* comerciante *m*; (*agent*) concessionário *m*; representante *m*

dealings /'di:lɪŋz/ *npl* relações *fpl*; (*comm*) negócios *mpl*

dealt /delt/ *see* **deal**

dean /di:n/ *n* decano *m*

dear /dɪə(r)/ *a* (**-er, -est**) (*cherished*) caro, querido; (*expensive*) caro □ *n* amor *m* □ *adv* caro □ *int* **oh ~!** meu Deus! **~ly** *adv* (*very much*) muito; (*pay*) caro

dearth /dɜ:θ/ *n* escassez *f*

death /deθ/ *n* morte *f*. **~ certificate** certidão *f* de óbito. **~ penalty** pena *f* de morte. **~ rate** taxa *f* de mortalidade. **~-trap** *n* lugar *m* perigoso, ratoeira *f*. **~ly** *a* de morte, mortal

debase /dɪ'beɪs/ *vt* degradar

debat|e /dɪ'beɪt/ *n* debate *m* □ *vt* debater. **~able** *a* discutível

debauchery /dɪ'bɔ:tʃərɪ/ *n* deboche *m*, devassidão *f*

debility /dɪ'bɪlətɪ/ *n* debilidade *f*

debit /'debɪt/ *n* débito *m* □ *vt* (*pt* **debited**) debitar

debris /'deɪbri:/ *n* destroços *mpl*

debt /det/ *n* dívida *f*. **in ~** endividado. **~or** *n* devedor *m*

debunk /di:'bʌŋk/ *vt* (*colloq*) desmitificar

début /'deɪbju:/ *n* (*of actor, play etc*) estréia *f*

decade /'dekeɪd/ *n* década *f*

decaden|t /'dekədənt/ *a* decadente. **~ce** *n* decadência *f*

decaffeinated /di:'kæfi:meɪtɪd/ *a* sem cafeína

decanter /dɪ'kæntə(r)/ *n* garrafa *f* para vinho, de vidro ou cristal

decapitate /dɪ'kæpɪteɪt/ *vt* decapitar

decay /dɪ'keɪ/ *vi* apodrecer, estragar-se; (*food, fig*) deteriorar-se; (*building*) degradar-se □ *n* apodrecimento *m*; (*of tooth*) cárie *f*; (*fig*) declínio *m*, decadência *f*

deceased /dɪ'si:st/ *a & n* falecido (*m*), defunto (*m*)

deceit /dɪ'si:t/ *n* engano *m*. **~ful** *a* enganador

deceive /dɪ'si:v/ *vt* enganar, iludir

December /dɪ'sembə(r)/ *n* dezembro *m*

decen|t /'di:snt/ *a* decente; (*colloq: good*) (bastante) bom; (*colloq: likeable*) simpático. **~cy** *n* decência *f*

decentralize /di:'sentrəlaɪz/ *vt* descentralizar

decept|ive /dɪ'septɪv/ *a* enganador, ilusório. **~ion** /-ʃn/ *n* engano *m*

decibel /'desɪbel/ n decibel m

decide /dɪ'saɪd/ vt/i decidir. ~ **on** decidir-se por. ~ **to do** decidir fazer. ~**d** /-ɪd/ a decidido; (clear) definido, nítido. ~**dly** /-ɪdlɪ/ adv decididamente

decimal /'desɪml/ a decimal □ n (fração f, (P) fracção f) decimal m. ~ **point** vírgula f decimal

decipher /dɪ'saɪfə(r)/ vt decifrar

decision /dɪ'sɪʒn/ n decisão f

decisive /dɪ'saɪsɪv/ a decisivo; (manner) decidido. ~**ly** adv decisivamente

deck /dek/ n convés m; (of cards) baralho m. ~**-chair** n espreguiçadeira f

declar|**e** /dɪ'kleə(r)/ vt declarar. ~**ation** /deklə'reɪʃn/ n declaração f

decline /dɪ'klaɪn/ vt (refuse) declinar, recusar delicadamente; (gram) declinar □ vi (deteriorate) declinar; (fall) baixar □ n declínio m; (fall) abaixamento m

decode /diː'kəʊd/ vt descodificar

decompos|**e** /diːkəm'pəʊz/ vt/i decompor(-se). ~**ition** /-ɒmpə'zɪʃn/ n decomposição f

décor /'deɪkɔː(r)/ n decoração f

decorat|**e** /'dekəreɪt/ vt decorar, enfeitar; (paint) pintar; (paper) pôr papel em. ~**ion** /-'reɪʃn/ n decoração f; (medal etc) condecoração f. ~**ive** /-ətɪv/ a decorativo

decorum /dɪ'kɔːrəm/ n decoro m

decoy[1] /'diːkɔɪ/ n chamariz m, engodo m; (trap) armadilha f

decoy[2] /dɪ'kɔɪ/ vt atrair, apanhar

decrease[1] /diː'kriːs/ vt/i diminuir

decrease[2] /'diːkriːs/ n diminuição f

decree /dɪ'kriː/ n decreto m; (jur) decisão f judicial □ vt decretar

decrepit /dɪ'krepɪt/ a decrépito

dedicat|**e** /'dedɪkeɪt/ vt dedicar. ~**ed** a dedicado. ~**ion** /-'keɪʃn/ n dedicação f; (in book) dedicatória f

deduce /dɪ'djuːs/ vt deduzir

deduct /dɪ'dʌkt/ vt deduzir; (from pay) descontar

deduction /dɪ'dʌkʃn/ n dedução f; (from pay) desconto m

deed /diːd/ n ato m; (jur) contrato m

deem /diːm/ vt julgar, considerar

deep /diːp/ a (-er, -est) profundo □ adv profundamente. ~**-freeze** n congelador m □ vt congelar. **take a** ~ **breath** respirar fundo. ~**ly** adv profundamente

deepen /'diːpən/ vt/i aprofundar (-se); (mystery, night) adensar-se

deer /dɪə(r)/ n (pl invar) veado m

deface /dɪ'feɪs/ vt danificar, degradar

defamation /defə'meɪʃn/ n difamação f

default /dɪ'fɔːlt/ vi faltar □ n **by** ~ à revelia. **win by** ~ (sport) ganhar por não comparecimento, (P) comparência □ n (comput) default m

defeat /dɪ'fiːt/ vt derrotar; (thwart) malograr □ n derrota f; (of plan, etc) malogro m

defect[1] /'diːfekt/ n defeito m. ~**ive** /dɪ'fektɪv/ a defeituoso

defect[2] /dɪ'fekt/ vi desertar. ~**ion** n defecção m. ~**or** n trânsfuga mf, dissidente mf; (political) asilado m político

defence /dɪ'fens/ n defesa f. ~**less** a indefeso

defend /dɪ'fend/ vt defender. ~**ant** n (jur) réu m, acusado m. ~**er** n advogado m de defesa, defensor m

defensive /dɪ'fensɪv/ a defensivo □ n **on the** ~ na defensiva f; (person, sport) na retranca f (colloq)

defer /dɪ'fɜː(r)/ vt (pt **deferred**) adiar, diferir □ vi ~ **to** ceder, deferir

deferen|**ce** /'defərəns/ n deferência f. ~**tial** /-'renʃl/ a deferente

defian|**ce** /dɪ'faɪəns/ n desafio m. **in** ~ **of** sem respeito por. ~**t** a de desafio. ~**tly** adv com ar de desafio

deficien|**t** /dɪ'fɪʃnt/ a deficiente. **be** ~**t in** ter falta de. ~**cy** n deficiência f

deficit /'defɪsɪt/ n déficit m

define /dɪ'faɪn/ vt definir

definite /'defɪnɪt/ a definido; (clear) categórico, claro; (certain) certo. ~**ly** adv decididamente; (clearly) claramente

definition /defɪ'nɪʃn/ n definição f

definitive /dɪ'fɪnətɪv/ a definitivo

deflat|**e** /dɪ'fleɪt/ vt esvaziar; (person) desemproar, desinchar. ~**ion** /-ʃn/ n esvaziamento m; (econ) deflação f

deflect /dɪ'flekt/ vt/i desviar(-se)

deform /dɪ'fɔːm/ vt deformar. ~**ed** a deformado, disforme. ~**ity** n deformidade f

defraud /dɪ'frɔːd/ vt defraudar

defrost /diː'frɒst/ vt descongelar

deft /deft/ a (-er, -est) hábil

defunct /dɪ'fʌŋkt/ a (law etc) caduco, extinto

defuse /diː'fjuːz/ vt (a bomb) desativar, (P) desactivar; (a situation) acalmar

defy /dɪ'faɪ/ vt desafiar; (attempts) resistir a; (the law) desobedecer a; (public opinion) opor-se a

degenerate /dɪ'dʒenəreɪt/ vi degenerar (**into** em)

degrad|**e** /dɪ'greɪd/ vt degradar. ~**ation** /degrə'deɪʃn/ n degradação f

degree /dɪ'griː/ n grau m; (univ) diploma m. **to a** ~ ao mais alto grau, muito

dehydrate /diːˈhaɪdreɪt/ *vt/i* desidratar(-se)

de-ice /diːˈaɪs/ *vt* descongelar, degelar; (*windscreen*) tirar o gelo de

deign /deɪn/ *vt* ~ **to do** dignar-se (a) fazer

deity /ˈdiːɪtɪ/ *n* divindade *f*

dejected /dɪˈdʒektɪd/ *a* abatido

delay /dɪˈleɪ/ *vt* atrasar; (*postpone*) retardar □ *vi* atrasar-se □ *n* atraso *m*, demora *f*

delegate[1] /ˈdelɪɡət/ *n* delegado *m*

delegat|**e**[2] /ˈdelɪɡeɪt/ *vt* delegar. ~**ion** /-ˈɡeɪʃn/ *n* delegação *f*

delet|**e** /dɪˈliːt/ *vt* riscar. ~**ion** /-ʃn/ *n* rasura *f*

deliberate[1] /dɪˈlɪbərət/ *a* deliberado; (*steps etc*) compassado. ~**ly** *adv* deliberadamente, de propósito

deliberat|**e**[2] /dɪˈlɪbəreɪt/ *vt/i* deliberar. ~**ion** /-ˈreɪʃn/ *n* deliberação *f*

delica|te /ˈdelɪkət/ *a* delicado. ~**cy** *n* delicadeza *f*; (*food*) guloseima *f*, iguaria *f*, (*P*) acepipe *m*

delicatessen /delɪkəˈtesn/ *n* (*shop*) mercearias *fpl* finas

delicious /dɪˈlɪʃəs/ *a* delicioso

delight /dɪˈlaɪt/ *n* grande prazer *m*, delícia *f*; (*thing*) delícia *f*, encanto *m* □ *vt* deliciar □ *vi* ~ **in** deliciar-se com. ~**ed** *a* deliciado, encantado. ~**ful** *a* delicioso, encantador

delinquen|t /dɪˈlɪŋkwənt/ *a* & *n* delinqüente *mf*, (*P*) delinquente *mf*. ~**cy** *n* delinqüência *f*, (*P*) delinquência *f*

deliri|ous /dɪˈlɪrɪəs/ *a* delirante. **be** ~**ous** delirar. ~**um** /-əm/ *n* delírio *m*

deliver /dɪˈlɪvə(r)/ *vt* entregar; (*letters*) distribuir; (*free*) libertar; (*med*) fazer o parto. ~**ance** *n* libertação *f*. ~**y** *n* entrega *f*; (*letters*) distribuição *f*; (*med*) parto *m*

delu|de /dɪˈluːd/ *vt* enganar. ~**de o.s.** ter ilusões. ~**sion** /-ʒn/ *n* ilusão *f*

deluge /ˈdeljuːdʒ/ *n* dilúvio *m* □ *vt* inundar

de luxe /dɪˈlʌks/ *a* de luxo

delve /delv/ *vi* ~ **into** pesquisar, rebuscar

demand /dɪˈmɑːnd/ *vt* exigir; (*ask to be told*) perguntar □ *n* exigência *f*; (*comm*) procura *f*; (*claim*) reivindicação *f*. **in** ~ procurado. ~**ing** *a* exigente; (*work*) puxado, custoso

demean /dɪˈmiːn/ *vt* ~ **o.s.** rebaixar-se

demeanour /dɪˈmiːnə(r)/ *n* comportamento *m*, conduta *f*

demented /dɪˈmentɪd/ *a* louco, demente. **become** ~ enlouquecer

demo /ˈdeməʊ/ *n* (*pl* **-os**) (*colloq*) manifestação *f*, (*P*) manif *f*

democracy /dɪˈmɒkrəsɪ/ *n* democracia *f*

democrat /ˈdeməkræt/ *n* democrata *mf*. ~**ic** /-ˈkrætɪk/ *a* democrático

demoli|sh /dɪˈmɒlɪʃ/ *vt* demolir. ~**tion** /deməˈlɪʃn/ *n* demolição *f*

demon /ˈdiːmən/ *n* demônio *m*

demonstrat|e /ˈdemənstreɪt/ *vt* demonstrar □ *vi* (*pol*) fazer uma manifestação, manifestar-se. ~**ion** /-ˈstreɪʃn/ *n* demonstração *f*; (*pol*) manifestação *f*. ~**or** *n* (*pol*) manifestante *mf*

demonstrative /dɪˈmɒnstrətɪv/ *a* demonstrativo

demoralize /dɪˈmɒrəlaɪz/ *vt* desmoralizar

demote /dɪˈməʊt/ *vt* fazer baixar de posto, rebaixar

demure /dɪˈmjʊə(r)/ *a* recatado, modesto

den /den/ *n* antro *m*, covil *m*; (*room*) cantinho *m*, recanto *m*

denial /dɪˈnaɪəl/ *n* negação *f*; (*refusal*) recusa *f*; (*statement*) desmentido *m*

denigrate /ˈdenɪɡreɪt/ *vt* denegrir

denim /ˈdenɪm/ *n* brim *m*. ~**s** (*jeans*) jeans *mpl*

Denmark /ˈdenmɑːk/ *n* Dinamarca *f*

denomination /dɪnɒmɪˈneɪʃn/ *n* denominação *f*; (*relig*) confissão *f*, seita *f*; (*money*) valor *m*

denote /dɪˈnəʊt/ *vt* denotar

denounce /dɪˈnaʊns/ *vt* denunciar

dens|e /dens/ *a* (**-er**, **-est**) denso; (*colloq: person*) obtuso. ~**ely** *adv* (*packed etc*) muito. ~**ity** *n* densidade *f*

dent /dent/ *n* mossa *f*, depressão *f* □ *vt* dentear

dental /ˈdentl/ *a* dentário, dental

dentist /ˈdentɪst/ *n* dentista *mf*. ~**ry** *n* odontologia *f*

denture /ˈdentʃə(r)/ *n* dentadura *f* (postiça)

denunciation /dɪnʌnsɪˈeɪʃn/ *n* denúncia *f*

deny /dɪˈnaɪ/ *vt* negar; (*rumour*) desmentir; (*disown*) renegar; (*refuse*) recusar

deodorant /diːˈəʊdərənt/ *n* & *a* desodorante (*m*), (*P*) desodorizante (*m*)

depart /dɪˈpɑːt/ *vi* partir. ~ **from** (*deviate*) afastar-se de, desviar-se de

department /dɪˈpɑːtmənt/ *n* departamento *m*; (*in shop, office*) seção *f*, (*P*) secção *f*; (*government*) repartição *f*. ~ **store** loja *f* de departamentos, (*P*) grande armazém *m*

departure /dɪˈpɑːtʃə(r)/ *n* partida *f*. **a** ~ **from** (*custom, diet etc*) uma mudança de. **a new** ~ uma nova orientação

depend /dɪˈpend/ *vi* ~ **on** depender de; (*trust*) contar com. ~**able** *a* de

d

confiança. ~ence *n* dependência *f*. ~ent (on) *a* dependente (de)

dependant /dɪ'pendənt/ *n* dependente *mf*

depict /dɪ'pɪkt/ *vt* descrever; (*in pictures*) representar

deplete /dɪ'pli:t/ *vt* reduzir; (*use up*) esgotar

deplor|e /dɪ'plɔ:(r)/ *vt* deplorar. ~able *a* deplorável

deport /dɪ'pɔ:t/ *vt* deportar. ~ation /di:pɔ:'teɪʃn/ *n* deportação *f*

depose /dɪ'pəʊz/ *vt* depor

deposit /dɪ'pɒzɪt/ *vt* (*pt* **deposited**) depositar □ *n* depósito *m*. ~ account conta *f* de depósito a prazo. ~or *n* depositante *mf*

depot /'depəʊ/ *n* (*mil*) depósito *m*; (*buses*) garagem *f*; (*Amer: station*) rodoviária *f*, estação *f* de trem, (*P*) de comboio

deprav|e /dɪ'preɪv/ *vt* depravar. ~ity /-'prævətɪ/ *n* depravação *f*

depreciat|e /dɪ'pri:ʃɪeɪt/ *vt/i* depreciar(-se). ~ion /-'eɪʃn/ *n* depreciação *f*

depress /dɪ'pres/ *vt* deprimir; (*press down*) carregar em. ~ion /-ʃn/ *n* depressão *f*

deprivation /deprɪ'veɪʃn/ *n* privação *f*

deprive /dɪ'praɪv/ *vt* ~ of privar de. ~d *a* privado; (*underprivileged*) deserdado (da sorte), destituído; (*child*) carente

depth /depθ/ *n* profundidade *f*. be out of one's ~ perder pé, (*P*) não ter pé; (*fig*) ficar desnorteado, estar perdido. in the ~(s) of no mais fundo de, nas profundezas de

deputation /depju'teɪʃn/ *n* delegação *f*

deputy /'depjʊtɪ/ *n* (*pl* -ies) delegado *m* □ *a* adjunto. ~ chairman vice-presidente *m*

derail /dɪ'reɪl/ *vt* descarrilhar. be ~ed descarrilhar. ~ment *n* descarrilhamento *m*

deranged /dɪ'reɪndʒd/ *a* (*mind*) transtornado, louco

derelict /'derəlɪkt/ *a* abandonado

deri|de /dɪ'raɪd/ *vt* escarnecer de. ~sion /-'rɪʒn/ *n* escárnio *m*. ~sive *a* escarninho. ~sory *a* escarninho; (*offer etc*) irrisório

derivative /dɪ'rɪvətɪv/ *a* derivado; (*work*) pouco original □ *n* derivado *m*

deriv|e /dɪ'raɪv/ *vt* ~e from tirar de □ *vi* ~e from derivar de. ~ation /derɪ'veɪʃn/ *n* derivação *f*

derogatory /dɪ'rɒgətrɪ/ *a* pejorativo; (*remark*) depreciativo

derv /dɜ:v/ *n* gasóleo *m*

descend /dɪ'send/ *vt/i* descer, descender. be ~ed from descender de. ~ant *n* descendente *mf*

descent /dɪ'sent/ *n* descida *f*; (*lineage*) descendência *f*, origem *f*

descri|be /dɪs'kraɪb/ *vt* descrever. ~ption /-'krɪpʃn/ *n* descrição *f*; ~ptive /-'krɪptɪv/ *a* descritivo

desecrat|e /'desɪkreɪt/ *vt* profanar. ~ion /-'kreɪʃn/ *n* profanação *f*

desert¹ /'dezət/ *a* & *n* deserto (*m*). ~ island ilha *f* deserta

desert² /dɪ'zɜ:t/ *vt/i* desertar. ~ed *a* abandonado. ~er *n* desertor *m*. ~ion /-ʃn/ *n* deserção *f*

deserv|e /dɪ'zɜ:v/ *vt* merecer. ~edly /dɪ'zɜ:vɪdlɪ/ *adv* merecidamente, a justo título. ~ing *a* (*person*) merecedor; (*action*) meritório

design /dɪ'zaɪn/ *n* desenho *m*; (*artistic*) design *m*; (*style of dress*) modelo *m*; (*pattern*) padrão *m*, motivo *m* □ *vt* desenhar; (*devise*) conceber. ~er *n* desenhador *m*; (*of dresses*) costureiro *m*; (*of machine*) inventor *m*

designat|e /'dezɪgneɪt/ *vt* designar. ~ion /-'neɪʃn/ *n* designação *f*

desir|e /dɪ'zaɪə(r)/ *n* desejo *m* □ *vt* desejar. ~able *a* desejável, atraente

desk /desk/ *n* secretária *f*; (*of pupil*) carteira *f*; (*in hotel*) recepção *f*; (*in bank*) caixa *f*

desolat|e /'desələt/ *a* desolado. ~ion /-'leɪʃn/ *n* desolação *f*

despair /dɪ'speə(r)/ *n* desespero *m* □ *vi* desesperar (of de)

desperate /'despərət/ *a* desesperado; (*criminal*) capaz de tudo. be ~ for ter uma vontade doida de. ~ly *adv* desesperadamente

desperation /despə'reɪʃn/ *n* desespero *m*

despicable /dɪ'spɪkəbl/ *a* desprezível

despise /dɪ'spaɪz/ *vt* desprezar

despite /dɪ'spaɪt/ *prep* apesar de, a despeito de, mau grado

desponden|t /dɪ'spɒndənt/ *a* desanimado. ~cy *n* desânimo *m*

despot /'despɒt/ *n* déspota *mf*

dessert /dɪ'zɜ:t/ *n* sobremesa *f*. ~-spoon *n* colher *f* de sobremesa

destination /destɪ'neɪʃn/ *n* destino *m*, destinação *f*

destine /'destɪn/ *vt* destinar

destiny /'destɪnɪ/ *n* destino *m*

destitute /'destɪtju:t/ *a* destituído, indigente

destr|oy /dɪ'strɔɪ/ *vt* destruir. ~uction /-'strʌkʃn/ *n* destruição *f*. ~uctive *a* destrutivo, destruidor

detach /dɪ'tætʃ/ *vt* separar, arrancar. ~able *a* separável; (*lining etc*) solto. ~ed *a* separado; (*impartial*) imparcial; (*unemotional*) desprendido.

~ed house casa *f* sem parede-meia com outra

detachment /dɪ'tætʃmənt/ *n* separação *f*; (*indifference*) desprendimento *m*; (*mil*) destacamento *m*; (*impartiality*) imparcialidade *f*

detail /'di:teɪl/ *n* pormenor *m*, detalhe *m* □ *vt* detalhar; (*troops*) destacar. ~ed *a* detalhado

detain /dɪ'teɪn/ *vt* reter; (*in prison*) deter. ~ee /di:teɪ'ni:/ *n* detido *m*

detect /dɪ'tekt/ *vt* detectar. ~ion /-ʃn/ *n* detecção *f*. ~or *n* detector *m*

detective /dɪ'tektɪv/ *n* detective *m*. ~ story romance *m* policial

detention /dɪ'tenʃn/ *n* detenção *f*. be given a ~ (*school*) ficar de castigo na escola

deter /dɪ'tɜ:(r)/ *vt* (*pt* deterred) dissuadir; (*hinder*) impedir

detergent /dɪ'tɜ:dʒənt/ *a* & *n* detergente (*m*)

deteriorat|e /dɪ'tɪərɪəreɪt/ *vi* deteriorar(-se). ~ion /-'reɪʃn/ *n* deterioração *f*

determin|e /dɪ'tɜ:mɪn/ *vt* determinar. ~e to do decidir fazer. ~ation /-'neɪʃn/ *n* determinação *f*. ~ed *a* determinado. ~ed to do decidido a fazer

deterrent /dɪ'terənt/ *n* dissuasivo *m*

detest /dɪ'test/ *vt* detestar. ~able *a* detestável

detonat|e /'detəneɪt/ *vt*/*i* detonar. ~ion /-'neɪʃn/ *n* detonação *f*. ~or *n* espoleta *f*, detonador *m*

detour /'di:tʊə(r)/ *n* desvio *m*

detract /dɪ'trækt/ *vi* ~ from depreciar, menosprezar

detriment /'detrɪmənt/ *n* detrimento *m*. ~al /-'mentl/ *a* prejudicial

devalu|e /di:'vælju:/ *vt* desvalorizar. ~ation /-'eɪʃn/ *n* desvalorização *f*

devastat|e /'devəsteɪt/ *vt* devastar; (*fig: overwhelm*) arrasar. ~ing *a* devastador; (*criticism*) de arrasar

develop /dɪ'veləp/ *vt*/*i* (*pt* developed) desenvolver(-se); (*get*) contrair; (*build on*) urbanizar; (*film*) revelar. ~ into tornar-se. ~ing country país *m* subdesenvolvido. ~ment *n* desenvolvimento *m*; (*film*) revelação *f*; (*of land*) urbanização *f*

deviat|e /'di:vɪeɪt/ *vi* desviar-se. ~ion /-'eɪʃn/ *n* desvio *m*

device /dɪ'vaɪs/ *n* dispositivo *m*; (*scheme*) processo *m*. left to one's own ~s entregue a si mesmo

devil /'devl/ *n* diabo *m*

devious /'di:vɪəs/ *a* tortuoso; (*fig: means*) escuso; (*fig: person*) pouco franco

devise /dɪ'vaɪz/ *vt* imaginar, inventar

devoid /dɪ'vɔɪd/ *a* ~ of desprovido de, destituído de

devot|e /dɪ'vəʊt/ *vt* dedicar, devotar. ~ed *a* dedicado, devotado. ~ion /-ʃn/ *n* devoção *f*

devotee /devə'ti:/ *n* ~ of adepto *m* de, entusiasta *mf* de

devour /dɪ'vaʊə(r)/ *vt* devorar

devout /dɪ'vaʊt/ *a* devota; (*prayer*) fervoroso

dew /dju:/ *n* orvalho *m*

dext|erity /dek'sterətɪ/ *n* destreza *f*, jeito *m*. ~rous /'dekstrəs/ *a* destro, hábil

diabet|es /daɪə'bi:ti:z/ *n* diabetes *f*. ~ic /-'betɪk/ *a* diabético

diabolical /daɪə'bɒlɪkl/ *a* diabólico

diagnose /'daɪəgnəʊz/ *vt* diagnosticar

diagnosis /daɪəg'nəʊsɪs/ *n* (*pl* -oses /-si:z/) diagnóstico *m*

diagonal /daɪ'ægənl/ *a* & *n* diagonal (*f*)

diagram /'daɪəgræm/ *n* diagrama *m*, esquema *m*

dial /'daɪəl/ *n* mostrador *m* □ *vt* (*pt* dialled) (*number*) marcar, discar. ~ling code código *m* de discagem. ~ling tone sinal *m* de discar

dialect /'daɪəlekt/ *n* dialeto *m*, (*P*) dialecto *m*

dialogue /'daɪəlɒg/ *n* diálogo *m*

diameter /daɪ'æmɪtə(r)/ *n* diâmetro *m*

diamond /'daɪəmənd/ *n* diamante *m*, brilhante *m*; (*shape*) losango *m*. ~s (*cards*) ouros *mpl*

diaper /'daɪəpə(r)/ *n* (*Amer*) fralda *f*

diaphragm /'daɪəfræm/ *n* diafragma *m*

diarrhoea /daɪə'rɪə/ *n* diarréia *f*, (*P*) diarreia *f*

diary /'daɪərɪ/ *n* agenda *f*; (*record*) diário *m*

dice /daɪs/ *n* (*pl invar*) dado *m*

dictat|e /dɪk'teɪt/ *vt*/*i* ditar. ~ion /-ʃn/ *n* ditado *m*

dictator /dɪk'teɪtə(r)/ *n* ditador *m*. ~ship *n* ditadura *f*

diction /'dɪkʃn/ *n* dicção *f*

dictionary /'dɪkʃənrɪ/ *n* dicionário *m*

did /dɪd/ *see* do

diddle /'dɪdl/ *vt* (*colloq*) trapacear, enganar

didn't /'dɪdnt/ = did not

die /daɪ/ *vi* (*pres p* dying) morrer. be dying to estar doido para. ~ down diminuir, baixar. ~ out desaparecer, extinguir-se

diesel /'di:zl/ *n* diesel *m*. ~ engine motor *m* diesel

diet /'daɪət/ *n* dieta *f* □ *vi* fazer dieta, estar de dieta

differ /'dɪfə(r)/ *vi* diferir; (*disagree*) discordar

differen|t /'dɪfrənt/ a diferente. **~ce** n diferença f; (disagreement) desacordo m. **~ly** adv diferentemente

differentiate /dɪfə'renʃɪeɪt/ vt/i diferençar(-se), diferenciar(-se)

difficult /'dɪfɪkəlt/ a difícil. **~y** n dificuldade f

diffiden|t /'dɪfɪdənt/ a acanhado, inseguro. **~ce** n acanhamento m, insegurança f

diffuse[1] /dɪ'fju:s/ a difuso

diffus|e[2] /dɪ'fju:z/ vt difundir. **~ion** /-ʒn/ n difusão f

dig /dɪg/ vt/i (pt dug, pres p digging) cavar; (thrust) espetar □ n (with elbow) cotovelada f; (with finger) cutucada f, (P) espetadela f; (remark) ferroada f; (archaeol) escavação f. **~s** (colloq) quarto m alugado. **~ up** desenterrar

digest /dɪ'dʒest/ vt/i digerir. **~ible** a digerível, digestível. **~ion** /-ʃn/ n digestão f

digestive /dɪ'dʒestɪv/ a digestivo

digit /'dɪdʒɪt/ n dígito m

digital /'dɪdʒɪtl/ a digital. **~ camera** câmara f digital. **~ clock** relógio m digital

dignif|y /'dɪgnɪfaɪ/ vt dignificar. **~ied** a digno

dignitary /'dɪgnɪtərɪ/ n dignitário m

dignity /'dɪgnətɪ/ n dignidade f

digress /daɪ'gres/ vi digressar, divagar. **~ from** desviar-se de. **~ion** /-ʃn/ n digressão f

dike /daɪk/ n dique m

dilapidated /dɪ'læpɪdeɪtɪd/ a (house) arruinado, degradado; (car) estragado

dilat|e /daɪ'leɪt/ vt/i dilatar(-se). **~ion** /-ʃn/ n dilatação f

dilemma /dɪ'lemə/ n dilema m

diligen|t /'dɪlɪdʒənt/ a diligente, aplicado. **~ce** n diligência f, aplicação f

dilute /daɪ'lju:t/ vt diluir □ a diluído

dim /dɪm/ a (dimmer, dimmest) (weak) fraco; (dark) sombrio; (indistinct) vago; (colloq: stupid) burro (colloq) □ vt/i (pt dimmed) (light) baixar. **~ly** adv (shine) fracamente; (remember) vagamente

dime /daɪm/ n (Amer) moeda f de dez centavos

dimension /daɪ'menʃn/ n dimensão f

diminish /dɪ'mɪnɪʃ/ vt/i diminuir

diminutive /dɪ'mɪnjʊtɪv/ a diminuto □ n diminutivo m

dimple /'dɪmpl/ n covinha f

din /dɪn/ n barulheira f, (P) chinfrim m

dine /daɪn/ vi jantar. **~r** /-ə(r)/ n (person) comensal m; (rail) vagão restaurante m; (Amer: restaurant) lanchonete f

dinghy /'dɪŋgɪ/ n (pl -ghies) bote m; (inflatable) bote m de borracha, (P) barco m de borracha

dingy /'dɪndʒɪ/ a (-ier, -iest) com ar sujo, esquálido

dining-room /'daɪnɪŋru:m/ n sala f de jantar

dinner /'dɪnə(r)/ n jantar m; (lunch) almoço m. **~-jacket** n smoking m

dinosaur /'daɪnəsɔ:(r)/ n dinossauro m

dip /dɪp/ vt/i (pt dipped) mergulhar; (lower) baixar □ n mergulho m; (bathe) banho m rápido, mergulho m; (slope) descida f; (culin) molho m. **~ into** (book) folhear. **~ one's headlights** baixar para médios

diphtheria /dɪf'θɪərɪə/ n difteria f

diphthong /'dɪfθɒŋ/ n ditongo m

diploma /dɪ'pləʊmə/ n diploma m

diplomacy /dɪ'pləʊməsɪ/ n diplomacia f

diplomat /'dɪpləmæt/ n diplomata mf. **~ic** /-'mætɪk/ a diplomático

dire /daɪə(r)/ a (-er, -est) terrível; (need, poverty) extremo

direct /dɪ'rekt/ a direto, (P) directo □ adv diretamente, (P) directamente □ vt dirigir. **~ sb to** indicar a alg o caminho para

direction /dɪ'rekʃn/ n direção f, (P) direcção f, sentido m. **~s** instruções fpl. **~s for use** modo m de emprego

directly /dɪ'rektlɪ/ adv diretamente, (P) directamente; (at once) imediatamente, logo

director /dɪ'rektə(r)/ n diretor m, (P) director m

directory /dɪ'rektərɪ/ n (telephone) ~ lista f telefônica, (P) telefónica

dirt /dɜ:t/ n sujeira f. **~ cheap** (colloq) baratíssimo

dirty /'dɜ:tɪ/ a (-ier, -iest) sujo; (word) obsceno □ vt/i sujar(-se). **~ trick** golpe m baixo, (P) boa partida f

disability /dɪsə'bɪlətɪ/ n deficiência f

disable /dɪs'eɪbl/ vt incapacitar. **~d** a inválido, deficiente

disadvantage /dɪsəd'va:ntɪdʒ/ n desvantagem f

disagree /dɪsə'gri:/ vi discordar (with de). **~ with** (food, climate) não fazer bem. **~ment** n desacordo m; (quarrel) desentendimento m

disagreeable /dɪsə'gri:əbl/ a desagradável

disappear /dɪsə'pɪə(r)/ vi desaparecer. **~ance** n desaparecimento m

disappoint /dɪsə'pɔɪnt/ vt desapontar, decepcionar. **~ment** n desapontamento m, decepção f

disapprov|e /dɪsə'pru:v/ vi **~e (of)** desaprovar. **~al** n desaprovação f

disarm /dɪˈsɑːm/ vt/i desarmar. **~ament** n desarmamento m

disast|er /dɪˈzɑːstə(r)/ n desastre m. **~rous** a desastroso

disband /dɪsˈbænd/ vt/i debandar; (troops) dispersar

disbelief /dɪsbɪˈliːf/ n incredulidade f

disc /dɪsk/ n disco m. **~ jockey** disc(o) jockey m

discard /dɪsˈkɑːd/ vt pôr de lado, descartar(-se) de; (old clothes etc) desfazer-se de

discern /dɪˈsɜːn/ vt discernir. **~ible** a perceptível. **~ing** a perspicaz. **~ment** n discernimento m, perspicácia f

discharge¹ /dɪsˈtʃɑːdʒ/ vt descarregar; (dismiss) despedir, mandar embora; (duty) cumprir; (liquid) vazar, (P) deitar; (patient) dar alta a; (prisoner) absolver, pôr em liberdade; (pus) purgar, (P) deitar

discharge² /ˈdɪstʃɑːdʒ/ n descarga f; (dismissal) despedimento m; (of patient) alta f; (of prisoner) absolvição f; (med) secreção f

disciple /dɪˈsaɪpl/ n discípulo m

disciplin|e /ˈdɪsɪplɪn/ n disciplina f ▢ vt disciplinar; (punish) castigar. **~ary** a disciplinar

disclaim /dɪsˈkleɪm/ vt (jur) repudiar; (deny) negar. **~er** n desmentido m

disclos|e /dɪsˈkləʊz/ vt revelar. **~ure** /-ʒə(r)/ n revelação f

disco /ˈdɪskəʊ/ n (pl -os) (colloq) discoteca f

discolour /dɪsˈkʌlə(r)/ vt/i descolorir(-se); (in sunlight) desbotar (-se)

discomfort /dɪsˈkʌmfət/ n mal- estar m; (lack of comfort) desconforto m

disconcert /dɪskənˈsɜːt/ vt desconcertar. **~ing** a desconcertante

disconnect /dɪskəˈnekt/ vt desligar

discontent /dɪskənˈtent/ n descontentamento m. **~ed** a descontente

discontinue /dɪskənˈtɪnjuː/ vt descontinuar, suspender

discord /ˈdɪskɔːd/ n discórdia f. **~ant** /-ˈskɔːdənt/ a discordante

discoth'que /ˈdɪskətek/ n discoteca f

discount¹ /ˈdɪskaʊnt/ n desconto m

discount² /dɪsˈkaʊnt/ vt descontar; (disregard) dar o desconto a

discourage /dɪsˈkʌrɪdʒ/ vt desencorajar

discourte|ous /dɪsˈkɜːtɪəs/ a indelicado. **~sy** /-sɪ/ n indelicadeza f

discover /dɪsˈkʌvə(r)/ vt descobrir. **~y** n descoberta f; (of island etc) descobrimento m

discredit /dɪsˈkredɪt/ vt (pt discredited) desacreditar ▢ n descrédito m

discreet /dɪsˈkriːt/ a discreto

discrepancy /dɪsˈkrepənsɪ/ n discrepância f

discretion /dɪsˈkreʃn/ n discrição f; (prudence) prudência f

discriminat|e /dɪsˈkrɪmɪneɪt/ vt/i discriminar. **~e against** tomar partido contra, fazer discriminação contra. **~ing** a discriminador; (having good taste) com discernimento. **~ion** /-ˈneɪʃn/ n discernimento m; (bias) discriminação f

discus /ˈdɪskəs/ n disco m

discuss /dɪsˈkʌs/ vt discutir. **~ion** /-ʃn/ n discussão f

disdain /dɪsˈdeɪn/ n desdém m ▢ vt desdenhar. **~ful** a desdenhoso

disease /dɪˈziːz/ n doença f. **~d** a (plant) atacado por doença; (person, animal) doente

disembark /dɪsɪmˈbɑːk/ vt/i desembarcar

disembodied /dɪsɪmˈbɒdɪd/ a desencarnado

disenchant /dɪsɪnˈtʃɑːnt/ vt desencantar. **~ment** n desencantamento m

disengage /dɪsɪnˈgeɪdʒ/ vt desprender, soltar; (mech) desengatar

disentangle /dɪsɪnˈtæŋgl/ vt desembaraçar, desenredar

disfavour /dɪsˈfeɪvə(r)/ n desfavor m, desgraça f

disfigure /dɪsˈfɪgə(r)/ vt desfigurar

disgrace /dɪsˈgreɪs/ n vergonha f; (disfavour) desgraça f ▢ vt desonrar. **~ful** a vergonhoso

disgruntled /dɪsˈgrʌntld/ a descontente

disguise /dɪsˈgaɪz/ vt disfarçar ▢ n disfarce m. **in ~** disfarçado

disgust /dɪsˈgʌst/ n repugnância f ▢ vt repugnar. **~ing** a repugnante

dish /dɪʃ/ n prato m ▢ vt **~ out** (colloq) distribuir. **~ up** servir. **the ~es** (crockery) a louça f

dishcloth /ˈdɪʃklɒθ/ n pano m de prato

dishearten /dɪsˈhɑːtn/ vt desencorajar, desalentar

dishevelled /dɪˈʃevld/ a desgrenhado

dishonest /dɪsˈɒnɪst/ a desonesto. **~y** n desonestidade f

dishonour /dɪsˈɒnə(r)/ n desonra f ▢ vt desonrar. **~able** a desonroso

dishwasher /ˈdɪʃwɒʃə(r)/ n lavadora f de pratos, (P) máquina f de lavar a louça

disillusion /dɪsɪˈluːʒn/ vt desiludir. **~ment** n desilusão f

disinfect /dɪsɪnˈfekt/ vt desinfetar, (P) desinfectar. **~ant** n desinfetante m, (P) desinfectante m

disinherit /dɪsɪnˈherɪt/ vt deserdar

disintegrate /dɪsˈɪntɪɡreɪt/ *vt/i*
desintegrar(-se)

disinterested /dɪsˈɪntrəstɪd/ *a*
desinteressado

disjointed /dɪsˈdʒɔɪntɪd/ *a* (*talk*)
descosido, desconexo

disk /dɪsk/ *n* (*comput*) disco *m*; (*Amer*) =
disc. ~ **drive** unidade *f* de disco

dislike /dɪsˈlaɪk/ *n* aversão *f*, antipatia *f*
□ *vt* não gostar de, antipatizar com

dislocat|e /ˈdɪsləkeɪt/ *vt* (*limb*) deslocar.
~**ion** /-ˈkeɪʃn/ *n* deslocação *f*

dislodge /dɪsˈlɒdʒ/ *vt* desalojar

disloyal /dɪsˈlɔɪəl/ *a* desleal. ~**ty** *n*
deslealdade *f*

dismal /ˈdɪzməl/ *a* tristonho

dismantle /dɪsˈmæntl/ *vt* desmantelar

dismay /dɪsˈmeɪ/ *n* consternação *f* □ *vt*
consternar

dismiss /dɪsˈmɪs/ *vt* despedir; (*from
mind*) afastar, pôr de lado. ~**al** *n*
despedimento *m*

dismount /dɪsˈmaʊnt/ *vi* desmontar

disobedien|t /dɪsəˈbiːdɪənt/ *a*
desobediente. ~**ce** *n* desobediência *f*

disobey /dɪsəˈbeɪ/ *vt/i* desobedecer (a)

disorder /dɪsˈɔːdə(r)/ *n* desordem *f*;
(*med*) perturbações *fpl*, disfunção *f*.
~**ly** *a* desordenado; (*riotous*)
desordeiro

disorganize /dɪsˈɔːɡənaɪz/ *vt*
desorganizar

disorientate /dɪsˈɔːrɪənteɪt/ *vt*
desorientar

disown /dɪsˈəʊn/ *vt* repudiar

disparaging /dɪsˈpærɪdʒɪŋ/ *a*
depreciativo

disparity /dɪsˈpærətɪ/ *n* disparidade *f*

dispatch /dɪsˈpætʃ/ *vt* despachar □ *n*
despacho *m*

dispel /dɪsˈpel/ *vt* (*pt* **dispelled**) dissipar

dispensary /dɪsˈpensərɪ/ *n* dispensário
m, farmácia *f*

dispense /dɪsˈpens/ *vt* dispensar □ *vi* ~
with dispensar, passar sem. ~**r** /-ə(r)/
n (*container*) distribuidor *m*

dispers|e /dɪsˈpɜːs/ *vt/i* dispersar (-se).
~**al** *n* dispersão *f*

dispirited /dɪsˈpɪrɪtɪd/ *a* desanimado

displace /dɪsˈpleɪs/ *vt* deslocar; (*take the
place of*) substituir. ~**d person**
deslocado *m* de guerra

display /dɪsˈpleɪ/ *vt* exibir, mostrar;
(*feeling*) manifestar, dar mostras de
□ *n* exposição *f*; (*of computer*)
apresentação *f* visual; (*comm*) objetos
mpl expostos

displeas|e /dɪsˈpliːz/ *vt* desagradar a.
~**ed with** descontente com. ~**ure**
/-ˈpleʒə(r)/ *n* desagrado *m*

disposable /dɪsˈpəʊzəbl/ *a* descartável

dispos|e /dɪsˈpəʊz/ *vt* dispor □ *vi* ~**e of**
desfazer-se de. **well** ~**ed towards** bem
disposto para com. ~**al** *n* (*of waste*)
eliminação *f*. **at sb's** ~**al** à disposição
de alg

disposition /dɪspəˈzɪʃn/ *n* disposição *f*;
(*character*) índole *f*

disproportionate /dɪsprəˈpɔːʃənət/ *a*
desproporcionado

disprove /dɪsˈpruːv/ *vt* refutar

dispute /dɪsˈpjuːt/ *vt* contestar; (*fight for,
quarrel*) disputar □ *n* disputa *f*;
(*industrial, pol*) conflito *m*. **in** ~ em
questão

disqualif|y /dɪsˈkwɒlɪfaɪ/ *vt* tornar
inapto; (*sport*) desqualificar. ~**y from
driving** apreender a carteira de
motorista. ~**ication** /-ɪˈkeɪʃn/ *n*
desqualificação *f*

disregard /dɪsrɪˈɡɑːd/ *vt* não fazer caso
de □ *n* indiferença *f* (**for** por)

disrepair /dɪsrɪˈpeə(r)/ *n* mau estado *m*,
abandono *m*, degradação *f*

disreputable /dɪsˈrepjʊtəbl/ *a* pouco
recomendável; (*in appearance*) com
mau aspecto; (*in reputation*)
vergonhoso, de má fama

disrepute /dɪsrɪˈpjuːt/ *n* descrédito *m*

disrespect /dɪsrɪˈspekt/ *n* falta *f* de
respeito. ~**ful** *a* desrespeitoso,
irreverente

disrupt /dɪsˈrʌpt/ *vt* perturbar; (*plans*)
transtornar; (*break up*) dividir. ~**ion**
/-ʃn/ *n* perturbação *f*. ~**ive** *a*
perturbador

dissatisf|ied /dɪsˈsætɪsfaɪd/ *a*
descontente. ~**action** /dɪsætɪsˈfækʃn/
n descontentamento *m*

dissect /dɪsˈsekt/ *vt* dissecar. ~**ion** /-ʃn/ *n*
dissecação *f*

dissent /dɪsˈsent/ *vi* dissentir, discordar
□ *n* dissensão *f*, desacordo *m*

dissertation /dɪsəˈteɪʃn/ *n* dissertação *f*

disservice /dɪsˈsɜːvɪs/ *n* **do sb a** ~
prejudicar alg

dissident /ˈdɪsɪdənt/ *a* & *n* dissidente
(*mf*)

dissimilar /dɪsˈsɪmɪlə(r)/ *a* diferente

dissipate /ˈdɪsɪpeɪt/ *vt* dissipar; (*efforts,
time*) desperdiçar. ~**d** *a* dissoluto

dissociate /dɪsˈsəʊʃɪeɪt/ *vt* dissociar,
desassociar

dissolution /dɪsəˈluːʃn/ *n* dissolução *f*

dissolve /dɪsˈzɒlv/ *vt/i* dissolver (-se)

dissuade /dɪsˈsweɪd/ *vt* dissuadir

distance /ˈdɪstəns/ *n* distância *f*. **from a**
~ de longe. **in the** ~ ao longe, à
distância

distant /ˈdɪstənt/ *a* distante; (*relative*)
afastado

distaste /dɪsˈteɪst/ n aversão f. ~**ful** a desagradável

distemper /dɪsˈtempə(r)/ n pintura f a têmpera; (*animal disease*) cinomose f ◻ vt pintar a têmpera

distend /dɪˈstend/ vt/i distender (-se)

distil /dɪˈstɪl/ vt (pt **distilled**) destilar. ~**lation** /-ˈleɪʃn/ n destilação f

distillery /dɪˈstɪləri/ n destilaria f

distinct /dɪˈstɪŋkt/ a distinto; (*marked*) claro, nítido. ~**ion** /-ʃn/ n distinção f. ~**ive** a distintivo, característico. ~**ly** adv distintamente; (*markedly*) claramente

distinguish /dɪˈstɪŋgwɪʃ/ vt/i distinguir. ~**ed** a distinto

distort /dɪˈstɔːt/ vt distorcer; (*misrepresent*) deturpar. ~**ion** /-ʃn/ n distorção f; (*misrepresentation*) deturpação f

distract /dɪˈstrækt/ vt distrair. ~**ed** a (*distraught*) desesperado, fora de si. ~**ing** a enlouquecedor. ~**ion** /-ʃn/ n distração f, (P) distracção f

distraught /dɪˈstrɔːt/ a desesperado, fora de si

distress /dɪˈstres/ n (*physical*) dor f; (*anguish*) aflição f; (*poverty*) miséria f; (*danger*) perigo m ◻ vt afligir. ~**ing** a aflitivo, doloroso

distribut|e /dɪˈstrɪbjuːt/ vt distribuir. ~**ion** /-ˈbjuːʃn/ n distribuição f. ~**or** n distribuidor m

district /ˈdɪstrɪkt/ n região f; (*of town*) zona f

distrust /dɪsˈtrʌst/ n desconfiança f ◻ vt desconfiar de

disturb /dɪˈstɜːb/ vt perturbar; (*move*) desarrumar; (*bother*) incomodar. ~**ance** n (*noise, disorder*) distúrbio m. ~**ed** a perturbado. ~**ing** a perturbador

disused /dɪsˈjuːzd/ a fora de uso, desusado, em desuso

ditch /dɪtʃ/ n fosso m ◻ vt (sl: *abandon*) abandonar, largar

dither /ˈdɪðə(r)/ vi hesitar

ditto /ˈdɪtəʊ/ adv idem

div|e /daɪv/ vi mergulhar; (*rush*) precipitar-se ◻ n mergulho m; (*of plane*) picada f; (sl: *place*) espelunca f. ~**er** n mergulhador m. ~**ing-board** n prancha f de saltos. ~**ing-suit** n escafandro m

diverge /daɪˈvɜːdʒ/ vi divergir

divergent /daɪˈvɜːdʒənt/ a divergente

diverse /daɪˈvɜːs/ a diverso

diversify /daɪˈvɜːsɪfaɪ/ vt diversificar

diversity /daɪˈvɜːsətɪ/ n diversidade f

diver|t /daɪˈvɜːt/ vt desviar; (*entertain*) divertir. ~**sion** /-ʃn/ n diversão f; (*traffic*) desvio m

divide /dɪˈvaɪd/ vt/i dividir(-se). ~ **in two** (*branch, river, road*) bifurcar-se

dividend /ˈdɪvɪdend/ n dividendo m

divine /dɪˈvaɪn/ a divino

divinity /dɪˈvɪnətɪ/ n divindade f; (*theology*) teologia f

division /dɪˈvɪʒn/ n divisão f

divorce /dɪˈvɔːs/ n divórcio m ◻ vt/i divorciar(-se) de. ~**d** a divorciado

divorcee /dɪvɔːˈsiː/ n divorciado m

divulge /daɪˈvʌldʒ/ vt divulgar

DIY abbr see **do-it-yourself**

dizz|y /ˈdɪzɪ/ a (-**ier**, -**iest**) tonto. be or feel ~**y** ter tonturas, sentir-se tonto. ~**iness** n tontura f, vertigem f

do /duː/ vt/i (3 sing pres **does**, pt **did**, pp **done**) fazer; (*be suitable*) servir; (*be enough*) bastar (a); (sl: *swindle*) enganar, levar (*colloq*). **how** ~ **you** ~? como vai? **well done** muito bem!, (P) bravo!; (*culin*) bem passado. **done for** (*colloq*) liquidado (*colloq*), (P) anumado (*colloq*) ◻ v aux ~ **you see?** vê?; **I** ~ **not smoke** não fumo. **don't you?, doesn't he?** etc não é? ◻ n (pl **dos** or **do's**) festa f. ~**-it-yourself** a faça-você-mesmo. ~ **away with** eliminar, suprimir. ~ **in** (sl) matar, liquidar (*colloq*). ~ **out** limpar. ~ **up** (*fasten*) fechar; (*house*) renovar. **I could** ~ **with a cup of tea** apetecia-me uma xícara de chá. **it could** ~ **with a wash** precisa de uma lavagem

docile /ˈdəʊsaɪl/ a dócil

dock[1] /dɒk/ n doca f ◻ vt levar à doca ◻ vi entrar na doca. ~**er** n estivador m

dock[2] /dɒk/ n (jur) banco m dos réus

dockyard /ˈdɒkjɑːd/ n estaleiro m

doctor /ˈdɒktə(r)/ n médico m, doutor m; (*univ*) doutor m ◻ vt (*cat*) capar; (*fig*) adulterar, falsificar

doctorate /ˈdɒktərət/ n doutorado m, (P) doutoramento m

doctrine /ˈdɒktrɪn/ n doutrina f

document /ˈdɒkjʊmənt/ n documento m ◻ vt documentar. ~**ary** /-ˈmentrɪ/ a documental ◻ n documentário m

dodge /dɒdʒ/ vt/i esquivar(-se), furtar(-se) a ◻ n (*colloq*) truque m

dodgy /ˈdɒdʒɪ/ a (-**ier**, -**iest**) (*colloq*) delicado, difícil, embaraçoso

does /dʌz/ see **do**

doesn't /ˈdʌznt/ = **does not**

dog /dɒg/ n cão m ◻ vt (pt **dogged**) ir no encalço de, perseguir. ~**-eared** a com os cantos dobrados

dogged /ˈdɒgɪd/ a obstinado, persistente

dogma /ˈdɒgmə/ n dogma m. ~**tic** /-ˈmætɪk/ a dogmático

dogsbody /ˈdɒgzbɒdɪ/ n (*colloq*) pau-para-toda-obra m (*colloq*), factótum m

doldrums /'dɒldrəmz/ *npl* **be in the ~** estar com a neura; (*business*) estar parado

dole /dəʊl/ *vt* **~ out** distribuir ◻ *n* (*colloq*) auxílio *m* desemprego. **on the ~** (*colloq*) desempregado (titular de auxílio)

doleful /'dəʊlfl/ *a* tristonho, melancólico

doll /dɒl/ *n* boneca *f* ◻ *vt/i* **~ up** (*colloq*) embonecar(-se)

dollar /'dɒlə(r)/ *n* dólar *m*

dolphin /'dɒlfɪn/ *n* golfinho *m*

domain /dəʊ'meɪn/ *n* domínio *m*

dome /dəʊm/ *n* cúpula *f*; (*vault*) abóbada *f*

domestic /də'mestɪk/ *a* (*of home, animal, flights*) doméstico; (*trade*) interno; (*news*) nacional. **~ated** /-keɪtɪd/ *a* (*animal*) domesticado; (*person*) que gosta de trabalhos caseiros

dominant /'dɒmɪnənt/ *a* dominante

dominat|e /'dɒmɪneɪt/ *vt/i* dominar. **~ion** /-'neɪʃn/ *n* dominação *f*, domínio *m*

domineer /dɒmɪ'nɪə(r)/ *vi* **~ over** mandar (em), ser autocrático (para com). **~ing** *a* mandão, autocrático

dominion /də'mɪnjən/ *n* domínio *m*

domino /'dɒmɪnəʊ/ *n* (*pl* **-oes**) dominó *m*

donat|e /dəʊ'neɪt/ *vt* fazer doação de, doar, dar. **~ion** /-ʃn/ *n* donativo *m*

done /dʌn/ *see* **do**

donkey /'dɒŋkɪ/ *n* burro *m*

donor /'dəʊnə(r)/ *n* (*of blood*) doador *m*, (*P*) dador *m*

don't /dəʊnt/ = **do not**

doodle /'duːdl/ *vi* rabiscar

doom /duːm/ *n* ruína *f*; (*fate*) destino *m*. **be ~ed to** ser/estar condenado a. **~ed (to failure)** condenado ao fracasso

door /dɔː(r)/ *n* porta *f*

doorman /'dɔːmən/ *n* (*pl*-**men**) porteiro *m*

doormat /'dɔːmæt/ *n* capacho *m*

doorstep /'dɔːstep/ *n* degrau *m* da porta

doorway /'dɔːweɪ/ *n* vão *m* da porta, (*P*) entrada *f*

dope /dəʊp/ *n* (*colloq*) droga *f*; (*sl: idiot*) imbecil *mf* ◻ *vt* dopar, drogar

dormant /'dɔːmənt/ *a* dormente; (*inactive*) inativo, (*P*) inactivo; (*latent*) latente

dormitory /'dɔːmɪtrɪ/ *n* dormitório *m*; (*Amer univ*) residência *f*

dos|e /dəʊs/ *n* dose *f* ◻ *vt* medicar. **~age** *n* dosagem *f*; (*on label*) posologia *f*

doss /dɒs/ *vi* **~ (down)** dormir sem conforto. **~-house** *n* pensão *f* miserável, asilo *m* noturno, (*P*) nocturno. **~er** *n* vagabundo *m*

dot /dɒt/ *n* ponto *m*. **on the ~** no momento preciso ◻ *vt* **be ~ted with** estar semeado de. **~ted line** linha *f* pontilhada

dot-com /dɒt'kɒm/ *n* empresa *f* dot.com

dote /dəʊt/ *vi* **~ on** ser louco por

double /'dʌbl/ *a* duplo; (*room, bed*) de casal ◻ *adv* duas vezes mais ◻ *n* dobro *m*. **~s** (*tennis*) dupla *f*, (*P*) pares *mpl* ◻ *vt/i* dobrar, duplicar; (*fold*) dobrar em dois. **at the ~** a passo acelerado. **~-bass** *n* contrabaixo *m*. **~-chin** papada *f*. **~-cross** *vt* enganar. **~-dealing** *n* jogo *m* duplo. **~-decker** *n* ônibus *m*, (*P*) autocarro *m* de dois andares. **~ Dutch** algaraviada *f*, fala *f* incompreensível. **~ glazing** (janela *f* de) vidro (*m*) duplo. **doubly** *adv* duplamente

doubt /daʊt/ *n* dúvida *f* ◻ *vt* duvidar de. **~ if** *or* **that** duvidar que. **~ful** *a* duvidoso; (*hesitant*) que tem dúvidas. **~less** *adv* sem dúvida, indubitavelmente

dough /dəʊ/ *n* massa *f*

doughnut /'dəʊnʌt/ *n* sonho *n*, (*P*) bola *f* de Berlim

dove /dʌv/ *n* pomba *f*

dowdy /'daʊdɪ/ *a* (**-ier, -iest**) sem graça, sem gosto

down[1] /daʊn/ *n* (*feathers, hair*) penugem *f*

down[2] /daʊn/ *adv* (*to lower place*) abaixo, para baixo; (*in lower place*) em baixo. **be ~** (*level, price*) descer; (*sun*) estar posto ◻ *prep* por (+)(*n*) (*n*+) abaixo. **~ the hill/street** *etc* pelo monte/pela rua *etc* abaixo ◻ *vt* (*colloq: knock down*) jogar abaixo; (*colloq: drink*) esvaziar. **come** *or* **go ~** descer. **~-and-out** *n* marginal *m*. **~-hearted** *a* desencorajado, desanimado. **~-to-earth** *a* terra-a-terra *invar*. **~ under** na Austrália. **~ with** abaixo

downcast /'daʊnkɑːst/ *a* abatido, deprimido, desmoralizado

downfall /'daʊnfɔːl/ *n* queda *f*, ruína *f*

downhill /daʊn'hɪl/ *adv* **go ~** descer; (*fig*) ir abaixo ◻ *a* /'daʊnhɪl/ a descer, descendente

download /daʊn'ləʊd/ *vt* (*comput*) baixar

downpour /'daʊnpɔː(r)/ *n* aguaceiro *m* forte, (*P*) chuvada *f*

downright /'daʊnraɪt/ *a* franco; (*utter*) autêntico, verdadeiro ◻ *adv* positivamente

downstairs /daʊn'steəz/ *adv* (*at/to*) em/para baixo, no/para o andar de baixo ◻ *a* /'daʊnsteəz/ (*flat etc*) de baixo, do andar de baixo

downstream /'daʊnstriːm/ *adv* rio abaixo

downtown /'daʊntaʊn/ *a & adv* (de, em, para) o centro da cidade. **~ Boston** o centro de Boston

downtrodden /'daʊntrɒdn/ *a* espezinhado, oprimido

downward /'daʊnwəd/ *a* descendente. **~(s)** *adv* para baixo

dowry /'daʊərɪ/ *n* dote *m*

doze /dəʊz/ *vi* dormitar. **~ off** cochilar □ *n* soneca *f*, cochilo *m*

dozen /'dʌzn/ *n* dúzia *f*. **~s of** (*colloq*) dezenas de, dúzias de

Dr *abbr* (*Doctor*) Dr

drab /dræb/ *a* insípido; (*of colour*) morto, apagado

draft[1] /dra:ft/ *n* rascunho *m*; (*comm*) ordem *f* de pagamento □ *vt* fazer o rascunho de; (*draw up*) redigir. **the ~** (*Amer: mil*) recrutamento *m*

draft[2] /dra:ft/ *n* (*Amer*) = **draught**

drag /dræg/ *vt/i* (*pt* **dragged**) arrastar(-se); (*river*) dragar; (*pull away*) arrancar □ *n* (*colloq: task*) chatice *f* (*sl*); (*colloq: person*) estorvo *m*; (*sl: clothes*) travesti *m*

dragon /'drægən/ *n* dragão *m*

dragonfly /'drægənflaɪ/ *n* libélula *f*

drain /dreɪn/ *vt* drenar; (*vegetables*) escorrer; (*glass, tank*) esvaziar; (*use up*) esgotar □ *vi* **~ (off)** escoar-se □ *n* cano *m*. **~s** *npl* (*sewers*) esgotos *mpl*. **~age** *n* drenagem *f*. **~(-pipe)** cano *m* de esgoto. **~ing-board** *n* escorredouro *m*

drama /'dra:mə/ *n* arte *f* dramática; (*play, event*) drama *m*. **~tic** /drə'mætɪk/ *a* dramático. **~tist** /'dræmətɪst/ *n* dramaturgo *m*. **~tize** /'dræmətaɪz/ *vt* dramatizar

drank /dræŋk/ *see* **drink**

drape /dreɪp/ *vt* **~ round/over** dispor (tecido) em pregas à volta de *or* sobre. **~s** *npl* (*Amer*) cortinas *fpl*

drastic /'dræstɪk/ *a* drástico, violento

draught /dra:ft/ *n* corrente *f* de ar; (*naut*) calado *m*. **~s** (*game*) (jogo *m* das) damas *fpl*. **~ beer** chope *m*, (*P*) cerveja *f* à caneca, imperial *f* (*colloq*). **~y** *a* com correntes de ar, ventoso

draughtsman /'dra:ftsmən/ *n* (*pl*-**men**) desenhista *m*, (*P*) desenhador *m*

draw /drɔ:/ *vt* (*pt* **drew**, *pp* **drawn**) puxar; (*attract*) atrair; (*picture*) desenhar; (*in lottery*) tirar à sorte; (*line*) traçar; (*open curtains*) abrir; (*close curtains*) fechar □ *vi* desenhar; (*sport*) empatar; (*come*) vir □ *n* (*sport*) empate *m*; (*lottery*) sorteio *m*. **~ back** recuar. **~ in** (*of days*) diminuir. **~ near** aproximar-se. **~ out** (*money*) levantar. **~ up** deter-se, parar; (*document*) redigir; (*chair*) aproximar, chegar

drawback /'drɔ:bæk/ *n* inconveniente *m*, desvantagem *f*

drawer /drɔ:(r)/ *n* gaveta *f*

drawing /'drɔ:ɪŋ/ *n* desenho *m*. **~-board** *n* prancheta *f*. **~-pin** *n* percevejo *m*

drawl /drɔ:l/ *n* fala *f* arrastada

drawn /drɔ:n/ *see* **draw**

dread /dred/ *n* terror *m* □ *vt* temer

dreadful /'dredfl/ *a* medonho, terrível. **~ly** *adv* terrivelmente

dream /dri:m/ *n* sonho *m* □ *vt/i* (*pt* **dreamed** *or* **dreamt**) sonhar (**of** com) □ *a* (*ideal*) dos seus sonhos. **~ up** imaginar. **~er** *n* sonhador *m*, *a* sonhador; (*music*) romântico

dreary /'drɪərɪ/ *a* (**-ier**, **-iest**) tristonho; (*boring*) aborrecido

dredge /dredʒ/ *n* draga *f* □ *vt/i* dragar. **~r** /-ə(r)/ *n* draga *f*; (*for sugar*) polvilhador *m*

dregs /dregz/ *npl* depósito *m*, sedimento *m*; (*fig*) escória *f*

drench /drentʃ/ *vt* encharcar

dress /dres/ *n* vestido *m*; (*clothing*) roupa *f* □ *vt/i* vestir(-se); (*food*) temperar; (*wound*) fazer curativo, (*P*) pensar, (*P*) tratar. **~ rehearsal** ensaio *m* geral. **~ up as** fantasiar-se de. **get ~ed** vestir-se

dresser /'dresə(r)/ *n* (*furniture*) guarda-louça *m*

dressing /'dresɪŋ/ *n* (*sauce*) tempero *m*; (*bandage*) curativo *m*, (*P*) penso *m*. **~-gown** *n* roupão *m*. **~-room** *n* (*sport*) vestiário *m*; (*theat*) camarim *m*. **~-table** *n* toucador *m*

dressmak|er /'dresmeɪkə(r)/ *n* costureira *f*, modista *f*. **~ing** *n* costura *f*

dressy /'dresɪ/ *a* (**-ier**, **-iest**) elegante, chique *invar*

drew /dru:/ *see* **draw**

dribble /'drɪbl/ *vi* pingar; (*person*) babar-se; (*football*) driblar

dried /draɪd/ *a* (*fruit etc*) seco

drier /'draɪə(r)/ *n* secador *m*

drift /drɪft/ *vi* ir à deriva; (*pile up*) amontoar-se □ *n* força *f* da corrente; (*pile*) monte *m*; (*of events*) rumo *m*; (*meaning*) sentido *m*. **~er** *n* pessoa *f* sem rumo

drill /drɪl/ *n* (*tool*) broca *f*; (*training*) exercício *m*, treino *m*; (*routine procedure*) exercícios *mpl* □ *vt* furar, perfurar; (*train*) treinar; (*tooth*) abrir □ *vi* treinar-se

drink /drɪŋk/ *vt/i* (*pt* **drank**, *pp* **drunk**) beber □ *n* bebida *f*. **a ~ of water** um copo de água. **~able** *a* potável; (*palatable*) bebível. **~er** *n* bebedor *m*. **~ing water** água *f* potável

drip /drɪp/ *vi* (*pt* **dripped**) pingar □ *n* pingar *m*; (*sl: person*) banana *mf* (*colloq*). **~-dry** *vt* deixar escorrer □ *a* que não precisa passar

dripping /'drɪpɪŋ/ *n* gordura *f* do assado

drive /draɪv/ *vt* (*pt* **drove**, *pp* **driven** /'drɪvn/) empurrar, impelir, levar; (*car, animal*) dirigir, conduzir, (*P*) guiar; (*machine*) acionar □ *vi* dirigir, conduzir, (*P*) guiar □ *n* passeio *m* de carro; (*private road*) entrada *f* para veículos; (*fig*) energia *f*; (*psych*) drive *m*, compulsão *f*, impulso *m*; (*campaign*) campanha *f*. **~ at** chegar a. **~ away** (*car*) partir. **~ in** (*force in*) enterrar. **~-in** *n* (*bank, cinema etc*) banco *m*, cinema *m etc* em que se é atendido no carro, drive-in *m*. **~ mad** (fazer) enlouquecer, pôr fora de si

drivel /'drɪvl/ *n* baboseira *f*, bobagem *f*

driver /'draɪvə(r)/ *n* condutor *m*; (*of taxi, bus*) chofer *m*, motorista *mf*

driving /'draɪvɪŋ/ *n* condução *f*. **~-licence** *n* carteira *f* de motorista, (*P*) carta *f* de condução. **~ school** auto-escola *f*; (*P*) **escola** *f* **de condução.** **~ test** exame *m* de motorista, (*P*) de condução

drizzle /'drɪzl/ *n* chuvisco *m* □ *vi* chuviscar

drone /drəʊn/ *n* zumbido *m*; (*male bee*) zangão *m* □ *vi* zumbir; (*fig*) falar monotonamente

drool /druːl/ *vi* babar(-se)

droop /druːp/ *vi* pender, curvar-se

drop /drɒp/ *n* gota *f*; (*fall*) queda *f*; (*distance*) altura *f* de queda □ *vt/i* (*pt* **dropped**) (deixar) cair; (*fall, lower*) baixar. **~ (off)** (*person from car*) deixar, largar. **~ a line** escrever duas linhas (**to** a). **~ in** passar por (**on** em casa de). **~ off** (*doze*) adormecer. **~ out** (*withdraw*) retirar-se; (*of student*) abandonar. **~-out** *n* marginal *mf*, marginalizado *m*

droppings /'drɒpɪŋz/ *npl* excrementos *mpl* de animal; (*of birds*) cocô *m* (*colloq*), porcaria *f* (*colloq*)

dross /drɒs/ *n* escória *f*; (*refuse*) lixo *m*

drought /draʊt/ *n* seca *f*

drove /drəʊv/ *see* **drive**

drown /draʊn/ *vt/i* afogar(-se)

drowsy /'draʊzɪ/ *a* sonolento. **be** *or* **feel ~** ter vontade de dormir

drudge /drʌdʒ/ *n* mouro *m* de trabalho. **~ry** /-ərɪ/ *n* trabalho *m* penoso e monótono, estafa *f*

drug /drʌg/ *n* droga *f*; (*med*) medicamento *m*, remédio *m* □ *vt* (*pt* **drugged**) drogar. **~ addict** drogado *m*, tóxico-dependente *m*

drugstore /'drʌgstɔː(r)/ *n* (*Amer*) farmácia *f* que vende também sorvetes etc

drum /drʌm/ *n* (*mus*) tambor *m*; (*for oil*) barril *m*, tambor *m*. **~s** (*mus*) bateria *f* □ *vi* (*pt* **drummed**) tocar tambor; (*with one's fingers*) tamborilar □ *vt* **~ into sb** fazer entrar na cabeça de alg. **~ up** (*support*) conseguir obter; (*business*) criar. **~mer** *n* tambor *m*; (*in pop group etc*) baterista *m*, (*P*) bateria *m*

drunk /drʌŋk/ *see* **drink** □ *a* embriagado, bêbedo. **get ~** embebedar-se, embriagar-se □ *n* bêbedo *m*. **~ard** *n* alcoólico *m*, bêbedo *m*. **~en** *a* embriagado, bêbedo; (*habitually*) bêbedo

dry /draɪ/ *a* (**drier, driest**) seco; (*day*) sem chuva □ *vt/i* secar. **be** *or* **feel ~** ter sede. **~-clean** *vt* limpar a seco. **~-cleaner's** *n* (loja de) lavagem *f* a seco, lavanderia *f*. **~ up** (*dishes*) secar a louça *f*; (*of supplies*) esgotar-se. **~ness** *n* secura *f*

dual /'djuːəl/ *a* duplo. **~ carriageway** estrada *f* dividida por faixa central. **~-purpose** *a* com fim duplo

dub /dʌb/ *vt* (*pt* **dubbed**) (*film*) dobrar; (*nickname*) apelidar de

dubious /'djuːbɪəs/ *a* duvidoso; (*character, compliment*) dúbio. **feel ~ about** ter dúvidas quanto a

duchess /'dʌtʃɪs/ *n* duquesa *f*

duck /dʌk/ *n* pato *m* □ *vi* abaixar-se rapidamente □ *vt* (*head*) baixar; (*person*) batizar, pregar uma amona em. **~ling** *n* patinho *m*

duct /dʌkt/ *n* canal *m*, tubo *m*

dud /dʌd/ *a* (*sl: thing*) que não presta ou não funciona; (*sl: coin*) falso; (*sl: cheque*) sem fundos, (*P*) careca (*sl*)

due /djuː/ *a* devido; (*expected*) esperado □ *adv* **~ east**/*etc* exatamente, (*P*) exactamente a leste/*etc* □ *n* devido *m*. **~s** direitos *mpl*; (*of club*) cota *f*. **~ to** devido a, por causa de. **in ~ course** no tempo devido

duel /'djuːəl/ *n* duelo *m*

duet /djuː'et/ *n* dueto *m*

duffel /'dʌfl/ *a* **~ bag** saco *m* de lona. **~-coat** *n* casaco *m* de tecido de lã

dug /dʌg/ *see* **dig**

duke /djuːk/ *n* duque *m*

dull /dʌl/ *a* (**-er, -est**) (*boring*) enfadonho; (*colour*) morto; (*mirror*) embaçado; (*weather*) encoberto; (*sound*) surdo; (*stupid*) burro

duly /'djuːlɪ/ *adv* devidamente; (*in due time*) no tempo devido

dumb /dʌm/ *a* (**-er, -est**) mudo; (*colloq: stupid*) bronco, burro

dumbfound /dʌm'faʊnd/ *vt* pasmar

dummy /'dʌmɪ/ n imitação f, coisa f
simulada; (of tailor) manequim m; (of
baby) chupeta f

dump /dʌmp/ vt (rubbish) jogar fora; (put
down) deixar cair; (colloq: abandon)
largar □ n monte m de lixo; (tip) lixeira
f; (mil) depósito m; (colloq) buraco m

dunce /dʌns/ n burro m. **~'s cap** orelhas
fpl de burro

dune /dju:n/ n duna f

dung /dʌŋ/ n esterco m; (manure)
estrume m

dungarees /dʌŋgə'ri:z/ npl macacão m,
(P) fato m de macaco

dungeon /'dʌndʒən/ n calabouço m,
masmorra f

dupe /dju:p/ vt enganar □ n trouxa m

duplicate[1] /'dju:plɪkət/ n duplicado m □ a
idêntico

duplicate[2] /'dju:plɪkeɪt/ vt duplicar, fazer
em duplicado; (on machine) fotocopiar

duplicity /dju:'plɪsətɪ/ n duplicidade f

durable /'djʊərəbl/ a resistente;
(enduring) duradouro, durável

duration /dju'reɪʃn/ n duração f

duress /dju'res/ n **under ~** sob coação f,
(P) coacção f

during /'djʊərɪŋ/ prep durante

dusk /dʌsk/ n crepúsculo m, anoitecer m

dusky /'dʌskɪ/ a (-ier, -iest) escuro,
sombrio

dust /dʌst/ n pó m, poeira f □ vt limpar o
pó de; (sprinkle) polvilhar. **~-jacket** n
sobrecapa f de livro

dustbin /'dʌstbɪn/ n lata f do lixo, (P)
caixote m

duster /'dʌstə(r)/ n pano m do pó

dustman /'dʌstmən/ n (pl -men) lixeiro
m, (P) homem m do lixo

dusty /'dʌstɪ/ a (-ier, -iest) poeirento,
empoeirado

Dutch /dʌtʃ/ a holandês □ n (lang)
holandês m. **~man** n holandês m.
~woman n holandesa f. **go ~** pagar
cada um a sua despesa

dutiful /'dju:tɪfl/ a cumpridor; (showing
respect) respeitador

dut|y /'dju:tɪ/ n dever m; (tax) impostos
mpl. **~ies** (of official etc) funções fpl. **off
~y** de folga. **on ~y** de serviço. **~y-free**
a isento de impostos. **~y-free shop**
free shop m

duvet /'dju:veɪ/ n edredom m, (P) edredão
m de penas

dwarf /dwɔ:f/ n (pl -fs) anão m

dwell /dwel/ vi (pt dwelt) morar. **~ on**
alongar-se sobre. **~er** n habitante.
~ing n habitação f

dwindle /'dwɪndl/ vi diminuir,
reduzir-se

dye /daɪ/ vt (pres p dyeing) tingir □ n
tinta f

dying /'daɪɪŋ/ see **die**

dynamic /dar'næmɪk/ a dinâmico

dynamite /'daɪnəmaɪt/ n dinamite f □ vt
dinamitar

dynamo /'daɪnəməʊ/ n (pl -os) dínamo m

dynasty /'dɪnəstɪ/ n dinastia f

dysentery /'dɪsəntrɪ/ n disenteria f

dyslex|ia /dɪs'leksɪə/ n dislexia f. **~ic** a
disléxico

d

e

··

Ee

··

each /i:tʃ/ a & pron cada. **~ one** cada um.
~ other um ao outro, uns aos outros.
they like ~ other gostam um do
outro/uns dos outros. **know/love/etc ~
other** conhecer-se/amar-se/etc

eager /'i:gə(r)/ a ansioso (**to** por),
desejoso (**for** de); (supporter)
entusiástico. **be ~ to** ter vontade de.
~ly adv com impaciência,
ansiosamente; (keenly) com
entusiasmo. **~ness** n ansiedade f,
desejo m; (keenness) entusiasmo m

eagle /'i:gl/ n águia f

ear /ɪə(r)/ n ouvido m; (external part)
orelha f. **~-drum** n tímpano m. **~-ring**
n brinco m

earache /'ɪəreɪk/ n dor f de ouvidos

earl /ɜ:l/ n conde m

early /'ɜ:lɪ/ (-ier, -iest) adv cedo □ a
primeiro; (hour) matinal; (fruit)
temporão; (retirement) antecipado.
have an ~ dinner jantar cedo. **in ~
summer** no princípio do verão

earmark /'ɪəma:k/ vt destinar, reservar
(**for** para)

earn /ɜ:n/ vt ganhar; (deserve) merecer

earnest /'ɜ:nɪst/ a sério. **in ~** a sério

earnings /'ɜ:nɪŋz/ npl salário m; (profits)
ganhos mpl, lucros mpl

earshot /'ɪəʃɒt/ n **within ~** ao alcance
da voz

earth /ɜ:θ/ n terra f □ vt (electr) ligar à
terra. **why on ~?** por que diabo?, por
que cargas d'água? **~ly** a terrestre,
terreno

earthenware /'ɜ:θənweə(r)/ n louça f de
barro, faiança f

earthquake /'ɜ:θkweɪk/ n tremor m de
terra, terremoto m

earthy /'ɜ:θɪ/ a terroso, térreo; (coarse)
grosseiro

earwig /ˈɪəwɪg/ n lacrainha f, (P) bicha-cadela f

ease /iːz/ n facilidade f; (comfort) bem-estar m □ vt/i (from pain, anxiety) acalmar(-se); (slow down) afrouxar; (slide) deslizar. **at** ~ à vontade; (mil) descansar. **ill at** ~ pouco à vontade. **with** ~ facilmente. ~ **in/out** fazer entrar/sair com cuidado

easel /ˈiːzl/ n cavalete m

east /iːst/ n este m, leste m, oriente m. the **E**~ o Oriente □ a este, (de) leste, oriental □ adv a/para leste. ~ **of** para o leste de ~**erly** a oriental, leste, a/de leste. ~**ward** a, ~**ward(s)** adv para leste

Easter /ˈiːstə(r)/ n Páscoa f. ~ **egg** ovo m de Páscoa

eastern /ˈiːstən/ a oriental, leste

easy /ˈiːzɪ/ a (-ier, -iest) fácil; (relaxed) natural, descontraído. **take it** ~ levar as coisas com calma. ~ **chair** poltrona f. ~-**going** a bonacheirão. **easily** adv facilmente

eat /iːt/ vt/i (pt ate, pp eaten) comer. ~ **into** corroer. ~**able** a comestível

eaves /iːvz/ npl beiral m

eavesdrop /ˈiːvzdrɒp/ vi (pt -dropped) escutar por detrás da porta

e-book /ˈiːbʊk/ n livro m eletrônico

ebb /eb/ n vazante f, baixa-mar m □ vi vazar; (fig) declinar

EC /iːˈsiː/ n (abbr of European Commission) CE f

eccentric /ɪkˈsentrɪk/ a & n excêntrico (m). ~**ity** /eksenˈtrɪsətɪ/ n excentricidade f

ecclesiastical /ɪkliːzɪˈæstɪkl/ a eclesiástico

echo /ˈekəʊ/ n (pl -oes) eco m □ vt/i (pt echoed, pres p echoing) ecoar; (fig) repetir

eclipse /ɪˈklɪps/ n eclipse m □ vt eclipsar

ecolog|**y** /iːˈkɒlədʒɪ/ n ecologia f. ~ **ical** /iːkəˈlɒdʒɪkl/ a ecológico

e-commerce /ˈiːkɒmɜːs/ n comércio m eletrônico

economic /iːkəˈnɒmɪk/ a econômico; (profitable) rentável. ~**al** a econômico. ~**s** n economia f política

economist /ɪˈkɒnəmɪst/ n economista mf

econom|**y** /ɪˈkɒnəmɪ/ n economia f. ~**ize** vt/i economizar

ecstasy /ˈekstəsɪ/ n êxtase m

ecstatic /ɪkˈstætɪk/ a extático

ecu /ˈeɪkjuː/ n unidade f monetária européia

eczema /ˈeksɪmə/ n eczema m

edge /edʒ/ n borda f, beira f; (of town) periferia f, limite m; (of knife) fio m □ vt

debruar □ vi (move) avançar pouco a pouco

edging /ˈedʒɪŋ/ n borda f, (P) bordadura f

edgy /ˈedʒɪ/ a irritadiço, nervoso

edible /ˈedɪbl/ a comestível

edict /ˈiːdɪkt/ n édito m

edifice /ˈedɪfɪs/ n edifício m

edit /ˈedɪt/ vt (pt edited) (newspaper) dirigir; (text) editar

edition /ɪˈdɪʃn/ n edição f

editor /ˈedɪtə(r)/ n (of newspaper) diretor m, (P) director m, editor m responsável; (of text) organizador m de texto. **the** ~ (**in chief**) redator-chefe m, (P) redactor-chefe m. ~**ial** /edɪˈtɔːrɪəl/ a & n editorial (m)

educat|**e** /ˈedʒʊkeɪt/ vt instruir; (mind, public) educar. ~**ed** a instruído; educado. ~**ion** /-ˈkeɪʃn/ n educação f; (schooling) ensino m. ~**ional** /-ˈkeɪʃənl/ a educativo, pedagógico

EEC /iːiːˈsiː/ n (abbr of European Economic Community) CEE f

eel /iːl/ n enguia f

eerie /ˈɪərɪ/ a (-ier, -iest) arrepiante, misterioso

effect /ɪˈfekt/ n efeito m □ vt efetuar, (P) efectuar. **come into** ~ entrar em vigor. **in** ~ na realidade. **take** ~ ter efeito

effective /ɪˈfektɪv/ a eficaz, eficiente; (striking) sensacional; (actual) efetivo, (P) efectivo. ~**ly** adv (efficiently) eficazmente; (strikingly) de forma sensacional; (actually) efetivamente, (P) efectivamente. ~**ness** n eficácia f

effeminate /ɪˈfemɪnət/ a efeminado, afeminado

effervescent /efəˈvesnt/ a efervescente

efficien|**t** /ɪˈfɪʃnt/ a eficiente, eficaz. ~**cy** n eficiência f. ~**tly** adv eficientemente

effigy /ˈefɪdʒɪ/ n efígie f

effort /ˈefət/ n esforço m. ~**less** a fácil, sem esforço

effrontery /ɪˈfrʌntərɪ/ n desfaçatez f

effusive /ɪˈfjuːsɪv/ a efusivo, expansivo

e.g. /iːˈdʒiː/ abbr por ex

egg[1] /eg/ n ovo m. ~-**cup** n copinho m para ovo quente, oveiro m. ~-**plant** n beringela f

egg[2] /eg/ vt ~ **on** (colloq) incitar

eggshell /ˈegʃel/ n casca f de ovo

ego /ˈegəʊ/ n (pl -os) ego m, eu m. ~**ism** n egoísmo m. ~**ist** n egoísta mf. ~**tism** n egotismo m. ~**tist** n egotista mf

Egypt /ˈiːdʒɪpt/ n Egito m. ~**ian** /ɪˈdʒɪpʃn/ a & n egípcio (m)

eh /eɪ/ int (colloq) hã?

eiderdown /ˈaɪdədaʊn/ n edredão m, edredom m

eight /eɪt/ a & n oito (m). **eighth** /eɪtθ/ a & n oitavo (m)

eighteen /eɪ'ti:n/ a & n dezoito (m). ~**th** a & n décimo oitavo (m)

eight|y /'eɪtɪ/ a & n oitenta (m). ~ **ieth** a & n octogésimo (m)

either /'aɪðə(r)/ a & pron um e outro; (with negative) nem um nem outro; (each) cada □ adv também não □ conj ~ ... **or** ou ... ou; (with negative) nem ... nem

ejaculate /ɪ'dʒækjʊleɪt/ vt/i ejacular; (exclaim) exclamar

eject /ɪ'dʒekt/ vt expelir; (expel) expulsar, despejar

elaborate[1] /ɪ'læbərət/ a elaborado, rebuscado, minucioso

elaborate[2] /ɪ'læbəreɪt/ vt elaborar □ vi entrar em pormenores. ~**on** estender-se sobre

elapse /ɪ'læps/ vi decorrer

elastic /ɪ'læstɪk/ a & n elástico (m). ~ **band** elástico m

elat|ed /ɪ'leɪtɪd/ a radiante, exultante. ~ **ion** n exultação f

elbow /'elbəʊ/ n cotovelo m

elder[1] /'eldə(r)/ a mais velho. ~**s** npl pessoas fpl mais velhas

elder[2] /'eldə(r)/ n (tree) sabugueiro m

elderly /'eldəlɪ/ a idoso. **the** ~ as pessoas de idade

eldest /'eldɪst/ a & n o mais velho (m)

elect /ɪ'lekt/ vt eleger □ a eleito. ~**ion** /-kʃn/ n eleição f

electric /ɪ'lektrɪk/ a elétrico, (P) eléctrico.

electrician /ɪlek'trɪʃn/ n eletricista m, (P) electricista m

electricity /ɪlek'trɪsətɪ/ n eletricidade f, (P) electricidade f

electrify /ɪ'lektrɪfaɪ/ vt eletrificar, (P) electrificar; (fig: excite) eletrizar, (P) electrizar

electrocute /ɪ'lektrəkju:t/ vt eletrocutar, (P) electrocutar

electronic /ɪlek'trɒnɪk/ a eletrônico, (P) electrónico. ~**s** n eletrônica f, (P) electrónica f

elegan|t /'elɪɡənt/ a elegante. ~**ce** n elegância f. ~**tly** adv elegantemente, com elegância

element /'elɪmənt/ n elemento m; (of heater etc) resistência f. ~**ary** /-'mentrɪ/ a elementar; (school) primário

elephant /'elɪfənt/ n elefante m

elevat|e /'elɪveɪt/ vt elevar. ~**ion** /-'veɪʃn/ n elevação f

elevator /'elɪveɪtə(r)/ n (Amer: lift) elevador m, ascensor m

eleven /ɪ'levn/ a & n onze (m). ~**th** a & n décimo primeiro (m). **at the** ~**th hour** à última hora

elicit /ɪ'lɪsɪt/ vt extrair, obter

eligible /'elɪdʒəbl/ a (for office) idôneo, (P) idóneo (**for** para); (desirable) aceitável. **be** ~ **for** (entitled to) ter direito a

eliminat|e /ɪ'lɪmɪneɪt/ vt eliminar. ~**ion** /-'neɪʃn/ n eliminação f

élite /er'li:t/ n elite f

ellip|se /ɪ'lɪps/ n elipse f. ~**tical** a elíptico

elm /elm/ n olmo m, ulmeiro m

elocution /elə'kju:ʃn/ n elocução f

elongate /'i:lɒŋɡeɪt/ vt alongar

elope /ɪ'ləʊp/ vi fugir. ~**ment** n fuga f (de amantes), (P) (de amorosos)

eloquen|t /'eləkwənt/ a eloqüente, (P) eloquente. ~**ce** n eloqüência f, (P) eloquência f

else /els/ adv mais. **everybody** ~ todos os outros. **nobody** ~ mais ninguém. **nothing** ~ nada mais. **or** ~ ou então, senão. **somewhere** ~ noutro lado qualquer. ~**where** adv noutro lado

elude /ɪ'lu:d/ vt escapar a; (a question) evadir

elusive /ɪ'lu:sɪv/ a (person) esquivo, difícil de apanhar; (answer) evasivo

emaciated /ɪ'meɪʃɪeɪtɪd/ a emaciado, macilento

email /'i:meɪl/ n correio m eletrônico, e-mail m; ~ **address** endereço m de e-mail

emancipat|e /ɪ'mænsɪpeɪt/ vt emancipar. ~**ion** /-'peɪʃn/ n emancipação f

embalm /ɪm'ba:m/ vt embalsamar

embankment /ɪm'bæŋkmənt/ n (of river) dique m; (of railway) terrapleno m, talude m, (P) aterro m

embargo /ɪm'ba:ɡəʊ/ n (pl -oes) embargo m

embark /ɪm'ba:k/ vt/i embarcar. ~ **on** (business etc) embarcar em, meter-se em (colloq); (journey) começar

embarrass /ɪm'bærəs/ vt embaraçar, confundir. ~**ment** n embaraço m, atrapalhação f

embassy /'embəsɪ/ n embaixada f

embellish /ɪm'belɪʃ/ vt embelezar, enfeitar. ~**ment** n embelezamento m, enfeite m

embezzle /ɪm'bezl/ vt desviar (fundos). ~**ment** n desfalque m

embitter /ɪm'bɪtə(r)/ vt (person) amargurar; (situation) azedar

emblem /'embləm/ n emblema m

embod|y /ɪm'bɒdɪ/ vt encarnar; (include) incorporar, incluir. ~**iment** n personificação f

emboss /ɪmˈbɒs/ *vt* (*metal*) gravar em relevo; (*paper*) gofrar

embrace /ɪmˈbreɪs/ *vt/i* abraçar (-se); (*offer, opportunity*) acolher □ ~*n* abraço *m*

embroider /ɪmˈbrɔɪdə(r)/ *vt* bordar. ~y *n* bordado *m*

embryo /ˈembrɪəʊ/ *n* (*pl* -os) embrião *m*. ~nic /-ˈɒnɪk/ *a* embrionário

emerald /ˈemərəld/ *n* esmeralda *f*

emerge /ɪˈmɜːdʒ/ *vi* emergir, surgir

emergency /ɪˈmɜːdʒənsɪ/ *n* emergência *f*. (*urgent case*) urgência *f*. ~ **exit** saída *f* de emergência. **in an** ~ em caso de urgência

emigrant /ˈemɪɡrənt/ *n* emigrante *mf*

emigrat|e /ˈemɪɡreɪt/ *vi* emigrar. ~ion /-ˈɡreɪʃn/ *n* emigração *f*

eminen|t /ˈemɪnənt/ *a* eminente. ~tly *adv* eminentemente

emi|t /ɪˈmɪt/ *vt* (*pt* **emitted**) emitir. ~ssion /-ʃn/ *n* emissão *f*

emotion /ɪˈməʊʃn/ *n* emoção *f*. ~al *a* (*person, shock*) emotivo; (*speech, scene*) emocionante

emperor /ˈempərə(r)/ *n* imperador *m*

emphasis /ˈemfəsɪs/ *n* ênfase *f*. **lay** ~ **on** pôr em relevo

emphasize /ˈemfəsaɪz/ *vt* enfatizar, sublinhar; (*syllable, word*) acentuar

emphatic /ɪmˈfætɪk/ *a* enfático; (*manner*) enérgico. ~ally *adv* enfaticamente

empire /ˈempaɪə(r)/ *n* império *m*

employ /ɪmˈplɔɪ/ *vt* empregar. ~ee /emplɔɪˈiː/ *n* empregado *m*. ~er *n* patrão *m*. ~ment *n* emprego *m*. ~ment **agency** agência *f* de empregos

empower /ɪmˈpaʊə(r)/ *vt* autorizar (**to do** a fazer)

empress /ˈemprɪs/ *n* imperatriz *f*

empt|y /ˈemptɪ/ *a* vazio; (*promise*) falso □ *vt/i* esvaziar(-se). **on an** ~y **stomach** com o estômago vazio, em jejum. ~**ies** *npl* garrafas *fpl* vazias. ~**iness** *n* vazio *m*

emulate /ˈemjʊleɪt/ *vt* imitar, rivalizar com, emular com

emulsion /ɪˈmʌlʃn/ *n* emulsão *f*

enable /ɪˈneɪbl/ *vt* ~ **sb to do** permitir a alg fazer

enact /ɪˈnækt/ *vt* (*jur*) decretar; (*theat*) representar

enamel /ɪˈnæml/ *n* esmalte *m* □ *vt* (*pt* **enamelled**) esmaltar

enamoured /ɪˈnæməd/ *a* ~ **of** enamorado de, apaixonado por

encase /ɪnˈkeɪs/ *vt* encerrar (**in** em); (*cover*) revestir (**in** de)

enchant /ɪnˈtʃɑːnt/ *vt* encantar. ~**ing** *a* encantador. ~**ment** *n* encantamento *m*

encircle /ɪnˈsɜːkl/ *vt* cercar, rodear

enclose /ɪnˈkləʊz/ *vt* (*land*) cercar; (*with letter*) enviar incluso/junto. ~**d** *a* (*space*) fechado; (*with letter*) anexo, incluso, junto

enclosure /ɪnˈkləʊʒə(r)/ *n* cercado *m*, recinto *m*; (*with letter*) documento *m* anexo

encompass /ɪnˈkʌmpəs/ *vt* abranger

encore /ɒŋˈkɔː(r)/ *int* & *n* bis (*m*)

encounter /ɪnˈkaʊntə(r)/ *vt* encontrar, deparar com □ *n* encontro *m*

encourage /ɪnˈkʌrɪdʒ/ *vt* encorajar. ~**ment** *n* encorajamento *m*

encroach /ɪnˈkrəʊtʃ/ *vi* ~ **on** (*land*) invadir; (*time*) abusar de

encumb|er /ɪnˈkʌmbə(r)/ *vt* estorvar; (*burden*) sobrecarregar. ~**rance** *n* estorvo *m*, empecilho *m*; (*burden*) ônus *m*, (*P*) ónus *m*, encargo *m*

encyclop|ed|ia /ɪnsaɪkləˈpiːdɪə/ *n* enciclopédia *f*. ~**ic** *a* enciclopédico

end /end/ *n* fim *m*; (*farthest part*) extremo *m*, ponta *f* □ *vt/i* acabar, terminar. ~ **up** (*arrive finally*) ir parar (**in** a/em). ~ **up doing** acabar por fazer. **in the** ~ por fim. **no** ~ **of** (*colloq*) muito, enorme, imenso. **on** ~ (*upright*) em pé; (*consecutive*) a fio, de seguida

endanger /ɪnˈdeɪndʒə(r)/ *vt* pôr em perigo

endear|ing /ɪnˈdɪərɪŋ/ *a* cativante. ~**ment** *n* palavra *f* meiga; (*act*) carinho *m*

endeavour /ɪnˈdevə(r)/ *n* esforço *m* □ *vi* esforçar-se (**to** por)

ending /ˈendɪŋ/ *n* fim *m*; (*of word*) terminação *f*

endless /ˈendlɪs/ *a* interminável; (*times*) sem conta; (*patience*) infinito

endorse /ɪnˈdɔːs/ *vt* (*document*) endossar; (*action*) aprovar. ~**ment** *n* (*auto*) averbamento *m*

endow /ɪnˈdaʊ/ *vt* doar. ~**ment** *n* doação *f*

endur|e /ɪnˈdjʊə(r)/ *vt* suportar □ *vi* durar. ~**able** *a* suportável. ~ **ance** *n* resistência *f*

enemy /ˈenəmɪ/ *n* & *a* inimigo (*m*)

energetic /enəˈdʒetɪk/ *a* enérgico

energy /ˈenədʒɪ/ *n* energia *f*

enforce /ɪnˈfɔːs/ *vt* aplicar

engage /ɪnˈɡeɪdʒ/ *vt* (*staff*) contratar; (*mech*) engrenar □ *vi* ~ **in** envolver-se em, lançar-se em. ~ **d** *a* noivo; (*busy*) ocupado. ~**ment** *n* noivado *m*; (*undertaking, appointment*) compromisso *m*; (*mil*) combate *m*

engender /ɪnˈdʒendə(r)/ *vt* engendrar, produzir, causar

engine /ˈendʒɪn/ *n* motor *m*; (*of train*) locomotiva *f*

engineer /endʒɪ'nɪə(r)/ n
engenheiro m □ vt engenhar. ~ing
n engenharia f

England /'ɪŋglənd/ n Inglaterra f

English /'ɪŋglɪʃ/ a inglês □ n (lang)
inglês m. **the** ~ os ingleses mpl. ~**man**
n inglês m. ~**-speaking** a de lingua
inglesa f. ~**woman** n inglesa f

engrav|e /ɪn'greɪv/ vt gravar. ~**ing**
n gravura f

engrossed /ɪn'grəʊst/ a absorto (**in** em)

engulf /ɪn'gʌlf/ vt engolfar, tragar

enhance /ɪn'hɑːns/ vt aumentar;
(heighten) realçar

enigma /ɪ'nɪgmə/ n enigma m. ~**tic**
/enɪg'mætɪk/ a enigmático

enjoy /ɪn'dʒɔɪ/ vt gostar de; (benefit from)
gozar de. ~ **o.s.** divertir-se. ~**able** a
agradável. ~**ment** n prazer m

enlarge /ɪn'lɑːdʒ/ vt/i aumentar.
~ **upon** alargar-se sobre. ~**-ment**
n ampliação f

enlighten /ɪn'laɪtn/ vt esclarecer.
~**ment** n esclarecimento m,
elucidação f

enlist /ɪn'lɪst/ vt recrutar; (fig) aliciar,
granjear □ vi alistar-se

enliven /ɪn'laɪvn/ vt animar

enmity /'enmətɪ/ n inimizade f

enormous /ɪ'nɔːməs/ a enorme

enough /ɪ'nʌf/ a, adv & n bastante (m),
suficiente (m) □ int basta!, chega! **have**
~ **of** estar farto de

enquir|e /ɪn'kwaɪə(r)/ vt/i perguntar,
indagar. ~**e about** informar-se de,
pedir informações sobre. ~**y** n pedido
m de informações

enrage /ɪn'reɪdʒ/ vt enfurecer,
enraivecer

enrich /ɪn'rɪtʃ/ vt enriquecer

enrol /ɪn'rəʊl/ vt/i (pt enrolled)
inscrever(-se); (schol)
matricular(-se). ~**ment** n inscrição f;
(schol) matrícula f

ensemble /ɒn'sɒmbl/ n conjunto m

ensign /'ensən/ n pavilhão m; (officer)
guarda-marinha m

ensu|e /ɪn'sjuː/ vi seguir-se. ~**ing** a
decorrente

ensure /ɪn'ʃʊə(r)/ vt assegurar. ~ **that**
assegurar-se de que

entail /ɪn'teɪl/ vt acarretar

entangle /ɪn'tæŋgl/ vt emaranhar,
enredar

enter /'entə(r)/ vt (room, club etc) entrar
em; (register) registar; (data) entrar
com □ vi entrar (**into** em). ~ **for**
inscrever-se em

enterprise /'entəpraɪz/ n empresa f,
empreendimento m; (fig) iniciativa f

enterprising /'entəpraɪzɪŋ/ a
empreendedor

entertain /entə'teɪn/ vt entreter; (guests)
receber; (ideas) alimentar, nutrir. ~**er**
n artista mf. ~**ment** n entretenimento
m; (performance) espetáculo m, (P)
espectáculo m

enthral /ɪn'θrɔːl/ vt (pt enthralled)
fascinar

enthuse /ɪn'θjuːz/ vi ~ **over**
entusiasmar-se por

enthusias|m /ɪn'θjuːzɪæzm/ n
entusiasmo m. ~**t** n entusiasta mf.
~**tic** /-'æstɪk/ a entusiástico. ~**tically**
/-'æstɪkəlɪ/ adv entusiasticamente

entice /ɪn'taɪs/ vt atrair. ~ **to do** induzir a
fazer. ~**ment** n tentação f, engodo m

entire /ɪn'taɪə(r)/ a inteiro. ~**ly** adv
inteiramente

entirety /ɪn'taɪərətɪ/ n **in its** ~ por
inteiro, na (sua) totalidade

entitle /ɪn'taɪtl/ vt dar direito.
~**d** a (book) intitulado. **be** ~**d to**
sth ter direito a alg coisa. ~**ment** n
direito m

entity /'entətɪ/ n entidade f

entrance /'entrəns/ n entrada f (**to** para);
(right to enter) admissão f

entrant /'entrənt/ n (sport) concorrente
mf; (in exam) candidato m

entreat /ɪn'triːt/ vt rogar, suplicar. ~**y** n
rogo m, súplica f

entrench /ɪn'trentʃ/ vt (mil)
entrincheirar; (fig) fincar

entrust /ɪn'trʌst/ vt confiar

entry /'entrɪ/ n entrada f; (on list) item m;
(in dictionary) verbete m. ~ **form** ficha
f de inscrição, (P) boletim m de
inscrição. **no** ~ entrada proibida

enumerate /ɪ'njuːməreɪt/ vt enumerar

envelop /ɪn'veləp/ vt (pt enveloped)
envolver

envelope /'envələʊp/ n envelope m,
sobrescrito m

enviable /'envɪəbl/ a invejável

envious /'envɪəs/ a invejoso. **be** ~ **of** ter
inveja de. ~**ly** adv invejosamente, com
inveja

environment /ɪn'vaɪərənmənt/ n meio
m; (ecological) meio- ambiente m. ~**al**
/-'mentl/ a do meio; (ecological) do
ambiente

envisage /ɪn'vɪzɪdʒ/ vt encarar; (foresee)
prever

envoy /'envɔɪ/ n enviado m

envy /'envɪ/ n inveja f □ vt invejar, ter
inveja de

enzyme /'enzaɪm/ n enzima f

epic /'epɪk/ n epopéia f □ a épico

epidemic /epɪ'demɪk/ n epidemia f

e

epilep|sy /'epɪlepsɪ/ n epilepsia f. **~tic** /-'leptɪk/ a & n epiléptico (m)

episode /'epɪsəʊd/ n episódio m

epitaph /'epɪtɑːf/ n epitáfio m

epithet /'epɪθet/ n epíteto m

epitom|e /ɪ'pɪtəmɪ/ n (summary) epítome m; (embodiment) modelo m. **~ize** vt (fig) representar, encarnar; (summarize) resumir

epoch /'iːpɒk/ n época f. **~-making** a que marca uma época

equal /'iːkwəl/ a & n igual (m) □ vt (pt **equalled**) igualar, ser igual a. **~ to** (task) à altura de. **~ity** /iː'kwɒlətɪ/ n igualdade f. **~ly** adv igualmente; (similarly) de igual modo

equalize /'iːkwəlaɪz/ vt/i igualar; (sport) empatar

equanimity /ekwə'nɪmətɪ/ n equanimidade f, serenidade f

equate /ɪ'kweɪt/ vt equacionar (**with** com); (treat as equal) equiparar (**with** a)

equation /ɪ'kweɪʒn/ n equação f

equator /ɪ'kweɪtə(r)/ n equador m. **~ial** /ekwə'tɔːrɪəl/ a equatorial

equilibrium /iːkwɪ'lɪbrɪəm/ n equilíbrio m

equip /ɪ'kwɪp/ vt (pt **equipped**) equipar (**with** com), munir (**with** de). **~ment** n equipamento m

equitable /'ekwɪtəbl/ a eqüitativo, (P) equitativo

equity /'ekwətɪ/ n eqüidade f, (P) equidade f

equivalent /ɪ'kwɪvələnt/ a & n eqüivalente (m), (P) equivalente (m)

equivocal /ɪ'kwɪvəkl/ a equívoco

era /'ɪərə/ n era f, época f

eradicate /ɪ'rædɪkeɪt/ vt erradicar, suprimir

erase /ɪ'reɪz/ vt apagar. **~r** /-ə(r)/ n borracha f (de apagar)

erect /ɪ'rekt/ a ereto, (P) erecto □ vt erigir. **~ion** /-ʃn/ n ereção f, (P) erecção f; (building) construção f, edifício m

ero|de /ɪ'rəʊd/ vt corroer. **~sion** /ɪ'rəʊʒn/ n erosão f

erotic /ɪ'rɒtɪk/ a erótico

err /ɜː(r)/ vi (pt **erred**) errar

errand /'erənd/ n recado m

erratic /ɪ'rætɪk/ a errático, irregular; (person) variável, imprevisível

erroneous /ɪ'rəʊnɪəs/ a errôneo, (P) erróneo, errado

error /'erə(r)/ n erro m

erudit|e /'eruːdaɪt/ a erudito. **~ion** /-'dɪʃn/ n erudição f

erupt /ɪ'rʌpt/ vi (war, fire) irromper; (volcano) entrar em erupção. **~ion** /-ʃn/ n erupção f

escalat|e /'eskəleɪt/ vt/i intensificar(-se); (of prices) subir em espiral. **~ion** /-'leɪʃn/ n escalada f

escalator /'eskəleɪtə(r)/ n escada f rolante

escapade /eskə'peɪd/ n peripécia f

escape /ɪ'skeɪp/ vi escapar-se □ vt escapar a □ n fuga f; (of prisoner) evasão f, fuga f. **~ from sb** escapar de alguém. **~ to** fugir para. **have a lucky** or **narrow ~** escapar por um tris

escapism /ɪ'skeɪpɪzəm/ n escapismo m

escort[1] /'eskɔːt/ n escolta f; (of woman) cavalheiro m, acompanhante m

escort[2] /ɪ'skɔːt/ vt escoltar; (accompany) acompanhar

escudo /es'kjuːdəʊ/ n (pl -os) escudo m

Eskimo /'eskɪməʊ/ n (pl -os) esquimó mf

especial /ɪ'speʃl/ a especial. **~ly** adv especialmente

espionage /'espɪənɑːʒ/ n espionagem f

espouse /ɪ'spaʊz/ vt (a cause etc) abraçar

espresso /e'spresəʊ/ n (pl -os) (coffee) expresso m

essay /'eseɪ/ n ensaio m; (schol) redação f, (P) redacção f

essence /'esns/ n essência f

essential /ɪ'senʃl/ a essencial □ n **the ~s** o essencial m. **~ly** adv essencialmente

establish /ɪ'stæblɪʃ/ vt estabelecer; (business, state) fundar; (prove) provar, apurar. **~ment** n estabelecimento m; (institution) instituição f. **the E~ment** o Establishment m, a classe f dirigente

estate /ɪ'steɪt/ n propriedade f; (possessions) bens mpl; (inheritance) herança f. **~ agent** agente m imobiliário. **(housing) ~** conjunto m habitacional. **~ car** perua f

esteem /ɪ'stiːm/ vt estimar □ n estima f

estimate[1] /'estɪmət/ n cálculo m, avaliação f; (comm) orçamento m, estimativa f

estimat|e[2] /'estɪmeɪt/ vt calcular, estimar. **~ion** /-'meɪʃn/ n opinião f

estuary /'estʃʊərɪ/ n estuário m

etc abbr = **et cetera** /ɪt'setərə/ etc

etching /'etʃɪŋ/ n água-forte f

eternal /ɪ'tɜːnl/ a eterno

eternity /ɪ'tɜːnətɪ/ n eternidade f

ethic /'eθɪk/ n ética f. **~s** ética f. **~al** a ético

ethnic /'eθnɪk/ a étnico

etiquette /'etɪket/ n etiqueta f

etymology /etɪ'mɒlədʒɪ/ n etimologia f

eulogy /'juːlədʒɪ/ n elogio m

euphemism /ˈjuːfəmɪzəm/ n eufemismo m

euphoria /juːˈfɔːrɪə/ n euforia f

euro /ˈjʊərəʊ/ n euro m

Europe /ˈjʊərəp/ n Europa f. **~an** /-ˈpɪən/ a & n europeu (m). **~an Union** União f Européia

euthanasia /juːθəˈneɪzɪə/ n eutanásia f

evacuat|e /ɪˈvækjʊeɪt/ vt evacuar. **~ion** /-ˈeɪʃn/ n evacuação f

evade /ɪˈveɪd/ vt evadir

evaluate /ɪˈvæljʊeɪt/ vt avaliar

evangelical /iːvænˈdʒelɪkl/ a evangélico

evaporat|e /ɪˈvæpəreɪt/ vt/i evaporar(-se). **~ed milk** leite m evaporado. **~ion** /-ˈreɪʃn/ n evaporação f

evasion /ɪˈveɪʒn/ n evasão f

evasive /ɪˈveɪsɪv/ a evasivo

eve /iːv/ n véspera f

even /ˈiːvn/ a regular; (surface) liso, plano; (amounts) igual; (number) par ▢ vt/i **~ up** igualar(-se), acertar ▢ adv mesmo. **~ better** ainda melhor. **get ~ with** ajustar contas com. **~ly** adv uniformemente

evening /ˈiːvnɪŋ/ n entardecer m, anoitecer m; (whole evening) serão m. **~ class** aula f à noite (para adultos). **~ dress** traje m de cerimônia, (P) trajo m de cerimônia or de rigor; (woman's) vestido m de noite

event /ɪˈvent/ n acontecimento m. **in the ~ of** no caso de. **~ful** a movimentado, memorável

eventual /ɪˈventʃʊəl/ a final. **~ity** /-ˈælətɪ/ n eventualidade f. **~ly** adv por fim; (in future) eventualmente

ever /ˈevə(r)/ adv jamais; (at all times) sempre. **do you ~ go?** você já foi alguma vez?, vais alguma vez? **the best I ~ saw** o melhor que já vi. **~ since** adv desde então ▢ prep desde ▢ conj desde que. **~ so** (colloq) muitíssimo, tão. **hardly ~** quase nunca

evergreen /ˈevəgriːn/ n sempre-verde f, planta f de folhas persistentes ▢ a persistente

everlasting /ˈevəlɑːstɪŋ/ a eterno

every /ˈevrɪ/ a cada. **~ now and then** de vez em quando, volta e meia. **~ one** cada um. **~ other day** dia sim dia não, de dois em dois dias. **~ three days** de três em três dias

everybody /ˈevrɪbɒdɪ/ pron todo mundo, todos

everyday /ˈevrɪdeɪ/ a cotidiano, (P) quotidiano, diário; (common) do dia a dia, vulgar

everyone /ˈevrɪwʌn/ pron todo mundo, todos

everything /ˈevrɪθɪŋ/ pron tudo

everywhere /ˈevrɪweə(r)/ adv (position) em todo lugar, em toda parte; (direction) a todo lugar, a toda parte

evict /ɪˈvɪkt/ vt expulsar, despejar. **~ion** /-ʃn/ n despejo m

evidence /ˈevɪdəns/ n evidência f; (proof) prova f; (testimony) testemunho m, depoimento m. **~ of** sinal de. **give ~** testemunhar. **in ~** em evidência

evident /ˈevɪdənt/ a evidente. **~ly** adv evidentemente

evil /ˈiːvl/ a mau ▢ n mal m

evo|ke /ɪˈvəʊk/ vt evocar. **~cative** /ɪˈvɒkətɪv/ a evocativo

evolution /iːvəˈluːʃn/ n evolução f

evolve /ɪˈvɒlv/ vi evolucionar, evoluir ▢ vt desenvolver, produzir

ex- /eks/ pref ex-

exacerbate /ɪɡˈzæsəbeɪt/ vt exacerbar

exact /ɪɡˈzækt/ a exato, (P) exacto ▢ vt exigir (**from** de). **~ing** a exigente; (task) difícil. **~ly** adv exatamente, (P) exactamente

exaggerat|e /ɪɡˈzædʒəreɪt/ vt/i exagerar. **~ion** /-ˈreɪʃn/ n exagero m

exam /ɪɡˈzæm/ n (colloq) exame m

examination /ɪɡzæmɪˈneɪʃn/ n exame m; (jur) interrogatório m

examine /ɪɡˈzæmɪn/ vt examinar; (witness etc) interrogar. **~r** /-ə(r)/ n examinador m

example /ɪɡˈzɑːmpl/ n exemplo m. **for ~** por exemplo. **make an ~ of** castigar para servir de exemplo

exasperat|e /ɪɡˈzæspəreɪt/ vt exasperar. **~ion** /-ˈreɪʃn/ n exaspero m

excavat|e /ˈekskəveɪt/ vt escavar; (uncover) desenterrar. **~ion** /-ˈveɪʃn/ n escavação f

exceed /ɪkˈsiːd/ vt exceder; (speed limit) ultrapassar, exceder

excel /ɪkˈsel/ vi (pt **excelled**) distinguir-se ▢ vt superar, ultrapassar

excellen|t /ˈeksələnt/ a excelente. **~ce** n excelência f. **~tly** adv excelentemente

except /ɪkˈsept/ prep exceto, (P) excepto, fora ▢ vt excetuar, (P) exceptuar. **~ for** a não ser, menos, salvo. **~ing** prep à exceção de, (P) à excepção de. **~ion** /-ʃn/ n exceção f, (P) excepção f. **take ~ion to** (object to) achar inaceitável; (be offended by) achar ofensivo

exceptional /ɪkˈsepʃənl/ a excepcional. **~ly** adv excepcionalmente

excerpt /ˈeksɜːpt/ n trecho m, excerto m

excess[1] /ɪkˈses/ n excesso m

excess[2] /ˈekses/ a excedente, em excesso. **~ fare** excesso m, suplemento m. **~ luggage** excesso m de peso

excessive /ɪkˈsesɪv/ a excessivo. ~ly adv excessivamente

exchange /ɪksˈtʃeɪndʒ/ vt trocar □ n troca f; (of currency) câmbio m. **(telephone)** ~ central f telefônica, (P) telefónica. ~ **rate** taxa f de câmbio

excise /ˈeksaɪz/ n imposto m (indireto, (P) indirecto)

excit|e /ɪkˈsaɪt/ vt excitar; (rouse) despertar; (enthuse) entusiasmar. ~**able** a excitável. ~**ed** a excitado. **get** ~**ed** excitar-se, entusiasmar-se. ~**ement** n excitação f. ~**ing** a excitante, emocionante

exclaim /ɪkˈskleɪm/ vi exclamar

exclamation /ekskləˈmeɪʃn/ n exclamação f. ~ **mark** ponto m de exclamação

exclu|de /ɪkˈsklu:d/ vt excluir. ~**ding** prep excluído. ~**sion** /ɪkˈsklu:ʒn/ n exclusão f

exclusive /ɪkˈsklu:sɪv/ a (rights etc) exclusivo; (club etc) seleto, (P) selecto; (news item) (em) exclusivo. ~ **of** sem incluir. ~**ly** adv exclusivamente

excruciating /ɪkˈskru:ʃɪeɪtɪŋ/ a excruciante, atroz

excursion /ɪkˈskɜ:ʃn/ n excursão f

excus|e¹ /ɪkˈskju:z/ vt desculpar. ~**e me!** desculpe!, com licença! ~**e from** (exempt) dispensar de. ~**able** a desculpável

excuse² /ɪkˈskju:s/ n desculpa f

ex-directory /eksdɪˈrektərɪ/ a que não vem no anuário, (P) na lista

execute /ˈeksɪkju:t/ vt executar

execution /eksɪˈkju:ʃn/ n execução f

executive /ɪgˈzekjʊtɪv/ a & n executivo (m)

exemplary /ɪgˈzemplərɪ/ a exemplar

exemplify /ɪgˈzemplɪfaɪ/ vt exemplificar, ilustrar

exempt /ɪgˈzempt/ a isento (**from** de) □ vt dispensar, eximir. ~**ion** /-ʃn/ n isenção f

exercise /ˈeksəsaɪz/ n exercício m □ vt (powers, restraint etc) exercer; (dog) levar para passear □ vi fazer exercício. ~ **book** caderno m

exert /ɪgˈzɜ:t/ vt empregar, exercer. ~ **o.s.** esforçar-se, fazer um esforço. ~**ion** /-ʃn/ n esforço m

exhaust /ɪgˈzɔ:st/ vt esgotar □ n (auto) (tubo de) escape m. ~**ed** a esgotado, exausto. ~**ion** /-stʃən/ n esgotamento m, exaustão f

exhaustive /ɪgˈzɔ:stɪv/ a exaustivo, completo

exhibit /ɪgˈzɪbɪt/ vt exibir, mostrar; (thing, collection) expor □ n objeto m, (P) objecto m exposto

exhibition /eksɪˈbɪʃn/ n exposição f; (act of showing) demonstração f

exhilarat|e /ɪgˈzɪləreɪt/ vt regozijar; (invigorate) animar, estimular. ~**ion** /-ˈreɪʃn/ n animação f, alegria f

exhort /ɪgˈzɔ:t/ vt exortar

exile /ˈeksaɪl/ n exílio m; (person) exilado m □ vt exilar, desterrar

exist /ɪgˈzɪst/ vi existir. ~**ence** n existência f. **be in** ~**ence** existir

exit /ˈeksɪt/ n saída f

exonerate /ɪgˈzɒnəreɪt/ vt exonerar

exorbitant /ɪgˈzɔ:bɪtənt/ a exorbitante

exorcize /ˈeksɔ:saɪz/ vt esconjurar, exorcisar

exotic /ɪgˈzɒtɪk/ a exótico

expan|d /ɪkˈspænd/ vt/i expandir (-se); (extend) estender(-se), alargar(-se); (gas, liquid, metal) dilatar(-se). ~**sion** /ɪkˈspænʃn/ n expansão f; (extension) alargamento m; (of gas etc) dilatação f

expanse /ɪkˈspæns/ n extensão f

expatriate /eksˈpætrɪət/ a & n expatriado (m)

expect /ɪkˈspekt/ vt esperar; (suppose) crer, supor; (require) contar com, esperar; (baby) esperar. ~ **to do** contar fazer. ~**ation** /ekspekˈteɪʃn/ n expectativa f

expectan|t /ɪkˈspektənt/ a ~**t mother** gestante f. ~**cy** n expectativa f

expedient /ɪkˈspi:dɪənt/ a oportuno □ n expediente m

expedition /ekspɪˈdɪʃn/ n expedição f

expel /ɪkˈspel/ vt (pt **expelled**) expulsar; (gas, poison etc) expelir

expend /ɪkˈspend/ vt despender. ~**able** a descartável

expenditure /ɪkˈspendɪtʃə(r)/ n despesa f, gasto m

expense /ɪkˈspens/ n despesa f; (cost) custo m. **at sb's** ~ à custa de alg. **at the** ~ **of** (fig) à custa de

expensive /ɪkˈspensɪv/ a caro, dispendioso; (tastes, habits) de luxo

experience /ɪkˈspɪərɪəns/ n experiência f □ vt experimentar; (feel) sentir. ~**d** a experiente

experiment /ɪkˈsperɪmənt/ n experiência f □ vi /ɪkˈsperɪment/ fazer uma experiência. ~**al** /-ˈmentl/ a experimental

expert /ˈekspɜ:t/ a & n perito (m). ~**ly** adv com perícia, habilmente

expertise /ekspɜ:ˈti:z/ n perícia f, competência f

expir|e /ɪkˈspaɪə(r)/ vi expirar. ~**y** n fim m de prazo, expiração f

expl|ain /ɪkˈspleɪn/ vt explicar. ~**anation** /ekspləˈneɪʃn/ n explicação f. ~**anatory** /ɪkˈsplæ-nətrɪ/ a explicativo

expletive /ɪk'spli:tɪv/ n imprecação f, praga f

explicit /ɪk'splɪsɪt/ a explícito

explo|de /ɪk'spləʊd/ vt/i (fazer) explodir. ~**sion** /ɪk'spləʊʒn/ n explosão f. ~**sive** a & n explosivo (m)

exploit[1] /'eksplɔɪt/ n façanha f

exploit[2] /ɪk'splɔɪt/ vt explorar. ~**ation** /eksplɔɪ'teɪʃn/ n exploração f

exploratory /ɪk'splɒrətrɪ/ a exploratório; (talks) preliminar

explor|e /ɪk'splɔ:(r)/ vt explorar; (fig) examinar. ~**ation** /eksplə'reɪʃn/ n exploração f. ~**er** n explorador m

exponent /ɪk'spəʊnənt/ n (person) expoente mf; (math) expoente m

export[1] /ɪk'spɔ:t/ vt exportar. ~**er** n exportador m

export[2] /'ekspɔ:t/ n exportação f. ~**s** npl exportações fpl

expos|e /ɪk'spəʊz/ vt expor; (disclose) revelar; (unmask) desmascarar. ~**ure** /-ʒə(r)/ n exposição f; (cold) frio m

expound /ɪk'spaʊnd/ vt explanar, expor

express[1] /ɪk'spres/ a expresso, categórico; (mail) expresso □ n (train) rápido m, expresso m. ~**ly** adv expressamente

express[2] /ɪk'spres/ vt exprimir. ~**ion** /-ʃn/ n expressão f. ~**ive** a expressivo

expulsion /ɪk'spʌlʃn/ n expulsão f

exquisite /'ekskwɪzɪt/ a requintado

extempore /ek'stempərɪ/ a improvisado □ adv de improviso, sem preparação prévia

exten|d /ɪk'stend/ vt (stretch) estender; (enlarge) aumentar, ampliar; (prolong) prolongar; (grant) oferecer □ vi (stretch) estender-se; (in time) prolongar-se. ~**sion** /ɪk'stenʃn/ n (incl phone) extensão f; (of deadline) prorrogação f; (building) anexo m

extensive /ɪk'stensɪv/ a extenso; (damage, study) vasto. ~**ly** adv muito

extent /ɪk'stent/ n extensão f; (degree) medida f. **to some** ~ até certo ponto, em certa medida. **to such an** ~ **that** a tal ponto que

exterior /ɪk'stɪərɪə(r)/ a & n exterior (m)

exterminat|e /ɪk'stɜ:mɪneɪt/ vt exterminar. ~**ion** /-'neɪʃn/ n exterminação f, extermínio m

external /ɪk'stɜ:nl/ a externo. ~**ly** adv exteriormente

extinct /ɪk'stɪŋkt/ a extinto. ~**ion** /-ʃn/ n extinção f

extinguish /ɪk'stɪŋgwɪʃ/ vt extinguir, apagar. ~**er** n extintor m

extol /ɪk'stəʊl/ vt (pt **extolled**) exaltar, elogiar, louvar

extort /ɪk'stɔ:t/ vt extorquir (**from** a). ~**ion** /-ʃn/ n extorsão f

extortionate /ɪk'stɔ:ʃənət/ a exorbitante

extra /'ekstrə/ a extra, adicional □ adv extra, excepcionalmente. ~ **strong** extra-forte □ n extra m; (cine, theat) extra mf, figurante mf. ~ **time** (football) prorrogação f

extra- /'ekstrə/ pref extra-

extract[1] /ɪk'strækt/ vt extrair; (promise, tooth) arrancar; (fig) obter. ~**ion** /-ʃn/ n extração f, (P) extracção f; (descent) origem f

extract[2] /'ekstrækt/ n extrato m, (P) extracto m

extradit|e /'ekstrədaɪt/ vt extraditar. ~**ion** /-'dɪʃn/ n extradição f

extramarital /ekstrə'mærɪtl/ a extraconjugal, extramatrimonial

extraordinary /ɪk'strɔ:dnrɪ/ a extraordinário

extravagan|t /ɪk'strævəgənt/ a extravagante; (wasteful) esbanjador. ~**ce** n extravagância f; (wastefulness) esbanjamento m

extrem|e /ɪk'stri:m/ a & n extremo (m). ~**ely** adv extremamente. ~**ist** n extremista mf

extremity /ɪk'stremətɪ/ n extremidade f

extricate /'ekstrɪkeɪt/ vt desembaraçar, livrar

extrovert /'ekstrəvɜ:t/ n extrovertido m

exuberan|t /ɪg'zju:bərənt/ a exuberante. ~**ce** n exuberância f

exude /ɪg'zju:d/ vt (charm etc) destilar, ressumar, (P) transpirar

exult /ɪg'zʌlt/ vi exultar

eye /aɪ/ n olho m □ vt (pt **eyed**, pres p **eyeing**) olhar. **keep an** ~ **on** vigiar. **see** ~ **to** ~ concordar inteiramente. ~-**opener** n revelação f. ~-**shadow** n sombra f

eyeball /'aɪbɔ:l/ n globo m ocular

eyebrow /'aɪbraʊ/ n sobrancelha f

eyelash /'aɪlæʃ/ n pestana f

eyelid /'aɪlɪd/ n pálpebra f

eyesight /'aɪsaɪt/ n vista f

eyesore /'aɪsɔ:(r)/ n monstruosidade f, horror m

eyewitness /'aɪwɪtnɪs/ n testemunha f ocular

Ff

fable /'feɪbl/ n fábula f

fabric /'fæbrɪk/ n tecido m; (*structure*) edifício m

fabricat|e /'fæbrɪkeɪt/ vt fabricar; (*invent*) urdir, inventar. ~ion /-'keɪʃn/ n fabrico m; (*invention*) invenção f

fabulous /'fæbjʊləs/ a fabuloso

façade /fə'sɑːd/ n fachada f

face /feɪs/ n face f, cara f, rosto m; (*expression*) face f; (*grimace*) careta f; (*of clock*) mostrador m □ vt (*look towards*) encarar; (*confront*) enfrentar □ vi (*be opposite*) estar de frente para. ~ up to enfrentar. ~ to face cara a cara, frente a frente. in the ~ of em vista de. on the ~ of it a julgar pelas aparências. pull ~s fazer caretas. ~-cloth n toalha f de rosto, (P) toalhete m de rosto. ~-lift n cirurgia f plástica do rosto. ~-pack n máscara de beleza f

faceless /'feɪslɪs/ a (*fig*) anônimo, (P) anónimo

facet /'fæsɪt/ n faceta f

facetious /fə'siːʃəs/ a faceto; (*pej*) engraçadinho (*colloq pej*)

facial /'feɪʃl/ a facial

facile /'fæsaɪl/ a fácil; (*superficial*) superficial

facilitate /fə'sɪlɪteɪt/ vt facilitar

facilit|y /fə'sɪlətɪ/ n facilidade f. ~ies (*means*) facilidades fpl; (*installations*) instalações fpl

facing /'feɪsɪŋ/ n revestimento m

facsimile /fæk'sɪmɪlɪ/ n facsímile m

fact /fækt/ n fato m, (P) facto m. in ~, as a matter of ~ na realidade

faction /'fækʃn/ n facção f

factor /'fæktə(r)/ n fator m, (P) factor m

factory /'fæktərɪ/ n fábrica f

factual /'fæktʃʊəl/ a concreto, real

faculty /'fækltɪ/ n faculdade f

fad /fæd/ n capricho m, mania f; (*craze*) moda f

fade /feɪd/ vt/i (*colour*) desbotar; (*sound*) diminuir; (*disappear*) apagar(-se)

fag /fæg/ n (*colloq: chore*) estafa f; (*sl: cigarette*) cigarro m. ~ged a estafado

fail /feɪl/ vt/i falhar; (*in an examination*) reprovar; (*omit, neglect*) deixar de; (*comm*) falir □ n without ~ sem falta

failing /'feɪlɪŋ/ n deficiência f □ prep na falta de, à falta de

failure /'feɪljə(r)/ n fracasso m, (P) falhanço m; (*of engine*) falha f; (*of electricity*) falta f; (*person*) fracassado m.

faint /feɪnt/ a (-er, -est) (*indistinct*) apagado; (*weak*) fraco; (*giddy*) tonto □ vi desmaiar □ n desmaio m. ~-hearted a tímido. ~ly adv vagamente. ~ness n debilidade f; (*indistinctness*) apagado m

fair[1] /feə(r)/ n feira f. ~-ground n parque m de diversões, (P) largo m de feira

fair[2] /feə(r)/ a (-er, -est) (*hair*) louro; (*weather*) bom; (*of moderate quality*) razoável; (*just*) justo. ~ play jogo m limpo, fair play m. ~ly adv razoavelmente. ~ness n justiça f

fairy /'feərɪ/ n fada f. ~ story, ~ tale conto m de fadas

faith /feɪθ/ n fé f; (*religion*) religião f; (*loyalty*) lealdade f. in good ~ de boa fé, (P) à boa fé. ~-healer n curandeiro m

faithful /'feɪθfl/ a fiel. ~ly adv fielmente. yours ~ly atenciosamente. ~ness n fidelidade f

fake /feɪk/ n (*thing*) imitação f; (*person*) impostor m □ a falsificado □ vt falsificar; (*pretend*) simular, fingir

falcon /'fɔːlkən/ n falcão m

fall /fɔːl/ vi (*pt* fell, *pp* fallen) cair □ n quedas f; (*Amer: autumn*) outono m. ~s npl (*waterfall*) queda-d'água f. ~ back bater em retirada. ~ back on recorrer a. ~ behind atrasar-se (with em). ~ down or off cair. ~ flat falhar, não resultar. ~ flat on one's face estatelar-se. ~ for (*a trick*) cair em, deixar-se levar por; (*colloq: a person*) apaixonar-se por, ficar caído por (*colloq*). ~ in (*roof*) ruir; (*mil*) alinhar-se, pôr-se em forma. ~ out zangar-se (with com). ~-out n poeira f radioativa, (P) radioactiva. ~ through (*of plans*) falhar

fallac|y /'fæləsɪ/ n falácia f, engano m. ~ious /fə'leɪʃəs/ a errôneo

fallen /'fɔːlən/ *see* fall

fallible /'fæləbl/ a falível

fallow /'fæləʊ/ a (*of ground*) de pousio; (*uncultivated*) inculto

false /fɔːls/ a falso. ~ teeth dentadwa f. ~ly adv falsamente. ~ness n falsidade f

falsehood /'fɔːlshʊd/ n falsidade f, mentira f

falsify /'fɔːlsɪfaɪ/ vt (*pt* -fied) falsificar; (*a story*) deturpar

falter /'fɔːltə(r)/ vi vacilar; (*of the voice*) hesitar

fame /feɪm/ n fama f. ~d a afamado

familiar /fə'mɪlɪə(r)/ a familiar; (*intimate*) íntimo. **be ~ with** estar familiarizado com

familiarity /fəmɪlɪ'ærɪtɪ/ n familiaridade f

familiarize /fə'mɪlɪəraɪz/ vt familiarizar (**with/to** com); (*make well known*) tornar conhecido

family /'fæməlɪ/ n família f. **~ doctor** médico m da familia. **~ tree** árvore f genealógica

famine /'fæmɪn/ n fome f

famished /'fæmɪʃt/ a esfomeado, faminto. **be ~** (*colloq*) estar morrendo de fome, (*P*) estar a morrer de fome

famous /'feɪməs/ a famoso

fan[1] /fæn/ n (*in the hand*) leque m; (*mechanical*) ventilador m, (*P*) ventoínha f □ vt (*pt* fanned) abanar; (*a fire; fig*) atiçar □ vi **~ out** abrir-se em leque. **~ belt** correia f da ventoínhas

fan[2] /fæn/ n (*colloq*) fã mf. **~ mail** correio m de fãs

fanatic /fə'nætɪk/ n fanático m. **~al** a fanático. **~ism** /-sɪzəm/ n fanatismo m

fanciful /'fænsɪfl/ a fantasioso, fantasista

fancy /'fænsɪ/ n fantasia f; (*liking*) gosto m □ a extravagante, fantástico; (*of buttons etc*) de fantasia; (*of prices*) exorbitante □ vt imaginar; (*colloq: like*) gostar de; (*colloq: want*) apetecer. **it took my ~** gostei disso, (*P*) deu-me no gosto. **a passing ~** um entusiasmo passageiro. **~ dress** traje m fantasia, (*P*) trajo m de fantasia

fanfare /'fænfeə(r)/ n fanfarra f

fang /fæŋ/ n presa f, dente m canino

fantastic /fæn'tæstɪk/ a fantástico

fantas|y /'fæntəsɪ/ n fantasia f. **~ize** vt fantasiar, imaginar

far /fɑː(r)/ adv longe; (*much, very*) muito □ a distante, longínquo; (*end, side*) outro. **~ away, ~ off** ao longe. **as ~ as** (*up to*) até. **as ~ as I know** tanto quanto saiba. **the F~ East** o Extremo-Oriente m. **~-away** a distante, longínquo. **~-fetched** a forçado; (*unconvincing*) pouco plausível. **~-reaching** a de grande alcance

farc|e /fɑːs/ n farsa f. **~ical** a de farsa; ridículo

fare /feə(r)/ n preço m da passagem; (*in taxi*) tarifa f, preço m da corrida; (*passenger*) passageiro m; (*food*) comida f □ vi (*get on*) dar-se

farewell /feə'wel/ int & n adeus (m)

farm /fɑːm/ n quinta f, fazenda f □ vt cultivar □ vi ser fazendeiro, (*P*) lavrador. **~ out** (*of work*) delegar a tarefeiros. **~-hand** n trabalhador m

rural. **~er** n fazendeiro m, (*P*) lavrador m. **~ing** n agricultura f, lavoura f

farmhouse /'fɑːmhaʊs/ n casa f da fazenda, (*P*) quinta f

farmyard /'fɑːmjɑːd/ n quintal de fazenda m, (*P*) pátio m de quinta

farth|er /'fɑːðə(r)/ adv mais longe □ a mais distante. **~est** adv mais longe □ a o mais distante

fascinat|e /'fæsɪneɪt/ vt fascinar. **~ion** /-'neɪʃn/ n fascínio m, fascinação f

fascis|t /'fæʃɪst/ n fascista mf. **~m** /-zəm/ n fascismo m

fashion /'fæʃn/ n moda f; (*manner*) maneira f □ vt amoldar, (*P*) moldar. **~able** a na moda, (*P*) à moda. **~ably** adv na moda, (*P*) à moda

fast[1] /fɑːst/ a (**-er, -est**) rápido; (*colour*) fixo, que não desbota □ adv depressa; (*firmly*) firmemente. **be ~** (*of clock*) adiantar-se, estar adiantado. **~ asleep** profundamente adormecido, ferrado no sono. **~ food** n fast-food f

fast[2] /fɑːst/ vi jejuar □ n jejum m

fasten /'fɑːsn/ vt/i prender; (*door, window*) fechar(-se); (*seat-belt*) apertar. **~er, ~ing** ns fecho m

fastidious /fə'stɪdɪəs/ a exigente

fat /fæt/ n gordura f □ a (**fatter, fattest**) gordo. **~ness** n gordura f

fatal /'feɪtl/ a fatal. **~ injuries** ferimentos mpl mortais. **~ity** /fə'tælətɪ/ n fatalidade f. **~ly** adv fatalmente, mortalmente

fate /feɪt/ n (*destiny*) destino m; (*one's lot*) destino m, sorte f. **~ful** a fatídico

fated /'feɪtɪd/ a predestinado; (*doomed*) condenado (**to,** a)

father /'fɑːðə(r)/ n pai m □ vt gerar. **~-in-law** n (*pl* **~s-in-law**) sogro m. **~ly** a paternal

fathom /'fæðəm/ n braça f □ vt **~ (out)** (*comprehend*) compreender

fatigue /fə'tiːg/ n fadiga f □ vt fatigar

fatten /'fætn/ vt/i engordar. **~ing** a que engorda

fatty /'fætɪ/ a (**-ier, -iest**) gorduroso; (*tissue*) adiposo

fault /fɔːlt/ n defeito m, falha f; (*blame*) falta f, culpa f; (*geol*) falha f. **at ~** culpado. **it's your ~** é culpa sua. **~less** a impecável. **~y** a defeituoso

favour /'feɪvə(r)/ n favor m □ vt favorecer; (*prefer*) preferir. **do sb a ~** fazer um favor a alg. **~able** a favorável. **~ably** adv favoravelmente

favourit|e /'feɪvərɪt/ a & n favorito (m). **~ism** /-ɪzəm/ n favoritismo m

fawn[1] /fɔːn/ n cervo m novo □ a (*colour*) castanho claro

fawn[2] /fɔːn/ vi **~ on** adular, bajular

fax /fæks/ n fax m, fac-símile m ▢ vt
mandar um fax. **∼ machine** fax m

fear /fɪə(r)/ n medo m, receio m, temor m;
(*likelihood*) perigo m ▢ vt recear, ter
medo de. **for ∼ of/that** com medo
de/que. **∼ful** a (*terrible*) medonho;
(*timid*) medroso, receoso. **∼less** a
destemido, intrépido

feasib|le /ˈfiːzəbl/ a factível, praticável;
(*likely*) plausível. **∼ility** /-ˈbɪlətɪ/ n
possibilidade f; (*plausibility*)
plausibilidade f

feast /fiːst/ n festim m; (*relig; fig*) festa f
▢ vt/i festejar; (*eat and drink*)
banquetear-se. **∼ on** regalar-se com

feat /fiːt/ n feito m, façanha f

feather /ˈfeðə(r)/ n pena, pluma f

feature /ˈfiːtʃə(r)/ n feição f, traço m;
(*quality*) característica f; (*film*) longa
metragem f; (*article*) artigo m em
destaque ▢ vt representar; (*film*) ter
como protagonista ▢ vi figurar

February /ˈfebruərɪ/ n Fevereiro m

fed /fed/ see **feed** ▢ a **be ∼ up** estar farto
(*collog*) (**with** de)

federa|l /ˈfedərəl/ a federal. **∼tion**
/-ˈreɪʃn/ n federação f

fee /fiː/ n preço m. **∼(s)** (*of doctor, lawyer
etc*) honorários mpl; (*member's
subscription*) quota f; (*univ*) (P)
propinas fpl; (*enrolment/registration*)
matrícula f; **school ∼s** mensalidades
fpl escolares, (P) mensalidades fpl

feeble /ˈfiːbl/ a (-er, -est) débil, fraco.
∼-minded a débil mental, (P)
deficiente

feed /fiːd/ vt (*pt* fed) alimentar, dar de
comer a; (*suckle*) alimentar; (*supply*)
alimentar, abastecer ▢ vi alimentar-se
▢ n comida f; (*breast-feeding*) mamada
f; (*mech*) alimentação f

feedback /ˈfiːdbæk/ n reação f, (P)
reacção f; (*electr*) regeneração f

feel /fiːl/ vt (*pt* felt) sentir; (*touch*)
apalpar, tatear ▢ vi (*tired, lonely etc*)
sentir-se. **∼ hot/thirsty** ter calor/sede.
∼ as if ter a impressão (de) que. **∼ like**
ter vontade de

feeler /ˈfiːlə(r)/ n antena f

feeling /ˈfiːlɪŋ/ n sentimento m;
(*physical*) sensação f

feet /fiːt/ see **foot**

feign /feɪn/ vt fingir

feline /ˈfiːlaɪn/ a felino

fell[1] /fel/ vt abater, derrubar

fell[2] /fel/ see **fall**

fellow /ˈfeləʊ/ n companheiro m,
camarada m; (*of society, college*) membro
m; (*collog*) cara m, (P) tipo m (*collog*).
∼-traveller n companheiro m de
viagem. **∼ -ship** n companheirismo m,
camaradagem f; (*group*) associação f

felt[1] /felt/ n feltro m

felt[2] /felt/ see **feel**

female /ˈfiːmeɪl/ a (*animal etc*) fêmea f;
(*voice, sex etc*) feminino ▢ n mulher f;
(*animal*) fêmea f

feminin|e /ˈfemənɪn/ a & n feminino (m).
∼ity /-ˈnɪnətɪ/ n feminilidade f

feminist /ˈfemɪnɪst/ n feminista mf

fenc|e /fens/ n tapume m, cerca f ▢ vt
cercar ▢ vi esgrimir. **∼er** n esgrimista
mf. **∼ing** n esgrima f; (*fences*)
tapume m

fend /fend/ vi **∼ for o.s.** defender-se,
virar-se (*collog*), governar-se ▢ vt
∼ off defender-se de

fender /ˈfendə(r)/ n guarda-fogo m;
(*Amer: mudguard*) pára-lama m,
guarda-lama m, (P) pára-choques m

fennel /ˈfenl/ n (*herb*) funcho m, erva-
doce f

ferment[1] /fəˈment/ vt/i fermentar; (*excite*)
excitar. **∼ation** /fɜːmenˈteɪʃn/ n
fermentação f

ferment[2] /ˈfɜːment/ n fermento m; (*fig*)
efervescência f

fern /fɜːn/ n feto m

feroc|ious /fəˈrəʊʃəs/ a feroz. **∼ity**
/-ˈrɒsətɪ/ n ferocidade f

ferret /ˈferɪt/ n furão m ▢ vi (*pt* ferreted)
caçar com furões ▢ vt **∼ out**
desenterrar

ferry /ˈferɪ/ n barco m de travessia,
ferry(-boat) m ▢ vt transportar

fertil|e /ˈfɜːtaɪl/ a fértil, fecundo. **∼ity**
/fəˈtɪlətɪ/ n fertilidade f, fecundidade f.
∼ize /-əlaɪz/ vt fertilizar, fecundar

fertilizer /ˈfɜːtəlaɪzə(r)/ n adubo m,
fertilizante m

fervent /ˈfɜːvənt/ a fervoroso

fervour /ˈfɜːvə(r)/ n fervor m, ardor m

fester /ˈfestə(r)/ vt/i infectar; (*fig*)
envenenar

festival /ˈfestɪvl/ n festival m; (*relig*)
festa f

festiv|e /ˈfestɪv/ a festivo. **∼e season**
período m das festas. **∼ity** /feˈstɪvətɪ/ n
festividade f, regozijo m. **∼ities** festas
fpl, festividades fpl

festoon /feˈstuːn/ vt engrinaldar

fetch /fetʃ/ vt (*go for*) ir buscar; (*bring*)
trazer; (*be sold for*) vender-se por, render

fetching /ˈfetʃɪŋ/ a atraente

fête /feɪt/ n festa for feira f de caridade
ao ar livre ▢ vt festejar

fetish /ˈfetɪʃ/ n fetiche m, ídolo m;
(*obsession*) mania f

fetter /ˈfetə(r)/ vt agrilhoar. **∼s** npl ferros
mpl, grilhões mpl, grilhetas fpl

feud /fjuːd/ n discórdia f, inimizade f.
∼al a feudal

fever /ˈfiːvə(r)/ n febre f. **∼ish** a febril

few /fju:/ *a & n* poucos (*mpl*). ∼ **books** poucos livros. **they are** ∼ são poucos. **a** ∼ *a* alguns (*mpl*). **a good** ∼, **quite a** ∼ bastantes. ∼**er** *a & n* menos (de). **they were** ∼**er** eram menos numerosos. ∼**est** *a & n* o menor número (de)

fiancé /fɪ'ɑnseɪ/ *n* noivo *m*. ∼**e** *n* noiva *f*

fiasco /fɪ'æskəʊ/ *n* (*pl* -**os**) fiasco *m*

fib /fɪb/ *n* lorota *f*, cascata *f*, peta *f*, (*P*) mentira *f* □ *vi* (*pt* **fibbed**) mentir

fibre /'faɪbə(r)/ *n* fibra *f*

fibreglass /'faɪbəglɑ:s/ *n* fibra *f* de vidro

fickle /'fɪkl/ *a* leviano, inconstante

fiction /'fɪkʃn/ *n* ficção *f*. **(works of)** ∼ romances *mpl*, obras *fpl* de ficção. ∼**al** *a* de ficção, fictício

fictitious /fɪk'tɪʃəs/ *a* fictício

fiddle /'fɪdl/ *n* (*colloq*) violino *m*; (*sl: swindle*) trapaça *f* □ *vi* (*sl*) trapacear (*sl*) □ *vt* (*sl: falsify*) falsificar, cozinhar (*sl*). ∼ **with** (*colloq*) brincar com, remexer em, (*P*) estar a brincar com, estar a (re)mexer em. ∼**r** /-ə(r)/ *n* (*colloq*) violinista *m/f*

fidelity /fɪ'delətɪ/ *n* fidelidade *f*

fidget /'fɪdʒɪt/ *vi* (*pt* **fidgeted**) estar irrequieto, remexer-se. ∼ **with** remexer em. ∼**y** *a* irrequieto; (*impatient*) impaciente

field /fi:ld/ *n* campo *m* □ *vt/i* (*cricket*) (estar pronto para) apanhar ou interceptar a bola. ∼-**day** *n* grande dia *m*. ∼-**glasses** *npl* binóculo *m*. **F**∼ **Marshal** marechal-de-campo *m*

fieldwork /'fi:ldwɜ:k/ *n* trabalho *m* de campo; (*mil*) fortificação *f* de campanha

fiend /fi:nd/ *n* diabo *m*, demônio *m*, (*P*) demónio *m*. ∼**ish** *a* diabólico

fierce /fɪəs/ *a* (-**er**, -**est**) feroz; (*storm, attack*) violento; (*heat*) intenso, abrasador. ∼**ness** *n* ferocidade *f*; (*of storm, attack*) violência *f*; (*of heat*) intensidade *f*

fiery /'faɪərɪ/ *a* (-**ier**, -**iest**) ardente; (*temper, speech*) inflamado

fifteen /fɪf'ti:n/ *a & n* quinze (*m*). ∼**th** *a & n* décimo quinto (*m*)

fifth /fɪfθ/ *a & n* quinto (*m*)

fift|y /'fɪftɪ/ *a & n* cinqüenta (*m*), (*P*) cinquenta (*m*). ∼**y**-∼**y** *a* meias. ∼**ieth** *a & n* qüinquagésimo (*m*), (*P*) quinquagésimo (*m*)

fig /fɪg/ *n* figo *m*. ∼-**tree** *n* figueira *f*

fight /faɪt/ *vi* (*pt* **fought**) lutar, combater □ *vt* lutar contra, combater □ *n* luta *f*; (*quarrel, brawl*) briga *f*. ∼ **over sth** lutar por alg coisa. ∼ **shy of** esquivar-se de, fugir de. ∼**er** *n* lutador *m*; (*mil*) combatente *mf*; (*plane*) caça *m*. ∼**ing** *n* combate *m*

figment /'fɪgmənt/ *n* ∼ **of the imagination** fruto *m or* produto *m* da imaginação

figurative /'fɪgjərətɪv/ *a* figurado. ∼**ly** *adv* em sentido figurado

figure /'fɪgə(r)/ *n* (*number*) algarismo *m*; (*diagram, body*) figura *f*. ∼**s** *npl* (*arithmetic*) contas *fpl*, aritmética *f* □ *vt* imaginar, supor □ *vi* (*appear*) figurar (**in** em). ∼ **of speech** figura *f* de retórica. ∼ **out** compreender. ∼-**head** *n* figura *f* de proa; (*pej: person*) testa-de-ferro *m*, chefe *m* nominal

filament /'fɪləmənt/ *n* filamento *m*

fil|e¹ /faɪl/ *n* (*tool*) lixa *f*, lima *f* □ *vt* lixar, limar. ∼**ings** *npl* limalha *f*

fil|e² /faɪl/ *n* fichário *m*, (*P*) dossier *m*; (*box, drawer*) fichário *m*, (*P*) ficheiro *m*; (*comput*) arquivo *m*; (*line*) fila *f* □ *vt* arquivar □ *vi* ∼**e (past)** desfilar, marchar em fila. ∼**e in/out** entrar/sair em fila. **(in) single** ∼**e** (em) fila indiana. ∼**ing cabinet** fichário *m*, (*P*) ficheiro *m*

fill /fɪl/ *vt/i* encher(-se); (*vacancy*) preencher □ *n* **eat one's** ∼ comer o que quiser. **have one's** ∼ estar farto. ∼ **in** (*form*) preencher. ∼ **out** (*get fat*) engordar. ∼ **up** encher até cima; (*auto*) encher o tanque

fillet /'fɪlɪt/ *n* (*meat, fish*) filé *m*, (*P*) filete *m* □ *vt* (*pt* **filleted**) (*meat, fish*) cortar em filés, (*P*) filetes

filling /'fɪlɪŋ/ *n* recheio *m*; (*of tooth*) obturação *f*, (*P*) chumbo *m*. ∼ **station** posto *m* de gasolina

film /fɪlm/ *n* filme *m* □ *vt/i* filmar. ∼ **star** estrela *f or* vedete *f or* (*P*) vedeta *f* de cinema, astro *m*

filter /'fɪltə(r)/ *n* filtro *m* □ *vt/i* filtrar(-se). ∼ **coffee** café *m* filtro. ∼-**tip** *n* cigarro *m* com filtro

filth /fɪlθ/ *n* imundície *f*; (*fig*) obscenidade *f*. ∼**y** *a* imundo; (*fig*) obsceno

fin /fɪn/ *n* barbatana *f*

final /'faɪnl/ *a* final; (*conclusive*) decisivo □ *n* (*sport*) final *f*. ∼**s** *npl* (*exams*) finais *fpl*. ∼**ist** *n* finalista *mf*. ∼**ly** *adv* finalmente, por fim; (*once and for all*) definitivamente

finale /fɪ'nɑ:lɪ/ *n* final *m*

finalize /'faɪnəlaɪz/ *vt* finalizar

financ|e /'faɪnæns/ *n* finança(s) *f* (*pl*) □ *a* financeiro □ *vt* financiar. ∼**ier** /-'nænsɪə(r)/ *n* financeiro *m*

financial /faɪ'nænʃl/ *a* financeiro. ∼**ly** *adv* financeiramente

find /faɪnd/ *vt* (*pt* **found**) (*sth lost*) achar, encontrar; (*think*) achar; (*discover*) descobrir; (*jur*) declarar □ *n* achado *m*.

f

~ **out** *vt* apurar, descobrir □ *vi* informar-se (**about** sobre)

fine[1] /fam/ *n* multa *f* □ *vt* multar

fine[2] /fam/ *a* (**-er, -est**) fino; (*splendid*) belo, lindo □ *adv* (muito) bem; (*small*) fino, fininho. ~ **arts** belas artes *fpl*. ~ **weather** bom tempo. ~**ly** *adv* lindamente; (*cut*) fininho, aos bocadinhos

finesse /fi'nes/ *n* finura *f*, sutileza *f*

finger /'fɪŋɡə(r)/ *n* dedo *m* □ *vt* apalpar. ~**-mark** *n* dedada *f*. ~**-nail** *n* unha *f*

fingerprint /'fɪŋɡəprɪnt/ *n* impressão *f* digital

fingertip /'fɪŋɡətɪp/ *n* ponta *f* do dedo

finicky /'fɪnɪkɪ/ *a* meticuloso, miudinho

finish /'fɪnɪʃ/ *vt/i* acabar, terminar □ *n* fim *m*; (*of race*) chegada *f*; (*on wood, clothes*) acabamento *m*. ~ **doing** acabar de fazer. ~ **up doing** acabar por fazer. ~ **up in** ir parar a, acabar em

finite /'famaɪt/ *a* finito

Fin|land /'fɪnlənd/ *n* Finlândia *f*. ~**n** *n* finlandês *m*. ~**nish** *a & n* (*lang*) finlandês (*m*)

fir /fɜː(r)/ *n* abeto *m*

fire /'faɪə(r)/ *n* fogo *m*; (*conflagration*) incêndio *m*; (*heater*) aquecedor *m* □ *vt* (*bullet, gun, etc*) disparar; (*dismiss*) despedir; (*fig: stimulate*) inflamar □ *vi* atirar, fazer fogo (**at** sobre). **on** ~ em chamas. **set** ~ **to** pôr fogo em. ~**-alarm** *n* alarme *m* de incêndio. ~ **brigade** bombeiros *mpl*. ~**-engine** *n* carro *m* de bombeiro, (*P*) da bomba. ~**-escape** *n* saída *f* de incêndio. ~ **extinguisher** *n* extintor *m* de incêndio. ~ **station** quartel *m* dos bombeiros

firearm /'faɪərɑːm/ *n* arma *f* de fogo

fireman /'faɪəmən/ *n* (*pl* **-men**) bombeiro *m*

fireplace /'faɪəpleɪs/ *n* chaminé *f*, lareira *f*

firewood /'faɪəwʊd/ *n* lenha *f*

firework /'faɪəwɜːk/ *n* fogo *m* de artifício

firing-squad /'faɪərɪŋskwɒd/ *n* pelotão *m* de execução

firm[1] /fɜːm/ *n* firma *f* comercial

firm[2] /fɜːm/ *a* (**-er, -est**) firme; (*belief*) firme, inabalável. ~**ly** *adv* firmemente. ~**ness** *n* firmeza *f*

first /fɜːst/ *a & n* primeiro (*m*); (*auto*) primeira (*f*) □ *adv* primeiro, em primeiro lugar. **at** ~ a princípio, no início. ~ **of all** antes de mais nada. **for the** ~ **time** pela primeira vez. ~ **aid** primeiros socorros *mpl*. ~ **class** *a* de primeira classe. ~ **name** nome de batismo *m*, (*P*) baptismo *m*. ~**-rate** *a* excelente. ~**ly** *adv* primeiramente, em primeiro lugar

fiscal /'fɪskl/ *a* fiscal

fish /fɪʃ/ *n* (*pl usually invar*) peixe *m* □ *vt/i* pescar. ~ **out** (*colloq*) tirar. ~**ing** *n* pesca *f*. **go** ~**ing** ir pescar, (*P*) ir à pesca. ~**ing-rod** *n* vara *f* de pescar. ~**y** *a* de peixe; (*fig: dubious*) suspeito

fisherman /'fɪʃəmən/ *n* (*pl* **-men**) pescador *m*

fishmonger /'fɪʃmʌŋɡə(r)/ *n* dono *m*/empregado *m* de peixaria. ~**'s** (**shop**) peixaria *f*

fission /'fɪʃn/ *n* fissão *f*, cisão *f*

fist /fɪst/ *n* punho *m*, mão *f* fechada, (*P*) punho *m*

fit[1] /fɪt/ *n* acesso *m*, ataque *m*; (*of generosity*) rasgo *m*

fit[2] /fɪt/ *a* (**fitter, fittest**) de boa saúde, em forma; (*proper*) próprio; (*good enough*) em condições; (*able*) capaz □ *vt/i* (*pt* **fitted**) (*clothes*) assentar, ficar bem (**a**); (*into space*) caber; (*match*) ajustar(-se) (**a**); (*install*) instalar □ *n* **be a good** ~ assentar bem. **be a tight** ~ estar justo. ~ **out** equipar. ~**ted carpet** carpete *m*, (*P*) alcatifa *f*. ~**ness** *n* saúde *f*, (*P*) condição *f* física

fitful /'fɪtfl/ *a* intermitente

fitment /'fɪtmənt/ *n* móvel *m* de parede

fitting /'fɪtɪŋ/ *a* apropriado □ *n* (*clothes*) prova *f*. ~**s** (*fixtures*) instalações *fpl*; (*fitments*) mobiliário *m*. ~ **room** cabine *f*

five /faɪv/ *a & n* cinco (*m*)

fix /fɪks/ *vt* fixar; (*mend, prepare*) arranjar □ *n* **in a** ~ em apuros, (*P*) numa alhada. ~ **sb up with sth** conseguir alg coisa para alguém. ~**ed** *a* fixo

fixation /fɪk'seɪʃn/ *n* fixação *f*; (*obsession*) obsessão *f*

fixture /'fɪkstʃə(r)/ *n* equipamento *m*, instalação *f*; (*sport*) (data *f* marcada para) competição *f*

fizz /fɪz/ *vi* efervescer, borbulhar □ *n* efervescência *f*. ~**y** *a* gasoso

fizzle /'fɪzl/ *vi* ~ **out** (*plan etc*) acabar em nada *or* (*P*) em águas de bacalhau (*colloq*)

flab /flæb/ *n* (*colloq*) gordura *f*, banha *f* (*colloq*). ~**by** *a* flácido

flabbergasted /'flæbəɡɑːstɪd/ *a* (*colloq*) espantado, pasmado (*colloq*)

flag[1] /flæɡ/ *n* bandeira *f* □ *vt* (*pt* **flagged**) fazer sinal. ~ **down** fazer sinal para parar. ~**-pole** *n* mastro *m* (de bandeira)

flag[2] /flæɡ/ *vi* (*pt* **flagged**) (*droop*) cair, pender, tombar; (*of person*) esmorecer

flagrant /'fleɪɡrənt/ *a* flagrante

flagstone /'flæɡstəʊn/ *n* laje *f*

flair /fleə(r)/ *n* jeito *m*, habilidade *f*

flak|e /fleɪk/ n floco m; (paint) lasca f □ vi descamar-se, lascar-se. ~y a (paint) descamado, lascado

flamboyant /flæmˈbɔɪənt/ a flamejante; (showy) flamante, vistoso; (of manner) extravagante

flame /fleɪm/ n chama f, labareda f □ vi flamejar. **burst into** ~s incendiar-se

flamingo /fləˈmɪŋɡəʊ/ n (pl -os) flamingo m

flammable /ˈflæməbl/ a inflamável

flan /flæn/ n torta f, (P) tarte f

flank /flæŋk/ n flanco m □ vt flanquear

flannel /ˈflænl/ n flanela f; (for face) toalha f, (P) toalhete m de rosto

flap /flæp/ vt/i (pt flapped) bater □ vt ~ **its wings** bater as asas □ n (of table, pocket) aba f; (sl: panic) pânico m

flare /fleə(r)/ vi ~ **up** irromper em chamas; (of war) rebentar; (fig: of person) enfurecer-se □ n chamejar m; (dazzling light) clarão m; (signal) foguete m de sinalização. ~**d** a (skirt) évasé

flash /flæʃ/ vi brilhar subitamente; (on and off) piscar; (auto) fazer sinal com o pisca-pisca □ vt fazer brilhar; (send) lançar, dardejar; (flaunt) fazer alarde de, ostentar □ n clarão m, lampejo m; (photo) flash m. ~ **past** passar como uma bala, (P) passar como um bólide

flashback /ˈflæʃbæk/ n cena f retrospectiva, flashback m

flashlight /ˈflæʃlaɪt/ n lanterna f elétrica, (P) eléctrica

flashy /ˈflæʃɪ/ a espalhafatoso, que dá na vista

flask /flɑːsk/ n frasco m; (vacuum flask) garrafa f térmica, (P) garrafa f termos

flat /flæt/ a (**flatter, flattest**) plano, chato; (tyre) arriado, vazio; (battery) fraco; (refusal) categórico; (fare, rate) fixo; (monotonous) monótono; (mus) bemol; (out of tune) desafinado □ n apartamento m; (colloq: tyre) furo m no pneu; (mus) bemol m. ~ **out** (drive) em alta velocidade; (work) a dar tudo por tudo. ~**ly** adv categoricamente

flatter /ˈflætə(r)/ vt lisonjear, adular. ~**er** n lisonjeiro m, adulador m. ~**ing** a lisonjeiro, adulador. ~**y** n lisonja f

flatulence /ˈflætjʊləns/ n flatulência f

flaunt /flɔːnt/ vt/i pavonear(-se), ostentar

flavour /ˈfleɪvə(r)/ n sabor m (of a) □ vt dar sabor a, temperar. ~**ing** n aroma m sintético; (seasoning) tempero m

flaw /flɔː/ n falha f, imperfeição f. ~**ed** a imperfeito. ~**less** a perfeito

flea /fliː/ n pulga f

fled /fled/ see **flee**

fledged /fledʒd/ a **fully-**~ (fig) treinado, experiente

flee /fliː/ vi (pt fled) fugir □ vt fugir de

fleece /fliːs/ n lã f de carneiro, velo m □ vt (fig) esfolar, roubar

fleet /fliːt/ n (of warships) esquadra f; (of merchant ships, vehicles) frota f

fleeting /ˈfliːtɪŋ/ a curto, fugaz

Flemish /ˈflemɪʃ/ a & n (lang) flamengo (m)

flesh /fleʃ/ n carne f; (of fruit) polpa f. ~**y** a carnudo

flew /fluː/ see **fly**[2]

f

flex[1] /fleks/ vt flexionar

flex[2] /fleks/ n (electr) fio f flexível

flexib|le /ˈfleksəbl/ a flexível. ~**ility** /-ˈbɪlətɪ/ n flexibilidade f

flexitime /ˈfleksɪtaɪm/ n horário m flexível

flick /flɪk/ n (light blow) safanão m; (with fingertip) piparote m □ vt dar um safanão em; (with fingertip) dar um piparote a. ~-**knife** n navalha f de ponta e mola. ~ **through** folhear

flicker /ˈflɪkə(r)/ vi vacilar, oscilar, tremular □ n oscilação f, tremular m; (light) luz f oscilante

flier /ˈflaɪə(r)/ n = **flyer**

flies /flaɪz/ npl (of trousers) braguilha f

flight[1] /flaɪt/ n (flying) voo m. ~ **of stairs** lance m, (P) lanço m de escada. ~-**deck** n cabine f, (P) cabina f

flight[2] /flaɪt/ n (fleeing) fuga f. **put to** ~ pôr em fuga. **take** ~ pôr-se em fuga

flimsy /ˈflɪmzɪ/ a (-**ier**, -**iest**) (material) fino; (object) frágil; (excuse etc) fraco, esfarrapado

flinch /flɪntʃ/ vi (wince) retrair-se; (draw back) recuar; (hesitate) hesitar

fling /flɪŋ/ vt/i (pt flung) atirar(-se), arremessar(-se); (rush) precipitar-se

flint /flɪnt/ n sílex m; (for lighter) pedra f

flip /flɪp/ vt (pt flipped) fazer girar com o dedo e o polegar □ n pancadinha f. ~ **through** folhear

flippant /ˈflɪpənt/ a irreverente, petulante

flipper /ˈflɪpə(r)/ n (of seal) nadadeira f; (of swimmer) pé-de-pato m

flirt /flɜːt/ vt namoriscar, flertar, (P) flartar □ n namorador m, namoradeira f. ~**ation** /-ˈteɪʃn/ n namorico m, flerte m, (P) flirt m. ~**atious** a namorador m, namoradeira f

flit /flɪt/ vi (pt flitted) esvoaçar

float /fləʊt/ vt/i (fazer) flutuar; (company) lançar □ n bóia f; (low cart) carro m de alegórico

flock /flɒk/ n (of sheep; congregation) rebanho m; (of birds) bando m; (crowd) multidão f □ vi afluir, juntar-se

flog /flɒg/ *vt* (*pt* **flogged**) açoitar; (*sl: sell*) vender

flood /flʌd/ *n* inundação *f*, cheia *f*; (*of tears*) dilúvio *m* □ *vt* inundar, alagar □ *vi* estar inundado; (*river*) transbordar; (*fig: people*) afluir

floodlight /'flʌdlaɪt/ *n* projetor *m*, (P) projector *m*, holofote *m* □ *vt* (*pt* **floodlit**) iluminar

floor /flɔː(r)/ *n* chão *m*, soalho *m*; (*for dancing*) pista *f*; (*storey*) andar *m* □ *vt* assoalhar; (*baffle*) desconcertar, embatucar

flop /flɒp/ *vi* (*pt* **flopped**) (*drop*) (deixar-se) cair; (*move helplessly*) debater-se; (*sl: fail*) ser um fiasco □ *n* (*sl*) fiasco *m*. ~**py** *a* mole, tombado. ~**py (disk)** disquete *m*

floral /'flɔːrəl/ *a* floral

florid /'flɒrɪd/ *a* florido

florist /'flɒrɪst/ *n* florista *mf*

flounce /flaʊns/ *n* babado *m*, debrum *m*

flounder /'flaʊndə(r)/ *vi* esbracejar, debater-se; (*fig*) meter os pés pelas mãos

flour /'flaʊə(r)/ *n* farinha *f*. ~**y** *a* farinhento

flourish /'flʌrɪʃ/ *vi* florescer, prosperar □ *vt* brandir □ *n* floreado *m*; (*movement*) gesto *m* elegante. ~**ing** *a* próspero

flout /flaʊt/ *vt* escarnecer (de)

flow /fləʊ/ *vi* correr, fluir; (*traffic*) mover-se; (*hang loosely*) flutuar; (*gush*) jorrar □ *n* corrente *f*; (*of tide; fig*) enchente *f*. ~ **into** (*of river*) desaguar em. ~ **chart** organograma *m*, (P) organigrama *m*

flower /'flaʊə(r)/ *n* flor *f* □ *vi* florir, florescer. ~**bed** *n* canteiro *m*. ~**ed** *a* de flores, (P) florido, às flores. ~**y** *a* florido

flown /fləʊn/ *see* **fly**[2]

flu /fluː/ *n* (*colloq*) gripe *f*

fluctuat|e /'flʌktjʊeɪt/ *vi* flutuar, oscilar. ~**ion** /-'eɪʃn/ *n* flutuação *f*, oscilação *f*

flue /fluː/ *n* cano *m* de chaminé

fluen|t /'fluːənt/ *a* fluente. **be** ~**t (in a language)** falar correntemente (uma língua). ~**cy** *n* fluência *f*. ~**tly** *adv* fluentemente

fluff /flʌf/ *n* cotão *m*; (*down*) penugem *f* □ *vt* (*colloq: bungle*) estender-se em (*sl*), executar mal. ~**y** *a* penugento, fofo

fluid /'fluːɪd/ *a* & *n* fluido (*m*)

fluke /fluːk/ *n* bambúrrio (*colloq*) *m*, golpe *m* de sorte

flung /flʌŋ/ *see* **fling**

flunk /flʌŋk/ *vt/i* (*Amer colloq*) levar pau (*colloq*), (P) chumbar (*colloq*)

fluorescent /flʊə'resnt/ *a* fluorescente

fluoride /'flʊəraɪd/ *n* flúor *m*, fluor *m*

flurry /'flʌrɪ/ *n* rajada *f*, rabanada *f*, lufada *f*; (*fig*) atrapalhação *f*, agitação *f*

flush[1] /flʌʃ/ *vi* corar, ruborizar-se □ *vt* lavar com água, (P) lavar a jorros de água □ *n* rubor *m*, vermelhidão *f*; (*fig*) excitação *f*; (*of water*) jorro *m* □ *a* ~ **with** ao nível de, rente a. ~ **the toilet** dar descarga

flush[2] /flʌʃ/ *vt* ~ **out** desalojar

fluster /'flʌstə(r)/ *vt* atarantar, perturbar, enervar

flute /fluːt/ *n* flauta *f*

flutter /'flʌtə(r)/ *vi* esvoaçar; (*wings*) bater; (*heart*) palpitar □ *vt* bater. ~ **one's eyelashes** pestanejar □ *n* (*of wings*) batimento *m*; (*fig*) agitação *f*

flux /flʌks/ *n* **in a state of** ~ em mudança *f* contínua

fly[1] /flaɪ/ *n* mosca *f*

fly[2] /flaɪ/ *vi* (*pt* **flew**, *pp* **flown**) voar; (*passengers*) ir de/viajar de avião; (*rush*) correr □ *vt* pilotar; (*passengers, goods*) transportar por avião; (*flag*) hastear, (P) arvorar □ *n* (*of trousers*) braguilha *f*

flyer /'flaɪə(r)/ *n* aviador *m*; (*Amer: circular*) prospecto *m*

flying /'flaɪɪŋ/ *a* voador. **with** ~ **colours** com grande êxito, esplendidamente. ~ **saucer** disco *m* voador. ~ **start** bom arranque *m*. ~ **visit** visita *f* de médico

flyleaf /'flaɪliːf/ *n* (*pl* -**leaves**) guarda *f*, folha *f* em branco

flyover /'flaɪəʊvə(r)/ *n* viaduto *m*

foal /fəʊl/ *n* potro *m*

foam /fəʊm/ *n* espuma *f* □ *vi* espumar. ~ (**rubber**) *n* espuma *f* de borracha

fob /fɒb/ *vt* (*pt* **fobbed**) ~ **off** iludir, entreter com artifícios. ~ **off on** impingir a

focus /'fəʊkəs/ *n* (*pl* -**cuses** *or* -**ci** /-saɪ/) foco *m* □ *vt/i* (*pt* **focused**) focar; (*fig*) concentrar(-se). **in** ~ focado, em foco. **out of** ~ desfocado

fodder /'fɒdə(r)/ *n* forragem *f*

foetus /'fiːtəs/ *n* (*pl* -**tuses**) feto *m*

fog /fɒg/ *n* nevoeiro *m* □ *vt/i* (*pt* **fogged**) enevoar(-se). ~**horn** *n* sereia *f* de nevoeiro. ~**gy** *a* enevoado, brumoso. **it is** ~**gy** está nevoento

foible /'fɔɪbl/ *n* fraqueza *f*, ponto *m* fraco

foil[1] /fɔɪl/ *n* papel *m* de alumínio; (*fig*) contraste *m*

foil[2] /fɔɪl/ *vt* frustrar

foist /fɔɪst/ *vt* impingir (**on** a)

fold /fəʊld/ *vt/i* dobrar(-se); (*arms*) cruzar; (*colloq: fail*) falir □ *n* dobra *f*. ~**er** *n* pasta *f*; (*leaflet*) prospecto *m* (desdobrável). ~**ing** *a* dobrável, dobradiço

foliage /'fəʊlɪɪdʒ/ *n* folhagem *f*

folk /fəʊk/ *n* povo *m*. ~**s** (*family, people*) gente *f* (*colloq*) □ *a* folclórico, popular. ~**lore** *n* folclore *m*

follow /'fɒləʊ/ *vt/i* seguir. **it ~s that** quer dizer que. **~ suit** (*cards*) servir o naipe jogado; (*fig*) seguir o exemplo, fazer o mesmo. **~ up** (*letter etc*) dar seguimento a. **~er** *n* partidário *m*, seguidor *m*. **~ing** *n* partidários *mpl* □ *a* seguinte □ *prep* em seguimento a

folly /'fɒlɪ/ *n* loucura *f*

fond /fɒnd/ *a* (-er -est) carinhoso; (*hope*) caro. **be ~ of** gostar de, ser amigo de. **~ness** *n* (*for people*) afeição *f*; (*for thing*) gosto *m*

fondle /'fɒndl/ *vt* acariciar

font /fɒnt/ *n* pia *f* batismal, (*P*) baptismal

food /fu:d/ *n* alimentação *f*, comida *f*; (*nutrient*) alimento *m* □ *a* alimentar. **~ poisoning** envenenamento *m* alimentar

fool /fu:l/ *n* idiota *mf*, parvo *m* □ *vt* enganar □ *vi* **~ around** andar sem fazer nada

foolhardy /'fu:lha:dɪ/ *a* imprudente, atrevido

foolish /'fu:lɪʃ/ *a* idiota, parvo. **~ly** *adv* parvamente. **~ness** *n* idiotice *f*, parvoice *f*

foolproof /'fu:lpru:f/ *a* infalível

foot /fut/ *n* (*pl* **feet**) (*of person, bed, stairs*) pé *m*; (*of animal*) pata *f*; (*measure*) pé *m* (= 30,48 cm) □ *vt* **~ the bill** pagar a conta. **on ~** a pé. **on** *or* **to one's feet** de pé. **put one's ~ in it** fazer uma gafe. **to be under sb's feet** atrapalhar alg. **~-bridge** *n* passarela *f*

football /'futbɔ:l/ *n* bola *f* de futebol; (*game*) futebol *m*. **~ pools** loteria *f* esportiva, (*P*) totobola *m*. **~er** *n* futebolista *mf*, jogador *m* de futebol

foothills /'futhɪlz/ *npl* contrafortes *mpl*

foothold /'futhəʊld/ *n* ponto *m* de apoio

footing /'futɪŋ/ *n*: **firm ~** apoio seguro **on an equal ~** em pé de igualdade

footlights /'futlaɪts/ *npl* ribalta *f*

footnote /'futnəʊt/ *n* nota *f* de rodapé

footpath /'futpa:θ/ *n* (*pavement*) calçada *f*, (*P*) passeio *m*; (*in open country*) atalho *m*, caminho *m*

footprint /'futprɪnt/ *n* pegada *f*

footstep /'futstep/ *n* passo *m*

footwear /'futweə(r)/ *n* calçado *m*

for /fə(r)/; *emphatic* /fɔ:(r)/ *prep* para; (*in favour of; in place of*) por; (*during*) durante □ *conj* porque, visto que. **a liking ~** gosto por. **he has been away ~ two years** há dois anos que ele está fora. **~ ever** para sempre

forage /'fɒrɪdʒ/ *vi* forragear; (*rummage*) remexer à procura (de) □ *n* forragem *f*

forbade /fə'bæd/ *see* **forbid**

forbear /fɔ:'beə(r)/ *vt/i* (*pt* **forbore**, *pp* **forborne**) abster-se (**from** de). **~ance** *n* paciência *f*, tolerância *f*

forbid /fə'bɪd/ *vt* (*pt* **forbade**, *pp* **forbidden**) proibir. **you are ~den to smoke** você está proibido de fumar, (*P*) estás proibido de fumar. **~ding** *a* severo, intimidante

force /fɔ:s/ *n* força *f* □ *vt* forçar. **~ into** fazer entrar à força. **~ on** impor a. **come into ~** entrar em vigor. **the ~s** as Forças Armadas. **~d** *a* forçado. **~ful** *a* enérgico

force-feed /'fɔ:sfi:d/ *vt* (*pt* -**fed**) alimentar à força

forceps /'fɔ:seps/ *n* (*pl invar*) fórceps *m*

forcibl|e /'fɔ:səbl/ *a* convincente; (*done by force*) à força. **~y** *adv* à força

ford /fɔ:d/ *n* vau *m* □ *vt* passar a vau, vadear

fore /fɔ:(r)/ *a* dianteiro □ *n* **to the ~** em evidência

forearm /'fɔ:ra:m/ *n* antebraço *m*

foreboding /fɔ:'bəʊdɪŋ/ *n* pressentimento *m*

forecast /'fɔ:ka:st/ *vt* (*pt* **forecast**) prever □ *n* previsão *f*. **weather ~** boletim *m* meteorológico, previsão *f* do tempo

forecourt /'fɔ:kɔ:t/ *n* pátio *m* de entrada; (*of garage*) área *f* das bombas de gasolina

forefinger /'fɔ:fɪŋgə(r)/ *n* (dedo) indicador *m*

forefront /'fɔ:frʌnt/ *n* vanguarda *f*

foregone /'fɔ:gɒn/ *a* **~ conclusion** resultado *m* previsto

foreground /'fɔ:graʊnd/ *n* primeiro plano *m*

forehead /'fɒrɪd/ *n* testa *f*

foreign /'fɒrən/ *a* estrangeiro; (*trade*) externo; (*travel*) ao/no estrangeiro. **F~ Office** Ministério *m* dos Negócios Estrangeiros. **~er** *n* estrangeiro *m*.

foreman /'fɔ:mən/ *n* (*pl* **foremen**) contramestre *m*; (*of jury*) primeiro jurado *m*

foremost /'fɔ:məʊst/ *a* principal, primeiro □ *adv* **first and ~** antes de mais nada, em primeiro lugar

forename /'fɔ:neɪm/ *n* prenome *m*

forensic /fə'rensɪk/ *a* forense. **~ medicine** medicina *f* legal

forerunner /'fɔ:rʌnə(r)/ *n* precursor *m*

foresee /fɔ:'si:/ *vt* (*pt* -**saw**, *pp* -**seen**) prever. **~able** *a* previsível

foreshadow /fɔ:'ʃædəʊ/ *vt* prefigurar, pressagiar

foresight /'fɔ:saɪt/ *n* previsão *f*, previdência *f*

forest /'fɒrɪst/ *n* floresta *f*

forestall /fɔːˈstɔːl/ vt (do first) anteciparse a; (prevent) prevenir; (anticipate) antecipar

forestry /ˈfɒrɪstrɪ/ n silvicultura f

foretell /fɔːˈtel/ vt (pt **foretold**) predizer, profetizar

forever /fəˈrevə(r)/ adv (endlessly) constantemente

foreword /ˈfɔːwɜːd/ n prefácio m

forfeit /ˈfɔːfɪt/ n penalidade f, preço m; (in game) prenda f □ vt perder

forgave /fəˈɡeɪv/ see **forgive**

forge[1] /fɔːdʒ/ vi ~ **ahead** tomar a dianteira, avançar

forge[2] /fɔːdʒ/ n forja f □ vt (metal, friendship) forjar; (counterfeit) falsificar, forjar. ~**r** /-ə(r)/ n falsificador m, forjador m. ~**ry** /-ərɪ/ n falsificação f

forget /fəˈɡet/ vt/i (pt **forgot**, pp **forgotten**) esquecer. ~ **o.s.** portar-se com menos dignidade, esquecer-se de quem é. ~**-me-not** n miosótis m. ~**ful** a esquecido. ~**fulness** n esquecimento m

forgive /fəˈɡɪv/ vt (pt **forgave**, pp **forgiven**) perdoar (sb for sth alg coisa a alg). ~**ness** n perdão m

forgo /fɔːˈɡəʊ/ vt (pt **forwent**, pp **forgone**) renunciar a

fork /fɔːk/ n garfo m; (for digging etc) forquilha f; (in road) bifurcação f □ vi bifurcar. ~ **out** (sl) desembolsar. ~**-lift truck** empilhadeira f. ~**ed** a bifurcado; (lightning) em ziguezague

forlorn /fəˈlɔːn/ a abandonado, desolado

form /fɔːm/ n forma f; (document) impresso m, formulário m; (schol) classe f □ vt/i formar(-se)

formal /ˈfɔːml/ a formal; (dress) de cerimônia, (P) cerimónia. ~**ity** /-ˈmælətɪ/ n formalidade f. ~**ly** adv formalmente

format /ˈfɔːmæt/ n formato m □ vt (pl **formatted**) (disk) formatar

formation /fɔːˈmeɪʃn/ n formação f

former /ˈfɔːmə(r)/ a antigo; (first of two) primeiro. **the** ~ aquele. ~**ly** adv antigamente

formidable /ˈfɔːmɪdəbl/ a formidável, tremendo

formula /ˈfɔːmjʊlə/ n (pl -**ae** /-iː/or -**as**) fórmula f

formulate /ˈfɔːmjʊleɪt/ vt formular

forsake /fəˈseɪk/ vt (pt **forsook**, pp **forsaken**) abandonar

fort /fɔːt/ n (mil) forte m

forth /fɔːθ/ adv adiante, para a frente. **and so** ~ e assim por diante, etcetera. **go back and** ~ andar de trás para diante.

forthcoming /fɔːθˈkʌmɪŋ/ a que está para vir, próximo; (communicative) comunicativo, receptivo; (book) no prelo

forthright /ˈfɔːθraɪt/ a franco, direto, (P) directo

fortif|y /ˈfɔːtɪfaɪ/ vt fortificar. ~**ication** /-ɪˈkeɪʃn/ n fortificação f

fortitude /ˈfɔːtɪtjuːd/ n fortitude f, fortaleza f

fortnight /ˈfɔːtnaɪt/ n quinze dias mpl, (P) quinzena f. ~**ly** a quinzenal □ adv de quinze em quinze dias

fortress /ˈfɔːtrɪs/ n fortaleza f

fortuitous /fɔːˈtjuːɪtəs/ a fortuito, acidental

fortunate /ˈfɔːtʃənət/ a feliz, afortunado. **be** ~ ter sorte. ~**ly** adv felizmente

fortune /ˈfɔːtʃən/ n sorte f; (wealth) fortuna f. **have the good** ~ to ter a sorte de. ~**-teller** n cartomante mf

fort|y /ˈfɔːtɪ/ a & n quarenta (m). ~**ieth** a &n quadragésimo (m)

forum /ˈfɔːrəm/ n fórum m, foro m

forward /ˈfɔːwəd/ a (in front) dianteiro; (towards the front) para a frente; (advanced) adiantado; (pert) atrevido □ n (sport) atacante m, (P) avançado m □ adv ~(**s**) para a frente, para diante □ vt (letter) remeter; (goods) expedir; (fig: help) favorecer. **come** ~ apresentar-se. **go** ~ avançar. ~**ness** n adiantamento m; (pertness) atrevimento m

fossil /ˈfɒsl/ a & n fóssil (m)

foster /ˈfɒstə(r)/ vt fomentar; (child) criar. ~**-child** n filho m adotivo, (P) adoptivo. ~**-mother** n mãe f adotiva, (P) adoptiva

fought /fɔːt/ see **fight**

foul /faʊl/ a (-**er**, -**est**) infecto; (language) obsceno; (weather) mau □ n (football) falta f □ vt sujar, emporcalhar. ~**-mouthed** a de linguagem obscena. ~ **play** jogo m desleal; (crime) crime m

found[1] /faʊnd/ see **find**

found[2] /faʊnd/ vt fundar. ~**ation** /-ˈdeɪʃn/ n fundação f; (basis) fundamento m. ~**ations** npl (of building) alicerces mpl

founder[1] /ˈfaʊndə(r)/ n fundador m

founder[2] /ˈfaʊndə(r)/ vi afundar-se

foundry /ˈfaʊndrɪ/ n fundição f

fountain /ˈfaʊntɪn/ n fonte f. ~**-pen** n caneta-tinteiro f, (P) caneta f de tinta permanente

four /fɔː(r)/ a & n quatro (m). ~**fold** a quádruplo □ adv quadruplamente. ~**th** a & n quarto (m)

foursome /ˈfɔːsəm/ n grupo m de quatro pessoas

fourteen /fɔːˈtiːn/ a & n catorze (m). ~**th** a & n décimo quarto (m)

fowl /faʊl/ n ave f de capoeira

fox /fɒks/ n raposa f □ vt (colloq) mistificar, enganar. **be** ~**ed** ficar perplexo

foyer /ˈfɔɪeɪ/ n foyer m

fraction /ˈfrækʃn/ n fracção f, (P) fracção f; (small bit) bocadinho m, partícula f

fracture /ˈfræktʃə(r)/ n fratura f, (P) fractura f □ vt/i fraturar(-se), (P) fracturar(-se)

fragile /ˈfrædʒaɪl/ a frágil

fragment /ˈfrægmənt/ n fragmento m. ~**ary** /ˈfrægməntrɪ/ a fragmentário

fragran|t /ˈfreɪɡrənt/ a fragrante, perfumado. ~**ce** n fragrância f, perfume m

frail /freɪl/ a (-er, -est) frágil

frame /freɪm/ n (techn; of spectacles) armação f; (of picture) moldura f; (of window) caixilho m; (body) corpo m, (P) estrutura f □ vt colocar a armação em; (picture) emoldurar; (fig) formular; (sl) incriminar falsamente, tramar. ~ **of mind** estado m de espírito

framework /ˈfreɪmwɜːk/ n estrutura f; (context) quadro m, esquema m

France /frɑːns/ n França f

franchise /ˈfræntʃaɪz/ n (pol) direito m de voto; (comm) concessão f, franchise f

frank[1] /fræŋk/ a franco. ~**ly** adv francamente. ~**ness** n franqueza f

frank[2] /fræŋk/ vt franquear

frantic /ˈfræntɪk/ a frenético

fraternal /frəˈtɜːnl/ a fraternal

fraternize /ˈfrætənaɪz/ vi confraternizar

fraud /frɔːd/ n fraude f; (person) impostor m. ~**ulent** /ˈfrɔːdjʊlənt/ a fraudulento

fraught /frɔːt/ a ~ **with** cheio de

fray[1] /freɪ/ n rixa f

fray[2] /freɪ/ vt/i desfiar(-se), puir, esgarçar(-se)

freak /friːk/ n aberração f, anomalia f □ a anormal. ~ **of nature** aborto m da natureza. ~**ish** a anormal

freckle /ˈfrekl/ n sarda f. ~**d** a sardento

free /friː/ a (**freer**, **freest**) livre; (gratis) grátis; (lavish) liberal □ vt (pt **freed**) libertar (**from** de); (rid) livrar (**of** de). ~ **of charge** grátis, de graça. **a** ~ **hand** carta f branca. ~**-lance** a independente, free-lance. ~**-range** a (egg) de galinha criada em galinheiro. ~**ly** adv livremente

freedom /ˈfriːdəm/ n liberdade f

freez|e /friːz/ vt/i (pt **froze**, pp **frozen**) gelar; (culin; finance) congelar(-se) □ n gelo m; (culin; finance) congelamento m. ~**er** n congelador m. ~**ing** a gélido, glacial. **below** ~**ing** abaixo de zero

freight /freɪt/ n frete m

French /frentʃ/ a francês □ n (lang) francês m. **the** ~ os franceses. ~**man** n francês m. ~**-speaking** a francófono. ~ **window** porta f envidraçada. ~**woman** n francesa f

frenz|y /ˈfrenzɪ/ n frenesi m. ~**ied** a frenético

frequen|t[1] /ˈfriːkwənt/ a freqüente, (P) frequente. ~**cy** n freqüência f, (P) frequência f. ~**tly** adv freqüentemente, (P) frequentemente

frequent[2] /frɪˈkwent/ vt freqüentar, (P) frequentar

fresh /freʃ/ a (-er, -est) fresco; (different, additional) novo; (colloq: cheeky) descarado, atrevido. ~**ly** adv recentemente. ~**ness** n frescura f

freshen /ˈfreʃn/ vt/i refrescar. ~ **up** refrescar-se

fret /fret/ vt/i (pt **fretted**) ralar (-se). ~**ful** a rabugento

friar /ˈfraɪə(r)/ n frade m; (before name) frei m

friction /ˈfrɪkʃn/ n fricção f

Friday /ˈfraɪdɪ/ n sexta-feira f. **Good** ~ sexta-feira f santa

fridge /frɪdʒ/ n (colloq) geladeira f, (P) frigorífico m

fried /fraɪd/ see **fry** □ a frito

friend /frend/ n amigo m. ~**ship** n amizade f

friendl|y /ˈfrendlɪ/ a (-ier, -iest) amigável, amigo, simpático. ~**iness** n simpatia f, gentileza f

frieze /friːz/ n friso m

frigate /ˈfrɪɡət/ n fragata f

fright /fraɪt/ n medo m, susto m. **give sb a** ~ pregar um susto em alguém. ~**ful** a medonho, assustador

frighten /ˈfraɪtn/ vt assustar. ~ **off** afugentar. ~**ed** a assustado. **be** ~**ed** (**of**) ter medo (de)

frigid /ˈfrɪdʒɪd/ a frígido. ~**ity** /-ˈdʒɪdətɪ/ n frigidez f, frieza f; (psych) frigidez f

frill /frɪl/ n babado m, (P) folho m

fringe /frɪndʒ/ n franja f; (of area) borda f; (of society) margem f. ~ **benefits** (work) regalias fpl extras. ~ **theatre** teatro m alternativo, teatro m de vanguarda

frisk /frɪsk/ vt pular, brincar □ vt revistar

fritter[1] /ˈfrɪtə(r)/ n bolinho m frito, (P) frito m

fritter[2] /ˈfrɪtə(r)/ vt ~ **away** desperdiçar

frivol|ous /ˈfrɪvələs/ a frívolo. ~**ity** /-ˈvɒlətɪ/ n frivolidade f

fro /frəʊ/ see **to and fro**

frock /frɒk/ n vestido m

f

frog /frɒg/ *n* rã *f*

frogman /'frɒgmən/ *n* (*pl* -**men**) homem-rã *m*

frolic /'frɒlɪk/ *vi* (*pt* **frolicked**) brincar, fazer travessuras □ *n* brincadeira *f*, travessura *f*

from /frɒm/; *emphatic* /frɒm/ *prep* de; (*with time, prices etc*) de, a partir de; (*according to*) por, a julgar por

front /frʌnt/ *n* (*meteo, mil, pol; of car, train*) frente *f*; (*of shirt*) peitilho *m*; (*of building; fig*) fachada *f*; (*promenade*) calçada *f* à beira-mar □ *a* da frente; (*first*) primeiro. **in ~ (of)** em frente (de). **~ door** porta *f* da rua. **~-wheel drive** *n* tração *f*, (*P*) tracção *f* dianteira. **~age** *n* frontaria *f*. **~al** *a* **frontal**

frontier /'frʌntɪə(r)/ *n* fronteira *f*

frost /frɒst/ *n* gelo *m*, temperatura *f* abaixo de zero; (*on ground, plants etc*) geada *f* □ *vt/i* cobrir (-se) de geada. **~-bite** *n* queimadura *f* de frio. **~-bitten** *a* queimado pelo frio. **~ed** *a* (*glass*) fosco. **~y** *a* glacial

froth /frɒθ/ *n* espuma *f* □ *vi* espumar, fazer espuma. **~y** *a* espumoso

frown /fraʊn/ *vi* franzir as sobrancelhas □ *n* franzir *m* de sobrancelhas. **~ on** desaprovar

froze, frozen /frəʊz, 'frəʊzn/ *see* **freeze**

frugal /'fru:gl/ *a* poupado; (*meal*) frugal. **~ly** *adv* frugalmente

fruit /fru:t/ *n* fruto *m*; (*collectively*) fruta *f*. **~ machine** caça-níqueis *ms*/*pl*. **~ salad** salada *f* de frutas. **~y** *a* que tem gosto *or* cheiro de fruta

fruit|ful /'fru:tfl/ *a* frutífero, produtivo. **~less** *a* infrutífero

fruition /fru:'ɪʃn/ *n* **come to ~** realizar-se

frustrat|e /frʌ'streɪt/ *vt* frustrar. **~ion** /-ʃn/ *n* frustração *f*

fry /fraɪ/ *vt/i* (*pt* **fried**) fritar. **~ing-pan** *n* frigideira *f*

fudge /fʌdʒ/ *n* (*culin*) doce *m* de leite, (*P*) doce *m* acaramelado □ *vt/i* **~ (the issue)** lançar a confusão

fuel /'fju:əl/ *n* combustível *m*; (*for car*) carburante *m* □ *vt* (*pt* **fuelled**) abastecer de combustível; (*fig*) atear.

fugitive /'fju:dʒətɪv/ *a & n* fugitivo (*m*)

fulfil /fʊl'fɪl/ *vt* (*pt* **fulfilled**) cumprir, realizar; (*condition*) satisfazer. **~ o.s.** realizar-se. **~ling** *a* satisfatório. **~ment** *n* realização *f*; (*of condition*) satisfação *f*

full /fʊl/ *a* (-**er**, -**est**) cheio; (*meal*) completo; (*price*) total, por inteiro; (*skirt*) rodado □ *adv* **in ~** integralmente. **at ~ speed** a toda velocidade. **to the ~** ao máximo. **be ~ up** (*colloq: after eating*) estar cheio

(*colloq*). **~ moon** lua *f* cheia. **~-scale** *a* em grande. **~-size** *a* em tamanho natural. **~ stop** ponto *m* final. **~-time** *a & adv* a tempo integral, full-time. **~y** *adv* completamente

fulsome /'fʊlsəm/ *a* excessivo

fumble /'fʌmbl/ *vi* tatear, (*P*) tactear; (*in the dark*) andar tateando. **~ with** estar atrapalhado com, andar às voltas com

fume /fju:m/ *vi* defumar, (*P*) deitar fumo, fumegar; (*with anger*) ferver. **~s** *npl* gases *mpl*

fumigate /'fju:mɪgeɪt/ *vt* fumigar

fun /fʌn/ *n* divertimento *m*. **for ~** de brincadeira. **make ~ of** zombar de, fazer troça de. **~-fair** *n* parque *m* de diversões, (*P*) feira *f* de diversões, (*P*) feira *f* popular

function /'fʌŋkʃn/ *n* função *f* □ *vi* funcionar. **~al** *a* funcional

fund /fʌnd/ *n* fundos *mpl* □ *vt* financiar

fundamental /fʌndə'mentl/ *a* fundamental

funeral /'fju:nərəl/ *n* enterro *m*, funeral *m* □ *a* fúnebre

fungus /'fʌŋgəs/ *n* (*pl*-**gi** /-gaɪ/) fungo *m*

funnel /'fʌnl/ *n* funil *m*; (*of ship*) chaminé *f*

funn|y /'fʌnɪ/ *a* (-**ier**, -**iest**) engraçado, divertido; (*odd*) esquisito. **~ily** *adv* comicamente; (*oddly*) estranhamente. **~ily enough** por incrível que pareça

fur /fɜ:(r)/ *n* pêlo *m*; (*for clothing*) pele *f*; (*in kettle*) depósito *m*, crosta *f*. **~ coat** casaco *m* de pele

furious /'fjʊərɪəs/ *a* furioso. **~ly** *adv* furiosamente

furnace /'fɜ:nɪs/ *n* fornalha *f*

furnish /'fɜ:nɪʃ/ *vt* mobiliar, (*P*) mobilar; (*supply*) prover (**with** de). **~ings** *npl* mobiliário *m* e equipamento *m*

furniture /'fɜ:nɪtʃə(r)/ *n* mobília *f*

furrow /'fʌrəʊ/ *n* sulco *m*; (*wrinkle*) ruga *f* □ *vt* sulcar; (*wrinkle*) enrugar

furry /'fɜ:rɪ/ *a* (-**ier**, -**iest**) peludo; (*toy*) de pelúcia

furth|er /'fɜ:ðə(r)/ *a* mais distante; (*additional*) adicional, suplementar □ *adv* mais longe; (*more*) mais □ *vt* promover. **~er education** ensino *m* supletivo, cursos *mpl* livres, (*P*) educação *f* superior. **~est** *a* o mais distante □ *adv* mais longe

furthermore /fɜ:ðə'mɔ:(r)/ *adv* além disso

furtive /'fɜ:tɪv/ *a* furtivo

fury /'fjʊərɪ/ *n* fúria *f*, furor *m*

fuse[1] /fju:z/ *vt/i* fundir(-se); (*fig*) amalgamar □ *n* fusível *m*. **the lights ~d** os fusíveis queimaram

fuse[2] /fju:z/ *n* (*of bomb*) espoleta *f*

fuselage /'fju:zəla:ʒ/ *n* fuselagem *f*

fusion /'fju:ʒn/ *n* fusão *f*

fuss /fʌs/ *n* história(s) *f* (*pl*), escarcéu *m* □ *vi* preocupar-se com ninharias. **make a ~ of** ligar demasiado para, criar caso com, fazer um espalhafato com. **~y** *a* exigente, complicado

futile /'fju:taɪl/ *a* fútil

future /'fju:tʃə(r)/ *a & n* futuro (*m*). **in ~** no futuro, de agora em diante

futuristic /fju:tʃə'rɪstɪk/ *a* futurista, futurístico

fuzz /fʌz/ *n* penugem *f*; (*hair*) cabelo *m* frisado

fuzzy /'fʌzɪ/ *a* (*hair*) frisado; (*photo*) pouco nítido, desfocado

....

Gg

....

gab /gæb/ *n* (*colloq*) **have the gift of the ~** ter o dom da palavra

gabble /'gæbl/ *vt/i* tagarelar, falar, ler muito depressa □ *n* tagarelice *f*, algaravia *f*

gable /'geɪbl/ *n* empena *f*, oitão *m*

gad /gæd/ *vi* (*pt* **gadded**) **~ about** (*colloq*) badalar

gadget /'gædʒɪt/ *n* pequeno utensílio *m*; (*fitting*) dispositivo *m*; (*device*) engenhoca *f* (*colloq*)

Gaelic /'geɪlɪk/ *n* galês *m*

gaffe /gæf/ *n* gafe *f*

gag /gæg/ *n* mordaça *f*; (*joke*) gag *m*, piada *f* □ *vt* (*pt* **gagged**) amordaçar

gaiety /'geɪətɪ/ *n* alegria *f*

gaily /'geɪlɪ/ *adv* alegremente

gain /geɪn/ *vt* ganhar □ *vi* (*of clock*) adiantar-se. **~ weight** aumentar de peso. **~ on** (*get closer to*) aproximar-se de □ *n* ganho *m*; (*increase*) aumento *m*. **~ful** *a* lucrativo, proveitoso

gait /geɪt/ *n* (modo de) andar *m*

gala /'gɑ:lə/ *n* gala *m*; (*sport*) festival *m*

galaxy /'gæləksɪ/ *n* galáxia *f*

gale /geɪl/ *n* vento *m* forte

gall /gɔ:l/ *n* bílis *f*; (*fig*) fel *m*; (*sl: impudence*) descaramento *m*, desplante *m*, (*P*) lata *f* (*sl*). **~-bladder** *n* vesícula *f* biliar. **~-stone** *n* cálculo *m* biliar

gallant /'gælənt/ *a* galhardo, valente; (*chivalrous*) galante, cortês. **~ry** *n* galhardia *f*, valentia *f*; (*chivalry*) galanteria *f*, cortesia *f*

gallery /'gælərɪ/ *n* galeria *f*

galley /'gælɪ/ *n* (*pl* **-eys**) galera *f*; (*ship's kitchen*) cozinha *f*

gallivant /gælɪ'vænt/ *vi* (*colloq*) vadiar, (*P*) andar na paródia

gallon /'gælən/ *n* galão *m* (= *4,546 litros; Amer = 3.785 litros*)

gallop /'gæləp/ *n* galope *m* □ *vi* (*pt* **galloped**) galopar

gallows /'gæləʊz/ *npl* forca *f*

galore /gə'lɔ:(r)/ *adv* a beça, em abundância

galvanize /'gælvənaɪz/ *vt* galvanizar

gambit /'gæmbɪt/ *n* gambito *m*

gamble /'gæmbl/ *vt/i* jogar □ *n* jogo (de azar) *m*; (*fig*) risco *m*. **~e on** apostar em. **~er** *n* jogador *m*. **~ing** *n* jogo *m* (de azar)

game /geɪm/ *n* jogo *m*; (*football*) desafio *m*; (*animals*) caça *f* □ *a* bravo. **~ for** pronto para

gamekeeper /'geɪmki:pə(r)/ *n* guarda-florestal *m*

gammon /'gæmən/ *n* presunto *m* defumado

gamut /'gæmət/ *n* gama *f*

gang /gæŋ/ *n* bando *m*, gang *m*; (*of workmen*) turma *f*, (*P*) grupo *m* □ *vi* **~ up** ligar-se (**on** contra)

gangling /'gæŋglɪŋ/ *a* desengonçado

gangrene /'gæŋgri:n/ *n* gangrena *f*

gangster /'gæŋstə(r)/ *n* gângster *m*, bandido *m*

gangway /'gæŋweɪ/ *n* passagem *f*; (*aisle*) coxia *f*; (*on ship*) portaló *m*; (*from ship to shore*) passadiço *m*

gaol /dʒeɪl/ *n & vt* = **jail**

gap /gæp/ *n* abertura *f*, brecha *f*; (*in time*) intervalo *m*; (*deficiency*) lacuna *f*

gape /geɪp/ *vi* ficar boquiaberto *or* embasbacado. **~ing** *a* escancarado

garage /'gæra:ʒ/ *n* garagem *f*; (*service station*) posto *m* de gasolina, (*P*) estação *f* de serviço □ *vt* pôr na garagem

garbage /'gɑ:bɪdʒ/ *n* lixo *m*. **~ can** (*Amer*) lata *f* do lixo, (*P*) caixote *m* do lixo

garble /'gɑ:bl/ *vt* deturpar

garden /'gɑ:dn/ *n* jardim *m* □ *vi* jardinar. **~er** *n* jardineiro *m*. **~ing** *n* jardinagem *f*

gargle /'gɑ:gl/ *vi* gargarejar □ *n* gargarejo *m*

gargoyle /'gɑ:gɔɪl/ *n* gárgula *f*

garish /'geərɪʃ/ *a* berrante, espalhafatoso

garland /'gɑ:lənd/ *n* grinalda *f*

garlic /'gɑ:lɪk/ *n* alho *m*

garment /'gɑ:mənt/ *n* peça *f* de vestuário, roupa *f*

garnish /'gɑ:nɪʃ/ *vt* enfeitar, guarnecer □ *n* guarnição *f*

garrison /'gærɪsn/ n guarnição f □ vt guarnecer

garrulous /'gærələs/ a tagarela

garter /'ga:tə(r)/ n liga f. ~-**belt** n (Amer) cinta f de ligas

gas /gæs/ n (pl gases) gás m; (med) anestésico m; (Amer colloq: petrol) gasolina f □ vt (pt gassed) asfixiar; (mil) gasear □ vi (colloq) fazer conversa fiada. ~ **fire** aquecedor m a gás. ~ **mask** máscara f anti-gás. ~ **meter** medidor m do gás

gash /gæʃ/ n corte m, lanho m □ vt cortar

gasket /'gæskɪt/ n junta f

gasoline /'gæsəli:n/ n (Amer) gasolina f

gasp /ga:sp/ vi arfar, arquejar; (fig: with rage, surprise) ficar sem ar □ n arquejo m

gassy /'gæsɪ/ a gasoso; (full of gas) cheio de gás

gastric /'gæstrɪk/ a gástrico

gastronomy /gæ'strɒnəmɪ/ n gastronomia f

gate /geɪt/ n portão m; (of wood) cancela f; (barrier) barreira f; (airport) porta f

gateau /'gætəu/ n (pl ~x /-təuz/) bolo m grande com creme

gatecrash /'geɪtkræʃ/ vt/i entrar (numa festa) sem convite

gateway /'geɪtweɪ/ n (porta de) entrada f

gather /'gæðə(r)/ vt reunir, juntar; (pick up, collect) apanhar; (amass, pile up) acumular, juntar; (conclude) deduzir; (cloth) franzir □ vi reunir-se; (pile up) acumular-se. ~ **speed** ganhar velocidade. ~**ing** n reunião f

gaudy /'gɔ:dɪ/ a (-ier, -iest) (bright) berrante; (showy) espalhafatoso

gauge /geɪdʒ/ n medida f padrão; (device) indicador m; (railway) bitola f □ vt medir, avaliar

gaunt /gɔ:nt/ a emagrecido, macilento; (grim) lúgubre, desolado

gauntlet /'gɔ:ntlɪt/ n run the ~ of (fig) expor-se a. throw down the ~ lançar um desafio, (P) atirar a luva

gauze /gɔ:z/ n gaze f

gave /geɪv/ see give

gawky /'gɔ:kɪ/ a (-ier, -iest) desajeitado

gay /geɪ/ a (-er, -est) alegre; (colloq: homosexual) homosexual, gay

gaze /geɪz/ vi ~ (at) olhar fixamente (para) □ n contemplação f

gazelle /gə'zel/ n gazela f

GB abbr of **Great Britain**

gear /gɪə(r)/ n equipamento m; (techn) engrenagem f; (auto) velocidade f □ vt equipar; (adapt) adaptar. in ~ engrenado. out of ~ em ponto morto. ~-**lever** n alavanca f de mudanças

gearbox /'gɪəbɒks/ n caixa f de mudança, caixa f de transmissão, (P) caixa f de velocidades

geese /gi:s/ see **goose**

gel /dʒel/ n geléia f, (P) geleia f

gelatine /'dʒeləti:n/ n gelatina f

gelignite /'dʒelɪgnaɪt/ n gelignite f

gem /dʒem/ n gema f, pedra f preciosa

Gemini /'dʒemɪnaɪ/ n (astr) Gêmeos mpl, (P) Gémeos mpl

gender /'dʒendə(r)/ n gênero m, (P) género m

gene /dʒi:n/ n gene m

genealogy /dʒi:nɪ'ælədʒɪ/ n genealogia f

general /'dʒenrəl/ a geral □ n general m. ~ **election** eleições fpl legislativas. ~ **practitioner** n clínico-geral m, (P) médico m de família. in ~ em geral. ~**ly** adv geralmente

generaliz|e /'dʒenrəlaɪz/ vt/i generalizar. ~**ation** /-'zeɪʃn/ n generalização f

generate /'dʒenəreɪt/ vt gerar, produzir

generation /dʒenə'reɪʃn/ n geração f

generator /'dʒenəreɪtə(r)/ n gerador m

gener|ous /'dʒenərəs/ a generoso; (plentiful) abundante. ~**osity** /-'rɒsətɪ/ n generosidade f

genetic /dʒɪ'netɪk/ a genético. ~**s** n genética f

genial /'dʒi:nɪəl/ a agradável

genital /'dʒenɪtl/ a genital. ~**s** npl órgãos mpl genitais

genius /'dʒi:nɪəs/ n (pl -uses) gênio m, (P) génio m

genocide /'dʒenəsaɪd/ n genocídio m

gent /dʒent/ n the **G~s** (colloq) banheiros mpl de homens, (P) lavabos mpl para homens

genteel /dʒen'ti:l/ a elegante, fino, refinado

gentl|e /'dʒentl/ a (~**er**, ~**est**) brando, suave. ~**eness** n brandura f, suavidade f. ~**y** adv brandamente, suavemente

gentleman /'dʒentlmən/ n (pl -men) senhor m; (well-bred) cavalheiro m

genuine /'dʒenjom/ a genuíno, verdadeiro; (belief) sincero

geograph|y /dʒɪ'ɒgrəfɪ/ n geografia f. ~**er** n geógrafo m. ~**ical** /dʒɪə'græfɪkl/ a geográfico

geolog|y /dʒɪ'ɒlədʒɪ/ n geologia f. ~**ical** /dʒɪə'lɒdʒɪkl/ a geológico. ~**ist** n geólogo m

geometr|y /dʒɪ'ɒmətrɪ/ n geometria f. ~**ic(al)** /dʒɪə'metrɪk(l)/ a geométrico

geranium /dʒə'reɪnɪəm/ n gerânio m

geriatric /dʒerɪ'ætrɪk/ a geriátrico

germ /dʒɜ:m/ n germe m, micróbio m

German /'dʒɜːmən/ a & n alemão (m), alemã (f); (lang) alemão (m). **~ measles** rubéola f. **~ic** /dʒə'mænɪk/ a germânico. **~y** n Alemanha f

germinate /'dʒɜːmɪneɪt/ vi germinar

gestation /dʒe'steɪʃn/ n gestação f

gesticulate /dʒe'stɪkjʊleɪt/ vi gesticular

gesture /'dʒestʃə(r)/ n gesto m

get /get/ vt (pt **got**, pres p **getting**) (have) ter; (receive) receber; (catch) apanhar; (earn, win) ganhar; (fetch) ir buscar; (find) achar; (colloq: understand) entender. **~ sb to do sth** fazer com que alguém faça alg coisa □ vi ir, chegar; (become) ficar. **~ married/ready** casar-se/aprontar-se. **~ about** andar dum lado para o outro. **~ across** atravessar. **~ along** or by (manage) ir indo. **~ along** or on with entender-se com. **~ at** (reach) chegar a; (attack) atacar; (imply) insinuar. **~ away** ir-se embora; (escape) fugir. **~ back** vi voltar □ vt recuperar. **~ by** (pass) passar, escapar; (manage) aguentar-se. **~ down** descer. **~ in** entrar. **~ off** vi descer; (leave) partir; (jur) ser absolvido □ vt (remove) tirar. **~ on** (succeed) fazer progressos, ir; (be on good terms) dar-se bem. **~ out** sair. **~ out of** (fig) fugir de. **~ over** (illness) restabelecer-se de. **~ round** (person) convencer; (rule) contornar. **~ up** vi levantar-se □ vt (mount) montar. **~-up** n (colloq) apresentação f

getaway /'getəweɪ/ n fuga f

geyser /'giːzə(r)/ n aquecedor m; (geol) gêiser m, (P) géiser m

Ghana /'gɑːnə/ n Gana m

ghastly /'gɑːstlɪ/ a (-ier, -iest) horrível; (pale) lívido

gherkin /'gɜːkɪn/ n pepino m pequeno para conservas, cornichão m

ghetto /'getəʊ/ n (pl -os) gueto m, ghetto m

ghost /gəʊst/ n fantasma m, espectro m. **~ly** a fantasmagórico, espectral

giant /'dʒaɪənt/ a & n gigante (m)

gibberish /'dʒɪbərɪʃ/ n algaravia f, linguagem f incompreensível

gibe /dʒaɪb/ n zombaria f □ vi **~ (at)** zombar (de)

giblets /'dʒɪblɪts/ npl miúdos mpl, miudezas fpl

giddy /'gɪdɪ/ a (-ier, -iest) estonteante, vertiginoso. **be** or **feel ~** ter tonturas or vertigens

gift /gɪft/ n presente m, dádiva f; (ability) dom m, dote m. **~-wrap** vt (pt -wrapped) fazer um embrulho de presente

gifted /'gɪftɪd/ a dotado

gig /gɪg/ n (colloq) show m, sessão f de jazz etc

gigantic /dʒar'gæntɪk/ a gigantesco

giggle /'gɪgl/ vi dar risadinhas nervosas □ n risinho m nervoso

gild /gɪld/ vt dourar

gills /gɪlz/ npl guelras fpl

gilt /gɪlt/ a & n dourado (m). **~-edged** a de toda a confiança

gimmick /'gɪmɪk/ n truque m, artifício m

gin /dʒɪn/ n gin m, genebra f

ginger /'dʒɪndʒə(r)/ n gengibre m □ a louro-avermelhado, ruivo. **~ ale**, **~ beer** cerveja f de gengibre, (P) ginger ale m

gingerbread /'dʒɪndʒəbred/ n pão m de gengibre

gingerly /'dʒɪndʒəlɪ/ adv cautelosamente

gipsy /'dʒɪpsɪ/ n = **gypsy**

giraffe /dʒɪ'rɑːf/ n girafa f

girder /'gɜːdə(r)/ n trave f, viga f

girdle /'gɜːdl/ n cinto m; (corset) cinta f □ vt rodear

girl /gɜːl/ n (child) menina f; (young woman) moça f, (P) rapariga f. **~-friend** n amiga f; (of boy) namorada f. **~hood** n (of child) meninice f; (youth) juventude f

giro /'dʒaɪrəʊ/ n sistema m de transferência de crédito entre bancos; (cheque) cheque m pago pelo governo a desempregados ou doentes

girth /gɜːθ/ n circumferência f, perímetro m

gist /dʒɪst/ n essencial m

give /gɪv/ vt/i (pt **gave**, pp **given**) dar; (bend, yield) ceder. **~ away** dar; (secret) revelar, trair. **~ back** devolver. **~ in** dar-se por vencido, render-se. **~ off** emitir. **~ out** vt anunciar □ vi esgotar-se. **~ up** vt/i desistir (de), renunciar (a). **~ o.s. up** entregar-se. **~ way** ceder; (traffic) dar prioridade; (collapse) dar de si

given /'gɪvn/ see **give** □ a dado. **~ name** nome m de batismo, (P) baptismo

glacier /'glæsɪə(r)/ n glaciar m, geleira f

glad /glæd/ a contente. **~ly** adv com (todo o) prazer

gladden /'glædn/ vt alegrar

glam|our /'glæmə(r)/ n fascinação f, encanto m. **~orize** vt tornar fascinante. **~orous** a fascinante, sedutor

glance /glɑːns/ n relance m, olhar m □ vi **~ at** dar uma olhada a. **at first ~** à primeira vista

gland /glænd/ n glândula f

glar|e /gleə(r)/ vi brilhar intensamente, faiscar □ n luz f crua; (fig) olhar m feroz. **~e at** olhar ferozmente para. **~ing** a brilhante; (obvious) flagrante

glass /glɑːs/ n vidro m; (*vessel, its contents*) copo m; (*mirror*) espelho m. **~es** óculos mpl. **~y** a vítreo

glaze /gleɪz/ vt (*door etc*) envidraçar; (*pottery*) vidrar □ n vidrado m

gleam /gliːm/ n raio m de luz frouxa; (*fig*) vislumbre m □ vi luzir, brilhar

glean /gliːn/ vt catar

glee /gliː/ n alegria f. **~ful** a cheio de alegria

glib /glɪb/ a que tem a palavra fácil, verboso. **~ly** adv fluentemente, sem hesitação. **~ness** n verbosidade f

glide /glaɪd/ vi deslizar; (*bird, plane*) planar. **~r** /-ə(r)/ n planador m

glimmer /'glɪmə(r)/ n luz f trêmula □ vi tremular

glimpse /glɪmps/ n vislumbre m. **catch a ~ of** entrever, ver de relance

glint /glɪnt/ n brilho m, reflexo m □ vi brilhar, cintilar

glisten /'glɪsn/ vi reluzir

glitter /'glɪtə(r)/ vi luzir, resplandecer □ n esplendor m, cintilação f

gloat /gləʊt/ vi **~ over** ter um prazer maligno em, exultar com

global /'gləʊbl/ a global

globe /gləʊb/ n globo m

gloom /gluːm/ n obscuridade f; (*fig*) tristeza f. **~y** a sombrio; (*sad*) triste; (*pessimistic*) pessimista

glorif|**y** /'glɔːrɪfaɪ/ vt glorificar. **a ~ied waitress**/*etc* pouco mais que uma garçonete/*etc*

glorious /'glɔːrɪəs/ a glorioso

glory /'glɔːrɪ/ n glória f; (*beauty*) esplendor m □ vi **~ in** orgulhar-se de

gloss /glɒs/ n brilho m □ a brilhante □ vt **~ over** minimizar, encobrir. **~y** a brilhante

glossary /'glɒsərɪ/ n (*pl* **-ries**) glossário m

glove /glʌv/ n luva f. **~ compartment** porta-luvas m. **~d** a enluvado

glow /gləʊ/ vi arder; (*person*) resplandecer □ n brasa f. **~ing** a (*fig*) entusiástico

glucose /'gluːkəʊs/ n glucose f

glue /gluː/ n cola f □ vt (*pres p* **gluing**) colar

glum /glʌm/ a (**glummer, glummest**) sorumbático; (*dejected*) abatido

glut /glʌt/ n superabundância f

glutton /'glʌtn/ n glutão m. **~ous** a glutão. **~y** n gula f

GMO /dʒiːɛm'əʊ/ n OGM, organismo m geneticamente modificado

gnarled /naːld/ a nodoso

gnash /næʃ/ vt **~ one's teeth** ranger os dentes

gnat /næt/ n mosquito m

gnaw /nɔː/ vt/i roer

gnome /nəʊm/ n gnomo m

go /gəʊ/ vi (*pt* **went**, *pp* **gone**) ir; (*leave*) ir, ir-se; (*mech*) andar, funcionar; (*become*) ficar; (*be sold*) vender-se; (*vanish*) ir-se, desaparecer □ n (*pl* **goes**) (*energy*) dinamismo m; (*try*) tentativa f; (*success*) sucesso m; (*turn*) vez f. **~ riding** ir andar *or* montar a cavalo. **~ shopping** ir às compras. **be ~ing to do** ir fazer. **~ ahead** ir para diante. **~ away** ir-se embora. **~ back** voltar atrás (**on** com). **~ bad** estragar-se. **~ by** (*pass*) passar. **~ down** descer; (*sun*) pôr-se; (*ship*) afundar-se. **~ for** ir buscar; (*like*) gostar de; (*sl: attack*) atirar-se a, irse a (*colloq*). **~ in** entrar. **~ in for** (*exam*) apresentar-se a. **~ off** ir-se; (*explode*) rebentar; (*sound*) soar; (*decay*) estragar-se. **~ on** continuar; (*happen*) acontecer. **~ out** sair; (*light*) apagar-se. **~ over** *or* **through** verificar, examinar. **~ round** (*be enough*) chegar. **~ under** ir abaixo. **~ up** subir. **~ without** passar sem. **on the ~** em grande atividade. **~-ahead** n luz f verde □ a dinâmico, empreendedor. **~-between** n intermediário m. **~-kart** n kart m. **~-slow** n operação f tartaruga, (*P*) greve f de zelo

goad /gəʊd/ vt aguilhoar, espicaçar

goal /gəʊl/ n meta f; (*area*) baliza f; (*score*) gol m, (*P*) golo m. **~-post** n trave f

goalkeeper /'gəʊlkiːpə(r)/ n goleiro m, (*P*) guarda-redes m

goat /gəʊt/ n cabra f

gobble /'gɒbl/ vt comer com sofreguidão, devorar

goblet /'gɒblɪt/ n taça f, cálice m

goblin /'gɒblɪn/ n duende m

God /gɒd/ n Deus m. **~-forsaken** a miserável, abandonado

god /gɒd/ n deus m. **~-daughter** n afilhada f. **~dess** n deusa f. **~father** n padrinho m. **~ly** a devoto. **~mother** n madrinha f. **~son** n afilhado m

godsend /'gɒdsend/ n achado m, dádiva f do céu

goggles /'gɒglz/ npl óculos mpl de proteção, (*P*) protecção

going /'gəʊɪŋ/ n **it is slow/hard ~** é demorado/difícil □ a (*price, rate*) corrente, atual, (*P*) actual. **~s-on** npl acontecimentos mpl estranhos

gold /gəʊld/ n ouro m □ a de/em ouro. **~-mine** n mina f de ouro

golden /'gəʊldən/ a de ouro; (*like gold*) dourado; (*opportunity*) único. **~ wedding** bodas fpl de ouro

goldfish /'gəʊldfɪʃ/ n peixe m dourado/vermelho

goldsmith /'gəʊldsmɪθ/ *n* ourives *m inv*

golf /gɒlf/ *n* golfe *m*. ~ **club** clube *m* de golfe, associação *f* de golfe; (*stick*) taco *m*. ~-**course** *n* campo *m* de golfe. ~**er** *n* jogador *m* de golfe

gone /gɒn/ *see* **go** □ *a* ido, passado. ~ **six o'clock** depois das seis

gong /gɒŋ/ *n* gongo *m*

good /gʊd/ *a* (**better, best**) bom □ *n* bem *m*. **as** ~ **as** praticamente. **for** ~ para sempre. **it is no** ~ **shouting**/*etc* não adianta gritar/*etc*. ~ **afternoon** *int* boa(s) tarde(s). ~ **evening/night** *int* boa(s) noite(s). **G**~ **Friday** Sexta-feira *f* Santa. ~-**looking** *a* bonito. ~ **morning** *int* bom dia. ~ **name** bom nome *m*

goodbye /gʊd'baɪ/ *int & n* adeus (*m*)

goodness /'gʊdnɪs/ *n* bondade *f*. **my** ~**ness!** meu Deus!

goods /gʊdz/ *npl* (*comm*) mercadorias *fpl*. ~ **train** trem *m* de carga, (*P*) comboio *m* de mercadorias

goodwill /gʊd'wɪl/ *n* boa vontade *f*

goose /gu:s/ *n* (*pl* **geese**) ganso *m*. ~-**flesh,** ~-**pimples** *ns* pele *f* de galinha

gooseberry /'gʊzbərɪ/ *n* (*fruit*) groselha *f*; (*bush*) groselheira *f*

gore¹ /gɔ:(r)/ *n* sangue *m* coagulado

gore² /gɔ:(r)/ *vt* perfurar

gorge /gɔ:dʒ/ *n* desfiladeiro *m*, garganta *f* □ *vt* ~ **o.s.** empanturrar-se

gorgeous /'gɔ:dʒəs/ *a* magnífico, maravilhoso

gorilla /gə'rɪlə/ *n* gorila *m*

gormless /'gɔ:mlɪs/ *a* (*sl*) estúpido

gorse /gɔ:s/ *n* giesta *f*, tojo *m*, urze *f*

gory /'gɔ:rɪ/ *a* (**-ier, -iest**) sangrento

gosh /gɒʃ/ *int* puxa!, (*P*) caramba!

gospel /'gɒspl/ *n* evangelho *m*

gossip /'gɒsɪp/ *n* bisbilhotice *f*, fofoca *f*; (*person*) bisbilhoteiro *m*, fofoqueiro *m* □ *vi* (*pt* **gossiped**) bisbilhotar. ~**y** *a* bisbilhoteiro, fofoqueiro

got /gɒt/ *see* **get**. **have** ~ ter. **have** ~ **to do** ter de *or* que fazer

Gothic /'gɒθɪk/ *a* gótico

gouge /gaʊdʒ/ *vt* ~ **out** arrancar

gourmet /'gʊəmeɪ/ *n* gastrônomo *m*, (*P*) gastrónomo *m*, gourmet *m*

gout /gaʊt/ *n* gota *f*

govern /'gʌvn/ *vt/i* governar. ~**ess** *n* preceptora *f*. ~**or** *n* governador *m*; (*of school, hospital etc*) diretor *m*, (*P*) director *m*

government /'gʌvənmənt/ *n* governo *m*. ~**al** /-'mentl/ *a* governamental

gown /gaʊn/ *n* vestido *m*; (*of judge, teacher*) toga *f*

GP *abbr see* **general practitioner**

grab /græb/ *vt* (*pt* **grabbed**) agarrar, apanhar

grace /greɪs/ *n* graça *f* □ *vt* honrar; (*adorn*) ornar. **say** ~ dar graças. ~**ful** *a* gracioso

gracious /'greɪʃəs/ *a* gracioso; (*kind*) amável, afável

grade /greɪd/ *n* categoria *f*; (*of goods*) classe *f*, qualidade *f*; (*on scale*) grau *m*; (*school mark*) nota *f* □ *vt* classificar

gradient /'greɪdɪənt/ *n* gradiente *m*, declive *m*

gradual /'grædʒʊəl/ *a* gradual, progressivo. ~**ly** *adv* gradualmente

graduate¹ /'grædʒʊət/ *n* diplomado *m*, graduado *m*, licenciado *m*

graduat|e² /'grædʒʊeɪt/ *vt/i* formar(-se). ~**ion** /-'eɪʃn/ *n* colação *f* de grau, (*P*) formatura *f*

graffiti /grə'fi:ti:/ *npl* graffiti *mpl*

graft /gra:ft/ *n* (*med, bot*) enxerto *m*; (*work*) batalha *f* □ *vt* enxertar; (*work*) batalhar

grain /greɪn/ *n* grão *m*; (*collectively*) cereais *mpl*; (*in wood*) veio *m*. **against the** ~ (*fig*) contra a maneira de ser

gram /græm/ *n* grama *m*

gramm|ar /'græmə(r)/ *n* gramática *f*. ~**atical** /grə'mætɪkl/ *a* gramatical

grand /grænd/ *a* (**-er, -est**) grandioso, magnífico; (*duke, master*) grão. ~ **piano** piano *m* de cauda.

grand|child /'græntʃaɪld/ *n* (*pl* **-children**) neto *m*. ~**daughter** *n* neta *f*. ~**father** *n* avô *m*. ~**mother** *n* avó *f*. ~**parents** *npl* avós *mpl*. ~**son** *n* neto *m*

grandeur /'grændʒə(r)/ *n* grandeza *f*

grandiose /'grændɪəʊs/ *a* grandioso

grandstand /'grændstænd/ *n* tribuna *f* principal

granite /'grænɪt/ *n* granito *m*

grant /gra:nt/ *vt* conceder; (*a request*) ceder a; (*admit*) admitir (**that** que) □ *n* subsídio *m*; (*univ*) bolsa *f*. **take for** ~**ed** ter como coisa garantida, contar com

grape /greɪp/ *n* uva *f*

grapefruit /'greɪpfru:t/ *n inv* grapefruit *m*, toronja *f*

graph /gra:f/ *n* gráfico *m*

graphic /'græfɪk/ *a* gráfico; (*fig*) vívido. ~**s** *npl* (*comput*) gráficos *mpl*

grapple /'græpl/ *vi* ~ **with** estar engalfinhado com; (*fig*) estar às voltas com

grasp /gra:sp/ *vt* agarrar; (*understand*) compreender □ *n* domínio *m*; (*reach*) alcance *m*; (*fig: understanding*) compreensão *f*

grasping /'gra:spɪŋ/ *a* ganancioso

grass /gra:s/ *n* erva *f*; (*lawn*) grama *f*, (*P*) relva *f*; (*pasture*) pastagem *f*; (*sl*:

g

informer) delator *m* □ *vt* cobrir com
grama; (*sl: betray*) delatar. ~ **roots**
(*pol*) bases *fpl*. ~**y** *a* coberto de erva

grasshopper /'grɑ:shɒpə(r)/ *n*
gafanhoto *m*

grate[1] /greɪt/ *n* (*fireplace*) lareira *f*;
(*frame*) grelha *f*

grate[2] /greɪt/ *vt* ralar □ *vi* ranger. ~ **one's**
teeth ranger os dentes. ~**r** /-ə(r)/ *n*
ralador *m*

grateful /'greɪtfl/ *a* grato, agradecido.
~**ly** *adv* com reconhecimento, com
gratidão

gratify /'grætɪfaɪ/ *vt* (*pt* -**fied**) contentar,
satisfazer. ~**ing** *a* gratificante

grating /'greɪtɪŋ/ *n* grade *f*

gratis /'greɪtɪs/ *a & adv* grátis (*invar*), de
graça

gratitude /'grætɪtju:d/ *n* gratidão *f*,
reconhecimento *m*

gratuitous /grə'tju:ɪtəs/ *a* gratuito;
(*uncalled-for*) sem motivo

gratuity /grə'tju:ətɪ/ *n* gratificação *f*,
gorjeta *f*

grave[1] /greɪv/ *n* cova *f*, sepultura *f*,
túmulo *m*

grave[2] /greɪv/ *a* (-**er**, -**est**) grave, sério.
~**ly** *adv* gravemente

grave[3] /grɑ:v/ *a* ~ **accent** acento *m* grave

gravel /'grævl/ *n* cascalho *m* miúdo,
saibro *m*

gravestone /'greɪvstəʊn/ *n* lápide *f*,
campa *f*

graveyard /'greɪvjɑ:d/ *n* cemitério *m*

gravity /'grævɪtɪ/ *n* gravidade *f*

gravy /'greɪvɪ/ *n* molho *m* (de carne)

graze[1] /greɪz/ *vt/i* pastar

graze[2] /greɪz/ *vt* roçar; (*scrape*) esfolar
□ *n* esfoladura *f*, (*P*) esfoladela *f*

grease |e /gri:s/ *n* gordura *f* □ *vt*
engordurar; (*culin*) untar; (*mech*)
lubrificar. ~**e-proof paper** papel *m*
vegetal. ~**y** *a* gorduroso

great /greɪt/ *a* (-**er**, -**est**) grande; (*colloq:
splendid*) esplêndido. **G**~ **Britain** Grã-
Bretanha *f*. ~**grandfather** *n* bisavô
m. ~**grandmother** *f* bisavó *f*. ~**ly**
adv grandemente, muito. ~- **ness** *n*
grandeza *f*

Great Britain /greɪt'brɪtən/ *n* Grã-
Bretanha *f*

Greece /gri:s/ *n* Grécia *f*

greed /gri:d/ *n* cobiça *f*, ganância *f*; (*for
food*) gula *f*. ~**y** *a* cobiçoso,
ganancioso; (*for food*) guloso

Greek /gri:k/ *a & n* grego (*m*)

green /gri:n/ *a* (-**er**, -**est**) verde □ *n* verde
m; (*grass*) gramado *m*, (*P*) relvado *m*.
~**s** hortaliças *fpl*. ~ **belt** zona *f* verde,
paisagem *f* protegida. ~ **light** luz *f*
verde. ~**ery** *n* verdura *f*

greengrocer /'gri:ngrəʊsə(r)/ *n*
quitandeiro *m*, (*P*) vendedor *m* de
hortaliças

greenhouse /'gri:nhaʊs/ *n* estufa *f*.
~ **effect** efeito estufa

Greenland /'gri:nlənd/ *n* Groenlândia *f*

greet /gri:t/ *vt* acolher. ~**ing** *n* saudação
f; (*welcome*) acolhimento *m*. ~**ings** *npl*
cumprimentos *mpl*; (*Christmas etc*)
votos *mpl*, desejos *mpl*

gregarious /grɪ'geərɪəs/ *a* gregário;
(*person*) sociável

grenade /grɪ'neɪd/ *n* granada *f*

grew /gru:/ *see* **grow**

grey /greɪ/ *a* (-**er**, -**est**) cinzento; (*of hair*)
grisalho □ *n* cinzento *m*

greyhound /'greɪhaʊnd/ *n* galgo *m*

grid /grɪd/ *n* (*grating*) gradeamento *m*,
grade *f*; (*electr*) rede *f*

grief /gri:f/ *n* dor *f*. **come to** ~ acabar
mal

grievance /'gri:vns/ *n* razão *f* de queixa

grieve /gri:v/ *vt* sofrer, afligir □ *vi* sofrer.
~ **for** chorar por

grill /grɪl/ *n* grelha *f*; (*food*) grelhado *m*;
(*place*) grill *m* □ *vt* grelhar; (*question*)
submeter a interrogatório cerrado,
apertar com perguntas □ *vi* grelhar

grille /grɪl/ *n* grade *f*; (*of car*) grelha *f*

grim /grɪm/ *a* (**grimmer**, **grimmest**)
sinistro; (*without mercy*) implacável

grimace /grɪ'meɪs/ *n* careta *f* □ *vi* fazer
careta(s)

grim|**e** /graɪm/ *n* sujeira *f*. ~**y** *a*
encardido, sujo

grin /grɪm/ *vi* (*pt* **grinned**) sorrir
abertamente, dar um sorriso largo □ *n*
sorriso *m* aberto

grind /graɪnd/ *vt* (*pt* **ground**) triturar;
(*coffee*) moer; (*sharpen*) amolar, afiar.
~ **one's teeth** ranger os dentes. ~ **to a**
halt parar freando lentamente

grip /grɪp/ *vt* (*pt* **gripped**) agarrar;
(*interest*) prender □ *n* (*of hands*) aperto
m; (*control*) controle *m*, domínio *m*.
come to ~**s with** arcar com. ~**ping** *a*
apaixonante

grisly /'grɪzlɪ/ *a* (-**ier**, -**iest**) macabro,
horrível

gristle /'grɪsl/ *n* cartilagem *f*

grit /grɪt/ *n* areia *f*, grão *m* de areia; (*fig:
pluck*) coragem *f*, fortaleza *f* □ *vt* (*pt*
gritted) (*road*) jogar areia em; (*teeth*)
cerrar

groan /grəʊn/ *vi* gemer □ *n* gemido *m*

grocer /'grəʊsə(r)/ *n* dono/a *m/f* de
mercearia. ~**ies** *npl* artigos *mpl* de
mercearia. ~**y** (*shop*) mercearia *f*

groggy /'grɒgɪ/ *a* (-**ier**, -**iest**) grogue,
fraco das pernas

groin /grɔɪn/ *n* virilha *f*

groom /gru:m/ *n* noivo *m*; (*for horses*) moço *m* de estrebaria □ *vt* (*horse*) tratar de; (*fig*) preparar

groove /gru:v/ *n* ranhura *f*; (*for door, window*) calha *f*; (*in record*) estria *f*; (*fig*) rotina *f*

grope /grəʊp/ *vi* tatear. ~ **for** procurar às cegas

gross /grəʊs/ *a* (-**er**, -**est**) (*vulgar*) grosseiro; (*flagrant*) flagrante; (*of error*) crasso; (*of weight, figure etc*) bruto □ *n* (*pl invar*) grosa *f*. ~**ly** *adv* grosseiramente; (*very*) extremamente

grotesque /grəʊ'tesk/ *a* grotesco

grotty /'grɒtɪ/ *a* (*sl*) sórdido

grouch /graʊtʃ/ *vi* (*colloq*) ralhar. ~**y** *a* (*colloq*) rabugento

ground[1] /graʊnd/ *n* chão *m*, solo *m*; (*area*) terreno *m*; (*reason*) razão *f*, motivo *m*. ~**s** jardins *mpl*; (*of coffee*) borra(s) *f*(*pl*) □ *vt/i* (*naut*) encalhar; (*plane*) reter em terra. ~ **floor** térreo *m*, (*P*) rés-do-chão *m*. ~**less** *a* infundado, sem fundamento

ground[2] /graʊnd/ *see* **grind**

grounding /'graʊndɪŋ/ *n* bases *fpl*, conhecimentos *mpl* básicos

groundsheet /'graʊndʃi:t/ *n* impermeável *m* para o chão

groundwork /'graʊndwɜ:k/ *n* trabalhos *mpl* de base *or* preliminares

group /gru:p/ *n* grupo *m* □ *vt/i* agrupar(-se)

grouse[1] /graʊs/ *n* (*pl invar*) galo *m* silvestre

grouse[2] /graʊs/ *vi* (*colloq: grumble*) resmungar; (*colloq: complain*) queixar-se

grovel /'grɒvl/ *vi* (*pt* **grovelled**) humilhar-se; (*fig*) rebaixar-se

grow /grəʊ/ *vi* (*pt* **grew**, *pp* **grown**) crescer; (*become*) tornar-se □ *vt* cultivar. ~ **old** envelhecer. ~ **up** crescer, tornar-se adulto. ~**er** *n* cultivador *m*, produtor *m*. ~**ing** *a* crescente

growl /graʊl/ *vi* rosnar □ *n* rosnadela *f*

grown /grəʊn/ *see* **grow** □ *a* ~ **man** homem feito. ~-**up** *a* adulto □ *n* pessoa *f* adulta

growth /grəʊθ/ *n* crescimento *m*; (*increase*) aumento *m*; (*med*) tumor *m*

grub /grʌb/ *n* larva *f*; (*sl: food*) bóia *f*, rango *m*, (*P*) comida *f*

grubby /'grʌbɪ/ *a* (-**ier**, -**iest**) sujo, porco

grudge /grʌdʒ/ *vt* dar/reconhecer de má vontade □ *n* má vontade *f*. ~ **doing** fazer de má vontade. ~ **sb sth** dar alg a alguém má vontade. **have a** ~ **against** ter ressentimento contra. **grudgingly** *adv* relutantemente

gruelling /'gru:əlɪŋ/ *a* estafante, extenuante

gruesome /'gru:səm/ *a* macabro

gruff /grʌf/ *a* (-**er**, -**est**) carrancudo, rude

grumble /'grʌmbl/ *vi* resmungar (**at** contra, por)

grumpy /'grʌmpɪ/ *a* (-**ier**, -**iest**) mal-humorado, rabugento

grunt /grʌnt/ *vi* grunhir □ *n* grunhido *m*

guarantee /gærən'ti:/ *n* garantia *f* □ *vt* garantir

guard /ga:d/ *vt* guardar, proteger □ *vi* ~ **against** precaver-se contra □ *n* guarda *f*; (*person*) guarda *m*; (*on train*) condutor *m*. ~**ian** *n* guardião *m*, defensor *m*; (*of orphan*) tutor *m*

guarded /'ga:dɪd/ *a* cauteloso, circunspeto, (*P*) circunspecto

guerrilla /gə'rɪlə/ *n* guerrilheiro *m*, (*P*) guerrilha *m*. ~ **warfare** guerrilha *f*, guerra *f* de guerrilhas

guess /ges/ *vt/i* adivinhar; (*suppose*) supor □ *n* suposição *f*, conjetura *f*, (*P*) conjectura *f*

guesswork /'geswɜ:k/ *n* suposição *f*, conjetura(s) *f*(*pl*), (*P*) conjectura(s) *f*(*pl*)

guest /gest/ *n* convidado *m*; (*in hotel*) hóspede *mf*. ~**-house** *n* pensão *f*

guffaw /gə'fɔ:/ *n* gargalhada *f* □ *vi* rir à(s) gargalhada(s)

guidance /'gaɪdns/ *n* orientação *f*, direção *f*, (*P*) direcção *f*

guide /gaɪd/ *n* guia *mf* □ *vt* guiar. ~**d missile** míssil *m* guiado; (*remote-control*) míssil *m* teleguiado. ~-**dog** *n* cão *m* de cego, cão-guia *m*. ~-**lines** *npl* diretrizes *fpl*, (*P*) directrizes *fpl*

Guide /gaɪd/ *n* Guia *f*

guidebook /'gaɪdbʊk/ *n* guia *m* (turístico)

guild /gɪld/ *n* corporação *f*

guile /gaɪl/ *n* astúcia *f*, manha *f*

guilt /gɪlt/ *n* culpa *f*. ~**y** *a* culpado

guinea-pig /'gɪnɪpɪg/ *n* cobaia *f*, porquinho-da-India *m*

guitar /gɪ'ta:(r)/ *n* guitarra *f*, violão *m*, (*P*) viola *f*. ~**ist** *n* guitarrista *mf*, tocador *m* de violão, (*P*) de viola

gulf /gʌlf/ *n* golfo *m*; (*hollow*) abismo *m*

gull /gʌl/ *n* gaivota *f*

gullible /'gʌləbl/ *a* crédulo

gully /'gʌlɪ/ *n* barranco *m*; (*drain*) sarjeta *f*

gulp /gʌlp/ *vt* engolir, devorar □ *vi* engolir em seco □ *n* trago *m*

gum[1] /gʌm/ *n* (*anat*) gengiva *f*

gum[2] /gʌm/ *n* goma *f*; (*chewing-gum*) chiclete *m*, goma *f* elástica, (*P*) pastilha *f* □ *vt* (*pt* **gummed**) colar

gumboot /'gʌmbu:t/ *n* bota *f* de borracha

gumption /'gʌmpʃn/ n (colloq) iniciativa f e bom senso m, cabeça f, juizo m

gun /gʌn/ n (pistol) pistola f; (rifle) espingarda f; (cannon) canhão m □ vt (pt **gunned**) ~ **down** abater a tiro

gunfire /'gʌnfaɪə(r)/ n tiroteio m

gunman /'gʌnmən/ n (pl -men) bandido m armado

gunpowder /'gʌnpaʊdə(r)/ n pólvora f

gunshot /'gʌnʃɒt/ n tiro m

gurgle /'gɜːgl/ n gorgolejo m □ vi gorgolejar

gush /gʌʃ/ vi jorrar □ n jorro m. ~**ing** a efusivo, derretido

gust /gʌst/ n (of wind) rajada f; (of smoke) nuvem f. ~**y** a ventoso

gusto /'gʌstəʊ/ n gosto m, entusiasmo m

gut /gʌt/ n tripa f. ~**s** (belly) barriga f; (colloq: courage) coragem f □ vt (pt **gutted**) estripar; (fish) limpar; (fire) destruir o interior de

gutter /'gʌtə(r)/ n calha f, canaleta f; (in street) sarjeta f, valeta f

guy /gaɪ/ n (sl: man) cara m, (P) tipo m (colloq)

guzzle /'gʌzl/ vt/i comer/beber com sofreguidão, encher-se (de)

gym /dʒɪm/ n (colloq: gymnasium) ginásio m; (colloq: gymnastics) ginástica f. ~**slip** n uniforme m escolar

gym|nasium /dʒɪm'neɪzɪəm/ n ginásio m. ~**nast** /'dʒɪmnæst/ n ginasta mf. ~**nastics** /-'næstɪks/ npl ginástica f

gynaecolog|y /gaɪnɪ'kɒlədʒɪ/ n ginecologia f. ~**ist** n ginecologista mf

gypsy /'dʒɪpsɪ/ n cigano m

gyrate /dʒaɪ'reɪt/ vi girar

....

Hh

....

haberdashery /'hæbədæʃərɪ/ n armarinho m, (P) retrosaria f

habit /'hæbɪt/ n hábito m, costume m; (costume) hábito m. **be in/get into the ~ of** ter/apanhar o hábito de

habit|able /'hæbɪtəbl/ a habitável. ~**ation** /-'teɪʃn/ n habitação f

habitat /'hæbɪtæt/ n habitat m

habitual /hə'bɪtʃʊəl/ a habitual, costumeiro; (smoker, liar) inveterado. ~**ly** adv habitualmente

hack[1] /hæk/ n (horse) cavalo m de aluguel; (writer) escrevinhador (pej) m. ~**er** (comput) micreiro m

hack[2] /hæk/ vt cortar, despedaçar. ~ **to pieces** cortar em pedaços

hackneyed /'hæknɪd/ a banal, batido

had /hæd/ see **have**

haddock /'hædək/ n invar hadoque m, eglefim m. **smoked ~** hadoque m fumado

haemorrhage /'hemərɪdʒ/ n hemorragia f

haemorrhoids /'hemərɔɪdz/ npl hemorróidas fpl

haggard /'hægəd/ a desfigurado, com o rosto desfeito, magro e macilento

haggle /'hægl/ vi ~ **(over)** regatear

hail[1] /heɪl/ vt saudar; (taxi) fazer sinal para, chamar □ vi ~ **from** vir de

hail[2] /heɪl/ n granizo m, (P) saraiva f, (P) chuva de pedra f □ vi chover granizo, (P) saraivar

hailstone /'heɪlstəʊn/ n pedra f de granizo

hair /heə(r)/ n (on head) cabelo(s) m(pl); (on body) pêlos mpl; (single strand) cabelo m; (of animal) pêlo m. ~**do** n (colloq) penteado m. ~**dryer** n secador m de cabelo. ~**raising** a horripilante, de pôr os cabelos em pé. ~**style** n estilo m de penteado

hairbrush /'heəbrʌʃ/ n escova f para o cabelo

haircut /'heəkʌt/ n corte m de cabelo

hairdresser /'heədresə(r)/ n cabeleireiro m, cabeleireira f

hairpin /'heəpɪn/ n grampo m, (P) gancho m para o cabelo. ~ **bend** curva f techada, quase em W

hairy /'heərɪ/ a (-ier, -iest) peludo, cabeludo; (sl: terrifying) de pôr os cabelos em pé, horripilante

hake /heɪk/ n (pl invar) abrótea f

half /haːf/ n (pl **halves** /haːvz/) metade f, meio m □ a meio □ adv ao meio. ~ **a dozen** meia dúzia. ~ **an hour** meia hora. ~**caste** n mestiço m. ~**hearted** a sem grande entusiasmo. ~**term** n férias fpl no meio do trimestre. ~**time** n meio-tempo m. ~**way** a & adv a meio caminho. ~**wit** n idiota mf. **go halves** dividir as despesas

halibut /'hælɪbət/ n (pl invar) halibute m

hall /hɔːl/ n sala f; (entrance) vestíbulo m, entrada f; (mansion) solar m. ~ **of residence** resi-dência f de estudantes

hallmark /'hɔːlmaːk/ n (on gold etc) marca f do contraste; (fig) cunho m, selo m

hallo /hə'ləʊ/ int & n (greeting, surprise) olá; (on phone) está

hallow /'hæləʊ/ vt consagrar, santificar

Halloween /hæləʊ'iːn/ n véspera f do Dia de Todos os Santos

hallucination /həlu:sɪˈneɪʃn/ n alucinação f

halo /ˈheɪləʊ/ n (pl -oes) halo m, auréola f

halt /hɔ:lt/ n parada f, (P) paragem f □ vt deter, fazer parar □ vi fazer alto, parar

halve /ha:v/ vt dividir ao meio; (time etc) reduzir à metade

ham /hæm/ n presunto m

hamburger /ˈhæmbɜ:gə(r)/ n hambúrguer m, (P) hamburgo m

hamlet /ˈhæmlɪt/ n aldeola f, lugarejo m

hammer /ˈhæmə(r)/ n martelo m □ vt/i martelar; (fig) bater com força

hammock /ˈhæmək/ n rede f (de dormir)

hamper[1] /ˈhæmpə(r)/ n cesto m, (P) cabaz m

hamper[2] /ˈhæmpə(r)/ vt dificultar, atrapalhar

hamster /ˈhæmstə(r)/ n hamster m

hand /hænd/ n mão f; (of clock) ponteiro m; (writing) letra f; (worker) trabalhador m; (cards) mão f; (measure) palmo m. (helping) ~ ajuda f, mão f □ vt dar, entregar. **at** ~ à mão. ~**baggage** n bagagem f de mão. **in** or **over** entregar. ~ **out** distribuir. ~**out** n impresso m, folheto m; (money) esmola f, donativo m. **on the one** ~ . . . **on the other** ~ por um lado . . . por outro. **out of** ~ incontrolável. **to** ~ à mão

handbag /ˈhændbæg/ n carteira f, bolsa de mão f, mala de mão f

handbook /ˈhændbʊk/ n manual m

handbrake /ˈhændbreɪk/ n freio m de mão, (P) travão m de mão

handcuffs /ˈhændkʌfs/ npl algemas fpl

handful /ˈhændfʊl/ n mão-cheia f, punhado m; (a few) punhado m; (difficult task) mão-de-obra f. **she's a** ~ (colloq) ela é danada

handicap /ˈhændɪkæp/ n (in competition) handicap m; (disadvantage) desvantagem f □ vt (pt handicapped) prejudicar. ~**ped** a deficiente. **mentally** ~**ped** deficiente mental

handicraft /ˈhændɪkra:ft/ n artesanato m, trabalho m manual

handiwork /ˈhændɪwɜ:k/ n obra f, trabalho m

handkerchief /ˈhæŋkətʃɪf/ n lenço m

handle /ˈhændl/ n (of door etc) maçaneta f, puxador m; (of cup etc) asa f; (of implement) cabo m; (of pan etc) alça f, (P) pega f □ vt (touch) manusear, tocar; (operate with hands) manejar; (deal in) negociar em; (deal with) tratar de; (person) lidar com. **fly off the** ~ (colloq) perder as estribeiras

handlebar /ˈhændlba:(r)/ n guidão m, (P) guiador m

handmade /ˈhændmeɪd/ a feito à mão

handshake /ˈhændʃeɪk/ n aperto m de mão

handsome /ˈhænsəm/ a bonito; (fig) generoso

handwriting /ˈhændraɪtɪŋ/ n letra f, caligrafia f

handy /ˈhændɪ/ a (-ier, -iest) a (convenient, useful) útil, prático; (person) jeitoso; (near) à mão

handyman /ˈhændɪmæn/ n (pl -men) faz-tudo m

hang /hæŋ/ vt (pt hung) pendurar, suspender; (head) baixar; (pt hanged) (criminal) enforcar □ vi estar dependurado, pender; (criminal) ser enforcado. **get the** ~ **of** (colloq) pegar o jeito de, (P) apanhar. ~ **about** andar por ai. ~ **back** hesitar. ~**gliding** n asa f delta. ~ **on** (wait) aguardar. ~ **on to** (hold tightly) agarrar-se a. ~ **out** (sl: live) morar. ~ **up** (phone) desligar. ~**up** n (sl) complexo m

hangar /ˈhæŋə(r)/ n hangar m

hanger /ˈhæŋə(r)/ n (for clothes) cabide m. ~**on** n parasita mf

hangover /ˈhæŋəʊvə(r)/ n (from drinking) ressaca f

hanker /ˈhæŋkə(r)/ vi ~ **after** ansiar por, suspirar por

haphazardly /hæpˈhæzədlɪ/ adv ao acaso, à sorte, a fortuito, casual

happen /ˈhæpən/ vi acontecer, suceder. **he** ~**s to be out** por acaso ele não está. ~**ing** n acontecimento m

happ|y /ˈhæpɪ/ a (-ier, -iest) feliz. **be** ~**y with** estar contente com. ~**y-go-lucky** a despreocupado. ~**ily** adv com satisfação; (fortunately) felizmente. **she smiled** ~**ily** ela sorriu feliz. ~**iness** n felicidade f

harass /ˈhærəs/ vt amofinar, atormentar, perseguir. ~**ment** n amofinação f, perseguição f. **sexual** ~**ment** assédio m sexual

harbour /ˈha:bə(r)/ n porto m; (shelter) abrigo m □ vt abrigar, dar asilo a; (fig: in the mind) ocultar, obrigar

hard /ha:d/ a (-er, -est) duro; (difficult) difícil □ adv muito, intensamente; (look) fixamente; (pull) com força; (think) a fundo, a sério. ~**back** n livro m encadernado. ~**-boiled egg** ovo m cozido. ~ **by** muito perto. ~ **disk** disco m rígido, (P) duro. ~**-headed** a realista, prático. ~ **of hearing** meio surdo. ~ **shoulder** acostamento m, (P) berma f alcatroada. ~ **up** (colloq) sem dinheiro, teso (sl), liso (sl). ~ **water** água f dura

h

hardboard /'ha:dbɔ:d/ n madeira f compensada, madeira f prensada, (P) tabopan m

harden /'ha:dn/ vt/i endurecer. ~ed a (callous) calejado; (robust) enrijado

hardly /'ha:dlɪ/ adv mal, dificilmente, a custo. ~ ever quase nunca

hardship /'ha:dʃɪp/ n provação f, adversidade f; (suffering) sofrimento m; (financial) privação f

hardware /'ha:dweə(r)/ n ferragens fpl; (comput) hardware m

hardy /'ha:dɪ/ a (-ier, -iest) resistente

hare /heə(r)/ n lebre f

hark /ha:k/ vi ~ back to voltar a, recordar

harm /ha:m/ n mal m □ vt prejudicar, fazer mal a. ~ful a prejudicial, nocivo. ~less a inofen-sivo. out of ~'s way a salvo. there's no ~ in não há mal em

harmonica /ha:'mɒnɪkə/ n gaita f de boca, (P) beiços

harmon|y /'ha:mənɪ/ n harmonia f. ~ious /-'məʊnɪəs/ a harmonioso. ~ize vt/i harmonizar(-se)

harness /'ha:nɪs/ n arreios mpl □ vt arrear; (fig: use) aproveitar, utilizar

harp /ha:p/ n harpa f □ vi ~ on (about) repisar. ~ ist n harpista mf

harpoon /ha:'pu:n/ n arpão m

harpsichord /'ha:psɪkɔ:d/ n cravo m

harrowing /'hærəʊŋ/ a dilacerante, lancinante

harsh /ha:ʃ/ a (-er, -est) duro, severo; (texture, voice) áspero; (light) cru; (colour) gritante; (climate) rigoroso. ~ly adv duramente. ~ness n dureza f

harvest /'ha:vɪst/ n colheita f, ceifa f □ vt colher, ceifar

has /hæz/ see **have**

hash /hæʃ/ n picadinho m, carne f cozida; (fig: jumble) bagunça f. **make a ~ of** fazer uma bagunça

hashish /'hæʃɪʃ/ n haxixe m

hassle /'hæsl/ n (colloq: quarrel) discussão f; (colloq: struggle) dificuldade f □ vt (colloq) aborrecer

haste /heɪst/ n pressa f. **make ~** apressar-se

hasten /'heɪsn/ vt/i apressar(-se)

hast|y /'heɪstɪ/ a (-ier, -iest) apressado; (too quick) precipitado. ~ily adv às pressas, precipitadamente

hat /hæt/ n chapéu m

hatch[1] /hætʃ/ n (for food) postigo m; (naut) escotilha f

hatch[2] /hætʃ/ vt/i chocar; (a plot etc) tramar, urdir

hatchback /'hætʃbæk/ n carro m de três ou cinco portas

hatchet /'hætʃɪt/ n machadinha f

hate /heɪt/ n ódio m □ vt odiar, detestar. ~ful a odioso, detestável

hatred /'heɪtrɪd/ n ódio m

haughty /'hɔ:tɪ/ a (-ier, -iest) altivo, soberbo, arrogante

haul /hɔ:l/ vt arrastar, puxar; (goods) transportar em camião □ n (booty) presa f; (fish caught) apanha f; (distance) percurso m. ~age n transporte m de cargas. ~ier n (firm) transportadora f rodoviária; (person) fretador m

haunt /hɔ:nt/ vt rondar, freqüentar, (P) frequentar; (ghost) assombrar; (thought) obcecar □ n lugar m favorito. ~ed house casa f mal-assombrada

have /hæv/ vt/i (3 sing pres has, pt had) ter; (bath etc) tomar; (meal) fazer; (walk) dar □ v aux ter. ~ done ter feito. ~ it out (with) pôr a coisa em pratos limpos, pedir uma explicação (para). ~ sth done mandar fazer alg coisa

haven /'heɪvn/ n porto m; (refuge) refúgio m

haversack /'hævəsæk/ n mochila f

havoc /'hævək/ n estragos mpl. **play ~ with** causar estragos em

hawk[1] /hɔ:k/ n falcão m

hawk[2] /hɔ:k/ vt vender de porta em porta. ~er n vendedor m ambulante

hawthorn /'hɔ:θɔ:n/ n pirilteiro m, estrepeiro m

hay /heɪ/ n feno m. ~ **fever** febre f do feno

haystack /'heɪstæk/ n palheiro m, (P) meda f de feno

haywire /'heɪwaɪə(r)/ a **go ~** (colloq) ficar transtornado

hazard /'hæzəd/ n risco m □ vt arriscar. ~ **warning lights** pisca-alerta m. ~ous a arriscado

haze /heɪz/ n bruma f, neblina f, cerração f

hazel /'heɪzl/ n aveleira f. ~-**nut** n avelã f

hazy /'heɪzɪ/ a (-ier, -iest) brumoso, encoberto; (fig: vague) vago

he /hi:/ pron ele □ n macho m

head /hed/ n cabeça f; (chief) chefe m; (of beer) espuma f □ a principal □ vt encabeçar, estar à frente de □ vi ~ **for** dirigir-se para. ~**dress** n toucador m. ~ **first** de cabeça. ~**-on** a frontal □ adv de frente. ~**s or tails?** cara ou coroa? ~ **waiter** chefe de garçons m, (P) dos criados. ~**er** n (football) cabeçada f

headache /'hedeɪk/ n dor f de cabeça

heading /'hedɪŋ/ n cabeçalho m, título m; (subject category) rubrica f

headlamp /'hedlæmp/ n farol m

headland /'hedlənd/ n promontório m

headlight /'hedlaɪt/ n farol m

headline /'hedlam/ n título m, cabeçalho m

headlong /'hedlɒŋ/ a de cabeça; (rash) precipitado □ adv de cabeça; (rashly) precipitadamente

head|master /hed'ma:stə(r)/ n diretor m, (P) director m. ~**mistress** n diretora f, (P) directora f

headphone /'hedfəʊn/ n fone m de cabeça, (P) auscultador m

headquarters /hed'kwɔ:təz/ npl sede f; (mil) quartel m general

headrest /'hedrest/ n apoio m para a cabeça

headroom /'hedru:m/ n (auto) espaço m para a cabeça; (bridge) limite m de altura, altura f máxima

headstrong /'hedstrɒŋ/ a teimoso

headway /'hedweɪ/ n progresso m. make ~ fazer progressos

heady /'hedɪ/ a (-ier, -iest) empolgante

heal /hi:l/ vt/i curar(-se), sarar; (wound) cicatrizar

health /helθ/ n saúde f. ~ centre posto m de saúde. ~ foods alimentos mpl naturais. ~y a saudável, sadio

heap /hi:p/ n monte m, pilha f □ vt amontoar, empilhar. ~s of money (colloq) dinheiro aos montes (colloq)

hear /hɪə(r)/ vt/i (pt heard /hɜ:d/) ouvir. ~, hear! apoiado! ~ from ter notícias de. ~ of or about ouvir falar de. I won't ~ of it nem quero ouvir falar nisso. ~ing n ouvido m, audição f; (jur) audiência f. ~ing-aid n aparelho m de audição

hearsay /'hɪəseɪ/ n boato m. it's only ~ é só por ouvir dizer

hearse /hɜ:s/ n carro m funerário

heart /ha:t/ n coração m. ~s (cards) copas fpl. at ~ no fundo. by ~ de cor. ~ attack ataque m de coração. ~-beat n pulsação f, batida f. ~-breaking a de cortar o coração. ~-broken a com o coração partido, desfeito. ~-to-heart a com o coração nas mãos. lose ~ perder a coragem, desanimar

heartburn /'ha:tbɜ:n/ n azia f

hearten /'ha:tn/ vt animar, encorajar

heartfelt /'ha:tfelt/ a sincero, sentido

hearth /ha:θ/ n lareira f

heartless /'ha:tlɪs/ a insensível, desalmado, cruel

heart|y /'ha:tɪ/ a (-ier, -iest) caloroso; (meal) abundante. ~ily adv calorosamente; (eat, laugh) com vontade

heat /hi:t/ n calor m; (fig) ardor m; (contest) eliminatória f □ vt/i aquecer. ~stroke n insolação f. ~wave n onda

f de calor. ~er n aquecedor m. ~ing n aquecimento m

heated /'hi:tɪd/ a (fig) acalorado, aceso

heathen /'hi:ðn/ n pagão m, pagã f

heather /'heðə(r)/ n urze f

heave /hi:v/ vt/i (lift) içar; (a sigh) soltar; (retch) ter náuseas; (colloq: throw) atirar

heaven /'hevn/ n céu m. ~ly a celestial; (colloq) divino

heav|y /'hevɪ/ a (-ier, -iest) pesado; (blow, rain) forte; (cold, drinker) grande; (traffic) intenso. ~ily adv pesadamente; (drink, smoke etc) inveterado

heavyweight /'hevɪweɪt/ n (boxing) peso-pesado m

Hebrew /'hi:bru:/ a hebreu, hebraico □ n (lang) hebreu m

h

heckle /'hekl/ vt interromper, interpelar

hectic /'hektɪk/ a muito agitado, febril

hedge /hedʒ/ n sebe f □ vt cercar □ vi (in answering) usar de evasivas. ~ one's bets (fig) resguardar-se

hedgehog /'hedʒhɒg/ n ouriço-cacheiro m

heed /hi:d/ vt prestar atenção a, escutar □ n pay ~ to prestar atenção a, dar ouvidos a. ~less a ~less of indiferente a, sem prestar atenção a

heel /hi:l/ n calcanhar m; (of shoe) salto m; (sl) canalha m

hefty /'heftɪ/ a (-ier, -iest) robusto e corpulento

height /haɪt/ n altura f; (of mountain, plane) altitude f; (fig) auge m, cúmulo m

heighten /'haɪtn/ vt/i aumentar, elevar(-se)

heir /eə(r)/ n herdeiro m. ~ess n herdeira f

heirloom /'eəlu:m/ n peça f de família, (P) relíquia f de família

held /held/ see hold¹

helicopter /'helɪkɒptə(r)/ n helicóptero m

hell /hel/ n inferno m. for the ~ of it só por gozo. ~-bent a decidido a todo o custo (on a). ~ish a infernal

hello /hə'ləʊ/ int & n = hallo

helm /helm/ n leme m

helmet /'helmɪt/ n capacete m

help /help/ vt/i ajudar □ n ajuda f. home ~ empregada f, faxineira f, (P) mulher f a dias. ~ o.s. to servir-se de. he cannot ~ laughing ele não pode conter o riso. it can't be ~ed não há remédio. ~er n ajudante mf. ~ful a útil; (serviceable) de grande ajuda. ~less a impotente

helping /'helpɪŋ/ n porção f, dose f

hem /hem/ *n* bainha *f* □ *vt* (*pt* **hemmed**) fazer a bainha. **~ in** cercar, encurralar

hemisphere /'hemɪsfɪə(r)/ *n* hemisfério *m*

hemp /hemp/ *n* cânhamo *m*

hen /hen/ *n* galinha *f*

hence /hens/ *adv* (*from now*) a partir desta altura; (*for this reason*) daí, por isso. **a week ~** daqui a uma semana. **~forth** *adv* de agora em diante, doravante

henpecked /'henpekt/ *a* mandado, (*P*) dominado pela mulher

her /hɜː(r)/ *pron* a (a ela); (*after prep*) ela. **(to) ~** lhe. **I know ~** conheço-a □ *a* seu(s), sua(s); dela

herald /'herəld/ *vt* anunciar

heraldry /'herəldrɪ/ *n* heráldica *f*

herb /hɜːb/ *n* erva *f* culinária *or* medicinal

herd /hɜːd/ *n* manada *f*; (*of pigs*) vara *f* □ □ *vi* **~ together** juntar-se em rebanho

here /hɪə(r)/ *adv* aqui □ *int* tome; aqui está. **to/from ~** para aqui/daqui

hereafter /hɪər'ɑːftə(r)/ *adv* de/para o futuro, daqui em diante □ *n* **the ~** a vida de além-túmulo, (*P*) a vida futura

hereby /hɪə'baɪ/ *adv* (*jur*) pelo presente ato ou decreto, etc, (*P*) pelo presente acto ou decreto, etc

hereditary /hɪ'redɪtrɪ/ *a* hereditário

heredity /hɪ'redətɪ/ *n* hereditariedade *f*

here|sy /'herəsɪ/ *n* heresia *f*. **~tic** *n* herege *mf*. **~tical** /hɪ'retɪkl/ *a* herético

heritage /'herɪtɪdʒ/ *n* herança *f*, patrimônio *m*, (*P*) património *m*

hermit /'hɜːmɪt/ *n* eremita *m*

hernia /'hɜːnɪə/ *n* hérnia *f*

hero /'hɪərəʊ/ *n* (*pl* -oes) herói *m*

heroic /hɪ'rəʊɪk/ *a* heróico

heroin /'herəʊɪn/ *n* heroína *f*

heroine /'herəʊɪn/ *n* heroína *f*

heroism /'herəʊɪzəm/ *n* heroísmo *m*

heron /'herən/ *n* garça *f*

herring /'herɪŋ/ *n* arenque *m*

hers /hɜːz/ *poss pron* o(s) seu(s), a(s) sua(s), o(s) dela, a(s) dela. **it is ~** é (o) dela *or* o seu

herself /hɜː'self/ *pron* ela mesma; (*reflexive*) se. **by ~** sozinha. **for ~** para si mesma. **to ~** a/para si mesma. **Mary ~ said so** foi a própria Maria que o disse

hesitant /'hezɪtənt/ *a* hesitante

hesitat|e /'hezɪteɪt/ *vt* hesitar. **~ion** /-'teɪʃn/ *n* hesitação *f*

heterosexual /hetərəʊ'seksjʊəl/ *a* & *n* heterossexual (*mf*)

hexagon /'heksəgən/ *n* hexágono *m*. **~al** /-'ægənl/ *a* hexagonal

hey /heɪ/ *int* eh, olá

heyday /'heɪdeɪ/ *n* auge *m*, apogeu *m*

hi /haɪ/ *int* olá, viva

hibernat|e /'haɪbəneɪt/ *vi* hibernar. **~ion** /-'neɪʃn/ *n* hibernação *f*

hiccup /'hɪkʌp/ *n* soluço *m* □ *vi* soluçar, estar com soluços

hide[1] /haɪd/ *vt/i* (*pt* **hid**, *pp* **hidden**) esconder(-se) (**from** de). **~-and-seek** *n* (*game*) esconde-esconde *m*. **~-out** *n* (*colloq*) esconderijo *m*

hide[2] /haɪd/ *n* pele *f*, couro *m*

hideous /'hɪdɪəs/ *a* horrendo, medonho

hiding /'haɪdɪŋ/ *n* (*colloq: thrashing*) sova *f*, surra *f*. **go into ~** esconder-se. **~-place** *n* esconderijo *m*

hierarchy /'haɪərɑːkɪ/ *n* hierarquia *f*

hi-fi /haɪ'faɪ/ *a* & *n* (de) alta fidelidade (*f*)

high /haɪ/ *a* (-**er**, -**est**) alto; (*price, number*) elevado; (*voice, pitch*) agudo □ *n* alta *f* □ *adv* alto. **two metres ~** com dois metros de altura. **~ chair** cadeira *f* alta para crianças. **~-handed** *a* autoritário, prepotente. **~ jump** salto *m* em altura. **~-rise building** edifício *m* alto, (*P*) torre *f*. **~ school** escola *f* secundária. **in the ~ season** em plena estação. **~-speed** *a* ultra-rápido. **~-spirited** *a* animado, vivo. **~ spot** (*sl*) ponto *m* culminante. **~ street** rua *f* principal. **~ tide** maré *f* alta. **~er education** ensino *m* superior

highbrow /'haɪbraʊ/ *a* & *n* (*colloq*) intelectual (*m*)

highlight /'haɪlaɪt/ *n* (*fig*) ponto *m* alto □ *vt* salientar, pôr em relevo, realçar

highly /'haɪlɪ/ *adv* altamente, extremamente. **~-strung** *a* muito sensível, nervoso, tenso. **speak ~ of** falar bem de

Highness /'haɪnɪs/ *n* Alteza *f*

highway /'haɪweɪ/ *n* estrada *f*, rodovia *f*. **H~ Code** Código *m* Nacional de Trânsito

hijack /'haɪdʒæk/ *vt* seqüestrar, (*P*) sequestrar □ *n* seqüestro *m*, (*P*) sequestro *m*. **~er** *n* (*of plane*) pirata *m* (do ar)

hike /haɪk/ *n* caminhada no campo *f* □ *vi* fazer uma caminhada. **~r** /-ə(r)/ *n* excursionista *mf*, caminhante *mf*

hilarious /hɪ'leərɪəs/ *a* divertido, desopilante

hill /hɪl/ *n* colina *f*, monte *m*; (*slope*) ladeira *f*, subida *f*. **~y** *a* acidentado

hillside /'hɪlsaɪd/ *n* encosta *f*, vertente *f*

hilt /hɪlt/ *n* punho *m*. **to the ~** completamente, inteiramente

him /hɪm/ *pron* o (a ele); (*after prep*) ele. **(to)** ~ lhe. **I know** ~ conheço-o

himself /hɪm'self/ *pron* ele mesmo; (*reflexive*) se. **by** ~ sozinho. **for** ~ para si mesmo. **to** ~ a/para si mesmo. **Peter** ~ **saw it** foi o próprio Pedro que o viu

hind /haɪnd/ *a* traseiro, posterior

hind|er /'hɪndə(r)/ *vt* empatar, estorvar; (*prevent*) impedir. ~**rance** *n* estorvo *m*

hindsight /'haɪndsaɪt/ *n* **with** ~ em retrospecto

Hindu /hɪn'duː/ *n & a* hindu (*mf*). ~**ism** /-ɪzəm/ *n* hinduísmo *m*

hinge /hɪndʒ/ *n* dobradiça *f* □ *vi* ~ **on** depender de

hint /hɪnt/ *n* insinuação *f*, indireta *f*, (*P*) indirecta *f*; (*advice*) sugestão *f*, dica *f* (*colloq*) □ *vt* dar a entender, insinuar □ *vi* ~ **at** fazer alusão a

hip /hɪp/ *n* quadril *m*

hippie /'hɪpɪ/ *n* hippie *mf*

hippopotamus /hɪpə'pɒtəməs/ *n* (*pl* -**muses**) hipopótamo *m*

hire /'haɪə(r)/ *vt* alugar; (*person*) contratar □ *n* aluguel *m*, (*P*) aluguer *m*. ~-**purchase** *n* compra *f* a prestações, (*P*) crediário *m*

hirsute /'hɜːsjuːt/ *a* hirsuto

his /hɪz/ *a* seu(s), sua(s), dele □ *poss pron* o(s) seu(s), a(s) sua(s), o(s) dele, a(s) dele. **it is** ~ é (o) dele *or* o seu

Hispanic /hɪs'pænɪk/ *a* hispânico

hiss /hɪs/ *n* silvo *m*; (*for disapproval*) assobio *m*, vaia *f* □ *vt/i* sibilar; (*for disapproval*) assobiar, vaiar

historian /hɪ'stɔːrɪən/ *n* historiador *m*

histor|y /'hɪstərɪ/ *n* história *f*. ~**ic(al)** /hɪ'stɒrɪk(l)/ *a* histórico

hit /hɪt/ *vt* (*pt* **hit**, *pres p* **hitting**) atingir, bater em; (*knock against, collide with*) chocar com, ir de encontro a; (*strike a target*) acertar em; (*find*) descobrir; (*affect*) atingir □ *vi* ~ **on** dar com □ *n* pancada *f*; (*fig: success*) sucesso *m*. ~ **it off** dar-se bem (**with** com). ~-**and-run** *a* (*driver*) que foge depois do desastre. ~-**or-miss** *a* ao acaso

hitch /hɪtʃ/ *vt* atar, prender; (*to a hook*) enganchar □ *n* sacão *m*; (*snag*) problema *m*. ~ **a lift**, ~-**hike** viajar de carona, (*P*) boleia. ~-**hiker** *n* o que viaja de carona, boleia. ~ **up** puxar para cima

hive /haɪv/ *n* colméia *f* □ *vt* ~ **off** separar e tornar independente

hoard /hɔːd/ *vt* juntar, açambarcar □ *n* provisão *f*; (*of valuables*) tesouro *m*

hoarding /'hɔːdɪŋ/ *n* tapume *m*, outdoor *m*

hoarse /hɔːs/ *a* (-**er**, -**est**) rouco. ~**ness** *n* rouquidão *f*

hoax /həʊks/ *n* (*malicious*) logro *m*, embuste *m*; (*humorous*) trote *m* □ *vt* (*malicious*) enganar, lograr; passar um trote, pregar uma peça em

hob /hɒb/ *n* placa *f* de aquecimento (do fogão)

hobble /'hɒbl/ *vi* coxear □ *vt* pear

hobby /'hɒbɪ/ *n* passatempo *m* favorito. ~-**horse** *n* (*fig*) tópico *m* favorito

hock /hɒk/ *n* vinho *m* branco do Reno

hockey /'hɒkɪ/ *n* hóquei *m*

hoe /həʊ/ *n* enxada *f* □ *vt* trabalhar com enxada

hog /hɒg/ *n* porco *m*; (*greedy person*) glutão *m* □ *vt* (*pt* **hogged**) (*colloq*) açambarcar

hoist /hɔɪst/ *vt* içar □ *n* guindaste *m*, (*P*) monta-cargas *m*

hold¹ /həʊld/ *vt* (*pt* **held**) segurar; (*contain*) levar; (*possess*) ter, possuir; (*occupy*) ocupar; (*keep, maintain*) conservar, manter; (*affirm*) manter □ *vi* (*of rope etc*) agüentar(-se), (*P*) aguentar(-se) □ *n* (*influence*) domínio *m*. **get** ~ **of** pôr as mãos em; (*fig*) apanhar. ~ **back** reter. ~ **on** (*colloq*) esperar. ~ **on to** guardar; (*cling to*) agarrar-se a. ~ **one's breath** suster a respiração. ~ **one's tongue** calar-se. ~ **the line** não desligar. ~ **out** resistir. ~ **up** (*support*) sustentar; (*delay*) demorar; (*rob*) assaltar. ~-**up** *n* atraso *m*; (*auto*) engarrafamento *m*; (*robbery*) assalto *m*. ~ **with** agüentar, (*P*) aguentar. ~**er** *n* detentor *m*; (*of post, title etc*) titular *mf*; (*for object*) suporte *m*

hold² /həʊld/ *n* (*of ship, plane*) porão *m*

holdall /'həʊldɔːl/ *n* saco *m* de viagem

holding /'həʊldɪŋ/ *n* (*land*) propriedade *f*; (*comm*) acções *fpl*, (*P*) acções *fpl*, valores *mpl*, holding *m*

hole /həʊl/ *n* buraco *m* □ *vt* abrir buraco(s) em, esburacar

holiday /'hɒlədeɪ/ *n* férias *fpl*; (*day off; public*) feriado *m* □ *vi* passar férias. ~-**maker** *n* pessoa *f* em férias; (*in summer*) veranista *mf*, (*P*) veraneante *mf*

holiness /'həʊlɪnɪs/ *n* santidade *f*

Holland /'hɒlənd/ *n* Holanda *f*

hollow /'hɒləʊ/ *a* oco, vazio; (*fig*) falso; (*cheeks*) fundo; (*sound*) surdo □ *n* (*in the ground*) cavidade *f*; (*in the hand*) cova *f*

holly /'hɒlɪ/ *n* azevinho *m*

holster /'həʊlstə(r)/ *n* coldre *m*

holy /'həʊlɪ/ *a* (-**ier**, -**iest**) santo, sagrado; (*water*) benta. **H**~ **Ghost**, **H**~ **Spirit** Espírito *m* Santo

homage /'hɒmɪdʒ/ *n* homenagem *f*. **pay** ~ **to** prestar homenagem a

home /həʊm/ n casa f, lar m; (institution) lar m, asilo m; (country) país m natal □ a caseiro, doméstico; (of family) de família; (pol) nacional, interno; (football match) em casa □ adv (at) ~ em casa. **come/go** ~ vir/ir para casa. **make oneself at** ~ não fazer cerimônia, (P) cerimónia. ~-**made** a caseiro. **H**~ **Office** Ministério m do Interior. ~ **town** cidade f or terra f natal. ~ **truth** dura verdade f, verdade(s) f (pl) amarga(s). ~**less** a sem casa, desabrigado

homeland /ˈhəʊmlænd/ n pátria f

homely /ˈhəʊmlɪ/ a (-ier, -iest) (simple) simples; (Amer: ugly) sem graça

homesick /ˈhəʊmsɪk/ a **be** ~ ter saudades

homeward /ˈhəʊmwəd/ a (journey) de regresso

homework /ˈhəʊmwɜːk/ n trabalho m de casa, dever m de casa

homicide /ˈhɒmɪsaɪd/ n homicídio m; (person) homicida mf

homoeopath|y /ˈhəʊmɪˈɒpəθɪ/ n homeopatia f. ~**ic** a homeopático

homosexual /ˌhɒməˈsekʃʊəl/ a & n homossexual (mf)

honest /ˈɒnɪst/ a honesto; (frank) franco. ~**ly** adv honestamente; (frankly) francamente. ~**y** n honestidade f

honey /ˈhʌnɪ/ n mel m; (colloq: darling) querido m, querida f, meu bem m

honeycomb /ˈhʌnɪkəʊm/ n favo m de mel

honeymoon /ˈhʌnɪmuːn/ n lua de mel f

honorary /ˈɒnərərɪ/ a honorário

honour /ˈɒnə(r)/ n honra f □ vt honrar. ~**able** a honrado, honroso

hood /hʊd/ n capuz m; (car roof) capota f, (P) tejadilho m; (Amer: bonnet) capô m, (P) capot m

hoodwink /ˈhʊdwɪŋk/ vt enganar

hoof /huːf/ n (pl -fs) casco m

hook /hʊk/ n gancho m; (on garment) colchete m; (for fishing) anzol m □ vt enganchar; (fish) apanhar, pescar. **off the** ~ livre de dificuldades; (phone) desligado

hooked /hʊkt/ a **be** ~ **on** (sl) ter o vício de, estar viciado em

hookey /ˈhʊkɪ/ n **play** ~ (Amer sl) fazer gazeta

hooligan /ˈhuːlɪɡən/ n desordeiro m

hoop /huːp/ n arco m; (of cask) cinta f

hooray /huːˈreɪ/ int & n = **hurrah**

hoot /huːt/ n (of owl) pio m de mocho; (of horn) buzinada f; (jeer) apupo m □ vi (of owl) piar; (of horn) buzinar; (jeer) apupar. ~**er** n buzina f; (of factory) sereia f

Hoover /ˈhuːvə(r)/ n aspirador de pó m, (P) aspirador m □ vt passar o aspirador

hop[1] /hɒp/ vi (pt hopped) saltar num pé só, (P) ao pé coxinho □ n salto m. ~ **in** (colloq) subir, saltar (colloq). ~ **it** (sl) pôr-se a andar (colloq). ~ **out** (colloq) descer, saltar (colloq)

hop[2] /hɒp/ n (plant) lúpulo m. ~**s** espigas fpl de lúpulo

hope /həʊp/ n esperança f □ vt/i esperar. ~ **for** esperar (ter). ~-**ful** a esperançoso; (promising) promissor. **be** ~**ful (that)** ter esperança (que), confiar (em que). ~**fully** adv esperançosamente; (it is hoped that) é de esperar que. ~**less** a desesperado, sem esperança; (incompetent) incapaz

horde /hɔːd/ n horda f

horizon /həˈraɪzn/ n horizonte m

horizontal /ˌhɒrɪˈzɒntl/ a horizontal

hormone /ˈhɔːməʊn/ n hormônio m, (P) hormona f

horn /hɔːn/ n chifre m, corno m; (of car) buzina f; (mus) trompa f. ~**y** a caloso, calejado

hornet /ˈhɔːnɪt/ n vespão m

horoscope /ˈhɒrəskəʊp/ n horóscopo m, (P) horoscópio m

horrible /ˈhɒrəbl/ a horrível, horroroso

horrid /ˈhɒrɪd/ a horrível, horripilante

horrific /həˈrɪfɪk/ a horrífico

horr|or /ˈhɒrə(r)/ n horror m □ a (film etc) de terror. ~**ify** vt horrorizar, horripilar

horse /hɔːs/ n cavalo m. ~-**chest-nut** n castanha f da India. ~ **racing** n corrida f de cavalos, hipismo m. ~-**radish** n rábano m

horseback /ˈhɔːsbæk/ n **on** ~ a cavalo

horseplay /ˈhɔːspleɪ/ n brincadeira f grosseira, abrutalhada f

horsepower /ˈhɔːspaʊə(r)/ n cavalo-vapor m

horseshoe /ˈhɔːsʃuː/ n ferradura f

horticultur|e /ˈhɔːtɪkʌltʃə(r)/ n horticultura f. ~**al** /-ˈkʌltʃərəl/ a hortícola

hose /həʊz/ n ~-(**pipe**) mangueira f □ vt regar com a mangueira

hospice /ˈhɒspɪs/ n hospício m; (for travellers) hospedaria f

hospit|able /həˈspɪtəbl/ a hospitaleiro. ~**ality** /-ˈtæləti/ n hospitalidade f

hospital /ˈhɒspɪtl/ n hospital m

host[1] /həʊst/ n anfitrião m, dono m da casa. ~**ess** n anfitriã f, dona f da casa

host[2] /həʊst/ n **a** ~ **of** uma multidão de, um grande número de

host[3] /həʊst/ n (relig) hóstia f

hostage /ˈhɒstɪdʒ/ n refém m

hostel /'hɒstl/ *n* residência *f* de estudantes *etc*

hostil|e /'hɒstaɪl/ *a* hostil. **~ity** /hɒ'stɪlətɪ/ *n* hostilidade *f*

hot /hɒt/ *a* (**hotter, hottest**) quente; (*culin*) picante. **be** *or* **feel ~** estar com *or* ter calor. **it is ~** está *or* faz calor □ *vt/i* (*pt* **hotted**) **~ up** (*colloq*) aquecer. **~ dog** cachorro-quente *m*. **~ line** linha direta *f*, (*P*) directa esp entre chefes de estado. **~-water bottle** saco *m* de água quente

hotbed /'hɒtbed/ *n* (*fig*) foco *m*

hotchpotch /'hɒtʃpɒtʃ/ *n* misturada *f*, (*P*) salgalhada *f*

hotel /həʊ'tel/ *n* hotel *m*. **~ier** /-ɪə(r)/ *n* hoteleiro *m*

hound /haʊnd/ *n* cão *m* de caça e de corrida, sabujo *m* □ *vt* acossar, perseguir

hour /'aʊə(r)/ *n* hora *f*. **~ly** *adv* de hora em hora □ *a* de hora em hora. **~ly pay** retribuição *f* horária. **paid ~ly** pago por hora

house[1] /haʊs/ *n* (*pl* **~s** /'haʊzɪz/) *n* casa *f*; (*pol*) câmara *f*. **on the ~** por conta da casa. **~-warming** *n* inauguração *f* da casa

house[2] /haʊz/ *vt* alojar; (*store*) arrecadar, guardar

houseboat /'haʊsbəʊt/ *n* casa *f* flutuante

household /'haʊshəʊld/ *n* família *f*, agregado *m* familiar. **~er** *n* ocupante *mf*; (*owner*) proprietário *m*

housekeep|er /'haʊskiːpə(r)/ *n* governanta *f*. **~ing** *n* (*work*) tarefas *fpl* domésticas

housewife /'haʊswaɪf/ *n* (*pl* **-wives**) dona *f* de casa

housework /'haʊswɜːk/ *n* tarefas *fpl* domésticas

housing /'haʊzɪŋ/ *n* alojamento *m*. **~ estate** zona *f* residencial

hovel /'hɒvl/ *n* casebre *m*, tugúrio *m*

hover /'hɒvə(r)/ *vi* pairar; (*linger*) deixar-se ficar, demorar-se

hovercraft /'hɒvəkrɑːft/ *n invar* aerobarco *m*, hovercraft *m*

how /haʊ/ *adv* como. **~ long/old is...?** que comprimento/idade tem...? **~ far?** a que distância? **~ many?** quantos? **~ much?** quanto? **~ often?** com que freqüência, (*P*) frequência? **~ pretty it is** como é lindo. **~ about a walk?** e se fôssemos dar uma volta? **~ are you?** como vai? **~ do you do?** muito prazer! **and ~!** oh se é!

however /haʊ'evə(r)/ *adv* de qualquer maneira; (*though*) contudo, no entanto, todavia. **~ small it may be** por menor que seja

howl /haʊl/ *n* uivo *m* □ *vi* uivar

HP *abbr see* **hire-purchase**

hp *abbr see* **horsepower**

hub /hʌb/ *n* cubo *m* da roda; (*fig*) centro *m*. **~-cap** *n* calota *f*, (*P*) tampão *m* da roda

hubbub /'hʌbʌb/ *n* chinfrim *m*

huddle /'hʌdl/ *vt/i* apinhar(-se). **~ together** aconchegar-se

hue[1] /hjuː/ *n* matiz *f*, tom *m*

hue[2] /hjuː/ *n* **~ and cry** clamor *m*, alarido *m*

huff /hʌf/ *n* **in a ~** com raiva, zangado

hug /hʌg/ *vt* (*pt* **hugged**) abraçar, apertar nos braços; (*keep close to*) chegar-se a □ *n* abraço *m*

huge /hjuːdʒ/ *a* enorme

hulk /hʌlk/ *n* casco (esp de navio desmantelado) *m*. **~ing** *a* (*colloq*) desajeitadão (*colloq*)

hull /hʌl/ *n* (*of ship*) casco *m*

hullo /hə'ləʊ/ *int* & *n* = **hallo**

hum /hʌm/ *vt/i* (*pt* **hummed**) cantar com a boca fechada; (*of insect, engine*) zumbir □ *n* zumbido *m*

human /'hjuːmən/ *a* humano □ *n* **~ (being)** ser *m* humano

humane /hjuː'meɪn/ *a* humano, compassivo

humanitarian /hjuːmænɪ'teərɪən/ *a* humanitário

humanity /hjuː'mænətɪ/ *n* humanidade *f*

humbl|e /'hʌmbl/ *a* (**-er, -est**) humilde □ *vt* humilhar. **~y** *adv* humildemente

humdrum /'hʌmdrʌm/ *a* monótono, rotineiro

humid /'hjuːmɪd/ *a* úmido, (*P*) húmido. **~ity** /-'mɪdətɪ/ *n* umidade *f*, (*P*) humidade *f*

humiliat|e /hjuː'mɪlɪeɪt/ *vt* humilhar. **~ion** /-'eɪʃn/ *n* humilhação *f*

humility /hjuː'mɪlətɪ/ *n* humildade *f*

humorist /'hjuːmərɪst/ *n* humorista *mf*

hum|our /'hjuːmə(r)/ *n* humor *m* □ *vt* fazer a vontade de. **~orous** *a* humorístico; (*person*) divertido, espirituoso

hump /hʌmp/ *n* corcova *f*; (*of the back*) corcunda *f* □ *vt* corcovar, arquear. **the ~** (*sl*) a neura (*colloq*)

hunch[1] /hʌntʃ/ *vt* curvar. **~ed up** curvado

hunch[2] /hʌntʃ/ *n* (*colloq*) palpite *m*

hunchback /'hʌntʃbæk/ *n* corcunda *mf*

hundred /'hʌndrəd/ *a* cem □ *n* centena *f*, cento *m*. **~s of** centenas de. **~fold** *a* cêntuplo □ *adv* cem vezes mais. **~th** *a* & *n* centésimo *m*

hundredweight /'hʌndrədweɪt/ *n* quintal *m* (= *50,8 kg; Amer 45,36 kg*)

hung /hʌŋ/ *see* **hang**

Hungar|y /'hʌŋgərɪ/ *n* Hungria *f.* ∼**ian**
/-'geərɪən/ *a* & *n* húngaro (*m*)

hunger /'hʌŋgə(r)/ *n* fome *f* □ *vi* ∼ **for** ter
fome de; (*fig*) desejar vivamente,
ansiar por

hungr|y /'hʌŋgrɪ/ *a* (**ier, -iest**)
esfomeado, faminto. **be** ∼**y** ter fome,
estar com fome. ∼**ily** *adv* avidamente

hunk /hʌŋk/ *n* grande naco *m*

hunt /hʌnt/ *vt/i* caçar □ *n* caça *f.* ∼ **for**
andar à caça de, andar à procura de.
∼**er** *n* caçador *m*. ∼**ing** *n* caça *f*,
caçada *f*

hurdle /'hɜ:dl/ *n* obstáculo *m*

hurl /hɜ:l/ *vt* arremessar, lançar com
força

hurrah, hurray /hʊ'rɑ:, hʊ'reɪ/ *int* & *n*
hurra (*m*), viva (*m*)

hurricane /'hʌrɪkən/ *n* furacão *m*

hurried /'hʌrɪd/ *a* apressado. ∼**ly** *adv*
apressadamente, às pressas

hurry /'hʌrɪ/ *vt/i* apressar(-se),
despachar(-se) □ *n* pressa *f.* **be in a**
∼ estar com *or* ter pressa. **do sth in a**
∼ fazer alg coisa às pressas. ∼**up!** ande
logo

hurt /hɜ:t/ *vt* (*pt* **hurt**) fazer mal a;
(*injure, offend*) magoar, ferir □ *vi* doer
□ *a* magoado, ferido □ *n* mal *m*;
(*feelings*) mágoa *f.* ∼**ful** *a* prejudicial;
(*remark etc*) que magoa

hurtle /'hɜ:tl/ *vi* despenhar-se; (*move
rapidly*) precipitar-se □ *vt* arremessar

husband /'hʌzbənd/ *n* marido *m*,
esposo *m*

hush /hʌʃ/ *vt* (fazer) calar. ∼! silencio!
□ *vi* calar-se □ *n* silêncio *m*. ∼-**hush** *a*
(*colloq*) muito em segredo. ∼ **up**
abafar, encobrir

husk /hʌsk/ *n* casca *f*

husky /'hʌskɪ/ *a* (**-ier, -iest**) (*hoarse*)
rouco, enrouquecido; (*burly*)
corpulento □ *n* cão *m* esquimó

hustle /'hʌsl/ *vt* empurrar, dar
encontrões a □ *n* empurrão *m*. ∼ **and
bustle** grande movimento *m*

hut /hʌt/ *n* cabana *f*, barraca *f* de madeira

hutch /hʌtʃ/ *n* coelheira *f*

hyacinth /'haɪəsɪnθ/ *n* jacinto *m*

hybrid /'haɪbrɪd/ *a* & *n* híbrido (*m*)

hydrant /'haɪdrənt/ *n* hidrante *m*

hydraulic /haɪ'drɔ:lɪk/ *a* hidráulico

hydroelectric /haɪdrəʊ'lektrɪk/ *a*
hidrelétrico, (*P*) hidroelectrico

hydrofoil /'haɪdrəʊfɔɪl/ *n* hidrofoil *m*

hydrogen /'haɪdrədʒən/ *n* hidrogênio *m*,
(*P*) hidrogénio *m*

hyena /haɪ'i:nə/ *n* hiena *f*

hygiene /'haɪdʒi:n/ *n* higiene *f*

hygienic /haɪ'dʒi:nɪk/ *a* higiénico, (*P*)
higiénico

hymn /hɪm/ *n* hino *m*, cântico *m*

hyper- /'haɪpə(r)/ *pref* hiper-

hypermarket /'haɪpəmɑ:kɪt/ *n*
hipermercado *m*

hyphen /'haɪfn/ *n* hífen *m*, traço-de-
união *m*. ∼**ate** *vt* unir com hifen

hypno|sis /hɪp'nəʊsɪs/ *n* hipnose *f.* ∼**tic**
/-'nɒtɪk/ *a* hipnótico

hypnot|ize /'hɪpnətaɪz/ *vt* hipnotizar.
∼**ism** /-ɪzəm/ *n* hipnotismo *m*

hypochondriac /haɪpə'kɒndrɪæk/ *n*
hipocondríaco *m*

hypocrisy /hɪ'pɒkrəsɪ/ *n* hipocrisia *f*

hypocrit|e /'hɪpəkrɪt/ *n* hipócrita *mf.*
∼**ical** /-'krɪtɪkl/ *a* hipócrita

hypodermic /haɪpə'dɜ:mɪk/ *a*
hipodérmico □ *n* seringa *f*

hypothe|sis /haɪ'pɒθəsɪs/ *n* (*pl* -**theses**
/-si:z/) hipótese *f.* ∼**tical** /-ə'θetɪkl/ *a*
hipotético

hyster|ia /hɪ'stɪərɪə/ *n* histeria *f.* ∼**ical**
/hɪ'sterɪkl/ *a* histérico

Ii

I /aɪ/ *pron* eu

Iberian /aɪ'bɪərɪən/ *a* ibérico □ *n*
íbero *m*

ice /aɪs/ *n* gelo *m* □ *vt/i* gelar; (*cake*) cobrir
com glacê □ *vi* ∼ **up** gelar. ∼-**box** *n*
(*Amer*) geladeira *f*, (*P*) frigorífico *m*.
∼(-**cream**) *n* sorvete *m*, (*P*) gelado
m. ∼-**cube** *n* cubo *m* or pedra *f* de gelo.
∼ **hockey** hóquei *m* sobre o gelo.
∼ **lolly** picolé *m*. ∼-**pack** *n* saco *m* de
gelo. ∼-**rink** *n* rinque *m* de patinação,
(*P*) patinagem *f* no gelo. ∼ **skating** *n*
patinação *f*, (*P*) patinagem *f* no gelo

iceberg /'aɪsbɜ:g/ *n* iceberg *m*; (*fig*)
pedaço *m* de gelo

Iceland /'aɪslənd/ *n* Islândia *f.* ∼**er**
n islandês *m*. ∼**ic** /-'lændɪk/ *a* & *n*
islandês (*m*)

icicle /'aɪsɪkl/ *n* pingente *m* de gelo

icing /'aɪsɪŋ/ *n* (*culin*) cobertura *f* de
açúcar, glacê *m*

icy /'aɪsɪ/ *a* (**-ier, -iest**) gelado, gélido,
glacial; (*road*) com gelo

idea /aɪ'dɪə/ *n* idéia *f*, (*P*) ideia *f*

ideal /aɪ'dɪəl/ *a* & *n* ideal (*m*). ∼**ize** *vt*
idealizar. ∼**ly** *adv* idealmente

idealis|t /aɪ'dɪəlɪst/ *n* idealista *mf.* ∼**m**
/-zəm/ *n* idealismo *m*. ∼**tic** /-'lɪstɪk/ *a*
idealista

identical /aɪ'dentɪkl/ *a* idêntico

identif|y /aɪˈdentɪfaɪ/ *vt* identificar □ *vi*
~**y with** identificar-se com. ~**ication**
/-ɪˈkeɪʃn/ *n* identificação *f*; (*papers*)
documentos *mpl* de identificação

identity /aɪˈdentəti/ *n* identidade *f*.
~ **card** carteira *f* de identidade, (*P*)
bilhete *m*. de identidade

ideolog|y /aɪdɪˈblɒdʒi/ *n* ideologia *f*.
~**ical** *a* /-ɪəˈlɒdʒɪkl/ *a* ideológico

idiom /ˈɪdɪəm/ *n* idioma *m*; (*phrase*)
expressão *f* idiomática. ~**atic**
/-ˈmætɪk/ *a* idiomático

idiosyncrasy /ɪdɪəˈsɪŋkrəsi/ *n*
idiossincrasia *f*, peculiaridade *f*

idiot /ˈɪdɪət/ *n* idiota *mf*. ~**ic** /-ˈɒtɪk/ *a*
idiota

idl|e /ˈaɪdl/ *a* (**-er**, **-est**) (*not active; lazy*)
ocioso; (*unemployed*) sem trabalho; (*of
machines*) parado; (*fig: useless*) inútil
□ *vt*/*i* (*of engine*) estar em ponto
morto, *P* estar no ralenti. ~**eness** *n*
ociosidade *f*. ~**y** *adv* ociosamente

idol /ˈaɪdl/ *n* ídolo *m*. ~**ize** *vt* idolatrar

idyllic /ɪˈdɪlɪk/ *a* idílico

i.e. *abbr* isto é, quer dizer

if /ɪf/ *conj* se

igloo /ˈɪɡluː/ *n* iglu *m*

ignite /ɪɡˈnaɪt/ *vt*/*i* inflamar(-se),
acender; (*catch fire*) pegar fogo; (*set fire
to*) atear fogo a, (*P*) deitar fogo a

ignition /ɪɡˈnɪʃn/ *n* (*auto*) ignição *f*.
~ (**key**) chave *f* de ignição

ignoran|t /ˈɡnərənt/ *a* ignorante. ~**ce** *n*
ignorância *f*. **be** ~**t of** ignorar

ignore /ɪɡˈnɔː(r)/ *vt* não fazer caso de,
passar por cima de; (*person in the street
etc*) fingir não ver

ill /ɪl/ *a* (*sick*) doente; (*bad*) mau □ *adv*
mal □ *n* mal *m*. ~**-advised** *a* pouco
aconselhável. ~ **at ease** pouco à
vontade. ~**-bred** *a* mal educado.
~**-fated** *a* malfadado. ~**-treat** *vt*
maltratar. ~ **will** má vontade *f*,
animosidade *f*

illegal /ɪˈliːɡl/ *a* ilegal

illegible /ɪˈledʒəbl/ *a* ilegível

illegitima|te /ɪlɪˈdʒɪtɪmət/ *a* ilegítimo.
~**cy** *n* ilegitimidade *f*

illitera|te /ɪˈlɪtərət/ *a* analfabeto;
(*uneducated*) iletrado. ~**cy** *n*
analfabetismo *m*

illness /ˈɪlnɪs/ *n* doença *f*

illogical /ɪˈlɒdʒɪkl/ *a* ilógico

illuminat|e /ɪˈluːmɪneɪt/ *vt* iluminar;
(*explain*) esclarecer. ~**ion** /-ˈneɪʃn/ *n*
iluminação *f*. ~**ions** *npl* luminárias *fpl*

illusion /ɪˈluːʒn/ *n* ilusão *f*

illusory /ɪˈluːsəri/ *a* ilusório

illustrat|e /ˈɪləstreɪt/ *vt* ilustrar. ~**ion**
/-ˈstreɪʃn/ *n* ilustração *f*. ~**ive** /-ətɪv/ *a*
ilustrativo

illustrious /ɪˈlʌstrɪəs/ *a* ilustre

image /ˈɪmɪdʒ/ *n* imagem *f*. (**public**)
~ imagem *f* pública

imaginary /ɪˈmædʒɪnəri/ *a* imaginário

imaginat|ion /ɪmædʒɪˈneɪʃn/ *n*
imaginação *f*. ~**ive** /ɪˈmædʒɪnətɪv/ *a*
imaginativo

imagin|e /ɪˈmædʒɪn/ *vt* imaginar. ~**able**
a imaginável

imbalance /ɪmˈbæləns/ *n* desequilíbrio *m*

imbecile /ˈɪmbəsiːl/ *a* & *n* imbecil (*mf*)

imbue /ɪmˈbjuː/ *vt* imbuir, impregnar

imitat|e /ˈɪmɪteɪt/ *vt* imitar. ~**ion** /-ˈteɪʃn/
n imitação *f*

immaculate /ɪˈmækjʊlət/ *a* imaculado;
(*impeccable*) impecável

immaterial /ɪməˈtɪərɪəl/ *a* (*of no
importance*) irrelevante. **that's** ~ **to
me** para mim tanto faz

immature /ɪməˈtjʊə(r)/ *a* imaturo

immediate /ɪˈmiːdɪət/ *a* imediato. ~**ly**
adv imediatamente □ *conj* logo que,
assim que

immens|e /ɪˈmens/ *a* imenso. ~**ely** /-slɪ/
adv imensamente. ~**ity** *n* imensidade *f*

immers|e /ɪˈmɜːs/ *vt* mergulhar, imergir.
be ~**ed in** (*fig*) estar imerso em.
~**ion** /-ʃn/ *n* imersão *f*. ~**ion heater**
aquecedor *m* de água elétrico, (*P*)
eléc-trico

immigr|ate /ˈɪmɪɡreɪt/ *vi* imigrar. ~**ant**
n & *a* imigrante (*mf*), imigrado (*m*).
~**ation** /-ˈɡreɪʃn/ *n* imigração *f*

imminen|t /ˈɪmɪnənt/ *a* iminente. ~**ce** *n*
iminência *f*

immobil|e /ɪˈməʊbaɪl/ *a* imóvel. ~**ize**
/-əlaɪz/ *vt* imobilizar

immoderate /ɪˈmɒdərət/ *a* imoderado,
descomedido

immoral /ɪˈmɒrəl/ *a* imoral. ~**ity**
/ɪməˈrælətɪ/ *n* imoralidade *f*

immortal /ɪˈmɔːtl/ *a* imortal. ~**ity**
/-ˈtælətɪ/ *n* imortalidade *f*. ~**ize** *vt*
imortalizar

immun|e /ɪˈmjuːn/ *a* imune, imunizado
(**from**, **to** contra). ~**ity** *n* imunidade *f*

imp /ɪmp/ *n* diabrete *m*

impact /ˈɪmpækt/ *n* impacto *m*

impair /ɪmˈpeə(r)/ *vt* deteriorar;
(*damage*) prejudicar

impale /ɪmˈpeɪl/ *vt* empalar

impart /ɪmˈpɑːt/ *vt* comunicar,
transmitir (**to** a)

impartial /ɪmˈpɑːʃl/ *a* imparcial. ~**ity**
/-ʃɪˈrælətɪ/ *n* imparcialidade *f*

impassable /ɪmˈpɑːsəbl/ *a* (*road, river*)
impraticável, intransitável; (*barrier
etc*) intransponível

impasse /ˈæmpɑːs/ *n* impasse *m*

impatien|t /ɪmˈpeɪʃənt/ a impaciente. ∼**ce** n impaciência f. ∼**tly** adv impacientemente

impeach /ɪmˈpiːtʃ/ vt incriminar, acusar

impeccable /ɪmˈpekəbl/ a impecável

impede /ɪmˈpiːd/ vt impedir, estorvar

impediment /ɪmˈpedɪmənt/ n impedimento m, obstáculo m. **(speech)** ∼ defeito m (na fala)

impel /ɪmˈpel/ vt (pt **impelled**) impelir, forçar (**to do** a fazer)

impending /ɪmˈpendɪŋ/ a iminente

impenetrable /ɪmˈpenɪtrəbl/ a impenetrável

imperative /ɪmˈperətɪv/ a imperativo; (*need etc*) imperioso ◻ n imperativo m

imperceptible /ɪmpəˈseptəbl/ a imperceptível

imperfect /ɪmˈpɜːfɪkt/ a imperfeito. ∼**ion** /-əˈfekʃn/ n imperfeição f

imperial /ɪmˈpɪəriəl/ a imperial; (*of measures*) legal (*na* GB). ∼**ism** /-lɪzəm/ n imperialismo m

imperious /ɪmˈpɪəriəs/ a imperioso

impersonal /ɪmˈpɜːsənl/ a impessoal

impersonat|e /ɪmˈpɜːsəneɪt/ vt fazer-se passar por; (*theat*) fazer or representar (o papel) de. ∼**ion** /-ˈneɪʃn/ n imitação f

impertinen|t /ɪmˈpɜːtɪnənt/ a impertinente. ∼**ce** n impertinência f. ∼**tly** adv com impertinência

impervious /ɪmˈpɜːvɪəs/ a ∼ **to** (*water*) impermeável a; (*fig*) insensível a

impetuous /ɪmˈpetʃʊəs/ a impetuoso

impetus /ˈɪmpɪtəs/ n ímpeto m

impinge /ɪmˈpɪndʒ/ vi ∼ **on** afetar, *P* afectar; (*encroach*) infringir

impish /ˈɪmpɪʃ/ a travesso, malicioso

implacable /ɪmˈplækəbl/ a implacável

implant /ɪmˈplɑːnt/ vt implantar

implement[1] /ˈɪmplɪmənt/ n instrumento m, utensílio m

implement[2] /ˈɪmplɪment/ vt implementar, executar

implicat|e /ˈɪmplɪkeɪt/ vt implicar. ∼**ion** /-ˈkeɪʃn/ n implicação f

implicit /ɪmˈplɪsɪt/ a implícito; (*unquestioning*) absoluto, incondicional

implore /ɪmˈplɔː(r)/ vt implorar, suplicar, rogar

imply /ɪmˈplaɪ/ vt implicar; (*hint*) sugerir, dar a entender, insinuar

impolite /ɪmpəˈlaɪt/ a indelicado, incorreto, (*P*) incorrecto

import[1] /ɪmˈpɔːt/ vt importar. ∼**ation** /-ˈteɪʃn/ n importação f. ∼**er** n importador m

import[2] /ˈɪmpɔːt/ n importação f; (*meaning*) significado m; (*importance*) importância f

importan|t /ɪmˈpɔːtnt/ a importante. ∼**ce** n importância f

impos|e /ɪmˈpəʊz/ vt impôr; (*inflict*) infligir ◻ vi ∼**e on** abusar de. ∼**ition** /-əˈzɪʃn/ n imposição f; (*unfair burden*) abuso m

imposing /ɪmˈpəʊzɪŋ/ a imponente

impossib|le /ɪmˈpɒsəbl/ a impossível. ∼**ility** /-ˈbɪlətɪ/ n impossibilidade f

impostor /ɪmˈpɒstə(r)/ n impostor m

impoten|t /ˈɪmpətənt/ a impotente. ∼**ce** n impotência f

impound /ɪmˈpaʊnd/ vt apreender, confiscar

impoverish /ɪmˈpɒvərɪʃ/ vt empobrecer

impracticable /ɪmˈpræktɪkəbl/ a impraticável

impractical /ɪmˈpræktɪkl/ a pouco prático

imprecise /ɪmprɪˈsaɪs/ a impreciso

impregnable /ɪmˈpregnəbl/ a inexpugnável; (*fig*) inabalável, irrefutável

impregnate /ˈɪmpregneɪt/ vt impregnar (**with** de)

impresario /ɪmprɪˈsaːrɪəʊ/ n (*pl* -**os**) empresário m

impress /ɪmˈpres/ vt impressionar, causar impressão a; (*imprint*) imprimir. ∼ **sth on s.o.** inculcar algo em alguém

impression /ɪmˈpreʃn/ n impressão f. ∼**able** a impressionável. ∼**ist** n impressionista mf

impressive /ɪmˈpresɪv/ a impressionante, imponente

imprint[1] /ˈɪmprɪnt/ n impressão f, marca f

imprint[2] /ɪmˈprɪnt/ vt imprimir

imprison /ɪmˈprɪzn/ vt prender, aprisionar. ∼**ment** n aprisionamento m, prisão f

improbab|le /ɪmˈprɒbəbl/ a improvável. ∼**ility** /-ˈbɪlətɪ/ n improbabilidade f

impromptu /ɪmˈprɒmptjuː/ a & adv de improviso ◻ n impromptu m

improper /ɪmˈprɒpə(r)/ a impróprio; (*indecent*) indecente, pouco decente; (*wrong*) incorreto, (*P*) incorrecto

improve /ɪmˈpruːv/ vt/i melhorar. ∼ **on** aperfeiçoar. ∼**ment** n melhoria f; (*in house etc*) melhoramento m; (*in health*) melhoras fpl

improvis|e /ˈɪmprəvaɪz/ vt/i improvisar. ∼**ation** /-ˈzeɪʃn/ n improvisação f

imprudent /ɪmˈpruːdnt/ a imprudente

impuden|t /ˈɪmpjʊdənt/ a descarado, insolente. ∼**ce** n descaramento m, insolência f

impulse /ˈɪmpʌls/ n impulso m

impulsive /ɪmˈpʌlsɪv/ a impulsivo

impur|e /ɪm'pjʊə(r)/ a impuro. **~ity** n impureza f

in /ɪn/ prep em, dentro de □ adv dentro; (at home) em casa; (in fashion) na moda. **~ Lisbon/English** em Lisboa/inglês. **~ winter** no inverno. **~ an hour** (at end of, within) numa hora. **~ the rain** na chuva. **~ doing** ao fazer. **~ the evening** à tardinha. **the best ~** o melhor em. **we are ~ for** vamos ter. **~-laws** npl (colloq) sogros mpl. **~-patient** n doente m internado. **the ~s and outs** meandros mpl

inability /ɪnə'bɪlətɪ/ n incapacidade f (**to do** para fazer)

inaccessible /ɪnæk'sesəbl/ a inacessível

inaccura|te /ɪn'ækjərət/ a inexato, (P) inexacto. **~cy** n inexatidão f, (P) inexactidão f, falta f de rigor

inaction /ɪn'ækʃn/ n inação f, (P) inacção f

inactiv|e /ɪn'æktɪv/ a inativo, (P) inactivo. **~ity** /-'tɪvətɪ/ n inação f, (P) inacção f

inadequa|te /ɪn'ædɪkwət/ a inadequado, impróprio; (insufficient) insuficiente. **~cy** n inadequação f; (insufficiency) insuficiência f

inadmissible /ɪnəd'mɪsəbl/ a inadmissível

inadvertently /ɪnəd'vɜːtəntlɪ/ adv inadvertidamente, (unintentionally) sem querer, sem ser por mal

inadvisable /ɪnəd'vaɪzəbl/ a desaconselhável, não aconselhável

inane /ɪ'neɪn/ a tolo, oco

inanimate /ɪn'ænɪmət/ a inanimado

inappropriate /ɪnə'prəʊprɪət/ a impróprio, inadequado

inarticulate /ɪnɑː'tɪkjʊlət/ a inarticulado; (of person) incapaz de se exprimir claramente

inattentive /ɪnə'tentɪv/ a desatento

inaugural /ɪ'nɔːgjʊrəl/ a inaugural

inaugurat|e /ɪ'nɔːgjʊreɪt/ vt inaugurar. **~ion** /-'reɪʃn/ n inauguração f

inauspicious /ɪnɔː'spɪʃəs/ a pouco auspicioso

inborn /ɪn'bɔːn/ a inato

inbred /ɪn'bred/ a inato, congênito, (P) congénito

incalculable /ɪn'kælkjʊləbl/ a incalculável

incapable /ɪn'keɪpəbl/ a incapaz

incapacit|y /ɪnkə'pæsətɪ/ n incapacidade f. **~ate** vt incapacitar

incarnat|e /ɪn'kɑːneɪt/ a encarnado. **the devil ~e** o diabo em pessoa. **~ion** /-'neɪʃn/ n encarnação f

incendiary /ɪn'sendɪərɪ/ a incendiário □ n bomba f incendiária

incense[1] /'ɪnsens/ n incenso m

incense[2] /ɪn'sens/ vt exasperar, enfurecer

incentive /ɪn'sentɪv/ n incentivo, estímulo

incessant /ɪn'sesənt/ a incessante. **~ly** adv incessantemente, sem cessar

incest /'ɪnsest/ n incesto m. **~uous** /ɪn'sestjʊəs/ a incestuoso

inch /ɪntʃ/ n polegada f (= 2.54 cm) □ vt/i avançar palmo a palmo or pouco a pouco. **within an ~ of** a um passo de

incidence /'ɪnsɪdəns/ n incidência f; (rate) percentagem f

incident /'ɪnsɪdənt/ n incidente m

incidental /ɪnsɪ'dentl/ a incidental, acessório; (casual) acidental; (expenses) eventuais; (music) de cena, incidental. **~ly** adv incidentalmente; (by the way) a propósito

incinerat|e /ɪn'sɪnəreɪt/ vt incinerar. **~or** n incinerador m

incision /ɪn'sɪʒn/ n incisão f

incisive /ɪn'saɪsɪv/ a incisivo

incite /ɪn'saɪt/ vt incitar, instigar. **~ment** n incitamento m

inclination /ɪnklɪ'neɪʃn/ n inclinação f, tendência f

incline[1] /ɪn'klaɪn/ vt/i inclinar (-se). **be ~d to** inclinar-se para; (have tendency) ter tendência para

incline[2] /'ɪnklaɪn/ n inclinação f, declive m

inclu|de /ɪn'kluːd/ vt incluir; (in letter) enviar junto or em anexo. **~ding** prep inclusive. **~sion** n inclusão f

inclusive /ɪn'kluːsɪv/ a & adv inclusive. **be ~ of** incluir

incognito /ɪnkɒg'niːtəʊ/ a & adv incógnito

incoherent /ɪnkə'hɪərənt/ a incoerente

income /'ɪŋkʌm/ n rendimento m. **~ tax** imposto sobre a renda, (P) sobre o rendimento

incoming /'ɪnkʌmɪŋ/ a (tide) enchente; (tenant etc) novo

incomparable /ɪn'kɒmpərəbl/ a incomparável

incompatible /ɪnkəm'pætəbl/ a incompatível

incompeten|t /ɪn'kɒmpɪtənt/ a incompetente. **~ce** n incompetência f

incomplete /ɪnkəm'pliːt/ a incompleto

incomprehensible /ɪnkɒmprɪ-'hensəbl/ a incompreensível

inconceivable /ɪnkən'siːvəbl/ a inconcebível

inconclusive /ɪnkən'kluːsɪv/ a inconcludente

incongruous /ɪnˈkɒŋgrʊəs/ a incongruente; (absurd) absurdo

inconsequential /ɪnkɒnsɪˈkwenʃl/ a sem importância

inconsiderate /ɪnkənˈsɪdərət/ a impensado, inconsiderado; (lacking in regard) pouco atencioso, sem consideração (pelos sentimentos etc de outrem)

inconsisten|t /ɪnkənˈsɪstənt/ a incoerente; (at variance) contraditório. ~t with incompatível com. ~cy n incoerência f. ~cies npl contradições fpl

inconspicuous /ɪnkənˈspɪkjʊəs/ a que não dá nas vistas, que não chama a atenção

incontinen|t /ɪnˈkɒntɪmənt/ a incontinente. ~ce n incontinência f

inconvenien|t /ɪnkənˈviːnɪənt/ a inconveniente, incômodo. ~ce n inconveniência f; (drawback) inconveniente m □ vt incomodar

incorporate /ɪnˈkɔːpəreɪt/ vt incorporar; (include) incluir

incorrect /ɪnkəˈrekt/ a incorreto, (P) incorrecto

incorrigible /ɪnˈkɒrɪdʒəbl/ a incorrigível

increas|e¹ /ɪnˈkriːs/ vt/i aumentar. ~ing a crescente. ~ingly adv cada vez mais

increase² /ˈɪnkriːs/ n aumento m. on the ~ aumentando, crescendo

incredible /ɪnˈkredəbl/ a incrível

incredulous /ɪnˈkredjʊləs/ a incrédulo

increment /ˈɪŋkrəmənt/ n incremento m, aumento m

incriminat|e /ɪnˈkrɪmɪneɪt/ vt incriminar. ~ing a comprometedor

incubat|e /ˈɪnkjʊbeɪt/ vt incubar. ~ion /-ˈbeɪʃn/ n incubação f. ~or n incubadora f

inculcate /ˈɪnkʌlkeɪt/ vt inculcar

incumbent /ɪnˈkʌmbənt/ n (pol, relig) titular mf □ a be ~ on incumbir a, caber a

incur /ɪnˈkɜːr/ vt (pt incurred) (displeasure, expense etc) incorrer em; (debts) contrair

incurable /ɪnˈkjʊərəbl/ a incurável, que não tem cura

indebted /ɪnˈdetɪd/ a ~ to s.o. em dívida (para) com alg (for por)

indecen|t /ɪnˈdiːsnt/ a indecente. ~t assault atentado m contra o pudor. ~cy n indecência f

indecision /ɪndɪˈsɪʒn/ n indecisão f

indecisive /ɪndɪˈsaɪsɪv/ a inconcludente, não decisivo; (hesitating) indeciso

indeed /ɪnˈdiːd/ adv realmente, deveras, mesmo; (in fact) de fato, (P) facto. **very much** ~ muitíssimo

indefinite /ɪnˈdefnət/ a indefinido; (time) indeterminado. ~ly adv indefinidamente

indelible /ɪnˈdeləbl/ a indelével

indemnify /ɪnˈdemnɪfaɪ/ vt indenizar, (P) indemnizar (for de); (safeguard) garantir (against contra)

indemnity /ɪnˈdemnəti/ n (legal exemption) isenção f; (compensation) indenização f, (P) indemnização f; (safeguard) garantia f

indent /ɪnˈdent/ vt (notch) recortar; (typ) entrar. ~ation /-ˈteɪʃn/ n recorte m; (typ) entrada f

independen|t /ɪndɪˈpendənt/ a independente. ~ce n independência f. ~tly adv independentemente

indescribable /ɪndɪˈskraɪbəbl/ a indescritível

indestructible /ɪndɪˈstrʌktəbl/ a indestrutível

indeterminate /ɪndɪˈtɜːmmət/ a indeterminado

index /ˈɪndeks/ n (pl indexes) n (in book) índice m; (in library) catálogo m □ vt indexar. ~ card ficha f (de fichário). ~ finger index m, (dedo) indicador m. ~-linked a ligado ao índice de inflação

India /ˈɪndiə/ n India f. ~n a & n (of India) indiano (m); (American) índio (m)

indicat|e /ˈɪndɪkeɪt/ vt indicar. ~ion /-ˈkeɪʃn/ n indicação f. ~or n indicador m; (auto) pisca-pisca m; (board) quadro m

indicative /ɪnˈdɪkətɪv/ a & n indicativo (m)

indict /ɪnˈdaɪt/ vt acusar. ~ment n acusação f

indifferen|t /ɪnˈdɪfrənt/ a indiferente; (not good) medíocre. ~ce n indiferença f

indigenous /ɪnˈdɪdʒməs/ a indígena, natural, nativo (to de)

indigest|ion /ɪndɪˈdʒestʃən/ n indigestão f. ~ible /-təbl/ a indigesto

indign|ant /ɪnˈdɪgnənt/ a indignado. ~ation /-ˈneɪʃn/ n indignação f

indirect /ɪndɪˈrekt/ a indireto, (P) indirecto. ~ly adv indiretamente, (P) indirectamente

indiscr|eet /ɪndɪˈskriːt/ a indiscreto; (not wary) imprudente. ~etion /-ˈeʃn/ n indiscrição f; (action, remark etc) deslize m

indiscriminate /ɪndɪˈskrɪmmət/ a que tem falta de discernimento; (random) indiscriminado. ~ly adv sem discernimento; (at random) indiscriminadamente, ao acaso

indispensable /ɪndɪˈspensəbl/ *a* indispensável

indispos|ed /ɪndɪˈspəʊzd/ *a* indisposto. **∼ition** /-əˈzɪʃn/ *n* indisposição *f*

indisputable /ɪndɪˈspjuːtəbl/ *a* indisputável, incontestável

indistinct /ɪndɪˈstɪŋkt/ *a* indistinto

indistinguishable /ɪndɪˈstɪŋgwɪʃ-əbl/ *a* indistinguível, imperceptível; (*identical*) indiferenciável

individual /ɪndɪˈvɪdʒʊəl/ *a* individual □ *n* indivíduo *m*. **∼ity** /-ˈæləti/ *n* individualidade *f*. **∼ly** *adv* individualmente

indivisible /ɪndɪˈvɪzəbl/ *a* indivisível

indoctrinat|e /ɪnˈdɒktrɪneɪt/ *vt* (en)doutrinar. **∼ion** /-ˈneɪʃn/ *n* (en)doutrinação *f*

indolen|t /ˈɪndələnt/ *a* indolente. **∼ce** *n* indolência *f*

indoor /ˈɪndɔː(r)/ *a* (de) interior, interno; (*under cover*) coberto; (*games*) de salão. **∼s** /ɪnˈdɔːz/ *adv* dentro de casa, no interior

induce /ɪnˈdjuːs/ *vt* induzir, levar; (*cause*) causar, provocar. **∼ment** *n* incentivo *m*, encorajamento *m*

indulge /ɪnˈdʌldʒ/ *vt* satisfazer; (*spoil*) fazer a(s) vontade(s) de □ *vi* **∼ in** entregar-se a

indulgen|t /ɪnˈdʌldʒənt/ *a* indulgente. **∼ce** *n* (*leniency*) indulgência *f*; (*desire*) satisfação *f*

industrial /ɪnˈdʌstrɪəl/ *a* industrial; (*unrest etc*) trabalhista; (*action*) reivindicativo. **∼ estate** zona *f* industrial. **∼ist** *n* industrial *m*. **∼ized** *a* industrializado

industrious /ɪnˈdʌstrɪəs/ *a* trabalhador, aplicado

industry /ˈɪndəstrɪ/ *n* indústria *f*; (*zeal*) aplicação *f*, diligência *f*, zelo *m*

inebriated /ɪˈniːbrɪeɪtɪd/ *a* embriagado, ébrio

inedible /ɪˈnedɪbl/ *a* não comestível

ineffective /ɪnɪˈfektɪv/ *a* ineficaz; (*person*) ineficiente, incapaz

ineffectual /ɪnɪˈfektʃʊəl/ *a* ineficaz, improfícuo

inefficien|t /ɪnɪˈfɪʃnt/ *a* ineficiente. **∼cy** *n* ineficiência *f*

ineligible /ɪnˈelɪdʒəbl/ *a* inelegível; (*undesirable*) indesejável. **be ∼ for** não ter direito a

inept /ɪˈnept/ *a* inepto

inequality /ɪnɪˈkwɒlətɪ/ *n* desigualdade *f*

inert /ɪˈnɜːt/ *a* inerte. **∼ia** /-ʃə/ *n* inércia *f*

inevitable /ɪnˈevɪtəbl/ *a* inevitável, fatal

inexcusable /ɪnɪkˈskjuːzəbl/ *a* indesculpável, imperdoável

inexhaustible /ɪnɪgˈzɔːstəbl/ *a* inesgotável, inexaurível

inexorable /ɪnˈeksərəbl/ *a* inexorável

inexpensive /ɪnɪkˈspensɪv/ *a* barato, em conta

inexperience /ɪnɪkˈspɪərɪəns/ *n* inexperiência *f*, falta de experiência *f*. **∼d** *a* inexperiente

inexplicable /ɪnˈeksplɪkəbl/ *a* inexplicável

inextricable /ɪnˈekstrɪkəbl/ *a* inextricável

infallib|le /ɪnˈfæləbl/ *a* infalível. **∼ility** /-ˈbɪlətɪ/ *n* infalibilidade *f*

infam|ous /ˈɪnfəməs/ *a* infame. **∼y** *n* infâmia *f*

infan|t /ˈɪnfənt/ *n* bebê *m*, (*P*) bebé *m*; (*child*) criança *f*. **∼cy** *n* infância *f*; (*babyhood*) primeira infância *f*

infantile /ˈɪnfəntaɪl/ *a* infantil

infantry /ˈɪnfəntrɪ/ *n* infantaria *f*

infatuat|ed /ɪnˈfætʃʊeɪtɪd/ *a* **∼ed with** cego *or* perdido por. **∼ion** /-ˈeɪʃn/ *n* cegueira *f*, paixão *f*

infect /ɪnˈfekt/ *vt* infectar. **∼ s.o. with** contagiar *or* contaminar alg com. **∼ion** /-ʃn/ *n* infecção *f*, contágio *m*. **∼ious** /-ʃəs/ *a* infeccioso, contagioso

infer /ɪnˈfɜː(r)/ *vt* (*pt* **inferred**) inferir, deduzir. **∼ence** /ˈɪnfərəns/ *n* inferência *f*

inferior /ɪnˈfɪərɪə(r)/ *a* inferior; (*work etc*) de qualidade inferior □ *n* inferior *mf*; (*in rank*) subalterno *m*. **∼ity** /-ˈɒrətɪ/ *n* inferioridade *f*

infernal /ɪnˈfɜːnl/ *a* infernal

infertil|e /ɪnˈfɜːtaɪl/ *a* infértil, estéril. **∼ity** /-əˈtɪlətɪ/ *n* infertilidade *f*, esterilidade *f*

infest /ɪnˈfest/ *vt* infestar (**with** de). **∼ation** *n* infestação *f*

infidelity /ɪnfɪˈdelətɪ/ *n* infidelidade *f*

infiltrat|e /ˈɪnfɪltreɪt/ *vt/i* infiltrar (-se). **∼ion** /-ˈtreɪʃn/ *n* infiltração *f*

infinite /ˈɪnfɪnət/ *a & n* infinito (*m*). **∼ly** *adv* infinitamente

infinitesimal /ɪnfɪnɪˈtesɪml/ *a* infinitesimal, infinitésimo

infinitive /ɪnˈfɪnətɪv/ *n* infinitivo *m*

infinity /ɪnˈfɪnətɪ/ *n* infinidade *f*, infinito *m*

infirm /ɪnˈfɜːm/ *a* débil, fraco. **∼ity** /-ɪtɪ/ *n* (*illness*) enfermidade *f*; (*weakness*) fraqueza *f*

inflam|e /ɪnˈfleɪm/ *vt* inflamar. **∼mable** /-æməbl/ *a* inflamável. **∼mation** /-əˈmeɪʃn/ *n* inflamação *f*

inflate /ɪnˈfleɪt/ *vt* (*balloon etc*) encher de ar; (*prices*) causar inflação de

inflation /ɪnˈfleɪʃn/ *n* inflação *f*. **∼ary** *a* inflacionário

inflection /ɪnˈflekʃn/ n inflexão f; (gram) flexão f, desinência f

inflexible /ɪnˈfleksəbl/ a inflexível

inflict /ɪnˈflɪkt/ vt infligir, impor (**on** a)

influence /ˈɪnfluəns/ n influência f ▫ vt influenciar, influir sobre

influential /ɪnfluˈenʃl/ a influente

influenza /ɪnfluˈenzə/ n gripe f

influx /ˈɪnflʌks/ n afluência f, influxo m

inform /ɪnˈfɔːm/ vt informar. ~ **against** or **on** denunciar. **keep** ~**ed** manter ao corrente or a par. ~**ant** n informante mf. ~ **er** n delator m, denunciante mf

informal /ɪnˈfɔːml/ a informal; (simple) simples, sem cerimônia, (P) cerimónia; (unofficial) oficioso; (colloquial) familiar; (dress) de passeio, à vontade; (dinner, gathering) íntimo. ~**ity** /-ˈmæləti/ n informalidade f; (simplicity) simplicidade f; (intimacy) intimidade f. ~**ly** adv informalmente, sem cerimônia, (P) cerimónia, à vontade

information /ɪnfəˈmeɪʃn/ n informação f; (facts, data) informações fpl. ~ **technology** tecnologia f da informação

informative /ɪnˈfɔːmətɪv/ a informativo

infra-red /ɪnfrəˈred/ a infravermelho

infrequent /ɪnˈfriːkwənt/ a pouco freqüente, (P) frequente. ~**ly** adv raramente

infringe /ɪnˈfrɪndʒ/ vt infringir. ~ **on** transgredir; (rights) violar. ~**ment** n infração f, (P) infracção f; (rights) violação f

infuriate /ɪnˈfjʊərɪeɪt/ vt enfurecer, enraivecer. ~**ing** a enfurecedor, de enfurecer, de dar raiva

infus|e /ɪnˈfjuːz/ vt infundir, incutir; (herbs, tea) pôr de infusão. ~**ion** /-ʒn/ n infusão f

ingen|ious /ɪnˈdʒiːnɪəs/ a engenhoso, bem pensado. ~**uity** /-ˈnjuːəti/ n engenho m, habilidade f, imaginação f

ingenuous /ɪnˈdʒenjʊəs/ a cândido, ingênuo, (P) ingénuo

ingot /ˈɪŋɡət/ n barra f, lingote m

ingrained /ɪnˈɡreɪnd/ a arraigado, enraizado; (dirt) entranhado

ingratiate /ɪnˈɡreɪʃɪeɪt/ vt ~ **o.s. with** insinuar-se junto de, cair nas or ganhar as boas graças de

ingratitude /ɪnˈɡrætɪtjuːd/ n ingratidão f

ingredient /ɪnˈɡriːdɪənt/ n ingrediente m

inhabit /ɪnˈhæbɪt/ vt habitar. ~**-able** a habitável. ~**ant** n habitante mf

inhale /ɪnˈheɪl/ vt inalar, aspirar. ~**r** /-ə(r)/ n inalador m

inherent /ɪnˈhɪərənt/ a inerente. ~**ly** adv inerentemente, em si

inherit /ɪnˈherɪt/ vt herdar (**from** de). ~**ance** n herança f

inhibit /ɪnˈhɪbɪt/ vt inibir; (prevent) impedir. **be** ~**ed** ser (um) inibido. ~**ion** /-ˈbɪʃn/ n inibição f

inhospitable /ɪnˈhɒspɪtəbl/ a inóspito; (of person) inospitaleiro, pouco/nada hospitaleiro

inhuman /ɪnˈhjuːmən/ a desumano. ~**ity** /-ˈmænəti/ n desumanidade f

inhumane /ɪnhjuːˈmeɪn/ a inumano, cruel

inimitable /ɪˈnɪmɪtəbl/ a inimitável

iniquitous /ɪˈnɪkwɪtəs/ a iníquo

initial /ɪˈnɪʃl/ a & n inicial (f) ▫ vt (pt **initialled**) assinar com as iniciais, rubricar. ~**ly** adv inicialmente

initiat|e /ɪˈnɪʃɪeɪt/ vt iniciar (**into** em); (scheme) lançar. ~**ion** /-ˈeɪʃn/ n iniciação f; (start) início m

initiative /ɪˈnɪʃətɪv/ n iniciativa f

inject /ɪnˈdʒekt/ vt injetar, (P) injectar; (fig) insuflar. ~**ion** /-ʃn/ n injeção f, (P) injecção f

injure /ˈɪndʒə(r)/ vt (harm) fazer mal a, prejudicar, lesar; (hurt) ferir

injury /ˈɪndʒərɪ/ n ferimento m, lesão f; (wrong) mal m

injustice /ɪnˈdʒʌstɪs/ n injustiça f

ink /ɪŋk/ n tinta f. ~**-well** n tinteiro m. ~**y** a sujo de tinta

inkling /ˈɪŋklɪŋ/ n idéia f, (P) ideia f, suspeita f

inlaid /ɪnˈleɪd/ see **inlay**[1]

inland /ˈɪnlənd/ a interior ▫ adv /ɪnˈlænd/ no interior, para o interior. **the I~ Revenue** o Fisco, a Receita Federal

inlay[1] /ɪnˈleɪ/ vt (pt **inlaid**) embutir, incrustar

inlay[2] /ˈɪnleɪ/ n incrustação f, obturação f

inlet /ˈɪnlet/ n braço m de mar, enseada f; (techn) admissão f

inmate /ˈɪnmeɪt/ n residente mf; (in hospital) internado m; (in prison) presidiário m

inn /ɪn/ n estalagem f

innards /ˈɪnədz/ npl (colloq) tripas (colloq) fpl

innate /ɪˈneɪt/ a inato

inner /ˈɪnə(r)/ a interior, interno; (fig) íntimo. ~ **city** centro m da cidade. ~**most** a mais profundo, mais íntimo. ~ **tube** n câmara f de ar

innings /ˈɪnɪŋz/ n (cricket) vez f de bater; (pol) período m no poder

innocen|t /ˈɪnəsnt/ a & n inocente (mf). ~**ce** n inocência f

innocuous /ɪˈnɒkjʊəs/ a inócuo, inofensivo

innovat|e /'ɪnəveɪt/ *vi* inovar. **∼ion**
/-'veɪʃn/ *n* inovação *f*. **∼or** *n* inovador *m*

innuendo /ɪnjuː'endəʊ/ *n* (*pl* -**oes**)
insinuação *f*, indireta *f*, (*P*) indirecta *f*

innumerable /ɪ'njuːmərəbl/ *a*
inumerável

inoculat|e /ɪ'nɒkjʊleɪt/ *vt* inocular. **∼ion**
/-'leɪʃn/ *n* inoculação *f*, vacina *f*

inoffensive /ɪnə'fensɪv/ *a* inofensivo

inoperative /ɪn'ɒpərətɪv/ *a* inoperante,
ineficaz

inopportune /ɪn'ɒpətjuːn/ *a* inoportuno

inordinate /ɪ'nɔːdɪnət/ *a* excessivo,
desmedido. **∼ly** *adv* excessivamente,
desmedidamente

input /'ɪnpʊt/ *n* (*data*) dados *mpl*; (*electr:
power*) energia *f*; (*computer process*)
entrada *f*, dados *mpl*

inquest /'ɪnkwest/ *n* inquérito *m*

inquir|e /ɪn'kwaɪə(r)/ *vi* informar-se
□ *vt* perguntar, indagar, inquirir.
∼e about procurar informações sobre,
indagar. **∼e into** inquirir, indagar.
∼ing *a* (*look*) interrogativo; (*mind*)
inquisitivo. **∼y** *n* (*question*) pergunta
f. (*jur*) inquérito *m*; (*investigation*)
investigação *f*

inquisition /ɪnkwɪ'zɪʃn/ *n* inquisição *f*

inquisitive /ɪn'kwɪzətɪv/ *a* curioso,
inquisitivo; (*prying*) intrometido,
bisbilhoteiro

insan|e /ɪn'seɪn/ *a* louco, doido. **∼ity**
/ɪn'sænəti/ *n* loucura *f*, demência *f*

insanitary /ɪn'sænɪtrɪ/ *a* insalubre,
anti-higiênico, (*P*) anti-higiénico

insatiable /ɪn'seɪʃəbl/ *a* insaciável

inscri|be /ɪn'skraɪb/ *vt* inscrever; (*book*)
dedicar. **∼ption** /-ɪpʃn/ *n* inscrição *f*;
(*in book*) dedicatória *f*

inscrutable /ɪn'skruːtəbl/ *a*
impenetrável, misterioso

insect /'ɪnsekt/ *n* inseto *m*, (*P*) insecto *m*

insecur|e /ɪnsɪ'kjʊə(r)/ *a* (*not firm*)
inseguro, mal seguro; (*unsafe; psych*)
inseguro. **∼ity** *n* insegurança *f*, falta *f*
de segurança

insensible /ɪn'sensəbl/ *a* insensível;
(*unconscious*) inconsciente

insensitive /ɪn'sensətɪv/ *a* insensível

inseparable /ɪn'seprəbl/ *a* inseparável

insert[1] /ɪn'sɜːt/ *vt* inserir; (*key*) meter,
colocar; (*add*) pôr, inserir. **∼ion** /-ʃn/ *n*
inserção *f*

insert[2] /'ɪnsɜːt/ *n* coisa *f* inserida

inside /ɪn'saɪd/ *n* interior *m*. **∼s** (*colloq*)
tripas *fpl* (*colloq*) □ *a* interior, interno
□ *adv* no interior, dentro, por dentro
□ *prep* dentro de; (*of time*) em menos de.
∼ out de dentro para fora, do avesso;
(*thoroughly*) por dentro e por fora, a
fundo

insidious /ɪn'sɪdɪəs/ *a* insidioso

insight /'ɪnsaɪt/ *n* penetração *f*,
perspicácia *f*; (*glimpse*) vislumbre *m*

insignificant /ɪnsɪg'nɪfɪkənt/ *a*
insignificante

insincer|e /ɪnsɪn'sɪə(r)/ *a* insincero.
∼ity /-'serətɪ/ *n* insinceridade *f*, falta *f*
de sinceridade

insinuat|e /ɪn'sɪnjʊeɪt/ *vt* insinuar. **∼ion**
/-'eɪʃn/ *n* (*act*) insinuação *f*; (*hint*)
indireta *f*, (*P*) indirecta *f*, insinuação *f*

insipid /ɪn'sɪpɪd/ *a* insípido, sem sabor

insist /ɪn'sɪst/ *vt/i* **∼ (on/that)** insistir
(em/em que)

insisten|t /ɪn'sɪstənt/ *a* insistente. **∼ce** *n*
insistência *f*. **∼tly** *adv*
insistentemente

insolen|t /'ɪnsələnt/ *a* insolente. **∼ce** *n*
insolência *f*

insoluble /ɪn'sɒljʊbl/ *a* insolúvel

insolvent /ɪn'sɒlvənt/ *a* insolvente

insomnia /ɪn'sɒmnɪə/ *n* insônia *f*,
(*P*) insónia *f*

inspect /ɪn'spekt/ *vt* inspecionar, (*P*)
inspeccionar, examinar; (*tickets*)
fiscalizar; (*passport*) controlar;
(*troops*) passar revista a. **∼ion** /-ʃn/ *n*
inspeção *f*, (*P*) inspecção *f*, exame *m*;
(*ticket*) fiscalização *f*; (*troops*) revista *f*.
∼or *n* inspetor *m*, (*P*) inspector *m*; (*on
train*) fiscal *m*

inspir|e /ɪn'spaɪə(r)/ *vt* inspirar. **∼ation**
/-ə'reɪʃn/ *n* inspiração *f*

instability /ɪnstə'bɪlətɪ/ *n* instabilidade *f*

install /ɪn'stɔːl/ *vt* instalar; (*heater etc*)
montar, instalar. **∼ation** /-ə'leɪʃn/ *n*
instalação *f*

instalment /ɪn'stɔːlmənt/ *n* prestação *f*;
(*of serial*) episódio *m*

instance /'ɪnstəns/ *n* exemplo *m*, caso *m*.
for ∼ por exemplo. **in the first ∼** em
primeiro lugar

instant /'ɪnstənt/ *a* imediato; (*food*)
instantâneo □ *n* instante *m*. **∼ly** *adv*
imediatamente, logo

instantaneous /ɪnstən'teɪnɪəs/ *a*
instantâneo

instead /ɪn'sted/ *adv* em vez disso, em
lugar disso. **∼ of** em vez de, em lugar de

instigat|e /'ɪnstɪgeɪt/ *vt* instigar, incitar.
∼ion /-'geɪʃn/ *n* instigação *f*. **∼or** *n*
instigador *m*

instil /ɪn'stɪl/ *vt* (*pt* **instilled**) instilar,
insuflar

instinct /'ɪnstɪŋkt/ *n* instinto *m*. **∼ive**
/ɪn'stɪŋktɪv/ *a* instintivo

institut|e /'ɪnstɪtjuːt/ *n* instituto *m* □ *vt*
instituir; (*legal proceedings*) intentar;
(*inquiry*) ordenar. **∼ion** /-'tjuːʃn/ *n*
instituição *f*; (*school*) estabelecimento

m de ensino; (*hospital*)
estabelecimento *m* hospitalar

instruct /m'strʌkt/ *vt* instruir; (*order*)
mandar, ordenar; (*a solicitor etc*) dar
instruções a. **~ s.o. in sth** ensinar alg
coisa a alguém. **~ion** /-ʃn/ *n* instrução
f. **~ions** /-ʃnz/ *npl* instruções *fpl*, modo
m de emprego; (*orders*) ordens *fpl*. **~ive**
a instrutivo. **~or** *n* instrutor *m*

instrument /'ɪnstrʊmənt/ *n*
instrumento *m*. **~ panel** painel *m* de
instrumentos

instrumental /ɪnstrʊ'mentl/ *a*
instrumental. **be ~ in** ter um papel
decisivo em. **~ist** *n* instrumentalista *mf*

insubordinat|e /ɪnsə'bɔːdɪnət/ *a*
insubordinado. **~ion** /-'neɪʃn/ *n*
insubordinação *f*

insufferable /ɪn'sʌfrəbl/ *a* intolerável,
insuportável

insufficient /ɪnsə'fɪʃnt/ *a* insuficiente

insular /'ɪnsjʊlə(r)/ *a* insular; (*fig:
narrow-minded*) bitolado, limitado, (*P*)
tacanho

insulat|e /'ɪnsjʊleɪt/ *vt* isolar. **~ing tape**
fita *f* isolante. **~ion** /-'leɪʃn/ *n*
isolamento *m*

insulin /'ɪnsjʊlɪn/ *n* insulina *f*

insult[1] /ɪn'sʌlt/ *vt* insultar, injuriar.
~ing *a* insultante, injurioso

insult[2] /'ɪnsʌlt/ *n* insulto *m*, injúria *f*

insur|e /ɪn'ʃʊə(r)/ *vt* segurar, pôr no
seguro; (*Amer*) = **ensure**. **~ance** *n*
seguro *m*. **~ance policy** apólice *f* de
seguro

insurmountable /ɪnsə'maʊntəbl/ *a*
insuperável

intact /ɪn'tækt/ *a* intato, (*P*) intacto

intake /'ɪnteɪk/ *n* admissão *f*; (*techn*)
admissão *f*, entrada *f*; (*of food*) ingestão *f*

intangible /ɪn'tændʒəbl/ *a* intangível

integral /'ɪntɪɡrəl/ *a* integral. **be an
~ part of** ser parte integrante de

integrat|e /'ɪntɪɡreɪt/ *vt/i* integrar (-se).
~ed circuit circuito *m* integrado.
~ion /-'ɡreɪʃn/ *n* integração *f*

integrity /ɪn'teɡrəti/ *n* integridade *f*

intellect /'ɪntəlekt/ *n* intelecto *m*,
inteligência *f*. **~ual** /-'lektʃʊəl/ *a* & *n*
intelectual (*mf*)

intelligen|t /ɪn'telɪdʒənt/ *a* inteligente.
~ce *n* inteligência *f*; (*mil*)
informações *fpl*. **~tly** *adv*
inteligentemente

intelligible /ɪn'telɪdʒəbl/ *a* inteligível

intend /ɪn'tend/ *vt* tencionar; (*destine*)
reservar, destinar. **~ed** *a* intencional,
propositado

intens|e /ɪn'tens/ *a* intenso; (*person*)
emotivo. **~ely** *adv* intensamente;

(*very*) extremamente. **~ity** *n*
intensidade *f*

intensif|y /ɪn'tensɪfaɪ/ *vt* intensificar.
~ication /-ɪ'keɪʃn/ *n* intensificação *f*

intensive /ɪn'tensɪv/ *a* intensivo. **~ care**
tratamento *m* intensivo

intent /ɪn'tent/ *n* intento *m*, desígnio *m*,
propósito *m* □ *a* atento, concentrado.
~ on absorto em; (*intending to*)
decidido a. **~ly** *adv* atentamente

intention /ɪn'tenʃn/ *n* intenção *f*. **~al** *a*
intencional. **~ally** *adv* de propósito

inter /ɪn'tɜː(r)/ *vt* (*pt* interred) enterrar

inter- /'ɪntə(r)/ *pref* inter-

interact /ɪntə'rækt/ *vi* agir uns sobre os
outros. **~ion** /-ʃn/ *n* interação *f*, (*P*)
interacção *f*

intercede /ɪntə'siːd/ *vi* interceder

intercept /ɪntə'sept/ *vt* interceptar

interchange[1] /ɪntə'tʃeɪndʒ/ *vt* permutar,
trocar. **~able** *a* permutável

interchange[2] /'ɪntətʃeɪndʒ/ *n* permuta *f*,
intercâmbio *m*; (*road junction*) trevo *m*
de trânsito, (*P*) nó *m*

intercom /'ɪntəkɒm/ *n* interfone *m*, (*P*)
intercomunicador *m*

interconnected /ɪntəkə'nektɪd/ *a* (*facts,
events etc*) ligado

intercourse /'ɪntəkɔːs/ *n* (*sexual*)
relações *fpl* sexuais

interest /'ɪntrəst/ *n* interesse *m*; (*legal
share*) título *m*; (*in finance*) juro(s)
m(*pl*). **rate of ~** taxa *f* de juros □ *vt*
interessar. **~ed** *a* interessado. **be ~ed
in** interessar-se por. **~ing** *a* interessante

interface /'ɪntəfeɪs/ *n* interface *f*

interfer|e /ɪntə'fɪə(r)/ *vi* interferir,
intrometer-se (**in** em); (*meddle, hinder*)
interferir (**with** com); (*tamper*) mexer
indevidamente (**with** em). **~ence** *n*
interferência *f*

interim /'ɪntərɪm/ *n* **in the ~** nesse/
neste interim *m*, (*P*) interim *m* □ *a*
interino, provisório

interior /ɪn'tɪərɪə(r)/ *a* & *n* interior (*m*)

interjection /ɪntə'dʒekʃn/ *n* interjeição *f*

interlock /ɪntə'lɒk/ *vt/i* entrelaçar;
(*pieces of puzzle etc*) encaixar(-se);
(*mech: wheels*) engrenar, engatar

interloper /'ɪntələʊpə(r)/ *n* intruso *m*

intermarr|iage /ɪntə'mærɪdʒ/ *n*
casamento *m* entre membros de
diferentes famílias, raças etc; (*between
near relations*) casamento *m*
consangüíneo, (*P*) consanguíneo. **~y**
vi ligar-se por casamento

intermediary /ɪntə'miːdɪərɪ/ *a* & *n*
intermediário (*m*)

intermediate /ɪntə'miːdɪət/ *a*
intermédio, intermediário

interminable /ɪnˈtɜːmɪnəbl/ *a* interminável, infindável

intermission /ɪntəˈmɪʃn/ *n* intervalo *m*

intermittent /ɪntəˈmɪtnt/ *a* intermitente. **~ly** *adv* intermitentemente

intern /ɪnˈtɜːn/ *vt* internar. **~ee** /-ˈniː/ *n* internado *m*. **~ment** *n* internamento *m*

internal /ɪnˈtɜːnl/ *a* interno, interior. (*Amer.*) the **I ~** Revenue o Fisco, a Receita Federal (*B*) **~ly** *adv* internamente, interiormente

international /ɪntəˈnæʃnəl/ *a & n* internacional (*mf*)

Internet /ˈɪntənet/ *n* Internet *f*

interpret /ɪnˈtɜːprɪt/ *vt/i* interpretar. **~ation** /-ˈteɪʃn/ *n* interpretação *f*. **~er** *n* intérprete *mf*

interrelated /ɪntərɪˈleɪtɪd/ *a* inter-relacionado, correlacionado

interrogat|e /ɪnˈterəgeɪt/ *vt* interrogar. **~ion** /-ˈgeɪʃn/ *n* interrogação *f*; (*of police etc*) interrogatório *m*

interrogative /ɪntəˈrɒgətɪv/ *a* interrogativo □ *n* (*pronoun*) pronome *m* interrogativo

interrupt /ɪntəˈrʌpt/ *vt* interromper. **~ion** /-ʃn/ *n* interrupção *f*

intersect /ɪntəˈsekt/ *vt/i* intersectar(-se); (*roads*) cruzar-se. **~ion** /-ʃn/ *n* intersecção *f*; (*crossroads*) cruzamento *m*

intersperse /ɪntəˈspɜːs/ *vt* entremear, intercalar; (*scatter*) espalhar

interval /ˈɪntəvl/ *n* intervalo *m*. **at ~s** a intervalos

interven|e /ɪntəˈviːn/ *vi* (*interfere*) intervir; (*of time*) decorrer; (*occur*) sobrevir, intervir. **~tion** /-ˈvenʃn/ *n* intervenção *f*

interview /ˈɪntəvjuː/ *n* entrevista *f* □ *vt* entrevistar. **~ee** *n* entrevistado *m*. **~er** *n* entrevistador *m*

intestin|e /ɪnˈtestɪn/ *n* intestino *m*. **~al** *a* intestinal

intima|te[1] /ˈɪntɪmət/ *a* íntimo; (*detailed*) profundo. **~cy** *n* intimidade *f*. **~tely** *adv* intimamente

intimate[2] /ˈɪntɪmeɪt/ *vt* (*announce*) dar a conhecer, fazer saber; (*imply*) dar a entender

intimidat|e /ɪnˈtɪmɪdeɪt/ *vt* intimidar. **~ion** /-ˈdeɪʃn/ *n* intimidação *f*

into /ˈɪntə/; *emphatic* /ˈɪntʊ/ *prep* para dentro de. **divide ~ three** dividir em três. **~ pieces** aos bocados. **translate ~** traduzir para

intolerable /ɪnˈtɒlərəbl/ *a* intolerável, insuportável

intoleran|t /ɪnˈtɒlərənt/ *a* intolerante. **~ce** *n* intolerância *f*

intonation /ɪntəˈneɪʃn/ *n* entonação *f*, entoação *f*, inflexão *f*

intoxicat|ed /ɪnˈtɒksɪkeɪtɪd/ *a* embriagado, etilizado. **~ion** /-ˈkeɪʃn/ *n* embriaguez *f*

intra- /ˈɪntrə/ *pref* intra-

intractable /ɪnˈtræktəbl/ *a* intratável, difícil

intranet /ˈɪntrənet/ *n* rede *f* corporativa

intransigent /ɪnˈtrænsɪdʒənt/ *a* intransigente

intransitive /ɪnˈtrænsətɪv/ *a* (*verb*) intransitivo

intravenous /ɪntrəˈviːnəs/ *a* intravenoso

intrepid /ɪnˈtrepɪd/ *a* intrépido, arrojado

intrica|te /ˈɪntrɪkət/ *a* intrincado, complexo. **~cy** *n* complexidade *f*

intrigu|e /ɪnˈtriːg/ *vt/i* intrigar □ *n* intriga *f*. **~ing** *a* intrigante, curioso

intrinsic /ɪnˈtrɪnsɪk/ *a* intrínseco. **~ally** /-klɪ/ *adv* intrinsecamente

introduce /ɪntrəˈdjuːs/ *vt* (*programme, question*) apresentar; (*bring in, insert*) introduzir; (*initiate*) iniciar. **~ sb to sb** (*person*) apresentar alg a alguém

introduct|ion /ɪntrəˈdʌkʃn/ *n* introdução *f*; (*of/to person*) apresentação *f*. **~ory** /-tərɪ/ *a* introdutório, de introdução; (*letter, words*) de apresentação

introspective /ɪntrəˈspektɪv/ *a* introspectivo

introvert /ˈɪntrəvɜːt/ *n & a* introvertido (*m*)

intru|de /ɪnˈtruːd/ *vi* intrometer-se, ser a mais. **~der** *n* intruso *m*. **~sion** *n* intrusão *f*. **~sive** *a* intruso

intuit|ion /ɪntjuːˈɪʃn/ *n* intuição *f*. **~ive** /ɪnˈtjuːɪtɪv/ *a* intuitivo

inundate /ˈɪnʌndeɪt/ *vt* inundar (**with** de)

invade /ɪnˈveɪd/ *vt* invadir. **~r** /-ə(r)/ *n* invasor *m*

invalid[1] /ˈɪnvəlɪd/ *n* inválido *m*

invalid[2] /ɪnˈvælɪd/ *a* inválido. **~ate** *vt* invalidar

invaluable /ɪnˈvæljʊəbl/ *a* inestimável

invariabl|e /ɪnˈveərɪəbl/ *a* invariável. **~y** *adv* invariavelmente

invasion /ɪnˈveɪʒn/ *n* invasão *f*

invective /ɪnˈvektɪv/ *n* invectiva *f*

invent /ɪnˈvent/ *vt* inventar. **~ion** *n* invenção *f*. **~ive** *a* inventivo. **~or** *n* inventor *m*

inventory /ˈɪnvəntrɪ/ *n* inventário *m*

inverse /ɪnˈvɜːs/ *a & n* inverso (*m*). **~ly** *adv* inversamente

inver|t /ɪnˈvɜːt/ *vt* inverter. **~ted commas** aspas *fpl*. **~sion** *n* inversão *f*

invest /ɪnˈvest/ *vt* investir; (*time, effort*) dedicar □ *vi* fazer um investimento. **~ in** (*colloq: buy*) gastar dinheiro em.

~ment n investimento m. ~or n investidor m, financiador m

investigat|e /m'vestɪɡeɪt/ vt investigar. ~ion /-'ɡeɪʃn/ n investigação f. under ~ion em estudo. ~or n investigador m

inveterate /m'vetərət/ a inveterado

invidious /m'vɪdɪəs/ a antipático, odioso

invigorate /m'vɪɡəreɪt/ vt revigorar; (encourage) estimular

invincible /m'vɪnsəbl/ a invencível

invisible /m'vɪzəbl/ a invisível

invit|e /m'vaɪt/ vt convidar; (bring on) pedir, provocar. ~ation /ɪnvɪ'teɪʃn/ n convite m. ~ing a (tempting) tentador; (pleasant) acolhedor, convidativo

invoice /'ɪnvɔɪs/ n fatura f, (P) factura f □ vt faturar, (P) facturar

invoke /m'vəʊk/ vt invocar

involuntary /m'vɒləntrɪ/ a involuntário

involve /m'vɒlv/ vt implicar, envolver. ~d a (complex) complicado; (at stake) em jogo; (emotionally) envolvido. ~d in implicado em. ~ment n envolvimento m, participação f

invulnerable /m'vʌlnərəbl/ a invulnerável

inward /'mwəd/ a interior; (thought etc) íntimo. ~(s) adv para dentro, para o interior. ~ly adv interiormente, intimamente

iodine /'aɪədiːn/ n iodo m; (antiseptic) tintura f de iodo

IOU /aɪəʊ'juː/ n abbr vale m

IQ /aɪ'kjuː/ abbr (intelligence quotient) QI m

Iran /ɪ'rɑːn/ n Irã m. ~ian /ɪ'remɪən/ a & n iraniano (m)

Iraq /ɪ'rɑːk/ n Iraque m. ~i a & n iraquiano (m)

irascible /ɪ'ræsəbl/ a irascível

irate /aɪ'reɪt/ a irado, enraivecido

Ireland /'aɪələnd/ n Irlanda f

iris /'aɪərɪs/ n (anat, bot) íris f

Irish /'aɪərɪʃ/ a & n (language) irlandês (m). ~man n irlandês m. ~woman n irlandesa f

irk /ɜːk/ vt aborrecer, incomodar. ~some a aborrecido

iron /'aɪən/ n ferro m; (appliance) ferro m de engomar □ a de ferro □ vt passar a ferro. ~ out fazer desaparecer; (fig) aplanar, resolver. ~ing n do the ~ing passar a roupa. ~ing-board n tábua f de passar roupa, (P) tábua f de engomar

ironic(al) /aɪ'rɒnɪk(l)/ a irónico, (P) irónico

ironmonger /'aɪənmʌŋɡə(r)/ n ferreiro m, (P) ferrageiro m. ~'s n (shop) loja f de ferragens

irony /'aɪərənɪ/ n ironia f

irrational /ɪ'ræʃənl/ a irracional; (person) ilógico, que não raciocina

irreconcilable /ɪrekən'saɪləbl/ a irreconciliável

irrefutable /ɪrɪ'fjuːtəbl/ a irrefutável

irregular /ɪ'reɡjʊlə(r)/ a irregular. ~ity /-'lærətɪ/ n irregularidade f

irrelevant /ɪ'reləvənt/ a irrelevante, que não é pertinente

irreparable /ɪ'repərəbl/ a irreparável, irremediável

irreplaceable /ɪrɪ'pleɪsəbl/ a insubstituível

irresistible /ɪrɪ'zɪstəbl/ a irresistível

irresolute /ɪ'rezəluːt/ a irresoluto

irrespective /ɪrɪ'spektɪv/ a ~ of sem levar em conta, independente de

irresponsible /ɪrɪ'spɒnsəbl/ a irresponsável

irretrievable /ɪrɪ'triːvəbl/ a irreparável

irreverent /ɪ'revərənt/ a irreverente

irreversible /ɪrɪ'vɜːsəbl/ a irreversível; (decision) irrevogável

irrigat|e /'ɪrɪɡeɪt/ vt irrigar. ~ion /-'ɡeɪʃn/ n irrigação f

irritable /'ɪrɪtəbl/ a irritável, irascível

irritat|e /'ɪrɪteɪt/ vt irritar. ~ion /-'teɪʃn/ n irritação f

is /ɪz/ see be

Islam /'ɪzlɑːm/ n Islã m. ~ic /ɪz'læmɪk/ a islâmico

island /'aɪlənd/ n ilha f. traffic ~ abrigo m de pedestres, (P) placa f de refugio

isolat|e /'aɪsəleɪt/ vt isolar. ~ion /-'leɪʃn/ n isolamento m

Israel /'ɪzreɪl/ n Israel m. ~i /ɪz'reɪlɪ/ a & n israelense (mf), (P) israelita (mf)

issue /'ɪʃuː/ n questão f; (outcome) resultado m; (of magazine etc) número m; (of stamps, money etc) emissão f □ vt distribuir, dar; (stamps, money etc) emitir; (orders) dar □ vi ~ from sair de. at ~ em questão. take ~ with entrar em discussão com, discutir com

it /ɪt/ pron (subject) ele, ela; (object) o, a; (non-specific) isto, isso, aquilo. ~ is cold está or faz frio. ~ is the 6th of May hoje é seis de maio. that's ~ é isso. take ~ leva isso. who is ~? quem é?

italic /ɪ'tælɪk/ a itálico. ~s npl itálico m

Ital|y /'ɪtəlɪ/ n Itália f. ~ian /ɪ'tælɪən/ a & n (person, lang) italiano (m)

itch /ɪtʃ/ n coceira f, (P) comichão f; (fig: desire) desejo m ardente □ vi coçar, sentir comichão, comichar. my arm ~es estou com coceira no braço. I am ~ing to estou morto por (colloq). ~y a que dá coceira

item /'aɪtəm/ n item m, artigo m; (on programme) número m; (on agenda) ponto *m*. **news ~** notícia *f*. **~ize** /-aɪz/ *vt* divulgar, especificar

itinerant /aɪˈtɪnərənt/ *a* itinerante; (*musician, actor*) ambulante

itinerary /aɪˈtɪnərərɪ/ *n* itinerário *m*

its /ɪts/ *a* seu, sua, seus, suas

it's /ɪts/ = **it is, it has**

itself /ɪtˈself/ *pron* ele mesmo, ele próprio, ela mesma, ela própria; (*reflexive*) se; (*after prep*) si mesmo, si próprio, si mesma, si própria. **by ~** sozinho, por si

ivory /ˈaɪvərɪ/ *n* marfim *m*

ivy /ˈaɪvɪ/ *n* hera *f*

Jj

jab /dʒæb/ *vt* (*pt* **jabbed**) espetar ◻ *n* espetadela *f*; (*colloq: injection*) picada *f*

jabber /ˈdʒæbə(r)/ *vi* tagarelar; (*indistinctly*) falar confusamente ◻ *n* tagarelice *f*; (*indistinct speech*) algaravia *f*; (*indistinct voices*) algaraviada *f*

jack /dʒæk/ *n* (*techn*) macaco *m*; (*cards*) valete *m* ◻ *vt* **~ up** levantar com macaco. **the Union J~** a bandeira *f* inglesa

jackal /ˈdʒækl/ *n* chacal *m*

jackdaw /ˈdʒækdɔː/ *n* gralha *f*

jacket /ˈdʒækɪt/ *n* casaco (curto) *m*; (*of book*) sobrecapa *f*; (*of potato*) casca *f*

jack-knife /ˈdʒæknaɪf/ *vi* (*lorry*) perder o controle

jackpot /ˈdʒækpɒt/ *n* sorte *f* grande. **hit the ~** ganhar a sorte grande

Jacuzzi /dʒəˈkuːzɪ/ *n* (*P*) jacuzzi *m*, banheira *f* de hidromassagem

jade /dʒeɪd/ *n* (*stone*) jade *m*

jaded /ˈdʒeɪdɪd/ *a* (*tired*) estafado; (*bored*) enfastiado

jagged /ˈdʒægɪd/ *a* recortado, denteado; (*sharp*) pontiagudo

jail /dʒeɪl/ *n* prisão *f* ◻ *vt* prender, colocar na cadeia. **~er** *n* carcereiro *m*

jam¹ /dʒæm/ *n* geléia *f*, compota *f*

jam² /dʒæm/ *vt/i* (*pt* **jammed**) (*wedge*) entalar; (*become wedged*) entalar-se; (*crowd*) apinhar(-se); (*mech*) bloquear; (*radio*) provocar interferências em ◻ *n* (*crush*) aperto *m*; (*traffic*) engarrafamento *m*; (*colloq: difficulty*) apuro *m*, aperto *m*. **~ one's brakes on** (*colloq*) pôr o pé no freio, (*P*) no travão subitamente, apertar o freio

subitamente. **~-packed** *a* (*colloq*) abarrotado (**with** de)

Jamaica /dʒəˈmeɪkə/ *n* Jamaica *f*

jangle /ˈdʒæŋgl/ *n* som *m* estridente ◻ *vi* retinir

janitor /ˈdʒænɪtə(r)/ *n* porteiro *m*; (*caretaker*) zelador *m*

January /ˈdʒænjʊərɪ/ *n* Janeiro *m*

Japan /dʒəˈpæn/ *n* Japão *m*. **~ese** /dʒæpəˈniːz/ *a & n* japonês (*m*)

jar¹ /dʒɑː(r)/ *n* pote *m*. **jam-~** *n* frasco *m* de geléia

jar² /dʒɑː(r)/ *vt/i* (*pt* **jarred**) ressoar, bater ruidosamente (**against** contra); (*of colours*) destoar; (*disagree*) discordar (**with** de) ◻ *n* (*shock*) choque *m*. **~ring** *a* dissonante

jargon /ˈdʒɑːgən/ *n* jargão *m*, gíria *f* profissional

jaundice /ˈdʒɔːndɪs/ *n* icterícia *f*. **~d** *a* (*fig*) invejoso, despeitado

jaunt /dʒɔːnt/ *n* (*trip*) passeata *f*

jaunty /ˈdʒɔːntɪ/ *a* (**-ier, -iest**) (*cheerful*) alegre, jovial; (*sprightly*) desenvolto

javelin /ˈdʒævlɪn/ *n* dardo *m*

jaw /dʒɔː/ *n* maxilar *m*, mandíbula *f*

jay /dʒeɪ/ *n* gaio *m*. **~-walker** *n* pedestre *m* imprudente, (*P*) peão *m* indisciplinado

jazz /dʒæz/ *n* jazz *m* ◻ *vt* **~ up** animar. **~y** *a* (*colloq*) espalhafatoso

jealous /ˈdʒeləs/ *a* ciumento; (*envious*) invejoso. **~y** *n* ciúme *m*; (*envy*) inveja *f*

jeans /dʒiːnz/ *npl* (blue-)jeans *mpl*, calça *f* de zuarte, (*P*) calças *fpl* de ganga

jeep /dʒiːp/ *n* jipe *m*

jeer /dʒɪə(r)/ *vt/i* **~ at** (*laugh*) fazer troça de; (*scorn*) escarnecer de; (*boo*) vaiar ◻ *n* (*mockery*) troça *f*; (*booing*) vaia *f*

jell /dʒel/ *vi* tomar consistência, gelatinizar-se

jelly /ˈdʒelɪ/ *n* gelatina *f*.

jellyfish /ˈdʒelɪfɪʃ/ *n* água-viva *f*

jeopard|y /ˈdʒepədɪ/ *n* perigo *m*. **~ize** *vt* comprometer, pôr em perigo

jerk /dʒɜːk/ *n* solavanco *m*, (*P*) sacão *m*; (*sl: fool*) idiota *mf* ◻ *vt/i* sacudir; (*move jerkily*) mover-se aos solavancos, (*P*) mover(-se) aos sacões. **~y** *a* sacudido

jersey /ˈdʒɜːzɪ/ *n* (*pl* **-eys**) camisola *f*, pulôver *m*, suéter *m*; (*fabric*) jérsei *m*

jest /dʒest/ *n* gracejo *m*, graça *f* ◻ *vi* gracejar, brincar

Jesus /ˈdʒiːzəs/ *n* Jesus *m*

jet¹ /dʒet/ *n* azeviche *m*. **~-black** *a* negro de azeviche

jet² /dʒet/ *n* jato *m*, (*P*) jacto *m*; (*plane*) (avião a) jato *m*, (*P*) jacto *m*. **~ lag** cansaço *m* provocado pela diferença de fuso horário. **~-propelled** *a* de propulsão a jato, (*P*) jacto

jettison /'dʒetɪsn/ vt alijar; (discard)
desfazer-se de; (fig) abandonar

jetty /'dʒetɪ/ n (breakwater) quebra-mar
m; (landing-stage) desembarcadouro
m, cais m

Jew /dʒuː/ n judeu m

jewel /'dʒuːəl/ n jóia f. **~ler** n joalheiro
m. **~ler's (shop)** joalheria f. **~lery** n
jóias fpl

Jewish /'dʒuːɪʃ/ a judeu

jib /dʒɪb/ vi (pt jibbed) recusar-se a
avançar; (of a horse) empacar. **~ at**
(fig) opor-se a, ter relutância em □ n
(sail) bujarrona f

jig /dʒɪg/ n jiga f

jiggle /'dʒɪgl/ vt (rock) balançar; (jerk)
sacolejar

jigsaw /'dʒɪgsɔː/ n **~(-puzzle)** puzzle m,
quebra-cabeça m, (P) quebra-cabeças
m

jilt /dʒɪlt/ vt deixar, abandonar, dar um
fora em (colloq), (P) mandar passear
(colloq)

jingle /'dʒɪŋgl/ vt/i tilintar, tinir □ n
tilintar m, tinido m; (advertising etc)
música f de anúncio

jinx /dʒɪŋks/ n (colloq) pessoa f or coisa f
azarenta; (fig: spell) azar m

jitter|s /'dʒɪtəz/ npl **the ~s** (colloq)
nervos mpl. **~y** /-ərɪ/ a **be ~y** (colloq)
estar nervoso, ter os nervos à flor da
pele (colloq)

job /dʒɒb/ n trabalho m; (post) emprego
m. **have a ~ doing** ter dificuldade em
fazer. **it is a good ~ that** felizmente
que. **~less** a desempregado

jobcentre /'dʒɒbsentə(r)/ n posto m de
desemprego

jockey /'dʒɒkɪ/ n (pl -eys) jóquei m

jocular /'dʒɒkjʊlə(r)/ a jocoso,
galhofeiro, brincalhão

jog /dʒɒg/ vt (pt jogged) dar um leve
empurrão em, tocar em; (memory)
refrescar □ vi (sport) fazer jogging.
~ging n jogging m

join /dʒɔɪn/ vt/i juntar, unir; (become
member) fazer-se sócio de, entrar para.
~ sb juntar-se a alg □ vi (of roads)
juntar-se, entroncar-se; (of rivers)
confluir □ n junção f, junta f. **~ in** vt/i
participar (em). **~ up** alistar-se

joiner /'dʒɔɪnə(r)/ n marceneiro m

joint /dʒɔɪnt/ a comum, conjunto; (effort)
conjunto □ n junta f, junção f; (anat)
articulação f; (culin) quarto m; (roast
meat) carne f assada; (sl: place)
espelunca f. **~ author** co-autor m. **~ly**
adv conjuntamente

joist /dʒɔɪst/ n trave f, barrote m

jok|e /dʒəʊk/ n piada f, gracejo m □ vi
gracejar. **~er** n brincalhão m; (cards)

curinga f de baralho, (P) diabo m.
~ingly adv brincadeira

joll|y /'dʒɒlɪ/ a (-ier, -iest) alegre, bem
disposto □ adv (colloq) muito. **~ity** n
festança f, pândega f

jolt /dʒəʊlt/ vt sacudir, sacolejar □ vi ir
aos solavancos □ n solavanco m; (shock)
choque m, sobressalto m

jostle /'dʒɒsl/ vt dar um encontrão or
encontrões em, empurrar □ vi
empurrar, acotovelar-se

jot /dʒɒt/ n (not a) **~** nada □ vt (pt jotted)
~ (down) apontar, tomar nota de.
~ter n (pad) bloco m de notas

journal /'dʒɜːnl/ n diário m; (newspaper)
jornal m; (periodical) periódico m,
revista f. **~ism** n jornalismo m. **~ist** n
jornalista mf

journey /'dʒɜːnɪ/ n (pl -eys) viagem f;
(distance) trajeto m, (P) trajecto m □ vi
viajar

jovial /'dʒəʊvɪəl/ a jovial

joy /dʒɔɪ/ n alegria f. **~-ride** n passeio m
em carro roubado. **~ful, ~ous** adjs
alegre

jubil|ant /'dʒuːbɪlənt/ a cheio de alegria,
jubiloso. **~ation** /-'leɪʃn/ n júbilo m,
regozijo m

jubilee /'dʒuːbɪliː/ n jubileu m

Judaism /'dʒuːdeɪɪzəm/ n judaísmo m

judder /'dʒʌdə(r)/ vi trepidar, vibrar □ n
trepidação f, vibração f

judge /dʒʌdʒ/ n juiz m □ vt julgar. **~ment**
n (judging) julgamento m, juízo m;
(opinion) juízo m; (decision) julgamento
m

judic|iary /dʒuː'dɪʃərɪ/ n magistratura f;
(system) judiciário m. **~ial** a judiciário

judicious /dʒuː'dɪʃəs/ a judicioso

judo /'dʒuːdəʊ/ n judô m, (P) judo m

jug /dʒʌg/ n (tall) jarro m; (round) botija
f; **milk-~** n leiteira f

juggernaut /'dʒʌgənɔːt/ n (lorry)
jainanta f, (P) camião m TIR

juggle /'dʒʌgl/ vt/i fazer malabarismos
(**with** com). **~r** /-ə(r)/ n malabarista mf

juic|e /dʒuːs/ n suco m, (P) sumo m. **~y** a
suculento; (colloq: story etc) picante

juke-box /'dʒuːkbɒks/ n juke-box m, (P)
máquina f de música

July /dʒuː'laɪ/ n julho m

jumble /'dʒʌmbl/ vt misturar □ n
mistura f. **~ sale** venda f de caridade
de objetos usados

jumbo /'dʒʌmbəʊ/ a **~ jet** (avião) jumbo
m

jump /dʒʌmp/ vt/i saltar; (start)
sobressaltar(-se); (of prices etc) subir
repentinamente □ n salto m; (start)
sobressalto m; (of prices) alta f. **~ at**
aceitar imediatamente. **~ the gun** agir

prematuramente. ~ **the queue** furar a fila. ~ **to conclusions** tirar conclusões apressadas

jumper /'dʒʌmpə(r)/ *n* pulôver *m*, suéter *m*, (*P*) camisada *f* de lã

jumpy /'dʒʌmpɪ/ *a* nervoso

junction /'dʒʌŋkʃn/ *n* junção *f*; (*of roads etc*) entroncamento *m*

June /dʒuːn/ *n* junho *m*

jungle /'dʒʌŋgl/ *n* selva *f*, floresta *f*

junior /'dʒuːnɪə(r)/ *a* júnior; (*in age*) mais novo (**to** que); (*in rank*) subalterno; (*school*) primária □ *n* o mais novo *m*; (*sport*) júnior *mf*. ~ **to** (*in rank*) abaixo de

junk /dʒʌŋk/ *n* ferro-velho *m*, velharias *fpl*; (*rubbish*) lixo *m*. ~ **food** comida *f* sem valor nutritivo. ~ **mail** material *m* impresso, enviado por correio, sem ter sido solicitado. ~ **shop** loja *f* de ferro-velho, bricabraque *m*

junkie /'dʒʌŋkɪ/ *n* (*sl*) drogado *m*

jurisdiction /dʒʊərɪs'dɪkʃn/ *n* jurisdição *f*

juror /'dʒʊərə(r)/ *n* jurado *m*

jury /'dʒʊərɪ/ *n* júri *m*

just /dʒʌst/ *a* justo □ *adv* justamente, exatamente, (*P*) exactamente; (*only*) só. **he has** ~ **left** ele acabou de sair. ~ **listen!** escuta só! ~ **as** assim como; (*with time*) assim que. ~ **as tall as** exatamente, (*P*) exactamente tão alto quanto. ~ **as well that** ainda bem que. ~ **before** um momento antes (de). ~**ly** *adv* com justiça, justamente

justice /'dʒʌstɪs/ *n* justiça *f*. **J**~ **of the Peace** juiz *m* de paz

justifiabl|e /'dʒʌstɪfaɪəbl/ *a* justificável. ~**y** *adv* com razão, justificadamente

justif|y /'dʒʌstɪfaɪ/ *vt* justificar. ~**ication** /-ɪ'keɪʃn/ *n* justificação *f*

jut /dʒʌt/ *vi* (*pt* **jutted**) ~ **out** fazer saliência, sobressair

juvenile /'dʒuːvənaɪl/ *a* (*youthful*) juvenil; (*childish*) pueril; (*delinquent*) jovem; (*court*) de menores □ *n* jovem *mf*

juxtapose /dʒʌkstə'pəʊz/ *vt* justapor

kaleidoscope /kə'laɪdəskəʊp/ *n* caleidoscópio *m*

kangaroo /kæŋgə'ruː/ *n* canguru *m*

karate /kə'rɑːtɪ/ *n* karatê *m*

kebab /kə'bæb/ *n* churrasquinho *m*, espetinho *m*

keel /kiːl/ *n* quilha *f* □ *vi* ~ **over** virar-se

keen /kiːn/ *a* (*-er, -est*) (*sharp*) agudo; (*eager*) entusiástico; (*of appetite*) devorador; (*of intelligence*) vivo; (*of wind*) cortante. ~**ly** *adv* vivamente; (*eagerly*) com entusiasmo. ~**ness** *n* vivacidade *f*; (*enthusiasm*) entusiasmo *m*

keep /kiːp/ *vt* (*pt* **kept**) *vt* guardar; (*family*) sustentar; (*animals*) ter, criar; (*celebrate*) festejar; (*conceal*) esconder; (*delay*) demorar; (*prevent*) impedir (**from** de); (*promise*) cumprir; (*shop*) ter □ *vi* manter-se, conservar-se; (*remain*) ficar. ~ **(on)** continuar (**doing** fazendo) □ *n* sustento *m*; (*of castle*) torre *f* de menagem. ~ **back** *vt* (*withhold*) reter □ *vi* manter-se afastado. ~ **in/out** impedir de entrar/ de sair. ~ **up** conservar. ~ **up (with)** acompanhar. ~**er** *n* guarda *mf*

keeping /'kiːpɪŋ/ *n* guarda *f*, cuidado *m*. **in** ~ **with** em harmonia com, (*P*) de harmonia com

keepsake /'kiːpseɪk/ *n* (*thing*) lembrança *f*, recordação *f*

keg /keg/ *n* barril *m* pequeno

kennel /'kenl/ *n* casota *f* (de cão). ~**s** *npl* canil *m*

kept /kept/ *see* **keep**

kerb /kɜːb/ *n* meio fio *m*, (*P*) borda *f* do passeio

kernel /'kɜːnl/ *n* (*of nut*) miolo *m*

kerosene /'kerəsiːn/ *n* (*paraffin*) querosene *m*, (*P*) petróleo *m*; (*aviation fuel*) gasolina *f*

ketchup /'ketʃəp/ *n* molho *m* de tomate, ketchup *m*

kettle /'ketl/ *n* chaleira *f*

key /kiː/ *n* chave *f*; (*of piano etc*) tecla *f*; (*mus*) clave *f* □ *a* chave (*m*). ~**-ring** *n* chaveiro *m*, porta-chaves *m invar* □ *vt* ~ **in** digitar, bater. ~**ed up** tenso

keyboard /'kiːbɔːd/ *n* teclado *m*

keyhole /'kiːhəʊl/ *n* buraco *m* da fechadura

khaki /'kɑːkɪ/ *a & n* cáqui (*invar m*), (*P*) caqui (*invar m*)

kick /kɪk/ *vt/i* dar um pontapé *or* pontapés (**a, em**); (*ball*) chutar (**em**); (*of horse*) dar um coice *or* coices, escoicear □ *n* pontapé *m*; (*of gun, horse*) coice *m*; (*colloq: thrill*) excitação *f*, prazer *m*. ~**-off** *n* chute *m* inicial, kick-off. ~ **out** (*colloq*) pôr na rua. ~ **up** (*colloq: fuss, racket*) fazer

kid /kɪd/ *n* (*goat*) cabrito *m*; (*sl: child*) garoto *m*; (*leather*) pelica *f* □ *vt/i* (*pt* **kidded**) (*colloq*) brincar (com)

kidnap /'kɪdnæp/ *vt* (*pt* **kidnapped**) raptar. ~**ping** *n* rapto *m*

kidney /'kɪdnɪ/ *n* rim *m*

kill /kɪl/ vt matar; (fig: put an end to) acabar com ◻ n matança f. **~er** n assassino m. **~ing** n matança f, massacre m; (of game) caçada f ◻ a (colloq: funny) de morrer de rir; (colloq: exhausting) de morte

killjoy /'kɪldʒɔɪ/ n desmancha- prazeres mf

kiln /kɪln/ n forno m

kilo /'ki:ləʊ/ n (pl -os) quilo m

kilogram /'kɪləɡræm/ n quilograma m

kilometre /'kɪləmi:tə(r)/ n quilômetro m, (P) quilómetro m

kilowatt /'kɪləwɒt/ n quilowatt m, (P) quilovate m

kilt /kɪlt/ n kilt m, saiote m escocês

kin /kɪn/ n família f, parentes mpl. **next of ~** os parentes mais próximos

kind[1] /kaɪnd/ n espécie f, gênero m, (P) género m, natureza f. **in ~** em gêneros, (P) géneros; (fig: in the same form) na mesma moeda. **~ of** (colloq: somewhat) de certo modo, um pouco

kind[2] /kaɪnd/ a (-er, -est) (good) bom; (friendly) gentil, amável. **~-hearted** a bom, bondoso. **~ness** n bondade f

kindergarten /'kɪndəɡa:tn/ n jardim de infância m, (P) infantil

kindle /'kɪndl/ vt/i acender(-se), atear(-se)

kindly /'kaɪndlɪ/ a (-ier, -iest) benévolo, bondoso ◻ adv bondosamente, gentilmente, com sim-patia. **~ wait** tenha a bondade de esperar

kindred /'kɪndrɪd/ a aparentado; (fig: connected) afim. **~ spirit** espírito m congênere, alma f gêmea

kinetic /kɪ'netɪk/ a cinético

king /kɪŋ/ n rei m. **~-size(d)** a de tamanho grande

kingdom /'kɪŋdəm/ n reino m

kingfisher /'kɪŋfɪʃə(r)/ n pica-peixe m, martim-pescador m

kink /kɪŋk/ n (in rope) volta f, nó m; (fig) perversão f. **~y** a (colloq) excêntrico, pervertido; (of hair) encarapinhado

kiosk /'ki:ɒsk/ n quiosque m. **telephone ~** cabine telefônica, (P) telefônica

kip /kɪp/ n (sl) sono m ◻ vi (pt kipped) (sl) dormir

kipper /'kɪpə(r)/ n arenque m defumado

kiss /kɪs/ n beijo m ◻ vt/i beijar (-se)

kit /kɪt/ n equipamento m; (set of tools) ferramenta f; (for assembly) kit m ◻ vt (pt kitted) **~ out** equipar

kitbag /'kɪtbæɡ/ n mochila f (de soldado etc); saco m de viagem

kitchen /'kɪtʃɪn/ n cozinha f. **~ garden** horta f. **~ sink** pia f, (P) lava-louças m

kite /kaɪt/ n (toy) pipa f, (P) papagaio m de papel

kith /kɪθ/ n **~ and kin** parentes e amigos mpl

kitten /'kɪtn/ n gatinho m

kitty /'kɪtɪ/ n (fund) fundo m comum, vaquinha f; (cards) bolo m

knack /næk/ n jeito m

knapsack /'næpsæk/ n mochila f

knead /ni:d/ vt amassar

knee /ni:/ n joelho m

kneecap /'ni:kæp/ n rótula f

kneel /ni:l/ vi (pt knelt) **~ (down)** ajoelhar(-se)

knelt /nelt/ see **kneel**

knew /nju:/ see **know**

knickers /'nɪkəz/ npl calcinhas (de senhora) fpl

knife /naɪf/ n (pl knives) faca f ◻ vt esfaquear, apunhalar

knight /naɪt/ n cavaleiro m; (chess) cavalo m. **~hood** n grau m de cavaleiro

knit /nɪt/ vt (pt knitted or knit) tricotar ◻ vi tricotar, fazer tricô; (fig: unite) unir-se; (of bones) soldar-se. **~ one's brow** franzir as sobrancelhas. **~ting** n malha f, tricô m

knitwear /'nɪtweə(r)/ n roupa f de malha, malhas fpl

knob /nɒb/ n (of door) maçaneta f; (of drawer) puxador m; (of radio, TV etc) botão m; (of butter) noz f. **~bly** a nodoso

knock /nɒk/ vt/i bater (em); (sl : criticize) desancar (em). **~ about** vt tratar mal ◻ vi (wander) andar a esmo. **~ down** (chair, pedestrian) deitar no chão, derrubar; (demolish) deitar abaixo; (colloq: reduce) baixar, reduzir; (at auction) adjudicar (**to** a). **~-down** a (price) muito baixo. **~-kneed** a de pernas de tesoura. **~ off** vt (colloq: complete quickly) despachar; (sl: steal) roubar ◻ vi (colloq) parar de trabalhar, fechar a loja (colloq). **~ out** pôr fora de combate, eliminar; (stun) assombrar. **~-out** n (boxing) nocaute m, KO m. **~ over** entornar. **~ up** (meal etc) arranjar às pressas. **~er** n aldrava f

knot /nɒt/ n nó m ◻ vt (pt knotted) atar com nó, dar nó or nós em

knotty /'nɒtɪ/ a (-ier, -iest) nodoso, cheio de nós; (difficult) complicado, espinhoso

know /nəʊ/ vt/i (pt knew, pp known) saber (that que); (person, place) conhecer ◻ n **in the ~** (colloq) por dentro. **~ about** (cars etc) saber sobre, saber de. **~-all** n sabe-tudo m (colloq). **~-how** n know-how m, conhecimentos mpl técnicos, culturais etc. **~ of** ter conhecimento de, ter ouvido falar de. **~ingly** adv com ar conhecedor; (consciously) conscientemente

knowledge /'nɒlɪdʒ/ n conhecimento m; (learning) saber m. **~able** a conhecedor, entendido, versado

known /nəʊn/ see **know** □ a conhecido

knuckle /'nʌkl/ n nó m dos dedos □ vi **~ under** ceder, submeter-se

Koran /kə'ra:n/ n Alcorão m, Corão m

Korea /kə'rɪə/ n Coréia f

kosher /'kəʊʃə(r)/ a aprovado pela lei judaica; (colloq) como deve ser

kowtow /kaʊ'taʊ/ vi prosternar-se (**to** diante de); (act obsequiously) bajular

....

Ll

....

lab /læb/ n (colloq) laboratório m

label /'leɪbl/ n (on bottle etc) rótulo m; (on clothes, luggage) etiqueta f □ vt (pt **labelled**) rotular; etiquetar, pôr etiqueta em

laboratory /lə'bɒrətrɪ/ n laboratório m

laborious /lə'bɔ:rɪəs/ a laborioso, trabalhoso

labour /'leɪbə(r)/ n trabalho m, labuta f; (workers) mão-de-obra f □ vi trabalhar; (try hard) esforçar-se □ vt alongar-se sobre, insistir em. **in ~** em trabalho de parto. **~ed** a (writing) laborioso, sem espontaneidade; (breathing, movement) difícil. **~-saving** a que poupa trabalho

Labour /'leɪbə(r)/ n (party) Partido m Trabalhista, os trabalhistas □ a trabalhista

labourer /'leɪbərə(r)/ n trabalhador m; (on farm) trabalhador m rural

labyrinth /'læbərɪnθ/ n labirinto m

lace /leɪs/ n renda f; (of shoe) cordão m de sapato, (P) atacador m □ vt atar; (drink) juntar um pouco de (aguardente, rum etc)

lacerate /'læsəreɪt/ vt lacerar, rasgar

lack /læk/ n falta f □ vt faltar (a), não ter. **be ~ing** faltar. **be ~ing in** carecer de

lackadaisical /lækə'deɪzɪkl/ a lânguido, apático, desinteressado

laconic /lə'kɒnɪk/ a lacônico, (P) lacónico

lacquer /'lækə(r)/ n laca f

lad /læd/ n rapaz m, moço m

ladder /'lædə(r)/ n escada de mão f, (P) escadote m; (in stocking) fio m corrido, (P) malha f caída □ vi deixar correr um fio, (P) cair uma malha □ vt fazer malhas em

laden /'leɪdn/ a carregado (**with** de)

ladle /'leɪdl/ n concha (de sopa) f

lady /'leɪdɪ/ n senhora f; (title) Lady f. **~-in-waiting** n dama f de companhia, (P) dama f de honor. **young ~** jovem f. **~-like** a senhoril, elegante. **Ladies** n (toilets) toalete m das Senhoras

ladybird /'leɪdɪbɜ:d/ n joaninha f

lag[1] /læg/ vi (pt **lagged**) atrasar-se, ficar para trás □ n atraso m

lag[2] /læg/ vt (pt **lagged**) (pipes etc) revestir com isolante térmico

lager /'la:gə(r)/ n cerveja f leve e clara, loura f (sl)

lagoon /lə'gu:n/ n lagoa f

laid /leɪd/ see **lay**[2]

lain /leɪn/ see **lie**[2]

lair /leə(r)/ n toca f, covil m

laity /'leɪətɪ/ n leigos mpl

lake /leɪk/ n lago m

lamb /læm/ n cordeiro m, carneiro m; (meat) carneiro m

lambswool /'læmzwʊl/ n lã f

lame /leɪm/ a (-er, -est) coxo; (fig: unconvincing) fraco. **~ness** n claudicação f, coxeadura f

lament /lə'ment/ n lamento m, lamentação f □ vt/i lamentar(-se) (de). **~able** a lamentável

laminated /'læmɪneɪtɪd/ a laminado

lamp /læmp/ n lâmpada f

lamppost /'læmppəʊst/ n poste m (do candeeiro) (de iluminação pública)

lampshade /'læmpʃeɪd/ n abajur m, quebra-luz m

lance /la:ns/ n lança f □ vt lancetar

lancet /'la:nsɪt/ n bisturi m, (P) lanceta f

land /lænd/ n terra f; (country) país m; (plot) terreno m; (property) terras fpl □ a de terra, terrestre; (policy etc) agrário □ vt/i desembarcar; (aviat) aterrissar, (P) aterrar; (fall) ir parar (**on** em); (colloq: obtain) arranjar; (a blow) aplicar, mandar. **~-locked** a rodeado de terra

landing /'lændɪŋ/ n desembarque m; (aviat) aterrissagem f, (P) aterragem f; (top of stairs) patamar m. **~-stage** n cais m flutuante

land|lady /'lændleɪdɪ/ n (of rented house) senhoria f, proprietária f; (who lets rooms) dona f da casa; (of boarding-house) dona f da pensão; (of inn etc) proprietária f, estalajadeira f. **~lord** n (of rented house) senhorio m, proprietário m; (of inn etc) proprietário m, estalajadeiro m

landmark /'lændma:k/ n (conspicuous feature) ponto m de referência; (fig) marco m

k

l

landscape /'lændskeɪp/ n paisagem f
□ vt projetar, (P) projectar
paisagisticamente

landslide /'lændslaɪd/ n desabamento m
or desmoronamento m de terras; (fig:
pol) vitoria f esmagadora

lane /leɪn/ n senda f, caminho m; (in
country) estrada f pequena; (in town)
viela f, ruela f; (of road) faixa f, pista f;
(of traffic) fila f; (aviat) corredor m;
(naut) rota f

language /'læŋgwɪdʒ/ n língua f;
(speech, style) linguagem f. **bad** ~
linguagem f grosseira. ~ **lab**
laboratório m de línguas

languid /'læŋgwɪd/ a lânguido

languish /'læŋgwɪʃ/ vi elanguescer

lank /læŋk/ a (of hair) escorrido, liso

lanky /'læŋkɪ/ a (-ier, -iest)
desengonçado, escanifrado

lantern /'læntən/ n lanterna f

lap[1] /læp/ n colo m; (sport) volta f
completa. ~-**dog** n cãozinho m de
estimação

lap[2] /læp/ vt ~ **up** beber lambendo □ vi
marulhar

lapel /lə'pel/ n lapela f

lapse /læps/ vi decair, degenerar-se;
(expire) caducar □ n lapso m; (jur)
prescrição f. ~ **into** (thought)
mergulhar em; (bad habit) adquirir

larceny /'la:sənɪ/ n furto m

lard /la:d/ n banha de porco f

larder /'la:də(r)/ n despensa f

large /la:dʒ/ a (-er, -est) grande. **at** ~ à
solta, em liberdade. **by and** ~ em geral.
~**ly** adv largamente, em grande parte.
~**ness** n grandeza f

lark[1] /la:k/ n (bird) cotovia f

lark[2] /la:k/ n (colloq) pândega f,
brincadeira f □ vi ~ **about** (colloq)
fazer travessuras, brincar

larva /'la:və/ n (pl -vae /-vi:/) larva f

laryngitis /lærɪn'dʒaɪtɪs/ n laringite f

larynx /'lærɪŋks/ n laringe f

lascivious /lə'sɪvɪəs/ a lascivo, sensual

laser /'leɪzə(r)/ n laser m. ~ **printer**
impressora f a laser

lash /læʃ/ vt chicotear, açoitar; (rain)
fustigar □ n chicote m; (stroke)
chicotada f; (eyelash) pestana f, cílio m.
~ **out** atacar, atirar-se a; (colloq: spend)
esbanjar dinheiro em algo

lashings /'læʃɪŋz/ npl ~ **of** (sl) montes de
(colloq)

lasso /læ'su:/ n (pl -os) laço m □ vt laçar

last[1] /la:st/ a último □ adv no fim, em
último lugar; (most recently) a última
vez □ n último m. **at** (long) ~ por fim,
finalmente. ~-**minute** a de última
hora. ~ **night** ontem à noite, a noite

passada. **the** ~ **straw** a gota d'água. **to**
the ~ até o fim. ~**ly** adv finalmente, em
último lugar

last[2] /la:st/ vt/i durar, continuar. ~**ing** a
duradouro, durável

latch /lætʃ/ n trinco m

late /leɪt/ a (-er, -est) atrasado; (recent)
recente; (former) antigo, ex-, anterior;
(hour, fruit etc) tardio; (deceased)
falecido □ adv tarde. **in** ~ **july** no fim
de julho. **of** ~ ultimamente. **at the** ~**st**
o mais tardar. ~**ness** n atraso m

lately /'leɪtlɪ/ adv nos últimos tempos,
ultimamente

latent /'leɪtnt/ a latente

lateral /'lætərəl/ a lateral

lathe /leɪð/ n torno m

lather /'la:ðə(r)/ n espuma f de sabão □ vt
ensaboar □ vi fazer espuma

Latin /'lætɪn/ n (lang) latim m □ a latino.
~ **America** n América f Latina.
~ **American** a & n latino-americano (m)

latitude /'lætɪtju:d/ n latitude f

latter /'lætə(r)/ a último, mais recente
□ n **the** ~ este, esta. ~**ly** adv
recentemente

lattice /'lætɪs/ n treliça f, (P)
gradeamento m de ripas

laudable /'lɔ:dəbl/ a louvável

laugh /la:f/ vi rir (**at** de). ~ **off** disfarçar
com uma piada □ n riso m. ~**able** a
irrisório, ridículo. ~**ing-stock** n
objeto m, (P) objecto m de troça

laughter /'la:ftə(r)/ n riso m, risada f

launch[1] /lɔ:ntʃ/ vt lançar □ n lançamento
m. ~ **into** lançar-se or meter-se em.
~**ing pad** plataforma f de lançamento

launch[2] /lɔ:ntʃ/ n (boat) lancha f

launder /'lɔ:ndə(r)/ vt lavar e passar

launderette /lɔ:n'dret/ n lavandaria f
automática

laundry /'lɔ:ndrɪ/ n lavandaria f;
(clothes) roupa f. **do the** ~ lavar a roupa

laurel /'lɒrəl/ n loureiro m, louro m

lava /'la:və/ n lava f

lavatory /'lævətrɪ/ n privada f, (P)
retrete f; (room) toalete m, (P) lavabo m

lavender /'lævəndə(r)/ n alfazema f,
lavanda f

lavish /'lævɪʃ/ a pródigo; (plentiful)
copioso, generoso; (lush) suntuoso □ vt
ser pródigoem, encher de. ~**ly** adv
prodigamente; copiosamente;
suntuosamente

law /lɔ:/ n lei f, (profession, study) direito
m. ~-**abiding** a cumpridor da lei,
respeitador da lei. ~ **and order** ordem
f pública. ~-**breaker** n transgressor m
da lei. ~**ful** a legal, legítimo. ~**fully**
adv legalmente. ~**less** a sem lei; (act)
ilegal; (person) rebelde

lawcourt /'lɔːkɔːt/ n tribunal m

lawn /lɔːn/ n gramado m, (P) relvado m. **~-mower** n cortador m de grama, (P) máquina f de cortar a relva

lawsuit /'lɔːsuːt/ n processo m, ação f, (P) acção f judicial

lawyer /'lɔːjə(r)/ n advogado m

lax /læks/ a negligente; (*discipline*) frouxo; (*morals*) relaxado. **~ity** n negligência f; (*of discipline*) frouxidão f; (*of morals*) relaxamento m

laxative /'læksətɪv/ n laxante m, laxativo m

lay[1] /leɪ/ a leigo. **~ opinion** opinião f de um leigo

lay[2] /leɪ/ vt (pt **laid**) pôr, colocar; (*trap*) preparar, pôr; (*eggs, table, siege*) pôr; (*plan*) fazer □ vi pôr (ovos). **~ aside** pôr de lado. **~ down** pousar; (*condition, law, rule*) impôr; (*arms*) depor; (*one's life*) oferecer; (*policy*) ditar. **~ hold of** agarrar(-se a). **~ off** vt (*worker*) suspender do trabalho □ vi (*colloq*) parar, desistir. **~-off** n suspensão f temporária. **~ on** (*gas, water etc*) instalar, ligar; (*entertainment etc*) organizar, providenciar; (*food*) servir. **~ out** (*design*) traçar, planejar; (*spread out*) estender, espalhar; (*money*) gastar. **~ up** vt (*store*) juntar; (*ship, car*) pôr fora de serviço

lay[3] /leɪ/ see **lie**

layabout /'leɪəbaʊt/ n (sl) vadio m

lay-by /'leɪbaɪ/ n acostamento m, (P) berma f

layer /'leɪə(r)/ n camada f

layman /'leɪmən/ n (pl **-men**) leigo m

layout /'leɪaʊt/ n disposição f; (*typ*) composição f

laze /leɪz/ vi descansar, vadiar

laz|y /'leɪzɪ/ a (**-ier, -iest**) preguiçoso. **~iness** n preguiça f. **~y-bones** n (*colloq*) vadio m, vagabundo m

lead[1] /liːd/ vt/i (pt **led**) conduzir, guiar, levar; (*team etc*) chefiar, liderar; (*life*) levar; (*choir, band etc*) dirigir □ n (*distance*) avanço m; (*first place*) dianteira f; (*clue*) indício m, pista f; (*leash*) coleira f; (*electr*) cabo m; (*theatr*) papel m principal; (*example*) exemplo m. **in the ~** na frente. **~ away** levar. **~ on** (*fig*) encorajar. **~ the way** ir na frente. **~ up to** conduzir a

lead[2] /led/ n chumbo m; (*of pencil*) grafite f. **~en** a de chumbo; (*of colour*) plúmbeo

leader /'liːdə(r)/ n chefe m, líder m; (*of country, club, union etc*) dirigente mf; (*pol*) líder; (*of orchestra*) regente mf, maestro m; (*in newspaper*) editorial m. **~ship** n direção f, (P) direcção f, liderança f

leading /'liːdɪŋ/ a principal. **~ article** artigo m de fundo, editorial m

leaf /liːf/ n (pl **leaves**) folha f; (*flap of table*) aba f □ vi **~ through** folhear. **~y** a frondoso

leaflet /'liːflɪt/ n prospecto m, folheto m informativo

league /liːg/ n liga f; (*sport*) campeonato m da Liga. **in ~ with** de coligação com, em conluio com

leak /liːk/ n (*escape*) fuga f; (*hole*) buraco m □ vt/i (*roof, container*) pingar; (*electr, gas*) ter um escapamento, (P) ter uma fuga; (*naut*) fazer água. **~ out** (*fig: divulge*) divulgar; (*fig: become known*) transpirar, divulgar-se. **~age** n vazamento m. **~y** a que tem um vazamento

lean[1] /liːn/ a (**-er, -est**) magro. **~ness** n magreza f

lean[2] /liːn/ vt/i (pt **leaned** or **leant** /lent/) encostar(-se), apoiar-se (**on** em); (*be slanting*) inclinar(-se). **~ back/forward** or **over** inclinar-se para trás/para a frente. **~ on** (*colloq*) pressionar. **~-to** n alpendre m

leaning /'liːnɪŋ/ a inclinado □ n inclinação f

leap /liːp/ vt (pt **leaped** or **leapt** /lept/) galgar, saltar por cima de □ vi saltar □ n salto m, pulo m. **~-frog** n eixo-badeixo m, (P) jogo m do eixo. **~ year** ano m bissexto

learn /lɜːn/ vt/i (pt **learned** or **learnt**) aprender; (*be told*) vir a saber, ouvir dizer. **~er** n principiante mf, aprendiz m

learn|ed /'lɜːnɪd/ a erudito. **~ing** n saber m, erudição f

lease /liːs/ n arrendamento m, aluguel m, (P) aluguer m □ vt arrendar, (P) alugar

leash /liːʃ/ n coleira f

least /liːst/ a o menor □ n o mínimo m, o menos m □ adv o menos. **at ~** pelo menos. **not in the ~** de maneira alguma

leather /'leðə(r)/ n couro m, cabedal m

leave /liːv/ vt/i (pt **left**) deixar; (*depart from*) sair/partir (de), ir-se (de) □ n licença f, permissão f. **be left (over)** restar, sobrar. **~ alone** deixar em paz, não tocar. **~ out** omitir. **~ of absence** licença f. **on ~** (*mil*) de licença. **take one's ~** despedir-se (**of** de)

leavings /'liːvɪŋz/ npl restos mpl

Leban|on /'lebənən/ n Líbano m. **~ese** /-'niːz/ a & n libanês (m)

lecherous /'letʃərəs/ a lascivo

lectern /'lektən/ n estante f (de coro de igreja)

lecture /'lektʃə(r)/ n conferência f; (*univ*) aula f teórica; (*fig*) sermão m

□ *vi* dar uma conferência; (*univ*) dar aula(s) □ *vt* pregar um sermão a alg (*colloq*). ~r /-ə(r)/ *n* conferente *mf*, conferencista *mf*; (*univ*) professor *m*

led /led/ *see* **lead**¹

ledge /ledʒ/ *n* rebordo *m*, saliência *f*; (*of window*) peitoril *m*

ledger /'ledʒə(r)/ *n* livro-mestre *m*, razão *m*

leech /liːtʃ/ *n* sanguessuga *f*

leek /liːk/ *n* alho-poró *m*, (*P*) alho-porro *m*

leer /lɪə(r)/ *vi* ~ (**at**) olhar de modo malicioso *or* manhoso (para) □ *n* olhar *m* malicioso *or* manhoso

leeway /'liːweɪ/ *n* (*naut*) deriva *f*; (*fig*) liberdade *f* de ação, (*P*) acção, margem *f* (*colloq*)

left¹ /left/ *see* **leave**. ~ **luggage (office)** depósito *m* de bagagens. ~**overs** *npl* restos *mpl*, sobras *fpl*

left² /left/ *a* à esquerdo; (*pol*) de esquerda □ *n* esquerda *f* □ *adv* à/para a esquerda. ~**-hand** *a* da esquerda; (*position*) à esquerda. ~**-handed** *a* canhoto. ~**-wing** *a* (*pol*) de esquerda

leg /leg/ *n* perna *f*; (*of table*) pé *m*, perna *f*; (*of journey*) etapa *f*. **pull sb's** ~s brincar *or* mexer com alg. **stretch one's** ~s esticar as pernas. ~**-room** *n* espaço *m* para as pernas

legacy /'legəsɪ/ *n* legado *m*

legal /'liːgl/ *a* legal; (*affairs etc*) jurídico. ~ **adviser** advogado *m*. ~**ity** /liːˈgælətɪ/ *n* legalidade *f*. ~**ly** *adv* legalmente

legalize /'liːgəlaɪz/ *vt* legalizar

legend /'ledʒənd/ *n* lenda *f*. ~**ary** /'ledʒəndrɪ/ *a* lendário

leggings /'legɪnz/ *npl* perneiras *fpl*; (*women's*) legging *m*

legib|le /'ledʒəbl/ *a* legível. ~**ility** /-'bɪlətɪ/ *n* legibilidade *f*

legion /'liːdʒən/ *n* legião *f*

legislat|e /'ledʒɪsleɪt/ *vi* legislar. ~**ion** /-'leɪʃn/ *n* legislação *f*

legislat|ive /'ledʒɪslətɪv/ *a* legislativo. ~**ure** /-eɪtʃə(r)/ *n* corpo *m* legislativo

legitima|te /lɪˈdʒɪtɪmət/ *a* legítimo. ~**cy** *n* legitimidade *f*

leisure /'leʒə(r)/ *n* lazer *m*, tempo livre *m*. **at one's** ~ ao bel prazer, (*P*) a seu belo prazer. ~ **centre** centro *m* de lazer. ~**ly** *a* pausado, compassado □ *adv* sem pressa, devagar

lemon /'lemən/ *n* limão *m*

lemonade /lemə'neɪd/ *n* limonada *f*

lend /lend/ *vt* (*pt* **lent**) emprestar; (*contribute*) dar. ~ **a hand to** (*help*) ajudar. ~ **itself to** prestar-se a. ~**er** *n* pessoa *f* que empresta. ~**ing** *n* empréstimo *m*

length /leŋθ/ *n* comprimento *m*; (*in time*) período *m*; (*of cloth*) corte *m*. **at** ~ extensamente; (*at last*) por fim, finalmente. ~**y** *a* longo, demorado

lengthen /'leŋθən/ *vt/i* alongar (-se)

lengthways /'leŋθweɪz/ *adv* ao comprido, em comprimento, longitudinalmente

lenien|t /'liːnɪənt/ *a* indulgente, clemente. ~**cy** *n* indulgência *f*, clemência *f*

lens /lenz/ *n* (*of spectacles*) lente *f*; (*photo*) objetiva *f*, (*P*) objectiva *f*

lent /lent/ *see* **lend**

Lent /lent/ *n* Quaresma *f*

lentil /'lentl/ *n* lentilha *f*

Leo /'liːəʊ/ *n* (*astr*) Leão *m*

leopard /'lepəd/ *n* leopardo *m*

leotard /'liːətɑːd/ *n* collant(s) *m* (*pl*), (*P*) maillot *m* de ginástica ou dança

leper /'lepə(r)/ *n* leproso *m*

leprosy /'leprəsɪ/ *n* lepra *f*

lesbian /'lezbɪən/ *a* lésbico □ *n* lésbica *f*

less /les/ *a* (*in number*) menor (**than** que); (*in quantity*) menos (**than** que) □ *n*, *adv* & *prep* menos. ~ **and** ~ cada vez menos

lessen /'lesn/ *vt/i* diminuir

lesser /'lesə(r)/ *a* menor. **to a** ~ **degree** em menor grau

lesson /'lesn/ *n* lição *f*

let /let/ *vt* (*pt* **let**, *pres p* **letting**) deixar, permitir; (*lease*) alugar, arrendar □ *v aux* ~'**s go** vamos. ~ **him do it** que o faça ele. ~ **me know** diga-me, avise-me □ *n* aluguel *m*, (*P*) aluguer *m*. ~ **alone** deixar em paz; (*not to mention*) sem falar em, para não falar em. ~ **down** baixar; (*deflate*) esvaziar; (*disappoint*) desapontar; (*fail to help*) deixar na mão. ~**-down** *n* desapontamento *m*. ~ **go** *vt/i* soltar. ~ **in** deixar entrar. ~ **o.s. in for** (*task, trouble*) meter-se em. ~ **off** (*gun*) disparar; (*firework*) soltar, (*P*) deitar; (*excuse*) desculpar. ~ **on** (*colloq*) *vt* revelar (**that** que) □ *vi* descoser-se (*colloq*), (*P*) descair-se (*colloq*). ~ **out** deixar sair. ~ **through** deixar passar. ~ **up** (*colloq*) abrandar, diminuir. ~**-up** *n* (*colloq*) pausa *f*, trégua *f*

lethal /'liːθl/ *a* fatal, mortal

letharg|y /'leθədʒɪ/ *n* letargia *f*, apatia *f*. ~**ic** /lɪ'θɑːdʒɪk/ *a* letárgico, apático

letter /'letə(r)/ *n* (*symbol*) letra *f*; (*message*) carta *f*. ~**-bomb** *n* carta-bomba *f*. ~**-box** *n* caixa *f* do correio. ~**ing** *n* letras *fpl*

lettuce /'letɪs/ *n* alface *f*

leukaemia /luːˈkiːmɪə/ *n* leucemia *f*

level /'levl/ *a* plano; (*on surface*) horizontal; (*in height*) no mesmo nível (**with** que); (*spoonful etc*) raso □ *n* nível *m* □ *vt* (*pt* **levelled**) nivelar; (*gun, missile*) apontar; (*accusation*) dirigir. **on the ~** (*colloq*) franco, sincero. **~ crossing** passagem *f* de nível. **~-headed** *a* equilibrado, sensato

lever /'li:və(r)/ *n* alavanca *f* □ *vt* **~ up** levantar com alavanca

leverage /'li:vərɪdʒ/ *n* influência *f*

levity /'levətɪ/ *n* frivolidade *f*, leviandade *f*

levy /'levɪ/ *vt* (*tax*) cobrar □ *n* imposto *m*

lewd /lu:d/ *a* (**-er, -est**) libidinoso, obsceno

liabilit|y /laɪə'bɪlətɪ/ *n* responsabilidade *f*; (*colloq: handicap*) desvantagem *f*. **~ies** dívidas *fpl*

liable /'laɪəbl/ *a* **~ to do** suscetível, (P) susceptível de fazer; **~ to** (*illness etc*) suscetível, (P) susceptível a; (*fine*) sujeito a. **~ for** responsável por

liaise /lɪ'eɪz/ *vi* (*colloq*) servir de intermediário (**between** entre), fazer a ligação (**with** com)

liaison /lɪ'eɪzn/ *n* ligação *f*

liar /'laɪə(r)/ *n* mentiroso *m*

libel /'laɪbl/ *n* difamação *f* □ *vt* (*pt* **libelled**) difamar

liberal /'lɪbərəl/ *a* liberal. **~ly** *adv* liberalmente

Liberal /'lɪbərəl/ *a & n* liberal (*mf*)

liberat|e /'lɪbəreɪt/ *vt* libertar. **~ion** /-'reɪʃn/ *n* libertação *f*; (*of women*) emancipação *f*

libert|y /'lɪbətɪ/ *n* liberdade *f*. **at ~y to** livre de. **take ~ies** tomar liberdades

libido /lɪ'bi:dəʊ/ *n* (*pl* **-os**) libido *m*

Libra /'li:brə/ *n* (*astr*) Balança *f*, Libra *f*

librar|y /'laɪbrərɪ/ *n* biblioteca *f*. **~ian** /-'breərɪən/ *n* bibliotecário *m*

Libya /'lɪbɪə/ *n* Líbia *f*. **~n** *a & n* líbio (*m*)

lice /laɪs/ *n see* **louse**

licence /'laɪsns/ *n* licença *f*; (*for TV*) taxa *f*; (*for driving*) carteira *f*, (P) carta *f*; (*behaviour*) libertinagem *f*

license /'laɪsns/ *vt* dar licença para, autorizar □ *n* (*Amer*) = **licence**. **~ plate** placa *f* do carro, (P) placa *f* de matrícula

licentious /laɪ'senʃəs/ *a* licencioso

lichen /'laɪkən/ *n* líquen *m*

lick /lɪk/ *vt* lamber; (*sl: defeat*) bater (*colloq*), dar uma surra em (*colloq*) □ *n* lambidela *f*. **a ~ of paint** uma mão de pintura

lid /lɪd/ *n* tampa *f*

lido /'li:dəʊ/ *n* (*pl* **~os**) piscina *f* pública ao ar livre

lie[1] /laɪ/ *n* mentira *f* □ *vi* (*pt* **lied**, *pres p* **lying**) mentir. **give the ~ to** desmentir

lie[2] /laɪ/ *vi* (*pt* **lay**, *pp* **lain**, *pres p* **lying**) estar deitado; (*remain*) ficar; (*be situated*) estar, encontrar-se; (*in grave, on ground*) jazer. **~ down** descansar. **~ in, have a ~-in** dormir até tarde. **~ low** (*colloq: hide*) andar escondido

lieu /lu:/ *n* **in ~ of** em vez de

lieutenant /lef'tenənt/ *n* (*army*) tenente *m*; (*navy*) 1° tenente *m*

life /laɪf/ *n* (*pl* **lives**) vida *f*. **~ cycle** ciclo *m* vital. **~ expectancy** probabilidade *f* de vida. **~-guard** *n* salva-vidas *m*. **~ insurance** seguro *m* de vida. **~-jacket** *n* colete *m* salva-vidas. **~-size(d)** *a* (de) tamanho natural *invar*

lifebelt /'laɪfbelt/ *n* cinto *m* salva-vidas, (P) cinto *m* de salvação

lifeboat /'laɪfbəʊt/ *n* barco *m* salva-vidas

lifebuoy /'laɪfbɔɪ/ *n* bóia *f* salva-vidas, (P) bóia *f* de salvação

lifeless /'laɪflɪs/ *a* sem vida

lifelike /'laɪflaɪk/ *a* natural, real; (*of portrait*) muito parecido

lifelong /'laɪflɒŋ/ *a* de toda a vida, perpétuo

lifestyle /'laɪfstaɪl/ *n* estilo *m* de vida

lifetime /'laɪftaɪm/ *n* vida *f*. **the chance of a ~** uma oportunidade única

lift /lɪft/ *vt/i* levantar(-se), erguer (-se); (*colloq: steal*) roubar, surripiar (*colloq*); (*of fog*) levantar, dispersar-se □ *n* ascensor *m*, elevador *m*. **give a ~ to** dar carona, (P) boleia a (*colloq*). **~-off** *n* decolagem *f*, (P) descolagem *f*

ligament /'lɪgəmənt/ *n* ligamento *m*

light[1] /laɪt/ *n* luz *f*; (*lamp*) lâmpada *f*; (*on vehicle*) farol *m*; (*spark*) lume *m* □ *a* claro □ *vt* (*pt* **lit** *or* **lighted**) (*ignite*) acender; (*illuminate*) iluminar. **bring to ~** trazer à luz, revelar. **come to ~** vir à luz. **~ up** iluminar(-se), acender(-se). **~-year** *n* ano-luz *m*

light[2] /laɪt/ *a & adv* (**-er, -est**) leve. **~-headed** *a* (*dizzy*) estonteado, tonto; (*frivolous*) leviano. **~-hearted** *a* alegre, despreocupado. **~ly** *adv* de leve, levemente, ligeiramente. **~ness** *n* leveza *f*

lighten[1] /'laɪtn/ *vt/i* iluminar(-se); (*make brighter*) clarear

lighten[2] /'laɪtn/ *vt/i* (*load etc*) aligeirar(-se), tornar mais leve

lighter /'laɪtə(r)/ *n* isqueiro *m*

lighthouse /'laɪthaʊs/ *n* farol *m*

lighting /'laɪtɪŋ/ *n* iluminação *f*

lightning /'laɪtnɪŋ/ *n* relâmpago *m*; (*thunderbolt*) raio *m* □ *a* muito rápido. **like ~** como um relâmpago

lightweight /'laɪtweɪt/ *a* leve

like¹ /laɪk/ *a* parecido (com) □ *prep* como □ *conj* (colloq) como □ *n* igual *m*, coisa *f* parecida. ~**-minded** *a* da mesma opinião. **the** ~**s of you** gente como você(s).

like² /laɪk/ *vt* gostar (de). ~**s** *npl* gostos *mpl*. **I would** ~ gostaria (de), queria. **if you** ~ se quiser. **would you** ~? gostaria?, queria? ~**able** *a* simpático

like|ly /'laɪklɪ/ *a* (-ier, -iest) provável □ *adv* provavelmente. **he is** ~**ly to come** é provável que ele venha. **not** ~**ly!** (colloq) nem morto, nem por sonhos. ~**lihood** *n* probabilidade *f*

liken /'laɪkn/ *vt* comparar (**to** com)

likeness /'laɪknɪs/ *n* semelhança *f*

likewise /'laɪkwaɪz/ *adv* também; (in the same way) da mesma maneira

liking /'laɪkɪŋ/ *n* gosto *m*, inclinação *f*; (for person) afeição *f*. **take a** ~ **to** (thing) tomar gosto por; (person) simpatizar com

lilac /'laɪlək/ *n* lilás *m* □ *a* lilás invar

lily /'lɪlɪ/ *n* lírio *m*, lis *m*. ~ **of the valley** lírio *m* do vale

limb /lɪm/ *n* membro *m*

limber /'lɪmbə(r)/ *vi* ~ **up** fazer exercícios para desenferrujar (colloq)

lime¹ /laɪm/ *n* cal *f*

lime² /laɪm/ *n* (fruit) limão *m*

lime³ /laɪm/ *n* ~**(-tree)** tília *f*

limelight /'laɪmlaɪt/ *n* **be in the** ~ estar em evidência

limerick /'lɪmərɪk/ *n* poema *m* humorístico (de cinco versos)

limit /'lɪmɪt/ *n* limite *m* □ *vt* limitar. ~**ation** /-'teɪʃn/ *n* limitação *f*. ~**ed company** sociedade *f* anônima, (P) anónima de responsabilidade limitada

limousine /'lɪməzi:n/ *n* limusine *f*

limp¹ /lɪmp/ *vi* mancar, coxear □ *n* **have a** ~ coxear

limp² /lɪmp/ *a* (-er, -est) mole, frouxo

line¹ /laɪn/ *n* linha *f*; (string) fio *m*; (rope) corda *f*; (row) fila *f*; (of poem) verso *m*; (wrinkle) ruga *f*; (of business) ramo *m*; (of goods) linha *f*; (Amer: queue) bicha *f* □ *vt* marcar com linhas; (streets etc) ladear, enfileirar-se ao longo de. ~**d paper** papel *m* pautado. **in** ~ **with** de acordo com. ~ **up** alinhar(-se), enfileirar(-se); (in queue) pôr(-se) em fila, (P) bicha. ~**-up** *n* (players) formação *f*

line² /laɪn/ *vt* (garment) forrar (**with** de)

lineage /'lɪnɪɪdʒ/ *n* linhagem *f*

linear /'lɪnɪə(r)/ *a* linear

linen /'lɪnɪn/ *n* (sheets etc) roupa *f* (branca) de cama; (material) linho *m*

liner /'laɪnə(r)/ *n* navio *m* de linha regular, (P) paquete *m*

linesman /'laɪnzmən/ *n* (football, tennis) juiz *m* de linha

linger /'lɪŋgə(r)/ *vi* demorar-se, deixar-se ficar; (of smells etc) persistir

lingerie /'lænʒərɪ/ *n* roupa *f* de baixo (de senhora), lingerie *f*

linguist /'lɪŋgwɪst/ *n* lingüista *mf*, (P) linguista *mf*

linguistic /lɪŋ'gwɪstɪk/ *a* lingüístico, (P) linguístico. ~**s** *n* lingüística *f*, (P) linguística *f*

lining /'laɪnɪŋ/ *n* forro *m*

link /lɪŋk/ *n* laço *m*; (of chain; fig) elo *m* □ *vt* unir, ligar; (relate) ligar; (arm) enfiar. ~ **up** (of roads) juntar-se (**with** a). ~**age** *n* ligação *f*

lino, linoleum /'laɪnəʊ, lɪ'nəʊlɪəm/ *n* linóleo *m*

lint /lɪnt/ *n* (med) curativo *m* de fibra de algodão; (fluff) cotão *m*

lion /'laɪən/ *n* leão *m*. ~**ess** *n* leoa *f*

lip /lɪp/ *n* lábio *m*, beiço *m*; (edge) borda *f*; (of jug etc) bico *m*. ~**read** *vt/i* entender pelos movimentos dos lábios. **pay** ~**-service to** fingir pena, admiração etc

lipstick /'lɪpstɪk/ *n* batom *m*, (P) bâton *m*

liquefy /'lɪkwɪfaɪ/ *vt/i* liquefazer(-se)

liqueur /lɪ'kjʊə(r)/ *n* licor *m*

liquid /'lɪkwɪd/ *n & a* líquido (*m*). ~**ize** *vt* liqüidificar, (P) liquidificar. ~**izer** *n* liqüidificador *m*, (P) liquidificador *m*

liquidat|e /'lɪkwɪdeɪt/ *vt* liquidar. ~**ion** /-'deɪʃn/ *n* liquidação *f*

liquor /'lɪkə(r)/ *n* bebida *f* alcoólica

liquorice /'lɪkərɪs/ *n* alcaçuz *m*

Lisbon /'lɪzbən/ *n* Lisboa *f*

lisp /lɪsp/ *n* ceceio *m* □ *vi* cecear

list¹ /lɪst/ *n* lista *f* □ *vt* fazer uma lista de; (enter) pôr na lista

list² /lɪst/ *vi* (of ship) adernar □ *n* adernamento *m*

listen /'lɪsn/ *vi* escutar, prestar atenção. ~ **to,** ~ **in (to)** escutar, pôr-se à escuta. ~**er** *n* ouvinte *mf*

listless /'lɪstlɪs/ *a* sem energia, apático

lit /lɪt/ *see* **light¹**

literal /'lɪtərəl/ *a* literal. ~**ly** *adv* literalmente

litera|te /'lɪtərət/ *a* alfabetizado. ~**cy** *n* alfabetização *f*, instrução *f*

literature /'lɪtrətʃə(r)/ *n* literatura *f*; (colloq: leaflets etc) folhetos *mpl*

lithe /laɪð/ *a* ágil, flexível

litigation /lɪtɪ'geɪʃn/ *n* litígio *m*

litre /'li:tə(r)/ *n* litro *m*

litter /'lɪtə(r)/ *n* lixo *m*; (animals) ninhada *f* □ *vt* cobrir de lixo. ~**ed with**

coberto de. **~-bin** *n* lata *f*, (*P*) caixote *m* do lixo

little[1] /'lɪtl/ *a* pequeno; (*not much*) pouco □ *n* pouco *m* □ *adv* pouco, mal, nem. **a ~** um pouco (de). **he ~ knows** ele mal/nem sabe. **~ by ~** pouco a pouco

liturgy /'lɪtədʒɪ/ *n* liturgia *f*

live[1] /laɪv/ *a* vivo; (*wire*) eletrizado; (*broadcast*) em direto, (*P*) directo, ao vivo

live[2] /lɪv/ *vt/i* viver; (*reside*) habitar, morar, viver. **~ down** fazer esquecer. **~ it up** cair na farra. **~ on** viver de; (*continue*) continuar a viver. **~ up to** mostrar-se à altura de; (*fulfil*) cumprir

livelihood /'laɪvlɪhʊd/ *n* modo *m* de vida

livel|**y** /'laɪvlɪ/ *a* (**-ier, -iest**) vivo, animado. **~iness** *n* vivacidade *f*, animação *f*

liven /'laɪvn/ *vt/i* **~ up** animar (-se)

liver /'lɪvə(r)/ *n* fígado *m*

livery /'lɪvərɪ/ *n* libré *f*

livestock /'laɪvstɒk/ *n* gado *m*

livid /'lɪvɪd/ *a* lívido; (*colloq: furious*) furioso

living /'lɪvɪŋ/ *a* vivo □ *n* vida *f*; (*livelihood*) modo de vida *m*, sustento *m*. **earn** *or* **make a ~** ganhar a vida. **standard of ~** nível *m* de vida. **~-room** *n* sala *f* de estar

lizard /'lɪzəd/ *n* lagarto *m*

llama /'lɑ:mə/ *n* lama *m*

load /ləʊd/ *n* carga *f*; (*of lorry, ship*) carga *f*, carregamento *m*; (*weight, strain*) peso *m*. **~s of** (*colloq*) montes de (*colloq*) □ *vt* carregar. **~ed** *a* (*dice*) viciado; (*sl: rich*) cheio da nota

loaf[1] /ləʊf/ *n* (*pl* **loaves**) pão *m*

loaf[2] /ləʊf/ *vi* vadiar. **~er** *n* preguiçoso *m*, vagabundo *m*

loan /ləʊn/ *n* empréstimo *m* □ *vt* emprestar. **on ~** emprestado

loath /ləʊθ/ *a* sem vontade de, pouco disposto a, relutante em

loath|**e** /ləʊð/ *vt* detestar. **~ing** *n* repugnância *f*, aversão *f*.

lobby /'lɒbɪ/ *n* entrada *f*, vestíbulo *m*; (*pol*) lobby *m*, grupo *m* de pressão □ *vt* fazer pressão sobre

lobe /ləʊb/ *n* lóbulo *m*

lobster /'lɒbstə(r)/ *n* lagosta *f*

local /'ləʊkl/ *a* local; (*shops etc*) do bairro □ *n* pessoa *f* do lugar; (*colloq: pub*) taberna *f*/pub *m* do bairro. **~ government** administração *f* municipal. **~ly** *adv* localmente

locale /ləʊˈkɑ:l/ *n* local *m*

locality /ləʊˈkælətɪ/ *n* localidade *f*; (*position*) lugar *m*

localization /ləʊəˈlaɪzeɪʃn/ *n* localização *f*

localized /'ləʊkəlaɪzd/ *a* localizado

locat|**e** /ləʊˈkeɪt/ *vt* localizar; (*situate*) situar. **~ion** /-ʃn/ *n* localização *f*. **on ~ion** (*cinema*) em external, (*P*) no exterior

lock[1] /lɒk/ *n* (*hair*) mecha *f* de cabelo

lock[2] /lɒk/ *n* (*on door etc*) fecho *m*, fechadura *f*; (*on canal*) comporta *f* □ *vt/ i* fechar à chave; (*auto: wheels*) imobilizar(-se). **~ in** fechar à chave, encerrar. **~ out** fechar a porta para, deixar na rua. **~-out** *n* lockout *m*. **~ up** fechar a casa. **under ~ and key** a sete chaves

locker /'lɒkə(r)/ *n* compartimento *m* com chave

locket /'lɒkɪt/ *n* medalhão *m*

locksmith /'lɒksmɪθ/ *n* serralheiro *m*, chaveiro *m*

locomotion /ləʊkəˈməʊʃn/ *n* locomoção *f*

locomotive /'ləʊkəməʊtɪv/ *n* locomotiva *f*

locum /'ləʊkəm/ *n* (*med*) substituto *m*

locust /'ləʊkəst/ *n* gafanhoto *m*

lodge /lɒdʒ/ *n* casa *f* do guarda numa propriedade; (*of porter*) portaria *f* □ *vt* alojar; (*money*) depositar. **~ a complaint** apresentar uma queixa □ *vi* estar alojado (**with** em casa de); (*become fixed*) alojar-se. **~r** /-ə(r)/ *n* hóspede *mf*

lodgings /'lɒdʒɪŋz/ *n* quarto *m* mobiliado; (*flat*) apartamento *m*

loft /lɒft/ *n* sótão *m*

lofty /'lɒftɪ/ *a* (**-ier, -iest**) elevado; (*haughty*) altivo

log /lɒg/ *n* tronco *m*, toro *m*. **~ (-book)** *n* (*naut*) diário *m* de bordo; (*aviat*) diario *m* de vôo. **sleep like a ~** dormir como uma pedra □ *vt* (*pt* **logged**) (*naut/aviat*) lançar no diário de bordo. **~ off** acabar de usar. **~ on** começar a usar

loggerheads /'lɒgəhedz/ *npl* **at ~** às turras (**with** com)

logic /'lɒdʒɪk/ *a* lógico. **~al** *a* lógico. **~ally** *adv* logicamente

logistics /ləˈdʒɪstɪks/ *n* logística *f*

logo /'ləʊgəʊ/ *n* (*pl* **-os**) (*colloq*) emblema *m*, logotipo *m*, (*P*) logótipo *m*

loin /lɔɪn/ *n* (*culin*) lombo *m*, alcatra *f*

loiter /'lɔɪtə(r)/ *vi* andar vagarosamente; (*stand about*) rondar

loll /lɒl/ *vi* refestelar-se

loll|**ipop** /'lɒlɪpɒp/ *n* pirulito *m*, (*P*) chupa-chupa *m*. **~y** *n* (*colloq*) pirulito *m*, (*P*) chupa-chupa *m*; (*sl: money*) grana *f*

London /'lʌndən/ *n* Londres

lone /ləʊn/ *a* solitário. **~r** /-ə(r)/ *n* solitário *m*. **~some** *a* solitário

lonely /'ləʊnlɪ/ a (-ier, -iest) solitário; (*person*) só, solitário

long[1] /lɒŋ/ a (-er, -est) longo, comprido □ adv muito tempo, longamente. **how ~ is. . .?** (*in size*) qual é o comprimento de. . .? **how ~?** (*in time*) quanto tempo? **he will not be ~** ele não vai demorar. **a ~ time** muito tempo. **a ~ way** longe. **as or so ~ as** contanto que, desde que. **~ ago** há muito tempo. **before ~** (*future*) daqui a pouco, dentro em pouco; (*past*) pouco (tempo) depois. **in the ~ run** no fim de contas. **~ before** muito (tempo) antes. **~-distance** a (*flight*) de longa distância; (*phone call*) interurbano. **~ face** cara f triste. **~ jump** salto m em distância. **~-playing record** LP m. **~-range** a de longo alcance; (*forecast*) a longo prazo. **~-sighted** a que enxerga mal a distância. **~-standing** a de longa data. **~-suffering** a com paciência exemplar/de santo. **~-term** a a longo prazo. **~ wave** ondas fpl longas. **~-winded** a prolixo. **so ~!** (*colloq*) até logo!

long[2] /lɒŋ/ vi **~ for** ansiar por, ter grande desejo de. **~ to** desejar. **~ing** n desejo m ardente

longevity /lɒn'dʒevɪtɪ/ n longevidade f, vida f longa

longhand /'lɒŋhænd/ n escrita f à mão

longitude /'lɒndʒɪtjuːd/ n longitude f

loo /luː/ n (*colloq*) banheiro m, (P) casa f de banho

look /lʊk/ vt/i olhar; (*seem*) parecer □ n olhar m; (*appearance*) ar m, aspecto m. **(good) ~s** beleza f. **~ after** tomar conta de, olhar por. **~ at** olhar para. **~ down on** desprezar. **~ for** procurar. **~ forward to** aguardar com impaciência. **~ in on** visitar. **~ into** examinar, investigar. **~ like** parecer-se com, ter ar de. **~ on** (*as spectator*) ver, assistir; (*regard as*) considerar. **~ out** ter cautela. **~ out for** procurar; (*watch*) estar à espreita de. **~-out** n (*mil*) posto m de observação; (*watcher*) vigia m. **~ round** olhar em redor. **~ up** (*word*) procurar; (*visit*) ir ver. **~ up to** respeitar

loom[1] /luːm/ n tear m

loom[2] /luːm/ vi surgir indistintamente; (*fig*) ameaçar

loony /'luːnɪ/ n & a (*sl*) maluco (m), doido (m)

loop /luːp/ n laçada f; (*curve*) volta f, arco m; (*aviat*) loop m □ vt dar uma laçada

loophole /'luːphəʊl/ n (*in rule*) saída f, furo m

loose /luːs/ a (-er, -est) (*knot etc*) frouxo; (*page etc*) solto; (*clothes*) folgado; (*not packed*) a granel; (*inexact*) vago; (*morals*) dissoluto, imoral. **at a ~ end** sem saber o que fazer, sem ocupação definida. **break ~** soltar-se. **~ly** adv sem apertar; (*roughly*) vagamente

loosen /'luːsn/ vt (*slacken*) soltar, desapertar; (*untie*) desfazer, desatar

loot /luːt/ n saque m □ vt pilhar, saquear. **~er** n assaltante mf. **~ing** n pilhagem f, saque m

lop /lɒp/ vt (*pt* lopped) **~ off** cortar, podar

lop-sided /lɒp'saɪdɪd/ a torto, inclinado para um lado

lord /lɔːd/ n senhor m; (*title*) lord m. **the L~** o Senhor. **the L~'s Prayer** o Pai-Nosso. **(good) L~!** meu Deus! **~ly** a magnifico, nobre; (*haughty*) altivo, arrogante

lorry /'lɒrɪ/ n camião m, caminhão m

lose /luːz/ vt/i (*pt* lost) perder. **get lost** perder-se. **get lost** (*sl*) vai passear! (*colloq*) **~r** /-ə(r)/ n perdedor m

loss /lɒs/ n perda f. **be at a ~** estar perplexo. **at a ~ for words** sem saber o que dizer

lost /lɒst/ *see* lose □ a perdido. **~ property** objetos mpl, (P) objectos mpl perdidos (e achados)

lot[1] /lɒt/ n sorte f; (*at auction, land*) lote m. **draw ~s** tirar à sorte

lot[2] /lɒt/ n **the ~** tudo; (*people*) todos mpl. **a ~ (of), ~s of** (*colloq*) uma porção (de) (*colloq*). **quite a ~ (of)** (*colloq*) uma boa porção (de) (*colloq*)

lotion /'ləʊʃn/ n loção f

lottery /'lɒtərɪ/ n loteria f, (P) lotaria f

loud /laʊd/ a (-er, -est) alto, barulhento, ruidoso; (*of colours*) berrante □ adv alto. **~-hailer** n megafone m. **out ~** em voz alta. **~ly** adv alto

loudspeaker /laʊd'spiːkə(r)/ n alto-falante m

lounge /laʊndʒ/ vi recostar-se preguiçosamente □ n sala f, salão m

louse /laʊs/ n (*pl* lice) piolho m

lousy /'laʊzɪ/ a (-ier, -iest) piolhento; (*sl: very bad*) péssimo

lout /laʊt/ n pessoa f grosseira, arruaceiro m

lovable /'lʌvəbl/ a amoroso, adorável

love /lʌv/ n amor m; (*tennis*) zero m, nada m □ vt amar, estar apaixonado por; (*like greatly*) gostar muito de. **in ~** apaixonado (**with** por). **~ affair** aventura f amorosa. **she sends you her ~** ela lhe manda lembranças

lovely /'lʌvlɪ/ a (-ier, -iest) lindo; (*colloq: delightful*) encantador, delicioso

lover /'lʌvə(r)/ n namorado m, apaixonado m; (*illicit*) amante m; (*devotee*) admirador m, apreciador m

lovesick /'lʌvsɪk/ *a* perdido de amor
loving /'lʌvɪŋ/ *a* amoroso, terno, extremoso
low /ləʊ/ *a* (-er, -est) baixo ◻ *adv* baixo ◻ *n* baixa *f*; (*low pressure*) área de baixa pressão *f*. ~**-cut** *a* decotado. ~**-down** *a* baixo, reles ◻ *n* (*colloq*) a verdade autêntica, (*P*) a verdade nua e crua. ~**-fat** *a* de baixo teor de gordura. ~**-key** *a* (*fig*) moderado, discreto
lower /'ləʊə(r)/ *a* & *adv see* **low** ◻ *vt* baixar. ~ **o.s.** (re)baixar-se (**to** *a*)
lowlands /'ləʊləndz/ *npl* planície(s) *f* (*pl*)
lowly /'ləʊlɪ/ *a* (-ier, -iest) humilde, modesto
loyal /'lɔɪəl/ *a* leal. ~**ly** *adv* lealmente. ~**ty** *n* lealdade *f*
lozenge /'lɒzɪndʒ/ *n* (*shape*) losango *m*; (*tablet*) pastilha *f*
LP *abbr see* **long-playing record**
lubric|ate /'lu:brɪkeɪt/ *vt* lubrificar. ~**ant** *n* lubrificante *m*. ~**ation** /-'keɪʃn/ *n* lubrificação *f*
lucid /'lu:sɪd/ *a* lúcido. ~**ity** /lu:-'sɪdətɪ/ *n* lucidez *f*
luck /lʌk/ *n* sorte *f*. **bad** ~ pouca sorte *f*. **for** ~ para dar sorte. **good** ~! boa sorte
luck|y /'lʌkɪ/ *a* (-ier, -iest) sortudo, com sorte; (*event etc*) feliz; (*number etc*) que dá sorte. ~**ily** *adv* felizmente
lucrative /'lu:krətɪv/ *a* lucrativo, rentável
ludicrous /'lu:dɪkrəs/ *a* ridículo, absurdo
lug /lʌg/ *vt* (*pt* **lugged**) arrstar
luggage /'lʌgɪdʒ/ *n* bagagem *f*. ~**-rack** *n* porta-bagagem *m*. ~**-van** *n* furgão *m*
lukewarm /'lu:kwɔ:m/ *a* morno; (*fig*) sem entusiasmo, indiferente
lull /lʌl/ *vt* (*send to sleep*) embalar; (*suspicions*) acalmar ◻ *n* calmarica *f*, (*P*) acalmia *f*
lullaby /'lʌləbaɪ/ *n* canção *f* de embalar
lumbago /lʌm'beɪgəʊ/ *n* lumbago *m*
lumber /'lʌmbə(r)/ *n* trastes *mpl* velhos; (*wood*) madeira *f* cortada ◻ *vt* ~ **sb with** sobre carregar alguém com
luminous /'lu:mɪnəs/ *a* luminoso
lump /lʌmp/ *n* bocado *m*; (*swelling*) caroço *m*; (*in the throat*) nó *m*; (*in liquid*) grumo *m*; (*of sugar*) torrão *m* ◻ *vt* ~ **together** amontoar, juntar indiscriminadamente. ~ **sum** quantia *f* total; (*payment*) pagamento

m de uma vez. ~**y** *a* grumoso, encaroçado
lunacy /'lu:nəsɪ/ *n* loucura *f*
lunar /'lu:nə(r)/ *a* lunar
lunatic /'lu:nətɪk/ *n* lunático *m*. ~ **asylum** manicômio *m*, (*P*) manicômio *m*
lunch /lʌntʃ/ *n* almoço *m* ◻ *vi* almoçar. ~**-time** *n* hora *f* do almoço
luncheon /'lʌntʃən/ *n* (*formal*) almoço *m*. ~ **meat** carne *f* enlatada, (*P*) 'merenda' *f*. ~ **voucher** senha *f* de almoço
lung /lʌŋ/ *n* pulmão *m*
lunge /lʌndʒ/ *n* mergulho *m*, movimento *m* súbito para a frente; (*thrust*) arremetida *f* ◻ *vi* mergulhar, arremessar-se (**at** para cima de, contra)
lurch[1] /lɜ:tʃ/ **leave sb in the** ~ deixar alg em apuros
lurch[2] /lɜ:tʃ/ *vi* ir aos ziguezagues, dar guinadas; (*stagger*) cambalear
lure /lʊə(r)/ *vt* atrair, tentar ◻ *n* chamariz *m*, engodo *m*. **the** ~ **of the sea** a atração, (*P*) atracção do mar
lurid /'lʊərɪd/ *a* berrante; (*fig: sensational*) sensacional; (*fig: shocking*) horrífico
lurk /lɜ:k/ *vi* esconder-se à espreita; (*prowl*) rondar; (*be latent*) estar latente
luscious /'lʌʃəs/ *a* apetitoso; (*voluptuous*) desejável
lush /lʌʃ/ *a* víoso, luxuriante
Lusitanian /lusɪ'temɪən/ *a* & *n* lusitano (*m*)
lust /lʌst/ *n* luxúria *f*, sensualidade *f*; (*fig*) cobía *f*, desejo *m* ardente ◻ *vi* ~ **after** cobíar, desejar ardentemente. ~**ful** *a* sensual
lustre /'lʌstə(r)/ *n* lustre *m*; (*fig*) prestígio *m*
lusty /'lʌstɪ/ *a* (-ier, -iest) robusto
lute /lu:t/ *n* alaúde *m*
Luxemburg /'lʌksəmbɜ:g/ *n* Luxemburgo *m*
luxuriant /lʌg'ʒʊərɪənt/ *a* luxuriante
luxurious /lʌg'ʒʊərɪəs/ *a* luxuoso
luxury /'lʌkʃərɪ/ *n* luxo *m* ◻ *a* de luxo
lying /'laɪŋ/ *see* **lie**[1], **lie**[2]
lynch /lɪntʃ/ *vt* linchar
lynx /lɪŋks/ *n* lince *m*
lyre /'laɪə(r)/ *n* lira *f*
lyric /'lɪrɪk/ *a* lírico. ~**s** *npl* (*mus*) letra *f*. ~**al** *a* lírico

Mm

MA *abbr see* **Master of Arts**

mac /mæk/ n (*colloq*) impermeável m, gabardine f

macabre /mə'ka:brə/ a macabro

macaroni /mækə'rəʊnɪ/ n macarrão m

macaroon /mækə'ru:n/ n bolinho m seco de amêndoa ralada

mace[1] /meɪs/ n (*staff*) maça f

mace[2] /meɪs/ n (*spice*) macis m

machination /mækɪ'neɪʃn/ n maquinação f

machine /mə'ʃi:n/ n máquina f □ ~ vt fazer à máquina; (*sewing*) coser à máquina. ~-**gun** n metralhadora f. ~-**readable** a em linguagem de máquina. ~ **tool** máquina-ferramenta f

machinery /mə'ʃi:nərɪ/ n maquinaria f; (*working parts; fig*) mecanismo m

machinist /mə'ʃi:nɪst/ n maquinista m

macho /'mætʃəʊ/ a machista

mackerel /'mækrəl/ n (*pl invar*) cavala f

mackintosh /'mækɪntɒʃ/ n impermeável m, gabardine f

mad /mæd/ a (**madder, maddest**) doido, louco; (*dog*) raivoso; (*colloq: angry*) furioso (*colloq*). ~ **cow disease** doença f da vaca louca. **be ~ about** ser doido por. **like a ~** como (um) doido. ~**ly** *adv* loucamente; (*frantically*) enlouquecidamente. ~**ness** n loucura f

Madagascar /mædə'gæskə(r)/ n Madagáscar m

madam /'mædəm/ n senhora f. **no, ~** não senhora

madden /'mædn/ vt endoidecer, enlouquecer. **it's ~ing** é de enlouquecer

made /meɪd/ *see* **make**. ~ **to measure** feito sob medida

Madeira /mə'dɪərə/ n Madeira f; (*wine*) Madeira m

madman /'mædmən/ n (*pl* -**men**) doido m

madrigal /'mædrɪgl/ n madrigal m

Mafia /'mæfɪə/ n Máfia f

magazine /mægə'zi:n/ n revista f, magazine m; (*of gun*) carregador m

magenta /mə'dʒentə/ a & n magenta (m), carmin (m)

maggot /'mægət/ n larva f. ~**y** a bichento

Magi /'meɪdʒaɪ/ npl **the ~** os Reis mpl Magos

magic /'mædʒɪk/ n magia f □ ~ a mágico. ~**al** a mágico

magician /mə'dʒɪʃn/ n (*conjuror*) prestidigitador m; (*wizard*) feiticeiro m

magistrate /'mædʒɪstreɪt/ n magistrado m

magnanim|ous /mæg'nænɪməs/ a magnânimo. ~**ity** /-ə'nɪmətɪ/ n magnanimidade f

magnate /'mægneɪt/ n magnata m

magnet /'mægnɪt/ n íma m, (P) íman m. ~**ic** /-'netɪk/ a magnético. ~**ism** /-ɪzəm/ n magnetismo m. ~**ize** vt magnetizar

magnificen|t /mæg'nɪfɪsnt/ a magnífico. ~**ce** n magnificência f

magnif|y /'mægnɪfaɪ/ vt aumentar; (*sound*) ampliar, amplificar. ~**ication** /-ɪ'keɪʃn/ n aumento m, ampliação f. ~**ying glass** lupa f

magnitude /'mægnɪtju:d/ n magnitude f

magpie /'mægpaɪ/ n pega f

mahogany /mə'hɒgənɪ/ n mogno m

maid /meɪd/ n criada f, empregada f. **old ~** solteirona f

maiden /'meɪdn/ n (*old use*) donzela f □ a (*aunt*) solteira; (*speech, voyage*) inaugural. ~ **name** nome m de solteira

mail[1] /meɪl/ n correio m; (*letters*) correio m, correspondência f □ a postal □ vt postar, pôr no correio; (*send by mail*) mandar pelo correio. ~-**bag** n mala f postal. ~-**box** n (*Amer*) caixa f do correio. ~**ing-list** n lista f de endereços. ~ **order** n encomenda f por correspondência, (P) por correio

mail[2] /meɪl/ n (*armour*) cota f de malha

mailman /'meɪlmæn/ n (*pl* -**men**) (*Amer*) carteiro m

maim /meɪm/ vt mutilar, aleijar

main[1] /meɪn/ a principal □ n **in the ~** em geral, essencialmente. ~ **road** estrada f principal. ~**ly** *adv* principalmente, sobretudo

main[2] /meɪn/ n (**water/gas**) ~ cano m de água/gás. **the ~s** (*electr*) a rede f elétrica

mainland /'meɪnlənd/ n continente m

mainstay /'meɪnsteɪ/ n (*fig*) esteio m

mainstream /'meɪnstri:m/ n tendência f dominante, linha f principal

maintain /meɪn'teɪn/ vt manter, sustentar; (*rights*) defender, manter

maintenance /'meɪntənəns/ n (*care, continuation*) manutenção f; (*allowance*) pensão f

maisonette /meɪzə'net/ n dúplex m

maize /meɪz/ n milho m

majestic /mə'dʒestɪk/ a majestoso. ~**ally** *adv* majestosamente

majesty /'mædʒəstɪ/ n majestade f

major /'meɪdʒə(r)/ *a* maior; (*very important*) de vulto □ *n* major *m* □ *vi* **~in** (*Amer: univ*) especializar-se em. **~ road** estrada *f* principal

Majorca /məˈdʒɔːkə/ *n* Maiorca *f*

majority /məˈdʒɒrətɪ/ *n* maioria *f*; (*age*) maioridade *f* □ *a* majoritário, (*P*) maioritário. **the ~ of people** a maioria *or* a maior parte das pessoas

make /meɪk/ *vt/i* (*pt* **made**) fazer; (*decision*) tomar; (*destination*) chegar a; (*cause to*) fazer (+ *inf*) *or* (com) que (+ *subj*). **you ~ me angry** você me aborrece □ *n* (*brand*) marca *f*. **on the ~** (*sl*) oportunista. **be made of** ser feito de. **~ o.s. at home** estar à vontade/como em sua casa. **~ it** chegar; (*succeed*) triunfar. **I ~ it two o'clock** são duas pelo meu relógio. **~ as if to** fazer *ou* fingir que. **~ believe** fingir. **~-believe** *a* fingido □ *n* fantasia *f*. **~ do with** arranjar-se com, contentar-se com. **~ for** dirigir-se para; (*contribute to*) ajudar a. **~ good** *vi* triunfar □ *vt* compensar; (*repair*) reparar. **~ off** fugir (**with** com). **~ out** avistar, distinguir; (*understand*) entender; (*claim*) pretender; (*a cheque*) passar, emitir. **~ over** ceder, transferir. **~ up** *vt* fazer, compor; (*story*) inventar; (*deficit*) suprir □ *vi* fazer as pazes. **~ up (one's face)** maquilar-se, (*P*) maquilhar-se. **~-up** *n* maquilagem *f*, (*P*) maquilhagem *f*; (*of object*) composição *f*; (*psych*) maneira *f* de ser, natureza *f*. **~ up for** compensar. **~ up one's mind** decidir-se

maker /'meɪkə(r)/ *n* fabricante *mf*

makeshift /'meɪkʃɪft/ *n* solução *f* temporária □ *a* provisório

making /'meɪkɪŋ/ *n* **be the ~ of** fazer, ser a causa do sucesso de. **in the ~** em formação. **he has the ~s of** ele tem as qualidades essenciais de

maladjusted /mælə'dʒʌstɪd/ *a* desajustado, inadaptado

maladministration /mælədmɪnɪ-'streɪʃn/ *n* mau governo *m*, má gestão *f*

malaise /mæ'leɪz/ *n* mal-estar *m*

malaria /mə'leərɪə/ *n* malária *f*

Malay /mə'leɪ/ *a* & *n* malaio (*m*). **~sia** /-ʒə/ *n* Malásia *f*

male /meɪl/ *a* (*voice, sex*) masculino; (*biol, techn*) macho □ *n* (*human*) homem *m*, indivíduo *m* do sexo masculino; (*arrival*) macho *m*

malevolen|t /mə'levələnt/ *a* malévolo. **~ce** *n* malevolência *f*, má vontade *f*

malform|ation /mælfɔː'meɪʃn/ *n* malformação *f*, deformidade *f*. **~ed** *a* deformado

malfunction /mæl'fʌŋkʃn/ *n* mau funcionamento *m* □ *vi* funcionar mal

malice /'mælɪs/ *n* maldade *f*, malícia *f*. **bear sb ~** guardar rancor a alg

malicious /mə'lɪʃəs/ *a* maldoso, malicioso. **~ly** *adv* maldosamente, maliciosamente

malign /mə'laɪn/ *vt* caluniar, difamar

malignan|t /mə'lɪɡnənt/ *a* (*tumour*) maligno; (*malevolent*) malévolo. **~cy** *n* malignidade *f*; malevolência *f*

malinger /mə'lɪŋɡə(r)/ *vi* fingir-se doente. **~er** *n* pessoa *f* que se finge doente

mallet /'mælɪt/ *n* maço *m*

malnutrition /mælnjuː'trɪʃn/ *n* desnutrição *f*, subalimentação *f*

malpractice /mæl'præktɪs/ *n* abuso *m*; (*incompetence*) incompetência *f* profissional, negligência *f*

malt /mɔːlt/ *n* malte *m*

Malt|a /'mɔːltə/ *n* Malta *f*. **~ese** /-'tiːz/ *a* & *n* maltês (*m*)

maltreat /mæl'triːt/ *vt* maltratar. **~ment** *n* mau(s) trato(s) *m*(*pl*)

mammal /'mæml/ *n* mamífero *m*

mammoth /'mæməθ/ *n* mamute *m* □ *a* gigantesco, colossal

man /mæn/ *n* (*pl* **men**) homem *m*; (*in sports team*) jogador *m*; (*chess*) peça *f* □ *vt* (*pt* **manned**) prover de pessoal; (*mil*) guarnecer; (*naut*) guarnecer, equipar, tripular; (*be on duty at*) estar de serviço em. **~ in the street** o homem da rua. **~-hour** *n* hora *f* de trabalho per capita, homem-hora *f*. **~-hunt** *n* caça *f* ao homem. **~-made** *a* artificial. **~ to man** de homem para homem

manage /'mænɪdʒ/ *vt* (*household*) governar; (*tool*) manejar; (*boat, affair, crowd*) manobrar; (*shop*) dirigir, gerir. **I could ~ another drink** (*colloq*) até que tomaria mais um drinque (*colloq*) □ *vi* arranjar-se. **~ to do** conseguir fazer. **~able** *a* manejável; (*easily controlled*) controlável. **~ment** *n* gerência *f*, direção *f*, (*P*) direcção *f*. **managing director** diretor *m*, (*P*) director *m* geral

manager /'mænɪdʒə(r)/ *n* diretor *m*, (*P*) director *m*; (*of bank, shop*) gerente *m*; (*of actor*) empresário *m*; (*sport*) treinador *m*. **~ess** /-'res/ *n* diretora *f*, (*P*) directora *f*; gerente *f*. **~ial** /-'dʒɪərɪəl/ *a* diretivo, (*P*) directivo, administrativo. **~ial staff** gestores *mpl*

mandarin /'mændərɪn/ *n* mandarim *m*. **~ (orange)** mandarina *f*, tangerina *f*

mandate /'mændeɪt/ *n* mandato *m*

mandatory /'mændətrɪ/ *a* obrigatório

m

mane /meɪn/ n crina f; (of lion) juba f

mangle[1] /'mæŋgl/ n calandra f □ vt espremer (com a calandra)

mangle[2] /'mæŋgl/ vt (mutilate) mutilar, estropiar

mango /'mæŋgəʊ/ n (pl -oes) manga f

manhandle /'mænhændl/ vt mover à força de braço; (treat roughly) tratar com brutalidade

manhole /'mænhəʊl/ n poço m de inspeção, (P) inspecção

manhood /'mænhʊd/ n idade adulta f; (quality) virilidade f

mania /'meɪnɪə/ n mania f. ~c /-ræk/ n maníaco m

manicur|e /'mænɪkjʊə(r)/ n manicure f □ vt fazer. ~ist n manicure m

manifest /'mænɪfest/ a manifesto □ vt manifestar. ~ation /-'steɪʃn/ n manifestação f

manifesto /mænɪ'festəʊ/ n (pl -os) manifesto m

manipulat|e /mə'nɪpjʊleɪt/ vt manipular. ~ion /-'leɪʃn/ n manipulação f

mankind /mæn'kaɪnd/ n humanidade f, gênero m, (P) género m humano

manly /'mænlɪ/ a viril, másculo

manner /'mænə(r)/ n maneira f, modo m; (attitude) modo(s) m (pl); (kind) espécie f. ~s maneiras fpl. bad ~s má-criação f, falta f de educação. good ~s (boa) educação f. ~ed a afetado.

mannerism /'mænərɪzəm/ n maneirismo m

manoeuvre /mə'nu:və(r)/ n manobra f □ vt/i manobrar

manor /'mænə(r)/ n solar m

manpower /'mænpaʊə(r)/ n mão-de-obra f

mansion /'mænʃn/ n mansão f

manslaughter /'mænslɔ:tə(r)/ n homicídio m involuntário

mantelpiece /'mæntlpi:s/ n (shelf) consolo m da lareira, (P) prateleira f da chaminé

manual /'mænjʊəl/ a manual □ n manual m

manufacture /mænjʊ'fæktʃə(r)/ vt fabricar □ n fabrico m, fabricação f. ~r /-ə(r)/ n fabricante mf

manure /mə'njʊə(r)/ n estrume m

manuscript /'mænjʊskrɪpt/ n manuscrito m

many /'menɪ/ a (more, most) muitos □ n muitos; (many people) muita gente f. a great ~ muitíssimos. ~ a man/tear/ etc muitos homens/muitas lágrimas/ etc. you may take as ~ as you want você pode levar quantos quiser. of us/them/you muitos de nós/deles/de

vocês. how ~? quantos? one too ~ um a mais

map /mæp/ n mapa m □ vt (pt mapped) fazer mapa de. ~ out planear em pormenor; (route) traçar

maple /'meɪpl/ n bordo m

mar /ma:(r)/ vt (pt marred) estragar; (beauty) desfigurar

marathon /'mærəθən/ n maratona f

marble /'ma:bl/ n mármore m; (for game) bola f de gude, (P) berlinde m

March /ma:tʃ/ n março m

march /ma:tʃ/ vi marchar □ vt ~off fazer marchar, conduzir à força. **he was ~ed off to prison** fizeram-no marchar para a prisão □ n marcha f. ~past n desfile m em revista militar

mare /meə(r)/ n égua f

margarine /ma:dʒə'ri:n/ n margarina f

margin /'ma:dʒɪn/ n margem f. ~al a marginal. ~al seat (pol) lugar m ganho com pequena maioria. ~ally adv por uma pequena margem, muito pouco

marigold /'mærɪɡəʊld/ n cravo-de-defunto m, (P) malmequer m

marijuana /mærɪ'wa:nə/ n maconha f

marina /mə'ri:nə/ n marina f

marinade /mærɪ'neɪd/ n vinha d'alho, escalabeche m □ vt pôr na vinha d'alho

marine /mə'ri:n/ a marinho; (of ship, trade etc) marítimo □ n (shipping) marinha f; (sailor) fuzileiro m naval

marionette /mærɪə'net/ n fantoche m, marionete f

marital /'mærɪtl/ a marital, conjugal, matrimonial. ~ status estado m civil

maritime /'mærɪtaɪm/ a marítimo

mark[1] /ma:k/ n (currency) marco m

mark[2] /ma:k/ n marca f; (trace) marca f, sinal m; (stain) mancha f; (schol) nota f; (target) alvo m □ vt marcar; (exam etc) marcar, classificar. ~ out marcar. ~ out for escolher para, designar para. ~ time marcar passo. **make one's ~** ganhar nome. ~er n marcador m. ~ing n marcas fpl, marcação f

marked /ma:kt/ a marcado. ~ly /-ɪdlɪ/ adv manifestamente, visivelmente

market /'ma:kɪt/ n mercado m □ vt vender; (launch) comercializar, lançar. ~ garden horta f de legumes para venda. ~place n mercado m. ~ research pesquisa f de mercado. on the ~ à venda. ~ing n marketing m

marksman /'ma:ksmən/ n (pl -men) atirador m especial

marmalade /'ma:məleɪd/ n compota f de laranja

maroon /mə'ru:n/ a & n bordô (m), (P) bordeaux (m)

marooned /məˈruːnd/ a abandonado em ilha, costa deserta etc; (*fig: stranded*) encalhado (*fig*)

marquee /maːˈkiː/ n barraca f ou tenda f grande; (*Amer: awning*) toldo m

marriage /ˈmærɪdʒ/ n casamento m, matrimónio m, (P) matrimónio m. ~ **certificate** certidão f de casamento. ~**able** a casadouro

marrow /ˈmærəʊ/ n (*of bone*) tutano m, medula f; (*vegetable*) abóbora f. **chilled to the** ~ gelado até os ossos

marr|y /ˈmærɪ/ vt casar(-se) com; (*give or unite in marriage*) casar ▢ vi casar-se. ~**ied** a casado; (*life*) de casado, conjugal. **get** ~**ied** casar-se

Mars /maːz/ n Marte m

marsh /maːʃ/ n pântano m. ~**y** a pantanoso

marshal /ˈmaːʃl/ n (*mil*) marechal m; (*steward*) mestre m de cerimónias, (P) cerimónias ▢ vt (*pt* **marshalled**) dispor em ordem, ordenar; (*usher*) conduzir, escoltar

marshmallow /maːʃˈmæləʊ/ n marshmallow m

martial /ˈmaːʃl/ a marcial. ~ **law** lei f marcial

martyr /ˈmaːtə(r)/ n mártir mf ▢ vt martirizar. ~**dom** n martírio m

marvel /ˈmaːvl/ n maravilha f, prodígio m ▢ vi (*pt* **marvelled**) (*feel wonder*) maravilhar-se (**at** com); (*be astonished*) pasmar (**at** com)

marvellous /ˈmaːvələs/ a maravilhoso

Marxis|t /ˈmaːksɪst/ a & n marxista (mf). ~**m** /-zəm/ n marxismo m

marzipan /ˈmaːzɪpæn/ n maçapão m

mascara /mæˈskaːrə/ n rímel m

mascot /ˈmæskət/ n mascote f

masculin|e /ˈmæskjʊlɪn/ a masculino ▢ n masculino m. ~**ity** /-ˈlɪnətɪ/ n masculinidade f

mash /mæʃ/ n (*pulp*) papa f ▢ vt esmagar. ~**ed potatoes** purê m de batata(s)

mask /maːsk/ n máscara f ▢ vt mascarar

masochis|t /ˈmæsəkɪst/ n masoquista mf. ~**m** /-zəm/ n masoquismo m

mason /ˈmeɪsn/ n maçom m; (*building*) pedreiro m. ~**ry** n maçonaria f; (*building*) alvenaria f

Mason /ˈmeɪsn/ n Maçónico m, (P) Maçónico m. ~**ic** /məˈsɒnɪk/ a Maçónico, (P) Maçónico

masquerade /mæːskəˈreɪd/ n mascarada f ▢ vi ~ **as** mascarar-se de, disfarçar-se de

mass[1] /mæs/ n (*relig*) missa f

mass[2] /mæs/ n massa f; (*heap*) montão m ▢ vt/i aglomerar(-se), reunir(-se) em

massa. ~- **produce** vt produzir em série. **the** ~**es** as massas, a grande massa

massacre /ˈmæsəkə(r)/ n massacre m ▢ vt massacrar

massage /ˈmæsaːʒ/ n massagem f ▢ vt massagear, fazer massagens em, (P) dar massagens a

masseu|r /mæˈsɜː(r)/ n massagista m. ~**se** /mæˈsɜːz/ n massagista f

massive /ˈmæsɪv/ a (*heavy*) maciço; (*huge*) enorme

mast /maːst/ n mastro m; (*for radio etc*) antena f

master /ˈmaːstə(r)/ n (*in school*) professor m, mestre m; (*expert*) mestre m; (*boss*) patrão m; (*owner*) dono m. **M~** (*boy*) menino m ▢ vt dominar. ~**-key** n chave-mestra f. ~**-mind** n (*of scheme etc*) cérebro m ▢ vt planejar, dirigir. **M~ of Arts**/etc Licenciado m em Letras/etc. ~- **stroke** n golpe m de mestre. ~**y** n domínio m (**over** sobre); (*knowledge*) conhecimento m; (*skill*) perícia f

masterly /ˈmaːstəlɪ/ a magistral

masterpiece /ˈmaːstəpiːs/ n obraprima f

masturbat|e /ˈmæstəbeɪt/ vi masturbar-se. ~**ion** /-ˈbeɪʃn/ n masturbação f

mat /mæt/ n tapete m pequeno; (*at door*) capacho m. (**table-**)~ n (*of cloth*) paninho m de mesa; (*for hot dishes*) descanso m para pratos

match[1] /mætʃ/ n fósforo m

match[2] /mætʃ/ n (*contest*) competição f, torneio m; (*game*) partida f; (*equal*) par m, parceiro m, igual mf; (*fig: marriage*) casamento m; (*marriage partner*) partido m ▢ vt/i (*set against*) contrapôr (**against** a); (*equal*) igualar; (*go with*) condizer; (*be alike*) ir com, emparceirar com. **her shoes** ~**ed her bag** os sapatos dela combinavam com a bolsa. ~**ing** a condizente, a condizer

matchbox /ˈmætʃbɒks/ n caixa f de fósforos

mat|e[1] /meɪt/ n companheiro m, camarada mf; (*of birds, animals*) macho m, fêmea f; (*assistant*) ajudante mf ▢ vt/i acasalar(-se) (**with** com). ~**ing season** n época f de cio

mate[2] /meɪt/ n (*chess*) mate m, xeque-mate m

material /məˈtɪərɪəl/ n material m; (*fabric*) tecido m; (*equipment*) apetrechos mpl ▢ a material; (*significant*) importante

materialis|m /məˈtɪərɪəlɪzəm/ n materialismo m. ~**tic** /-ˈlɪstɪk/ a materialista

materialize /məˈtɪərɪəlaɪz/ vi realizar-se, concretizar-se; (*appear*) aparecer

maternal /məˈtɜːnəl/ a maternal

maternity /məˈtɜːnətɪ/ *n* maternidade *f* □ *a* (*clothes*) de grávida. ~ **hospital** maternidade *f*. ~ **leave** licença *f* de maternidade

mathematic|s /mæθəˈmætɪks/ *n* matemática *f*. ~**al** *a* matemático. ~**ian** /-əˈtɪʃn/ *n* matemático *m*.

maths /mæθs/ *n* (*colloq*) matemática *f*

matinée /ˈmætmeɪ/ *n* matinê *f*, (*P*) matinée *f*

matrimon|y /ˈmætrɪmənɪ/ *n* matrimônio *m*, (*P*) matrimónio *m*. ~**ial** /-ˈməʊnɪəl/ *a* matrimonial, conjugal

matrix /ˈmeɪtrɪks/ *n* (*pl* **matrices** /-siːz/) matriz *f*

matron /ˈmeɪtrən/ *n* matrona *f*; (*in school*) inspetora *f*; (*former use: senior nursing officer*) enfermeira-chefe *f*. ~**ly** *a* respeitável, muito digno

matt /mæt/ *a* fosco, sem brilho

matted /ˈmætɪd/ *a* emaranhado

matter /ˈmætə(r)/ *n* (*substance*) matéria *f*; (*affair*) assunto *m*, caso *m*, questão *f*; (*pus*) pus *m* □ *vi* importar. **as a ~ of fact** na verdade. **it does not ~** não importa. ~**-of-fact** *a* prosaico, terra-a-terra. **no ~ what happens** não importa o que acontecer. **what is the ~?** o que há? **what is the ~ with you?** o que é que você tem?

mattress /ˈmætrɪs/ *n* colchão *m*

matur|e /məˈtjʊə(r)/ *a* maduro, amadurecido □ *vt/i* amadurecer; (*comm*) vencer-se. ~**ity** *n* madureza *f*, maturidade *f*; (*comm*) vencimento *m*

maul /mɔːl/ *vt* maltratar, atacar

Mauritius /məˈrɪʃəs/ *n* Ilha *f* Maurícia

mausoleum /mɔːsəˈlɪəm/ *n* mausoléu *m*

mauve /məʊv/ *a & n* lilás (*m*)

maxim /ˈmæksɪm/ *n* máxima *f*

maxim|um /ˈmæksɪməm/ *a & n* (*pl* -**ima**) máximo (*m*). ~**ize** *vt* aumentar ao máximo, maximizar

may /meɪ/ *v aux* (*pt* **might**) poder. **he ~/might come** talvez venha/viesse. **you might have** podia ter. **you ~ leave** pode ir. ~ **I smoke?** posso fumar?, dá licença que eu fume? ~ **he be happy** que ele seja feliz. **I ~ or might as well go** talvez seja *or* fosse melhor eu ir

May /meɪ/ *n* maio *n*. ~ **Day** o primeiro de maio

maybe /ˈmeɪbɪ/ *adv* talvez

mayhem /ˈmeɪhem/ *n* (*disorder*) distúrbios *mpl* violentos; (*havoc*) estragos *mpl*

mayonnaise /meɪəˈneɪz/ *n* maionese *f*

mayor /meə(r)/ *n* prefeito *m*. ~**ess** *n* prefeita *f*; (*mayor's wife*) mulher *f* do prefeito

maze /meɪz/ *n* labirinto *m*

me /miː/ *pron* me; (*after prep*) mim. **with ~** comigo. **he knows ~** ele me conhece. **it's ~** sou eu

meadow /ˈmedəʊ/ *n* prado *m*, campina *f*

meagre /ˈmiːgə(r)/ *a* (*thin*) magro; (*scanty*) escasso

meal¹ /miːl/ *n* refeição *f*

meal² /miːl/ *n* (*grain*) farinha *f* grossa

mean¹ /miːn/ *a* (-**er**, -**est**) mesquinho; (*unkind*) mau. ~**ness** *n* mesquinhez *f*

mean² /miːn/ *a* médio □ *n* média *f*. **Greenwich ~ time** tempo *m* médio de Greenwich

mean³ /miːn/ *vt* (*pt* **meant**) (*intend*) tencionar *or* ter (a) intenção (**to** de); (*signify*) querer dizer, significar; (*entail*) dar em resultado, resultar provavelmente em; (*refer to*) referir-se a. **be meant for** destinar-se a. **I didn't ~ it** desculpe, foi sem querer. **he ~s what he says** ele está falando sério

meander /mɪˈændə(r)/ *vi* serpentear; (*wander*) perambular

meaning /ˈmiːnɪŋ/ *n* sentido *m*, significado *m*. ~**ful** *a* significativo. ~**less** *a* sem sentido

means /miːnz/ *n* meio(s) *m*(*pl*) □ *npl* meios *mpl* pecuniários, recursos *mpl*. **by all ~** com certeza. **by ~ of** por meio de, através de. **by no ~** de modo nenhum

meant /ment/ *see* **mean³**

mean|time /ˈmiːntaɪm/ *adv* (**in the**) ~**time** entretanto. ~ **while** /-waɪl/ *adv* entretanto

measles /ˈmiːzlz/ *n* sarampo *m*. **German ~** rubéola *f*

measly /ˈmiːzlɪ/ *a* (*sl*) miserável, ínfimo

measurable /ˈmeʒərəbl/ *a* mensurável

measure /ˈmeʒə(r)/ *n* medida *f* □ *vt/i* medir. **made to ~** feito sob medida. ~ **up to** mostrar-se à altura de. ~**d** *a* medido, calculado. ~**ment** *n* medida *f*

meat /miːt/ *n* carne *f*. ~**y** *a* carnudo; (*fig: substantial*) substancial

mechanic /mɪˈkænɪk/ *n* mecânico *m*

mechanic|al /mɪˈkænɪkl/ *a* mecânico. ~**s** *n* mecânica *f*; *npl* mecanismo *m*

mechan|ism /ˈmekənɪzəm/ *n* mecanismo *m*. ~**ize** *vt* mecanizar

medal /ˈmedl/ *n* medalha *f*. ~**list** *n* condecorado *m*. **be a gold ~-list** ser medalha de ouro

medallion /mɪˈdælɪən/ *n* medalhão *m*

meddle /ˈmedl/ *vi* (*interfere*) imiscuir-se, intrometer-se (**in** em); (*tinker*) mexer (**with** em). ~**some** *a* intrometido, abelhudo

media /ˈmiːdɪə/ *see* **medium** □ *npl* **the ~** a média, os meios de comunicação social *or* de massa

mediat|e /'mi:dɪeɪt/ *vi* servir de
intermediário, mediar. **~ion** /-'eɪʃn/ *n*
mediação *f*. **~or** *n* mediador *m*,
intermediário *m*

medical /'medɪkl/ *a* médico □ *n* (*colloq:
examination*) exame *m* médico

medicat|ed /'medɪkeɪtɪd/ *a* medicinal.
~ion /-'keɪʃn/ *n* medicamentação *f*

medicinal /mɪ'dɪsɪnl/ *a* medicinal

medicine /'medsn/ *n* medicina *f*;
(*substance*) remédio *m*, medicamento *m*

medieval /medɪ'i:vl/ *a* medieval

mediocr|e /mi:dɪ'əʊkə(r)/ *a* medíocre.
~ity /-'ɒkrətɪ/ *n* mediocridade *f*

meditat|e /'medɪteɪt/ *vt/i* meditar. **~ion**
/-'teɪʃn/ *n* meditação *f*

Mediterranean /medɪtə'reɪnɪən/ *a*
mediterrâneo □ *n* **the ~** o
Mediterrâneo

medium /'mi:dɪəm/ *n* (*pl* **media**) meio *m*;
(*pl* **mediums**) (*person*) médium *mf* □ *a*
médio. **~ wave** (*radio*) onda *f* média.
the happy ~ o meio-termo

medley /'medlɪ/ *n* (*pl* **-eys**) miscelânea *f*

meek /mi:k/ *a* (**-er, -est**) manso,
submisso, sofrido

meet /mi:t/ *vt* (*pt* **met**) encontrar;
(*intentionally*) encontrar-se com, ir ter
com; (*at station etc*) ir esperar, ir
buscar; (*make the acquaintance of*)
conhecer; (*conform with*) ir ao encontro
de, satisfazer; (*opponent, obligation etc*)
fazer face a; (*bill, expenses*) pagar □ *vi*
encontrar-se; (*get acquainted*)
familiarizar-se; (*in session*) reunir-se.
~ with encontrar; (*accident,
misfortune*) sofrer, ter

meeting /'mi:tɪŋ/ *n* reunião *f*, encontro
m; (*between two people*) encontro *m*.
~-place *n* ponto *m* de encontro

megalomania /megələʊ'meɪnɪə/ *n*
megalomania *f*, mania *f* de grandezas

megaphone /'megəfəʊn/ *n* megafone *m*,
porta-voz *m*

melancholy /'melənkɒlɪ/ *n* melancolia *f*
□ *a* melancólico

mellow /'meləʊ/ *a* (**-er, -est**) (*fruit,
person*) amadurecido, maduro; (*sound,
colour*) quente, suave □ *vt/i*
amadurecer; (*soften*) suavizar

melodious /mɪ'ləʊdɪəs/ *a* melodioso

melodrama /'melədra:mə/ *n* melodrama
m. **~tic** /-ə'mætɪk/ *a* melodramático

melod|y /'melədɪ/ *n* melodia *f*. **~ic**
/mɪ'lɒdɪk/ *a* melódico

melon /'melən/ *n* melão *m*

melt /melt/ *vt/i* (*metals*) fundir (-se);
(*butter, snow etc*) derreter (-se); (*fade
away*) desvanecer (-se). **~ing-pot** *n*
cadinho *m*

member /'membə(r)/ *n* membro *m*; (*of
club etc*) sócio *m*. **M~ of Parliament**
deputado *m*. **~ship** *n* qualidade *f* de
sócio; (*members*) número *m* de sócios;
(*fee*) cota *f*. **~ship card** carteira *f*, (*P*)
cartão *m* de sócio

membrane /'membreɪn/ *n* membrana *f*

memento /mɪ'mentəʊ/ *n* (*pl* **-oes**)
lembrança *f*, recordação *f*

memo /'meməʊ/ *n* (*pl* **-os**) (*colloq*) nota *f*,
apontamento *m*, lembrete *m*

memoir /'memwa:(r)/ *n* (*record, essay*)
memória *f*, memorial *m*; **~s** *npl*
memórias *fpl*

memorable /'memərəbl/ *a* memorável

memorandum /memə'rændəm/ *n* (*pl*
-da *or* **-dums**) nota *f*, lembrete *m*;
(*diplomatic*) memorando *m*

memorial /mɪ'mɔ:rɪəl/ *n* monumento *m*
comemorativo □ *a* comemorativo

memorize /'meməraɪz/ *vt* decorar,
memorizar, aprender de cor

memory /'memərɪ/ *n* memória *f*. **from ~**
de memória, de cor. **in ~ of** em
memória de **~ stick** pente *m*. de
memória

men /men/ *see* **man**

menac|e /'menəs/ *n* ameaça *f*; (*nuisance*)
praga *f*, chaga *f* □ *vt* ameaçar. **~ingly**
adv ameaçadoramente, de modo
ameaçador

menagerie /mɪ'nædʒərɪ/ *n* coleção *f*, (*P*)
colecção *f* de animais ferozes em jaulas

mend /mend/ *vt* consertar, reparar;
(*darn*) remendar □ *n* conserto *m*; (*darn*)
remendo *m*. **~ one's ways** corrigir-se,
emendar-se. **on the ~** melhorando

menial /'mi:nɪəl/ *a* humilde

meningitis /menɪn'dʒaɪtɪs/ *n* meningite
f

menopause /'menəpɔ:z/ *n* menopausa *f*

menstruation /menstrʊ'eɪʃn/ *n*
menstruação *f*

mental /'mentl/ *a* mental; (*hospital*) de
doentes mentais, psiquiátrico

mentality /men'tælətɪ/ *n* mentalidade *f*

mention /'menʃn/ *vt* mencionar □ *n*
menção *f*. **don't ~ it**! não tem de quê, de
nada

menu /'menju:/ *n* (*pl* **-us**) menu *m*, (*P*)
ementa *f*

mercenary /'mɜ:snərɪ/ *a & n* mercenário
(*m*)

merchandise /'mɜ:tʃəndaɪz/ *n*
mercadorias *fpl* □ *vt/i* negociar

merchant /'mɜ:tʃənt/ *n* mercador *m* □ *a*
(*ship, navy*) mercante. **~ bank** banco *m*
comercial

merciful /'mɜ:sɪfl/ *a* misericordioso

merciless /'mɜ:sɪlɪs/ *a* impiedoso, sem dó

mercury /'mɜ:kjʊrɪ/ *n* mercúrio *m*

m

mercy /'mɜːsɪ/ n piedade f, misericórdia
f. **at the ~ of** à mercê de

mere /mɪə(r)/ a mero, simples. **~ly** adv
meramente, simplesmente, apenas

merge /mɜːdʒ/ vt/i fundir(-se),
amalgamar(-se); (comm: companies)
fundir(-se). **~r** /-ə(r)/ n fusão f

meringue /məˈræŋ/ n merengue m,
suspiro m

merit /'merɪt/ n mérito m □ vt (pt
merited) merecer

mermaid /'mɜːmeɪd/ n sereia f

merriment /'merɪmənt/ n divertimento
m, alegria f, folguedo m

merry /'merɪ/ a (-ier, -iest) alegre,
divertido. **~ Christmas** Feliz Natal.
~-go-round n carrossel m. **~-making**
n festa f, divertimento m. **merrily**
adv alegremente

mesh /meʃ/ n malha f. **~es** npl (network;
fig) malhas fpl.

mesmerize /'mezməraɪz/ vt hipnotizar

mess /mes/ n (disorder) desordem f,
trapalhada f; (trouble) embrulhada f,
trapalhada f; (dirt) porcaria f; (mil:
place) cantina f; (mil: food) rancho m
□ vt **~ up** (make untidy) desarrumar;
(make dirty) sujar; (confuse) atrapalhar,
estragar □ vi **~ about** com perder tempo;
(behave foolishly) fazer asneiras. **~
about with** (tinker with) entreter-se
com, andar às voltas com. **make a ~ of**
estragar

message /'mesɪdʒ/ n mensagem f;
(informal) recado m

messenger /'mesɪndʒə(r)/ n mensageiro
m

Messiah /mɪˈsaɪə/ n Messias m

messy /'mesɪ/ a (-ier, -iest)
desarrumado, bagunçado; (dirty) sujo,
porco

met /met/ see meet

metabolism /mɪˈtæbəlɪzm/ n
metabolismo m

metal /'metl/ n metal m □ a de metal.
~lic /mɪˈtælɪk/ a metálico; (paint,
colour) metalizado

metamorphosis /metəˈmɔːfəsɪs/ n (pl
-phoses /-siːz/) metamorfose f

metaphor /'metəfə(r)/ n metáfora f.
~ical /-ˈfɒrɪkl/ a metafórico

meteor /'miːtɪə(r)/ n meteoro m

meteorolog|y /miːtɪəˈrɒlədʒɪ/ n
meteorologia f. **~ical** /-əˈlɒdʒɪkl/ a
meteorológico

meter¹ /'miːtə(r)/ n contador m

meter² /'miːtə(r)/ n (Amer) = metre

method /'meθəd/ n método m

methodical /mɪˈθɒdɪkl/ a metódico

Methodist /'meθədɪst/ n metodista mf

methylated /'meθɪleɪtɪd/ a **~ spirit**
álcool m metílico

meticulous /mɪˈtɪkjʊləs/ a meticuloso

metre /'miːtə(r)/ n metro m

metric /'metrɪk/ a métrico. **~ation**
/-ˈkeɪʃn/ n conversão f para o sistema
métrico

metropol|is /məˈtrɒpəlɪs/ n metrópole f.
~itan /metrəˈpɒlɪtən/ a metropolitano

mettle /'metl/ n têmpera f, caráter m, (P)
carácter m; (spirit) brio m

mew /mjuː/ n miado m □ vi miar

Mexic|o /'meksɪkəʊ/ n México m. **~an** a
& n mexicano (m)

miaow /miːˈaʊ/ n & vi = mew

mice /maɪs/ see mouse

mickey /'mɪkɪ/ n **take the ~ out of** (sl)
fazer troça de, gozar (colloq)

micro- /'maɪkrəʊ/ pref micro-

microbe /'maɪkrəʊb/ n micróbio m

microchip /'maɪkrəʊtʃɪp/ n microchip m

microcomputer /'maɪkrəʊkəmpjuːtə(r)/
n microcomputador m

microfilm /'maɪkrəʊfɪlm/ n microfilme
m

microlight /'maɪkrəʊlaɪt/ n (aviat)
ultraleve m

microphone /'maɪkrəfəʊn/ n microfone
m

microprocessor /maɪkrəʊˈprəʊsesə(r)/
n microprocessador m

microscop|e /'maɪkrəskəʊp/ n
microscópio m. **~ic** /-ˈskɒpɪk/ a
microscópico

microwave /'maɪkrəʊweɪv/ n
microonda f. **~ oven** forno m de
microondas

mid /mɪd/ a meio. **in ~-air** no ar, em
pleno vôo. **in ~-March** em meados de
março

midday /mɪdˈdeɪ/ n meio-dia m

middle /'mɪdl/ a médio, meio; (quality)
médio, mediano □ n meio m. **in the ~
of** no meio de. **~-aged** a de meia idade.
M~ Ages Idade f Média. **~ class**
classe f média. **~-class** a burguês. **M~
East** Médio Oriente m. **~ name**
segundo nome m

middleman /'mɪdlmæn/ n (pl -men)
intermediário m

midge /mɪdʒ/ n mosquito m

midget /'mɪdʒɪt/ n anão m □ a minúsculo

Midlands /'mɪdləndz/ npl região f do
centro da Inglaterra

midnight /'mɪdnaɪt/ n meia-noite f

midriff /'mɪdrɪf/ n diafragma m;
(abdomen) ventre m

midst /mɪdst/ n **in the ~ of** no meio de

midsummer /mɪdˈsʌmə(r)/ n pleno
verão m; (solstice) solstício m do verão

midway /mɪd'weɪ/ adv a meio caminho

midwife /'mɪdwaɪf/ n (pl **-wives**) parteira f

might¹ /maɪt/ n potência f; (strength) força f. ∼**y** a poderoso; (fig: great) imenso ▫ adv (colloq) muito

might² /maɪt/ see **may**

migraine /'mi:greɪn/ n enxaqueca f

migrant /'maɪgrənt/ a migratório ▫ n (person) migrante mf, emigrante mf

migrat|e /maɪ'greɪt/ vi migrar. ∼**ion** /-ʃn/ n migração f

mike /maɪk/ n (colloq) microfone m

mild /maɪld/ a (-er, -est) brando, manso; (illness, taste) leve; (climate) temperado; (weather) ameno. ∼**ly** adv brandamente, mansamente. **to put it** ∼**ly** para não dizer coisa pior. ∼**ness** n brandura f

mildew /'mɪldju:/ n bolor m, mofo m; (in plants) míldio m

mile /maɪl/ n milha f (= 1.6 km). ∼**s too big**/etc (colloq) grande demais. ∼**age** n (loosely) quilometragem f

milestone /'maɪlstəʊn/ n marco m miliário; (fig) data f or acontecimento m importante

militant /'mɪlɪtənt/ a & n militante (mf)

military /'mɪlɪtrɪ/ a militar

militate /'mɪlɪteɪt/ vi militar. ∼ **against** militar contra

milk /mɪlk/ n leite m ▫ a (product) lácteo ▫ vt ordenhar; (fig: exploit) explorar. ∼**-shake** n milk-shake m, leite m batido. ∼**y** a (like milk) leitoso; (tea etc) com muito leite. **M**∼ **Way** Via f Láctea

milkman /'mɪlkmən/ n (pl **-men**) leiteiro m

mill /mɪl/ n moinho m; (factory) fábrica f ▫ vt moer ▫ vi ∼ **around** aglomerar-se; (crowd) apinhar-se, (P) agitar-se. ∼**er** n moleiro m. **pepper-**∼ n moedor m de pimenta

millennium /mɪ'lenɪəm/ n (pl **-iums** or **-ia**) milênio m, (P) milénio m

millet /'mɪlɪt/ n painço m, milhete m

milli- /'mɪlɪ/ pref mili-

milligram /'mɪlɪgræm/ n miligrama m

millilitre /'mɪlɪli:tə(r)/ n mililitro m

millimetre /'mɪlɪmi:tə(r)/ n milímetro m

million /'mɪlɪən/ n milhão m. **a** ∼ **pounds** um milhão de libras. ∼**aire** /-'neə(r)/ n milionário m

millstone /'mɪlstəʊn/ n mó f. **a** ∼ **round one's neck** um peso nos ombros

mime /maɪm/ n mímica f; (actor) mímico m ▫ vt/i exprimir por mímica, mimar

mimic /'mɪmɪk/ vt (pt **mimicked**) imitar ▫ n imitador m, parodiante mf. ∼**ry** n imitação f.

mince /mɪns/ vt picar ▫ n carne f moída, (P) carne f picada. ∼**-pie** n pastel m recheado com massa de passas, amêndoas, especiarias etc. ∼**r** n máquina f de moer

mincemeat /'mɪnsmi:t/ n massa f de passas, amêndoas, especiarias etc usada para recheio. **make** ∼ **of** (colloq) arrasar, aniquilar

mind n espírito m, mente f; (intellect) intelecto m; (sanity) razão f ▫ vt (look after) tomar conta de, tratar de; (heed) prestar atenção a; (object to) importar-se com, incomodar-se com. **do you** ∼ **if I smoke?** você se incomoda que eu fume? **do you** ∼ **helping me?** quer fazer o favor de me ajudar? **never** ∼ não se importe, não tem importância. **to be out of one's** ∼ estar fora de si. **have a good** ∼ **to** estar disposto a. **make up one's** ∼ decidir-se. **presence of** ∼ presença f de espírito. **to my** ∼ a meu ver. ∼**ful** of atento a, consciente de. ∼**less** a insensato

minder /'maɪndə(r)/ n pessoa f que toma conta mf; (bodyguard) guarda-costa mf, (P) guarda-costas mf

mine¹ /maɪn/ poss pron o(s) meu(s), a(s) minha(s). **it is** ∼ é (o) meu or (a) minha

min|e² /maɪn/ n mina f ▫ vt escavar, explorar; (extract) extrair; (mil) minar. ∼**er** n mineiro m. ∼**ing** n exploração f mineira ▫ a mineiro

minefield /'maɪnfi:ld/ n campo m minado

mineral /'mɪnərəl/ n mineral m; (soft drink) bebida f gasosa. ∼ **water** água f mineral

minesweeper /'maɪnswi:pə(r)/ n caça-minas m

mingle /'mɪŋgl/ vt/i misturar(-se) (**with** com)

mingy /'mɪndʒɪ/ a (-ier, -iest) (colloq) sovina, unha(s)-de-fome (colloq)

mini- /'mɪnɪ/ pref mini-

miniature /'mɪnɪtʃə(r)/ n miniatura f ▫ a miniatural

minibus /'mɪnɪbʌs/ n (public) microônibus m, (P) autocarro m pequeno

minim /'mɪnɪm/ n (mus) mínima f

minim|um /'mɪnɪməm/ a & n (pl **-ma**) mínimo (m). ∼**al** a mínimo. ∼**ize** vt minimizar, dar pouca importância a

miniskirt /'mɪnɪskɜːt/ n minissaia f

minist|er /'mɪnɪstə(r)/ n ministro m; (relig) pastor m. ∼**erial** /-'stɪərɪəl/ a ministerial. ∼**ry** n ministério m

mink /mɪŋk/ n (fur) marta f, visão m

minor /'maɪnə(r)/ a & n menor (mf)

minority /maɪ'nɒrətɪ/ n minoria f ▫ a minoritário

m

mint[1] /mɪnt/ *n* the M~ a Casa da Moeda. **a ~** uma fortuna □ *vt* cunhar. **in ~ condition** em perfeito estado, como novo, impecável

mint[2] /mɪnt/ *n* (*plant*) hortelã *f*; (*sweet*) pastilha *f* de hortelã

minus /'maɪnəs/ *prep* menos; (*colloq: without*) sem □ *n* menos *m*

minute[1] /'mɪnɪt/ *n* minuto *m*. ~**s** (*of meeting*) ata *f*, (P) acta *f*

minute[2] /maɪ'njuːt/ *a* diminuto, minúsculo; (*detailed*) minucioso

mirac|le /'mɪrəkl/ *n* milagre *m*. ~**ulous** /mɪ'rækjʊləs/ *a* milagroso, miraculoso

mirage /'mɪrɑːʒ/ *n* miragem *f*

mire /maɪə(r)/ *n* lodo *m*, lama *f*

mirror /'mɪrə(r)/ *n* espelho *m*; (*in car*) retrovisor *m* □ *vt* refletir, (P) reflectir, espelhar

mirth /mɜːθ/ *n* alegria *f*, hilaridade *f*

misadventure /mɪsəd'ventʃə(r)/ *n* desgraça *f*. **death by ~** morte *f* acidental

misanthropist /mɪs'ænθrəpɪst/ *n* misantropo *m*

misapprehension /mɪsæprɪ'henʃn/ *n* mal-entendido *m*

misbehav|e /mɪsbɪ'heɪv/ *vi* portar-se mal, proceder mal. ~**iour** /-'heɪvɪə(r)/ *n* mau comportamento *m*, má conduta *f*

miscalculat|e /mɪs'kælkjʊleɪt/ *vi* calcular mal, enganar-se. ~**ion** /-'leɪʃn/ *n* erro *m* de cálculo

miscarr|y /mɪs'kærɪ/ *vi* abortar, ter um aborto; (*fail*) falhar, malograr-se. ~**iage** /-ɪdʒ/ *n* aborto *m*. ~**iage of justice** erro *m* judiciário

miscellaneous /mɪsə'leɪnɪəs/ *a* variado, diverso

mischief /'mɪstʃɪf/ *n* (*of children*) diabrura *f*, travessura *f*; (*harm*) mal *m*, dano *m*. **get into ~** fazer disparates. **make ~** criar *or* semear discórdias

mischievous /'mɪstʃɪvəs/ *a* endiabrado, travesso

misconception /mɪskən'sepʃn/ *n* idéia *f* errada, falso conceito *m*

misconduct /mɪs'kɒndʌkt/ *n* conduta *f* imprópria

misconstrue /mɪskən'struː/ *vt* interpretar mal

misdeed /mɪs'diːd/ *n* má ação *f*, (P) acção *f*; (*crime*) crime *m*

misdemeanour /mɪsdɪ'miːnə(r)/ *n* delito *m*

miser /'maɪzə(r)/ *n* avarento *m*, sovina *mf*. ~**ly** *a* avarento, sovina

miserable /'mɪzrəbl/ *a* infeliz; (*wretched, mean*) desgraçado, miserável

misery /'mɪzərɪ/ *n* infelicidade *f*

misfire /mɪs'faɪə(r)/ *vi* (*plan, gun, engine*) falhar

misfit /'mɪsfɪt/ *n* inadaptado *m*

misfortune /mɪs'fɔːtʃən/ *n* desgraça *f*, infelicidade *f*, pouca sorte *f*

misgiving(s) /mɪs'gɪvɪŋ(z)/ *n*(*pl*) dúvida(s) *f*(*pl*), receio(s) *m*(*pl*)

misguided /mɪs'gaɪdɪd/ *a* (*mistaken*) desencaminhado; (*misled*) mal aconselhado, enganado

mishap /'mɪshæp/ *n* contratempo *m*, desastre *m*

misinform /mɪsɪn'fɔːm/ *vt* informar mal

misinterpret /mɪsɪn'tɜːprɪt/ *vt* interpretar mal

misjudge /mɪs'dʒʌdʒ/ *vt* julgar mal

mislay /mɪs'leɪ/ *vt* (*pt* **mislaid**) perder, extraviar

mislead /mɪs'liːd/ *vt* (*pt* **misled**) induzir em erro, enganar. ~**ing** *a* enganador

mismanage /mɪs'mænɪdʒ/ *vt* dirigir mal. ~**ment** *n* má gestão *f*, desgoverno *m*

misnomer /mɪs'nəʊmə(r)/ *n* termo *m* impróprio

misogynist /mɪ'sɒdʒɪnɪst/ *n* misógino *m*

misprint /'mɪsprɪnt/ *n* erro *m* tipográfico

mispronounce /mɪsprə'naʊns/ *vt* pronunciar mal

misquote /mɪs'kwəʊt/ *vt* citar incorretamente

misread /mɪs'riːd/ *vt* (*pt* **misread** /-'red/) ler *or* interpretar mal

misrepresent /mɪsreprɪ'zent/ *vt* deturpar, desvirtuar

miss /mɪs/ *vt/i* (*chance, bus etc*) perder; (*target*) errar, falhar; (*notice the loss of*) dar pela falta de; (*regret the absence of*) sentir a falta de, ter saudades de. **he ~es her/Portugal**/*etc* ele sente a falta *or* tem saudades dela/de Portugal/*etc* □ *n* falha *f*. **it was a near ~** foi *or* escapou por um triz. ~ **out** omitir. ~ **the point** não compreender

Miss /mɪs/ *n* (*pl* **Misses**) Senhorita *f*, (P) Senhora *f*

misshapen /mɪs'ʃeɪpn/ *a* disforme

missile /'mɪsaɪl/ *n* míssil *m*; (*object thrown*) projétil *m*, (P) projéctil *m*

missing /'mɪsɪŋ/ *a* que falta; (*lost*) perdido; (*person*) desaparecido. **a book with a page ~** um livro com uma página a menos

mission /'mɪʃn/ *n* missão *f*

missionary /'mɪʃənrɪ/ *n* missionário *m*

misspell /mɪs'spel/ *vt* (*pt* **misspelt** *or* **misspelled**) escrever mal

mist /mɪst/ *n* neblina *f*, névoa *f*, bruma *f*; (*fig*) névoa *f* □ *vt/i* enevoar(-se); (*window*) embaçar(-se)

mistake /mɪ'steɪk/ *n* engano *m*, erro *m* □ *vt* (*pt* **mistook**, *pp* **mistaken**) compreender mal; (*choose wrongly*) enganar-se em. ~ **for** confundir com,

tomar por. ~n /-ən/ a errado. be ~n
enganar-se. ~nly /-ənlɪ/ adv por
engano

mistletoe /'mɪsltəʊ/ n visco m

mistreat /mɪs'triːt/ vt maltratar. ~ment
n mau trato m

mistress /'mɪstrɪs/ n senhora f, dona f;
(teacher) professora f; (lover) amante f

mistrust /mɪs'trʌst/ vt desconfiar de,
duvidar de □ n desconfiança f

misty /'mɪstɪ/ a (-ier, -iest) enevoado,
brumoso; (window) embaçado;
(indistinct) indistinto

misunderstand /mɪsʌndə'stænd/ vt (pt
-stood) compreender mal. ~ing n mal-
entendido m

misuse[1] /mɪs'juːz/ vt empregar mal;
(power etc) abusar de

misuse[2] /mɪs'juːs/ n mau uso m; (abuse)
abuso m; (of funds) desvio m

mitigat|e /'mɪtɪɡeɪt/ vt atenuar, mitigar.
~ing circumstances circunstâncias
fpl atenuantes

mitten /'mɪtn/ n luva f com uma única
divisão entre o polegar e os dedos

mix /mɪks/ vt/i misturar(-se) □ n mistura
f. ~ up misturar bem; (fig: confuse)
confundir. ~-up n trapalhada f,
confusão f. ~ with associar-se com.
~er n (culin) batedeira f

mixed /mɪkst/ a (school etc) misto;
(assorted) sortido. be ~ up (colloq)
estar confuso

mixture /'mɪkstʃə(r)/ n mistura f. cough
~ xarope m para a tosse

moan /məʊn/ n gemido m □ vi gemer;
(complain) queixar-se, lastimar-se
(about de). ~er n pessoa f lamurienta

moat /məʊt/ n fosso m

mob /mɒb/ n multidão f; (tumultuous)
turba f; (sl: gang) bando m □ vt (pt
mobbed) cercar, assediar

mobil|e /'məʊbaɪl/ a móvel. ~e
home caravana f, trailer m. ~e phone
telemóvel m. ~ity /-'bɪlətɪ/ n
mobilidade f

mobiliz|e /'məʊbɪlaɪz/ vt/i mobilizar.
~ation /-'zeɪʃn/ n mobilização f

moccasin /'mɒkəsɪn/ n mocassim m

mock /mɒk/ vt/i zombar de, gozar □ a
falso. ~-up n maqueta f

mockery /'mɒkərɪ/ n troça f, gozação f. a
~ of uma gozação de

mode /məʊd/ n modo m; (fashion) moda
f

model /'mɒdl/ n modelo m □ a modelo;
(exemplary) exemplar; (toy) em
miniatura □ vt (pt modelled) modelar;
(clothes) apresentar □ vi ser or
trabalhar como modelo

modem /'məʊdem/ n modem m

moderate[1] /'mɒdərət/ a & n moderado
(m). ~ly adv moderadamente. ~ly
good sofrível

moderat|e[2] /'mɒdəreɪt/ vt/i moderar(-se).
~ion /-'reɪʃn/ n moderação f. in ~ion
com moderação

modern /'mɒdn/ a moderno.
~ languages línguas fpl vivas. ~ize
vt modernizar

modest /'mɒdɪst/ a modesto. ~y n
modéstia f. ~ly adv modestamente

modicum /'mɒdɪkəm/ n a ~ of um pouco
de

modif|y /'mɒdɪfaɪ/ vt modificar.
~ication /-ɪ'keɪʃn/ n modificação f

modulat|e /'mɒdjʊleɪt/ vt/i modular.
~ion /-'leɪʃn/ n modulação f

module /'mɒdjuːl/ n módulo m

mohair /'məʊheə(r)/ n mohair m

moist /mɔɪst/ a (-er, -est) úmido, (P)
húmido. ~ure /'mɔɪstʃə(r)/ n umidade
f, (P) humidade f. ~urizer
/-tʃəraɪzə(r)/ n creme m hidratante

moisten /'mɔɪsn/ vt/i umedecer, (P)
humedecer

molasses /mə'læsɪz/ n melaço m

mole[1] /məʊl/ n (on skin) sinal na pele m

mole[2] /məʊl/ n (animal) toupeira f

molecule /'mɒlɪkjuːl/ n molécula f

molest /mə'lest/ vt meter-se com,
molestar

mollusc /'mɒləsk/ n molusco m

mollycoddle /'mɒlɪkɒdl/ vt mimar

molten /'məʊltən/ a fundido

moment /'məʊmənt/ n momento m

momentar|y /'məʊməntrɪ/ a
momentâneo. ~ily /'məʊməntrəlɪ/ adv
momentaneamente

momentous /mə'mentəs/ a grave,
importante

momentum /mə'mentəm/ n ímpeto m,
velocidade f adquirida

Monaco /'mɒnəkəʊ/ n Mônaco m

monarch /'mɒnək/ n monarca mf. ~y n
monarquia f

monast|ery /'mɒnəstrɪ/ n mosteiro m,
convento m. ~ic /mə-'næstɪk/ a
monástico

Monday /'mʌndɪ/ n segunda-feira f

monetary /'mʌnɪtrɪ/ a monetário

money /'mʌnɪ/ n dinheiro m. ~-box n
cofre m. ~-lender n agiota mf. ~ order
vale m postal

mongrel /'mʌŋɡrəl/ n (cão) vira-lata m,
(P) rafeiro m

monitor /'mɒnɪtə(r)/ n chefe m de turma;
(techn) monitor m □ vt controlar; (a
broadcast) monitorar (a transmissão)

monk /mʌŋk/ n monge m, frade m

m

monkey /'mʌŋkɪ/ n (pl -eys) macaco m.
~**-nut** n amendoim m. ~**-wrench** n
chave f inglesa

mono /'mɒnəʊ/ n (pl -os) gravação f
mono ▢ a mono invar

monocle /'mɒnəkl/ n monóculo m

monogram /'mɒnəgræm/ n
monograma m

monologue /'mɒnəlɒg/ n monólogo m

monopol|y /mə'nɒpəlɪ/ n monopólio m.
~**ize** vt monopolizar

monosyllab|le /'mɒnəsɪləbl/ n
monossílabo m. ~**ic** /-'læbɪk/ a
monossilábico

monotone /'mɒnətəʊn/ n tom m
uniforme

monoton|ous /mə'nɒtənəs/ a monótono.
~**y** n monotonia f

monsoon /mɒn'su:n/ n monção f

monst|er /'mɒnstə(r)/ n monstro m.
~**rous** a monstruoso

monstrosity /mɒn'strɒsətɪ/ n
monstruosidade f

month /mʌnθ/ n mês m

monthly /'mʌnθlɪ/ a mensal ▢ adv
mensalmente ▢ n (periodical) revista f
mensal

monument /'mɒnjʊmənt/ n monumento
m. ~**al** /-'mentl/ a monumental

moo /mu:/ n mugido m ▢ vi mugir

mood /mu:d/ n humor m, disposição f.
in a good/bad ~ de bom/mau humor.
~**y** a de humor instável; (sullen)
carrancudo

moon /mu:n/ n lua f

moon|light /'mu:nlaɪt/ n luar m. ~**lit** a
iluminado pela lua, enluarado

moonlighting /'mu:nlaɪtɪŋ/ n (colloq)
segundo emprego m, esp à noite

moor[1] /mʊə(r)/ n charneca f

moor[2] /mʊə(r)/ vt amarrar, atracar.
~**ings** npl amarras fpl; (place)
amarradouro m, fundeadouro m

moose /mu:s/ n (pl invar) alce m

moot /mu:t/ a discutível ▢ vt levantar

mop /mɒp/ n esfregão m ▢ vt (pt
mopped) ~ (**up**) limpar. ~ **of hair**
trunfa f

mope /məʊp/ vi estar or andar abatido e
triste

moped /'məʊped/ n (bicicleta)
motorizada f

moral /'mɒrəl/ a moral ▢ n moral f. ~**s**
moral f, bons costumes mpl. ~**ize** vi
moralizar. ~**ly** adv moralmente

morale /mə'ra:l/ n moral m

morality /mə'rælətɪ/ n moralidade f

morass /mə'ræs/ n pântano m

morbid /'mɔ:bɪd/ a mórbido

more /mɔ:(r)/ a & adv mais (**than** (do)
que) ▢ n mais m. (**some**) ~ **tea/pens/**
etc mais chá/canetas/etc. **there is no**
~ **bread** não há mais pão. **or less** mais
ou menos

moreover /mɔ:'rəʊvə(r)/ adv além disso,
de mais a mais

morgue /mɔ:g/ n morgue f, necrotério m

moribund /'mɒrɪbʌnd/ a moribundo,
agonizante

morning /'mɔ:nɪŋ/ n manhã f. **in the**
~ de manhã

Morocc|o /mə'rɒkəʊ/ n Marrocos m. ~**an**
a & n marroquino (m)

moron /'mɔ:rɒn/ n idiota mf

morose /mə'rəʊs/ a taciturno e
insociável, carrancudo

morphine /'mɔ:fi:n/ n morfina f

Morse /mɔ:s/ n ~ (**code**) (alfabeto)
Morse m

morsel /'mɔ:sl/ n bocado m (esp de
comida)

mortal /'mɔ:tl/ a & n mortal (mf). ~**ity**
/mɔ:'tælətɪ/ n mortalidade f

mortar /'mɔ:tə(r)/ n argamassa f; (bowl)
almofariz m; (mil) morteiro m

mortgage /'mɔ:gɪdʒ/ n hipoteca f ▢ vt
hipotecar

mortify /'mɔ:tɪfaɪ/ vt mortificar

mortuary /'mɔ:tʃərɪ/ n casa f mortuária

mosaic /məʊ'zeɪk/ n mosaico m

Moscow /'mɒskəʊ/ n Moscou m, (P)
Moscovo m

mosque /mɒsk/ n mesquita f

mosquito /mə'ski:təʊ/ n (pl -oes)
mosquito m

moss /mɒs/ n musgo m. ~**y** a musgoso

most /məʊst/ a o mais, o maior;
(majority) a maioria de, a maior parte
de ▢ n mais m; (majority) a maioria, a
maior parte, o máximo ▢ adv o mais;
(very) muito. **at** ~ no máximo. **for the**
~ **part** na maior parte, na grande
maioria. **make the** ~ **of** aproveitar
ao máximo, tirar o melhor partido de.
~**ly** adv sobretudo

motel /məʊ'tel/ n motel m

moth /mɒθ/ n mariposa f, (P) borboleta
f nocturna. (**clothes-**)~ n traça f.
~**-ball** n bola f de naftalina. ~**-eaten** a
roído por traças

mother /'mʌðə(r)/ n mãe f ▢ vt tratar
como a um filho. ~**hood** n
maternidade f. ~**-in-law** n (pl
~**s-in-law**) sogra f. ~**-of-pearl** n
madrepérola f. **M**~**'s Day** o Dia das
Mães. ~**-to-be** n futura mãe f. ~**ly** a
maternal

motif /məʊ'ti:f/ n tema m

motion /ˈməʊʃn/ n movimento m; (*proposal*) moção f □ vt/i ~ **(to) sb to** fazer sinal a alg para. ~**less** a imóvel

motivat|e /ˈməʊtɪveɪt/ vt motivar. ~**ion** /-ˈveɪʃn/ n motivação f

motive /ˈməʊtɪv/ n motivo m

motor /ˈməʊtə(r)/ n motor m; (*car*) automóvel m □ a (*anat*) motor; (*boat*) a motor □ vi ir de automóvel. ~ **bike** (*colloq*) moto f (*colloq*). ~ **car** carro m. ~ **cycle** motocicleta f. ~ **cyclist** motociclista mf. ~ **vehicle** veículo m automóvel. ~**ing** n automobilismo m. ~**ized** a motorizado

motorist /ˈməʊtərɪst/ n motorista mf, automobilista mf

motorway /ˈməʊtəweɪ/ n auto-estrada f

mottled /ˈmɒtld/ a sarapintado, pintalgado

motto /ˈmɒtəʊ/ n (pl -**oes**) divisa f, lema m

mould[1] /məʊld/ n (*container*) forma f, molde m; (*culin*) forma f □ vt moldar. ~**ing** n (*archit*) moldura f

mould[2] /məʊld/ n (*fungi*) bolor m, mofo m. ~**y** a bolorento

moult /məʊlt/ vi estar na muda

mound /maʊnd/ n monte m de terra or de pedras; (*small hill*) montículo m

mount /maʊnt/ vt/i montar □ n (*support*) suporte m; (*for gem etc*) engaste m. ~ **up** aumentar, subir

mountain /ˈmaʊntɪn/ n montanha f. ~ **bike** mountain bike f. ~ **ous** a montanhoso

mountaineer /maʊntɪˈnɪə(r)/ n alpinista mf. ~**ing** n alpinismo m

mourn /mɔːn/ vt/i ~ **(for)** chorar (a morte de). ~ **(over)** sofrer (por). ~**er** n pessoa f que acompanha o enterro. ~**ing** n luto m. **in** ~**ing** de luto

mournful /ˈmɔːnfl/ a triste; (*sorrowful*) pesaroso

mouse /maʊs/ n (pl **mice**) camundongo m

mousetrap /ˈmaʊstræp/ n ratoeira f

mousse /muːs/ n mousse f

moustache /məˈstɑːʃ/ n bigode m

mouth[1] /maʊθ/ n boca f. ~**-organ** n gaita f de boca, (P) beiços

mouth[2] /maʊð/ vt/i declamar; (*silently*) articular sem som

mouthful /ˈmaʊθfʊl/ n bocado m

mouthpiece /ˈmaʊθpiːs/ n (*mus*) bocal m, boquilha f; (*fig: person*) porta-voz mf

mouthwash /ˈmaʊθwɒʃ/ n líquido m para bochecho

movable /ˈmuːvəbl/ a móvel

move /muːv/ vt/i mover(-se), mexer(-se), deslocar(-se); (*emotionally*) comover; (*incite*) convencer, levar a; (*act*) agir; (*propose*) propor; (*depart*) ir, partir; (*go forward*) avançar. ~ **(out)** mudar-se, sair □ n movimento m; (*in game*) jogada f; (*player's turn*) vez f; (*house change*) mudança f. ~ **back** recuar. ~ **forward** avançar. ~ **in** mudar-se para. ~ **on!** circulem! ~ **over, please** chegue-se para lá, por favor. **on the** ~ em marcha

movement /ˈmuːvmənt/ n movimento m

movie /ˈmuːvɪ/ n (*Amer*) filme m. **the** ~**s** o cinema

moving /ˈmuːvɪŋ/ a (*touching*) comovente; (*movable*) móvil; (*in motion*) em movimento

mow /məʊ/ vt (pp **mowed** or **mown**) ceifar; (*lawn*) cortar a grama, (P) relva. ~ **down** ceifar. ~**er** n (*for lawn*) máquina f de cortar a grama, (P) relva

MP abbr see **Member of Parliament**

Mr /ˈmɪstə(r)/ n (pl **Messrs**) Senhor m. ~ **Smith** o Sr Smith

Mrs /ˈmɪsɪz/ n Senhora f. ~ **Smith** a Sra Smith. **Mr and** ~ **Smith** o Sr Smith e a mulher

Ms /mɪz/ n Senhora D f

much /mʌtʃ/ (**more, most**) a, adv & n muito (m). **very** ~ muito, muitíssimo. **you may have as** ~ **as you need** você pode levar o que precisar. ~ **of it** muito or grande parte dela. **so** ~ **the better/worse** tanto melhor/pior. **how** ~? quanto? **not** ~ não muito. **too** ~ demasiado, demais. **he's not** ~ **of a gardener** não é lá grande jardineiro

muck /mʌk/ n estrume m; (*colloq: dirt*) porcaria f □ vi ~ **about** (*sl*) entreter-se, perder tempo. ~ **in** (*sl*) ajudar, dar uma mão □ vt ~ **up** (*sl*) estragar. ~**y** a sujo

mucus /ˈmjuːkəs/ n muco m

mud /mʌd/ n lama f. ~**dy** a lamacento, enlameado

muddle /ˈmʌdl/ vt baralhar, atrapalhar, confundir □ vi ~ **through** sair-se bem, desenrascar-se (*sl*) □ n desordem f; (*mix-up*) confusão f, trapalhada f

mudguard /ˈmʌdgɑːd/ n para-lama m

muff /mʌf/ n (*for hands*) regalo m

muffle /ˈmʌfl/ vt abafar. ~ **(up)** agasalhar(-se). ~**d sounds** sons mpl abafados. ~**r** /-ə(r)/ n cachecol m

mug /mʌg/ n caneca f; (*sl: face*) cara f; (*sl: fool*) trouxa mf (*colloq*) □ vt (pt **mugged**) assaltar, agredir. ~**ger** n assaltante mf. ~**ging** n assalto m

muggy /ˈmʌgɪ/ a abafado

mule /mjuːl/ n mulo m; (*female*) mula f

mull /mʌl/ vt ~ **over** ruminar; (*fig*) matutar em

multi- /ˈmʌltɪ/ pref mult(i)-

multicoloured /ˈmʌltɪkʌləd/ a multicolor

m

multinational /mʌltɪ'næʃnəl/ a & n multinacional (f)

multiple /'mʌltɪpl/ a & n múltiplo (m)

multipl|y /'mʌltɪplaɪ/ vt/i multiplicar (-se). ~**ication** /-ɪ'keɪʃn/ n multiplicação f

multi-storey /mʌltɪ'stɔːrɪ/ a (car park) em vários níveis

multitude /'mʌltɪtjuːd/ n multidão f

mum[1] /mʌm/ a keep ~ (colloq) ficar calado

mum[2] /mʌm/ (B) mamãe f(colloq) n (colloq) (P) mamã

mumble /'mʌmbl/ vt/i resmungar, resmonear

mummy[1] /'mʌmɪ/ n (body) múmia f

mummy[2] /'mʌmɪ/ n (esp child's lang) mamã (B) mamãe f(colloq) (P) mãezinha f(colloq), (P)

mumps /mʌmps/ n parotidite f, papeira f

munch /mʌntʃ/ vt mastigar

mundane /mʌn'deɪn/ a banal; (worldly) mundano

municipal /mjuː'nɪsɪpl/ a municipal. ~**ity** /-'pælətɪ/ n municipalidade f

munitions /mjuː'nɪʃnz/ npl munições fpl

mural /'mjʊərəl/ a & n mural (m)

murder /'mɜːdə(r)/ n assassínio m, assassinato m □ vt assassinar. ~**er** n assassino m, assassina f. ~**ous** a assassino, sanguinário; (of weapon) mortífero

murky /'mɜːkɪ/ a (-ier, -iest) escuro, sombrio

murmur /'mɜːmə(r)/ n murmúrio m □ vt/i murmurar

muscle /'mʌsl/ n músculo m □ vi ~ **in** (colloq) impor-se, intrometer-se

muscular /'mʌskjʊlə(r)/ a muscular; (brawny) musculoso

muse /mjuːz/ vi meditar, cismar

museum /mjuː'zɪəm/ n museu m

mush /mʌʃ/ n papa f de farinha de milho. ~**y** a mole; (sentimental) piegas inv

mushroom /'mʌʃrʊm/ n cogumelo m □ vi pulular, multiplicar-se com rapidez

music /'mjuːzɪk/ n música f. ~**al** a musical □ n (show) comédia f musical, musical m. ~**al box** n caixa f de música. ~**stand** n estante f de música

musician /mjuː'zɪʃn/ n músico m

musk /mʌsk/ n almíscar m

Muslim /'mʊzlɪm/ a & n muçulmano (m)

muslin /'mʌzlɪn/ n musselina f

mussel /'mʌsl/ n mexilhão m

must /mʌst/ v aux dever. **you** ~ **go** é necessário que você parta. **he** ~ **be old** ele deve ser velho. **I** ~ **have done it** eu devo tê-lo feito □ n **be a** ~ (colloq) ser imprescindível

mustard /'mʌstəd/ n mostarda f

muster /'mʌstə(r)/ vt/i juntar(-se), reunir(-se). **pass** ~ ser aceitável

musty /'mʌstɪ/ a (-ier, -iest) mofado, bolorento

mutation /mjuː'teɪʃn/ n mutação f

mute /mjuːt/ a & n mudo (m)

muted /'mjuːtɪd/ a (sound) em surdina; (colour) suave

mutilat|e /'mjuːtɪleɪt/ vt mutilar. ~**ion** /-'leɪʃn/ n mutilação f

mutin|y /'mjuːtɪnɪ/ n motim f □ vi amotinar-se. ~**ous** a amotinado

mutter /'mʌtə(r)/ vt/i resmungar

mutton /'mʌtn/ n (carne de) carneiro m

mutual /'mjuːtʃʊəl/ a mútuo; (colloq: common) comum. ~**ly** adv mutuamente

muzzle /'mʌzl/ n focinho m; (device) focinheira f; (of gun) boca f □ vt amordaçar; (dog) pôr focinheira em

my /maɪ/ a meu(s), minha(s)

myself /maɪ'self/ pron eu mesmo, eu próprio; (reflexive) me; (after prep) mim (próprio, mesmo). **by** ~ sozinho

mysterious /mɪ'stɪərɪəs/ a misterioso

mystery /'mɪstərɪ/ n mistério m

mystic /'mɪstɪk/ a & n místico (m). ~**al** a místico. ~**ism** /-sɪzəm/ n misticismo m

mystify /'mɪstɪfaɪ/ vt deixar perplexo

mystique /mɪ'stiːk/ n mística f

myth /mɪθ/ n mito m. ~**ical** a mítico

mytholog|y /mɪ'θɒlədʒɪ/ n mitologia f. ~**ical** /mɪθə'lɒdʒɪkl/ a mitológico

Nn

nab /næb/ vt (pt nabbed) (sl) apanhar em flagrante, apanhar com a boca na botija (colloq), pilhar

nag /næg/ vt/i (pt nagged) implicar (com), criticar constantemente; (pester) apoquentar

nagging /'nægɪŋ/ a implicante; (pain) constante, contínuo

nail /neɪl/ n prego m; (of finger, toe) unha f □ vt pregar. ~**-brush** n escova f de unhas. ~**-file** n lixa f de unhas. ~**polish** esmalte m, (P) verniz m para as unhas. **hit the** ~ **on the head** acertar em cheio. **on the** ~ sem demora

naïve /naɪ'iːv/ a ingênuo, (P) ingénuo

naked /'neɪkɪd/ a nu. **to the** ~ **eye** a olho nu, à vista desarmada ~**ness** f nudez f

name /neɪm/ n nome m; (fig) reputação f, fama f □ vt (mention; appoint) nomear; (give a name to) chamar, dar o nome de; (a date) marcar. **be ~d after** ter o nome de. **~less** a sem nome, anônimo, (P) anónimo

namely /'neɪmlɪ/ adv a saber

namesake /'neɪmseɪk/ n homônimo m, (P) homónimo m

nanny /'nænɪ/ n ama f, babá f

nap[1] /næp/ n soneca f □ vi (pt **napped**) dormitar, tirar um cochilo. **catch ~ping** apanhar desprevenido

nap[2] /næp/ n (of material) felpa f

nape /neɪp/ n nuca f

napkin /'næpkɪn/ n guardanapo m; (for baby) fralda f

nappy /'næpɪ/ n fralda f. **~-rash** n assadura f

narcotic /na:'kɒtɪk/ a & n narcótico (m)

narrat|e /nə'reɪt/ vt narrar. **~ion** /-ʃn/ n narrativa f. **~or** n narrador m

narrative /'nærətɪv/ n narrativa f □ a narrativo

narrow /'nærəʊ/ a (-er, -est) estreito; (fig) restrito □ vt/i estreitar(-se); (limit) limitar(-se). **~ly** adv (only just) por pouco; (closely, carefully) de perto, com cuidado. **~-minded** a bitolado, de visão limitada. **~ness** n estreiteza f

nasal /'neɪzl/ a nasal

nast|y /'na:stɪ/ a (-ier, -iest) (malicious, of weather) mau; (unpleasant) desagradável, intra-gável; (rude) grosseiro. **~ily** adv maldosamente; (unpleasantly) desagradavelmente. **~iness** f (malice) maldade f; (rudeness) grosseria f

nation /'neɪʃn/ n nação f. **~-wide** a em todo o país, em escala or a a nível nacional

national /'næʃnəl/ a nacional □ n natural mf. **~ anthem** hino m nacional. **~ism** n nacionalismo m. **~ize** vt nacionalizar. **~ly** adv em escala nacional

nationality /næʃə'nælətɪ/ n nacionalidade f

native /'neɪtɪv/ n natural mf, nativo m □ a nativo; (country) natal; (inborn) inato. **be a ~ of** ser natural de. **~ language** língua f materna. **~ speaker of Portuguese** pessoa f de língua portuguesa, falante m nativo de Português

Nativity /nə'tɪvətɪ/ n **the ~** a Natividade f

natter /'nætə(r)/ vi fazer conversa fiada, falar à toa, tagarelar

natural /'nætʃrəl/ a natural. **~ history** história f natural. **~ist** n naturalista

mf. **~ly** adv naturalmente; (by nature) por natureza

naturaliz|e /'nætʃrəlaɪz/ vt/i naturalizar(-se); (animal, plant) aclimatar(-se). **~ation** /-'zeɪʃn/ n naturalização f

nature /'neɪtʃə(r)/ n natureza f; (kind) gênero m, (P) género m; (of person) indole f

naughty /'nɔ:tɪ/ a (-ier, -iest) (child) levado; (indecent) picante

nause|a /'nɔ:sɪə/ n náusea f. **~ate** /'nɔ:sɪeɪt/ vt nausear. **~ating, ~ous** a nauseabundo, repugnante

nautical /'nɔ:tɪkl/ a náutico. **~ mile** milha f marítima

naval /'neɪvl/ a naval; (officer) de marinha

nave /neɪv/ n nave f

navel /'neɪvl/ n umbigo m

navigable /'nævɪgəbl/ a navegável

navigat|e /'nævɪgeɪt/ vt (sea etc) navegar; (ship) pilotar □ vi navegar. **~ion** /-'geɪʃn/ n navegação f. **~or** n navegador m

navy /'neɪvɪ/ n marinha f de guerra. **~ (blue)** azul-marinho m invar

near /nɪə(r)/ adv perto, quaze □ prep perto de □ a próximo □ vt aproximar-se de, chegar-se a. **draw ~** aproximar(-se) (**to de**). **~ by** adv perto, próximo. **N~ East** Oriente m Próximo. **~ to** perto de. **~ness** n proximidade f

nearby /'nɪəbaɪ/ a & adv próximo, perto

nearly /'nɪəlɪ/ adv quase, por pouco. **not ~ as pretty/etc as** longe de ser tão bonita/etc como

neat /ni:t/ a (-er, -est) (bem) cuidado; (room) bem arrumado; (spirits) puro, sem gelo. **~ly** adv (with care) com cuidado; (cleverly) habilmente. **~ness** n aspecto m cuidado

nebulous /'nebjʊləs/ a nebuloso; (vague) vago, confuso

necessar|y /'nesəsərɪ/ a necessário. **~ily** adv necessariamente

necessitate /nɪ'sesɪteɪt/ vt exigir, obrigar a, tornar necessário

necessity /nɪ'sesətɪ/ n necessidade f; (thing) coisa f indispensável, artigo m de primeira neces-sidade

neck /nek/ n pescoço m; (of dress) gola f. **~ and neck** emparelhados

necklace /'neklɪs/ n colar m

neckline /'neklaɪn/ n decote m

nectarine /'nektərɪn/ n pêssego m

née /neɪ/ a em solteira. **Ann Jones ~ Drewe** Ann Jones cujo nome de solteira era Drewe

need /ni:d/ n necessidade f □ vt precisar de, necessitar de. **you ~ not come** não tem de or não precisa vir. **~less** a

inútil, desnecessário. **~lessly** *adv*
inutilmente, sem necessidade

needle /'niːdl/ *a* agulha *f* □ *vt* (*colloq:*
provoke) provocar

needlework /'niːdlwɜːk/ *n* costura *f*;
(*embroidery*) bordado *m*

needy /'niːdɪ/ *a* (**-ier, -iest**) necessitado,
carenciado

negation /nɪ'ɡeɪʃn/ *n* negação *f*

negative /'neɡətɪv/ *a* negativo □ *n*
negativa *f*, negação *f*; (*photo*) negativo
m. **in the ~** (*answer*) na negativa;
(*gram*) na forma negativa. **~ly** *adv*
negativamente

neglect /nɪ'ɡlekt/ *vt* descuidar;
(*opportunity*) desprezar; (*family*) não
cuidar de (*duty*) não cumprir □ *n* falta *f*
de cuidado(s), descuido *m*. **(state of)**
~ abandono *m*. **~ to** (*omit to*) esquecer-
se de. **~ful** *a* negligente

negligen|t /'neɡlɪdʒənt/ *a* negligente.
~ce *n* negligência *f*, desleixo *m*

negligible /'neɡlɪdʒəbl/ *a* insignificante,
ínfimo

negotiable /nɪ'ɡəʊʃəbl/ *a* negociável

negotiat|e /nɪ'ɡəʊʃɪeɪt/ *vt/i* negociar;
(*obstacle*) transpor; (*difficulty*) vencer.
~ion /-sɪ'eɪʃn/ *n* negociação *f*. **~or** *n*
negociador *m*

Negro /'niːɡrəʊ/ *a* & *n* (*pl* **-oes**) negro
(*m*), preto (*m*)

neigh /neɪ/ *n* relincho *m* □ *vi* relinchar

neighbour /'neɪbə(r)/ *n* vizinho *m*.
~hood *n* vizinhança *f*. **~ing** *a* vizinho.
~ly *a* de boa vizinhança

neither /'naɪðə(r)/ *a* & *pron* nenhum(a)
(de dois *ou* duas), nem um nem outro,
nem uma nem outra □ *adv* tampouco,
também não □ *conj* nem. **~ big nor**
small nem grande nem
pequeno. **~ am I** nem eu

neon /'niːɒn/ *n* néon *m*

nephew /'nevjuː/ *n* sobrinho *m*

nerve /nɜːv/ *n* nervo *m*; (*fig: courage*)
coragem *f*; (*colloq: impudence*)
descaramento *m*, (*P*) lata *f* (*colloq*). **get**
on sb's nerves irritar, dar nos nervos
de alg. **~-racking** *a* de arrasar os
nervos, enervante

nervous /'nɜːvəs/ *a* nervoso. **be** *or* **feel**
~ (*afraid*) ter receio/um certo medo.
~ breakdown esgotamento *m*
nervoso. **~ly** *adv* nervosamente.
~ness *n* nervosismo *m*; (*fear*) receio *m*

nest /nest/ *n* ninho *m* □ *vi* aninhar-se,
fazer *or* ter ninho. **~-egg** *n* pé-
de-meia *m*

nestle /'nesl/ *vi* aninhar-se

net¹ /net/ *n* rede *f* □ *vt* (*pt* **netted**)
apanhar na rede. **~ting** *n* rede *f*. **wire**
~ting rede *f* de arame

net² /net/ *a* (*weight etc*) líquido

Netherlands /'neðələndz/ *npl* **the ~** os
Países Baixos

netsurfer /'netsɜːfə(r)/ *n* internauta *m/f*

nettle /'netl/ *n* urtiga *f*

network /'netwɜːk/ *n* rede *f*, cadeia *f*

neuro|sis /njʊə'rəʊsɪs/ *n* (*pl* **-oses** /-siːz/)
neurose *f*. **~tic** /-'rɒtɪk/ *a* & *n*
neurótico (*m*)

neuter /'njuːtə(r)/ *a* & *n* neutro (*m*) □ *vt*
castrar, capar

neutral /'njuːtrəl/ *a* neutro. **~ (gear)**
ponto *m* morto. **~ity** /-'trælətɪ/ *n*
neutralidade *f*

never /'nevə(r)/ *adv* nunca; (*colloq: not*)
não. **he ~ refuses** ele nunca recusa.
I ~ saw him (*colloq*) nunca o vi.
~ mind não faz mal, deixe para lá.
~-ending *a* interminável

nevertheless /nevəðə'les/ *adv* & *conj*
contudo, no entanto

new /njuː/ *a* (**-er, -est**) novo. **~-born** *a*
recém-nascido. **~ moon** lua *f* nova. **~**
year ano *m* novo. **N~ Year's Day** dia *m*
de Ano Novo. **N~ Year's Eve** véspera *f*
de Ano Novo. **N~ Zealand** Nova
Zelândia *f*. **N~ Zealander** neo-zelandês
m. **~ness** *n* novidade *f*

newcomer /'njuːkʌmə(r)/ *n* recém-
chegado *m*, (*P*) recém-vindo *m*

newfangled /njuː'fæŋɡld/ *a* (*pej*)
moderno

newly /'njuːlɪ/ *adv* há pouco,
recentemente. **~-weds** *npl* recém-
casados *mpl*

news /njuːz/ *n* notícia(s) *f*(*pl*); (*radio*)
noticiário *m*, notícias *fpl*; (*TV*)
telejornal *m*. **~-caster, ~-reader** *n*
locutor *m*. **~-flash** *n* notícia *f* de
última hora

newsagent /'njuːzeɪdʒənt/ *n* jornaleiro *m*

newsletter /'njuːzletə(r)/ *n* boletim *m*
informativo

newspaper /'njuːzpeɪpə(r)/ *n* jornal *m*

newsreel /'njuːzriːl/ *n* atualidades *fpl*, (*P*)
actualidades *fpl*

newt /njuːt/ *n* tritão *m*

next /nekst/ *a* próximo; (*adjoining*)
pegado, ao lado, contíguo; (*following*)
seguinte □ *adv* a seguir □ *n* seguinte
mf. **~-door** *a* do lado. **~ of kin** parente
m mais próximo. **~ to** ao lado de. **~ to**
nothing quase nada

nib /nɪb/ *n* bico *m*, (*P*) aparo *m*

nibble /'nɪbl/ *vt* mordiscar, dar
dentadinhas em

nice /naɪs/ *a* (**-er, -est**) agradável, bom;
(*kind*) simpático, gentil; (*pretty*)
bonito; (*respectable*) bem educado,
correto, (*P*) correcto; (*subtle*) fino,
subtil. **~ly** *adv* agradavelmente; (*well*)
bem

nicety /'naɪsətɪ/ n sutileza f, (P) subtileza f

niche /nɪtʃ/ n nicho m; (fig) bom lugar m

nick /nɪk/ n corte m, chanfradura f; (sl: prison) cadeia f □ vt dar um corte em; (sl: steal) roubar, limpar (colloq); (sl: arrest) apanhar, pôr a mão em (colloq). **in good** ∼ (colloq) em boa forma, em bom estado. **in the** ∼ **of time** mesmo a tempo

nickel /'nɪkl/ n níquel m; (Amer) moeda f de cinco cêntimos

nickname /'nɪkneɪm/ n apelido m, (P) alcunha f; (short form) diminutivo m □ vt apelidar de

nicotine /'nɪkəti:n/ n nicotina f

niece /ni:s/ n sobrinha f

Nigeria /naɪ'dʒɪərɪə/ n Nigéria f. ∼n a & n nigeriano (m)

niggardly /'nɪgədlɪ/ a miserável

night /naɪt/ n noite f □ a de noite, noturno, (P) nocturno. **at** ∼ à/ de noite. **by** ∼ de noite. ∼**cap** n (drink) bebida f na hora de deitar. ∼**club** n boate f, (P) boîte f. ∼**dress**, ∼**gown** ns camisola f de dormir, (P) camisa f de noite. ∼**life** n vida f noturna, (P) nocturna. ∼**school** n escola f noturna, (P) nocturna. ∼**time** n noite f. ∼**watchman** n guarda-noturno m, (P) guarda-nocturno m

nightfall /'naɪtfɔ:l/ n anoitecer m

nightingale /'naɪtɪŋgeɪl/ n rouxinol m

nightly /'naɪtlɪ/ a noturno, (P) nocturno □ adv de noite, à noite, todas as noites

nightmare /'naɪtmeə(r)/ n pesadelo m

nil /nɪl/ n nada m; (sport) zero m □ a nulo

nimble /'nɪmbl/ a (-er, -est) ágil, ligeiro

nin|e /naɪn/ a & n nove (m). ∼**th** a & n nono (m)

nineteen /naɪn'ti:n/ a & n dezenove (m), (P) dezanove (m). ∼**th** a & n décimo nono (m)

ninet|y /'naɪntɪ/ a & n noventa (m). ∼**ieth** a & n nonagésimo (m)

nip /nɪp/ vt/i (pt nipped) apertar, beliscar; (colloq: rush) ir correndo, ir num pulo (colloq) □ n aperto m, beliscão m; (drink) gole m, trago m. **a** ∼ **in the air** um frio cortante. ∼ **in the bud** cortar pela raiz

nipple /'nɪpl/ n mamilo m

nippy /'nɪpɪ/ a (-ier, -iest) (colloq: quick) rápido; (colloq: chilly) cortante

nitrogen /'naɪtrədʒən/ n azoto m, nitrogênio m, (P) nitrogénio m

nitwit /'nɪtwɪt/ n (colloq) imbecil m

no /nəʊ/ a nenhum □ adv não □ n (pl noes) não m. ∼ **entry** entrada f proibida. ∼ **money/time/** etc nenhum dinheiro/tempo/etc. ∼ **man's land**

terra f de ninguém. ∼ **one = nobody**. ∼ **smoking** é proibido fumar. ∼ **way!** (colloq) de modo nenhum!

nob|le /'nəʊbl/ a (-er, -est) nobre. ∼**ility** /-'bɪlətɪ/ n nobreza f

nobleman /'nəʊblmən/ n (pl -men) nobre m, fidalgo m

nobody /'nəʊbədɪ/ pron ninguém □ n nulidade f. **he knows** ∼ ele não conhece ninguém. ∼ **is there** não tem ninguém lá

nocturnal /nɒk'tɜ:nl/ a noturno, (P) nocturno

nod /nɒd/ vt/i (pt nodded) ∼ (one's head) acenar (com) a cabeça; ∼ (off) cabecear □ n aceno m com a cabeça (para dizer que sim or para cumprimentar)

noise /nɔɪz/ n ruído m, barulho m. ∼**less** a silencioso

nois|y /'nɔɪzɪ/ a (-ier, -iest) ruidoso, barulhento. ∼**ily** adv ruidosamente

nomad /'nəʊmæd/ n nómade mf, (P) nómada mf. ∼**ic** /-'mædɪk/ a nómade, (P) nómada

nominal /'nɒmɪnl/ a nominal; (fee, sum) simbólico

nominat|e /'nɒmɪneɪt/ vt (appoint) nomear; (put forward) propor. ∼**ion** /-'neɪʃn/ n nomeação f

non- /nɒn/ pref não, sem, in-, a-, anti-, des-. ∼**-skid** a antiderrapante. ∼**-stick** a não-aderente

nonchalant /'nɒnʃələnt/ a indiferente, desinteressado

non-commissioned /nɒnkə-'mɪʃnd/ a ∼ **officer** sargento m, cabo m

non-committal /nɒnkə'mɪtl/ a evasivo

nondescript /'nɒndɪskrɪpt/ a insignificante, medíocre, indefinível

none /nʌn/ pron (person) nenhum, ninguém; (thing) nenhum, nada. ∼ **of us** nenhum de nós. **I have** ∼ não tenho nenhum. ∼ **of that!** nada disso! □ adv ∼ **too** não muito. **he is** ∼ **the happier** nem por isso ele é mais feliz. ∼ **the less** contudo, no entanto, apesar disso

nonentity /nɒ'nentətɪ/ n nulidade f, zero m à esquerda, João Ninguém m

non-existent /nɒnɪg'zɪstənt/ a inexistente

nonplussed /nɒn'plʌst/ a perplexo, pasmado

nonsens|e /'nɒnsns/ n absurdo m, disparate m. ∼**ical** /-'sensɪkl/ a absurdo, disparatado

non-smoker /nɒn'sməʊkə(r)/ n não-fumante m, (P) não-fumador m

non-stop /nɒn'stɒp/ a ininterrupto, contínuo; (train) direto, (P) directo; (flight) sem escala □ adv sem parar

n

noodles /'nu:dlz/ *npl* talharim *m*, (*P*) macarronete *m*

nook /nʊk/ *n* (re)canto *m*

noon /nu:n/ *n* meio-dia *m*

noose /nu:s/ *n* laço *m* corrediço

nor /nɔ:(r)/ *conj & adv* nem, também não. ~ **do I** nem eu

norm /nɔ:m/ *n* norma *f*

normal /'nɔ:ml/ *a & n* normal (*m*). **above/below** ~ acima/abaixo do normal. ~**ity** /nɔ:'mælətɪ/ *n* normalidade *f*. ~**ly** *adv* normalmente

north /nɔ:θ/ *n* norte *m* □ *a* norte, do norte; (*of country, people etc*) setentrional □ *adv* a, ao/para o norte. **N**~ **America** América *f* do Norte. **N**~ **American** *a & n* norte-americano (*m*). ~**-east** *n* nordeste *m*. ~**erly** /'nɔ:ðəlɪ/ *a* do norte. ~**ward** *a* ao norte. ~**ward(s)** *adv* para o norte. ~**west** *n* noroeste *m*

northern /'nɔ:ðən/ *a* do norte

Norw|ay /'nɔ:weɪ/ *n* Noruega *f*. ~**egian** /nɔ:'wi:dʒən/ *a & n* norueguês (*m*)

nose /nəʊz/ *n* nariz *m*; (*of animal*) focinho *m* □ *vi* ~ **about** farejar. **pay through the** ~ pagar um preço exorbitante

nosebleed /'nəʊzbli:d/ *n* hemorragia *f* nasal *or* pelo nariz

nosedive /'nəʊzdaɪv/ *n* vôo *m* picado

nostalg|ia /nɒ'stældʒə/ *n* nostalgia *f*. ~**ic** *a* nostálgico

nostril /'nɒstrəl/ *n* narina *f*; (*of horse*) venta *f* (*usually pl*)

nosy /'nəʊzɪ/ *a* (**-ier, -iest**) (*colloq*) bisbilhoteiro

not /nɒt/ *adv* não. ~ **at all** nada, de modo nenhum; (*reply to thanks*) de nada. **he is** ~ **at all bored** ele não está nem um pouco entediado. ~ **yet** ainda não. **I suppose** ~ creio que não

notable /'nəʊtəbl/ *a* notável □ *n* notabilidade *f*

notably /'nəʊtəblɪ/ *adv* notavelmente; (*particularly*) especialmente

notch /nɒtʃ/ *n* corte *m* em V □ *vt* marcar com cortes. ~ **up** (*score etc*) marcar

note /nəʊt/ *n* nota *f*; (*banknote*) nota (de banco) *f*; (*short letter*) bilhete *m* □ *vt* notar

notebook /'nəʊtbʊk/ *n* livrinho *m* de notas, (*P*) bloco-notas *m*

noted /'nəʊtɪd/ *a* conhecido, famoso

notepaper /'nəʊtpeɪpə(r)/ *n* papel *m* de carta

noteworthy /'nəʊtwɜ:ðɪ/ *a* notável

nothing /'nʌθɪŋ/ *n* nada *m*; (*person*) nulidade *f*, zero *m* □ *adv* nada, de modo algum *or* nenhum, de maneira alguma *or* nenhuma. **he eats** ~ ele não come nada. ~ **big/***etc* nada (de) grande/*etc*.

~ **else** nada mais. ~ **much** pouca coisa. **for** ~ (*free*) de graça; (*in vain*) em vão

notice /'nəʊtɪs/ *n* anúncio *m*, notícia *f*; (*in street, on wall*) letreiro *m*; (*warning*) aviso *m*; (*attention*) atenção *f*. **(advance)** ~ pré-aviso *m* □ *vt* notar, reparar. **at short** ~ num prazo curto. **a week's** ~ o prazo de uma semana. ~**-board** *n* quadro *m* para afixar anúncios etc. **hand in one's** ~ pedir demissão. **take** ~ reparar (**of** em). **take no** ~ não fazer caso de (**of** de)

noticeabl|e /'nəʊtɪsəbl/ *a* visível. ~**y** *adv* visivelmente

notif|y /'nəʊtɪfaɪ/ *vt* participar, notificar. ~**ication** /-ɪ'keɪʃn/ *n* participação *f*, notificação *f*

notion /'nəʊʃn/ *n* noção *f*

notor|ious /nəʊ'tɔ:rɪəs/ *a* notório. ~**iety** /-ə'raɪətɪ/ *n* fama *f*

notwithstanding /nɒtwɪθ'stændɪŋ/ *prep* apesar de, não obstante □ *adv* mesmo assim, ainda assim □ *conj* embora, conquanto, apesar de que

nougat /'nu:ga:/ *n* nugá *m*, torrone *m*

nought /nɔ:t/ *n* zero *m*

noun /naʊn/ *n* substantivo *m*, nome *m*

nourish /'nʌrɪʃ/ *vt* alimentar, nutrir. ~**ing** *a* alimentício, nutritivo. ~**ment** *n* alimento *m*, sustento *m*

novel /'nɒvl/ *n* romance *m* □ *a* novo, original. ~**ist** *n* romancista *mf*. ~**ty** *n* novidade *f*

November /nəʊ'vembə(r)/ *n* novembro *m*

novice /'nɒvɪs/ *n* (*beginner*) noviço *m*, novato *m*; (*relig*) noviço *m*

now /naʊ/ *adv* agora □ *conj* ~ **(that)** agora que. **by** ~ a estas horas, por esta altura. **from** ~ **on** de agora em diante. ~ **and again,** ~ **and then** de vez em quando. **right** ~ já

nowadays /'naʊədeɪz/ *adv* hoje em dia, presentemente, atualmente, (*P*) actualmente

nowhere /'nəʊweə(r)/ *adv* (*position*) em lugar nenhum, em lado nenhum; (*direction*) a lado nenhum, a parte alguma *or* nenhuma

nozzle /'nɒzl/ *n* bico *m*, bocal *m*; (*of hose*) agulheta *f*

nuance /'nju:a:ns/ *n* nuance *f*, matiz *m*

nuclear /'nju:klɪə(r)/ *a* nuclear

nucleus /'nju:klɪəs/ *n* (*pl* **-lei** /-lɪaɪ/) núcleo *m*

nud|e /nju:d/ *a & n* nu (*m*). **in the** ~**e** nu. ~**ity** *n* nudez *f*

nudge /nʌdʒ/ *vt* tocar com o cotovelo, cutucar □ *n* ligeira cotovelada *f*, cutucada *f*

nudis|t /'nju:dɪst/ *n* nudista *mf*. **∼m**
/-zəm/ *n* nudismo *m*

nuisance /'nju:sns/ *n* aborrecimento *m*,
chatice *f* (*sl*); (*person*) chato *m* (*sl*)

null /nʌl/ *a* nulo. **∼ and void** (*jur*) irrito
e nulo. **∼ify** *vt* anular, invalidar

numb /nʌm/ *a* entorpecido, dormente
□ *vt* entorpecer, adormecer

number /'nʌmbə(r)/ *n* número *m*;
(*numeral*) algarismo *m* □ *vt* numerar;
(*amount to*) ser em número de; (*count*)
contar, incluir. **∼-plate** *n* chapa (do
carro) *f*

numeral /'nju:mərəl/ *n* número *m*,
algarismo *m*

numerate /'nju:mərət/ *a* que tem
conhecimentos básicos de matemática

numerical /nju:'merɪkl/ *a* numérico

numerous /'nju:mərəs/ *a* numeroso

nun /nʌn/ *n* freira *f*, religiosa *f*

nurs|e /nɜ:s/ *n* enfermeira *f*, enfermeiro
m; (*nanny*) ama(-seca) *f*, babá *f* □ *vt*
cuidar de, tratar de; (*hopes etc*)
alimentar, acalentar. **∼ing** *n*
enfermagem *f*. **∼ing home** clínica *f* de
repouso

nursery /'nɜ:sərɪ/ *n* quarto *m* de
crianças; (*for plants*) viveiro *m*. **(day)
∼** creche *f*. **∼ rhyme** poema *m* or
canção *f* infantil. **∼ school** jardim *m*
de infância

nurture /'nɜ:tʃə(r)/ *vt* educar

nut /nʌt/ *n* (*bot*) noz *f*; (*techn*) porca *f* de
parafuso

nutcrackers /'nʌtkrækəz/ *npl* quebra-
nozes *m invar*

nutmeg /'nʌtmeg/ *n* noz-moscada *f*

nutrient /'nju:trɪənt/ *n* substância *f*
nutritiva, nutriente *m*

nutrit|ion /nju:'trɪʃn/ *n* nutrição *f*.
∼ious *a* nutritivo

nutshell /'nʌtʃel/ *n* casca *f* de noz. **in a ∼**
em poucas palavras

nuzzle /'nʌzl/ *vt* esfregar com o focinho

nylon /'naɪlɒn/ *n* nylon *m*. **∼s** meias *fpl*
de nylon

Oo

oaf /əʊf/ *n* (*pl* oafs) imbecil *m*, idiota *m*

oak /əʊk/ *n* carvalho *m*

OAP *abbr see* old-age pensioner

oar /ɔ:(r)/ *n* remo *m*

oasis /əʊ'eɪsɪs/ *n* (*pl* oases /-si:z/) oásis *m*

oath /əʊθ/ *n* juramento *m*; (*swear-word*)
praga *f*

oatmeal /'əʊtmi:l/ *n* farinha *f* de aveia;
(*porridge*) papa *f* de aveia

oats /əʊts/ *npl* aveia *f*

obedien|t /ə'bi:dɪənt/ *a* obediente. **∼ce**
n obediência *f*. **∼tly** *adv*
obedientemente

obes|e /əʊ'bi:s/ *a* obeso. **∼ity** *n*
obesidade *f*

obey /ə'beɪ/ *vt/i* obedecer (a)

obituary /ə'bɪtʃʊərɪ/ *n* necrológico *m*, (*P*)
necrologia *f*

object¹ /'ɒbdʒɪkt/ *n* objeto *m*, (*P*) objecto
m; (*aim*) objetivo *m*, (*P*) objectivo *m*;
(*gram*) complemento *m*

object² /əb'dʒekt/ *vt/i* objetar, (*P*) objectar
(que). **∼ to** opor-se a, discordar de.
∼ion /-ʃn/ *n* objeção *f*, (*P*) objecção *f*

objectionable /əb'dʒekʃnəbl/ *a*
censurável; (*unpleasant*) desagradável

objectiv|e /əb'dʒektɪv/ *a* objetivo, (*P*)
objectivo. **∼ity** /-'tɪvətɪ/ *n* objetividade
f, (*P*) objectividade *f*

obligation /ɒblɪ'geɪʃn/ *n* obrigação *f*. **be
under an ∼ to sb** dever favores a alg

obligatory /ə'blɪgətrɪ/ *a* obrigatório

oblig|e /ə'blaɪdʒ/ *vt* obrigar; (*do a favour*)
fazer um favor a, obsequiar. **∼ed** *a*
obrigado (**to** a). **∼ed to sb** em dívida
(para) com alg. **∼ing** *a* prestável,
amável. **∼ingly** *adv* amavelmente

oblique /ə'bli:k/ *a* oblíquo

obliterat|e /ə'blɪtəreɪt/ *vt* obliterar. **∼ion**
/-'reɪʃn/ *n* obliteração *f*

oblivion /ə'blɪvɪən/ *n* esquecimento *m*

oblivious /ə'blɪvɪəs/ *a* esquecido, sem
consciência (**of/to** de)

oblong /'ɒblɒŋ/ *a* oblongo □ *n* retângulo
m, (*P*) rectângulo *m*

obnoxious /əb'nɒkʃəs/ *a* ofensivo,
detestável

oboe /'əʊbəʊ/ *n* oboé *m*

obscen|e /əb'si:n/ *a* obsceno. **∼ity**
/-'enətɪ/ *n* obscenidade *f*

obscur|e /əb'skjʊə(r)/ *a* obscuro □ *vt*
obscurecer; (*conceal*) encobrir. **∼ity** *n*
obscuridade *f*

obsequious /əb'si:kwɪəs/ *a* demasiado
obsequioso, subserviente

observan|t /əb'zɜ:vənt/ *a* observador.
∼ce *n* observância *f*, cumprimento *m*

observatory /əb'zɜ:vətrɪ/ *n* observatório
m

observ|e /əb'zɜ:v/ *vt* observar. **∼ation**
/ɒbzə'veɪʃn/ *n* observação *f*. **keep
under ∼ation** vigiar. **∼er** *n*
observador *m*

obsess /əb'ses/ *vt* obcecar. **∼ion** /-ʃn/ *n*
obsessão *f*. **∼ive** *a* obsessivo

obsolete /'ɒbsəli:t/ *a* obsoleto, antiguado

obstacle /'ɒbstəkl/ *n* obstáculo *m*

n

o

obstetric|s /əb'stetrɪks/ *n* obstetrícia *f*. **~ian** /ɒbstɪ'trɪʃn/ *n* obstetra *mf*

obstina|te /'ɒbstɪnət/ *a* obstinado. **~cy** *n* obstinação *f*

obstruct /əb'strʌkt/ *vt* obstruir, bloquear; (*hinder*) estorvar, obstruir. **~ion** /-ʃn/ *n* obstrução *f*; (*thing*) obstáculo *m*

obtain /əb'teɪn/ *vt* obter □ *vi* prevalecer, estar em vigor. **~able** *a* que se pode obter

obtrusive /əb'truːsɪv/ *a* importuno; (*thing*) demasiadamente em evidência, que dá muito na vista (*colloq*)

obvious /'ɒbvɪəs/ *a* óbvio, evidente. **~ly** *adv* obviamente

occasion /ə'keɪʒn/ *n* ocasião *f*; (*event*) acontecimento *m* □ *vt* ocasionar. **on ~** de vez em quando, ocasionalmente

occasional /ə'keɪʒənl/ *a* ocasional. **~ly** *adv* de vez em quando, ocasionalmente

occult /ɒ'kʌlt/ *a* oculto

occupation /ɒkjʊ'peɪʃn/ *n* ocupação *f*. **~al** *a* profissional; (*therapy*) ocupacional

occup|y /'ɒkjʊpaɪ/ *vt* ocupar. **~ant**, **~ier** *ns* ocupante *mf*

occur /ə'kɜː(r)/ *vi* (*pt* occurred) ocorrer, acontecer, dar-se; (*arise*) apresentar-se, aparecer. **~ to sb** ocorrer a alg

occurrence /ə'kʌrəns/ *n* acontecimento *m*, ocorrência *f*

ocean /'əʊʃn/ *n* oceano *m*

o'clock /ə'klɒk/ *adv* **it is one ~** é uma hora. **it is six ~** são seis horas

octagon /'ɒktəgən/ *n* octógono *m*. **~al** /-'tægənl/ *a* octogonal

octave /'ɒktɪv/ *n* oitava *f*

October /ɒk'təʊbə(r)/ *n* outubro *m*

octopus /'ɒktəpəs/ *n* (*pl* -puses) polvo *m*

odd /ɒd/ *a* (-er, -est) estranho, singular; (*number*) ímpar; (*left over*) de sobra; (*not of set*) desemparelhado; (*occasional*) ocasional. **~ jobs** (*paid*) biscates *mpl*; (*in garden etc*) trabalhos *mpl* diversos. **twenty ~** vinte e tantos. **~ity** *n* singularidade *f*; (*thing*) curiosidade *f*. **~ly** *adv* de modo estranho

oddment /'ɒdmənt/ *n* resto *m*, artigo *m* avulso

odds /ɒdz/ *npl* probabilidades *fpl*; (*in betting*) ganhos *mpl* líquidos. **at ~** em desacordo; (*quarrelling*) de mal, brigado. **it makes no ~** não faz diferença. **~ and ends** artigos *mpl* avulsos, coisas *fpl* pequenas

odious /'əʊdɪəs/ *a* odioso

odour /'əʊdə(r)/ *n* odor *m*. **~less** *a* inodoro

of /əv/; *emphatic* /ɒv/ *prep* de. **a friend ~ mine** um amigo meu. **the fifth ~ June** (no dia) cinco de junho. **take six ~ them** leve seis deles

off /ɒf/ *adv* embora, fora; (*switched off*) apagado, desligado; (*taken off*) tirado, desligado; (*cancelled*) cancelado; (*food*) estragado □ *prep* (fora) de; (*distant from*) a alguma distância de. **be ~** (*depart*) ir-se embora, partir. **be well ~** ser abastado. **be better/worse ~** estar em melhor/ pior situação. **a day ~** um dia de folga. **20% ~** redução de 20%. **on the ~ chance that** no caso de. **~ colour** indisposto, adoentado. **~-licence** *n* loja *f* de bebidas alcoólicas. **~-load** *vt* descarregar. **~-putting** *a* desconcertante. **~-stage** *adv* fora de cena. **~-white** *a* branco-sujo

offal /'ɒfl/ *n* miudezas *fpl*, fressura *f*

offence /ə'fens/ *n* (*feeling*) ofensa *f*; (*crime*) delito *m*, transgressão *f*. **give ~ to** ofender. **take ~** ofender-se (**at** com)

offend /ə'fend/ *vt* ofender. **be ~ed** ofender-se (**at** com). **~er** *n* delinqüente *mf*, (P) delinquente *mf*

offensive /ə'fensɪv/ *a* ofensivo; (*disgusting*) repugnante □ *n* ofensiva *f*

offer /'ɒfə(r)/ *vt* (*pt* offered) oferecer □ *n* oferta *f*. **on ~** em promoção. **~ing** *n* oferenda *f*

offhand /ɒf'hænd/ *a* espontâneo; (*curt*) seco □ *adv* de improviso, sem pensar

office /'ɒfɪs/ *n* escritório *m*; (*post*) cargo *m*; (*branch*) filial *f*. **~ hours** horas *fpl* de expediente. **in ~** no poder. **take ~** assumir o cargo

officer /'ɒfɪsə(r)/ *n* oficial *m*; (*policeman*) agente *m*

official /ə'fɪʃl/ *a* oficial □ *n* funcionário *m*. **~ly** *adv* oficialmente

officiate /ə'fɪʃɪeɪt/ *vi* (*relig*) oficiar. **~ as** presidir, exercer as funções de

officious /ə'fɪʃəs/ *a* intrometido

offing /'ɒfɪŋ/ *n* **in the ~** (*fig*) em perspectiva

offset /'ɒfset/ *vt* (*pt*-set, *pres p*-setting) compensar, contrabalançar

offshoot /'ɒfʃuːt/ *n* rebento *m*; (*fig*) efeito *m* secundário

offshore /'ɒfʃɔː(r)/ *a* ao largo da costa

offside /ɒf'saɪd/ *a & adv* offside, em impedimento, (P) fora de jogo

offspring /'ɒfsprɪŋ/ *n* (*pl invar*) descendência *f*, prole *f*

often /'ɒfn/ *adv* muitas vezes, freqüentemente, (P) frequentemente. **every so ~** de vez em quando. **how ~?** quantas vezes?

oh /əʊ/ *int* oh, ah

oil /ɔɪl/ n óleo m; (petroleum) petróleo m □ vt lubrificar. **~-painting** n pintura f a óleo. **~ rig** plataforma f de poço de petróleo. **~ well** poço m de petróleo. **~y** a oleoso; (food) gorduroso

oilfield /ˈɔɪlfiːld/ n campo m petrolífero

oilskins /ˈɔɪlskɪnz/ npl roupa f de oleado

ointment /ˈɔɪntmənt/ n pomada f

OK /əʊˈkeɪ/ a & adv (colloq) (está) bem, (está) certo, (está) legal

old /əʊld/ a (-er, -est) velho; (person) velho, idoso; (former) antigo. **how ~ is he?** que idade tem ele? **he is eight years ~** ele tem oito anos (de idade). **of ~** (d)antes, antigamente. **~ age** velhice f. **~-age pensioner** reformado m, aposentado m, pessoa f de terceira idade. **~ boy** antigo aluno m. **~-fashioned** a fora de moda. **~ girl** antiga aluna f. **~ maid** solteirona f. **~ man** homem m idoso, velho m. **~-time** a antigo. **~ woman** mulher f idosa, velha f

olive /ˈɒlɪv/ n azeitona f □ a de azeitona. **~ oil** azeite m

Olympic /əˈlɪmpɪk/ a olímpico. **~s** npl Olimpíadas fpl. **~ Games** Jogos mpl Olímpicos

omelette /ˈɒmlɪt/ n omelete f

omen /ˈəʊmən/ n agouro m

ominous /ˈɒmɪnəs/ a agourento

omi|t /əˈmɪt/ vt (pt omitted) omitir. **~ssion** /-ʃn/ n omissão f

on /ɒn/ prep sobre, em cima de, de, em □ adv para diante, para a frente; (switched on) aceso, ligado; (tap) aberto; (machine) em funcionamento; (put on) posto; (happening) em curso. **~ arrival** na chegada, ao chegar. **~ foot** etc a pé etc. **~ doing** ao fazer. **~ time** na hora, dentro do horário. **~ Tuesday** na terça-feira. **~ Tuesdays** às terças-feiras. **walk**/etc **~** continuar a andar/ etc. **be ~ at** (film, TV) estar levando or passando. **~ and off** de vez em quando. **~ and ~** sem parar

once /wʌns/ adv uma vez; (formerly) noutro(s) tempo(s) □ conj uma vez que, desde que. **all at ~** de repente; (simultaneously) todos ao mesmo tempo. **just this ~** só esta vez. **~ (and) for all** duma vez para sempre. **~ upon a time** era uma vez. **~-over** n (colloq) vista f de olhos

oncoming /ˈɒnkʌmɪŋ/ a que se aproxima, próximo. **the ~ traffic** o trânsito que vem do sentido oposto, (P) no sentido contrário

one /wʌn/ a um(a); (sole) único □ n um(a) m f & pron um(a) m f; (impersonal) se. **~ by ~** um a um. **a big/red**/etc **~** um grande/vermelho/etc. **this/that ~**

este/esse. **~ another** um ao outro, uns aos outros. **~-sided** a parcial. **~-way** a (street) mão única; (ticket) simples

oneself /wʌnˈself/ pron si, si mesmo/ próprio; (reflexive) se. **by ~** sozinho

onion /ˈʌnɪən/ n cebola f

on-line /ɒnˈlaɪn/ adj conectado (à Internet)

onlooker /ˈɒnlʊkə(r)/ n espectador m, circunstante mf

only /ˈəʊnlɪ/ a único □ adv apenas, só, somente □ conj só que. **an ~ child** um filho único. **he ~ has six** ele só tem seis. **not ~ . . . but also** não só . . . mas também. **~ too** muito, mais que

onset /ˈɒnset/ n começo m; (attack) ataque m

onslaught /ˈɒnslɔːt/ n ataque m violento, assalto m

onward(s) /ˈɒnwəd(z)/ adv para a frente/ diante

ooze /uːz/ vt/i escorrer, verter

opal /ˈəʊpl/ n opala f

opaque /əʊˈpeɪk/ a opaco, tosco

open /ˈəʊpən/ a aberto; (view) aberto, amplo; (free to all) aberto ao público; (attempt) franco □ vt/i abrir(-se); (of shop, play) abrir. **in the ~ air** ao ar livre. **keep ~ house** receber muito, abrir a porta para todos. **~ on to** dar para. **~ out or up** abrir(-se). **~-heart** a (of surgery) de coração aberto. **~-minded** a imparcial. **~-plan** a sem divisórias. **~ secret** segredo m de polichinelo. **~ sea** mar m alto. **~ness** n abertura f; (frankness) franqueza f

opener /ˈəʊpənə(r)/ n (tins) abridor m de latas; (bottles) saca-rolhas m invar

opening /ˈəʊpənɪŋ/ n abertura f; (beginning) começo m; (opportunity) oportunidade f; (job) vaga f

openly /ˈəʊpənlɪ/ adv abertamente

opera /ˈɒprə/ n ópera f. **~-glasses** npl binóculo (de teatro) m, (P) binóculos mpl. **~tic** /ɒpəˈrætɪk/ a de ópera

operat|e /ˈɒpəreɪt/ vt/i operar; (techn) (pôr a) funcionar. **~e on** (med) operar. **~ing-theatre** n (med) anfiteatro m, sala f de operações. **~ion** /-ˈreɪʃn/ n operação f. **in ~ion** em vigor; (techn) em funcionamento. **~ional** /-ˈreɪʃnl/ a operacional. **~or** n operador m; (telephonist) telefonista mf

operative /ˈɒpərətɪv/ a (surgical) operatório; (law etc) em vigor

opinion /əˈpɪnɪən/ n opinião f, parecer m. **in my ~** a meu ver. **~ poll** n sondagem (de opinião) f. **~ated** /-eɪtɪd/ a dogmático

opium /ˈəʊpɪəm/ n ópio m

Oporto /əˈpɔːtəʊ/ n Porto m

o

opponent /ə'pəʊnənt/ *n* adversário *m*, antagonista *mf*, oponente *mf*

opportune /'ɒpətjuːn/ *a* oportuno

opportunity /ɒpə'tjuːnətɪ/ *n* oportunidade *f*

oppos|e /ə'pəʊz/ *vt* opor-se a. **~ed to** oposto a. **~ing** *a* oposto

opposite /'ɒpəzɪt/ *a* & *n* oposto (*m*), contrário (*m*) □ *adv* em frente □ *prep* **~ (to)** em frente de

opposition /ɒpə'zɪʃn/ *n* oposição *f*

oppress /ə'pres/ *vt* oprimir. **~ion** /-ʃn/ *n* opressão *f*. **~ive** *a* opressivo. **~or** *n* opressor *m*

opt /ɒpt/ *vi* **~ for** optar por. **~ out** recusar-se a participar (of de). **~ to do** escolher fazer

optical /'ɒptɪkl/ *a* óptico. **~ illusion** ilusão *f* óptica

optician /ɒp'tɪʃn/ *n* oculista *mf*

optimis|t /'ɒptɪmɪst/ *n* otimista *mf*, (*P*) optimista *mf*. **~m** /-zəm/ *n* otimismo *m*, (*P*) optimismo *m*. **~tic** /-'mɪstɪk/ *a* otimista, (*P*) optimista. **~tically** /-'mɪstɪklɪ/ *adv* com otimismo, (*P*) optimismo

optimum /'ɒptɪməm/ *a* & *n* (*pl* **-ima**) ótimo (*m*), (*P*) óptimo (*m*)

option /'ɒpʃn/ *n* escolha *f*, opção *f*. **have no ~ (but)** não ter outro remédio (senão)

optional /'ɒpʃənl/ *a* opcional, facultativo

opulen|t /'ɒpjʊlənt/ *a* opulento. **~ce** *n* opulência *f*

or /ɔː(r)/ *conj* ou; (*with negative*) nem. **~ else** senão

oracle /'ɒrəkl/ *n* oráculo *m*

oral /'ɔːrəl/ *a* oral

orange /'ɒrɪndʒ/ *n* laranja *f*; (*colour*) laranja *m*, cor *f* de laranja □ *a* de laranja; (*colour*) alaranjado, cor de laranja

orator /'ɒrətə(r)/ *n* orador *m*. **~y** *n* oratória *f*

orbit /'ɔːbɪt/ *n* órbita *f* □ *vt* (*pt* **orbited**) gravitar em torno de

orchard /'ɔːtʃəd/ *n* pomar *m*

orchestra /'ɔːkɪstrə/ *n* orquestra *f*. **~l** /-'kestrəl/ *a* orquestral

orchestrate /'ɔːkɪstreɪt/ *vt* orquestrar

orchid /'ɔːkɪd/ *n* orquídea *f*

ordain /ɔː'deɪn/ *vt* decretar; (*relig*) ordenar

ordeal /ɔː'diːl/ *n* prova *f*, provação *f*

order /'ɔːdə(r)/ *n* ordem *f*, (*comm*) encomenda *f*, pedido *m* □ *vt* ordenar; (*goods etc*) encomendar. **in ~ that** para que. **in ~ to** para

orderly /'ɔːdəlɪ/ *a* ordenado, em ordem; (*not unruly*) ordeiro □ *n* (*mil*)

ordenança *f*; (*med*) servente *m* de hospital

ordinary /'ɔːdɪnrɪ/ *a* normal, ordinário, vulgar. **out of the ~** fora do comum

ordination /ɔːdɪ'neɪʃn/ *n* (*relig*) ordenação *f*

ore /ɔː(r)/ *n* minério *m*

organ /'ɔːgən/ *n* órgão *m*. **~ist** *n* organista *mf*

organic /ɔː'gænɪk/ *a* orgânico

organism /'ɔːgənɪzəm/ *n* organismo *m*

organiz|e /'ɔːgənaɪz/ *vt* organizar. **~ation** /-'zeɪʃn/ *n* organização *f*. **~er** *n* organizador *m*

orgasm /'ɔːgæzəm/ *n* orgasmo *m*

orgy /'ɔːdʒɪ/ *n* orgia *f*

Orient /'ɔːrɪənt/ *n* **the ~** o Oriente *m*. **~al** /-'entl/ *a* & *n* oriental (*mf*)

orientat|e /'ɔːrɪənteɪt/ *vt* orientar. **~ion** /-'teɪʃn/ *n* orientação *f*

orifice /'ɒrɪfɪs/ *n* orifício *m*

origin /'ɒrɪdʒɪn/ *n* origem *f*

original /ə'rɪdʒənl/ *a* original; (*not copied*) original. **~ity** /-'nælətɪ/ *n* originalidade *f*. **~ly** *adv* originalmente; (*in the beginning*) originariamente

originat|e /ə'rɪdʒəneɪt/ *vt*/*i* originar(-se). **~e from** provir de. **~or** *n* iniciador *m*, criador *m*, autor *m*

ornament /'ɔːnəmənt/ *n* ornamento *m*; (*object*) peça *f* decorativa. **~al** /-'mentl/ *a* ornamental. **~ation** /-en'teɪʃn/ *n* ornamentação *f*

ornate /ɔː'neɪt/ *a* florido, floreado

ornitholog|y /ɔːnɪ'θɒlədʒɪ/ *n* ornitologia *f*. **~ist** *n* ornitólogo *m*

orphan /'ɔːfn/ *n* órfã(o) *f*(*m*) □ *vt* deixar órfão. **~age** *n* orfanato *m*

orthodox /'ɔːθədɒks/ *a* ortodoxo

orthopaedic /ɔːθə'piːdɪk/ *a* ortopédico

oscillate /'ɒsɪleɪt/ *vi* oscilar, vacilar

ostensibl|e /ɒs'tensəbl/ *a* aparente, pretenso. **~y** *adv* aparentemente, pretensamente

ostentati|on /ɒsten'teɪʃn/ *n* ostentação *f*. **~ous** /-'teɪʃəs/ *a* ostentoso, ostensivo

osteopath /'ɒstɪəpæθ/ *n* osteopata *mf*

ostracize /'ɒstrəsaɪz/ *vt* pôr de lado, marginalizar

ostrich /'ɒstrɪtʃ/ *n* avestruz *mf*

other /'ʌðə(r)/ *a*, *n* & *pron* outro (*m*) □ *adv* **~ than** diferente de, senão. (**some**) **~s** outros. **the ~ day** no outro dia. **the ~ one** o outro

otherwise /'ʌðəwaɪz/ *adv* de outro modo □ *conj* senão, caso contrário

otter /'ɒtə(r)/ *n* lontra *f*

ouch /aʊtʃ/ *int* ai!, ui!

o

ought /ɔːt/ *v aux* (*pt* **ought**) dever. **you ~ to stay** você devia ficar. **he ~ to succeed** ele deve vencer. **I ~ to have done it** eu devia tê-lo feito

ounce /aʊns/ *n* onça *f* (= *28,35g*)

our /'aʊə(r)/ *a* nosso(s), nossa(s)

ours /'aʊəz/ *poss pron* o(s) nosso(s), a(s) nossa(s)

ourselves /aʊə'selvz/ *pron* nós mesmos/ próprios; (*reflexive*) nos. **by ~** sozinhos

oust /aʊst/ *vt* expulsar, obrigar a sair

out /aʊt/ *adv* fora; (*of light, fire*) apagado; (*in blossom*) aberto, desabrochado; (*of tide*) baixo. **be ~** não estar em casa, estar fora (de casa); (*wrong*) enganar-se. **be ~ to** estar resolvido a. **run**/*etc* **~ sair correndo**/*etc*. **~-and-~** *a* completo, rematado. **~ of** fora de; (*without*) sem. **~ of pity**/*etc* por pena/ *etc*. **made ~ of** feito de *or* em. **take ~ of** tirar de. **5 ~ of 6** 5 (de) entre 6. **~ of date** fora de moda; (*not valid*) fora do prazo. **~ of doors** ao ar livre. **~ of one's mind** doido. **~ of order** quebrado. **~ of place** deslocado. **~ of the way** afastado. **~-patient** *n* doente *mf* de consulta externa

outboard /'aʊtbɔːd/ *a* **~ motor** motor *m* de popa

outbreak /'aʊtbreɪk/ *n* (*of flu etc*) surto *m*, epidemia *f*; (*of war*) deflagração *f*

outburst /'aʊtbɜːst/ *n* explosão *f*

outcast /'aʊtkɑːst/ *n* pária *m*

outcome /'aʊtkʌm/ *n* resultado *m*

outcry /'aʊtkraɪ/ *n* clamor *m*; (*protest*) protesto *m*

outdated /aʊt'deɪtɪd/ *a* fora da moda, ultrapassado

outdo /aʊt'duː/ *vt* (*pt* **-did**, *pp* **-done**) ultrapassar, superar

outdoor /'aʊtdɔː(r)/ *a* ao ar livre. **~s** /-'dɔːz/ *adv* fora de casa, ao ar livre

outer /'aʊtə(r)/ *a* exterior. **~ space** espaço (cósmico) *m*

outfit /'aʊtfɪt/ *n* equipamento *m*; (*clothes*) roupa *f*

outgoing /'aʊtgəʊɪŋ/ *a* que vai sair; (*of minister etc*) demissionário; (*fig*) sociável. **~s** *npl* despesas *fpl*

outgrow /aʊt'grəʊ/ *vt* (*pt* **-grew**, *pp* **-grown**) crescer mais do que; (*clothes*) já não caber em

outhouse /'aʊthaʊs/ *n* anexo *m*, dependência *f*

outing /'aʊtɪŋ/ *n* saída *f*, passeio *m*

outlandish /aʊt'lændɪʃ/ *a* exótico, estranho

outlaw /'aʊtlɔː/ *n* fora-da-lei *mf*, bandido *m* ▫ *vt* banir, proscrever

outlay /'aʊtleɪ/ *n* despesa(s) *f*(*pl*)

outlet /'aʊtlet/ *n* saída *f*, escoadouro *m*; (*for goods*) mercado *m*, saída *f*; (*for feelings*) escape *m*, vazão *m*; (*electr*) tomada *f*

outline /'aʊtlaɪn/ *n* contorno *m*; (*summary*) plano *m* geral, esquema *m*, esboço *m* ▫ *vt* contornar; (*summarize*) descrever em linhas gerais

outlive /aʊt'lɪv/ *vt* sobreviver a

outlook /'aʊtlʊk/ *n* (*view*) vista *f*; (*mental attitude*) visão *f*; (*future prospects*) perspectiva(s) *f*(*pl*)

outlying /'aʊtlaɪɪŋ/ *a* afastado, remoto

outnumber /aʊt'nʌmbə(r)/ *vt* ultrapassar em número

outpost /'aʊtpəʊst/ *n* posto *m* avançado

output /'aʊtpʊt/ *n* rendimento *m*; (*of computer*) saída *f*, output *m*

outrage /'aʊtreɪdʒ/ *n* atrocidade *f*, crime *m*; (*scandal*) escândalo *m* ▫ *vt* ultrajar

outrageous /aʊt'reɪdʒəs/ *a* (*shocking*) escandaloso; (*very cruel*) atroz

outright /'aʊtraɪt/ *adv* completamente; (*at once*) imediatamente; (*frankly*) abertamente ▫ *a* completo; (*refusal*) claro

outset /'aʊtset/ *n* início *m*, começo *m*, princípio *m*

outside¹ /aʊt'saɪd/ *n* exterior *m* ▫ *adv* (lá) (por) fora ▫ *prep* (para) fora de, além de; (*in front of*) diante de. **at the ~** no máximo

outside² /'aʊtsaɪd/ *a* exterior

outsider /aʊt'saɪdə(r)/ *n* estranho *m*; (*in race*) cavalo *m* com poucas probabilidades, azarão *m*

outsize /'aʊtsaɪz/ *a* tamanho extra *invar*

outskirts /'aʊtskɜːts/ *npl* arredores *mpl*, subúrbios *mpl*

outspoken /aʊt'spəʊkn/ *a* franco

outstanding /aʊt'stændɪŋ/ *a* saliente, proeminente; (*debt*) por saldar; (*very good*) notável, destacado

outstretched /aʊt'stretʃt/ *a* (*arm*) estendido, esticado

outstrip /aʊt'strɪp/ *vt* (*pt* **-stripped**) ultrapassar, passar à frente de

outward /'aʊtwəd/ *a* para o exterior; (*sign etc*) exterior; (*journey*) de ida. **~ly** *adv* exteriormente. **~s** *adv* para o exterior

outwit /aʊt'wɪt/ *vt* (*pt* **-witted**) ser mais esperto que, enganar

oval /'əʊvl/ *n & a* oval (*m*)

ovary /'əʊvərɪ/ *n* ovário *m*

ovation /əʊ'veɪʃn/ *n* ovação *f*

oven /'ʌvn/ *n* forno *m*

over /'əʊvə(r)/ *prep* sobre, acima de, por cima de; (*across*) de para o/do outro lado de; (*during*) durante, em; (*more than*) mais de ▫ *adv* por cima; (*too*)

O

demais, demasiadamente; (*ended*)
acabado. **the film is** ~ o filme já
acabou. **jump**/*etc* ~ saltar/*etc* por
cima. **he has some** ~ ele tem uns de
sobra. **all** ~ **the country** em/por todo
o país. **all** ~ **the table** por toda a mesa.
~ **and above** (*besides, in addition to*)
(para) além de. ~ **and** ~ repetidas
vezes. ~ **there** ali, lá, acolá

over- /ˈəʊvə(r)/ *pref* sobre-, super-;
(*excessively*) demais, demasiado

overall[1] /ˈəʊvərɔːl/ *n* bata *f*. ~**s** macacão
m, (*P*) fato-macaco *m*

overall[2] /ˌəʊvərˈɔːl/ *a* global; (*length etc*)
total □ *adv* globalmente

overawe /əʊvərˈɔː/ *vt* intimidar

overbalance /əʊvəˈbæləns/ *vt/i* (fazer)
perder o equilíbrio

overbearing /əʊvəˈbeərɪŋ/ *a* autoritário,
despótico; (*arrogant*) arrogante

overboard /ˈəʊvəbɔːd/ *adv* (pela) borda
fora

overcast /əʊvəˈkɑːst/ *a* encoberto,
nublado

overcharge /əʊvəˈtʃɑːdʒ/ *vt* ~ **sb (for)**
cobrar demais a alg (por)

overcoat /ˈəʊvəkəʊt/ *n* casacão *m*; (*for
men*) sobretudo *m*

overcome /əʊvəˈkʌm/ *vt* (*pt* **-came**, *pp*
-come) superar, vencer. ~ **by**
sucumbindo a, dominado *or* vencido
por

overcrowded /əʊvəˈkraʊdɪd/ *a*
apinhado, superlotado; (*country*)
superpovoado

overdo /əʊvəˈduː/ *vt* (*pt* **-did**, *pp* **-done**)
exagerar, levar longe demais. ~**ne**
(*culin*) cozinhado demais

overdose /ˈəʊvədəʊs/ *n* dose *f* excessiva

overdraft /ˈəʊvədrɑːft/ *n* saldo *m*
negativo

overdraw /əʊvəˈdrɔː/ *vt* (*pt* **-drew**,
pp **-drawn**) sacar a descoberto

overdue /əʊvəˈdjuː/ *a* em atraso,
atrasado; (*belated*) tardio

overestimate /əʊvərˈestɪmeɪt/ *vt*
sobreestimar, atribuir valor
excessivo a

overexpose /əʊvərɪkˈspəʊz/ *vt* expor
demais

overflow[1] /əʊvəˈfləʊ/ *vt/i* extravasar,
transbordar (**with** de)

overflow[2] /ˈəʊvəfləʊ/ *n* (*outlet*) descarga
f; (*excess*) excesso *m*

overgrown /əʊvəˈɡrəʊn/ *a* que cresceu
demais; (*garden etc*) invadido pela
vegetação

overhang /əʊvəˈhæŋ/ *vt* (*pt* **-hung**) estar
sobranceiro a, pairar sobre □ *vi*
projetar-se, (*P*) projectar-se para fora
□ *n* saliência *f*

overhaul[1] /əʊvəˈhɔːl/ *vt* fazer uma
revisão em

overhaul[2] /ˈəʊvəhɔːl/ *n* revisão *f*

overhead[1] /əʊvəˈhed/ *adv* em *or* por
cima, ao *or* no alto

overhead[2] /ˈəʊvəhed/ *a* aéreo. ~**s** *npl*
despesas *fpl* gerais

overhear /əʊvəˈhɪə(r)/ *vt* (*pt* **-heard**)
(*eavesdrop*) ouvir sem conhecimento
do falante; (*hear by chance*) ouvir por
acaso

overjoyed /əʊvəˈdʒɔɪd/ *a* radiante,
felicíssimo

overlap /əʊvəˈlæp/ *vt/i* (*pt* **-lapped**)
sobrepor(-se) parcialmente; (*fig*)
coincidir

overleaf /əʊvəˈliːf/ *adv* no verso

overload /əʊvəˈləʊd/ *vt* sobrecarregar

overlook /əʊvəˈlʊk/ *vt* deixar passar; (*of
window*) dar para; (*of building*)
dominar

overnight /əʊvəˈnaɪt/ *adv* durante a
noite; (*fig*) dum dia para o outro □ *a*
(*train*) da noite; (*stay, journey, etc*) noite,
noturno; (*fig*) súbito

overpass /əʊvəˈpɑːs/ *n* passagem *f*
superior

overpay /əʊvəˈpeɪ/ *vt* (*pt* **-paid**) pagar em
excesso

overpower /əʊvəˈpaʊə(r)/ *vt* dominar,
subjugar; (*fig*) esmagar. ~**ing** *a*
esmagador; (*heat*) sufocante,
insuportável

overpriced /əʊvəˈpraɪst/ *a* muito caro

overrate /əʊvəˈreɪt/ *vt* sobreestimar,
exagerar o valor de

overrid|e /əʊvəˈraɪd/ *vt* (*pt* **-rode**, *pp*
-ridden) prevalecer sobre, passar por
cima de. ~**ing** *a* primordial,
preponderante; (*importance*) maior

overripe /ˈəʊvəraɪp/ *a* demasiado
maduro

overrule /əʊvəˈruːl/ *vt* anular, rejeitar;
(*claim*) indeferir

overrun /əʊvəˈrʌn/ *vt* (*pt* **-ran**, *pp* **-run**,
pres p **-running**) invadir; (*a limit*)
exceder, ultrapassar

overseas /əʊvəˈsiːz/ *a* ultramarino;
(*abroad*) estrangeiro □ *adv* no
ultramar, no estrangeiro

oversee /əʊvəˈsiː/ *vt* (*pt* **-saw** *pp* **-seen**)
supervisionar. ~**r** /ˈəʊvəsɪə(r)/ *n*
capataz *m*

overshadow /əʊvəˈʃædəʊ/ *vt* (*fig*)
eclipsar, ofuscar

oversight /ˈəʊvəsaɪt/ *n* lapso *m*

oversleep /əʊvəˈsliːp/ *vi* (*pt* **-slept**)
acordar tarde, dormir demais

overt /ˈəʊvɜːt/ *a* manifesto, claro, patente

overtake /əʊvəˈteɪk/ *vt/i* (*pt* **-took**, *pp*
-taken) ultrapassar

331 | overthrow | palace

overthrow /əʊvəˈθrəʊ/ vt (pt -threw, pp -thrown) derrubar □ n /ˈəʊvəθrəʊ/ (pol) derrubada f

overtime /ˈəʊvətaɪm/ n horas fpl extras

overtones /ˈəʊvətəʊnz/ npl (fig) tom m, implicação f

overture /ˈəʊvətjʊə(r)/ n (mus) abertura f; (fig) proposta f, abordagem f

overturn /əʊvəˈtɜːn/ vt/i virar (-se); (car, plane) capotar, virar-se

overweight /əʊvəˈweɪt/ a be ~ ter excesso de peso

overwhelm /əʊvəˈwelm/ vt oprimir; (defeat) esmagar; (amaze) assoberbar. ~ing a esmagador; (urge) irresistível

overwork /əʊvəˈwɜːk/ vt/i sobrecarregar(-se) com trabalho □ n excesso m de trabalho

overwrought /əʊvəˈrɔːt/ a muito agitado, superexcitado

ow|e /əʊ/ vt dever. ~ing a devido. ~ing to devido a

owl /aʊl/ n coruja f

own[1] /əʊn/ a próprio. a house/etc of one's ~ uma casa/etc própria. get one's ~ back (colloq) ir à forra, (P) desforrar-se. hold one's ~ agüentar-se, (P) aguentar-se. on one's ~ sozinho

own[2] /əʊn/ vt possuir. ~ up (to) (colloq) confessar. ~er n proprietário m, dono m. ~ership n posse f, propriedade f

ox /ɒks/ n (pl oxen) boi m

oxygen /ˈɒksɪdʒən/ n oxigênio m, (P) oxigénio m

oyster /ˈɔɪstə(r)/ n ostra f

ozone /ˈəʊzəʊn/ n ozônio m, (P) ozono m. ~ layer camada f de ozônio, (P) ozono m

Pp

pace /peɪs/ n passo m; (fig) ritmo m □ vt percorrer passo a passo □ vi ~ up and down andar de um lado para o outro. keep ~ with acompanhar, manter-se a par de

pacemaker /ˈpeɪsmeɪkə(r)/ n (med) marcapasso m, (P) pacemaker m

Pacific /pəˈsɪfɪk/ a pacífico □ n ~ (Ocean) (Oceano) Pacífico m

pacifist /ˈpæsɪfɪst/ n pacifista mf

pacify /ˈpæsɪfaɪ/ vt pacificar, apaziguar

pack /pæk/ n pacote m; (mil) mochila f; (of hounds) matilha f; (of lies) porção f; (of cards) baralho m □ vt empacotar; (suitcase) fazer; (box, room) encher;

(press down) atulhar, encher até não caber mais □ vi fazer as malas. ~ into (cram) apinhar em, comprimir em. send ~ing pôr a andar, mandar passear. ~ed a apinhado. ~ed lunch merenda f

package /ˈpækɪdʒ/ n pacote m, embrulho m □ vt embalar. ~ deal pacote m de propostas. ~ holiday pacote m turístico, (P) viagem f organizada

packet /ˈpækɪt/ n pacote m; (of cigarettes) maço m

pact /pækt/ n pacto m

pad /pæd/ n (in clothing) chumaço m; (for writing) bloco m de papel/de notas; (for ink) almofada (de carimbo) f. (launching) ~ rampa f de lançamento □ vt (pt padded) enchumaçar, acolchoar; (fig: essay etc) encher linguiça. ~ding n chumaço m; (fig) linguiça f

paddle[1] /ˈpædl/ n remo m de canoa. ~-steamer n vapor m movido a rodas

paddl|e[2] /ˈpædl/ vi chapinhar, molhar os pés. ~ing pool piscina f de plástico para crianças

paddock /ˈpædək/ n cercado m; (at racecourse) paddock m

padlock /ˈpædlɒk/ n cadeado m □ vt fechar com cadeado

paediatrician /piːdɪəˈtrɪʃn/ n pediatra mf

pagan /ˈpeɪɡən/ a & n pagão (m), pagã (f)

page[1] /peɪdʒ/ n (of book etc) página f

page[2] /peɪdʒ/ vt mandar chamar

pageant /ˈpædʒənt/ n espetáculo m, (P) espectáculo m (histórico); (procession) cortejo m. ~ry n pompa f

pagoda /pəˈɡəʊdə/ n pagode m

paid /peɪd/ see pay □ a put ~ to (colloq: end) pôr fim a

pail /peɪl/ n balde m

pain /peɪn/ n dor f. ~s esforços mpl □ vt magoar. be in ~ sofrer, ter dores. ~-killer n analgésico m. take ~s to esforçar-se por. ~ful a doloroso; (grievous, laborious) penoso. ~less a sem dor, indolor

painstaking /ˈpeɪnzteɪkɪŋ/ a cuidadoso, esmerado, meticuloso

paint /peɪnt/ n tinta f. ~s (in box) tintas fpl □ vt/i pintar. ~er n pintor m. ~ing n pintura f

paintbrush /ˈpeɪntbrʌʃ/ n pincel m

pair /peə(r)/ n par m. a ~ of scissors uma tesoura. a ~ of trousers um par de calças. in ~s aos pares □ vi ~ off formar pares

Pakistan /pɑːkɪˈstɑːn/ n Paquistão m. ~i a & n paquistanês (m)

pal /pæl/ n (colloq) colega mf, amigo m

palace /ˈpælɪs/ n palácio m

palat|e /ˈpælət/ n palato m. ~**able** a saboroso, gostoso; (fig) agradável

palatial /pəˈleɪʃl/ a suntuoso, (P) sumptuoso

pale /peɪl/ a (-er, -est) pálido; (colour) claro □ vi empalidecer. ~**ness** n palidez f

Palestin|e /ˈpælɪstaɪn/ n Palestina f. ~**ian** /-ˈstɪnɪən/ a & n palestino (m)

palette /ˈpælɪt/ n paleta f. ~-**knife** n espátula f

pall /pɔːl/ vi tornar-se enfadonho, perder o interesse (**on** para)

pallid /ˈpælɪd/ a pálido

palm /paːm/ n (of hand) palma f; (tree) palmeira f □ vt ~ **off** impingir (**on** a). **P~ Sunday** Domingo m de Ramos

palpable /ˈpælpəbl/ a palpável

palpitat|e /ˈpælpɪteɪt/ vi palpitar. ~**ion** /-ˈteɪʃn/ n palpitação f

paltry /ˈpɔːltrɪ/ a (-ier, -iest) irrisório

pamper /ˈpæmpə(r)/ vt mimar, paparicar

pamphlet /ˈpæmflɪt/ n panfleto m, folheto m

pan /pæn/ n panela f; (for frying) frigideira f □ vt (pt panned) (colloq) criticar severamente

panacea /pænəˈsɪə/ n panacéia f

panache /pæˈnæʃ/ n brio m, estilo m, panache m

pancake /ˈpænkeɪk/ n crepe m, panqueca f

pancreas /ˈpæŋkrɪəs/ n pâncreas m

panda /ˈpændə/ n panda m

pandemonium /pændɪˈməʊnɪəm/ n pandemônio m, (P) pandemónio m, caos m

pander /ˈpændə(r)/ vi ~ **to** prestar-se a servir, ir ao encontro de, fazer concessões a

pane /peɪn/ n vidraça f

panel /ˈpænl/ n painel m; (jury) júri m; (speakers) convidados mpl. (**instrument**) ~ painel m de instrumentos, (P) de bordo. ~**led** a apainelado. ~**ling** n apainelamento m. ~**list** n convidado m

pang /pæŋ/ n pontada f, dor f aguda e súbita. ~**s** (of hunger) ataques mpl de fome. ~**s of conscience** remorsos mpl

panic /ˈpænɪk/ n pânico m □ vt/i (pt panicked) desorientar(-se), (fazer) entrar em pânico. ~-**stricken** a tomado de pânico

panoram|a /pænəˈraːmə/ n panorama m. ~**ic** /-ˈræmɪk/ a panorâmico

pansy /ˈpænzɪ/ n amor-perfeito m

pant /pænt/ vi ofegar, arquejar

panther /ˈpænθə(r)/ n pantera f

panties /ˈpæntɪz/ npl (colloq) calcinhas fpl

pantomime /ˈpæntəmaɪm/ n pantomima f

pantry /ˈpæntrɪ/ n despensa f

pants /pænts/ npl (colloq: underwear) cuecas fpl; (colloq: trousers) calças fpl

papal /ˈpeɪpl/ a papal

paper /ˈpeɪpə(r)/ n papel m; (newspaper) jornal m; (exam) prova f escrita; (essay) comunicação f. ~**s** npl (for identification) documentos mpl □ vt forrar com papel. **on** ~ por escrito. ~-**clip** n clipe m

paperback /ˈpeɪpəbæk/ a & n ~ (book) livro m de capa mole

paperweight /ˈpeɪpəweɪt/ n pesa-papéis m invar, (P) pisa-papéis m invar

paperwork /ˈpeɪpəwɜːk/ n trabalho m de secretária; (pej) papelada f

paprika /ˈpæprɪkə/ n páprica f

par /paː(r)/ n **be below** ~ estar abaixo do padrão desejado. **on a** ~ **with** em igualdade com

parable /ˈpærəbl/ n parábola f

parachut|e /ˈpærəʃuːt/ n pára-quedas m invar □ vi descer de pára-quedas. ~**ist** n pára-quedista mf

parade /pəˈreɪd/ n (mil) parada f militar; (procession) procissão f □ vi desfilar □ vt alardear

paradise /ˈpærədaɪs/ n paraíso m

paradox /ˈpærədɒks/ n paradoxo m. ~**ical** /-ˈdɒksɪkl/ a paradoxal

paraffin /ˈpærəfɪn/ n querosene m, (P) petróleo m

paragon /ˈpærəgən/ n modelo m de perfeição

paragraph /ˈpærəgraːf/ n parágrafo m

parallel /ˈpærəlel/ a & n paralelo (m) □ vt (pt parelleled) comparar(-se) a

paralyse /ˈpærəlaɪz/ vt paralisar

paraly|sis /pəˈræləsɪs/ n paralisia f. ~**tic** /-ˈlɪtɪk/ a & n paralítico (m)

paramedic /pærəˈmedɪk/ n paramédico m

parameter /pəˈræmɪtə(r)/ n parâmetro m

paramount /ˈpærəmaʊnt/ a supremo, primordial

parapet /ˈpærəpɪt/ n parapeito m

paraphernalia /pærəfəˈneɪlɪə/ n equipamento m, tralha f (colloq)

paraphrase /ˈpærəfreɪz/ n paráfrase f □ vt parafrasear

paraplegic /pærəˈpliːdʒɪk/ n paraplégico m

parasite /ˈpærəsaɪt/ n parasita mf

parasol /ˈpærəsɒl/ n sombrinha f; (on table) pára-sol m, guarda-sol m

parcel /ˈpaːsl/ n embrulho m; (for post) encomenda f

parch /paːtʃ/ vt ressecar. **be** ~**ed** estar com muita sede

parchment /'pɑːtʃmənt/ n pergaminho m

pardon /'pɑːdn/ n perdão m; (jur) perdão m, indulto m □ vt (pt **pardoned**) perdoar. **I beg your** ~ perdão, desculpe. **(I beg your)** ~? como?

pare /peə(r)/ vt aparar, cortar; (peel) descascar

parent /'peərənt/ n pai m, mãe f. ~s npl pais mpl. ~**al** /pə'rentl/ a dos pais, paterno, materno

parenthesis /pə'renθəsɪs/ n (pl -**theses** /-siːz/ parêntese m, parêntesis m

Paris /'pærɪs/ n Paris m

parish /'pærɪʃ/ n paróquia f; (municipal) freguesia f. ~**ioner** /pə'rɪʃənə(r)/ n paroquiano m

parity /'pærətɪ/ n paridade f

park /pɑːk/ n parque m □ vt estacionar. ~**ing** n estacionamento m. **no** ~**ing** estacionamento proibido. ~**ing-meter** n parquímetro m

parliament /'pɑːləmənt/ n parlamento m, assembléia f. ~**ary** /-'mentrɪ/ a parlamentar

parochial /pə'rəʊkɪəl/ a paroquial; (fig) provinciano, tacanho

parody /'pærədɪ/ n paródia f □ vt parodiar

parole /pə'rəʊl/ n **on** ~ em liberdade condicional □ vt pôr em liberdade condicional

parquet /'pɑːkeɪ/ n parquê m, parquete m

parrot /'pærət/ n papagaio m

parry /'pærɪ/ vt (a)parar □ n parada f

parsimonious /pɑːsɪ'məʊnɪəs/ a parco; (mean) avarento

parsley /'pɑːslɪ/ n salsa f

parsnip /'pɑːsnɪp/ n cherovia f, pastinaga f

parson /'pɑːsn/ n pároco m, pastor m

part /pɑːt/ n parte f; (of serial) episódio m; (of machine) peça f; (theatre) papel m; (side in dispute) partido m □ a parcial □ adv em parte □ vt/i separar (-se) (**from** de). **in** ~ em parte. **on the** ~ **of** da parte de. ~-**exchange** n troca f parcial. ~ **of speech** categoria f gramatical. ~-**time** a & adv a tempo parcial, part-time. **take** ~ **in** tomar parte em. **these** ~s estas partes

partial /'pɑːʃl/ a (incomplete, biased) parcial. **be** ~ **to** gostar de. ~**ity** /-ɪ'ælətɪ/ n parcialidade f; (liking) predileção f, (P) predilecção f (**for** por). ~**ly** adv parcialmente

particip|ate /pɑː'tɪsɪpeɪt/ vi participar (**in** em). ~**ant** n /-ənt/ participante mf. ~**ation** /-'peɪʃn/ n participação f

participle /'pɑːtɪsɪpl/ n particípio m

particle /'pɑːtɪkl/ n partícula f; (of dust) grão m; (fig) mínimo m

particular /pə'tɪkjʊlə(r)/ a especial, particular; (fussy) exigente; (careful) escrupuloso. ~**s** npl pormenores mpl. **in** ~ adv em especial, particularmente. ~**ly** adv particularmente

parting /'pɑːtɪŋ/ n separação f; (in hair) risca f □ a de despedida

partisan /pɑːtɪ'zæn/ n partidário m; (mil) guerrilheiro m

partition /pɑː'tɪʃn/ n (of room) tabique m, divisória f; (pol: division) partilha f, divisão f □ vt dividir, repartir. ~ **off** dividir por meio de tabique

partly /'pɑːtlɪ/ adv em parte

partner /'pɑːtnə(r)/ n sócio m; (cards, sport) parceiro m; (dancing) par m. ~**ship** n associação f; (comm) sociedade f

partridge /'pɑːtrɪdʒ/ n perdiz f

party /'pɑːtɪ/ n festa f, reunião f; (group) grupo m; (pol) partido m; (jur) parte f. ~ **line** (telephone) linha f coletiva, (P) colectiva

pass /pɑːs/ vt/i (pt **passed**) passar; (overtake) ultrapassar; (exam) passar; (approve) passar; (law) aprovar. ~ **(by)** passar por □ n (permit, sport) passe m; (geog) desfiladeiro m, garganta f; (in exam) aprovação f. **make a** ~ **at** (colloq) atirar-se para (colloq). ~ **away** falecer. ~ **out** or **round** distribuir. ~ **out** (colloq: faint) perder os sentidos, desmaiar. ~ **over** (disregard, overlook) passar por cima de. ~ **up** (colloq: forgo) deixar perder

passable /'pɑːsəbl/ a passável; (road) transitável

passage /'pæsɪdʒ/ n passagem f; (voyage) travessia f; (corridor) corredor m, passagem f

passenger /'pæsɪndʒə(r)/ n passageiro m

passer-by /pɑːsə'baɪ/ n (pl **passers-by**) transeunte mf

passion /'pæʃn/ n paixão f. ~**ate** a apaixonado, exaltado

passive /'pæsɪv/ a passivo. ~**ness** n passividade f

Passover /'pɑːsəʊvə(r)/ n Páscoa f dos judeus

passport /'pɑːspɔːt/ n passaporte m

password /'pɑːswɜːd/ n senha f

past /pɑːst/ a passado; (former) antigo □ n passado □ prep para além de; (in time) mais de; (in front of) diante de □ adv em frente. **be** ~ **it** já não ser capaz. **it's five** ~ **eleven** são onze e cinco. **these** ~ **months** estes últimos meses

pasta /'pæstə/ n prato m de massa(s)

paste /peɪst/ n cola f; (culin) massa(s) f (pl); (dough) massa f; (jewellery) strass m □ vt colar

p

pastel /'pæstl/ *n* pastel *m* □ *a* pastel *invar*

pasteurize /'pæstʃəraɪz/ *vt* pasteurizar

pastille /'pæstl/ *n* pastilha *f*

pastime /'pɑːstaɪm/ *n* passatempo *m*

pastoral /'pɑːstərəl/ *a & n* pastoral (*f*)

pastry /'peɪstrɪ/ *n* massa *f* (de pastelaria); (*tart*) pastel *m*

pasture /'pɑːstʃə(r)/ *n* pastagem *f*

pasty[1] /'pæstɪ/ *n* empadinha *f*

pasty[2] /'peɪstɪ/ *a* pastoso

pat /pæt/ *vt* (*pt* **patted**) (*hit gently*) dar pancadinhas em; (*caress*) fazer festinhas a □ *n* pancadinha *f*; (*caress*) festinha *f* □ *adv* a propósito; (*readily*) prontamente □ *a* preparado, pronto

patch /pætʃ/ *n* remendo *m*; (*over eye*) tapa-ôlho *m*; (*spot*) mancha *f*; (*small area*) pedaço *m*; (*of vegetables*) canteiro *m*, (P) leira *f* □ *vt* ~ **up** remendar. ~ **up a quarrel** fazer as pazes. **bad** ~ mau bocado *m*. **not be a** ~ **on** não chegar aos pés de. ~-**work** *n* obra *f* de retalhos. ~**y** *a* desigual

pâté /'pæteɪ/ *n* patê *m*

patent /'peɪtnt/ *a & n* patente (*f*) □ *vt* patentear. ~ **leather** verniz *m*, polimento *m*. ~**ly** *adv* claramente

paternal /pə'tɜːnl/ *a* paternal; (*relative*) paterno

paternity /pə'tɜːnətɪ/ *n* paternidade *f*

path /pɑːθ/ *n* (*pl* -s /pɑːðz/) caminho *m*, trilha *f*; (*in park*) aléia *f*; (*of rocket*) trajetória *f*, (P) trajectória *f*

pathetic /pə'θetɪk/ *a* patético; (*colloq: contemptible*) desgraçado (*colloq*)

patholog|**y** /pə'θɒlədʒɪ/ *n* patologia *f*. ~**ist** *n* patologista *mf*

pathos /'peɪθɒs/ *n* patos *m*, patético *m*

patience /'peɪʃns/ *n* paciência *f*

patient /'peɪʃnt/ *a* paciente □ *n* doente *mf*, paciente *mf*. ~**ly** *adv* pacientemente

patio /'pætɪəʊ/ *n* (*pl* -os) pátio *m*

patriot /'pætrɪət/ *n* patriota *mf*. ~**ic** /-'ɒtɪk/ *a* patriótico. ~**ism** /-ɪzəm/ *n* patriotismo *m*

patrol /pə'trəʊl/ *n* patrulha *f* □ *vt/i* patrulhar. ~ **car** carro *m* de patrulha

patron /'peɪtrən/ *n* (*of the arts etc*) patrocinador *m*, protetor *m*, (P) protector *m*; (*of charity*) benfeitor *m*; (*customer*) freguês *m*, cliente *mf*. ~ **saint** padroeiro *m*, patrono *m*

patron|**age** /'pætrənɪdʒ/ *n* freguesia *f*, clientela *f*; (*support*) patrocínio *m*. ~**ize** *vt* ser cliente de; (*support*) patrocinar; (*condescend*) tratar com ares de superioridade

patter[1] /'pætə(r)/ *n* (*of rain*) tamborilar *m*, rufo *m*. ~ **of steps** som *m* leve de passos miúdos, corridinha *f* leve

patter[2] /'pætə(r)/ *n* (*of class, profession*) gíria *f*, jargão *m*; (*chatter*) conversa *f* fiada

pattern /'pætn/ *n* padrão *m*; (*for sewing*) molde *m*; (*example*) modelo *m*

paunch /pɔːntʃ/ *n* pança *f*

pause /pɔːz/ *n* pausa *f* □ *vi* pausar, fazer (uma) pausa

pav|**e** /peɪv/ *vt* pavimentar. ~**e the way** preparar o caminho (**for** para). ~**ing-stone** *n* paralelepípedo *m*, laje *f*

pavement /'peɪvmənt/ *n* passeio *m*

pavilion /pə'vɪlɪən/ *n* pavilhão *m*

paw /pɔː/ *n* pata *f* □ *vt* dar patadas em; (*horse*) escarvar; (*colloq: person*) pôr as patas em cima de

pawn[1] /pɔːn/ *n* (*chess*) peão *m*; (*fig*) joguete *m*

pawn[2] /pɔːn/ *vt* empenhar. ~-**shop** casa *f* de penhores, prego *m* (*colloq*)

pawnbroker /'pɔːnbrəʊkə(r)/ *n* penhorista *mf*, dono *m* de casa de penhores, agiota *mf*

pay /peɪ/ *vt/i* (*pt* **paid**) pagar; (*interest*) render; (*visit, compliment*) fazer □ *n* pagamento *m*; (*wages*) vencimento *m*, ordenado *m*, salário *m*. **in the** ~ **of** em pagamento de. ~ **attention** prestar atenção. ~ **back** restituir. ~ **for** pagar. ~ **homage** prestar homenagem. ~ **in** depositar. ~-**slip** *n* contracheque *m*, (P) folha *f* de pagamento

payable /'peɪəbl/ *a* pagável

payment /'peɪmənt/ *n* pagamento *m*; (*fig: reward*) recompensa *f*

payroll /'peɪrəʊl/ *n* folha *f* de pagamentos. **be on the** ~ fazer parte da folha de pagamento de uma firma

pea /piː/ *n* ervilha *f*

peace /piːs/ *n* paz *f*. **disturb the** ~ perturbar a ordem pública. ~**able** *a* pacífico

peaceful /'piːsfl/ *a* pacífico; (*calm*) calmo, sereno

peacemaker /'piːsmeɪkə(r)/ *n* mediador *m*, pacificador *m*

peach /piːtʃ/ *n* pêssego *m*

peacock /'piːkɒk/ *n* pavão *m*

peak /piːk/ *n* pico *m*, cume *m*, cimo *m*; (*of cap*) pala *f*; (*maximum*) máximo *m*. ~ **hours** horas *fpl* de ponta; (*electr*) horas *fpl* de carga máxima. ~**ed cap** boné *m* de pala

peaky /'piːkɪ/ *a* com ar doentio

peal /piːl/ *n* (*of bells*) repique *m*; (*of laughter*) gargalhada *f*, risada *f*

peanut /'piːnʌt/ *n* amendoim *m*. ~**s** (*sl: small sum*) uma bagatela *f*

pear /peə(r)/ *n* pera *f*

pearl /pɜːl/ *n* pérola *f*. ~**y** *a* nacarado

peasant /'peznt/ *n* camponês *m*, aldeão *m*

peat /piːt/ n turfa f

pebble /'pebl/ n seixo m, calhau m

peck /pek/ vt/i bicar; (attack) dar bicadas (em) ▫ n bicada f; (colloq: kiss) beijo m seco. ~**ing order** hierarquia f, ordem f de importância

peckish /'pekɪʃ/ a be ~ (colloq) ter vontade de comer

peculiar /pɪ'kjuːlɪə(r)/ a bizarro, singular; (special) peculiar (**to** a), característico (**to** de). ~**ity** /-'ærətɪ/ n singularidade f; (feature) peculiaridade f

pedal /'pedl/ n pedal m ▫ vi (pt **pedalled**) pedalar

pedantic /pɪ'dæntɪk/ a pedante

peddle /'pedl/ vt vender de porta em porta; (drugs) fazer tráfico de

pedestal /'pedɪstl/ n pedestal m

pedestrian /pɪ'destrɪən/ n pedestre mf, (P) peão m ▫ a pedestre; (fig) prosaico. ~ **crossing** faixa f para pedestres, (P) passadeira f

pedigree /'pedɪɡriː/ n estirpe f, linhagem f; (of animal) raça f ▫ a de raça

pedlar /'pedlə(r)/ n vendedor m ambulante

peek /piːk/ vi espreitar ▫ n espreitadela f

peel /piːl/ n casca f ▫ vt descascar ▫ vi (skin) pelar; (paint) escamar-se, descascar; (wallpaper) descolar-se. ~**ings** npl cascas fpl

peep /piːp/ vi espreitar ▫ n espreitadela f. ~**-hole** n vigia f; (in door) olho m mágico

peer[1] /pɪə(r)/ vi ~ **at/into** (searchingly) perscrutar; (with difficulty) esforçar-se por ver

peer[2] /pɪə(r)/ n (equal, noble) par m. ~**age** n pariato m

peeved /piːvd/ a (sl) irritado, chateado (sl)

peevish /'piːvɪʃ/ a irritável

peg /peɡ/ n cavilha f; (for washing) pregador m de roupa, (P) mola f; (for coats etc) cabide m; (for tent) estaca f ▫ vt (pt **pegged**) prender com estacas. **off the** ~ prêt-à-porter

pejorative /pɪ'dʒɒrətɪv/ a pejorativo

pelican /'pelɪkən/ n pelicano m. ~ **crossing** passagem f com sinais manobrados pelos pedestres

pellet /'pelɪt/ n bolinha f; (for gun) grão m de chumbo

pelt[1] /pelt/ n pele f

pelt[2] /pelt/ vt bombardear (**with** com) ▫ vi chover a cântaros; (run fast) correr em disparada

pelvis /'pelvɪs/ n (anat) pélvis m, bacia f

pen[1] /pen/ n (enclosure) cercado m. **play-~** n cercado m, (P) pargue m ▫ vt (pt **penned**) encurralar

pen[2] /pen/ n caneta f ▫ vt (pt **penned**) escrever. ~**friend** n correspondente mf. ~**name** n pseudónimo m, (P) pseudónimo m

penal /'piːnl/ a penal. ~**ize** vt impôr uma penalidade a; (sport) penalizar

penalty /'penltɪ/ n pena f; (fine) multa f; (sport) penalidade f. ~ **kick** pênalti m, (P) grande penalidade f

penance /'penəns/ n penitência f

pence /pens/ see **penny**

pencil /'pensl/ n lápis m ▫ vt (pt **pencilled**) escrever or desenhar a lápis. ~**sharpener** n apontador m, (P) apara-lápis m invar

pendant /'pendənt/ n berloque m

pending /'pendɪŋ/ a pendente ▫ prep (during) durante; (until) até

pendulum /'pendjʊləm/ n pêndulo m

penetrat|e /'penɪtreɪt/ vt/i penetrar (em). ~**ing** a penetrante. ~**ion** /-'treɪʃn/ n penetração f

penguin /'peŋɡwɪn/ n pingüim m, (P) pinguim m

penicillin /penɪ'sɪlɪn/ n penicilina f

peninsula /pə'nɪnsjʊlə/ n península f

penis /'piːnɪs/ n pênis m, (P) pénis m

peniten|t /'penɪtənt/ a & n penitente (mf). ~**ce** n /-əns/ contrição f, penitência f

penitentiary /penɪ'tenʃərɪ/ n (Amer) penitenciária f, cadeia f

penknife /'pennaɪf/ n (pl -knives) canivete m

penniless /'penɪlɪs/ a sem vintém, sem um tostão

penny /'penɪ/ n (pl **pennies** or **pence**) pêni m, (P) péni m; (fig) centavo m, vintém m

pension /'penʃn/ n pensão f; (in retirement) aposentadoria f, (P) reforma f ▫ vt ~ **off** reformar, aposentar. ~**er** n (old-age) ~**er** reformado m

pensive /'pensɪv/ a pensativo

Pentecost /'pentɪkɒst/ n Pentecostes m

penthouse /'penthaʊs/ n cobertura f, (P) apartamento de luxo (no último andar)

pent-up /'pentʌp/ a reprimido

penultimate /pen'ʌltɪmət/ a penúltimo

people /'piːpl/ npl pessoas fpl ▫ n gente f, povo m ▫ vt povoar. **the Portuguese** ~ os portugueses mpl. ~ **say** dizem, diz-se

pep /pep/ n vigor m ▫ vt ~ **up** animar. ~ **talk** discurso m de encorajamento

pepper /'pepə(r)/ n pimenta f; (vegetable) pimentão m, (P) pimento m □ vt apimentar. ~y a apimentado, picante

peppermint /'pepəmɪnt/ n hortelã-pimenta f; (sweet) bala f, (P) pastilha f de hortelã-pimenta

per /pɜ:(r)/ prep por. ~ **annum** por ano. ~ **cent** por cento. ~ **kilo**/etc o quilo/etc

perceive /pə'si:v/ vt perceber; (notice) aperceber-se de

percentage /pə'sentɪdʒ/ n percentagem f

perceptible /pə'septəbl/ a perceptível

percept|ion /pə'sepʃn/ n percepção f. ~**ive** /-tɪv/ a perceptivo, penetrante, perspicaz

perch[1] /pɜ:tʃ/ n poleiro m □ vi empoleirar-se, pousar

perch[2] /pɜ:tʃ/ n (fish) perca f

percolat|e /'pɜ:kəleɪt/ vt/i filtrar (-se), passar. ~**or** n máquina f de café com filtro, cafeteira f

percussion /pə'kʌʃn/ n percussão f

peremptory /pə'remptərɪ/ a peremptório, decisivo

perennial /pə'renɪəl/ a perene; (plant) perene

perfect[1] /'pɜ:fɪkt/ a perfeito. ~**ly** adv perfeitamente

perfect[2] /pə'fekt/ vt aperfeiçoar. ~**ion** /-ʃn/ n perfeição f. ~**ionist** n perfeccionista m

perforat|e /'pɜ:fəreɪt/ vt perfurar. ~**ion** /-'reɪʃn/ n perfuração f; (line of holes) pontilhado m, picotado m

perform /pə'fɔ:m/ vt (a task; mus) executar; (a function; theat) desempenhar □ vi representar; (function) funcionar. ~**ance** n (of task; mus) execução f; (of function; theat) desempenho m; (of car) performance f, comportamento m, rendimento m; (colloq: fuss) drama m, cena f. ~**er** n artista mf

perfume /'pɜ:fju:m/ n perfume m

perfunctory /pə'fʌŋktərɪ/ a superficial, negligente

perhaps /pə'hæps/ adv talvez

peril /'perəl/ n perigo m. ~**ous** a perigoso

perimeter /pə'rɪmɪtə(r)/ n perímetro m

period /'pɪərɪəd/ n período m, época f; (era) época f; (lesson) hora f de aula, período m letivo, (P) lectivo; (med) período m; (full stop) ponto (final) m □ a (of novel) de costumes; (of furniture) de estilo. ~**ic** /-'ɒdɪk/ a periódico. ~**ical** /-'ɒdɪkl/ n periódico m. ~**ically** /-'ɒdɪklɪ/ adv periodicamente

peripher|y /pə'rɪfərɪ/ n periferia f. ~**al** a periférico; (fig) marginal, à margem

perish /'perɪʃ/ vi morrer, perecer; (rot) estragar-se, deteriorar-se. ~**able** a (of goods) deteriorável

perjur|e /'pɜ:dʒə(r)/ vpr ~**e o.s.** jurar falso, perjurar. ~**y** n perjúrio m

perk[1] /pɜ:k/ vt/i ~ **up** (colloq) arrebitar(-se). ~**y** a (colloq) vivo, animado

perk[2] /pɜ:k/ n (colloq) regalia f, extra m

perm /pɜ:m/ n permanente f □ vt **have one's hair** ~**ed** fazer uma permanente

permanen|t /'pɜ:mənənt/ a permanente. ~**ce** n permanência f. ~**tly** adv permanentemente, a título permanente

permeable /'pɜ:mɪəbl/ a permeável

permeate /'pɜ:mɪeɪt/ vt/i permear, penetrar

permissible /pə'mɪsəbl/ a permissível, admissível

permission /pə'mɪʃn/ n permissão f, licença f

permissive /pə'mɪsɪv/ a permissivo. ~ **society** sociedade f permissiva. ~**ness** n permissividade f

permit[1] /pə'mɪt/ vt (pt permitted) permitir, consentir (**sb to** a alguém que)

permit[2] /'pɜ:mɪt/ n licença f; (pass) passe m

permutation /pɜ:mju:'teɪʃn/ n permutação f

pernicious /pə'nɪʃəs/ a pernicioso, prejudicial

perpendicular /pɜ:pən'dɪkjʊlə(r)/ a & n perpendicular (f)

perpetrat|e /'pɜ:pɪtreɪt/ vt perpetrar. ~**or** n autor m

perpetual /pə'petʃʊəl/ a perpétuo

perpetuate /pə'petʃʊeɪt/ vt perpetuar

perplex /pə'pleks/ vt deixar perplexo. ~**ed** a perplexo. ~**ing** a confuso. ~**ity** n perplexidade f

persecut|e /'pɜ:sɪkju:t/ vt perseguir. ~**ion** n /-'kju:ʃn/ n perseguição f

persever|e /pɜ:sɪ'vɪə(r)/ vi perseverar. ~**ance** n perseverança f

Persian /'pɜ:ʃn/ a & n (lang) persa (m)

persist /pə'sɪst/ vi persistir (**in doing** em fazer). ~**ence** n persistência f. ~**ent** a persistente; (obstinate) teimoso; (continual) constante. ~**ently** adv persistentemente

person /'pɜ:sn/ n pessoa f. **in** ~ em pessoa

personal /'pɜ:sənl/ a pessoal; (secretary) particular. ~ **stereo** estereo m pessoal. ~**ly** adv pessoalmente

personality /pɜ:sə'nælətɪ/ n personalidade f; (on TV) vedete f

personify /pə'sɒnɪfaɪ/ vt personificar

personnel /pɜːsə'nel/ n pessoal m

perspective /pə'spektɪv/ n perspectiva f

perspir|e /pə'spaɪə(r)/ vi transpirar.
∼**ation** /-ə'reɪʃn/ n transpiração f

persua|de /pə'sweɪd/ vt persuadir (**to** a).
∼**sion** /-'sweɪʒn/ n persuasão f; (belief)
crença f, convicção f. ∼**sive** /-'sweɪsɪv/
a persuasivo

pert /pɜːt/ a (saucy) atrevido, descarado;
(lively) vivo

pertain /pə'teɪn/ vi ∼ **to** pertencer a; (be
relevant) ser pertinente a, (P) ser
próprio de

pertinent /'pɜːtɪmənt/ a pertinente

perturb /pə'tɜːb/ vt perturbar,
transtornar

Peru /pə'ruː/ n Peru m. ∼**vian** a & n
peruano (m), (P) peruviano (m)

peruse /pə'ruːz/ vt ler com atenção

perva|de /pə'veɪd/ vt espalhar-se por,
invadir. ∼**sive** a penetrante

pervers|e /pə'vɜːs/ a que insiste no erro;
(wicked) perverso; (wayward)
caprichoso. ∼**ity** n obstinação f;
(wickedness) perversidade f;
(waywardness) capricho m, birra f

perver|t[1] /pə'vɜːt/ vt perverter. ∼**sion** n
perversão f

pervert[2] /'pɜːvɜːt/ n pervertido m

peseta /pə'seɪtə/ n peseta f

pessimis|t /'pesɪmɪst/ n pessimista mf.
∼**m** /-zəm/ n pessimismo m. ∼**tic**
/-'mɪstɪk/ a pessimista

pest /pest/ n inseto m, (P) insecto m
nocivo; (animal) animal m daninho;
(person) peste f

pester /'pestə(r)/ vt incomodar (colloq)

pesticide /'pestɪsaɪd/ n pesticida m

pet /pet/ n animal m de estimação;
(favourite) preferido m, querido m □ a
(rabbit etc) de estimação □ vt (pt
petted) acariciar. ∼ **name** nome m
usado em família

petal /'petl/ n pétala f

peter /'piːtə(r)/ vi ∼ **out** extinguir-se,
acabar pouco a pouco, morrer (fig)

petition /pɪ'tɪʃn/ n petição f □ vt requerer

petrify /'petrɪfaɪ/ vt petrificar

petrol /'petrəl/ n gasolina f. ∼ **pump**
bomba f de gasolina. ∼ **station** posto m
de gasolina. ∼ **tank** tanque m de
gasolina

petroleum /pɪ'trəʊlɪəm/ n petróleo m

petticoat /'petɪkəʊt/ n combinação f,
anágua f

petty /'petɪ/ a (-**ier**, -**iest**) pequeno,
insignificante; (mean) mesquinho.
∼ **cash** fundo m para pequenas
despesas, caixa f pequena

petulan|t /'petjʊlənt/ a irritável. ∼**ce** n
irritabilidade f

pew /pjuː/ n banco (de igreja) m

pewter /'pjuːtə(r)/ n estanho m

phallic /'fælɪk/ a fálico

phantom /'fæntəm/ n fantasma m

pharmaceutical /faːmə'sjuːtɪkl/ a
farmacêutico

pharmac|y /'faːməsɪ/ n farmácia f. ∼**ist**
n farmacêutico m

phase /feɪz/ n fase f □ vt ∼ **in/out**
introduzir/retirar progressivamente

PhD abbr of **Doctor of Philosophy** n
doutorado m

pheasant /'feznt/ n faisão m

phenomen|on /fɪ'nɒmɪnən/ n (pl -**ena**)
fenômeno m, (P) fenómeno m. ∼**al** a
fenomenal

philanthrop|ist /fɪ'lænθrəpɪst/ n
filantropo m. ∼**ic** /-ən'θrɒpɪk/ a
filantrópico

Philippines /'fɪlɪpiːnz/ npl the ∼ as
Filipinas fpl

philistine /'fɪlɪstaɪn/ n filisteu m

philosoph|y /fɪ'lɒsəfɪ/ n filosofia f. ∼**er** n
filósofo m. ∼**ical** /-ə'sɒfɪkl/ a filosófico

phlegm /flem/ n (med) catarro m,
fleuma f

phobia /'fəʊbɪə/ n fobia f

phone /fəʊn/ n (colloq) telefone m □ vt/i
(colloq) telefonar (para). **on the** ∼ no
telefone. ∼ **back** voltar a telefonar,
ligar de volta. ∼ **book** lista f telefônica,
(P) telefónica. ∼ **box** cabine f
telefónica, (P) telefónica. ∼ **call**
chamada f, telefonema m. ∼**-in** n
programa m de rádio ou tv com
participação dos ouvintes

phonecard /'fəʊnkaːd/ n cartão m para
uso em telefone público

phonetic /fə'netɪk/ a fonetico. ∼**s** n
fonética f

phoney /'fəʊnɪ/ a (-**ier**, -**iest**) (sl) falso,
fingido □ n (sl: person) fingido m; (sl:
thing) falso m, (P) falsificação f

phosphate /'fɒsfeɪt/ n fosfato m

phosphorus /'fɒsfərəs/ n fósforo m

photo /'fəʊtəʊ/ n (pl -**os**) (colloq) retrato
m, foto f

photocop|y /'fəʊtəʊkɒpɪ/ n fotocópia f
□ vt fotocopiar. ∼**ier** n fotocopiadora f

photogenic /fəʊtəʊ'dʒenɪk/ a fotogênico,
(P) fotogénico

photograph /'fəʊtəgraːf/ n fotografia
f □ vt fotografar. ∼**er** /fə-'tɒgrəfə(r)/
n fotógrafo m. ∼**ic** /-'græfɪk/
a fotográfico. ∼**y** /fə-'tɒgrəfɪ/ n
fotografia f

phrase /freɪz/ n expressão f, frase f;
(gram) locução f, frase f elíptica □ vt
exprimir. ∼**-book** n livro m de
expressões idiomáticas

physical /'fɪzɪkl/ a físico

p

physician /fɪ'zɪʃn/ n médico m

physicist /'fɪzɪsɪst/ n físico m

physics /'fɪzɪks/ n física f

physiology /fɪzɪ'ɒlədʒɪ/ n fisiologia f

physiotherap|y /fɪzɪəʊ'θerəpɪ/ n fisioterapia f. ~**ist** n fisioterapeuta mf

physique /fɪ'zi:k/ n físico m

pian|o /prænəʊ/ n (pl -os) piano m. ~**ist** /'pɪənɪst/ n pianista mf

pick[1] /pɪk/ n (tool) picareta f

pick[2] /pɪk/ vt escolher; (flowers, fruit etc) colher; (lock) forçar; (teeth) palitar □ n escolha f; (best) o/a melhor. ~ **a quarrel with** puxar uma briga com. ~ **holes in an argument** descobrir os pontos fracos dum argumento. ~ **sb's pocket** bater a carteira de alg. ~ **off** tirar, arrancar. ~ **on** implicar com. ~ **out** escolher; (identify) identificar, reconhecer. ~ **up** vt apanhar; (speed) ganhar. **take one's** ~ escolher livremente

pickaxe /'pɪkæks/ n picareta f

picket /'pɪkɪt/ n piquete m; (single striker) grevista mf de piquete □ vt (pt **picketed**) colocar um piquete em □ vi fazer piquete

pickings /'pɪkɪŋz/ npl restos mpl

pickle /'pɪkl/ n vinagre m. ~**s** picles mpl, (P) pickles mpl □ vt conservar em vinagre. **in a** ~ (colloq) numa encrenca (colloq)

pickpocket /'pɪkpɒkɪt/ n batedor m de carteiras, (P) carteirista m

picnic /'pɪknɪk/ n piquenique m □ vi (pt **picnicked**) piquenicar, (P) fazer um piquenique

pictorial /pɪk'tɔːrɪəl/ a ilustrado

picture /'pɪktʃə(r)/ n imagem f; (illustration) estampa f, ilustração f; (painting) quadro m, pintura f; (photo) fotografia f, retrato m; (drawing) desenho m; (fig) descrição f, quadro m □ vt imaginar; (describe) pintar, descrever. **the** ~**s** o cinema

picturesque /pɪktʃə'resk/ a pitoresco

pidgin /'pɪdʒɪn/ a ~ **English** inglês m estropiado

pie /paɪ/ n torta f, (P) tarte f, (of meat) empada f

piece /piːs/ n pedaço m, bocado m; (of machine, in game) peça f; (of currency) moeda f □ vt ~ **together** juntar, montar. **a** ~ **of advice/furniture**/etc um conselho/um móvel/etc. ~-**work** n trabalho m por, (P) a peça or por, (P) a tarefa. **take to** ~**s** desmontar

piecemeal /'piːsmiːl/ a aos poucos, pouco a pouco

pier /pɪə(r)/ n molhe m

pierc|e /pɪəs/ vt furar, penetrar. ~**ing** a penetrante; (of scream, pain) lancinante

piety /'paɪətɪ/ n piedade f, devoção f

pig /pɪg/ n porco m. ~-**headed** a cabeçudo, teimoso

pigeon /'pɪdʒɪn/ n pombo m. ~-**hole** n escaninho m

piggy /'pɪgɪ/ a como um porco. ~-**back** adv nas costas. ~ **bank** cofre m de criança

pigment /'pɪgmənt/ n pigmento m. ~**ation** /-'teɪʃn/ n pigmentação f

pigsty /'pɪgstaɪ/ n pocilga f, chiqueiro m

pigtail /'pɪgteɪl/ n trança f

pike /paɪk/ n (pl invar) (fish) lúcio m

pilchard /'pɪltʃəd/ n peixe m pequeno da família do arenque, sardinha f européia

pile /paɪl/ n pilha f; (of carpet) pêlo m □ vt/i amontoar(-se), empilhar(-se) (into em). **a** ~ **of** (colloq) um monte de (colloq). ~ **up** acumular(-se). ~-**up** n choque m em cadeia

piles /paɪlz/ npl hemorróidas fpl

pilfer /'pɪlfə(r)/ vt furtar. ~**age** n furto m (de coisas pequenas or em pequenas quantidades)

pilgrim /'pɪlgrɪm/ n peregrino m, romeiro m. ~**age** n peregrinação f, romaria f

pill /pɪl/ n pílula f, comprimido m

pillage /'pɪlɪdʒ/ n pilhagem f, saque m □ vt pilhar, saquear

pillar /'pɪlə(r)/ n pilar m. ~-**box** n marco m do correio

pillion /'pɪlɪən/ n assento m traseiro de motorizada. **ride** ~ ir no assento de trás

pillow /'pɪləʊ/ n travesseiro m

pillowcase /'pɪləʊkeɪs/ n fronha f

pilot /'paɪlət/ n piloto m □ vt (pt **piloted**) pilotar. ~-**light** n piloto m; (electr) lâmpada f testemunho; (gas) piloto m

pimento /pɪ'mentəʊ/ n (pl -os) pimentão m vermelho

pimple /'pɪmpl/ n borbulha f, espinha f

pin /pɪn/ n alfinete m; (techn) cavilha f □ vt (pt **pinned**) pregar or prender com alfinete(s); (hold down) prender, segurar. **have** ~**s and needles** estar com cãibra. ~ **sb down** (fig) obrigar alg a definir-se, apertar alg (fig). ~-**point** vt localizar com precisão. ~-**stripe** a de listras finas. ~ **up** pregar. ~-**up** n (colloq) pin-up f

pinafore /'pɪnəfɔː(r)/ n avental m. ~ **dress** veste f

pincers /'pɪnsəz/ npl (tool) torquês f, (P) alicate m; (med) pinça f; (zool) pinça(s) f(pl), tenaz(es) f(pl)

pinch /pɪntʃ/ vt apertar; (sl: steal) surripiar (colloq) □ n aperto m; (tweak) beliscão m; (small amount) pitada f. **at a ~** em caso de necessidade

pine[1] /paɪn/ n (tree) pinheiro m; (wood) pinho m

pine[2] /paɪn/ vi **~ away** definhar, consumir-se. **~ for** suspirar por

pineapple /'paɪnæpl/ n abacaxi m, (P) ananás m

ping-pong /'pɪŋpɒŋ/ n pingue-pongue m

pink /pɪŋk/ a & n rosa (m)

pinnacle /'pɪnəkl/ n pináculo m

pint /paɪnt/ n quartilho m (= 0,57l; Amer = 0,47l)

pioneer /paɪə'nɪə(r)/ n pioneiro m □ vt ser o pioneiro em, preparar o caminho para

pious /'paɪəs/ a piedoso, devoto

pip /pɪp/ n (seed) pevide f

pipe /paɪp/ n cano m, tubo m; (of smoker) cachimbo m □ vt encanar, canalizar. **~ down** calar a boca

pipeline /'paɪplaɪn/ n (for oil) oleoduto m; (for gas) gaseoduto m, (P) gasoduto m. **in the ~** (fig) encaminhado

piping /'paɪpɪŋ/ n tubagem f. **~ hot** muito quente

piquant /'pi:kənt/ a picante

pira|te /'paɪərət/ n pirata m. **~cy** n pirataria f

Pisces /'paɪsi:z/ n (astr) Peixe m, (P) Pisces m

pistol /'pɪstl/ n pistola f

piston /'pɪstən/ n êmbolo m, pistão m

pit /pɪt/ n (hole) cova f, fosso m; (mine) poço m; (quarry) pedreira f □ vt (pt **pitted**) picar, esburacar; (fig) opor. **~ o.s. against** (struggle) medir-se com

pitch[1] /pɪtʃ/ n breu m. **~-black** a escuro como breu

pitch[2] /pɪtʃ/ vt (throw) lançar; (tent) armar □ vi cair □ n (slope) declive m; (of sound) som m; (of voice) altura f; (sport) campo m

pitchfork /'pɪtʃfɔ:k/ n forcado m

pitfall /'pɪtfɔ:l/ n (fig) cilada f, perigo m inesperado

pith /pɪθ/ n (of orange) parte f branca da casca, mesocarpo m; (fig: essential part) cerne m, âmago m

pithy /'pɪθɪ/ a (-ier, -iest) preciso, conciso

piti|ful /'pɪtɪfl/ a lastimoso; (contemptible) miserável. **~less** a impiedoso

pittance /'pɪtns/ n salário m miserável, miséria f

pity /'pɪtɪ/ n dó m, pena f, piedade f □ vt compadecer-se de. **it's a ~** é uma pena.

take ~ on ter pena de. **what a ~!** que pena!

pivot /'pɪvət/ n eixo m □ vt (pt **pivoted**) girar em torno de

placard /'plæka:d/ n (poster) cartaz m

placate /plə'keɪt/ vt apaziguar, aplacar

place /pleɪs/ n lugar m, sítio m; (house) casa f; (seat, rank etc) lugar m □ vt colocar, pôr. **~ an order** fazer uma encomenda. **at/to my ~** em a or na minha casa. **~-mat** n pano m de mesa individual, (P) napperon m à americana

placid /'plæsɪd/ a plácido

plagiar|ize /'pleɪdʒəraɪz/ vt plagiar. **~ism** n plágio m

plague /pleɪg/ n peste f; (of insects) praga f □ vt atormentar, atazanar

plaice /pleɪs/ n (pl invar) solha f

plain /pleɪn/ a (-er, -est) claro; (candid) franco; (simple) simples; (not pretty) sem beleza; (not patterned) liso □ adv com franqueza □ n planície f. **in ~ clothes** à paisana. **~ly** adv claramente; (candidly) francamente

plaintiff /'pleɪntɪf/ n queixoso m

plaintive /'pleɪntɪv/ a queixoso

plait /plæt/ vt entrançar □ n trança f

plan /plæn/ n plano m, projeto m, (P) projecto m; (of a house, city etc) plano m, planta f □ vt (pt **planned**) planear, planejar □ vi fazer planos. **~ to do** ter a intenção de fazer

plane[1] /pleɪn/ n (level) plano m; (aeroplane) avião m □ a plano

plane[2] /pleɪn/ n (tool) plaina f □ vt aplainar

planet /'plænɪt/ n planeta m

plank /plæŋk/ n prancha f

planning /'plænɪŋ/ n planeamento m, planejamento m. **~ permission** permissão f para construir

plant /pla:nt/ n planta f; (techn) aparelhagem f, (factory) fábrica f □ vt plantar. **~ a bomb** colocar uma bomba. **~ation** /-'teɪʃn/ n plantação f

plaque /pla:k/ n placa f; (on teeth) tártaro m, pedra f

plaster /'pla:stə(r)/ n reboco m; (adhesive) esparadrapo m, band-aid m □ vt rebocar; (cover) cobrir (**with** com, de). **in ~** engessado. **~ of Paris** gesso m. **~er** n rebocador m, caiador m

plastic /'plæstɪk/ a plástico □ n plástica f. **~ surgery** cirurgia f plástica

plate /pleɪt/ n prato m; (in book) gravura f □ vt revestir de metal

plateau /'plætəʊ/ n (pl **-eaux** /-əʊz/) planalto m, platô m

platform /'plætfɔ:m/ n estrado m; (for speaking) tribuna f; (rail) plataforma

p

f, cais *m*; (*fig*) programa *m* de partido político. **~ ticket** bilhete *m* de gare

platinum /'plætnəm/ *n* platina *f*

platitude /'plætɪtjuːd/ *n* banalidade *f*, lugar-comum *m*

platonic /plə'tɒnɪk/ *a* platônico, (P) platónico

plausible /'plɔːzəbl/ *a* plausível; (*person*) convincente

play /pleɪ/ *vt/i* (*for amusement*) brincar; (*instrument*) tocar; (*cards, game*) jogar; (*opponent*) jogar contra; (*match*) disputar □ *n* jogo *m*; (*theatre*) peça *f*; (*movement*) folga *f*, margem *f*. **~ down** minimizar. **~ on** (*take advantage of*) aproveitar-se de. **~ safe** jogar pelo seguro. **~ up** (*colloq*) dar problemas (a). **~-group** *n* jardim *m* de infância, (P) jardim *m* infantil. **~-pen** *n* cercado *m* para crianças

playboy /'pleɪbɔɪ/ *n* play-boy *m*

player /'pleɪə(r)/ *n* jogador *m*; (*theat*) artista *mf*; (*mus*) artista *mf*, executante *mf*, instrumentista *mf*

playful /'pleɪfl/ *a* brincalhão *m*

playground /'pleɪɡraʊnd/ *n* pátio *m* de recreio

playing /'pleɪɪŋ/ *n* atuação *f*, (P) actuação *f*. **~-card** *n* carta *f* de jogar. **~-field** *n* campo *m* de jogos

playwright /'pleɪraɪt/ *n* dramaturgo *m*

plc *abbr* (*of public limited company*) SARL

plea /pliː/ *n* súplica *f*; (*reason*) pretexto *m*, desculpa *f*; (*jur*) alegação *f* da defesa

plead /pliːd/ *vt/i* pleitear; (*as excuse*) alegar. **~ guilty** confessar-se culpado. **~ with** implorar a

pleasant /'pleznt/ *a* agradável

pleas|e /pliːz/ *vt/i* agradar (a), dar prazer (a) □ *adv* por favor, (P) se faz favor. **~e themselves, they do as they ~e** eles fazem como bem entendem. **~ed** *a* contente, satisfeito (**with** com). **~ing** *a* agradável

pleasur|e /'pleʒə(r)/ *n* prazer *m*. **~able** *a* agradável

pleat /pliːt/ *n* prega *f* □ *vt* preguear

pledge /pledʒ/ *n* penhor *m*, garantia *f*; (*fig*) promessa *f* □ *vt* prometer; (*pawn*) empenhar

plentiful /'plentɪfl/ *a* abundante

plenty /'plentɪ/ *n* abundância *f*, fartura *f*. **~ (of)** muito (de); (*enough*) bastante (de)

pliable /'plaɪəbl/ *a* flexível

pliers /'plaɪəz/ *npl* alicate *m*

plight /plaɪt/ *n* triste situação *f*

plimsoll /'plɪmsəl/ *n* alpargata *f*, tênis *m*, (P) ténis *m*

plinth /plɪnθ/ *n* plinto *m*

plod /plɒd/ *vi* (*pt* **plodded**) caminhar lentamente; (*work*) trabalhar, marrar (*sl*). **~der** *n* trabalhador *m* lento mas perseverante. **~ding** *a* lento

plonk /plɒŋk/ *n* (*sl*) vinho *m* ordinário, (P) carrascão *m*

plot /plɒt/ *n* complô *m*, conspiração *f*; (*of novel etc*) trama *f*; (*of land*) lote *m* □ *vt/i* (*pt* **plotted**) conspirar; (*mark out*) traçar

plough /plaʊ/ *n* arado *m* □ *vt/i* arar. **~ back** reinvestir. **~ into** colidir. **~ through** abrir caminho por

ploy /plɔɪ/ *n* (*colloq*) estratagema *m*

pluck /plʌk/ *vt* apanhar; (*bird*) depenar; (*eyebrows*) depilar; (*mus*) tanger □ *n* coragem *f*. **~ up courage** ganhar coragem. **~y** *a* corajoso

plug /plʌɡ/ *n* tampão *m*; (*electr*) tomada *f*, (P) ficha *f* □ *vt* (*pt* **plugged**) tapar com tampão; (*colloq: publicize*) fazer grande propaganda de □ *vi* **~ away** (*colloq*) trabalhar com afinco. **~ in** (*electr*) ligar. **~-hole** *n* buraco *m* do cano

plum /plʌm/ *n* ameixa *f*

plumb /plʌm/ *adv* exatamente, (P) exactamente, mesmo □ *vt* sondar. **~-line** *n* fio *m* de prumo

plumb|er /'plʌmə(r)/ *n* bombeiro *m*, encanador *m*, (P) canalizador *m*. **~ing** *n* encanamento *m*, (P) canalização *f*

plummet /'plʌmɪt/ *vi* (*pt* **plummeted**) despencar

plump /plʌmp/ *a* (-er, -est) rechonchudo, roliço □ *vi* **~ for** optar por. **~ness** *n* gordura *f*

plunder /'plʌndə(r)/ *vt* pilhar, saquear □ *n* pilhagem *f*, saque *m*; (*goods*) despojo *m*

plunge /plʌndʒ/ *vt/i* mergulhar, atirar(-se), afundar(-se) □ *n* mergulho *m*. **take the ~** (*fig*) decidir-se, dar o salto (*fig*)

plunger /'plʌndʒə(r)/ *n* (*of pump*) êmbolo *m*, pistão *m*; (*for sink etc*) desentupidor *m*

pluperfect /pluː'pɜːfɪkt/ *n* mais-que-perfeito *m*

plural /'plʊərəl/ *a* plural; (*noun*) no plural □ *n* plural *m*

plus /plʌs/ *prep* mais □ *a* positivo □ *n* sinal +; (*fig*) qualidade *f* positiva

plush /plʌʃ/ *n* pelúcia *f* □ *a* de pelúcia; (*colloq*) de luxo

ply /plaɪ/ *vt* (*tool*) manejar; (*trade*) exercer □ *vi* (*ship, bus*) fazer carreira entre dois lugares. **~ sb with drink** encher alguém de bebidas

plywood /'plaɪwʊd/ *n* madeira *f* compensada

p.m. /piː'em/ *adv* da tarde, da noite

pneumatic /njuːˈmætɪk/ *a* pneumático. **~ drill** broca *f* pneumática

pneumonia /njuːˈməʊnɪə/ *n* pneumonia *f*

PO *abbr see* **Post Office**

poach /pəʊtʃ/ *vt/i* (*steal*) caçar/pescar em propriedade alheia; (*culin*) fazer pochê, (*P*) escalfar. **~ed eggs** ovos *mpl* pochês, (*P*) ovos *mpl* escalfados

pocket /ˈpɒkɪt/ *n* bolso *m*, algibeira *f* □ *a* de algibeira □ *vt* meter no bolso. **~-book** *n* (*notebook*) livro *m* de apontamentos; (*Amer: handbag*) carteira *f*. **~-money** *n* (*monthly*) mesada *f*; (*weekly*) semanada *f*, dinheiro *m* para pequenas despesas

pod /pɒd/ *n* vagem *f*

poem /ˈpəʊɪm/ *n* poema *m*

poet /ˈpəʊɪt/ *n* poeta *m*, poetisa *f*. **~ic** /-ˈetɪk/ *a* poético

poetry /ˈpəʊɪtrɪ/ *n* poesia *f*

poignant /ˈpɔɪnjənt/ *a* pungente, doloroso

point /pɔɪnt/ *n* ponto *m*; (*tip*) ponta *f*; (*decimal point*) vírgula *f*; (*meaning*) sentido *m*, razão *m*; (*electr*) tomada *f*. **~s** (*rail*) agulhas *fpl* □ *vt/i* (*aim*) apontar (**at** para); (*show*) apontar, indicar (**at/to** para). **on the ~ of** prestes a, quase a. **~-blank** *a & adv* à *queima-roupa*; (*fig*) categórico. **~ of view** ponto *m* de vista. **~ out** apontar, fazer ver. **that is a good ~** (*remark*) é uma boa observação. **to the ~** a propósito. **what is the ~?** de que adianta?

pointed /ˈpɔɪntɪd/ *a* ponteagudo; (*of remark*) intencional, contundente

pointer /ˈpɔɪntə(r)/ *n* ponteiro *m*; (*colloq: hint*) sugestão *f*

pointless /ˈpɔɪntlɪs/ *a* inútil, sem sentido

poise /pɔɪz/ *n* equilíbrio *m*; (*carriage*) porte *m*; (*fig: self-possession*) presença *f*, segurança *f*. **~d** *a* equilibrado; (*person*) seguro de si

poison /ˈpɔɪzn/ *n* veneno *m*, peçonha *f* □ *vt* envenenar. **blood-~ing** *n* envenenamento *m* do sangue. **food-~ing** *n* intoxicação *f* alimentar. **~ous** *a* venenoso

poke /pəʊk/ *vt/i* espetar; (*with elbow*) acotovelar; (*fire*) atiçar □ *n* espetadela *f*; (*with elbow*) cotovelada *f*. **~ about** esgaravatar, remexer, procurar. **~ fun at** fazer troça/pouco de. **~ out** (*head*) enfiar

poker[1] /ˈpəʊkə(r)/ *n* atiçador *m*

poker[2] /ˈpəʊkə(r)/ *n* (*cards*) pôquer *m*, (*P*) póquer *m*

poky /ˈpəʊkɪ/ *a* (**-ier, -iest**) acanhado, apertado

Poland /ˈpəʊlənd/ *n* Polônia *f*, (*P*) Polónia *f*

polar /ˈpəʊlə(r)/ *a* polar. **~ bear** urso *m* branco

polarize /ˈpəʊləraɪz/ *vt* polarizar

pole[1] /pəʊl/ *n* vara *f*; (*for flag*) mastro *m*; (*post*) poste *m*

pole[2] /pəʊl/ *n* (*geog*) pólo *m*

Pole /pəʊl/ *n* polaco *m*

polemic /pəˈlemɪk/ *n* polêmica *f*, (*P*) polémica *f*

police /pəˈliːs/ *n* polícia *f* □ *vt* policiar. **~ state** estado *m* policial. **~ station** distrito *m*, delegacia *f*, (*P*) esquadra *f* de polícia

police|man /pəˈliːsmən/ *n* (*pl* **-men**) policial *m*, (*P*) polícia *m*, guarda *m*, agente *m* de polícia. **~-woman** (*pl* **-women**) *n* polícia *f* feminina, (*P*) mulher-policia *f*

policy[1] /ˈpɒlɪsɪ/ *n* (*plan of action*) política *f*

policy[2] /ˈpɒlɪsɪ/ *n* (*insurance*) apólice *f* de seguro

polio /ˈpəʊlɪəʊ/ *n* polio *f*

polish /ˈpɒlɪʃ/ *vt* polir, dar lustro em; (*shoes*) engraxar; (*floor*) encerar □ *n* (*for shoes*) graxa *f*; (*for floor*) cera *f*; (*for nails*) esmalte *m*, (*P*) verniz *m*; (*shine*) polimento *m*; (*fig*) requinte *m*. **~ off** acabar (rapidamente). **~ up** (*language*) aperfeiçoar. **~ed** *a* requintado, elegante

Polish /ˈpəʊlɪʃ/ *a & n* polonês (*m*), (*P*) polaco (*m*)

polite /pəˈlaɪt/ *a* polido, educado, delicado. **~ly** *adv* delicadamente. **~ness** *n* delicadeza *f*, cortesia *f*

political /pəˈlɪtɪkl/ *a* político

politician /pɒlɪˈtɪʃn/ *n* político *m*

politics /ˈpɒlətɪks/ *n* política *f*

polka /ˈpɒlkə/ *n* polca *f*. **~ dots** bolas *fpl*

poll /pəʊl/ *n* votação *f*; (*survey*) sondagem *f*, pesquisa *f* □ *vt* (*votes*) obter. **go to the ~s** votar, ir às urnas. **~ing-booth** *n* cabine *f* de voto

pollen /ˈpɒlən/ *n* pólen *m*

pollut|e /pəˈluːt/ *vt* poluir. **~ion** /-ʃn/ *n* poluição *f*

polo /ˈpəʊləʊ/ *n* pólo *m*. **~ neck** gola *f* rolê

polyester /pɒlɪˈestə/ *n* poliéster *m*

polytechnic /pɒlɪˈteknɪk/ *n* politécnica *f*

polythene /ˈpɒlɪθiːn/ *n* politeno *m*. **~ bag** *n* saco *m* de plástico

pomegranate /ˈpɒmɪɡrænɪt/ *n* romã *f*

pomp /pɒmp/ *n* pompa *f*

pompon /ˈpɒmpɒn/ *n* pompom *m*

pomp|ous /ˈpɒmpəs/ *a* pomposo. **~osity** /-ˈpɒsətɪ/ *n* imponência *f*

pond /pɒnd/ *n* lagoa *f*, lago *m*; (*artificial*) tanque *m*, lago *m*

ponder /ˈpɒndə(r)/ *vt/i* ponderar, meditar (**over** sobre)

p

pong /pɒŋ/ n (sl) pivete m □ vi (sl) cheirar mal, tresandar

pony /'pəʊnɪ/ n pônei m, (P) pónei m. ~-tail n rabo m de cavalo. ~-trekking n passeio m de pônei, (P) pónei

poodle /'puːdl/ n cão m de água, caniche m

pool[1] /puːl/ n (puddle) charco m, poça f; (for swimming) piscina f

pool[2] /puːl/ n (fund) fundo m comum; (econ, comm) bolsa m; (game) forma f de bilhar. ~s loteca f, (P) totobola m □ vt pôr num fundo comum

poor /pʊə(r)/ a (-er, -est) pobre; (not good) medíocre. ~ly adv mal □ a doente

pop[1] /pɒp/ n estalido m, ruído m seco □ vt/i (pt popped) dar um estalido, estalar; (of cork) saltar. ~ in/out/off entrar/sair/ir-se embora. ~ up aparecer de repente, saltar

pop[2] /pɒp/ n música f pop □ a pop invar

popcorn /'pɒpkɔːn/ n pipoca f

pope /pəʊp/ n papa m

poplar /'pɒplə(r)/ n choupo m, álamo m

poppy /'pɒpɪ/ n papoula f

popular /'pɒpjʊlə(r)/ a popular; (in fashion) em voga, na moda. be ~ with ser popular entre. ~ity /-'lærətɪ/ n popularidade f. ~ize vt popularizar, vulgarizar

populat|e /'pɒpjʊleɪt/ vt povoar. ~ion /-'leɪʃn/ n população f

populous /'pɒpjʊləs/ a populoso

porcelain /'pɔːslɪn/ n porcelana f

porch /pɔːtʃ/ n alpendre m; (Amer) varanda f

porcupine /'pɔːkjʊpaɪn/ n porcoespinho m

pore[1] /pɔː(r)/ n poro m

pore[2] /pɔː(r)/ vi ~ over examinar, estudar

pork /pɔːk/ n carne f de porco

pornograph|y /pɔː'nɒɡrəfɪ/ n pornografia f. ~ic /-ə'ɡræfɪk/ a pornográfico

porous /'pɔːrəs/ a poroso

porpoise /'pɔːpəs/ n toninha f, (P) golfinho m

porridge /'pɒrɪdʒ/ n (papa f de) flocos mpl de aveia

port[1] /pɔːt/ n (harbour) porto m

port[2] /pɔːt/ n (wine) (vinho do) Porto m

portable /'pɔːtəbl/ a portátil

porter[1] /'pɔːtə(r)/ n (carrier) carregador m

porter[2] /'pɔːtə(r)/ n (doorkeeper) porteiro m

portfolio /pɔːt'fəʊlɪəʊ/ n (pl -os) (case, post) pasta f; (securities) carteira f de investimentos

porthole /'pɔːthəʊl/ n vigia f

portion /'pɔːʃn/ n (share, helping) porção f; (part) parte f

portly /'pɔːtlɪ/ a (-ier, -iest) corpulento e digno

portrait /'pɔːtrɪt/ n retrato m

portray /pɔː'treɪ/ vt retratar, pintar; (fig) descrever. ~al n retrato m

Portug|al /'pɔːtjʊɡl/ n Portugal m. ~uese /-'ɡiːz/ a & n invar português (m)

pose /pəʊz/ vt/i (fazer) posar; (question) fazer □ n pose f, postura f. ~ as fazer-se passar por

poser /'pəʊzə(r)/ n quebra-cabeças m

posh /pɒʃ/ a (sl) chique invar

position /pə'zɪʃn/ n posição f; (job) lugar m, colocação f; (state) situação f □ vt colocar

positive /'pɒzətɪv/ a positivo; (definite) categórico, definitivo; (colloq: downright) autêntico. she's ~ that ela tem certeza que. ~ly adv positivamente; (absolutely) completamente

possess /pə'zes/ vt possuir. ~ion /-ʃn/ n posse f; (thing possessed) possessão f. ~or n possuidor m

possessive /pə'zesɪv/ a possessivo

possib|le /'pɒsəbl/ a possível. ~ility /-'bɪlətɪ/ n possibilidade f

possibly /'pɒsəblɪ/ adv possivelmente, talvez. if I ~ can se me fôr possível. I cannot ~ leave estou impossibilitado de partir

post[1] /pəʊst/ n (pole) poste m □ vt (notice) afixar, pregar

post[2] /pəʊst/ n (station, job) posto m □ vt colocar; (appoint) colocar

post[3] /pəʊst/ n (mail) correio m □ a postal □ vt mandar pelo correio. keep ~ed manter informado. ~-code n código m postal. P~ Office agência f dos correios, (P) estação f dos correios; (corporation) Departamento m dos Correios e Telégrafos, (P) Correios, Telégrafos e Telefones mpl (CTT)

post- /pəʊst/ pref pós-

postage /'pəʊstɪdʒ/ n porte m

postal /'pəʊstl/ a postal. ~ order vale m postal

postcard /'pəʊstkaːd/ n cartão-postal m, (P) (bilhete) postal m

poster /'pəʊstə(r)/ n cartaz m

posterity /pɒ'sterətɪ/ n posteridade f

postgraduate /pəʊst'ɡrædʒʊet/ n pós-graduado m

posthumous /'pɒstjʊməs/ a póstumo. ~ly adv a título póstumo

postman /'pəʊstmən/ n (pl -men) carteiro m

postmark /'pəʊstmaːk/ n carimbo m do correio

post-mortem /pəʊst'mɔːtəm/ n autópsia f

postpone /pə'spəʊn/ vt adiar. ∼ment n adiamento m

postscript /'pəʊsskrɪpt/ n post scriptum m

postulate /'pɒstjʊleɪt/ vt postular

posture /'pɒstʃə(r)/ n postura f, posição f □ vi posar

post-war /'pəʊstwɔː(r)/ a de após-guerra

posy /'pəʊzɪ/ n raminho m de flores

pot /pɒt/ n pote m; (for cooking) panela f; (for plants) vaso m; (sl: marijuana) maconha f □ vt (pt potted) ∼ (up) plantar em vaso. go to ∼ (sl: business) arruinar, degringolar (colloq); (sl: person) estar arruinado or liquidado. ∼-belly n pança f, barriga f. take ∼ luck aceitar o que houver. take a ∼-shot dar um tiro de perto (at em); (at random) dar um tiro a esmo (at em)

potato /pə'teɪtəʊ/ n (pl -oes) batata f

poten|t /'pəʊtnt/ a potente, poderoso; (drink) forte. ∼cy n potência f

potential /pə'tenʃl/ a & n potencial (m). ∼ly adv potencialmente

pothol|e /'pɒthəʊl/ n caverna f, caldeirão m; (in road) buraco m. ∼ing n espeleologia f

potion /'pəʊʃn/ n poção f

potted /'pɒtɪd/ a (of plant) de vaso; (preserved) de conserva

potter[1] /'pɒtə(r)/ n oleiro m, ceramista mf. ∼y n olaria f, cerâmica f

potter[2] /'pɒtə(r)/ vi entreter-se com isto ou aquilo

potty[1] /'pɒtɪ/ a (-ier, -iest) (sl) doido, pirado (sl), (P) chanfrado (colloq)

potty[2] /'pɒtɪ/ n (-ties) (colloq) penico m de criança

pouch /paʊtʃ/ n bolsa f; (for tobacco) tabaqueira f

poultice /'pəʊltɪs/ n cataplasma f

poultry /'pəʊltrɪ/ n aves fpl domésticas

pounce /paʊns/ vi atirar-se (on sobre, para cima de) □ n salto m

pound[1] /paʊnd/ n (weight) libra f (= 453 g); (money) libra f

pound[2] /paʊnd/ n (for dogs) canil municipal m; (for cars) parque de viaturas rebocadas m

pound[3] /paʊnd/ vt/i (crush) esmagar, pisar; (of heart) bater com força; (bombard) bombardear; (on piano etc) martelar

pour /pɔː(r)/ vt deitar □ vi correr; (rain) chover torrencialmente. ∼ in/out (of people) afluir/sair em massa. ∼ off or out esvaziar, vazar. ∼ing rain chuva f torrencial

pout /paʊt/ vt/i ∼ (one's lips) (sulk) fazer beicinho; (in annoyance) ficar de trombas □ n beicinho m

poverty /'pɒvətɪ/ n pobreza f, miséria f. ∼-stricken a pobre

powder /'paʊdə(r)/ n pó m; (for face) pó-de-arroz m □ vt polvilhar; (face) empoar. ∼ed a em pó. ∼-room n toalete m, toucador m. ∼y a como pó

power /'paʊə(r)/ n poder m; (maths, mech) potência f; (energy) energia f; (electr) corrente f. ∼ cut corte m de energia, blecaute m. ∼ station central f elétrica, (P) eléctrica. ∼ed by movido a; (jet etc) de propulsão. ∼ful a poderoso; (mech) potente. ∼less a impotente

practicable /'præktɪkəbl/ a viável

practical /'præktɪkl/ a prático. ∼ joke brincadeira f de mau gosto

practically /'præktɪklɪ/ adv praticamente

practice /'præktɪs/ n prática f; (of law etc) exercício m; (sport) treino m; (clients) clientela f. in ∼ (in fact) na prática; (well-trained) em forma. out of ∼ destreinado, sem prática. put into ∼ pôr em prática

practis|e /'præktɪs/ vt/i (skill, sport) praticar, exercitar-se em; (profession) exercer; (put into practice) pôr em prática. ∼ed a experimentado, experiente. ∼ing a (Catholic etc) praticante

practitioner /præk'tɪʃənə(r)/ n praticante mf. **general** ∼ médico m de clínica geral or de família

pragmatic /præg'mætɪk/ a pragmático

prairie /'preərɪ/ n pradaria f

praise /preɪz/ vt louvar, elogiar □ n elogio(s) m(pl), louvor(es) m(pl)

praiseworthy /'preɪzwɜːðɪ/ a louvável, digno de louvor

pram /præm/ n carrinho m de bebê, (P) bebé

prance /praːns/ vi (of horse) curvetear, empinar-se; (of person) pavonear-se

prank /præŋk/ n brincadeira f de mau gosto

prattle /'prætl/ vi tagarelar

prawn /prɔːn/ n camarão m grande, (P) gamba f

pray /preɪ/ vi rezar, orar

prayer /preə(r)/ n oração f. the Lord's P∼ o Padre-Nosso. ∼-book n missal m

pre- /priː/ pref pré-

preach /priːtʃ/ vt/i pregar (at, to a). ∼er n pregador m

preamble /priː'æmbl/ n preâmbulo m

prearrange /priːə'reɪndʒ/ vt combinar or arranjar de antemão

p

precarious /prɪˈkeərɪəs/ a precário; (*of position*) instável, inseguro

precaution /prɪˈkɔːʃn/ n precaução f. ∼**ary** a de precaução

preced|e /prɪˈsiːd/ vt preceder. ∼**ing** a precedente

precedent /ˈpresɪdənt/ n precedente m

precinct /ˈpriːsɪŋkt/ n precinto m; (*Amer: district*) circunscrição f. (**pedestrian**) ∼ área f de pedestres, (P) zona f para peões

precious /ˈpreʃəs/ a precioso

precipice /ˈpresɪpɪs/ n precipício m

precipitat|e /prɪˈsɪpɪteɪt/ vt precipitar □ a /-ɪtət/ precipitado. ∼**ion** /-ˈteɪʃn/ n precipitação f

precis|e /prɪˈsaɪs/ a preciso; (*careful*) meticuloso. ∼**ely** adv precisamente. ∼**ion** /-ˈsɪʒn/ n precisão f

preclude /prɪˈkluːd/ vt evitar, excluir, impedir

precocious /prɪˈkəʊʃəs/ a precoce

preconc|eived /priːkənˈsiːvd/ a preconcebido. ∼**eption** /priːkənˈsepʃn/ n idéia f preconcebida

precursor /prɪˈkɜːsə(r)/ n precursor m

predator /ˈpredətə(r)/ n animal m de rapina, predador m. ∼**y** a predatório

predecessor /ˈpriːdɪsesə(r)/ n predecessor m

predicament /prɪˈdɪkəmənt/ n situação f difícil

predict /prɪˈdɪkt/ vt predizer, prognosticar. ∼**able** a previsível. ∼**ion** /-ʃn/ n predição f, prognóstico m

predominant /prɪˈdɒmɪnənt/ a predominante, preponderante. ∼**ly** adv predominantemente, preponderantemente

predominate /prɪˈdɒmɪneɪt/ vi predominar

pre-eminent /priːˈemɪnənt/ a preeminente, superior

pre-empt /priːˈempt/ vt adquirir por preempção. ∼**ive** a antecipado; (*mil*) preventivo

preen /priːn/ vt alisar. ∼ **o.s.** enfeitar-se

prefab /ˈpriːfæb/ n (*colloq*) casa f pré-fabricada. ∼**ricated** /-ˈfæbrɪkeɪtɪd/ a pré-fabricado

preface /ˈprefɪs/ n prefácio m

prefect /ˈpriːfekt/ n aluno m autorizado a disciplinar outros; (*official*) prefeito m

prefer /prɪˈfɜː(r)/ vt (*pt preferred*) preferir. ∼**able** a /ˈprefrəbl/ a preferível

preferen|ce /ˈprefrəns/ n preferência f. ∼**tial** /-əˈrenʃl/ a preferencial, privilegiado

prefix /ˈpriːfɪks/ n (*pl* -**ixes**) prefixo m

pregnan|t /ˈpregnənt/ a (*woman*) grávida; (*animal*) prenhe. ∼**cy** n gravidez f

prehistoric /priːhɪˈstɒrɪk/ a pré-histórico

prejudice /ˈpredʒʊdɪs/ n preconceito m, idéia f preconcebida, prejuízo m; (*harm*) prejuízo m □ vt influenciar. ∼**d** a com preconceitos

preliminar|y /prɪˈlɪmɪnərɪ/ a preliminar. ∼**ies** npl preliminares mpl, preâmbulos mpl

prelude /ˈpreljuːd/ n prelúdio m

premarital /priːˈmærɪtl/ a antes do casamento, pré-marital

premature /ˈpremətjʊə(r)/ a prematuro

premeditated /priːˈmedɪteɪtɪd/ a premeditado

premier /ˈpremɪə(r)/ a primeiro □ n (*pol*) primeiro-ministro m

premises /ˈpremɪsɪz/ npl local m, edifício m. **on the** ∼ neste estabelecimento, no local

premium /ˈpriːmɪəm/ n prêmio m, (P) prémio m. **at a** ∼ a peso de ouro

premonition /priːməˈnɪʃn/ n pressentimento m

preoccup|ation /priːɒkjʊˈpeɪʃn/ n preocupação f. ∼**ied** /-ˈɒkjʊpaɪd/ a preocupado

preparation /prepəˈreɪʃn/ n preparação f. ∼**s** preparativos mpl

preparatory /prɪˈpærətrɪ/ a preparatório. ∼ **school** escola f primária particular

prepare /prɪˈpeə(r)/ vt/i preparar(-se) (**for** para). ∼**d to** pronto a, preparado para

preposition /prepəˈzɪʃn/ n preposição f

preposterous /prɪˈpɒstərəs/ a absurdo, disparatado, ridículo

prerequisite /priːˈrekwɪzɪt/ n condição f prévia

prerogative /prɪˈrɒgətɪv/ n prerrogativa f

Presbyterian /prezbɪˈtɪərɪən/ a & n presbiteriano (m)

prescri|be /prɪˈskraɪb/ vt prescrever; (*med*) receitar, prescrever. ∼**ption** /-ɪpʃn/ n prescrição f; (*med*) receita f

presence /ˈprezns/ n presença f. ∼ **of mind** presença f de espírito

present[1] /ˈpreznt/ a & n presente (*mf*). **at** ∼ no momento, presentemente

present[2] /ˈpreznt/ n (*gift*) presente m

present[3] /prɪˈzent/ vt apresentar; (*film etc*) dar. ∼ **sb with** oferecer a alg. ∼**able** a apresentável. ∼**ation** /prezn'teɪʃn/ n apresentação f. ∼**er** n apresentador m

presently /'prezntlɪ/ adv dentro em pouco, daqui a pouco; (Amer: now) neste momento

preservative /prɪ'zɜ:vətɪv/ n preservativo m

preserv|e /prɪ'zɜ:v/ vt preservar; (maintain; culin) conservar □ n reserva f; (fig) área f, terreno m; (jam) compota f. ~ation /prezə'veɪʃn/ n conservação f

preside /prɪ'zaɪd/ vi presidir (**over** a)

presiden|t /'prezɪdənt/ n presidente mf. ~cy n presidência f. ~tial /-'denʃl/ a presidencial

press /pres/ vt/i carregar (**on** em); (squeeze) espremer; (urge) pressionar; (iron) passar a ferro □ n imprensa f; (mech) prensa f; (for wine) lagar m. ~ed for estar apertado com falta de. ~ on (with) continuar (com), prosseguir (com). ~ conference entrevista f coletiva. ~-stud n mola f, botão m de pressão

pressing /'presɪŋ/ a premente, urgente

pressure /'preʃə(r)/ n pressão f □ vt fazer pressão sobre. ~-cooker n panela f de pressão. ~ group grupo m de pressão

pressurize /'preʃəraɪz/ vt pressionar, fazer pressão sobre

prestige /pre'sti:ʒ/ n prestígio m

prestigious /pre'stɪdʒəs/ a prestigioso

presumably /prɪ'zju:məblɪ/ adv provavelmente

presum|e /prɪ'zju:m/ vt presumir. ~e to tomar a liberdade de, atrever-se a. ~ption /-'zʌmpʃn/ n presunção f

presumptuous /prɪ'zʌmptʃʊəs/ a presunçoso

pretence /prɪ'tens/ n fingimento m; (claim) pretensão f; (pretext) desculpa f, pretexto m

pretend /prɪ'tend/ vt/i fingir (**to do** fazer). ~ to (lay claim to) ter pretensões a, ser pretendente a; (profess to have) pretender ter

pretentious /prɪ'tenʃəs/ a pretencioso

pretext /'pri:tekst/ n pretexto m

pretty /'prɪtɪ/ a (**-ier, -iest**) bonito, lindo □ adv bastante

prevail /prɪ'veɪl/ vi prevalecer. ~ on sb to convencer alguéma. ~ing a dominante

prevalen|t /'prevələnt/ a geral, dominante. ~ce n frequência f

prevent /prɪ'vent/ vt impedir (**from doing** de fazer). ~able a que se pode evitar, evitável. ~ion /-ʃn/ n prevenção f. ~ive a preventivo

preview /'pri:vju:/ n pré-estréia f, (P) ante-estréia f

previous /'pri:vɪəs/ a precedente, anterior. ~ to antes de. ~ly adv antes, anteriormente

pre-war /pri:'wɔ:(r)/ a do pré-guerra, (P) de antes da guerra

prey /preɪ/ n presa f □ vi ~ on dar caça a; (worry) preocupar, atormentar. **bird of** ~ ave f de rapina, predador m

price /praɪs/ n preço m □ vt marcar o preço de. ~less a inestimável; (colloq: amusing) impa-gável

prick /prɪk/ vt picar, furar □ n picada f. ~ up one's ears arrebitar a(s) orelha(s)

prickl|e /'prɪkl/ n pico m, espinho m; (sensation) picada f. ~y a espinhoso, que pica; (person) irritável

pride /praɪd/ n orgulho m □ vpr ~ o.s. on orgulhar-se de

priest /pri:st/ n padre m, sacerdote m. ~hood n sacerdócio m; (clergy) clero m

prim /prɪm/ a (**primmer, primmest**) formal, cheio de nove-horas; (prudish) pudico

primary /'praɪmərɪ/ a primário; (chief, first) primeiro. ~ school escola f primária

prime[1] /praɪm/ a primeiro, principal; (first-rate) de primeira qualidade. **P~ Minister** Primeiro-Ministro m. ~ number número m primo

prime[2] /praɪm/ vt aprontar, aprestar; (with facts) preparar; (surface) preparar, aparelhar. ~r /-ə(r)/ n (paint) aparelho m

primeval /praɪ'mi:vl/ a primitivo

primitive /'prɪmɪtɪv/ a primitivo

primrose /'prɪmrəʊz/ n primavera f, prímula f

prince /prɪns/ n príncipe m

princess /prɪn'ses/ n princesa f

principal /'prɪnsəpl/ a principal □ n (schol) diretor m, (P) director m. ~ly adv principalmente

principle /'prɪnsəpl/ n princípio m. **in/on** ~ em/por princípio

print /prɪnt/ vt imprimir; (write) escrever em letra de imprensa □ n marca f, impressão f; (letters) letra f de imprensa; (photo) prova (fotográfica) f; (engraving) gravura f. **out of** ~ esgotado. ~-out n cópia f impressa. ~ed matter impressos mpl

print|er /'prɪntə(r)/ n tipógrafo m; (comput) impressora f. ~ing n impressão f, tipografia f

prior /'praɪə(r)/ a anterior, precedente. ~ to antes de

priority /praɪ'ɒrətɪ/ n prioridade f

prise /praɪz/ vt forçar (com alavanca). ~ open arrombar

p

prison /'prɪzn/ n prisão f. ∼er n prisioneiro m

pristine /'prɪstiːn/ a primitivo; (*condition*) perfeito, como novo

privacy /'prɪvəsɪ/ n privacidade f, intimidade f; (*solitude*) isolamento m

private /'praɪvət/ a privado; (*confidential*) confidencial; (*lesson, life, house etc*) particular; (*ceremony*) íntimo □ n soldado m raso. **in** ∼ em particular; (*of ceremony*) na intimidade. ∼ly adv particularmente; (*inwardly*) no fundo, interiormente

privet /'prɪvɪt/ n (*bot*) alfena f, ligustro m

privilege /'prɪvəlɪdʒ/ n privilégio m. ∼d a privilegiado. **be** ∼**d to** ter o privilégio de

prize /praɪz/ n prêmio m, (P) prémio m □ a premiado; (*fool etc*) perfeito □ vt ter em grande apreço, apreciar muito. ∼-**giving** n distribuição f de prêmios, (P) prémios. ∼-**winner** n premiado m, vencedor m

pro[1] /prəʊ/ n **the** ∼**s and cons** os prós e os contras

pro- /prəʊ/ pref (*acting for*) pro-; (*favouring*) pró-

probab|le /'prɒbəbl/ a provável. ∼**ility** /-'bɪlətɪ/ n probabilidade f. ∼**ly** adv provavelmente

probation /prə'beɪʃn/ n (*testing*) estágio m, tirocínio m; (*jur*) liberdade f condicional. ∼**ary** a probatório

probe /prəʊb/ n (*med*) sonda f; (*fig: investigation*) inquérito m □ vt/i ∼ (**into**) sondar, investigar

problem /'prɒbləm/ n problema m □ a difícil. ∼**atic** /-'mætɪk/ a problemático

procedure /prə'siːdʒə(r)/ n procedimento m, processo m, norma f

proceed /prə'siːd/ vi prosseguir, ir para diante, avançar. ∼ **to do** passar a fazer. ∼ **with sth** continuar or avançar com alguma coisa. ∼**ing** n procedimento m

proceedings /prə'siːdɪŋz/ npl (*jur*) processo m; (*report*) ata f, (P) acta f

proceeds /'prəʊsiːdz/ npl produto m, luco m, proventos mpl

process /'prəʊses/ n processo m □ vt tratar; (*photo*) revelar. **in** ∼ em curso. **in the** ∼ **of doing** sendo feito

procession /prə'seʃn/ n procissão f, cortejo m

procl|aim /prə'kleɪm/ vt proclamar. ∼**amation** /prɒklə'meɪʃn/ n proclamação f

procure /prə'kjʊə(r)/ vt obter

prod /prɒd/ vt/i (*pt* **prodded**) (*push*) empurrar; (*poke*) espetar; (*fig: urge*) incitar □ n espetadela f; (*fig*) incitamento m

prodigal /'prɒdɪgl/ a pródigo

prodigious /prə'dɪdʒəs/ a prodigioso

prodigy /'prɒdɪdʒɪ/ n prodígio m

produc|e[1] /prə'djuːs/ vt/i produzir; (*bring out*) tirar, extrair; (*show*) apresentar, mostrar; (*cause*) causar, provocar; (*theat*) pôr em cena. ∼**er** n produtor m. ∼**tion** /-'dʌkʃn/ n produção f; (*theat*) encenação f

produce[2] /'prɒdjuːs/ n produtos (agrícolas) mpl

product /'prɒdʌkt/ n produto m

productiv|e /prə'dʌktɪv/ a produtivo. ∼**ity** /prɒdʌk'tɪvətɪ/ n produtividade f

profan|e /prə'feɪm/ a profano; (*blasphemous*) blasfemo. ∼**ity** /-'fænətɪ/ n profanidade f

profess /prə'fes/ vt professar. ∼ **to do** alegar fazer

profession /prə'feʃn/ n profissão f. ∼**al** a profissional; (*well done*) de profissional; (*person*) que exerce uma profissão liberal □ n profissional mf

professor /prə'fesə(r)/ n professor (universitário) m

proficien|t /prə'fɪʃnt/ a proficiente, competente. ∼**cy** n proficiência f, competência f

profile /'prəʊfaɪl/ n perfil m

profit /'prɒfɪt/ n proveito m; (*money*) lucro m □ vi (*pt* **profited**) ∼ **by** aproveitar-se de; ∼ **from** tirar proveito de. ∼**able** a proveitoso; (*of business*) lucrativo, rentável

profound /prə'faʊnd/ a profundo. ∼**ly** adv profundamente

profus|e /prə'fjuːs/ a profuso. ∼**ely** adv profusamente, em abundância. ∼**ion** /-ʒn/ n profusão f

program /'prəʊgræm/ n (**computer**) ∼ programa m □ vt (*pt* **programmed**) programar. ∼**mer** n programador m

programme /'prəʊgræm/ n programa m

progress[1] /'prəʊgres/ n progresso m. **in** ∼ em curso, em andamento

progress[2] /prə'gres/ vi progredir. ∼**ion** /-ʃn/ n progressão f

progressive /prə'gresɪv/ a progressivo; (*reforming*) progressista. ∼**ly** adv progressivamente

prohibit /prə'hɪbɪt/ vt proibir (**sb from doing** alg de fazer)

project[1] /prə'dʒekt/ vt projetar, (P) projectar □ vi ressaltar, sobressair. ∼**ion** /-ʃn/ n projeção f, (P) projecção f; (*protruding*) saliência f, ressalto m

project[2] /'prɒdʒekt/ n projeto m, (P) projecto m

projectile /prə'dʒektaɪl/ n projétil m, (P) projéctil m

projector /prə'dʒektə(r)/ n projetor m, (P) projector m

proletari|at /prəʊlɪ'teərɪət/ n proletariado m. ~**an** a & n proletário (m)

proliferat|e /prə'lɪfəreɪt/ vi proliferar. ~**ion** /-'reɪʃn/ n proliferação f

prolific /prə'lɪfɪk/ a prolífico

prologue /'prəʊlɒg/ n prólogo m

prolong /prə'lɒŋ/ vt prolongar

promenade /prɒmə'na:d/ n passeio m □ vt/i passear

prominen|t /'prɒmɪnənt/ a (projecting; important) proeminente; (conspicuous) bem à vista, conspícuo. ~**ce** n proeminência f. ~**tly** adv bem à vista

promiscu|ous /prə'mɪskjʊəs/ a promíscuo, de costumes livres. ~**ity** /prɒmɪs'kjuːətɪ/ n promiscuidade f, liberdade f de costumes

promis|e /'prɒmɪs/ n promessa f □ vt/i prometer. ~**ing** a prometedor, promissor

promot|e /prə'məʊt/ vt promover. ~**ion** /-'məʊʃn/ n promoção f

prompt /prɒmpt/ a pronto, rápido, imediato; (punctual) pontual □ adv em ponto □ vt levar; (theat) soprar, servir de ponto para. ~**er** n ponto m. ~**ly** adv prontamente; pontualmente. ~**ness** n prontidão f

prone /prəʊn/ a deitado (de bruços). ~ **to** propenso a

prong /prɒŋ/ n (of fork) dente m

pronoun /'prəʊnaʊn/ n pronome m

pron|ounce /prə'naʊns/ vt pronunciar; (declare) declarar. ~**ounced** a pronunciado. ~**ouncement** n declaração f. ~**unciation** /-ʌnsɪ'eɪʃn/ n pronúncia f

proof /pruːf/ n prova f; (of liquor) teor m alcóolico, graduação f □ a ~ **against** à prova de

prop[1] /prɒp/ n suporte m; (lit & fig) apoio m, esteio m □ vt (pt **propped**) sustentar, suportar, apoiar. ~ **against** apoiar contra

prop[2] /prɒp/ n (colloq: theat) acessório m, (P) adereço m

propaganda /prɒpə'gændə/ n propaganda f

propagat|e /'prɒpəgeɪt/ vt/i propagar (-se). ~**ion** /-'geɪʃn/ n propagação f

propel /prə'pel/ vt (pt **propelled**) propulsionar, impelir

propeller /prə'pelə(r)/ n hélice f

proper /'prɒpə(r)/ a correto, (P) correcto; (seemly) conveniente; (real) propriamente dito; (colloq: thorough) belo. ~ **noun** substantivo m próprio. ~**ly** adv corretamente, (P) correctamente; (rightly) com razão,

acertadamente; (accurately) propriamente

property /'prɒpətɪ/ n (house) imóvel m; (land, quality) propriedade f; (possessions) bens mpl

prophecy /'prɒfəsɪ/ n profecia f

prophesy /'prɒfɪsaɪ/ vt/i profetizar. ~ **that** predizer que

prophet /'prɒfɪt/ n profeta m. ~**ic** /prə'fetɪk/ a profético

proportion /prə'pɔːʃn/ n proporção f. ~**al**, ~**ate** adjs proporcional

proposal /prə'pəʊzl/ n proposta f; (of marriage) pedido m de casamento

propos|e /prə'pəʊz/ vt propor □ vi pedir em casamento. ~**e to do** propor-se fazer. ~**ition** /prɒpə'zɪʃn/ n proposição f; (colloq: matter) caso m, questão f

propound /prə'paʊnd/ vt propor

proprietor /prə'praɪətə(r)/ n proprietário m

propriety /prə'praɪətɪ/ n propriedade f, correção f, (P) correcção f

propulsion /prə'pʌlʃn/ n propulsão f

prosaic /prə'zeɪk/ a prosaico

prose /prəʊz/ n prosa f

prosecut|e /'prɒsɪkjuːt/ vt (jur) processar. ~**ion** /-'kjuːʃn/ n (jur) acusação f

prospect[1] /'prɒspekt/ n perspectiva f

prospect[2] /prə'spekt/ vt/i pesquisar, prospectar

prospective /prə'spektɪv/ a futuro; (possible) provável

prosper /'prɒspə(r)/ vi prosperar

prosper|ous /'prɒspərəs/ a próspero. ~**ity** /-'sperətɪ/ n prosperidade f

prostitut|e /'prɒstɪtjuːt/ n prostituta f. ~**ion** /-'tjuːʃn/ n prostituição f

prostrate /'prɒstreɪt/ a prostrado

protect /prə'tekt/ vt proteger. ~**ion** /-ʃn/ n proteção f, (P) protecção f. ~**ive** a protetor, (P) protector. ~**or** n protetor m, (P) protector m

protégé /'prɒtɪʒeɪ/ n protegido m. ~**e** n protegida f

protein /'prəʊtiːn/ n proteína f

protest[1] /'prəʊtest/ n protesto m

protest[2] /prə'test/ vt/i protestar. ~**er** n (pol) manifestante mf

Protestant /'prɒtɪstənt/ a & n protestante (mf). ~**ism** /-ɪzəm/ n protestantismo m

protocol /'prəʊtəkɒl/ n protocolo m

prototype /'prəʊtətaɪp/ n protótipo m

protract /prə'trækt/ vt prolongar, arrastar

protrud|e /prə'truːd/ vi sobressair, sair do alinhamento. ~**ing** a saliente

proud /praʊd/ a (er, -est) orgulhoso. ~ly adv orgulhosamente

prove /pruːv/ vt provar, demonstrar □ vi ~ (to be) easy/etc verificar-se ser fácil/ etc. ~ o.s. dar provas de si. ~n /-n/ a provado

proverb /ˈprɒvɜːb/ n provérbio m. ~ial /prəˈvɜːbɪəl/ a proverbial

provid|e /prəˈvaɪd/ vt prover, munir (sb with sth alg de alguma coisa) □ vi ~ for providenciar para; (person) prover de, cuidar de; (allow for) levar em conta. ~ed, ~ing (that) conj desde que, contanto que

providence /ˈprɒvɪdəns/ n providência f

province /ˈprɒvɪns/ n província f; (fig) competência f

provincial /prəˈvɪnʃl/ a provincial; (rustic) provinciano

provision /prəˈvɪʒn/ n provisão f; (stipulation) disposição f. ~s (pl (food) provisões fpl

provisional /prəˈvɪʒənl/ a provisório. ~ly adv provisoriamente

proviso /prəˈvaɪzəʊ/ n (pl -os) condição f

provo|ke /prəˈvəʊk/ vt provocar. ~cation /prɒvəˈkeɪʃn/ n provocação f. ~cative /-ˈvɒkətɪv/ a provocante

prowess /ˈpraʊɪs/ n proeza f, façanha f

prowl /praʊl/ vi rondar □ n be on the ~ andar à espreita. ~er n pessoa f que anda à espreita

proximity /prɒkˈsɪmətɪ/ n proximidade f

proxy /ˈprɒksɪ/ n by ~ por procuração

prude /pruːd/ n puritano m, pudico m

pruden|t /ˈpruːdnt/ a prudente. ~ce n prudência f

prune[1] /pruːn/ n ameixa f seca

prune[2] /pruːn/ vt podar

pry /praɪ/ vi bisbilhotar. ~ into meter o nariz em, intrometer-se em

psalm /saːm/ n salmo m

pseudo- /ˈsjuːdəʊ/ pref pseudo-

pseudonym /ˈsjuːdənɪm/ n pseudônimo m, (P) pseudónimo m

psychiatr|y /saɪˈkaɪətrɪ/ n psiquiatria f. ~ic /-ɪˈætrɪk/ a psiquiátrico. ~ist n psiquiatra mf

psychic /ˈsaɪkɪk/ a psíquico; (person) com capacidade de telepatia

psychoanalys|e /saɪkəʊˈænəlaɪz/ vt psicanalisar. ~t /-ɪst/ n psicanalista mf

psychoanalysis /saɪkəʊəˈnæləsɪs/ n psicanálise f

psycholog|y /saɪˈkɒlədʒɪ/ n psicologia f. ~ical /-əˈlɒdʒɪkl/ a psicológico. ~ist n psicólogo m

psychopath /ˈsaɪkəʊpæθ/ n psicopata mf

pub /pʌb/ n pub m

puberty /ˈpjuːbətɪ/ n puberdade f

public /ˈpʌblɪk/ a público; (holiday) feriado. in ~ em público. ~ house pub m. ~ relations relações fpl públicas. ~ school escola f particular; (Amer) escola f oficial. ~-spirited a de espírito cívico, patriótico. ~ly adv publicamente

publication /pʌblɪˈkeɪʃn/ n publicação f

publicity /pʌˈblɪsətɪ/ n publicidade f

publicize /ˈpʌblɪsaɪz/ vt fazer publicidade de

publish /ˈpʌblɪʃ/ vt publicar. ~er n editor m. ~ing n publicação f. ~ing house editora f

pucker /ˈpʌkə(r)/ vt/i franzir

pudding /ˈpʊdɪŋ/ n pudim m; (dessert) doce m

puddle /ˈpʌdl/ n poça f de água, charco m

puerile /ˈpjʊəraɪl/ a pueril

puff /pʌf/ n baforada f □ vt/i lançar baforadas; (breathe hard) arquejar, ofegar. ~ at (cigar etc) dar baforadas em. ~ out (swell) inchar(-se). ~-pastry n massa f folhada

puffy /ˈpʌfɪ/ a inchado

pugnacious /pʌgˈneɪʃəs/ a belicoso, combativo

pull /pʊl/ vt/i puxar; (muscle) distender □ n puxão m; (fig: influence) influência f, empenho m. give a ~ dar um puxão. ~ a face fazer uma careta. ~ one's weight (fig) fazer a sua quota-parte. ~ sb's leg brincar com alguém, meter-se com alguém. ~ away or out (auto) arrancar. ~ down puxar para baixo; (building) demolir. ~ in (auto) encostar-se. ~ off tirar; (fig) sair-se bem em, conseguir alcançar. ~ out partir; (extract) arrancar, tirar. ~ through sair-se bem. ~ o.s. together recompor-se, refazer-se. ~ up puxar para cima; (uproot) arrancar; (auto) parar

pulley /ˈpʊlɪ/ n roldana f

pullover /ˈpʊləʊvə(r)/ n pulôver m

pulp /pʌlp/ n polpa f; (for paper) pasta f de papel

pulpit /ˈpʊlpɪt/ n púlpito m

pulsat|e /pʌlˈseɪt/ vi pulsar, bater, palpitar. ~ion /-ˈseɪʃn/ n pulsação f

pulse /pʌls/ n pulso m. feel sb's ~ tirar o pulso de alguém

pulverize /ˈpʌlvəraɪz/ vt (grind, defeat) pulverizar

pummel /ˈpʌml/ vt (pt pummelled) esmurrar

pump[1] /pʌmp/ n bomba f □ vt/i bombear; (person) arrancar or extrair informações de. ~ up encher com bomba

pump[2] /pʌmp/ n (shoe) sapato m

pumpkin /'pʌmpkɪn/ n abóbora f

pun /pʌn/ n trocadilho m, jogo m de palavras

punch[1] /pʌntʃ/ vt esmurrar, dar um murro or soco; (perforate) furar, perfurar; (a hole) fazer □ n murro m, soco m; (device) furador m. ∼-line n remate m. ∼-up n (collog) pancadaria f

punch[2] /pʌntʃ/ n (drink) ponche m

punctual /'pʌŋktʃʊəl/ a pontual. ∼ity /-'ælətɪ/ n pontualidade f

punctuat|e /'pʌŋktʃʊert/ vt pontuar. ∼ion /-'eɪʃn/ n pontuação f

puncture /'pʌŋktʃə(r)/ n (in tyre) furo m □ vt/i furar

pundit /'pʌndɪt/ n autoridade f, sumidade f

pungent /'pʌndʒənt/ a acre, pungente

punish /'pʌnɪʃ/ vt punir, castigar. ∼able a punível. ∼ment n punição f, castigo m

punitive /'pju:nɪtɪv/ a (expedition, measure etc) punitivo; (taxation etc) penalizador

punt /pʌnt/ n (boat) chalana f

punter /'pʌntə(r)/ n (gambler) jogador m; (collog: customer) freguês m

puny /'pju:nɪ/ a (-ier, -iest) fraco, débil

pup(py) /'pʌp(ɪ)/ n cachorro m, cachorrinho m

pupil /'pju:pl/ n aluno m; (of eye) pupila f

puppet /'pʌpɪt/ n (lit &fig) fantoche m, marionete f

purchase /'pɜ:tʃəs/ vt comprar (from sb de alg) □ n compra f. ∼r /-ə(r)/ n comprador m

pur|e /'pjʊə(r)/ a (-er, -est) puro. ∼ely adv puramente. ∼ity n pureza f

purgatory /'pɜ:gətrɪ/ n purgatório m

purge /pɜ:dʒ/ vt purgar; (pol) sanear □ n (med) purgante m; (pol) saneamento m

purif|y /'pjʊərɪfaɪ/ vt purificar. ∼ication /-ɪ'keɪʃn/ n purificação f

puritan /'pjʊərɪtən/ n puritano m. ∼ical /-'tænɪkl/ a puritano

purple /'pɜ:pl/ a roxo, purpúreo □ n roxo m, púrpura f

purport /pə'pɔ:t/ vt dizer-se, (P) dar a entender. ∼ to be pretender ser

purpose /'pɜ:pəs/ n propósito m; (determination) firmeza f. on ∼ de propósito. to no ∼ em vão. ∼-built a construído especialmente.

purposely /'pɜ:pəslɪ/ adv de propósito, propositadamente

purr /pɜ:r/ n ronrom m □ vi ronronar

purse /pɜ:s/ n carteira f; (Amer) bolsa f □ vt franzir

pursue /pə'sju:/ vt perseguir; (go on with) prosseguir; (engage in) entregar-se a, dedicar-se a. ∼r /-ə(r)/ n perseguidor m

pursuit /pə'sju:t/ n perseguição f; (fig) atividade f, (P) actividade f

pus /pʌs/ n pus m

push /pʊʃ/ vt/i empurrar; (button) apertar; (thrust) enfiar; (collog: recommend) insistir □ n empurrão m; (effort) esforço m; (drive) energia f. be ∼ed for (time etc) estar com pouco. be ∼ing thirty/etc (collog) estar beirando os trinta/etc. give the ∼ to (sl) dar o fora em alguém. ∼ back repelir. ∼-chair n carrinho m (de criança). ∼er n fornecedor m (de droga). ∼ off (sl) dar o fora. ∼ on continuar. ∼-over n canja f, coisa f fácil. ∼ up (lift) levantar; (prices) forçar o aumento de. ∼-up n (Amer) flexão f. ∼y a (collog) agressivo, furão

put /pʊt/ vt/i (pt put, pres p putting) colocar, pôr; (question) fazer. ∼ the damage at a million estimar os danos em um milhão. I'd ∼ it at a thousand eu diria mil. ∼ sth tactfully dizer alg coisa com tato. ∼ across comunicar. ∼ away guardar. ∼ back repor; (delay) retardar, atrasar. ∼ by pôr de lado. ∼ down pôr em lugar baixo; (write) anotar; (pay) pagar; (suppress) sufocar, reprimir. ∼ forward (plan) submeter. ∼ in (insert) introduzir; (fix) instalar; (submit) submeter. ∼ in for fazer um pedido, candidatar-se. ∼ off (postpone) adiar; (disconcert) desanimar; (displease) desagradar. ∼ s.o. off sth tirar o gosto de alguém por alg coisa. ∼ on (clothes) pôr; (radio) ligar; (light) acender; (speed, weight) ganhar; (accent) adotar. ∼ out pôr para fora; (stretch) esticar; (extinguish) extinguir, apagar; (disconcert) desconcertar; (inconvenience) incomodar. ∼ up levantar; (building) erguer, cons-truir; (notice) colocar; (price) aumentar; (guest) hospedar; (offer) oferecer. ∼-up job embuste m. ∼ up with suportar

putrefy /'pju:trɪfaɪ/ vi putrefazer-se, apodrecer

putty /'pʌtɪ/ n massa de vidraceiro f, betume m

puzzl|e /'pʌzl/ n puzzle m, quebra-cabeça m □ vt deixar perplexo, intrigar □ vi quebrar a cabeça. ∼ing a intrigante

pygmy /'pɪgmɪ/ n pigmeu m

pyjamas /pə'dʒɑ:məz/ npl pijama m

pylon /'paɪlɒn/ n poste m

pyramid /'pɪrəmɪd/ n pirâmide f

python /'paɪθn/ n píton m

p

quack[1] /kwæk/ *n* (*of duck*) grasnido *m* □ *vi* grasnar

quack[2] /kwæk/ *n* charlatão *m*

quadrangle /'kwɒdræŋgl/ *n* quadrângulo *m*; (*of college*) pátio *m* quadrangular

quadruped /'kwɒdruped/ *n* quadrúpede *m*

quadruple /'kwɒdrʊpl/ *a & n* quádruplo (*m*) □ *vt/i* /kwɒ'drʊpl/ quadruplicar. **∼ts** /-plɪts/ *npl* quadrigêmeos *mpl*, (P) quadrigémeos *mpl*

quagmire /'kwægmaɪə(r)/ *n* pântano *m*, lamaçal *m*

quail /kweɪl/ *n* codorniz *f*

quaint /kweɪnt/ *a* (-er, -est) pitoresco; (*whimsical*) estranho, bizarro

quake /kweɪk/ *vi* tremer □ *n* (*colloq*) tremor *m* de terra

Quaker /'kweɪkə(r)/ *n* quaker *mf*, quacre *m*

qualification /kwɒlɪfɪ'keɪʃn/ *n* qualificação *f*; (*accomplishment*) habilitação *f*; (*diploma*) diploma *m*, título *m*; (*condition*) requisito *m*, condição *f*; (*fig*) restrição *f*, reserva *f*

qualif|y /'kwɒlɪfaɪ/ *vt* qualificar; (*fig: moderate*) atenuar, moderar; (*fig: limit*) pôr ressalvas *or* restrições a □ *vi* (*fig: be entitled to*) ter os requisitos (**for** para); (*sport*) classificar-se. **he ∼ied as a vet** ele formou-se em veterinária. **∼ied** *a* formado; (*able*) qualificado, habilitado; (*moderated*) atenuado; (*limited*) limitado

quality /'kwɒlətɪ/ *n* qualidade *f*

qualm /kwa:m/ *n* escrúpulo *m*

quandary /'kwɒndərɪ/ *n* dilema *m*

quantity /'kwɒntətɪ/ *n* quantidade *f*

quarantine /'kwɒrənti:n/ *n* quarentena *f*

quarrel /'kwɒrəl/ *n* zanga *f*, questão *f*, discussão *f* □ *vi* (*pt* quarrelled) zangar-se, questionar, discutir. **∼some** *a* conflituoso, brigão

quarry[1] /'kwɒrɪ/ *n* (*prey*) presa *f*, caça *f*

quarry[2] /'kwɒrɪ/ *n* (*excavation*) pedreira *f*

quarter /'kwɔːtə(r)/ *n* quarto *m*; (*of year*) trimestre *m*; (*Amer: coin*) quarto *m* de dólar, 25 cêtimos *mpl*; (*district*) bairro *m*, quarteirão *m*. **∼s** (*lodgings*) alojamento *m*, residência *f*; (*mil*) quartel *m* □ *vt* dividir em quarto; (*mil*) aquartelar. **from all ∼s** de todos os lados. **∼ of an hour** quarto *m* de hora. **(a) ∼ past six** seis e quinze. **(a) ∼ to seven** quinze para as sete. **∼-final** *n* (*sport*) quarta *f* de final. **∼ly** *a* trimestral □ *adv* trimestralmente

quartet /kwɔː'tet/ *n* quarteto *m*

quartz /kwɔːts/ *n* quartzo *m* □ *a* (*watch etc*) de quartzo

quash /kwɒʃ/ *vt* reprimir; (*jur*) revogar

quaver /'kweɪvə(r)/ *vi* tremer, tremular □ *n* (*mus*) colcheia *f*

quay /ki:/ *n* cais *m*

queasy /'kwi:zɪ/ *a* delicado. **feel ∼** estar enjoado

queen /kwi:n/ *n* rainha *f*; (*cards*) dama *f*

queer /kwɪə(r)/ *a* (-er, -est) estranho; (*slightly ill*) indisposto; (*sl: homosexual*) bicha, maricas (*sl*); (*dubious*) suspeito □ *n* (*sl*) bicha *m*, maricas *m* (*sl*)

quell /kwel/ *vt* reprimir, abafar, sufocar

quench /kwentʃ/ *vt* (*fire, flame*) apagar; (*thirst*) matar, saciar

query /'kwɪərɪ/ *n* questão *f* □ *vt* pôr em dúvida

quest /kwest/ *n* busca *f*, procura *f*. **in ∼ of** em demanda de

question /'kwestʃən/ *n* pergunta *f*, interrogação *f*; (*problem, affair*) questão *f* □ *vt* perguntar, interrogar; (*doubt*) pôr em dúvida *or* em causa. **in ∼** em questão *or* em causa. **out of the ∼** fora de toda a questão. **there's no ∼ of** nem pensar em. **without ∼** sem dúvida. **∼ mark** ponto *m* de interrogação. **∼able** *a* discutível

questionnaire /kwestʃə'neə(r)/ *n* questionário *m*

queue /kju:/ *n* fila *f*, (P) bicha *f* □ *vi* (*pres p* queuing) fazer fila, (P) fazer bicha

quibble /'kwɪbl/ *vi* tergiversar, usar de evasivas; (*raise petty objections*) discutir por coisas insignificantes

quick /kwɪk/ *a* (-er, -est) rápido □ *adv* depressa. **be ∼** despachar-se. **have a ∼ temper** exaltar-se facilmente. **∼ly** *adv* rapidamente, depressa. **∼ness** *n* rapidez *f*

quicken /'kwɪkən/ *vt/i* apressar (-se)

quicksand /'kwɪksænd/ *n* areia *f* movediça

quid /kwɪd/ *n invar* (*sl*) libra *f*

quiet /'kwaɪət/ *a* (-er, -est) quieto, sossegado, tranquilo □ *n* quietude *f*, sossego *m*, tranqüilidade *f*. **keep ∼** calar-se. **on the ∼** às escondidas, na calada. **∼ly** *adv* sossegadamente, silenciosamente. **∼ness** *n* sossego *m*, tranquilidade *f*, calma *f*

quieten /'kwaɪətn/ *vt/i* sossegar, acalmar(-se)

quilt /kwɪlt/ *n* coberta *f* acolchoada. **(continental)** ~ edredão *m* de penas □ *vt* acolchoar

quince /kwɪns/ *n* marmelo *m*

quintet /kwɪn'tet/ *n* quinteto *m*

quintuplets /kwɪn'tju:plɪts/ *npl* quíntuplos *mpl*

quip /kwɪp/ *n* piada *f* □ *vt* contar piadas

quirk /kwɜ:k/ *n* mania *f*, singularidade *f*

quit /kwɪt/ *vt* (*pt* **quitted**) deixar □ *vi* ir-se embora; (*resign*) demitir-se. ~ **doing** (*Amer*) parar de fazer

quite /kwaɪt/ *adv* completamente, absolutamente; (*rather*) bastante. ~ **(so)!** isso mesmo!, exatamente! ~ **a few** bastante, alguns/algumas. ~ **a lot** bastante

quiver /'kwɪvə(r)/ *vi* tremer, estremecer □ *n* tremor *m*, estremecimento *m*

quiz /kwɪz/ *n* (*pl* **quizzes**) teste *m*; (*game*) concurso *m* □ *vt* (*pt* **quizzed**) interrogar

quizzical /'kwɪzɪkl/ *a* zombeteiro

quorum /'kwɔ:rəm/ *n* quorum *m*

quota /'kwəʊtə/ *n* cota *f*, quota *f*

quotation /kwəʊ'teɪʃn/ *n* citação *f*; (*estimate*) orçamento *m*. ~ **marks** aspas *fpl*

quote /kwəʊt/ *vt* citar; (*estimate*) fazer um orçamento □ *n* (*colloq: passage*) citação *f*; (*colloq: estimate*) orçamento *m*

····································

Rr

····································

rabbi /'ræbaɪ/ *n* rabino *m*

rabbit /'ræbɪt/ *n* coelho *m*

rabble /'ræbl/ *n* turba *f*. **the** ~ a ralé, a gentalha, o povinho

rabid /'ræbɪd/ *a* (*fig*) fanático, ferrenho; (*dog*) raivoso

rabies /'reɪbi:z/ *n* raiva *f*

race[1] /reɪs/ *n* corrida *f* □ *vt* (*horse*) fazer correr □ *vi* correr, dar uma corrida; (*rush*) ir em grande *or* a toda (a) velocidade. ~**-track** *n* pista *f*

race[2] /reɪs/ *n* (*group*) raça *f* □ *a* racial

racecourse /'reɪskɔ:s/ *n* hipódromo *m*

racehorse /'reɪshɔ:s/ *n* cavalo *m* de corrida

racial /'reɪʃl/ *a* racial

racing /'reɪsɪŋ/ *n* corridas *fpl*. ~ **car** carro *m* de corridas

racis|t /'reɪsɪst/ *a* & *n* racista (*mf*). ~**m** /-zəm/ *n* racismo *m*

rack[1] /ræk/ *n* (*for luggage*) porta-bagagem *m*, bagageiro *m*; (*for plates*) escorredor *m* de prato □ *vt* ~ **one's brains** dar tratos à imaginação

rack[2] /ræk/ *n* **go to** ~ **and ruin** arruinar-se; (*of buildings etc*) cair em ruínas

racket[1] /'rækɪt/ *n* (*sport*) raquete *f*, (*P*) raqueta *f*

racket[2] /'rækɪt/ *n* (*din*) barulheira *f*; (*swindle*) roubalheira *f*; (*sl: business*) negociata *f* (*colloq*)

racy /'reɪsɪ/ *a* (**-ier, -iest**) vivo, vigoroso

radar /'reɪda:(r)/ *n* radar *m* □ *a* de radar

radian|t /'reɪdɪənt/ *a* radiante. ~**ce** *n* brilho *m*

radiator /'reɪdɪeɪtə(r)/ *n* radiador *m*

radical /'rædɪkl/ *a* & *n* radical (*m*)

radio /'reɪdɪəʊ/ *n* (*pl* **-os**) rádio *f*; (*set*) (aparelho de) rádio *m* □ *vt* transmitir pelo rádio. ~ **station** estação *f* de rádio, emissora *f*

radioactiv|e /reɪdɪəʊ'æktɪv/ *a* radioativo, (*P*) radioactivo. ~**ity** /-'tɪvətɪ/ *n* radioatividade *f*, (*P*) radioactividade *f*

radiograph|er /reɪdɪ'ɒgrəfə(r)/ *n* radiologista *mf*. ~**y** *n* radiografia *f*

radish /'rædɪʃ/ *n* rabanete *m*

radius /'reɪdɪəs/ *n* (*pl* **-dii** /-dɪaɪ/) raio *m*

raffle /'ræfl/ *n* rifa *f* □ *vt* rifar

raft /ra:ft/ *n* jangada *f*

rafter /'ra:ftə(r)/ *n* trave *f*, viga *f*

rag[1] /ræg/ *n* farrapo *m*; (*for wiping*) trapo *m*; (*pej: newspaper*) jornaleco *m*. ~**s** *npl* farrapos *mpl*, andrajos *mpl*. **in** ~**s** maltrapilho. ~ **doll** boneca *f* de trapos

rag[2] /ræg/ *vt* (*pt* **ragged**) zombar de

rage /reɪdʒ/ *n* raiva *f*, fúria *f* □ *vi* estar furioso; (*of storm*) rugir; (*of battle*) estar acesa. **be all the** ~ (*colloq*) fazer furor, estar na moda (*colloq*)

ragged /'rægɪd/ *a* (*clothes, person*) esfarrapado, roto; (*edge*) esfiapado, esgarçado

raid /reɪd/ *n* (*mil*) ataque *m*; (*by police*) batida *f*; (*by criminals*) assalto *m* □ *vt* fazer um ataque *or* uma batida *or* um assalto. ~**er** *n* atacante *m*, assaltante *m*

rail /reɪl/ *n* (*of stairs*) corrimão *m*; (*of ship*) amurada *f*; (*on balcony*) parapeito *m*; (*for train*) trilho *m*; (*for curtain*) varão *m*. **by** ~ por estrada, (*P*) caminho de fer-ro

railings /'reɪlɪŋz/ *npl* grade *f*

railroad /'reɪlrəʊd/ *n* (*Amer*) = **railway**

railway /'reɪlweɪ/ *n* estrada *f*, (*P*) caminho *m* de ferro. ~ **line** linha *f* do trem. ~ **station** estação *f* ferroviária, (*P*) estação *f* de caminho de ferro

rain /rem/ *n* chuva *f* □ *vi* chover. ~ **forest** floresta *f* tropical. ~**storm** *n* tempestade *f* com chuva. ~**water** *n* água *f* da chuva

rainbow /'rembəʊ/ *n* arco-íris *m*

raincoat /'remkəʊt/ *n* impermeável *m*

raindrop /'remdrɒp/ *n* pingo *m* de chuva

rainfall /'remfɔːl/ *n* precipitação *f*, pluviosidade *f*

rainy /'remɪ/ *a* (-**ier**, -**iest**) chuvoso

raise /reɪz/ *vt* levantar, erguer; (*breed*) criar; (*voice*) levantar; (*question*) fazer; (*price etc*) aumentar, subir; (*funds*) angariar; (*loan*) obter □ *n* (*Amer*) aumento *m*

raisin /'reɪzn/ *n* passa *f*

rake /reɪk/ *n* ancinho *m* □ *vt* juntar, alisar com ancinho; (*search*) revolver, remexer. ~ **in** (*money*) ganhar a rodos. ~-**off** *n* (*colloq*) percentagem *f* (*colloq*). ~ **up** desenterrar, ressuscitar

rally /'rælɪ/ *vt*/*i* reunir(-se); (*reassemble*) reagrupar(-se), reorganizar(-se); (*health*) restabelecer (-se); (*strength*) recuperar as forças □ *n* (*recovery*) recuperação *f*; (*meeting*) comício *m*, assembléia *f*; (*auto*) rally *m*, rali *m*

ram /ræm/ *n* (*sheep*) carneiro *m* □ *vt* (*pt* **rammed**) (*beat down*) calcar; (*push*) meter à força; (*crash into*) bater contra

rambl|e /'ræmbl/ *n* caminhada *f*, perambulação *f* □ *vi* perambular, vaguear. ~**e on** divagar. ~**er** *n* caminhante *mf*; (*plant*) trepadeira *f*. ~**ing** *a* (*speech*) desconexo

ramp /ræmp/ *n* rampa *f*

rampage /ræm'peɪdʒ/ *vi* causar distúrbios violentos

rampant /'ræmpənt/ *a* **be** ~ vicejar, florescer; (*diseases etc*) grassar

rampart /'ræmpɑːt/ *n* baluarte *m*; (*fig*) defesa *f*

ramshackle /'ræmʃækl/ *a* (*car*) desconjuntado; (*house*) caindo aos pedaços

ran /ræn/ *see* **run**

ranch /rɑːntʃ/ *n* rancho *m*, estância *f*. ~**er** *n* rancheiro *m*

rancid /'rænsɪd/ *a* rançoso

rancour /'ræŋkə(r)/ *n* rancor *m*

random /'rændəm/ *a* feito, tirado *etc* ao acaso □ *n* **at** ~ ao acaso, a esmo, aleatoriamente

randy /'rændɪ/ *a* (-**ier**, -**iest**) lascivo, sensual

rang /ræŋ/ *see* **ring**

range /reɪndʒ/ *n* (*distance*) alcance *m*; (*scope*) âmbito *m*; (*variety*) gama *f*, variedade *f*; (*stove*) fogão *m*; (*of voice*) registro *m*, (*P*) registo *m*; (*of temperature*) variação *f* □ *vt* dispor, ordenar □ *vi* estender-se; (*vary*) variar. ~ **of mountains** cordilheira *f*, serra *f*. ~**r** *n* guarda *m* florestal

rank[1] /ræŋk/ *n* fila *f*, fileira *f*; (*mil*) posto *m*; (*social position*) classe *f*, categoria *f* □ *vt*/*i* ~ **among** contar(-se) entre. **the** ~ **and file** a massa

rank[2] /ræŋk/ *a* (-**er**, -**est**) (*plants*) luxuriante; (*smell*) fétido; (*out-and-out*) total

ransack /'rænsæk/ *vt* (*search*) espionar, revistar, remexer; (*pillage*) pilhar, saquear

ransom /'rænsəm/ *n* resgate *m* □ *vt* resgatar. **hold to** ~ prender como refém

rant /rænt/ *vi* usar linguagem bombástica

rap /ræp/ *n* pancadinha *f* seca □ *vt*/*i* (*pt* **rapped**) bater, dar uma pancada seca em

rape /reɪp/ *vt* violar, estuprar □ *n* violação *f*, estupro *m*

rapid /'ræpɪd/ *a* rápido. ~**ity** /rə'pɪdətɪ/ *n* rapidez *f*

rapids /'ræpɪdz/ *npl* rápidos *mpl*

rapist /'reɪpɪst/ *n* violador *m*, estuprador *m*

rapport /ræ'pɔː(r)/ *n* bom relacionamento *m*

rapt /ræpt/ *a* absorto. ~ **in** mergulhado em

raptur|e /'ræptʃə(r)/ *n* êxtase *m*. ~**ous** *a* extático; (*welcome etc*) entusiástico

rar|e[1] /'reə(r)/ *a* (-**er**, -**est**) raro. ~**ely** *adv* raramente, raras vezes. ~**ity** *n* raridade *f*

rare[2] /reə(r)/ *a* (-**er**, -**est**) (*culin*) mal passado

rarefied /'reərɪfaɪd/ *a* rarefeito; (*refined*) requintado

raring /'reərɪŋ/ *a* ~ **to** (*colloq*) impaciente por, louco por (*colloq*)

rascal /'rɑːskl/ *n* (*dishonest*) patife *m*; (*mischievous*) maroto *m*

rash[1] /ræʃ/ *n* erupção *f* cutânea, irritação *f* na pele (*colloq*)

rash[2] /ræʃ/ *a* (-**er**, -**est**) imprudente, precipitado. ~**ly** *adv* imprudentemente, precipitadamente

rasher /'ræʃə(r)/ *n* fatia *f* (de presunto *or* de bacon)

rasp /rɑːsp/ *n* lixa *f* grossa, (*P*) lima *f* grossa

raspberry /'rɑːzbrɪ/ *n* framboesa *f*

rasping /'rɑːspɪŋ/ *a* áspero

rat /ræt/ *n* rato *m*, (*P*) ratazana *f*. ~ **race** (*fig*) luta renhida para vencer na vida, arrivismo *m*

r

rate /reɪt/ *n* (*ratio*) razão *f*; (*speed*) velocidade *f*; (*price*) tarifa *f*; (*of exchange*) (taxa *m* de) câmbio *m*; (*of interest*) taxa *f*. **~s** (*taxes*) impostos *mpl* municipais, taxas *fpl* □ *vt* avaliar; (*fig: consider*) considerar. **at any ~** de qualquer modo, pelo menos. **at the ~ of** à razão de. **at this ~** desse jeito, desse modo

ratepayer /'reɪtpeɪə(r)/ *n* contribuinte *mf*

rather /'rɑːðə(r)/ *adv* (*by preference*) antes; (*fairly*) muito, bastante; (*a little*) um pouco. **I would ~ go** preferia ir

ratif|y /'rætɪfaɪ/ *vt* ratificar. **~ication** /-ɪ'keɪʃn/ *n* ratificação *f*

rating /'reɪtɪŋ/ *n* (*comm*) rating *m*, (P) valor *m*; (*sailor*) praça *f*, marinheiro *m*; (*radio, TV*) índice *m* de audiência

ratio /'reɪʃɪəʊ/ *n* (*pl* **-os**) proporção *f*

ration /'ræʃn/ *n* ração *f* □ *vt* racionar

rational /'ræʃnəl/ *a* racional; (*person*) sensato, razoável. **~- ize** *vt* racionalizar

rattle /'rætl/ *vt/i* matraquear; (*of door, window*) bater; (*of bottles*) chocalhar; (*colloq*) agitar, mexer com os nervos de □ *n* (*baby's toy*) guizo *m*, chocalho *m*; (*of football fan*) matraca *f*; (*sound*) matraquear *m*, chocalhar *m*. **~ off** despejar (*colloq*)

rattlesnake /'rætlsneɪk/ *n* cobra *f* cascavel

raucous /'rɔːkəs/ *a* áspero, rouco

ravage /'rævɪdʒ/ *vt* devastar, causar estragos a. **~s** *npl* devastação *f*, estragos *mpl*

rave /reɪv/ *vi* delirar; (*in anger*) urrar. **~ about** delirar (de entusiasmo) com

raven /'reɪvn/ *n* corvo *m*

ravenous /'rævənəs/ *a* esfomeado; (*greedy*) voraz

ravine /rə'viːn/ *n* ravina *f*, barranco *m*

raving /'reɪvɪŋ/ *a* **~ lunatic** doido *m* varrido □ *adv* **~ mad** loucamente

ravish /'rævɪʃ/ *vt* (*rape*) violar; (*enrapture*) arrebatar, encantar. **~ing** *a* arrebatador, encantador

raw /rɔː/ *a* (**-er, -est**) cru; (*not processed*) bruto; (*wound*) em carne viva; (*weather*) frio e úmido, (P) húmido; (*immature*) inexperiente, verde. **~ deal** tratamento *m* injusto. **~ material** matéria-prima *f*

ray /reɪ/ *n* raio *m*

raze /reɪz/ *vt* arrasar

razor /'reɪzə(r)/ *n* navalha *f* de barba. **~-blade** *n* lâmina *f* de barbear

re /riː/ *prep* a respeito de, em referência a, relativo a

re- /riː/ *pref* re-

reach /riːtʃ/ *vt* chegar a atingir; (*contact*) contatar; (*pass*) passar □ *vi* estender-se, chegar □ *n* alcance *m*. **out of ~** fora de alcance. **~ for** estender a mão para agarrar. **within ~ of** ao alcance de; (*close to*) próximo de

react /rɪ'ækt/ *vi* reagir

reaction /rɪ'ækʃn/ *n* reação *f*, (P) reacção *f*. **~ary** *a* & *n* reacionário (*m*), (P) reaccionário (*m*)

reactor /rɪ'æktə(r)/ *n* reator *m*, (P) reactor *m*

read /riːd/ *vt/i* (*pt* **read** /red/) ler; (*fig: interpret*) interpretar; (*study*) estudar; (*of instrument*) marcar, indicar □ *n* (*colloq*) leitura *f*. **~ about** ler um artigo sobre. **~ out** ler em voz alta. **~able** *a* agradável *or* fácil de ler; (*legible*) legível. **~er** *n* leitor *m*; (*book*) livro *m* de leitura. **~ing** *n* leitura *f*; (*of instrument*) registro *m*, (P) registo *m*

readily /'redɪlɪ/ *adv* de boa vontade, prontamente; (*easily*) facilmente

readiness /'redɪnɪs/ *n* prontidão *f*. **in ~** pronto (**for** para)

readjust /riːə'dʒʌst/ *vt* reajustar □ *vi* readaptar-se

ready /'redɪ/ *a* (**-ier, -iest**) pronto □ *n* **at the ~** pronto para disparar. **~-made** *a* pronto. **~ money** dinheiro *m* vivo, (P) dinheiro *m* de contado, pagamento *m* à vista. **~-to-wear** *a* prêt-à-porter

real /rɪəl/ *a* real, verdadeiro; (*genuine*) autêntico □ *adv* (*Amer: colloq*) realmente. **~ estate** bens *mpl* imobiliários

realis|t /'rɪəlɪst/ *n* realista *mf*. **~m** /-zəm/ *n* realismo *m*. **~tic** /-'lɪstɪk/ *a* realista. **~tically** /-'lɪstɪkəlɪ/ *adv* realisticamente

reality /rɪ'ælətɪ/ *n* realidade *f*

realiz|e /'rɪəlaɪz/ *vt* dar-se conta de, aperceber-se de, perceber; (*fulfil; turn into cash*) realizar. **~ation** /-'zeɪʃn/ *n* consciência *f*, noção *f*; (*fulfilment*) realização *f*

really /'rɪəlɪ/ *adv* realmente, na verdade

realm /relm/ *n* reino *m*; (*fig*) domínio *m*, esfera *f*

reap /riːp/ *vt* (*cut*) ceifar; (*gather; fig*) colher

reappear /riːə'pɪə(r)/ *vi* reaparecer. **~ance** *n* reaparição *f*

rear[1] /rɪə(r)/ *n* traseira *f*, retaguarda *f* □ *a* traseiro, de trás, posterior. **bring up the ~** ir na retaguarda, fechar a marcha. **~-view mirror** espelho *m* retrovisor

rear[2] /rɪə(r)/ *vt* levantar, erguer; (*children, cattle*) criar □ *vi* (*of horse etc*) empinar-se. **~ one's head** levantar a cabeça

r

rearrange /riːəˈreɪndʒ/ vt arranjar doutro modo, reorganizar

reason /ˈriːzn/ n razão f □ vt/i raciocinar, argumentar. ~ **with sb** procurar convencer alguém. **within** ~ razoável. ~**ing** n raciocínio m

reasonable /ˈriːznəbl/ a razoável

reassur|e /riːəˈʃʊə(r)/ vt tranqüilizar, sossegar. ~**ance** n garantia f. ~**ing** a animador, reconfortante

rebate /ˈriːbeɪt/ n (refund) reimbolso m; (discount) desconto m, abatimento m

rebel[1] /ˈrebl/ n rebelde mf

rebel[2] /rɪˈbel/ vi (pt rebelled) rebelar-se, revoltar-se, sublevar-se. ~**lion** n rebelião f, revolta f. ~**lious** a rebelde

rebound[1] /rɪˈbaʊnd/ vi repercutir, ressoar; (fig: backfire) recair (on sobre)

rebound[2] /ˈriːbaʊnd/ n ricochete m

rebuff /rɪˈbʌf/ vt receber mal, repelir (colloq) □ n rejeição f

rebuild /riːˈbɪld/ vt (pt rebuilt) reconstruir

rebuke /rɪˈbjuːk/ vt repreender □ n reprimenda f

recall /rɪˈkɔːl/ vt chamar, mandar regressar; (remember) lembrar-se de □ n (summons) ordem f de regresso

recant /rɪˈkænt/ vi retratar-se, (P) retractar-se

recap /ˈriːkæp/ vt/i (pt recapped) (colloq) recapitular □ n recapitulação f

recapitulat|e /riːkəˈpɪtʃʊleɪt/ vt/i recapitular. ~**ion** /-ˈleɪʃn/ n recapitulação f

recede /rɪˈsiːd/ vi recuar, retroceder. **his hair is** ~**ing** ele está ficando com entradas. ~**ing** a (forehead, chin) recuado, voltado para dentro

receipt /rɪˈsiːt/ n recibo m; (receiving) recepção f. ~**s** (comm) receitas fpl

receive /rɪˈsiːv/ vt receber. ~**r** /-ə(r)/ n (of stolen goods) receptador m; (phone) fone m, (P) auscultador m; (radio/TV) receptor m. **(official)** ~**r** síndico m de massa falida

recent /ˈriːsnt/ a recente. ~**ly** adv recentemente

receptacle /rɪˈseptəkl/ n recipiente m, receptáculo m

reception /rɪˈsepʃn/ n recepção f; (welcome) acolhimento m. ~**ist** n recepcionista mf

receptive /rɪˈseptɪv/ a receptivo

recess /rɪˈses/ n recesso m; (of legislature) recesso m; (Amer: schol) recreio m

recession /rɪˈseʃn/ n recessão f, depressão f

recharge /riːˈtʃɑːdʒ/ vt tornar a carregar, recarregar

recipe /ˈresəpɪ/ n (culin) receita f

recipient /rɪˈsɪpɪənt/ n recipiente mf; (of letter) destinatário m

reciprocal /rɪˈsɪprəkl/ a recíproco

reciprocate /rɪˈsɪprəkeɪt/ vt/i reciprocar(-se), retribuir, fazer o mesmo

recital /rɪˈsaɪtl/ n (music etc) recital m

recite /rɪˈsaɪt/ vt recitar; (list) enumerar

reckless /ˈreklɪs/ a inconsciente, imprudente, estouvado

reckon /ˈrekən/ vt/i calcular; (judge) considerar; (think) supor, pensar. ~ **on** contar com, depender de. ~ **with** contar com, levar em conta. ~**ing** n conta(s) f(pl)

reclaim /rɪˈkleɪm/ vt (demand) reclamar; (land) recuperar

reclin|e /rɪˈklaɪn/ vt/i reclinar (-se). ~**ing** a (person) reclinado; (chair) reclinável

recluse /rɪˈkluːs/ n solitário m, recluso m

recognition /rekəgˈnɪʃn/ n reconhecimento m. **beyond** ~ irreconhecível. **gain** ~ ganhar nome, ser reconhecido

recogniz|e /ˈrekəgnaɪz/ vt reconhecer. ~**able** /ˈrekəgnaɪzəbl/ a reconhecível

recoil /rɪˈkɔɪl/ vi recuar; (gun) dar coice □ n recuo m; (gun) coice m. ~ **from doing** recusar-se a fazer

recollect /rekəˈlekt/ vt recordar-se de. ~**ion** /-ʃn/ n recordação f

recommend /rekəˈmend/ vt recomendar. ~**ation** /-ˈdeɪʃn/ n recomendação f

recompense /ˈrekəmpens/ vt recompensar □ n recompensa f

reconcil|e /ˈrekənsaɪl/ vt (people) reconciliar; (facts) conciliar. ~**e o.s. to** resignar-se a, conformar-se com. ~**iation** /-sɪlɪˈeɪʃn/ n reconciliação f

reconnaissance /rɪˈkɒnɪsns/ n reconhecimento m

reconnoitre /rekəˈnɔɪtə(r)/ vt/i (pres p -tring) (mil) reconhecer, fazer um reconhecimento (de)

reconsider /riːkənˈsɪdə(r)/ vt reconsiderar

reconstruct /riːkənˈstrʌkt/ vt reconstruir. ~**ion** /-ʃn/ n reconstrução f

record[1] /rɪˈkɔːd/ vt registar; (disc, tape etc) gravar. ~ **that** referir/relatar que. ~**ing** n (disc, tape etc) gravação f

record[2] /ˈrekɔːd/ n (register) registro m, (P) registo m; (mention) menção f, nota f; (file) arquivo m; (mus) disco m; (sport) record(e) m □ a record(e) invar. **have a (criminal)** ~ ter cadastro. **off the** ~ (unofficial) oficioso; (secret) confidencial. ~**player** n toca-discos m invar, (P) gira-discos m invar

recorder /rɪˈkɔːdə(r)/ n (mus) flauta f de ponta; (techn) instrumento m registrador

recount /rɪˈkaʊnt/ vt narrar em pormenor, relatar

re-count /ˈriːkaʊnt/ n (pol) nova contagem f

recoup /rɪˈkuːp/ vt compensar; (recover) recuperar

recourse /rɪˈkɔːs/ n recurso m. **have ~ to** recorrer a

recover /rɪˈkʌvə(r)/ vt recuperar □ vi restabelecer-se. ~**y** n recuperação f; (health) recuperação f, restabelecimento m

recreation /rekrɪˈeɪʃn/ n recreação f, recreio m; (pastime) passatempo m. ~**al** a recreativo

recrimination /rɪkrɪmɪˈneɪʃn/ n recriminação f

recruit /rɪˈkruːt/ n recruta m □ vt recrutar. ~**ment** n recrutamento m

rectangle /ˈrektæŋɡl/ n retângulo m, (P) rectângulo m. ~**ular** /-ˈtæŋɡjʊlə(r)/ a retangular, (P) rectangular

rectify /ˈrektɪfaɪ/ vt retificar, (P) rectificar

recuperate /rɪˈkjuːpəreɪt/ vt/i recuperar(-se)

recur /rɪˈkɜː(r)/ vi (pt recurred) repetir-se; (come back) voltar (**to** a)

recurren|t /rɪˈkʌrənt/ a freqüente, (P) frequente, repetido, periódico. ~**ce** n repetição f

recycle /riːˈsaɪkl/ vt reciclar

red /red/ a (**redder, reddest**) encarnado, vermelho; (hair) ruivo □ n encarnado m, vermelho m. **in the ~** em défict. ~ **carpet** (fig) recepção f solene, tratamento m especial. **R~ Cross** Cruz f Vermelha. ~**-handed** a em flagrante (delito), com a boca na botija (colloq). ~ **herring** (fig) pista f falsa. ~**-hot** a escaldante, incandescente. ~ **light** luz f vermelha. ~ **tape** (fig) papelada f, burocracia f. ~ **wine** vinho m tinto

redden /ˈredn/ vt/i avermelhar(-se); (blush) corar, ruborizar-se

redecorate /riːˈdekəreɪt/ vt decorar; pintar de novo

red|eem /rɪˈdiːm/ vt (sins etc) redimir; (sth pawned) tirar do prego (colloq); (voucher etc) resgatar. ~**emption** /rɪˈdempʃn/ n resgate m; (of honour) salvação f

redirect /riːdaɪˈrekt/ vt (letter) reendereçar

redness /ˈrednɪs/ n vermelhidão f, cor f vermelha

redo /riːˈduː/ vt (pt **-did**, pp **-done**) refazer

redress /rɪˈdres/ vt reparar; (set right) remediar, emendar. ~ **the balance** restabelecer o equilíbrio □ n reparação f

reduc|e /rɪˈdjuːs/ vt reduzir; (temperature etc) baixar. ~**tion** /rɪˈdʌkʃən/ n redução f

redundan|t /rɪˈdʌndənt/ a redundante, supérfluo; (worker) desempregado. **be made ~t** ficar desempregado. ~**cy** n demissão f por excesso de pessoal

reed /riːd/ n cara f, junco m; (mus) palheta f

reef /riːf/ n recife m

reek /riːk/ n mau cheiro m □ vi cheirar mal, tresandar. **he ~s of wine** ele está com cheiro de vinho

reel /riːl/ n carretel m; (spool) bobina f □ vi cambalear, vacilar □ vt ~ **off** recitar (colloq)

refectory /rɪˈfektərɪ/ n refeitório m

refer /rɪˈfɜː(r)/ vt/i (pt referred) ~ **to** referir-se a; (concern) aplicar-se a, dizer respeito a; (consult) consultar; (direct) remeter a

referee /refəˈriː/ n árbitro m; (for job) pessoa f que dá referências □ vt (pt **refereed**) arbitrar

reference /ˈrefrəns/ n referência f; (testimonial) referências fpl. **in ~ or with ~ to** com referência a. ~ **book** livro m de consulta

referendum /refəˈrendəm/ n (pl **-dums** or **-da**) referendo m, plebiscito m

refill[1] /riːˈfɪl/ vt encher de novo; (pen etc) pôr carga nova em

refill[2] /ˈriːfɪl/ n (pen etc) carga f nova, (P) recarga f

refine /rɪˈfaɪn/ vt refinar. ~**d** a refinado; (taste, manners etc) requintado. ~**ment** n (taste, manners etc) refinamento m, requinte m; (tech) refinação f. ~**ry** /-ərɪ/ n refinaria f

reflect /rɪˈflekt/ vt/i refletir, (P) reflectir (**on/upon** em). ~**ion** /-ʃn/ n reflexão f; (image) reflexo m. ~**or** n refletor m, (P) reflector m

reflective /rɪˈflektɪv/ a refletor, (P) reflector; (thoughtful) refletido, (P) reflectido, ponderado

reflex /ˈriːfleks/ a & n reflexo (m)

reflexive /rɪˈfleksɪv/ a (gram) reflexivo, (P) reflexo

reform /rɪˈfɔːm/ vt/i reformar(-se) □ n reforma f. ~**er** n reformador m

refract /rɪˈfrækt/ vt refratar, (P) refractar

refrain[1] /rɪˈfreɪn/ n refrão m, estribilho m

refrain[2] /rɪˈfreɪn/ vi abster-se (**from** de)

refresh /rɪˈfreʃ/ vt refrescar; (of rest etc) restaurar. ~ **one's memory** avivar or

refrescar a memória. ~ing *a*
refrescante; (*of rest etc*) reparador.
~ments *npl* refeição *f* leve; (*drinks*)
refrescos *mpl*
refresher /rɪˈfreʃə(r)/ *n* ~ **course** curso
m de reciclagem
refrigerat|e /rɪˈfrɪdʒəreɪt/ *vt* refrigerar.
~**or** *n* frigorífico *m*, refrigerador *m*,
geladeira *f*
refuel /riːˈfjuːəl/ *vt/i* (*pt* **refuelled**)
reabastecer(-se) (de combustível)
refuge /ˈrefjuːdʒ/ *n* refúgio *m*, asilo *m*.
take ~ refugiar-se
refugee /refjʊˈdʒiː/ *n* refugiado *m*
refund[1] /rɪˈfʌnd/ *vt* reembolsar
refund[2] /ˈriːfʌnd/ *n* reembolso *m*
refus|e[1] /rɪˈfjuːz/ *vt/i* recusar(-se). ~**al** *n*
recusa *f*. **first** ~**al** preferência *f*,
primeira opção *f*
refuse[2] /ˈrefjuːs/ *n* refugo *m*, lixo *m*.
~-**collector** *n* lixeiro *m*, (*P*) homem *m*
do lixo
refute /rɪˈfjuːt/ *vt* refutar
regain /rɪˈɡeɪn/ *vt* recobrar, recuperar
regal /ˈriːɡl/ *a* real, régio
regalia /rɪˈɡeɪlɪə/ *npl* insígnias *fpl*
regard /rɪˈɡɑːd/ *vt* considerar; (*gaze*)
olhar □ *n* consideração *f*, estima *f*;
(*gaze*) olhar *m*. ~**s** cumprimentos *mpl*;
(*less formally*) lembranças *fpl*,
saudades *fpl*. **as** ~**s**, ~**ing** *prep* no que
diz respeito a, quanto a. ~**less** *adv*
apesar de tudo. ~**less of** apesar de
regatta /rɪˈɡætə/ *n* regata *f*
regenerate /rɪˈdʒenəreɪt/ *vt* regenerar
regen|t /ˈriːdʒənt/ *n* regente *mf*. ~**cy** *n*
regência *f*
regime /reɪˈʒiːm/ *n* regime *m*
regiment /ˈredʒɪmənt/ *n* regimento *m*.
~**al** /-ˈmentl/ *a* de regimento,
regimental. ~**ation** /-enˈteɪʃn/ *n*
arregimentação *f*, disciplina *f*
excessiva
region /ˈriːdʒən/ *n* região *f*. **in the** ~ **of**
por volta de. ~**al** *a* regional
regist|er /ˈredʒɪstə(r)/ *n* registro *m*, (*P*)
registo *m* □ *vt* (*record*) anotar; (*notice*)
fixar, registar, prestar atenção a; (*birth,
letter*) registrar, (*P*) registar; (*vehicle*)
matricular; (*emotions etc*) exprimir
□ *vi* inscrever-se. ~**er office** registro
m, (*P*) registo *m*. ~**ration** /-ˈstreɪʃn/ *n*
registro *m*, (*P*) registo *m*; (*for course*)
inscrição *f*, matrícula *f*. ~**ration
(number)** número *m* de placa
registrar /redʒɪˈstrɑː(r)/ *n* oficial *m* do
registro, (*P*) registo civil; (*univ*)
secretário *m*
regret /rɪˈɡret/ *n* pena *f*, pesar *m*;
(*repentance*) remorso *m*. **I have no** ~**s**
não estou arrependido □ *vt* (*pt*

regretted) lamentar, sentir (**to do**
fazer); (*feel repentance*) arrepender-se
de, lamentar. ~**fully** *adv* com pena,
pesarosamente. ~**table** *a* lamentável.
~**tably** *adv* infelizmente
regular /ˈreɡjʊlə(r)/ *a* regular; (*usual*)
normal; (*colloq: thorough*) perfeito,
verdadeiro, autêntico □ *n* (*colloq:
client*) cliente *mf* habitual. ~**ity**
/-ˈlærətɪ/ *n* regularidade *f*. ~**ly** *adv*
regularmente
regulat|e /ˈreɡjʊleɪt/ *vt* regular. ~**ion**
/-ˈleɪʃn/ *n* regulação *f*; (*rule*)
regulamento *m*, regra *f*
rehabilitat|e /riːəˈbɪlɪteɪt/ *vt* reabilitar.
~**ion** /-ˈteɪʃn/ *n* reabilitação *f*
rehash[1] /riːˈhæʃ/ *vt* apresentar sob nova
forma, (*P*) cozinhar (*colloq*)
rehash[2] /ˈriːhæʃ/ *n* (*fig*) apanhado *m*, (*P*)
cozinhado *m* (*colloq*)
rehears|e /rɪˈhɜːs/ *vt* ensaiar. ~**al** *n*
ensaio *m*. **dress** ~**al** ensaio *m* geral
reign /reɪn/ *n* reinado *m* □ *vi* reinar
(**over** em)
reimburse /riːɪmˈbɜːs/ *vt* reembolsar.
~**ment** *n* reembolso *m*
rein /reɪn/ *n* rédea *f*
reincarnation /riːɪnkɑːˈneɪʃn/ *n*
reencarnação *f*
reindeer /ˈreɪndɪə(r)/ *n invar* rena *f*
reinforce /riːɪnˈfɔːs/ *vt* reforçar. ~**ment**
n reforço *m*. ~**ments** reforços *mpl*. ~**d
concrete** concreto *m* armado, (*P*)
cimento *m* or betão *m* armado
reinstate /riːɪnˈsteɪt/ *vt* reintegrar
reiterate /riːˈɪtəreɪt/ *vt* reiterar
reject[1] /rɪˈdʒekt/ *vt* rejeitar. ~**ion** /-ʃn/ *n*
rejeição *f*
reject[2] /ˈriːdʒekt/ *n* (artigo de) refugo *m*
rejoic|e /rɪˈdʒɔɪs/ *vi* regozijar-se (**at/over**
com). ~**ing** *n* regozijo *m*
rejuvenate /riːˈdʒuːvəneɪt/ *vt*
rejuvenescer
relapse /rɪˈlæps/ *n* recaída *f* □ *vi* recair
relate /rɪˈleɪt/ *vt* relatar; (*associate*)
relacionar □ *vi* ~ **to** ter relação com,
dizer respeito a; (*get on with*) entender-
se com. ~**d** *a* aparentado; (*ideas etc*)
afim, relacionado
relation /rɪˈleɪʃn/ *n* relação *f*; (*person*)
parente *mf*. ~**ship** *n* parentesco *m*;
(*link*) relação *f*; (*affair*) ligação *f*
relative /ˈrelətɪv/ *n* parente *mf* □ *a*
relativo. ~**ly** *adv* relativamente
relax /rɪˈlæks/ *vt/i* relaxar(-se); (*fig*)
descontrair(-se). ~**ation** /riːlækˈseɪʃn/
n relaxamento *m*; (*fig*) descontração *f*,
(*P*) descontracção *f*; (*recreation*)
distração *f*, (*P*) distracção *f*. ~**ing** *a*
relaxante

relay¹ /'ri:leɪ/ n turma f, (P) turno m. ~ **race** corrida f de revezamento, (P) estafetas

relay² /rɪ'leɪ/ vt (message) retransmitir

release /rɪ'li:s/ vt libertar, soltar; (mech) desengatar, soltar; (bomb, film, record) lançar; (news) dar, publicar; (gas, smoke) soltar □ n libertação f; (mech) desengate m; (bomb, film, record) lançamento m; (news) publicação f; (gas, smoke) emissão f. **new** ~ estréia f

relegate /'relɪgeɪt/ vt relegar

relent /rɪ'lent/ vi ceder. ~**less** a implacável, inexorável, inflexível

relevan|t /'reləvənt/ a relevante, pertinente, a propósito. **be** ~ **to** ter a ver com. ~**ce** n pertinência f, relevância f

reliab|le /rɪ'laɪəbl/ a de confiança, com que se pode contar; (source etc) fidedigno; (machine etc) seguro, confiável. ~**ility** /-'bɪlətɪ/ n confiabilidade f

reliance /rɪ'laɪəns/ n (dependence) segurança f; (trust) confiança f, fé f (**on** em)

relic /'relɪk/ n relíquia f. ~**s** vestígios mpl, ruínas fpl

relief /rɪ'li:f/ n alívio m; (assistance) auxílio m, assistência f; (outline, design) relevo m. ~ **road** estrada f alternativa

relieve /rɪ'li:v/ vt aliviar; (help) socorrer; (take over from) revezar, substituir; (mil) render

religion /rɪ'lɪdʒən/ n religião f

religious /rɪ'lɪdʒəs/ a religioso

relinquish /rɪ'lɪŋkwɪʃ/ vt abandonar, renunciar a

relish /'relɪʃ/ n prazer m, gosto m; (culin) molho m condimentado □ vt saborear, apreciar, gostar de

relocate /ri:ləʊ'keɪt/ vt/i transferir(-se), mudar(-se)

reluctan|t /rɪ'lʌktənt/ a relutante (**to** em), pouco inclinado (**to** a). ~**ce** n relutância f. ~**tly** adv a contragosto, relutantemente

rely /rɪ'laɪ/ vi ~ **on** contar com; (depend) depender de

remain /rɪ'meɪn/ vi ficar, permanecer. ~**s** npl restos mpl; (ruins) ruínas fpl. ~**ing** a restante

remainder /rɪ'meɪndə(r)/ n restante m, remanescente m

remand /rɪ'ma:nd/ vt reconduzir à prisão para detenção provisória □ n **on** ~ sob prisão preventiva

remark /rɪ'ma:k/ n observação f, comentário m □ vt observar, comentar □ vi ~ **on** fazer observações or comentários sobre. ~**able** a notável

remarr|y /ri:'mærɪ/ vt/i tornar a casar(-se) (com). ~**iage** n novo casamento m

remed|y /'remədɪ/ n remédio m □ vt remediar. ~**ial** /rɪ'mi:dɪəl/ a (med) corretivo, (P) correctivo

rememb|er /rɪ'membə(r)/ vt lembrar-se de, recordar-se de. ~**rance** n lembrança f, recordação f

remind /rɪ'maɪnd/ vt (fazer) lembrar (**sb of sth** alg coisa a alguém). ~ **sb to do** lembrar a alguém que faça. ~**er** n o que serve para fazer lembrar; (note) lembrete m

reminisce /remɪ'nɪs/ vi (re)lembrar (coisas passadas). ~**nces** npl reminiscências fpl

reminiscent /remɪ'nɪsnt/ a ~ **of** que faz lembrar, evocativo de

remiss /rɪ'mɪs/ a negligente, descuidado

remission /rɪ'mɪʃn/ n remissão f; (jur) comutação f (de pena)

remit /rɪ'mɪt/ vt (pt remitted) (money) remeter. ~**tance** n remessa f (de dinheiro)

remnant /'remnənt/ n resto m; (trace) vestígio m; (of cloth) retalho m

remorse /rɪ'mɔ:s/ n remorso m. ~**ful** a arrependido, com remorsos. ~**less** a implacável

remote /rɪ'məʊt/ a remoto, distante; (person) distante; (slight) vago, leve. ~ **control** comando m à distância, telecomando m. ~**ly** adv de longe; vagamente

remov|e /rɪ'mu:v/ vt tirar, remover; (lead away) levar; (dismiss) demitir; (get rid of) eliminar. ~**al** n remoção f; (dismissal) demissão f; (from house) mudança f

remunerat|e /rɪ'mju:nəreɪt/ vt remunerar. ~**ion** /-'reɪʃn/ n remuneração f

rename /ri:'neɪm/ vt rebatizar, (P) rebaptizar

render /'rendə(r)/ vt retribuir; (services) prestar; (mus) interpretar; (translate) traduzir. ~**ing** n (mus) interpretação f; (plaster) reboco m

renegade /'renɪgeɪd/ n renegado m

renew /rɪ'nju:/ vt renovar; (resume) retomar. ~**able** a renovável. ~**al** n renovação f; (resumption) reatamento m

renounce /rɪ'naʊns/ vt renunciar a; (disown) renegar, repudiar

renovat|e /'renəveɪt/ vt renovar. ~**ion** /-'veɪʃn/ n renovação f

renown /rɪ'naʊn/ n renome m. ~**ed** a conceituado, célebre, de renome

rent /rent/ n aluguel m, (P) aluguer m, renda f □ vt alugar, arrendar. ~**al** n

r

(*charge*) aluguel *m*, (*P*) aluguer *m*,
renda *f*; (*act of renting*) aluguel *m*, (*P*)
aluguer *m*

renunciation /rɪnʌnsɪ'eɪʃn/ *n* renúncia *f*

reopen /ri:'əʊpən/ *vt/i* reabrir (-se). ∼**ing**
n reabertura *f*

reorganize /ri:'ɔ:gənaɪz/ *vt/i*
reorganizar(-se)

rep /rep/ *n* (*colloq*) vendedor *m*, caixeiro-
viajante *m*

repair /rɪ'peə(r)/ *vt* reparar, consertar
☐ *n* reparo *m*, conserto *m*. **in good**
∼ em bom estado (de conservação)

repartee /repa:'ti:/ *n* resposta *f* pronta e
espirituosa

repatriat|**e** /ri:'pætrɪeɪt/ *vt* repatriar.
∼**ion** /-'eɪʃn/ *n* repatriamento *m*

repay /ri:'peɪ/ *vt* (*pt* **repaid**) pagar,
devolver, reembolsar; (*reward*)
recompensar. ∼**ment** *n* pagamento *m*,
reembolso *m*

repeal /rɪ'pi:l/ *vt* revogar ☐ *n* revogação *f*

repeat /rɪ'pi:t/ *vt/i* repetir(-se) ☐ *n*
repetição *f*; (*broadcast*) retransmissão
f. ∼**edly** *adv* repetidas vezes,
repetidamente

repel /rɪ'pel/ *vt* (*pt* **repelled**) repelir.
∼**lent** *a* & *n* repelente (*m*)

repent /rɪ'pent/ *vi* arrepender-se (**of** de).
∼**ance** *n* arrependimento *m*. ∼**ant** *a*
arrependido

repercussion /ri:pə'kʌʃn/ *n*
repercussão *f*

repertoire /'repətwa:(r)/ *n* repertório *m*

repertory /'repətrɪ/ *n* repertório *m*

repetit|**ion** /repɪ'tɪʃn/ *n* repetição *f*.
∼**ious** /-'tɪʃəs/, ∼**ive** /rɪ-'petətɪv/ *a*
repetitivo

replace /rɪ'pleɪs/ *vt* colocar no mesmo
lugar, repor; (*take the place of*)
substituir. ∼**ment** *n* reposição *f*;
(*substitution*) substituição *f*; (*person*)
substituto *m*

replenish /rɪ'plenɪʃ/ *vt* voltar a encher,
reabastecer; (*renew*) renovar

replica /'replɪkə/ *n* réplica *f*, cópia *f*,
reprodução *f*

reply /rɪ'plaɪ/ *vt/i* responder, replicar ☐ *n*
resposta *f*, réplica *f*

report /rɪ'pɔ:t/ *vt* relatar; (*notify*)
informar; (*denounce*) denunciar,
apresentar queixa de ☐ *vi* fazer um
relatório. ∼ (**on**) (*news item*) fazer uma
reportagem (sobre). ∼ **to** (*go*)
apresentar-se a ☐ *n* (*in newspapers*)
reportagem *f*; (*of company, doctor*)
relatório *m*; (*schol*) boletim *m* escolar;
(*sound*) detonação *f*; (*rumour*) rumores
mpl. ∼**edly** *adv* segundo consta. ∼**er** *n*
repórter *m*

repose /rɪ'pəʊz/ *n* repouso *m*

repossess /ri:pə'zes/ *vt* reapossar-se de,
retomar de

represent /reprɪ'zent/ *vt* representar.
∼**ation** /-'teɪʃn/ *n* representação *f*

representative /reprɪ'zentətɪv/ *a*
representativo ☐ *n* representante *mf*

repress /rɪ'pres/ *vt* reprimir. ∼**ion** /-ʃn/ *n*
repressão *f*. ∼**ive** *a* repressor,
repressivo

reprieve /rɪ'pri:v/ *n* suspensão *f*
temporária; (*temporary relief*) tréguas
fpl ☐ *vt* suspender temporariamente;
(*fig*) dar tréguas a

reprimand /'reprɪma:nd/ *vt* repreender
☐ *n* repreensão *f*, reprimenda *f*

reprint /'ri:prɪnt/ *n* reimpressão *f*,
reedição *f* ☐ *vt* /ri:'prɪnt/ reimprimir

reprisals /rɪ'praɪzlz/ *npl* represálias *fpl*

reproach /rɪ'prəʊtʃ/ *vt* censurar,
repreender (**sb for sth** alguém por alg
coisa, alg coisa a alguém) ☐ *n* censura
f. **above** ∼ irrepreensível. ∼**ful** *a*
repreensivo, reprovador. ∼**fully** *adv*
reprovadoramente

reproduc|**e** /ri:prə'dju:s/ *vt/i*
reproduzir(-se). ∼**tion** /-'dʌkʃn/ *n*
reprodução *f*. ∼**tive** /-'dʌktɪv/ *a*
reprodutivo, reprodutor

reptile /'reptaɪl/ *n* réptil *m*

republic /rɪ'pʌblɪk/ *n* república *f*. ∼**an** *a*
& *n* republicano (*m*)

repudiate /rɪ'pju:dɪeɪt/ *vt* repudiar,
rejeitar

repugnan|**t** /rɪ'pʌgnənt/ *a* repugnante.
∼**ce** *n* repugnância *f*

repuls|**e** /rɪ'pʌls/ *vt* repelir, repulsar.
∼**ion** /-ʃn/ *n* repulsa *f*. ∼**ive** *a*
repulsivo, repelente, repugnante

reputable /'repjʊtəbl/ *a* respeitado,
honrado; (*firm, make etc*) de renome,
conceituado

reputation /repjʊ'teɪʃn/ *n* reputação *f*

repute /rɪ'pju:t/ *n* reputação *f*. ∼**d** /-ɪd/ *a*
suposto, putativo. ∼**d to be** tido como,
tido na conta de. ∼**dly** /-ɪdlɪ/ *adv*
segundo consta, com fama de

request /rɪ'kwest/ *n* pedido *m* ☐ *vt* pedir,
solicitar (**of, from** a)

requiem /'rekwɪəm/ *n* réquiem *m*; (*mass*)
missa *f* de réquiem

require /rɪ'kwaɪə(r)/ *vt* requerer. ∼**d** *a*
requerido; (*needed*) necessário,
preciso. ∼**ment** *n* (*fig*) requisito *m*;
(*need*) necessidade *f*; (*demand*)
exigência *f*

requisite /'rekwɪzɪt/ *a* necessário ☐ *n*
coisa necessária *f*, requisito *m*. ∼**s** (*for
travel etc*) artigos *mpl*

requisition /rekwɪ'zɪʃn/ *n* requisição *f*
☐ *vt* requisitar

resale /'ri:seɪl/ *n* revenda *f*

rescue /'reskju:/ *vt* salvar, socorrer (**from** de). □ *n* salvamento *m*; (*help*) socorro *m*, ajuda *f*. **~r** /-ə(r)/ *n* salvador *m*

research /rɪ'sɜːtʃ/ *n* pesquisa *f*, investigação *f* □ *vt/i* pesquisar, fazer investigação (**into** sobre). **~er** *n* investigador *m*

resembl|e /rɪ'zembl/ *vt* assemelhar-se a, parecer-se com. **~ance** *n* semelhança *f*, similaridade *f* (**to** com)

resent /rɪ'zent/ *vt* ressentir(-se de), ficar ressentido com. **~ful** *a* ressentido. **~ment** *n* ressentimento *m*

reservation /rezə'veɪʃn/ *n* (*booking*) reserva *f*; (*Amer*) reserva *f* (de índios)

reserve /rɪ'zɜːv/ *vt* reservar □ *n* reserva *f*; (*sport*) suplente *mf*. **in ~** de reserva. **~d** *a* reservado

reservoir /'rezəvwɑː(r)/ *n* (*lake, supply etc*) reservatório *m*; (*container*) depósito *m*

reshape /riː'ʃeɪp/ *vt* remodelar

reshuffle /riː'ʃʌfl/ *vt* (*pol*) remodelar □ *n* (*pol*) reforma *f* (do Ministério)

reside /rɪ'zaɪd/ *vi* residir

residen|t /'rezɪdənt/ *a* residente □ *n* morador *m*, habitante *mf*; (*foreigner*) residente *mf*; (*in hotel*) hóspede *mf*. **~ce** *n* residência *f*; (*of students*) residência *f*, lar *m*. **~ce permit** visto *m* de residência

residential /rezɪ'denʃl/ *a* residencial

residue /'rezɪdjuː/ *n* resíduo *m*

resign /rɪ'zam/ *vt* (*post*) demitir-se. **~ o.s. to** resignar-se a □ *vi* demitir-se de. **~ation** /rezɪg'neɪʃn/ *n* resignação *f*; (*from job*) demissão *f*. **~ed** *a* resignado

resilien|t /rɪ'zɪlɪənt/ *a* (*springy*) elástico; (*person*) resistente. **~ce** *n* elasticidade *f*; (*of person*) resistência *f*

resin /'rezɪn/ *n* resina *f*

resist /rɪ'zɪst/ *vt/i* resistir (a). **~ance** *n* resistência *f*. **~ant** *a* resistente

resolut|e /'rezəluːt/ *a* resoluto. **~ion** /-'luːʃn/ *n* resolução *f*

resolve /rɪ'zɒlv/ *vt* resolver. **~ to do** resolver fazer □ *n* resolução *f*. **~d** *a* (*resolute*) resoluto; (*decided*) resolvido (**to** a)

resonan|t /'rezənənt/ *a* ressonante. **~ce** *n* ressonância *f*

resort /rɪ'zɔːt/ *vi* **~ to** recorrer a, valer-se de □ *n* recurso *m*; (*place*) estância *f*, local *m* turístico. **as a last ~** em último recurso. **seaside ~** praia *f*, balneário *m*, (*P*) estância *f* balnear

resound /rɪ'zaʊnd/ *vi* reboar, ressoar (**with** com). **~ing** *a* ressoante; (*fig*) retumbante

resource /rɪ'sɔːs/ *n* recurso *m*. **~s** recursos *mpl*, riquezas *fpl*. **~ful** *a* expedito, engenhoso, desembaraçado. **~fulness** *n* expediente *m*, engenho *m*

respect /rɪ'spekt/ *n* respeito *m* □ *vt* respeitar. **with ~ to** a respeito de, com respeito a, relativamente a. **~ful** *a* respeitoso

respectab|le /rɪ'spektəbl/ *a* respeitável; (*passable*) passável, aceitável. **~ility** /-'bɪlətɪ/ *n* respeitabilidade *f*

respective /rɪ'spektɪv/ *a* respectivo. **~ly** *adv* respectivamente

respiration /respə'reɪʃn/ *n* respiração *f*

respite /'respaɪt/ *n* pausa *f*, trégua *f*, folga *f*

respond /rɪ'spɒnd/ *vi* responder (**to** a); (*react*) reagir (**to** a)

response /rɪ'spɒns/ *n* resposta *f*; (*reaction*) reação *f*, (*P*) reacção *f*

responsib|le /rɪ'spɒnsəbl/ *a* responsável; (*job*) de responsabilidade. **~ility** /-'bɪlətɪ/ *n* responsabilidade *f*

responsive /rɪ'spɒnsɪv/ *a* receptivo, que reage bem. **~ to** sensível a

rest[1] /rest/ *vt/i* descansar, repousar; (*lean*) apoiar(-se) □ *n* descanso *m*, repouso *m*; (*support*) suporte *m*. **~-room** *n* (*Amer*) banheiro *m*, (*P*) toaletes *mpl*

rest[2] /rest/ *vi* (*remain*) ficar □ *n* (*remainder*) resto *m* (**of** de). **the ~** (**of the**) (*others*) os outros. **it ~s with him** cabe a ele

restaurant /'restrɒnt/ *n* restaurante *m*

restful /'restfl/ *a* sossegado, repousante, tranquilo, (*P*) tranquilo

restitution /restɪ'tjuːʃn/ *n* restituição *f*; (*for injury*) indenização *f*, (*P*) indemnização *f*

restless /'restlɪs/ *a* agitado, desassossegado

restor|e /rɪ'stɔː(r)/ *vt* restaurar; (*give back*) restituir, devolver. **~ation** /restə'reɪʃn/ *n* restauração *f*

restrain /rɪ'streɪn/ *vt* conter, reprimir. **~ o.s.** controlar-se. **~ sb from** impedir alguém de. **~ed** *a* comedido, reservado. **~t** *n* controle *m*; (*moderation*) moderação *f*, comedimento *m*

restrict /rɪ'strɪkt/ *vt* restringir, limitar. **~ion** /-ʃn/ *n* restrição *f*. **~ive** *a* restritivo

result /rɪ'zʌlt/ *n* resultado *m* □ *vi* resultar (**from** de). **~ in** resultar em

resum|e /rɪ'zjuːm/ *vt/i* reatar, retomar; (*work, travel*) recomeçar. **~ption** /rɪ'zʌmpʃn/ *n* reatamento *m*, retomada *f*; (*of work*) recomeço *m*

résumé /'rezjuːmeɪ/ *n* resumo *m*

resurgence /rɪˈsɜːdʒəns/ n reaparecimento m, ressurgimento m

resurrect /rezəˈrekt/ vt ressuscitar. ∼**ion** /-ʃn/ n ressureição f

resuscitat|e /rɪˈsʌsɪteɪt/ vt ressuscitar, reanimar. ∼**ion** /-ˈteɪʃn/ n reanimação f

retail /ˈriːteɪl/ n retalho m □ a & adv a retalho □ vt/i vender(-se) a retalho. ∼**er** n retalhista mf

retain /rɪˈteɪn/ vt reter; (keep) conservar, guardar

retaliat|e /rɪˈtælieɪt/ vi retaliar, exercer represálias, desforrar-se. ∼**ion** /-ˈeɪʃn/ n retaliação f, represália f, desforra f

retarded /rɪˈtɑːdɪd/ a retardado, atrasado

retch /retʃ/ vi fazer esforço para vomitar, estar com ânsias de vômito

retention /rɪˈtenʃn/ n retenção f

retentive /rɪˈtentɪv/ a retentivo. ∼ **memory** boa memória f

reticen|t /ˈretɪsnt/ a reticente. ∼**ce** n reticência f

retina /ˈretɪnə/ n retina f

retinue /ˈretɪnjuː/ n séquito m, comitiva f

retire /rɪˈtaɪə(r)/ vi reformar-se, aposentar-se; (withdraw) retirar-se; (go to bed) ir deitar-se □ vt reformar, aposentar. ∼**d** a reformado, aposentado. ∼**ment** n reforma f, aposentadoria f, (P) aposentação f

retiring /rɪˈtaɪərɪŋ/ a reservado, retraído

retort /rɪˈtɔːt/ vt/i retrucar, retorquir □ n réplica f

retrace /riːˈtreɪs/ vt ∼ one's steps refazer o mesmo caminho; (fig) recordar, recapitular

retract /rɪˈtrækt/ vt/i retratar (-se); (wheels) recolher; (claws) encolher, recolher

retreat /rɪˈtriːt/ vi retirar-se; (mil) retirar, bater em retirada □ n retirada f; (seclusion) retiro m

retrial /riːˈtraɪəl/ n novo julgamento m

retribution /retrɪˈbjuːʃn/ n castigo (merecido) m; (vengeance) vingança f

retriev|e /rɪˈtriːv/ vt ir buscar; (rescue) salvar; (recover) recuperar; (put right) reparar. ∼**al** n recuperação f. **information** ∼**al** (comput) acesso m à informação. ∼**er** n (dog) perdigueiro m, (P) cobrador m

retrograde /ˈretrəɡreɪd/ a retrógrado □ vt retroceder, recuar

retrospect /ˈretrəspekt/ n **in** ∼ em retrospecto, (P) retrospectivamente. ∼**ive** /-ˈspektɪv/ a retrospectivo; (of law, payment) retroativo, (P) retroactivo

return /rɪˈtɜːn/ vi voltar, regressar, retornar (**to**, a) □ vt devolver; (compliment, visit) retribuir; (put back) pôr de volta □ n volta f, regresso m, retorno m; (profit) lucro m, rendimento m; (restitution) devolução f. **in** ∼ **for** em troca de. ∼ **journey** viagem f de volta. ∼ **match** (sport) desafio m de desforra. ∼ **ticket** bilhete m de ida e volta. **many happy** ∼**s (of the day)** muitos parabéns

reunion /riːˈjuːnɪən/ n reunião f

reunite /riːjuːˈnaɪt/ vt reunir

rev /rev/ n (colloq: auto) rotação f □ vt/i (pt revved) ∼ (**up**) (colloq: auto) acelerar (o motor)

reveal /rɪˈviːl/ vt revelar; (display) expor. ∼**ing** a revelador

revel /ˈrevl/ vi (pt revelled) divertir-se. ∼ **in** deleitar-se com. ∼**ry** n festas fpl, festejos mpl

revelation /revəˈleɪʃn/ n revelação f

revenge /rɪˈvendʒ/ n vingança f; (sport) desforra f □ vt vingar

revenue /ˈrevənjuː/ n receita f, rendimento m. **Inland R**∼ Fisco m

reverberate /rɪˈvɜːbəreɪt/ vi ecoar, repercutir

revere /rɪˈvɪə(r)/ vt reverenciar, venerar

reverend /ˈrevərənd/ a reverendo. **R**∼ Reverendo

reveren|t /ˈrevərənt/ a reverente. ∼**ce** n reverência f, veneração f

revers|e /rɪˈvɜːs/ a contrário, inverso □ n contrário m; (back) reverso m; (gear) marcha f à ré, (P) atrás □ vt virar ao contrário; (order) inverter; (turn inside out) virar do avesso; (decision) anular □ vi (auto) fazer marcha à ré, (P) atrás. ∼**al** n inversão f, mudança f em sentido contrário; (of view etc) mudança f

revert /rɪˈvɜːt/ vi ∼ **to** reverter a

review /rɪˈvjuː/ n (inspection; magazine) revista f; (of a situation) revisão f; (critique) crítica f □ vt revistar, passar revista em; (situation) rever; (book, film etc) fazer a crítica de. ∼**er** n crítico m

revis|e /rɪˈvaɪz/ vt rever; (amend) corrigir. ∼**ion** /-ʒn/ n revisão f; (amendment) correção f

reviv|e /rɪˈvaɪv/ vt/i ressuscitar, reavivar; (play) reapresentar; (person) reanimar(-se). ∼**al** n reflorescimento m, renascimento m

revoke /rɪˈvəʊk/ vt revogar, anular, invalidar

revolt /rɪˈvəʊlt/ vt/i revoltar(-se) □ n revolta f

revolting /rɪˈvəʊltɪŋ/ a (disgusting) repugnante

revolution /revəˈluːʃn/ n revolução f. ∼**ary** a & n revolucionário (m). ∼**ize** vt revolucionar

revolv|e /rɪ'vɒlv/ *vi* girar. **~ing door** porta *f* giratória

revolver /rɪ'vɒlvə(r)/ *n* revólver *m*

revulsion /rɪ'vʌlʃn/ *n* repugnância *f*, repulsa *f*

reward /rɪ'wɔːd/ *n* prêmio *m*, (*P*) prémio *m*; (*for criminal, for lost/stolen property*) recompensa *f* □ *vt* recompensar. **~ing** *a* compensador; (*task etc*) gratificante

rewind /riː'waɪnd/ *vt* (*pt* **rewound**) rebobinar

rewrite /riː'raɪt/ *vt* (*pt* **rewrote**, *pp* **rewritten**) reescrever

rhetoric /'retərɪk/ *n* retórica *f*. **~al** /rɪ'tɒrɪkl/ *a* retórico; (*question*) pro forma

rheumati|c /ruː'mætɪk/ *a* reumático. **~sm** /'ruːmətɪzm/ *n* reumatismo *m*

rhinoceros /raɪ'nɒsərəs/ *n* (*pl* **-oses**) rinoceronte *m*

rhubarb /'ruːbɑːb/ *n* ruibarbo *m*

rhyme /raɪm/ *n* rima *f*; (*poem*) versos *mpl* □ *vt/i* (fazer) rimar

rhythm /'rɪðəm/ *n* ritmo *m*. **~ic(al)** /'rɪðmɪk(l)/ *a* rítmico, compassado

rib /rɪb/ *n* costela *f*

ribbon /'rɪbən/ *n* fita *f*. **in ~s** em tiras

rice /raɪs/ *n* arroz *m*

rich /rɪtʃ/ *a* (-er, -est) rico; (*food*) rico em açúcar e gordura. **~es** *npl* riquezas *fpl*. **~ly** *adv* ricamente. **~ness** *n* riqueza *f*

rickety /'rɪkətɪ/ *a* (*shaky*) desconjuntado

ricochet /'rɪkəʃeɪ/ *n* ricochete *m* □ *vi* (*pt* **ricocheted** -ʃeɪd/) fazer ricochete, ricochetear

rid /rɪd/ *vt* (*pt* **rid**, *pres p* **ridding**) desembaraçar (**of** de). **get ~ of** desembaraçar-se de, livrar-se de

riddance /'rɪdns/ *n* **good ~**! que alívio!, vai com Deus!

ridden /'rɪdn/ *see* ride

riddle¹ /'rɪdl/ *n* enigma *m*; (*puzzle*) charada *f*

riddle² /'rɪdl/ *vt* **~ with** crivar de

ride /raɪd/ *vi* (*pt* **rode**, *pp* **ridden**) andar (de bicicleta, a cavalo, de carro) □ *vt* (*horse*) montar; (*bicycle*) andar de; (*distance*) percorrer □ *n* passeio *m or* volta *f* (de carro, a cavalo etc); (*distance*) percurso *m*. **~r** /-ə(r)/ *n* cavaleiro *m*, amazona *f*; (*cyclist*) ciclista *mf*; (*in document*) aditamento *m*

ridge /rɪdʒ/ *n* aresta *f*; (*of hill*) cume *m*

ridicule /'rɪdɪkjuːl/ *n* ridículo *m* □ *vt* ridicularizar

ridiculous /rɪ'dɪkjʊləs/ *a* ridículo

riding /'raɪdɪŋ/ *n* equitação *f*

rife /raɪf/ *a* **be ~** estar espalhado; (*of illness*) grassar. **~ with** cheio de

riff-raff /'rɪfræf/ *n* gentinha *f*, povinho *m*, ralé *f*

rifle /'raɪfl/ *n* espingarda *f* □ *vt* revistar e roubar, saquear

rift /rɪft/ *n* fenda *f*, brecha *f*; (*fig: dissension*) desacordo *m*, desavença *f*, desentendimento *m*

rig¹ /rɪg/ *vt* (*pt* **rigged**) equipar □ *n* (*for oil*) plataforma *f* de poço de petróleo. **~ out** enfarpelar (*colloq*). **~-out** *n* (*colloq*) roupa *f*, farpela *f* (*colloq*). **~ up** arranjar

rig² /rɪg/ *vt* (*pt* **rigged**) (*pej*) manipular. **~ged** *a* (*election*) fraudulento

right /raɪt/ *a* (*correct, moral*) certo, correto, (*P*) correcto; (*fair*) justo; (*not left*) direito; (*suitable*) certo, próprio □ *n* (*entitlement*) direito *m*; (*not left*) direita *f*; (*not evil*) o bem □ *vt* (*a wrong*) reparar; (*sth fallen*) endireitar □ *adv* (*not left*) à direita; (*directly*) direito; (*exactly*) mesmo, bem; (*completely*) completamente. **be ~** (*person*) ter razão (**to em**). **be in the ~** ter razão. **on the ~** à direita. **put ~** acertar, corrigir. **~ of way** (*auto*) prioridade *f*. **~ angle** *n* ângulo reto *m*, (*P*) recto. **~ away** logo, imediatamente. **~-hand** *a* à *or* de direita. **~-handed** *a* (*person*) destro. **~-wing** *a* (*pol*) de direita

righteous /'raɪtʃəs/ *a* justo, virtuoso

rightful /'raɪtfl/ *a* legítimo. **~ly** *adv* legitimamente, legalmente

rightly /'raɪtlɪ/ *adv* devidamente, corretamente, (*P*) correctamente; (*with reason*) justificadamente

rigid /'rɪdʒɪd/ *a* rígido. **~ity** /rɪ'dʒɪdətɪ/ *n* rigidez *f*

rigmarole /'rɪgmərəʊl/ *n* (*speech: procedure*) embrulhada *f*

rig|our /'rɪgə(r)/ *n* rigor *m*. **~orous** *a* rigoroso

rile /raɪl/ *vt* (*colloq*) irritar, exasperar

rim /rɪm/ *n* borda *f*; (*of wheel*) aro *m*

rind /raɪnd/ *n* (*on cheese, fruit*) casca *f*; (*on bacon*) pele *f*

ring¹ /rɪŋ/ *n* (*on finger*) anel *m*; (*for napkin, key etc*) argola *f*, (*circle*) roda *f*, círculo *m*; (*boxing*) ringue *m*; (*arena*) arena *f*; (*of people*) quadrilha *f* □ *vt* rodear, cercar. **~ road** *n* estrada *f* periférica *or* perimetral

ring² /rɪŋ/ *vt/i* (*pt* **rang**, *pp* **rung**) tocar; (*of words etc*) soar □ *n* toque *m*; (*colloq: phone call*) telefonadela *f* (*colloq*). **~ the bell** tocar a campainha. **~ back** telefonar de volta. **~ off** desligar. **~ up** telefonar (a)

ringleader /'rɪŋliːdə(r)/ *n* cabeça *m*, cérebro *m*

rink /rɪŋk/ *n* rinque *m* de patinação

rinse /rɪns/ *vt* enxaguar □ *n* enxaguada *f*, (*P*) enxaguadela *f*; (*hair tint*) rinsagem *f*

riot /'raɪət/ *n* distúrbio *m*, motim *m*; (*of colours*) festival *m* □ *vi* fazer distúrbios *or* motins. **run ~** desenfrear-se, descontrolar-se; (*of plants*) crescer em matagal. **~er** *n* desordeiro *m*

riotous /'raɪətəs/ *a* desenfreado, turbulento, desordeiro

rip /rɪp/ *vt/i* (*pt* **ripped**) rasgar (-se) □ *n* rasgão *m*. **~ off** (*sl*: *defraud*) defraudar, enrolar (*sl*). **~-off** *n* (*sl*) roubalheira *f* (*colloq*)

ripe /raɪp/ *a* (**-er**, **-est**) maduro. **~ness** *n* madureza *f*, (*P*) amadurecimento *m*

ripen /'raɪpən/ *vt/i* amadurecer

ripple /'rɪpl/ *n* ondulação *f* leve; (*sound*) murmúrio *m* □ *vt/i* encrespar(-se), agitar(-se), ondular

rise /raɪz/ *vi* (*pt* **rose**, *pp* **risen**) subir, elevar-se; (*stand up*) erguer-se, levantar-se; (*rebel*) sublevar-se; (*sun*) nascer; (*curtain, prices*) subir □ *n* (*increase*) aumento *m*; (*slope*) subida *f*, ladeira *f*; (*origin*) origem *f*. **give ~ to** originar, causar, dar origem a. **~r** /-ə(r)/ *n* **early ~r** madrugador *m*

rising /'raɪzɪŋ/ *n* (*revolt*) insurreição *f* □ *a* (*sun*) nascente

risk /rɪsk/ *n* risco *m* □ *vt* arriscar. **at ~** em risco, em perigo. **at one's own ~** por sua conta e risco. **~ doing** (*venture*) arriscar-se a fazer. **~y** *a* arriscado

risqué /'riːskeɪ/ *a* picante

rite /raɪt/ *n* rito *m*. **last ~s** últimos sacramentos *mpl*

ritual /'rɪtʃʊəl/ *a* & *n* ritual (*m*)

rival /'raɪvl/ *n* & *a* rival (*mf*); (*fig*) concorrente (*mf*), competidor (*m*) □ *vt* (*pt* **rivalled**) rivalizar com. **~ry** *n* rivalidade *f*

river /'rɪvə(r)/ *n* rio *m* □ *a* fluvial

rivet /'rɪvɪt/ *n* rebite *m* □ *vt* (*pt* **riveted**) rebitar; (*fig*) prender, cravar. **~ing** *a* fascinante

road /rəʊd/ *n* estrada *f*; (*in town*) rua *f*; (*small; fig*) caminho *m*. **~-block** *n* barricada *f*. **~-map** *n* mapa *m* das estradas. **~ sign** *n* sinal *m*, placa *f* de sinalização. **~ tax** *n* imposto *m* de circulação. **~-works** *npl* obras *fpl*

roadside /'rəʊdsaɪd/ *n* beira *f* da estrada

roadway /'rəʊdweɪ/ *n* pista *f* de rolamento, (*P*) rodagem *f*

roadworthy /'rəʊdwɜːðɪ/ *a* em condições de ser utilizado na rua/estrada

roam /rəʊm/ *vi* errar, andar sem destino □ *vt* percorrer

roar /rɔː(r)/ *n* berro *m*, rugido *m*; (*of thunder*) ribombo *m*, troar *m*; (*of sea,*

wind) bramido *m* □ *vt/i* berrar, rugir; (*of lion*) rugir; (*of thunder*) ribombar, troar; (*of sea, wind*) bramir. **~ with laughter** rir às gargalhadas

roaring /'rɔːrɪŋ/ *a* (*trade*) florescente; (*success*) enorme; (*fire*) com grandes chamas

roast /rəʊst/ *vt/i* assar □ *a* & *n* assado (*m*)

rob /rɒb/ *vt* (*pt* **robbed**) roubar (**sb of sth** alg coisa de alguém); (*bank*) assaltar; (*deprive*) privar (**of** de). **~ber** *n* ladrão *m*. **~bery** *n* roubo *m*; (*of bank*) assalto *m*

robe /rəʊb/ *n* veste *f* comprida e solta; (*dressing-gown*) robe *m*. **~s** *npl* (*of judge etc*) toga *f*

robin /'rɒbɪn/ *n* papo-roxo *m*, (*P*) pintarroxo *m*

robot /'rəʊbɒt/ *n* robô *m*, (*P*) robot *m*, autómano *m*, (*P*) autómato *m*

robust /rəʊ'bʌst/ *a* robusto

rock[1] /rɒk/ *n* rocha *f*; (*boulder*) penhasco *m*, rochedo *m*; (*sweet*) pirulito *m*, (*P*) chupa-chupa *m* comprido. **on the ~s** (*colloq: of marriage*) em crise; (*colloq: of drinks*) com gelo. **~-bottom** *n* ponto *m* mais baixo □ *a* (*of prices*) baixíssimo (*colloq*)

rock[2] /rɒk/ *vt/i* balouçar(-se); (*shake*) abanar, sacudir; (*child*) embalar □ *n* (*mus*) rock *m*. **~ing-chair** *n* cadeira *f* de balanço, (*P*) cadeira *f* de balouço. **~ing-horse** *n* cavalo *m* de balanço, (*P*) cavalo *m* de balouço

rocket /'rɒkɪt/ *n* foguete *m*

rocky /'rɒkɪ/ *a* (**-ier**, **-iest**) (*ground*) pedregoso; (*hill*) rochoso; (*colloq: unsteady*) instável; (*colloq: shaky*) tremido (*colloq*)

rod /rɒd/ *n* vara *f*, vareta *f*; (*mech*) haste *f*; (*for curtains*) bastão *m*, (*P*) varão *m*; (*for fishing*) vara (de pescar) *f*

rode /rəʊd/ *see* **ride**

rodent /'rəʊdnt/ *n* roedor *m*

rodeo /rəʊ'deɪəʊ/ *n* (*pl* **-os**) rode(i)o *m*

roe /rəʊ/ *n* ova(s) *f* (*pl*) de peixe

rogue /rəʊg/ *n* (*dishonest*) patife *m*, velhaco *m*; (*mischievous*) brincalhão *m*

role /rəʊl/ *n* papel *m*

roll /rəʊl/ *vt/i* (*fazer*) rolar; (*into ball or cylinder*) enrolar(-se) □ *n* rolo *m*; (*list*) rol *m*, lista *f*; (*bread*) pãozinho *m*; (*of ship*) balanço *m*; (*of drum*) rufar *m*; (*of thunder*) ribombo *m*. **be ~ing in money** (*colloq*) nadar em dinheiro (*colloq*). **~ over** (*turn over*) virar-se ao contrário. **~ up** *vi* (*colloq*) aparecer □ *vt* (*sleeves*) arregaçar; (*umbrella*) fechar. **~-call** *n* chamada *f*. **~ing-pin** *n* rolo *m* de pastel

roller /'rəʊlə(r)/ *n* cilindro *m*; (*wave*) vagalhão *m*; (*for hair*) rolo *m*. **~-blind**

n estore *m*. **~-coaster** *n* montanha *f* russa. **~-skate** *n* patim *m* de rodas

rolling /ˈrəʊlɪŋ/ *a* ondulante

Roman /ˈrəʊmən/ *a* & *n* romano (*m*). **R~ Catholic** *a* & *n* católico (*m*). **~ numerals** algarismos *mpl* romanos

romance /rəʊˈmæns/ *n* (*love affair*) romance *m*; (*fig*) poesia *f*

Romania /rʊˈmeɪnɪə/ *n* Romênia *f*, (*P*) Roménia *f*. **~n** *a* & *n* romeno (*m*)

romantic /rəʊˈmæntɪk/ *a* romântico. **~ally** *adv* românticamente. **~ism** *n* romantismo *m*. **~ize** *vi* fazer romance □ *vt* romantizar

romp /rɒmp/ *vi* brincar animadamente □ *n* brincadeira *f* animada. **~ers** *npl* macacão *m* de bebê, (*P*) fato *m* de bebé

roof /ruːf/ *n* (*pl* roofs) telhado *m*; (*of car*) teto *m*, (*P*) capota *f*; (*of mouth*) palato *m*, céu *m* da boca □ *vt* cobrir com telhado. **hit the ~** (*colloq*) ficar furioso. **~ing** *n* material *m* para telhados. **~-rack** *n* porta-bagagem *m*. **~-top** *n* cimo *m* do telhado

rook[1] /rʊk/ *n* (*bird*) gralha *f*

rook[2] /rʊk/ *n* (*chess*) torre *f*

room /ruːm/ *n* quarto *m*, divisão *f*; (*bedroom*) quarto *m* de dormir; (*large hall*) sala *f*; (*space*) espaço *m*, lugar *m*. **~s** (*lodgings*) apartamento *m*, cômodos *mpl*. **~-mate** *n* companheiro *m* de quarto. **~y** *a* espaçoso; (*clothes*) amplo, largo

roost /ruːst/ *n* poleiro *m* □ *vi* empoleirar-se. **~er** *n* (*Amer*) galo *m*

root[1] /ruːt/ *n* raiz *f*; (*fig*) origem *f* □ *vt/i* enraizar(-se), radicar(-se). **~ out** extirpar, erradicar. **take ~** criar raízes. **~less** *a* sem raízes, desenraizado

root[2] /ruːt/ *vi* **~ about** revolver, remexer. **~ for** (*Amer sl*) torcer por

rope /rəʊp/ *n* corda *f* □ *vt* atar. **know the ~s** estar por dentro (do assunto). **~ in** convencer a participar de

rosary /ˈrəʊzərɪ/ *n* rosário *m*

rose[1] /rəʊz/ *n* rosa *f*; (*nozzle*) ralo *m* (de regador). **~-bush** *n* roseira *f*

rose[2] /rəʊz/ *see* rise

rosé /ˈrəʊzeɪ/ *n* rosé *m*

rosette /rəʊˈzet/ *n* roseta *f*

rosewood /ˈrəʊzwʊd/ *n* pau-rosa *m*

roster /ˈrɒstə(r)/ *n* lista (de serviço) *f*, escala *f* (de serviço)

rostrum /ˈrɒstrəm/ *n* tribuna *f*; (*for conductor*) estrado *m*; (*sport*) podium *m*

rosy /ˈrəʊzɪ/ *a* (-ier, -iest) rosado; (*fig*) risonho

rot /rɒt/ *vt/i* (*pt* rotted) apodrecer □ *n* putrefação *f*, podridão *f*; (*sl: nonsense*) disparate *m*, asneiras *fpl*

rota /ˈrəʊtə/ *n* escala *f* de serviço

rotary /ˈrəʊtərɪ/ *a* rotativo, giratório

rotat|e /rəʊˈteɪt/ *vt/i* (fazer) girar, (fazer) revolver; (*change round*) alternar. **~ing** *a* rotativo. **~ion** /-ʃn/ *n* rotação *f*

rote /rəʊt/ *n* **by ~** de cor, maquinalmente

rotten /ˈrɒtn/ *a* podre; (*corrupt*) corrupto; (*colloq: bad*) mau, ruim. **~ eggs** ovos *mpl* podres. **feel ~** (*ill*) não se sentir nada bem

rotund /rəʊˈtʌnd/ *a* rotundo, redondo

rough /rʌf/ *a* (-er, -est) rude; (*to touch*) áspero, rugoso; (*of ground*) acidentado, irregular; (*violent*) violento; (*of sea*) agitado, encapelado; (*of weather*) tempestuoso; (*not perfect*) tosco, rudimentar; (*of estimate etc*) aproximado □ *n* (*ruffian*) rufia *m*, desordeiro *m* □ *adv* (*live*) ao relento; (*play*) bruto □ *vt* **~ it** viver de modo primitivo, não ter onde morar (*colloq*). **~ out** fazer um esboço preliminar de. **~-and-ready** *a* grosseiro mas eficiente. **~ paper** rascunho *m*, borrão *m*. **~ly** *adv* asperamente, rudemente; (*approximately*) aproximadamente. **~ness** *n* rudeza *f*, aspereza *f*; (*violence*) brutalidade *f*

roughage /ˈrʌfɪdʒ/ *n* alimentos *mpl* fibrosos

roulette /ruːˈlet/ *n* roleta *f*

round /raʊnd/ *a* (-er, -est) redondo □ *n* (*circle*) círculo *m*; (*slice*) fatia *f*; (*postman's*) entrega *f*; (*patrol*) ronda *f*; (*of drinks*) rodada *f*; (*competition*) partida *f*, rodada *f*; (*boxing*) round *m*; (*of talks*) ciclo *m*, série *f* □ *prep* & *adv* em volta (de), em torno (de) □ *vt* arredondar; (*cape, corner*) dobrar, virar. **come ~** (*into consciousness*) voltar a si. **go** *or* **come ~ to** (*a friend etc*) dar um pulo na casa de. **~ about** (*nearby*) por aí; (*fig*) mais ou menos. **~ of applause** salva *f* de palmas. **~ off** terminar. **~-shouldered** *a* curvado. **~ the clock** noite e dia sem parar. **~ trip** viagem *f* de ida e volta. **~ up** (*gather*) juntar; (*a figure*) arredondar. **~-up** *n* (*of cattle*) rodeio *m*; (*of suspects*) captura *f*

roundabout /ˈraʊndəbaʊt/ *n* carrossel *m*; (*for traffic*) rotatória *f*, (*P*) rotunda *f* □ *a* indireto, (*P*) indirecto

rous|e /raʊz/ *vt* acordar, despertar. **be ~ed** (*angry*) exaltar-se, inflamar-se, ser provocado. **~ing** *a* (*speech*) inflamado, exaltado; (*music*) vibrante; (*cheers*) frenético

rout /raʊt/ *n* derrota *f*; (*retreat*) debandada *f* □ *vt* derrotar; (*cause to retreat*) pôr em debandada

route /ruːt/ *n* percurso *m*, itinerário *m*; (*naut, aviat*) rota *f*

routine /ruːˈtiːn/ n rotina f; (theat) número m ▫ a de rotina, rotineiro.
daily ~ rotina f diária

rov|e /rəʊv/ vt/i errar (por), vaguear (em/por). ~**ing** a (life) errante

row[1] /rəʊ/ n fila f, fileira f; (in knitting) carreira f. **in a** ~ (consecutive) em fila

row[2] /rəʊ/ vt/i remar. ~**ing** n remo m. ~**ing-boat** n barco m a remo

row[3] /raʊ/ n (colloq: noise) barulho m, bagunça f, banzé m (colloq); (colloq: quarrel) discussão f, briga f. ~ **(with)** vi (colloq) brigar (com), discutir (com)

rowdy /ˈraʊdɪ/ a (-ier, -iest) desordeiro

royal /ˈrɔɪəl/ a real

royalty /ˈrɔɪəltɪ/ n família real f; (payment) direitos mpl (de autor, de patente, etc)

rub /rʌb/ vt/i (pt rubbed) esfregar; (with ointment etc) esfregar, friccionar ▫ n esfrega f; (with ointment etc) fricção f. ~ **it in** repisar/insistir em. ~ **off on** comunicar-se a, transmitir-se a. ~ **out** (with rubber) apagar

rubber /ˈrʌbə(r)/ n borracha f. ~ **band** elástico m. ~ **stamp** carimbo m. ~**-stamp** vt aprovar sem questionar. ~**y** a semelhante à borracha

rubbish /ˈrʌbɪʃ/ n (refuse) lixo m; (nonsense) disparates mpl. ~ **dump** n lixeira f. ~**y** a sem valor

rubble /ˈrʌbl/ n entulho m

ruby /ˈruːbɪ/ n rubi m

rucksack /ˈrʌksæk/ n mochila f

rudder /ˈrʌdə(r)/ n leme m

ruddy /ˈrʌdɪ/ a (-ier, -iest) avermelhado; (of cheeks) corado, vermelho; (sl: damned) maldito (colloq)

rude /ruːd/ a (-er, -est) mal-educado, malcriado, grosseiro. ~**ly** adv grosseiramente, malcriadamente. ~**ness** n má-educação f, má-criação f, grosseria f

rudiment /ˈruːdɪmənt/ n rudimento m. ~**ary** /-ˈmentrɪ/ a rudimentar

rueful /ˈruːfl/ a contrito, pesaroso

ruffian /ˈrʌfɪən/ n desordeiro m

ruffle /ˈrʌfl/ vt (feathers) eriçar; (hair) despentear; (clothes) amarrotar; (fig) perturbar ▫ n (frill) franzido m, (P) folho m

rug /rʌg/ n tapete m; (covering) manta f

rugged /ˈrʌgɪd/ a rude, irregular; (coast, landscape) acidentado; (character) forte; (features) marcado

ruin /ˈruːɪn/ n ruína f ▫ vt arruinar; (fig) estragar. ~**ous** a desastroso

rule /ruːl/ n regra f; (regulation) regulamento m; (pol) governo m ▫ vt governar; (master) dominar; (jur) decretar; (decide) decidir ▫ vi governar.
as a ~ regra geral, por via de regra. ~ **out** excluir. ~**d paper** papel m pautado. ~**r** /-ə(r)/ n (sovereign) soberano m; (leader) governante m; (measure) régua f

ruling /ˈruːlɪŋ/ a (class) dirigente; (pol) no poder ▫ n decisão f

rum /rʌm/ n rum m

rumble /ˈrʌmbl/ vi ribombar, ressoar; (of stomach) roncar ▫ n ribombo m, estrondo m

rummage /ˈrʌmɪdʒ/ vt revistar, remexer

rumour /ˈruːmə(r)/ n boato m, rumor m ▫ vt **it is** ~**ed that** corre o boato de que, consta que

rump /rʌmp/ n (of horse etc) garupa f; (of fowl) mitra f. ~ **steak** n bife m de alcatra

run /rʌn/ vi (pt ran, pp run, pres p running) correr; (flow) correr; (pass) passar; (function) andar, funcionar; (melt) derreter, pingar; (bus etc) circular; (play) estar em cartaz; (colour) desbotar; (in election) candidatar-se (for a) ▫ vt (manage) dirigir, gerir; (a risk) correr; (a race) participar em; (water) deixar correr; (a car) ter, manter ▫ n corrida f; (excursion) passeio m, ida f; (rush) corrida f, correria f; (in cricket) ponto m. **be on the** ~ estar foragido. **have the** ~ **of** ter à sua disposição. **in the long** ~ a longo prazo. ~ **across** encontrar por acaso, dar com. ~ **away** fugir. ~ **down** descer correndo; (of vehicle) atropelar; (belittle) dizer mal de, denegrir. **be** ~ **down** estar exausto. ~ **in** (engine) ligar. ~ **into** (meet) encontrar por acaso; (hit) bater em, ir de encontro a. ~ **off** vt (copies) tirar; (water) deixar correr ▫ vi fugir. ~**-of-the-mill** a vulgar. ~ **out** esgotar-se; (lease) expirar. **I ran out of sugar** o açúcar acabou. ~ **over** (of vehicle) atropelar. ~ **up** deixar acumular. **the** ~**-up to** o período que precede

runaway /ˈrʌnəweɪ/ n fugitivo m ▫ a fugitivo; (horse) desembestado; (vehicle) desavorado; (success) grande

rung[1] /rʌŋ/ n (of ladder) degrace m

rung[2] /rʌŋ/ see **ring**[2]

runner /ˈrʌnə(r)/ n (person) corredor m; (carpet) passadeira f. ~ **bean** feijão m verde. ~**-up** n segundo classificado m

running /ˈrʌnɪŋ/ n corrida f; (functioning) funcionamento m ▫ a consecutivo, seguido; (water) corrente. **be in the** ~ (competitor) ter probabilidades de êxito. **four days** ~ quatro dias seguidos or a fio. ~ **commentary** reportagem f, comentário m

runny /ˈrʌnɪ/ a derretido

runway /'rʌnweɪ/ n pista f de decolagem, (P) descolagem

rupture /'rʌptʃə(r)/ n ruptura f; (med) hérnia f □ vt/i romper (-se), rebentar

rural /'rʊərəl/ a rural

ruse /ruːz/ n ardil m, estratagema m, manha f

rush[1] /rʌʃ/ n (plant) junco m

rush[2] /rʌʃ/ vi (move) precipitar-se, (be in a hurry) apressar-se □ vt fazer, mandar etc a toda a pressa; (person) pressionar; (mil) tomar de assalto □ n tropel m; (haste) pressa f. **in a ~** as pressas. **~ hour** rush m, (P) hora f de ponta

rusk /rʌsk/ n bolacha f, biscoito m

russet /'rʌsɪt/ a castanho avermelhado □ n maçã f reineta

Russia /'rʌʃə/ n Rússia f. **~n** a & n russo (m)

rust /rʌst/ n (on iron, plants) ferrugem f □ vt/i enferrujar(-se). **~-proof** a inoxidável. **~y** a ferrugento, enferrujado; (fig) enferrujado

rustic /'rʌstɪk/ a rústico

rustle /'rʌsl/ vt/i restolhar, (fazer) farfalhar; (Amer: steal) roubar. **~ up** (colloq: food etc) arranjar

rut /rʌt/ n sulco m; (fig) rotina f. **in a ~** numa vida rotineira

ruthless /'ruːθlɪs/ a implacável

rye /raɪ/ n centeio m

. . . .

Ss

. . . .

sabbath /'sæbəθ/ n (Jewish) sábado m; (Christian) domingo m

sabbatical /sə'bætɪkl/ n (univ) período m de licença

sabot|age /'sæbətɑːʒ/ n sabotagem f □ vt sabotar. **~eur** /-'tɜː(r)/ n sabotador m

sachet /'sæʃeɪ/ n saché m

sack /sæk/ n saco m, saca f □ vt (colloq) despedir. **get the~** (colloq) ser despedido

sacrament /'sækrəmənt/ n sacramento m

sacred /'seɪkrɪd/ a sagrado

sacrifice /'sækrɪfaɪs/ n sacrifício m; (fig) sacrifício m □ vt sacrificar

sacrileg|e /'sækrɪlɪdʒ/ n sacrilégio m. **~ious** /-'lɪdʒəs/ a sacrílego

sad /sæd/ a (sadder, saddest) (person) triste; (story, news) triste. **~ly** adv tristemente; (unfortunately) infelizmente. **~ness** n tristeza f

sadden /'sædn/ vt entristecer

saddle /'sædl/ n sela f □ vt (horse) selar. **~ sb with** sobrecarregar alguém com

sadis|m /'seɪdɪzəm/ n sadismo m. **~t** /-ɪst/ n sádico m. **~tic** /sə'dɪstɪk/ a sádico

safe /seɪf/ a (-er, -est) (not dangerous) seguro; (out of danger) fora de perigo; (reliable) confiável. **~ from** salvo de risco de □ n cofre m, caixa-forte f. **~ and sound** são e salvo. **~ conduct** salvo-conduto m. **~ keeping** custódia f, (P) protecção f. **to be on the ~ side** por via das dúvidas. **~ly** adv (arrive etc) em segurança; (keep) seguro

safeguard /'seɪfgɑːd/ n salvaguarda f □ vt salvaguardar

safety /'seɪftɪ/ n segurança f. **~-belt** n cinto m de segurança. **~-pin** n alfinete m de fralda. **~-valve** n válvula f de segurança

sag /sæg/ vi (pt sagged) afrouxar

saga /'sɑːgə/ n saga f

sage[1] /seɪdʒ/ n (herb) salva f

sage[2] /seɪdʒ/ a sensato, prudente □ ~ n sábio m

Sagittarius /sædʒɪ'teərɪəs/ n (astrol) Sagitário m

said /sed/ see **say**

sail /seɪl/ n vela f; (trip) viagem f em barco à vela □ vi navegar; (leave) partir; (sport) velejar □ vt navegar. **~ing** n navegação f à vela. **~ing-boat** n barco m à vela

sailor /'seɪlə(r)/ n marinheiro m

saint /seɪnt/ n santo m. **~ly** a santo, santificado

sake /seɪk/ n **for the ~ of** em consideração a. **for my/your/ its own ~** por mim/por você/por isso

salad /'sæləd/ n salada f. **~-dressing** n molho m para salada

salary /'sælərɪ/ n salário m

sale /seɪl/ n venda f; (at reduced prices) liquidação f. **for ~** vende-se. **on ~** à venda. **~s assistant**, (Amer) **~s clerk** vendedor m. **~s department** departamento m de vendas

sales|man /'seɪlzmən/ n (pl -men) (in shop) vendedor m; (traveller) caixeiro-viajante m. **~woman** n (pl -women) (in shop) vendedora f; (traveller) caixeira-viajante f

saline /'seɪlaɪn/ a salino □ n salina f

saliva /sə'laɪvə/ n saliva f

sallow /'sæləʊ/ a (-er, -est) amarelado

salmon /'sæmən/ n (pl invar) salmão m

saloon /sə'luːn/ n (on ship) salão m; (bar) botequim m. **~ (car)** sedã m

r

s

salt /sɔːlt/ *n* sal *m* □ *a* salgado □ *vt* (*season*) salgar; (*cure*) pôr em salmoura. **~-cellar** *n* saleiro *m*. **~ water** água *f* salgada, água *f* do mar. **~y** *a* salgado

salutary /'sæljʊtrɪ/ *a* salutar

salute /sə'luːt/ *n* saudação *f* □ *vt/i* saudar

salvage /'sælvɪdʒ/ *n* (*naut*) salvamento *m*; (*of waste*) reciclagem *f* □ *vt* salvar

salvation /sæl'veɪʃn/ *n* salvação *f*

same /seɪm/ *a* mesmo (**as** que) □ *pron* **the ~** o mesmo □ *adv* **the ~** o mesmo. **all the ~** (*nevertheless*) mesmo assim, apesar de tudo. **at the ~ time** (*at once*) ao mesmo tempo

sample /'saːmpl/ *n* amostra *f* □ *vt* experimentar, provar

sanatorium /sænə'tɔːrɪəm/ *n* (*pl* **-iums**) sanatório *m*

sanctify /'sæŋktɪfaɪ/ *vt* santificar

sanctimonious /sæŋktɪ'məʊnɪəs/ *a* santarrão, carola

sanction /'sæŋkʃn/ *n* (*approval*) aprovação *f*; (*penalty*) pena *f*, sanção *f* □ *vt* sancionar

sanctity /'sæŋktɪtɪ/ *n* santidade *f*

sanctuary /'sæŋktʃʊərɪ/ *n* (*relig*) santuário *m*; (*refuge*) refúgio *m*; (*for animals*) reserva *f*

sand /sænd/ *n* areia *f*; (*beach*) praia *f* □ *vt* (*with sandpaper*) lixar

sandal /'sændl/ *n* sandália *f*

sandbag /'sændbæg/ *n* saco *m* de areia

sandbank /'sændbæŋk/ *n* banco *m* de areia

sandcastle /'sændkaːsl/ *n* castelo *m* de areia

sandpaper /'sændpeɪpə(r)/ *n* lixa *f* □ *vt* lixar

sandpit /'sændpɪt/ *n* caixa *f* de areia

sandwich /'sænwɪdʒ/ *n* sanduíche *m*, (*P*) sandes *f invar* □ *vt* **~ed between** encaixado entre. **~ course** curso *m* profissionalizante envolvendo estudo teórico e estágio em local de trabalho

sandy /'sændɪ/ *a* (**-ier, iest**) arenoso; (*beach*) arenoso; (*hair*) ruivo

sane /seɪn/ *a* (**-er, -est**) (*not mad*) são *m*; (*sensible*) sensato, ajuizado

sang /sæŋ/ *see* **sing**

sanitary /'sænɪtrɪ/ *a* sanitário; (*system*) sanitário. **~ towel**, (*Amer*) **~ napkin** toalha *f* absorvente

sanitation /sænɪ'teɪʃn/ *n* condições *fpl* sanitárias, saneamento *m*

sanity /'sænɪtɪ/ *n* sanidade *f*

sank /sæŋk/ *see* **sink**

Santa Claus /'sæntəklɔːz/ *n* Papai Noel *m*

sap /sæp/ *n* seiva *f* □ *vt* (*pt* **sapped**) esgotar, minar

sapphire /'sæfaɪə(r)/ *n* safira *f*

sarcas|m /'saːrkæzəm/ *n* sarcasmo *m*. **~tic** /saːr'kæstɪk/ *a* sarcástico

sardine /saː'diːn/ *n* sardinha *f*

sardonic /saː'dɒnɪk/ *a* sardônico

sash /sæʃ/ *n* (*around waist*) cinto *m*; (*over shoulder*) faixa *f*. **~-window** *n* janela *f* de guilhotina

sat /sæt/ *see* **sit**

satanic /sə'tænɪk/ *a* satânico

satchel /'sætʃl/ *n* sacola *f*

satellite /'sætəlaɪt/ *n* satélite *m*. **~ dish** antena *f* de satélite. **~ television** televisão *f* via satélite

satin /'sætɪn/ *n* cetim *m*

satir|e /'sætaɪə(r)/ *n* sátira *f*. **~ical** /sə'tɪrɪkl/ *a* satirical. **~ist** /'sætərɪst/ *n* satirista *mf*. **~ize** *vt* satirizar

satisfact|ion /sætɪs'fækʃn/ *n* satisfação *f*. **~ory** /-'fæktərɪ/ *a* satisfatório

satisfy /'sætɪsfaɪ/ *vt* satisfazer; (*convince*) convencer; (*fulfil*) atender. **~ing** *a* satisfatório

saturat|e /'sætʃəreɪt/ *vt* saturar; (*fig*) cansar. **~ed** *a* (*wet*) encharcado; (*fat*) saturado. **~ion** /-'reɪʃn/ *n* saturação *f*

Saturday /'sætədɪ/ *n* sábado *m*

sauce /sɔːs/ *n* molho *m*; (*colloq: cheek*) atrevimento *m*

saucepan /'sɔːspən/ *n* panela *f*, (*P*) caçarola *f*

saucer /'sɔːsə(r)/ *n* pires *m invar*

saucy /'sɔːsɪ/ *a* (**-ier, -iest**) picante

Saudi Arabia /saʊdɪə'reɪbɪə/ *n* Arábia *f* Saudita

sauna /'sɔːnə/ *n* sauna *f*

saunter /'sɔːntə(r)/ *vi* perambular

sausage /'sɒsɪdʒ/ *n* salsicha *f*, linguiça *f*; (*precooked*) salsicha *f*

savage /'sævɪdʒ/ *a* (*wild*) selvagem; (*fierce*) cruel; (*brutal*) brutal □ *n* selvagem *mf* □ *vt* atacar ferozmente. **~ry** *n* selvageria *f*, ferocidade *f*

sav|e /seɪv/ *vt* (*rescue*) salvar; (*keep*) guardar; (*collect*) (*P*) colecionar; (*money*) economizar; (*time*) ganhar; (*prevent*) evitar, impedir (**from** de) □ *n* (*sport*) salvamento *m* □ *prep* salvo, exceto. **~er** *n* poupador *m*. **~ing** *n* economia *f*, poupança *f*. **~ings** *npl* economias *fpl*

saviour /'seɪvɪə(r)/ *n* salvador *m*

savour /'seɪvə(r)/ *n* sabor *m* □ *vt* saborear. **~y** *a* (*tasty*) saboroso; (*not sweet*) salgado

saw[1] /sɔː/ *see* **see**[1]

saw[2] /sɔː/ *n* serra *f* □ *vt* (*pt* **sawed**, *pp* **sawn** *or* **sawed**) serrar

sawdust /'sɔːdʌst/ *n* serragem *f*

saxophone /'sæksəfəʊn/ *n* saxofone *m*

say /seɪ/ *vt/i* (*pt* **said** /sed/) dizer, falar □ *n* **have a ~ (in sth)** opinar sobre alg

coisa. **have one's** ~ exprimir sua
opinião. **I** ~! olhe! *or* escute! ~**ing** *n*
ditado *m*, provérbio *m*

scab /skæb/ *n* casca *f*, crosta *f*; (*colloq:
blackleg*) fura-greve *mf invar*

scaffold /'skæfəʊld/ *n* cadafalso *m*,
andaime *m*. ~**ing** /-əldɪŋ/ *n* andaime *m*

scald /skɔːld/ *vt* escaldar, queimar □ *n*
escaldadura *f*

scale[1] /skeɪl/ *n* (*of fish etc*) escama *f*

scale[2] /skeɪl/ *n* (*ratio, size*) escala *f*; (*mus*)
escala *f*; (*of salaries, charges*) tabela *f*.
on a small/large/*etc* ~ numa
pequena/grande/*etc* escala □ *vt* (*climb*)
escalar. ~ **down** reduzir

scales /skeɪlz/ *npl* (*for weighing*)
balança *f*

scallop /'skɒləp/ *n* (*culin*) concha *f* de
vieira; (*shape*) concha *f* de vieira

scalp /skælp/ *n* couro *m* cabeludo □ *vt*
escalpar

scalpel /'skælpl/ *n* bisturi *m*

scamper /'skæmpə(r)/ *vi* sair correndo

scampi /'skæmpɪ/ *npl* camarões *mpl*
fritos

scan /skæn/ *vt* (*pt* **scanned**) (*intently*)
perscrutar, esquadrinhar; (*quickly*)
passar os olhos em; (*med*) examinar;
(*radar*) explorar □ *n* (*med*) exame *m*

scandal /'skændl/ *n* (*disgrace*) escândalo
m; (*gossip*) fofoca *f*. ~**ous** *a*
escandaloso

Scandinavia /skændɪ'neɪvɪə/ *n*
Escandinávia *f*. ~ **n** *a* & *n* escandinavo
(*m*)

scanty /'skæntɪ/ *a* (**-ier, -iest**) escasso;
(*clothing*) sumário

scapegoat /'skeɪpɡəʊt/ *n* bode *m*
expiatório

scar /skɑː(r)/ *n* cicatriz *f* □ *vt* (*pt*
scarred) marcar; (*fig*) deixar marcas

scarce /skeəs/ *a* (**-er, -est**) escasso, raro.
make o.s. ~**e** (*colloq*) sumir, dar o fora
(*colloq*). ~**ity** *n* escassez *f*. ~**ely** *adv*
mal, apenas

scare /skeə(r)/ *vt* assustar, apavorar. **be**
~**d** estar com medo (**of** de) □ *n* pavor *m*,
pânico *m*. **bomb** ~ pânico *m* causado
por suspeita de bomba num local

scarecrow /'skeəkrəʊ/ *n* espantalho *m*

scarf /skɑːf/ *n* (*pl* **scarves**) (*oblong*)
cachecol *m*; (*square*) lenço *m* de cabelo

scarlet /'skɑːlət/ *a* escarlate *m*

scary /'skeərɪ/ *a* (**-ier, -iest**) (*colloq*)
assustador, apavorante

scathing /'skeɪðɪŋ/ *a* mordaz

scatter /'skætə(r)/ *vt* (*strew*) espalhar;
(*disperse*) dispersar □ *vi* espalhar-se

scavenge /'skævɪndʒ/ *vi* procurar
comida *etc* no lixo. ~**r** /-ə(r)/ *n* (*person*)

que procura comida *etc* no lixo;
(*animal*) que se alimenta de carniça

scenario /sɪ'nɑːrɪəʊ/ *n* (*pl* **-os**) sinopse *f*,
resumo *m* detalhado

scene /siːn/ *n* cena *f*; (*of event*) cenário *m*;
(*sight*) vista *f*, panorama *m*. **behind
the** ~**s** nos bastidores. **make a** ~ fazer
um escândalo

scenery /'siːnərɪ/ *n* cenário *m*, paisagem
f; (*theat*) cenário *m*

scenic /'siːnɪk/ *a* pitoresco, cênico

scent /sent/ *n* (*perfume*) perfume *m*,
fragrância *f*; (*trail*) rastro *m*, pista *f* □ *vt*
(*discern*) sentir. ~**ed** *a* perfumado

sceptic /'skeptɪk/ *n* cético *m*. ~**al** *a*
cético. ~**ism** /-sɪzəm/ *n* ceticismo *m*

schedule /'ʃedjuːl/ *n* programa *m*;
(*timetable*) horário *m* □ *vt* marcar,
programar. **according to** ~ conforme
planejado. **behind** ~ atrasado. **on**
~ (*train*) na hora; (*work*) em dia. ~**d**
flight *n* vôo *m* regular

scheme /skiːm/ *n* esquema *m*; (*plan of
work*) plano *m*; (*plot*) conspiração *f*,
maquinação *f* □ *vi* planejar, (*P*)
planear; (*pej*) intrigar, maquinar,
tramar

schism /'sɪzəm/ *n* cisma *m*

schizophreni|**a** /skɪtsəʊ'friːnɪə/ *n*
esquizofrenia *f*. ~**c** /-'frenɪk/ *a*
esquizofrênico, (*P*) esquizofrénico

scholar /'skɒlə(r)/ *n* erudito *m*, estudioso
m, escolar *m*. ~**ly** *a* erudito. ~**ship** *n*
erudição *f*, saber *m*; (*grant*) bolsa *f* de
estudo

school /skuːl/ *n* escola *f*; (*of university*)
escola *f*, faculdade *f* □ *a* (*age, year,
holidays*) escolar □ *vt* ensinar; (*train*)
treinar, adestrar. ~**ing** *n* instrução *f*;
(*attendance*) escolaridade *f*

school|**boy** /'skuːlbɔɪ/ *n* aluno *m*. ~**girl** *n*
aluna *f*

school|**master** /'skuːlmɑːstə(r)/,
~**mistress**, ~**teacher** *ns* professor *m*,
professora *f*

schooner /'skuːnə(r)/ *n* escuna *f*; (*glass*)
copo *m* alto

sciatica /saɪ'ætɪkə/ *n* ciática *f*

scien|**ce** /'saɪəns/ *n* ciência *f*. ~**ce fiction**
ficção *f* científica. ~**tific** /-'tɪfɪk/ *a*
científico

scientist /'saɪəntɪst/ *n* cientista *mf*

scintillate /'sɪntɪleɪt/ *vi* cintilar; (*fig:
person*) brilhar

scissors /'sɪzəz/ *npl* (**pair of** ~) tesoura *f*

scoff[1] /skɒf/ *vi* ~ **at** zombar de, (*P*)
troçar de

scoff[2] /skɒf/ *vt* (*sl: eat*) devorar, tragar

scold /skəʊld/ *vt* ralhar com. ~**ing** *n*
repreensão *f*, (*P*) descompostura *f*

S

scone /skɒn/ *n* (*culin*) scone *m*, bolinho *m* para o chá

scoop /sku:p/ *n* (*for grain, sugar etc*) pá *f*; (*ladle*) concha *f*; (*news*) furo *m* □ *vt* ~ **out** (*hollow out*) escavar, tirar com concha *or* pá. ~ **up** (*lift*) apanhar

scoot /sku:t/ *vi* (*colloq*) fugir, mandar-se (*colloq*), (*P*) pôr-se a milhas (*colloq*)

scooter /'sku:tə(r)/ *n* (*child's*) patinete *f*, (*P*) trotinete *m*; (*motor cycle*) motoreta *f*, lambreta *f*

scope /skəʊp/ *n* âmbito *m*; (*fig: opportunity*) oportunidade *f*

scorch /skɔ:tʃ/ *vt/i* chamuscar (-se), queimar de leve. ~**ing** *a* (*colloq*) escaldante, abrasador

score /skɔ:(r)/ *n* (*sport*) contagem *f*, escore *m*; (*mus*) partitura *f* □ *vt* marcar com corte(s), riscar; (*a goal*) marcar; (*mus*) orquestrar □ *vi* marcar pontos; (*keep score*) fazer a contagem; (*football*) marcar um gol, (*P*) golo. **a** ~ **(of)** (*twenty*) uma vintena (de), vinte. ~**s** muitos, dezenas. **on that** ~ nesse respeito, quanto a isso. ~**board** *n* marcador *m*. ~**r** /-ə(r)/ *n* (*score-keeper*) marcador *m*; (*of goals*) autor *m*

scorn /skɔ:n/ *n* desprezo *m* □ *vt* desprezar. ~**ful** *a* desdenhoso, escarninho. ~**fully** *adv* com desdém, desdenhosamente

Scorpio /'skɔ:pɪəʊ/ *n* (*astr*) Escorpião *m*

scorpion /'skɔ:pɪən/ *n* escorpião *m*

Scot /skɒt/ *n*, ~**tish** *a* escocês (*m*)

Scotch /skɒtʃ/ *a* escocês □ *n* uísque *m*

scotch /skɒtʃ/ *vt* pôr fim a, frustrar

scot-free /skɒt'fri:/ *a* impune □ *adv* impunemente

Scotland /'skɒtlənd/ *n* Escócia *f*

Scots /skɒts/ *a* escocês. ~**man** *n* escocês *m*. ~**woman** *n* escocesa *f*

scoundrel /'skaʊndrəl/ *n* patife *m*, canalha *m*

scour[1] /'skaʊə(r)/ *vt* (*clean*) esfregar, arear. ~**er** *n* esfregão *m* de palha de aço *or* de nylon

scour[2] /'skaʊə(r)/ *vt* (*search*) percorrer, esquadrinhar

scourge /skɜ:dʒ/ *n* açoite *m*; (*fig*) flagelo *m*

scout /skaʊt/ *n* (*mil*) explorador *m* □ *vi* ~ **about (for)** andar à procura de

Scout /skaʊt/ *n* escoteiro *m*, (*P*) escuteiro *m*. ~**ing** *n* escotismo *m*, (*P*) escutismo *m*

scowl /skaʊl/ *n* carranca *f*, ar *m* carrancudo □ *vi* fazer um ar carrancudo

scraggy /'skrægɪ/ *a* (-**ier**, -**iest**) descarnado, ossudo

scramble /'skræmbl/ *vi* trepar; (*crawl*) avançar de rastros, rastejar, arrastar-se □ *vt* (*eggs*) mexer □ *n* luta *f*, confusão *f*

scrap[1] /skræp/ *n* bocadinho *m*. ~**s** *npl* restos *mpl* □ *vt* (*pt* **scrapped**) jogar fora, (*P*) deitar fora; (*plan etc*) abandonar, pôr de lado. ~**book** *n* álbum *m* de recortes. ~ **heap** monte *m* de ferro-velho. ~**iron** *n* ferro *m* velho, sucata *f*. ~ **merchant** sucateiro *m*. ~**paper** *n* papel *m* de rascunho. ~**py** *a* fragmentário

scrap[2] /skræp/ *n* (*colloq: fight*) briga *f*, pancadaria *f* (*colloq*), rixa *f*

scrape /skreɪp/ *vt* raspar; (*graze*) esfolar, arranhar □ *vi* (*graze, rub*) roçar □ *n* (*act of scraping*) raspagem *f*; (*mark*) raspão *m*, esfoladura *f*; (*fig*) encrenca *f*, maus lençóis *mpl*. ~ **through** escapar pela tangente, (*P*) à tangente; (*exam*) passar pela tangente, (*P*) à tangente. ~ **together** conseguir juntar. ~**r** /-ə(r)/ *n* raspadeira *f*

scratch /skrætʃ/ *vt/i* arranhar (-se); (*a line*) riscar; (*to relieve itching*) coçar(-se) □ *n* arranhão *m*; (*line*) risco *m*; (*wound with claw, nail*) unhada *f*. **start from** ~ começar do princípio. **up to** ~ à altura, ao nível requerido

scrawl /skrɔ:l/ *n* rabisco *m*, garrancho *m*, garatuja *f* □ *vt/i* rabiscar, fazer garranchos, garatujar

scrawny /'skrɔ:nɪ/ *a* (-**ier**, -**iest**) descarnado, ossudo, magricela

scream /skri:m/ *vt/i* gritar □ *n* grito *m* (agudo)

screech /skri:tʃ/ *vi* guinchar, gritar; (*of brakes*) chiar, guinchar □ *n* guincho *m*, grito *m* agudo

screen /skri:n/ *n* écran *m*, tela *f*; (*folding*) biombo *m*; (*fig: protection*) manto *m* (*fig*), capa *f* (*fig*) □ *vt* resguardar, tapar; (*film*) passar; (*candidates etc*) fazer a triagem de. ~**ing** *n* (*med*) exame *m* médico

screw /skru:/ *n* parafuso *m* □ *vt* aparafusar, atarraxar. ~ **up** (*eyes, face*) franzir; (*sl: ruin*) estragar. ~ **up one's courage** cobrar coragem

screwdriver /'skru:draɪvə(r)/ *n* chave *f* de parafusos *or* de fenda

scribble /'skrɪbl/ *vt/i* rabiscar, garatujar □ *n* rabisco *m*, garatuja *f*

script /skrɪpt/ *n* escrita *f*; (*of film*) roteiro *m*, (*P*) guião *m*. ~**writer** *n* (*film*) roteirista *m*, (*P*) autor *m* do guião

Scriptures /'skrɪptʃəz/ *npl* **the** ~ a Sagrada Escritura

scroll /skrəʊl/ *n* rolo *m* (de papel ou pergaminho); (*archit*) voluta *f* □ *vt/i* (*comput*) passar na tela

scrounge /skraʊndʒ/ vt (colloq: cadge) filar (sl), (P) cravar (sl) ▫ vi (beg) parasitar, viver às custas de alguém. **~r** /-ə(r)/ n parasita mf, filão m (sl), (P) crava mf (sl)

scrub[1] /skrʌb/ n (land) mato m

scrub[2] /skrʌb/ vt/i (pt **scrubbed**) esfregar, lavar com escova e sabão; (colloq: cancel) cancelar ▫ n esfrega f

scruff /skrʌf/ n **by the ~ of the neck** pelo cangote, (P) pelo cachaço

scruffy /'skrʌfi/ a (-ier, -iest) desmazelado, desleixado, mal ajambrado (colloq)

scrum /skrʌm/ n rixa f; (Rugby) placagem f

scruple /'skruːpl/ n escrúpulo m

scrupulous /'skruːpjʊləs/ a escrupuloso. **~ly** adv escrupulosamente. **~ly clean** impecavelmente limpo

scrutin|y /'skruːtɪnɪ/ n averiguação f, escrutínio m. **~ize** vt examinar em detalhes

scuff /skʌf/ vt (scrape) esfolar, safar ▫ n esfoladura f

scuffle /'skʌfl/ n tumulto m, briga f

sculpt /skʌlpt/ vt/i esculpir. **~or** n escultor m. **~ure** /-tʃə(r)/ n escultura f ▫ vt/i esculpir

scum /skʌm/ n (on liquid) espuma f; (pej: people) gentinha f, escumalha f, ralé f

scurf /skɜːf/ n películas fpl; (dandruff) caspa f

scurrilous /'skʌrɪləs/ a injurioso, insultuoso

scurry /'skʌrɪ/ vi dar corridinhas; (hurry) apressar- se. **~ off** escapulir-se

scurvy /'skɜːvɪ/ n escorbuto m

scuttle[1] /'skʌtl/ n (bucket, box) balde m para carvão

scuttle[2] /'skʌtl/ vt (ship) afundar abrindo rombos or as torneiras de fundo

scuttle[3] /'skʌtl/ vi **~ away** or **off** fugir, escapulir-se

scythe /saɪð/ n gadanha f, foice f grande

sea /siː/ n mar m ▫ a do mar, marinho, marítimo. **at ~** no alto mar, ao largo. **all at ~** desnorteado. **by ~** por mar. **~ bird** ave f marinha. **~-green** a verde-mar. **~ horse** cavalo-marinho m, hipocampo m. **~ level** nível m do mar. **~lion** leão-marinho m. **~ shell** concha f. **~-shore** n litoral m; (beach) praia f. **~ water** água f do mar

seaboard /'siːbɔːd/ n litoral m, costa f

seafarer /'siːfeərə(r)/ n marinheiro m, navegante m

seafood /'siːfuːd/ n marisco(s) m (pl)

seagull /'siːɡʌl/ n gaivota f

seal[1] /siːl/ n (animal) foca f

seal[2] /siːl/ n selo m, sinete m ▫ vt selar; (with wax) lacrar. **~ing-wax** n lacre m. **~off** (area) vedar

seam /siːm/ n (in cloth etc) costura f; (of mineral) veio m, filão m. **~less** a sem costura

seaman /'siːmən/ n (pl **-men**) marinheiro m, marítimo m

seamy /'siːmɪ/ a **~ side** lado m (do) avesso; (fig) lado m sórdido

seance /'seɪɑːns/ n sessão f espírita

seaplane /'siːpleɪn/ n hidroavião m

seaport /'siːpɔːt/ n porto m de mar

search /sɜːtʃ/ vt/i revistar, dar busca (a); (one's heart, conscience etc) examinar ▫ n revista f, busca f; (quest) procura f, busca f; (official) inquérito m. **in ~ of** à procura de. **~ for** procurar. **~-party** n equipe f de busca. **~-warrant** n mandado m de busca. **~ing** a (of look) penetrante; (of test etc) minucioso

searchlight /'sɜːtʃlaɪt/ n holofote m

seasick /'siːsɪk/ a enjoado. **~ness** n enjôo m, P enjoo m

seaside /'siːsaɪd/ n costa f, praia f, beira-mar f. **~ resort** n balneário m, praia f

season /'siːzn/ n (of year) estação f; (proper time) época f; (cricket, football etc) temporada f ▫ vt temperar; (wood) secar. **in ~** na época. **~able** a próprio da estação. **~al** a sazonal. **~ed** a (of people) experimentado. **~ing** n tempero m. **~-ticket** n (train etc) passe m; (theatre etc) assinatura f

seat /siːt/ n assento m; (place) lugar m; (of bicycle) selim m; (of chair) assento m; (of trousers) fundilho m ▫ vt sentar; (have seats for) ter lugares sentados para. **be ~ed, take a ~** sentar-se. **~ of learning** centro m de cultura. **~-belt** n cinto m de segurança

seaweed /'siːwiːd/ n alga f marinha

seaworthy /'siːwɜːðɪ/ a navegável, em condições de navegabilidade

secateurs /'sekətsːz/ npl tesoura f de poda

seclu|de /sɪ'kluːd/ vt isolar. **~ded** a isolado, retirado. **~sion** /sɪ'kluːʒn/ n isolamento m

second[1] /'sekənd/ a segundo ▫ n segundo m; (in duel) testemunha f. **~ (gear)** (auto) segunda f (velocidade). **the ~ of April** dois de Abril. **~s** (goods) artigos mpl de segunda or de refugo ▫ adv (in race etc) em segundo lugar ▫ vt secundar. **~-best** a escolhido em segundo lugar. **~-class** a de segunda classe. **~-hand** a de segunda mão ▫ n (on clock) ponteiro m dos segundos. **~-rate** a medíocre, de segunda ordem. **~ thoughts** dúvidas fpl. **on**

S

~ **thoughts** pensando melhor. ~**ly** *adv* segundo, em segundo lugar

second² /sɪ'kɒnd/ *vt* (*transfer*) destacar (**to** para)

secondary /'sekəndrɪ/ *a* secundário. ~ **school** escola *f* secundária

secrecy /'si:krəsɪ/ *n* segredo *m*

secret /'si:krɪt/ *a* secreto □ *n* segredo *m*. **in** ~ em segredo. ~ **agent** *n* agente *mf* secreto. ~**ly** *adv* em segredo, secretamente

secretar|y /'sekrətrɪ/ *n* secretário *m*, secretária *f*. **S**~**y of State** ministro *m* de Estado, (*P*) Secretário *m* de Estado; (*Amer*) ministro *m* dos Negócios Estrangeiros. ~**ial** /-'teərɪəl/ *a* (*work, course etc*) de secretária

secret|e /sɪ'kri:t/ *vt* segregar; (*hide*) esconder. ~**ion** /-ʃn/ *n* secreção *f*

secretive /'si:krətɪv/ *a* misterioso, reservado

sect /sekt/ *n* seita *f*. ~**arian** /-'teərɪən/ *a* sectário

section /'sekʃn/ *n* seção *f*, (*P*) secção *f*; (*of country, community etc*) setor *m*, (*P*) sector *m*; (*district of town*) zona *f*

sector /'sektə(r)/ *n* setor *m*, (*P*) sector *m*

secular /'sekjʊlə(r)/ *a* secular, leigo, *P* laico; (*art, music etc*) profano

secure /sɪ'kjʊə(r)/ *a* seguro, em segurança; (*firm*) seguro, sólido; (*in mind*) tranqüilo, *P* tranquilo □ *vt* prender bem *or* com segurança; (*obtain*) conseguir, arranjar; (*ensure*) assegurar; (*windows, doors*) fechar bem. ~**ly** *adv* solidamente; (*safely*) em segurança

securit|y /sɪ'kjʊərətɪ/ *n* segurança *f*; (*for loan*) fiança *f*, caução *f*. ~ **ies** *npl* (*finance*) títulos *mpl*

sedate /sɪ'deɪt/ *a* sereno, comedido □ *vt* (*med*) tratar com sedativos

sedation /sɪ'deɪʃn/ *n* (*med*) sedação *f*. **under** ~ sob o efeito de sedativos

sedative /'sedətɪv/ *n* (*med*) sedativo *m*

sedentary /'sedntrɪ/ *a* sedentário

sediment /'sedɪmənt/ *n* sedimento *m*, depósito *m*

seduce /sɪ'dju:s/ *vt* seduzir

seduct|ion /sɪ'dʌkʃn/ *n* sedução *f*. ~**ive** /-tɪv/ *a* sedutor, aliciante

see¹ /si:/ *vt/i* (*pt* saw, *pp* seen) ver; (*escort*) acompanhar. ~ **about** *or* **to** tratar de, encarregar-se de. ~ **off** *vt* (*wave goodbye*) ir despedir-se de; (*chase*) acompanhar. ~ **through** (*task*) levar a cabo; (*not be deceived by*) não se deixar enganar por. ~ (**to it**) **that** assegurar que, tratar de fazer com que. ~**ing that** visto que, uma vez que. ~ **you later!** (*colloq*) até logo! (*colloq*)

see² /si:/ *n* sé *f*, bispado *m*

seed /si:d/ *n* semente *f*; (*fig: origin*) germe(n) *m*; (*tennis*) cabeça *f* de série; (*pip*) caroço *m*. **go to** ~ produzir sementes; (*fig*) desmazelar-se (*colloq*). ~**ling** *n* planta *f* brotada a partir da semente

seedy /'si:dɪ/ *a* (-**ier**, -**iest**) (com um ar) gasto, surrado; (*colloq: unwell*) abatido, deprimido, em baixo astral (*colloq*)

seek /si:k/ *vt* (*pt* sought) procurar; (*help etc*) pedir

seem /si:m/ *vi* parecer. ~**ingly** *adv* aparentemente, ao que parece

seemly /'si:mlɪ/ *adv* decente, conveniente, próprio

seen /si:n/ *see* see¹

seep /si:p/ *vi* (*ooze*) filtrar-se; (*trickle*) pingar, escorrer, passar. ~**age** *n* infiltração *f*

see-saw /'si:sɔ:/ *n* gangorra *f*, (*P*) balanço *m*

seethe /si:ð/ *vi* ~ **with** (*anger*) ferver de; (*people*) fervilhar de

segment /'segmənt/ *n* segmento *m*; (*of orange*) gomo *m*

segregat|e /'segrɪgeɪt/ *vt* segregar, separar. ~**ion** /-'geɪʃn/ *n* segregação *f*

seize /si:z/ *vt* agarrar, (*P*) deitar a mão a, apanhar; (*take possession by force*) apoderar-se de; (*by law*) apreender, confiscar, (*P*) apresar □ *vi* ~ **on** (*opportunity*) aproveitar. ~ **up** (*engine etc*) grimpar, emperrar. **be** ~**d with** (*fear, illness*) ter um ataque de

seizure /'si:ʒə(r)/ *n* (*med*) ataque *m*, crise *f*; (*law*) apreensão *f*, captura *f*

seldom /'seldəm/ *adv* raras vezes, raramente, raro

select /sɪ'lekt/ *vt* escolher, selecionar, (*P*) seleccionar □ *a* seleto, (*P*) selecto. ~**ion** /-ʃn/ *n* seleção *f*, (*P*) selecção *f*; (*comm*) sortido *m*

selective /sɪ'lektɪv/ *a* seletivo, (*P*) selectivo

self /self/ *n* (*pl* selves) **the** ~ o eu, o ego

self- /self/ *pref* ~**assurance** *n* segurança *f*. ~**assured** *a* seguro de si. ~**catering** *a* em que os hóspedes têm facilidades de cozinhar. ~**centred** *a* egocêntrico. ~**confidence** *n* autoconfiança *f*, confiança *f* em si mesmo. ~**confident** *a* que tem confiança em si mesmo. ~**conscious** *a* inibido, constrangido. ~**contained** *a* independente. ~**control** *n* autodomínio *m*. ~**controlled** *a* senhor de si. ~**defence** *n* legítima defesa *f*. ~**denial** *n* abnegação *f*. ~**employed** *a* autónomo. ~**esteem** *n* amor *m* próprio. ~**evident** *a* evidente. ~**indulgent** *a* que não resiste a tentações; (*for ease*) comodista.

~**-interest** *n* interesse *m* pessoal.
~**-portrait** *n* auto-retrato *m*.
~**-possessed** *a* senhor de si. ~**-reliant**
a independente, seguro de si. ~**-respect**
n amor *m* próprio. ~**-righteous** *a* que
se tem em boa conta. ~**-sacrifice** *n*
abnegação *f*, sacrifício *m*. ~**-satisfied**
a cheio de si, convencido (*colloq*).
~**-seeking** *a* egoísta. ~**-service** *a* auto-
serviço, self-service. ~**-styled** *a*
pretenso. ~**-sufficient** *a* auto-
suficiente. ~**-willed** *a* voluntarioso

selfish /'selfɪʃ/ *a* egoísta; (*motive*)
interesseiro. ~**ness** *n* egoísmo *m*

selfless /'selflɪs/ *a* desinteressado

sell /sel/ *vt/i* (*pt* **sold**) vender(-se). ~**-by
date** válido até. ~ **off** liquidar. **be sold
out** estar esgotado. ~**-out** *n* (*show*)
sucesso *m*; (*colloq: betrayal*) traição *f*.
~**er** *n* vendedor *m*

Sellotape /'seləʊteɪp/ *n* fita *f* adesiva, (*P*)
fitacola *f*

semantic /sɪ'mæntɪk/ *a* semântico. ~**s** *n*
semântica *f*

semblance /'sembləns/ *n* aparência *f*

semen /'si:mən/ *n* sêmen *m*, (*P*) sémen
m, esperma *m*

semester /sɪ'mestə(r)/ *n* (*Amer: univ*)
semestre *m*

semi- /'semɪ/ *pref* semi-, meio

semibreve /'semɪbri:v/ *n* (*mus*)
semibreve *f*

semicirc|le /'semɪsɜ:kl/ *n* semicírculo *m*.
~**ular** /-sɜ:kjʊlə(r)/ *a* semicircular

semicolon /semɪ'kəʊlən/ *n* ponto-e-
vírgula *m*

semi-detached /semɪdɪ'tætʃt/ *a* ~ **house**
casa *f* geminada

semifinal /semɪ'faɪnl/ *n* semifinal *f*, (*P*)
meiafinal *f*

seminar /'semɪnɑ:(r)/ *n* seminário *m*

semiquaver /'semɪkweɪvə(r)/ *n* (*mus*)
semicolcheia *f*

Semit|e /'si:maɪt/ *a & n* semita (*mf*). ~**ic**
/sɪ'mɪtɪk/ *a & n* (*lang*) semítico (*m*)

semitone /'semɪtəʊn/ *n* (*mus*) semitom *m*

semolina /semə'li:nə/ *n* sêmola *f*, (*P*)
sémola *f*, semolina *f*

senat|e /'senɪt/ *n* senado *m*. ~**or** /-ətə(r)/
n senador *m*

send /send/ *vt/i* (*pt* **sent**) enviar, mandar.
~ **back** devolver. ~ **for** (*person*)
chamar, mandar vir; (*help*) pedir.
~ (*away or* **off**) **for** encomendar,
mandar vir (por carta). ~**-off** *n*
despedida *f*, bota-fora *m*. ~ **up** (*colloq*)
parodiar. ~**er** *n* expedidor *m*,
remetente *m*

senil|e /'si:naɪl/ *a* senil. ~**ity** /sɪ'nɪlətɪ/ *n*
senilidade *f*

senior /'si:nɪə(r)/ *a* mais velho, mais
idoso (**to** que); (*in rank*) superior; (*in
service*) mais antigo; (*after surname*)
sênior, (*P*) sénior □ *n* pessoa *f* mais
velha; (*schol*) finalista *mf*. ~ **citizen**
pessoa *f* de idade *or* da terceira idade.
~**ity** /-'ɒrətɪ/ *n* (*in age*) idade *f*; (*in
service*) antiguidade *f*

sensation /sen'seɪʃn/ *n* sensação *f*. ~**al** *a*
sensacional. ~**alism** *n*
sensacionalismo *m*

sense /sens/ *n* sentido *m*; (*wisdom*) bom
senso *m*; (*sensation*) sensação *f*;
(*mental impression*) sentimento *m*. ~**s**
(*sanity*) razão *f* □ *vt* pressentir. **make**
~ fazer sentido. **make** ~ **of**
compreender. ~**less** *a* disparatado,
sem sentido; (*med*) sem sentidos,
inconsciente

sensible /'sensəbl/ *a* sensato, razoável;
(*clothes*) prático

sensitiv|e /'sensətɪv/ *a* sensível (**to** a);
(*touchy*) susceptível. ~**ity** /-'tɪvətɪ/ *n*
sensibilidade *f*

sensory /'sensərɪ/ *a* sensorial

sensual /'senʃʊəl/ *a* sensual. ~**ity**
/-'ælətɪ/ *n* sensualidade *f*

sensuous /'senʃʊəs/ *a* sensual

sent /sent/ *see* **send**

sentence /'sentəns/ *n* frase *f*; (*jur:
decision*) sentença *f*; (*punishment*)
pena *f* □ *vt* ~ **to** condenar a

sentiment /'sentɪmənt/ *n* sentimento *m*;
(*opinion*) modo *m* de ver

sentimental /sentɪ'mentl/ *a*
sentimental. ~**ity** /-men'tælətɪ/ *n*
sentimentalidade *f*, sentimentalismo *m*.
~ **value** valor *m* estimativo

sentry /'sentrɪ/ *n* sentinela *f*

separable /'sepərəbl/ *a* separável

separate¹ /'seprət/ *a* separado, diferente.
~**s** *npl* (*clothes*) conjuntos *mpl*. ~**ly** *adv*
separadamente, em separado

separat|e² /'sepəreɪt/ *vt/i* separar (-se).
~**ion** /-'reɪʃn/ *n* separação *f*   **S**

September /sep'tembə(r)/ *n* setembro *m*

septic /'septɪk/ *a* séptico, infectado

sequel /'si:kwəl/ *n* resultado *m*, seqüela
f, (*P*) sequela *f*; (*of novel, film*)
continuação *f*

sequence /'si:kwəns/ *n* seqüência *f*, (*P*)
sequência *f*

sequin /'si:kwɪn/ *n* lantejoula *f*

serenade /serə'neɪd/ *n* serenata *f* □ *vt*
fazer uma serenata para

seren|e /sɪ'ri:n/ *a* sereno. ~**ity** /-'enətɪ/ *n*
serenidade *f*

sergeant /'sɑ:dʒənt/ *n* sargento *m*

serial /'sɪərɪəl/ *n* folhetim *m* □ *a*
(*number*) de série. ~**ize** /-laɪz/ *vt*
publicar em folhetim

series /'sɪərɪːz/ *n invar* série *f*

serious /'sɪərɪəs/ *a* sério; (*very bad, critical*) grave, sério. **~ly** *adv* seriamente, gravemente, a sério. **take ~ly** levar a sério. **~ness** *n* seriedade *f*, gravidade *f*

sermon /'sɜːmən/ *n* sermão *m*

serpent /'sɜːpənt/ *n* serpente *f*

serrated /sɪ'reɪtɪd/ *a* (*edge*) serr(e)ado, com serrilha

serum /'sɪərəm/ *n* (*pl* -a) soro *m*

servant /'sɜːvənt/ *n* criado *m*, criada *f*, empregado *m*, empregada *f*

serv|e /sɜːv/ *vt/i* servir; (*a sentence*) cumprir; (*jur: a writ*) entregar; (*mil*) servir, prestar serviço; (*apprenticeship*) fazer ▢ *n* (*tennis*) saque *m*, (*P*) serviço *m*. **~e as/to** servir de/para. **~e its purpose** servir para o que é (*colloq*), servir os seus fins. **it ~es you/him** *etc* **right** é bem feito. **~ing** *n* (*portion*) dose *f*, porção *f*

server /'sɜːvə(r)/ *n* (*comput*) servidor *m*

service /'sɜːvɪs/ *n* serviço *m*; (*relig*) culto *m*; (*tennis*) saque *m*, (*P*) serviço *m*; (*maintenance*) revisão *f*. **~s** (*mil*) forças *fpl* armadas ▢ *vt* (*car etc*) fazer a revisão de. **of ~ to** útil a, de utilidade a. **~ area** área *f* de serviço. **~ charge** serviço *m*. **~ station** posto *m* de gasolina

serviceable /'sɜːvɪsəbl/ *a* útil, prático; (*durable*) resistente

serviceman /'sɜːvɪsmən/ *n* (*pl* -men) militar *m*

serviette /sɜːvɪ'et/ *n* guardanapo *m*

session /'seʃn/ *n* sessão *f*; (*univ*) ano *m* académico, (*P*) académico; (*Amer: univ*) semestre *m*. **in ~** (*sitting*) em sessão, reunidos

set /set/ *vt* (*pt* set, *pres p* setting) pôr, colocar; (*put down*) pousar; (*limit etc*) fixar; (*watch, clock*) regular; (*example*) dar; (*exam, task*) marcar; (*in plaster*) engessar ▢ *vi* (*of sun*) pôr-se; (*of jelly*) endurecer, solidificar(-se) ▢ *n* (*of people*) círculo *m*, roda *f*; (*of books*) colecção *f*, (*P*) colecção *f*; (*of tools, chairs etc*) jogo *m*; (*TV, radio*) aparelho *m*; (*hair*) mise *f*; (*theat*) cenário *m*; (*tennis*) partida *f*, set *m* ▢ *a* fixo; (*habit*) inveterado; (*jelly*) duro, sólido; (*book*) do programa, (*P*) adoptado; (*meal*) a preço fixo. **be ~ on doing** estar decidido a fazer. **~ about** *or* **to** começar a, pôr-se a. **~ back** (*plans etc*) atrasar; (*sl: cost*) custar. **~-back** *n* revés *m*, contratempo *m*, atraso *m* de vida (*colloq*). **~ fire to** atear fogo a, (*P*) deitar fogo a. **~free** pôr em liberdade. **~ in** (*rain etc*) pegar. **~off** *or* **out** partir, começar a viajar. **~ off** (*mechanism*)

pôr para funcionar, (*P*) pôr a funcionar; (*bomb*) explodir; (*by contrast*) realçar. **~ out** (*state*) expor; (*arrange*) dispôr. **~ sail** partir, içar as velas. **~ square** esquadro *m*. **~ the table** pôr a mesa. **~ theory** teoria *f* de conjuntos. **~-to** *n* briga *f*. **~ up** (*establish*) fundar, estabelecer. **~-up** *n* (*system*) sistema *m*, organização *f*; (*situation*) situação *f*

settee /se'tiː/ *n* sofá *m*

setting /'setɪŋ/ *n* (*framework*) quadro *m*; (*of jewel*) engaste *m*; (*typ*) composição *f*; (*mus*) arranjo *m* musical

settle /'setl/ *vt* (*arrange*) resolver; (*date*) marcar; (*nerves*) acalmar; (*doubts*) esclarecer; (*new country*) colonizar, povoar; (*bill*) pagar ▢ *vi* assentar; (*in country*) estabelecer-se; (*in house, chair etc*) instalar-se; (*weather*) estabilizar-se. **~ down** acalmar-se; (*become orderly*) assentar; (*sit, rest*) instalar-se. **~ for** aceitar. **~ up (with)** fazer contas (com); (*fig*) ajustar contas (com). **~r** /-ə(r)/ *n* colono *m*, colonizador *m*

settlement /'setlmənt/ *n* (*agreement*) acordo *m*; (*payment*) pagamento *m*; (*colony*) colónia *f*, (*P*) colónia *f*; (*colonization*) colonização *f*

seven /'sevn/ *a & n* sete (*m*). **~th** *a & n* sétimo (*m*)

seventeen /sevn'tiːn/ *a & n* dezessete (*m*), (*P*) dezassete (*m*). **~th** *a & n* décimo sétimo (*m*)

sevent|y /'sevntɪ/ *a & n* setenta (*m*). **~ieth** *a & n* septuagésimo (*m*)

sever /'sevə(r)/ *vt* cortar. **~ance** *n* corte *m*

several /'sevrəl/ *a & pron* vários, diversos

sever|e /sɪ'vɪə(r)/ *a* (-er, -est) severo; (*pain*) forte, violento; (*illness*) grave; (*winter*) rigoroso. **~ely** *adv* severamente; (*seriously*) gravemente. **~ity** /sɪ'verɪtɪ/ *n* severidade *f*; (*seriousness*) gravidade *f*

sew /səʊ/ *vt/i* (*pt* sewed, *pp* sewn *or* sewed) coser, costurar. **~ing** *n* costura *f*. **~ing-machine** *n* máquina *f* de costura

sewage /'sjuːɪdʒ/ *n* efluentes *mpl* dos esgotos, detritos *mpl*

sewer /'sjuːə(r)/ *n* cano *m* de esgoto

sewn /səʊn/ *see* sew

sex /seks/ *n* sexo *m* ▢ *a* sexual. **have ~** ter relações. **~ maniac** tarado *m* sexual. **~y** *a* sexy *invar*, que tem sex-appeal

sexist /'seksɪst/ *a & n* sexista *mf*

sexual /'sekʃʊəl/ *a* sexual. **~ harassment** assédio *m* sexual. **~ intercourse** relações *fpl* sexuais. **~ity** /-'ælətɪ/ *n* sexualidade *f*

shabb|y /'ʃæbɪ/ a (-ier, -iest) (clothes, object) gasto, surrado; (person) maltrapilho, mal vestido; (mean) miserável. **~ily** adv miseravelmente

shack /ʃæk/ n cabana f, barraca f

shackles /'ʃæklz/ npl grilhões mpl, algemas fpl

shade /ʃeɪd/ n sombra f; (of colour) tom m, matiz m; (of opinion) matiz m; (for lamp) abat-jour m, quebra-luz m; (Amer: blind) estore m □ vt resguardar da luz; (darken) sombrear. **a ~ bigger/etc** ligeiramente maior/etc. **in the ~** à sombra

shadow /'ʃædəʊ/ n sombra f □ vt cobrir de sombra; (follow) seguir, vigiar. **S~ Cabinet** gabinete m formado pelo partido da oposição. **~y** a ensombrado, sombreado; (fig) vago, indistinto

shady /'ʃeɪdɪ/ a (-ier, -iest) sombreiro, (P) que dá sombra; (in shade) à sombra; (fig: dubious) suspeito, duvidoso

shaft /ʃɑːft/ n (of arrow, spear) haste f; (axle) eixo m, veio m; (of mine, lift) poço m; (of light) raio m

shaggy /'ʃægɪ/ a (-ier, -iest) (beard) hirsuto; (hair) desgrenhado; (animal) peludo, felpudo

shake /ʃeɪk/ vt (pt shook, pp shaken) abanar, sacudir; (bottle) agitar; (belief, house etc) abalar □ vi estremecer, tremer □ n (violent) abanão m, safanão m; (light) sacudidela f. **~ hands with** apertar a mão de. **~ off** (get rid of) sacudir, livrar-se de. **~ one's head** (to say no) fazer que não com a cabeça. **~ up** agitar. **~-up** n (upheaval) reviravolta f

shaky /'ʃeɪkɪ/ a (-ier, -iest) (hand, voice) trêmulo, (P) trémulo; (unsteady, unsafe) pouco firme, inseguro; (weak) fraco

shall /ʃæl/; unstressed /ʃəl/ v aux **I/we ~ do** (future) farei/faremos. **I/you/he ~ do** (command) eu hei de/você há de/ tu hás de/ele há de fazer

shallot /ʃə'lɒt/ n cebolinha f, (P) chalota f

shallow /'ʃæləʊ/ a (-er, -est) pouco fundo, raso; (fig) superficial

sham /ʃæm/ n fingimento m; (jewel etc) imitação f; (person) impostor m, fingido m □ a fingido; (false) falso □ vt (pt shammed) fingir

shambles /'ʃæmblz/ npl (colloq: mess) balbúrdia f, trapalhada f

shame /ʃeɪm/ n vergonha f □ vt (fazer) envergonhar. **it's a ~** é uma pena. **what a ~!** que pena! **~ful** a vergonhoso. **~less** a sem vergonha, descarado; (immodest) despudorado, desavergonhado

shamefaced /'ʃeɪmfeɪst/ a envergonhado

shampoo /ʃæm'puː/ n xampu m, (P) champô m, shampoo m □ vt lavar com xampu, (P) champô or shampoo

shan't /ʃɑːnt/ = **shall not**

shanty /'ʃæntɪ/ n barraca f. **~ town** favela f, (P) bairro(s) m(pl) da lata

shape /ʃeɪp/ n forma f □ vt moldar □ vi **~ (up)** andar bem, fazer progressos. **take ~** concretizar-se, avançar. **~less** a informe, sem forma; (of body) deselegante, disforme

shapely /'ʃeɪplɪ/ a (-ier, -iest) (leg, person) bem feito, elegante

share /ʃeə(r)/ n parte f, porção f; (comm) ação f, (P) acção f □ vt/i partilhar (**with** com, **in** de)

shareholder /'ʃeəhəʊldə(r)/ n acionista mf, (P) accionista mf

shark /ʃɑːk/ n tubarão m

sharp /ʃɑːp/ a (-er, -est) (knife, pencil etc) afiado; (pin, point etc) pontiagudo, aguçado; (words, reply) áspero; (of bend) fechado; (acute) agudo; (sudden) brusco; (dishonest) pouco honesto; (well-defined) nítido; (brisk) rápido, vigoroso; (clever) vivo □ adv (stop) de repente □ n (mus) sustenido m. **six o'clock ~** seis horas em ponto. **~ly** adv (harshly) rispidamente; (suddenly) de repente

sharpen /'ʃɑːpən/ vt aguçar; (pencil) fazer a ponta de, (P) afiar; (knife etc) afiar, amolar. **~er** n afiadeira f; (for pencil) apontador m, (P) apára-lápis m, (P) afia-lápis m

shatter /'ʃætə(r)/ vt/i despedaçar (-se), esmigalhar(-se); (hopes) destruir(-se); (nerves) abalar(-se). **~ed** a (upset) passado; (exhausted) estafado (colloq)

shav|e /ʃeɪv/ vt/i barbear(-se), fazer a barba (de) □ n **have a ~e** barbear-se. **have a close ~** (fig) escapar por um triz. **~en** a raspado, barbeado. **~er** n aparelho m de barbear, (P) máquina f de barbear. **~ing-brush** n pincel m para a barba. **~ing-cream** n creme m de barbear

shaving /'ʃeɪvɪŋ/ n apara f

shawl /ʃɔːl/ n xale m, (P) xaile m

she /ʃiː/ pron ela □ n fêmea f

sheaf /ʃiːf/ n (pl sheaves) feixe m; (of papers) maço m, molho m

shear /ʃɪə(r)/ vt (pp shorn or sheared) (sheep etc) tosquiar

shears /ʃɪəz/ npl tesoura f para jardim

sheath /ʃiːθ/ n (pl ~s /ʃiːðz/) bainha f; (condom) preservativo m, camisa-de-Vénus f

sheathe /ʃiːð/ vt embainhar

shed[1] /ʃed/ n (hut) casinhola f; (for cows) estábulo m

S

shed[2] /ʃed/ (*pt* **shed**, *pres p* **shedding**) perder, deixar cair; (*spread*) espalhar; (*blood, tears*) deitar, derramar. ~ **light on** lançar luz sobre

sheen /ʃi:n/ *n* brilho *m*, lustre *m*

sheep /ʃi:p/ *n* (*pl invar*) carneiro *m*, ovelha *f*. ~**dog** *n* cão *m* de pastor

sheepish /ʃi:pɪʃ/ *a* encabulado. ~**ly** *adv* com um ar encabulado

sheepskin /ʃi:pskɪn/ *n* pele *f* de carneiro; (*leather*) carneira *f*

sheer /ʃɪə(r)/ *a* mero, simples; (*steep*) íngreme, a pique; (*fabric*) diáfano, transparente □ *adv* a pique, verticalmente

sheet /ʃi:t/ *n* lençol *m*; (*of glass, metal*) chapa *f*, placa *f*; (*of paper*) folha *f*

sheikh /ʃeɪk/ *n* xeque *m*, sheik *m*

shelf /ʃelf/ *n* (*pl* **shelves**) prateleira *f*

shell /ʃel/ *n* (*of egg, nut etc*) casca *f*; (*of mollusc*) concha *f*; (*of ship, tortoise*) casco *m*; (*of building*) estrutura *f*, armação *f*; (*of explosive*) cartucho *m* □ *vt* descascar; (*mil*) bombardear

shellfish /ʃelfɪʃ/ *n* (*pl invar*) crustáceo *m*; (*as food*) marisco *m*

shelter /ʃeltə(r)/ *n* abrigo *m*, refúgio *m* □ *vt* abrigar; (*protect*) proteger; (*harbour*) dar asilo a □ *vi* abrigar-se, refugiar-se. ~**ed** *a* (*life etc*) protegido; (*spot*) abrigado

shelve /ʃelv/ *vt* pôr em prateleiras; (*fit with shelves*) pôr prateleiras em; (*fig*) engavetar, pôr de lado

shelving /ʃelvɪŋ/ *n* (*shelves*) prateleiras *fpl*

shepherd /ʃepəd/ *n* pastor *m* □ *vt* guiar. ~'s **pie** empadão *m* de batata e carne moída

sheriff /ʃerɪf/ *n* xerife *m*

sherry /ʃerɪ/ *n* Xerez *m*

shield /ʃi:ld/ *n* (*armour, heraldry*) escudo *m*; (*screen*) antepara *m* □ *vt* proteger (**from** contra, de)

shift /ʃɪft/ *vt*/*i* mudar de posição, deslocar(-se); (*exchange, alter*) mudar de □ *n* mudança *f*; (*workers; work*) turno *m*. **make** ~ arranjar-se

shiftless /ʃɪftlɪs/ *a* (*lazy*) molengão, preguiçoso

shifty /ʃɪftɪ/ *a* (**-ier**, **-iest**) velhaco, duvidoso

shimmer /ʃɪmə(r)/ *vi* luzir suavemente □ *n* luzir *m*

shin /ʃɪn/ *n* perna *f*. ~**bone** *n* tíbia *f*, canela *f*. ~**pad** *n* (*football*) caneleira *f*

shin|e /ʃaɪn/ *vt*/*i* (*pt* **shone**) (fazer) brilhar, (fazer) reluzir; (*shoes*) engraxar □ *n* lustro *m*. ~**e a torch (on)** iluminar com uma lanterna de mão. **the sun is** ~**ing** faz sol

shingle /ʃɪŋgl/ *n* (*pebbles*) seixos *mpl*

shingles /ʃɪŋglz/ *npl med* zona *f*, herpes-zóster *f*

shiny /ʃaɪnɪ/ *a* (**-ier**, **-iest**) brilhante; (*of coat, trousers*) lustroso

ship /ʃɪp/ *n* barco *m*, navio *m* □ *vt* (*pt* **shipped**) transportar; (*send*) mandar por via marítima; (*load*) embarcar. ~**ment** *n* (*goods*) carregamento *m*; (*shipping*) embarque *m*. ~**per** *n* expedidor *m*. ~**ping** *n* navegação *f*; (*ships*) navios *mpl*

shipbuilding /ʃɪpbɪldɪŋ/ *n* construção *f* naval

shipshape /ʃɪpʃeɪp/ *adv* & *a* em (perfeita) ordem, impecável

shipwreck /ʃɪprek/ *n* naufrágio *m*. ~**ed** *a* naufragado. **be** ~**ed** naufragar

shipyard /ʃɪpja:d/ *n* estaleiro *m*

shirk /ʃɜ:k/ *vt* fugir a, furtar-se a, (*P*) baldar-se a (*sl*). ~**er** *n* parasita *mf*

shirt /ʃɜ:t/ *n* camisa *f*; (*of woman*) blusa *f*. **in** ~**sleeves** em mangas de camisa

shiver /ʃɪvə(r)/ *vi* arrepiar-se, tiritar □ *n* arrepio *m*

shoal /ʃəʊl/ *n* (*of fish*) cardume *m*

shock /ʃɒk/ *n* choque *m*, embate *m*; (*electr*) choque *m* elétrico, (*P*) eléctrico; (*med*) choque *m* □ *a* de choque □ *vt* chocar. ~ **absorber** (*mech*) amortecedor *m*. ~**ing** *a* chocante; (*colloq: very bad*) horrível

shod /ʃɒd/ *see* **shoe**

shodd|y /ʃɒdɪ/ *a* (**-ier**, **-iest**) mal feito, ordinário, de má qualidade. ~**ily** *adv* mal

shoe /ʃu:/ *n* sapato *m*; (*footwear*) calçado *m*; (*horse*) ferradura *f*; (*brake*) sapata *f*, (*P*) calço *m* (de travão) □ *vt* (*pt* **shod**, *pres p* **shoeing**) (*horse*) ferrar. ~**polish** *n* pomada *f*, (*P*) graxa *f* para sapatos. ~**shop** *n* sapataria *f*. **on a** ~**string** (*colloq*) com/por muito pouco dinheiro, na pindaíba (*colloq*)

shoehorn /ʃu:hɔ:n/ *n* calçadeira *f*

shoelace /ʃu:leɪs/ *n* cordão *m* de sapato, (*P*) atacador *m*

shoemaker /ʃu:meɪkə(r)/ *n* sapateiro *m*

shone /ʃɒn/ *see* **shine**

shoo /ʃu:/ *vt* enxotar □ *int* xô

shook /ʃʊk/ *see* **shake**

shoot /ʃu:t/ *vt* (*pt* **shot**) (*gun*) disparar; (*glance, missile*) lançar; (*kill*) matar a tiro; (*wound*) ferir a tiro; (*execute*) executar, fuzilar; (*hunt*) caçar; (*film*) filmar, rodar □ *vi* disparar, atirar (**at** contra, sobre); (*bot*) rebentar; (*football*) rematar □ *n* (*bot*) rebento *m*. ~ **down** abater (a tiro). ~ **in/out** (*rush*) entrar/sair correndo *or* disparado. ~ **up** (*spurt*) jorrar; (*grow quickly*) crescer a olhos vistos, dar um pulo;

(*prices*) subir em disparada. ∼**ing** *n*
(*shots*) tiroteio *m*. ∼**ing-range** *n*
carreira *f* de tiro. ∼**ing star** estrela *f*
cadente

shop /ʃɒp/ *n* loja *f*; (*workshop*) oficina *f*
□ *vi* (*pt* **shopped**) fazer compras.
∼ **around** procurar, ver o que há.
∼ **assistant** empregado *m*, caixeiro *m*;
vendedor *m*. ∼**-floor** *n* (*workers*)
trabalhadores *mpl*. ∼**per** *n* comprador
m. ∼**-soiled**, (*Amer*) ∼**-worn** *adjs*
enxovalhado. ∼ **steward** delegado *m*
sindical. ∼ **window** vitrina *f*, (*P*)
montra *f*. **talk** ∼ falar de coisas
profissionais

shopkeeper /ˈʃɒpkiːpə(r)/ *n* lojista *mf*,
comerciante *mf*

shoplift|er /ˈʃɒplɪftə(r)/ *n* gatuno *m* de
lojas. ∼**ing** *n* furto *m* em lojas

shopping /ˈʃɒpɪŋ/ *n* (*goods*) compras *fpl*.
go ∼ ir às compras. ∼ **bag** sacola *f* de
compras. ∼ **centre** centro *m* comercial

shore /ʃɔː(r)/ *n* (*of sea*) praia *f*, costa *f*; (*of
lake*) margem *f*

shorn /ʃɔːn/ *see* **shear** □ *a* tosquiado.
∼ **of** despojado de

short /ʃɔːt/ *a* (**-er, -est**) curto; (*person*)
baixo; (*brief*) breve, curto; (*curt*) seco,
brusco. **be** ∼ **of** (*lack*) ter falta de
□ *adv* (*abruptly*) bruscamente, de
repente. **cut** ∼ abreviar; (*interrupt*)
interromper □ *n* (*electr*) curto-circuito
m; (*film*) curta-metragem *f*, short *m*.
∼**s** (*trousers*) calção *m*, (*P*) calções *mpl*,
short *m*, (*P*) shorts *mpl*. **a** ∼ **time**
pouco tempo. **he is called Tom for** ∼ o
diminutivo de é Tom. **in** ∼ em
suma. ∼**-change** *vt* (*cheat*) enganar.
∼ **circuit** (*electr*) curto-circuito *m*
∼**-circuit** *vt*/*i* (*electr*) fazer or dar um
curto-circuito (em). ∼ **cut** atalho *m*.
∼**-handed** *a* com falta de pessoal.
∼ **list** (*trousers*) pré-seleção *f*, (*P*) pré-selecção *f*.
∼**-lived** *a* de pouca duração.
∼**-sighted** *a* míope, (*P*) curto de
vista. ∼**-tempered** *a* irritadiço.
∼ **story** conto *m*. ∼ **wave** (*radio*)
onda(s) *f*(*pl*) curta(s)

shortage /ˈʃɔːtɪdʒ/ *n* falta *f*, escassez *f*

shortbread /ˈʃɔːtbred/ *n* shortbread *m*,
biscoito *m* de massa amanteigada

shortcoming /ˈʃɔːtkʌmɪŋ/ *n* falha *f*,
imperfeição *f*

shorten /ˈʃɔːtn/ *vt*/*i* encurtar(-se),
abreviar(-se), diminuir

shorthand /ˈʃɔːthænd/ *n* estenografia *f*.
∼ **typist** estenodactilógrafa *f*

shortly /ˈʃɔːtlɪ/ *adv* (*soon*) em breve,
dentro em pouco

shot /ʃɒt/ *see* **shoot** □ *n* (*firing, bullet*)
tiro *m*; (*person*) atirador *m*; (*pellets*)
chumbo *m*; (*photograph*) fotografia *f*;

(*injection*) injeção *f*, (*P*) injecção *f*;
(*in golf, billiards*) tacada *f*. **go like a**
∼ ir disparado. **have a** ∼ **(at sth)**
experimentar (fazer alg coisa). ∼**-gun**
n espingarda *f*, caçadeira *f*

should /ʃʊd/ *unstressed* /ʃəd/ *v aux*
you ∼ **help me** você devia me ajudar.
I ∼ **have stayed** devia ter ficado.
I ∼ **like to** gostaria de *or* gostava de. **if**
he ∼ **come** se ele vier

shoulder /ˈʃəʊldə(r)/ *n* ombro *m* □ *vt*
(*responsibility*) tomar, assumir;
(*burden*) carregar, arcar com. ∼**-blade**
n (*anat*) omoplata *f*. ∼**-pad** *n*
enchimento *m* de ombro, ombreira *f*

shout /ʃaʊt/ *n* grito *m*, brado *m*; (*very*
loud) berro *m* □ *vt*/*i* gritar (**at** com);
(*very loudly*) berrar (**at** com). ∼ **down**
fazer calar com gritos. ∼**ing** *n* gritaria
f, berraria *f*

shove /ʃʌv/ *n* empurrão *m* □ *vt*/*i*
empurrar; (*colloq: put*) meter, enfiar.
∼ **off** (*colloq: depart*) começar a andar
(*colloq*), dar o fora (*colloq*), (*P*) cavar
(*colloq*)

shovel /ˈʃʌvl/ *n* pá *f*; (*machine*) es-
cavadora *f* □ *vt* (*pt* **shovelled**) remover
com pá

show /ʃəʊ/ *vt* (*pt* **showed**, *pp* **shown**)
mostrar; (*of dial, needle*) marcar; (*put*
on display) expor; (*film*) dar, passar
□ *vi* ver-se, aparecer, estar à vista □ *n*
mostra *f*, demonstração *f*,
manifestação *f*; (*ostentation*) alarde *m*,
espalhafato *m*; (*exhibition*) mostra *f*,
exposição *f*; (*theatre, cinema*)
espetáculo *m*, (*P*) espectáculo *m*, show
m. **for** ∼ para fazer vista. **on** ∼ exposto,
em exposição. ∼**-down** *n* confrontação
f. ∼**-jumping** *n* concurso *m* hípico. ∼ **in**
mandar entrar. ∼ **off** *vt* exibir, ostentar
□ *vi* exibir-se, querer fazer figura. ∼**-off**
n exibicionista *mf*. ∼ **out** acompanhar à
porta. ∼**-piece** *n* peça *f* digna de ser
expor. ∼ **up** ser claramente visível, ver-
se bem; (*colloq: arrive*) aparecer. ∼**ing** *n*
(*performance*) atuação *f*, performance
f; (*cinema*) exibição *f*

shower /ˈʃaʊə(r)/ *n* (*of rain*) aguaceiro *m*,
chuvarada *f*; (*of blows etc*) saraivada *f*;
(*in bathroom*) chuveiro *m*, ducha *f*,
(*P*) duche *m* □ *vt* ∼ **with** cumular de,
encher de □ *vi* tomar um banho de
chuveiro *or* uma ducha, (*P*) um duche.
∼**y** *a* chuvoso

showerproof /ˈʃaʊəpruːf/ *a*
impermeável

shown /ʃəʊn/ *see* **show**

showroom /ˈʃəʊrʊm/ *n* espaço *m* de
exposição, show-room *m*; (*for cars*)
stand *m*

showy /ˈʃəʊɪ/ *a* (**-ier, -iest**) vistoso; (*too*
bright) berrante; (*pej*) espalhafatoso

s

shrank /ʃrænk/ *see* **shrink**

shred /ʃred/ *n* tira *f*, retalho *m*, farrapo *m*; (*fig*) mínimo *m*, sombra *f* □ *vt* (*pt* **shredded**) reduzir a tiras, estrançalhar; (*culin*) desfiar. **∼der** *n* trituradora *f*; (*for paper*) fragmentadora *f*

shrewd /ʃruːd/ *a* (**-er, -est**) astucioso, fino, perspicaz. **∼ness** *n* astúcia *f*, perspicácia *f*

shriek /ʃriːk/ *n* grito *m* agudo, guincho *m* □ *vt/i* gritar, guinchar

shrift /ʃrɪft/ *n* **give sb short ∼** tratar alguém com brusquidão, despachar alguém sem mais cerimônias, (*P*) cerimónias

shrill /ʃrɪl/ *a* estridente, agudo

shrimp /ʃrɪmp/ *n* camarão *m*

shrine /ʃraɪn/ *n* (*place*) santuário *m*; (*tomb*) túmulo *m*; (*casket*) re licário *m*

shrink /ʃrɪŋk/ *vt/i* (*pt* **shrank**, *pp* **shrunk**) encolher; (*recoil*) encolher-se. **∼ from** esquivar-se a, fugir a (+ *inf*)/de (+ *noun*), retrair-se de. **∼age** *n* encolhimento *m*; (*comm*) contração *f*

shrivel /ʃrɪvl/ *vt/i* (*pt* **shrivelled**) encarquilhar(-se)

shroud /ʃraʊd/ *n* mortalha *f* □ *vt* (*veil*) encobrir, envolver

Shrove /ʃrəʊv/ *n* **∼ Tuesday** Terça-feira *f* gorda *or* de Carnaval

shrub /ʃrʌb/ *n* arbusto *m*. **∼bery** *n* arbustos *mpl*

shrug /ʃrʌg/ *vt* (*pt* **shrugged**) **∼ one's shoulders** encolher os ombros □ *n* encolher *m* de ombros. **∼ off** não dar importância a

shrunk /ʃrʌŋk/ *see* **shrink**. **∼en** *a* encolhido; (*person*) mirrado, chupado

shudder /ʃʌdə(r)/ *vi* arrepiar-se, estremecer, tremer □ *n* arrepio *m*, tremor *m*, estremecimento *m*. **I ∼ to think** tremo só de pensar

shuffle /ʃʌfl/ *vt* (*feet*) arrastar; (*cards*) embaralhar □ *vi* arrastar os pés □ *n* marcha *f* arrastada

shun /ʃʌn/ *vt* (*pt* **shunned**) evitar, fugir de

shunt /ʃʌnt/ *vt/i* (*train*) mudar de linha, manobrar

shut /ʃʌt/ *vt* (*pt* **shut**, *pres p* **shutting**) fechar □ *vi* fechar-se; (*shop, bank etc*) encerrar, fechar. **∼ down** *or* **up** fechar. **∼-down** *n* encerramento *m*. **∼ in** *or* **up** trancar. **∼ up** *vi* (*colloq: stop talking*) calar-se □ *vt* (*colloq: silence*) mandar calar. **∼ up!** (*colloq*) cale-se!, cale a boca!

shutter /ʃʌtə(r)/ *n* taipais *mpl*, (*P*) portada *f* de madeira; (*of laths*) persiana *f*; (*in shop*) taipais *mpl*; (*photo*) obturador *m*

shuttle /ʃʌtl/ *n* (*of spaceship*) ônibus *m* espacial. **∼ service** (*plane*) ponte *f* aérea; (*bus*) navete *f*

shuttlecock /ʃʌtlkɒk/ *n* volante *m*

shy /ʃaɪ/ *a* (**-er, -est**) tímido, acanhado, envergonhado □ *vi* (*horse*) espantar-se (**at** com); (*fig*) assustar-se (**at** *or* **away from** com). **∼ness** *n* timidez *f*, acanhamento *m*, vergonha *f*

Siamese /saɪəˈmiːz/ *a* & *n* siamês (*m*). **∼ cat** gato *m* siamês

Sicily /ˈsɪsɪlɪ/ *n* Sicília *f*

sick /sɪk/ *a* doente; (*humour*) negro. **be ∼** (*vomit*) vomitar. **be ∼ of** estar farto de. **feel ∼** estar enjoado. **∼-bay** *n* enfermaria *f*. **∼-leave** *n* licença *f* por doença **∼-room** *n* quarto *m* de doente

sicken /ˈsɪkn/ *vt* (*distress*) desesperar; (*disgust*) repugnar □ *vi* **be ∼ing for flu** *etc* começar a pegar uma gripe (*colloq*)

sickle /ˈsɪkl/ *n* foice *f*

sickly /ˈsɪklɪ/ *a* (**-ier, -iest**) (*person*) doentio, achacado; (*smell*) enjoativo; (*pale*) pálido

sickness /ˈsɪknɪs/ *n* doença *f*; (*vomiting*) náusea *f*, vômito *m*, (*P*) vómito *m*

side /saɪd/ *n* lado *m*; (*of road, river*) beira *f*; (*of hill*) encosta *f*; (*sport*) equipe *f*, (*P*) equipa *f* □ *a* lateral □ *vi* **∼ with** tomar o partido de. **on the ∼** (*extra*) nas horas vagas; (*secretly*) pela calada. **∼ by side** lado a lado. **∼-car** *n* sidecar *m*. **∼-effect** *n* efeito *m* secundário. **∼-show** *n* espetáculo *m*, (*P*) espectáculo *m* suplementar. **∼-step** *vt* (*pt* **-stepped**) evitar. **∼-track** *vt* (fazer) desviar dum propósito

sideboard /ˈsaɪdbɔːd/ *n* aparador *m*

sideburns /ˈsaɪdbɜːnz/ *npl* suíças *fpl*, costeletas *fpl*, (*P*) patilhas *fpl*

sidelight /ˈsaɪdlaɪt/ *n* (*auto*) luz *f* lateral, (*P*) farolim *m*

sideline /ˈsaɪdlaɪn/ *n* atividade *f*, (*P*) actividade *f* secundária; (*sport*) linha *f* lateral

sidelong /ˈsaɪdlɒŋ/ *adv* & *a* de lado

sidewalk /ˈsaɪdwɔːk/ *n* (*Amer*) passeio *m*

sideways /ˈsaɪdweɪz/ *adv* & *a* de lado

siding /ˈsaɪdɪŋ/ *n* desvio *m*, ramal *m*

sidle /ˈsaɪdl/ *vi* **∼ up (to)** avançar furtivamente (para), chegar-se furtivamente (a)

siege /siːdʒ/ *n* cerco *m*

siesta /sɪˈestə/ *n* sesta *f*

sieve /sɪv/ *n* peneira *f*; (*for liquids*) coador *m* □ *vt* peneirar; (*liquids*) passar, coar

sift /sɪft/ *vt* peneirar; (*sprinkle*) polvilhar. **∼ through** examinar minuciosamente, esquadrinhar

sigh /saɪ/ *n* suspiro *m* □ *vt/i* suspirar

sight /saɪt/ *n* vista *f*; (*scene*) cena *f*; (*on gun*) mira *f* □ *vt* avistar, ver, divisar. **at** *or* **on ~** à vista. **catch ~ of** avistar. **in ~** à vista, visível. **lose ~ of** perder de vista. **out of ~** longe dos olhos

sightsee|ing /ˈsaɪtsiːɪŋ/ *n* visita *f*, turismo *m*. **go ~ing** visitar lugares turísticos. **~r** /ˈsaɪtsiːə(r)/ *n* turista *mf*

sign /saɪn/ *n* sinal *m*; (*symbol*) signo *m* □ *vt* (*in writing*) assinar □ *vi* (*make a sign*) fazer sinal. **~ on** *or* **up** (*worker*) assinar contrato. **~-board** *n* tabuleta *f*. **~ language** *n* mímica *f*

signal /ˈsɪɡnəl/ *n* sinal *m* □ *vi* (*pt* **signalled**) fazer signal □ *vt* comunicar (por sinais); (*person*) fazer sinal para. **~-box** *n* cabine *f* de sinalização

signature /ˈsɪɡnətʃə(r)/ *n* assinatura *f*. **~ tune** indicativo *m* musical

signet-ring /ˈsɪɡnɪtrɪŋ/ *n* anel *m* de sinete

significan|t /sɪɡˈnɪfɪkənt/ *a* importante; (*meaningful*) significativo. **~ce** *n* importância *f*; (*meaning*) significado *m*. **~tly** *adv* (*much*) sensivelmente

signify /ˈsɪɡnɪfaɪ/ *vt* significar

signpost /ˈsaɪnpəʊst/ *n* poste *m* de sinalização □ *vt* sinalizar

silence /ˈsaɪləns/ *n* silêncio *m* □ *vt* silenciar, calar. **~r** /-ə(r)/ *n* (*on gun*) silenciador *m*; (*on car*) silencioso *m*

silent /ˈsaɪlənt/ *a* silencioso; (*not speaking*) calado; (*film*) mudo. **~ly** *adv* silenciosamente

silhouette /sɪluˈet/ *n* silhueta *f* □ *vt* **be ~d against** estar em silhueta contra

silicon /ˈsɪlɪkən/ *n* silicone *m*. **~ chip** circuito *m* integrado

silk /sɪlk/ *n* seda *f*. **~en**, **~y** *adjs* sedoso

sill /sɪl/ *n* (*of window*) parapeito *m*; (*of door*) soleira *f*, limiar *m*

sill|y /ˈsɪlɪ/ *a* (**-ier**, **-iest**) tolo, idiota. **~iness** *n* tolice *f*, idiotice *f*

silo /ˈsaɪləʊ/ *n* (*pl* **-os**) silo *m*

silt /sɪlt/ *n* aluvião *m*, sedimento *m*

silver /ˈsɪlvə(r)/ *n* prata *f*; (*silverware*) prataria *f*, pratas *fpl* □ *a* de prata. **~ paper** papel *m* prateado. **~ wedding** bodas *fpl* de prata. **~y** *a* prateado; (*sound*) argentino

silversmith /ˈsɪlvəsmɪθ/ *n* ourives *m*

silverware /ˈsɪlvəweə(r)/ *n* prataria *f*, pratas *fpl*

similar /ˈsɪmɪlə(r)/ *a* **~ (to)** semelhante (a), parecido (com). **~ity** /-əˈlærətɪ/ *n* semelhança *f*. **~ly** *adv* de igual modo, analogamente

simile /ˈsɪmɪlɪ/ *n* símile *m*, comparação *f*

simmer /ˈsɪmə(r)/ *vt/i* cozinhar em fogo brando; (*fig: smoulder*) ferver, fremir; **~ down** acalmar(-se)

simpl|e /ˈsɪmpl/ *a* (**-er**, **-est**) simples. **~e-minded** *a* simples; (*feeble-minded*) pobre de espírito, tolo. **~icity** /-ˈplɪsətɪ/ *n* simplicidade *f*. **~y** *adv* simplesmente; (*absolutely*) absolutamente, simplesmente

simpleton /ˈsɪmpltən/ *n* simplório *m*

simplif|y /ˈsɪmplɪfaɪ/ *vt* simplificar. **~ication** /-ɪˈkeɪʃn/ *n* simplificação *f*

simulat|e /ˈsɪmjʊleɪt/ *vt* simular, imitar. **~ion** /-ˈleɪʃn/ *n* simulação *f*, imitação *f*

simultaneous /sɪmlˈteɪnɪəs/ *a* simultâneo, concomitante. **~ly** *adv* simultaneamente

sin /sɪn/ *n* pecado *m* □ *vi* (*pt* **sinned**) pecar

since /sɪns/ *prep* desde □ *adv* desde então □ *conj* desde que; (*because*) uma vez que, visto que. **~ then** desde então

sincer|e /sɪnˈsɪə(r)/ *a* sincero. **~ely** *adv* sinceramente. **~ity** /-ˈserətɪ/ *n* sinceridade *f*

sinew /ˈsɪnjuː/ *n* (*anat*) tendão *m*. **~s** músculos *mpl*. **~y** *a* forte, musculoso

sinful /ˈsɪnfl/ *a* (*wicked*) pecaminoso; (*shocking*) escandaloso

sing /sɪŋ/ *vt/i* (*pt* **sang**, *pp* **sung**) cantar. **~er** *n* cantor *m*

singe /sɪndʒ/ *vt* (*pres p* **singeing**) chamuscar

single /ˈsɪŋɡl/ *a* único, só; (*unmarried*) solteiro; (*bed*) de solteiro; (*room*) individual; (*ticket*) de ida, simples □ *n* (*ticket*) bilhete *m* de ida *or* simples; (*record*) disco *m* de 45 r.p.m. **~s** (*tennis*) singulares *mpl* □ *vt* **~ out** escolher. **in ~ file** em fila indiana. **~-handed** *a* sem ajuda, sozinho. **~-minded** *a* decidido, aferrado à sua idéia, tenaz. **~ parent** pai *m* solteiro, mãe *f* solteira. **singly** *adv* um a um, um por um

singsong /ˈsɪŋsɒŋ/ *n* **have a ~** cantar em coro □ *a* (*voice*) monótono, monocórdico

singular /ˈsɪŋɡjʊlə(r)/ *n* singular *m* □ *a* (*uncommon; gram*) singular; (*noun*) no singular. **~ly** *adv* singularmente

sinister /ˈsɪnɪstə(r)/ *a* sinistro

sink /sɪŋk/ *vt* (*pt* **sank**, *pp* **sunk**) (*ship*) afundar, ir a pique; (*well*) abrir; (*invest money*) empatar; (*lose money*) enterrar □ *vi* afundar-se; (*of ground*) ceder; (*of voice*) baixar □ *n* pia *f*, (*P*) lava-louça *m*. **~ in** (*fig*) ficar gravado, entrar (*colloq*). **~ or swim** ou vai ou racha

sinner /ˈsɪnə(r)/ *n* pecador *m*

sinuous /ˈsɪnjʊəs/ *a* sinuoso

sinus /ˈsaɪnəs/ *n* (*pl* **-es**) (*anat*) seio (nasal) *m*. **~itis** /saɪnəˈsaɪtɪs/ *n* sinusite *f*

sip /sɪp/ *n* gole *m* □ *vt* (*pt* **sipped**) bebericar, beber aos golinhos

siphon /'saɪfn/ n sifão m □ vt ~ **off** extrair por meio de sifão

sir /sɜ:(r)/ n senhor m. **S~** (title) Sir m. **Dear S~** Exmo Senhor. **excuse me,** ~ desculpe(-se); (of committee etc) **no,** ~ não, senhor

siren /'saɪərən/ n sereia f, sirene f

sirloin /'sɜ:lɔɪn/ n lombo m de vaca

sissy /'sɪsɪ/ n maricas m

sister /'sɪstə(r)/ n irmã f; (nun) irmã f, freira f; (nurse) enfermeira-chefe f. **~-in-law** (pl ~s-in-law) cunhada f. **~ly** a fraterno, fraternal

sit /sɪt/ vt/i (pt sat, pres p sitting) sentar(-se); (of committee etc) reunir-se. ~ **for an exam** fazer um exame, prestar uma prova. **be** ~ting estar sentado. ~ **around** não fazer nada. ~ **down** sentar-se. ~-**in** n ocupação f. ~ting n reunião f, sessão f; (in restaurant) serviço m. ~ting-room n sala f de estar. ~ **up** endireitar-se na cadeira; (not go to bed) passar a noite acordado

site /saɪt/ n local m. (**building**) ~ terreno m para construção, lote m □ vt localizar, situar

situat|e /'sɪtʃʊeɪt/ vt situar. **be** ~ed estar situado. ~ion /-'eɪʃn/ n (position, condition) situação f; (job) emprego m, colocação f

six /sɪks/ a & n seis (m). ~th a & n sexto (m)

sixteen /sɪk'sti:n/ a & n dezesseis m, (P) dezasseis (m). ~th a & n décimo sexto (m)

sixt|y /'sɪkstɪ/ a & n sessenta (m). ~ieth a & n sexagésimo (m)

size /saɪz/ n tamanho m; (of person, garment etc) tamanho m, medida f; (of shoes) número m; (extent) grandeza f □ vt ~ **up** calcular o tamanho de; (colloq: judge) formar um juízo sobre, avaliar. ~**able** a bastante grande, considerável

sizzle /'sɪzl/ vi chiar, rechinar

skate¹ /skeɪt/ n (pl invar) (fish) (ar)raia f

skat|e² /skeɪt/ n patim m □ vi patinar. ~**er** n patinador m. ~**ing** n patinação f. ~**ing-rink** n rinque m de patinação

skateboard /'skeɪtbɔ:d/ n skate m

skelet|on /'skelɪtən/ n esqueleto m; (framework) armação f. ~**on crew** or **staff** pessoal m reduzido. ~**on key** n chave f mestra. ~**al** a esquelético

sketch /sketʃ/ n esboço m, croqui(s) m; (theat) sketch m, peça f curta e humorística; (outline) idéia f geral, esboço m □ vt esboçar, delinear □ vi fazer esboços. ~-**book** n caderno m de desenho

sketchy /'sketʃɪ/ a (-ier, -iest) incompleto, esboçado

skewer /'skjʊə(r)/ n espeto m

ski /ski:/ n (pl -s) esqui m □ vi (pt ski'd or skied, pres p skiing) esquiar; (go skiing) fazer esqui. ~**er** n esquiador m. ~**ing** n esqui m

skid /skɪd/ vi (pt skidded) derrapar, patinar □ n derrapagem f

skilful /'skɪlfl/ a hábil, habilidoso. ~**ly** adv habilmente, com perícia

skill /skɪl/ n habilidade f, jeito m; (craft) arte f. ~**s** aptidões fpl. ~**ed** a hábil, habilidoso; (worker) especializado

skim /skɪm/ vt (pt skimmed) tirar a espuma de; (milk) desnatar, tirar a nata de; (pass or glide over) deslizar sobre, roçar □ vi ~ **through** ler por alto, passar os olhos por. ~**med milk** leite m desnatado

skimp /skɪmp/ vt (use too little) poupar em □ vi ser poupado

skimpy /'skɪmpɪ/ a (-ier, -iest) (clothes) sumário; (meal) escasso, racionado (fig)

skin /skɪn/ n (of person, animal) pele f; (of fruit) casca f □ vt (pt skinned) (animal) esfolar, tirar a pele de; (fruit) descascar. ~-**diving** n mergulho m, caça f submarina

skinny /'skɪnɪ/ a (-ier, -iest) magricela, escanzelado

skint /skɪnt/ a (sl) sem dinheiro, na última lona (sl), (P) nas lonas

skip¹ /skɪp/ vi (pt skipped) saltar, pular; (jump about) saltitar; (with rope) pular corda □ vt (of page) saltar; (class) faltar a □ n salto m. ~**ping rope** n corda f de pular

skip² /skɪp/ n (container) container m grande para entulho

skipper /'skɪpə(r)/ n capitão m

skirmish /'skɜ:mɪʃ/ n escaramuça f

skirt /skɜ:t/ n saia f □ vt contornar, ladear. ~**ing-board** n rodapé m

skit /skɪt/ n (theat) paródia f, sketch m satírico

skittle /'skɪtl/ n pino m. ~**s** npl boliche m, (P) jogo m de laranjinha

skive /skaɪv/ vi (sl) eximir-se de um dever, evitar trabalhar (sl)

skulk /skʌlk/ vi (move) rondar furtivamente; (hide) esconder-se

skull /skʌl/ n caveira f, crânio m

skunk /skʌŋk/ n (animal) gambá m

sky /skaɪ/ n céu m. ~-**blue** a & n azul-celeste (m)

skylight /'skaɪlaɪt/ n clarabóia f

skyscraper /'skaɪskreɪpə(r)/ n arranha-céus m invar

slab /slæb/ n (of marble) placa f; (of paving-stone) laje f; (of metal) chapa f; (of cake) fatia f grossa

slack /slæk/ a (**-er, -est**) (*rope*) bambo, frouxo; (*person*) descuidado, negligente; (*business*) parado, fraco; (*period, season*) morto □ n **the ~** (*in rope*) a parte bamba □ vt/i (*be lazy*) estar com preguiça, fazer cera (*fig*)

slacken /'slækən/ vt/i (*speed, activity etc*) afrouxar, abrandar

slacks /slæks/ npl calças fpl

slag /slæg/ n escória f

slain /slem/ see **slay**

slam /slæm/ vt (*pt* **slammed**) bater violentamente com; (*throw*) atirar; (*sl: criticize*) criticar, malhar □ vi (*door etc*) bater violentamente □ n (*noise*) bater m, pancada f

slander /'sla:ndə(r)/ n calúnia f, difamação f □ vt caluniar, difamar. **~ous** a calunioso, difamatório

slang /slæŋ/ n calão m, gíria f. **~y** a de calão

slant /sla:nt/ vt/i inclinar(-se); (*news*) apresentar de forma tendenciosa □ n inclinação f; (*bias*) tendência f; (*point of view*) ângulo m. **be ~ing** ser/estar inclinado or em declive

slap /slæp/ vt (*pt* **slapped**) (*strike*) bater, dar uma palmada em; (*on face*) esbofetear, dar uma bofetada em; (*put forcefully*) atirar com □ n palmada f, bofetada f □ adv em cheio. **~-up** a (*sl: excellent*) excelente

slapdash /'slæpdæʃ/ a descuidado; (*impetuous*) precipitado

slapstick /'slæpstɪk/ n farsa f com palhaçadas

slash /slæʃ/ vt (*cut*) retalhar, dar golpes em; (*sever*) cortar; (*a garment*) golpear; (*fig: reduce*) reduzir drasticamente, fazer um corte radical em □ n corte m, golpe m

slat /slæt/ n (*in blind*) ripa f, (P) lâmina f

slate /sleɪt/ n ardósia f □ vt (*colloq: criticize*) criticar severamente

slaughter /'slɔ:tə(r)/ vt chacinar, massacrar; (*animals*) abater □ n chacina f, massacre m, mortandade f; (*animals*) abate m

slaughterhouse /'slɔ:təhaʊs/ n matadouro m

slave /sleɪv/ n escravo m □ vi mourejar, trabalhar como um escravo. **~-driver** n (*fig*) o que obriga os outros a trabalharem como escravos, condutor m de escravos. **~ry** /-ərɪ/ n escravatura f

slavish /'sleɪvɪʃ/ a servil

slay /sleɪ/ vt (*pt* **slew**, *pp* **slain**) matar

sleazy /'sli:zɪ/ a (**-ier, -iest**) (*colloq*) esquálido, sórdido

sledge /sledʒ/ n trenó m. **~-hammer** n martelo m de forja, marreta f

sleek /sli:k/ a (**-er, -est**) liso, macio e lustroso

sleep /sli:p/ n sono m □ vi (*pt* **slept**) dormir □ vt ter lugar para, alojar. **go to ~** ir dormir, adormecer. **put to ~** (*kill*) mandar matar. **~ around** ser promíscuo. **~er** n aquele que dorme; (*rail: beam*) dormente m; (*berth*) couchette f. **~ing-bag** n saco m de dormir. **~ing-car** n carro-dormitório m, carruagem-cama f, (P) vagon-lit m. **~less** a insone; (*night*) em claro, insone. **~-walker** n sonâmbulo m

sleep|y /'sli:pɪ/ a (**-ier, -iest**) sonolento. **be ~y** ter or estar com sono. **~ily** adv meio dormindo

sleet /sli:t/ n geada f miúda □ vi cair geada miúda

sleeve /sli:v/ n manga f; (*of record*) capa f. **up one's ~** de reserva, escondido. **~less** a sem mangas

sleigh /sleɪ/ n trenó m

sleight /slaɪt/ a **~ of hand** prestidigitação f, passe m de mágica

slender /'slendə(r)/ a esguio, esbelto; (*fig: scanty*) escasso. **~ness** n aspecto m esguio, esbelteza f, elegância f; (*scantiness*) escassez f

slept /slept/ see **sleep**

sleuth /slu:θ/ n (*colloq*) detective m

slew¹ /slu:/ vi (*turn*) virar-se

slew² /slu:/ see **slay**

slice /slaɪs/ n fatia f □ vt cortar em fatias; (*golf, tennis*) cortar

slick /slɪk/ a (*slippery*) escorregadio; (*cunning*) astuto, habilidoso; (*unctuous*) melífluo □ n (**oil**) **~** mancha f de óleo

slid|e /slaɪd/ vt/i (*pt* **slid**) escorregar, deslizar □ n escorregadela f, escorregão m; (*in playground*) escorrega m; (*for hair*) prendedor m, (P) travessa f; (*photo*) diapositivo m, slide m. **~e-rule** n régua f de cálculo. **~ing** a (*door, panel*) corrediço, de correr. **~ing scale** escala f móvel

slight /slaɪt/ a (**-er, -est**) (*slender, frail*) delgado, franzino; (*inconsiderable*) leve, ligeiro □ vt desconsiderar, desfeitear □ n desconsideração f, desfeita f. **the ~est** a o/a menor. **not in the ~est** em absoluto. **~ly** adv ligeiramente, um pouco

slim /slɪm/ a (**slimmer, slimmest**) magro, esbelto; (*chance*) pequeno, remoto □ vi (*pt* **slimmed**) emagrecer. **~ness** n magreza f, esbelteza f

slim|e /slaɪm/ n lodo m. **~y** a lodoso; (*slippery*) escorregadio; (*fig: servile*) servil, bajulador

sling /slɪŋ/ n (*weapon*) funda f; (*for arm*) tipóia f □ vt (*pt* **slung**) atirar, lançar

S

slip /slɪp/ *vt/i* (*pt* **slipped**) escorregar; *(move quietly)* mover-se de mansinho □ *n* escorregadela *f*, escorregão *m*; *(mistake)* engano *m*, lapso *m*; *(petticoat)* combinação *f*; *(of paper)* tira *f* de papel. **give the ~ to** livrar-se de, escapar(-se) de. **~ away** esgueirar-se. **~ by** passar sem se dar conta, passar despercebido. **~-cover** *n* (*Amer*) capa *f* para móveis. **~ into** (*go*) entrar de mansinho, enfiar-se em; *(clothes)* enfiar. **~ of the tongue** lapso *m*. **~ped disc** disco *m* deslocado. **~ road** *n* acesso *m* a autoestrada. **~ sb's mind** passar pela cabeça de alguém. **~ up** *(colloq)* cometer uma gafe. **~up** *n* (*colloq*) gafe *f*

slipper /'slɪpə(r)/ *n* chinelo *m*

slippery /'slɪpərɪ/ *a* escorregadio; (*fig: person*) que não é de confiança, sem escrúpulos

slipshod /'slɪpʃɒd/ *a* (*person*) desleixado, desmazelado; *(work)* feito sem cuidado, desleixado

slit /slɪt/ *n* fenda *f*; *(cut)* corte *m*; *(tear)* rasgão *m* □ *vt* (*pt* **slit**, *pres p* **slitting**) fender; *(cut)* fazer um corte em, cortar

slither /'slɪðə(r)/ *vi* escorregar, resvalar

sliver /'slɪvə(r)/ *n* (*of cheese etc*) fatia *f*; *(splinter)* lasca *f*

slobber /'slɒbə(r)/ *vi* babar-se

slog /slɒg/ *vt* (*pt* **slogged**) (*hit*) bater com força □ *vi* (*walk*) caminhar com passos pesados e firmes; *(work)* trabalhar duro □ *n* (*work*) trabalheira *f*; *(walk, effort)* estafa *f*

slogan /'sləʊgən/ *n* slogan *m*, lema *m*, palavra *f* de ordem

slop /slɒp/ *vt/i* (*pt* **slopped**) transbordar, entornar. **~s** *npl* (*dirty water*) água(s) *f* (*pl*) suja(s); *(liquid refuse)* despejos *mpl*

slop|e /sləʊp/ *vt/i* inclinar(-se), formar declive □ *n* (*of mountain*) encosta *f*; *(of street)* rampa *f*, ladeira *f*. **~ing** *a* inclinado, em declive

sloppy /'slɒpɪ/ *a* (**-ier, -iest**) (*ground*) molhado, com poças de água; (*food*) aguado; *(clothes)* desleixado; *(work)* descuidado, feito de qualquer jeito *or* maneira *(colloq)*; (*person*) desmazelado; *(maudlin)* piegas

slosh /slɒʃ/ *vt* entornar; *(colloq: splash)* esparrinhar; (*sl: hit*) bater em, dar (uma) sova em □ *vi* chapinhar

slot /slɒt/ *n* ranhura *f*; *(in timetable)* horário *m*; *(TV)* espaço *m*; *(aviat)* slot *m* □ *vt/i* (*pt* **slotted**) enfiar(-se), meter(-se), encaixar (-se). **~-machine** *n* (*for stamps, tickets etc*) distribuidor *m* automático; (*for gambling*) caça-níqueis *m*, (*P*) slot machine *f*

sloth /sləʊθ/ *n* preguiça *f*, indolência *f*; *(zool)* preguiça *f*

slouch /slaʊtʃ/ *vi* (*stand, move*) andar com as costas curvadas; *(sit*) sentar em má postura

slovenly /'slʌvnlɪ/ *a* desmazelado, desleixado

slow /sləʊ/ *a* (**-er, -est**) lento, vagaroso □ *adv* devagar, lentamente □ *vt/i* **~ (up *or* down)** diminuir a velocidade, afrouxar; *(auto)* desacelerar. **be ~** *(clock etc)* atrasar-se, estar atrasado. **in ~ motion** em câmara lenta. **~ly** *adv* devagar, lentamente, vagarosamente

slow|coach /'sləʊkəʊtʃ/, (*Amer*) **~poke** *ns* lesma *m*/*f*, pastelão *m* (*fig*)

sludge /slʌdʒ/ *n* lama *f*, lodo *m*

slug /slʌg/ *n* lesma *f*

sluggish /'slʌgɪʃ/ *a* (*slow*) lento, moroso; *(lazy)* indolente, preguiçoso

sluice /slu:s/ *n* (*gate*) comporta *f*; *(channel*) canal *m* □ *vt* lavar com jorros de água

slum /slʌm/ *n* favela *f*, (*P*) bairro *m* da lata; *(building)* cortiço *m*

slumber /'slʌmbə(r)/ *n* sono *m* □ *vi* dormir

slump /slʌmp/ *n* (*in prices*) baixa *f*, descida *f*; *(in demand)* quebra *f* na procura; *(econ)* depressão *f* □ *vi* (*fall limply*) cair, afundar-se; *(of price)* baixar bruscamente

slung /slʌŋ/ *see* **sling**

slur /slɜ:(r)/ *vt/i* (*pt* **slurred**) (*speech*) pronunciar indistintamente, mastigar □ *n* (*in speech*) som *m* indistinto; *(discredit)* nódoa *f*, estigma *m*

slush /slʌʃ/ *n* (*snow*) neve *f* meio derretida. **~fund** (*comm*) fundo *m* para subornos. **~y** *a* (*road*) coberto de neve derretida, lamacento

slut /slʌt/ *n* (*dirty woman*) porca *f*, desmazelada *f*; *(immoral woman)* desavergonhada *f*

sly /slaɪ/ *a* (**slyer, slyest**) (*crafty*) manhoso; *(secretive)* sonso □ *n* **on the ~** na calada. **~ly** *adv* (*craftily*) astutamente; *(secretively)* sonsamente

smack[1] /smæk/ *n* palmada *f*; *(on face)* bofetada *f* □ *vt* dar uma palmada *or* tapa em; *(on the face)* esbofetear, dar uma bofetada em □ *adv* (*colloq*) em cheio, direto

smack[2] /smæk/ *vi* **~ of sth** cheirar a alg coisa

small /smɔːl/ *a* (**-er, -est**) pequeno □ *n* **~ of the back** zona *f* dos rins □ *adv* (*cut etc*) em pedaços pequenos, aos bocadinhos. **~ change** trocado *m*, dinheiro *m* miúdo. **~ talk** conversa *f* fiada, bate-papo *m*. **~ness** *n* pequenez *f*

smallholding /'smɔːlhəʊldɪŋ/ *n* pequena propriedade *f*

smallpox /'smɔːlpɒks/ *n* varíola *f*

smarmy /'smaːmɪ/ *a* (**-ier, -iest**) (*colloq*) bajulador, puxa-saco (*colloq*)

smart /smaːt/ *a* (**-er, -est**) elegante; (*clever*) esperto, vivo; (*brisk*) rápido □ *vi* (*sting*) arder, picar. ~**ly** *adv* elegantemente, com elegância; (*cleverly*) com esperteza, vivamente; (*briskly*) rapidamente. ~**ness** *n* elegância *f*

smarten /'smaːtn/ *vt/i* ~ (**up**) arranjar, dar um ar mais cuidado a. ~ (**o.s.**) **up** embelezar-se, arrumar-se, (*P*) pôr-se elegante/bonito; (*tidy*) arranjar-se

smash /smæʃ/ *vt/i* (*to pieces*) despedaçar(-se), espatifar(-se) (*colloq*); (*a record*) quebrar; (*opponent*) esmagar; (*ruin*) fazer falir; (*of vehicle*) espatifar (-se) □ *n* (*noise*) estrondo *m*; (*blow*) pancada *f* forte, golpe *m*; (*collision*) colisão *f*; (*tennis*) smash *m*

smashing /'smæʃɪŋ/ *a* (*colloq*) formidável, estupendo (*colloq*)

smattering /'smætərɪŋ/ *n* leves noções *fpl*

smear /smɪə(r)/ *vt* (*stain; discredit*) manchar; (*coat*) untar, besuntar □ *n* mancha *f*, nódoa *f*; (*med*) esfregaço *m*

smell /smel/ *n* cheiro *m*, odor *m*; (*sense*) cheiro *m*, olfato *m*, (*P*) olfacto *m* □ *vt/i* (*pt* **smelt** *or* **smelled**) ~ (**of**) cheirar (a). ~**y** *a* malcheiroso

smelt[1] /smelt/ *see* **smell**

smelt[2] /smelt/ *vt* (*ore*) fundir

smil|e /smaɪl/ *n* sorriso *m* □ *vi* sorrir. ~**ing** *a* sorridente, risonho

smirk /smɜːk/ *n* sorriso *m* falso *or* afetado, (*P*) afectado

smithereens /smɪðə'riːnz/ *npl* to *or* in ~ em pedaços *mpl*

smock /smɒk/ *n* guarda-pó *m*

smog /smɒg/ *n* mistura *f* de nevoeiro e fumaça, smog *m*

smoke /sməʊk/ *n* fumo *m*, fumaça *f* □ *vt* fumar; (*bacon etc*) fumar, defumar □ *vi* fumar, fumegar. ~-**screen** *n* (*lit & fig*) cortina *f* de fumaça. ~**less** *a* (*fuel*) sem fumo. ~**r** /-ə(r)/ *n* (*person*) fumante *mf*, (*P*) fumador *m*. **smoky** *a* (*air*) enfumaçado, fumacento

smooth /smuːð/ *a* (**-er, -est**) liso; (*soft*) macio; (*movement*) regular, suave; (*manners*) lisonjeiro, conciliador, suave □ *vt* alisar. ~ **out** (*fig*) aplanar, remover. ~**ly** *adv* suavemente, facilmente

smother /'smʌðə(r)/ *vt* (*stifle*) abafar, sufocar; (*cover, overwhelm*) cobrir (**with** de); (*suppress*) abafar, reprimir

smoulder /'sməʊldə(r)/ *vi* (*lit & fig*) arder, abrasar-se

smudge /smʌdʒ/ *n* mancha *f*, borrão *m* □ *vt/i* sujar(-se), manchar(-se), borrar(-se)

smug /smʌg/ *a* (**smugger, smuggest**) presunçoso, convencido (*colloq*). ~**ly** *adv* presunçosamente. ~**ness** *n* presunção *f*

smuggl|e /'smʌgl/ *vt* contrabandear, fazer contrabando de. ~**er** *n* contrabandista *mf*. ~**ing** *n* contrabando *m*

smut /smʌt/ *n* fuligem *f*. ~**ty** *a* cheio de fuligem; (*colloq: obscene*) indecente, sujo (*colloq*)

snack /snæk/ *n* refeição *f* ligeira. ~-**bar** *n* lanchonete *f*, (*P*) snack(-bar) *m*

snag /snæg/ *n* (*obstacle*) obstáculo *m*; (*drawback*) problema *m*, contra *m*; (*in cloth*) rasgão *m*; (*in stocking*) fio *m* puxado

snail /sneɪl/ *n* caracol *m*. **at a** ~**'s pace** em passo de tartaruga

snake /sneɪk/ *n* serpente *f*, cobra *f*

snap /snæp/ *vt/i* (*pt* **snapped**) (*whip, fingers*) fazer) estalar; (*break*) estalar(-se), partir(-se) com um estalo, rebentar; (*say*) dizer irritadamente □ *n* estalo *m*; (*photo*) instantâneo *m*; (*Amer: fastener*) mola *f* □ *a* súbito, repentino. ~ **at** (*bite*) abocanhar, tentar morder; (*speak angrily*) retrucar asperamente. ~ **up** (*buy*) comprar rapidamente

snappish /'snæpɪʃ/ *a* irritadiço

snappy /'snæpɪ/ *a* (**-ier, -iest**) (*colloq*) vivo, animado. **make it** ~ (*colloq*) vai rápido!, apresse-se! (*colloq*)

snapshot /'snæpʃɒt/ *n* instantâneo *m*

snare /sneə(r)/ *n* laço *m*, cilada *f*, armadilha *f*

snarl /snaːl/ *vi* rosnar □ *n* rosnadela *f*

snatch /snætʃ/ *vt* (*grab*) agarrar, apanhar; (*steal*) roubar. ~ **from sb** arrancar de alguém □ *n* (*theft*) roubo *m*; (*bit*) bocado *m*, pedaço *m*

sneak /sniːk/ *vi* (*slink*) esgueirar-se furtivamente; (*sl: tell tales*) fazer queixa, delatar □ *vt* (*sl: steal*) rapinar (*colloq*) □ *n* (*sl*) dedo-duro *m*, queixinhas *mf* (*sl*). ~**ing** *a* secreto. ~**y** *a* sonso

sneer /snɪə(r)/ *n* sorriso *m* de desdém □ *vi* sorrir desdenhosamente

sneeze /sniːz/ *n* espirro *m* □ *vi* espirrar

snide /snaɪd/ *a* (*colloq*) sarcástico

sniff /snɪf/ *vi* fungar □ *vt/i* ~ (**at**) (*smell*) cheirar; (*dog*) farejar. ~ **at** (*fig: in contempt*) desprezar □ *n* fungadela *f*

snigger /'snɪgə(r)/ *n* riso *m* abafado □ *vi* rir dissimuladamente

S

snip /snɪp/ vt (pt **snipped**) cortar com tesoura □ n pedaço m, retalho m; (sl: bargain) pechincha f

snipe /snaɪp/ vi dar tiros de emboscada. ~**r** /-ə(r)/ n franco-atirador m

snivel /'snɪvl/ vi (pt **snivelled**) choramingar, lamuriar-se

snob /snɒb/ n esnobe mf, (P) snob mf. ~**bery** n esnobismo m, (P) snobismo m. ~**bish** a esnobe, (P) snob

snooker /'snuːkə(r)/ n snooker m, sinuca f

snoop /snuːp/ vi (colloq) bisbilhotar, meter o nariz em toda a parte. ~ **on** espiar, espionar. ~**er** n bisbilhoteiro m

snooty /'snuːtɪ/ a (-ier, -iest) (colloq) convencido, arrogante (colloq)

snooze /snuːz/ n (colloq) soneca f (colloq) □ vi (colloq) tirar uma soneca

snore /snɔː(r)/ n ronco m □ vi roncar

snorkel /'snɔːkl/ n tubo m de respiração, snorkel m

snort /snɔːt/ n resfôlego m , bufido m □ vi resfolegar, bufar

snout /snaʊt/ n focinho m

snow /snəʊ/ n neve f □ vi nevar. be ~**ed under** (fig: be overwhelmed) estar sobrecarregado (fig). ~**board** n snowboard m ~**bound** a bloqueado pela neve. ~**drift** n banco m de neve. ~**plough** n limpa-neve m. ~**y** a nevado, coberto de neve

snowball /'snəʊbɔːl/ n bola f de neve □ vi atirar bolas de neve (em); (fig) acumular-se, ir num crescendo, aumentar rapidamente

snowdrop /'snəʊdrɒp/ n (bot) fura-neve m

snowfall /'snəʊfɔːl/ n nevada f, (P) nevão m

snowflake /'snəʊfleɪk/ n floco m de neve

snowman /'snəʊmæn/ n (pl -**men**) boneco m de neve

snub /snʌb/ vt (pt **snubbed**) desdenhar, tratar com desdém □ n desdém m

snuff[1] /'snʌf/ n rapé m

snuff[2] /snʌf/ vt ~ **out** (candles, hopes etc) apagar, extinguir

snuffle /'snʌfl/ vi fungar

snug /snʌg/ a (**snugger**, **snuggest**) (cosy) aconchegado; (close-fitting) justo

snuggle /'snʌgl/ vt/i (nestle) aninhar-se, aconchegar-se; (cuddle) aconchegar

so /səʊ/ adv tão, de tal modo; (thus) assim, deste modo □ conj por isso, portanto, por conseguinte. ~ **am I** eu também. ~ **does he** ele também. **that is** ~ é isso. **I think** ~ acho que sim. **five or** ~ uns cinco. ~ **as to** de modo a. ~ **far** até agora, até aqui. ~ **long!** (colloq) até já! (colloq). ~ **many** tantos. ~**much** tanto.

~ **that** para que, de modo que. ~**-and-** ~ fulano m. ~**-called** a pretenso, soi-disant. ~**-so** a & adv assim assim, mais ou menos

soak /səʊk/ vt/i molhar(-se), ensopar(-se), enchacar(-se). **leave to** ~ pôr de molho. ~ **in** or **up** vt absorver, embeber. ~ **through** repassar. ~**ing** a ensopado, encharcado

soap /səʊp/ n sabão m. (**toilet**) ~ sabonete m □ vt ensaboar. ~ **opera** (radio) novela f radiofônica, (P) radiofónica; (TV) telenovela f. ~ **flakes** flocos mpl de sabão. ~ **powder** sabão m em pó. ~**y** a ensaboado

soar /sɔː(r)/ vi voar alto; (go high) elevar-se; (hover) pairar

sob /sɒb/ n soluço m □ vi (pt **sobbed**) soluçar

sober /'səʊbə(r)/ a (not drunk, calm, of colour) sóbrio; (serious) sério, grave □ vt/i ~ **up** (fazer) ficar sóbrio, (fazer) curar a bebedeira (colloq)

soccer /'sɒkə(r)/ n (colloq) futebol m

sociable /'səʊʃəbl/ a sociável

social /'səʊʃl/ a social; (sociable) sociável; (gathering, life) de sociedade □ n reunião f social. ~**ly** adv socialmente; (meet) em sociedade. ~ **security** previdência f social; (for old age) pensão f. ~ **worker** assistente mf social

socialis|t /'səʊʃəlɪst/ n socialista mf. ~**m** /-zəm/ n socialismo m

socialize /'səʊʃəlaɪz/ vi socializar-se, reunir-se em sociedade. ~ **with** freqüentar, (P) frequentar, conviver com

society /sə'saɪətɪ/ n sociedade f

sociolog|y /səʊsɪ'ɒlədʒɪ/ n sociologia f. ~**ical** /-ə'lɒdʒɪkl/ a sociológico. ~**ist** n sociólogo m

sock[1] /sɒk/ n meia f curta; (men's) meia f (curta), (P) peuga f; (women's) soquete f

sock[2] /sɒk/ vt (sl: hit) esmurrar, dar um murro em (colloq)

socket /'sɒkɪt/ n cavidade f; (for lamp) suporte m; (electr) tomada f; (of tooth) alvéolo m

soda /'səʊdə/ n soda f. (**baking**) ~ (culin) bicarbonato m de soda. ~**(-water**) água f gasosa, soda f limonada, (P) água f gaseificada

sodden /'sɒdn/ a ensopado, empapado

sodium /'səʊdɪəm/ n sódio m

sofa /'səʊfə/ n sofá m

soft /sɒft/ a (-**er**, -**est**) (not hard, feeble) mole; (not rough, not firm) macio; (gentle, not loud, not bright) suave; (tender-hearted) sensível; (fruit) sem caroço; (wood) de coníferas; (drink) não alcoólico. ~**-boiled** a (egg) quente.

~**spot** (*fig*) fraco *m*. ~**ly** *adv* docemente. ~**ness** *n* moleza *f*; (*to touch*) maciez *f*; (*gentleness*) suavidade *f*, brandura *f*

soften /'sɒfn/ *vt/i* amaciar, amolecer; (*tone down, lessen*) abrandar

software /'sɒftweə(r)/ *n* software *m*

soggy /'sɒgɪ/ *a* (-**ier**, -**iest**) ensopado, empapado

soil¹ /sɔɪl/ *n* solo *m*, terra *f*

soil² /sɔɪl/ *vt/i* sujar(-se). ~**ed** *a* sujo

solace /'sɒlɪs/ *n* consolo *m*; (*relief*) alívio *m*

solar /'səʊlə(r)/ *a* solar

sold /səʊld/ *see* **sell** □ *a* ~ **out** esgotado

solder /'səʊldə(r)/ *n* solda *f* □ *vt* soldar

soldier /'səʊldʒə(r)/ *n* soldado *m* □ *vi* ~ **on** (*colloq*) perseverar com afinco, batalhar (*colloq*)

sole¹ /səʊl/ *n* (*of foot*) planta *f*, sola *f* do pé; (*of shoe*) sola *f*

sole² /səʊl/ *n* (*fish*) solha *f*

sole³ /səʊl/ *a* único. ~**ly** *adv* unicamente

solemn /'sɒləm/ *a* solene. ~**ity** /sə'lemnətɪ/ *n* solenidade *f*. ~**ly** *adv* solenemente

solicit /sə'lɪsɪt/ *vt* (*seek*) solicitar □ *vi* (*of prostitute*) aproximar-se de homens na rua

solicitor /sə'lɪsɪtə(r)/ *n* advogado *m*

solicitous /sə'lɪsɪtəs/ *a* solícito

solid /'sɒlɪd/ *a* sólido; (*not hollow*) maciço, cheio, compacto; (*gold etc*) maciço; (*meal*) substancial □ *n* sólido *m* ~**s** (*food*) alimentos *mpl* sólidos. ~**ity** /sə'lɪdətɪ/ *n* solidez *f*. ~**ly** *adv* solidamente

solidarity /sɒlɪ'dærətɪ/ *n* solidariedade *f*

solidify /sə'lɪdɪfaɪ/ *vt/i* solidificar (-se)

soliloquy /sə'lɪləkwɪ/ *n* monólogo *m*, solilóquio *m*

solitary /'sɒlɪtrɪ/ *a* solitário, só; (*only one*) um único. ~ **confinement** prisão *f* celular, solitária *f*

solitude /'sɒlɪtjuːd/ *n* solidão *f*

solo /'səʊləʊ/ *n* (*pl* -**os**) solo *m* □ *a* solo. ~ **flight** vôo *m* solo. ~**ist** *n* solista *mf*

soluble /'sɒljʊbl/ *a* solúvel

solution /sə'luːʃn/ *n* solução *f*

solv|e /sɒlv/ *vt* resolver, solucionar. ~**able** *a* resolúvel, solúvel

solvent /'sɒlvənt/ *a* (dis)solvente; (*comm*) solvente □ *n* (dis)solvente *m*

sombre /'sɒmbə(r)/ *a* sombrio

some /sʌm/ *a* (*quantity*) algum(a); (*number*) alguns, algumas, uns, umas; (*unspecified, some or other*) um(a)… qualquer, uns… quaisquer, umas… quaisquer; (*a little*) um pouco de, algum; (*a certain*) um certo; (*contrasted with others*) uns, umas, alguns, algumas, certos, certas □ *pron* uns, umas, algum(a), alguns, algumas; (*a little*) um pouco, algum □ *adv* (*approximately*) uns, umas. **will you have** ~ **coffee**/*etc*? você quer café/*etc*? ~ **day** algum dia. ~ **of my friends** alguns dos meus amigos. ~ **people say…** algumas pessoas dizem… ~ **time ago** algum tempo atrás

somebody /'sʌmbədɪ/ *pron* alguém □ *n* **be a** ~ ser alguém

somehow /'sʌmhaʊ/ *adv* (*in some way*) de algum modo, de alguma maneira; (*for some reason*) por alguma razão

someone /'sʌmwʌn/ *pron & n* = **somebody**

somersault /'sʌməsɔːlt/ *n* cambalhota *f*; (*in the air*) salto *m* mortal □ *vi* dar uma cambalhota/um salto mortal

something /'sʌmθɪŋ/ *pron & n* uma /alguma/qualquer coisa *f*, algo. ~ **good**/*etc* uma coisa boa/*etc*, qualquer coisa de bom/*etc*. ~ **like** um pouco como

sometime /'sʌmtaɪm/ *adv* a certa altura, um dia □ *a* (*former*) antigo. ~ **last summer** a certa altura no verão passado. **I'll go** ~ hei de ir um dia

sometimes /'sʌmtaɪmz/ *adv* às vezes, de vez em quando

somewhat /'sʌmwɒt/ *adv* um pouco, um tanto (ou quanto)

somewhere /'sʌmweə(r)/ *adv* (*position*) em algum lugar; (*direction*) para algum lugar

son /sʌn/ *n* filho *m*. ~-**in-law** *n* (*pl* ~**s-in-law**) genro *m*

sonar /'səʊnɑː(r)/ *n* sonar *m*

sonata /sə'nɑːtə/ *n* (*mus*) sonata *f*

song /sɒŋ/ *n* canção *f*. ~-**bird** *n* ave *f* canora

sonic /'sɒnɪk/ *a* ~ **boom** estrondo *m* sônico, (*P*) sónico

sonnet /'sɒnɪt/ *n* soneto *m*

soon /suːn/ *adv* (-**er**, -**est**) em breve, dentro em pouco, daqui a pouco; (*early*) cedo. **as** ~ **as possible** o mais rápido possível. **I would** ~**er stay** preferia ficar. ~ **after** pouco depois. ~**er or later** mais cedo ou mais tarde

soot /sʊt/ *n* fuligem *f*. ~**y** *a* coberto de fuligem

sooth|e /suːð/ *vt* acalmar, suavizar; (*pain*) aliviar. ~**ing** *a* (*remedy*) calmante, suavizante; (*words*) confortante

sophisticated /sə'fɪstɪkeɪtɪd/ *a* sofisticado, refinado, requintado; (*machine etc*) sofisticado

soporific /sɒpə'rɪfɪk/ *a* soporífico

sopping /'sɒpɪŋ/ *a* encharcado, ensopado

soppy /'sɒpɪ/ a (-ier, -iest) (colloq: sentimental) piegas; (colloq: silly) bobo

soprano /sə'prɑ:nəʊ/ n (pl ∼s) & adj soprano (mf)

sorbet /'sɔ:beɪ/ n (water-ice) sorvete m feito sem leite

sorcerer /'sɔ:sərə(r)/ n feiticeiro m

sordid /'sɔ:dɪd/ a sórdido

sore /sɔ:(r)/ a (-er, -est) dolorido; (vexed) aborrecido (at, with com) □ n ferida f. have a ∼ throat ter a garganta inflamada, ter dores de garganta

sorely /'sɔ:lɪ/ adv fortemente, seriamente

sorrow /'sɒrəʊ/ n dor f, mágoa f, pesar m. ∼ful a pesaroso, triste

sorry /'sɒrɪ/ a (-ier, -iest) (state, sight etc) triste. be ∼ to/that (regretful) sentir muito/que, lamentar que; be ∼ about/for (repentant) ter pena de, estar arrependido de. feel ∼ for ter pena de. ∼! desculpe!, perdão!

sort /sɔ:t/ n gênero m, (P) género m, espécie f, qualidade f. of ∼s (colloq) uma espécie de (colloq, pej). out of ∼s indisposto □ vt separar por grupos; (tidy) arrumar. ∼ out (problem) resolver; (arrange, separate) separar, distribuir

soufflé /'su:fleɪ/ n (culin) suflê m, (P) soufflé m

sought /sɔ:t/ see seek

soul /səʊl/ n alma f. the life and ∼ of (fig) a alma f de (fig)

soulful /'səʊlfl/ a emotivo, expressivo, cheio de sentimento

sound¹ /saʊnd/ n som m, barulho m, ruído m □ vt/i soar; (seem) dar a impressão de, parecer (as if que). ∼ a horn tocar uma buzina, buzinar. ∼ barrier barreira f de som. ∼ like parecer ser, soar como. ∼-proof a à prova de som □ vt fazer o isolamento sonoro de, isolar. ∼-track n (of film) trilha f sonora, (P) banda f sonora

sound² /saʊnd/ a (-er, -est) (healthy) saudável, sadio; (sensible) sensato, acertado; (secure) firme, sólido. ∼ asleep profundamente adormecido. ∼ly adv solidamente

sound³ /saʊnd/ vt (test) sondar; (med; views) auscultar

soup /su:p/ n sopa f

sour /saʊə(r)/ a (-er, -est) azedo □ vt/i azedar, envinagrar

source /sɔ:s/ n fonte f; (of river) nascente f

souse /saʊs/ vt (throw water on) atirar água em cima de; (pickle) pôr em vinagre; (salt) pôr em salmoura

south /saʊθ/ n sul m □ a sul, do sul; (of country, people etc) meridional □ adv a, ao/para o sul. S∼ Africa/America

África f/América f do Sul. S∼ African/American a & n sul-africano (m)/sul-americano (m). ∼-east n sudeste m. ∼erly /'sʌðəlɪ/ a do sul, meridional. ∼ward a ao sul. ∼ward(s) adv para o sul. ∼-west n sudoeste m

southern /'sʌðən/ a do sul, meridional, austral

souvenir /su:və'nɪə(r)/ n recordação f, lembrança f

sovereign /'sɒvrɪn/ n & a soberano (m). ∼ty n soberania f

Soviet /'səʊvɪət/ a soviético. the S∼ Union a União Soviética

sow¹ /səʊ/ vt (pt sowed, pp sowed or sown) semear

sow² /saʊ/ n (zool) porca f

soy /'sɔɪ/ n ∼ sauce molho m de soja

soya /'sɔɪə/ n soja f. ∼-bean semente f de soja

spa /spɑ:/ n termas fpl

space /speɪs/ n espaço m; (room) lugar m; (period) espaço m, período m □ a (research etc) espacial □ vt ∼ out espaçar

space|craft /'speɪskrɑ:ft/ n (pl invar), ∼ship n nave espacial f

spacious /'speɪʃəs/ a espaçoso

spade /speɪd/ n (gardener's) pá f de ferro; (child's) pá f. ∼s (cards) espadas fpl

spadework /'speɪdwɜ:k/ n (fig) trabalho m preliminar

spaghetti /spə'getɪ/ n espaguete m, (P) esparguete m

Spain /spem/ n Espanha f

span¹ /spæn/ n (of arch) vão m; (of wings) envergadura f; (of time) espaço m, duração f; (measure) palmo m □ vt (pt spanned) (extend across) transpor; (measure) medir em palmos; (in time) abarcar, abranger, estender-se por

span² /spæn/ see spick

Spaniard /'spænɪəd/ n espanhol m

Spanish /'spænɪʃ/ a espanhol □ n (lang) espanhol m

spaniel /'spænɪəl/ n spaniel m, epagneul m

spank /spæŋk/ vt dar palmadas or chineladas no. ∼ing n (with hand) palmada f; (with slipper) chinelada f

spanner /'spænə(r)/ n (tool) chave f de porcas; (adjustable) chave f inglesa

spar /spɑ:(r)/ vi (pt sparred) jogar boxe, esp para treino; (fig: argue) discutir

spare /speə(r)/ vt (not hurt; use with restraint) poupar; (afford to give) dispensar, ceder □ a (in reserve) de reserva, de sobra; (tyre) sobressalente; (bed) extra; (room) de hóspedes □ n (part) sobressalente m. ∼ time horas fpl vagas. have an hour to ∼ dispôr de uma hora. **have no time to** ∼ não ter tempo a perder

sparing /'speərɪŋ/ a poupado. **be** ∼ **of** poupar em, ser poupado com. ∼**ly** adv frugalmente

spark /spɑːk/ n centelha f, faísca f □ vt lançar faíscas. ∼ **off** (initiate) desencadear, provocar. ∼**(ing)-plug** n vela f de ignição

sparkle /'spɑːkl/ vi cintilar, brilhar □ n brilho m, cintilação f

sparkling /'spɑːklɪŋ/ a (wine) espumante

sparrow /'spærəʊ/ n pardal m

sparse /spɑːs/ a esparso; (hair) ralo. ∼**ly** adv (furnished etc) escassamente

spasm /'spæzəm/ n (of muscle) espasmo m; (of coughing, anger etc) ataque m, acesso m

spasmodic /spæz'mɒdɪk/ a espasmódico; (at irregular intervals) intermitente

spastic /'spæstɪk/ n deficiente mf motor

spat /spæt/ see **spit**[1]

spate /speɪt/ n (in river) enxurrada f, cheia f. **a** ∼ **of** (letters etc) uma avalanche de

spatter /'spætə(r)/ vt salpicar (**with** de, com)

spawn /spɔːn/ n ovas fpl □ vi desovar □ vt gerar em quantidade

speak /spiːk/ vt/i (pt **spoke**, pp **spoken**) falar (**to/up with sb about sth** com alguém de/sobre alg coisa); (say) dizer. ∼ **out/up** falar abertamente; (louder) falar mais alto. ∼ **one's mind** dizer o que se pensa. **so to** ∼ por assim dizer. **English/Portuguese spoken** fala-se português/inglês

speaker /'spiːkə(r)/ n (in public) orador m; (loudspeaker) alto-falante m; (of a language) pessoa f de língua nativa

spear /spɪə(r)/ n lança f

spearhead /'spɪəhed/ n ponta f de lança □ vt (lead) estar à frente de, encabeçar

special /'speʃl/ a especial. ∼**ity** /-ɪ'rælətɪ/ n especialidade f. ∼**ly** adv especialmente. ∼**ty** n especialidade f

specialist /'speʃəlɪst/ n especialista mf

specialize /'speʃəlaɪz/ vi especializar-se (**in** em). ∼**d** a especializado

species /'spiːʃɪz/ n (pl invar) espécie f

specific /spə'sɪfɪk/ a específico. ∼**ally** adv especificamente, explicitamente

specif|y /'spesɪfaɪ/ vt especificar. ∼**ication** /-ɪ'keɪʃn/ n especificação f. ∼**ications** npl (of work etc) caderno m de encargos

specimen /'spesɪmɪn/ n espécime(n) m, amostra f

speck /spek/ n (stain) mancha f pequena; (dot) pontinho m, pinta f; (particle) grão m

speckled /'spekld/ a salpicado, manchado

specs /speks/ npl (colloq) óculos mpl

spectacle /'spektəkl/ n espetáculo m, (P) espetáculo m. (**pair of**) ∼**s** (par m de) óculos mpl

spectacular /spek'tækjʊlə(r)/ a espetacular, (P) espectacular

spectator /spek'teɪtə(r)/ n espectador m

spectre /'spektə(r)/ n espectro m, fantasma m

spectrum /'spektrəm/ n (pl -tra) espectro m; (of ideas etc) faixa f, gama f, leque m

speculat|e /'spekjʊleɪt/ vi especular, fazer especulações or conjeturas, (P) conjecturas (**about** sobre); (comm) especular, fazer especulação (**in** em). ∼**ion** /-'leɪʃn/ n especulação f, conjetura f, (P) conjectura f; (comm) especulação f. ∼**or** n especulador m

speech /spiːtʃ/ n (faculty) fala f; (diction) elocução f; (dialect) falar m; (address) discurso m. ∼**less** a mudo, sem fala (**with** com, de)

speed /spiːd/ n velocidade f, rapidez f □ vt/i (pt **sped** /sped/) (move) ir depressa or a grande velocidade; (send) despedir, mandar; (pt **speeded**) (drive too fast) ultrapassar o limite de velocidade. ∼ **camera** radar m. ∼ **limit** limite m de velocidade. ∼ **up** acelerar (-se). ∼**ing** n excesso m de velocidade

speedometer /spiː'dɒmɪtə(r)/ n velocímetro m, (P) conta-quilómetros m inv

speed|y /'spiːdɪ/ a (-**ier**, -**iest**) rápido; (prompt) pronto. ∼**ily** adv rapidamente; (promptly) prontamente

spell[1] /spel/ n (magic) sortilégio m

spell[2] /spel/ vt/i (pt **spelled** or **spelt**) escrever; (fig: mean) significar, ter como resultado. ∼ **out** soletrar; (fig: explain) explicar claramente. ∼**ing** n ortografia f

spell[3] /spel/ n (short period) período m curto, breve espaço m de tempo; (turn) turno m

spend /spend/ vt (pt **spent**) (money, energy) gastar (**on** em); (time, holiday) passar. ∼**er** n gastador m

spendthrift /'spendθrɪft/ n perdulário m, esbanjador m

spent /spent/ see **spend** □ a gasto

sperm /spɜːm/ n (pl **sperms** or **sperm**) (semen) esperma m, sêmen m, (P) sémen m; (cell) espermatozóide m

spew /spjuː/ vt/i vomitar, lançar

sphere /sfɪə(r)/ n esfera f

spherical /'sferɪkl/ a esférico

S

spic|e /spaɪs/ *n* especiaria *f*, condimento *m*; (*fig*) picante *m* ▫ *vt* condimentar. ~**y** *a* condimentado; (*fig*) picante

spick /spɪk/ *a* ~ **and span** novo em folha, impecável

spider /'spaɪdə(r)/ *n* aranha *f*

spik|e /spaɪk/ *n* (*of metal etc*) bico *m*, espigão *m*, ponta *f*. ~**y** *a* guarnecido de bicos *or* pontas

spill /spɪl/ *vt/i* (*pt* **spilled** *or* **spilt**) derramar(-se), entornar (-se), espalhar(-se). ~ **over** transbordar, extravasar

spin /spɪn/ *vt/i* (*pt* **spun**, *pres p* **spinning**) (*wool, cotton*) fiar; (*web*) tecer; (*turn*) (fazer) girar, (fazer) rodopiar. ~ **out** (*money, story*) fazer durar; (*time*) (fazer) parar ▫ *n* volta *f*; (*aviat*) parafuso *m*. **go for a** ~ dar uma volta *or* um giro. ~**-drier** *n* centrifugadora *f* para a roupa, secadora *f*. ~**ning-wheel** *n* roda *f* de fiar. ~**-off** *n* bônus *m*, (*P*) bónus *m* inesperado; (*by-product*) derivado *m*

spinach /'spɪnɪdʒ/ *n* (*plant*) espinafre *m*; (*as food*) espinafres *mpl*

spinal /'spaɪnl/ *a* vertebral. ~ **cord** espina *f* dorsal

spindl|e /'spɪndl/ *n* roca *f*, fuso *m*; (*mech*) eixo *m*. ~**y** *a* alto e magro; (*of plant*) espigado

spine /spaɪn/ *n* espinha *f*, coluna *f* vertebral; (*prickle*) espinho *m*, pico *m*; (*of book*) lombada *f*

spineless /'spaɪnlɪs/ *a* (*fig: cowardly*) covarde, sem fibra (*fig*)

spinster /'spɪnstə(r)/ *n* solteira *f*; (*pej*) solteirona *f*

spiral /'spaɪərəl/ *a* (em) espiral; (*staircase*) em caracol ▫ *n* espiral *f* ▫ *vi* (*pt* **spiralled**) subir em espiral

spire /'spaɪə(r)/ *n* agulha *f*, flecha *f*

spirit /'spɪrɪt/ *n* espírito *m*; (*boldness*) coragem *f*, brio *m*. ~**s** (*morale*) moral *m*; (*drink*) bebidas *fpl* alcoólicas, (*P*) bebidas *fpl* espirituosas. **in high** ~**s** alegre ▫ *vt* ~ **away** dar sumiço em, arrebatar. ~**-level** *n* nível *m* de bolha de ar

spirited /'spɪrɪtɪd/ *a* fogoso; (*attack, defence*) vigoroso, enérgico

spiritual /'spɪrɪtʃʊəl/ *a* espiritual

spiritualism /'spɪrɪtʃʊəlɪzəm/ *n* espiritismo *m*

spit[1] /spɪt/ *vt/i* (*pt* **spat** *or* **spit**, *pres p* **spitting**) cuspir; (*of rain*) chuviscar; (*of cat*) bufar ▫ *n* cuspe *m*, (*P*) cuspo *m*. **the** ~**ting image of** o retrato vivo de, a cara chapada de (*colloq*)

spit[2] /spɪt/ *n* (*for meat*) espeto *m*; (*of land*) restinga *f*, (*P*) língua *f* de terra

spite /spaɪt/ *n* má vontade *f*, despeito *m*, rancor *m* ▫ *vt* aborrecer, mortificar. **in** ~ **of** a despeito de, apesar de. ~**ful** *a* rancoroso, maldoso. ~**fully** *adv* rancorosamente, maldosamente

spittle /'spɪtl/ *n* cuspe *m*, (*P*) cuspo *m*, saliva *f*

splash /splæʃ/ *vt* salpicar, respingar ▫ *vi* esparrinhar, esparramar-se. ~ **(about)** chapinhar ▫ *n* (*act, mark*) salpico *m*; (*sound*) chape *m*; (*of colour*) mancha *f*. **make a** ~ (*striking display*) fazer um vistão, causar furor

spleen /spli:n/ *n* (*anat*) baço *m*. **vent one's** ~ **on sb** descarregar a neura em alguém (*colloq*)

splendid /'splendɪd/ *a* esplêndido, magnífico; (*excellent*) estupendo (*colloq*), ótimo, (*P*) óptimo

splendour /'splendə(r)/ *n* esplendor *m*

splint /splɪnt/ *n* (*med*) tala *f*

splinter /'splɪntə(r)/ *n* lasca *f*, estilhaço *m*; (*under the skin*) farpa *f*, lasca *f* ▫ *vi* estilhaçar-se, lascar-se. ~ **group** grupo *m* dissidente

split /splɪt/ *vt/i* (*pt* **split**, *pres p* **splitting**) rachar, fender(-se); (*divide, share*) dividir; (*tear*) romper(-se) ▫ *n* racha *f*, fenda *f*; (*share*) quinhão *m*, parte *f*; (*pol*) cisão *f*. ~ **on** (*sl: inform on*) denunciar. ~ **one's sides** rebentar de risa. ~ **up** (*of couple*) separar-se. **a** ~ **second** uma fração de segundo. ~**ting headache** *n* dor *f* de cabeça forte

splurge /splɜ:dʒ/ *n* (*colloq*) espalhafato *m*, estardalhaço *m* ▫ *vi* (*colloq: spend*) gastar os tubos, (*P*) gastar à doida (*colloq*)

spool /spu:l/ *n* (*of sewing machine*) bobina *f*; (*for cotton thread*) carretel *m*, carrinho *m*; (*naut; fishing*) carretel *m*

splutter /'splʌtə(r)/ *vi* falar cuspindo; (*engine*) cuspir; (*fat*) crepitar

spoil /spɔɪl/ *vt* (*pt* **spoilt** *or* **spoiled**) estragar; (*pamper*) mimar ▫ *n* ~**(s)** (*plunder*) despojo(s) *m(pl*), espólios *mpl*. ~**-sport** *n* desmancha-prazeres *mf invar*. ~**t** *a* (*pampered*) mimado, estragado com mimos

spoke[1] /spəʊk/ *n* raio *m*

spoke[2], **spoken** /spəʊk, 'spəʊkən/ *see* **speak**

spokes|man /'spəʊksmən/ *n* (*pl* -**men**) ~**woman** *n* (*pl* -**women**) porta-voz *mf*

sponge /spʌndʒ/ *n* esponja *f* ▫ *vt* (*clean*) lavar com esponja; (*wipe*) limpar com esponja ▫ *vi* ~ **on** (*colloq: cadge*) viver à custa de. ~ **bag** bolsa *f* de toalete. ~**cake** pão-de-ló *m*. ~**r** /-ə(r)/ *n* parasita *mf* (*colloq*) (*sl*). **spongy** *a* esponjoso

sponsor /'spɒnsə(r)/ *n* patrocinador *m*; (*for membership*) (sócio) proponente *m*

□ *vt* patrocinar; (*for membership*) propor. ~**ship** *n* patrocínio *m*

spontaneous /spɒn'teɪnɪəs/ *a* espontâneo

spoof /spuːf/ *n* (*colloq*) paródia *f*

spooky /'spuːkɪ/ *a* (-**ier**, -**iest**) (*colloq*) fantasmagórico, que dá arrepios

spool /spuːl/ *n* (*of sewing machine*) bobina *f*; (*for thread, line*) carretel *m*, (P) carrinho *m*

spoon /spuːn/ *n* colher *f*. ~**feed** *vt* (*pt* -**fed**) alimentar de colher; (*fig: help*) dar na bandeja para (*fig*). ~**ful** *n* (*pl* ~**fuls**) colherada *f*

sporadic /spə'rædɪk/ *a* esporádico, acidental

sport /spɔːt/ *n* esporte *m*, (P) desporto *m*. (**good**) ~ (*sl: person*) gente *f* fina, (P) bom tipo *m* (*colloq*), (P) tipo *m* bestial □ *vt* (*display*) exibir, ostentar. ~**s car/coat** carro *m*/casaco *m* esporte, (P) de desporto. ~**y** *a* (*colloq*) esportivo, (P) desportivo

sporting /'spɔːtɪŋ/ *a* esportivo, (P) desportivo. **a** ~ **chance** uma certa possibilidade de sucesso, uma boa chance

sports|**man** /'spɔːtsmən/ *n* (*pl* -**men**), ~**woman** (*pl* -**women**) desportista *mf*. ~**manship** (*spirit*) espírito *m* esportivo, (P) desportivo; (*activity*) esportismo *m*, (P) desportismo *m*

spot /spɒt/ *n* (*mark, stain*) mancha *f*; (*in pattern*) pinta *f*, bola *f*; (*drop*) gota *f*; (*place*) lugar *m*, ponto *m*; (*pimple*) borbulha *f*, espinha *f*; (*TV*) spot *m* televisivo □ *vt* (*pt* **spotted**) manchar; (*colloq: detect*) descobrir, detectar (*colloq*). **a** ~ **of** (*colloq*) um pouco de. **be in a** ~ (*colloq*) estar numa encrenca (*colloq*), (P) estar metido numa alhada (*colloq*). **on the** ~ no local; (*there and then*) ali mesmo, logo ali. ~-**on** *a* (*colloq*) certo. ~ **check** inspeção *f*, (P) inspecção *f* de surpresa; (*of cars*) fiscalização *f* de surpresa. ~**ted** *a* manchado; (*with dots*) de pintas, de bolas; (*animal*) malhado. ~**ty** *a* (*with pimples*) com borbulhas

spotless /'spɒtlɪs/ *a* impecável, imaculado

spotlight /'spɒtlaɪt/ *n* foco *m*; (*cine, theat*) refletor *m*, holofote *m*

spouse /spaʊz/ *n* cônjuge *mf*, esposo *m*

spout /spaʊt/ *n* (*of vessel*) bico *m*; (*of liquid*) esguicho *m*, jorro *m*; (*pipe*) cano *m* □ *vi* jorrar, esguichar. **up the** ~ (*sl: ruined*) liquidado (*sl*)

sprain /spreɪn/ *n* entorse *f*, mau jeito *m* □ *vt* torcer, dar um mau jeito a

sprang /spræŋ/ *see* **spring**

sprawl /sprɔːl/ *vi* (*sit*) estirar-se, esparramar-se; (*fall*) estatelar-se; (*town*) estender-se, espraiar-se

spray[1] /spreɪ/ *n* (*of flowers*) raminho *m*, ramalhete *m*

spray[2] /spreɪ/ *n* (*water*) borrifo *m*, salpico *m*; (*from sea*) borrifo *m* de espuma; (*device*) bomba *f*, aerossol *m*; (*for perfume*) vaporizador *m*, atomizador *m* □ *vt* aspergir, borrifar, pulverizar; (*with insecticide*) pulverizar. ~**gun** *n* (*for paint*) pistola *f*

spread /spred/ *vt/i* (*pt* **spread**) (*extend, stretch*) estender(-se); (*news, fear, illness etc*) alastrar (-se) espalhar(-se), propagar(-se); (*butter etc*) passar; (*wings*) abrir □ *n* (*expanse*) expansão *f*, extensão *f*; (*spreading*) propagação *f*; (*paste*) pasta *f* para passar pão; (*colloq: meal*) banquete *m*. ~-**eagled** *a* de braços e pernas abertos. ~**sheet** *n* (*comput*) folha *f* de cálculo

spree /spriː/ *n* **go on a** ~ (*colloq*) cair na farra

sprig /sprɪɡ/ *n* raminho *m*

sprightly /'spraɪtlɪ/ *a* (-**ier**, -**iest**) vivo, animado

spring /sprɪŋ/ *vi* (*pt* **sprang**, *pp* **sprung**) (*arise*) nascer; (*jump*) saltar, pular □ *vt* (*produce suddenly*) sair-se com; (*a surprise*) fazer (**on sb** a alguém) □ *n* salto *m*, pulo *m*; (*device*) mola *f*; (*season*) primavera *f*; (*of water*) fonte *f*, nascente *f*. ~ **from** vir de, originar-se de, provir de. ~-**clean** *vt* fazer limpeza geral. ~ **onion** cebolinha *f*. ~ **up** surgir

springboard /'sprɪŋbɔːd/ *n* trampolim *m*

springtime /'sprɪŋtaɪm/ *n* primavera *f*

springy /'sprɪŋɪ/ *a* (-**ier**, -**iest**) elástico

sprinkle /'sprɪŋkl/ *vt* (*with liquid*) borrifar, salpicar; (*with salt, flour*) polvilhar (**with** de). ~ **sand**/*etc* espalhar areia/*etc*. ~**r** /-ə(r)/ *n* (*in garden*) regador *m*; (*for fires*) sprinkler *m*

sprinkling /'sprɪŋklɪŋ/ *n* (*amount*) pequena quantidade *f*; (*number*) pequeno número *m*

sprint /sprɪnt/ *n* (*sport*) corrida *f* de pequena distância, sprint *m* □ *vi* correr em sprint *or* a toda a velocidade; (*sport*) correr

sprout /spraʊt/ *vt/i* brotar, germinar; (*put forth*) deitar □ *n* (*on plant etc*) broto *m*. (**Brussels**) ~**s** couves *f* de Bruxelas

spruce /spruːs/ *a* bem arrumado □ *vt* ~ **o.s. up** arrumar(-se)

sprung /sprʌŋ/ *see* **spring** □ *a* (*mattress etc*) de molas

spry /spraɪ/ *a* (**spryer**, **spryest**) vivo, ativo, (P) activo; (*nimble*) ágil

spud /spʌd/ *n* (*sl*) batata *f*

spun /spʌn/ *see* **spin**

spur /spɜ:(r)/ n (of rider) espora f; (fig: stimulus) aguilhão m; (fig) espora f (fig) □ vt (pt **spurred**) esporear, picar com esporas; (fig: incite) aguilhoar, esporear. **on the ~ of the moment** impulsivamente

spurious /'spjʊərɪəs/ a falso, espúrio

spurn /spɜ:n/ vt desdenhar, desprezar, rejeitar

spurt /spɜ:t/ vi jorrar, esguichar; (fig: accelerate) acelerar subitamente, dar um arranco súbito □ n jorro m, esguicho m; (of energy, speed) arranco m, surto m

spy /spaɪ/ n espião m □ vt (make out) avistar, descortinar □ vi ~ **(on)** espiar, espionar. ~ **out** descobrir. ~**ing** n espionagem f

squabble /'skwɒbl/ vi discutir, brigar □ n briga f, disputa f

squad /skwɒd/ n (mil) pelotão m; (team) equipe f, (P) equipa f. **firing** ~ pelotão m de fuzilamento. **flying** ~ brigada f móvel

squadron /'skwɒdrən/ n (mil) esquadrão m; (aviat) esquadrilha f; (naut) esquadra f

squal|id /'skwɒlɪd/ a esquálido, sórdido. ~**or** n sordidez f

squall /skwɔ:l/ n borrasca f

squander /'skwɒndə(r)/ vt desperdiçar

square /skweə(r)/ n quadrado m; (in town) largo m, praça f; (T-square) régua-tê f; (set-square) esquadro m □ a (of shape) quadrado; (metre, mile etc) quadrado; (honest) direito, honesto; (of meal) abundante, substancial. **(all)** ~ **(quits)** quite(s) □ vt (settle) acertar □ vi (math) elevar ao quadrado; (settle) acertar □ vi (agree) concordar. **go back to** ~ **one** recomeçar tudo do princípio, voltar à estaca zero. ~ **brackets** parênteses mpl retos, (P) rectos. ~ **up to** enfrentar. ~**ly** adv diretamente, (P) directamente; (fairly) honestamente

squash /skwɒʃ/ vt (crush) esmagar; (squeeze) espremer; (crowd) comprimir, apertar □ n (game) squash m; (Amer: marrow) abóbora f. **lemon** ~ limonada f. **orange** ~ laranjada f. ~**y** a mole

squat /skwɒt/ vi (pt **squatted**) acocorar-se, agachar-se; (be a squatter) ser ocupante ilegal □ a (dumpy) atarracado. ~**ter** n ocupante mf ilegal de casa vazia, posseiro m

squawk /skwɔ:k/ n grasnido m, crocito m □ vi grasnar, crocitar

squeak /skwi:k/ n guincho m, chio m; (of door, shoes etc) rangido m □ vi guinchar, chiar; (of door, shoes etc) ranger. ~**y** a (shoe etc) que range; (voice) esganiçado

squeal /skwi:l/ vi dar gritos agudos, guinchar □ n grito m agudo, guincho m. ~ **(on)** (sl: inform on) delatar, (P) denunciar

squeamish /'skwi:mɪʃ/ a (nauseated) que enjoa à toa

squeeze /skwi:z/ vt (lemon, sponge etc) espremer; (hand, arm) apertar; (extract) arrancar, extorquir **(from** de) □ vi (force one's way) passar à força, meter-se por □ n aperto m, apertão m; (hug) abraço m; (comm) restrições fpl de crédito

squelch /skweltʃ/ vi chapinhar or fazer chape-chape na lama

squid /skwɪd/ n lula f

squiggle /'skwɪgl/ n rabisco m, floreado m

squint /skwɪnt/ vi ser estrábico or vesgo; (with half-shut eyes) franzir os olhos □ n (med) estrabismo m

squirm /skwɜ:m/ vi (re)torcer-se, contorcer-se

squirrel /'skwɪrəl/ n esquilo m

squirt /skwɜ:t/ vt/i esguichar □ n esguicho m

stab /stæb/ vt (pt **stabbed**) apunhalar; (knife) esfaquear □ n punhalada f; (with knife) facada f; (of pain) pontada f; (colloq: attempt) tentativa f

stabilize /'steɪbəlaɪz/ vt estabilizar

stab|le[1] /'steɪbl/ a (-er, -est) estável. ~**ility** /stə'bɪləti/ n estabilidade f

stable[2] /'steɪbl/ n cavalariça f, estrebaria f. ~-**boy** n moço m de estrebaria

stack /stæk/ n pilha f, montão m; (of hay etc) meda f □ vt ~ **(up)** empilhar, amontoar

stadium /'steɪdɪəm/ n estádio m

staff /sta:f/ n pessoal m; (in school) professores mpl; (mil) estado-maior m; (stick) bordão m, cajado m; (mus) (pl **staves**) pauta f □ vt prover de pessoal

stag /stæg/ n veado (macho) m, cervo m. ~-**party** n (colloq) reunião f masculina; (before wedding) despedida f de solteiro

stage /steɪdʒ/ n (theatre) palco m; (phase) fase f, ponto m; (platform in hall) estrado m □ vt encenar, pôr em cena; (fig: organize) organizar. **go on the** ~ seguir a carreira teatral, ir para o teatro (colloq). ~ **door** entrada f dos artistas. ~-**fright** n nervosismo m

stagger /'stægə(r)/ vi vacilar, cambalear □ vt (shock) atordoar, chocar; (holidays etc) escalonar. ~**ing** a atordoador, chocante

stagnant /'stægnənt/ a estagnado, parado

stagnat|e /stæg'neɪt/ vi estagnar. ~**ion** /-ʃn/ n estagnação f

staid /steɪd/ *a* sério, sensato, estável

stain /steɪn/ *vt* manchar, pôr nódoa em; (*colour*) tingir, dar cor a □ *n* mancha *f*, nódoa *f*; (*colouring*) corante *m*. ~**ed glass window** vitral *m*. ~**less steel** aço *m* inoxidável

stair /steə(r)/ *n* degrau *m*. ~**s** escada(s) *f*(*pl*)

stair|case /'steəkeɪs/, ~**way** /-weɪ/ *ns* escada(s) *f*(*pl*), escadaria *f*

stake /steɪk/ *n* estaca *f*, poste *m*; (*wager*) parada *f*, aposta *f* □ *vt* (*area*) demarcar, delimitar; (*wager*) jogar, apostar. **at** ~ em jogo. **have a** ~ **in** ter interesse em. ~ **a claim to** reivindicar

stale /steɪl/ *a* (**-er, -est**) estragado, velho; (*bread*) duro, mofado; (*smell*) rançoso; (*air*) viciado; (*news*) velho

stalemate /'steɪlmeɪt/ *n* (*chess*) empate *m*; (*fig: deadlock*) impasse *m*, beco-sem-saída *m*

stalk[1] /stɔ:k/ *n* (*of plant*) caule *m*

stalk[2] /stɔ:k/ *vi* andar com ar empertigado □ *vt* (*prey*) perseguir furtivamente, tocaiar

stall /stɔ:l/ *n* (*in stable*) baia *f*; (*in market*) tenda *f*, barraca *f*. ~**s** (*theat*) poltronas *fpl* de orquestra; (*cinema*) platéia *f*, (*P*) plateia *f* □ *vt/i* (*auto*) enguiçar, (*P*) ir abaixo. ~ (**for time**) ganhar tempo

stalwart /'stɔ:lwət/ *a* forte, rijo; (*supporter*) fiel

stamina /'stæmɪnə/ *n* resistência *f*

stammer /'stæmə(r)/ *vt/i* gaguejar □ *n* gagueira *f*, (*P*) gaguez *f*

stamp /stæmp/ *vt/i* ~ (**one's foot**) bater com o pé (no chão), pisar com força □ *vt* estampar; (*letter*) estampilhar, selar; (*with rubber stamp*) carimbar. ~ **out** (*fire, rebellion etc*) esmagar; (*disease*) erradicar □ *n* estampa *f*; (*for postage*) selo *m*; (*fig: mark*) cunho *m*. (**rubber**) ~ carimbo *m*. ~-**collecting** *n* filatelia *f*

stampede /stæm'pi:d/ *n* (*scattering*) debandada *f*; (*of horses, cattle etc*) debandada *f*; (*fig: rush*) corrida *f* □ *vt/i* (fazer) debandar; (*horses, cattle etc*) tresmalhar

stance /stæns/ *n* posição *f*, postura *f*

stand /stænd/ *vi* (*pt* **stood**) estar em pé; (*keep upright position*) ficar em pé; (*rise*) levantar-se; (*be situated*) encontrar-se, ficar, situar-se; (*pol*) candidatar-se (**for** por) □ *vt* pôr (de pé), colocar; (*tolerate*) suportar, agüentar, (*P*) aguentar □ *n* posição *f*; (*support*) apoio *m*; (*mil*) resistência *f*; (*at fair*) stand *m*, pavilhão *m*; (*in street*) quiosque *m*; (*for spectators*) arquibancada *f*, (*P*) bancada *f*; (*Amer: witness-box*) banco *m* das testemunhas.

~ **a chance** ter uma possibilidade. ~ **back** recuar. ~ **by** *or* **around** estar parado sem fazer nada. ~ **by** (*be ready*) estar a postos; (*promise, person*) manter-se fiel a. ~ **down** desistir, retirar-se. ~ **for** representar, simbolizar; (*colloq: tolerate*) aturar. ~ **in for** substituir. ~ **out** (*be conspicuous*) sobressair. ~ **still** estar/ ficar imóvel. ~ **still!** não se mexa!, quieto! ~ **to reason** ser lógico. ~ **up** levantar-se, pôr-se em *or* de pé. ~ **up for** defender, apoiar. ~ **up to** enfrentar.

~-**by** *a* (*for emergency*) de reserva; (*ticket*) de stand-by □ *n* (*at airport*) stand-by *m*. **on** ~-**by** (*mil*) de prontidão; (*med*) de plantão. ~-**in** *n* substituto *m*, suplente *mf*. ~-**offish** *a* (*colloq: aloof*) reservado, distante

standard /'stændəd/ *n* norma *f*, padrão *m*; (*level*) nível *m*; (*flag*) estandarte *m*, bandeira *f*. ~**s** (*morals*) princípios *mpl* □ *a* regulamentar; (*average*) standard, normal. ~ **lamp** abajur *m* de pé. ~ **of living** padrão *m* de vida, (*P*) nível *m* de vida

standardize /'stændədaɪz/ *vt* padronizar

standing /'stændɪŋ/ *a* em pé, de pé *invar*; (*army, committee etc*) permanente □ *n* posição *f*; (*reputation*) prestígio *m*; (*duration*) duração *f*. ~ **order** (*at bank*) ordem *f* permanente. ~-**room** *n* lugares *mpl* em pé

standpoint /'stændpɔɪnt/ *n* ponto *m* de vista

standstill /'stændstɪl/ *n* paralisação *f*. **at a** ~ parado, paralisado. **bring/come to a** ~ (fazer) parar, paralisar(-se), imobilizar (-se)

stank /stæŋk/ *see* **stink**

staple[1] /'steɪpl/ *n* (*for paper*) grampo *m*, (*P*) agrafo *m* □ *vt* (*paper*) grampear, (*P*) agrafar. ~**r** /-ə(r)/ *n* grampeador *m*, (*P*) agrafador *m*

staple[2] /'steɪpl/ *a* principal, básico □ *n* (*comm*) artigo *m* básico

star /sta:(r)/ *n* estrela *f*; (*cinema*) estrela *f*, vedete *f*; (*celebrity*) celebridade *f* □ *vt* (*pt* **starred**) (*of film*) ter no papel principal, (*P*) ter como actor principal □ *vi* ~ **in** ser a vedete *or* ter o papel principal em. ~**dom** *n* celebridade *f*, estrelato *m*

starch /sta:tʃ/ *n* amido *m*, fécula *f*; (*for clothes*) goma *f* □ *vt* pôr em goma, engomar. ~**y** *a* (*of food*) farináceo, feculento; (*fig: of person*) rígido, formal

stare /steə(r)/ *vi* ~ **at** olhar fixamente □ *n* olhar *m* fixo

starfish /'sta:fɪʃ/ *n* (*pl invar*) estrela-do-mar *f*

S

stark /stɑːk/ a (-er, -est) (*desolate*) árido, desolado; (*severe*) austero, severo; (*utter*) completo, rematado; (*fact etc*) brutal □ *adv* completamente. ~ **naked** nu em pêlo, (P) em pelota (*colloq*)

starling /'stɑːlɪŋ/ n estorninho m

starlit /'stɑːlɪt/ a estrelado

starry /'stɑːrɪ/ a estrelado. ~-**eyed** a (*colloq*) sonhador, idealista

start /stɑːt/ vt/i começar; (*machine*) ligar, pôr em andamento; (*fashion etc*) lançar; (*leave*) partir; (*cause*) causar, provocar; (*jump*) sobressaltar-se, estremecer; (*of car*) arrancar, partir □ n começo m, início m; (*of race*) largada f, partida f; (*lead*) avanço m; (*jump*) sobressalto m, estremecimento m. **by fits and ~s** aos arrancos, intermitentemente. **for a ~** para começar. **give sb a ~** sobressaltar alguém, pregar um susto a alguém. ~ **to do** começar a *or* pôr-se a fazer. ~**er** n (*auto*) arranque m; (*competitor*) corredor m; (*culin*) entrada f. ~**ing-point** n ponto m de partida

startl|e /'stɑːtl/ vt (*make jump*) sobressaltar, pregar um susto a; (*shock*) alarmar, chocar. ~**ing** a alarmante; (*surprising*) surpreendente

starv|e /stɑːv/ vi (*suffer*) passar fome; (*die*) morrer de fome. **be ~ing** (*colloq: very hungry*) ter muita fome, morrer de fome (*colloq*) □ vt fazer passar fome a; (*deprive*) privar. ~**ation** /-'veɪʃn/ n fome f

stash /stæʃ/ vt (*sl*) guardar, esconder, enfurnar (*colloq*)

state /steɪt/ n estado m, condição f; (*pomp*) pompa f, gala f; (*pol*) Estado m □ a de Estado, do Estado; (*school*) público; (*visit etc*) oficial □ vt afirmar (**that** que); (*views*) exprimir; (*fix*) marcar, fixar. **in a ~** muito abalado

stateless /'steɪtlɪs/ a apátrida

stately /'steɪtlɪ/ a (-ier, -iest) majestoso. ~ **home** solar m, palácio m

statement /'steɪtmənt/ n declaração f; (*of account*) extrato m, (P) extracto m de conta

statesman /'steɪtsmən/ n (pl -**men**) homem m de estado, estadista m

static /'stætɪk/ a estático □ n (*radio,TV*) estática f, interferência f

station /'steɪʃn/ n (*position*) posto m; (*rail, bus, radio*) estação f; (*rank*) condição f, posição f social □ vt colocar. ~-**wagon** n perua f, (P) carrinha f. ~**ed at** *or* **in** (*mil*) estacionado em

stationary /'steɪʃnrɪ/ a estacionário, parado, imóvel; (*vehicle*) estacionado, parado

stationer /'steɪʃənə(r)/ n dono m de papelaria. ~**'s shop** papelaria f. ~**y** n artigos mpl de papelaria; (*writing-paper*) papel m de carta

statistic /stə'tɪstɪk/ n dado m estatístico. ~**s** n (*as a science*) estatística f. ~**al** a estatístico

statue /'stætʃuː/ n estátua f

stature /'stætʃə(r)/ n estatura f

status /'steɪtəs/ n (pl -**uses**) situação f, posição f, categoria f; (*prestige*) prestígio m, importância f, status m. ~ **quo** status quo m. ~ **symbol** símbolo m de status

statut|e /'stætjuːt/ n estatuto m, lei f. ~**ory** /-ʊtrɪ/ a estatutário, regulamentar; (*holiday*) legal

staunch /stɔːntʃ/ a (-er, -est) (*friend*) fiel, leal

stave /steɪv/ n (*mus*) pauta f □ vt ~ **off** (*keep off*) conjurar, evitar; (*delay*) adiar

stay /steɪ/ vi estar, ficar, permanecer; (*dwell temporarily*) ficar, alojar-se, hospedar-se; (*spend time*) demorar-se □ vt (*hunger*) enganar □ n estada f, visita f, permanência f. ~ **behind** ficar para trás. ~ **in** ficar em casa. ~ **put** (*colloq*) não se mexer (*colloq*). ~ **up** (*late*) deitar-se tarde. ~**ing-power** n resistência f

stead /sted/ n **in my/your/**etc ~ no meu/teu/etc lugar. **stand in good ~** ser muito útil

steadfast /'stedfɑːst/ a firme, constante

stead|y /'stedɪ/ a (-ier, -iest) (*stable*) estável, firme, seguro; (*regular*) regular, constante; (*hand, voice*) firme □ vt firmar, fixar, estabilizar; (*calm*) acalmar. **go ~y with** (*colloq*) namorar. ~**ily** adv firmemente; (*regularly*) regularmente, de modo constante

steak /steɪk/ n bife m

steal /stiːl/ vt/i (pt **stole**, pp **stolen**) roubar (**from sb** de alguém). ~ **away** /**in/**etc sair/entrar/etc furtivamente, esgueirar-se. ~ **the show** pôr os outros na sombra

stealth /stelθ/ n **by ~** furtivamente, na calada, às escondidas. ~**y** a furtivo

steam /stiːm/ n vapor m de água; (*on window*) condensação f □ vt (*cook*) cozinhar a vapor. ~ **up** (*window*) embaciar □ vi soltar vapor, fumegar; (*move*) avançar. ~-**engine** n máquina f a vapor; (*locomotive*) locomotiva f a vapor. ~ **iron** ferro m a vapor. ~**y** a (*heat*) úmido, (P) húmido

steamer /'stiːmə(r)/ n (*ship*) (barco a) vapor m; (*culin*) utensílio m para cozinhar a vapor

steamroller /'stiːmrəʊlə(r)/ n cilindro m a vapor, rolo m compressor

steel /stiːl/ n aço m ▫ a de aço ▫ vpr
~ **o.s.** endurecer-se, fortalecer-se.
~ **industry** siderurgia f

steep¹ /stiːp/ vt (soak) mergulhar, pôr de
molho; (permeate) passar, impregnar.
~**ed in** (fig: vice, misery etc)
mergulhado em; (fig: knowledge,
wisdom etc) impregnado de,
repassado de

steep² /stiːp/ a (-er, -est) íngreme,
escarpado; (colloq) exagerado,
exorbitante. **rise** ~**ly** (slope) subir a
pique; (price) disparar

steeple /ˈstiːpl/ n campanário m, torre f

steeplechase /ˈstiːpltʃeɪs/ n (race)
corrida f de obstáculos

steer /stɪə(r)/ vt/i guiar, conduzir, dirigir;
(ship) governar; (fig) guiar, orientar. ~
clear of evitar passar perto de. ~**ing**
n (auto) direção f, (P) direcção f.
~**ing-wheel** n (auto) volante m

stem¹ /stem/ n caule m, haste f; (of glass)
pé m; (of pipe) boquilha f; (of word)
radical m ▫ vi (pt **stemmed**) ~ **from**
provir de, vir de

stem² /stem/ vt (pt **stemmed**) (check)
conter; (stop) estancar

stench /stentʃ/ n mau cheiro m, fedor m

stencil /ˈstensl/ n estêncil m, (P) stencil
m ▫ vt (pt **stencilled**) (document)
policopiar

step /step/ vi (pt **stepped**) ir andar ▫ vt
~ **up** aumentar ▫ n passo m, passada f;
(of stair, train) degrau m; (action)
medida f, passo m. ~**s** (ladder) escada
f. **in** ~ no mesmo passo, a passo certo;
(fig) em conformidade (**with** com).
~ **down** (resign) demitir-se. ~ **in**
(intervene) intervir. ~**ladder** n escada
f portátil. ~**ping-stone** n (fig: means to
an end) ponte f, trampolim m

stepbrother /ˈstepbrʌðə(r)/ n meio-
irmão m. ~**daughter** n nora f, (P)
enteada f. ~**father** n padrasto m.
~**mother** n madrasta f. ~**sister** n
meio-irmã f. ~**son** n genro m, (P)
enteado m

stereo /ˈsterɪəʊ/ n (pl -os) estéreo m;
(record-player etc) aparelhamento m or
sistema m estéreo ▫ a estéreo invar.
~**phonic** /-əˈfɒnɪk/ a estereofônico, (P)
estereofónico

stereotype /ˈsterɪətaɪp/ n estereótipo m.
~**d** a estereotipado

steril|e /ˈsteraɪl/ a estéril. ~**ity**
/stəˈrɪlətɪ/ n esterilidade f

steriliz|e /ˈsterəlaɪz/ vt esterilizar.
~**ation** /-ˈzeɪʃn/ n esterilização f

sterling /ˈstɜːlɪŋ/ n libra f esterlina ▫ a
esterlino; (silver) de lei; (fig) excelente,
de (primeira) qualidade

stern¹ /stɜːn/ a (-er, -est) severo

stern² /stɜːn/ n (of ship) popa f, ré f

stethoscope /ˈsteθəskəʊp/ n estetoscópio
m

stew /stjuː/ vt/i estufar, guisar; (fruit)
cozer ▫ n ensopado m. ~**ed fruit**
compota f

steward /ˈstjʊəd/ n (of club etc) ecônomo
m, (P) ecónomo m, administrador m;
(on ship etc) camareiro m (de bordo), (P)
criado m (de bordo). ~**ess** /-ˈdes/ n
aeromoça f, (P) hospedeira f

stick¹ /stɪk/ n pau m; (for walking)
bengala f; (of celery) talo m

stick² /stɪk/ vt (pt **stuck**) (glue) colar;
(thrust) cravar, espetar; (colloq: put)
enfiar, meter; (sl: endure) agüentar, (P)
aguentar, aturar, suportar ▫ vi (adhere)
colar, aderir; (remain) ficar enfiado or
metido; (be jammed) emperrar, ficar
engatado. ~ **in one's mind** ficar na
memória. **be stuck with sb/sth**
(colloq) não conseguir descartar-se de
alguém/alguma coisa (colloq). ~ **out** vt
(head) esticar; (tongue etc) mostrar ▫ vi
(protrude) sobressair. ~ **to** (promise)
ser fiel a. ~**up** n (sl) assalto m à mão
armada. ~ **up for** (colloq) tomar o
partido de, defender. ~**ing-plaster** n
esparadrapo m, (P) adesivo m

sticker /ˈstɪkə(r)/ n adesivo m, etiqueta f
(adesiva)

stickler /ˈstɪklə(r)/ n **be a** ~ **for** fazer
grande questão de, insistir em

sticky /ˈstɪkɪ/ a (-ier, -iest) pegajoso;
(label, tape) adesivo; (weather) abafado,
mormacento

stiff /stɪf/ a (-er, -est) teso, hirto, rígido;
(limb, joint) duro; (unbending)
inflexível; (price) elevado, puxado
(colloq); (penalty) severo; (drink)
forte; (manner) reservado, formal. **be
bored/scared** ~ (colloq) estar muito
aborrecido/com muito medo (colloq).
~ **neck** torcicolo m. ~**ness** n rigidez f

stiffen /ˈstɪfn/ vt/i (harden) endurecer;
(limb, joint) emperrar

stifl|e /ˈstaɪfl/ vt/i abafar, sufocar. ~**ing** a
sufocante

stigma /ˈstɪɡmə/ n estigma m. ~**tize** vt
estigmatizar

stile /staɪl/ n degrau m para passar por
cima de cerca

stiletto /strˈletəʊ/ n (pl -os) estilete m.
~ **heel** n salto m alto fino

still¹ /stɪl/ a imóvel, quieto;
(quiet) sossegado ▫ n silêncio m,
sossego m ▫ adv ainda; (nevertheless)
apesar disso, apesar de tudo. **keep** ~!
fique quieto!, não se mexa! ~ **life**
natureza f morta. ~**ness** n calma f

still² /stɪl/ n (apparatus) alambique m

S

stillborn /'stɪlbɔːn/ a natimorto, (P) nado-morto

stilted /'stɪltɪd/ a afetado, (P) afectado

stilts /stɪlts/ npl pernas de pau fpl, (P) andas fpl

stimul|ate /'stɪmjʊleɪt/ vt estimular. ∼ant n estimulante m. ∼ating a estimulante. ∼ation /-'leɪʃn/ n estimulação f

stimulus /'stɪmjʊləs/ n (pl -li /-laɪ/) (spur) estímulo m

sting /stɪŋ/ n picada f; (organ) ferrão m □ vt (pt stung) picar □ vi picar, arder. ∼ing nettle urtiga f

stingy /'stɪndʒɪ/ a (-ier, -iest) pão-duro m, sovina (with com)

stink /stɪŋk/ n fedor m, catinga f, mau cheiro m □ vi (pt stank or stunk, pp stunk) ∼ (of) cheirar (a), tresandar (a) □ vt ∼ out (room etc) empestar. ∼ing a malcheiroso. ∼ing rich (sl) podre de rico (colloq)

stinker /'stɪŋkə(r)/ n (sl: person) cara m horroroso (colloq); (sl: sth difficult) osso m duro de moer

stint /stɪnt/ vi ∼ on poupar em, apertar em □ n (work) tarefa f, parte f, quinhão m

stipulat|e /'stɪpjʊleɪt/ vt estipular. ∼ion /-'leɪʃn/ n condição f, estipulação f

stir /stɜːr/ vt/i (pt stirred) (move) mexer(-se), mover(-se); (excite) excitar; (a liquid) mexer □ n agitação f, rebuliço m. ∼ up (trouble etc) provocar, fomentar. ∼ring a excitante

stirrup /'stɪrəp/ n estribo m

stitch /stɪtʃ/ n (in sewing; med) ponto m; (in knitting) malha f, ponto m; (pain) pontada f □ vt coser. in ∼es (colloq) às gargalhadas (colloq)

stoat /stəʊt/ n arminho m

stock /stɒk/ n (comm) estoque m, (P) stock m, provisão f; (finance) valores mpl, fundos mpl; (family) família f, estirpe f; (culin) caldo m; (flower) goivo m □ a (goods) corrente, comum; (hackneyed) estereotipado □ vt (shop etc) abastecer, fornecer; (sell) vender □ vi ∼ up with abastecer-se de. in ∼ em estoque. out of ∼ esgotado. take ∼ (fig) fazer um balanço. ∼-car n stock-car m. ∼-cube n cubo m de caldo. ∼ market Bolsa f (de Valores). ∼-still a, adv imóvel. ∼-taking n (comm) inventário m

stockbroker /'stɒkbrəʊkə(r)/ n corretor m da Bolsa

stocking /'stɒkɪŋ/ n meia f

stockist /'stɒkɪst/ n armazenista m

stockpile /'stɒkpaɪl/ n reservas fpl □ vt acumular reservas de, estocar

stocky /'stɒkɪ/ a (-ier, -iest) atarracado

stodg|e /stɒdʒ/ n (colloq) comida f pesada (colloq). ∼y a (of food, book) pesado, maçudo

stoic /'stəʊɪk/ n estóico m. ∼al a estoico. ∼ism /-sɪzəm/ n estoicismo m

stoke /stəʊk/ vt (boiler, fire) alimentar, carregar

stole[1] /stəʊl/ n (garment) estola m

stole[2], **stolen** /stəʊl, 'stəʊlən/ see **steal**

stomach /'stʌmək/ n estômago m; (abdomen) barriga f, ventre m □ vt (put up with) aturar. ∼-ache n dor f de estômago; (abdomen) dores fpl de barriga

ston|e /stəʊn/ n pedra f; (pebble) seixo m; (in fruit) caroço m; (weight) 6,348 kg; (med) cálculo m, pedra f □ vt apedrejar; (fruit) tirar o caroço de. within a ∼e's throw (of) muito perto (de). ∼e-cold gelado. ∼e-deaf totalmente surdo. ∼ed a (colloq: drunk) bebão m (colloq); (colloq: drugged) drogado. ∼y a pedregoso. ∼y-broke a (sl) duro, liso (sl)

stonemason /'stəʊnmeɪsn/ n pedreiro m

stood /stʊd/ see **stand**

stooge /stuːdʒ/ n (colloq: actor) ajudante mf; (colloq: puppet) antoche m, (P) comparsa mf, parceiro m

stool /stuːl/ n banco m, tamborete m

stoop /stuːp/ vi (bend) curvar-se, baixar-se; (condescend) condescender, dignar-se. ∼ to sth rebaixar-se para (fazer) coisa □ n walk with a ∼ andar curvado

stop /stɒp/ vt/i (pt stopped) parar; (prevent) impedir (from de); (hole, leak etc) tapar, vedar; (pain, noise etc) parar; (colloq: stay) ficar □ n (of bus) parada f, (P) paragem f; (full stop) ponto m final. put a ∼ to pôr fim a. ∼ it! acabe logo com isso! ∼-over n (break in journey) parada f, (P) paragem f; (port of call) escala f. ∼press n notícia f de última hora. ∼-watch n cronômetro m, (P) cronómetro m

stopgap /'stɒpgæp/ n substituto m provisório, tapa-buracos mpl (colloq) □ a temporário

stoppage /'stɒpɪdʒ/ n parada f, (P) paragem f; (of work) paralisação f de trabalho; (of pay) suspensão f

stopper /'stɒpə(r)/ n rolha f, tampa f

storage /'stɔːrɪdʒ/ n (of goods, food etc) armazenagem f, armazenamento m. in cold ∼ em frigorífico

store /stɔː(r)/ n reserva f, provisão f; (warehouse) armazém m, entreposto m; (shop) grande armazém m; (Amer) loja f; (in computer) memória f □ vt (for future) pôr de reserva, juntar, fazer provisão de; (in warehouse) armazenar.

be in ~ estar guardado. **have in** ~ **for** reservar para. **set** ~ **by** dar valor a. ~**-room** n depósito m, almortarifado m, (P) armazém m

storey /'stɔːrɪ/ n (pl **-eys**) andar m

stork /stɔːk/ n cegonha f

storm /stɔːm/ n tempestade f □ vt tomar de assalto □ vi enfurecer-se. **a** ~ **in a teacup** uma tempestade num copo de água. ~**y** a tempestuoso

story /'stɔːrɪ/ n estória f, (P) história f; (in press) artigo m, matéria f; (Amer: storey) andar m; (colloq: lie) cascata f, (P) peta f. ~**-teller** n contador m de estórias, (P) histórias

stout /staʊt/ a (**-er, -est**) (fat) gordo, corpulento; (strong, thick) resistente, sólido, grosso; (brave) resoluto □ n cerveja f preta forte

stove /stəʊv/ n (for cooking) fogão m (de cozinha)

stow /stəʊ/ vt ~ (**away**) (put away) guardar, arrumar; (hide) esconder □ vi ~ **away** viajar clandestinamente

stowaway /'stəʊəweɪ/ n passageiro m clandestino

straddle /'strædl/ vt (sit) escarranchar-se em, montar; (stand) pôr-se de pernas abertas sobre

straggle /'strægl/ vi (lag behind) desgarrar-se, ficar para trás; (spread) estender-se desordenadamente. ~**r** /-ə(r)/ n retardatário m

straight /streɪt/ a (**-er, -est**) direito; (tidy) em ordem; (frank) franco, direto, (P) directo; (of hair) liso; (of drink) puro □ adv (in straight line) reto; (directly) direito, direto, (P) directo, diretamente, (P) directamente □ n linha f reta, (P) recta. ~ **ahead** or **on** (sempre) em frente. ~ **away** logo, imediatamente. **go** ~ viver honestamente. **keep a** ~ **face** não se desmanchar, manter um ar sério

straighten /'streɪtn/ vt endireitar; (tidy) arrumar, pôr em ordem

straightforward /streɪt'fɔːwəd/ a franco, sincero; (easy) simples

strain¹ /streɪn/ n (breed) raça f; (streak) tendência f, veia f

strain² /streɪn/ vt (rope) esticar, puxar; (tire) cansar; (filter) filtrar, passar; (vegetables, tea etc) coar; (med) distender, torcer; (fig) forçar, pôr à prova □ vi esforçar-se □ n tensão f; (fig: effort) esforço m; (med) distensão f. ~**s** (music) melodias fpl. ~ **one's ears** apurar o ouvido. ~**ed** a forçado; (relations) tenso. ~**er** n coador m, (P) passador m

strait /streɪt/ n estreito m. ~**s** estreito m; (fig) apuros mpl, dificuldades fpl.

~**-jacket** n camisa-de-força f. ~**-laced** a severo, puritano

strand /strænd/ n (thread) fio m; (lock of hair) mecha f, madeixa f

stranded /'strændɪd/ a (person) em dificuldades, deixado para trás, abandonado

strange /streɪndʒ/ a (**-er, -est**) estranho. ~**ly** adv estranhamente. ~**ness** n estranheza f

stranger /'streɪndʒə(r)/ n estranho m, desconhecido m

strangle /'stræŋgl/ vt estrangular, sufocar

stranglehold /'stræŋglhəʊld/ n **have a** ~ **on** ter dominio sobre

strangulation /stræŋgjʊ'leɪʃn/ n estrangulamento m

strap /stræp/ n (of leather etc) correia f; (of dress) alça f; (of watch) pulseira f com correia □ vt (pt **strapped**) prender com correia

strapping /'stræpɪŋ/ a robusto, grande

strata /'streɪtə/ see **stratum**

stratagem /'strætədʒəm/ n estratagema m

strategic /strə'tiːdʒɪk/ a estratégico; (of weapons) de longo alcance

strategy /'strætədʒɪ/ n estratégia f

stratum /'straːtəm/ n (pl **strata**) estrato m, camada f

straw /strɔː/ n palha f; (for drinking) canudo m, (P) palhinha f. **the last** ~ a última gota f

strawberry /'strɔːbrɪ/ n (fruit) morango m; (plant) morangueiro m

stray /streɪ/ vi (deviate from path etc) extraviar-se, desencaminhar-se, afastar-se (**from** de); (lose one's way) perder-se; (wander) vagar, errar □ a perdido, extraviado; (isolated) isolado, raro, esporádico □ n animal m perdido or vadio

streak /striːk/ n risca f, lista f; (strain) veia f; (period) período m. ~ **of lightning** relâmpago m □ vt listrar, riscar □ vi ir como um raio. ~**er** n (colloq) pessoa f que corre nua em lugares públicos. ~**y** a listrado, riscado. ~**y bacon** toucinho m entremeado com gordura

stream /striːm/ n riacho m, córrego m, regato m; (current) corrente f; (fig: flow) jorro m, torrente f; (schol) nível m, grupo m □ vi correr; (of banner, hair) flutuar; (sweat) escorrer, pingar

streamer /'striːmə(r)/ n (of paper) serpentina f; (flag) flâmula f, bandeirola f

streamline /'striːmlaɪn/ vt dar forma aerodinâmica a; (fig) racionalizar. ~**d** a (shape) aerodinâmico

street /striːt/ n rua f. **the man in the ~** (fig) o homem da rua. **~ lamp** poste m de iluminação

streetcar /ˈstriːtkɑː(r)/ n (Amer) bonde m, (P) carro m eléctrico

strength /streŋθ/ n força f; (of wall) solidez f; (of fabric etc) resistência f. **on the ~ of** à base de, em virtude de

strengthen /ˈstreŋθn/ vt fortificar, fortalecer, reforçar

strenuous /ˈstrenjʊəs/ a enérgico; (arduous) árduo, estrénuo, (P) estrénuo; (tiring) fatiganﬆe, esgotante. **~ly** adv esforçadamente, energicamente

stress /stres/ n acento m; (pressure) pressão f, tensão f; (med) stress m □ vt acentuar, sublinhar; (sound) acentuar. **~ful** a estressante

stretch /stretʃ/ vt (pull taut) esticar; (arm, leg, neck) estender, esticar; (clothes) alargar; (truth) forçar, torcer □ vi estender-se; (after sleep etc) espreguiçar-se; (of clothes) alargar-se □ n extensão f, trecho m; (period) período m; (of road) troço m □ a (of fabric) com elasticidade. **at a ~** sem parar. **~ one's legs** esticar as pernas

stretcher /ˈstretʃə(r)/ n maca f, padiola f. **~-bearer** n padioleiro m, (P) maqueiro m

strew /struː/ vt (pt strewed, pp strewed or strewn) (scatter) espalhar; (cover) juncar, cobrir

stricken /ˈstrɪkən/ a **~ with** atacado or acometido de

strict /strɪkt/ a (-er, -est) estrito, rigoroso. **~ly** adv estritamente. **~ly speaking** a rigor. **~ness** n severidade f, rigor m

stride /straɪd/ vi (pt strode, pp stridden) caminhar a passos largos □ n passada f. **make great ~s** (fig) fazer grandes progressos. **take sth in one's ~** fazer alg coisa sem esforço

strident /ˈstraɪdnt/ a estridente

strife /straɪf/ n conflito m, dissensão f, luta f

strike /straɪk/ vt (pt struck) bater (em); (blow) dar; (match) riscar, acender; (gold etc) descobrir; (of clock) soar, dar, bater (horas); (of lightning) atingir □ vi fazer greve; (attack) atacar □ n (of workers) greve f; (mil) ataque m; (find) descoberta f. **on ~** em greve. **~ a bargain** fechar negócio. **~ off or out** riscar. **~ up** (mus) começar a tocar; (friendship) travar

striker /ˈstraɪkə(r)/ n grevista mf

striking /ˈstraɪkɪŋ/ a notável, impressionante; (attractive) atraente

string /strɪŋ/ n corda f, fio m; (of violin, racket etc) corda f; (of pearls) fio m; (of onions, garlic) réstia f; (of lies etc) série f; (row) fila f □ vt (pt strung) (thread) enfiar. **pull ~s** usar pistolão, (P) puxar os cordelinhos. **~ out** espaçar-se. **~ed** a (instrument) de cordas. **~y** a filamentoso, fibroso; (meat) com nervos

stringent /ˈstrɪndʒənt/ a rigoroso, estrito

strip[1] /strɪp/ vt/i (pt stripped) (undress) despir(-se); (machine) desmontar; (deprive) despojar, privar. **~per** n artista mf de strip-tease; (solvent) removedor m

strip[2] /strɪp/ n tira f; (of land) faixa f. **comic ~** história f em quadrinhos, (P) banda f desenhada. **~ light** tubo m de luz fluorescente

stripe /straɪp/ n risca f, lista f, barra f. **~d** a listrado, com listras

strive /straɪv/ vi (pt strove, pp striven) esforçar-se (to por)

strode /strəʊd/ see **stride**

stroke[1] /strəʊk/ n golpe m; (of pen) penada f, (P) traço m; (in swimming) braçada f; (in rowing) remada f; (med) ataque m, congestão f. **~ of genius** rasgo m de genialidade. **~ of luck** golpe m de sorte

stroke[2] /strəʊk/ vt (with hand) acariciar, fazer festas em

stroll /strəʊl/ vi passear, dar uma volta □ n volta f, (P) giro m. **~ in/etc** entrar/etc tranquilamente

strong /strɒŋ/ a (-er, -est) forte; (shoes, fabric etc) resistente. **be a hundred/etc ~** ser em número de cem/etc. **~-box** n cofre-forte m. **~ language** linguagem f grosseira, palavrões mpl. **~-minded** a resoluto, firme. **~-room** n casa-forte f. **~ly** adv (greatly) fortemente, grandemente; (with energy) com força; (deeply) profundamente

stronghold /ˈstrɒŋhəʊld/ n fortaleza f; (fig) baluarte m, bastião m

strove /strəʊv/ see **strive**

struck /strʌk/ see **strike** □ a **~ on** (sl) apaixonado por

structur|e /ˈstrʌktʃə(r)/ n estrutura f; (of building etc) edifício m, construção f. **~al** a estrutural, de estrutura, de construção

struggle /ˈstrʌɡl/ vi (to get free) debater-se; (contend) lutar; (strive) esforçar-se (to, for por) □ n luta f; (effort) esforço m. **have a ~ to** ter dificuldade em. **~ to one's feet** levantar-se a custo

strum /strʌm/ vt (pt strummed) (banjo etc) dedilhar

strung /strʌŋ/ see **string**

strut /strʌt/ n (*support*) suporte m, escora f ◻ vi (*pt* **strutted**) (*walk*) pavonear-se

stub /stʌb/ n (*of pencil, cigarette*) ponta f; (*of tree*) cepo m, toco m; (*counterfoil*) talão m, canhoto m ◻ vt (*pt* **stubbed**) ∼ **one's toe** dar uma topada. ∼ **out** esmagar

stubble /ˈstʌbl/ n (*on chin*) barba f por fazer; (*of crop*) restolho m

stubborn /ˈstʌbən/ a teimoso, obstinado. ∼**ly** adv obstinadamente, teimosamente. ∼**ness** n teimosia f, obstinação f

stubby /ˈstʌbɪ/ a (**-ier, -iest**) (*finger*) curto e grosso; (*person*) atarracado

stuck /stʌk/ *see* **stick**[2] □ a emperrado. ∼**up** a (*colloq: snobbish*) convencido, esnobe

stud[1] /stʌd/ n tacha f; (*for collar*) botão m de colarinho ◻ vt (*pt* **studded**) enfeitar com tachas. ∼**ded with** salpicado de

stud[2] /stʌd/ n (*horses*) haras m. ∼**(-farm)** n coudelaria f. ∼**(-horse)** n garanhão m

student /ˈstjuːdnt/ n (*univ*) estudante mf, aluno m; (*schol*) aluno m □ a (*life, residence*) universitário

studied /ˈstʌdɪd/ a estudado

studio /ˈstjuːdɪəʊ/ n (*pl* **-os**) estúdio m. ∼ **flat** estúdio m

studious /ˈstjuːdɪəs/ a (*person*) estudioso; (*deliberate*) estudado. ∼**ly** adv (*carefully*) cuidadosamente

study /ˈstʌdɪ/ n estudo m; (*office*) escritório m ◻ vt/i estudar

stuff /stʌf/ n substância f, matéria f; (*sl: things*) coisa(s) f (pl) □ vt encher; (*animal*) empalhar; (*cram*) apinhar, encher ao máximo; (*culin*) rechear; (*block up*) entupir; (*put*) enfiar, meter. ∼**ing** n enchimento m; (*culin*) recheio m

stuffy /ˈstʌfɪ/ a (**-ier, -iest**) abafado, mal arejado; (*dull*) enfadonho

stumble /ˈstʌmbl/ vi tropeçar. ∼**e across** or on dar com, encontrar por acaso, topar com. ∼**ing-block** n obstáculo m

stump /stʌmp/ n (*of tree*) cepo m, toco m; (*of limb*) coto m; (*of pencil, cigar*) ponta f

stumped /stʌmpt/ a (*colloq: baffled*) atrapalhado, perplexo

stun /stʌn/ vt (*pt* **stunned**) aturdir, estontear

stung /stʌŋ/ *see* **sting**

stunk /stʌŋk/ *see* **stink**

stunning /ˈstʌnɪŋ/ a atordoador; (*colloq: delightful*) fantástico, sensacional

stunt[1] /stʌnt/ vt (*growth*) atrofiar. ∼**ed** a atrofiado

stunt[2] /stʌnt/ n (*feat*) façanha f, proeza f; (*trick*) truque m; (*aviat*) acrobacia f aérea. ∼ **man** n dublê m, (*P*) duplo m

stupefy /ˈstjuːpɪfaɪ/ vt estupefazer, (*P*) estupeficar

stupendous /stjuːˈpendəs/ a estupendo, assombroso, prodigioso

stupid /ˈstjuːpɪd/ a estúpido, obtuso. ∼**ity** /-ˈpɪdətɪ/ n estupidez f. ∼**ly** adv estupidamente

stupor /ˈstjuːpə(r)/ n estupor m, torpor m

sturdy /ˈstɜːdɪ/ a (**-ier, -iest**) robusto, vigoroso, forte

stutter /ˈstʌtə(r)/ vi gaguejar ◻ n gagueira f, (*P*) gaguez f

sty /staɪ/ n (*pigsty*) pocilga f, chiqueiro m

stye /staɪ/ n (*on eye*) terçol m, terçolho m

style /staɪl/ n estilo m; (*fashion*) moda f; (*kind*) gênero m, (*P*) género m, tipo m; (*pattern*) feitio m, modelo m ◻ vt (*design*) desenhar, criar. **in** ∼**e** (*live*) em grande estilo; (*do things*) com classe. ∼**e sb's hair** fazer um penteado em alguém. ∼**ist** n (*of hair*) cabeleireiro m

stylish /ˈstaɪlɪʃ/ a elegante, na moda

stylized /ˈstaɪlaɪzd/ a estilizado

stylus /ˈstaɪləs/ n (*pl* **-uses**) (*of record-player*) agulha f, safira f

suave /swɑːv/ a polido, de fala mansa, (*P*) melífluo

sub- /sʌb/ *pref* sub-

subconscious /sʌbˈkɒnʃəs/ a & n subconsciente (*m*)

subcontract /sʌbkənˈtrækt/ vt dar de subempreitada

subdivide /sʌbdɪˈvaɪd/ vt subdividir

subdue /səbˈdjuː/ vt (*enemy, feeling*) dominar, subjugar; (*sound, voice*) abrandar. ∼**d** a (*weak*) submisso; (*quiet*) recolhido; (*light*) velado

subject[1] /ˈsʌbdʒɪkt/ a (*state etc*) dominado □ n sujeito m; (*schol, univ*) disciplina f, matéria f; (*citizen*) súdito m. ∼**-matter** n conteúdo m, tema m, assunto m. ∼ **to** sujeito a

subject[2] /səbˈdʒekt/ vt submeter. ∼**ion** /-kʃn/ n submissão f

subjective /sʌbˈdʒektɪv/ a subjetivo, (*P*) subjectivo

subjunctive /səbˈdʒʌŋktɪv/ a & n subjuntivo (*m*), (*P*) conjuntivo (*m*)

sublime /səˈblaɪm/ a sublime

submarine /sʌbməˈriːn/ n submarino m

submerge /səbˈmɜːdʒ/ vt submergir ◻ vi submergir, mergulhar

submissive /səbˈmɪsɪv/ a submisso

submit /səbˈmɪt/ vt/i (*pt* **submitted**) submeter(-se) (**to** a); (*jur: argue*) alegar. ∼**ssion** /-ˈmɪʃn/ n submissão f

subnormal /sʌbˈnɔːml/ a subnormal; (*temperature*) abaixo do normal

S

subordinate[1] /sə'bɔ:dmət/ a subordinado, subalterno; (*gram*) subordinado □ n subordinado m, subalterno m

subordinate[2] /sə'bɔ:dmeɪt/ vt subordinar (**to** a)

subpoena /səb'pi:nə/ n (*pl* -**as**) (*jur*) citação f, intimação f

subscribe /səb'skraɪb/ vt/i subscrever, contribuir (**to** para). ~ **to** (*theory, opinion*) subscrever, aceitar; (*newspaper*) assinar. ~**r** /-ə(r)/ n subscritor m, assinante m

subscription /səb'skrɪpʃn/ n subscrição f; (*to newspaper*) assinatura f

subsequent /'sʌbsɪkwənt/ a subsequente, (P) subsequente, posterior. ~**ly** adv subsequentemente, a seguir, posteriormente

subservient /səb'sɜ:vɪənt/ a servil, subserviente

subside /səb'saɪd/ vi (*flood, noise etc*) baixar; (*land*) ceder, afundar; (*wind, storm, excitement*) abrandar. ~**nce** /-əns/ n (*of land*) afundamento m

subsidiary /səb'sɪdɪərɪ/ a subsidiário □ n (*comm*) filial f, sucursal f

subsid|y /'sʌbsədɪ/ n subsídio m, subvenção f. ~**ize** /-ɪdaɪz/ vt subsidiar, subvencionar

subsist /səb'sɪst/ vi subsistir. ~ **on** viver de. ~**ence** n subsistência f. ~**ence allowance** ajudas fpl de custo

substance /'sʌbstəns/ n substância f

substandard /sʌb'stændəd/ a de qualidade inferior

substantial /səb'stænʃl/ a substancial. ~**ly** adv substancialmente

substantiate /səb'stænʃɪeɪt/ vt comprovar, fundamentar

substitut|e /'sʌbstɪtju:t/ n (*person*) substituto m, suplente mf (**for** de); (*thing*) substituto m (**for** de) □ vt substituir (**for** por). ~**ion** /-'tju:ʃn/ n substituição f

subterfuge /'sʌbtəfju:dʒ/ n subterfúgio m

subtitle /'sʌbtaɪtl/ n subtítulo m

subtle /'sʌtl/ a (-**er**, -**est**) sutil, (P) subtil. ~**ty** n sutileza f, (P) subtileza f

subtotal /'sʌbtəʊtl/ n soma f parcial

subtract /səb'trækt/ vt subtrair, diminuir. ~**ion** /-kʃn/ n subtração f, diminuição f

suburb /'sʌbɜ:b/ n subúrbio m, arredores mpl. ~**an** /sə'bɜ:bən/ a dos subúrbios, suburbano. ~**ia** /sə'bɜ:bɪə/ n (*pej*) os arredores

subver|t /səb'vɜ:t/ vt subverter. ~**sion** /-ʃn/ n subverção f. ~**sive** /-sɪv/ a subversivo

subway /'sʌbweɪ/ n passagem f subterrânea; (*Amer: underground*) metropolitano m

succeed /sək'si:d/ vi ser bem sucedido, ter êxito. ~ **in doing sth** conseguir fazer alg coisa □ vt (*follow*) suceder a. ~**ing** a seguinte, sucessivo

success /sək'ses/ n sucesso m, êxito m

succession /sək'seʃn/ n sucessão f; (*series*) série f. **in** ~ seguidos, consecutivos

successive /sək'sesɪv/ a sucessivo, consecutivo

successor /sək'sesə(r)/ n sucessor m

succinct /sək'sɪŋkt/ a sucinto

succulent /'sʌkjʊlənt/ a suculento

succumb /sə'kʌm/ vi sucumbir

such /sʌtʃ/ a & pron tal, semelhante, assim; (*so much*) tanto □ adv tanto. ~ **a book**/etc un tal livro/etc or um livro/etc assim. ~ **books**/etc tais livros/etc or livros/etc assim. ~ **courage**/ etc tanta coragem/etc. ~ **a big house** uma casa tão grande. **as** ~ como tal. ~ **as** como, tal como. **there's no** ~ **thing** uma coisa dessa não existe. ~-**and-such** a & pron tal e tal

suck /sʌk/ vt chupar; (*breast*) mamar. ~ **in** or **up** (*absorb*) absorver, aspirar; (*engulf*) tragar. ~ **up to** puxar o saco a (*colloq*). ~ **one's thumb** chupar o dedo. ~**er** n (*sl: greenhorn*) trouxa mf (*colloq*); (*bot*) broto m

suckle /'sʌkl/ vt amamentar, dar de mamar a

suction /'sʌkʃn/ n sucção f

sudden /'sʌdn/ a súbito, repentino. **all of a** ~ de repente, de súbito. ~**ly** adv subitamente, repentinamente. ~**ness** n subitaneidade f, brusquidão f

suds /sʌdz/ npl espuma f de sabão; (*soapy water*) água f de sabão

sue /su:/ vt (*pres p* **suing**) processar

suede /sweɪd/ n camurça f

suet /'su:ɪt/ n sebo m

suffer /'sʌfə(r)/ vt/i sofrer; (*tolerate*) tolerar, suportar. ~**er** n sofredor m, o que sofre; (*patient*) doente mf, vítima f. ~**ing** n sufrimento m

suffice /sə'faɪs/ vi bastar, chegar, ser suficiente

sufficien|t /sə'fɪʃnt/ a suficiente, bastante. ~**cy** n suficiência f, quantidade f suficiente. ~**tly** adv suficientemente

suffix /'sʌfɪx/ n sufixo m

suffocat|e /'sʌfəkeɪt/ vt/i sufocar. ~**ion** /-'keɪʃn/ n sufocação f, asfixia f. ~**ing** a sufocante, asfixiante

sugar /'ʃʊgə(r)/ n açucar m □ vt adoçar, pôr açúcar em. ~-**bowl** n açucareiro m.

∼-**lump** n torrão m de açúcar, (P) quadradinho m de açúcar. **brown** ∼ açúcar m preto, (P) açúcar m amarelo. ∼**y** a açucarado; (fig: too sweet) delicodoce

suggest /səˈdʒest/ vt sugerir. ∼**ion** /-tʃn/ n sugestão f. ∼**ive** a sugestivo; (improper) brejeiro, picante. **be** ∼**ive of** sugerir, fazer lembrar

suicid|**e** /ˈsuːɪsaɪd/ n suicídio m. **commit** ∼**e** suicidar-se. ∼**al** /-ˈsaɪdl/ a suicida

suit /suːt/ n terno m, (P) fato m; (woman's) costume m, (P) saia-casaco m; (cards) naipe m □ vt convir a; (of garment, style) ficar bem em; (adapt) adaptar. **follow** ∼ (fig) seguir o exemplo. ∼-**ability** n (of action) conveniência f, oportunidade f; (of candidate) aptidão f. ∼**able** a conveniente, apropriado (**for** para). ∼**ably** adv convenientemente. ∼**ed to** a **be** ∼**ed to** ser feito para, servir para. **be well** ∼**ed** (matched) combinar-se bem; (of people) ser o ideal

suitcase /ˈsuːtkeɪs/ n mala f (de viagem)

suite /swiːt/ n (of rooms; mus) suíte f, (P) suíte f; (of furniture) mobília f

suitor /ˈsuːtə(r)/ n pretendente m

sulk /sʌlk/ vi amuar, ficar emburrado. ∼**y** a amuado, emburrado (colloq)

sullen /ˈsʌlən/ a carrancudo

sulphur /ˈsʌlfə(r)/ n enxofre m. ∼**ic** /-ˈfjʊərɪk/ a ∼**ic acid** ácido m sulfúrico

sultan /ˈsʌltən/ n sultão m

sultana /sʌlˈtɑːnə/ n (fruit) passa f branca, (P) sultana f

sultry /ˈsʌltrɪ/ a (-**ier**, -**iest**) abafado, opressivo; (fig) sensual

sum /sʌm/ n soma f; (amount of money) soma f, quantia f, importância f; (in arithmetic) conta f □ vt (pt **summed**) somar. ∼ **up** recapitular, resumir; (assess) avaliar, medir

summar|**y** /ˈsʌmərɪ/ n sumário m, resumo m □ a sumário. ∼**ize** vt resumir

summer /ˈsʌmə(r)/ n verão m, estio m □ a de verão. ∼-**time** n verão m, época f de verão. ∼**y** a estival, próprio de verão

summit /ˈsʌmɪt/ n cume m, cimo m. ∼ **conference** (pol) conferência f de cúpula, (P) reunião f de cimeira

summon /ˈsʌmən/ vt mandar chamar; (to meeting) convocar. ∼ **up** (strength, courage etc) chamar a si, fazer apelo a

summons /ˈsʌmənz/ n (jur) citação f, intimação f □ vt citar, intimar

sump /sʌmp/ n (auto) cárter m

sumptuous /ˈsʌmptʃʊəs/ a suntuoso, (P) sumptuoso, luxuoso

sun /sʌn/ n sol m □ vt (pt **sunned**) ∼ **o.s.** aquecer-se ao sol. ∼**glasses** npl óculos mpl de sol. ∼-**roof** n teto m solar. ∼-**tan**

n bronzeado m. ∼-**tanned** a bronzeado. ∼-**tan oil** n óleo m de bronzear

sunbathe /ˈsʌnbeɪð/ vi tomar um banho de sol

sunburn /ˈsʌnbɜːn/ n queimadura f de sol. ∼**t** a queimado pelo sol

Sunday /ˈsʌndɪ/ n domingo m. ∼ **school** catecismo m

sundial /ˈsʌndaɪəl/ n relógio m de sol

sundown /ˈsʌndaʊn/ n = **sunset**

sundr|**y** /ˈsʌndrɪ/ a vários, diversos. ∼**ies** npl artigos mpl diversos. **all and** ∼**y** todo o mundo

sunflower /ˈsʌnflaʊə(r)/ n girassol m

sung /sʌŋ/ see **sing**

sunk /sʌŋk/ see **sink**

sunken /ˈsʌŋkən/ a (ship etc) afundado; (eyes) fundo

sunlight /ˈsʌnlaɪt/ n luz f do sol, sol m

sunny /ˈsʌnɪ/ a (-**ier**, -**iest**) (room, day etc) ensolarado

sunrise /ˈsʌnraɪz/ n nascer m do sol

sunset /ˈsʌnset/ n pôr m do sol

sunshade /ˈsʌnʃeɪd/ n (awning) toldo m; (parasol) pára-sol m, (P) guarda-sol m

sunshine /ˈsʌnʃaɪn/ n sol m, luz f do sol

sunstroke /ˈsʌnstrəʊk/ n (med) insolação f

super /ˈsuːpə(r)/ a (colloq: excellent) formidável

superb /suːˈpɜːb/ a soberbo, esplêndido

supercilious /suːpəˈsɪlɪəs/ a (haughty) altivo; (disdainful) desdenhoso

superficial /suːpəˈfɪʃl/ a superficial. ∼**ity** /-ɪˈælɪt/ n superficialidade f. ∼**ly** adv superficialmente

superfluous /suːˈpɜːflʊəs/ a supérfluo

superhuman /suːpəˈhjuːmən/ a sobrehumano

superimpose /suːpərɪmˈpəʊz/ vt sobrepor (**on** a)

superintendent /suːpərɪnˈtendənt/ n superintendente m; (of police) comissário m, chefe m de polícia

superior /suːˈpɪərɪə(r)/ a & n superior (m). ∼**ity** /-ˈɒrətɪ/ n superioridade f

superlative /suːˈpɜːlətɪv/ a supremo, superlativo □ n (gram) superlativo m

supermarket /ˈsuːpəmɑːkɪt/ n supermercado m

supernatural /suːpəˈnætʃrəl/ a sobrenatural

superpower /ˈsuːpəpaʊə(r)/ n superpotência f

supersede /suːpəˈsiːd/ vt suplantar, substituir

supersonic /suːpəˈsɒnɪk/ a supersônico, (P) supersónico

superstiti|**on** /suːpəˈstɪʃn/ n superstição f. ∼**ous** a /-ˈstɪʃəs/ supersticioso

S

superstore /'su:pəstɔ:(r)/ n
hipermercado m

supertanker /'su:pətæŋkə(r)/ n
superpetroleiro m

supervis|e /'su:pəvaɪz/ vt supervisar,
fiscalizar. **~ion** /-'vɪʒn/ n supervisão f.
~or n supervisor m; (shop) chefe mf de
seção; (firm) chefe mf de serviço. **~ory**
/'su:pəvaɪzərɪ/ a de supervisão

supper /'sʌpə(r)/ n jantar m; (late at
night) ceia f

supple /'sʌpl/ a flexível, maleável

supplement[1] /'sʌplɪmənt/ n suplemento
m. **~ary** /-'mentrɪ/ a suplementar

supplement[2] /'sʌplɪment/ vt
suplementar

supplier /sə'plaɪə(r)/ n fornecedor m

suppl|y /sə'plaɪ/ vt suprir, prover; (comm)
fornecer, abastecer □ n provisão f; (of
goods, gas etc) fornecimento m,
abastecimento m □ a (teacher)
substituto. **~ies** (food) víveres mpl;
(mil) suprimentos mpl. **~y and
demand** oferta e procura

support /sə'pɔ:t/ vt (hold up, endure)
suportar; (provide for) sustentar,
suster; (back) apoiar, patrocinar;
(sport) torcer por □ n apoio m; (techn)
suporte m. **~er** n partidário m; (sport)
torcedor m

suppos|e /sə'pəʊz/ vt/i supor. **~e that**
supondo que, na hipótese de que. **~ed** a
suposto. **he's ~ed to do** ele deve fazer;
(believed to) consta que ele faz. **~edly**
/-ɪdlɪ/ adv segundo dizem; (probably)
supostamente, em princípio. **~ing** conj
se. **~ition** /sʌpə-'zɪʃn/ n suposição f

suppress /sə'pres/ vt (put an end to)
suprimir, (restrain) conter, reprimir;
(stifle) abafar, sufocar; (psych)
recalcar. **~ion** /-ʃn/ n supressão f;
(restraint) repressão f; (psych)
recalque m, (P) recalcamento m

suprem|e /su:'pri:m/ a supremo. **~acy**
/-eməsɪ/ n supremacia f

surcharge /'sɜ:tʃɑ:dʒ/ n sobretaxa f; (on
stamp) sobrecarga f

sure /ʃʊə(r)/ a (-er, -est) seguro, certo
□ adv (colloq: certainly) deveras, não há
dúvida que, de certeza. **be ~ about** or
of ter a certeza de. **be ~ to** (not fail) não
deixar de. **he is ~ to find out** ele vai
descobrir com certeza. **make ~**
assegurar. **~ly** adv com certeza,
certamente

surety /'ʃʊərətɪ/ n (person) fiador m;
(thing) garantia f

surf /sɜ:f/ n (waves) ressaca f,
rebentação f. **~er** n surfista mf. **~ing** n
surfe m, (P) surf m, jacaré-na-praia m

surface /'sɜ:fɪs/ n superfície f □ a
superficial □ vt/i revestir; (rise, become

known) emergir. **~ mail** via f
marítima

surfboard /'sɜ:fbɔ:d/ n prancha f de
surfe, (P) surf

surfeit /'sɜ:fɪt/ n excesso m (of de)

surge /sɜ:dʒ/ vi (waves) ondular,
encapelar-se; (move forward) avançar
□ n (wave) onda f, vaga f; (motion)
arremetida f

surgeon /'sɜ:dʒən/ n cirurgião m

surg|ery /'sɜ:dʒərɪ/ n cirurgia f; (office)
consultório m; (session) consulta f;
(consulting hours) horas fpl de
consulta. **~ical** a cirúrgico

surly /'sɜ:lɪ/ a (-ier, -iest) carrancudo,
trombudo

surmise /sə'maɪz/ vt imaginar, supor,
calcular □ n conjetura f, (P)
conjectura f; hipótese f

surmount /sə'maʊnt/ vt sobrepujar,
vencer, (P) superar

surname /'sɜ:neɪm/ n sobrenome m, (P)
apelido m

surpass /sə'pɑ:s/ vt superar, ultrapassar,
exceder

surplus /'sɜ:pləs/ n excedente m, excesso
m; (finance) saldo m positivo □ a
excedente, em excesso

surpris|e /sə'praɪz/ n surpresa f □ vt
surpreender. **~ed** a surpreendido,
admirado (at com). **~ing** a
surpreendente. **~ingly** adv
surpreendentemente

surrender /sə'rendə(r)/ vi render-se □ vt
(hand over; mil) entregar □ n (mil)
rendição f; (of rights) renúncia f

surreptitious /sʌrep'tɪʃəs/ a sub-
reptício, furtivo

surrogate /'sʌrəgeɪt/ n delegado m. **~
mother** mãe f de aluguel, (P) aluguer

surround /sə'raʊnd/ vt rodear, cercar;
(mil etc) cercar. **~ing** a circundante,
vizinho. **~ings** npl arredores mpl;
(setting) meio m, ambiente m

surveillance /sɜ:'veɪləns/ n vigilância f

survey[1] /sə'veɪ/ vt (landscape etc)
observar; (review) passar em revista;
(inquire about) pesquisar; (land) fazer
o levantamento de; (building) vistoriar,
inspecionar, (P) inspeccionar. **~or** n
(of buildings) fiscal m; (of land)
agrimensor m

survey[2] /'sɜ:veɪ/ n (inspection) vistoria f,
inspeção f, (P) inspecção f; (general
view) panorâmica f; (inquiry)
pesquisa f

survival /sə'vaɪvl/ n sobrevivência f;
(relic) relíquia f, vestígio m

surviv|e /sə'vaɪv/ vt/i sobreviver (a). **~or**
n sobrevivente mf

susceptib|le /sə'septəbl/ a (prone)
suscetível (to a); (sensitive,

impressionable) susceptível, sensível. **~ility** /-'bɪlətɪ/ *n* susceptibilidade *f*

suspect[1] /sə'spekt/ *vt* suspeitar; (*doubt, distrust*) desconfiar de, suspeitar de

suspect[2] /'sʌspekt/ *a & n* suspeito (*m*)

suspen|d /sə'spend/ *vt* (*hang, stop*) suspender; (*from duty etc*) suspender. **~ded sentence** suspensão *f* de pena. **~sion** *n* suspensão *f*. **~sion bridge** ponte *f* suspensa *or* pênsil

suspender /sə'spendə(r)/ *n* (presilha de) liga *f*. **~ belt** *n* cinta-liga *f*, (P) cinta *f* de ligas. **~s** (*Amer: braces*) suspensórios *mpl*

suspense /sə'spens/ *n* ansiedade *f*, incerteza *f*; (*in book etc*) suspense *m*, tensão *f*

suspicion /sə'spɪʃn/ *n* suspeita *f*; (*distrust*) desconfiança *f*; (*trace*) vestígio *m*, (P) traço *m*

suspicious /səs'pɪʃəs/ *a* desconfiado; (*causing suspicion*) suspeito. **be ~ of** desconfiar de. **~ly** *adv* de modo suspeito

sustain /sə'stem/ *vt* (*support*) suster, sustentar; (*suffer*) sofrer; (*keep up*) sustentar; (*jur: uphold*) sancionar; (*interest, effort*) manter. **~ed effort** esforço *m* contínuo

sustenance /'sʌstməns/ *n* (*food*) alimento *m*, sustento *m*

swagger /'swægə(r)/ *vi* pavonear-se, andar com arrogância

swallow[1] /'swɒləʊ/ *vt/i* engolir. **~ up** (*absorb, engulf*) devorar, tragar

swallow[2] /'swɒləʊ/ *n* (*bird*) andorinha *f*

swam /swæm/ *see* **swim**

swamp /swɒmp/ *n* pântano *m*, brejo *m* □ *vt* (*flood, overwhelm*) inundar, submergir. **~y** *a* pantanoso

swan /swɒn/ *n* cisne *m*

swank /swæŋk/ *vi* (*colloq: show off*) gabar-se, mostrar-se (*colloq*)

swap /swɒp/ *vt/i* (*pt* **swapped**) (*colloq*) trocar (**for** por) □ *n* (*colloq*) troca *f*

swarm /swɔːm/ *n* (*of insects, people*) enxame *m* □ *vi* formigar. **~ into** *or* **round** invadir

swarthy /'swɔːðɪ/ *a* (-**ier**, -**iest**) moreno, trigueiro

swat /swɒt/ *vt* (*pt* **swatted**) (*fly etc*) esmagar, esborrachar

sway /sweɪ/ *vt/i* oscilar, balançar (-se); (*influence*) mover, influenciar □ *n* oscilação *f*, balanceio *m*; (*rule*) domínio *m*, poder *m*

swear /sweə(r)/ *vt/i* (*pt* **swore**, *pp* **sworn**) jurar; (*curse*) praguejar, rogar pragas (**at** contra). **~ by** jurar por; (*colloq: recommend*) ter grande fé em. **~word** *n* palavrão *m*

sweat /swet/ *n* suor *m* □ *vi* suar. **~y** *a* suado

sweater /'swetə(r)/ *n* suéter *m*, (P) camisola *f*

sweatshirt /'swetʃɜːt/ *n* suéter *m* de malha *or* algodão

swede /swiːd/ *n* couve-nabo *f*

Swed|e /swiːd/ *n* sueco *m*. **~en** *n* Suécia *f*. **~ish** *a & n* sueco (*m*)

sweep /swiːp/ *vt/i* (*pt* **swept**) varrer; (*go majestically*) avançar majestosamente; (*carry away*) arrastar; (*chimney*) limpar □ *n* (*with broom*) varredela *f*; (*curve*) curva *f*; (*movement*) gesto *m* largo. (**chimney-**)**~** limpa-chaminés *m*. **~ing** *a* (*gesture*) largo; (*action*) de grande alcance. **~ing statement** generalização *f* fácil

sweet /swiːt/ *a* (-**er**, -**est**) doce; (*colloq: charming*) doce, gracinha; (*colloq: pleasant*) agradável □ *n* doce *m*. **~ corn** milho *m*. **~ pea** ervilha-de-cheiro *f*. **~ shop** confeitaria *f*. **have a ~ tooth** gostar de doce. **~ly** *adv* docemente. **~ness** *n* doçura *f*

sweeten /'swiːtn/ *vt* adoçar; (*fig: mitigate*) suavizar. **~er** *n* (*for tea, coffee*) adoçante *m* (artificial); (*colloq: bribe*) agrado *m*

sweetheart /'swiːthɑːt/ *n* namorado *m*, namorada *f*; (*term of endearment*) querido *m*, querida *f*, amor *m*

swell /swel/ *vt/i* (*pt* **swelled**, *pp* **swollen** *or* **swelled**) (*expand*) inchar; (*increase*) aumentar □ *n* (*of sea*) ondulação *f* □ *a* (*colloq: excellent*) excelente; (*colloq: smart*) chique. **~ing** *n* (*med*) inchação *f*, inchaço *m*

swelter /'sweltə(r)/ *vi* fazer um calor abrasador; (*person*) abafar (com calor)

swept /swept/ *see* **sweep**

swerve /swɜːv/ *vi* desviar-se, dar uma guinada

swift /swɪft/ *a* (-**er**, -**est**) rápido, veloz. **~ly** *adv* rapidamente. **~ness** *n* rapidez *f*

swig /swɪg/ *vt* (*pt* **swigged**) (*colloq: drink*) emborcar, beber em longos tragos □ *n* (*colloq*) trago *m*, gole *m*

swill /swɪl/ *vt* passar por água □ *n* (*pig-food*) lavagem *f*, (P) lavadura *f*

swim /swɪm/ *vi* (*pt* **swam**, *pp* **swum**, *pres p* **swimming**) nadar; (*room, head*) rodar □ *vt* atravessar a nado; (*distance*) nadar □ *n* banho *m*. **~mer** *n* nadador *m*. **~ming** *n* natação *f*. **~ming-bath**, **~ming-pool** *ns* piscina *f*. **~ming-cap** *n* touca *f* de banho. **~ming-costume**, **~suit** *ns* maiô *m*, (P) fato *m* de banho. **~ming-trunks** *npl* calção *m* de banho

S

swindle /'swɪndl/ vt trapacear, fraudar, (P) vigarizar ◻ n vigarice f. ~r /-ə(r)/ n vigarista mf

swine /swaɪn/ npl (pigs) porcos mpl ◻ n (pl invar) (colloq: person) animal m, canalha m (colloq)

swing /swɪŋ/ vt/i (pt swung) balançar(-se); (turn round) girar ◻ n (seat) balanço m; (of opinion) reviravolta f; (mus) swing m; (rhythm) ritmo m. **in full** ~ no máximo, em plena atividade, (P) actividade. ~ **round** (of person) virar-se. ~-**bridge/door** ns ponte f/porta f giratória

swipe /swaɪp/ vt (colloq: hit) bater em, dar uma pancada em (colloq); (colloq: steal) afanar, roubar (colloq) ◻ n (colloq: hit) pancada f (colloq). ~ **card** cartão m magnético

swirl /swɜːl/ vi rodopiar, redemoinhar ◻ n turbilhão m, redemoinho m

swish /swɪʃ/ vt/i sibilar, zunir, (fazer) cortar o ar; (with brushing sound) roçar ◻ a (colloq) chique

Swiss /swɪs/ a & n suíço (m)

switch /swɪtʃ/ n interruptor m; (change) mudança f ◻ vt (transfer) transferir; (exchange) trocar ◻ vi desviar-se. ~ **off** desligar

switchboard /'swɪtʃbɔːd/ n (telephone) PBX m, mesa f telefônica

Switzerland /'swɪtsələnd/ n Suíça f

swivel /'swɪvl/ vt/i (pt swivelled) (fazer) girar. ~ **chair** cadeira f giratória

swollen /'swəʊlən/ see **swell** ◻ a inchado

swoop /swuːp/ vi (bird) lançar-se, cair (**down** on sobre); (police) dar uma batida policial, (P) rusga

sword /sɔːd/ n espada f

swore /swɔː(r)/ see **swear**

sworn /swɔːn/ see **swear** ◻ a (enemy) jurado, declarado; (ally) fiel

swot /swɒt/ vt/i (pt swotted) (colloq: study) estudar muito, (P) marrar (sl) ◻ n (colloq) estudante m muito aplicado, (P) marrão m (sl)

swum /swʌm/ see **swim**

swung /swʌŋ/ see **swing**

sycamore /'sɪkəmɔː(r)/ n (maple) sicômoro m, (P) sicómoro m; (Amer: plane) plátano m

syllable /'sɪləbl/ n sílaba f

syllabus /'sɪləbəs/ n (pl -uses) programa m

symbol /'sɪmbl/ n símbolo m. ~**ic(al)** /-'bɒlɪk(l)/ a simbólico. ~**ism** n simbolismo m

symbolize /'sɪmbəlaɪz/ vt simbolizar

symmetr|y /'sɪmətrɪ/ n simetria f. ~**ical** /sɪ'metrɪkl/ a simétrico

sympathize /'sɪmpəθaɪz/ vi ~ **with** ter pena de, condoer-se de; (fig) compartilhar os sentimentos de. ~**r** n simpatizante mf

sympath|y /'sɪmpəθɪ/ n (pity) pena f, compaixão f; (solidarity) solidariedade f; (condolences) pêsames mpl, condolências fpl. **be in** ~**y with** estar de acordo com. ~**etic** /-'θetɪk/ a compreensivo, simpático; (likeable) simpático; (showing pity) compassivo. ~**etically** /-'θetɪklɪ/ adv compassivamente; (fig) compreensivamente

symphon|y /'sɪmfənɪ/ n sinfonia f ◻ a sinfônico, (P) sinfónico. ~**ic** /-'fɒnɪk/ a sinfônico, (P) sinfónico

symptom /'sɪmptəm/ n sintoma m. ~**atic** /-'mætɪk/ a sintomático (**of** de)

synagogue /'sɪnəgɒg/ n sinagoga f

synchronize /'sɪŋkrənaɪz/ vt sincronizar

syndicate /'sɪndɪkət/ n sindicato m

syndrome /'sɪndrəʊm/ n (med) síndrome m, (P) sindroma m

synonym /'sɪnənɪm/ n sinônimo m, (P) sinónimo m. ~**ous** /sɪ'nɒnɪməs/ a sinônimo, (P) sinónimo (**with** de)

synopsis /sɪ'nɒpsɪs/ n (pl -opses /-siːz/) sinopse f, resumo m

syntax /'sɪntæks/ n sintaxe f

synthesis /'sɪnθəsɪs/ n (pl -theses /-siːz/) síntese f

synthetic /sɪn'θetɪk/ a sintético

syphilis /'sɪfɪlɪs/ n sífilis f

Syria /'sɪrɪə/ n Síria f. ~**n** a & n sírio (m)

syringe /sɪ'rɪndʒ/ n seringa f ◻ vt seringar

syrup /'sɪrəp/ n (liquid) xarope m; (treacle) calda f de açúcar. ~**y** a (fig) melado, enjoativo

system /'sɪstəm/ n sistema m; (body) organismo m; (order) método m. ~**atic** /sɪstə'mætɪk/ a sistemático

Tt

tab /tæb/ n (*flap*) lingueta f; (*for fastening, hanging*) aba f; (*label*) etiqueta f; (*loop*) argola f; (*Amer colloq: bill*) conta f. **keep ~s on** (*colloq*) vigiar

table /'teɪbl/ n mesa f; (*list*) tabela f, lista f □ vt (*submit*) apresentar; (*postpone*) adiar. **at ~** à mesa. **lay** or **set the ~** pôr a mesa. **~ of contents** índice m (das matérias). **turn the ~s** inverter as posições. **~-cloth** n toalha de mesa f. **~-mat** n descanso m. **~ tennis** pingue-pongue m

tablespoon /'teɪblspuːn/ n colher f grande de sopa. **~ful** n (*pl* **~fuls**) colher f de sopa cheia

tablet /'tæblɪt/ n (*of stone*) lápide f, placa f; (*drug*) comprimido m

tabloid /'tæblɔɪd/ n tablóide m. **~ journalism** (*pej*) jornalismo m sensacionalista, imprensa f marron

taboo /tə'buː/ n & a tabu (m)

tacit /'tæsɪt/ a tácito

taciturn /'tæsɪtɜːn/ a taciturno

tack /tæk/ n (*nail*) tacha f; (*stitch*) ponto m de alinhavo; (*naut*) amura f; (*fig: course of action*) rumo m □ vt (*nail*) pregar com tachas; (*stitch*) alinhavar □ vi (*naut*) bordejar. **~ on** (*add*) acrescentar, juntar

tackle /'tækl/ n equipamento m, apetrechos mpl; (*sport*) placagem f □ vt (*problem etc*) atacar; (*sport*) placar; (*a thief etc*) agarrar-se a

tacky /'tækɪ/ a (-ier, -iest) peganhento, pegajoso

tact /tækt/ n tato m, (*P*) tacto m. **~ful** a cheio de tato, (*P*) tacto, diplomático. **~fully** adv com tato, (*P*) tacto. **~less** a sem tato, (*P*) tacto. **~lessly** adv sem tato, (*P*) tacto

tactic /'tæktɪk/ n (*expedient*) tática f, (*P*) táctica f. **~s** n(pl) (*procedure*) tática f, (*P*) táctica f. **~al** a tático, (*P*) táctico

tadpole /'tædpəʊl/ n girino m

tag /tæg/ n (*label*) etiqueta f; (*on shoelace*) agulheta f; (*phrase*) chavão m, clichê m □ vi (*pt* tagged) etiquetar; (*add*) juntar □ vi **~ along** (*colloq*) andar atrás, seguir

Tagus /'teɪɡʌs/ n Tejo m

tail /teɪl/ n cauda f, rabo m; (*of shirt*) fralda f. **~s!** (*tossing coin*) coroa! □ vt (*follow*) seguir, vigiar □ vi **~ away** or **off** diminuir, baixar. **~-back** n (*traffic*) fila f, (*P*) bicha f. **~-end** n parte f traseira, cauda f. **~-light** n (*auto*)

farolete m traseiro, (*P*) farolim m da rectaguarda

tailor /'teɪlə(r)/ n alfaiate m □ vt (*garment*) fazer; (*fig: adapt*) adaptar. **~-made** a feito sob medida, (*P*) por medida. **~-made for** (*fig*) feito para, talhado para

tainted /'teɪntɪd/ a (*infected*) contaminado; (*decayed*) estragado; (*fig*) manchado

take /teɪk/ vt/i (*pt* took, *pp* taken) (*get hold of*) agarrar em, pegar em; (*capture*) tomar; (*a seat, a drink; train, bus etc*) tomar; (*carry*) levar (**to** a, para); (*contain, escort*) levar; (*tolerate*) suportar, agüentar, (*P*) aguentar; (*choice, exam*) fazer; (*photo*) tirar; (*require*) exigir. **be ~n by** or **with** ficar encantado com. **be ~n ill** adoecer. **it ~s time to** leva tempo para. **~ after** parecer-se a. **~-away** n (*meal*) comida f para levar, take-away m; (*shop*) loja f que só vende comida para ser consumida em outro lugar. **~ away** levar. **~ away from sb/sth** tirar de alguém/de alg coisa. **~ back** aceitar de volta; (*return*) devolver; (*accompany*) acompanhar; (*statement*) retirar, retratar. **~ down** (*object*) tirar para baixo; (*notes*) tirar, tomar. **~ in** (*garment*) meter para dentro; (*include*) incluir; (*cheat*) enganar, levar (*colloq*); (*grasp*) compreender; (*receive*) receber. **~ it that** supor que. **~ off** vt (*remove*) tirar; (*mimic*) imitar, macaquear □ vi (*aviat*) decolar, levantar vôo. **~-off** n imitação f; (*aviat*) decolagem f, (*P*) descolagem f. **~ on** (*task*) encarregar-se de; (*staff*) admitir, contratar. **~ out** tirar; (*on an outing*) levar para sair. **~ over** vt tomar conta de, assumir a direção, (*P*) direcção de □ vi tomar o poder. **~ over from** (*relieve*) render, substituir; (*succeed*) suceder a. **~-over** n (*pol*) tomada f de poder; (*comm*) take-over m. **~ part** participar or tomar parte (**in** em). **~ place** ocorrer, suceder. **~ sides** tomar partido. **~ sides with** tomar o partido de. **~ to** gostar de, simpatizar com; (*activity*) tomar gosto por, entregar-se a. **~ up** (*object*) apanhar, pegar em; (*hobby*) dedicar-se a; (*occupy*) ocupar, tomar

takings /'teɪkɪnz/ npl receita f

talcum /'tælkəm/ n talco m. **~ powder** pó m talco

tale /teɪl/ n conto m, história f

talent /'tælənt/ n talento m. **~ed** a talentoso, bem dotado

talk /tɔ:k/ vt/i falar; (chat) conversar □ n conversa f; (mode of speech) fala f; (lecture) palestra f. **small ~** conversa f banal. **~ into doing** convencer a fazer. **~ nonsense** dizer disparates. **~ over** discutir. **~ shop** falar de assuntos profissionais. **~to o.s.** falar sozinho, falar com os seus botões. **there's ~ of** fala-se de. **~er** n conversador m. **~ing-to** n (colloq) descompostura f

talkative /'tɔ:kətɪv/ a falador, conversador, tagarela

tall /tɔ:l/ a (-er, -est) alto. **~ story** (colloq) história f do arco-da-velha

tallboy /'tɔ:lbɔɪ/ n cômoda f, (P) cómoda f alta

tally /'tælɪ/ vi corresponder (**with** a), conferir (**with** com)

tambourine /tæmbə'ri:n/ n tamborim m, pandeiro m

tame /teɪm/ a (-er, -est) manso; (domesticated) domesticado; (dull) insípido □ vt amansar, domesticar

tamper /'tæmpə(r)/ vi **~ with** mexer indevidamente em; (text) alterar

tampon /'tæmpən/ n (med) tampão m; (sanitary towel) toalha f higiênica

tan /tæn/ vt/i (pt tanned) queimar, bronzear; (hide) curtir □ n bronzeado m □ a castanho amarelado

tandem /'tændəm/ n (bicycle) tandem m. **in ~** em tandem, um atrás do outro

tang /tæŋ/ n (taste) sabor m or gosto m característico; (smell) cheiro m característico

tangent /'tændʒənt/ n tangente f

tangerine /tændʒə'ri:n/ n tangerina f

tangible /'tændʒəbl/ a tangível

tangle /'tæŋgl/ vt emaranhar, enredar □ n emaranhado m. **become ~d** emaranhar-se, enredar-se

tank /tæŋk/ n tanque m, reservatório m; (for petrol) tanque m, (P) depósito m; (for fish) aquário m; (mil) tanque m

tankard /'tæŋkəd/ n caneca f grande

tanker /'tæŋkə(r)/ n carro-tanque m, camião-cisterna m; (ship) petroleiro m

tantaliz|**e** /'tæntəlaɪz/ vt atormentar, tantalizar. **~ing** a tentador

tantamount /'tæntəmaʊnt/ a **be ~ to** equivaler a

tantrum /'tæntrəm/ n chilique m, ataque m de mau gênio, (P) génio, birra f

tap[1] /tæp/ n (for water etc) torneira f □ vt (pt tapped) (resources) explorar; (telephone) grampear. **on ~** (colloq. available) disponível

tap[2] /tæp/ vt/i (pt tapped) bater levemente. **~-dance** n sapateado m

tape /teɪp/ n (for dressmaking) fita f; (sticky) fita f adesiva. **(magnetic) ~** fita f (magnética) □ vt (tie) atar, prender; (stick) colar; (record) gravar. **~-measure** n fita f métrica. **~ recorder** gravador m

taper /'teɪpə(r)/ n vela f comprida e fina □ vt/i **~ (off)** estreitar (-se), afilar(-se). **~ed, ~ing** adjs (fingers etc) afilado; (trousers) afunilado

tapestry /'tæpɪstrɪ/ n tapeçaria f

tapioca /tæpɪ'əʊkə/ n tapioca f

tar /ta:(r)/ n alcatrão m □ vt (pt tarred) alcatroar

target /'ta:gɪt/ n alvo m □ vt ter como alvo

tariff /'tærɪf/ n tarifa f; (on import) direitos mpl aduaneiros

Tarmac /'ta:mæk/ n macadame (alcatroado) m; (runway) pista f

tarnish /'ta:nɪʃ/ vt/i (fazer) perder o brilho; (stain) manchar

tarpaulin /ta:'pɔ:lɪn/ n lona f impermeável (alcatroada or encerada)

tart[1] /ta:t/ a (-er, -est) ácido; (fig: cutting) mordaz, azedo

tart[2] /ta:t/ n (culin) torta f de fruta, (P) tarte f; (sl: prostitute) prostituta f, mulher f da vida (sl) □ vt **~ up** (colloq) embonecar(-se)

tartan /'ta:tn/ n tecido m escocês □ a escocês

tartar /'ta:tə(r)/ n (on teeth) tártaro m, (P) pedra f. **~ sauce** molho m tártaro

task /ta:sk/ n tarefa f, trabalho m. **take to ~** repreender, censurar. **~ force** (mil) força-tarefa f

tassel /'tæsl/ n borla f

taste /teɪst/ n gosto m; (fig: sample) amostra f □ vt (eat, enjoy) saborear; (try) provar; (perceive taste of) sentir o gosto de □ vi **~ of** or **like** ter o sabor de. **have a ~ of** (experience) provar. **~ful** a de bom gosto. **~fully** adv com bom gosto. **~less** a insípido, insosso; (fig: not in good taste) sem gosto; (fig: in bad taste) de mau gosto

tasty /'teɪstɪ/ a (-ier, -iest) saboroso, gostoso

tat /tæt/ see **tit**[2]

tatter|**s** /'tætəz/ npl farrapos mpl. **~ed** /-əd/ a esfarrapado

tattoo /tə'tu:/ vt tatuar □ n tatuagem f

tatty /'tætɪ/ a (-ier, -iest) (colloq) enxovalhado, em mau estado

taught /tɔ:t/ see **teach**

taunt /tɔ:nt/ vt escarnecer de, zombar de □ n escárnio m. **~ing** a escarninho

Taurus /'tɔ:rəs/ n (astr) Touro m, (P) Taurus m

taut /tɔːt/ a esticado, retesado; (*fig: of nerves*) tenso

tawdry /'tɔːdrɪ/ a (-ier, -iest) espalhafatoso e ordinário

tawny /'tɔːnɪ/ a fulvo

tax /tæks/ n taxa f, imposto m; (*on income*) imposto m de renda, (P) sobre o rendimento ◻ vt taxar, lançar impostos sobre, tributar; (*fig: put to test*) pôr à prova. ~**-collector** n cobrador m de impostos. ~**-free** a isento de imposto. ~ **relief** isenção f de imposto. ~ **return** declaração f do imposto de renda, (P) sobre o rendimento. ~ **year** ano m fiscal. ~**able** a tributável, passível de imposto. ~**ation** /-'seɪʃn/ n impostos mpl, tributação f. ~**ing** a penoso, difícil

taxi /'tæksɪ/ n (pl -is) táxi m ◻ vi (pt **taxied**, pres p **taxiing**) (*aviat*) rolar na pista, taxiar. ~**-cab** n táxi m. ~**-driver** n motorista mf de táxi. ~ **rank**, (*Amer*) ~ **stand** ponto m de táxis, (P) praça f de táxis

taxpayer /'tækspeɪə(r)/ n contribuinte mf

tea /tiː/ n chá m. high ~ refeição f leve à noite. ~**-bag** n saquinho m de chá. ~**-break** n intervalo m para o chá. ~**-cosy** n abafador m. ~**-leaf** n folha f de chá. ~**-set** n serviço m de chá. ~**-shop** n salão m or casa f de chá. ~**-time** n hora f do chá. ~ **towel** n pano m de prato

teach /tiːtʃ/ vt (pt **taught**) ensinar, lecionar, (P) leccionar (**sb sth** alg coisa a alguém) ◻ vi ensinar, ser professor. ~**er** n professor m. ~**ing** n ensino m; (*doctrines*) ensinamento(s) m (pl) a pedagógico, de ensino; (*staff*) docente

teacup /'tiːkʌp/ n xícara f de chá, (P) chávena f

teak /tiːk/ n teca f

team /tiːm/ n equipe f, (P) equipa f; (*of oxen*) junta f; (*of horses*) parelha f ◻ vi ~ **up** juntar-se, associar-se (**with** a). ~**-work** n trabalho m de equipe, (P) equipa

teapot /'tiːpɒt/ n bule m

tear[1] /teə(r)/ vt/i (pt **tore**, pp **torn**) rasgar(-se); (*snatch*) arrancar, puxar; (*rush*) lançar-se, ir numa correria; (*fig*) dividir ◻ n rasgão m. ~ **o.s. away** arrancar-se (**from** de)

tear[2] /tɪə(r)/ n lágrima f. ~**-gas** n gases mpl lacrimogênios, (P) lacrimogénios

tearful /'tɪəfl/ a lacrimoso, choroso. ~**ly** adv choroso, com (as) lágrimas nos olhos

tease /tiːz/ vt implicar; (*make fun of*) caçoar de

teaspoon /'tiːspuːn/ n colher f de chá. ~**ful** n (pl -fuls) colher f de chá cheia

teat /tiːt/ n (*of bottle*) bico m; (*of animal*) teta f

technical /'teknɪkl/ a técnico. ~**ity** /-'kælətɪ/ n questão f de ordem técnica. ~**ly** adv tecnicamente

technician /tek'nɪʃn/ n técnico m

technique /tek'niːk/ n técnica f

technolog|**y** /tek'nɒlədʒɪ/ n tecnologia f. ~**ical** /-ə'lɒdʒɪkl/ a tecnológico

teddy /'tedɪ/ a ~ (**bear**) ursinho m de pelúcia, (P) peluche

tedious /'tiːdɪəs/ a maçante

tedium /'tiːdɪəm/ n tédio m

tee /tiː/ n (*golf*) tee m

teem[1] /tiːm/ vi ~ (**with**) (*swarm*) pulular (de), fervilhar (de), abundar (em)

teem[2] /tiːm/ vi ~ (**with rain**) chover torrencialmente

teenage /'tiːneɪdʒ/ a juvenil, de/para adolescente. ~**r** /-ə(r)/ n jovem mf, adolescente mf

teens /tiːnz/ npl **in one's** ~ na adolescência, entre os 13 e os 19 anos

teeter /'tiːtə(r)/ vi cambalear

teeth /tiːθ/ see **tooth**

teeth|**e** /tiːð/ vi começar a ter dentes. ~**ing troubles** (*fig*) problemas mpl iniciais

teetotaller /tiː'təʊtlə(r)/ n abstêmio m, (P) abstémio m

telecommunications /ˌtelɪkəmjuːnɪ'keɪʃnz/ npl telecomunicações fpl

telegram /'telɪgræm/ n telegrama m

telegraph /'telɪgrɑːf/ n telégrafo m ◻ a telegráfico. ~**ic** /-'græfɪk/ a telegráfico

telepath|**y** /tɪ'lepəθɪ/ n telepatia f. ~**ic** /telɪ'pæθɪk/ a telepático

telephone /'telɪfəʊn/ n telefone m ◻ vt (*person*) telefonar a; (*message*) telefonar ◻ vi telefonar. ~ **book** lista f telefônica, (P) telefónica, guia m telefônico, (P) telefónico. ~ **box**, ~ **booth** cabine f telefônica, (P) telefónica. ~ **call** chamada f. ~ **directory** lista f telefônica, (P) telefónica, guia m telefônico, (P) telefónico. ~ **number** número m de telefone

telephonist /tɪ'lefənɪst/ n (*in exchange*) telefonista mf

telephoto /telɪ'fəʊtəʊ/ n ~ **lens** teleobjetiva f, (P) teleobjectiva f

telescop|**e** /'telɪskəʊp/ n telescópio m ◻ vt/i encaixar(-se). ~**ic** /-'skɒpɪk/ a telescópico

teletext /'telɪtekst/ n teletexto m

televise /'telɪvaɪz/ vt televisionar

t

television /'telɪvɪʒn/ n televisão f. ~ **set** aparelho m de televisão, televisor m

teleworking /'telɪwɜːkɪŋ/ n teletrabalho m

telex /'teleks/ n telex m □ vt transmitir por telex, telexar

tell /tel/ vt (pt **told**) dizer (**sb sth** alg coisa a alguém); (story) contar; (distinguish) distinguir, diferençar □ vi (know) ver-se, saber. **I told you so** bem lhe disse. ~ **of** falar de. ~ **off** (colloq: scold) ralhar, dar uma bronca em. ~ **on** (have effect on) afetar, (P) afectar; (colloq: inform on) fazer queixa de (colloq). ~**-tale** n mexeriqueiro m, fofoqueiro m □ a (revealing) revelador. ~ **tales** mexericar, fofocar

telly /'telɪ/ n (colloq) TV f (colloq)

temp /temp/ n (colloq) empregado m temporário

temper /'tempə(r)/ n humor m, disposição f; (anger) mau humor m □ vt temperar. **keep/lose one's** ~ manter a calma/perder a calma or a cabeça, zangar-se

temperament /'temprəmənt/ n temperamento m. ~**al** /-'mentl/ a caprichoso

temperance /'tempərəns/ n (in drinking) sobriedade f

temperate /'tempərət/ a moderado, comedido; (climate) temperado

temperature /'temprətʃə(r)/ n temperatura f. **have a** ~ estar com or ter febre

tempest /'tempɪst/ n tempestade f, temporal m

tempestuous /tem'pestʃʊəs/ a tempestuoso

template /'templ(e)ɪt/ n molde m

temple[1] /'templ/ n templo m

temple[2] /'templ/ n (anat) têmpora f, fonte f

tempo /'tempəʊ/ n (pl -os) (mus) tempo m; (pace) ritmo m

temporar|y /'temprərɪ/ a temporário, provisório. ~**ily** adv temporariamente, provisoriamente

tempt /tempt/ vt tentar. ~ **sb to do** dar a alguém vontade de fazer, tentar alguém a fazer. ~**ation** /-'teɪʃn/ n tentação f. ~**ing** a tentador

ten /ten/ a & n dez (m)

tenac|ious /tɪ'neɪʃəs/ a tenaz. ~**ity** /-æsətɪ/ n tenacidade f

tenant /'tenənt/ n inquilino m, locatário m

tend[1] /tend/ vt tomar conta de, cuidar de

tend[2] /tend/ vi ~ **to** (be apt to) tender a, ter tendência para

tendency /'tendənsɪ/ n tendência f

tender[1] /'tendə(r)/ a (soft, delicate) terno; (sore, painful) sensível, dolorido; (loving) terno, meigo. ~**-hearted** a compassivo. ~**ly** adv (lovingly) ternamente, meigamente; (delicately) delicadamente. ~**ness** n (love) ternura f, meiguice f

tender[2] /'tendə(r)/ vt (money) oferecer; (apologies, resignation) apresentar □ vi ~ **(for)** apresentar orçamento (para) □ n (comm) orçamento m. **legal** ~ (money) moeda f corrente

tendon /'tendən/ n tendão m

tenement /'tenəmənt/ n prédio m de apartamentos de renda moderada; (Amer: slum) prédio m pobre

tenet /'tenɪt/ n princípio m, dogma m

tennis /'tenɪs/ n tênis m, (P) ténis m. ~ **court** quadra f de tênis, (P) court m de ténis

tenor /'tenə(r)/ n (meaning) teor m; (mus) tenor m

tense[1] /tens/ n (gram) tempo m

tense[2] /tens/ a (-er, -est) tenso □ vt (muscles) retesar

tension /'tenʃn/ n tensão f

tent /tent/ n tenda f, barraca f. ~**-peg** n estaca f

tentacle /'tentəkl/ n tentáculo m

tentative /'tentətɪv/ a provisório; (hesitant) hesitante. ~**ly** adv tentativamente, a título experimental; (hesitantly) hesitantemente

tenterhooks /'tentəhʊks/ npl **on** ~ em suspense

tenth /tenθ/ a & n décimo (m)

tenuous /'tenjʊəs/ a tênue, (P) ténue

tepid /'tepɪd/ a tépido, morno

term /tɜːm/ n (word) termo m; (limit) prazo m, termo m; (schol etc) período m, trimestre m; (Amer) semestre m; (of imprisonment) (duração de) pena f. ~**s** (conditions) condições fpl □ vt designar, denominar, chamar. **on good/bad** ~**s** de boas/más relações. **not on speaking** ~**s** de relações cortadas. **come to** ~**s with** chegar a um acordo com; (become resigned to) resignar-se a. ~ **of office** (pol) mandato m

terminal /'tɜːmɪnl/ a terminal, final; (illness) fatal, mortal □ n (oil, computer) terminal m; (rail) estação f terminal; (electr) borne m. **(air)** ~ terminal m (de avião)

terminat|e /'tɜːmɪneɪt/ vt terminar, pôr termo a □ vi terminar. ~**ion** /-'neɪʃn/ n término m, (P) terminação f, termo m

terminology /tɜːmɪ'nɒlədʒɪ/ n terminologia f

terminus /'tɜːmɪnəs/ n (pl -ni /-naɪ/) (rail, coach) estação f terminal

terrace /'terəs/ n terraço m; (in cultivation) socalco m; (houses) casas fpl em fileira contínua, lance m de casas. **the ~s** (sport) arquibancada f. **~d house** casa f ladeada por outras casas

terrain /te'rem/ n terreno m

terribl|e /'terəbl/ a terrível. **~y** adv terrivelmente; (colloq: very) extremamente, espantosamente

terrific /tə'rɪfɪk/ a terrífico, tremendo; (colloq: excellent; great) tremendo. **~ally** adv (colloq: very) tremendamente (colloq); (colloq: very well) lindamente, maravilhosamente

terrif|y /'terɪfaɪ/ vt aterrar, aterrorizar. **be ~ied of** ter pavor de

territorial /terɪ'tɔːrɪəl/ a territorial

territory /'terɪtərɪ/ n território m

terror /'terə(r)/ n terror m, pavor m

terroris|t /'terərɪst/ n terrorista mf. **~m** /-zəm/ n terrorismo m

terrorize /'terəraɪz/ vt aterrorizar, aterrar

terse /tɜːs/ a conciso, lapidar; (curt) lacónico, (P) lacónico

test /test/ n teste m, exame m, prova f; (schol) teste m, prova f; (of goods) controle m; (of machine etc) ensaio m; (of strength) prova f □ vt examinar; (check) controlar; (try) ensaiar; (pupil) interrogar. **put to the ~** pôr à prova. **~ match** jogo m internacional. **~-tube** n proveta f. **~-tube baby** bebê m de proveta

testament /'testəmənt/ n testamento m. **Old/New T~** Antigo/Novo Testamento m

testicle /'testɪkl/ n testículo m

testify /'testɪfaɪ/ vt/i testificar, testemunhar, depôr

testimonial /testɪ'məʊnɪəl/ n carta f de recomendação

testimony /'testɪmənɪ/ n testemunho m

tetanus /'tetənəs/ n tétano m

tether /'teðə(r)/ vt prender com corda □ n **be at the end of one's ~** estar nas últimas

text /tekst/ n texto m. **~ message** mensagem f escrita □ vt enviar um mensagem de texto a

textbook /'tekstbʊk/ n compêndio m, manual m, livro m de texto

textile /'tekstaɪl/ n & a têxtil (m)

texture /'tekstʃə(r)/ n (of fabric) textura f; (of paper) grão m

Thai /taɪ/ a & n tailandês (m). **~-land** n Tailândia f

Thames /temz/ n Tâmisa m

than /ðæn/; unstressed /ðən/ conj que, do que; (with numbers) de. **more/less ~ ten** mais/menos de dez

thank /θæŋk/ vt agradecer. **~ you!** obrigado! **~s!** (colloq) (P) obrigadinho! (colloq). **~s** npl agradecimentos mpl. **~s to** graças a. **T~sgiving (Day)** (Amer) Dia m de Ação, (P) Acção de Graças

thankful /'θæŋkfl/ a grato, agradecido, reconhecido (**for** por). **~ly** adv com gratidão; (happily) felizmente

thankless /'θæŋklɪs/ a ingrato

that /ðæt/; unstressed /ðət/ a & pron (pl **those**) esse/essa, esses/essas; (more distant) aquele/aquela, aqueles/aquelas; (neuter) isso invar; (more distant) aquilo invar □ adv tão, tanto, de tal modo □ rel pron que □ conj que. **~ boy** esse/aquele rapaz. **what is ~**? o que é isso? **who is ~**? quem é? **is ~ you**? é você? **give me ~** (one) dá-me esse. **~ is (to say)** isto é, quer dizer. **after ~** depois disso. **the day ~** o dia em que. **~ much** tanto assim, tanto como isto

thatch /θætʃ/ n colmo m. **~ed** a de colmo. **~ed cottage** casa f com telhado de colmo

thaw /θɔː/ vt/i derreter(-se), degelar; (food) descongelar □ n degelo m, derretimento m

the /before vowel ðɪ, before consonant ðə, stressed ðiː/ a o, a (pl os, as). **of ~, from ~** do, da (pl dos, das). **at ~, to ~** ao, à (pl aos, às), para o/a/os/as. **in ~** no, na (pl nos, nas). **by ~ hour** a cada hora □ adv **all ~ better** tanto melhor. **~ more… ~ more…** quanto mais… tanto mais…

theatre /'θɪətə(r)/ n teatro m

theatrical /θɪ'ætrɪkl/ a teatral

theft /θeft/ n roubo m

their /ðeə(r)/ a deles, delas, seu

theirs /ðeəz/ poss pron o(s) seu(s), a(s) sua(s), o(s) dele(s), a(s) delas. **it is ~** é (o) deles/delas or o seu

them /ðem/; unstressed /ðəm/ pron os, as; (after prep) eles, elas. **(to) ~** lhes

theme /θiːm/ n tema m. **~ park** parque m temático

themselves /ðəm'selvz/ pron eles mesmos/próprios, elas mesmas/ próprias; (reflexive) se; (after prep) si (mesmos, próprios). **by ~** sozinhos. **with ~** consigo

then /ðen/ adv (at that time) então, nessa altura; (next) depois, em seguida; (in that case) então, nesse caso; (therefore) então, portanto, por conseguinte

theolog|y /θɪ'ɒlədʒɪ/ n teologia f. **~ian** /θɪə'ləʊdʒən/ n teólogo m

t

theorem /'θɪərəm/ n teorema m

theor|y /'θɪərɪ/ n teoria f. ∼**etical** /-'retɪkl/ a teórico

therapeutic /θerə'pju:tɪk/ a terapêutico

therap|y /'θerəpɪ/ n terapia f. ∼**ist** n terapeuta mf

there /ðeə(r)/ adv aí, ali, lá; (over there) lá, acolá □ int (triumphant) pronto, aí está; (consoling) então, vamos lá. **he goes** ∼ ele vai aí or lá. ∼ **he goes** aí vai ele. ∼ **is,** ∼ **are** há. ∼ **you are** (giving) toma. ∼ **and then** logo ali. ∼**abouts** adv por aí. ∼**after** adv daí em diante, depois disso. ∼**by** adv desse modo

therefore /'ðeəfɔ:(r)/ adv por isso, portanto, por conseguinte

thermal /'θɜ:ml/ a térmico

thermometer /θə'mɒmɪtə(r)/ n termômetro m, (P) termómetro m

Thermos /'θɜ:məs/ n garrafa f térmica, (P) termo m

thermostat /'θɜ:məstæt/ n termostato m

thesaurus /θɪ'sɔ:rəs/ n (pl -ri /-raɪ/) dicionário m de sinônimos, (P) sinónimos

these /ði:z/ see **this**

thesis /'θi:sɪs/ n (pl theses /-si:z/) tese f

they /ðeɪ/ pron eles, elas. ∼ **say (that)** ... diz-se or dizem que ...

thick /θɪk/ a (-er, -est) espesso, grosso; (colloq: stupid) estúpido □ adv = **thickly** □ n **in the** ∼ **of** no meio de. ∼**-skinned** a insensível. ∼**ly** adv espessamente; (spread) em camada espessa. ∼**ness** n espessura f, grossura f

thicken /'θɪkən/ vt/i engrossar, espessar (-se). **the plot** ∼**s** o enredo complica-se

thickset /θɪk'set/ a (person) atarracado

thief /θi:f/ n (pl thieves /θi:vz/) ladrão m, gatuno m

thigh /θaɪ/ n coxa f

thimble /'θɪmbl/ n dedal m

thin /θɪn/ a (thinner, thinnest) (slender) estreito, fino, delgado; (lean, not plump) magro; (sparse) ralo, escasso; (flimsy) leve, fino; (soup) aguado; (hair) ralo □ adv = **thinly** □ vt/i (pt thinned) (of liquid) diluir(-se); (of fog etc) dissipar(-se); (of hair) rarear. ∼ **out** (in quantity) diminuir, reduzir; (seedlings etc) desbastar. ∼**ly** adv (sparsely) esparsamente. ∼**ness** n (of board, wire etc) finura f; (of person) magreza f

thing /θɪŋ/ n coisa f. ∼**s** (belongings) pertences mpl. **the best** ∼ **is to** o melhor é. **for one** ∼ em primeiro lugar. **just the** ∼ exatamente o que era preciso. **poor** ∼ coitado

think /θɪŋk/ vt/i (pt thought) pensar (about, of em); (carefully) refletir, (P)

reflectir (about, of em). **I** ∼ **so** eu acho que sim. ∼ **better of it** (change one's mind) pensar melhor. ∼ **nothing of** achar natural. ∼ **of** (hold opinion of) pensar de, achar de. ∼ **over** pensar bem em. ∼**-tank** n comissão f de peritos. ∼ **up** inventar. ∼**er** n pensador m

third /θɜ:d/ a terceiro □ n terceiro m; (fraction) terço m. ∼**-party insurance** seguro m contra terceiros. ∼**-rate** a inferior, medíocre. **T**∼ **World** Terceiro Mundo m. ∼**ly** adv em terceiro lugar

thirst /θɜ:st/ n sede f. ∼**y** a sequioso, sedento. **be** ∼**y** estar com or ter sede. ∼**ily** adv sofregamente

thirteen /θɜ:'ti:n/ a & n treze (m). ∼**th** a & n décimo terceiro (m)

thirt|y /'θɜ:tɪ/ a & n trinta (m). ∼**ieth** a & n trigésimo (m)

this /ðɪs/ a & pron (pl these) este, esta □ pron isto invar. ∼ **one** este, esta. **these ones** estes, estas. ∼ **boy** este rapaz. ∼ **is** isto é. **after** ∼ depois disto. **like** ∼ assim. ∼ **is the man** este é o homem. ∼ **far** até aqui. ∼ **morning** esta manhã. ∼ **Wednesday** esta quarta-feira

thistle /'θɪsl/ n cardo m

thorn /θɔ:n/ n espinho m, pico m. ∼**y** a espinhoso; (fig) bicudo, espinhoso

thorough /'θʌrə/ a conscienciôso; (deep) completo, profundo; (cleaning, washing) a fundo. ∼**ly** adv (clean, study etc) completo, a fundo; (very) perfeitamente, muito bem

thoroughbred /'θʌrəbred/ n (horse etc) puro-sangue m invar

thoroughfare /'θʌrəfeə(r)/ n artéria f. **no** ∼ passagem f proibida

those /ðəʊz/ see **that**

though /ðəʊ/ conj se bem que, embora, conquanto □ adv (colloq) contudo, no entanto

thought /θɔ:t/ see **think** □ n pensamento m; idéia f. **on second** ∼**s** pensando bem

thoughtful /'θɔ:tfl/ a pensativo; (considerate) atencioso, solícito. ∼**ly** adv pensativamente; (considerately) com consideração, atenciosamente

thoughtless /'θɔ:tlɪs/ a irrefletido, (P) irreflectido; (inconsiderate) pouco atencioso. ∼**ly** adv sem pensar; (inconsiderately) sem consideração

thousand /'θaʊznd/ a & n mil (m). ∼**s of** milhares de. ∼**th** a & n milésimo (m)

thrash /θræʃ/ vt surrar, espancar; (defeat) dar uma surra or sova em. ∼ **about** debater-se. ∼ **out** debater a fundo, discutir bem

thread /θred/ n fio m; (for sewing) linha f de coser; (of screw) rosca f ▢ vt enfiar. ~ **one's way** abrir caminho, furar

threadbare /'θredbeə(r)/ a puído, surrado

threat /θret/ n ameaça f

threaten /'θretn/ vt/i ameaçar. ~**ingly** adv com ar ameaçador, ameaçadoramente

three /θri:/ a & n três (m)

thresh /θreʃ/ vt (corn etc) malhar, debulhar

threshold /'θreʃəʊld/ n limiar m, soleira f; (fig) limiar m

threw /θru:/ see **throw**

thrift /θrɪft/ n economia f, poupança f. ~**y** a económico, (P) económico, poupado

thrill /θrɪl/ n arrepio m de emoção, frêmito m, (P) frémito m ▢ vt excitar(-se), emocionar(-se), (fazer) vibrar. **be ~ed** estar/ficar encantado. ~**ing** a excitante, emocionante

thriller /'θrɪlə(r)/ n livro m or filme m de suspense

thriv|e /θraɪv/ vi (pt **thrived** or **throve**, pp **thrived** or **thriven**) prosperar, florescer; (grow strong) crescer, dar-se bem (**on** com). ~**ing** a próspero

throat /θrəʊt/ n garganta f. **have a sore ~** ter dores de garganta

throb /θrɒb/ vi (pt **throbbed**) (wound, head) latejar; (heart) palpitar, bater; (engine; fig) vibrar, trepidar ▢ n (of pain) latejo m, espasmo m; (of heart) palpitação f, batida f; (of engine) vibração f, trepidação f. ~**bing** a (pain) latejante

throes /θrəʊz/ npl **in the ~ of** (fig) às voltas com, no meio de

thrombosis /θrɒm'bəʊsɪs/ n trombose f

throne /θrəʊn/ n trono m

throng /θrɒŋ/ n multidão f ▢ vt/i apinhar(-se); (arrive) afluir

throttle /'θrɒtl/ n (auto) válvula-borboleta f, estrangulador m, acelerador m de mão ▢ vt estrangular

through /θru:/ prep através de, por; (during) durante; (by means or way of, out of) por; (by reason of) por, por causa de ▢ adv através; (entirely) completamente, até o fim ▢ a (train, traffic etc) direto, (P) directo. **be ~** ter acabado (**with** com); (telephone) estar ligado. **come** or **go ~** (cross, pierce) atravessar. **get ~** (exam) passar. **be wet ~** estar ensopado or encharcado

throughout /θru:'aʊt/ prep durante, por todo. ~ **the country** por todo o país afora. ~ **the day** durante todo a dia, pelo dia afora ▢ adv completamente;

(place) por toda a parte; (time) durante todo o tempo

throw /θrəʊ/ vt (pt **threw**, pp **thrown**) atirar, jogar, lançar; (colloq: baffle) desconcertar ▢ n lançamento m; (of dice) lance m. ~ **a party** (colloq) dar uma festa. ~ **away** jogar fora, (P) deitar fora. ~ **off** (get rid of) livrar-se de. ~ **out** (person) expulsar; (reject) rejeitar. ~ **over** (desert) abandonar, deixar. ~ **up** (one's arms) levantar; (resign from) abandonar; (colloq: vomit) vomitar

thrush /θrʌʃ/ n (bird) tordo m

thrust /θrʌst/ vt (pt **thrust**) arremeter, empurrar, impelir ▢ n empurrão m, arremetida f. ~ **into** (put) meter em, mergulhar em. ~ **upon** (force on) impôr a

thud /θʌd/ n som m surdo, baque m

thug /θʌg/ n bandido m, facínora m, malfeitor m

thumb /θʌm/ n polegar m ▢ vt (book) manusear. ~ **a lift** pedir carona, (P) boleia. **under sb's ~** completamente dominado por alguém. ~-**index** n índice m de dedo

thumbtack /'θʌmtæk/ n (Amer) percevejo m

thump /θʌmp/ vt/i bater (em), dar pancadas (em); (with fists) dar murros (em); (piano) martelar (em); (of heart) bater com força ▢ n pancada f; (thud) baque m. ~**ing** a (colloq) enorme

thunder /'θʌndə(r)/ n trovão m, trovoada f; (loud noise) estrondo m ▢ vi (weather, person) trovejar. ~ **past** passar como um raio. ~**y** a (weather) tempestuoso

thunderbolt /'θʌndəbəʊlt/ n raio m e ribombo m de trovão; (fig) raio m fulminante (fig)

thunderstorm /'θʌndəstɔ:m/ n tempestade f com trovoadas, temporal m

Thursday /'θɜ:zdɪ/ n quinta-feira f

thus /ðʌs/ adv assim, desta maneira. ~ **far** até aqui

thwart /θwɔ:t/ vt frustrar, contrariar

thyme /taɪm/ n tomilho m

tiara /tɪ'ɑ:rə/ n tiara f, diadema m

tic /tɪk/ n tique m

tick[1] /tɪk/ n (sound) tique-taque m; (mark) sinal m; (colloq: moment) instantinho m ▢ vi fazer tique-taque ▢ vt ~ (**off**) marcar com sinal. ~ **off** (colloq: scold) dar uma bronca em (colloq). ~ **over** (engine, factory) funcionar em marcha lenta, (P) no "ralenti"

tick[2] /tɪk/ n (insect) carrapato m

t

ticket /ˈtɪkɪt/ n bilhete m; (label)
etiqueta f; (for traffic offence) aviso m
de multa. **~-collector** n (railway)
guarda m. **~-office** n bilheteira f

tickle /ˈtɪkl/ vt fazer cócegas; (fig: amuse)
divertir □ n cócegas fpl, comichão m

ticklish /ˈtɪklɪʃ/ a coceguento, sensível a
cócegas; (fig) delicado, melindroso

tidal /ˈtaɪdl/ a de marés, que tem marés.
~ wave onda f gigantesca; (fig) onda f
de sentimento popular

tiddly-winks /ˈtɪdlɪwɪŋks/ n (game) jogo
m da pulga

tide /taɪd/ n maré f; (of events) marcha f,
curso m. **high ~** maré f cheia, preia-
mar f. **low ~** maré f baixa, baixa-mar
f □ vt **~ over** (help temporarily)
aguentar, (P) aguentar

tid|y /ˈtaɪdɪ/ a (-ier, -iest) (room)
arrumado; (appearance, work) asseado,
cuidado; (methodical) bem ordenado;
(colloq: amount) belo (colloq) □ vt
arrumar, arranjar. **~ily** adv com
cuidado. **~iness** n arrumação f,
ordem f

tie /taɪ/ vt (pres p **tying**) atar, amarrar,
prender; (link) ligar, vincular; (a knot)
dar, fazer □ vi (sport) empatar □ n fio m,
cordel m; (necktie) gravata f, (link) laço
m, vínculo m; (sport) empate m. **~ in
with** estar ligado com, relacionar-se
com. **~ up** amarrar, atar; (animal)
prender; (money) imobilizar; (occupy)
ocupar

tier /tɪə(r)/ n cada fila f, camada f,
prateleira f etc colocada em cima de
outra; (in stadium) bancada f; (of cake)
andar m; (of society) camada f

tiff /tɪf/ n arrufo m

tiger /ˈtaɪgə(r)/ n tigre m

tight /taɪt/ a (-er, -est) (clothes) apertado,
justo; (rope) esticado, tenso; (control)
rigoroso; (knot, schedule, lid) apertado;
(colloq: drunk) embriagado (colloq)
□ adv = **tightly. be in a ~ corner** (fig)
estar em apuros or num aperto, (P)
estar entalado (colloq). **~-fisted** a
sovina, pão-duro, (P) agarrado (colloq).
~ly adv bem; (squeeze) com força

tighten /ˈtaɪtn/ vt/i (rope) esticar; (bolt,
control) apertar. **~ up on** apertar o
cinto

tightrope /ˈtaɪtrəʊp/ n corda f (de
acrobacias). **~ walker** funâmbulo m

tights /taɪts/ npl collants mpl, meias-
colant fpl

tile /taɪl/ n (on wall, floor) ladrilho m,
azulejo m; (on roof) telha f □ vt
ladrilhar, pôr azulejos em; (roof)
telhar, cobrir com telhas

till[1] /tɪl/ vt (land) cultivar

till[2] /tɪl/ prep & conj = **until**

till[3] /tɪl/ n caixa (registadora) f

tilt /tɪlt/ vt/i inclinar(-se), pender □ n
(slope) inclinação f. **(at) full ~** a toda a
velocidade

timber /ˈtɪmbə(r)/ n madeira f (de
construção); (trees) árvores fpl

time /taɪm/ n tempo m; (moment)
momento m; (epoch) época f, tempo m;
(by clock) horas fpl; (occasion) vez f;
(rhythm) compasso m. **~s** (multiplying)
vezes □ vt escolher a hora para;
(measure) marcar o tempo de; (sport)
cronometrar; (regulate) acertar. **at ~s**
às vezes. **for the ~ being** por agora,
por enquanto. **from ~ to ~** de vez em
quando. **have a good ~** divertir-se.
have no ~ for não ter paciência
para. **in no ~** num instante. **in ~** a
tempo; (eventually) com o tempo. **in
two days' ~** daqui a dois dias. **on ~** na
hora, (P) a horas. **take your ~** não se
apresse. **what's the ~?** que horas são?
~ bomb bomba-relógio f. **~-limit** n
prazo m. **~ off** tempo m livre.
~-sharing n time-sharing m. **~ zone**
fuso m horário

timeless /ˈtaɪmlɪs/ a intemporal;
(unending) eterno

timely /ˈtaɪmlɪ/ a oportuno

timer /ˈtaɪmə(r)/ n (techn) relógio m;
(with sand) ampulheta f

timetable /ˈtaɪmteɪbl/ n horário m

timid /ˈtɪmɪd/ a tímido; (fearful)
assustadiço, medroso. **~ly** adv
timidamente

timing /ˈtaɪmɪŋ/ n (measuring)
cronometragem f; (of artist) ritmo m;
(moment) cálculo m do tempo, timing
m. **good/bad ~** (moment) momento m
bem/mal escolhido

tin /tɪn/ n estanho m; (container) lata f
□ vt (pt **tinned**) estanhar; (food)
enlatar. **~ foil** papel m de alumínio.
~-opener n abridor m de latas, (P)
abre-latas m. **~ plate** lata f,
folha(-de-Flandes) f. **~ned foods**
conservas fpl. **~ny** a (sound) metálico

tinge /tɪndʒ/ vt **~ (with)** tingir (de); (fig)
dar um toque (de) □ n tom m, matiz m;
(fig) toque m

tingle /ˈtɪŋgl/ vi (sting) arder; (prickle)
picar □ n ardor m; (prickle) picadela f

tinker /ˈtɪŋkə(r)/ n latoeiro m ambulante
□ vi **~ (with)** mexer (em), tentar
consertar

tinkle /ˈtɪŋkl/ n tinido m, tilintar m □ vt/i
tilintar

tinsel /ˈtɪnsl/ n fio m prateado/dourado,
enfeites mpl metálicos de Natal; (fig)
falso brilho m, ouropel m

tint /tɪnt/ n tom m, matiz m; (for hair)
tintura f, tinta f □ vt tingir, colorir

tiny /'taɪnɪ/ a (-ier, -iest) minúsculo, pequenino

tip¹ /tɪp/ n ponta f. **(have sth) on the ~ of one's tongue** ter alg coisa na ponta de língua

tip² /tɪp/ vt/i (pt tipped) (tilt) inclinar(-se); (overturn) virar(-se); (pour) colocar, (P) deitar; (empty) despejar(-se) □ n (money) gorjeta f; (advice) sugestão f, dica f(colloq); (for rubbish) lixeira f. **~ off** avisar, prevenir. **~-off** n (warning) aviso m; (information) informação f

tipsy /'tɪpsɪ/ a ligeiramente embriagado, alegre, tocado

tiptoe /'tɪptəʊ/ n **on ~** na ponta dos pés

tir|e¹ /'taɪə(r)/ vt/i cansar(-se) (of de). **~eless** a incansável, infatigável. **~ing** a fatigante, cansativo

tire² /'taɪə(r)/ n (Amer) pneu m

tired /'taɪəd/ a cansado, fatigado. **~ of** (sick of) farto de. **~ out** morto de cansaço

tiresome /'taɪəsəm/ a maçador, aborrecido, chato (sl)

tissue /'tɪʃuː/ n tecido m; (handkerchief) lenço m de papel. **~-paper** n papel m de seda

tit¹ /tɪt/ n (bird) chapim m, canário-da-terra m

tit² /tɪt/ **give ~ for tat** pagar na mesma moeda

titbit /'tɪtbɪt/ n petisco m

titillate /'tɪtɪleɪt/ vt excitar, titilar, (P) dar gozo a

title /'taɪtl/ n título m. **~-deed** n título m de propriedade. **~-page** n página f de rosto, (P) frontispício m. **~-role** n papel m principal

titter /'tɪtə(r)/ vi rir com riso abafado

to /tuː/; unstressed /tə/ prep a, para; (as far as) até; (towards) para; (of attitude) para (com) □ adv **push** or **pull ~** (close) fechar. **~ Portugal** (for a short time) a Portugal; (to stay) para Portugal. **~ the baker's** para o padeiro, (P) ao padeiro. **~ do/sit/etc** (infinitive) fazer/sentar-se/etc; (expressing purpose) para fazer/para se sentar/etc. **it's ten ~ six** são dez para as seis, faltam dez para as seis. **go ~ and** fro andar de um lado para outro. **husband/etc-~-be** n futuro marido m/etc. **~-do** n (fuss) agitação f, alvoroço m

toad /təʊd/ n sapo m

toadstool /'təʊdstuːl/ n cogumelo m venenoso

toady /'təʊdɪ/ n lambe-botas mf, puxa-saco m □ vi puxar saco

toast /təʊst/ n fatia f de pão torrado, torrada f; (drink) brinde m, saúde f □ vt

(bread) torrar; (drink to) brindar, beber à saúde de. **~er** n torradeira f

tobacco /tə'bækəʊ/ n tabaco m

tobacconist /tə'bækənɪst/ n vendedor m de tabaco, homem m da tabacaria (colloq). **~'s shop** tabacaria f

toboggan /tə'bɒgən/ n tobogã m, (P) toboggan m

today /tə'deɪ/ n & adv hoje (m)

toddler /'tɒdlə(r)/ n criança f que está aprendendo a andar

toe /təʊ/ n dedo m do pé; (of shoe, stocking) biqueira f □ vt **~ the line** andar na linha. **on one's ~s** alerta, vigilante. **~-hold** n apoio (precário) m. **~-nail** n unha f do dedo do pé

toffee /'tɒfɪ/ n puxa-puxa m, (P) caramelo m. **~-apple** n maçã f caramelizada

together /tə'geðə(r)/ adv junto, juntamente, juntos; (at the same time) ao mesmo tempo. **~ with** juntamente com. **~ness** n camaradagem f, companheirismo m

toil /tɔɪl/ vi labutar □ n labuta f, labor m

toilet /'tɔɪlɪt/ n banheiro m, (P) casa f de banho; (grooming) toalete f. **~-paper** n papel m higiénico, (P) higiénico. **~-roll** n rolo m de papel higiénico, (P) higiénico. **~ water** água-de-colônia f

toiletries /'tɔɪlɪtrɪz/ npl artigos mpl de toalete

token /'təʊkən/ n sinal m, prova f; (voucher) cheque m; (coin) ficha f □ a simbólico

told /təʊld/ see tell □ a **all ~** (all in all) ao todo

tolerabl|e /'tɒlərəbl/ a tolerável; (not bad) sofrível, razoável. **~y** adv (work, play) razoavelmente

toleran|t /'tɒlərənt/ a tolerante (of para com). **~ce** n tolerância f. **~tly** adv com tolerância

tolerate /'tɒləreɪt/ vt tolerar

toll¹ /təʊl/ n pedágio m, (P) portagem f. **~ death** n número m de mortos. **take its ~ (of age)** fazer sentir o seu peso

toll² /təʊl/ vt/i (of bell) dobrar

tomato /tə'mɑːtəʊ/ n (pl -oes) tomate m

tomb /tuːm/ n túmulo m, sepultura f

tomboy /'tɒmbɔɪ/ n menina f levada (e masculinizada), (P) maria-rapaz f

tombstone /'tuːmstəʊn/ n lápide f, pedra f tumular

tome /təʊm/ n tomo m, volume m

tomfoolery /tɒm'fuːlərɪ/ n disparates mpl, imbecilidades fpl

tomorrow /tə'mɒrəʊ/ n & adv amanhã (m). **~ morning/night** amanhã de manhã/à noite

ton /tʌn/ n tonelada f (= 1016 kg). **(metric) ~** tonelada f (= 1000 kg). **~s of**

(*colloq*) montes de (*colloq*), (*P*) carradas de (*colloq*)

tone /təʊn/ *n* tom *m*; (*of radio, telephone etc*) sinal *m*; (*colour*) tom *m*, tonalidade *f*; (*med*) tonicidade *f* □ *vt* ~ **down** atenuar □ *vi* ~ **in** combinar-se, harmonizar-se (**with** com). ~ **up** (*muscles*) tonificar. ~**-deaf** *a* sem ouvido musical

tongs /tɒŋz/ *n* tenaz *f*; (*for sugar*) pinça *f*; (*for hair*) pinça *f*

tongue /tʌŋ/ *n* língua *f*. ~**-in-cheek** *a* & *adv* sem ser a sério, com ironia. ~**-tied** *a* calado. ~**-twister** *n* travalíngua *m*

tonic /'tɒnɪk/ *n* (*med*) tônico *m*, (*P*) tónico *m*; (*mus*) tónica *f*, (*P*) tónica *f* □ *a* tônico, (*P*) tónico

tonight /tə'naɪt/ *adv* & *n* hoje à noite, logo à noite, esta noite (*f*)

tonne /tʌn/ *n* (*metric*) tonelada *f*

tonsil /'tɒnsl/ *n* amígdala *f*

tonsillitis /tɒnsɪ'laɪtɪs/ *n* amigdalite *f*

too /tu:/ *adv* demasiado, demais; (*also*) também, igualmente; (*colloq: very*) muito. ~ **many** *a* demais, demasiados. ~ **much** *a* & *adv* demais, demasiado

took /tʊk/ *see* take

tool /tu:l/ *n* (*carpenter's, plumber's etc*) ferramenta *f*; (*gardener's*) utensílio *m*; (*fig: person*) joguete *m*. ~**-bag** *n* saco *m* de ferramenta

toot /tu:t/ *n* toque *m* de buzina □ *vt/i* ~ (**the horn**) buzinar

tooth /tu:θ/ *n* (*pl* **teeth**) dente *m*. ~**less** *a* desdentado

toothache /'tu:θeɪk/ *n* dor *f* de dentes

toothbrush /'tu:θbrʌʃ/ *n* escova *f* de dentes

toothpaste /'tu:θpeɪst/ *n* pasta *f* de dentes, dentifrício *m*

toothpick /'tu:θpɪk/ *n* palito *m*

top[1] /tɒp/ *n* (*highest point; upper part*) alto *m*, cimo *m*, topo *m*; (*of hill; fig*) cume *m*; (*upper surface*) cimo *m*, topo *m*; (*surface of table*) tampo *m*; (*lid*) tampa *f*; (*of bottle*) rolha *f*; (*of list*) cabeça *f* □ *a* (*shelf etc*) de cima, superior; (*in rank*) primeiro; (*best*) melhor; (*distinguished*) eminente; (*maximum*) máximo □ *vt* (*pt* **topped**) (*exceed*) ultrapassar, ir acima de. **from** ~ **to bottom** de alto a baixo. **on** ~ **of** em cima de; (*fig*) além de. **on** ~ **of that** ainda por cima. ~ **gear** (*auto*) a velocidade mais alta. ~ **hat** chapéu *m* alto. ~**-heavy** *a* mais pesado na parte de cima. ~ **secret** ultra-secreto. ~ **up** encher; (*mobiles*) recarregar ~**ped with** coberto de

top[2] /tɒp/ *n* (*toy*) pião *m*. **sleep like a** ~ dormir como uma pedra

topic /'tɒpɪk/ *n* tópico *m*, assunto *m*

topical /'tɒpɪkl/ *a* da atualidade, (*P*) actualidade, corrente

topless /'tɒplɪs/ *a* com o peito nu, topless

topple /'tɒpl/ *vt/i* (fazer) desabar, (fazer) tombar, (fazer) cair

torch /tɔ:tʃ/ *n* (*electric*) lanterna *f* elétrica, (*P*) eléctrica; (*flaming*) archote *m*, facho *m*

tore /tɔ:(r)/ *see* tear[1]

torment[1] /'tɔ:mənt/ *n* tormento *m*

torment[2] /tɔ:'ment/ *vt* atormentar, torturar; (*annoy*) aborrecer, chatear

torn /tɔ:n/ *see* tear[1]

tornado /tɔ:'neɪdəʊ/ *n* (*pl* **-oes**) tornado *m*

torpedo /tɔ:'pi:dəʊ/ *n* (*pl* **-oes**) torpedo *m* □ *vt* torpedear

torrent /'tɒrənt/ *n* torrente *f*. ~**ial** /tə'renʃl/ *a* torrencial

torrid /'tɒrɪd/ *a* (*climate etc*) tórrido; (*fig*) intenso, ardente

torso /'tɔ:səʊ/ *n* (*pl* **-os**) torso *m*

tortoise /'tɔ:təs/ *n* tartaruga *f*

tortoiseshell /'tɔ:təsʃel/ *n* (*for ornaments etc*) tartaruga *f*

tortuous /'tɔ:tʃʊəs/ *a* (*of path etc*) que dá muitas voltas, sinuoso; (*fig*) tortuoso, retorcido

torture /'tɔ:tʃə(r)/ *n* tortura *f*, suplício *m* □ *vt* torturar. ~**r** /-ə(r)/ *n* carrasco *m*, algoz *m*, torturador *m*

Tory /'tɔ:rɪ/ *a* & *n* (*colloq*) conservador (*m*), (*P*) tóri (*m*)

toss /tɒs/ *vt* atirar, jogar, (*P*) deitar; (*shake*) agitar, sacudir □ *vi* agitar-se, debater-se. ~ **a coin**, ~ **up** tirar cara ou coroa

tot[1] /tɒt/ *n* criancinha *f*; (*colloq: glass*) copinho *m*

tot[2] /tɒt/ *vt/i* (*pt* **totted**) ~ **up** (*colloq*) somar

total /'təʊtl/ *a* & *n* total (*m*) □ *vt* (*pt* **totalled**) (*find total of*) totalizar; (*amount to*) elevar-se a, montar a. ~**ity** /-'tælətɪ/ *n* totalidade *f*. ~**ly** *adv* totalmente

totalitarian /təʊtælɪ'teərɪən/ *a* totalitário

totter /'tɒtə(r)/ *vi* cambalear, andar aos tombos; (*of tower etc*) oscilar

touch /tʌtʃ/ *vt/i* tocar; (*of ends, gardens etc*) tocar-se; (*tamper with*) mexer em; (*affect*) comover □ *n* (*sense*) tato *m*, (*P*) tacto *m*; (*contact*) toque *m*; (*of colour*) toque *m*, retoque *m*. **a** ~ **of** (*small amount*) um pouco de. **get in** ~ **with** entrar em contato, (*P*) contacto com. **lose** ~ perder contato, (*P*) contacto. ~ **down** (*aviat*) aterrissar, (*P*) aterrar. ~ **off** disparar; (*cause*) dar início a, desencadear. ~ **on** (*mention*) tocar em.

~ **up** retocar. ~**-and-go** *a* (*risky*) arriscado; (*uncertain*) duvidoso, incerto. ~**-line** *n* linha *f* lateral

touching /'tʌtʃɪŋ/ *a* comovente, comovedor

touchy /'tʌtʃɪ/ *a* melindroso, suscetível, (*P*) susceptível, que se ofende facilmente

tough /tʌf/ *a* (**-er, -est**) (*hard, difficult; relentless*) duro; (*strong*) forte, resistente □ *n* ~ **(guy)** valentão *m*, durão *m* (*colloq*). ~ **luck!** (*colloq*) pouca sorte! ~**ness** *n* dureza *f*; (*strength*) força *f*, resistência *f*

toughen /'tʌfn/ *vt*/*i* (*person*) endurecer; (*strengthen*) reforçar

tour /tʊə(r)/ *n* viagem *f*; (*visit*) visita *f*; (*by team etc*) tournée *f* □ *vt* visitar. **on** ~ em tournée

tourism /'tʊərɪzəm/ *n* turismo *m*

tourist /'tʊərɪst/ *n* turista *mf* □ *a* turístico. ~ **office** agência *f* de turismo

tournament /'tʊərnəmənt/ *n* torneio *m*

tousle /'taʊzl/ *vt* despentear, esguedelhar

tout /taʊt/ *vi* angariar clientes (**for** para) □ *vt* (*try to sell*) tentar revender □ *n* (*hotel etc*) angariador *m*; (*ticket*) cambista *m*, (*P*) revendedor *m*

tow /təʊ/ *vt* rebocar □ *n* reboque *m*. **on** ~ a reboque. ~ **away** (*vehicle*) rebocar. ~**-path** *n* caminho *m* de sirga. ~**-rope** *n* cabo *m* de reboque

toward(s) /tə'wɔ:d(z)/ *prep* para, em direção, (*P*) direcção a, na direção, (*P*) direcção de; (*of attitude*) para com; (*time*) por volta de

towel /'taʊəl/ *n* toalha *f*; (*tea towel*) pano *m* de prato □ *vt* (*pt* **towelled**) esfregar com a toalha. ~**-rail** *n* toalheiro *m*. ~**ling** *n* atoalhado *m*, (*P*) pano *m* turco

tower /'taʊə(r)/ *n* torre *f* □ *vi* ~ **above** dominar. ~ **block** prédio *m* alto. ~**ing** *a* muito alto; (*fig: of rage etc*) violento

town /taʊn/ *n* cidade *f*. **go to** ~ (*colloq*) perder a cabeça (*colloq*). ~ **council** município *m*. ~ **hall** câmara *f* municipal. ~ **planning** urbanização *f*

toxic /'tɒksɪk/ *a* tóxico

toy /tɔɪ/ *n* brinquedo *m* □ *vi* ~ **with** (*object*) brincar com; (*idea*) considerar, cogitar

trace /treɪs/ *n* traço *m*, rastro *m*, sinal *m*; (*small quantity*) traço *m*, vestígio *m* □ *vt* seguir *or* encontrar a pista de; (*draw*) traçar; (*with tracing-paper*) decalcar

tracing /'treɪsɪŋ/ *n* decalque *m*, desenho *m*. ~**-paper** *n* papel *m* vegetal

track /træk/ *n* (*of person etc*) rastro *m*, pista *f*; (*race-track, of tape*) pista *f*; (*record*) faixa *f*; (*path*) trilho *m*, carreiro *m*; (*rail*) via *f* □ *vt* seguir a pista *or* a trajetória, (*P*) trajectória de. **keep** ~ **of** manter-se em contato com; (*keep oneself informed*) seguir. ~ **down** (*find*) encontrar, descobrir; (*hunt*) seguir a pista de. ~ **suit** conjunto *m* de jogging, (*P*) fato *m* de treino

tract /trækt/ *n* (*land*) extensão *f*; (*anat*) aparelho *m*

tractor /'træktə(r)/ *n* trator *m*, (*P*) tractor *m*

trade /treɪd/ *n* comércio *m*; (*job*) ofício *m*, profissão *f*; (*swap*) troca *f* □ *vt*/*i* comerciar (em), negociar (em) □ *vt* (*swap*) trocar. ~ **in** (*used article*) trocar. ~**-in** *n* troca *f*. ~ **mark** marca *f* de fábrica. ~ **on** (*exploit*) tirar partido de, abusar de. ~ **union** sindicato *m*. ~**r** /-ə(r)/ *n* negociante *mf*, comerciante *mf*

tradesman /'treɪdzmən/ *n* (*pl* **-men**) comerciante *m*

trading /'treɪdɪŋ/ *n* comércio *m*. ~ **estate** zona *f* industrial

tradition /trə'dɪʃn/ *n* tradição *f*. ~**al** *a* tradicional

traffic /'træfɪk/ *n* (*trade*) tráfego *m*, tráfico *m*; (*on road*) trânsito *m*, tráfego *m*; (*aviat*) tráfego *m* □ *vi* (*pt* **trafficked**) traficar (**in** em). ~ **circle** (*Amer*) giratória *f*, (*P*) rotunda *f*. ~ **island** ilha *f* de pedestres, (*P*) refúgio *m* para peões. ~ **jam** engarrafamento *m*. ~**-lights** *npl* sinal *m* luminoso, (*P*) semáforo *m*. ~ **warden** guarda *mf* de trânsito. ~**ker** *n* traficante *mf*

tragedy /'trædʒədɪ/ *n* tragédia *f*.

tragic /'trædʒɪk/ *a* trágico

trail /treɪl/ *vt*/*i* arrastar(-se), rastejar; (*of plant, on ground*) rastejar; (*of plant, over wall*) trepar; (*track*) seguir □ *n* (*of powder, smoke etc*) esteira *f*, rastro *m*, (*P*) rasto *m*; (*track*) pista *f*; (*beaten path*) trilho *m*

trailer /'treɪlə(r)/ *n* reboque *m*; (*Amer: caravan*) reboque *m*, caravana *f*, trailer *m*; (*film*) trailer *m*, apresentação *f* de filme

train /treɪn/ *n* (*rail*) trem *m*, (*P*) comboio *m*; (*procession*) fila *f*; (*of dress*) cauda *f*; (*retinue*) comitiva *f* □ *vt* (*instruct, develop*) educar, formar, treinar; (*plant*) guiar; (*sportsman, animal*) treinar; (*aim*) assestar, apontar □ *vi* estudar, treinar-se. ~**ed** *a* (*skilled*) qualificado; (*doctor etc*) diplomado. ~**er** *n* (*sport*) treinador *m*; (*shoe*) tênis *m*. ~**ing** *n* treino *m*

trainee /treɪ'ni:/ *n* estagiário *m*

trait /treɪ(t)/ *n* traço *m*, característica *f*

traitor /'treɪtə(r)/ *n* traidor *m*

tram /træm/ *n* bonde *m*, (*P*) (carro) eléctrico *m*

tramp /træmp/ *vi* marchar (com passo pesado) □ *vt* percorrer, palmilhar □ *n* som *m* de passos pesados; (*vagrant*) vagabundo *m*, andarilho *m*; (*hike*) longa caminhada *f*

trample /'træmpl/ *vt/i* ~ **(on)** pisar com força; (*fig*) menosprezar

trampoline /'træmpəli:n/ *n* (lona *f* usada como) trampolim *m*

trance /tra:ns/ *n* (*hypnotic*) transe *m*; (*ecstasy*) êxtase *m*, arrebatamento *m*; (*med*) estupor *m*

tranquil /'træŋkwɪl/ *a* tranqüilo, (*P*) tranquilo, sossegado. ~**lity** /-'kwɪlətɪ/ *n* tranqüilidade *f*, (*P*) tranquilidade *f*, sossego *m*

tranquillizer /'træŋkwɪlaɪzə(r)/ *n* (*drug*) tranqüilizante *m*, (*P*) tranquilizante *m*, calmante *m*

transact /træn'zækt/ *vt* (*business*) fazer, efetuar, (*P*) efectuar. ~**ion** /-kʃn/ *n* transação *f*, (*P*) transacção *f*

transcend /træn'send/ *vt* transcender. ~**ent** *a* transcendente

transcri|be /træn'skraɪb/ *vt* transcrever. ~**pt**, ~**ption** /-ɪpʃn/ *ns* transcrição *f*

transfer[1] /træns'fɜ:(r)/ *vt* (*pt* **transferred**) transferir; (*power, property*) transmitir □ *vi* mudar, ser transferido; (*change planes etc*) fazer transferência. ~ **the charges** (*telephone*) ligar a cobrar

transfer[2] /'trænsfə(r)/ *n* transferência *f*; (*of power, property*) transmissão *f*; (*image*) decalcomania *f*

transfigure /træns'fɪgə(r)/ *vt* transfigurar

transform /træns'fɔ:m/ *vt* transformar. ~**ation** /-ə'meɪʃn/ *n* transformação *f*. ~**er** *n* (*electr*) transformador *m*

transfusion /træns'fju:ʒn/ *n* (*of blood*) transfusão *f*

transient /'trænzɪənt/ *a* transitório, transiente, efêmero, (*P*) efémero, passageiro

transistor /træn'zɪstə(r)/ *n* (*device, radio*) transistor *m*

transit /'trænsɪt/ *n* trânsito *m*. **in** ~ em trânsito

transition /træn'zɪʃn/ *n* transição *f*. ~**al** *a* transitório

transitive /'trænsətɪv/ *a* transitivo

transitory /'trænsɪtərɪ/ *a* transitório

translat|e /trænz'leɪt/ *vt* traduzir. ~**ion** /-ʃn/ *n* tradução *f*. ~**or** *n* tradutor *m*

translucent /trænz'lu:snt/ *a* translúcido

transmi|t /trænz'mɪt/ *vt* (*pt* **transmitted**) transmitir. ~**ssion** *n* transmissão *f*. ~**tter** *n* transmissor *m*

transparen|t /træns'pærənt/ *a* transparente. ~**cy** *n* transparência *f*; (*photo*) diapositivo *m*

transpire /træn'spaɪə(r)/ *vi* (*secret etc*) transpirar; (*happen*) suceder, acontecer

transplant[1] /træns'pla:nt/ *vt* transplantar

transplant[2] /'trænspla:nt/ *n* (*med*) transplantação *f*, transplante *m*

transport[1] /træn'spɔ:t/ *vt* (*carry, delight*) transportar. ~**ation** /-'teɪʃn/ *n* transporte *m*

transport[2] /'trænspɔ:t/ *n* (*of goods, delight etc*) transporte *m*

transpose /træn'spəʊz/ *vt* transpor

transverse /'trænzvɜ:s/ *a* transversal

transvestite /trænz'vestaɪt/ *n* travesti *mf*

trap /træp/ *n* armadilha *f*, ratoeira *f*, cilada *f* □ *vt* (*pt* **trapped**) apanhar na armadilha; (*cut off*) prender, bloquear. ~**per** *n* caçador *m* de armadilha (esp de peles)

trapdoor /træp'dɔ:(r)/ *n* alçapão *m*

trapeze /trə'pi:z/ *n* trapézio *m*

trash /træʃ/ *n* (*worthless stuff*) porcaria *f*; (*refuse*) lixo *m*; (*nonsense*) disparates *mpl*. ~ **can** *n* (*Amer*) lata *f* do lixo, (*P*) caixote *m* do lixo. ~**y** *a* que não vale nada, porcaria

trauma /'trɔ:mə/ *n* trauma *m*, traumatismo *m*. ~**tic** /-'mætɪk/ *a* traumático

travel /'trævl/ *vi* (*pt* **travelled**) viajar; (*of vehicle, bullet, sound*) ir □ *vt* percorrer □ *n* viagem *f*. ~ **agent** agente *mf* de viagem. ~**ler** *n* viajante *mf*. ~**ler's cheque** cheque *m* de viagem. ~**ling** *n* viagem *f*, viagens *fpl*, viajar *m*

travesty /'trævəstɪ/ *n* paródia *f*, caricatura *f*

trawler /'trɔ:lə(r)/ *n* traineira *f*, (*P*) arrastão *m*

tray /treɪ/ *n* tabuleiro *m*, bandeja *f*

treacherous /'tretʃərəs/ *a* traiçoeiro

treachery /'tretʃərɪ/ *n* traição *f*, perfídia *f*, deslealdade *f*

treacle /'tri:kl/ *n* melaço *m*

tread /tred/ *vt/i* (*pt* **trod**, *pp* **trodden**) (*step*) pisar; (*walk*) andar, caminhar; (*walk along*) seguir □ *n* passo *m*, maneira *f* de andar; (*of tyre*) trilho *m*. ~ **sth into** (*carpet*) esmigalhar alg coisa sobre/em

treason /'tri:zn/ *n* traição *f*

treasure /'treʒə(r)/ *n* tesouro *m* □ *vt* ter o maior apreço por; (*store*) guardar bem guardado. ~**r** *n* tesoureiro *m*

treasury /'treʒərɪ/ *n* (*building*) tesouraria *f*; (*department*) Ministério *m* das Finanças *or* da Fazenda; (*fig*) tesouro *m*

treat /tri:t/ *vt/i* tratar □ *n* (*pleasure*) prazer *m*, regalo *m*; (*present*) mimo *m*, gentileza *f*. ∼ **sb to sth** convidar alguém para alg coisa

treatise /'tri:tɪz/ *n* tratado *m*

treatment /'tri:tmənt/ *n* tratamento *m*

treaty /'tri:tɪ/ *n* (*pact*) tratado *m*

trebl|e /'trebl/ *a* triplo □ *vt/i* triplicar □ *n* (*mus: voice*) soprano *m*. ∼**y** *adv* triplamente

tree /tri:/ *n* árvore *f*

trek /trek/ *n* viagem *f* penosa; (*walk*) caminhada *f* □ *vi* (*pt* **trekked**) viajar penosamente; (*walk*) caminhar

trellis /'trelɪs/ *n* grade *f* para trepadeiras, treliça *f*

tremble /'trembl/ *vi* tremer

tremendous /trɪ'mendəs/ *a* (*fearful, huge*) tremendo; (*colloq: excellent*) fantástico, formidável

tremor /'tremə(r)/ *n* tremor *m*, estremecimento *m*. (**earth**) ∼ abalo (sísmico) *m*, tremor *m* de terra

trench /trentʃ/ *n* fossa *f*, vala *f*; (*mil*) trincheira *f*

trend /trend/ *n* tendência *f*; (*fashion*) moda *f*. ∼**y** *a* (*colloq*) na última moda, (*P*) na berra (*colloq*)

trepidation /trepɪ'deɪʃn/ *n* (*fear*) receio *m*, apreensão *f*

trespass /'trespəs/ *vi* entrar ilegalmente (**on** em). **no** ∼**ing** entrada *f* proibida. ∼**er** *n* intruso *m*

trestle /'tresl/ *n* cavalete *m*, armação *f* de mesa. ∼**-table** *n* mesa *f* de cavaletes

trial /'traɪəl/ *n* (*jur*) julgamento *m*, processo *m*; (*test*) ensaio *m*, experiência *f*, prova *f*; (*ordeal*) provação *f*. **on** ∼ em julgamento. ∼ **and error** tentativas *fpl*

triang|le /'traɪæŋgl/ *n* triângulo *m*. ∼**ular** /-'æŋgjʊlə(r)/ *a* triangular

trib|e /traɪb/ *n* tribó *f*. ∼**al** *a* tribal

tribulation /trɪbjʊ'leɪʃn/ *n* tribulação *f*

tribunal /traɪ'bju:nl/ *n* tribunal *m*

tributary /'trɪbjʊtərɪ/ *n* afluente *m*, tributário *m*

tribute /'trɪbju:t/ *n* tributo *m*. **pay** ∼ **to** prestar homenagem a, render tributo a

trick /trɪk/ *n* truque *m*; (*prank*) partida *f*; (*habit*) jeito *m* □ *vt* enganar. **do the** ∼ (*colloq: work*) dar resultado

trickery /'trɪkərɪ/ *n* trapaça *f*

trickle /'trɪkl/ *vi* pingar, gotejar, escorrer □ *n* fio *m* de água *etc*; (*fig: small number*) punhado *m*

tricky /'trɪkɪ/ *a* (*crafty*) manhoso; (*problem*) delicado, complicado

tricycle /'traɪsɪkl/ *n* triciclo *m*

trifle /'traɪfl/ *n* ninharia *f*, bagatela *f*; (*sweet*) sobremesa *f* feita de pão-de-ló e frutas e creme □ *vi* ∼ **with** brincar com. **a** ∼ um pouquinho, (*P*) um poucochinho

trifling /'traɪflɪŋ/ *a* insignificante

trigger /'trɪgə(r)/ *n* (*of gun*) gatilho *m* □ *vt* ∼ (**off**) (*initiate*) desencadear, despoletar

trill /trɪl/ *n* trinado *m*, gorjeio *m*

trilogy /'trɪlədʒɪ/ *n* trilogia *f*

trim /trɪm/ *a* (**trimmer, trimmest**) bem arranjado, bem cuidado; (*figure*) elegante, esbelto □ *vt* (*pt* **trimmed**) (*cut*) aparar; (*sails*) orientar, marear; (*ornament*) enfeitar, guarnecer (**with** com) □ *n* (*cut*) aparadela *f*, corte *m* leve; (*decoration*) enfeite *m*; (*on car*) acabamento(s) *m*(*pl*), estofado *m*. **in** ∼ em ordem; (*fit*) em boa forma. ∼**ming(s)** *n*(*pl*) (*dress*) enfeite *m*; (*culin*) guarnição *f*, acompanhamento *m*

Trinity /'trɪnətɪ/ *n* **the (Holy)** ∼ a Santíssima Trindade

trinket /'trɪŋkɪt/ *n* bugiganga *f*; (*jewel*) bijuteria *f*, berloque *m*

trio /'tri:əʊ/ *n* (*pl* -**os**) trio *m*

trip /trɪp/ *vi* (*pt* **tripped**) (*stumble*) tropeçar, dar um passo em falso; (*go or dance lightly*) andar/dançar com passos leves □ *vt* ∼ (**up**) fazer tropeçar, passar uma rasteira a □ *n* (*journey*) viagem *f*; (*outing*) passeio *m*, excursão *f*; (*stumble*) tropeção *m*, passo *m* em falso

tripe /traɪp/ *n* (*food*) dobrada *f*, tripas *fpl*; (*colloq: nonsense*) disparates *mpl*

triple /'trɪpl/ *a* triplo, tríplice □ *vt/i* triplicar. ∼**ts** /-plɪts/ *npl* trigémeos *mpl*, (*P*) trigémeos *mpl*

triplicate /'trɪplɪkət/ *n* **in** ∼ em triplicata

tripod /'traɪpɒd/ *n* tripé *m*

trite /traɪt/ *a* banal, corriqueiro

triumph /'traɪəmf/ *n* triunfo *m* □ *vi* triunfar (**over** sobre); (*exult*) exultar, rejubilar-se. ∼**al** /-'ʌmfl/ *a* triunfal. ∼**ant** /-'ʌmfənt/ *a* triunfante. ∼**antly** /-'ʌmfəntlɪ/ *adv* em triunfo, triunfantemente

trivial /'trɪvɪəl/ *a* insignificante

trod, trodden /trɒd, 'trɒdn/ *see* **tread**

trolley /'trɒlɪ/ *n* carrinho *m*. (**tea-**) ∼ carrinho *m* de chá

trombone /trɒm'bəʊn/ *n* (*mus*) trombone *m*

troop /tru:p/ *n* bando *m*, grupo *m*. ∼**s** (*mil*) tropas *fpl* □ *vi* ∼ **in/out** entrar/ sair em bando *or* grupo. ∼**ing the colour** a saudação da bandeira. ∼**er** *n* soldado *m* de cavalaria

trophy /'trəʊfɪ/ *n* troféu *m*

tropic /'trɒpɪk/ *n* trópico *m*. ∼**s** trópicos *mpl*. ∼**al** *a* tropical

t

trot /trɒt/ n trote m ◻ vi (pt **trotted**) trotar; (of person) correr em passos curtos, ir num or a trote (colloq). **on the ~** (colloq) a seguir, a fio. **~ out** (colloq: produce) exibir; (colloq: state) desfiar

trouble /'trʌbl/ n (difficulty) dificuldade(s) f (pl), problema(s) m (pl); (distress) desgosto(s) m (pl), aborrecimento(s) m (pl); (pains, effort) cuidado m, trabalho m, maçada f; (inconvenience) transtorno m, incómodo m, (P) incómodo m; (med) doença f. **~(s)** (unrest) agitação f, conflito(s) m (pl) ◻ vt/i (bother) incomodar(-se), (P) maçar(-se); (worry) preocupar(-se); (agitate) perturbar. **be in ~** estar em apuros, estar em dificuldades. **get into ~** meter-se em encrenca/apuros. **it is not worth the ~** não vale a pena. **~-maker** n desordeiro m, provocador m. **~-shooter** n mediador m, negociador m. **~d** a agitado, perturbado; (of sleep) agitado; (of water) turvo

troublesome /'trʌblsəm/ a problemático, importuno, (P) maçador

trough /trɒf/ n (drinking) bebedouro m; (feeding) comedouro m. **~ (of low pressure)** depressão f, linha f de baixa pressão

trounce /traʊns/ vt (defeat) esmagar; (thrash) espancar

troupe /tru:p/ n (theat) companhia f, troupe f

trousers /'traʊzəz/ npl calça f, (P) calças fpl. **short ~** calções mpl

trousseau /'tru:səʊ/ n (pl -s /-əʊz/) (of bride) enxoval m de noiva

trout /traʊt/ n (pl invar) truta f

trowel /'traʊəl/ n (garden) colher f de jardineiro; (for mortar) trolha f

truan|t /'tru:ənt/ n absenteísta mf, (P) absentista mf; (schol) gazeteiro m. **play ~t** fazer gazeta. **~cy** n absenteísmo m, (P) absentismo m

truce /tru:s/ n trégua(s) f (pl), armistício m

truck /trʌk/ n (lorry) camião m; (barrow) carro m de bagageiro; (wagon) vagão m aberto. **~-driver** n motorista mf de camião, (P) camionista mf

truculent /'trʌkjʊlənt/ a agressivo, brigão

trudge /trʌdʒ/ vi caminhar com dificuldade, caminhar a custo, arrastar-se

true /tru:/ a (-er, -est) verdadeiro; (accurate) exato, (P) exacto; (faithful) fiel. **come ~** (happen) realizar-se, concretizar-se. **it is ~** é verdade

truffle /'trʌfl/ n trufa f

truism /'tru:izəm/ n truísmo m, verdade f evidente, (P) verdade f do Amigo Banana (colloq)

truly /'tru:lɪ/ adv verdadeiramente; (faithfully) fielmente; (truthfully) sinceramente

trump /trʌmp/ n trunfo m ◻ vt jogar trunfo, trunfar. **~ up** forjar, inventar. **~ card** carta f de trunfo; (colloq: valuable resource) trunfo m

trumpet /'trʌmpɪt/ n trombeta f

truncheon /'trʌntʃən/ n cassetete m, (P) cassetête m

trundle /'trʌndl/ vt/i (fazer) rolar ruidosamente/pesadamente

trunk /trʌŋk/ n (of tree, body) tronco m; (of elephant) tromba f; (box) mala f grande; (Amer, auto) mala f. **~s** (for swimming) calção m de banho. **~ call** n chamada f interurbana. **~ road** n estrada f nacional

truss /trʌs/ n (med) funda f ◻ vt atar, amarrar

trust /trʌst/ n confiança f; (association) truste m, (P) trust m, consórcio m; (foundation) fundação f; (responsibility) responsabilidade f; (jur) fideicomisso m ◻ vt (rely on) ter confiança em, confiar em; (hope) esperar ◻ vi **~ in** or **to** confiar em. **in ~** em fideicomisso. **on ~** (without proof) sem verificação prévia; (on credit) a crédito. **~ sb with** confiar em alguém. **~ed** a (friend etc) de confiança, seguro. **~ful, ~ing** adjs confiante. **~y** a fiel

trustee /trʌs'ti:/ n administrador m; (jur) fideicomissório m

trustworthy /'trʌstwɜːðɪ/ a (digno) de confiança

truth /tru:θ/ n (pl -s /tru:ðz/) verdade f. **~ful** a (account etc) verídico; (person) verdadeiro, que fala verdade. **~fully** adv sinceramente

try /traɪ/ vt/i (pt **tried**) tentar, experimentar; (be a strain on) cansar, pôr à prova; (jur) julgar ◻ n (attempt) tentativa f, experiência f; (Rugby) ensaio m. **~ for** (post, scholarship) candidatar-se a; (record) tentar alcançar. **~ on** (clothes) provar. **~ out** experimentar. **~ to do** tentar fazer. **~ing** a difícil

tsar /zɑː(r)/ n czar m

T-shirt /'tiːʃɜːt/ n T-shirt f, camiseta f de algodão de mangas curtas

tub /tʌb/ n selha f; (colloq: bath) tina f, banheira f

tuba /'tjuːbə/ n (mus) tuba f

tubby /'tʌbɪ/ a (-ier, -iest) baixote e gorducho

tub|e /tjuːb/ n tubo m; (colloq: railway) metrô m. **inner ~e** câmara f de ar. **~ing** n tubos mpl, tubagem f

tuber /'tjuːbə(r)/ n tubérculo m

tuberculosis /tjuːbɜːkjuˈləʊsɪs/ n tuberculose f

tubular /ˈtjuːbjʊlə(r)/ a tubular

tuck /tʌk/ n (fold) prega f cosida; (for shortening or ornament) refego m □ vt/i fazer pregas; (put) guardar, meter, enfiar; (hide) esconder. ~ **in** or **into** (colloq: eat) atacar. ~ **in** (shirt) meter as fraldas para dentro; (blanket) prender em; (person) cobrir bem, aconchegar. ~**-shop** n (schol) loja f de balas, (P) pastelaria f (junto à escola)

Tuesday /ˈtjuːzdɪ/ n terça-feira f

tuft /tʌft/ n tufo m

tug /tʌg/ vt/i (pt **tugged**) puxar com força; (vessel) rebocar □ n (boat) rebocador m; (pull) puxão m. ~ **of war** cabo-de-guerra m, (P) jogo m da guerra

tuition /tjuːˈɪʃn/ n ensino m

tulip /ˈtjuːlɪp/ n tulipa f

tumble /ˈtʌmbl/ vi tombar, baquear, dar um trambolhão □ n tombo m, trambolhão m. ~**-drier** n máquina f de secar (roupa)

tumbledown /ˈtʌmbldaʊn/ a em ruínas

tumbler /ˈtʌmblə(r)/ n copo m

tummy /ˈtʌmɪ/ n (colloq: stomach) estômago m; (colloq: abdomen) barriga f. ~**ache** n (colloq) dor f de barriga/de estômago

tumour /ˈtjuːmə(r)/ n tumor m

tumult /ˈtjuːmʌlt/ n tumulto m. ~**uous** /-ˈmʌltʃʊəs/ a tumultuado, barulhento, agitado

tuna /ˈtjuːnə/ n (pl invar) atum m

tune /tjuːn/ n melodia f □ vt (engine) regular; (piano etc) afinar □ vi ~ **in** (**to**) (radio, TV) ligar (em), (P) sintonizar. ~ **up** afinar. **be in** ~/**out of** ~ (instrument) estar afinado/ desafinado; (singer) cantar afinado/ desafinado. ~**ful** a melodioso, harmonioso. ~**r** n afinador m; (radio) sintonizador m

tunic /ˈtjuːnɪk/ n túnica f

Tunisia /tjuːˈnɪzɪə/ n Tunísia f. ~**n** a & n tunisiano (m), (P) tunisino (m)

tunnel /ˈtʌnl/ n túnel m □ vi (pt **tunnelled**) abrir um túnel (**into** em)

turban /ˈtɜːbən/ n turbante m

turbine /ˈtɜːbaɪn/ n turbina f

turbo- /ˈtɜːbəʊ/ pref turbo-

turbot /ˈtɜːbət/ n rodovalho m

turbulen|t /ˈtɜːbjʊlənt/ a turbulento. ~**ce** n turbulência f

tureen /təˈriːn/ n terrina f

turf /tɜːf/ n (pl **turfs** or **turves**) gramado m, (P) relva f, relvado m □ vt ~ **out** (colloq) jogar fora, (P) deitar fora. **the** ~ (racing) turfe m, hipismo m. ~ **accountant** corretor m de apostas

turgid /ˈtɜːdʒɪd/ a (speech, style) pomposo, empolado

Turk /tɜːk/ n turco m. ~**ey** n Turquia f. ~**ish** a turco m □ n (lang) turco m

turkey /ˈtɜːkɪ/ n peru m

turmoil /ˈtɜːmɔɪl/ n agitação f, confusão f, desordem f. **in** ~ em ebulição

turn /tɜːn/ vt/i virar(-se), voltar (-se), girar; (change) transformar (-se) (**into** em); (become) ficar, tornar-se; (corner) virar, dobrar; (page) virar, voltar □ n volta f; (in road) curva f; (of mind, events) mudança f; (occasion, opportunity) vez f; (colloq) ataque m, crise f; (colloq: shock) susto m. **do a good** ~ prestar (um) serviço. **in** ~ por sua vez, sucessivamente. **speak out of** ~ dizer o que não se deve, cometer uma indiscrição. **take** ~**s** revezar-se. ~ **of the century** virada f do século. ~ **against** virar-se or voltar-se contra. ~ **away** vi virar-se or voltar-se para o outro lado □ vt (avert) desviar; (reject) recusar; (send back) mandar embora. ~ **back** vi (return) voltar; (vehicle) dar meia volta, voltar para trás □ vt (fold) dobrar para trás. ~ **down** recusar; (fold) dobrar para baixo; (reduce) baixar. ~ **in** (hand in) entregar; (colloq: go to bed) deitar-se. ~ **off** (light etc) apagar; (tap) fechar; (road) virar (para rua transversal). ~ **on** (light etc) acender, ligar; (tap) abrir. ~ **out** vt (light) apagar; (empty) esvaziar, despejar; (pocket) virar do avesso; (produce) produzir □ vi (transpire) vir a saber-se, descobrir-se; (colloq: come) aparecer. ~ **round** virar-se, voltar-se. ~ **up** vi aparecer, chegar; (be found) aparecer □ vt (find) desenterrar; (increase) aumentar; (collar) levantar. ~**-out** n assistência f. ~**-up** n (of trousers) dobra f

turning /ˈtɜːnɪŋ/ n rua f transversal; (corner) esquina f. ~**-point** n momento m decisivo

turnip /ˈtɜːnɪp/ n nabo m

turnover /ˈtɜːnəʊvə(r)/ n (pie, tart) pastel m, empada f; (money) faturamento m, (P) facturação f; (of staff) rotatividade f

turnpike /ˈtɜːnpaɪk/ n (Amer) auto-estrada f com pedágio, (P) portagem

turnstile /ˈtɜːnstaɪl/ n (gate) torniquete m, borboleta f

turntable /ˈtɜːnteɪbl/ n (for record) prato m do toca-disco, (P) giradiscos; (record-player) toca-disco m, (P) giradiscos m

turpentine /ˈtɜːpəntaɪn/ n terebentina f, aguarrás m

turquoise /ˈtɜːkwɔɪz/ a turquesa invar

turret /ˈtʌrɪt/ n torreão m, torrinha f

t

turtle /'tɜ:tl/ n tartaruga-do-mar f.
~**-neck** a de gola alta

tusk /tʌsk/ n (tooth) presa f; (elephant's)
defesa f, dente m

tussle /'tʌsl/ n luta f, briga f

tutor /'tju:tə(r)/ n professor m particular;
(univ) professor m universitário

tutorial /tju:'tɔ:rɪəl/ n (univ) seminário m

TV /ti:'vi:/ n tevê f

twaddle /'twɒdl/ n disparates mpl

twang /twæŋ/ n (mus) som m duma corda
esticada; (in voice) nasalação f □ vt/i
(mus) (fazer) vibrar, dedilhar

tweet /twi:t/ n pio m, pipilom □ ~vi
pipilar

tweezers /'twi:zəz/ npl pinça f

twel|ve /twelv/ a & n doze (m). ~
(**o'clock**) doze horas. ~**fth** a & n
décimo segundo (m). **T~fth Night**
véspera f de Reis

twent|y /'twentɪ/ a & n vinte (m). ~**ieth** a
& n vigésimo (m)

twice /twaɪs/ adv duas vezes

twiddle /'twɪdl/ vt/i ~ (**with**) (fiddle
with) torcer, brincar (com). ~ **one's
thumbs** girar os polegares

twig /twɪg/ n galho m, graveto m

twilight /'twaɪlaɪt/ n crepúsculo m □ a
crepuscular

twin /twɪn/ n & a gêmeo (m), (P) gémeo
(m) □ vt (pt **twinned**) (pair)
emparelhar, emparceirar. ~ **beds** par
m de camas de solteiro. ~**ning** n
emparelhamento m

twine /twaɪn/ n guita f, cordel m □ vt/i
(weave together) entrançar; (wind)
enroscar(-se)

twinge /twɪndʒ/ n dor f aguda e súbita,
pontada f; (fig) pontada f, (P) ferroada f

twinkle /'twɪŋkl/ vi cintilar, brilhar □ n
cintilação f, brilho m

twirl /twɜ:l/ vt/i (fazer) girar;
(moustache) torcer

twist /twɪst/ vt torcer; (weave together)
entrançar; (roll) enrolar; (distort)
torcer, deturpar □ vi (rope etc) torcer-
se, enrolar-se; (road) dar voltas ou
curvas, serpentear □ n (act of twisting)
torcedura f, (P) torcedela f; (of rope) nó
m; (of events) reviravolta f. ~ **sb's arm**
(fig) forçar alguém

twit /twɪt/ n (colloq) idiota mf

twitch /twɪtʃ/ vt/i contrair(-se) □ n (tic)
tique m; (jerk) puxão m

two /tu:/ a & n dois (m). **in** or **of** ~ **minds**
indeciso. **put** ~ **and** ~ **together** tirar
conclusões. ~**-faced** a de duas caras,
hipócrita. ~**-piece** n (garment)
duas-peças m invar. ~**-seater** n (car)
carro m de dois lugares. ~**-way** a (of
road) mão dupla

twosome /'tu:səm/ n par m

tycoon /taɪ'ku:n/ n magnata m

tying /'taɪŋ/ see **tie**

type /taɪp/ n (example, print) tipo m;
(kind) tipo m, gênero m, (P) género m;
(colloq: person) cara m, (P) tipo m
(colloq) □ vt/i (write) bater à máquina,
datilografar, (P) dactilografar

typescript /'taɪpskrɪpt/ n texto m
datilografado, (P) dactilografado

typewrit|er /'taɪpraɪtə(r)/ n máquina f
de escrever. ~**ten** /-ɪtn/ a batido à
máquina, datilografado, (P)
dactilografado

typhoid /'taɪfɔɪd/ n ~ (**fever**) febre f
tifóide

typhoon /taɪ'fu:n/ n tufão m

typical /'tɪpɪkl/ a típico. ~**ly** adv
tipicamente

typify /'tɪpɪfaɪ/ vt ser o (protó)tipo de,
tipificar

typing /'taɪpɪŋ/ n datilografia f, (P)
dactilografia f

typist /'taɪpɪst/ n datilógrafa f, (P)
dactilógrafa f

tyrann|y /'tɪrənɪ/ n tirania f. ~**ical**
/tɪ'rænɪkl/ a tirânico

tyrant /'taɪərənt/ n tirano m

tyre /'taɪə(r)/ n pneu m

Uu

ubiquitous /ju:'bɪkwɪtəs/ a ubíquo,
onmipresente

udder /'ʌdər/ n úbere m

UFO /'ju:fəʊ/ n OVNI m

ugl|y /'ʌglɪ/ a (-ier, -iest) feio. ~**iness** n
feiúra f, (P) fealdade f

UK abbr see **United Kingdom**

ulcer /'ʌlsə(r)/ n úlcera f

ulterior /ʌl'tɪərɪə(r)/ a ulterior. ~ **motive**
razão f inconfessada, segundas
intenções fpl

ultimate /'ʌltɪmət/ a último, derradeiro;
(definitive) definitivo; (maximum)
supremo; (basic) fundamental. ~**ly** adv
finalmente

ultimatum /ʌltɪ'meɪtəm/ n (pl -**ums**)
ultimato n

ultra- /'ʌltrə/ pref ultra-, super-

ultraviolet /ʌltrə'vaɪələt/ a ultravioleta

umbilical /ʌm'bɪlɪkl/ a ~ **cord** cordão m
umbilical

umbrage /'ʌmbrɪdʒ/ n take ~ (at sth)
ofender-se or melindrar-se (com alg
coisa)

umbrella /ʌm'brelə/ *n* guarda-chuva *m*

umpire /'ʌmpaɪə(r)/ *n* (*sport*) àrbitro *m*
□ *vt* arbitrar

umpteen /'ʌmpti:n/ *a* (*sl*) sem conta, montes de (*colloq*). **for the ~th time** (*sl*) pela centésima *or* enésima vez

UN *abbr* (*United Nations*) ONU *f*

un- /ʌn/ *pref* não, pouco

unable /ʌn'eɪbl/ *a* **be ~ to do** ser incapaz de/não poder fazer

unabridged /ʌnə'brɪdʒd/ *a* (*text*) integral

unacceptable /ʌnək'septəbl/ *a* inaceitável, inadmissível

unaccompanied /ʌnə'kʌmpənɪd/ *a* só, desacompanhado

unaccountable /ʌnə'kaʊntəbl/ *a* (*strange*) inexplicável; (*not responsible*) que não tem que dar contas

unaccustomed /ʌnə'kʌstəmd/ *a* desacostumado. **~ to** não acostumado *or* não habituado a

unadulterated /ʌnə'dʌltəreɪtɪd/ *a* (*pure, sheer*) puro

unaided /ʌn'eɪdɪd/ *a* sem ajuda, sozinho, por si só

unanim|ous /ju:'nænɪməs/ *a* unânime. **~ity** /-ə'nɪmətɪ/ *n* unanimidade *f*. **~ously** *adv* unânimemente, por unanimidade

unarmed /ʌn'a:md/ *a* desarmado, indefeso

unashamed /ʌnə'ʃeɪmd/ *a* desavergonhado, sem vergonha. **~ly** /-ɪdlɪ/ *adv* sem vergonha

unassuming /ʌnə'sju:mɪŋ/ *a* modesto, despretencioso

unattached /ʌnə'tætʃt/ *a* (*person*) livre

unattainable /ʌnə'teɪnəbl/ *a* inacessível

unattended /ʌnə'tendɪd/ *a* (*person*) desacompanhado; (*car, luggage*) abandonado

unattractive /ʌnə'træktɪv/ *a* sem atrativos, (*P*) atractivos; (*offer*) de pouco interesse

unauthorized /ʌn'ɔ:θəraɪzd/ *a* não-autorizado, sem autorização

unavoidabl|e /ʌnə'vɔɪdəbl/ *a* inevitável. **~y** *adv* inevitavelmente

unaware /ʌnə'weə(r)/ *a* **be ~ of** desconhecer, ignorar, não ter consciência de. **~s** /-eəz/ *adv* (*unexpectedly*) inesperadamente. **catch sb ~s** apanhar alguém desprevenido

unbalanced /ʌn'bælənst/ *a* (*mind, person*) desequilibrado

unbearable /ʌn'beərəbl/ *a* insuportável

unbeat|able /ʌn'bi:təbl/ *a* imbatível. **~en** *a* não vencido, invicto; (*unsurpassed*) insuperado

unbeknown(st) /ʌnbɪ'nəʊn(st)/ *a* **~ to** (*colloq*) sem o conhecimento de

unbelievable /ʌnbɪ'li:vəbl/ *a* inacreditável, incrível

unbend /ʌn'bend/ *vi* (*pt* **unbent**) (*relax*) descontrair. **~ing** *a* inflexível

unbiased /ʌn'baɪəst/ *a* imparcial

unblock /ʌn'blɒk/ *vt* desbloquear, desobstruir; (*pipe*) desentupir

unborn /ʌn'bɔ:n/ *a* por nascer; (*future*) vindouro, futuro

unbounded /ʌn'baʊndɪd/ *a* ilimitado

unbreakable /ʌn'breɪkəbl/ *a* inquebrável

unbridled /ʌn'braɪdld/ *a* desequilibrado, (*P*) desenfreado

unbroken /ʌn'brəʊkən/ *a* (*intact*) intato, (*P*) intacto, inteiro; (*continuous*) ininterrupto

unburden /ʌn'bɜ:dn/ *vpr* **~ o.s.** (*open one's heart*) desabafar (**to** com)

unbutton /ʌn'bʌtn/ *vt* desabotoar

uncalled-for /ʌn'kɔ:ldfɔ:(r)/ *a* injustificável, gratuito

uncanny /ʌn'kænɪ/ *a* (**-ier, -iest**) estranho, misterioso

unceasing /ʌn'si:sɪŋ/ *a* incessante

unceremonious /ʌnserɪ'məʊnɪəs/ *a* sem cerimónia, (*P*) cerimónia, brusco

uncertain /ʌn'sɜ:tn/ *a* incerto. **be ~ whether** não saber ao certo se, estar indeciso quanto a. **~ty** *n* incerteza *f*

unchang|ed /ʌn'tʃeɪndʒd/ *a* inalterado, sem modificação. **~ing** *a* inalterável, imutável

uncivilized /ʌn'sɪvɪlaɪzd/ *a* não civilizado, bárbaro

uncle /'ʌŋkl/ *n* tio *m*

uncomfortable /ʌn'kʌmfətəbl/ *a* (*thing*) desconfortável, incómodo, (*P*) incómodo; (*unpleasant*) desagradável. **feel** *or* **be ~** (*uneasy*) sentir-se *or* estar pouco à vontade

uncommon /ʌn'kɒmən/ *a* pouco vulgar, invulgar, fora do comum. **~ly** *adv* invulgarmente, excepcionalmente

uncompromising /ʌn'kɒmprəmaɪzɪŋ/ *a* intransigente

unconcerned /ʌnkən'sɜ:nd/ *a* (*indifferent*) indiferente (**by** a)

unconditional /ʌnkən'dɪʃənl/ *a* incondicional

unconscious /ʌn'kɒnʃəs/ *a* inconsciente (**of** de). **~ly** *adv* inconscientemente. **~ness** *n* inconsciência *f*

unconventional /ʌnkən'venʃənl/ *a* não convencional, fora do comum

uncooperative /ʌnkəʊ'ɒpərətɪv/ *a* (*person*) pouco cooperativo, do contra (*colloq*)

u

uncork /ʌnˈkɔːk/ *vt* desarrolhar, tirar a rolha de

uncouth /ʌnˈkuːθ/ *a* rude, grosseiro

uncover /ʌnˈkʌvə(r)/ *vt* descobrir, revelar

unctuous /ˈʌŋktʃʊəs/ *a* untuoso, gorduroso; (*fig*) melifluo

undecided /ʌndɪˈsaɪdɪd/ *a* (*irresolute*) indeciso; (*not settled*) por decidir, pendente

undeniable /ʌndɪˈnaɪəbl/ *a* inegável, incontestável

under /ˈʌndə(r)/ *prep* debaixo de, sob; (*less than*) com menos de; (*according to*) conforme, segundo □ *adv* por baixo, debaixo. ~ **age** menor de idade. ~ **way** em preparo

under- /ˈʌndə(r)/ *pref* sub-

undercarriage /ˈʌndəkærɪdʒ/ *n* (*aviat*) trem *m* de aterrissagem, (*P*) trem *m* de aterragem

underclothes /ˈʌndəkləʊðz/ *npl see* **underwear**

undercoat /ˈʌndəkəʊt/ *n* (*of paint*) primeira mão *f*, (*P*) primeira demão *f*

undercover /ʌndəˈkʌvə(r)/ *a* (*agent, operation*) secreto

undercurrent /ˈʌndəkʌrənt/ *n* corrente *f* subterrânea; (*fig*) filão *m* (*fig*), tendência *f* oculta

undercut /ʌndəˈkʌt/ *vt* (*pt* **undercut**, *pres p* **undercutting**) (*comm*) vender a preços mais baixos que

underdeveloped /ʌndədɪˈveləpt/ *a* atrofiado; (*country*) subdesenvolvido

underdog /ˈʌndədɒg/ *n* desprotegido *m*, o mais fraco (*colloq*)

underdone /ˈʌndədʌn/ *a* (*of meat*) mal passado

underestimate /ʌndəˈrestɪmeɪt/ *vt* subestimar, não dar o devido valor a

underfed /ʌndəˈfed/ *a* subalimentado, subnutrido

underfoot /ʌndəˈfʊt/ *adv* debaixo dos pés; (*on the ground*) no chão

undergo /ʌndəˈgəʊ/ *vt* (*pt* **-went**, *pp* **-gone**) (*be subjected to*) sofrer; (*treatment*) ser submetido a

undergraduate /ʌndəˈgrædʒʊət/ *n* estudante *mf* universitário

underground[1] /ʌndəˈgraʊnd/ *adv* debaixo da terra; (*fig: secretly*) clandestinamente

underground[2] /ˈʌndəgraʊnd/ *a* subterrâneo; (*fig: secret*) clandestino □ *n* (*rail*) metro(politano) *m*

undergrowth /ˈʌndəgrəʊθ/ *n* mato *m*

underhand /ˈʌndəhænd/ *a* (*deceitful*) sonso, dissimulado

under|lie /ʌndəˈlaɪ/ *vt* (*pt* **-lay**, *pp* **-lain**, *pres p* **-lying**) estar por baixo de. **~lying** *a* subjacente

underline /ʌndəˈlaɪn/ *vt* sublinhar

undermine /ʌndəˈmaɪn/ *vt* minar, solapar

underneath /ʌndəˈniːθ/ *prep* sob, debaixo de, por baixo de □ *adv* abaixo, em baixo, por baixo

underpaid /ʌndəˈpeɪd/ *a* mal pago

underpants /ˈʌndəpænts/ *npl* (*man's*) cuecas *fpl*

underpass /ˈʌndəpaːs/ *n* (*for cars, people*) passagem *f* inferior

underprivileged /ʌndəˈprɪvɪlɪdʒd/ *a* desfavorecido

underrate /ʌndəˈreɪt/ *vt* subestimar, depreciar

underside /ˈʌndəsaɪd/ *n* lado *m* inferior, base *f*

underskirt /ˈʌndəskɜːt/ *n* anágua *f*

understand /ʌndəˈstænd/ *vt/i* (*pt* **-stood**) compreender, entender. **~able** *a* compreensível. **~ing** *a* compreensivo □ *n* compreensão *f*; (*agreement*) acordo *m*, entendimento *m*

understatement /ˈʌndəsteɪtmənt/ *n* versão *f* atenuada da verdade, litotes *f*

understudy /ˈʌndəstʌdɪ/ *n* substituto *m*

undertak|e /ʌndəˈteɪk/ *vt* (*pt* **-took**, *pp* **-taken**) empreender; (*responsibility*) assumir. **~e to** encarregar-se de. **~ing** *n* (*task*) empreendimento *m*; (*promise*) compromisso *m*

undertaker /ˈʌndəteɪkə(r)/ *n* agente *m* funerário, papa-defuntos *m* (*colloq*)

undertone /ˈʌndətəʊn/ *n* **in an ~** a meia voz

undervalue /ʌndəˈvælju:/ *vt* avaliar por baixo, subestimar

underwater /ʌndəˈwɔːtə(r)/ *a* submarino □ *adv* debaixo de água

underwear /ˈʌndəweə(r)/ *n* roupa *f* interior *or* de baixo

underweight /ˈʌndəweɪt/ *a* **be ~** estar com o peso abaixo do normal, ter peso a menos

underwent /ʌndəˈwent/ *see* **undergo**

underworld /ˈʌndəwɜːld/ *n* (*of crime*) submundo *m*, bas-fonds *mpl*

underwriter /ˈʌndəraɪtə(r)/ *n* segurador *m*; (*marine*) underwriter *m*

undeserved /ʌndɪˈzɜːvd/ *a* imerecido, injusto

undesirable /ʌndɪˈzaɪərəbl/ *a* indesejável, inconveniente

undies /ˈʌndɪz/ *npl* (*colloq*) roupa *f* de baixo *or* interior

undignified /ʌnˈdɪgnɪfaɪd/ *a* pouco digno, sem dignidade

undisputed /ʌndɪˈspjuːtɪd/ *a* incontestado

undo /ʌnˈduː/ *vt* (*pt* -**did**, *pp* -**done** /dʌn/) desfazer; (*knot*) desfazer, desatar; (*coat, button*) abrir. **leave ~ne** não fazer, deixar por fazer. **~ing** *n* desgraça *f*, ruína *f*

undoubted /ʌnˈdaʊtɪd/ *a* indubitável. **~ly** *adv* indubitavelmente

undress /ʌnˈdres/ *vt/i* despir(-se). **get ~ed** despir-se

undu|e /ʌnˈdjuː/ *a* excessivo, indevido. **~ly** *adv* excessivamente, indevidamente

undulate /ˈʌndjʊleɪt/ *vi* ondular

undying /ʌnˈdaɪɪŋ/ *a* eterno, perene

unearth /ʌnˈɜːθ/ *vt* desenterrar; (*fig*) descobrir

unearthly /ʌnˈɜːθlɪ/ *a* sobrenatural, misterioso. **~ hour** (*colloq*) hora *f* absurda *or* inconveniente

uneasy /ʌnˈiːzɪ/ *a* (*ill at ease*) pouco à vontade; (*worried*) preocupado

uneconomic /ʌniːkəˈnɒmɪk/ *a* antieconômico. **~al** *a* antieconômico

uneducated /ʌnˈedʒʊkeɪtɪd/ *a* (*person*) inculto, sem instrução

unemploy|ed /ʌnɪmˈplɔɪd/ *a* desempregado. **~ment** *n* desemprego *m*. **~ment benefit** auxílio-desemprego *m*

unending /ʌnˈendɪŋ/ *a* interminável, sem fim

unequal /ʌnˈiːkwəl/ *a* desigual. **~led** *a* sem igual, inigualável

unequivocal /ʌnɪˈkwɪvəkl/ *a* inequívoco, claro

uneven /ʌnˈiːvn/ *a* desigual, irregular

unexpected /ʌnɪkˈspektɪd/ *a* inesperado. **~ly** *a* inesperadamente

unfair /ʌnˈfeə(r)/ *a* injusto (**to** com). **~ness** *n* injustiça *f*

unfaithful /ʌnˈfeɪθfl/ *a* infiel

unfamiliar /ʌnfəˈmɪlɪə(r)/ *a* estranho, desconhecido. **be ~ with** desconhecer, não conhecer, não estar familiarizado com

unfashionable /ʌnˈfæʃənəbl/ *a* fora de moda

unfasten /ʌnˈfɑːsn/ *vt* (*knot*) desatar, soltar; (*button*) abrir

unfavourable /ʌnˈfeɪvərəbl/ *a* desfavorável

unfeeling /ʌnˈfiːlɪŋ/ *a* insensível

unfinished /ʌnˈfɪnɪʃt/ *a* incompleto, inacabado

unfit /ʌnˈfɪt/ *a* sem preparo físico, fora de forma; (*unsuitable*) impróprio (**for** para)

unfold /ʌnˈfəʊld/ *vt* desdobrar; (*expose*) expor, revelar □ *vi* desenrolar-se

unforeseen /ʌnfɔːˈsiːn/ *a* imprevisto, inesperado

unforgettable /ʌnfəˈgetəbl/ *a* inesquecível

unforgivable /ʌnfəˈgɪvəbl/ *a* imperdoável, indesculpável

unfortunate /ʌnˈfɔːtʃənət/ *a* (*unlucky*) infeliz; (*regrettable*) lamentável. **it was very ~ that** foi uma pena que **~ly** *adv* infelizmente

unfounded /ʌnˈfaʊndɪd/ *a* (*rumour etc*) infundado, sem fundamento

unfriendly /ʌnˈfrendlɪ/ *a* pouco amável, antipático, frio

unfurnished /ʌnˈfɜːnɪʃt/ *a* sem mobília

ungainly /ʌnˈgeɪnlɪ/ *a* desajeitado, desgracioso

ungodly /ʌnˈgɒdlɪ/ *a* ímpio. **~ hour** (*colloq*) hora *f* absurda, às altas horas (*colloq*)

ungrateful /ʌnˈgreɪtfl/ *a* ingrato

unhapp|y /ʌnˈhæpɪ/ *a* (-**ier**, -**iest**) infeliz, triste; (*not pleased*) descontente, pouco contente (**with** com). **~ily** *adv* infelizmente. **~iness** *n* infelicidade *f*, tristeza *f*

unharmed /ʌnˈhɑːmd/ *a* incólume, são e salvo, ileso

unhealthy /ʌnˈhelθɪ/ *a* (-**ier**, -**iest**) (*climate etc*) doentio, insalubre; (*person*) adoentado, com pouca saúde

unheard-of /ʌnˈhɜːdɒv/ *a* inaudito, sem precedentes

unhinge /ʌnˈhɪndʒ/ *vt* (*person, mind*) desequilibrar

unholy /ʌnˈhəʊlɪ/ *a* (-**ier**, -**iest**) (*person, act etc*) ímpio; (*colloq: great*) incrível, espantoso

unhook /ʌnˈhʊk/ *vt* desenganchar; (*dress*) desapertar

unhoped /ʌnˈhəʊpt/ *a* **~ for** inesperado

unhurt /ʌnˈhɜːt/ *a* ileso, incólume

unicorn /ˈjuːnɪkɔːn/ *n* unicórnio *m*

uniform /ˈjuːnɪfɔːm/ *n* uniforme *m* □ *a* uniforme, sempre igual. **~ity** /-ˈfɔːmətɪ/ *n* uniformidade *f*. **~ly** *adv* uniformemente

unif|y /ˈjuːnɪfaɪ/ *vt* unificar. **~ication** /-ɪˈkeɪʃn/ *n* unificação *f*

unilateral /juːnɪˈlætrəl/ *a* unilateral

unimaginable /ʌnɪˈmædʒɪnəbl/ *a* inimaginável

unimportant /ʌnɪmˈpɔːtnt/ *a* sem importância, insignificante

uninhabited /ʌnɪnˈhæbɪtɪd/ *a* desabitado

unintentional /ʌnɪnˈtenʃənl/ *a* involuntário, não propositado

uninterest|ed /ʌnˈɪntrəstɪd/ *a* desinteressado (**in** em), indiferente

u

(in a). **~ing** a desinteressante, sem interesse

union /'ju:nɪən/ n união f; (trade union) sindicato m. **~ist** n sindicalista mf; (pol) unionista mf. **U~ Jack** bandeira f británica

unique /ju:'ni:k/ a único, sem igual

unisex /'ju:nɪseks/ a unisexo

unison /'ju:nɪsn/ n in ~ em uníssono

unit /'ju:nɪt/ n unidade f; (of furniture) peça f, unidade f, (P) módulo m

unite /ju:'naɪt/ vt/i unir(-se). **U~d Kingdom** n Reino m Unido. **U~d Nations (Organization)** n Organização f das Nações Unidas. **U~ States (of America)** Estados mpl Unidos (da América)

unity /'ju:nətɪ/ n unidade f; (fig: harmony) união f

universal /ju:nɪ'vɜ:sl/ a universal

universe /'ju:nɪvɜ:s/ n universo m

university /ju:nɪ'vɜ:sətɪ/ n universidade f □ a universitário; (student, teacher) universitário, da universidade

unjust /ʌn'dʒʌst/ a injusto

unkempt /ʌn'kempt/ a desmazelado, desleixado; (of hair) despenteado, desgrenhado

unkind /ʌn'kaɪnd/ a desagradável, duro. **~ly** adv mal

unknowingly /ʌn'nəʊɪŋlɪ/ adv sem saber, inconscientemente

unknown /ʌn'nəʊn/ a desconhecido □ n the ~ o desconhecido

unleaded /ʌn'ledɪd/ a sem chumbo

unless /ʌn'les/ conj a não ser que, a menos que, salvo se, se não

unlike /ʌn'laɪk/ a diferente □ prep ao contrário de

unlikely /ʌn'laɪklɪ/ a improvável

unlimited /ʌn'lɪmɪtɪd/ a ilimitado

unload /ʌn'ləʊd/ vt descarregar

unlock /ʌn'lɒk/ vt abrir (com chave)

unluck|y /ʌn'lʌkɪ/ a (-ier, -iest) infeliz, sem sorte; (number) que dá azar. **be ~y** ter pouca sorte. **~ily** adv infelizmente

unmarried /ʌn'mærɪd/ a solteiro, celibatário

unmask /ʌn'mɑ:sk/ vt desmascarar

unmistakable /ʌnmɪs'teɪkəbl/ a (voice etc) inconfundível; (clear) claro, inequívoco

unmitigated /ʌn'mɪtɪgeɪtɪd/ a (absolute) completo, absoluto

unmoved /ʌn'mu:vd/ a impassível; (indifferent) indiferente (by a), insensível (by a)

unnatural /ʌn'nætʃrəl/ a que não é natural; (wicked) desnaturado

unnecessary /ʌn'nesəserɪ/ a desnecessário; (superfluous) supérfluo, dispensável

unnerve /ʌn'nɜ:v/ vt desencorajar, desmoralizar, intimidar

unnoticed /ʌn'nəʊtɪst/ a go ~ passar despercebido

unobtrusive /ʌnəb'tru:sɪv/ a discreto

unofficial /ʌnə'fɪʃl/ a oficioso, que não é oficial; (strike) ilegal, inautorizado

unorthodox /ʌn'ɔ:θədɒks/ a pouco ortodoxo, não ortodoxo

unpack /ʌn'pæk/ vt (suitcase etc) desfazer; (contents) desembalar, desempacotar □ vi desfazer a mala

unpaid /ʌn'peɪd/ a não remunerado; (bill) a pagar

unpalatable /ʌn'pælətəbl/ a (food, fact etc) desagradável, intragável

unparalleled /ʌn'pærəleld/ a sem paralelo, incomparável

unpleasant /ʌn'pleznt/ a desagradável (to com); (person) antipático

unplug /ʌn'plʌg/ vt (pt-plugged) (electr) desligar a tomada, (P) tirar a ficha da tomada

unpopular /ʌn'pɒpjʊlə(r)/ a impopular

unprecedented /ʌn'presɪdentɪd/ a sem precedentes, inaudito, nunca visto

unpredictable /ʌnprə'dɪktəbl/ a imprevisível

unprepared /ʌnprɪ'peəd/ a sem preparação, improvisado; (person) desprevenido

unpretentious /ʌnprɪ'tenʃəs/ a despretencioso, sem pretensões

unprincipled /ʌn'prɪnsəpld/ a sem princípios, sem escrúpulos

unprofessional /ʌnprə'feʃənl/ a (work) de amador; (conduct) sem consciência profissional

unprofitable /ʌn'prɒfɪtəbl/ a não lucrativo

unqualified /ʌn'kwɒlɪfaɪd/ a sem habilitações; (success etc) total, absoluto. **be ~ to** não estar habilitado para

unquestionable /ʌn'kwestʃənəbl/ a incontestável, indiscutível

unravel /ʌn'rævl/ vt (pt unravelled) desenredar, desemaranhar; (knitting) desmanchar

unreal /ʌn'rɪəl/ a irreal

unreasonable /ʌn'ri:znəbl/ a pouco razoável, disparatado; (excessive) excessivo

unrecognizable /ʌn'rekəgnaɪzəbl/ a irreconhecível

unrelated /ʌnrɪ'leɪtɪd/ a (facts) desconexo, sem relação (to com); (people) não aparentado (to com)

unreliable /ʌnrɪˈlaɪəbl/ *a* que não é de confiança

unremitting /ʌnrɪˈmɪtɪŋ/ *a* incessante, infatigável

unreservedly /ʌnrɪˈzɜːvɪdlɪ/ *adv* sem reservas

unrest /ʌnˈrest/ *n* agitação *f*, distúrbios *mpl*

unrivalled /ʌnˈraɪvld/ *a* sem igual, incomparável

unroll /ʌnˈrəʊl/ *vt* desenrolar

unruffled /ʌnˈrʌfld/ *a* calmo, tranqüilo, imperturbável

unruly /ʌnˈruːlɪ/ *a* indisciplinado, turbulento

unsafe /ʌnˈseɪf/ *a* (*dangerous*) que não é seguro, perigoso; (*person*) em perigo

unsaid /ʌnˈsed/ *a* **leave ~** não mencionar, não dizer, deixar algo por dizer

unsatisfactory /ʌnsætɪsˈfæktərɪ/ *a* insatisfatório, pouco satisfatório

unsavoury /ʌnˈseɪvərɪ/ *a* desagradável, repugnante

unscathed /ʌnˈskeɪðd/ *a* ileso, incólume

unscrew /ʌnˈskruː/ *vt* desenroscar, desparafusar

unscrupulous /ʌnˈskruːpjʊləs/ *a* sem escrúpulos, pouco escrupuloso, sem consciência

unseemly /ʌnˈsiːmlɪ/ *a* inconveniente, indecoroso, impróprio

unsettle /ʌnˈsetl/ *vt* perturbar, agitar. **~d** *a* perturbado; (*weather*) instável, variável; (*bill*) não saldado

unshakeable /ʌnˈʃeɪkəbl/ *a* (*person, belief etc*) inabalável

unshaven /ʌnˈʃeɪvn/ *a* com a barba por fazer, por barbear

unsightly /ʌnˈsaɪtlɪ/ *a* feio

unskilled /ʌnˈskɪld/ *a* inexperiente; (*work, worker*) não especializado; (*labour*) mão-de-obra *f* não especializada

unsociable /ʌnˈsəʊʃəbl/ *a* insociável, misantropo

unsophisticated /ʌnsəˈfɪstɪkeɪtɪd/ *a* insofisticado, simples

unsound /ʌnˈsaʊnd/ *a* pouco sólido. **of ~ mind** (*jur*) não estar em plena posse das suas faculdades mentais (*jur*)

unspeakable /ʌnˈspiːkəbl/ *a* indescritível; (*bad*) inqualificável

unspecified /ʌnˈspesɪfaɪd/ *a* não especificado, indeterminado

unstable /ʌnˈsteɪbl/ *a* instável

unsteady /ʌnˈstedɪ/ *a* (*step*) vacilante, incerto; (*ladder*) instável; (*hand*) pouco firme

unstuck /ʌnˈstʌk/ *a* (*not stuck*) descolado. **come ~** (*colloq: fail*) falhar

unsuccessful /ʌnsəkˈsesfl/ *a* (*candidate*) mal sucedido; (*attempt*) malogrado, fracassado. **be ~** não ter êxito. **~ly** *adv* em vão

unsuit|able /ʌnˈs(j)uːtəbl/ *a* impróprio, pouco apropriado, inadequado (**for** para). **~ed** *a* inadequado (**to** para)

unsure /ʌnˈʃʊə(r)/ *a* incerto

unsuspecting /ʌnsəˈspektɪŋ/ *a* sem desconfiar de nada, insuspeitado

untangle /ʌnˈtæŋgl/ *vt* desemaranhar, desenredar

unthinkable /ʌnˈθɪŋkəbl/ *a* impensável, inconcebível

untid|y /ʌnˈtaɪdɪ/ *a* (**-ier, -iest**) (*room, desk etc*) desarrumado; (*appearance*) desleixado, desmazelado; (*hair*) despenteado. **~ily** *adv* sem cuidado. **~iness** *n* desordem *f*; (*of appearance*) desmazelo *m*

untie /ʌnˈtaɪ/ *vt* (*knot, parcel*) desatar, desfazer; (*person*) desamarrar

until /ənˈtɪl/ *prep* até. **not ~** não antes de □ *conj* até que

untimely /ʌnˈtaɪmlɪ/ *a* inoportuno, intempestivo; (*death*) prematuro

untold /ʌnˈtəʊld/ *a* incalculável

untoward /ʌntəˈwɔːd/ *a* inconveniente, desagradável

untrue /ʌnˈtruː/ *a* falso

unused[1] /ʌnˈjuːzd/ *a* (*new*) novo, por usar; (*not in use*) não utilizado

unused[2] /ʌnˈjuːst/ *a* **~ to** não habituado a, não acostumado a

unusual /ʌnˈjuːʒəl/ *a* insólito, fora do comum. **~ly** *adv* excepcionalmente

unveil /ʌnˈveɪl/ *vt* descobrir; (*statue, portrait etc*) desvelar

unwanted /ʌnˈwɒntɪd/ *a* (*useless*) que já não serve; (*child*) indesejado

unwarranted /ʌnˈwɒrəntɪd/ *a* injustificado

unwelcome /ʌnˈwelkəm/ *a* desagradável; (*guest*) indesejável

unwell /ʌnˈwel/ *a* indisposto

unwieldy /ʌnˈwiːldɪ/ *a* difícil de manejar, pouco jeitoso

unwilling /ʌnˈwɪlɪŋ/ *a* relutante (**to** em), pouco disposto (**to** a)

unwind /ʌnˈwaɪnd/ *vt/i* (*pt* **unwound** /ʌnˈwaʊnd/) desenrolar (-se); (*colloq: relax*) descontrair (-se)

unwise /ʌnˈwaɪz/ *a* imprudente, insensato

unwittingly /ʌnˈwɪtɪŋlɪ/ *adv* sem querer

unworthy /ʌnˈwɜːðɪ/ *a* indigno

unwrap /ʌnˈræp/ *vt* (*pt* **unwrapped**) desembrulhar, abrir, desfazer

unwritten /ʌnˈrɪtn/ *a* (*agreement*) verbal, tácito

u

up /ʌp/ adv (to higher place) cima, para cima, para o alto; (in higher place) em cima, no alto; (out of bed) acordado, de pé; (up and dressed) pronto; (finished) acabado; (sun) alto ◻ prep no cimo de, em cima de, no alto de. ∼ **the street/river**/etc pela rua/pelo rio/etc acima ◻ vt (pt **upped**) (increase) aumentar. **be ∼ against** defrontar, enfrentar. **be ∼ in** (colloq) saber. **be ∼ to** (do) estar fazendo; (plot) estar tramando; (task) estar à altura de. **feel ∼ to doing** (able) sentir-se capaz de fazer. **it is ∼ to you** depende de você. **come** or **go ∼** subir. **have ∼s and downs** (fig) ter (os seus) altos e baixos. **walk ∼ and down** andar dum lado para o outro or para a frente e para trás. **∼-and-coming** a promoter. **∼-market** a requintado, fino

upbringing /'ʌpbrɪŋɪŋ/ n educação f

update /ʌp'deɪt/ vt atualizar, (P) actualizar

upheaval /ʌp'hiːvl/ n pandemônio m, (P) pandemónio m, revolução f (fig); (social, political) convulsão f

uphill /'ʌphɪl/ a ladeira acima, ascendente; (fig: difficult) árduo ◻ adv /ʌp'hɪl/ **go ∼** subir

uphold /ʌp'həʊld/ vt (pt **upheld**) sustentar, manter, apoiar

upholster /ʌp'həʊlstə(r)/ vt estofar. **∼y** n estofados mpl, (P) estofo(s) m(pl)

upkeep /'ʌpkiːp/ n manutenção f

upon /ə'pɒn/ prep sobre

upper /'ʌpə(r)/ a superior ◻ n (of shoe) gáspea f. **have the ∼ hand** estar por cima, estar em posição de superioridade. **∼ class** aristocracia f. **∼most** a (highest) o mais alto, superior

upright /'ʌpraɪt/ a vertical; (honourable) honesto, honrado, (P) recto

uprising /'ʌpraɪzɪŋ/ n insurreição f, sublevação f, levantamento m

uproar /'ʌprɔː(r)/ n tumulto m, alvoroço m

uproot /ʌp'ruːt/ vt desenraizar; (fig) erradicar, desarraigar

upset[1] /ʌp'set/ vt (pt **upset**, pres p **upsetting**) (overturn) entornar, virar; (plan) contrariar, transtornar; (stomach) desarranjar; (person) contrariar, transtornar, incomodar ◻ a aborrecido

upset[2] /'ʌpset/ n transtorno m; (of stomach) indisposição f; (distress) choque m

upshot /'ʌpʃɒt/ n resultado m

upside-down /ʌpsaɪd'daʊn/ adv (lit & fig) ao contrário, de pernas para o ar

upstairs /ʌp'steəz/ adv (at/to) em/para cima, no/para o andar de cima ◻ a /'ʌpsteəz/ (flat etc) de cima, do andar de cima

upstart /'ʌpstɑːt/ n arrivista mf

upstream /ʌp'striːm/ adv rio acima, contra a corrente

upsurge /'ʌpsɜːdʒ/ n recrudescência f, recrudescimento m; (of anger) acesso m, ataque m

uptake /'ʌpteɪk/ n **be quick on the ∼** pegar rapidamente as coisas; (fig) ser de compreensão rápida, ser vivo

up-to-date /'ʌptədeɪt/ a moderno, atualizado, (P) actualizado

upturn /'ʌptɜːn/ n melhoria f

upward /'ʌpwəd/ a ascendente, voltado para cima. **∼s** adv para cima

uranium /jʊ'reɪnɪəm/ n urânio m

urban /'ɜːbən/ a urbano

urbane /ɜː'beɪn/ a delicado, cortês, urbano

urge /ɜːdʒ/ vt aconselhar vivamente (to a) ◻ n (strong desire) grande vontade f. **∼ on** (impel) incitar

urgen|t /'ɜːdʒənt/ a urgente. **be ∼t** urgir. **∼cy** n urgência f

urinal /jʊə'raɪnl/ n urinol m

urin|e /'jʊərɪn/ n urina f. **∼ate** vi urinar

urn /ɜːn/ n urna f; (for tea, coffee) espécie f de samovar

us /ʌs/; unstressed /əs/ pron nos; (after preps) nós. **with ∼** conosco. **he knows ∼** ele nos conhece

US abbr **United States**

USA abbr **United States of America**

USB port /juːesbiː'pɔːt/ n porto m USB

usable /'juːzəbl/ a utilizável

usage /'juːzɪdʒ/ n uso m

use[1] /juːz/ vt usar, utilizar, servir-se de; (exploit) servir-se de; (consume) gastar, usar, consumir. **∼ up** esgotar, consumir. **∼r /-ə(r)/** n usuário m, (P) utente mf. **∼r-friendly** a fácil de usar

use[2] /juːs/ n uso m, emprego m. **in ∼** em uso. **it is no ∼ shouting**/etc não serve de nada or não adianta gritar/etc. **make ∼ of** servir-se de. **of ∼** útil

used[1] /juːzd/ a (second-hand) usado

used[2] /juːst/ pt **he ∼ to** ele costumava, ele tinha por costume or hábito ◻ a **∼ to** acostumado a, habituado a

use|ful /'juːsfl/ a útil. **∼less** a inútil; (person) incompetente

usher /'ʌʃə(r)/ n vagalume m, (P) arrumador m ◻ vt **∼ in** mandar entrar. **∼ette** n vagalume m, (P) arrumadora f

usual /'juːʒʊəl/ a usual, habitual, normal. **as ∼** como de costume, como habitualmente. **at the ∼ time** na hora de costume, (P) à(s) hora(s) de costume. **∼ly** adv habitualmente, normalmente

USSR abbr **URSS**

usurp /juːˈzɜːp/ *vt* usurpar

utensil /juːˈtensl/ *n* utensílio *m*

uterus /ˈjuːtərəs/ *n* útero *m*

utilitarian /juːtɪlɪˈteərɪən/ *a* utilitário

utility /juːˈtɪlətɪ/ *n* utilidade *f*. **(public)** ~ service *m* público. ~ **room** área *f* de serviço (para as máquinas de lavar a roupa e a louça)

utilize /ˈjuːtɪlaɪz/ *vt* utilizar

utmost /ˈʌtməʊst/ *a* (*furthest, most intense*) extremo. **the** ~ **care**/*etc* (*greatest*) o maior cuidado/*etc* □ *n* **do one's** ~ fazer todo o possível

utter[1] /ˈʌtə(r)/ *a* completo, absoluto. ~**ly** *adv* completamente

utter[2] /ˈʌtə(r)/ *vt* proferir; (*sigh, shout*) dar. ~**ance** *n* expressão *f*

U-turn /ˈjuːtɜːn/ *n* retorno *m*

vacan|t /ˈveɪkənt/ *a* (*post, room, look*) vago; (*mind*) vazio; (*seat, space, time*) desocupado, livre. ~**cy** *n* (*post*) vaga *f*; (*room in hotel*) vago *m*

vacate /vəˈkeɪt/ *vt* vagar, deixar vago

vacation /vəˈkeɪʃn/ *n* férias *fpl*

vaccinat|e /ˈvæksmeɪt/ *vt* vacinar. ~**ion** /-ˈneɪʃn/ *n* vacinação *f*

vaccine /ˈvæksiːn/ *n* vacina *f*

vacuum /ˈvækjʊəm/ *n* (*pl* -**cuums** *or* -**cua**) vácuo *m*, vazio *m*. ~ **flask** garrafa *f* térmica, (P) termo(s) *m*. ~ **cleaner** aspirador *m* de pó

vagina /vəˈdʒaɪnə/ *n* vagina *f*

vagrant /ˈveɪɡrənt/ *n* vadio *m*, vagabundo *m*

vague /veɪɡ/ *a* (-**er**, -**est**) vago; (*outline*) impreciso. **be** ~ **about** ser vago acerca de, não precisar. ~**ly** *adv* vagamente

vain /veɪn/ *a* (-**er**, -**est**) (*conceited*) vaidoso; (*useless*) vão, inútil; (*fruitless*) infrutífero. **in** ~ em vão. ~**ly** *adv* em vão

valentine /ˈvæləntaɪn/ *n* (*card*) cartão *m* do dia de São Valentin

valet /ˈvælɪt, ˈvæleɪ/ *n* (*manservant*) criado *m* de quarto; (*of hotel*) camareiro *m* □ *vt* (*car*) lavar e limpar o interior

valiant /ˈvælɪənt/ *a* corajoso, valente

valid /ˈvælɪd/ *a* válido. ~**ity** /vəˈlɪdətɪ/ *n* validade *f*

validate /ˈvælɪdeɪt/ *vt* validar, confirmar, ratificar

valley /ˈvælɪ/ *n* vale *m*

valuable /ˈvæljʊəbl/ *a* (*object*) valioso, de valor; (*help, time etc*) precioso. ~**s** *npl* objetos *mpl*, (P) objectos *mpl* de valor

valuation /væljʊˈeɪʃn/ *n* avaliação *f*

value /ˈvæljuː/ *n* valor *m* □ *vt* avaliar; (*cherish*) dar valor a. ~ **added tax** imposto *m* de valor adicional, (P) acrescentado. ~**r** /-ə/(r)/ *n* avaliador *m*

valve /vælv/ *n* (*anat, techn, of car tyre*) válvula *f*; (*of bicycle tyre*) pipo *m*; (*of radio*) lâmpada *f*, válvula *f*

vampire /ˈvæmpaɪə(r)/ *n* vampiro *m*

van /væn/ *n* (*large*) camião *m*; (*small*) camionete *f*, comercial *m*; (*milkman's, baker's etc*) camionete *f*; (*rail*) bagageiro *m*, (P) furgão *m*

vandal /ˈvændl/ *n* vândalo *m*. ~**ism** /-əlɪzəm/ *n* vandalismo *m*

vandalize /ˈvændəlaɪz/ *vt* destruir, estragar

vanguard /ˈvænɡɑːd/ *n* vanguarda *f*

vanilla /vəˈnɪlə/ *n* baunilha *f*

vanish /ˈvænɪʃ/ *vi* desaparecer, sumir-se, desvanecer-se

vanity /ˈvænətɪ/ *n* vaidade *f*. ~ **case** bolsa *f* de maquilagem

vantage-point /ˈvɑːntɪdʒpɔɪnt/ *n* (bom) ponto *m* de observação

vapour /ˈveɪpə(r)/ *n* vapor *m*; (*mist*) bruma *f*

vari|able /ˈveərɪəbl/ *a* variável. ~**ation** /-ˈeɪʃn/ *n* variação *f*. ~**ed** /-ɪd/ *a* variado

variance /ˈveərɪəns/ *n* **at** ~ em desacordo (**with** com)

variant /ˈveərɪənt/ *a* diverso, diferente □ *n* variante *f*

varicose /ˈværɪkəʊs/ *a* ~ **veins** varizes *fpl*

variety /vəˈraɪətɪ/ *n* variedade *f*; (*entertainment*) variedades *fpl*

various /ˈveərɪəs/ *a* vários, diversos, variados

varnish /ˈvɑːnɪʃ/ *n* verniz *m* □ *vt* envernizar; (*nails*) pintar

vary /ˈveərɪ/ *vt/i* variar. ~**ing** *a* variado

vase /vɑːz/ *n* vaso *m*, jarra *f*

vast /vɑːst/ *a* vasto, imenso. ~**ly** *adv* imensamente, infinitamente. ~**ness** *n* vastidão *f*, imensidão *f*, imensidade *f*

vat /væt/ *n* tonel *m*, dorna *f*, cuba *f*

VAT /viːerˈtiː, væt/ *abbr* ICM *m*, (P) IVA *m*

vault[1] /vɔːlt/ *n* (*roof*) abóbada *f*; (*in bank*) casa-forte *f*; (*tomb*) cripta *f*; (*cellar*) adega *f*

vault[2] /vɔːlt/ *vt/i* saltar □ *n* salto *m*

vaunt /vɔːnt/ *vt/i* gabar(-se), ufanar(-se) (de), vangloriar(-se)

VD *abbr see* **venereal disease**

VDU *abbr see* **visual display unit**

veal /viːl/ *n* (*meat*) vitela *f*

u

v

veer /vɪə(r)/ *vi* virar, mudar de direção, (P) direcção

vegan /'viːgən/ *a & n* vegetariano (*m*) estrito

vegetable /'vedʒɪtəbl/ *n* hortaliça *f*, legume *m* □ *a* vegetal

vegetarian /vedʒɪ'teərɪən/ *a & n* vegetariano (*m*)

vegetate /'vedʒɪteɪt/ *vi* vegetar

vegetation /vedʒɪ'teɪʃn/ *n* vegetação *f*

vehement /'viːəmənt/ *a* veemente. **~ly** *adv* veementemente

vehicle /'viːɪkl/ *n* veículo *m*

veil /veɪl/ *n* véu *m* □ *vt* velar, cobrir com véu; (*fig*) esconder, disfarçar

vein /veɪn/ *n* (*in body; mood*) veia *f*; (*in rock*) veio *m*, filão *m*; (*of leaf*) nervura *f*

velocity /vɪ'lɒsətɪ/ *n* velocidade *f*

velvet /'velvɪt/ *n* veludo *m*. **~y** *a* aveludado

vendetta /ven'detə/ *n* vendeta *f*

vending-machine /'vendɪŋməʃiːn/ *n* vendedora *f* automática, (P) máquina *f* de distribuição

vendor /'vendə(r)/ *n* vendedor *m*. **street ~** vendedor *m* ambulante

veneer /və'nɪə(r)/ *n* folheado *m*; (*fig*) fachada *f*, máscara *f*

venerable /'venərəbl/ *a* venerável

venereal /və'nɪərɪəl/ *a* venéreo. **~ disease** doença *f* venérea

venetian /və'niːʃn/ *a* **~ blinds** persiana *f*

Venezuela /venɪz'weɪlə/ *n* Venezuela *f*. **~n** *a & n* venezuelano (*m*)

vengeance /'vendʒəns/ *n* vingança. **with a ~** furiosamente, em excesso, com mais força do que se pretende

venison /'venɪzn/ *n* carne *f* de veado

venom /'venəm/ *n* veneno *m*. **~ous** /'venəməs/ *a* venenoso

vent[1] /vent/ *n* (*in coat*) abertura *f*

vent[2] /vent/ *n* (*hole*) orifício *m*, abertura *f*; (*for air*) respiradouro *m* □ *vt* (*anger*) descarregar (**on** para cima de). **give ~ to** (*fig*) desabafar, dar vazão a

ventilat|e /'ventɪleɪt/ *vt* ventilar. **~ion** /-'leɪʃn/ *n* ventilação *f*. **~or** *n* ventilador *m*

ventriloquist /ven'trɪləkwɪst/ *n* ventríloquo *m*

venture /'ventʃə(r)/ *n* empreendimento *m* arriscado, aventura *f* □ *vt/i* arriscar(-se)

venue /'venjuː/ *n* porto *m* de encontro

veranda /və'rændə/ *n* varanda *f*

verb /vɜːb/ *n* verbo *m*

verbal /'vɜːbl/ *a* verbal; (*literal*) literal

verbatim /vɜː'beɪtɪm/ *adv* literalmente, palavra por palavra

verbose /vɜː'bəʊs/ *a* palavroso, prolixo

verdict /'vɜːdɪkt/ *n* veredicto *m*; (*opinion*) opinião *f*

verge /vɜːdʒ/ *n* beira *f*, borda *f* □ *vi* **~ on** estar à beira de. **on the ~ of doing** prestes a fazer

verify /'verɪfaɪ/ *vt* verificar

veritable /'verɪtəbl/ *a* autêntico, verdadeiro

vermicelli /vɜːmɪ'selɪ/ *n* aletria *f*

vermin /'vɜːmɪn/ *n* animais *mpl* nocivos; (*lice, fleas etc*) parasitas *mpl*

vermouth /'vɜːməθ/ *n* vermute *m*

vernacular /və'nækjʊlə(r)/ *n* vernáculo *m*; (*dialect*) dialeto *m*, (P) dialecto *m*

versatil|e /'vɜːsətaɪl/ *a* versátil; (*tool*) que serve para vários fins. **~ity** /-'tɪlətɪ/ *n* versatilidade *f*

verse /vɜːs/ *n* (*poetry*) verso *m*, poesia *f*; (*stanza*) estrofe *f*; (*of Bible*) versículo *m*

versed /vɜːst/ *a* **~ in** versado em, conhecedor de

version /'vɜːʃn/ *n* versão *f*

versus /'vɜːsəs/ *prep* contra

vertebra /'vɜːtɪbrə/ *n* (*pl* **-brae** /-briː/) vértebra *f*

vertical /'vɜːtɪkl/ *a* vertical. **~ly** *adv* verticalmente

vertigo /'vɜːtɪgəʊ/ *n* vertigem *f*

verve /vɜːv/ *n* verve *f*, vivacidade *f*

very /'verɪ/ *adv* muito □ *a* (*actual*) mesmo, próprio; (*exact*) preciso, exato, (P) exacto. **the ~ day/etc** o próprio *or* o mesmo dia/*etc*. **at the ~ end** mesmo *or* precisamente no fim. **the ~ first/best/etc** (*emph*) o primeiro/melhor/*etc* de todos. **~ much** muito. **~ well** muito bem

vessel /'vesl/ *n* vaso *m*

vest[1] /vest/ *n* corpete *m*, (P) camisola *f* interior; (*Amer: waistcoat*) colete *m*

vest[2] /vest/ *vt* conferir (**in** a). **~ed interests** interesses *mpl*

vestige /'vestɪdʒ/ *n* vestígio *m*

vestry /'vestrɪ/ *n* sacristia *f*

vet /vet/ *n* (*colloq*) veterinário *m* □ *vt* (*pt* **vetted**) (*candidate etc*) examinar atentamente, estudar

veteran /'vetərən/ *n* veterano *m*. **(war) ~** veterano *m* de guerra

veterinary /'vetərɪnərɪ/ *a* veterinário. **~ surgeon** veterinário *m*

veto /'viːtəʊ/ *n* (*pl* **-oes**) veto *m*; (*right*) direito *m* de veto □ *vt* vetar, opor o veto a

vex /veks/ *vt* aborrecer, irritar, contrariar. **~ed question** questão *f* muito debatida, assunto *m* controverso

via /'vaɪə/ *prep* por, via

viab|le /'vaɪəbl/ *a* viável. **~ility** /-'bɪlətɪ/ *n* viabilidade *f* viaduct /'vaɪədʌkt/ n viaduto m

vibrant /'vaɪbrənt/ a vibrante

vibrat|e /vaɪ'breɪt/ vt/i (fazer) vibrar. ~ion /-ʃn/ n vibração f

vicar /'vɪkə(r)/ n (Anglican) pastor m; (Catholic) vigário m, pároco m. ~age n presbitério m

vicarious /vɪ'keərɪəs/ a vivido indiretamente, (P) indirectamente

vice¹ /vaɪs/ n (depravity) vício m

vice² /vaɪs/ n (techn) torno m

vice- /vaɪs/ pref vice-. ~- chairman vice-presidente m. ~-chancellor n vice-chanceler m; (univ) reitor m. ~-consul n vice-cônsul m. ~-president n vice-presidente mf

vice versa /'vaɪsɪ'vɜːsə/ adv vice-versa

vicinity /vɪ'smətɪ/ n vizinhança f, cercania(s) fpl, arredores mpl. in the ~ of nos arredores de

vicious /'vɪʃəs/ a (spiteful) mau, maldoso; (violent) brutal, feroz. ~ circle círculo m vicioso. ~ly adv maldosamente; (violently) brutalmente, ferozmente

victim /'vɪktɪm/ n vítima f

victimiz|e /'vɪktɪmaɪz/ vt perseguir. ~ation /-'zeɪʃn/ n perseguição f

victor /'vɪktə(r)/ n vencedor m

victor|y /'vɪktərɪ/ n vitória f. ~ious /-'tɔːrɪəs/ a vitorioso

video /'vɪdɪəʊ/ a vídeo ▫ n (pl -os) (colloq) vídeo m ▫ vt (record) gravar em vídeo. ~ cassette videocassete m ~ recorder videocassete m

vie /vaɪ/ vi (pres p vying) rivalizar, competir (with com)

view /vjuː/ n vista f ▫ vt ver; (examine) examinar; (consider) considerar, ver; (a house) visitar, ver. in my ~ a meu ver, na minha opinião. in ~ of em vista de. on ~ em exposição, à mostra; (open to the public) aberto ao público. with a ~ to com a intenção de, com o fim de. ~er n (TV) telespectador m; (for slides) visor m

viewfinder /'vjuːfaɪndə(r)/ n visor m

viewpoint /'vjuːpɔɪnt/ n ponto m de vista

vigil /'vɪdʒɪl/ n vigília f; (over corpse) velório m; (relig) vigília f

vigilan|t /'vɪdʒɪlənt/ a vigilante. ~ce /-'vɪdʒɪ'lænti/ n vigilante m

vig|our /'vɪgə(r)/ n vigor m. ~orous /'vɪgərəs/ a vigoroso

vile /vaɪl/ a (base) infame, vil; (colloq: bad) horroroso, péssimo

villa /'vɪlə/ n vivenda f, vila f; (country residence) casa f de campo

village /'vɪlɪdʒ/ n aldeia f, povoado m. ~r n aldeão m, aldeã f

villain /'vɪlən/ n patife m, mau-caráter m. ~y n infâmia f, vilania f

vindicat|e /'vɪndɪkeɪt/ vt vindicar, justificar. ~ion /-'keɪʃn/ n justificação f

vindictive /vɪn'dɪktɪv/ a vingativo

vine /vaɪn/ n (plant) vinha f

vinegar /'vɪnɪgə(r)/ n vinagre m

vineyard /'vɪnjəd/ n vinha f, vinhedo m

vintage /'vɪntɪdʒ/ n (year) ano m de colheita de qualidade excepcional ▫ a (wine) de colheita excepcional e de um determinado ano; (car) de museu (colloq), fabricado entre 1917 e 1930

vinyl /'vaɪnɪl/ n vinil m

viola /vɪ'əʊlə/ n (mus) viola f, violeta f

violat|e /'vaɪəleɪt/ vt violar. ~ion /-'leɪʃn/ n violação f

violen|t /'vaɪələnt/ a violento. ~ce n violência f. ~tly adv violentamente, com violência

violet /'vaɪələt/ n (bot) violeta f; (colour) violeta m ▫ a violeta

violin /vaɪə'lɪn/ n violino m. ~ist n violinista mf

VIP /viːaɪ'piː/ abbr (very important person) VIP m, personalidade f importante

viper /'vaɪpə(r)/ n víbora f

virgin /'vɜːdʒɪn/ a & n virgem (f); ~ity /vəˈdʒɪnətɪ/ n virgindade f

Virgo /'vɜːgəʊ/ n (astr) Virgem f, (P) virgo m

viril|e /'vɪraɪl/ a viril, varonil. ~ity /vɪˈrɪlətɪ/ n virilidade f

virtual /'vɜːtʃʊəl/ a que é na prática embora não em teoria, verdadeiro. a ~ failure/etc praticamente um fracasso/etc. ~ly adv praticamente

virtue /'vɜːtʃuː/ n (goodness, chastity) virtude f; (merit) mérito m. by or in ~ of por or em virtude de

virtuos|o /vɜːtʃʊ'əʊsəʊ/ n (pl -si /-siː/) virtuoso m, virtuose mf. ~ity /-'ɒsətɪ/ n virtuosidade f, virtuosismo m

virtuous /'vɜːtʃʊəs/ a virtuoso

virulen|t /'vɪrʊlənt/ a virulento. ~ce /-ləns/ n virulência f

virus /'vaɪərəs/ n (pl -es) vírus m; (colloq: disease) virose f

visa /'viːzə/ n visto m

viscount /'vaɪkaʊnt/ n visconde m. ~ess /-ɪs/ n viscondessa f

viscous /'vɪskəs/ a viscoso

vise /vaɪs/ n (Amer: vice) torno m

visib|le /'vɪzəbl/ a visível. ~ility /-'bɪlətɪ/ n visibilidade f. ~ly adv visivelmente

vision /'vɪʒn/ n (dream, insight) visão f; (seeing, sight) vista f, visão f

v

visionary /'vɪʒənərɪ/ a visionário; (plan, scheme etc) fantasista, quimérico □ n visionário m

visit /'vɪzɪt/ vt (pt visited) (person) visitar, fazer uma visita a; (place) visitar □ vi estar de visita □ n (tour, call) visita f, (stay) estada f, visita f. ~or n visitante mf; (guest) visita f

visor /'vaɪzə(r)/ n viseira f; (in vehicle) visor m

vista /'vɪstə/ n vista f, panorama m

visual /'vɪʒʊəl/ a visual. ~ display unit terminal m de vídeo. ~ly adv visualmente

visualize /'vɪʒʊəlaɪz/ vt visualizar; (foresee) imaginar, prever

vital /'vaɪtl/ a vital. ~ statistics estatísticas fpl demográficas; (colloq: woman) medidas fpl

vitality /var'tælətɪ/ n vitalidade f

vitamin /'vɪtəmɪn/ n vitamina f

vivacious /vɪ'veɪʃəs/ a cheio de vida, vivo, animado. ~ity /-'væsətɪ/ n vivacidade f, animação f

vivid /'vɪvɪd/ a vívido; (imagination) vivo. ~ly adv vividamente

vivisection /vɪvɪ'sekʃn/ n vivissecção f

vixen /'vɪksn/ n raposa f fêmea

vocabulary /və'kæbjʊlərɪ/ n vocabulário m

vocal /'vəʊkl/ a vocal; (fig: person) eloquente, (P) eloquente. ~ cords cordas fpl vocais. ~ist n vocalista mf

vocation /və'keɪʃn/ n vocação f; (trade) profissão f. ~al a vocacional, profissional

vociferous /və'sɪfərəs/ a vociferante

vodka /'vɒdkə/ n vodka m

vogue /vəʊg/ n voga f, moda f, popularidade f. in ~ em voga, na moda

voice /vɔɪs/ n voz f □ vt (express) exprimir

void /vɔɪd/ a vazio; (jur) nulo, sem validade □ n vácuo m, vazio m. make ~ anular, invalidar. ~ of sem, destituído de

volatile /'vɒlətaɪl/ a (substance) volátil; (fig: changeable) instável

volcano /vɒl'keɪnəʊ/ n (pl -oes) vulcão m. ~ic /-ænɪk/ a vulcânico

volition /və'lɪʃn/ n of one's own ~ de sua própria vontade

volley /'vɒlɪ/ n (of blows etc) saraivada f; (of gunfire) salva f; (tennis) voleio m. ~ball n voleibol m, vôlei m

volt /vəʊlt/ n volt m. ~age n voltagem f

voluble /'vɒljʊbl/ a falante, loquaz

volume /'vɒljuːm/ n (book, sound) volume m; (capacity) capacidade f

voluntary /'vɒləntərɪ/ a voluntário; (unpaid) não-remunerado. ~ily /-trəlɪ/ adv voluntariamente

volunteer /vɒlən'tɪə(r)/ n voluntário m □ vi oferecer-se (to do para fazer); (mil) alistar-se como voluntário □ vt oferecer espontaneamente

voluptuous /və'lʌptʃʊəs/ a voluptuoso, sensual

vomit /'vɒmɪt/ vt/i (pt vomited) vomitar □ n vômito m, (P) vómito m

voodoo /'vuːduː/ n vodu m

voracious /və'reɪʃəs/ a voraz. ~ously adv vorazmente. ~ty /və'ræsətɪ/ n voracidade f

vote /vəʊt/ n voto m; (right) direito m de voto □ vt/i votar. ~er n eleitor m. ~ing n votação f; (poll) escrutínio m

vouch /vaʊtʃ/ vi ~ for responder por, garantir

voucher /'vaʊtʃə(r)/ n (for meal, transport) vale m; (receipt) comprovante m

vow /vaʊ/ n voto m □ vt (loyalty etc) jurar (to a). ~ to do jurar fazer

vowel /'vaʊəl/ n vogal f

voyage /'vɔɪɪdʒ/ n viagem (por mar) f. ~r /-ə(r)/ n viajante m

vulgar /'vʌlgə(r)/ a ordinário, grosseiro; (in common use) vulgar. ~ity /-'gærətɪ/ n (behaviour) grosseria f, vulgaridade f

vulnerable /'vʌlnərəbl/ a vulnerável. ~ility /-'bɪlətɪ/ n vulnerabilidade f

vulture /'vʌltʃə(r)/ n abutre m, urubu m

vying /'vaɪɪŋ/ see vie

Ww

wad /wɒd/ n bucha f, tampão m; (bundle) maço m, rolo m

wadding /'wɒdɪŋ/ n enchimento m

waddle /'wɒdl/ vi bambolear-se, rebolar-se, gingar

wade /weɪd/ vi ~ through (fig) avançar a custo por; (mud, water) patinhar em

wafer /'weɪfə(r)/ n (biscuit) bolacha f de baunilha; (relig) hóstia f

waffle[1] /'wɒfl/ n (colloq: talk) lengalenga f, papo m, conversa f; (colloq: writing) lenga-lenga □ vi (colloq) escrever muito sem dizer nada de importante

waffle[2] /'wɒfl/ n (culin) waffle m

waft /wɒft/ vi flutuar □ vt espalhar, levar suavemente

wag /wæg/ vt/i (pt wagged) abanar, agitar, sacudir

wage[1] /weɪdʒ/ vt (campaign, war) fazer

wage[2] /weɪdʒ/ n ~(s) (weekly, daily) salário m, ordenado m. ~-**claim** n pedido m de aumento de salário. ~-**earner** n trabalhador m assalariado. ~-**freeze** n congelamento m de salários

wager /'weɪdʒə(r)/ n (bet) aposta f ▫ vt apostar (**that** que)

waggle /'wægl/ vt/i abanar, agitar, sacudir

wagon /'wægən/ n (horse-drawn) carroça f; (rail) vagão m de mercadorias

waif /weɪf/ n criança f abandonada

wail /weɪl/ vi lamentar-se, gemer lamentosamente ▫ n lamentação f, gemido m lamentoso

waist /weɪst/ n cintura f. ~-**line** n cintura f

waistcoat /'weɪskəʊt/ n colete m

wait /weɪt/ vt/i esperar ▫ n espera f. ~ **for** esperar. ~ **on** servir. **lie in** ~ (**for**) estar escondido à espera (de), armar uma emboscada (para). **keep sb** ~**ing** fazer alguém esperar. ~**ing-list** n lista f de espera. ~**ing-room** n sala f de espera

wait|er /'weɪtə(r)/ n garçon m, (P) criado m (de mesa). ~**ress** n garçonete f, (P) criada f (de mesa)

waive /weɪv/ vt renunciar a, desistir de

wake[1] /weɪk/ vt/i (pt **woke**, pp **woken**) ~ (**up**) acordar, despertar ▫ n (before burial) velório m

wake[2] /weɪk/ n (ship) esteira f (de espuma) f. **in the** ~ **of** (following) atrás de, em seguida a

waken /'weɪkən/ vt/i acordar, despertar

Wales /weɪlz/ n País m de Gales

walk /wɔːk/ vi andar, caminhar; (not ride) ir a pé; (stroll) passear ▫ vt (streets) andar por, percorrer; (distance) andar, fazer a pé, percorrer; (dog) (levar para) passear ▫ n (stroll) passeio m, volta f; (excursion) caminhada f; (gait) passo m, maneira f de andar; (pace) passo m; (path) caminho m. **it's a 5-minute** ~ são 5 minutos a pé. ~ **of life** meio m, condição f social. ~ **out** (go away) sair; (go on strike) fazer greve. ~ **out on** abandonar. ~-**over** n vitória f fácil

walker /'wɔːkə(r)/ n caminhante mf

walkie-talkie /wɔːkɪ'tɔːkɪ/ n walkie-talkie m

walking /'wɔːkɪŋ/ n andar (a pé) m, marcha (a pé) f ▫ a (colloq: dictionary) vivo. ~-**stick** n bengala f

Walkman /'wɔːkmæn/ n walkman m

wall /wɔːl/ n parede f; (around land) muro m; (of castle, town; fig) muralha f; (of stomach etc) parede(s) f (pl) ▫ vt

(city) fortificar; (property) murar. **go to the** ~ sucumbir, falir; (firm) ir à falência. **up the** ~ (colloq) fora de si

wallet /'wɒlɪt/ n carteira f

wallflower /'wɔːlflaʊə(r)/ n (bot) goivo m. **be a** ~ (fig) tomar chá de cadeira, (P) levar banho de cadeira

wallop /'wɒləp/ vt (pt **walloped**) (sl) espancar (colloq) ▫ n (sl) pancada f forte

wallow /'wɒləʊ/ vi (in mud) chafurdar; (fig) regozijar-se

wallpaper /'wɔːlpeɪpə(r)/ n papel m de parede ▫ vt forrar com papel de parede

walnut /'wɔːlnʌt/ n (nut) noz f; (tree) nogueira f

walrus /'wɔːlrəs/ n morsa f

waltz /wɔːls/ n valsa f ▫ vi valsar

wan /wɒn/ a pálido

wand /wɒnd/ n (magic) varinha f mágica or de condão

wander /'wɒndə(r)/ vi andar ao acaso, vagar, errar; (river) serpentear; (mind, speech) divagar; (stray) extraviar-se. ~**er** n vagabundo m, andarilho m. ~**ing** a errante

wane /weɪn/ vi diminuir, minguar; (decline) declinar ▫ n **on the** ~ em declínio; (moon) no quarto minguante

wangle /'wæŋgl/ vt (colloq) conseguir algo através de pistolão

want /wɒnt/ vt querer (**to do** fazer); (need) precisar (de); (ask for) exigir, requerer ▫ vi ~ **for** ter falta de ▫ n (need) necessidade f, precisão f; (desire) desejo m; (lack) falta f, carência f. **for** ~ **of** por falta de. **I** ~ **you to go** eu quero que você vá. ~**ed** a (criminal) procurado pela polícia; (in ad) precisa(m)-se

wanting /'wɒntɪŋ/ a falho, falto (**in** de). **be found** ~ não estar à altura

wanton /'wɒntən/ a (playful) travesso, brincalhão; (cruelty, destruction etc) gratuito; (woman) despudorado

WAP /wæp/ a WAP

war /wɔː(r)/ n guerra f. **at** ~ em guerra. **on the** ~-**path** em pé de guerra

warble /'wɔːbl/ vt/i gorjear

ward /wɔːd/ n (in hospital) enfermaria f; (jur: minor) pupilo m; (pol) círculo m eleitoral ▫ vt ~ **off** (a blow) aparar; (anger) desviar; (danger) prevenir, evitar

warden /'wɔːdn/ n (of institution) diretor m, (P) director m; (of park) guarda m

warder /'wɔːdə(r)/ n guarda (de prisão) m, carcereiro m

wardrobe /'wɔːdrəʊb/ n (place) armário m, guarda-roupa m, (P) guarda-fato m,

w

(*P*) roupeiro *m*; (*clothes*) guarda-
roupa *m*

warehouse /'weəhaʊs/ *n* (*pl* **-s** /-haʊzɪz/)
armazém *m*, depósito *m* de
mercadorias

wares /weəz/ *npl* (*goods*) mercadorias
fpl, artigos *mpl*

warfare /'wɔːfeə(r)/ *n* guerra *f*

warhead /'wɔːhed/ *n* ogiva (de combate) *f*

warlike /'wɔːlaɪk/ *a* marcial, guerreiro;
(*bellicose*) belicoso

warm /wɔːm/ *a* (**-er**, **-est**) quente;
(*hearty*) caloroso, cordial. **be** *or* **feel**
~ estar com *or* ter *or* sentir calor □ *vt/i*
~ (**up**) aquecer(-se). ~**-hearted** *a*
afetuoso, (*P*) afectuoso, com calor
humano. ~**ly** *adv* (*heartily*)
calorosamente. **wrap up** ~**ly**
agasalhar-se bem. ~**th** *n* calor *m*

warn /wɔːn/ *vt* avisar, prevenir. ~ **sb off**
sth (*advise against*) pôr alguém de
prevenção *or* de pé atrás com alg coisa;
(*forbid*) proibir alg coisa a alguém.
~**ing** *n* aviso *m*. ~**ing light** lâmpada *f*
de advertência. **without** ~**ing** sem
aviso, sem prevenir

warp /wɔːp/ *vt/i* (*wood etc*) empenar; (*fig*:
pervert) torcer, deformar, desvirtuar.
~**ed** *a* (*fig*) deturpado, pervertido

warrant /'wɒrənt/ *n* autorização *f*; (*for
arrest*) mandato (de captura) *m*; (*comm*)
título *m* de crédito, warrant *m* □ *vt*
justificar; (*guarantee*) garantir

warranty /'wɒrəntɪ/ *n* garantia *f*

warring /'wɔːrɪŋ/ *a* em guerra; (*rival*)
contrário, antagônico, (*P*) antagónico

warrior /'wɒrɪə(r)/ *n* guerreiro *m*

warship /'wɔːʃɪp/ *n* navio *m* de guerra

wart /wɔːt/ *n* verruga *f*

wartime /'wɔːtaɪm/ *n* **in** ~ em tempo de
guerra

wary /'weərɪ/ *a* (**-ier**, **-iest**) cauteloso,
prudente

was /wɒz/; *unstressed* /wəz/ *see* **be**

wash /wɒʃ/ *vt/i* lavar(-se); (*flow over*)
molhar, inundar □ *n* lavagem *f*; (*dirty
clothes*) roupa *f* para lavar; (*of ship*)
esteira *f*; (*of paint*) fina camada *f* de
tinta. **have a** ~ lavar-se. ~**-basin** *n* pia
f, (*P*) lavatório *m*. ~**-cloth** *n* (*Amer*:
face-cloth) toalha *f* de rosto. ~ **one's
hands of** lavar as mãos de. ~ **out** (*cup
etc*) lavar; (*stain*) tirar lavando. ~**-out** *n*
(*sl*) fiasco *m*. ~**-room** *n* (*Amer*)
banheiro *m*, (*P*) casa *f* de banho. ~ **up**
lavar a louça; (*Amer*: *wash oneself*)
lavar-se. ~**able** *a* lavável. ~**ing** *n*
(*dirty*) roupa *f* suja; (*clean*) roupa *f*
lavada. ~**ing-machine** *n* máquina *f* de
lavar roupa. ~**ing-powder** *n*
detergente *m* em pó. ~**ing-up** *n*
lavagem *f* da louça

washed-out /wɒʃt'aʊt/ *a* (*faded*)
desbotado; (*exhausted*) exausto

washer /'wɒʃə(r)/ *n* (*machine*) máquina *f*
de lavar roupa, louça *f*, (*P*) loiça *f*;
(*ring*) anilha *f*

wasp /wɒsp/ *n* vespa *f*

wastage /'weɪstɪdʒ/ *n* desperdício *m*,
perda *f*. **natural** ~ desgaste *m* natural

waste /weɪst/ *vt* desperdiçar, esbanjar;
(*time*) perder □ *vi* ~ **away** consumir-se
□ *a* (*useless*) inútil; (*material*) de
refugo □ *n* desperdício *m*, perda *f*; (*of
time*) perda *f*; (*rubbish*) lixo *m*. **lay** ~
assolar, devastar. ~ (**land**) (*desolate*)
região *f* desolada, ermo *m*; (*unused*)
(terreno) baldio *m*. ~**-disposal unit**
triturador *m* de lixo. ~ **paper** papéis
mpl velhos. ~**-paper basket** cesto *m* de
papéis

wasteful /'weɪstfl/ *a* dispendioso;
(*person*) esbanjador, gastador,
perdulário

watch /wɒtʃ/ *vt/i* ver bem, olhar com
atenção, observar; (*game, TV*) ver;
(*guard, spy on*) vigiar; (*be careful
about*) tomar cuidado com □ *n* vigia *f*,
vigilância *f*; (*naut*) quarto *m*; (*for
telling time*) relógio *m*. ~**-dog** *n* cão *m*
de guarda. **on the** ~ (*look out*) estar à
espreita (**for** de); (*take care*) acautelar-
se. ~**-strap** *n* correia *f*, pulseira *f* do
relógio. ~**-tower** *n* torre *f* de
observação. ~**ful** *a* atento, vigilante

watchmaker /'wɒtʃmeɪkə(r)/ *n*
relojoeiro *m*

watchman /'wɒtʃmən/ *n* (*pl* **-men**)
(*of building*) guarda *m*. (**night-**)
~ guarda-noturno *m*

watchword /'wɒtʃwɜːd/ *n* lema *m*,
divisa *f*

water /'wɔːtə(r)/ *n* água *f* □ *vt* regar □ *vi*
(*of eyes*) lacrimejar, chorar. ~ **down**
juntar água a, diluir; (*milk, wine*)
aguar, batizar, (*P*) baptizar (*colloq*);
(*fig*: *tone down*) suavizar. ~**-closet** *n*
WC *m*, banheiro *m*, (*P*) lavabos *mpl*.
~**-colour** *n* aquarela *f*. ~**-ice** *n* sorvete
m. ~**-lily** *n* nenúfar *m*. ~**-main** *n* cano
m principal da rede. ~**-melon** *n*
melancia *f*. ~**-pistol** *n* pistola *f* de
água. ~ **polo** pólo *m* aquático.
~**-skiing** *n* esqui *m* aquático. ~**-wheel**
n roda *f* hidráulica

watercress /'wɔːtəkres/ *n* agrião *m*

waterfall /'wɔːtəfɔːl/ *n* queda *f* de água,
cascata *f*

watering-can /'wɔːtərɪŋkæn/ *n*
regador *m*

waterlogged /'wɔːtəlɒgd/ *a* saturado de
água; (*land*) empapado, alagado;
(*vessel*) inundado, alagado

W

watermark /'wɔːtəmaːk/ *n* (*in paper*) marca-d'água *f*, filigrana *f*

waterproof /'wɔːtəpruːf/ *a* impermeável; (*watch*) à prova d'água

watershed /'wɔːtəʃed/ *n* (*fig*) momento *m* decisivo; (*in affairs*) ponto *m* crítico

watertight /'wɔːtətaɪt/ *a* à prova d'água, hermético; (*fig: argument etc*) inequívoco, irrefutável

waterway /'wɔːtəweɪ/ *n* via *f* navegável

waterworks /'wɔːtəwɜːks/ *n* (*place*) estação *f* hidráulica

watery /'wɔːtərɪ/ *a* (*colour*) pálido; (*eyes*) lacrimoso; (*soup*) aguado; (*tea*) fraco

watt /wɒt/ *n* watt *m*

wav|e /weɪv/ *n* onda *f*; (*in hair; radio*) onda *f*; (*sign*) aceno *m* □ *vt* acenar com; (*sword*) brandir; (*hair*) ondular □ *vi* acenar (com a mão); (*hair etc*) ondular; (*flag*) tremular. **~eband** *n* faixa *f* de onda. **~e goodbye** dizer adeus. **~elength** *n* comprimento *m* de onda. **~y** *a* ondulado

waver /'weɪvə(r)/ *vi* vacilar; (*hesitate*) hesitar

wax[1] /wæks/ *n* cera *f* □ *vt* encerar; (*car*) polir. **~en, ~y** *adjs* de cera

wax[2] /wæks/ *vi* (*of moon*) aumentar, crescer

waxwork /'wækswɜːk/ *n* (*dummy*) figura *f* de cera. **~s** *npl* (*exhibition*) museu *m* de figuras de cera

way /weɪ/ *n* (*road, path*) caminho *m*, estrada *f*, rua *f* (**to** para); (*distance*) percurso *m*; (*direction*) (*P*) direcção *f*; (*manner*) modo *m*, maneira *f*; (*means*) meios *mpl*; (*respect*) respeito *m*. **~s** (*habits*) costumes *mpl* □ *adv* (*colloq*) consideravelmente, de longe. **be in the ~** atrapalhar. **be on one's** *or* **the ~** estar a caminho. **by the ~** a propósito. **by ~ of** por, via, através. **get one's own ~** conseguir o que quer. **give ~** (*yield*) ceder; (*collapse*) desabar; (*auto*) dar a preferência. **in a ~** de certo modo. **make one's ~** ir. **that ~** dessa maneira. **this ~** dessa maneira. **~ in** entrada *f*. **~ out** saída *f*. **~-out** *a* (*colloq*) excêntrico

waylay /weɪ'leɪ/ *vt* (*pt* -**laid**) (*assail*) armar uma cilada para; (*stop*) interceptar

wayward /'weɪwəd/ *a* (*wilful*) teimoso; (*perverse*) caprichoso, difícil

WC /dʌb(ə)ljuː'siː/ *n* WC *m*, banheiro *m*, (*P*) casa *f* de banho

we /wiː/ *pron* nós

weak /wiːk/ *a* (-**er**, -**est**) fraco; (*delicate*) frágil. **~en** *vt/i* enfraquecer; (*give way*) fraquejar. **~ly** *adv* fracamente. **~ness** *n* fraqueza *f*; (*fault*) ponto *m* fraco. **a ~ness for** (*liking*) um fraco por

weakling /'wiːklɪŋ/ *n* fraco *m*

wealth /welθ/ *n* riqueza *f*; (*riches, resources*) riquezas *fpl*; (*quantity*) abundância *f*

wealthy /'welθɪ/ *a* (-**ier**, -**iest**) rico

wean /wiːn/ *vt* (*baby*) desmamar; (*from habit etc*) desabituar

weapon /'wepən/ *n* arma *f*

wear /weə(r)/ *vt* (*pt* **wore**, *pp* **worn**) (*have on*) usar, trazer; (*put on*) pôr; (*expression*) ter; (*damage*) gastar. **~ black/red**/*etc* vestir-se de preto/vermelho/*etc* □ *vi* (*last*) durar; (*become old, damaged etc*) gastar-se □ *n* (*use*) uso *m*; (*deterioration*) gasto *m*, uso *m*; (*endurance*) resistência *f*; (*clothing*) roupa *f*. **~ and tear** desgaste *m*. **~ down** gastar; (*person*) extenuar. **~ off** passar. **~ on** (*time*) passar lentamente. **~ out** gastar; (*tire*) esgotar

wear|y /'wɪərɪ/ *a* (-**ier**, -**iest**) fatigado, cansado; (*tiring*) fatigante, cansativo □ *vi* **~y of** cansar-se de. **~ily** *adv* com lassidão, cansadamente. **~iness** *n* fadiga *f*

weasel /'wiːzl/ *n* doninha *f*

weather /'weðə(r)/ *n* tempo *m* □ *a* meteorológico □ *vt* (*survive*) agüentar, (*P*) aguentar, resistir a. **under the ~** (*colloq: ill*) indisposto, achacado. **~-beaten** *a* curtido pelo tempo. **~ forecast** *n* boletim *m* meteorológico. **~-vane** *n* cata-vento *m*

weathercock /'weðəkɒk/ *n* (*lit & fig*) cata-vento *m*

weav|e[1] /wiːv/ *vt* (*pt* **wove**, *pp* **woven**) (*cloth etc*) tecer; (*plot*) urdir, criar □ *n* (*style*) tipo *m* de tecido. **~er** /-ə(r)/ *n* tecelão *m*, tecelã *f*. **~ing** *n* tecelagem *f*

weave[2] /wiːv/ *vi* (*move*) serpear; (*through traffic, obstacles*) ziguezaguear

web /web/ *n* (*of spider*) teia *f*; (*fabric*) tecido *m*; (*comput*) web *m*; (*on foot*) membrana *f* interdigital. **~bed** *a* (*foot*) palmado. **~bing** *n* (*in chair*) tira *f* de tecido forte. **~-footed** *a* palmípede. **~page** página *f* web. **~site** site *m*

wed /wed/ *vt/i* (*pt* **wedded**) casar (-se)

wedding /'wedɪŋ/ *n* casamento *m*. **~-cake** *n* bolo *m* de noiva. **~-ring** *n* aliança (de casamento) *f*

wedge /wedʒ/ *n* calço *m*, cunha *f*; (*cake*) fatia *f*; (*of lemon*) quarto *m*; (*under wheel etc*) calço *m*, cunha *f* □ *vt* calçar; (*push*) meter *or* enfiar à força; (*pack in*) entalar

Wednesday /'wenzdɪ/ *n* quarta-feira *f*

weed /wiːd/ *n* erva *f* daninha *f* □ *vt/i* arrancar as ervas, capinar. **~-killer** *n* herbicida *m*. **~ out** suprimir, arrancar. **~y** *a* (*fig: person*) fraco

W

week /wiːk/ *n* semana *f*. **a ~ today/ tomorrow** de hoje/de amanhã a oito dias. **~ly** *a* semanal □ *a & n* (*periodical*) (jornal) semanário (*m*) □ *adv* semanalmente, todas as semanas

weekday /ˈwiːkdeɪ/ *n* dia *m* de semana

weekend /ˈwiːkend/ *n* fim-de- semana *m*

weep /wiːp/ *vt/i* (*pt* **wept**) chorar (**for sb** por alguém). **~ing willow** (salgueiro-)chorão *m*

weigh /weɪ/ *vt/i* pesar. **~ anchor** levantar âncora *or* ferro, zarpar. **~ down** (*weight*) sobrecarregar; (*bend*) envergar; (*fig*) acabrunhar. **~ up** (*colloq: examine*) pesar

weight /weɪt/ *n* peso *m*. **lose ~** emagrecer. **put on ~** engordar. **~less** *a* imponderável. **~-lifter** *n* halterofilista *m*. **~-lifting** *n* halterofilia *f*. **~y** *a* pesado; (*subject etc*) de peso; (*influential*) influente

weighting /ˈweɪtɪŋ/ *n* suplemento *m* salarial

weir /wɪə(r)/ *n* represa *f*, açude *m*

weird /wɪəd/ *a* (**-er, -est**) misterioso; (*strange*) estranho, bizarro

welcom|e /ˈwelkəm/ *a* agradável; (*timely*) oportuno □ *int* (seja) benvindo! □ *n* acolhimento *m* □ *vt* acolher, receber; (*as greeting*) dar as boas vindas a. **be ~e** ser bem-vindo. **you're ~e!** (*after thank you*) não tem de quê!, de nada! **~e to do** livre para fazer. **~ing** *a* acolhedor

weld /weld/ *vt* soldar □ *n* solda *f*. **~er** *n* soldador *m*. **~ing** *n* soldagem *f*, soldadura *f*

welfare /ˈwelfeə(r)/ *n* bem-estar *m*; (*aid*) assistência *f*, previdência *f* social. **W~ State** Estado-Providência *m*

well[1] /wel/ *n* (*for water, oil*) poço *m*; (*of stairs*) vão *m*; (*of lift*) poço *m*

well[2] /wel/ *adv* (**better, best**) bem □ *a* bem (*invar*) □ *int* bem! **as ~** também. **we may as ~ go** é melhor irnos andando. **as ~ as** tão bem como; (*in addition*) assim como. **be ~** (*healthy*) ir *or* passar bem. **do ~** (*succeed*) sair-se bem, ser bem sucedido. **very ~** muito bem. **~ done!** bravo!, muito bem! **~-behaved** *a* bem comportado, educado. **~-being** *n* bem-estar *m*. **~-bred** *a* (bem) educado. **~-done** *a* (*of meat*) bem passado. **~-dressed** *a* bem vestido. **~-heeled** *a* (*colloq: wealthy*) rico. **~-informed** *a* versado, bem informado. **~-known** *a* (bem-) conhecido. **~-meaning** *a* bem intencionado. **~-off** *a* rico, próspero. **~-read** *a* instruído. **~-spoken** *a* bem- falante. **~-timed** *a* oportuno. **~-to-do**

a rico. **~-wisher** *n* admirador *m*, simpatizante *m*

wellington /ˈwelɪŋtən/ *n* (*boot*) bota *f* alta de borracha

Welsh /welʃ/ *a* galês □ *n* (*lang*) galês *m*. **~man** *n* galês *m*. **~ woman** *n* galesa *f*

wend /wend/ *vt* **~ one's way** dirigir-se, seguir o seu caminho

went /went/ *see* **go**

wept /wept/ *see* **weep**

were /wɜː(r)/; *unstressed* /wə(r)/ *see* **be**

west /west/ *n* oeste *m*. **the W~** (*pol*) o Oeste, o Ocidente □ *a* ocidental, do oeste □ *adv* ao oeste, para o oeste. **W~ Indian** *a & n* antilhano (*m*). **the W~ Indies** as Antilhas. **~erly** *a* ocidental, oeste. **~ward** *a* para o oeste. **~ward(s)** *adv* para o oeste

western /ˈwestən/ *a* ocidental, do oeste; (*pol*) ocidental □ *n* (*film*) filme *m* de cowboys, bangue- bangue *m*

westernize /ˈwestənaɪz/ *vt* ocidentalizar

wet /wet/ *a* (**wetter, wettest**) molhado; (*of weather*) chuvoso, de chuva; (*colloq: person*) fraco. **get ~** molhar-se □ *vt* (*pt* **wetted**) molhar. **~ blanket** (*colloq*) desmancha-prazeres *mf invar* (*colloq*). **~ paint** pintado de fresco. **~ suit** roupa *f* de mergulho

whack /wæk/ *vt* (*colloq*) bater em □ *n* (*colloq*) pancada *f*. **~ed** *a* (*colloq*) morto de cansaço, rebentado (*colloq*). **~ing** *a* (*sl*) enorme, de todo o tamanho

whale /weɪl/ *n* baleia *f*

wharf /wɔːf/ *n* (*pl* **wharfs**) cais *m*

what /wɒt/ *a* (*interr, excl*) que. **~ time is it?** que horas são? **~ an idea!** que idéia! □ *pron* (*interr*) (o) quê, como, o que, qual, quais; (*object*) o que; (*after prep*) que; (*that which*) o que, aquilo que. **~?** (o) quê?, como? **~ is it?** o que é? **~ is your address?** qual é o seu endereço? **~ is your name?** como se chama? **~ can you see?** o que é que você pode ver? **this is ~ I write with** é com isto que escrevo. **that's ~ I need** é disso que eu preciso. **do ~ you want** faça o que *or* aquilo que quiser. **~ about me/him/etc?** e eu/ele/etc? **~ about doing sth?** e se fizéssemos alg coisa? **~ for?** para quê?

whatever /wɒtˈevə(r)/ *a* **~ book**/etc qualquer livro/etc que seja □ *pron* (*no matter what*) qualquer que seja; (*anything that*) o que quer que, tudo o que. **nothing ~** absolutamente nada. **~ happens** aconteça o que acontecer. **do ~ you like** faça o que quiser

whatsoever /wɒtsəʊˈevə(r)/ *a & pron* = **whatever**

wheat /wiːt/ *n* trigo *m*

W

wheedle /'wiːdl/ vt convencer, persuadir, levar a

wheel /wiːl/ n roda f ◻ vt empurrar ◻ vi rodar, rolar. **at the ∼** (of vehicle) ao volante; (helm) ao leme

wheelbarrow /'wiːlbærəʊ/ n carrinho m de mão

wheelchair /'wiːltʃeə(r)/ n cadeira f de rodas

wheeze /wiːz/ vi respirar ruidosamente ◻ n respiração f difícil

when /wen/ adv, conj & pron quando. **the day/moment ∼** o dia/momento em que

whenever /wen'evə(r)/ conj & adv (at whatever time) quando quer que, quando; (every time that) (de) cada vez que, sempre que

where /weə(r)/ adv, conj & pron onde, aonde; (in which place) em que, onde; (whereas) enquanto que, ao passo que. **∼ is he going?** aonde é que ele vai? **∼-abouts** adv onde ◻ n paradeiro m. **∼by** adv pelo que. **∼upon** adv após o que, depois do que

whereas /weər'æz/ conj enquanto que, ao passo que

wherever /weər'evə(r)/ conj & adv onde quer que. **∼ can it be?** onde pode estar?

whet /wet/ vt (pt whetted) (appetite, desire) aguçar, despertar

whether /'weðə(r)/ conj se. **not know ∼** não saber se. **∼ I go or not** caso eu vá ou não

which /wɪtʃ/ interr & pron qual, que. **∼ bag is yours?** qual das malas é a sua? **∼ is your coat?** qual é o seu casaco? **do you know ∼ he's taken?** sabe qual/quais é que ele levou? ◻ rel pron que, o qual; (referring to whole sentence) o que; (after prep) que, o qual, cujo. **at ∼** em qual/que. **from ∼** do qual/que. **of ∼** do qual/de que. **to ∼** para o qual/o que

whichever /wɪtʃ'evə(r)/ a ∼ **book/etc** qualquer livro/etc que seja, seja que livro/etc for. **take ∼ book you wish** leve o livro que quiser ◻ pron qualquer, quaisquer

whiff /wɪf/ n (of fresh air) sopro m, lufada f; (smell) baforada f

while /waɪl/ n (espaço de) tempo m, momento m. **once in a ∼** de vez em quando ◻ conj (when) enquanto; (although) embora; (whereas) enquanto que ◻ vt **∼ away** (time) passar

whim /wɪm/ n capricho m

whimper /'wɪmpə(r)/ vi gemer; (baby) choramingar ◻ n gemido m; (baby) choro m

whimsical /'wɪmzɪkl/ a (person) caprichoso; (odd) bizarro

whine /waɪn/ vi lamuriar-se, queixar-se; (dog) ganir ◻ n lamúria f, queixume m; (dog) ganido m

whip /wɪp/ n chicote m ◻ vt (pt whipped) chicotear; (culin) bater ◻ vi (move) ir a toda a pressa. **∼-round** n (colloq) coleta f, vaquinha f. **∼ up** excitar; (cause) provocar; (colloq: meal) preparar rapidamente. **∼ped cream** creme m chantilly

whirl /wɜːl/ vt/i (fazer) rodopiar, girar ◻ n rodopio m

whirlpool /'wɜːlpuːl/ n redemoinho m

whirlwind /'wɜːlwɪnd/ n redemoinho m de vento, turbilhão m

whirr /wɜː(r)/ vi zunir, zumbir

whisk /wɪsk/ vt/i (snatch) levar/tirar bruscamente; (culin) bater; (flies) sacudir ◻ n (culin) batedeira f. **∼ away** (brush away) sacudir

whisker /'wɪskə(r)/ n fio m de barba. **∼s** npl (of animal) bigode m; (beard) barba f; (sideboards) suíças fpl

whisky /'wɪskɪ/ n uísque m

whisper /'wɪspə(r)/ vt/i sussurrar, murmurar; (of stream, leaves) sussurrar ◻ n sussurro m, murmúrio m. **in a ∼** baixinho, em voz baixa

whist /wɪst/ n uíste m, (P) whist m

whistle /'wɪsl/ n assobio m; (instrument) apito m ◻ vt/i assobiar; (with instrument) apitar

Whit /wɪt/ a **∼ Sunday** domingo m de Pentecostes

white /waɪt/ a (-er, -est) branco, alvo; (pale) pálido ◻ n (colour; of eyes; person) branco m; (of egg) clara (de ovo) f. **go ∼** (turn pale) empalidecer; (of hair) branquear, embranquecer. **∼ coffee** café m com leite. **∼-collar worker** empregado m de escritório. **∼ elephant** (fig) trambolho m, elefante m branco. **∼ lie** mentirinha f. **∼ness** n brancura f, alvura f

whiten /'waɪtn/ vt/i branquear

whitewash /'waɪtwɒʃ/ n cal f; (fig) encobrimento m ◻ vt caiar; (fig) encobrir

Whitsun /'wɪtsn/ n Pentecostes m

whittle /'wɪtl/ vt **∼ down** aparar, cortar aparas; (fig) reduzir gradualmente

whiz /wɪz/ vi (pt whizzed) (through air) zunir, sibilar; (rush) passar a toda a velocidade. **∼-kid** n (colloq) prodígio m

who /huː/ interr pron quem ◻ rel pron que, o(a) qual, os(as) que

whoever /huː'evə(r)/ pron (no matter who) quem quer que, seja quem for; (the one who) aquele que

whole /həʊl/ a inteiro, todo; (not broken) intacto. **the ∼ house/etc** toda a casa/etc ◻ n totalidade f; (unit) todo m. **as a ∼ no**

conjunto, como um todo. **on the** ~ de um modo geral. **~-hearted** *a* de todo o coração; (*person*) dedicado. **~-heartedly** *adv* sem reservas, sinceramente

wholefood /'həʊlfuːd/ *n* comida *f* integral

wholemeal /'həʊlmiːl/ *a* ~ **bread** pão *m* integral

wholesale /'həʊlseɪl/ *n* venda *f* por grosso *or* por atacado □ *a* (*firm*) por grosso, por atacado; (*fig*) sistemático, em massa □ *adv* (*in large quantities*) por atacado; (*fig*) em massa, em grande escala. **~r** /-ə(r)/ *n* grossista *mf*, atacadista *mf*

wholesome /'həʊlsəm/ *a* sadio, saudável

wholewheat /'həʊlwiːt/ *a* = **wholemeal**

wholly /'həʊlɪ/ *adv* inteiramente, completamente

whom /huːm/ *interr pron* quem □ *rel pron* (*that*) que; (*after prep*) quem, que, o qual

whooping cough /'huːpɪŋkɒf/ *n* coqueluche *f*

whore /hɔː(r)/ *n* prostituta *f*

whose /huːz/ *rel pron & a* cujo, de quem □ *interr pron* de quem. ~ **hat is this?**, ~ **is this hat?** de quem é este chapéu? ~ **son are you?** de quem é que o senhor é filho?

why /waɪ/ *adv* porque, por que motivo, por que razão, porquê. **she doesn't know** ~ **he's here** ela não sabe porque *or* por que motivo ele está aqui. **she doesn't know** ~ ela não sabe porquê. **do you know** ~? você sabe porquê? □ *int* (*protest*) ora, ora essa; (*discovery*) oh. ~ **yes**/*etc* ah, sim

wick /wɪk/ *n* torcida *f*, mecha *f*, pavio *m*

wicked /'wɪkɪd/ *a* mau, malvado; (*mischievous, spiteful*) maldoso. **~ly** *adv* maldosamente. **~ness** *n* maldade *f*, malvadeza *f*

wicker /'wɪkə(r)/ *n* verga *f*, vime *m*. **~-work** *n* trabalho *m* de verga *or* de vime

wicket /'wɪkɪt/ *n* (*cricket*) arco *m*

wide /waɪd/ *a* (**-er, -est**) largo; (*extensive*) vasto, grande, extenso. **two metres** ~ com dois metros de largura □ *adv* longe; (*fully*) completamente. **open** ~ (*door, window*) abrir(-se) de par em par, escancarar(-se); (*mouth*) abrir bem. ~ **awake** desperto, acordado. **far and** ~ por toda a parte. **~ly** *adv* largamente; (*travel, spread*) muito; (*generally*) geralmente; (*extremely*) extremamente

widen /'waɪdn/ *vt/i* alargar(-se)

widespread /'waɪdspred/ *a* muito espalhado, difundido

widow /'wɪdəʊ/ *n* viúva *f*. **~ed** *a* (*man*) viúvo; (*woman*) viúva. **be ~ed** enviuvar, ficar viúvo *or* viúva. **~er** *n* viúvo *m*. **~hood** *n* viuvez *f*

width /wɪdθ/ *n* largura *f*

wield /wiːld/ *vt* (*axe etc*) manejar; (*fig: power*) exercer

wife /waɪf/ *n* (*pl* **wives**) mulher *f*, esposa *f*

wig /wɪg/ *n* cabeleira (postiça) *f*; (*judge's etc*) peruca *f*

wiggle /'wɪgl/ *vt/i* remexer(-se), retorcer(-se), mexer(-se) dum lado para outro

wild /waɪld/ *a* (**-er, -est**) selvagem; (*of plant*) silvestre; (*mad*) louco; (*enraged*) furioso, violento □ *adv* a esmo; (*without control*) à solta. ~**s** *npl* regiões *fpl* selvagens. **~-goose chase** falsa pista *f*, tentativa *f* inútil. **~ly** *adv* violentamente; (*madly*) loucamente

wildcat /'waɪldkæt/ *a* ~ **strike** greve *f* ilegal

wilderness /'wɪldənɪs/ *n* deserto *m*

wildlife /'waɪldlaɪf/ *n* animais *mpl* selvagens

wile /waɪl/ *n* artimanha *f*; (*cunning*) astúcia *f*, manha *f*

wilful /'wɪlfl/ *a* (*person*) voluntarioso; (*act*) intencional, propositado

will¹ /wɪl/ *v aux* **you** ~ **sing**/**he** ~ **do**/*etc* tu cantarás/ele fará/*etc*. (*1st person: future expressing will or intention*) **I** ~ **sing**/**we** ~ **do**/*etc* eu cantarei/nós faremos/*etc*. ~ **you have a cup of coffee?** quer tomar um cafézinho? ~ **you shut the door?** quer fazer o favor de fechar a porta?

will² /wɪl/ *n* vontade *f*; (*document*) testamento *m*. **at** ~ à vontade, quando *or* como se quiser □ *vt* (*wish*) querer; (*bequeath*) deixar em testamento. **~-power** *n* força *f* de vontade

willing /'wɪlɪŋ/ *a* pronto, de boa vontade. ~ **to** disposto a. **~ly** *adv* (*with pleasure*) de boa vontade, de bom grado; (*not forced*) voluntariamente. **~ness** *n* boa vontade *f*, disposição *f* (**to do** em fazer)

willow /'wɪləʊ/ *n* salgueiro *m*

willy-nilly /wɪlɪ'nɪlɪ/ *adv* de bom ou de mau grado, quer queira ou não

wilt /wɪlt/ *vi* murchar, definhar

wily /'waɪlɪ/ *a* (**-ier, -iest**) manhoso, matreiro

win /wɪn/ *vt/i* (*pt* **won**, *pres p* **winning**) ganhar □ *n* vitória *f*. ~ **over** *vt* convencer, conquistar

winc|e /wɪns/ *vi* estremecer, contrair-se.

winch /wɪntʃ/ *n* guincho *m* □ *vt* içar com guincho

wind¹ /wɪnd/ *n* vento *m*; (*breath*) fôlego *m*; (*flatulence*) gases *mpl*. **get** ~ **of** (*fig*) ouvir rumor de. **put the ~ up** (*sl*) assustar. **in the ~** no ar. **~ farm** central *f* eólica. **~ instrument** (*mus*) instrumento *m* de sopro. **~-swept** *a* varrido pelo vento

wind² /waınd/ *vt/i* (*pt* **wound**) enrolar(-se); (*wrap*) envolver, pôr em volta; (*of path, river*) serpentear. **~ (up)** (*clock etc*) dar corda em. **~ up** (*end*) terminar, acabar; (*fig: speech etc*) concluir; (*firm*) liquidar. **he'll ~ up in jail** (*colloq*) ele vai acabar na cadeia. **~ing** *a* (*path*) sinuoso; (*staircase*) em caracol

windfall /'wındfɔːl/ *n* fruta *f* caída; (*fig: money*) sorte *f* grande

windmill /'wındmıl/ *n* moinho *m* de vento

window /'wındəʊ/ *n* janela *f*; (*of shop*) vitrine *f*, (*P*) montra *f*; (*counter*) guichê *m*, (*P*) guichet *m*. **~-box** *n* jardineira *f*, (*P*) floreira *f*. **~-cleaner** *n* limpador *m* de janelas. **~-dressing** *n* decoração *f* de vitrines; (*fig*) apresentação *f* cuidadosa. **~-ledge** *n* peitoril *m*. **~-pane** *n* vidro *m*, vidraça *f*. **go ~-shopping** ir ver vitrines. **~-sill** *n* peitoril *m*

windpipe /'wındpaıp/ *n* traquéia *f*, (*P*) traqueia *f*

windscreen /'wındskriːn/ *n* pára-brisa *m*, (*P*) pára-brisas *m invar*. **~-wiper** /-waıpə(r)/ *n* limpador *m* de pára-brisa

windshield /'wındʃiːld/ *n* (*Amer*) = **windscreen**

windsurf|er /'wındsɜːfə(r)/ *n* surfista *mf*. **~ing** *n* surfe *m*

windy /'wındı/ *a* (**-ier, -iest**) ventoso. **it is very ~** está ventando muito

wine /waın/ *n* vinho *m*. **~ bar** bar *m* para degustação de vinhos. **~-cellar** *n* adega *f*, cave *f*. **~-grower** *n* vinicultor *m*. **~-growing** *n* vinicultura *f*. **~-list** *n* lista *f* de vinhos. **~-tasting** *n* prova *f* or degustação *f* de vinhos. **~ waiter** garçon *m*

wineglass /'waıngla:s/ *n* copo *m* de vinho; (*with stem*) cálice *m*

wing /wıŋ/ *n* asa *f*; (*mil*) flanco *m*; (*archit*) ala *f*; (*auto*) pára-lamas *m invar*, (*P*) guarda-lamas *m invar*. **~s** (*theat*) bastidores *mpl*. **under sb's ~** debaixo das asas de alguém. **~ed** *a* alado

wink /wıŋk/ *vi* piscar o olho; (*light, star*) cintilar, piscar □ *n* piscadela *f*. **not sleep a ~** não pregar olho

winner /'wınə(r)/ *n* vencedor *m*

winning /'wınıŋ/ *see* **win** □ *a* vencedor, vitorioso; (*number*) premiado; (*smile*) encantador, atraente. **~-post** *n* meta *f*, poste de chegada *f*. **~s** *npl* ganhos *mpl*

wint|er /'wıntə(r)/ *n* inverno *m* □ *vi* hibernar. **~ry** *a* de inverno, invernoso; (*smile*) glacial

wipe /waıp/ *vt* limpar; (*dry*) enxugar, limpar □ *n* limpadela *f*. **~ off** limpar. **~ out** (*destroy*) aniquilar, limpar (*colloq*); (*cancel*) cancelar. **~ up** enxugar

wir|e /'waıə(r)/ *n* arame *m*; (*colloq: telegram*) telegrama *m*. (**electric**) **~e** fio elétrico *m*, (*P*) eléctrico □ *vt* (*a house*) montar a instalação elétrica em; (*colloq: telegraph*) telegrafar. **~e netting** rede *f* de arame. **~ing** *n* (*electr*) instalação *f* elétrica, (*P*) eléctrica

wireless /'waıəlıs/ *n* rádio *f*; (*set*) rádio *m*

wiry /'waıərı/ *a* (**-ier, -iest**) magro e rijo

wisdom /'wızdəm/ *n* sagacidade *f*, sabedoria *f*; (*common sense*) bom senso *m*, sensatez *f*. **~ tooth** dente *m* (do) sizo

wise /waız/ *a* (**-er, -est**) (*person*) sábio, avisado, sensato; (*look*) entendedor. **~ guy** (*colloq*) sabichão *m* (*colloq*), sabe-tudo *m* (*colloq*). **none the ~r** sem entender nada. **~ly** *adv* sensatamente

wisecrack /'waızkræk/ *n* (*colloq*) (boa) piada *f*

wish /wıʃ/ *n* (*desire, aspiration*) desejo *m*, vontade *f*; (*request*) pedido *m*; (*greeting*) desejo *m*, voto *m*. **I have no ~ to go** não tenho nenhum desejo *or* nenhuma vontade de ir □ *vt* (*desire, bid*) desejar; (*want*) apetecer, ter vontade de, desejar (to **do** fazer) □ *vi* **~ for** desejar. **~ sb well** desejar felicidades a alguém. **I don't ~ to go** não me apetece ir, não tenho vontade de ir, não desejo ir. **I ~ he'd leave** eu gostaria que ele partisse. **with best ~es** (*formal: in letter*) com os melhores cumprimentos, com saudações cordiais; (*on greeting card*) com desejos *or* votos (**for** de)

wishful /'wıʃfl/ *a* **~ thinking** sonhar acordado

wishy-washy /'wıʃıwɒʃı/ *a* sem expressão, fraco, inexpressivo

wisp /wısp/ *n* (*of hair*) pequena mecha *f*; (*of smoke*) fio *m*

wistful /'wıstfl/ *a* melancólico, saudoso

wit /wıt/ *n* inteligência *f*; (*humour*) presença *f* de espírito, humor *m*; (*person*) senso *m* de humor. **be at one's ~'s** *or* **~'s end** não saber o que fazer. **keep one's ~s about one** estar alerta. **live by one's ~s** ganhar a vida de maneira suspeita. **scared out of one's ~s** apavorado

witch /wıtʃ/ *n* feiticeira *f*, bruxa *f*. **~craft** *n* feitiçaria *f*, bruxaria *f*, magia *f*

with /wɪð/ prep com; (having) de; (because of) de; (at the house of) em casa de. **the man** ∼ **the beard** o homem de barbas. **fill**/etc ∼ encher/etc de. **laughing/shaking/** etc ∼ a rir/a tremer/etc de. **I'm not** ∼ **you** (colloq) não estou compreendendo-o

withdraw /wɪð'drɔː/ vt/i (pt **withdrew,** pp **withdrawn**) retirar (-se); (money) tirar. ∼**al** n retirada f; (med) estado m de privação. ∼**n** a (person) retraído, fechado

wither /'wɪðə(r)/ vt/i murchar, secar. ∼**ed** a (person) mirrado. ∼**ing** a (fig: scornful) desdenhoso

withhold /wɪð'həʊld/ vt (pt **withheld**) negar, recusar; (retain) reter; (conceal, not tell) esconder (**from** de)

within /wɪ'ðɪn/ prep & adv dentro (de), por dentro (de); (in distances) a menos de. ∼ **a month** (before) dentro de um mês. ∼ **sight** à vista

without /wɪ'ðaʊt/ prep sem. ∼ **fail** sem falta. **go** ∼ **saying** não ser preciso dizer

withstand /wɪð'stænd/ vt (pt **withstood**) resistir a, opor-se a

witness /'wɪtnɪs/ n testemunha f; (evidence) testemunho m ▫ vt testemunhar, presenciar; (document) assinar como testemunha. **bear** ∼ **to** testemunhar, dar testemunho de. ∼**-box** n banco m das testemunhas

witticism /'wɪtɪsɪzəm/ n dito m espirituoso

witty /'wɪtɪ/ a (-**ier**, -**iest**) espirituoso

wives /waɪvz/ see **wife**

wizard /'wɪzəd/ n feiticeiro m; (fig: genius) gênio m, (P) génio m

wizened /'wɪznd/ a encarquilhado

wobbl|e /'wɒbl/ vi (of jelly, voice, hand) tremer; (stagger) cambalear, vacilar; (of table, chair) balançar. ∼**y** a (trembling) trêmulo; (staggering) cambaleante, vacilante; (table, chair) pouco firme

woe /wəʊ/ n dor f, infortúnio m

woke, woken /wəʊk, 'wəʊkən/ see **wake**[1]

wolf /wʊlf/ n (pl **wolves** /wʊlvz/) lobo m ▫ vt (food) devorar. **cry** ∼ dar alarme falso. ∼**-whistle** n assobio m de admiração

woman /'wʊmən/ n (pl **women**) mulher f. ∼**hood** n as mulheres, o sexo feminino; (maturity) maturidade f. ∼**ly** a feminino

womb /wuːm/ n seio m, ventre m; (med) útero m; (fig) seio m

women /'wɪmɪn/ see **woman**. ∼**'s movement** movimento m feminista

won /wʌn/ see **win**

wonder /'wʌndə(r)/ n admiração f; (thing) maravilha f ▫ vt perguntar-se a si mesmo (**if** se) ▫ vi admirar-se (**at** de, com), ficar admirado, espantar-se (**at** com); (reflect) pensar (**about** em). **it is no** ∼ não admira (**that** que)

wonderful /'wʌndəfl/ a maravilhoso. ∼**ly** adv maravilhosamente. **it works** ∼**ly** funciona às mil maravilhas

won't /wəʊnt/ = **will not**

wood /wʊd/ n madeira f, pau m; (for burning) lenha f. ∼(**s**) n (pl) (area) bosque m, mata f, floresta f. ∼**ed** a arborizado. ∼**en** a de or em madeira, de pau; (fig: stiff) rígido; (fig: inexpressive) inexpressivo, de pau

woodcut /'wʊdkʌt/ n gravura f em madeira

woodland /'wʊdlənd/ n região f arborizada, bosque m, mata f

woodlouse /'wʊdlaʊs/ n (pl -**lice** /laɪs/) baratinha f, tatuzinho m

woodpecker /'wʊdpekə(r)/ n (bird) pica-pau m

woodwind /'wʊdwɪnd/ n (mus) instrumentos mpl de sopro de madeira

woodwork /'wʊdwɜːk/ n (of building) madeiramento m; (carpentry) carpintaria f

woodworm /'wʊdwɜːm/ n caruncho m

woody /'wʊdɪ/ a (wooded) arborizado; (like wood) lenhoso

wool /wʊl/ n lã f. ∼**len** a de lã. ∼**lens** npl roupas fpl de lã. ∼**ly** a de lã; (vague) confuso ▫ n (colloq: garment) roupa f de lã

word /wɜːd/ n palavra f; (news) notícia(s) f(pl); (promise) palavra f ▫ vt exprimir, formular. **by** ∼ **of mouth** de viva voz. **have a** ∼ **with** dizer duas palavras a. **in other** ∼**s** em outras palavras. ∼**-perfect** a que sabe de cor seu papel, a lição etc. ∼ **processor** processador m de textos. ∼**ing** n termos mpl, redação f, (P) redacção f. ∼**y** a prolixo

wore /wɔː(r)/ see **wear**

work /wɜːk/ n trabalho m; (product, book etc) obra f; (building etc) obras fpl. **at** ∼ no trabalho. **out of** ∼ desempregado. ∼**s** npl (techn) mecanismo m; (factory) fábrica f ▫ vt/ i (of person) trabalhar; (techn) (fazer) funcionar, (fazer) andar; (of drug etc) agir, fazer efeito; (farm, mine) explorar; (land) lavrar. ∼ **sb** (make work) fazer alguém trabalhar. ∼ **in** introduzir, inserir. ~ **loose** soltar-se. ~ **off** (*get rid of*) descarregar. ~ **out** *vt* (*solve*) resolver; (*calculate*) calcular; (*devise*) planejar □ *vi* (*succeed*) resultar; (*sport*) treinar-se. ~**station** *n* estação *f* de trabalho. ~**-to-rule** *n* greve *f* de zelo. ~ **up** *vt* criar □ *vi* (*to climax*) ir num crescendo. ~**ed up** (*person*) enervado, transtornado, agitado

workable /'wɜːkəbl/ *a* viável, praticável

workaholic /wɜːkə'hɒlɪk/ *n* **be a** ~ (*colloq*) trabalhar como um possesso (*colloq*)

worker /'wɜːkə(r)/ *n* trabalhador *m*, trabalhadora *f*; (*factory*) operário *m*

working /'wɜːkɪŋ/ *a* (*a day, clothes, hypothesis, lunch etc*) de trabalho. **the** ~ **class(es)** a classe operária, a(s) class(es) trabalhadora(s), o proletariado. ~**class** *a* operário, trabalhador. ~ **mother** mãe *f* que trabalha. ~ **party** comissão *f* consultiva, de estudo *etc.* ~**s** *npl* mecanismo *m*. **in** ~ **order** em condições de funcionamento

workman /'wɜːkmən/ *n* (*pl* -**men**) trabalhador *m*; (*factory*) operário *m*. ~**ship** *n* trabalho *m*, execução *f*, mão-de-obra *f*; (*skill*) arte *f*, habilidade *f*

workshop /'wɜːkʃɒp/ *n* oficina *f*

world /wɜːld/ *n* mundo *m* □ *a* mundial. **a** ~ **of** muito(s), grande quantidade de, um mundo de. ~**-wide** *a* mundial, universal

worldly /'wɜːldlɪ/ *a* terreno; (*devoted to the affairs of life*) mundano. ~ **goods** bens *mpl* materiais. ~**-wise** *a* com experiência do mundo

worm /wɜːm/ *n* verme *m*; (*earthworm*) minhoca *f* □ *vt* ~ **one's way into** insinuar-se, introduzir-se, enfiar-se. ~**-eaten** *a* (*wood*) carunchoso; (*fruit*) bichado, bichoso

worn /wɔːn/ *see* **wear** □ *a* usado. ~**-out** *a* (*thing*) completamente gasto; (*person*) esgotado

worr|y /'wʌrɪ/ *vt/i* preocupar(-se) □ *n* preocupação *f*. **don't** ~**y** fique descansado, não se preocupe. ~**ied** *a* preocupado. ~**ying** *a* preocupante, inquietante

worse /wɜːs/ *a & adv* pior □ *n* pior *m*. **get** ~ piorar. **from bad to** ~ de mal a pior. ~ **luck** pouca sorte, pena

worsen /'wɜːsn/ *vt/i* piorar

worship /'wɜːʃɪp/ *n* (*reverence*) reverência *f*, veneração *f*; (*religious*) culto *m* □ *vt* (*pt* **worshipped**) adorar, venerar □ *vi* fazer as suas devoções, praticar o culto. ~**per** *n* (*in church*)

fiel *m*. **Your/His W**~ Vossa/Sua Excelência *f*

worst /wɜːst/ *a & n* (**the**) ~ (o/a) pior (*mf*) □ *adv* pior. **if the** ~ **comes to the** ~ se o pior acontecer, na pior das hipóteses. **do one's** ~ fazer todo o mal que se quiser. **get the** ~ **of** it ficar a perder. **the** ~ (**thing**) **that** o pior que

worth /wɜːθ/ *a* **be** ~ valer; (*deserving*) merecer □ *n* valor *m*, mérito *m*. **ten pounds** ~ **of** dez libras de. **it's** ~ **it**, it's ~ **while** vale a pena. **it's not** ~ **my while** não vale a pena. **it's** ~ **waiting**/*etc* vale a pena esperar/*etc*. **for all one's** ~ (*colloq*) dando tudo por tudo. ~**less** *a* sem valor

worthwhile /'wɜːθwaɪl/ *a* que vale a pena; (*cause*) louvável, meritório

worthy /'wɜːðɪ/ *a* (-**ier**, -**iest**) (*deserving*) digno, merecedor (**of** de); (*laudable*) meritório, louvável □ *n* (*person*) pessoa *f* ilustre

would /wʊd/; *unstressed* /wəd/ *v aux* **he** ~ **do/you** ~ **sing**/*etc* (*conditional tense*) ele faria/você cantaria/*etc*. **he** ~ **have done** ele teria feito. **she** ~ **come every day** (*used to*) ela vinha *or* costumava vir aqui todos os dias. ~ **you please come here?** chegue aqui por favor. ~ **you like some tea?** você quer um chazinho? **he** ~**n't go** (*refused to*) ele não queria ir. ~**-be author/doctor**/*etc* aspirante a autor/médico/*etc*

wound[1] /wuːnd/ *n* ferida *f* □ *vt* ferir. **the** ~**ed** os feridos *mpl*

wound[2] /waʊnd/ *see* **wind**[2]

wove, woven /wəʊv, 'wəʊvn/ *see* **weave**

wrangle /'ræŋgl/ *vi* disputar, discutir, brigar □ *n* disputa *f*, discussão *f*, briga *f*

wrap /ræp/ *vt* (*pt* **wrapped**) ~ (**up**) embrulhar (**in** em); (*in cotton wool, mystery etc*) envolver (**in** em) □ *vi* ~ **up** (*dress warmly*) abrigar-se bem, agasalhar-se bem □ *n* xale *m*. ~**ped up in** (*engrossed*) absorto em, mergulhado em. ~**per** *n* (*of sweet*) papel *m*; (*of book*) capa *f* de papel. ~**ing** *n* embalagem *f*

wrath /rɒθ/ *n* ira *f*. ~**ful** *a* irado

wreak /riːk/ *vt* ~ **havoc** (*of storm etc*) fazer estragos

wreath /riːθ/ *n* (*pl* -**s** /-ðz/) (*of flowers, leaves*) coroa *f*, grinalda *f*

wreck /rek/ *n* (*sinking*) naufrágio *m*; (*ship*) navio *m* naufragado; restos *mpl* de navio; (*remains*) destroços *mpl*; (*vehicle*) veículo *m* destroçado □ *vt* destruir; (*ship*) fazer naufragar, afundar; (*fig: hope*) acabar. **be a**

W

nervous ∼ estar com os nervos arrasados. ∼**age** n (pieces) destroços mpl

wren /ren/ n (bird) carriça f

wrench /rentʃ/ vt (pull) puxar; (twist) torcer; (snatch) arrancar (**from** a) ▫ n (pull) puxão m; (of ankle, wrist) torcedura f; (tool) chave f inglesa; (fig) dor f de separação

wrest /rest/ vt arrancar (**from** a)

wrestl|e /'resl/ vi lutar, debater-se (**with** com or contra). ∼**er** n lutador m. ∼**ing** n luta f

wretch /retʃ/ n desgraçado m, miserável mf; (rascal) miserável mf

wretched /'retʃɪd/ a (pitiful, poor) miserável; (bad) horrível, desgraçado

wriggle /'rɪgl/ vt/i remexer(-se), contorcer-se

wring /rɪŋ/ vt (pt wrung) (twist; clothes) torcer. ∼ **out of** (obtain from) arrancar a. ∼**ing wet** encharcado; (of person) encharcado até os ossos

wrinkle /'rɪŋkl/ n (on skin) ruga f; (crease) prega f ▫ vt/i enrugar (-se)

wrist /rɪst/ n pulso m. ∼-**watch** n relógio m de pulso

writ /rɪt/ n (jur) mandado m judicial

write /raɪt/ vt/i (pt wrote, pp written) escrever. ∼ **back** responder. ∼ **down** escrever, tomar nota de. ∼ **off** (debt) dar por liquidado; (vehicle) destinar à sucata. ∼-**off** n perda f total. ∼ **out** (in full) escrever por extenso. ∼ **up** (from notes) redigir. ∼-**up** n relato m; (review) crítica f

writer /'raɪtə(r)/ n escritor m, autor m

writhe /raɪð/ vi contorcer(-se)

writing /'raɪtɪŋ/ n escrita f. ∼**(s)** (works) escritos mpl, obras fpl. **in** ∼ por escrito. ∼-**paper** n papel m de carta

written /'rɪtn/ see write

wrong /rɒŋ/ a (incorrect, mistaken) mal, errado; (unfair) injusto; (wicked) mau; (amiss) que não está bem; (mus: note) falso; (clock) que não está certo ▫ adv mal ▫ n mal m; (injustice) injustiça f ▫ vt (do a wrong to) ser injusto com; (do a wrong to) fazer mal a. **what's** ∼? qual é o problema? **what's** ∼ **with it?** (amiss) o que é que não vai bem?; (morally) que mal há nisso?, que mal tem? **he's in the** ∼ (his fault) ele não tem razão. **go** ∼ (err) desencaminhar-se; (fail) ir mal; (vehicle) quebrar. ∼**ly** adv mal; (blame etc) sem razão, injustamente

wrongful /'rɒŋfl/ a injusto, ilegal

wrote /rəʊt/ see write

wrought /rɔːt/ a ∼ **iron** ferro m forjado. ∼-**up** a excitado

wrung /rʌŋ/ see wring

wry /raɪ/ a (wryer, wryest) torto; (smile) forçado. ∼ **face** careta f

Xx

Xerox /'zɪərɒks/ n fotocópia f, xerox m ▫ vt fotocopiar, xerocar, tirar um xerox de

Xmas /'krɪsməs/ n Christmas

X-ray /'eksreɪ/ n raio X m; (photograph) radiografia f ▫ vt radiografar. **have an** ∼ tirar uma radiografia

xylophone /'zaɪləfəʊn/ n xilofone m

Yy

yacht /jɒt/ n iate m. ∼**ing** n iatismo m, andar m de iate; (racing) regata f de iate

yank /jæŋk/ vt (colloq) puxar bruscamente ▫ n (colloq) puxão m

Yank /jæŋk/ n (colloq) ianque mf

yap /jæp/ vi (pt yapped) latir

yard¹ /jaːd/ n (measure) jarda f (= 0,9144 m). ∼**age** n medida f em jardas

yard² /jaːd/ n (of house) pátio m; (Amer: garden) jardim m; (for storage) depósito m

yardstick /'jaːdstɪk/ n jarda f; (fig) bitola f, craveira f

yarn /jaːn/ n (thread) fio m; (colloq: tale) longa história f

yawn /jɔːn/ vi bocejar; (be wide open) abrir-se, escancarar-se ▫ n bocejo m. ∼**ing** a escancarado

year /jɪə(r)/ n ano m. **school/tax** ∼ ano m escolar/fiscal. **be ten/**etc ∼**s old** ter dez/etc anos de idade. ∼-**book** n anuário m. ∼**ly** a anual ▫ adv anualmente

yearn /jɜːn/ vi ∼ **for, to** desejar, ansiar por, suspirar por. ∼**ing** n desejo m, anseio m (**for** de)

yeast /jiːst/ n levedura f

yell /jel/ vt/i gritar, berrar ▫ n grito m, berro m

yellow /'jeləʊ/ a amarelo; (*colloq: cowardly*) covarde, poltrão ▫ n amarelo m

yelp /jelp/ n (*of dog etc*) ganido m ▫ vi ganir

yen /jen/ n (*colloq: yearning*) grande vontade f (**for** de)

yes /jes/ n & adv sim (m). **~-man** (*colloq*) lambe-botas m invar, puxa-saco m

yesterday /'jestədɪ/ n & adv ontem (m). **~ morning/afternoon/evening** ontem de manhã/à tarde/à noite. **the day before ~** anteontem. **~ week** há oito dias, há uma semana

yet /jet/ adv ainda; (*already*) já ▫ conj contudo, no entanto. **as ~** até agora, por enquanto. **his best book ~** o seu melhor livro até agora

yew /ju:/ n teixo m

Yiddish /'jɪdɪʃ/ n ídiche m

yield /ji:ld/ vt (*produce*) produzir, dar; (*profit*) render; (*surrender*) entregar ▫ vi (*give way*) ceder ▫ n produção f; (*comm*) rendimento m

yoga /'jəʊɡə/ n ioga f

yoghurt /'jɒɡət/ n iogurte m

yoke /jəʊk/ n jugo m, canga f; (*of garment*) pala f ▫ vt jungir; (*unite*) unir, ligar

yokel /'jəʊkl/ n caipira m, labrego m

yolk /jəʊk/ n gema (de ovo) f

yonder /'jɒndə(r)/ adv acolá, além

you /ju:/ pron (*familiar*) tu, você (*pl* vocês); (*polite*) vós, o(s) senhor(es), a(s) senhora(s); (*object: familiar*) te, lhe (*pl* vocês); (*polite*) o(s), a(s), lhes, vós, o(s) senhor(es), a(s) senhora(s); (*after prep*) ti, si, você (*pl* vocês); (*polite*) vós, o senhor, a senhora (*pl* os senhores, as senhoras); (*indefinite*) se; (*after prep*) si, você. **with ~** (*familiar*) contigo, consigo, com você (*pl* com vocês); (*polite*) com o senhor/a senhora (*pl* convosco, com os senhores/as senhoras). **I know ~** (*familiar*) eu te conheço, eu o/a conheço (*pl* eu os/as conheço); (*polite*) eu vos conheço, conheço o senhor/a senhora (*pl* conheço os senhores/as senhoras). **~ can see the sea** você pode ver o mar

young /jʌŋ/ a (-**er**, -**est**) jovem, novo, moço ▫ n (*people*) jovens mpl, a juventude f, a mocidade f; (*of animals*) crias fpl, filhotes mpl

youngster /'jʌŋstə(r)/ n jovem mf, moço m, rapaz m

your /jɔː(r)/ a (*familiar*) teu, tua, seu, sua (*pl* teus, tuas, seus, suas); (*polite*) vosso, vossa, do senhor, da senhora (*pl* vossos, vossas, dos senhores, das senhoras)

yours /jɔːz/ poss pron (*familiar*) o teu, a tua, o seu, a sua (*pl* os teus, as tuas, os seus, as suas); (*polite*) o vosso, a vossa, o/a do senhor, o/a da senhora (*pl* os vossos, as vossas; os/as do(s) senhor(es), os/as da(s) senhora(s)). **a book of ~** um livro seu. **~ sincerely/faithfully** atenciosamente, com os cumprimentos de

yourself /jɔː'self/ pron (*pl* -**selves** /-'selvz/) (*familiar*) tu mesmo/a, você mesmo/a (*pl* vocês mesmos/as); (*polite*) vós mesmo/a, o senhor mesmo, a senhora mesma (*pl* vós mesmos/as, os senhores mesmos, as senhoras mesmas); (*reflexive: familiar*) a ti mesmo/a, se, a si mesmo/a (*pl* a vocês mesmos/as); (*polite*) ao senhor mesmo, à senhora mesma (*pl* aos senhores mesmos, às senhoras mesmas); (*after prep: familiar*) ti mesmo/a, si mesmo/a, você mesmo/a (*pl* vocês mesmos/as); (*after prep: polite*) vós mesmo/a, o senhor mesmo, a senhora mesma (*pl* vós mesmos/as, os senhores mesmos, as senhoras mesmas). **with ~** (*familiar*) contigo mesmo/a, consigo mesmo/a, com você (*pl* com vocês); (*polite*) convosco, com o senhor, com a senhora (*pl* com os senhores, com as senhoras). **by ~** sozinho

youth /ju:θ/ n (*pl* -s /-ðz/) mocidade f, juventude f; (*young man*) jovem m, moço m. **~ club** centro m de jovens. **~ hostel** albergue m da juventude. **~ful** a juvenil, jovem

yo-yo /'jəʊjəʊ/ n (*pl* -os) ioiô m

Yugoslav /'ju:ɡəslɑːv/ a & n iogoslavo (m), (P) jugoslavo (m). **~ia** /-'slɑːvɪə/ n Iogoslávia f, (P) Jugoslávia f

....

Zz

....

zany /'zeɪnɪ/ a (-**ier**, -**iest**) tolo, bobo

zeal /zi:l/ n zelo m

zealous /'zeləs/ a zeloso. **~ly** adv zelosamente

zebra /'zebrə, 'zi:brə/ n zebra f. **~ crossing** faixa f para pedestres, (P) passagem f para peões

zenith /'zenɪθ/ n zênite m, (P) zénite m, auge m

zero /'zɪərəʊ/ n (*pl* -os) zero m. **~ hour** hora H. **below ~** abaixo de zero

zest /zest/ n (*gusto*) entusiasmo m; (*fig: spice*) sabor m especial; (*lemon or*

y

z

orange peel) casca *f* de limão/laranja
ralada

zigzag /'zɪgzæg/ *n* ziguezague *m* ▢ *a* &
adv em ziguezague ▢ *vi* (*pt* **zigzagged**)
ziguezaguear

zinc /zɪŋk/ *n* zinco *m*

zip /zɪp/ *n* (*vigour*) energia *f*, alma *f*.
~(**-fastener**) fecho *m* ecler ▢ *vt* (*pt*
zipped) fechar o fecho eclerde ▢ *vi* ir a
toda a velocidade. **Z~ code** (*Amer*)
CEP de endereçamento postal *m*, (*P*)
código *m* postal

zipper /'zɪpə(r)/ *n* = **zip(-fastener)**

zodiac /'zəʊdɪæk/ *n* zodíaco *m*

zombie /'zɒmbɪ/ *n* zumbi *m*; (*colloq*)
zumbi *m*, (*P*) autómato *m*

zone /zəʊn/ *n* zona *f*

zoo /zu:/ *n* jardim *m* zoológico

zoolog|y /zəʊ'ɒlədʒɪ/ *n* zoologia *f*. ~**ical**
/-ə'lɒdʒɪkl/ *a* zoológico. ~**ist** *n*
zoólogo *m*

zoom /zu:m/ *vi* (*rush*) sair roando ~ **lens**
zum *m*, zoom *m*. ~ **off** *or* **past** passar
zunindo

zucchini /zu:'ki:nɪ/ *n* (*pl invar*) (*Amer*)
courgette *f*

Portuguese verbs

Portuguese verbs can be divided into three categories: regular verbs, those with spelling peculiarities determined by their sound and irregular verbs.

Regular verbs:

in -**ar** (e.g. **comprar**)

Present: compr|o, ~**as**, ~**a**, ~**amos**, ~**ais**, ~**am**

Future: comprar|**ei**, ~**ás**, ~**á**, ~**emos**, ~**eis**, ~**ão**

Imperfect: compr|**ava**, ~**avas**, ~**ava**, ~**ávamos**, ~**áveis**, ~**avam**

Preterite: compr|**ei**, ~**aste**, ~**ou**, ~**amos** (P: ~**ámos**), ~**astes**, ~**aram**

Pluperfect: compr|**ara**, ~**aras**, ~**ara**, ~**áramos**, ~**áreis**, ~**aram**

Present subjunctive: compr|**e**, ~**es**, ~**e**, ~**emos**, ~**eis**, ~**em**

Imperfect subjunctive: compr|**asse**, ~**asses**, ~**asse**, ~**ássemos**, ~**ásseis**, ~**assem**

Future subjunctive: compr|**ar**, ~**ares**, ~**ar**, ~**armos**, ~**ardes**, ~**arem**

Conditional: comprar|**ia**, ~**ias**, ~**ia**, ~**íamos**, ~**íeis**, ~**iam**

Personal infinitive: comprar, ~**es**, ~, ~**mos**, ~**des**, ~**em**

Present participle: comprando

Past participle: comprado

Imperative: compra, comprai

in ~**er** (e.g. **bater**)

Present: bat|o, ~**es**, ~**e**, ~**emos**, ~**eis**, ~**em**

Future: bater|**ei**, ~**ás**, ~**á**, ~**emos**, ~**eis**, ~**ão**

Imperfect: bat|**ia**, ~**ias**, ~**ia**, ~**íamos**, ~**íeis**, ~**iam**

Preterite: bat|**i**, ~**este**, ~**eu**, ~**emos**, ~**estes**, ~**eram**

Pluperfect: bat|**era**, ~**eras**, ~**era**, ~**êramos**, ~**êreis**, ~**eram**

Present subjunctive: bat|**a**, ~**as**, ~**a**, ~**amos**, ~**ais**, ~**am**

Imperfect subjunctive: bat|**esse**, ~**esses**, ~**esse**, ~**êssemos**, ~**êsseis**, ~**essem**

Future subjunctive: bat|**er**, ~**eres**, ~**er**, ~**ermos**, ~**erdes**, ~**erem**

Conditional: bater|**ia**, ~**ias**, ~**ia**, ~**íamos**, ~**íeis**, ~**iam**

Personal infinitive: bater, ~**es**, ~, ~**mos**, ~**des**, ~**em**

Present participle: batendo

Past participle: batido

Imperative: bate, batei

in ~**ir** (e.g. **admitir**)

Present: admit|o, ~**es**, ~**e**, ~**imos**, ~**is**, ~**em**

Future: admitir|**ei**, ~**ás**, ~**á**, ~**emos**, ~**eis**, ~**ão**

Imperfect: admit|**ia**, ~**ias**, ~**ia**, ~**íamos**, ~**íeis**, ~**iam**

Preterite: admit|**i**, ~**iste**, ~**iu**, ~**imos**, ~**istes**, ~**iram**

Pluperfect: admit|**ira**, ~**iras**, ~**ira**, ~**íramos**, ~**íreis**, ~**iram**

Present subjunctive: admit|**a**, ~**as**, ~**a**, ~**amos**, ~**ais**, ~**am**

Imperfect subjunctive: admit|**isse**, ~**isses**, ~**isse**, ~**íssemos**, ~**ísseis**, ~**issem**

Future subjunctive: admit|**ir**, ~**ires**, ~**ir**, ~**irmos**, ~**irdes**, ~**irem**

Conditional: admitir|**ia**, ~**ias**, ~**ia**, ~**íamos**, ~**íeis**, ~**iam**

Personal infinitive: admitir, ~**es**, ~, ~**mos**, ~**des**, ~**em**

Present participle: admitindo

Past participle: admitido

Imperative: admite, admiti

Regular verbs with spelling changes:

-ar verbs:

in -car (e.g. **ficar**)

Preterite: fiquei, ficaste, ficou, ficamos (P: ficámos), ficais, ficam
Present subjunctive: fique, fiques, fique, fiquemos, fiqueis, fiquem

in -çar (e.g. **abraçar**)

Preterite: abracei, abraçaste, abraçou, abraçamos (P: abraçámos), abraçastes, abraçaram
Present subjunctive: abrace, abraces, abrace, abracemos, abraceis, abracem

in -ear (e.g. **passear**)

Present: passeio, passeias, passeia, passeamos, passeais, passeiam
Present subjunctive: passeie, passeies, passeie, passeemos, passeeis, passeiem
Imperative: passeia, passeai

in -gar (e.g. **apagar**)

Preterite: apaguei, apagaste, apagou, apagamos (P: apagámos), apagastes, apagaram
Present subjunctive: apague, apagues, apague, apaguemos, apagueis, apaguem

in -oar (e.g. **voar**)

Present: vôo (P: voo), voas, voa, voamos, voais, voam

averiguar

Preterite: averigüei (P: averiguei), averiguaste, averiguou, averiguamos (P: averiguámos), averiguastes, averiguaram
Present subjunctive: averigúe, averigúes, averigúe, averigüemos

(P: averiguemos), averigüeis (P: averigueis), averigúem

enxaguar

Present: enxáguo, enxáguas, enxágua, enxaguamos, enxaguais, enxáguam
Preterite: enxagüei (P: enxaguei), enxaguaste, enxaguou, enxaguamos (P: enxaguámos), enxaguastes, enxaguaram
Present subjunctive: enxágüe, enxágües, enxágüe, enxagüemos, enxagüeis, enxágüem (P: enxágue, enxágues, enxágue, enxaguemos, enxagueis, enxáguem)
Similarly: aguar, desaguar

saudar

Present: saúdo, saúdas, saúda, saudamos, saudais, saúdam
Present subjunctive: saúde, saúdes, saúde, saudemos, saudeis, saúdem
Imperative: saúda, saudai

-er verbs:

in -cer (e.g. **tecer**)

Present: teço, teces, tece, tecemos, teceis, tecem
Present subjunctive: teça, teças, teça, teçamos, teçais, teçam

in -ger (e.g. **proteger**)

Present: protejo, proteges, protege, protegemos, protegeis, protegem
Present subjunctive: proteja, protejas, proteja, protejamos, protejais, protejam

in -guer (e.g. **erguer**)

Present: ergo, ergues, ergue, erguemos, ergueis, erguem
Present subjunctive: erga, ergas, erga, ergamos, ergais, ergam

in **-oer** (e.g. **roer**)

Present: rôo (P: roo), róis, rói, roemos, roeis, roem

Imperfect: roía, roías, roía, roíamos, roíeis, roíam

Preterite: roí, roeste, roeu, roemos, roestes, roeram

Past participle: roído

Imperative: rói, roei

-ir verbs:

in **-ir** with **-e-** in stem (e.g. **vestir**)

Present: visto, vestes, veste, vestimos, vestis, vestem

Present subjunctive: vista, vistas, vista, vistamos, vistais, vistam

Similarly: mentir, preferir, refletir, repetir, seguir, sentir, servir

in **-ir** with **-o-** in stem (e.g. **dormir**)

Present: durmo, dormes, dorme, dormimos, dormis, dormem

Present subjunctive: durma, durmas, durma, durmamos, durmais, durmam

Similarly: cobrir, descobrir, tossir

in **-ir** with **-u-** in stem (e.g. **subir**)

Present: subo, sobes, sobe, subimos, subis, sobem

Similarly: consumir, cuspir, fugir, sacudir, sumir

in **-air** (e.g. **sair**)

Present: saio, sais, sai, saímos, saís, saem

Imperfect: saía, saías, saía, saíamos, saíeis, saíam

Preterite: saí, saíste, saiu, saímos, saístes, saíram

Pluperfect: saíra, saíras, saíra, saíramos, saíreis, saíram

Present subjunctive: saia, saias, saia, saiamos, saiais, saiam

Imperfect subjunctive: saísse, saísses, saísse, saíssemos, saísseis, saíssem

Future subjunctive: sair, saíres, sair, sairmos, sairdes, saírem

Personal infinitive: sair, saíres, sair, sairmos, sairdes, saírem

Present participle: saindo

Past participle: saído

Imperative: sai, saí

in **-gir** (e.g. **dirigir**)

Present: dirijo, diriges, dirige, dirigimos, dirigis, dirigem

Present subjunctive: dirija, dirijas, dirija, dirijamos, dirijais, dirijam

in **-guir** (e.g. **distinguir**)

Present: distingo, distingues, distingue, distinguimos, distinguis, distinguem

Present subjunctive: distinga, distingas, distinga, distingamos, distingais, distingam

in **-uir** (e.g. **atribuir**)

Present: atribuo, atribuis, atribui, atribuímos, atribuís, atribuem

Imperfect: atribuía, atribuías, atribuía, atribuíamos, atribuíeis, atribuíam

Preterite: atribuí, atribuíste, atribuiu, atribuímos, atribuístes, atribuíram

Pluperfect: atribuíra, atribuíras, atribuíra, atribuíramos, atribuíreis, atribuíram

Present subjunctive: atribua, atribuas, atribua, atribuamos, atribuais, atribuam

Imperfect subjunctive: atribuísse, atribuísses, atribuísse, atribuíssemos, atribuísseis, atribuíssem

Future subjunctive: atribuir, atribuíres, atribuir, atribuirmos, atribuirdes, atribuírem

Personal infinitive: atribuir, atribuíres, atribuir, atribuirmos, atribuirdes, atribuírem

Present participle: atribuindo

Past participle: atribuído
Imperative: atribui, atribuí

proibir

Present: proíbo, proíbes, proíbe, proibimos, proibis, proíbem
Present subjunctive: proíba, proíbas, proíba, proibamos, proibais, proíbam
Imperative: proíbe, proibi
Similarly: coibir

reunir

Present: reúno, reúnes, reúne, reunimos, reunis, reúnem
Present subjunctive: reúna, reúnas, reúna, reunamos, reunais, reúnam
Imperative: reúne, reuni

in -struir (e.g. construir) – like atribuir except:

Present: construo, constróis/construis, constrói/construi, construímos, construís, constroem/construem
Imperative: constrói/construi, construí

in -duzir (e.g. produzir)

Present: produzo, produzes, produz, produzimos, produzis, produzem
Imperative: produz(e), produzi
Similarly: luzir, reluzir

Irregular verbs

caber

Present: caibo, cabes, cabe, cabemos, cabeis, cabem
Preterite: coube, coubeste, coube, coubemos, coubestes, couberam
Pluperfect: coubera, couberas, coubera, coubéramos, coubéreis, couberam
Present subjunctive: caiba, caibas, caiba, caibamos, caibais, caibam
Imperfect subjunctive: coubesse, coubesses, coubesse, coubéssemos, coubésseis, coubessem

Future subjunctive: couber, couberes, couber, coubermos, couberdes, couberem

dar

Present: dou, dás, dá, damos, dais, dão
Preterite: dei, deste, deu, demos, destes, deram
Pluperfect: dera, deras, dera, déramos, déreis, deram
Present subjunctive: dê, dês, dê, demos, deis, dêem
Imperfect subjunctive: desse, desses, desse, déssemos, désseis, dessem
Future subjunctive: der, deres, der, dermos, derdes, derem
Imperative: dá, dai

dizer

Present: digo, dizes, diz, dizemos, dizeis, dizem
Future: direi, dirás, dirá, diremos, direis, dirão
Preterite: disse, disseste, disse, dissemos, dissestes, disseram
Pluperfect: dissera, disseras, dissera, disséramos, disséreis, disseram
Present subjunctive: diga, digas, diga, digamos, digais, digam
Imperfect subjunctive: dissesse, dissesses, dissesse, disséssemos, dissésseis, dissessem
Future subjunctive: disser, disseres, disser, dissermos, disserdes, disserem
Conditional: diria, dirias, diria, diríamos, diríeis, diriam
Present participle: dizendo
Past participle: dito
Imperative: diz, dizei

estar

Present: estou, estás, está, estamos, estais, estão
Preterite: estive, estiveste, esteve, estivemos, estivestes, estiveram
Pluperfect: estivera, estiveras, estivera, estivéramos, estivéreis, estiveram

Present subjunctive: esteja, estejas, esteja, estejamos, estejais, estejam

Imperfect subjunctive: estivesse, estivesses, estivesse, estivéssemos, estivésseis, estivessem

Future subjunctive: estiver, estiveres, estiver, estivermos, estiverdes, estiverem

Imperative: está, estai

fazer

Present: faço, fazes, faz, fazemos, fazeis, fazem

Future: farei, farás, fará, faremos, fareis, farão

Preterite: fiz, fizeste, fez, fizemos, fizestes, fizeram

Pluperfect: fizera, fizeras, fizera, fizéramos, fizéreis, fizeram

Present subjunctive: faça, faças, faça, façamos, façais, façam

Imperfect subjunctive: fizesse, fizesses, fizesse, fizéssemos, fizésseis, fizessem

Future subjunctive: fizer, fizeres, fizer, fizermos, fizerdes, fizerem

Conditional: faria, farias, faria, faríamos, faríeis, fariam

Present participle: fazendo

Past participle: feito

Imperative: faz(e), fazei

frigir

Present: frijo, freges, frege, frigimos, frigis, fregem

Present subjunctive: frija, frijas, frija, frijamos, frijais, frijam

Imperative: frege, frigi

haver

Present: hei, hás, há, hemos/havemos, haveis/heis, hão

Preterite: houve, houveste, houve, houvemos, houvestes, houveram

Pluperfect: houvera, houveras, houvera, houvéramos, houvéreis, houveram

Present subjunctive: haja, hajas, haja, hajamos, hajais, hajam

Imperfect subjunctive: houvesse, houvesses, houvesse, houvéssemos, houvésseis, houvessem

Future subjunctive: houver, houveres, houver, houvermos, houverdes, houverem

Imperative: há, havei

ir

Present: vou, vais, vai, vamos, ides, vão

Imperfect: ia, ias, ia, íamos, íeis, iam

Preterite: fui, foste, foi, fomos, fostes, foram

Pluperfect: fora, foras, fora, fôramos, fôreis, foram

Present subjunctive: vá, vás, vá, vamos, vades, vão

Imperfect subjunctive: fosse, fosses, fosse, fôssemos, fôsseis, fossem

Future subjunctive: for, fores, for, formos, fordes, forem

Present participle: indo

Past participle: ido

Imperative: vai, ide

ler

Present: leio, lês, lê, lemos, ledes, lêem

Imperfect: lia, lias, lia, líamos, líeis, liam

Preterite: li, leste, leu, lemos, lestes, leram

Pluperfect: lera, leras, lera, lêramos, lêreis, leram

Present subjunctive: leia, leias, leia, leiamos, leiais, leiam

Imperfect subjunctive: lesse, lesses, lesse, lêssemos, lêsseis, lessem

Future subjunctive: ler, leres, ler, lermos, lerdes, lerem

Present participle: lendo

Past participle: lido

Imperative: lê, lede

Similarly: crer

odiar

Present: odeio, odeias, odeia, odiamos, odiais, odeiam

Present subjunctive: odeie, odeies, odeie, odiemos, odieis, odeiem
Imperative: odeia, odiai
Similarly: incendiar

ouvir

Present: ouço (P also: oiça), ouves, ouve, ouvimos, ouvis, ouvem
Present subjunctive: ouça, ouças, ouça, ouçamos, ouçais, ouçam (P also: oiça, oiças, oiça, oiçamos, oiçais, oiçam)

pedir

Present: peço, pedes, pede, pedimos, pedis, pedem
Present subjunctive: peça, peças, peça, peçamos, peçais, peçam
Similarly: despedir, impedir, medir

perder

Present: perco, perdes, perde, perdemos, perdeis, perdem
Present subjunctive: perca, percas, perca, percamos, percais, percam

poder

Present: posso, podes, pode, podemos, podeis, podem
Preterite: pude, pudeste, pôde, pudemos, pudestes, puderam
Pluperfect: pudera, puderas, pudera, pudéramos, pudéreis, puderam
Present subjunctive: possa, possas, possa, possamos, possais, possam
Imperfect subjunctive: pudesse, pudesses, pudesse, pudéssemos, pudésseis, pudessem
Future subjunctive: puder, puderes, puder, pudermos, puderdes, puderem

polir

Present: pulo, pules, pule, polimos, polis, pulem
Present subjunctive: pula, pulas, pula, pulamos, pulais, pulam
Imperative: pule, poli

pôr

Present: ponho, pões, põe, pomos, pondes, põem
Future: porei, porás, porá, poremos, poreis, porão
Imperfect: punha, punhas, punha, púnhamos, púnheis, punham
Preterite: pus, puseste, pôs, pusemos, pusestes, puseram
Pluperfect: pusera, puseras, pusera, puséramos, puséreis, puseram
Present subjunctive: ponha, ponhas, ponha, ponhamos, ponhais, ponham
Imperfect subjunctive: pusesse, pusesses, pusesse, puséssemos, pusésseis, pusessem
Future subjunctive: puser, puseres, puser, pusermos, puserdes, puserem
Conditional: poria, porias, poria, poríamos, poríeis, poriam
Present participle: pondo
Past participle: posto
Imperative: põe, ponde
Similarly: compor, depor, dispor, opor, supor etc

prover

Present: provejo, provês, provê, provemos, provedes, provêem
Present subjunctive: proveja, provejas, proveja, provejamos, provejais, provejam
Imperative: provê, provede

querer

Present: quero, queres, quer, queremos, quereis, querem
Preterite: quis, quiseste, quis, quisemos, quisestes, quiseram
Pluperfect: quisera, quiseras, quisera, quiséramos, quiséreis, quiseram
Present subjunctive: queira, queiras, queira, queiramos, queirais, queiram
Imperfect subjunctive: quisesse,

quisesses, quisesse, quiséssemos,
quisésseis, quisessem
Future subjunctive: quiser, quiseres,
quiser, quisermos, quiserdes,
quiserem
Imperative: quer, querei

requerer

Present: requeiro, requeres, requer,
requeremos, requereis, requerem
Present subjunctive: requeira, requeiras,
requeira, requeiramos, requeirais,
requeiram
Imperative: requer, requerei

rir

Present: rio, ris, ri, rimos, rides, riem
Present subjunctive: ria, rias, ria,
riamos, riais, riam
Imperative: ri, ride
Similarly: sorrir

saber

Present: sei, sabes, sabe, sabemos,
sabeis, sabem
Preterite: soube, soubeste, soube,
soubemos, soubestes, souberam
Pluperfect: soubera, souberas, soubera,
soubéramos, soubéreis, souberam
Present subjunctive: saiba, saibas, saiba,
saibamos, saibais, saibam
Imperfect subjunctive: soubesse,
soubesses, soubesse, soubéssemos,
soubésseis, soubessem
Future subjunctive: souber, souberes,
souber, soubermos, souberdes,
souberem
Imperative: sabe, sabei

ser

Present: sou, és, é, somos, sois, são
Imperfect: era, eras, era, éramos, éreis,
eram
Preterite: fui, foste, foi, fomos, fostes,
foram
Pluperfect: fora, foras, fora, fôramos,
fôreis, foram
Present subjunctive: seja, sejas, seja,

sejamos, sejais, sejam
Imperfect subjunctive: fosse, fosses,
fosse, fôssemos, fôsseis, fossem
Future subjunctive: for, fores, for,
formos, fordes, forem
Present participle: sendo
Past participle: sido
Imperative: sê, sede

ter

Present: tenho, tens, tem, temos,
tendes, têm
Imperfect: tinha, tinhas, tinha,
tínhamos, tínheis, tinham
Preterite: tive, tiveste, teve, tivemos,
tivestes, tiveram
Pluperfect: tivera, tiveras, tivera,
tivéramos, tivéreis, tiveram
Present subjunctive: tenha, tenhas,
tenha, tenhamos, tenhais, tenham
Imperfect subjunctive: tivesse, tivesses,
tivesse, tivéssemos, tivésseis,
tivessem
Future subjunctive: tiver, tiveres, tiver,
tivermos, tiverdes, tiverem
Present participle: tendo
Past participle: tido
Imperative: tem, tende

trazer

Present: trago, trazes, traz, trazemos,
trazeis, trazem
Future: trarei, trarás, trará, traremos,
trareis, trarão
Preterite: trouxe, trouxeste, trouxe,
trouxemos, trouxestes, trouxeram
Pluperfect: trouxera, trouxeras,
trouxera, trouxéramos, trouxéreis,
trouxeram
Present subjunctive: traga, tragas, traga,
tragamos, tragais, tragam
Imperfect subjunctive: trouxesse,
trouxesses, trouxesse,
trouxéssemos, trouxésseis,
trouxessem
Future subjunctive: trouxer, trouxeres,
trouxer, trouxermos, trouxerdes,
trouxerem

Conditional: traria, trarias, traria, traríamos, traríeis, trariam
Imperative: traze, trazei

valer

Present: valho, vales, vale, valemos, valeis, valem
Present subjunctive: valha, valhas, valha, valhamos, valhais, valham

ver

Present: vejo, vês, vê, vemos, vedes, vêem
Imperfect: via, vias, via, víamos, víeis, viam
Preterite: vi, viste, viu, vimos, vistes, viram
Pluperfect: vira, viras, vira, víramos, víreis, viram
Present subjunctive: veja, vejas, veja, vejamos, vejais, vejam
Imperfect subjunctive: visse, visses, visse, víssemos, vísseis, vissem

Future subjunctive: vir, vires, vir, virmos, virdes, virem
Present participle: vendo
Past participle: visto
Imperative: vê, vede

vir

Present: venho, vens, vem, vimos, vindes, vêm
Imperfect: vinha, vinhas, vinha, vínhamos, vínheis, vinham
Preterite: vim, vieste, veio, viemos, viestes, vieram
Pluperfect: viera, vieras, viera, viéramos, viéreis, vieram
Present subjunctive: venha, venhas, venha, venhamos, venhais, venham
Imperfect subjunctive: viesse, viesses, viesse, viéssemos, viésseis, viessem
Future subjunctive: vier, vieres, vier, viermos, vierdes, vierem
Present participle: vindo
Past participle: vindo
Imperative: vem, vinde

Verbos irregulares ingleses

Infinitivo	Pretérito	Particípio passado	Infinitivo	Pretérito	Particípio passado
be	was	been	**fight**	fought	fought
bear	bore	borne	**find**	found	found
beat	beat	beaten	**flee**	fled	fled
become	became	become	**fly**	flew	flown
begin	began	begun	**freeze**	froze	frozen
bend	bent	bent	**get**	got	got, gotten *US*
bet	bet, betted	bet, betted	**give**	gave	given
bid	bade, bid	bidden, bid	**go**	went	gone
bind	bound	bound	**grow**	grew	grown
bite	bit	bitten	**hang**	hung, hanged	hung, hanged
bleed	bled	bled			
blow	blew	blown	**have**	had	had
break	broke	broken	**hear**	heard	heard
breed	bred	bred	**hide**	hid	hidden
bring	brought	brought	**hit**	hit	hit
build	built	built	**hold**	held	held
burn	burnt, burned	burnt, burned	**hurt**	hurt	hurt
			keep	kept	kept
burst	burst	burst	**kneel**	knelt	knelt
buy	bought	bought	**know**	knew	known
catch	caught	caught	**lay**	laid	laid
choose	chose	chosen	**lead**	led	led
cling	clung	clung	**lean**	leaned, leant	leaned, leant
come	came	come			
cost	cost, costed *(vt)*	cost, costed	**learn**	learnt, learned	learnt, learned
cut	cut	cut	**leave**	left	left
deal	dealt	dealt	**lend**	lent	lent
dig	dug	dug	**let**	let	let
do	did	done	**lie**	lay	lain
draw	drew	drawn	**lose**	lost	lost
dream	dreamt, dreamed	dreamt, dreamed	**make**	made	made
			mean	meant	meant
drink	drank	drunk	**meet**	met	met
drive	drove	driven	**pay**	paid	paid
eat	ate	eaten	**put**	put	put
fall	fell	fallen	**read**	read	read
feed	fed	fed	**ride**	rode	ridden
feel	felt	felt	**ring**	rang	rung
			rise	rose	risen

Infinitivo	Pretérito	Particípio passado	Infinitivo	Pretérito	Particípio passado
run	ran	run	**spread**	spread	spread
say	said	said	**spring**	sprang	sprung
see	saw	seen	**stand**	stood	stood
seek	sought	sought	**steal**	stole	stolen
sell	sold	sold	**stick**	stuck	stuck
send	sent	sent	**sting**	stung	stung
set	set	set	**stride**	strode	stridden
sew	sewed	sewn, sewed	**strike**	struck	struck
shake	shook	shaken	**swear**	swore	sworn
shine	shone	shone	**sweep**	swept	swept
shoe	shod	shod	**swell**	swelled	swollen, swelled
shoot	shot	shot			
show	showed	shown	**swim**	swam	swum
shut	shut	shut	**swing**	swung	swung
sing	sang	sung	**take**	took	taken
sink	sank	sunk	**teach**	taught	taught
sit	sat	sat	**tear**	tore	torn
sleep	slept	slept	**tell**	told	told
sling	slung	slung	**think**	thought	thought
smell	smelt, smelled	smelt, smelled	**throw**	threw	thrown
			thrust	thrust	thrust
speak	spoke	spoken	**tread**	trod	trodden
spell	spelled, spelt	spelled, spelt	**understand**	understood	understood
spend	spent	spent	**wake**	woke	woken
spit	spat	spat	**wear**	wore	worn
spoil	spoilt, spoiled	spoilt, spoiled	**win**	won	won
			write	wrote	written